Encyclopedia of
Warrior Peoples and Fighting Groups

Encyclopedia of
Warrior Peoples and Fighting Groups

Second Edition

Paul K. Davis
and Allen Lee Hamilton

Grey House
Publishing

Millerton, NY

PUBLISHER:	Leslie Mackenzie
EDITORIAL DIRECTOR:	Laura Mars-Proietti
PRODUCTION EDITOR:	Toby Raymond
AUTHORS:	Paul K. Davis and Allen Lee Hamilton
COPY EDITOR:	Elaine Alibrandi
COMPOSITION:	ATLIS Graphics
MARKETING DIRECTOR:	Jessica Moody

Grey House Publishing, Inc.
185 Millerton Road
Millerton, NY 12546
518.789.8700
FAX 518.789.0545
www.greyhouse.com
e-mail: books @greyhouse.com

Publisher's Cataloging-In-Publication Data
(Prepared by The Donohue Group, Inc.)

Encyclopedia of warrior peoples and fighting groups / edited by Paul Davis & Allen Hamilton. – 2nd ed.

  p. : ill., maps ; 28 cm.

  ISBN: 1-59237-116-7
  Originally published: Santa Barbara, Calif. : ABC-CLIO, 1998.
  Includes bibliographical references and index.

1. Military history–Encyclopedias. I. Davis, Paul K., 1952- II. Hamilton, Allen Lee. III. Title: Warrior peoples and fighting groups

D25.A2 .E53 2006
355/.003

Encyclopedia of Warrior Peoples and Fighting Groups

Second Edition

SECTION ONE: ENTRIES

SECTION THREE: READINGS

PREFACE

Ever since mankind began organizing military forces, some have excelled in their craft. This came about either by fortuitous circumstances, outstanding leadership, or specialized instruction or training. In some cases, entire societies were geared toward military excellence. It is these populations and units that are the focus of this work.

We have selected four criteria for inclusion in this book: (1) Populations that dedicated themselves to a military structure in order to maintain societal discipline or dominate their neighbors. For example, the Spartans of ancient Greece or the Zulus of nineteenth-century Africa fit this criterion. (2) Soldiers who, through specialized training in the use of particular weapons or fighting styles, dominated the military forces of their times. Under this definition we would include knights, who controlled the military and social structure of medieval Europe, or submariners, who in modern times are carefully selected for their physical and psychological characteristics in operating undersea craft. (3) Units that did not necessarily set out to be noteworthy but who, through leadership or circumstance, made themselves famous. Here we include units such as the Minutemen of the American Revolution and Merrill's Marauders of World War II. (4) Units that recruit only high-quality soldiers with the intent of creating an elite force. The Varangian Guard of the Byzantine Empire and the Special Air Service of modern Great Britain fit into this category.

Some units that are well known are mentioned as subgroups of other topics. The famous Black Watch regiment of the British Army, for example, is included in the Highlanders entry, and the Comanche tribe is included with the Plains Indians. Certainly some readers will have personal favorites they feel we have overlooked. It has been our intent to include as many topics over as wide an area as possible, in terms both of eras and of parts of the world. No unit or group has been left out intentionally, but only as a matter of oversight.

We would like to thank several contributors who have eased our writing burden in the production of this work: Andy Galloway (St. Philip's College), Steve Davis (St. Mary's University), John Drake (University of Texas at San Antonio), along with Michael Forbes, Melvin C. (Mel) Wheat, David Beeson, Greg Regets, Trent Melcher, Nick Jourdan, Garrett Grohman, Robert Burke, Kyle Matheu, Tanya Alvarez (Vanderbilt University), Austin DeArmand (Georgetown University), Colleen Elizabeth Garcia (Georgetown University), and Clinton Chase Hamilton (Trinity University).

List of Contributors

Tanya Alvarez
David Beeson
Robert Burke
Steve Davis
Austin DeArmand
John Stephen Drake
Michael Forbes
Andy Galloway
Colleen Elizabeth Garcia
Garrett Grohman
Clinton Chase Hamilton
Nick Jourdan
Trent Melcher
Melvin C. Wheat

List of Maps

Title of General Maps at Back

SECTION ONE: ENTRIES

Afghans

A population of Afghanistan known for hostile and effective resistance to outside occupation.

For a few thousand years, Afghanistan was a crossroads for conquerors, with the countryside being overrun by Aryans, Greeks, Indians, Persians, Arabs, and Mongols. Over time, this constant influx of conquerors created a population of tough, independent-minded fighters that adopted a policy of maximum resistance to invaders. After the Sassanid Persians were removed from power, a local ruler, Ahmad Shah Durani, assumed control in 1747. He founded a ruling family that remained in power for 100 years before they—as do so many dynasties—became complacent and vulnerable. In 1824 Dost Mohammed overthrew this dissolute dynasty and became amir of Afghanistan, but soon began to feel pressure from major international powers both north and south of him.

The Persians, supported by the Russians, invaded Afghanistan in the 1830s. By chance, Eldred Pottinger, a British spy operating in Afghanistan, broke his cover, offered his assistance to the amir, and led the Afghan army in a successful defense of the country. Rather than establishing closer ties with Great Britain, which currently dominated India to the south, this incident instead provoked a British invasion. Britain did not fear Afghanistan itself, but worried that its domination by Russia would pose a potential threat to India. When Dost Mohammed refused to grant Britain the concessions it demanded, the British decided to put in place a more amenable ruler in his stead. Shah Shuja, Britain's chosen nominee, was of the ruling line Dost Mohammed had overthrown, but he was weak and therefore despised by the Afghan population. British forces invaded in late 1838 and by August 1839, Dost Mohammed was in exile and Shah Shuja was on the throne. The British army proceeded to put down pockets of resistance around the capital city of Kabul, and the tribes they did not defeat, they pacified with bribery. When in 1841 the bribes stopped, so did tribal cooperation. The British forces in Afghanistan found themselves surrounded in isolated forts, and the Afghans proved themselves able snipers, picking off unwary defenders. This uprising, coupled with the murder of the British ambassador, provoked another invasion.

The British in Kabul decided to flee for India. In January 1843, 4,500 British and Indian soldiers and civilians, along with some 10,000 Afghan supporters, abandoned the city. Only one British soldier made it to the border fort at Jelalabad; the rest were killed by the Afghans. The First Afghan War (as it came to be known) set a pattern for future intervention in the rugged country. A relief army from India forged the Khyber Pass, a feat no other power had ever accomplished, relieved the besieged Jelalabad, and then marched on Kabul. They released British prisoners held in Afghan confinement and burned the Great Bazaar, then marched home. Afghanistan was once again free of outside occupation, and Dost Mohammed returned to power.

The British failed to learn from history. In 1879, they once again attempted to place an envoy in Kabul, hoping to direct Afghanistan's foreign policy and keep out yet another Russian threat. One of Dost Mohammed's sons, Shere Ali, refused Britain's demands and, like his father, fled another army that marched into Kabul. Shere Ali died escaping to Russia, but one of his brothers, Yakub Khan, was installed as amir with British sufferance. By bowing to British pressure, Yakub Khan incurred the wrath of his people, who once again rose up, slaughtering the envoy and the British soldiers in the Residence of the British representative in the capital. Another relief force from India made its way to Kabul and exacted justice for the British envoy, but soon found itself surrounded and cut off from communication with India. A relief force from the fortress town of Kandahar fought through to Kabul, then learned that Kandahar had been besieged in their absence. Troops from Kabul marched back and recaptured the town. Now seemed like a good time to take everyone home, and the British retreated.

Once again rid of foreigners, the new Amir Abd-ar-Rahman Khan created a standing army and by diplomacy settled his borders with both Russia and British India. All was peaceful until 1919, when a new amir, supported by Afghan nobles, declared war on Britain. Since the British were busy with Indian independence movements, they quickly negotiated a settlement whereby Great Britain recognized

Afghan sovereignty. Free from outside threats, the Afghans turned upon each other. Rulers came and went over the next several years, all overthrown and either killed or forced into exile. Although the Afghans established friendly relations with Germany, Italy, and Japan in the 1930s when World War II broke out, they declared themselves neutral. After the war they joined the United Nations.

In 1947 another border dispute flared. The newly formed nation of Pakistan had a large ethnic Pathan population, people closely related to Afghans. When Pakistan would not allow the Pathans a referendum on self-rule, Afghanistan protested and began supporting Pathan insurgents demanding their own homeland, Pashtunistan (or Pathanistan). When the United States established friendly relations with Pakistan and offered military aid, Afghanistan began leaning toward the Soviet Union. With Soviet financial aid, the Afghan government began modernizing the country, but famine in the late 1960s and early 1970s brought aid from around the globe. Internal political squabbling led to more changes of government, still through violent means, until a revolutionary council established a socialist-style republic in 1978. When devout Muslims in this predominantly Shi'ite country revolted, the new government sought Soviet military assistance. In December 1979, a Soviet-supported coup killed Afghan Prime Minister Hafizullah Amin and Soviet troops occupied the country. Their experience, 100 years after the last British incursion, would be no more successful.

As many as 118,000 Soviet troops were sent to Afghanistan, but they could do little more than hold the major cities and roadways. The Afghan tribesmen, who had harassed and ultimately embarrassed the

British, proceeded to do the same to the Soviets. With covert military aid from the United States, the Muslim tribesmen controlled the mountainous countryside and the best Soviet attempts could not break them. In 1989, the disillusioned Soviet government withdrew all its combat troops, and once again the Afghans continued to fight among themselves. The blood of centuries of conquerors seems to have bred in the Afghan people the ability to fight; history has forced on them an ample opportunity to exercise that ability.

References: Adamec, Ludwig, *Dictionary of Afghan Wars, Revolutions, and Insurgencies* (Lanham, MD: Scarecrow Press, 1996); Bilgrami, Ashgar, *Afghanistan and British India* (New Delhi: Sterling Press, 1972); Farwell, Byron, *Queen Victoria's Little Wars* (New York: Harper and Row, 1972).

Afrika Korps

An outstanding unit of the Nazi army in North Africa in World War II.

Geography and terrain are always important when armies meet on the battlefield, and this was especially clear in North Africa during World War II. The desert environment determined the way war was fought in that campaign. Soldiers not only fought the enemy; they fought the elements as well. Temperatures rose above 100 degrees in the daytime and fell below freezing at night. Sand permeated everything from equipment to food and clothing. The fierce sun bleached uniforms and caused heat waves to dance on the sand, which sometimes prevented seeing farther than 1,000 yards.

The Mediterranean coastline with its sparkling waters was beautiful, but inland was a sterile, desolate, and forbidding desert. Rather than sand dunes, a hard crusty ground littered with rocks and boulders was typical. Maps were unreliable and the absence of landmarks made navigation difficult; men separated from their units could become lost and perish. Some parts of the desert rose in impassable escarpments or sank in depressions many miles across. Desert warfare employed new tactics using mechanized equipment—the tank, armored car, and self-propelled gun—in swift attacks. To take and hold territory required large quantities of supplies, so the main objective was simply to destroy the enemy. The opposing armies had to maneuver quickly, trying to flank their opponents and attack from the rear or side. The main consideration was always supplies. If an army raced forward too quickly, it might outrun its supply lines and become immobilized, which would lead to a counterattack.

Soldiers shared the desert with snakes, scorpions, lizards, and millions of flies and sand fleas. Large movements of vehicles and troops stirring up the dust gave away their positions. The dust got into the men's eyes, noses, and mouths, and penetrated into the food and water. Worse, it fouled engines and equipment, including rifles and cannons. Sandstorms were fierce and would stop most advances, causing the men to seek shelter in tents or vehicles until the storm passed. The sand, whipped by winds of 60 miles per hour or more, could strip the paint from vehicles and feel like pinpricks on the skin. It could reduce visibility to a few feet and make breathing impossible without covering the mouth and nose. Despite these conditions, the men of the German Afrika Korps under Field Marshall Erwin Rommel conducted a war in North Africa that almost beat the Allies.

Erwin Rommel, the "Desert Fox", leader of the Afrika Korps.

The men of the German Afrika Korps, who had been given no desert training, became hardened to the desert conditions as they fought. They were supplied at most only one gallon of water per man per day for drinking, cooking, and washing. They then saved the dirty water to be used in the vehicles. The army did not issue equipment for protection from the sun, such as sunglasses or lotion to protect the skin. Soldiers were originally issued pith helmets, but they soon discarded these in favor of cloth caps. They also wore shorts as part of the standard uniform. Soldiers soon found their skin chapped by the desert winds. Their lips cracked and their eyes became bloodshot from the piercing sunlight. Everyone was sunburned. Night brought no relief. The men, having sweated all day, would now shiver with the cold. Flies tormented the men by day, and sand fleas emerged at night to swarm the men, causing sores that were slow to heal.

The need for speed and mobility meant long, fast drives to reach a battle. Soldiers often steered their vehicles in a daze for lack of sleep. Sleeping at the wheel might only be interrupted by hitting another vehicle or a random boulder or being stuck in loose sand found off the main track. Moonless nights and the policy of driving without headlights caused men to lose sight of vehicles ahead of them and become lost in the vast desert. They would then be at the mercy of enemy air attacks when daylight came.

German soldiers were fed meager rations consisting of biscuits, cheese, and canned sardines. Canned meat was occasionally available, but was tough and tasteless. There was never enough water, and thirst was a constant companion; there were periods when water was rationed to one half cup per day. The Afrika Korps captured food and supplies from the enemy. Fuel was also obtained from enemy fuel dumps captured in battle. Both armies used captured vehicles, and cannibalized parts from vehicles that were no longer usable.

The equipment was as susceptible to the harsh conditions as the men. Tanks went only 1,500 miles before requiring an entire overhaul, one-fourth the time of those in a normal environment. Moreover, vehicles became bogged down in sand and the men had to wrestle with machines that the sun rendered too hot to touch with unprotected hands. The heat required columns to halt in order to allow engines to cool, and there were delays while crews cleaned clogged air and fuel filters. After a long night's drive and a daytime battle, men would refurbish their equipment and prepare for the next day's battle. The average

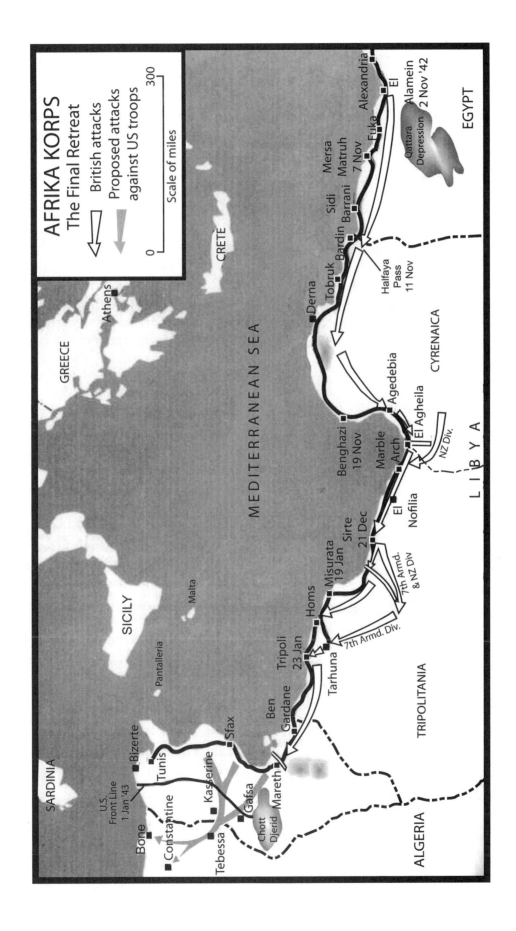

soldier might get three hours of sleep in every 24.

The desert's lack of cover made fighting very dangerous. Men in armored equipment had some protection, but the supporting infantries were at the mercy of enemy fire. Barbed wire and trenches surrounded emplacements. In addition, mines were laid in minefields that stretched for miles with only a few clear paths through them. Infantry advanced with armor, and in the confusion of battle the soldiers had to stay alert to avoid being run over by their own tanks. Infantry also tried to avoid the tanks because they invited enemy fire. Though the tank provided cover, an exploding tank could kill everyone around it.

Tank crews, although better protected than infantry, were not immune to destruction. Survival depended on the thickness of the tank's armor versus the shell being shot at it. A penetrating shell could ignite the ammunition or fuel in the vehicle, and all inside would perish. Tank crews worked in steel ovens. The big gun would add to the heat, and the tremendous noise required crews to talk with each other by intercom. Because the shimmering heat waves at midday cut visibility, the armies fought most battles at dawn or dusk. Fighting caused smoke and dust to obscure the battlefield. In addition, identification of the enemy was confusing because both armies used captured vehicles. Tank commanders needed good visibility, so they often opened the hatch and stood up in their turrets, risking death.

After nightfall, with the battle over, commanders shot flares into the sky to show lost units where to regroup. This was a time for tank crews to do maintenance or repair on the tanks and to rearm and refuel. There would also be guard duty or other tasks to perform, limiting the sleeping time of the troops to just a few hours because they frequently had to go back into action before dawn the next day. The British tank crews were usually on the line for a week before becoming exhausted, but Rommel kept his men in action for two weeks at a time or longer.

The Afrika Korps was an elite group led by an unusual leader. Rommel was revered by his men and acquired the nickname "Desert Fox." He had no hesitation about visiting the front. During one engagement, he piloted a light plane over the battlefield alone to understand the battle for himself. Rommel's assumption of command in North Africa changed the entire nature of the war there. The British, who had easily dominated the Italians and had success against earlier commanders, found Rommel's audacious moves almost impossible to counter. For example, the port city of Tobruk, which had resisted Axis capture for 26 months, fell to the Afrika Korps under Rommel in 26 hours. Repeatedly, Rommel defeated the Allied armies and caused England's prime minister, Winston Churchill, to remark that he was a formidable general. Rommel would not be stopped until September 1942 when a lack of supplies from Germany doomed his final drive on Alexandria and Cairo that threatened the Suez Canal. The combination of better-supplied British forces in Egypt and the arrival in early November 1942 of American forces to his rear doomed the Desert Fox to a fighting withdrawal and quashed the Axis plans to control North Africa.

John Drake

References: Barnett, Correlli, *The Desert Generals* (Bloomington: Indiana University Press, 1982); Bianco, Richard L., *Rommel, the Desert Warrior* (New York: Julian Messner, 1982);

Mitcham, Samuel W., *Rommel's Desert War: the Life and Death of the Afrika Korps* (New York: Stein and Day, 1982).

Akkadians

An ancient population that created through conquest the first known empire during the late third millennium BCE.

The people of the city of Akkad, or Agade, were Sumerians. The origin of the Sumerians, like many peoples of the ancient world, is somewhat hypothetical. They probably came from the area around the Caspian Sea, although there is no indication that they were Indo-European, like many later invaders from the north. They arrived in the fourth millennium BCE and settled the Tigris and Euphrates valleys, establishing the cities of Ur, Eridu, Mari, Nippur, Uruk, Kish, and Lagash. These communities collectively made up the population of Sumer, although they formed more of a confederation than a nation. They developed the cuneiform style of writing and were best known architecturally for the construction of ziggurats, step pyramids used as temples or altars. They also developed a monarchy, with a king in each city-state. The king was originally chosen for his military abilities, but over time the post became a permanent, and then a hereditary, position. As the military leader, the king commanded forces that fought in a phalanx-type formation, 11 men wide and six ranks deep. Most of the time the city-states fought among themselves in ever-shifting power struggles, or united against outside threats. That ended, however, with the monarchy of Sargon.

As with many ancient figures, Sargon's early years are somewhat of a mystery. He was born around 2350 BCE of undeter-mined parentage, though some theorize either a pastoral upbringing or that he was the child of a temple prostitute because he did not know his father. According to legend, Sargon began life as Moses did: cast adrift on a river by his mother—in this case, the Euphrates River. He was then reputedly rescued and raised by a farm family, not a royal one. He did manage, however, to become cupbearer to Ur-Za-baba, the king of Kish. Sargon came to power either by overthrowing the king himself or assuming the king's throne when Ur-Zababa was killed by the invading king of Sumer. Either way, at this point he took the name Sargon, meaning "King of Universal Dominion," and made war against Sumer.

Sargon united his Semitic people into history's first empire, the Akkadians. Sargon went about conquering and was quite successful at it. He captured cities up the Euphrates River, then crossed to the Tigris and worked his way up that river to Ashur. From there he conquered eastward to the Persian hills, then south to defeat Sumer, possibly gaining revenge for the death of Ur-Zababa. He symbolically washed his weapons in the Persian Gulf, marking the limit of his conquests in that direction. After consolidating his hold on Sumer, he marched west to conquer Mesopotamia and possibly as far as Syria and Lebanon, with rumors of conquests in lands as far-flung as Egypt, Asia Minor, and India.

In order to control this vast territory, Sargon appointed representatives of the conquered peoples to governing positions, answering only to him. He stationed troops in posts around the empire, garrisoning them with forces of all nations, although some soldiers were forced to join his armies. Sargon was successful in battle because he initiated new tactics. He aban-

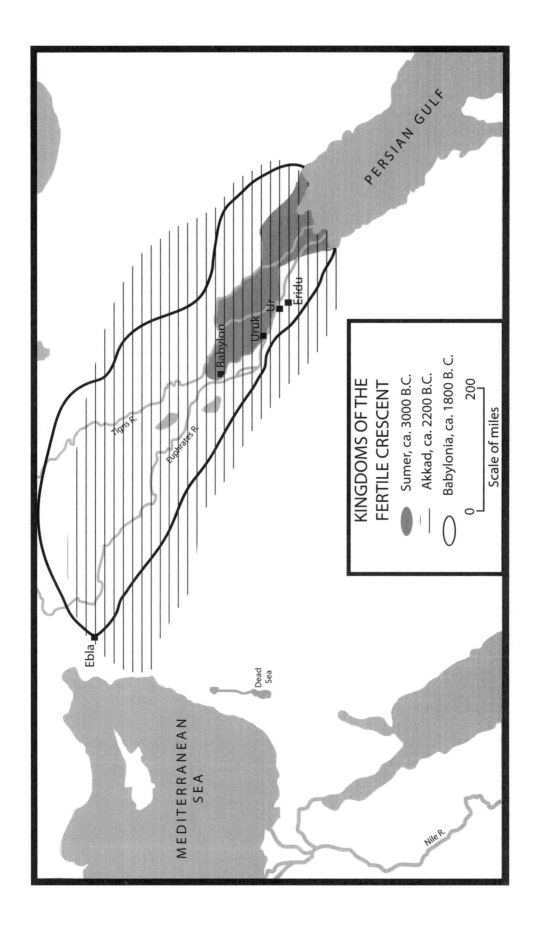

KINGDOMS OF THE
FERTILE CRESCENT

Sumer, ca. 3000 B.C.

Akkad, ca. 2200 B.C.

Babylonia, ca. 1800 B. C.

Scale of miles

0   200

PERSIAN GULF

Babylon

Uruk

Ur

Eridu

Tigris R.

Euphrates R.

Ebla

Dead
Sea

MEDITERRANEAN
SEA

Nile R.

doned the standard tight phalanx-style formation in favor of a looser one, and he adopted the use of javelins and arrows shot from compound bows. He also maintained the first standing army, a force of 5,400 men.

With so much land under one ruler, previously uncooperative peoples became more likely to open relations with neighboring tribes, and the freer exchange of goods and ideas resulted. New gods and religions were adopted from conquered peoples, as were cuneiform writing and art. The Akkadians were the first to use writing for more than keeping temple records. Because of this, we have the first recorded actions of royalty; hence, Sargon is regarded as the first clearly identified individual in history. He set an example for later royal chroniclers, as seen here: "He spread his terror-inspiring glamour over all the countries. He crossed the Sea in the East and he, himself, conquered the country of the West.... He marched against the country of Kazalla and turned Kazalla into ruin-hills and heaps of rubble. He even destroyed there every possible perching place for a bird" (Starr, 1965).

Having acquired vast amounts of land, Sargon's empire was exceedingly wealthy, controlling the known world's gold, silver, copper, and stone. With the abundant agriculture of Mesopotamia and abundant forage to the north, Sargon seemingly had it all. He maintained control by appointing loyal governors and visiting parts of his empire on occasion to let the people know he was interested in them. He ruled for 56 years, but ended his reign with parts of his empire in revolt. The Akkadian empire lasted some 200 years—only to be overthrown by its first conquest, a resurgent Sumerian society.

The Nellist Team following the Cabanatuan POW camp liberation. Back Row from left to right: Gil Cox, Wilber Wismer, Andy Smith. Front: Galen Kittleson, William Nellist. Reprinted with permission from the Alamo Scouts Association (www.alamoscouts.org).

References: Edwards, I. E. S., ed., *The Cambridge Ancient History* (Cambridge: Cambridge University Press, 1980); Gabriel, Richard, *The Culture of War* (New York: Greenwood Press, 1990); Gabriel, Richard, *From Sumer to Rome* (New York: Greenwood Press, 1991); Starr, Chester, *A History of the Ancient World* (New York: Oxford University Press, 1965).

Alamo Scouts

An elite United States Special Force Unit during World War II.

The Alamo Scouts originated on Fergusson Island, New Guinea, on November 28, 1943. Lt. General Walter Krueger, Commanding General of the Sixth U.S. Army, was responsible for creating this elite group of men. The name "Alamo Scouts" developed from Lt. Gen. Krueger's love of San Antonio and the city's famed Alamo. The Scouts were organized to perform reconnaissance behind enemy lines in the Southwest Pacific theater.

The men were all volunteers who were carefully selected for their level of intelligence, mental toughness and awareness, and physical capabilities. When men were interviewed, items were set out in front of them such as a brush, a pocket watch, matches, etc. As the person being interviewed was about to leave, the interviewer covered the items and asked the candidate to name the items. If he could not name them, he was disqualified and unable to continue on to the next stage of the selection process. The accepted men were trained to speak some of the foreign languages spoken in the area of operations, to maneuver a collapsible boat, to kill quietly, and to swim with full military gear. In January of 1944, the Alamo Scouts Training Center (ASTC) was ready for the first class of potential candidates to begin their training. The first class of men came from the 158th Regiment, known as the Bushmasters, who had undergone jungle warfare training in Panama. The facility on Fergusson Island, southeast of New Guinea, had been the site of a training camp for naval commandos, a unit which had recently been deactivated. Other camps were established on New Guinea and in the Philippines as the Allied offensive progressed.

There were only 138 men known to have had the honor to serve as an Alamo Scout. The Scouts completed 106 known missions behind enemy lines without the loss of a single life. Although the reconnaissance team had the option of declining any mission, they accepted every mission given to them and aborted only one. In only a few short months of serving in the field, the Scouts received 118 combat decorations, consisting of 44 Silver Stars, 33 Bronze Stars, four Soldier's Medals, and numerous Purple Hearts.

The Scout teams were usually led by a lieutenant and consisted of six or seven men on average. Among other accomplishments, they freed 197 Allied prisoners of war held captive in New Guinea and provided reconnaissance for the Ranger Battalion during the liberation of 511 prisoners of the Cabanatuan POW Camp in 1945. They also successfully captured 84 Japanese prisoners of war.

The Alamo Scouts' first mission consisted of five men led by Lt. John R. C. McGowan on February 27, 1944. The team was put ashore at the southeast point of Los Negros Island in the Admiralty Island chain. The Army Air Corps had searched the area before the Scouts arrived and had been unable to discover any enemy activity. Upon reconnoitering the island, the Scouts discovered Japanese troop activity. This new information prompted the decision to reinforce the invading unit, which staged a successful landing on the northeast tip of the island on February 29, 1944. The incident also led to the routine reconnaissance by the Scouts of enemy territory before each troop insertion, including those in New Guinea and the Philippines. The information gathered by the Scouts provided those up the chain of command with the information necessary to alter strategies and procedures to be used during assaults. Commanders who were fortunate enough to receive and use the information claimed that the Scouts saved many lives.

The raid on Cabanatuan is perhaps the most famous of all the Alamo Scouts' missions. On January 27, 1945, Lieutenants

William Nellist and Thomas Roundville led two teams to reconnoiter the POW camp at Cabanatuan in the Philippines. Lieutenant Colonel Henry Mucci and Captain Robert Prince of the Sixth Ranger Battalion, guided by Filipino guerrillas, led 107 Rangers through enemy territory. Juan Pajota was the captain of the guerrillas and helped the raid tremendously with his knowledge of the enemy and his firepower. Two of the Scouts, disguised as locals, were able to position themselves to closely observe and map the compound. The raid took place on January 30, 1945. Captain Prince's strategy for the raid was to have his men surprise and confuse the enemy by sneaking up to the compound and opening fire on them. While they raided the compound, Captain Pajota and his men would hold off any other Japanese soldiers coming for reinforcement. During the liberation of the prisoners, only two attackers were killed, while approximately 523 Japanese were killed or wounded. The liberation of the Cabanatuan POW camp was such a great victory that all the men were awarded medals. Lieutenant Colonel Mucci and Captain Prince received the Distinguished Service Cross, the other officers received the Silver Star, and all the enlisted personnel were awarded the Bronze Star. The Nellist and Roundville Scout teams also received a Presidential Unit Citation. Without the aid of the Alamo Scouts, the raid could well have been a fiasco.

With the Philippines secured, the Alamo Scouts began training for Operation Olympic, the invasion of the Japanese home islands. They were slated to perform their usual preinvasion secret reconnaissance, but the bombings of Hiroshima and Nagasaki made their mission unnecessary. They landed at Wakayama, Japan, in August 1945, but the unit was completely and without ceremony disbanded in November of 1945, at Kyoto.

Garrett Grohman

References:AlamoScouts,www.alamoscouts.org/special_forces/history.htm, 5 November 2005; Army Historical Foundation, "The Alamo Scouts," www.armyhistory.org/armyhistorical.aspx?pgID=868&id=79&exCompID=32, 4 November 2005; Nabbie, Eustace E., "The Alamo Scouts," CIA Historical Review Program, 22 September 1993, http://www.cia.gov/csi/kent_csi/docs/v03i4a08p_0001.htm; Zedric, Lance Q, *Silent Warriors of World War II: The Alamo Scouts Behind the Japanese Lines* (Oxnard, CA: Pathfinder Pub, 1995).

Almoravids

A Saharan Desert tribe known for its aggressive spread of fundamentalist Islam during the eleventh and twelfth centuries.

The nomads of the western Sahara, most notably the Sanhaja tribes, dominated the gold trade between Ghana and the Mediterranean in the eleventh century. This was a profitable pastime until Ghana seized control of the town of Awdaghust, at the southern end of the trade route. Owing to internal dissent, the Sanhaja tribes were unable to respond to this loss of revenue and power. The king of the tribes believed something needed to be done to unite his people, and he thought that religion was the key. Although Islam had been spread throughout western Africa since the eighth century, it was practiced with irregular piety. Among the Sanhaja tribes of the Sahara, the people seemed to be only nominally Muslim. When their king went on his pilgrimage to Mecca, he returned with the desire to increase his people's faithfulness. He brought with him a teach-

13

er, Ibn Yasin, to motivate his tribes to become better Muslims—a task Ibn Yasin was unable to accomplish.

Disgusted at the intransigence of the nomads, Ibn Yasin went into retreat along the west coast of Africa (some say near the mouth of the Senegal River, some say Mauritania or an island off the coast). Here he established a ribat, a fortified center for the study of religion and warfare, which attracted a following of people pious to the point of fanaticism. These "men of the ribat" came to be known as Almoravids (in Arabic, al-muribatun). When Ibn Yasin had about a thousand followers, mostly from the Sanhaja tribes, he declared a jihad, or holy war. Returning to the territory of the Sanhaja, he told his recruits to convert their people to a stronger belief or to visit God's wrath upon them. After a few defeats, the Sanhaja tribes embraced Ibn Yasin's fundamentalist stand and joined his forces, not just for religious reasons but for the promise of booty. With enlarged forces, Ibn Yasin moved north to Morocco, defeating the Berber inhabitants in 1054–1055. Here, in Ibn Yasin's homeland, the Almoravid state was established. After Ibn Yasin's death in battle in 1059, a dynasty was founded by Yusuf ibn Tashufin.

As the main Almoravid force was conquering Morocco, a smaller force attacked south with the intent of recapturing Awdaghust. They accomplished this in 1054 and ultimately attacked deeper into Ghanan territory, where they captured the capital in 1076. For a while the Almoravids instituted a strict Muslim rule in the west African state, forcing tribute and the payment of a head tax for non-Muslims. This control lasted only a few years, as the Almoravids were more concerned with pillage and profit than local improvement.

Even though they controlled both ends of the trans-Saharan trade route, they did not take advantage of it. When the Almoravids withdrew, Ghana remained disrupted, providing an opportunity for the expansion of Mali into the gold territory.

Meanwhile, the Almoravids in Morocco extended their campaign for Muslim fundamentalism into Spain. They attempted to revive the lethargic religious practices of the Islamic Spaniards and were welcomed by them to provide protection from the approaching Christian forces from Europe.

At their height, the Almoravids controlled territory from Spain through western Africa. That rule was short-lived, however. The Almoravids were in turn overthrown by another fundamentalist movement, the Almohads, who declared a jihad against them in 1122 and ultimately overthrew them in 1163. That defeat in Morocco, coupled with the inability to make a profit at the southern extreme of their holdings in the gold region of Ghana, brought the Almoravids to a rather abrupt end. The legacy of the Almoravid reign is mixed. It did not introduce Islam into Ghana, but it did accelerate the spread of the religion into the interior of western Africa along the Niger River to Mali and the Songhay empires. The Almoravids also acted as a solidifying influence for the tribes of the Maghrib in northwest Africa. By building their capital at Marrakesh, they laid the foundation for the modern nation of Morocco. Both in Morocco and in the Sahara, the tribes were firm in their Islamic faith, but the fundamentalism the Almoravids preached did not last much past their demise.

References: Fage, J. D., *A History of West Africa* (London: Cambridge University Press, 1969); Hallett, Robin, *Africa to 1875* (Ann Arbor: University of Michigan Press, 1970); Trimingham, *J. S., Islam in West Africa* (London: Oxford University Press, 1962).

Amazons

A legendary tribe of warrior women reported in ancient accounts.

No account of warriors would be complete without reference to the Amazons, who appear in the earliest Greek legends, predating Homer and the Trojan War. The most famous Amazon population supposedly resided in the Caucasus between the Black and Caspian Seas along the Thermidon River. Concrete evidence of their existence is lacking, but a society of female warriors in this region was also referred to in Chinese and Cherkessian folklore. If they were indeed mythical, an amazing amount of detail concerning their lifestyle is extant, differing mainly in detail rather than substance.

It is assumed by some that the society first appeared in the wake of warfare that seriously depleted the male population. The females, apparently trained for combat, turned away from a male-dominated society to establish a matriarchy in which males were either completely excluded or existed only around the edges of society. The most popular version of the fashion in which they maintained their population was that they would make annual forays into neighboring areas in order to engage in sexual activity strictly for the purposes of procreation. Female children born of these assignations would be retained while male children were either sent to their fathers, crippled and kept as slaves, or killed, depending on which account of the society one reads. The females reputedly were raised by the crippled slaves and nursed by mares, the mothers never feeding their children. At age eight they would have their right breasts seared by hot irons so that no mammary glands would grow. The reason for this was either to sublimate any masculine tendencies (which were believed to emanate from the right side) or to remove any obstacle to the use of a bow (assuming, one supposes, that all were right-handed). As hunters, Amazons nourished themselves by a diet of mare's milk, honey, blood, raw meat, and reeds. They apparently never acquired a taste for grain; indeed, one possible derivation of the word "amazon" is from the Greek *A-Maza*, meaning "no barley bread" or "one who lives without bread."

The Amazon society was supposedly ruled by a dual monarchy, one queen to command the armies and one to rule at the capital. They fought with double-headed axes (sagaris), a small crescent-shaped shield, bows and arrows, and short swords. They apparently adopted the lance after combat against the Greeks.

Greek folklore tells of a war with the Amazons waged by Theseus, one of the founders of Athens. He led an attack on the Amazon capital city of Themiscyra to acquire the queen's crystal and gold sword belt, the loss of which would symbolize the queen's ravishment. In one version of the story, Hercules aids Theseus in his attack on the capital while the Amazon army under Oreithyia is away defending its borders. The raiders overcame the city garrison and stole Queen Hippolyte's belt. Hercules seduced or kidnapped the queen's sister, Antiope. Oreithyia immediately launched a punitive expedition against Athens and occupied the Areopagus, besieging the Greeks on the Acropolis. The outcome of the battle is disputed, but after negotiations, the Amazons departed without having destroyed Athens. Later Greek historians located a number of sites where important events in the battle supposedly took place or where important casualties were buried.

Apparently, this marked the beginning of the end of Thermodontine Amazon power. They retained an eternal hatred of the Greeks and supposedly sent a detachment to King Priam to aid in the defense of Troy. Later populations that traveled or campaigned in western Asia reported stories of Amazon-style societies, fighting in Persia against Rome or in Russia against the Muscovites. These later descriptions often match the dress and fighting ability of the ancient Amazons, but no direct contact was ever established.

An earlier Amazon society was supposed to have existed in North Africa, the Libyan Amazons, although they did not live in the area of modern Libya, but along the Atlas Mountains of Morocco. According to legend, they derived much of their culture from a mainland colony of Atlantis. These women wore red leather armor and supposedly conquered as far as Ethiopia, Syria, and Phyrigia. There were two Amazon tribes, the Libyans and the Gorgons, who supposedly fought each other over the Atlantean colony. The Libyans under Myrine prevailed and the funeral pyres of the slain were the sites of monuments at the time of Diodorus. After this conflict, Myrine led the Libyans on campaigns into the Middle East. During their conquests, they established cities and conquered the Mediterranean islands of Samos, Lesbos, Pathmos, and Samothrace. They lost these lands later to a combined Thracian-Scythian force during which time Myrine was killed.

Strabo discussed the Amazon society of his day as maintaining a female-oriented military, but mainly for show rather than conquest. They did, however, still remove their right breast and had to remain unmarried while in the military. The society included men and marriage, but the men were relegated to domestic roles. Modern Berber and Tuareg societies emulate these practices in some ways.

Other Amazon-type societies have been reported around the world. The Gagans also lived in North Africa and killed baby boys until the group was converted to Christianity. They maintained a female-dominated government. Arabian sources describe a Hamitic Amazon tribe between the Nile and the Red Sea who fought with wonderfully wrought lances. Herodotus wrote of the Sauromatians on the far side of the Don River in Russia, a mixture of Amazon and Scythian, whose offspring, the Sarmatians, practiced Amazon ways. Pliny said they could not have children until they had first killed three male enemies. The earliest of the Amazon societies could have been an army led by Euryple, capturing Babylon in 1760 BCE. Pope Pius II, before he reached the pontificate, wrote in his *Historia Bohemica* of the kingdom of Libussa and Valeska in central Europe, describing a Bohemian girls' war. Finally, the Amazon River supposedly got its name from the resistance of a female army encountered by Portuguese explorers in the 1500s.

Did Amazons really exist? That can probably never be proven, but the multiple mentions throughout history and literature, with details overlapping in so many cultural references, imply the existence of some sort of female-dominated society as the basis for such a legend.

References: Diner, Helen, *Mothers and Amazons* (New York: The Julian Press, 1965); Herodotus, *The Histories,* trans. Aubrey de Selincourt (Baltimore: Penguin, 1954); Strabo, *Geography,* trans. Horace Leonard Jones (Cambridge: Harvard University Press, 1966).

ANZACs

Soldiers from Australia and New Zealand whose name derived from the words "Australia and New Zealand Army Corps."

When World War I began on August 4, 1914 Great Britain called on its empire for assistance. One of the first and largest responses came from Australia, which immediately promised 20,000 men. The number of volunteers was so much higher, however, that the authorities were able to select the cream of the crop of young Australian manhood. This meant that the members of the army, which came to be called the Australian Imperial Force (AIF), were in peak physical condition. By September 21, the troops were in uniform, organized into units, equipped, and ready to travel. It took until early November before sufficient transport could be arranged, however. When the AIF left western Australia, it had acquired a large number of New Zealand volunteers as well.

As the convoy approached the Suez Canal en route to Britain, force commander Major General Sir W. T. Bridges received word from London that the Ottoman Empire had just entered the war on the side of the Central Powers. General Bridges was instructed to debark in Egypt for training and to await orders for action against the Turks. The forces from the two nations of the British Empire were combined into the Australia and New Zealand Army Corps, hence the acronym "ANZAC." The ANZACs trained in the desert outside Cairo and adapted themselves to the drier climate of the Mediterranean. They were physically ready for action when orders came in the spring of 1915 to go into combat against the Turks.

The Turks had focused most of their attention on their traditional enemy, Russia, and the Russian government appealed to Britain and France to do something to ease the pressure. Britain already had an expedition in Mesopotamia working its way up the Tigris River. This diverted some Turkish troops, but a larger diversionary attack was necessary. Furthermore, the fighting in France had quickly turned from the rapid attack and response of the early weeks of the war into the stalemate of trench warfare. First Lord of the Admiralty Winston Churchill proposed a plan to both aid the Russians and accomplish a dramatic victory in the Mediterranean, a feat that was seemingly impossible in France. Churchill believed that a naval assault on the Dardanelles, the straits that connected the Mediterranean with the Ottoman capital of Constantinople, could possibly force Turkey out of the war completely and rob Germany of an ally. Although the naval bombardment of the forts guarding the Dardanelles was initially successful, minefields turned the ships back. The Allied governments then decided to send in the army to secure the area that the navy could not sail past. It was on the beaches of the Gallipoli peninsula, the western flank of the Dardanelles straits, to which the ANZACs were committed.

The invasion force, under the command of General Sir Ian Hamilton, consisted of a British and a French division as well, but it was the ANZACs who formed the bulk of the force and became the most famous force in the battle. Landing a mile north of their assigned target beach on April 25, 1915, the ANZACs found themselves on a narrow strand at the foot of a cliff from which well-placed Turkish machine guns

Anzac soldier giving water to a wounded Turk, in a photograph taken circa 1916.

swept the soldiers. The earlier naval assault had caught the Turks by surprise, but they were well prepared for the arrival of the army troops. Unable to return to their boats and unwilling to stand and be slaughtered, the ANZACs scaled the bluffs and dislodged the Turks from the top. They quickly followed the retreating Turks onto still higher ground a few hundred yards inland, and elements of the ANZAC force actually reached the highest elevation about a half mile inland, from where they could see the waters of the straits. However, the disarray caused by the mistake in the landings, as well as the almost individual nature of the fighting, caused the AN-ZAC commanders to order a withdrawal of the most forward elements in order for the force to regroup and prepare for Turkish reinforcements. Had the forward elements been reinforced instead, the invasion probably would have been a success. Instead, the Turks were allowed to bring in their reserves to the highest ground and the quick operation turned into a eight-month stalemate reminiscent of the fighting taking place in France.

The Australians and New Zealanders who fought at Gallipoli suffered from the weather as well as enemy assaults, and heavy casualties were reported. The poor logistical planning by the British commanders, as well as the difficulties of the rocky terrain, conspired against them.

Their determination and courage were so impressive to the Turks, however, that many of the positions the ANZACs defended retain to this day the names given to them by the foreigners during the battle. For example, the landing area where the men came ashore is still called ANZAC Cove. Colonel (later General) John Monash, a brigade commander at Gallipoli, wrote about the Australians in the force: "I have had plenty of opportunity of comparing them with the troops of British regular units and Territorials, and the British officers are the first to admit that for physique, dash, enterprise, and sublime courage, the Australians are head and shoulders above any others.... In spite, however, of our heavy losses (a total of over half the brigade) the men, as I say, are cheerful, not to say jolly, and are only too eagerly awaiting the next advance. I am convinced that there are no troops in the world equal to the Australians in cool daring, courage, and endurance" (Firkins, 1972). The New Zealanders performed just as well.

The most successful part of the entire Gallipoli operation from the Allied standpoint, however, was the withdrawal. Although the Turks had mounted a stout defense and were not unaware of the Allied retreat, the ANZACs withdrew from their positions, assembled on the beaches, and were ferried out to the transports, all without the loss of a single soldier. The casualties had been high: the New Zealanders lost approximately 3,000 dead and 5,000 wounded of the 10,000 men in the ANZAC force, while the Australians lost some 7,000 combined casualties. The anniversary of the landing, April 25, is called ANZAC Day and is a national holiday in both Australia and New Zealand, with memorial services and wreath-laying in almost every town in both countries.

The ANZACs were not through fighting after the Gallipoli fiasco. Some were posted to France and fought in the trenches, where they unfortunately came under the command of General Sir Hubert Gough, a particularly unimaginative commander with little regard for any soldiers who were not English. They continued to suffer heavy casualties, as did every unit in France during the war. Other Australians were sent to Mesopotamia where they were involved in the relief operations around the besieged Indian Army Sixth Division at Kut-al-Amara and for the rest of the campaign in that theater. The Australian First Light Horse Brigade served in Palestine and their charge at Beersheba in October 1918 was one of the last battles of World War I.

When World War II broke out in 1939, the empire again rapidly responded to Britain's call for aid. The Australians and New Zealanders who fought in North Africa in that war also came to be called ANZACs, but the term best denotes the World War I force. ANZAC Day observations, first practiced in 1916 in London, became annual soon thereafter and following World War II achieved the same importance as Memorial Day in the United States as an occasion to remember the dead of all the wars in which each country fought.

In one of history's tragic ironies, the Turkish republic established in 1924 joined the nations fighting the Axis in World War II and became an ally of Australia and New Zealand. The "father" of modern Turkey, Mustapha Kemal Ataturk, commanded the Turkish forces on the Gallipoli Peninsula. He oversaw the construction of a monument to the ANZACs and every year

ANZAC Day is observed in Turkey, with Turkish, Australian, and New Zealand officials in attendance. A 1934 quote of Ataturk is inscribed on the Turkish AN-ZAC memorial: "Those heroes that shed their blood and lost their lives; you are now lying in the soil of a friendly country. Therefore rest in peace. There is no difference between Johnnies and Mehemets to us where they lie side by side here in this country of ours. You, the mothers, who sent their sons from far-away countries, wipe away your tears; your sons are now lying in our bosom and are at peace. After having lost their lives on this land they have become our sons as well."

References: Firkins, Peter, *The Australians in Nine Wars* (London: Robert Hale & Co., 1972); Moorehead, Alan, *Gallipoli* (London: H. Hamilton, 1956); Thomson, Alastair, *ANZAC Memories* (New York: Oxford University Press, 1994).

Arab Legion

An elite defensive and peacekeeping force in Jordan from the 1920s to 1950s.

Although after World War I the winds of change blew strongly all over the globe, those winds felt even more intense to people in the Middle East, who were about to see their way of life completely inverted by the collapse of the Ottoman Empire and the occupation of their new countries by Europeans. Trans-Jordan, one of the Arab states whose status was about to be dramatically altered, responded to these changes by forming a unit that would become a permanent part of the history of the Middle East: the Arab Legion.

The Arab Legion was first created by Lt. Col. Frederick Peake, a British officer who had fought the Turks with T. E. Lawrence in the Egyptian Camel Corps, out of the need for a force to maintain order among the various Arab groups living in the British protectorate of Trans-Jordan. The British High Commissioner in Jerusalem gave Peake the task of organizing a force to guard the Amman-Palestine road from Arab raiders, and another force to guard the British officials in the southern city of Kerak. The Trans-Jordanian king, after receiving sovereignty from the British in 1923, merged his police force and army with Peake's force to form the Arab Legion.

They successfully kept order and things were quiet until Bedouin raiding parties, made up of religious zealots from Saudi Arabia called "Ikhwan," began raiding the southern villages of Trans-Jordan. In 1930, another British officer, John Bagot Glubb (called by his men Glubb Pasha), was charged with creating a force to end these raids. He went down to those southern villages and began trying to recruit the people of the villages to join his force. These people, called the Huwaitat, were tremendously uncooperative with Glubb because, after having suffered abuse by the Turkish government, they were suspicious of outsiders. He was finally able to win them over when he told them that if they didn't want to protect themselves, he would bring others to do it for them, and to the Huwaitat, this was unacceptable. Glubb was able to get 90 men to join his Desert Patrol, and by May 1931, he had significantly reduced the number of raids in the area. During this time, his southern force had also grown to about 250 men, a fifth of the entire Arab Legion.

In 1939, as World War II began, the Arab Legion underwent a significant change. Peake retired and was replaced by Glubb, who now commanded the 2,000-man Legion. As the Legion grew, it was also modernized, and it came to include a 350-man force of mechanized infantry. The Middle East was not isolated from the events of the raging war, and when a pro-German party seized power in Baghdad, Glubb's Arab Legion accompanied a British force in the campaign to quell the uprising. Along with assistance from the RAF, the Arab Legion and the British force won the battle and reestablished a pro-British government in Iraq.

As World War II continued, the Arab Legion continued to fight alongside British forces in Syria, and they also maintained the peace in the areas surrounding the Bedouin tribes. By the end of World War II, the force had arrived at a strength of 16,000, the highest it would reach. As the war ended and men returned home, the number decreased to 4,000 men. There was also a growing number of Arab officers in the Legion, which Glubb saw as the first stages of a British withdrawal from the Middle East.

This withdrawal thrust the region into a very trying time, because as the British removed themselves, the Jews were beginning to immigrate to Palestine, and talk of a new Jewish state was growing. As the Jews finally began fighting for independence, Glubb was forced back into battle. His Arab Legion was called into battle at Hebron, after Jewish forces attacked Arab reinforcements bound for Jerusalem. Seeing that this would be a difficult battle, Glubb padded his numbers with local villagers, who answered the call to jihad. The Jews fought hard and held the Arabs off for 24 hours of continuous fighting, but the Arabs prevailed. Without Glubb's knowledge, some of the villagers he had enlisted brutally killed men who had surrendered to them. This first battle made

Glubb realize the difficulty and brutality of the coming war.

As Arab diplomats met in Jerusalem, Glubb recommended they accept the U.N. proposal for a Jewish state, because he wanted to avoid the urban fighting that would certainly take place in Jerusalem if war did break out. The Arabs, though, felt victory would come easily, and they responded with violence to Israel's declaration of independence. King Abdullah of Trans-Jordan ordered Glubb to march his desert warriors into the streets of Jerusalem to combat the Jews.

The Arab Legion actually gained control of valuable strategic locations fairly quickly. After taking control of the Old City, they began wiping the Jewish forces out of the Judean hill country, an action Glubb knew would secure Jerusalem from any attacks from Jewish reinforcements. After doing this, Glubb launched an attack of the last stronghold of the Jews in the Old City, the Notre Dame Hospice. Despite heavy losses, he was able to force the Jews to deplete their supplies so significantly that they were compelled to surrender. Although other Arab forces around Palestine were beaten back, the Arab Legion had won Jerusalem for Trans-Jordan.

A cease fire was declared a few weeks after this battle, and Glubb, seeing his unit nearly out of supplies and in a position good for negotiations, wanted to have peace and take his land for Trans-Jordan. Other Arab nations refused to make peace, however, because they thought they could force all the Jews out of the area by total victory in this war. The war then continued, and the Israelis were able to mount a counterattack and take back some of their lost possessions. The war ended on January 9, 1949, and soon after King Abdullah renamed his nation the Arab Hashemite Kingdom of Jordan.

This kingdom also then severed its ties with Britain in its newfound sense of independence. Glubb returned with his legion to police the frontier, but when Abdullah was assassinated and a demand came from Jordanians to remove any British influences, the new king, Hussein, fired Glubb. Glubb, the mastermind of this great force, now had to retire to Britain, where he was knighted and devoted his life to study.

The Arab Legion was then absorbed into a new Jordanian army, made of both Legion forces and fresh conscripts. It no longer exists in name, but its spirit continues in the flag of Jordan, which to this day keeps the colors of green, red, and black, the same colors of the Arab Legion's pennant. The Legion participated in some of the most critical battles that have shaped our world today. The Arab-Israeli War is one of the major causes of the Arab world's hostility toward the West today, and had Glubb's forces achieved the total victory Arab leaders sought, the situation in the Middle East would certainly be different. In any case, the Arab Legion's hand in the development of independent Arab states is certainly noteworthy, for it established Jordan as a leading player in Middle Eastern politics, a position it still holds today.

Trent Melcher

References: Castlewitz, David M. "Glubb Pasha and the Arab Legion." Military History: Apr. 1998; Lunt, James, *The Arab Legion* (London: Constable and Robinson, 1999); Rothwell, Steve, "The Arab Legion," http://homepages.force9. net/rothwell/trans-jo.htm.

Army of Northern Virginia

The primary military force of the Confederate States of America (1861–1865).

The 11 states of the United States that seceded from the Union in 1860–1861 faced an almost impossible task. Creating a successful country with the governmental form of a confederation is difficult enough, but by firing on Union troops at Fort Sumter in Charleston Harbor, the seceding states provoked a war that they almost certainly could not win. The Confederacy's economy, based nearly exclusively on agriculture, lacked the resources necessary to fight an industrialized enemy, yet with a motivation that drew on the inspiration of the American Revolution, the rebellious states willingly engaged in the Civil War. Whatever the wisdom of their cause, the armies they fielded displayed remarkable courage and tenacity, with the Army of Northern Virginia leading the effort. The Confederacy named its armies after their theater of operations, hence their two primary forces were this and the Army of Tennessee. It was the leadership of its commander, Robert E. Lee, that imparted special status to the Army of Northern Virginia. Lee led that force from June 1862 through the final surrender in April 1865.

Lee was regarded by U.S. Army Commanding General Winfield Scott as the most talented of American military leaders, and he encouraged President Abraham Lincoln to appoint Lee commander of the Union armies. Lee, after extreme soul-searching, decided he could not make war against his home state of Virginia, so he resigned his commission and joined the Confederate army. He served in the background for the first year of the war, but

General Robert E. Lee. Library of Congress, Prints & Photographs Divison, Civil War Photographs [reproduction number LC-DIG-cwpbh-03115].

upon the wounding of General Joseph Johnston in the Peninsular Campaign of June 1862, Lee was appointed commander of the Army of Northern Virginia. He initially had a poor reputation with the Confederate troops owing to his dedication to digging defenses for the capital city of Richmond, Virginia—a project that brought him the nickname "King of Spades" and "Granny" Lee. Once having taken over from Johnston, however, Lee proved himself anything but conservative.

He knew his opponent, George McClellan, from West Point, and was aware of his overly cautious temperament. Lee therefore attacked McClellan's far larger force. Lee lost the opening battle, but McClellan withdrew. In the Seven Days Campaign that followed, Lee lost four of five battles, yet it was McClellan who retreated from the outskirts of Richmond back to the port city of Yorktown. By sheer aggression and audacity, Lee had convinced McClellan that the Union faced an overwhelming force. Lee's knowledge of his opponents, gathered from years of serving alongside them or knowing them from the U.S. Military Academy, enabled him time and again to outthink opposing generals. His daring, which he showed by attacking with smaller forces, dividing his forces in the face of the enemy, and launching surprise attacks, continually baffled his opponents and turned Lee into an icon of the Confederate army.

Lee's leadership emboldened his men who, like their enemies, came to believe Lee could perform any feat and outsmart any enemy. His men responded by fighting with ferocity born of confidence and loyalty. As the war progressed, however, that was the mainstay of the Confederate effort, for the effective Union blockade of Southern harbors made maintenance of the army increasingly difficult. The Confederacy's defensive strategy forced its armies to fight and live off its own land, which soon became unable to support them. Victories over Union generals John Pope in August 1862, Ambrose Burnside in December 1862, and Joseph Hooker in May 1863, as well as the inability of McClellan to operate effectively when opposed to Lee at Antietam in September 1862, all served to enhance the status of Lee's army. However, continued fighting without steady supplies made the army increasingly ragged. After his defeat of Hooker at Chancellorsville in 1863, Lee stated that feeding his men caused him much more concern than did fighting Union armies.

It was that need for supplies that convinced Lee to take the war to the North in June 1863, both to live off the enemy's land for a while and hopefully to encourage the Northern peace advocates as well as potential European allies. The Army of Northern Virginia marched through Maryland into Pennsylvania in late June. The residents of both states were appalled at the state of the Confederate troops and incredulous that such a rabble could defeat their Union soldiers. Rumors of a supply of shoes at the small town of Gettysburg, Pennsylvania, brought about a skirmish that led to the battle that changed the fortunes of the Confederacy. Lee was once again outnumbered, and finally the steadiness of new Union General Gordon Meade allowed that numerical superiority to tell. Unable to turn the flanks of the Union position on July 2, Lee gambled that the attacks had weakened the Union center sufficiently to allow a breakthrough there. He ordered some 10,000 men under the command of George Pickett to attack the Union position on Cemetery Ridge in a frontal assault. His men unhesitatingly followed his orders into the teeth of overwhelming artillery fire that caused almost 75 percent losses. When Lee openly wept and apologized to the survivors for ordering the assault, their response was to apologize to him for their failure and to volunteer to try again.

Lee withdrew from Gettysburg on July 4 back to defensive positions in Virginia. More than half of the 75,000 men he had taken into Gettysburg had failed to return with him to Virginia. He had failed in his plan to exploit northern supplies, but his army was allowed to recover by cautious Union generalship. Through the remainder of 1863 and into 1864, Lee labored to rebuild his shattered forces, while the legendary army held the Northern forces at bay by reputation alone. Only with the arrival of Ulysses Grant in May 1864 did Union caution come to an end. Grant brought more than 100,000 men into Virginia, almost double Lee's strength, and throughout the month of May lost battle after battle, yet continued to maneuver ever closer to Richmond. At the Wilderness, Spotsylvania, the North Anna River, and Cold Harbor, Confederate forces exacted a terrible toll on Union armies, yet Grant had replacements while Lee did not. In June, Grant was stymied at Petersburg, south of Richmond, and obliged to lay siege for nine months. Lee's army fought to maintain the railroad lines into Petersburg that brought whatever meager sustenance they received, but when the last line fell to Union troops in April 1865, the Army of Northern Virginia, down to less than 10,000 men, had no choice but to flee westward. Finally surrounded on April 8, Lee met with Grant to surrender at Appomattox Courthouse on April 9, 1865.

By the end of the war, the Army of Northern Virginia was fighting almost on courage alone, and in many cases even that failed. Desertions after Gettysburg and during the siege at Petersburg hurt the Confederate cause, but in reality had little effect on the final outcome. Still, Lee inspired almost fanatical devotion and even his opponents could not help but respect and praise him. His men came to call themselves "Lee's Miserables," referring to the recently published Hugo novel. They had suffered privations caused not only by the nature of warfare itself, but also by the inability of a confederation-style government to harness national resources and cooperation. In every battle the Army of Northern Virginia fought, it was outnumbered, but almost always inflicted greater casualties on its enemies than it received itself. Had Lee decided not to surrender but to disperse his men into the Virginia hills and fight a guerrilla war, those remaining would certainly have followed him. As one Texas soldier said of Lee after the battle of the Wilderness, "I'd charge Hell itself for that old man."

In Arlington National Cemetery, built on the grounds of Robert E. Lee's confiscated estate, stands a memorial to the Confederate dead. "Not for fame or reward, not for place or rank, not lured by ambition or goaded by necessity, but in simple obedience to duty as they understood it, these men suffered all, sacrificed all, endured all. . .and died."

References: Foote, Shelby, *The Civil War, a Narrative*, 3 vols. (New York: Vintage Books, 1958–1972); MacPherson, James, *Ordeal by Fire* (New York: McGraw-Hill, 1982); Smith, Page, *Trial by Fire* (New York: McGraw-Hill, 1982).

Aryans

An ancient Indo-European population that conquered and settled in India during the second millennium BCE.

The earliest known civilization in India was that of the Harappans, who established well-organized cities in the valley of the Indus River in the third millennium BCE. By about 2000 BCE, that civilization was beginning to fade, probably because of climatic changes that brought about shifts in the rivers and resultant widespread flooding. By sheer coincidence, as the Harappans were weakening, a group of invaders appeared from the steppes of the Caucasus. The Aryans were mostly nomadic, herding sheep, horses, and cattle, and (like most nomadic peoples) were more warlike than the agricultural inhabitants of northern India. Both by migration and by force of arms, they came to dominate the area of the upper Indus valley and over time spread eastward down the Ganges.

The Aryans took their name from the word in their language, Sanskrit, that means "noble." The Aryans themselves are identified as a language, not a racial group. The fact that their area of origin made them lighter-skinned than the people they conquered has nothing to do with the language they spoke, so equating "Aryan" with "white" is incorrect; this nineteenth-century concept was reinforced by some twentieth-century racists. The original Aryans did, however, institute a practice that called for separation of their people from the conquered. Aryan society comprised four classes that are the basis of the caste system that dominates India to this day: priests, warriors, merchants/artisans, and laborers. The conquered peoples of India became "outcast[e]s," or the "untouchables" of modern India.

Aryan weaponry included bows and arrows, hurling spears, and battle-axes. Aryans probably fought from chariots, thus easily overwhelming whatever type of foot soldier that may have opposed them in India. They did not conquer in order to spread culture, but to acquire wealth, especially cattle. In fact, their word for "war" is translated as "desire for more cows." Once they established themselves in India, each region was ruled by a king who was somewhat limited in his power by an advisory council of warriors. Near the top of the society they imposed were the warriors, or Kshatriyas, who (like the Vikings) believed that the ultimate honor was to die in battle; and the ultimate disgrace, to die in bed. Their primary god was Indra, whose hard-fighting and hard-living ways mirrored the Aryan warrior ideal. Contemporary literature described the Aryans as "a rowdy crew fond of beer, who engaged in bragging about their gambling, fighting, horse-racing, and womanizing" (Stearns et al., 1992).

The Aryans ultimately settled down to an agricultural way of life, but their early years in India were characterized by their primary herding ways. The plains of northern India provided good grazing land, and their horse and cattle herds grew. Cattle became the most valuable of commodities, possibly foreshadowing the sacredness of cattle in the Hindu faith. The Aryans' horsemanship was famous and was the reason for their military successes, as the Harappans had neither cavalry nor chariots. Considering the Aryans' Indo-European heritage, their common use of the horse is to be expected, as later steppe peoples like the Scythians were master riders as well.

The greatest legacy of the Aryans is the religious works passed down originally through the priesthood. The Vedas are a collection of religious rituals handed down through oral tradition and finally committed to writing when that skill was introduced about 700 BCE. The ceremonies practiced and the gods worshipped through the Vedas laid the groundwork for the introduction of the Hindu faith, the dominant religion of India for some 2,000 years.

As conquerors of northern India early in the second millennium BCE, and of the northeastern plains and Ganges River valley between 1000 and 500 BCE, the Aryans became the dominant inhabitants of India as they settled into agricultural pursuits. This less mobile pursuit bred—as it almost always does—a less martial society, but, thanks to their mountainous frontiers, the Indians managed to remain fairly isolated from later conquerors. Alexander the Great spent two years fighting and negotiating in northwestern India, installing a Greek administration in some areas. After his death, however, Chandragupta Maurya overthrew the bureaucracy and established an Indian empire. Not until the Islamic invasion of India in the 800s CE did outside forces have much luck in penetrating the subcontinent.

References: Gokhale, Balkrishna, *Ancient India: History and Culture* (Bombay and New York: Asia Publishing House, 1959); Stearns, Peter, et al., *World Civilizations* (New York: HarperCollins, 1992); Wheeler, Radha, *Early India and Pakistan* (New York: Praeger, 1959); Wolpert, Stanley, *India* (Englewood Cliffs, NJ: Prentice-Hall, 1965).

Ashanti

A West African tribe in the nineteenth century, known for its local dominance and resistance to European colonization.

The predecessors of the population that inhabits modern-day Ghana in northwestern Africa were the Akan tribe, probably descended from immigrants from the western Sudan region. They mined the gold available in the region and engaged in profitable trade with both Muslim and later European merchants. The cross-Sahara trade in gold to the Mediterranean coast made the source of that wealth almost mythical. When the Portuguese began exploring southward along the African continent's western shore, the area of the Akan people came to be called the Gold Coast.

The dominant tribe among the southern Akan peoples were the Ashanti (or Asante). In the mid-1600s the Ashanti expanded from their homeland around Lake Bosumtwi to encompass most of the central forest region of the country. The primary military leader in this era was Oti Akenten (reigned circa 1630–1660), who either conquered his neighbors or brought them into a confederation as allies. Under his descendant, Osei Tutu, at the end of the century, the confederacy was transformed into an empire, with its capital established at Kumasi. Osei Tutu took the title *asantehene*, or "King of the Ashanti." He allowed the subordinate tribes to retain their local customs and took the chief of each into a tribal council, both practices creating a relatively easy assimilation into the empire. The assimilated tribes exercised local autonomy, but in times of outside threat united under the asantehene's direction. By the 1820s, the Ashanti held sway over a huge area that encompassed three subordinate tribes and abutted the coastal possessions of the Fanti and other tribes that carried on trade with the Europeans.

The first Europeans, the Portuguese, built forts on the coast to protect their trading interests, which at first was gold but soon came to include slaves. Over time, the Portuguese were joined or supplanted by Dutch, Danish, and even Swedish interests. However, by the 1820s, the primary European power along the coast was Great Britain. All the Europeans stayed along the coast and traded with the interior tribes through local representatives. As long as the goods came to them, the Europeans were happy to leave the interior jungle well enough alone. The British bought out other European business interests and forts until, by the 1870s, they controlled the coastline completely and declared the Gold Coast a British colony. It was the decades-old British ban on slavery, however, that began to bring the British into affairs in the interior. That, coupled with the traditional Ashanti expansionist policies, guaranteed conflict.

In the first quarter of the nineteenth century, the Europeans dealt with the Ashanti peacefully, recognizing the preeminence of their inland empire. As long as trade goods arrived at the coast with a minimum of trouble, the Ashanti were free to do as they liked with their neighbors. It was when the British attempted to recruit coastal tribes to aid in the suppression of the slave trade that fighting started. Governor Charles MacCarthy tried to rouse the coastal Fanti and Ga tribes to resist Ashanti power, but in 1824 MacCarthy died leading native troops in a disastrous defeat. When the Ashanti attacked again in 1826 they were turned back, but their power was hardly diminished. The British attempted to consolidate the coastal tribes

into a protectorate, which was formalized by the signing of the Bond of 1844. This gave the British judicial authority over serious crimes, a greater voice in local administration, and a greater role in local defense. The British purchase of Elmina Castle, the last Dutch trading post, upset the Ashanti. They had viewed the Dutch as allies and good trading partners, and saw the British acquisition of Elmina as a closing of the Ashanti coastal trade outlet.

The Ashanti launched attacks on the coastal tribes and gained early successes, but the arrival of British reinforcements under the command of Major General Sir Garnet Wolseley set off what came to be called the Ashanti War. Wolseley brought with him an outstanding group of subordinates, most of whom later reached general's rank. He convinced the British government to supply him with battalions from three British regiments to supplement the First and Second West India Regiments and the few native troops he managed to coerce into accompanying him. As European troops fared notoriously badly in the climate of the Gold Coast, Wolseley planned his campaign to punish the Ashanti to take place in the dry months of December 1873 through February 1874. He planned on sending three columns to converge on the Ashanti capital at Komasi, but only his command encountered Ashanti forces and did any fighting; the other two columns served as little more than diversions. The single trail leading to Komasi ran through dense jungle, the occasional open ground being quite swampy. The track had, through years of use in wet weather, been worn as deep as a trench.

Wolseley tried to maintain his units in an open square formation, but the terrain kept them from holding their positions very well. Some 30 miles short of Komasi, the

British encountered their first major Ashanti force, before the village of Amoafu. Ashanti forces numbered possibly 40,000 and were positioned on the crests of low hills in a crescent formation. Their plan was to lure the British down the road into the open end of their position, then use their traditional enveloping tactics. The Ashanti used the high grass and tall trees to great advantage, but their muskets were not up to the quality of the rifles carried by Wolseley's men. Although the Ashanti warriors remained concealed, the smoke from their muskets gave away their positions and drew rifle, artillery, and rocket fire, for the British had four Congreve rocket launchers. Still, the Ashanti did have the advantage of superior numbers and knowledge of the terrain, and were also able at one point to send a body of men around the British rear. They were, in turn, outflanked by the British rear guard.

The two flanking forces of the British square made their way forward through dense jungle to take the high ground and blunt the Ashanti flanking units with rocket fire. The artillery in the center killed hundreds of Ashanti warriors. In spite of confusion (made worse by the echoing of the gunfire giving the impression of being attacked from all sides), the British and West Indian troops beat back the Ashanti force and captured Amoafu. They suffered some 250 casualties (although only three Europeans and one African dead) while inflicting possibly 2,000 casualties on the Ashanti, who had no fear of closing with their enemy if need be. The Ashanti could not, however, stand up to the artillery fire. However, they continued to harass the British column as it progressed northward, attacking at times in such great numbers that it seemed as if the entire jungle were moving. The British were able to take advantage of the deep-rutted track for cover and drove off all the Ashanti assaults.

When Wolseley's men reached Komasi, the town had been abandoned. The asantehene had fled, but left much loot behind. He also left behind evidence of why the local tribes feared the Ashanti more than they did the British: a large pile of skulls told the tale of widespread human sacrifice. Henry Stanley, traveling with the column as a war correspondent, estimated that the bones of 120,000 victims lay scattered around the area. The British burned the town, blew up the palace, and withdrew. They returned to the coast almost unmolested. The British were able after this victory to enforce a peace treaty whereby the Ashanti abandoned all their claims to coastal territories. They were also obliged to keep the road to Komasi open for trade. Gold and palm oil flowed fairly steadily to British merchants at the coast, but the Ashanti had been warriors too long to go quietly into oblivion. A rebellion in 1896 brought another British punitive expedition that again occupied Komasi, then abolished the position of asantehene. The Ashanti tried again in 1900 but another defeat broke their power for good. In 1902 the British proclaimed all Ashanti lands to be under their control, included in the jurisdiction of the governor of the Gold Coast.

Their contacts with Muslims and Europeans for centuries through the gold trade had given the Ashanti enough superior weaponry to dominate their tribal neighbors, but in the face of European arms, they could not stand. The Ashanti have been described as being an African version of the Prussians of nineteenth-century Europe in that they practiced universal military training and fielded a disciplined force that used the terrain and their numbers wisely. Had they been better armed, the outcome for them could have been quite different.

References: Farwell, Byron, *Queen Victoria's Little Wars* (New York: Harper & Row, 1972); Featherstone, Donald, *Colonial Small Wars* (Newton Abbot, Devon: David & Charles, 1973); Keegan, John, "Ashanti," in *War Monthly*, no. 7, 1974.

Assyrians

An ancient population known for its Middle Eastern empire built on terror and cruelty between the ninth and seventh centuries BCE.

Although many populations prior to the Assyrians engaged in war, the Assyrians were the first to make it a national pastime and the focus around which their society was built. Assyria's roots lay in four cities in the upper reaches of the Tigris River: Ashur, Arbela, Kalakh, and Nineveh. Their population was probably a mixture of Semites from the south, Hittites from the west, and Kurds from the north. They adopted the Sumerian language and artistic style, then further modified these by contact with Babylon. The cities grew up under the domination of the Kassites, with Shalmaneser regarded as the first Assyrian king. For the first few hundred years of their existence, the Assyrians depended on local levies to fill out the ranks of the army in time of need, with each city's governor having only a palace guard of perhaps 1,000 men as a standing force. These governors ultimately became the cadre of leaders when the Assyrians began to practice war more seriously.

The Assyrians first began to show aggressive tendencies in the latter half of the thirteenth century BCE, expanding westward toward the Euphrates and downriver to Babylon, which they held for a time. A hundred years later, Tiglath-Pileser I attacked as far as the Mediterranean, but could not hold his conquests. His successors fell into obscurity until the ninth century BCE. In the intervening 200 years, the Assyrians farmed, hunted, and defended themselves from their neighbors. King Adadnirari II began the return to expansionary ways and laid the groundwork for the coming Assyrian empire.

Through the administration of Adadnirari II's grandson, Ashurnasirpal II, the Assyrians raided downriver and westward, honing their army's skills. Babylon remained too strong in the south to conquer yet, and in the west Syria called on Phoenician and Israelite assistance to beat back an attack at the battle of Qarqar in 853 BCE. It was Tiglath-Pileser III (744–727 BCE) who finally began to conquer widely. He defeated Babylon and had himself crowned king of that city, then captured Damascus and solidified his control. It was this king who really became the first emperor, not only of the conquered territories but of his own land. No longer did each of the four cities exercise autonomy. The palace guards of earlier days became the core of a new standing army that was in almost constant action for more than 100 years.

Tiglath-Pileser III maintained forces primarily of infantry, but also of cavalry and chariots, in a ratio of approximately 100 infantry to 10 cavalry to one chariot. The infantry was mostly made up of Assyrian peasant stock, armed with spears and shields in a phalanx-type formation. The large rectangular shield was usually used to protect an archer, with the foot soldier and archer fighting in pairs. Carrying up to 50 arrows, massed archers could deliver extremely deadly fire. Lancers and slingers

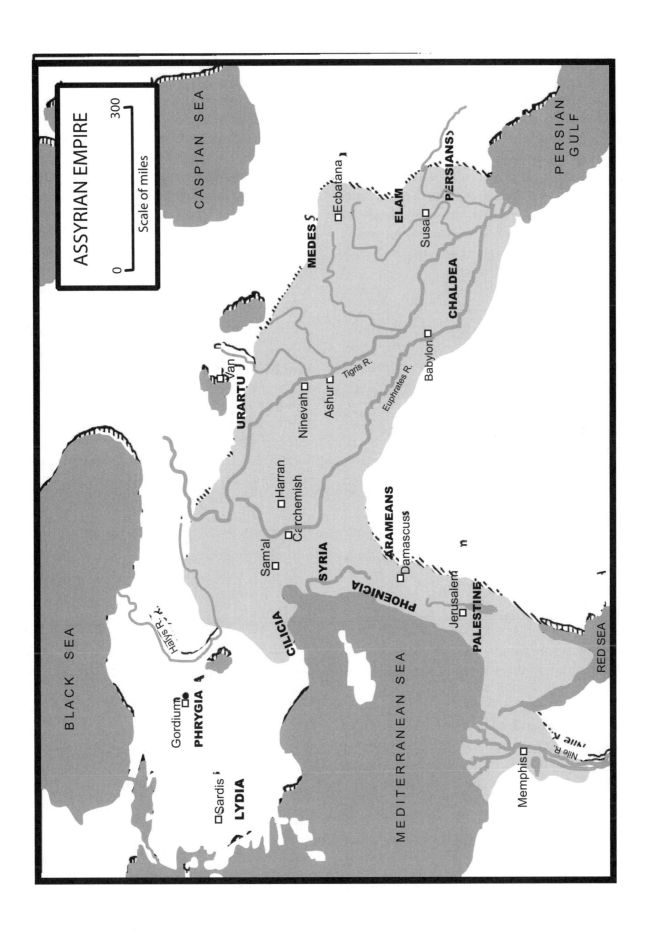

ASSYRIAN EMPIRE

Scale of miles

0   300

31

were also employed. The cavalry was of heavy and light types and employed en masse riding horses often bred especially for them by the government. The cavalry frequently rode in pairs, one rider controlling both horses and using his shield or lance while the other rider used his bow. Later, a third and then fourth man was added to carry shields for protecting the others. The chariots were used either in the attack as a shock force or around the flanks for harassment and pursuit.

When the Assyrians conquered a country, its surviving army was obliged to fight alongside them. This gave the Assyrian army a certain diversity in weaponry, depending on the nationality absorbed: Slingers, mounted archers, and light cavalry all joined the heavier-armed Assyrian forces. Perhaps the key element in Assyrian superiority, however, was the widespread use of iron, which had previously been less available and normally only used in the weapons of the nobility who could afford it. This gave the Assyrians a great edge over those societies still dependent on bronze. The Assyrians also perfected siege tactics that had been developed centuries earlier in other societies. Battering rams, along with sapping and mining of the city walls, were the preferred methods. Sometimes earthen ramps were constructed to allow the soldiers to overcome the walls.

Once a province was defeated, the Assyrians occupied it with a royally appointed governor and a garrison for whatever forts may have survived. All were under the direct control of the king, known to himself and his subjects as "the great king, the legitimate king, the king of the world, king of Assyria, king of all the four rims of the earth, king of kings, prince without rival, who rules from the Upper Sea to the Lower Sea." Kings were strong men, for

they had to both lead their armies in battle and guard against palace intrigues. They also kept a tight rein on their governors by appointing family members or by stationing spies (openly or covertly) to their entourage.

The Assyrians ruled their conquered territories ruthlessly, extracting money, supplies, and manpower. Royal records brag on the number of enemy soldiers slain and prisoners tortured. For example, Ashurnasirpal II boasted, "I destroyed them, tore down the walls and burned the town with fire; I caught the survivors and impaled them on stakes in front of their towns" (Starr, 1965). It was this treatment that proved the Assyrians' ultimate undoing.

Successive kings spread Assyrian power southeastward down the Tigris and Euphrates as far as the Persian Gulf and southwestward past the Mediterranean coast into Egypt as far up the Nile as Thebes. In spite of the terror they spread, they also spread urbanization, the culture of Babylon (which they had adopted as their own), and the worship of their gods (primarily Ashur). Trade and industry expanded and Assyrians began to make profits other than by looting. These were not enough, however, to replace the great wealth that plunder brought in, so the still weak economy could not stand on its own. Nevertheless, it was Assyrian high-handedness that caused such resentment that when the army was not engaged in conquering new territory, it was putting down revolts in provinces already occupied.

The constant warfare both on the frontiers and against captured peoples proved too much of a drain on the army. The Assyrian peasant, who was its backbone, came to be too rare a commodity, and dependence on an increasing number of foreign troops proved unfeasible. It was just too difficult to maintain loyalty with terror, and few troops were willing to voluntarily aid in the suppression of their own people. This weakening of the Assyrian army's quality, coupled with constant revolts against its rule, brought the Assyrians to a swift downfall. In 612 BCE, attacks by the Scythians from the Caucasus and the Medes to the east brought the Assyrian Empire down in a matter of weeks. The main beneficiary of the Assyrian rule proved to be Cyrus the Persian, whose benevolent manner was so radically different that cities and provinces often surrendered to his army without a fight in order to enjoy the relative blessings of his leadership. The Persian Empire inherited some of Assyria's military methods along with its imperial administration, and their establishment of control over what had been Assyria's dominion was swift, relatively painless, and profitable.

References: Starr, Chester, *A History of the Ancient World* (New York: Oxford University Press, 1965); Wise, Terence, *Ancient Armies of the Middle East* (London: Osprey Publishing, 1981); Wiseman, D. J., "The Assyrians," in John Hackett, ed., *Warfare in the Ancient World* (London: Sidgwick and Jackson, 1989).

Aztecs

The dominant population, conquering Mexico immediately prior to Spanish conquest and colonization of the fifteenth century.

Much of Central America was dominated by the Toltec peoples until their downfall about 1200 CE. The power vacuum that followed was coincidental with the arrival of nomadic tribes from the north. One of these tribes was from Aztlan and came to be known as Aztecs, or People from Aztlan. They drifted south into the valley of central Mexico and became subject to whatever power was able to achieve temporary hegemony. The Aztecs ultimately settled on the western side of Lake Texcoco, where they began to adapt themselves to the already established practice of building "floating gardens" of built-up silt. Here they established the city of Tenochtitlan in the mid-fourteenth century. A second city, Tlatelolco, was built by a second Aztec faction. The two cities put themselves under the protection of rival powers: Tenochtitlan under Culhuacan, Tlatelolco under the Tepanecs.

Through the latter part of the fourteenth century, the Tepanecs came to dominate the valley and expanded their power across the mountains to the west to encompass an area of perhaps 50,000 square kilometers. This consolidation was performed by the Tepanec king, Tezozomoc, but after his death in 1423 the various city-states he had dominated began to rebel. Three powers joined together into a Triple Alliance to replace the Tepanecs, and one of those three was the Aztecs of Tenochtitlan. Despite the occasional disagreement, the three worked fairly well together and dominated central Mexico for 90 years. From 1431 to 1465 they consolidated their hold over the former Tepanec domain, and then began a period of expansion. The Aztecs came to be the dominant partner in the triumvirate, but the three tribes collectively spread the empire from the Atlantic to the Pacific and as far southward as the modern-day border of Mexico and Guatemala. Only two tribes remained recalcitrant, the Tlaxaltecs and the Tarascans. The Aztecs established garrisons along disputed borders and occasionally warred with

Aztec priest performing the sacrificial offering of a living human's heart to the war god Huitzilopochtli, from the Codex Maglabecchi. Library of Congress, Prints & Photographs Division [reproduction number LC-USZC4-743]

them, although they never subjugated them.

The Aztecs led the expansion for a number of reasons. Mainly, they were expanding their trading routes while incorporating a larger tax base among the conquered peoples. They also fought for religious reasons. The Aztecs worshipped, among other gods, the god of the sun, Huitzilopochtli. The Aztec religion taught that history moved in cycles, the end of which came with the destruction of the sun. To stay healthy and shining, the sun god required sacrifices to eat, and the Aztecs went conquering for sacrificial offerings. The pyramids that dominated the city of Tenochtitlan were large altars that saw the daily execution of prisoners of

war. On days of special celebration, several thousand might be sacrificed. This need for offerings drove the Aztecs to conquest, but did not create loyal subjects.

The Aztecs developed a highly structured military organization, led by the nobility and the elite warriors. The warriors were in the front ranks, dressed in elaborate costumes festooned with feathers and animal skins. Their primary weapons were wooden swords with chunks of obsidian embedded along the edges to create a razor-sharp blade. Obsidian was also the primary material for spear heads and javelin points. The javelins were propelled by *atlatls* (spear throwers), which greatly increased their range. Slings and bows and arrows made up the missile weapons.

Peculiar to the Aztec society was the practice of "flower wars," or *xochiyaoyotl*. These were conflicts of relatively low intensity, in which small bands of warriors engaged in what was almost ritual combat. Both sides would agree in advance to fight at an appointed time and place and with an equal number of troops. Prior to the battle, ceremonies were performed to honor the gods. The two forces approached each other with battle cries and the pounding of swords on leather shields. Combat, once begun, broke into individual duels. The main object was not to inflict death and defeat but to wound and capture enemy soldiers to be used in sacrifices. Units would be rotated in and out of the battle every quarter hour or so, and the battles could last for days.

Sometimes these flower wars were preludes to invasion and conquest, but they could also be used both for training young soldiers and exercising political influence without the costs of a major war. As the Aztec Empire stretched over too much territory to be ruled directly, the threat of retribution was the chief Aztec tool in maintaining sufficient control to keep the tribute flowing. By winning these flower wars, the Aztecs could keep their warriors in shape and demonstrate their prowess to neighbors. Also, by using only a small number of troops in these conflicts, other units could be employed simultaneously capturing villages and towns allied to the formal enemy in the flower war. As the season for fighting in Central America was December to April, conquests generally had to be accomplished quickly. The Aztecs found that subversion of their opponents' allies, coupled with victory in the flower wars, was often the best way to keep potential rivals from growing too strong.

When needed, however, the Aztec army could fight serious wars of annihilation, as demonstrated against tribes ranging from 150 miles north of Tenochtitlan to the borders of modern-day Guatemala. When the Spanish arrived, Hernán Cortés found the Tlaxcallan people (living just east of Tenochtitlan) to be aggressive fighters that almost wiped out his small command. Only the discipline and fire power the Spaniards demonstrated kept them alive in several battles, and that impressed the Tlaxcallans enough to ally themselves with Cortés to fight against Montezuma and the Aztecs. Had they continued to harass the Spaniards to annihilation, the history of Spanish relations with Meso-america may have been quite different.

Once in control of their empire, the Aztecs expanded and beautified the city of Tenochtitlan. The city reached a population of perhaps 200,000, which may have numbered one-fifth of the Aztec population. The total number of subject peoples might have taken the empire's population as high as six million at the start of the sixteenth century. The capital city was laid out in logical order with straight streets and many canals, along which trade moved by boats. When Montezuma II came to power in 1502, the Aztec empire was well established and he was responsible for much of the lavish architecture and decoration in the city. Tenochtitlan's sister city, Tlatelolco, which the Tenochtitlan Aztecs took under their control in 1475, became the commercial center and contained the largest market in central America. The Spaniards under Cortés, who arrived in the city in 1519, estimated that 60,000 people attended the market days. The constant need for sacrificial victims created a resentment among all the subject peoples, however, and when the Spaniards arrived they were able to gain allies to assist them in their attacks on the Aztec empire. Although the Aztecs were in many ways more advanced than the Europeans, they lacked the necessary weaponry and resistance to foreign diseases to defeat their invaders. The Aztecs created outstanding works of art and developed an extensive hieroglyphic writing system. However, their scientific knowledge was extremely limited. Even without the arrival of the Spaniards, it is questionable how much longer the tribes of central America would have accepted the military dominance and religious practices of the Aztecs.

References: Hassig, Ross, *Aztec Warfare: Imperial Expansion and Political Control* (Norman: University of Oklahoma Press, 1995); Sahagun, Bernardino de, The War of Conquest, trans. *Arthur Anderson and Charles Dibble* (Salt Lake City: University of Utah Press, 1978); Townsend, Richard, *The Aztecs* (London: Thames and Hudson, 1992).

B

Berserkers

Individual Viking warriors known during the eighth through eleventh centuries for their ferocity.

The berserkers are one of the most interesting and least understood aspects of the Viking warrior society. These were individuals who fought in such a blinding fury that they lost all sense of self and became unconscious killing machines without discrimination.

The term *berserker* has a disputed derivation. It has been suggested that it comes from the term "bare-sark," meaning "bare of shirt," or without armor. Many references to the berserkers mention their lack of body armor. The other primary suggestion is "bear-sark," describing the wearing of animal skins. Bear skin would seem to be the logical choice of fur, but in some of the sagas the berserkers are called "Wolf-Skins" or "wolf-coats" (ulfhedinn). The berserkers are often associated with the Norse god Odin, or Wodan, whose name possibly comes from the German "wut," meaning "rage" or "fury," and the Gothic "wods," meaning "possessed."

This kinship with the chief Norse god is illustrated in many of the legends concerning berserkers. One is that, like Odin, they could alter their form and become animals, or at least assume wolflike or bearlike qualities. *Hrolf's Saga* describes the hero Bjarki taking the shape of a bear during battle and killing more men than any five warriors. Georges Dumezil, in *Gods of the Ancient Northmen* (1973), describes this phenomenon as the *hamnigja*, the spirit or soul of the animal appearing in dreams or visions as well as (so the Vikings believed) in reality. The berserkers were also reputed to have had an immunity to weapons, either naturally or through the performance of incantations. This quality is described in many of the sagas. It could possibly be explained by the thickness of the animal skins they wore as protection or their blind rage that dulled any feeling of pain or wounding. Either way, the sight of berserker warriors receiving what should be mortal wounds and continuing to fight certainly had a strong psychological effect on their enemies.

The berserkers may have belonged to a cult of Odin, whose practices and spells would have been revealed only to initiates. Emperor Constantine VII of Byzantium, who employed Vikings in his Varangian Guard, noted a dance his men engaged in while wearing animal skins. This could indicate the performance of cultish rites. Such a dance is also recorded in artwork on Swedish helmets, scabbards, and bracelets. A newly accepted member of the cult is sometimes described as having to undergo an initiation into a warrior band whereby he has to fight a bear. Such combats are also shown in artwork inscribed on Swedish helmets. In such a cult, a member probably would have learned the secrets of bringing on the fighting frenzy, and it has been suggested that the fury was a product of drugs or alcohol. One drug proposed to bring about this condition is the hallucinogenic mushroom *Amanita mucaria*. Other researchers put the killing frenzy down to mental illness, epilepsy, or self-induced hysteria.

The appearance of the berserker was also important in instilling fear in the enemy. The animal skin itself, especially if the head was still attached and worn over the warrior's head, could present a frightening sight. This, along with an already established reputation as shape changers, provoked fear in the berserkers' own forces at times. Sagas tell of warriors who in the evening would become moody and quiet before going off by themselves, and many in camp saw in this hints of a werewolf. Berserkers are also often described as being particularly ugly, to the point of being mistaken for trolls. Whether this came from genetic makeup, or intentional actions to make themselves look worse, is unknown.

Once battle was joined, the warrior would go into his frenzy, called *berserkergang*. The flow of adrenaline must have been immense, because the aftermath of the fight always left the berserker drained. *Hrolf's Saga* describes it thus: "On these giants fell sometimes such a fury that they could not control themselves, but killed men or cattle, whatever came in their way and did not take care of itself. While this fury lasted they were afraid of nothing, but when it left them they were so powerless that they did not have half of their strength, and were as feeble as if they had just come out of bed from a sickness. This fury lasted about one day" (Fabing, 1956). The berserkers screamed like animals and showed incredible strength. This also over

time could have contributed to their reputation as shape changers who turned into bears. Indeed, many of these warriors would assume a "bear name," by adding "bjorn" or "biorn" to their given names, for example, Arinbjorn or Esbjorn. They also are reputed to have drunk bear or wolf blood in order to take on some of the animals' characteristics.

The berserkers were admired as warriors, and in battle they were often the vanguard. Their ties to Odin gave their commanders some elevated status as well, for Odin was seen in many societies as patron of rulers and chieftains. However, the potential for killing their own comrades was great. This put the berserkers in a kind of social limbo, for killing ones' fellows was looked upon in Norse society as the meanest of crimes. Thus, in many sagas the berserkers are portrayed as villains. They were often accused of raping maidens or even other mens' wives. It is probably this factor that brought about the end of the berserkers. In 1015 King Erik had them outlawed, along with duels. Prior to this reform, berserkers often challenged men to duels and then killed them while in berserkergang. They then took their victims' possessions and families, as was allowed under Viking law. In Iceland, the church outlawed the practice as well, stating that if anyone went berserk they would receive three years' banishment. Being a berserker was equated with being a heathen and practicing magic, neither of which a Christian church or society would allow. Finally succumbing to these civilizing pressures, berserkergang came to an end in the twelfth century.

References: Dumezil, Georges, *Gods of the Ancient Northmen* (Los Angeles: University of California Press, 1973); Fabing, Howard D., "On Going Berserk: A Neurochemical Inquiry," in

The Battle of Belmont during the Boer-British War, November 23, 1899. Library of Congress, Prints & Photographs Division [reproduction number LC-USZ62-11455]

Scientific Monthly, November 1956, vol. 83; Jones, Gwen, Eirik the Red and Other Icelandic Sagas (New York: Ox ford University Press, 1961); Ward, Christy, "Description of the Ber-serk," (www.realtime.com/$flsim $gunnora).

Boers

Dutch South African population particularly known for its mastery of guerrilla warfare.

The southern portion of the African continent was the last to attract serious attention from Europeans. It is not surprising that the Dutch first settled people there, as they had most of the shipping going around the Cape of Good Hope en route to the East Indies. They established a way station there in 1652 from which a colony began to grow. The victualing station needed farmers to provide the food and soldiers to provide protection, so a number of Dutch moved there to start a new life of farming, ranching, or hunting. The inhabitants called themselves *Boers*, Dutch for "farmer." Over time the Boers expanded their population and moved northward, pressing back the native population with mixed results: The Hottentots became their laborers, the Bushmen became targets of genocide, and the numerous Bantu tribes, such as the Zulu and Matabele, became rivals for control of the land.

When French forces occupied the Netherlands in 1795, the British responded by occupying the Dutch colony at the Cape. Increased British trade with India could not be threatened by French forces in southern Africa, though the British saw no economic value in the colony itself. Still, they took it as their own in 1806 and that ownership was confirmed in the peace process in Europe after Napoleon's defeat. Keeping the colony would not prove nearly as easy as gaining it. As the British began to export settlers to the colony, the Boers resented the intrusion. They had grown used to settling huge ranches and did not want a foreign population robbing them of what they considered their lands. The British could not abide the relationship the Boers had with the Hottentots, which was one of virtual slavery. When the new British administration began to act in favor of native rights, the Boers decided it was time to move. They pushed northeastward, paralleling the coast, into the area known as Natal, recently left empty because of native wars. When the British would not or could not commit sufficient forces to defend the frontiers the Boers were expanding, the Dutch saw it as "kaffir-loving," a policy of favoring "colored" over white. They decided to move again, far enough to get away from British politicians. Thus began the Great Trek.

Starting in 1835, some 14,000 people ultimately migrated into the veld land farther north—lands occupied by native groups who did not want to leave. Here the Zulu and Ndebele tribes resisted. Their societies, which emphasized military training, were willing to fight the Boers at every turn. Superior fire power finally was the deciding factor, and small Boer republics sprang up wherever they settled to raise their crops and herd their livestock. The Boers became even more conservative in their views: They believed that they were a people chosen by God, the land was theirs to take, and the natives were an inferior race whom it was permissible to use or abuse as they saw fit. When the British

annexed Natal in 1842, some Boers stayed while others moved even farther north across the Vaal River, establishing the Transvaal Republic.

The two white communities began to tolerate each other. Then, major changes came to the area: In 1867 diamonds were discovered just south of the Vaal River. There was a mining rush, mainly by the British, and the Boers were able to keep few claims. The new wealth created problems. The discoveries were made in territory claimed by both Boertrekkers and British; the British bought out the Dutch claims just south of the Vaal. The main labor force in the mines was composed of natives who, although they worked for much less than white miners, still made plenty of money—money that they spent on firearms to take back to their tribes. The traditional hostility between native and Boer grew sharper, and the British policies were sufficiently irregular to keep the whites hostile to each other as well. The Boers believed the British were too conciliatory to the natives. At the same time, the British occasionally treated the Natal tribes much like the Americans treated their native tribes during the westward expansion, putting them on reservations, then persecuting them when the whites wanted the land. As native labor became more in demand, and therefore more expensive, the needs of white businessmen and the fears of black power grew.

In 1852, the British had recognized the independence of the Transvaal, but the Dutch did not manage their republic well. Owing to expensive campaigns against local tribes and a defaulted foreign loan, the republic was in dire financial straits. In 1877, the British offered to annex the Transvaal, delivering the Boers from their financial problems and providing protection on the frontiers. The local government reluctantly agreed to accept the annexation temporarily while its representatives traveled to London to have it reversed. The reversal did not happen, but the Boers were in no financial or military state to halt the course of events. Britain wanted the Cape Colony to federate all the lands available, much as in Canada, and the Transvaal was necessary for that goal. If the British could establish a united native policy throughout the federation, certainly peace and prosperity would follow. Necessary also was domination over all native lands. The British invaded Zululand in 1878–1879 on trumped-up excuses and established control there. When the Pedi were defeated and scattered a few months later, most of the other tribes saw the futility of resistance. Momentarily at least, the British had made good on their promise to protect the Boers from hostile natives.

Without a native threat, the Boers believed the British presence had become unnecessary and that the Transvaal should have its independence restored. When the British refused ("As long as the sun shines over South Africa, the British flag will fly over Pretoria" [Pakenham, 1991]), the Boers began cleaning their rifles. When the British provoked an incident over a Boer who would not pay his taxes, the Boers began organizing. Under the leadership of Paul Kruger (nicknamed "Oom," or "uncle"), who had gone to London to protest the annexation, the Boers declared their independence in November 1880. They raised a force of 7,000 men, three times what the British had in Transvaal, sent men to besiege British garrisons in Transvaal towns and began to fight a guerrilla war. In November and December 1880 and January 1881, they fought three battles and in

each defeated a superior British detachment. The embarrassed British government hastily approved negotiations to give the Boers independence. The general on the spot, Sir George Colley, disagreed with the government's offer and decided to press on. He died, with the majority of his force of 400 men, at the battle of Majuba Hill in late January 1881. Kruger accepted the offer to negotiate, and in late March the Transvaal was again independent, although the British did retain the right to direct the Boers' foreign policy. God, "Oom Paul" Kruger, and Mauser rifles had delivered the faithful.

As if to reinforce the belief in divine protection that the Boers enjoyed, gold was soon discovered in the Transvaal. In order to exploit the mines, foreign (uitlander) engineers had to be brought in, and these tended to be British. By the late 1890s, a large British population had migrated to the Boer republic to work the mines. In spite of the wealth they now enjoyed, the Boers remained wary. British expansionists, led by gold and diamond magnate Cecil Rhodes, had acquired land to the north of the Transvaal, effectively seizing the mineral rights, but more importantly denying the Boers any more room to expand. With British territory above and below them, the Boers felt sure that they would soon be obliged to defend their lands. When Rhodes sponsored a raid into the Transvaal, hoping futilely for a British uprising to grab the country and its riches for the empire, the Dutch farmers were confirmed in their fears. They responded by further denying political rights to uitlanders in their country, keeping them in the position of second-class citizens. The native population, of course, remained beyond the hope of even that lofty a status.

This was not a social position the British were prepared to accept. They appealed to the British government to protect them and, desiring not only wealth but the geographic position of Boer lands, the government responded. By controlling Egypt and having a dominant position in countries south of there, a transcontinental, Cape-to-Cairo railroad was possible. This would mean wealth and political power for the British Empire if it could build it. However, to do so the British needed to gain control of the right-of-way through the Boer republics of the Transvaal and the Orange Free State on its southern border. Additionally, some soldiers in the British army still chafed from the defeat the Boers dealt them in 1880–1881 and would truly savor revenge. The British public received a steady diet of anti-Boer propaganda to prepare them for the war that seemed inevitable.

Paul Kruger, now president of the Transvaal, saw the British designs and responded by launching preemptive attacks against British towns in Natal and along the southern and western borders of the Orange Free State. If the Boers could control Natal (which they believed the British stole from them after the Great Trek), the British would have a difficult time bringing in reinforcements. After all, the Cape Colony—even though long under British rule—had a Boer majority among its population.

Britain was again confident that the Boers could be easily overcome and again found themselves shocked. British garrisons were quickly besieged and Boer forces drove 100 miles into the Cape Colony. When the British finally began to arrive in large numbers in November of 1899, the Boers stopped to consolidate. When the British attacked in December, the Boers

thrashed them three times in one week. By Christmas, the British had suffered 7,000 casualties. In the face of growing British forces, however, the Boers were ultimately forced to resort to guerrilla tactics. As the British made their way into Boer territory, their enemy melted away into the hills and harassed them with ambushes. The British responded with the one proven method of dealing with a guerrilla movement. As Mao Tse-tung would later write, the population is the sea in which the guerrilla fish swims. Take away the population, and the guerrilla has no one to provide food, information, or refuge. The British rounded up the Boer population of women and children and placed them in concentration camps where they could provide no assistance. They then began a slow, expensive process to literally corral the Boers. They crisscrossed the countryside with barbed wire fencing and regularly placed strongpoints. By building more and more fences, they gradually lessened the area inside which the Boers could operate. Any attempt to break through brought quick responses from the strongpoints. With a smaller and smaller area in which to operate and gather supplies, the Boers were finally starved into submission.

The fighting went on until May 1902 when the exhausted Boers reached the bitter end and signed a peace treaty. They were promised self-government sometime in the future plus immediate financial relief for the losses they suffered—and losses there were. Owing to poor initial management of the concentration camps, huge numbers of civilians died from typhoid, dysentery, and measles—some 28,000 Boer women and children out of a total of just over 111,000, and 14,000 out of almost 44,000 native internees. Seven thousand Boer men were killed in combat. The

British lost 20,000 men and spent £200 million, but they had control over the land. The Boers and the British ultimately reached a relatively peaceful coexistence. When World War I came in 1914 the South African contingent helping the British was led by Jan Smuts, who had been one of the primary commanders of Boer forces.

References: Nuttingham, Anthony, *Scramble for Africa: The Great Trek to the Boer War* (London: Constable, 1970); Pakenham, Thomas, *The Scramble for Africa: White Man's Conquest of the Dark Continent* (New York: Random House, 1991); Reitz, Deneys, *Commando: A Boer Journal of the Boer War* (London: Faber & Faber, 1929).

Boxers

An ultranationalist Chinese faction, 1899–1900.

Throughout the nineteenth century, the ruling Manchu dynasty in China grew progressively weaker. This coincided with European colonial efforts in the Far East and resulted in first the British, and then other European powers, forcing concessions from the Chinese government. Not only were trade treaties forced on the Chinese, but port cities were virtually assigned to the various powers as they carved out economic spheres of influence in different parts of China. Britain, France, Russia, Germany, and Japan all had territory in which they held exclusive trade rights. Although the Chinese did profit from this trade, there were serious negative side effects. The traditionally xenophobic Chinese believed that their culture, as the oldest in the world, was therefore the best. Having foreigners dictate policy, profit on their own terms, and introduce alien ideas offended Chinese sensibilities. By the 1890s many Chinese could no longer stand being treated as inferiors and began organizing themselves to do something about it.

Secret societies formed, taking the name *I-ho-ch'üan* (translating as "Righteous and Harmonious Fists"). Many of their banners displayed a fist icon, so the Westerners called them the Boxers. They took an extreme nationalist stance, demanding that everything foreign be destroyed or expelled. As their stance was anti-Christian as well, the Boxers did have some religious overtones, but their aims were primarily political and social. The Chinese government was divided over its attitude toward this society. The Emperor Kuang Hsü wanted to modernize China, taking advantage of Western progress, as had Japan. He was, however, a weak ruler and did not control the government. His mother, Empress Tzu Hsi, responded to the urging of reactionary elements in the government and seized power from her son. Although with no official connection to the Boxers, the empress covertly aided and encouraged their activities. She could thus explain to foreign ambassadors that it was an independent movement over which she had no control.

Unaware of or ignoring any signs of unrest, the Westerners went about their business of engaging in trade and making demands for concessions from the government. In 1899 the United States entered the scene. American Secretary of State John Hay, wanting to gain inroads into the Chinese market but excluded because the Europeans controlled the ports, proposed what came to be called the Open Door Policy. Each nation could remain dominant in a single area, but all regions should be open to all foreign trading interests. This would open up markets currently

Boxer prisoners captured and brought in by 6th U.S. Cavalry, Tientsin, China, 1901. Library of Congress, Prints &
Photographs Division [reproduction number LC-USZ62-68811]

denied to the Europeans because of the sphere-of-interest practice. With an increased customer base and increased access to previously untapped local goods, Hay argued, profits would surely rise. The policy would also, of course, allow America to get in on the China trade as well. The Europeans accepted Hay's proposal, although with varying degrees of enthusiasm.

This economic cooperation agreement was not long in place when the Boxers began direct attacks on Westerners. In Shantung Province, American missionaries were attacked and their converts abused or killed. Appeals to diplomatic personnel in Washington or the Chinese capital of Peking brought little response. In May 1900, Boxers began acting more openly in Peking. Weaponry was produced and purchased throughout the city. Attacks on individuals began in May and the Boxers burned a railway station outside Peking on May 24. Placards around the city urged the Chinese to destroy the telegraph lines and the railroads as the first step toward ridding the country of the "foreign devils." Had the Boxers immediately followed up on this incident with assaults on the foreign embassies, they almost certainly would have massacred every European there. Instead, they continued to harass people in the streets for several weeks until the Europeans finally began to take seriously the threat to their safety. Chinese diplomats on June 19 ordered the Westerners out of Peking by the following day at 4:00 p.m. When the German ambassador left to register a protest with the Chinese government, he was shot and killed in the street. Precisely at 4:00 p.m. the shooting started, with a Chinese sniper killing a French sentry.

Throughout the previous days, the Methodist missionaries had been pleading with the diplomats to rescue them and their converts. Just in time they were given permission to gather in the borrowed palace of Prince Su, next door to the British embassy. Since all the legations were next to each other, the Europeans had a defensive position they could hold. Some 3,000 people were inside protected by only a few hundred military men with limited weaponry and ammunition. The Chinese attacked almost constantly, and when they were not assaulting the walls around the embassies, they were bombarding them or making noise. Although the Boxers were rarely armed with anything other than swords and knives, they were supported by Chinese imperial troops with modern weapons. How many Chinese were involved in the siege is a matter of speculation, but probably about 20,000 troops were involved, aided by thousands more Boxer volunteers.

Luckily for the defenders, the multinational group inside the embassy enclave rather quickly set aside national rivalries and elected the British ambassador, Sir Claude Macdonald, as their leader. Among the missionaries, diplomats, merchants, and travelers inside the compound were many with practical skills or military experience who could assist in the defense.

The chief Methodist missionary was Frank Gamewell, who before becoming a cleric was educated at Rensselaer Polytechnic in civil engineering. He was the only man in the entire group with any construction knowledge, and he was immediately given the task of building and maintaining defensive strongpoints. Embassy guards from France, Germany, Japan, Britain, Russia, and the United States were each given a section of wall to defend.

The Chinese artillery wrought havoc among the people inside the compound, but made little headway against the walls, which Reverend Gamewell kept as stoutly repaired as possible. The Boxers tried to burn out the defenders by setting fire to the Hanlin Library abutting the British Embassy. Because this contained a large collection of Chinese art and literary treasures, the Europeans were shocked to see the Chinese set it afire. With men, women, and children working the water bucket brigades (and aided certainly by some fortuitous winds), the British Embassy was saved from serious damage, but the fire destroyed the library. Bitter fighting took place along the Tartar Wall, the position held by American marines. The Boxers also mined under the French legation and collapsed part of its walls, but the French defenders occupied the rubble and held on.

Several messengers had been dispatched to the coast, begging for relief. Unknown to the defenders (as the telegraph lines had been cut), the first relief force had been defeated and driven back, and the Chinese held the key city of Tientsin. Although throughout the siege, the defenders on the walls looked toward Tientsin and were sure they saw signs of approaching armies, none came for weeks. The economic agreement Hay had negotiated the previous year among the Western powers now became the basis of military cooperation among them. All the interested countries sent troops in the first serious coalition effort since the defeat of Napoleon at Leipzig in 1814. On July 13, 1900, the multinational force attacked Tientsin and captured it after a 15-hour battle. With this in their possession to use as a base, the coalition forces set their sights on Peking, 75 miles away. They arrived on August 12, having fought harassing Boxers the entire way. No one was in supreme command, so the various national forces acted independently. The Russians attacked first and, although they forced an entrance into Peking, they soon found themselves in need of rescue. The individual forces assaulted various gates into the city, but the British, sent over from India, found themselves in front of the one most lightly defended. They broke through on the evening of August 13 and made their way through an undefended sluice gate into the diplomatic compound. The troops were greeted with hugs and kisses all around. The American forces arrived two hours later.

On August 14, the coalition forces captured the outer city and began driving inward. They soon entered the Imperial City, then broke through the final barrier into the Forbidden City. There they found that the government had fled, so few prisoners were taken. The invaders were not gentle in their treatment of the inhabitants of Peking, and looting was widespread. With the city under firm control, the British general, Gaselee, led his forces into the neighboring provinces to mop up what Boxer resistance he could find. After some weeks, the empress sent emissaries with an offer to negotiate: a return to the *status quo antebellum* in return for the withdrawal of foreign troops.

The negotiations dragged on for months and ultimately the Chinese government was forced to pay an indemnity of $333 million to the offended nations. The United States received $25 million, of which they accepted only half and dedicated the remainder to establishing a fund for Chinese students to study in America. This gesture may have had the longest-lasting effect of the entire incident. High damage claims and looting the Chinese expected from foreigners, but to have one of the invaders invest in the future of China was shocking. From that point, the United States enjoyed a much closer relationship with China than any other Western power—a relationship that lasted through World War II and until the victory of communism in 1949. The Chinese for the most part became no less xenophobic, but the organized resistance to foreign influence that the Boxers symbolized had only a brief life.

References: Lord, Walter, *The Good Years* (New York: Harper & Bros., 1960); McCormick, T. J., *China Market: America's Quest for Informal Empire* (Chicago: Quadrangle Books, 1967); Young, Marilyn, *The Rhetoric of Empire: American China Policy, 1895–1901* (Cambridge: Harvard University Press, 1968).

British East India Company

A trading company with a private army that dominated India in the eighteenth and nineteenth centuries.

After the defeat of the Spanish Armada in 1588, the British were able to gain enough freedom of action on the high seas in the 1600s to begin to explore, colonize, and seek international markets. They were already aware of the economic possibilities of India because the Portuguese had established trading posts there during the 1500s that had brought the spices and exotic goods of the East to western Europe. By the time the British began to probe the coasts of India, Portugal was a fading power, so setting up their own trading posts and warehouse facilities, or "factories" as they were called, was easy to do. The government in London had sponsored the creation of the East India Company, in which it owned shares and had a presence on the board of directors, but which was

The success of British-led forces under Robert Clive, depicted here in Lord Clive meeting with Mir Jafar after the Battle of Plassey, by Francis Hayman (c. 1762), determined the European dominance of India for almost two centuries.

primarily a private enterprise. The Company did, however, have the ability to call on the British government for support in times of trouble. In its early years, however, the protection of the factories in India fell not to soldiers of the king but to fighting men privately recruited and directed by the Company.

Three major factories were established in India: at Bengal on the northeastern coast, Madras near the tip of the subcontinent, and Bombay on the western coast. It was the men hired to protect these three trading centers that were to form the basis of the military force operated by "John Company" and that finally became the Indian army. Bengal's first troops were an ensign and 30 men along with a gunner and his crew hired in the late seventeenth century. At Madras, the watchmen and security guards were the basis of the military unit headquartered there. Most of the men recruited into these small units were native Indians who served under the leadership of Englishmen, a practice that remained in effect until Indian independence in 1947.

John Company was not the first to hire local men, however, for the French (also trying to establish an economic presence in India) first conceived of the idea. As the ruling Mogul Empire was in its final days and power vacuums existed across India, the French and other Europeans learned that even a small force trained in European tactics, armed with European weapons, and led by European officers could defeat Indian armies vastly superior in number. The first large-scale armies, therefore, were private ones raised by local princes and sultans to protect their territory and expand at the expense of their neighbors. French, as well as English, officers officially and unofficially offered their services to local rulers, not only to profit personally but to give their respective countries a foothold in local politics. This would provide them with leverage in trade concessions as well as physically challenge other European competitors, like the East India Company.

In 1748, the first regular European force in British service was officially formed from the three fledgling units raised by the three factories. They had now, however, established themselves to such an extent that the British government set up local administrations under the direction of officials sent from London, and the result was the presidencies of Bombay, Madras, and Bengal. To show their interest in maintaining the strongest presence in India, and certainly to intimidate the French, the British government sent a regiment of the British Army to serve with John Company, the Thirty-ninth Regiment of Foot (infantry).

The outbreak of the Seven Years War in Europe had international repercussions, as British and French forces fought battles around the world: in North America, the Caribbean, and in India. The units raised by European officers now fought each other not just for the local influence of a ruling monarch, but for European influence as well. The key battle in this conflict in India was Plassey in 1757, when British-led forces under Robert Clive defeated French-led forces in an engagement that determined the European dominance of India for almost two centuries. Although this broke French power in India and led to the eventual total withdrawal of the French from the subcontinent, it marked the beginning of serious expansion of the military forces in India. Although foreign competition was banished, local resistance to British expansion was widespread. Even where the Indian rajahs or princes did not actively antagonize the British, the overriding view of John Company was that peace was good for business. That meant that if a prince in a territory adjacent to British-dominated lands was oppressing his people or waging war against his neighbors, then British intervention was necessary to maintain order. By maintaining order from one province to another, the British expanded their influence across most of India. Expansion was never the official policy of the British government: It "just happened." Thus, through the end of the eighteenth century, the armies of the presidencies grew.

By 1795, a general reorganization was needed to set up the Company's army along the same lines as that employed by the British Army. In that year, some 13,000 Europeans lived in India, both civilian and military, while 33,000 Indians served in the Company's armed forces. Three separate commands were retained, but this move established a regular army, although still owned and operated by a private business. In Bengal, the forces consisted of three battalions of artillery, three battalions of British infantry, four regiments of native cavalry, and 12 regiments of native infantry. In Madras, two battalions of British infantry, two battalions of artillery, four regiments of native cavalry, and 11 regiments of native infantry made up the contingent. All the forces accepted recruits from across India, as well as some Afghans. The stigma of fighting against one's own people was no obstacle to these men, for most of them were misfits or exiles. In many cases the recruits were of the lowest castes in Hindu society and viewed the army as the only way out of a hopeless future. Most of the native cavalry units were made up of refugees from the private armies of defeated princes. For all of them, the promise of regular food and pay was something they could not achieve anywhere else. Moreover, as India was so divided among ethnic, religious, and political factions, rarely did one fight "one's own people."

The turn of the nineteenth century incited a new fervor in British administrators in India to grasp a firm hold on the subcontinent, as the rise of Napoleon in Europe threatened European interests worldwide. When Napoleon conquered a country in Europe, he immediately assumed control of all its colonies. This gave him opportunities to harass British colonies around the world. This, in turn, gave the British the excuse to "temporarily" occupy the colonies of other European nations, especially those of the Dutch in Africa and the Far East, in order to deny them to the French. Troops of the Company's army in those years served for the first time outside of India, establishing a precedent that lasted through World War II. Within India, French agents roused independent aristocrats to challenge British

power, and they found sympathetic ears in the province of Mysore and among the Mahratta Confederacy in central India. Under the direction of Marquis Wellesley, the Governor-General of the entire colony, British-Indian forces commanded by Wellesley's brother, Arthur (soon to become Duke of Wellington), along with those under Commander-in-Chief General Lord Lake, soundly defeated the native forces arrayed against them and established British control in the middle of India in 1803–1804. This experience brought Arthur Wellesley not only valuable command experience but official notice, both of which resulted in his transfer to Spain and victory against Napoleon's armies in Europe. Another war against the Mahrattas in 1817 destroyed the remaining pockets of discontent.

In the period of relative peace that followed, the Company's army was once again reorganized, and the new table of organization showed a vast increase in its size. Of particular interest in this larger, reorganized force was a huge disparity between the numbers of Indian regiments and British regiments, with the Indian infantry regiments outnumbering the British by nearly 24 to 1. In spite of this fact, all the Indian regiments had British officers. Also of note was the introduction of Indians to units of artillery. This had been avoided up until this time, as the British did not wish to share that decisive technology. But the need for artillery had proven so important that Indian units were organized. However, when the Sepoy Rebellion broke out in 1857, the Company had reason to regret their new policy of inclusiveness. In that rebellion, Indian artillery units in the rebel forces caused such great harm to the British and loyal Indian units that one of the first changes made after the rebellion was to ban all Indian artillery forces.

Through the decades of the 1820s through the 1850s the Company's army continued to grow and fight within India, maintaining order. Service in the military now was not just an escape for black sheep, but had become a respectable profession. It was the only organization in India, until the opening of the Civil Service to Indian employees, that took recruits from any background and mixed men of all social and religious standing. The only caste system inside the army was that of rank and of the British overlords and the Indian subordinates. As new provinces came under British control or influence, the best soldiers of that region were incorporated into the Company's forces. The army grew to include Mahrattas after the two wars against them, Sikhs after the two wars against them, and Gurkhas after the war against them—all in the four decades prior to 1857. The armies of the three presidencies enlisted men from every region and ethnic group in India. Men of ethnic and religious diversity recruited from a particular region usually served together. Furthermore, the Indians were not only trained in European tactics and weaponry, but they also wore European uniforms. Prior to the Sepoy Rebellion, most of the Indians wore the same red coats and white pants as their British counterparts. Later they adopted a variety of impressive and colorful dress uniforms. It was also in India, among the frontier units, that soldiers first began to wear khaki, a cloth that would come to be part of military dress worldwide.

The army of the East India Company lasted until the Sepoy Rebellion of 1857. By that time it numbered more than 311,000 Indian troops and just under 40,000 British troops, both regular army and Company soldiers. The reasons for the rebellion are not important here, but suffice it to say that in its wake the British government decided that the Company, which had been losing its economic as well as political power for some time, should be dismantled. What had been a semiofficial government became a fully fledged colonial administration. Reforms were instituted in the military, decreasing the ratio of British to Indian troops among other things, and the Indian Army emerged as a very professional and capable force. Its soldiers continued to serve the British Empire in campaigns throughout the world, and the army that an independent India inherited in 1947 was one of the best in Asia.

References: MacMunn, G. F., *The Armies of India* (London: Adam and Charles Black, 1911); Mason, Philip, *A Matter of Honour* (London: Jonathan Cape, 1974); Roberts, P. E., *History of British India* (London: Oxford University Press, 1952).

Buffalo Soldiers

African-American troops serving mainly in the American Southwest during the late nineteenth century.

During the American Civil War, more than 180,000 African-Americans served in the United States Army under white officers in segregated, so-called colored regiments. After the war, with the reduction in size of military forces, these troops were consolidated by Congress into four all-black units: the Ninth and Tenth Cavalry and the Twenty-fourth and Twenty-fifth Infantry Regiments. Although these units would eventually see action in Cuba during the Spanish-American War, in the Philippine Insurrection, and along the Mexican border before and during World War I, their

Buffalo soldiers of the 25th Infantry, Ft. Keogh, Montana, 1890. Library of Congress, Prints & Photographs Division [reproduction number LC-USZC4-6161]

chief fame is for their service on the western frontier in the late nineteenth century. There they earned the name "Buffalo Soldiers," either because Native Americans thought the black troopers' hair resembled that of the buffalo or because their fighting spirit reminded the Indians of the buffalo. Either way, the troopers proudly accepted the name as a sign of respect and honor, and it is still applied today to U.S. Army units that are linear descendants of the original Buffalo Soldiers.

Very high standards of recruitment were set by the regiments' commanders. Because a career in the army usually offered African-Americans better lives than they could lead as civilians at the time, four or five men applied for every opening in the regiments. Thus, the army had its choice of the best candidates, both physically and intellectually. While white soldiers frequently felt underpaid and ill treated, the Buffalo Soldiers were generally delighted with any pay (recruits received $13 a month, plus room, board, and clothing) and were far more accustomed to hard knocks than their white counterparts. Certainly, once in the army, the black troopers found much to their liking. Many of the men availed themselves of after-hours schools established by the regiments and run by their chaplains, so that they might overcome the illiteracy forced on them by slavery. They drank far less than their white counterparts and deserted at a rate of only one-tenth that of such "crack" regiments as Custer's Seventh Cavalry or Mackenzie's Fourth Cavalry. Indeed, the Tenth Cavalry posted the lowest desertion rate of any regiment in the U.S. Army in the late nineteenth century.

The Ninth and Tenth Cavalry were among the ten cavalry regiments thinly spread among more than 50 forts in the western states and territories. There they quickly established a reputation for bravery, daring, and incredible endurance. The troopers were constantly in the field, patrolling against hostile Indians over harsh terrain and in every extreme of weather. In over a hundred battles and skirmishes, from the Canadian border to south of the Rio Grande, they distinguished themselves against adversaries such as Geronimo, Sitting Bull, Victorio, Lone Wolf, Satank, and Satanta, not to mention Billy the Kid and Pancho Villa. Although the efforts of the black troopers were often belittled or simply ignored by the army administration and the newspapers, professional soldiers understood that the Buffalo Soldiers had developed into the most outstanding fighting units in the army. Toward the end of hostilities in the Sioux outbreak of 1890–1891, four companies of the Ninth Cavalry marched 108 miles through a howling blizzard to rescue twice their number of Seventh Cavalry troopers. Along the way they fought two engagements. For this they earned almost no official recognition.

The Buffalo Soldiers' duties were not limited to fighting. They escorted thousands of civilian contractors' trains and mail stages over the dangerous frontier. They aided local law officers in making arrests, pursued and captured rustlers and horse thieves, and transported criminals to the nearest civilian courts. They protected cattle herds moving west and kept the stage and wagon trails open. They built and maintained many army posts around which future towns and cities sprang to life, strung thousands of miles of telegraph wire, and guarded the United States-Mexican border. Finally, they explored and mapped some of the most rugged and inhospitable country in North America, opening up a large portion of the continent to settlement. For instance, the Tenth Cavalry scouted 34,420 miles of uncharted terrain and opened more than 300 miles of new roads. One patrol alone was out on the Staked Plains of the Texas Panhandle for 10 weeks in the fall and winter of 1877 covering over 1,360 miles without losing a single man or horse.

In spite of their abilities, the Buffalo Soldiers suffered frequent injustices, both from within and without the army. Many superior officers discriminated against the black regiments in housing, equipment, mounts, and assignments. Junior officers often refused to accept transfers to the units because they believed the commissions in the regiments to be socially degrading. Despite promises of fast promotion, officers such as George Armstrong Custer and Frederick Benteen refused commissions with African-American units. Because of such prejudice, the Buffalo Soldiers consistently received some of the worst assignments the army had to offer, but they carried out those assignments without complaint, and without faltering.

Among many civilians, the hatreds engendered by the Civil War and Reconstruction were still fresh, and in some minds former slaves carrying guns were all-too-painful reminders of Southern defeat and Northern victory. Many Texans saw the stationing of black troopers in their state as a deliberate attempt by the government to further humiliate them. Thus, relationships between troopers and locals were often antagonistic at best, and troopers frequently found themselves in siege-type situations, in danger as much from civilians in the settlements as from hostile native forces on the frontier. However, the Buffalo Soldiers managed to meet this prejudice with a stoic resolve and a devotion to duty that eventually surmounted such mistreatment. As one historian noted: "The protection afforded by the [black] cavalryman's carbines had a marvelous way of transcending the issue of race" (Hamilton, 1987).

With the outbreak of the Spanish-American War, the Buffalo Soldiers were sent to Cuba and, led by John J. Pershing, they participated in the desperate charge that secured San Juan and Kettle Hills, fighting alongside future president Theodore Roosevelt and his outfit, the Rough Riders. After their brilliant performance in Cuba, elements of all four black regiments saw action in the Philippine Insurrection. Scattered among army posts throughout the archipelago, black soldiers participated in military operations from northern Luzon to Samar, fighting against the hit-and-run guerrilla tactics of the Filipinos.

When the Mexican bandit-general Pancho Villa attacked Columbus, New Mexico, in 1916, a 7,000-man American force received permission from the Mexican government to pursue him. General John Pershing was given command, and he immediately added the Buffalo Soldiers to the expedition. When the United States withdrew from Mexico in 1917 in order to join the Allies fighting World War I, the Ninth and Tenth Cavalry stayed behind on the border to guard against possible Mexican invasion or German subversion. In 1918, they fought a pitched battle with Mexican forces at Nogales that ended any threat of German-inspired Mexican intervention.

In 1941, the Ninth and Tenth regiments were formed into the Fourth Cavalry Brigade, commanded by General Benjamin

Heraclius AV Solidus. Heraclius with Heraclius Constantine and Heraclonas, each holding globus cruciger VICTORIA AVSU, cross potent on three steps; Q/CONOB. DOC II 39h; MIB III 45. Coin from CNG coins (www.cngcoins.com), through Wildwinds. Used with permission.

O. Davis, Sr., at Camp Funston, Kansas. In 1944, all the horse cavalry regiments were disbanded and, with them, the long and proud service of the Buffalo Soldiers ended. With their sweat, blood, ability, and fidelity, the Buffalo Soldiers won the respect that often eluded them in civilian life at that time. In all, six officers and 15 enlisted men of the Buffalo Soldiers won the Congressional Medal of Honor for bravery and gallantry under fire. They were truly the elite soldiers of the late-nineteenth-century United States Army.

References: Carroll, John M., *The Black Military Experience in the American West* (New York: Liveright, 1971); Downey, Fairfax, *The Buffalo Soldiers in the Indian Wars* (New York: McGraw-Hill, 1969); Hamilton, Allen, *Sentinel of the Southern Plains* (Fort Worth: TCU Press, 1987).

Byzantines

Dominant military forces of the Middle East between the fourth and fifteenth centuries.

In 330 CE, Constantine I, Emperor of the Romans, founded a new capital for his empire on the triangular peninsula of land that divided the Bosphorus from the Sea of Marmara, commanding the narrow water passage from the Black Sea to the Mediterranean. He named it Constantinople, and in time it grew to be not only one of the greatest cities of antiquity, but the center of one of the most impressive civilizations the world has ever seen: the Byzantine Empire.

Within 200 years, the Byzantines (or Eastern Roman Empire, as they styled themselves) had grown to massive proportions, controlling all of Italy, the Balkans, Greece, Asia Minor, Syria, Egypt, North Africa, and Southern Spain. Such an empire could be held together only by a strong and efficient military, and for several centuries the Byzantine army had no equal anywhere in the world.

Although the empire had expanded enormously through conquest, the basic role of the Byzantine army was defensive. Fortifying the long borders was out of the question, and since raiders and invaders could strike anywhere along the empire's frontier, the army needed to be able to move quickly to meet these threats. Like their predecessors, the Roman legions, the Byzantine units formed a professional standing army which was trained to near-perfection as a fighting machine. Unlike the legions, however, the core of the army was cavalry and fast-moving foot archers. Speed and firepower had become the trademarks of the "new Romans."

The stirrup reached the empire from China early in the fifth century, and increased the effectiveness of the cavalry enormously. Therefore, the core of the Byzantine army became the heavy cavalry. A typical heavy cavalryman was armed with a long lance, a short bow, a small axe, a broadsword, a dagger, and a small shield. He wore a steel helmet, a plate mail corselet that reached from neck to thigh, leather gauntlets, and high boots. His horse's head and breast might be protected with light armor as well. By the later empire, armor for both rider and horse became almost complete, especially in the frontline units. In a secondary role, unarmored light cavalry horse archers on smaller mounts supported the heavy units with missile fire, while other light cavalry armed with a long lance and large shield protected their flanks.

The infantryman who usually accompanied the cavalry in the field was either a lightly armored archer who used a powerful long bow, a small shield, and a light axe, or an unarmored skirmisher armed with javelins and shield. Because most Byzantine operations depended on speed, tactically as well as strategically, heavy infantry seldom ventured beyond the camps or fortifications. The heavy infantryman wore a long mail coat and steel helmet and carried a large, round shield. He used a long spear and a short sword. The Varangian Guard, the emperor's personal bodyguards, were famous for their great two-handed axes which they wielded with great effect. Their armor was almost complete plate and mail from head to foot.

To the Byzantines, war was a science, and brains were prized over daring or strength. Military manuals such as the *Strategikon* (ca. 580) and the *Tactica* (ca. 900) laid down the basics of military strategy that really did not vary for almost a thousand years. The army was always small in number (field armies almost never exceeded 20,000 men, and the total force of the empire probably was never greater than 100,000) and, because of its training and equipment, very expensive to maintain. Huge losses in combat could be catastrophic, and seldom were great winner-take-all battles fought. The goal of any Byzantine general was to win with the least cost. If by delay, skirmishing, or withdrawing the local population and their goods into forts he could wear out an invading force and cause it to withdraw without a costly pitched battle, so much the better. Bribing an enemy to go away was also quite acceptable.

The warrior emperor Heraclius divided the empire into some 30 *themes*, or military districts, each under a separate military commander. Each *theme* provided and supported its own corps of cavalry and infantry, raised from self-supporting peasant warrior-farmers, enough to provide a small self-contained army that was capable of independent operation. For four centuries this system endured, and Byzantium remained strong. Only in the eleventh century, when the *theme* system and its free peasantry were abandoned, did the empire become weak and vulnerable.

Because *theme* commanders depended on accurate information about enemies and their movements, they maintained a very sophisticated intelligence service. Over time, espionage became so important to Byzantine operations that a part of the emperor's bureaucracy, known as the Office of Barbarians, was dedicated solely to gathering military intelligence and disseminating it to the commanders in the field.

Byzantine battlefield tactics, although highly flexible and adaptable, were based invariably on archery first, then shock assault as needed. Since everyone in the army except the heavy infantry carried a bow, an incredible amount of firepower could be directed against the enemy. The highly trained and disciplined cavalry units, supported by the light infantry archers, could pour volley after volley of arrows into enemy units and then, when those units began to lose cohesion, charge with lance and sword, rout them, and pursue them out of Byzantine territory.

Since Constantinople was a major port, surrounded by water on three sides, a strong navy was also necessary for the empire's survival. Byzantine ships were fairly typical oar-driven galleys of the time, but they possessed a great technological advantage over other navies: a weapon known as Greek fire. This was a highly flammable mixture that could be thrown on enemy ships in pots from catapults, or pumped by siphons directly on their decks, breaking into white-hot flames on contact. If water was poured on Greek fire, it burned even hotter. One of the great secrets of the ancient world is the exact composition of Greek fire, but it probably contained pitch, kerosene, sulfur, resin, naphtha, and quicklime. Whatever the mix, it was a terrifying weapon that was almost impossible to defend against. With Greek fire, the Byzantine navy reigned supreme for centuries on the Black Sea and the eastern Mediterranean.

The Byzantines were also fortunate in producing many great military leaders over the centuries: emperors such as Justinian I, Heraclius, Basil I, Leo III, Maurice, Leo VI "the Wise," and generals like Narses, Belisarius, and John Kurkuas. Their skills and insights maintained the Eastern Roman Empire for almost a thousand years after the fall of the western branch.

Although the Byzantines fought many peoples over the centuries, in campaigns of either conquest or defense, it was a religious opponent, the Muslims, who became their most intractable, and in the end, lethal, foe. For seven centuries, a succession of Muslim generals led Persian, Arab, and Turkish armies against the armies and walls of Constantinople. Gradually, the empire was eaten away, and its wealth and manpower base eroded. Not only did the Byzantines have to face the Muslim threat, but a growing schism between their church, the Greek Orthodox, and the Roman Catholic Church, isolated them from their fellow Christians. In 1071, the emperor Romanus IV violated one of the mainstays of Byzantine strategy when he concentrated most of his military power in one great battle against Alp Arslan and the Seljuk Turks at Manzikert in Armenia. The result was a devastating defeat, allowing the Turks to overrun most of Asia Minor, the heartland of the empire. Byzantium never really recovered from this debacle. In 1204, Christian crusaders, allied with the city-state of Venice, took advantage of internal Byzantine strife to seize and sack Constantinople. It was not until 1261 that the emperor Michael VIII Palaeologus recaptured Constantinople from the Latins, but the damage had been done. The empire's once great resources, and its ability to maintain itself, were almost gone. On May 29, 1453, Mohammed II, Sultan of the Ottoman Turks, using great cannons (weapons even more fearsome than Greek fire), broke through the seemingly eternal walls of Constantinople and brought the glorious Byzantine Empire to an end.

Certainly, Byzantines made many great contributions to civilization: Greek language and learning were preserved, the Roman imperial system and law was continued, the Greek Orthodox Church spread Christianity among many peoples, and a splendid new religious art form was created. But it is possible that their ideas on military science (mobility and firepower; delay and deception; espionage and statecraft; an emphasis on professionalism over the warrior ethos) might stand as the most significant aspect of their great legacy.

References: Diehl, Charles, *Byzantium: Greatness and Decline* (New Brunswick, NJ: Rutgers University Press, 1957); Griess, Thomas, *Ancient and Medieval Warfare* (West Point: U.S. Military Academy, 1984); Ostrogorsky, George, *History of the Byzantine State* (New Brunswick, NJ: Rutgers University Press, 1957).

C

Cavaliers and Roundheads

Units of the English Civil War, the Roundheads are noted as being the basis of the British Regular Army's "redcoats" for centuries.

The English Civil War raged from 1642 to 1646, although fighting sporadically continued for some years afterward. The issue was quite simple, and yet complex at the same time: Who or what was going to rule England, king or Parliament? King Charles I (1625–1648), like his Scottish father James I (1603–1625), believed in the divine right of kings. Unfortunately for them, Parliament had participated in the government of England for centuries, and its right to do so was well established in tradition. Further, Parliament had the power to vote taxes and used this right to defy Charles's attempts at autocratic rule. There were also religious concerns, as a strongly Protestant Parliament viewed Charles's Catholic leanings with alarm. Eventually, it became clear that the only way to resolve the differences between king and Parliament was through war. Almost everyone in England—lords, aristocrats, clergy, and commoners—fell into one camp or the other. The followers of the king were known as Royalists, or "cavaliers" (after the French word for horsemen), while the supporters of the Parliament were known as Parliamentarians, or "Roundheads" (supposedly because their shorter haircuts gave their heads a round appearance). Parliament had the early advantage of controlling the east and south of England, especially London, while the king's support tended to be strongest in the north and west of the country.

The soldiers who fought in the English Civil War were typical of those of the Thirty Years War era. Both sides tried to copy the Swedish army organization of Gustavus Adolphus, but instead ended up with forces distinctly more English than continental. The backbone of each army was the infantry, or foot, which consisted of pikemen and musketeers grouped together in regiments, with an ideal ratio of 2 musketeers to 1 pikeman. Typically, pikemen would form the middle of a regiment, with an equal number of musketeers on each flank. The armor of the pikemen would consist of iron helmets, back- and breastplates, with perhaps tassets (thigh guards) suspended from the breastplates, and thick leather gloves. Under this they wore long leather coats known as "buff-coats," thick enough to turn a sword cut. Their main weapon was the 16- to 18-foot English pike, with which they would try to dispatch other infantry and hold cavalry at bay. Obviously, individual pikemen were fairly helpless; only by operating in unison as a block could they be effective. Therefore, it was necessary for them to learn a complex set of maneuvers and drills in order to function as a unit on the battlefield. As in all wars, some regiments were better at this than others.

Musketeers furnished the infantry fire-power on the field. Typical firearms for both sides were 13-pound matchlocks or lighter harquebuses, usually supported by a forked rest. Both were slow and tedious to load, but could inflict terrible wounds on enemies at distances ranging up to 200 yards, although to be accurate it was necessary to be much closer, usually inside 40 yards. Aside from firearms, musketeers were equipped with bandoliers from which hung wooden or leather tubes filled with measured gunpowder charges (which often leaked, thus making each musketeer a potential walking bomb), short swords, and sometimes buffcoats. Musketeers were trained to fire by ranks, either by "intro-duction" (advancing) or "extraduction" (retiring), with one rank shooting, then reloading while the next stepped through. As bayonets were not yet invented, muske-teers would seek the protection of the pikemen's square when enemy pikes or cavalry came too near.

Infantry regiments were supposed to consist of 10 companies, although in prac-tice this number was seldom met. A com-pany could range from 100 to 200 men, so infantry regiments could be quite large. The only units in England that could be called "regulars" when the war broke out were the Trained Bands of London, which went over to Parliament's side; this gave the Roundheads an early and lasting ad-vantage in numbers and quality of infantry during the war.

Cavalry during the English Civil War, more so than on the continent during the Thirty Years War, ruled the battlefield. Equipment was almost never uniform or universal, but most heavy cavalrymen wore a buffcoat with back- and breastplate, a helmet with nasal guard and ear and neck protection, a metal gauntlet on the left hand and forearm to protect the bridle hand, and thick leather boots which exten-ded to the top of the thigh. Some very heavy cavalrymen known as cuirassiers wore an almost complete suit of armor like their predecessor, the heavy knight. Light-er cavalry could wear just a back- and breastplate, or simply a buffcoat.

The lance was seldom used by cavalry at this time, except for some units of light Scottish horse. Most heavy cavalry used the heavy straight broadsword with basket hilt as their shock weapon, and pistols or carbines as their secondary weapons. Fire-arms were wheel lock or firelock style, since a matchlock would be almost impos-sible to use or reload on horseback. Some light cavalry were organized as mounted infantry, or dragoons, so called because of the "dragons" or short muskets that they carried. They rode animals inferior to the cavalry horses and were trained to fight on foot as sharpshooters or skirmishers, using their horses to give them greater mobility. Cavalry regiments were organized in six to 12 troops of 70 to 100 men each. Thus, a regiment could consist of 1,200 men, but 800 were normal, and some units that had seen hard action were as small as 100 men.

The foremost cavalry regiment among the Roundheads was Oliver Cromwell's famous "Ironsides," whom he raised, trained, and led personally. Said to be twice the size of most cavalry regiments, the Ironsides were certainly the most tightly disciplined in the early war and more than a match for any one regiment the Royalists could throw against them. But, since most of the aristocracy preferred to fight on horseback and could afford the necessary horse and armor, the early advantage in horse quality and quantity lay with the Royalists. Under dashing leaders like Prince Rupert and Prince Maurice, who had both served in the Thirty Years War in Europe, wild Royalist cavalry charges usually swept the fields of Roundhead cavalry early in the war. Unfortunately, Cavalier horses were usually good for only one charge, impetuously chasing off after their fleeing enemies and leaving their infantry vulnerable. This lack of discipline, the inability to rally and charge a second time, became both a hallmark of the Royalist horse and the eventual undoing of the Royalist cause.

Armies of both sides had an artillery train, but the slow rate of fire of cannons of the times (about one round every three minutes) made them truly useful only during sieges. Field pieces weighed between 150 and 6,000 pounds and required 9 to 12 men to serve them. Heavy draught horses or oxen were needed to move these weapons between battles, so once they were set up, they tended to remain in place, win or lose.

In 1645, Parliament, at Cromwell's urging, authorized the raising of a "New Model Army," England's first regular standing army. It was to take the place of the militia, trained bands and private regiments of Parliamentary supporters. It was to be some 22,000 men strong, with 14,000 infantry, 6,600 horse, and 1,000 dragoons. Under Commander-in-Chief Thomas Fairfax and General of the Horse Oliver Cromwell, the army was tightly organized, thoroughly and professionally trained, highly disciplined, imbued with an almost religious fervor, and had regular rates of pay. They also adopted regular uniforms, the red coat that would become synonymous with the British Army for the next three centuries.

This New Model Army showed its worth on the field of Naseby on June 14, 1645. Although hard pressed by the more veteran Royalist foot, the Roundhead infantry held their own. Prince Rupert charged with his cavalry and broke the Parliamentary cavalry against him, but as usual they scattered out across the countryside, pursuing the fugitives over two miles back to their baggage train, and leaving his infantry vulnerable and without cavalry support. Meanwhile, Cromwell's horse had charged on the other flank and routed the Royalist cavalry against him. Instead of wildly pursuing, however, the training and discipline of the New Model Army paid off. Cromwell rallied his men, re-formed, and charged into the exposed flanks of the Royalist foot and for all purposes won the war. The victorious New Model Army proceeded to roll over one Royalist stronghold after another until, by the summer of 1646, all England was in their hands. Charles I surrendered to the Scots in late 1646, who handed him over to Parliament in 1647. He briefly escaped from captivity, spurring Royalist uprisings all over the country, but these were easily crushed, and he was recaptured in 1648. On January 30, 1649, Charles I, condemned as a "tyrant, traitor, murderer, and public enemy," was beheaded. A Puritan Commonwealth was proclaimed, and Oliver Cromwell came to rule England (with the backing of his New Model Army) as Lord Protector from 1653 until his death in 1658.

References: Ashley, Maurice, *The English Civil War* (London: Thames and Hudson, 1974); Haythornthwait, Philip, *The English Civil War* (London: Blandford Press, 1984); Young, Brigadier Sir Peter, and Wilfrid Emberton, *The Cavalier Army, Its Organization and Everyday Life* (London: George Allen and Unwin, 1974).

Celts

An ancient population dominating northern and western Europe prior to the Roman Empire.

The Celts were prehistoric Europeans, and little else can be said about them as far as unifying characteristics are concerned. A large number of tribes spread from the Atlantic coast to the Black Sea and they collectively came to be called Celts (from the Greek *Keltoi* or Latin *Celtae*) by their more literate, record-keeping southern neighbors. These tribes, described by the Greeks and Romans as barbarians, settled Europe in the ninth to sixth centuries BCE but were inexplicably overrun about 500 BCE. In the 400s BCE, European barbarian cultures reorganized and came to be called Gauls (from the Latin *Galli* or Greek *Galatae*).

As the numbers of tribes that stretched across Europe under these general headings were as numerous as the Celtic tribes, it is difficult to prove how related they all may have been. Described by archaeologists as the La Tene culture, there are some traces of common speech patterns over a wide span of territory from the British Isles to Asia Minor, as well as some common artistic and religious aspects.

The Celts attacked their Mediterranean neighbors starting around 400 BCE. They invaded past the Alps into Italy, sacking Rome in 390 BCE; however, after being driven back, they settled into the Po River valley in a region that came to be called Cisalpine Gaul. In 279 BCE, Galatians attacked into Greece as far as Delphi. Although driven back after a serious defeat, some Galatians crossed into Asia Minor and established a kingdom around modern Ankara. Traces of Celtic/Gallic culture and language appeared in Iberia in Roman times, but the chief remainder of Celtic heritage is found in the British Isles. Common tribal names and linguistic features connect Celtic populations from northwest Europe and the British Isles, as well as commonalities in defensive works, weaponry, artwork, and religion. The Picts of Scotland and the piratical Scotti of Ireland remained unconquered by the Romans, thus maintaining more of their Celtic languages.

It is from Greek and Roman sources that the first recorded observations of the Celts come, and they focus heavily on the Celtic passion for warfare. The Roman historian Strabo wrote, "The whole race. . .is madly fond of war, high-spirited and quick to battle, but otherwise straightforward and not of evil character. And so when they are stirred up they assemble in their bands for battle, quite openly and without forethought.... [When aroused] they are. . .ready to face danger even if they have nothing on their side but their own strength and courage" (Cunliffe, 1997). The display of individual valor was most important in Celtic society and was the prerequisite for leadership. The migration of Celtic tribes across Europe is believed to have been based on their ever-increasing need to find enemies to defeat and plunder. A raid of a neighboring village produced loot and status for the Celtic leader. He then held a feast and distributed the booty, attracting the attention of more warriors. He would then lead a second raid to acquire more loot, hold another feast to distribute it, and attract more warriors, and so on. This ever-growing cycle of loot-reward-recruit forced the tribes to range farther afield for greater glory and wealth.

The Celts were more of a warrior race than a militaristic population, in that they

An ancient Celtic dagger, scabbard and buckle.

depended more on individual effort and mass attacks than on well-planned strategies. The individual Celt carried a sword and a spear, occasionally bows and arrows, slings, or throwing clubs. The Celts carried shields and often wore metal helmets, but rarely wore body armor in the form of chain mail. Their swords were of iron with blades usually decorated with personal emblems. Spears were used both as thrusting and throwing weapons. The use of bows and arrows was rarely recorded, but arrowheads have been recovered in Celtic archaeological sites. In Britain, evidence of slings comes from the stockpiles of rocks discovered at key places in Celtic defensive positions, such as Maiden Castle in Dorset.

In battle, Celtic warriors often wore helmets decorated with attachments, such as animal figures. A helmet discovered in London has large protruding horns, while another unearthed in Romania has a large bird with hinged wings that flapped as the wearer ran. Although some indication of iron breastplates or chain mail exists, one of the most striking characteristics noted by ancient observers was the propensity of the Celts to go into battle naked, but for a helmet, sword belt, armlets, and a torc (a heavy necklace with religious significance). Contemporary artwork also depicts Celtic warriors fighting in the nude. In northern Britain the Picts were well known for painting their bodies blue before engaging in combat. Whether these practices were psychological ploys to intimidate foes or whether they held some religious significance is difficult to determine.

Celts usually fought as infantry, engaging in single combat, but have also been depicted in chariots. The two-horse chariot carried a driver and a warrior, and was probably used more for transportation to the battle and across the battlefield rather than as a fighting platform. Caesar does not mention any use of chariots by the Gauls, but they are often described in Roman combat against the inhabitants of Britain. The chariot driver was thus an auxiliary to the warrior, keeping close eye on him during combat to race the chariot to his position, to move him about the battlefield, or to rescue him when wounded. When Celtic cavalry is described, a unit of three is most common, the warrior being assisted by two bearers, much as appeared in feudal times with a knight, squire, and page.

Prior to battle, as the armies faced each other, individual Celtic warriors would offer challenges to single combat, usually with much boasting on their part and belittling of the enemy. This resulted in a series of combats that would either convince one side or the other to withdraw or provoke a general melee. As the Celts/Gauls became more accustomed to Mediterranean tactics, the challenges dwindled. Once the battle was to be joined, the Gauls blew masses of war trumpets, creating an awful din described by Diodorus: "Their trumpets again are of a peculiar barbarian kind; they blow into them and produce a harsh sound which suits the tumult of war" (Cunliffe, 1997). This sounding of the trumpets could have been a combination of psychological warfare and a summoning of the gods of war. Once the battle started, the strength of the Gallic attack was in its ferocity. If the enemy force could withstand the opening shock, the Gauls would often withdraw, having no other plan of battle and having expended their pent-up rage. In some battles, the warriors would continue the attack over the bodies of their fallen comrades, but that was more the exception than the rule.

It was their conflicts with the Romans that spelled the doom of the Gauls. The discipline of the Roman legions proved more than a match for the intensity of the Gallic fighting spirit, and the Gauls lost battle after battle. That, coupled with the arrival of Germanic tribes from the northeast, squeezed the European Gauls out of existence or onto the British Isles. The remoteness of Scotland and Ireland kept them free of Roman influence in society and language, and in Scotland the daunting terrain kept the migrant Scotti free from Scandinavian domination. Ultimately, the English, under Norman and later Tudor rule, conquered the islands and sublimated the Celtic heritage. Only since the eighteenth century with the discoveries of archaeological digs have the Celts come to modern attention. A renewed interest in their culture focuses more on language and society, rather than their vaunted military reputation.

References: Cunliffe, Barry, *The Ancient Celts* (Oxford: Oxford University Press, 1997); Dudley, Donald, *The Romans* (New York: Alfred Knopf, 1970); Jimenez, Ramon, *Caesar against the Celts* (New York: Sarpedon Publishers, 1995).

Charioteers

Specialists in warfare using horse-drawn wheeled vehicles for two millennia prior to the Roman Empire.

The earliest elite or specialized troops in history must have been chariot riders, who first appeared around 1700 BCE in the borderlands between the steppes of Asia and the river lands of Mesopotamia. True two-wheeled light chariots developed from Sumerian wooden carts or four-wheeled battle wagons drawn by onagers, as shown in the third millennium BCE Standard of Ur. However, they differ enormously from their early predecessors, and a great deal of technological advancement, specialization, and expense went into their development.

Before the chariot could become a practical means of conveyance, some method of harnessing the wild horse was necessary. Oxen, onagers, and donkeys all had their drawbacks as draught animals, being either too slow or uncontrollable. Early peoples must have quickly recognized the advantages that the horse offered in both areas. It was necessary, however, to work out a method of controlling the horse with a mouth bit and yoking it to a transport by means of a breast band or padded collar. Even then, horses could not pull heavy loads without these early collars choking them; therefore, chariots had to be developed that were as light as possible, with strong, yet open, frames and bent-wood spoked wheels (eventually the Egyptians built chariots that weighed no more than 75 pounds including harness). Furthermore, the axle that held the wheels had to be designed to pivot so the chariot's maneuverability and turning radius could be improved.

The expertise required to produce good chariots, together with the specialists necessary to maintain them and their horses in combat (grooms, saddlers, wheelwrights, etc.) meant that only wealthy armies could afford them. Moreover, the dominance these vehicles imparted on the battlefield quickly raised charioteers to a position of elite status among warriors of the ancient world.

Although javelins, maces, and swords are shown being used by charioteers in early artistic depictions, the composite bow was their most favored weapon and the one that made them most dangerous. Constructed of laminated wood and horn glued together in a curve, the short composite bow was the perfect weapon with which to rain down death upon masses of infantry and other charioteers as far as 300 yards away.

True chariots probably originated on the fringes of the agricultural world where the western steppe herdsmen met the settled peoples of the city-states of Mesopotamia.

No one knows who built the first chariot, but they almost certainly came from these borderlands. Here the knowledge of producing wheels, draughtpoles, and metal fittings for carts and wagons was pressed into service to meet the needs of nomadic sheep and goat herders for a fast-moving herding and hunting platform: the chariot. The advantages of the new vehicle must rapidly have become apparent. The chariot riders of the steppes discovered that their new weapon allowed them to hunt men as well as animals with equal ease. Around 1500 BCE, nomadic charioteers began to descend upon the civilized lands of the time: the Hyskos invaded Egypt, the Hurrians, Mittians, and Kassites swept into Mesopotamia, Aryans penetrated India, and the Shang overwhelmed northern China. All these invaders faced organized armies, but they were armies composed of infantry with perhaps a few of the clumsy battle wagons mentioned earlier. The chariot riders could circle these herds of men as they circled their herds of sheep on the steppes. One man drove the chariot while the other picked the enemy off with his compound bow, and both easily stayed out of reach of the infantry's short-ranged weapons. The assaulted infantry could not close with the far speedier chariots, nor could they retire. In such fashion charioteers consistently routed larger defending forces and carried off what they wished in food, gold, slaves, and other booty. In time, these aggressive nomads overthrew the very states they were raiding and established their own dynasties, based not on their numbers but on the sheer power of the chariot.

The rule of the invading charioteers was not long, however. All were overthrown or absorbed by the native populations, but their legacy lived on in the adoption of the chariot by the peoples they had conquered. The New Kingdom Egyptians and the Assyrians especially learned from the invaders and put what they had learned into practice: Their states became as aggressive and warlike as the nomads, only now they warred to protect their frontiers and to extend their boundaries in order to forestall new invasions. They made war a form of state policy, and the heart of their new mobile war machines was the two-wheeled chariot.

The New Kingdom Egyptian army had as its nucleus a chariot force, although not a large one. In reliefs and paintings, the pharaoh is always shown in his chariot, in the forefront of the battle, followed by a few nobles in their chariots and the mass of the army on foot. Despite artistic license and the need to portray the pharaoh in the best light, these depictions may be fairly accurate. In the earliest recorded battle in history, at Megiddo in 1469 BCE, the pharaoh Thutmosis III routed the Hyskos and forced their leaders to surrender. Only 83 Hyskos were killed in the battle, and another 340 taken prisoner, hardly the casualties one would expect, had a defeated army been pursued by a large chariot force. Two centuries later, in 1294 BCE, Rameses II fought the Hittites at Qadesh to a standstill with an army that, according to Egyptian accounts, numbered only 50 chariots and 5,000 infantry. However, those same accounts claim that the Hittites fielded 2,500 chariots—obviously an exaggeration. Still, the problems and expense inherent in maintaining a standing chariot force ensured that it would never be a large component of any army.

The Assyrians, too, as much as the Egyptians, are closely identified with the chariot. But the Assyrian army was far more professional and more organized for war as an imperial task than any of its contemporaries. Assyrian forces included specialized troops, armored infantry, engineers and siege units, and foreign troops who fought with their own unique weapons. However, Assyrian kings rode into battle in their chariots and the nobles, the cream of the Assyrian state, rode with them. At their core, they were charioteers.

The Egyptians, Assyrians, and most of their foes used a two-man crew—a fighter and his driver—in a light chariot pulled by two horses (Assyrians sometimes used four). This seems to have been the ideal compromise between speed, maneuverability, and fire power. After the ninth century BCE, the Assyrians seem to have added a third man, usually a shield bearer, to strengthen defenses. Some carvings and drawings from other ancient Middle Eastern nations depict four-, five-, and even six-man crews being pulled by four horses, although it is difficult to imagine how six men could actually fight from a chariot without constantly getting in each other's way. In these cases the chariot probably was being used as a means of transporting a combat team to the battlefield, rather than as an actual fighting vehicle. Both the Egyptians and the Assyrians moved the axle back from the center toward the rear of the car and allowed the axle a certain degree of movement within its brackets. Both innovations greatly increased the chariot's maneuverability. Assyrian ironsmiths even fitted a studded metal rim to the wheels to give the chariot more traction in turning.

Exactly how the chariot was used in combat is somewhat unclear. Certainly it acted as a mobile firing platform for archers, but its shock value must have been limited because the horses were unprotected and therefore vulnerable to hand weapons at close quarters. Despite the fact that kings and pharaohs are shown driving their vehicles over dead and dying enemies, anyone trying to fight from a chariot with a mace or sword must have encountered great difficulties. Furthermore, chariots could not maneuver over broken or wooded terrain. Over time, combatants would have learned how to counter chariot tactics, forming shoulder-to-shoulder ranks, using long spears to keep chariots away, protecting themselves with larger and stronger shields, and shooting chariot horses with their bows. Still, for over a thousand years, chariots offered the only real mobile fire power and speed in pursuit available, and this made them an indispensable component of the civilized armies of the time.

Eventually, the horse superseded the chariot in battle. The Assyrians had been breeding stronger horses, and by the eighth century BCE had produced a horse that could be ridden from the forward seat (with the weight over the animal's front shoulders), and thus be better controlled. Some Assyrian archers began to ride horses in battle. However, without stirrups, this was still a tenuous platform. On the steppes, some peoples may have already bred riding horses, or the animals may have been traded from Mesopotamia to nomads in the grasslands. Be that as it may, the nomads soon became mounted archers, and the days of the chariot were over. True cavalry simply possessed much more maneuverability than chariots and required far less trouble and expense to maintain. One of the final appearances of chariots in battle seems to have been at Gaugamela in 331 BCE, where the Persian king Darius had a field leveled and prepared so his chariots could charge unimpeded against the Macedonian pike phalanxes of Alexander the

Great. The results were disastrous for the Persians and Darius ultimately paid with his life. Some people, like the Bretons, continued to use chariots, but mostly as a sort of "battle taxi" in which to ride to and from combat. Once there, they fought on foot. This is the way Homer described their use in the *Iliad*, which was set around the twelfth century BCE but was probably written around the eighth or seventh century BCE. By the time of the Roman Empire, chariots had ceased to be weapons of war, or even to appear on battlefields, and instead became a quaint means of transport for the wealthy and a source of spectacle for the masses in great chariot races held in the Colosseum.

References: Ferrill, Arthur, *The Origins of War* (London: Thames and Hudson, 1985); Hackett, General Sir John, *Warfare in the Ancient World* (London: Sidgwick & Jackson, 1989); Keegan, John, *A History of Warfare* (New York: Random House, 1993).

Chindits

A special operations unit operating in Burma during World War II.

One of the more overlooked theaters of operations during World War II is the China-Burma-India theater, where Japanese forces ran amok in the early years of the war. After more than four years of combat in China, Japanese forces moved into Southeast Asia during 1940–1942. They were able to occupy Indochina with the assent of the German-directed Vichy French government, but they had to gain the remainder of the area by conquest. That conquest started December 8, 1941, within hours of the Japanese attack on the American naval base at Pearl Harbor, Hawaii. Japanese troops streamed through

British Brigadier Orde Charles Wingate. United States Department of Defense photograph.

the jungles of Malaya to capture Singapore, then turned eastward toward the greatest British possession: India. The occupation of Burma not only threatened the eastern frontier of India, but it also cut off the overland supply routes from the Indian Ocean to Chiang Kai-shek's nationalist Chinese forces. Extremely engaged in fighting in North Africa, the British could give little support to Indian defense. General Archibald Wavell was given command in India in February 1942, and he called upon the services of Orde Wingate, an eccentric British army officer, to strike at the Japanese.

Wingate was born into army life in India in 1903. Educated by his extremely religious parents, Wingate was a serious but not always successful student when he finally attended school in England. That

also characterized his record at the Royal Military Academy at Woolwich. Still, he managed to obtain a commission in 1926 and received his first assignment—to the Sudan. He learned Arabic on his own and was soon in demand for operations in the countryside where his language ability and study of the local customs stood him in good stead. He began to make a name for himself as a capable but erratic soldier. It was his transfer to Palestine in 1936 that marked the turning point in his career.

Palestine was then governed by the British under a League of Nations mandate, the country itself having been set aside as a Jewish homeland by the Versailles Treaty of 1919. The Arabs had little desire to give up the land to Jews, and constant harassment of emigrants took place. Wingate began to embrace Zionism and argued that the Jews should be allowed to organize self-defense forces. Upon being given that task, he created the Special Night Squads to combat Arab terrorist attacks. Wingate developed the tactics used by these irregular forces and became well known in the British Army for this specialty. It is to this early training that many trace the development of the modern Israeli defense forces.

Wingate's success in training these counterterrorist units brought him to the attention of Chaim Weizmann, a leading Zionist, who convinced him to assist in lobbying for Jewish causes in London. This overtly political action was regarded as out of place for a serving officer, and Wingate fell from favor with a number of higher-ranking officials. It was during this activity, though, that Wingate met and favorably impressed Winston Churchill, who would be his greatest supporter in years to come.

When Great Britain went to war in September 1939, Wingate was sent back to

Africa to aid in operations against Italian-held Ethiopia. In early 1941 he led his own specially trained "Gideon Force" as part of the British offensive to restore Emperor Haile Selassie. His mission was to disrupt the communications and bases of the Italian army, and in this, his force was extremely successful. Wingate's force of Ethiopians regularly defeated larger Italian units by bluff and superior maneuvering ability. Wingate escorted the emperor back into Addis Ababa in May 1942. In spite of the recognition he earned for his leadership abilities, he hurt himself by openly criticizing his superiors and theorizing about possible negative actions the British may have planned for Ethiopia. He was reduced in rank and shunned by his peers upon his return to Cairo and in July 1942 attempted suicide while suffering from a bout of malaria.

After his recovery and when in need of friends in high places, Wingate was called on by Wavell. He put Wingate in charge of the Bush Warfare School and soon the talents Wingate had developed in Palestine and Ethiopia were transferred and expanded in India. British public opinion was reeling from the loss of Singapore and the Japanese capture of Rangoon, Burma, with the threat that this posed to India. Badly in need of something to stoke morale, Wavell sent Wingate's men into Burma to disrupt Japanese rear areas. The force was composed originally of the Thirteenth King's Liverpool Regiment, the Third Battalion of the Second Regiment of the Gurkha Rifles, the 142nd Commando Company, with Royal Air Force support planes. As his troops also contained escaped Burmese and Burma was to be their area of operation, Wingate decided to give his soldiers a name to promote esprit de corps. He decided to name them *chinthe*, after the stone lions placed outside Burmese temples to ward off evil spirits, but this gradually was corrupted into "Chindits," the result of a mistake by a newspaper reporter for the London *Daily Express*. Wingate's first operation in Burma was a mixed success. He had no real knowledge of how to operate in the jungle and the dependence on resupply by air was an art in its infancy. Despite suffering from a variety of diseases as well as unfamiliarity with the terrain, the Chindits did indeed create havoc behind enemy lines, but it was more psychological than physical. Wingate returned after a few months in Burma with two-thirds of his force, but with valuable knowledge for future operations, including proof that the Japanese were not invincible in the jungles.

The morale boost for Britain was invaluable, and upon his return to London, Wingate immediately met with Churchill, now prime minister. Even more impressed with Wingate than previously, Churchill took him to meet with American politicians and military men at a conference in Quebec. Wingate's confidence won over President Roosevelt and some of the generals, and a joint operation was planned with the Chindits, British amphibious forces, and Chinese forces. The target was the central railroad junction of Myitkyina, into which Wingate's men were to be sent by glider to establish a number of strongholds from which to carry out guerrilla operations against the Japanese. What started out as a huge operation began to fall apart because of political concerns. In November 1943, the amphibious attack was canceled. That angered Chinese leader Chiang Kai-shek, who canceled the Chinese attack scheduled to be launched from the province of Yunnan. Other Chinese forces under command of American General Joseph Stilwell remained committed, but the overall operation was severely scaled back. Still, it proved fairly successful, and certainly well timed. The Japanese, in response to Wingate's first operation, decided to take the offensive against the Indian border cities of Imphal and Kohima. The commander of Japanese air forces in Burma warned against this major offensive, citing the British ability to place forces in the rear of the Japanese advance, but he was not heeded. Attacking in mid-March 1944, the Chindits soon secured their positions and harried the surprised Japanese, who had been focusing on their own offensive against India. The Chindit offensive coincided with attacks from the north under Stilwell's command.

Wingate directed the glider-borne landings, but the operations were severely hampered by an irregular supply of aircraft, occasional last-minute changes in forces, and the Japanese capture of one of the proposed landing zones. Still, the forces reached their appointed places and began operations against Japanese supply lines. On March 27 Wingate flew to meet with Colonel Philip Cochran, commander of the air support. The American B-25 bomber carrying him ran into heavy weather and never reached its destination. It was discovered days later buried in a mountainside, although whether it crashed owing to poor visibility or was shot down by Japanese aircraft has never been determined. Wingate's remains were identified and buried, oddly enough, at Arlington National Cemetery in the United States, because it was an American aircraft in which he died. The Chindits' operation continued under extremely difficult conditions. The Japanese focused a large number of men on the Chindits and soon outgunned them at the strongholds they were occupying for resupply by air. The Chindits were in action behind enemy lines from March through July 1944 and fought up to and past the point of endurance. The Chindits came under the command of General Stilwell, who was never a supporter of either the British or special operations. He ordered them to support his offensive even when the men were physically unable to continue. Stilwell's own medical officers told him the Chindits could no longer fight. Every one of them had suffered at least three attacks of malaria, the average loss of weight was 60 pounds per man, and they could no longer carry their supplies—much less continue to fight.

The British official history of the Burma campaign grants but slight credit to Wingate's forces, but the Japanese officers who survived the war told a different story. They were of the opinion that, had the Chindits not been active behind Japanese lines, the additional manpower and air power that the Japanese could have put to use in the planned attack on India would probably have been decisive. Even as it was, their offensive almost succeeded, but the forces diverted by the Chindits proved crucial. Furthermore, because Wingate's first operation inspired the Japanese to switch from a defensive to an offensive posture, their XV Army was almost completely destroyed in its failed offensive and during its subsequent retreat. Had the Japanese remained on the defensive, Stilwell's successful drive from the north would almost certainly have been thwarted and the overland supply route he established into China may not have been built.

References: Bidwell, Shelford, *The Chindit War* (New York: Macmillan, 1980); Rooney, David, *Burma Victory* (London: Arms and Armour Press, 1992); Slim, Field Marshal William, *Defeat into Victory* (London: Cassell and Company, 1956).

Condor Legion

A German air force unit operational during the Spanish Civil War (1936–1939).

In July 1936, conservative Spanish generals began an attempt to overthrow the liberal democratic government recently elected in Spain. The generals, under the leadership of Francisco Franco, faced a serious problem: Much of their army was not in Spain, but in Spanish Morocco. Because the Spanish navy remained loyal to the elected government, as did about half the army, the difficulty for the generals was how the Morocco-based troops could come to the aid of their fellow rebels at home. Representatives of Franco's forces traveled to Berlin to ask Nazi Chancellor Adolph Hitler if they could borrow planes from his air force, the *Luftwaffe*. Hitler hesitated, for failure would not only rob him of aircraft, but also of status. The convincing argument, however, was political and struck home with Hitler: The elected government was friendly with the Soviet Union. Hitler's hatred for communism almost matched his hatred for Jews, and the chance to strike a blow against international communism was too good to let pass. Hitler lent the Spaniards 20 Junkers, 52 transport aircraft, and six Heinkel 51 fighter escorts.

Thus began Operation Magic Fire. Luftwaffe pilots were "volunteered" to go to Spain and Morocco and train Spanish pilots, as well as to ferry Spanish troops. During the second week in August 1936, the airlift started—the first ever conducted. The Ju-52 was designed as a transport, but was used in Germany mainly as an airliner. Although the plane was designed to carry 17 passengers, the interiors were stripped of their seating and 40 soldiers were stuffed inside. German pilots flew as many as five round trips daily, carrying not only men but equipment and weapons, including 36 artillery pieces and 127 machine guns.

The planes flew without identifying markings at first. However, as the hastily trained Spanish pilots proved incompetent in handling the fighter planes, German pilots soon went into combat and the aircraft began displaying a black "X" on a white field on their rudders. On August 25, two German pilots each shot down a Loyalist aircraft for Franco's nationalist cause. At first these were individual decisions by the Germans, but when the airlift ended in October 1936 (after transporting 13,000 men), Hitler decided to expand his air force's role in Spain. He saw that Spain was not only a place to make a stand against communism, it was also a chance to combat-test new aircraft designs, as well as to give newly trained pilots on-the-job training. Thus was born the Condor Legion, so named by Luftwaffe chief Hermann Goering. The original complement was 48 bombers (converted Ju-52s) and 36 fighters. As new designs were manufactured, they were sent to Spain to update equipment. In addition, the Legion operated 12 reconnaissance planes, 14 reconnaissance-bomber float planes, antiaircraft cannon, and maintenance sections. Only the flying personnel were permitted to fight; army advisors were allowed only to train Franco's troops to use German tanks.

With the Legion fully organized, hundreds more "volunteers" were sent to Spain. They traveled as civilians, running the Loyalist blockade to land in Cadiz, then transferring to the nationalist headquarters of Seville. The strength of the Legion was around 5,000 men, usually rotating through on nine-month tours of duty. The unit was commanded by Hugo Sperrle, with Wolfram von Richthofen (cousin of World War I ace Manfred) as chief of staff. Richthofen was the Luftwaffe research and design chief, and he was able to view new aircraft in combat conditions and report any necessary changes to the factories. In addition to the Condor Legion, Italian dictator Benito Mussolini sent aircraft as well, but sent more infantry, ultimately almost 60,000 men.

The Germans faced a mixed group of opponents with a varied lot of aircraft. Much of the Loyalist air force was provided (at high cost) by the Soviet Union , who also provided manpower, artillery, and tanks. Many of the planes were flown by international volunteers, people from Europe and North America joining the Spanish to fight fascism. The material support from the Soviets provided a great boost in morale as well as combat effectiveness, and the Loyalists beat back Franco's major offensive against Madrid in November 1936. Frustrated by a lack of progress on the ground, Franco ordered the air force to bomb the city, a policy he had scrupulously avoided to that point. For five days German and Italian aircraft with German and Spanish crews bombed indiscriminately day and night, causing more than 1,000 casualties. Madrid continued to hold out. Franco then decided to attack supply lines into the city, and his German-trained tank crews went into battle with Condor Legion air support in the first hint of blitzkrieg tactics that the Germans employed so effectively in later years.

Unable to make headway against Madrid, Franco looked to occupy other Loyalist territory, focusing on the province of Vizcaya. The area was defended by a virtually impregnable series of defenses, and the Condor Legion got the assignment to break them. Newly arrived Heinkel 111s and Dornier 17s, the newest German bomber designs, gave the Germans an edge. The Ju-52s were too slow and had been easy prey for the Soviet I-15 fighter. The new German bombers could outrun the Russian planes. On March 31, 1937, the aerial offensive started, with bombs falling on the forts, nearby towns, and the harbor of Bilbao. Near Bilbao was the small farming town of Guernica. On April 26 the Condor Legion blasted it for three hours, although there was little there of strategic value other than a small arms factory on the edge of town. The bombers attacked everything, including hotels, hospitals, and schools. Low flying fighter planes machine-gunned running civilians. At least 70 percent of the town was destroyed and as many as 1,600 people died. The two structures of military value, the small arms factory and a bridge, were almost untouched. As much as the bombing of civilian areas of Madrid had brought international criticism, it was nothing compared to the loud condemnation from around the globe for the Guernica raid. Publicly, the Germans blamed communist terrorists for the fires that destroyed much of the town. Loyalist resistance in the area did weaken, however. Resistance around Bilbao broke under an armored assault in June in which German tankers fought alongside Spanish crews.

In the summer of 1937, both sides got upgraded aircraft. The Loyalists received Soviet I-16s, which they nicknamed *Moscas* (Spanish for "flies"). The Condor Legion received the latest German machine, the Messerschmitt 109. For a time the two opposing aircraft were well matched, but the engineers in Germany were faster at introducing modifications, and in early 1938, the latest Me-109 was almost 50 miles per hour faster than the I-16. The older aircraft, the He-51s, were dedicated to strafing missions. The pilots were not happy shooting ground targets, but the Loyalists became such good marksmen that the Germans had to develop new tactics to hit and run before the ground fire inflicted too much damage. Bombing became much more accurate with the introduction of the Junker 87, the infamous Stuka (short for *Sturmkampfflugzeug*). The dive bomber, although slow in level flight, was pinpoint accurate when bombing and became the most feared aircraft in the German arsenal as far as infantry was concerned.

Throughout 1939, the final year of the Spanish Civil War, the Condor Legion honed its skills. Close air support and rapid armored assaults became common practice, and the development of newer radios made the attacks even more effective as observers on the ground could direct the aircraft to particular targets. The Soviet tanks, heretofore far superior to the German panzers, found their match in the newly introduced German antiaircraft cannon, an 88-mm gun manufactured by the Krupp steel works. Although an extremely effective antiaircraft gun, this cannon also became the most effective tank-killer of World War II. By early 1939, Franco emerged victorious, and Germany had learned a number of valuable lessons. The Germans now had an air force that was not only well trained but combat-tested, and the close air support necessary to implement the blitzkrieg was finely tuned. Although Hitler's dream of Franco as an ally never came true, the German dictator had to be thankful for the opportunity the Spanish situation gave to his military to weld itself into a first-class fighting ma-

chine, which came close to conquering all of Europe.

References: Mason, Herbert Malloy, *The Rise of the Luftwaffe, 1918–1940* (New York: Dial Press, 1973); Thomas, Hugh, *The Spanish Civil War* (New York: Harper and Row, 1961); Time-Life series, *The Third Reich: Fists of Steel*, (Alexandria, VA: Time-Life, 1988).

Condottieri

Mercenary troops operating in the Italian peninsula from the twelfth through the fourteenth centuries.

The European practice of feudal society made a serf liable for 40 days' military service to his lord per year. The Crusades ended that practice, as troops were needed for years on end. European society of the time also experienced the growing power of the merchant classes, which came to dominate urban life but which had no military experience or inclination.

If the merchants were to protect their wealth and expand their power, they needed troops. In Italy these were "foreign" troops, although not necessarily from outside the peninsula. Anyone from a different city-state in Italy was considered foreign, and the five major powers (Florence, Venice, Milan, Naples, and the Papal states) all hired soldiers from outside their borders. It was considered prudent to hire these outsiders, the argument being that they would have no local ambitions, unlike citizens of the city-state. The city-state offered a *condotta*, or contract, for a soldier to raise the forces necessary, hence the term *condottiere*, or contractor (plural, *condottieri*).

The first mention of these mercenary companies in Italy comes in 1159 with the arrival of the "Company of Death" organized by Alberto di Giussano. These 900 knights fought for Pope Alexander against the Holy Roman Emperor Friedrich Barbarossa. The mercenaries practiced what would come to be the worst characteristic of the condottieri: living off the land and doing so as wantonly and destructively as possible. Profit came not just from the pay from their employers, but from whatever could be acquired along the way.

Most of the condottieri forces were predominantly cavalry, as the makeup of many of the forces were knights without lands or lords, known as free lances. The term "lance" came to designate the smallest unit of the condottieri force, made up of three men. The leader of this lance was the knight, who was supported by his squire, who looked after his armor and weapons, and a young page, who did the dirty work, such as laundry, cooking, and feeding horses. The knight and squire rode good warhorses; the page rode whatever animal was available. Five lances formed a *posta* and five *posta* formed a *bandiera*. A *caporale* commanded five lances, with other ranks commanding larger units through the senior officer, the captain general. Along with the forces went political advisors, or ambassadors, to negotiate with potential employers, and treasurers to handle payment of the troops.

The need for hired armies was so great that soldiering was one of the best methods for personal advancement at that time. Anyone with strength could fight, anyone with intelligence and strength could lead, and both made good money. The vast majority of the condottieri were peasants or the sons of artisans, many of whom rose to great wealth and influence, which they could never otherwise have obtained. The political atmosphere in Italy served the condottieri well, because two major factions struggled for dominance for more

than a century. The Guelph and Ghibelline parties represented the forces defending and attacking the power of the Catholic Church. The origins of this struggle came from Germany, where the Welf family fought the Hohenstauffens of Waiblingen over the relative role and power of the church and the Holy Roman Empire. The Catholic Church was constantly trying to extend its power—temporally as well as spiritually—past the bounds of the Papal States it had controlled since the era of Charlemagne at the start of the ninth century. All five city-states jockeyed for position in an ever-changing set of alliances. This meant that a condottieri force fighting *for* the Papal States may, in the next battle, be fighting *against* them, all the while receiving its pay from the same city-state that had just changed sides. Individual condottieri could also just as easily change sides themselves if the price was right, regardless of the political views of their employers.

Condottieri leaders sometimes became nobility and led the city-states themselves, as Francesco Sforza did in Milan. Pay included not just money, but lands and titles, and many times a young bride to seal the bargain. Marriage in the upper classes of Italian society at this time was more often than not a political or economic affair, not an amorous one. Thus did lower-class soldiers work their way to the social heights, because marriage into an established family gave one social legitimacy.

In order to reach these heights, of course, one had to be successful on the battlefield. Here is where the condottieri come under much criticism. They were trained soldiers in a population without such, and therefore they were valuable— too valuable to lose, in many cases. This fact meant that fighting between condottieri forces sometime verged on the ridiculous. The condotierri saw to it that sieges were long in order to save the lives of the soldiers as well as to draw more pay. Battles were sometimes negotiated rather than fought. The greatest contemporary critic of the condottieri, Niccolo Machiavelli, wrote disgustedly about the battle of Zagonara: "In this great defeat, famous throughout all Italy, no death occurred except those of Ludovico degli Obizi and two of his people, who, having fallen from their horses, were drowned in the mire" (Trease, 1971). Despite this gibe, the condottieri certainly fought often enough to prove their worth, and men died in real combat, but the condottieri are more remembered for their political maneuvers than their battles. Another mitigating factor for the condottieri is the fact that the condottieri units were dominated by heavy cavalry that needed open ground upon which to fight, precisely the type of terrain that is in short supply in Italy.

For professionals, the condottieri often had surprising difficulty adapting to new weaponry. During the era of the condottieri, gunpowder was introduced and artillery and personal firearms entered the military scene. At first, as knights, the condottieri were horrified at the matchlock muskets because—as the French nobility learned about longbows at Agincourt and Crécy—a peasant could easily take the life of a noble. One condottiere, Paolo Vitelli, put out the eyes and cut off the hands of prisoners who had handled these matchlocks against his forces. Still, one could not allow one's enemies to acquire such a weapon and use it against oneself, so firearm use spread. Artillery also achieved quick acceptance, once it was learned that the stone walls, which resisted catapults, could not stand before cannonballs. Fortress engineering hurried to catch up to, or stay ahead of, cannon development.

The age of the condottieri came to an end around the turn of the sixteenth century when the Italian peninsula was invaded by French troops. A professional force with national, not financial, motivations defeated the mercenaries repeatedly. This was proof that what Machiavelli had called for in his writings—a citizen army—was the wave of the future. Before the demise of the condottieri method, some condottieri had made themselves famous and rich. Francesco Sforza became duke of Milan. The English mercenary John Hawkwood was offered a lifetime contract to fight for Florence. Bartolomeo Colleone retired to become lord of Bergamo and rule his small state in a most enlightened manner. The other side of the coin was equally real: Francesco Carmagnola was beheaded by the Venetian authorities for his failure to win for his employers, and others met similar fates. Although mercenaries remained for centuries a regular source of fighting men, the condottieri were products of their time and quickly faded in the face of the rise of the citizen soldier.

References: Deiss, Joseph Jay, *Captains of Fortune* (New York: Thomas Crowell Company, 1967); Trease, Geoffrey, *The Condottieri* (New York: Holt, Rinehart, and Winston, 1971).

Conquistadors

A warrior class of Spain that defeated the Muslims and conquered Latin America during the fifteenth and sixteenth centuries.

In the seventh century CE, followers of the prophet Mohammed swept out of North Africa and invaded Spain. The Christian

Francisco Pizarro in the Battle of Cajamarca.

Spaniards were quickly overrun and driven into the mountainous provinces of Castile and Leon. Grimly, the Spanish Christians gathered their strength and struck back against the Muslims. This engendered a centuries-long war known as the *Reconquista*, the reconquest. To fight this war, the Spanish kings came to depend more and more on feudal heavy cavalry made up of aristocrats. These men were known as *hidalgos*; over time they also became known as *conquistadors*, or conquerors.

In early 1492, the last Muslim stronghold in Spain, the city of Grenada, fell to King Ferdinand and the Christians, and the Reconquista was at last over. This, however, brought up an old and reoccurring problem: What does a nation do with its military when the wars are over? Thousands of Spaniards knew no other art than war. Their entire lives had been devoted to the enterprise, and to expect them to turn to peaceful pursuits, such as agriculture or business, was naive at best. King Ferdinand found it increasingly difficult to control these bellicose fellows. Bands of unemployed soldiers began to wander the countryside, following popular captains and taking what—until then—had been freely given: the best of everything. Ferdinand

had a serious social problem on his hands. Then, in early 1493, one of his admirals, Christopher Columbus, returned from a voyage of exploration and reported finding a strange new world, which might be India, China, or even Japan. This news was a godsend to Ferdinand, who recognized in it the answer to what to do with his unemployed soldiers.

The New World (despite Columbus's insistence, it was not India, China, or Japan) became a beacon for the Spanish soldiers, for it offered them the chance to serve the mother country, spread the true faith, and possibly get rich in the process. This lure of "Glory, God, and Gold" proved almost irresistible. Soon the New World was teeming with heavily armed professional soldiers who proudly called themselves conquistadors.

Although some of the conquistadors were aristocrats and nobles, most were either young men from noble but poor backgrounds or common soldiers. What they all shared was a thirst for adventure, a dislike of discipline, and a great capacity for greed. Noble or commoner, all conquistadors were passionately individualistic; indeed, they raised individualism almost to a cult status. Their lust for power and wealth made them fierce rivals, and they frequently spent as much time fighting each other as they did the Native Americans. On the other hand, they also saw themselves as "bands of brothers" facing an unknown and hostile world. They were proud, daring, and reckless almost beyond belief, and their capacity for enduring heat, cold, hunger, and pain became legendary. The courage and hubris necessary for a few hundred of these men to march into the midst of hundreds of thousands of native warriors and demand their surrender is almost incomprehensible, as is the cruelty of which they were capable: They came to the New World with a cross in one hand and a sword in the other, and many of their deeds, committed ostensibly in the name of a benevolent religion, are horrifying in the extreme.

The weapons and training of the conquistadors were typical of late fifteenth-century Europe. Horses were always in short supply because of the difficulties in transporting them across the Atlantic. Consequently, cavalry was usually a minor arm in the conquistador forces, although it was very impressive psychologically to the Native Americans, who were terrified by this new, to them unknown, animal. Most conquistadors were heavy infantry, wearing iron cuirasses (breastplates) and helmets, as well as tassets to protect their thighs. Some wealthier men might have more complete arm and hand protection, and a few even wore suits of plate mail, although this was almost always restricted to cavalry. The conquistadors' weapons were rapiers and two-handed broadswords, pikes and halberds, crossbows and matchlock muskets, and a few cannons. In battle they always tried to seize the initiative, utilizing their superior weapons and defensive armor to shock and demoralize the natives, thus rendering them almost incapable of self-defense. When fighting alongside their own native allies, the conquistadors formed an irresistible spearhead on the attack, easily punching a hole in the enemy's lines through which their allies would pour, exploiting the flanks and rear of the enemy and breaking their formations. These simple tactics proved successful time and again in the conquest of the New World. The conquistadors' success is not surprising: Technologically speaking, the Spanish were almost 2,000 years in advance of any New World civilization.

None of the Native American peoples whom the Spanish encountered had developed iron working or the wheel, and without iron and steel weapons and armor, they were doomed.

Disease was also a very important factor in the defeat of the native populations. Native Americans had no immunity to diseases such as measles, smallpox, and the "Black Death" (bubonic plague). These diseases killed millions of them and left the survivors almost powerless to defend themselves from the Spanish onslaught. To many Native Americans, it seemed that their very gods had turned against them.

The true conquest of the New World began in 1519 when Hernan Cortés landed on the coast of Mexico with 550 men and 16 horses. He had heard rumors of a powerful tribe known as the Aztecs who ruled a vast and rich empire located to the west of Cuba in the interior Valley of Mexico. From their capital city of Tenochtitlan, which was built in the middle of a lake, the Aztecs, under their emperor Montezuma, controlled perhaps 11 million subject people. However, many of these people resented Aztec rule and, seeing Cortés as a possible savior, they allied with the strange newcomers. Playing on Aztec beliefs that he might be a god, Cortés boldly entered Tenochtitlan and captured Montezuma. Although he was driven from the city by a new emperor, Cortés received reinforcements, and in 1520 renewed his assaults.

Cortés's men built a fleet of small galleys on the shores of the lake and, with their Indian allies, instituted a siege of Tenochtitlan. An epidemic of smallpox was raging in the city, and—besieged from within and without—the Aztecs stood little chance. By 1521 Tenochtitlan had fallen, the conquest of the Aztec Empire was complete, and Cortés had literally become a king by his own hand. The surviving Indians found themselves virtual slaves, forced to labor in the silver mines and on the great estates of their new masters.

In 1530, another daring conquistador, Francisco Pizarro, set off to investigate rumors of another vast empire far south of Mexico. In present-day Peru he discovered the Incas, and used Cortés's methods as a blueprint for his own conquest. Although he had only 150 men, they boldly marched into the heart of the Inca nation to the capital city of Cajamarca. There they demanded an audience with the great Inca ruler Atahualpa. Although Atahualpa was backed by thousands of his professional soldiers, Pizarro and his 150 men seized the emperor and proceeded to slaughter over 7,000 Inca nobles and retainers without the loss of a single Spaniard. They then offered to ransom Atahualpa for a room full of gold and silver. Although it required several months, the ransom was finally assembled in 1533, at which point Pizarro ordered Atahualpa strangled. The Inca empire, deprived of its rightful ruler and most of its nobles and administrators, died with Atahualpa. Within two years the Inca people were subjugated, just as the Aztecs had been by their new overlords. Although Pizarro became rich and was named governor of Peru by the king, he did not outlive Atahualpa by much. In 1541 he was assassinated in his palace in Lima by rivals.

Other Spanish conquistadors explored the Americas searching for more rich empires to topple. In 1513 Ponce de Leon searched the swamps and everglades of Florida for the Fountain of Youth, a mythical spring reputed to cure ills and rejuvenate those who drank its waters. Hernando De Soto explored the Mississip-

pi River valley in 1539–1542. Francisco Coronado set off to find the Seven Cities of Gold in 1540, and explored and claimed most of present-day Arizona, Colorado, Kansas, and northern Texas. Other conquistadors pushed up the Pacific coast and established settlements in Los Angeles and San Francisco. Although these men failed to find any more Aztecs or Incas, they did help Spain claim an American empire that in time would prove more valuable than the gold of Mexico and Peru. All of this took place in a remarkably short time; within 40 years the great conquest was over. But because of the conquistadors, the world, for good or ill, would never be the same again.

References: Descola, Jean, *The Conquistadors, trans. Malcolm Barnes* (London: George Allen and Unwin, 1957); Fuentes, Patricia de, *The Conquistadors: First Person Accounts of the Conquest of Mexico* (New York: Orion, 1963); Innes, Hammond, *The Conquistadors* (New York: Knopf, 1969).

Cossacks

Horsemen of the west Asian steppes, known for their warlike nature from the sixteenth to the twentieth centuries.

Cossacks are a Russian tribal group that probably originated from the serfs in the Moscow area during the fourteenth and fifteenth centuries. They fled their peasant lives under the yoke of the aristocratic *boyars* and established farming and stock-raising communities along the Dnieper, Don, Kuban, and Ural Rivers and in Siberia. The name is probably Turkic in origin, *kazak*, translated variously as "freeman" or "wanderer." They first appeared as raiders and pirates in the 1500s and became both soldiers of the czar and

Two Cossack soldiers astride their ponies, December 1895. Library of Congress, Prints & Photographs Division, World's Transportation Commission Photograph Collection [reproduction number LC-W7-1165]

pioneers almost by accident. In 1581 they were hired by a merchant family, the Strogonoffs, to drive back Tatars who had been controlling Siberia and raiding into Muscovite lands. Siberia was seen as potentially a source of wealth in furs that the Strogonoffs, with royal support, could exploit. The Strogonoffs also hoped to turn the Cossacks, who had often raided their caravans, into allies or else to see them die at the hands of the Tatars, either of which would suit the Strogonoffs and Russian trade nicely.

Under the leadership of Yermak, their chief *(hetman or ataman)*, 800 Cossacks entered Siberia in September 1581. Why they launched their campaign with winter coming on is a mystery, for they suffered in the open. In spring of 1582 they pushed deeper into Siberia and met forces of the main Tatar chieftain, Kutchum Khan. At first the Cossacks fared well against superior forces, because they had harquebuses and the Tatars had no experience of gunpowder. With these matchlocks, Yermak defeated Kutchum's forces and captured

his capital at Sibir, but the Cossack chief had lost many of his men to disease, cold, and guerrilla action by the Tatars. Although Yermak died a year later (after most of his men), the power of the Tatars was broken and the Russian Czar Ivan IV expanded his country eastward.

The early Cossacks tended to move and raid by river, establishing villages and trading posts at river junctions, engaging in pillage and commerce much as did the early founders of Russia, the Vikings. The Cossacks tamed the frontier for their own purposes but at the same time acted as willing or tacit agents of the czar. By the 1630s, Cossacks had reached the Pacific Ocean and a generation later they had traversed the Aleutians into North America. Their wandering also took them southward toward the Caspian and Black Seas, with Russian authority and settlement moving in behind them. In 1650, the Russian Khabarov led a Cossack force across the Amur River in search of sables. They encountered Manchu tax collectors and soon thereafter Chinese troops. Russians sparred with Manchus along the frontier for almost 40 years, and the Cossacks were doing most of the fighting. After signing a treaty in 1689 ceding control of central Asia to the Manchus, the Cossack tradesmen looked toward the Pacific. Cossack fur traders explored and trapped Alaska, western Canada, and even the Rocky Mountains.

Meanwhile, Cossack and Russian interests were not always coinciding in the western lands. Although they served Czar Ivan IV in his campaigns in Astrakhan and the Crimea, with later czars, relations ebbed and flowed. During a conflict over the throne between Boris Gudonov and a pretender claiming to be Ivan IV's grandson, the Cossacks seized the opportunity to establish a homeland for themselves along the Don River. In 1648 the Cossacks began their longstanding conflict with Poland after the Poles attempted to acquire territory in the Ukraine populated by Zaporogue Cossacks. The Poles tried both to impose feudalism on the population and ban the Russian Orthodox faith. Under the leadership of hetman Bogdan Chmielnicki, a mixed Cossack and Muslim Tatar army from the Crimea routed a Polish army at Korsun. Believing that his people alone could not defeat the Poles, Chmielnicki offered his homeland, the Ukraine, to Czar Alexis. Under the Act of Pereyaslav, Russia took over the Ukraine in return for guaranteed local autonomy for the Cossacks. War between Russia and Poland continued until 1667, with the occasional interference of Sweden and the shifting loyalties of various Cossack and Tatar forces. Russia gained most of the Ukraine. When Czar Alexis proved tyrannical, Stenka Razin led a Cossack uprising that temporarily established an independent state around Astrakhan and Tsaritsyn (Stalingrad).

The Cossacks once again fought for the czar when Peter the Great in 1696 captured the Black Sea port of Azov, a battle in which the Don Cossacks played the major role. In 1705 Peter created a new army by drafting a peasant out of every 20 households for lifetime military service, but raised a separate force of 100,000 Cossacks. When Catherine the Great became czarina, she, too, had mixed relations with the Cossacks. Although she invited 54 Cossacks to be among the 564 representatives from across Russia to assist in drafting a new legal code, her reluctance to emancipate the serfs provoked a Cossack revolt. In 1772 Emelyan Pugachev, a Don Cossack and veteran of service in the Russian army against the Turks and Prussians, pro-claimed himself Peter III (who had died some years earlier) and stated he would overthrow the usurper Catherine. With the aid of almost every contingent in southern Russia that had a grudge against Catherine, Pugachev raised 20,000 men and captured a number of cities including Kazan and Saratov, then marched on Moscow. Catherine looked to the nobility for aid, and disciplined imperial troops defeated Pugachev's peasants. They surrendered their leader to Catherine, cementing the fate of serfs as well as the relationship between the monarch and the nobility.

Another role in which the Cossacks gained notoriety was in attacks upon Jews. During the war against Poland they had instituted pogroms in the territory they occupied, and when Czar Alexis joined with the Cossacks against Poland, his armies killed Jews as well. Again in Catherine the Great's time they slaughtered Jews along the Polish frontier. In 1734, 1750, and 1768 Cossacks ravaged Jewish communities in Kiev and throughout the Ukraine. In the last instance, they claimed to have a document from Catherine herself giving them authority "to exterminate the Poles and the Jews, the desecrators of our holy religion" (Durant, 1967). By this time the Cossacks had become master horsemen, and the image of the pogroms against the Jews was to be equated with the Cossack on horseback.

The Cossacks often proved useful to the czars, who in the nineteenth century began to use them not only as part of the army but also for suppressing political dissent. The reputation they had developed in the pogroms was reinforced by the appearance of Cossack cavalry breaking up meetings of whatever groups the government deemed dangerous. When large-scale revolt began in 1905, Cossack troops forced it into submission, but when the same happened in 1917, the Cossacks had had enough. Cossack horsemen fought for the czar during World War I, but would not do his bidding in suppressing the Menshevik revolt in March 1917. They did fight against the communists during the Russian Civil War, but were ultimately defeated and forced to submit to the communist system. They were forbidden after the Russian Revolution to serve in the military or even maintain their cavalry traditions, but in 1936 Stalin relented and formed Cossack units that fought against the Germans. Some, however, emulated other Ukrainians who welcomed the Nazis as liberators from the communists, and some Cossack units did serve with the Germans. Whether fighting for or against the invaders, Cossacks went into battle on horseback, probably the last time any large mounted units will ever operate in warfare.

In the wake of the decline and fall of the Soviet Union , the Cossack people have enjoyed something of a resurgence. In all their old territories, but mainly in Kazakhstan, various associations have formed to perpetuate their culture. Such organizations have spread as far northward as Moscow and St. Petersburg. They still seem to fight on both sides of the Russian government, however, by both demanding local autonomy yet protesting Russian cession of territory like the Kuril Islands. In 1992 Boris Yeltsin gave the Cossacks the status of an ethnic group and called for the use of Cossack troops to protect Russia's borders.

References: Durant, Will, and Ariel Durant, *Rousseau and Revolution* (New York: Simon and Schuster, 1967); Longworth, Philip, *The Cossacks* (New York: Holt, Rinehart and Winston, 1970); Seaton, Albert, *The Horsemen of the Steppes* (London: Hippocrene, 1985).

Czech Legion

Unit of Czechoslovak nationals caught between the Central Powers and Russian/Bolshevik forces in World War I.

When World War I broke out, Czech emigrés were scattered across the globe. Most of the men went looking for the nearest recruiter to join the army of whatever country they were in. France took a number of them into the Foreign Legion, while later in the war the British allowed them into the ranks of their army, and the Italians began using them as well. The largest number of emigrés, however, was in Russia, and they had no love for the Austro-Hungarian Empire that had long dominated their Bohemian homeland. Thus, the Czar was happy to recruit these motivated fighters into the Russian Army, and in 1915, the Czech Company was formed. Starting out in the role of scouts, their ranks were soon swelled by more men who were either captured in battle or defected from their forced service in the Austrian army. By May 1916, the force had grown to become the Czecho-Slovak Riflemen Regiment, then the Czecho-Slovak Riflemen Brigade. In return for this support, Czar Nicholas II hinted at national independence for a Czech state after the war.

While more and more Czechs came into the Russian camp, a Czech professor named Thomas Masaryk lobbied the Russian government to lead an entire Czech army within the Russian forces. Masaryk had no luck with this concept until the czar was overthrown in March 1917. The new, democratic Menshevik government gave Masaryk permission to organize the force. By September 1917, the force was at

Vladivostok, July 1920. A panzerzug armored train. It was with trains such as this that the Czechs kept the Red Army at bay and held the eastern end of the Trans-Siberian Railroad for more than a year while waiting for Allied ships to take them home. Courtesy Dr. Robert Faltin, Edmonton, Alberta, Canada.

division strength and the following month was designated the Czecho-Slovak Corps of some 40,000 men. It continued to grow until it finally reached a strength of 65,000–70,000 men. They fought very well, usually filling the gaps created by massive numbers of Russian desertions. The Russian war effort continued to deteriorate under Menshevik leadership until, in late October, Vladimir Lenin arrived and declared a communist government.

Through the remainder of 1917 and into early 1918, the Germans continued a steady advance into the Ukraine. The Czechs slowly retreated to Kiev, where they had to make a decision: Should they disband and each make his way homeward as best he could, or should they remain together and try to fight their way out of Russia in hopes of joining the Allies in France? They chose the latter course. Their first choice for escape was via Archangel on the northern coast, but that way was cut off by advancing German and Austrian armies, so they requisitioned whatever trains were available with the intent of heading eastward to Vladivostok. They fought an intense, two-day delaying action at Kiev to cover the withdrawal of the bulk of their force and rolled eastward on the Trans-Siberian Railway.

When Lenin's government signed the Treaty of Brest-Litovsk in March 1918, ending the Russian war against the Central Powers, it still had to contend with the counter-revolutionary White Army. Thus, it was in no position to help or hinder the Czechs and agreed to allow them free passage to Vladivostok. The Czechs in return declared themselves completely neutral and refused to aid any of the factions in the civil war. Their peaceful passage was short-lived, however, for soon Bolshevik units along the rail line (acting independently of any agreements made in Moscow) demanded arms and ammunition in return for the necessary train cars and safe passage. Seeing that if they cooperated they would soon be defenseless, the Czechs began fighting their way through. A skirmish between Bolshevik troops and Czechs at Tcheliabinsk convinced the former that the Czechs would surrender no more arms. This coincided with a message from Bolshevik War Minister Leon Trotsky (possibly under pressure from the Germans) to detain or destroy the Czech forces as anti-revolutionary.

Once past the Volga, the Czechs had virtually complete control of the railroad, but there were insufficient trains for the entire force to be transported en masse. Thus, they had to move forward in sections, with forward units holding stations while rear units caught up. They ran into some opposition and natural difficulties upon reaching Lake Baikal, where they confronted some naval units controlled by the Bolsheviks. The Czechs, having requisitioned anything that could float and mounted guns on all the boats they could,

succeeded in defeating the Red Navy units on the lake.

Their approach to the city of Ekaterinburg proved a blessing and a curse. Some units at the rear of the long stretch of railroad captured a train carrying eight cars full of gold from the Imperial reserve. Possession of that much gold made the Bolsheviks less likely to attack and more likely to negotiate. On the other hand, the royal family was being held in the city. When the Bolsheviks guarding them heard of the Czech approach, they assumed the force was coming to rescue Nicholas and his family. They immediately killed the family rather than have them be liberated. As it turned out, the Czechs never knew of the royal presence or even entered the city.

In order to maintain security, the Czechs gradually roamed farther and farther from the tracks, and by defeating whatever units of the Red Army approached, they provided inspiration to the counter-revolutionary movement. With the Red Army virtually destroyed in the region, Siberia declared itself an independent nation. Meanwhile, Thomas Masaryk had left the country and contacted the Allied leaders, who promised an independent Czechoslovakia if the Czechs would maintain control of the railway and aid the White Army. The Allies would also provide transport for them once they reached the Pacific coast. To make sure the Czechs knew they were serious, American forces landed in Siberia. Unfortunately, the White Army leadership was corrupt and increasingly brutal as they lost ground to the Bolsheviks, so the Allies withdrew their support, as did the Czechs. Some anti-communists among the Czechs stayed behind and joined the Whites, but they were wiped out with the rest of the army.

The Czechs, while waiting for transport, controlled the Trans-Siberian Railway along its entire eastern length, patrolling the countryside and maintaining order among the civilian population. The first ships began to arrive in April 1919, and the Czechs began withdrawing their men eastward to the port city. By May most had sailed away, heading for home via the United States or the Indian Ocean and Mediterranean Sea. The survivors made it home by 1920.

The Allies held up their end of the bargain and officially recognized the Czechs for their resistance to the Bolshevik regime. British Prime Minister David Lloyd George wrote to Masaryk, "The story of the adventures and triumphs of this small army is, indeed, one of the greatest epics of history. It has filled us all with admiration for the courage, persistence, and self-control of your countrymen, and shows what can be done to triumph over time, distance and lack of material resources by those holding the spirit of freedom in their hearts. Your nation has rendered inestimable service to Russia and to the Allies in their struggle to free the world from despotism." (Horne, nortvoods.net)

The Czechs returned to the Russians only seven of the eight cars of gold they had captured. The rest went for supplies during their stay in Siberia and to charter a bank in Prague when they got home. Thomas Masaryk was elected the first president of Czechoslovakia in 1920. When the Soviet Union took control of the country after World War II, survivors of the Czech Legion were persecuted. Since the collapse of the Soviet Union, however, a monument to the Legion has been erected in Vladivostok. The last survivor of the Czech Legion died in 2001.

References: Baerlein, Henry, *The March of the Seventy Thousand* (New York, Arno, 1971); Dupuy, Ernest, *Perish by the Sword* (Harrisburg, PA: Military Service Publishing, 1939); Horne, Charles F., "The Odyssey of the Checho-Slovaks: The Wandering War of the 'Army without a Country'", quoted by Dale Jones, nortvoods.net/rrs/siberia/czecharmy.

Delta Force

A United States Special Operations Force dedicated to counterterrorism.

The Delta Force, also known as the Combat Applications Group, was created by U.S. Army Colonel Charles Beckwith in 1977, in response to terrorist acts which occurred in the 1970s. Delta Force conducts missions similar to those of the British Special Air Service (after which Delta Force was modeled) because of Colonel Beckwith's year-long tour with the British force. The two forces share many similarities and sometimes train together.

Insignia patch of 1st Special Forces Operational Detachment Delta Unit

The existence of Delta Force is officially denied by the Pentagon, although many civilians allege that the unit took part in Operation Eagle Claw, the failed attempt to rescue American hostages from the U.S. Embassy in Iran in 1980. The Delta Force is also believed to be involved in numerous other operations, including Operation Urgent Fury (the invasion of Grenada in 1983), Operations Desert Shield and Desert Storm (Kuwait 1990–1991), Somalia (the infamous "Black Hawk Down" mission in 1993), Operation Uphold Democracy in Haiti (1994), Operations Enduring Freedom and Anaconda in Afghanistan (2001–2002), and Operation Iraqi Freedom. During the Iraqi Freedom operation, Delta Force allegedly entered Baghdad in advance, along with Navy SEALs, building networks of informants while eavesdropping on and sabotaging Iraqi communication lines. There is also a rumor that Delta operatives and Navy SEALs, after gaining access to the country prior to the invasion, planted explosive devices on important buildings and blew them up when the air raids began.

Counterterrorist missions in which they have supposedly been directly or indirectly involved include rescuing the passengers of a hijacked airliner in Bangkok in 1981 and saving American General James Dozier from Italian Red Brigade terrorists in 1982. They also responded to the hijacking of TWA Flight 847 in Beirut and the *S.S. Achille Lauro* in 1984, and the takeover of the Japanese Embassy in Lima, Peru, in 1997. Delta Force units have reportedly been employed in intelligence-gathering missions in Honduras (1982), Libya (1984), Lebanon (mid-late 1980s), Bosnia (1996), Kosovo (1998), and Afghanistan (since 2001). They also have had domestic duties, providing security for the Pan-American Games in Puerto Rico (1979), the Olympic Games in Los Angeles (1984) and Atlanta (1996), as well as more direct involvement in a prison riot in Atlanta (1987) and the Branch Davidian confrontation in Waco, Texas (1993).

Delta Force is believed to be divided into three different squadrons, subdivided into "troops," each of which specializes in a different skill, such as paratroopers (HALO and HAHO) or SCUBA. Delta Force is believed to recruit its members from the Army, usually from the Army Special Forces such as the Green Berets and the Rangers. They also recruit for the Army Reserve and the National Guard. Potential Delta Force operatives reportedly undergo an extremely rigorous training regime. Those soldiers who are initially selected are usually chosen in one of three ways: in response to advertisements posted at Army bases across the country; by personal recommendation from a trusted high-ranking officer; and, on occasion, by recruiting individuals who might not be interested in serving in the Delta Force, but whose skills, such as speaking a particular language or possessing extraordinary technical abilities, are pertinent to a mission.

Their main compound stands in a remote area of Fort Bragg, North Carolina, and is thought to house about 2,500 personnel. Reports of the compound mention numerous shooting facilities (both for close-quarters battle and longer-range sniping), a dive tank, an Olympic-size swimming pool, a huge climbing wall, and duplicates of buses, trains, and an airliner for counterterrorist training. Because the group never knows what mission they will need to accomplish next, they must train for any situation. To acquire field training, the Delta Force participates in exercises with other foreign elite units, such as Britain's 22 SAS Regiment and Germany's GSG-9, and equivalent units from France, Israel, and Australia. Delta troopers are also equipped with the most advanced weaponry and equipment available in the U.S. special operations arsenal. A significant portion of their gear is highly customized and cannot be found anywhere but on Delta Force members. An early example of this was a specially constructed HAHO parachute rig. The parachute had been adapted to allow jumpers to keep their hands at their sides during the descent rather than above their heads. This modification prevented the loss of mobility which can occur as a result of prolonged flight time in such an unnatural position. They could now land quickly and be more mobile to reduce the risk of being shot down.

Delta Force operators are granted an enormous amount of flexibility and independence. They reportedly do not maintain any general uniformed presence and civilian clothing is the standard attire on or off duty while at Ft. Bragg. This is done to conceal their identities as operatives of the Delta Force. If uniforms are worn, which is very rare, they display no ranks, names, or branch names. Hair is allowed to grow to civilian standards in order for the force to blend into their surroundings. Members of the force also call each other by name, not rank, thus reducing the risk of being recognized as military personnel and reinforcing a sense of brotherhood among the men.

Owing to the success of special operations units and the changing nature of warfare away from large-unit operations, the U.S. military has plans to increase its special forces, including the "non-existent" Delta Force.

Nick Jourdan

References: Beckwith, Charlie, *Delta Force* (New York: Harcourt, 1983); SpecWar.net, "Delta Force," http://www.specwarnet.net/americas/delta.htm, 1 November 2005; SpecialOperations.com, "1st Special Forces Operational Detachment—Delta (SFOD-D)," www.specialoperations.com; www.specialoperations.com/Army/Delta_Force/operations.htm, 1 November 2005; Tyson, Anne Scott, "Plan Seeks More Elite Forces to Fortify Military," *Washington Post*, 24 January 2006.

Dervishes, or Fuzzy-Wuzzy

A Sudanese tribe led by a radical Islamic leader in the late nineteenth century, best known for their tenacity in battle, especially against the British Army.

In the 1870s Egypt was a semi-autonomous possession of the Ottoman Empire and under the direction of an official known as the khedive. Ismail, the khedive, was a particularly corrupt individual who spent the country into such debt that the French and British sent in financial experts to take over the government and straighten out its tax collecting and bill paying. In order to support this action, in 1880 the Europeans sent in troops as well, with the British sending the lion's share. Having foreigners in their government and patrolling their streets did not sit well with the Egyptians, and the British found it neces-

sary to put down a revolt by an Egyptian officer named Arabi. Shortly afterward in the Sudan, the desert countryside south of Egypt, a religious leader rose to power to lead his followers against the infidels. This was Mohammed Ahmed, who called himself the *Mahdi*, or Messiah.

The idea of a Muslim messiah had been foretold for centuries, and occasionally a leader arose to gather the faithful against non-Muslim enemies. Thus, Mohammed Ahmed was one in a series of Mahdis who came to power either through self-promotion and exploitation of his followers or true religious fervor. In the Sudan the Mahdi started with a small group of followers and expanded his power through intimidation or by success against the British. The British called his followers dervishes. Technically, this is a term describing collections of Muslim Sufi mystics who often perform amazing feats while in a trance or the throes of religious ecstasy. The term seemed fitting to the British, because the Mahdi's followers fought with a fanatical courage and no fear of death.

The British government, under the direction of Prime Minister William Gladstone, had little interest in the Mahdi until the latter scored a stunning victory over an Egyptian force commanded by a British officer. In 1883 William Hicks led 10,000 ill-prepared men into the Sudanese desert and was ambushed and massacred at Kashgil south of the major city of Khartoum. This feat convinced many that the Mahdi was genuine, and his ranks swelled. One such tribe, the Hadendowa from the hills of eastern Sudan near the Red Sea coast, organized themselves under the leadership of Osman Digna. He had little to recommend him as a soldier, and apparently his men had little personal regard for him, but he was an excellent strategist and his raids kept his men in booty.

Digna's men slaughtered two Egyptian forces along the coast near the town of Saukin in late 1883, but Digna scored his most impressive victory on February 5, 1884. Hicks's replacement was Valentine Baker, formerly of both the British and Turkish armies. He commanded a relief force of 3,800, marching to rescue a garrison at the town of Tokar. Baker's force was a mixed lot: a few European officers, a number of high-quality black troops of southern Sudan who had been slave-soldiers, and a large number of untrained and unmotivated Egyptians. They were ambushed at El Teb by 1,200 Hadendowa tribesmen. The British called these men Fuzzy-Wuzzies, because of their practice of greasing their hair with sheep lard. However, that seemingly innocent name belied the rebels' fighting ability. Although they were armed with nothing but spears and clubs, the Fuzzy-Wuzzy attack was so determined and their reputation so fierce that the Egyptians immediately panicked and ran. The confusion made it difficult for the Sudanese soldiers to fight well and the Europeans who stood to fight were badly mauled. Baker's command lost 2,400 men and 3,000 rifles, along with half a million cartridges, four Krupp cannon, and two Gatling guns.

The British government was finally waking up to the very real threat arising in the Sudan, and Queen Victoria urged Gladstone to send troops. Within weeks a new force of 4,000 men under General Sir Gerald Graham was sailing down the Red Sea to land at Trinkitat, and from there to deal with Digna and his Fuzzy-Wuzzy. The Scottish Black Watch regiment distinguished itself in a second battle at El Teb on February 28, where, with a loss of fewer than 200 dead and wounded, the Scots inflicted more than 800 deaths on the Hadendowa. On March 9, Graham ordered the column to march on Tamai, supposed to be Digna's headquarters. Here the Fuzzy-Wuzzy, well armed with British rifles captured the previous month and with their usual fanaticism, made their mark on military history and literature.

The British advanced in their traditional square formation, which had proven unbreakable for decades. When they engaged the Fuzzy-Wuzzy on March 13, the British had early success. Graham ordered the Scots to advance, and in so doing they opened the square. The Fuzzy-Wuzzy immediately swarmed through a narrow gap in the British ranks and proceeded to stab, shoot, and club anyone within reach. Fighting was hand-to-hand, and even badly wounded tribesmen continued to hack at British soldiers. The quickly re-formed square kept out any further tribesmen while the inner ranks killed all those who had rushed inside. A trailing square quickly came up in support and drove off the remaining Fuzzy-Wuzzy, who lost some 2,400 men killed that day. Digna retreated to the hills and the British declined to follow him.

This action and these tribesmen were immortalized by the poet laureate of the Victorian British Army, Rudyard Kipling, in his poem "Fuzzy-Wuzzy."

In 'E rushes at the smoke when we let drive,
An', before we know, 'e's 'ackin' at our 'ead;
    'E's all 'ot sand an' ginger when alive,
An' 'e's generally shammin' when 'e's dead.
    'E's a daisy, 'e's a ducky, 'e's a lamb!
    'E's a injia-rubber idiot on the spree,
    'E's the on'y thing that doesn't give a damn
        For a Regiment o' British Infantree!
So 'ere's to you, Fuzzy-Wuzzy, at your 'ome in
        the Soudan;
    You're a pore benighted 'eathen, but a first-class
        fightin' man;
    An' 'ere's to you, Fuzzy-Wuzzy, with your
        'ayrick 'ead of 'air—
You big black boundin' beggar—for you broke a
        British square!

As the Highlanders still point out, the square really was not broken, just temporarily opened in order for them to advance as ordered, and the Hadendowa took advantage of the opportunity.

As these actions were taking place near the Red Sea coast, the main drama was unfolding at the Sudanese capital city of Khartoum. Rather than deal with the Mahdi and his followers, Gladstone decided to abandon the region and sent General Charles Gordon to oversee the removal of Europeans from the city. Gordon, who had made a reputation as an independent, charismatic figure when stationed in China, decided that Khartoum should not be abandoned, or perhaps he was slow in implementing his orders. The question is debated concerning his real intentions, but by design or bad luck he found himself surrounded by the Mahdi's forces. News of this siege created much controversy in London, where the government dallied over what to do. After some months, public and royal pressure forced Gladstone to send a relief force. The route south to Khartoum, however, is incredibly difficult. The Nile River is the natural route to follow, but a series of cataracts makes transporting supply boats nearly impossible. The expedition's commander, Garnet Wolseley, got off to a late start and then spent weeks constructing boats, bringing boatmen from Canada, training a camel corps—whatever seemed necessary to pass the rapids in the river and the desert beyond.

All the physical obstacles were overcome by January 1885. The advance force had fought the elements as well as the dervishes to be within striking distance of Khartoum, when the force commander, Sir Charles Wilson, stopped for three days to rest and tend his wounded. When ships arrived on the Nile at his camp, he boarded his men and steamed four days to Khartoum, there to find the Mahdi in control, as he had been for the previous two days. Gordon and the city had held back the besiegers with little more than courage for 317 days before being overcome and slaughtered. Many were blamed for his loss, but the brunt of the criticism fell on Gladstone. He finally got the troops withdrawn by deciding an incident in Afghanistan was more threatening.

The Mahdi died not long after his greatest triumph over the British, and his followers turned their allegiance to his second-in-command, known as the Khalifa (Caliph). The Sudanese were left undisturbed until 1897 when an expedition under the command of Horatio Kitchener marched south and extracted revenge for Gordon and Khartoum. Kitchener became a national hero, was elevated to Lord Kitchener of Khartoum, commanded the final offensives in South Africa against the Boers, and ultimately rose to the position of Minister of War during World War I. The dervishes and Fuzzy-Wuzzy had for a time, however, humbled the power of the British Empire and joined the Afghans and Zulus as one of the few native forces to do so.

References: Farwell, Byron, *Queen Victoria's Little Wars* (New York: Harper & Row, 1972); Kipling, Rudyard, "Fuzzy Wuzzy," *from The Complete Verses* (London: Kyle Cathie, 1995); Woolman, David, "The Day the Hadendowa Broke the British Square—or Did They?," *Military History*, vol. 11, no. 2. (June 1994).

E

Egyptians

An ancient population dominant in northeastern Africa and the Middle East, establishing a major Middle Eastern empire.

For a nation that had such an effect on the military atmosphere of the Middle East in the first millennium BCE, the Egyptians had a particularly non-military background. In the times of the Old Kingdom, more than 2,000 years before Christ, Egypt had virtually no military. Egypt was an isolated region protected on the north by the Mediterranean Sea, on the west by the Sahara Desert, on the south by the impassable cataracts of the Nile, and on the east by the Sinai Desert. With no outside threat, there was no need for an army. The only mention of military activity in the Old Kingdom was during the reign of Pepy, when he commissioned one of his chief subordinates to organize an army to expel some Bedouins. During the Middle Kingdom (2133–1786 BCE), the Egyptians built fortresses to guard potential invasion routes. These have been discovered along the frontier with Nubia to the south and near the Bitter Lakes at the approaches to the Sinai Peninsula.

Egyptians lived this isolated way for centuries until they learned the harsh lesson of living without an army, a lesson taught them by the Hyksos. These invaders from the east, probably from the neighbor-hood of Palestine, easily conquered the defenseless Egyptians about 1750 BCE and ruled until 1576 BCE. It was the Hyksos' chariots more than any other weapon that secured their victory, for until that time the Egyptians had not yet discovered the wheel. Almost two centuries of foreign rule wore thin, and the Egyptians secretly armed themselves and overthrew the Hyksos, who had become soft in the rich Nile Valley. From this point forward, during the time known as the New Kingdom, Egypt was a major power to be reckoned with in the politics of the known world.

With the exception of cavalry, the Egyptians developed every kind of military arm known at the time. The bulk of their forces were infantry, carrying shields and armed with lances or bows. Light infantry carried slings or javelins. For sidearms, the infantry usually carried short, double-edged swords. However, some pictures show them with a *khopesh*, which has a wide curved blade vaguely resembling a meat cleaver. Their shields were curved on top and straight or slightly curved along the sides, wooden and covered with leather. A shield was roughly about half the height of a man. Armor was unknown for the common soldier, his protection being little more than a quilted tunic and cap. The higher ranks are depicted in Egyptian artwork as wearing links of metal fastened loosely to permit freedom of movement. The king is usually depicted wearing a metal helmet and often carried a battle-axe

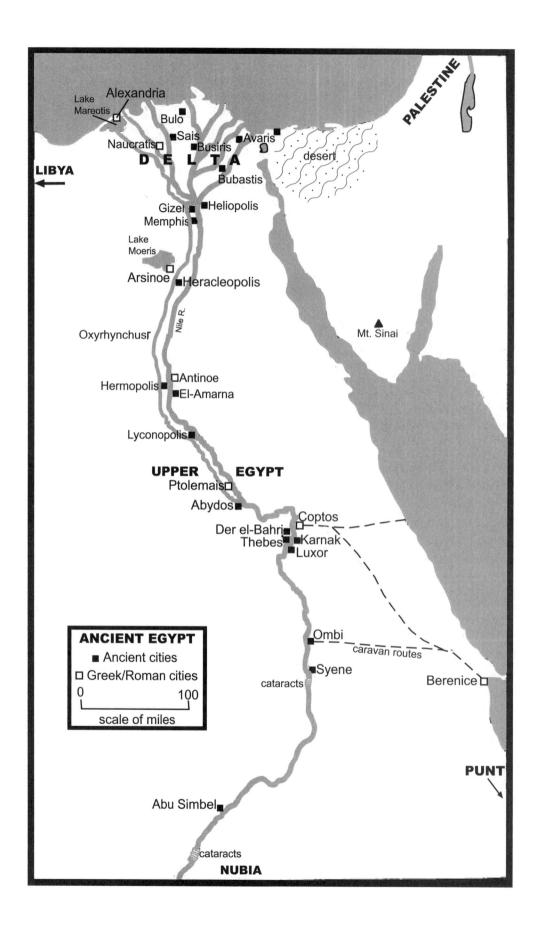

PALESTINE

Lake
Mareotis

Alexandria

Bulo

Sais

Busiris

Avaris

Naucratis

desert

LIBYA

DELTA

Bubastis

Gizeh ■Heliopolis

Memphis

Lake
Moeris

Arsinoe ■Heracleopolis

Nile R.

Oxyrhynchus

Mt. Sinai

□Antinoe

Hermopolis ■El-Amarna

Lyconopolis

UPPER   EGYPT

Ptolemais□

Abydos

Coptos

Der el-Bahri

Thebes ■Karnak

Luxor

Ombi

caravan routes

ANCIENT EGYPT

■ Ancient cities

□ Greek/Roman cities

0   100

scale of miles

Syene

cataracts

Berenice□

PUNT

Abu Simbel

cataracts

NUBIA

or a mace. More than any other weapon, however, the Egyptians depended on the bow. The one they employed was five to six feet long with arrows up to 30 inches long.

The glory of the Egyptian army was the chariot, the weapon they had adopted from the Hyksos. Tomb paintings almost always show the pharaoh in a chariot, usually alone with the reins tied about his midriff as he defeats his enemies. This is probably artistic license, as the two-wheeled vehicles they drove were designed to carry two men, a driver and an archer, and are usually shown with attached quivers of arrows and short spears. The horses were not only decorated with headdresses, but covered at their joints with metal ornaments doubling as protection. The most famous story concerning the use of chariots in Egypt is that of the Exodus, wherein the whole of Pharaoh's force of 600 chariots was employed in chasing the Hebrews. Although the Book of Exodus mentions cavalry, contemporary Egyptian artwork almost never shows men on horseback, and those who are depicted are usually foreigners.

The army of the New Kingdom was a thoroughly professional force, although conscripts were used: One man in 10 was liable for military service. Egyptian units were given names of gods for their titles (for example, Anubis, Phre, Thoth, etc.), which probably reflected the local divinity where the unit was raised. The divisions usually numbered 5,000, subdivided into 250-man companies and 50-man platoons. The artwork of ancient Egypt depicts the soldiers marching in order, but the battles seem to have no structure, just a melee. It is therefore difficult to know what military doctrines may have been developed in Egypt. However, as the point to the artwork was to glorify the pharaoh, the actions of the regular soldiers would not have mattered. In the depictions of attacks on fortifications, no reference exists for any sort of siege engines, like catapults or battering rams. In the pictures only arrows and extremely long pikes are being used in order to clear the walls of defenders, and scaling ladders are then employed. Artwork at Abu Simbel shows how the Egyptians set up camp when on campaign. They did not dig entrenchments, but surrounded the camp with a palisade made of the soldier's shields. The pharaoh's tent is in the center of the camp, surrounded by those of his officers. Separate sections hold the horses, the chariots, the mules, and the pack gear. A hospital section is depicted, as well as another area of camp for drill and punishment. Outside the camp, charioteers and infantry are shown exercising. In the center of the camp is a lion, although whether this is literal or the symbol of the pharaoh is disputed.

Once liberated from the Hyksos, the Egyptians apparently understood that the more distant the frontier they could defend, the safer would be the homeland. Thus, Egyptian campaigns began up the east coast of the Mediterranean toward modern Syria. Inscriptions of the time praise war as a high calling, whereas in previous days the main accomplishment of warfare was looting and the acquisition of wealth. (That, of course, remained a goal, and the pillage and tribute the Egyptians gathered financed the impressive buildings for which they are justly famous.) The problem they faced was that, unlike the nomads and bandits they had fought in earlier times, they now had to fight trained soldiers of other kings. The Egyptians apparently learned the art of war fairly quickly, however, for the contemporary inscriptions describe the joy the pharaoh felt when he got to go to war. "For the good god exults when he begins the fight, he is joyful when he has to cross the frontier, and is content when he sees blood. He cuts off the heads of his enemies, and an hour of fighting gives him more delight than a day of pleasure" (Erman, 1971).

The Egyptian military maintained a strong presence in the Palestine/Syria region for centuries, sometimes farther away and sometimes closer, depending on the nature of their opponents. They also expanded their borders southward at the expense of the Nubians. However, they found themselves occupied on occasion when they met too strong a foe, most notably the Assyrians. By the time of the Persian Empire in the seventh century BCE, the Egyptians were a fading power, and when they were conquered by Alexander in the fourth century they almost ceased to be important. As late as the first century BCE, however, Julius Caesar, Mark Antony, and Caesar Augustus found Egyptian wealth an important acquisition, even if the Egyptian army was of little use as an ally.

References: Erman, Adolf, trans. by H. M. Tirard, *Life in Ancient Egypt* (New York: Dover Publications, 1971 [1894]); Ferrill, Arther, *The Origins of War* (London: Thames and Hudson, 1985); Kenrick, John, *Ancient Egypt under the Pharoahs* New York: John B. Alden, 1883).

Ever Victorious Army

A Chinese army under British command during the Taiping Rebellion of the mid-nineteenth century.

In 1851 China was on the verge of civil war. A religious leader had arisen to unite various factions opposed to the increasingly oppressive rule of the Manchu dynasty. This leader was Hung Hsiu-ch'uan, who took the name Tien Wang, or "Heavenly King." He claimed to have had visions that took him to heaven and inspired the crusade against worldliness and corruption rampant in the Manchu court, especially on the part of the Emperor Hsien Feng. Tien Wang's religious message was a strange amalgam of Christianity and Taoism wherein he played the third part of the Trinity, replacing the Holy Spirit. His "New Christian Testament" appealed to many of China's poor, and Tien Wang also appealed to the established antigovernment Triad societies. Tien Wang's movement was dubbed the Taiping Tien-kuo, or "Heavenly Kingdom of Great Peace." Great slaughter, instead, was the result.

At first the Taiping Rebellion, as it came to be called, remained fairly true to the stated ideals, as the soldiers were bound to remain celibate while in the field and could not loot or pillage after victories. Both cowardice and opium smoking were capital offenses. Under this stringent discipline, the soldiers scored impressive early successes, conquering from their mountainous homeland into the Yangtze Valley. In 1853 the Taipings were in a position to march on the capital at Peking, which almost certainly would have fallen, but instead decided to occupy Nanking as the ancient capital of the Ming dynasty they claimed to want restored. Nanking fell easily because the defenders thought it prudent not to resist, but the Taipings still slaughtered so many inhabitants that their corpses blocked the river when Tien Wang arrived in his barge to take formal possession of the city. The imperial army held on to Peking with a hastily recruited unit that came to be called the Hunan Braves, reinforced with units recalled from Mongolia. The Taipings, however, captured Chinkiang, which put them into a position to threaten the major port city of Shanghai with its large European population.

By 1856, the Taiping movement began to slow. Tien Wang started to emulate the dissolute life of the emperor he was attempting to overthrow. Struggles between him and his generals intensified as some tried to challenge his authority, while Tien Wang used others to stave off the threats. The imperial court had its troubles as well. In 1857, the British and French sent in troops and ships in response to threats against their merchants and diplomatic personnel. The Westerners forced a new trade treaty from the emperor, but in 1860 they were back in force again to counter new Manchu demands. When the imperial army did not immediately allow the western force to march to Peking, the British and French shot their way toward the city. When the emperor proposed negotiations with the westerners at his gates, a new treaty was negotiated, but the British burned the emperor's summer palace as a warning against future vacillation.

This friction with the Manchu government put British troops in China, and they were there in time to assist with the new Manchu offensive against the Taipings. The Manchus had had some success with an army of mercenaries under the command of an American, Frederick Townshend Ward. They fought fairly well, and the Chinese awarded them the nickname of the Ever Victorious Army. When Ward was killed, whatever unit cohesion the force may have had fell apart. Because it had been successful, however, the Chinese hoped for a new commander to whip the force back into shape and continue its winning ways. The Manchu government appealed to the British commander in China, General Staveley, to appoint a new leader to restore the Ever Victorious Army

to its former glory. Staveley had on his staff a young engineer named Charles Gordon, with whom he had worked in the Crimean War. Gordon was keen to see action, and Staveley rather reluctantly appointed him to the position. Luckily, Gordon had already impressed the regional Manchu commander, General Li Hung-chang, so he proved a good choice and took command in March 1863 at age 30.

Gordon got right to work. While under Staveley's command he had overseen operations that cleared any Taipings out of a 30-mile circumference around Shanghai. He took the Ever Victorious Army, which had just been badly handled in an attack on the city of Taitsan northwest of Shanghai, and imposed his own form of discipline on it. Mainly by example, he created a strongly loyal force. Gordon showed no fear. He personally reconnoitered enemy positions, getting so close he often put himself under fire. When he went into battle he did not carry a weapon, but instead a bamboo walking stick. His force of 4,000 Chinese with western officers were given new uniforms of dark green serge with turbans, a pay raise, and timely payment of their wages.

His first move was to relieve a Taiping siege of Chanzu, where Taiping rebels had given their allegiance to the government and were now under attack by their former comrades. Gordon's army first captured the city of Fushan on the way to Chanzu. Seeing this, the Taipings decided to lift their siege rather than be caught between two forces. The major Taiping fortress of Taitsan fell to Gordon's artillery and a spirited assault through the breach, which the cannon fire produced. At Quinsan, Gordon attacked with a fleet of gunboats along the many canals that surrounded the town. Although Quinsan was a strongly walled city, Gordon's attack was such a surprise that the defenders fled after minimal fighting. Many were drowned in the canals.

The last major Taiping stronghold was Soo Chow, which was surrounded by a 12-mile-long wall. Gordon decided against an assault and laid siege. He also captured the city of Woo Kiang upriver in order to cut off any reinforcements or supplies to Soo Chow. The siege lasted from October through December 1863, when the defenders surrendered on condition of clemency for their leaders. Gordon granted it, but the imperial troops supporting his force killed them anyway. Gordon was so upset he considered marching his men against Peking, then decided instead to resign his commission. The Manchus finally were able to convince him to reconsider, but he refused to take any monetary reward from the emperor for his victories.

The Ever Victorious Army was disbanded in June 1864, having sustained almost 100 casualties among its officers and 1,440 among the rank and file, more than one-third its strength. Imperial troops were given the task of assaulting the final Taiping stronghold of Nanking. They surrounded the city with 80,000 men and the increasingly corrupt Tien Wang committed suicide rather than face capture and execution. The Taiping Rebellion lasted 15 years, and estimates of its cost reach as high as 30 million lives. Gordon's performance in China brought him to the attention of the government in London, where he became a popular public figure. He died in the Sudanese capital of Khartoum in 1885 when he was surrounded by the forces of another messianic figure, the Mahdi. Still, his nickname of "Chinese" Gordon, was earned in his first command.

References: Hanson, Lawrence, *Chinese Gordon* (New York: Funk and Wagnalls, 1954); Trench, Charles Chenevix, *The Road to Khartoum (New York: Norton, 1978); Wilson, Andrew, The Ever Victorious Army* (Edinburgh: Blackwood, 1868).

F

Flying Circus

An elite German fighter unit in World War I.

World War I was the first time aircraft were used in combat against each other. Before then the United States had used aircraft in scouting roles, and when World War I broke out, it was scouting that was the primary job of airmen on both sides. The need to stop aircraft from flying over one's own armies brought about the development of fighter aircraft. By early 1915, some six months after the war's inception, Roland Garros mounted a machine gun on the nose of his Morane airplane and bolted steel plates to the propeller to deflect whatever bullets failed to pass through. He was shot down behind German lines, and his idea was improved upon by a Dutch aircraft engineer, Anthony Fokker, who developed the interrupter gear. This allowed bullets to pass through the empty spaces of the propeller while interrupting the flow of bullets when the propeller's blades passed in front of the machine gun. The Fokker E-1 was the first widely used fighter aircraft, and for a while it devastated British and French aircraft.

The life of an airman proved tantalizing to many, especially those who had spent time in the mud of the trenches in northern France. One such soldier who transferred to the air service was a German aristocrat named Manfred von Richthofen, for the

Baron Captain Manfred von Richtofen, otherwise known as the "Red Baron", circa 1917. National Archives and Records Administration, Special Media Archives Services Division (NWCS-S), National Archives at College Park, 8601 Adelphi Road, College Park, MD. [Image 540163]

cavalry to which he originally was assigned was rapidly becoming obsolete. Richthofen learned to fly reconnaissance planes, with a cameraman in the rear seat to photograph enemy positions. This proved too tame for his temperament, and he learned to fly the Fokker E-1. His early experience in the aircraft was not positive, but he underwent fighter training and quickly improved. In the spring of 1916 he was assigned to a

Jagdstaffel, a German fighter squadron, which at full strength numbered 16 aircraft.

Like all young fighter pilots in the German air service, he idolized the "aces," men who had shot down at least five enemy aircraft. The leading aces, who rapidly became national heroes, were Oswald Boelcke and Max Immelman, both assigned to No. 62 Squadron. When Immelman was killed, the German government wanted to keep Boelcke alive for morale purposes and so assigned him to behind-the-lines tours. When in August 1916 he returned to command the newly formed *Jasta 2* ("Jasta" being an abbreviation of *Jagdstaffel*), he chose Richthofen as one of his pilots. Boelcke was regarded as the first serious theorist of fighter tactics, and Richthofen learned from the master. The British had been pioneering aggressive fighter tactics, but with the development of newer and faster German aircraft, the Germans took control of the air in the latter part of 1916.

By 1916, the war on the ground had turned into such a stalemate that there was a desperate need for heroes to maintain public morale. It was the fighter pilots who came to fill that role. The French press first invented the concept of the "ace," which the commanders of the Allied air services at first resisted. The British in particular stressed teamwork over individual accomplishments, but the ace concept took on a life of its own. The French were the first to develop an elite squadron, called Le Cignones (the Storks); each aircraft had a stork painted on its fuselage in a different pose. This gave each pilot his individual marking while also promoting unit esprit de corps. The Germans followed suit to an extent: Flight leaders began to paint parts of their aircraft bright colors in order to be better seen by the pilots flying with them.

Jasta 2 underwent a major change after Boelcke was killed in a flying accident in October 1916. In December the unit was renamed Jasta Boelcke. Richthofen was improving his skills and by the end of 1916 had shot down 15 enemy aircraft. In January 1917 he was given command of Jasta 11, and took delivery of the newest of the German fighter aircraft, the Albatross D.III. Jasta 11 had yet to score any victories in air-to-air combat, and Richthofen set about whipping his men into a first-class squadron. As squadron commander, he had followed the general practice of identifying his plane with bright red paint on the wheels and the tail section. Soon, he painted his entire aircraft a bright red. This was to serve a number of purposes. First, he made himself easily identifiable to his own pilots. Second, although he had experimented earlier in his career with camouflage and the German air service was also looking into the idea, his own flamboyance would not allow him to purposely remain inconspicuous. Third, he hoped that his becoming famous as an expert fighter pilot would make the red plane strike fear in his enemies. Soon, his entire squadron painted a portion of their own planes red, and the brightly colored planes came to be called the Flying Circus. Later, all the aircraft in the Jasta were painted solid red.

Richthofen's Jasta 11 came into its own in April 1917, by which time the Albatross D.III had become the standard aircraft in the German air service. Nothing the British or French had could match the Albatross, and the month came to be called by Allied airmen "Bloody April." In this month, Richthofen became Germany's highest-scoring ace, surpassing the mark of 41 kills set by his mentor Boelcke.

Both the Allies and the Germans developed increasingly faster and more maneuverable aircraft as the war progressed, and neither side was able to maintain superiority over the other for long. No matter what planes the Allies introduced, however, Richthofen continued to increase his score. Although wounded in combat and forced at another time by the high command to take leave, he rested only as long as he was required to do so. Combat seemed to have become an addiction with him. He and his squadron grew in notoriety—both inside Germany and out—and he was undoubtedly the best-known soldier in Germany. His younger brother, Lothar, flew with him and took command of the Jasta on Manfred's infrequent departures, and the family tie was one more item for the press to play up.

By April 1918, Manfred von Richthofen was the highest-scoring ace of the war, with 80 Allied aircraft confirmed destroyed. He had been promoted to command *Jagdge-schwader* 1 (Fighter Group 1). On April 21, however, he was killed in combat in circumstances argued to this day. Credit for bringing down the Red Baron, as he had come to be called, went at the time to Captain Arthur Royal "Roy" Brown. Brown attacked the scarlet Fokker Dr.1, the triplane Richthofen made famous, as it lined up on a British pilot on his first mission. Richthofen did not bring the enemy plane down quickly as he had become famous for doing, and he was shot down for flying too long in one direction. Richthofen's plane landed behind British lines and the smoothness of the landing seemed to indicate a wounded pilot. Richthofen, however, was dead with a single bullet through his chest. It has since been argued that he was killed in flight by an Australian machine gun crew firing from the Allied lines on the ground. However he

died, he was treated to a funeral with full honors by the British Royal Flying Corps.

Jasta 11 continued to operate under the command of Lothar von Richthofen, but he was never the public figure his brother had been. Manfred left behind the Air Combat *Operations Manual*, which described the necessary tactics for handling the larger Fighter Group he commanded at the end of his life. Ironically, it was the final dictum of that manual that he violated when he was shot down: "You should never stay with an opponent whom, through your bad shooting or his skillful turning, you have been unable to shoot down, the combat lasts for a long time and you are alone, outnumbered by adversaries." Manfred von Richthofen also left a legacy of intensity, dedication, and professionalism that fighter pilots ever since have striven to emulate.

References: Bickers, Richard Townshend, *Von Richthofen: The Legend Evaluated* (Annapolis, MD: Naval Institute Press, 1996); Gibbons, Floyd, *The Red Knight of Germany* (London: Cassell, 1932); Richthofen, Baron Manfred von, *Der Rote Kampfflieger* (Berlin: Ullstein, 1933).

Flying Tigers (American Volunteer Group)

An American fighter unit operating in China (1941–1942).

China was the victim of Japanese aggression as early as 1931 when Japanese forces overran and annexed Manchuria, renaming it the "independent" state of Manchukuo. The Chinese could do little to stop the annexation and made few preparations for any continuing conflict with Japan. Chinese Nationalist leader Chiang Kai-shek contracted with foreign air forces for advisors and instructors, but the quality of

The logo of the Flying Tigers.

training that the Chinese pilots received (mainly from Italian instructors) was extremely poor. Most of the period from 1932 to 1937 was spent, instead, with the Chinese Nationalist faction (Kuomintang) under Chiang fighting a civil war against the Communists under Mao Tse-tung. This internal division certainly encouraged the Japanese to expand their conquests by invading China proper in 1937. The Nationalists and Communists put their conflict on hold for the time being to concentrate on the external threat. Mao's forces fought out of northern China, while Chiang's units struggled in the southern part. Chiang appealed to the United States for assistance, which he got after the *Panay* incident. During the Japanese assault on the city of Nanking, the American gunboat, *Panay*, was bombed by Japanese aircraft and was sunk with heavy loss of life. The Japanese apologized and paid damages, but the United States began to pay much more serious attention to the war, although only indirect, under-the-table military aid was forthcoming owing to American neutrality agreements.

By 1940, war in Europe had broken out and American President Franklin Roosevelt was disposed to provide war material to resist aggressors, although the vast majority of the early aid went to Great Britain via Lend-Lease. He did nothing, however, to discourage Chiang Kai-shek from appealing directly to American cit-

izens for assistance. Chiang in 1937 had hired a retired maverick pilot of the United States Army Air Corps, Claire Chennault, to organize and train his air forces. Chennault, whose theories of fighter warfare conflicted with the generally accepted doctrine of the 1930s, jumped at the chance to leave retirement and put his theories to the test. In 1941, Chennault and Chinese General Mow visited the United States to organize a force of American volunteer pilots to come to China and fight the Japanese. Through 1941, Chennault approached pilots he knew well with the idea, but most pilots hesitated to give up their seniority and time toward retirement and promotion to join his group. Once assured that Chennault had the tacit support of the government, however, pilots in the Army Air Corps, navy, and Marines United States Marines resigned their positions to join him. The United States government also began to provide aircraft for the budding Chinese air forces.

Chennault recruited 100 pilots and nearly 200 ground crew for what came to be called the American Volunteer Group, or AVG. Acting in the role of modern-day hired gunfighters, the pilots were promised a generous base pay by the Chinese government, plus a $500 bonus for each Japanese plane they shot down that was confirmed by direct inspection of the wreckage. The training for the group's combat role was conducted by Chennault, who had spent the last few years fighting the Japanese air forces and learning the capabilities of their planes and pilots. He realized that the new fighter aircraft that the Japanese employed, the Mitsubishi Zero, was much faster and more maneuverable than the aircraft he was able to acquire from the U.S. government, the Curtis P-40B. Although it was the most modern

American fighter aircraft, it was no match for the Zero in one-on-one combat. Chennault therefore developed tactics to exploit the advantages the P-40 possessed, which were fire power, durability, and greater weight. If he could position his planes at a greater altitude than the Japanese, the speed that they would build up in a dive would be greater than that which the Zero could achieve. Attack out of the sun, use the greater fire power of the P-40 to inflict damage on enemy aircraft below, and escape with the superior speed developed in the dive: These were the tactics developed to outfight the Zero and destroy the Japanese bombers that were wreaking havoc on Chinese cities.

Chennault's men arrived at Rangoon, Burma, in July 1941 and trained through the fall at a base in Burma, Kyedow, well away from Japanese eyes. Because some of the pilots had flown only trainers or bombers, the transition to fighter aircraft was difficult and dangerous. Furthermore, the difficulty in transporting the aircraft, assembling them on-site, and trying to acquire spare parts was a massive undertaking. Accidents during training wrecked planes and killed pilots, and the primitive conditions of living and flying from a base carved out of the jungle was harrowing and demoralizing. Some men abandoned the project and returned to the United States in a matter of days after their arrival, but the rest persevered and learned not only how to fly the P-40s, but also how to fight using Chennault's tactics. They learned that individual action and heroics were to be spurned in favor of close teamwork.

The AVG was divided into three squadrons, deployed at separate air bases to minimize damage from Japanese attacks and to maximize the operational area. First Squadron was based at Kunming; its designation as the First Pursuit Squadron gave rise to their insignia: stick figures of Adam chasing Eve across an apple around which a snake was coiled, upon which was written "the First Pursuit." The Second Squadron, based also at Kunming, called themselves the Panda Bears. The Third Squadron, based at Rangoon, Burma, at a Royal Air Force airfield, designated themselves "Hell's Angels" and used red silhouettes of women with wings, in a variety of poses, as their insignia. The one feature all the squadrons had in common took advantage of the large air intake under the propeller of the P-40 aircraft: a full set of snarling teeth painted along the plane's nose up to the intake. This was not original with the AVG. British units operating in North Africa had painted this "shark's mouth" design on the P-40s that they acquired through the Lend-Lease program. It was this feature that gave the "Flying Tigers" their nickname and brought them much more notoriety than similarly painted aircraft elsewhere. This ferocious-looking paint job greatly appealed to the Chinese ground crews and workers at the airfields, who superstitiously believed it increased the fighting capabilities of the plane and pilot.

The Americans saw their first combat on December 20, 1941, well after the Japanese attack on Pearl Harbor brought the United States officially into the war. In action over Kunming, the Flying Tigers shot down six of an attacking force of 10 Japanese bombers and returned to base with no losses to themselves. Three days later, AVG pilots flying with British airmen at Rangoon intercepted a force of Japanese bombers and fighters with less spectacular results: 10 enemy aircraft destroyed for a loss of five British and four American planes. Fighting continued in Burma and China throughout

December, with Christmas Day's action proving especially heartening. Two major raids totaling 108 Japanese aircraft attacked Rangoon, and the defenders shot down 28 of them, losing two planes and no pilots in the process.

In the first six months of 1942, the Flying Tigers fought air-to-air combat against fighters and bombers, escorted British bombers on raids against Japanese targets, and assisted Chinese forces with ground attack. The constant strain wore on machines as well as men, for spare parts were impossible to find, unless cannibalized from damaged aircraft. The damage inflicted during combat seriously affected the performance of the planes, and the pilots' confidence began to waver. Finally, they refused to fly ground-support missions, as the intense antiaircraft fire was too damaging to their already battered planes. Still, in aerial combat, the pilots excelled. The leading "ace" in the AVG was Bob Neale, who shot down 16 Japanese aircraft; David "Tex" Hill destroyed 12; Bill Reed shot down 11. Six other pilots destroyed 10 Japanese planes each. Numerous pilots became aces by shooting down five or more. By July 4 ,1942, the three squadrons had 286 confirmed victories and possibly that many again shot down in locations that Chinese inspectors on the ground could not reach. In the six and a half months of operations, the American Volunteer Group suffered the loss of nine pilots in combat, four more missing and presumed dead, two killed by Japanese bombs, and nine killed in accidents. In that time they had significantly slowed the Japanese air forces, but could do little to stop the juggernaut of the Japanese army on the ground.

Action in Burma was designed not only to keep the country in British hands, but also to keep open the Burma Road, the one line of access China had to receive American Lend-Lease supplies. As the Japanese drove deeper into Burma, the Third Squadron withdrew from Rangoon to Magwe, then to Kunming with the rest of the AVG. With never more than 55 planes operational, the American volunteers were just too few.

The Tenth U.S. Army Air Force was created in April 1942. It was designed to replace the volunteers in Asia. Claire Chennault's commission was reactivated, and he was given the rank of brigadier general in what came to be called the China Air Task Force. When that was officially activated on July 4, the American Volunteer Group ceased to exist. Only five of the pilots chose to remain in service, the remainder wanting to go home, at least for a while, before reentering the service. This created some bad blood with the incoming personnel, but the difficulty of surviving the primitive base conditions and the stress of combat certainly seems to be sufficient justification for their decisions. Chennault stayed in China and served with the China Air Task Force and later the Fourteenth Air Force through January 1945.

The Flying Tigers were America's first heroes of World War II and, along with James Doolittle's surprise raid on Tokyo in April 1942, did much to raise the spirits of a nation just recovering from the shock of Pearl Harbor and the loss of so many men and possessions in the early days of the Pacific War.

References: Caidin, Martin, *The Ragged, Rugged Warriors* (New York: E.P. Dutton, 1966); Ford, Daniel, *Flying Tigers: Claire Chennault and the American Volunteer Group* (Washington, DC: Smithsonian Institution Press, 1991); Heiferman, Ron, *Flying Tigers: Chennault in China* (New York: Ballantine, 1971).

Franks

A population dominant in western Europe in the fifth to ninth centuries CE.

The Franks comprised a group of tribes living in the Rhine River area that were first recorded during the later Roman Empire. The earliest history of the Franks was written by Gregory of Tours, who was a contemporary of Clovis (481–511), one of the Franks' early great chieftains. Prior to Clovis, the history of the Franks is sketchy. The first recorded leader was Chlodio, who led the tribes into northern Gaul in the early fifth century. Chlodio was succeeded by Merovech, who fought alongside the Roman forces against Atilla the Hun at Mauriac Plain in eastern Gaul in 451. It is from Merovech that the first

101

recorded Frankish dynasty, the Merovingians, is named. His son, Childeric, was on the throne by 457 and seemed to remain a friend to the declining Roman Empire; he had perhaps been a captive of the Huns as a child. His Frankish forces again fought alongside Roman soldiers against the Visigoths at Orleans in 463 or 464, then kept later Gothic and Saxon invaders away from Roman Gaul.

In 481 Clovis came to be the Frankish king, although sources indicate that he was merely the chief of other Frankish chieftains, a first among equals. He made war against the remaining Roman leadership, under Sygarius, defeating him at Soissons in 486. Clovis soon thereafter defeated rival chieftains and claimed supreme authority among the major Frankish tribes, the Salians. Clovis can thus be considered the first real king of the Franks. With his victory at Soissons, he extended his authority to the Seine River and later reached the Loire. A decade later, Clovis went to the aid of the Ripaurian Franks around modern-day Bonn and defeated the Allemanni, thus extending Frankish power into Germany.

Clovis converted to Catholicism, possibly owing to the influence of his wife, Clotilda of Burgundy. Some sources suggest that he was a Christian when he won at Soissons, but many claim that he embraced the faith in 496. He chose Catholicism over the Arian version of Christianity (which denied Christ's equality with God the Father), although both were practiced among the Franks. This choice had profound effects, for it started the Franks on the road to becoming protectors of the Church of Rome.

First, however, there were other lands to capture and other enemies to fight. Clovis's expansion to the Loire River brought him into contact with the Visigoths, who controlled southern France and northern Spain. The Ostrogoth king, Theodoric, an Arian and related to Clovis by marriage, had long striven to maintain peace in southern Gaul, but Clovis went to war as the champion of Catholicism. He defeated the Visigothic forces under Alaric at Poitiers in 507 and sent his son to conquer as far as Burgundy. Frankish authority extended over all of France, with the exception of a southern coastal strip and the Breton peninsula. Clovis moved his capital to Paris and established a church to commemorate his victory over Alaric. Rumor has it that, in spite of his Christianity, Clovis plotted to murder the ruling family of the Ripaurian Franks. Whether this is true or not remains conjectural, but he was elected their king after his war against Alaric. With his power solidified, Clovis was recognized as king of the Franks by the Byzantine emperor, Anastasius. He was made a consul under the emperor's authority and treated as if he ruled in the emperor's name, which was hardly the case.

Clovis's four sons inherited parts of his kingdom and regularly made war against their neighbors. Under the leadership of Theudibert, the Germanic tribes were placed under tribute and the Burgunds were destroyed, which gave the Franks control over the Rhone River valley and the port city of Marseilles. Theudibert's expeditions into Italy weakened the Ostrogothic regime there to the extent that Byzantine forces came to control the peninsula.

The next great leader was Dagobert, who defeated the Avars, a Hunnish tribe threatening to expand past the Danube. He also raided into Spain and received tribute (or bribes) from Constantinople. Dagobert's reign also saw an expansion of Frankish trading power and the widespread coinage of gold and silver. He established a mint at the mouth of the Rhine and carried on extensive trade, mainly in the cloth of Frisia, in modern Belgium. He also supported the Church's efforts to convert the Frisians. The last great king of the Merovingian dynasty, Dagobert died in 639. His sons fought among themselves, and the eastern (Austrasian) and western (Neustrian) factions of the kingdom struggled for dominance.

In Roman times, Frankish soldiers armed and equipped themselves simply. Tacitus writes, "Only a few use swords or lances. The spears they carry— *framae* is the native word—have short and narrow heads, but are so sharp and easy to handle, that the same weapon serves at need for close or distant fighting. The horseman asks no more than his shield and spear, but the infantry have also javelins to shower, several per man, and can hurl them to a great distance; for they are either naked or only lightly clad in their cloaks. There is nothing ostentatious in their turn-out. Only the shields are picked out with carefully selected colors" (Norman, 1971). Tacitus describes few as wearing body armor and only a few with metal or leather headgear. He also says that the king was of noble birth, but the leaders in battle gained their rank through valor. Soldiers also carried an *angon*, a spear used for throwing or stabbing. It featured a barbed head and a long, metal-covered shaft, which proved impossible to remove from a shield once implanted. An enemy soldier thus attacked could not cut the long shaft with his sword because of the metal covering. Thus, the enemy's shield would become unusable, and the Frank would close in with a second spear or his axe. When the Franks formed field cavalry units, the horsemen carried

spears as much as two meters long with leaf-shaped heads.

Over time, real power in Frankish politics was exercised not by the king, but by the *majordomos* (mayors of the palace) who represented the tribal leaders before the king. It was Pepin II, one of the mayors, who founded the next Frankish ruling clan. He led Austrasian forces to victory over the Neustrians at the battle of Tertry in 687. This made him the dominant figure in Frankish politics, and he assumed the role of military leader, the defender of the Frankish lands from outside attack. Pepin's conquest of Frisia brought him into close cooperation with the Irish Catholic monks who were trying to convert the Frisians, and the connection between Pepin's family and the Catholic Church began to solidify. Pepin led campaigns against the Allemanni, Franconians, and Bavarians, and the missionaries followed his conquests. Pepin died in 714 as the most powerful man in Frankish politics, but still mayor of the palace.

Pepin's illegitimate son, Charles Martel, inherited the position of mayor. (His Latin name, Carolus, gave his heirs the title of Carolingians.) He led campaigns against the Saxons and Bavarians to secure the northern and eastern frontiers. He, like his father, worked closely with the church to extend Christianity. Charles developed a well-disciplined military based strongly on cavalry, and it was that arm that won for him his most recognizable victory. In 732, the Franks defeated a force of marauding Muslims from Spain at Poitiers in a battle widely regarded as saving Europe from Islamic influence. It was one of a series of battles in which the Franks forced the Muslims to settle south of the Pyrenees. In 737, the last Merovingian king died, but Charles remained mayor of the palace with no king to which he could represent the chieftains. He died in 741, dividing his extensive land holdings between his two sons; Carloman, to whom he granted his eastern holdings, and Pepin III, who inherited land in the west.

Carloman became increasingly interested in affairs of the soul, so much so that in 747 he ceded his lands to his brother and went to Monte Cassino to become a monk. Pepin, with tacit papal approval, removed the last pretenders to the Merovingian throne and made himself king of the Franks. His successful defense of Rome against Lombard invaders endeared him to the Catholic Church, which named Pepin III "King by the Grace of God." The Franks now became the official defenders of the Catholic Church. Pepin spent the 750s challenging the Muslims in Spain and reasserting Frankish claims on southern France. At his death, the greatest of the Carolingian monarchs, Charlemagne, came to the throne.

By the time of the majordomos, Frankish society was developing into feudalism and the use of horses became more widespread. Although Charles Martel defeated the Muslims at Poitiers mainly with infantry (described by Isidorus Pacensis as standing "like a wall motionless; they were like a belt of ice frozen together" [Norman, 1971]), he apparently came to appreciate cavalry, for later accounts report his expansion of that arm. It was Charlemagne, however, who brought in the next major changes in the Frankish military. First, he enforced a discipline on his men that had been infamously lacking in previous generations. Fines were imposed for desertion, drunkenness, and failure to report for duty. As for his troops, after warring both against and with the Lombards, Charlemagne seems to have incorporated their

cavalry practices. By the time his grandson, Charles the Bald, reined over the Franks, cavalry was the primary arm. By the end of the ninth century, Frankish infantry was almost nonexistent. By royal order, each horseman was to be armed with a spear, a shield, and a bow and arrows and protected by a chain mail shirt. Charlemagne also issued edicts concerning the establishment of supply trains (one of Charlemagne's chief accomplishments was development of logistical support), and he also made naval service obligatory for those living along the coastlines of his Holy Roman Empire.

The Franks dominated western Europe between the fall of the Roman Empire and the rise of the Vikings between the fifth and ninth centuries, and their development of feudalism, which ultimately resulted in the military development of knights on horseback, laid the groundwork for the Normans, who dominated everything from Britain to the Mediterranean until the Renaissance.

References: Gregory of Tours, trans. Ernest Brehaut, *History of the Franks* (New York: Norton, 1969); Lasko, Peter, *The Kingdom of the Franks* (New York: McGraw-Hill, 1971); Norman, A.V.B., *The Medieval Soldier* (New York: Thomas Crowell, 1971).

French Foreign Legion

An elite unit of foreign troops fighting for France since 1831

In 1830, King Charles X of France, needing an event to divert the population from the ineptitude of his governing, invaded Algeria. The bey of Algiers had insulted a French ambassador, and in the nineteenth century that was almost all that was necessary to start a colonial war. Although 37,000 men quickly captured the city of

Algiers and occupied the coastal cities, the hinterland was controlled by Berber tribesmen under the leadership of young and charismatic Abd el-Kader. In order to take the war into the countryside, the French government recruited a new organization on March 10, 1831, made up primarily of foreigners residing in France. It was an organization so desperate for officers that those who had failed in the regular French army had a chance to command in this new unit. Thus, from the beginning, the French Foreign Legion was a haven for any man of any nation to escape his past and serve an adopted country.

The first seven battalions were divided along national lines: First, Swiss; Second and Third, Swiss and German; Fourth, Spanish; Fifth, Italian; Sixth, Belgian and Dutch; and Seventh, Polish. The Legion got off to a particularly inauspicious start. Spurned by the regular army command, the Legionnaires had to scrounge for almost everything. Five thousand men sailed from France for Algeria, but they spent more time fighting among themselves than against Berbers. Finally committed to combat, they were sent into the mountains with too heavy wagons and too much ordnance. Abd el-Kader's tribesmen ambushed them in the passes and slaughtered

Three members of the Free French Foreign Legion, circa 1942. Library of Congress, Prints & Photographs Division, FSA.OWI Collection [reproduction number LC-USW33-055038-ZC]

105

hundreds, while Berber women emasculated and decapitated the wounded.

After this, the Legionnaires were posted to an even worse assignment. The Legion was transferred to Spain to support the child queen, Isabella, against the claims of Don Carlos for the Spanish monarchy. Now reduced to some 4,000 men, the Legion almost did not survive the ordeal, as it was torn apart by infighting and poor command as well as by the better-supplied forces of Don Carlos and the complete lack of logistical support from either France or Spain. The Legion's commander, Joseph Bernelle, was totally cowed by his shrewish wife Tharsile, who became the virtual commander of the French force through her affairs with many of the officers. She was universally despised from the ranks for her capricious ordering of punishment. The dissension this caused did nothing to enhance the Legion's awful tactical situation. Again fighting in mountainous terrain, they were regularly attacked by larger forces under Don Carlos's command. They received no pay or food, so the desertion rate grew as the Legion marched deeper into Spain and fought through a bitter winter. At Huesca, the bloodiest fighting occurred as the deserters fought their former comrades. At day's end, both sides had suffered more than 75 percent casualties. The Legion had virtually destroyed itself. Only 500 men were left when the force was finally given permission to withdraw.

The survivors, however, had finally found the element they needed for unity. Bernelle, for all his shortcomings, had wisely ended the system of segregating the battalions by nationality. From 1835 forward all enlistees had to speak French. The mixing of nationalities ended much of the infighting, and the shared experience of

surviving one of the worst campaigns any force ever fought created that spark of esprit de corps the Legion needed. Returned to Algeria, the Legion established itself as a fighting force. It was in the vanguard of an attack on the impregnable mountain fortress of Constantine. There the Legionnaires forced an entrance through the smallest of breaches in the walls created by days of pounding bombardment. Operating under the theory that became a Legion trademark, the men charged headlong into the breach in the belief that the closer to the enemy one gets, the fewer casualties one takes. Within two hours Algeria's strongest fortress was in French hands, thanks to the Legion, which, from that point forward, had the army's respect.

The Legion continued to operate in Algeria until that country's complete occupation, then aided the French effort in the Crimean War in 1854–1855. The Legion's next major campaign was in Mexico. The French Emperor Napoleon III occupied Mexico in 1863 after a failed attempt to collect debts. He installed Maximilian as Emperor of Mexico with the hopes of founding an empire in the Western Hemisphere. The Legion was sent to support Maximilian against Mexican resistance. On April 30, 1863, at the village of Camerone, Captain Jean Danjou and 65 men held a hacienda against several hundred Mexican cavalry later reinforced by three battalions of infantry. The battle raged all day until the Legionnaires finally ran out of ammunition. The remaining force—one officer and three men—surrendered. Because of the commitment shown there to fight to the death, the anniversary of the battle at Camerone is one of the Legion's premiere holidays, and Captain Danjou's wooden hand (he lost his left hand in an accident in

Algeria) is the Legion's prized relic. After the defense of the hacienda, one of the Mexican officers said, "These are not men, they are demons" (McLeave, 1973).

Perhaps the most famous of all Legion battles was Dien Bien Phu in 1954. The French colonial presence in Southeast Asia had provoked the formation of an underground movement called the Viet Minh, under the leadership of Ho Chi Minh and his chief commander Vo Nguyen Giap. Viet Minh forces had grown steadily after World War II until, by 1954, they were a full-fledged army. They occupied the high ground around the French base at Dien Bien Phu in Northern Indochina and pounded the base with artillery for weeks before finally occupying the position. Many of the Legionnaires were Germans, having joined the Legion to escape prosecution as Nazis or to continue as professional soldiers. Like Camerone, Dien Bien Phu was a defeat, but one that showed the Legion's dedication to fight to the end. Four thousand of the original 10,000 defenders survived the battle, which ended when their ammunition ran out. Hundreds more died in the jungle on the 600-kilometer march the Viet Minh forced them to undertake.

The Legion fought in all of France's colonial campaigns, for it violated French law for them to operate within French borders. For most of its existence, its headquarters were in Algeria, although now they are in Aubagne, near Marseilles. After World War II, the Legion received permission to reside in France, where today about 70 percent of the Legionnaires are based. To join the Legion, one must be prepared to commit for five years. Four months of training are given at Castelnaudary, home of the Fourth Regiment; then the volunteers are posted according to their talents: infantry, paratrooper, engineer, diver, etc. After three years of duty, French citizenship is available; after the five years, successive enlistments of up to three years are available. After 15 years, a pension is granted. The Legion currently has five bases in France, one each in Corsica, Guyana, the island of Mururoa in the Pacific, and Djibouti.

The Legion has become the primary unit in France for special operations, roughly paralleling the Special Air Service in Britain and the Green Berets in the United States. The paratroops, based in Corsica, are the best of the best. They have engaged in counterterrorist operations and served with the French contingent in Desert Storm. There, they waited six months for the war to get started, then were responsible for capturing Al Salman air base. After that, they were to block any westward retreat of the Iraqi Republican Guard. Three Legionnaires were lost during the campaign. Foreign Legion units also were committed to peacekeeping duties in Bosnia. Because of their unique composition, the Legion always has someone on hand who can speak the language of whatever country to which they are assigned. They undertook some clandestine operations in Bosnia between 1992–1995. Members of the Legion participated in Operation Restore Hope, alongside American units in Somalia in 1992. Rescue and peacekeeping operations have also been conducted in the Congo, Chad, and the Ivory Coast. The Third Regiment in Guyana is trained for jungle operations. The Sixth Regiment—the engineers based at Laudun in France—includes the *Detachment d'Intervention Operationelle Subaquatique* with men experienced in diving and underwater demolition.

The Legion has, of course, always been known as the refuge for men trying to get away from their past. These tend to fall into four broad categories. The first is men who are just looking to get a fresh start after their failures in previous endeavors. The second is those attempting to avoid a life of poverty and seeing the Legion as an alternative to homelessness and begging. The third category comprises those young men seeking adventure, while the fourth is made up of those who deserted from other armies but who still want to be soldiers. The training emphasizes endurance and practical combat skills, as well as intense esprit de corps. When one wears the traditional white kepi, he must conform to the Legion's code of honor: (1) You are a volunteer serving France faithfully and with honor. (2) Every Legionnaire is your brother-in-arms, irrespective of his nationality, race, or creed. You will demonstrate this by an unwavering and straightforward solidarity which must bind you as members of the same family. (3) Respectful of the Legion's traditions, honoring your superiors, discipline, and camaraderie are your strengths; courage and loyalty are your virtues. (4) Proud of your status as that of a Legionnaire, you will display this pride by your turnout, always impeccable; your behavior, ever worthy, though modest; your living quarters, always tidy. (5) An elite soldier, you will train vigorously, you will maintain your weapon as if it were your most precious possession, you will keep your body in the peak of condition, always fit. (6) A mission once given to you becomes sacred to you; you will accomplish it to the end at all cost. (7) In combat, you will act without relish of your task, or hatred; you will respect the vanquished enemy and will never abandon either your wounded or your dead, nor will you under any circumstances surrender your arms.

References: "11th Abn Brigade, French Foreign Legion, 2nd REP," Global Special Operations, 2006, http://www.globalspecialoperations.com/ffl.html, 4 March 2006; Cervens, Thierry de, "The French Foreign Legion," Legion Etranger, 2004, www.cervens.net/legion/home.htm, 3 March 2006; McLeave, Hugh, *The Damned Die Hard* (New York: Saturday Review Press, 1973); Porch, Douglas, *The French Foreign Legion* (New York: HarperCollins, 1991); Young, John Robert, *French Foreign Legion* (New York: Thames & Hudson, 1984).

G

Goths

A northern European tribe settling in southern Europe during the decline of the Roman Empire, known for their aggressive nature and introduction of cavalry as the primary military arm for the next several centuries.

The Goths were a Teutonic tribe, probably originating in Scandinavia, that arrived in northeastern Europe in the third century CE. The eastern Goths (Ostrogoths) and the western Goths (Visigoths) ravaged the lands of eastern Europe as far as Asia Minor and Greece. The first serious conflict between Goths and Romans came when a number of Gothic mercenaries aided the usurpation attempt of Procopius in Constantinople in 366. After Procopius's failed attempt and subsequent execution, the Roman emperor Valens launched an attack on the Goths across the Danube. After an inconclusive war, the two sides agreed on the Danube River as the boundary between their claims.

Around 370 the two Gothic groups separated, with the Visigoths occupying the land from the Dniester River to the Baltic Sea and the Ostrogoths living east of them to the Black Sea. In 376 the Goths found themselves threatened by the migration of the Huns from central Asia. The Ostrogoths fled westward to pressure the Visigoths, who appealed to Valens for protection and aid. Valens agreed to allow them across the Danube in return for their surrendering their weapons and their male children under military age. The Visigoths, under the leadership of Fritigern and Alavius, agreed and gave up their boys, but resisted giving up their weapons. The Romans abused the Visigoths and provoked their retaliation after killing Alavius during a parley. Fritigern attacked and defeated Roman forces at Marianopolis, in modern Bulgaria, then called on the Ostrogoths for assistance. Emperor Valens, fighting against the Persians, secured a truce there and moved to protect his northeastern frontier. Fritigern's Goths and Valens's Romans fought an indecisive battle at the mouth of the Danube in 377. Then the Goths withdrew after the battle and raised a general barbarian revolt along the frontier. By 378 the Romans finally began to regain control in the province of Thrace, but then met defeat while launching an attack on the Gothic forces near Adrianople. Spurning a request for peace talks, Valens attacked the Goths before reinforcements arrived. The Gothic force of perhaps 200,000 warriors (roughly half Visigothic infantry and half mixed barbarian cavalry) badly defeated Valens, who died in the battle along with some two-thirds of his 60,000 troops. The Visigothic king Fritigern was in overall command.

Valens's successor, Theodosius I, learned from his countryman's defeat and, after rebuilding an army and restoring order in Thrace, defeated the Goths and invited them into his army. The Visigoths served Theodosius, but upon his death in 395 they chose their own leader: Alaric. He had earlier raided Roman lands from across the Danube, but was captured and incorporated into the Roman army. Upon his election as king, Alaric led the Visigoths through Thrace and Greece. His only serious enemy was Stilicho, a Vandal general in Roman service who had served Theodosius. The Visigoths remained relatively unbothered, however, for the eastern Roman emperor, Arcadius, ordered Stilicho to remain in Italy. Alaric spent the mid-390s ravaging Greece, and then turned toward Italy.

Visigothic forces marched through Pannonia (along the eastern Adriatic coast) and crossed the Alps in October 401. Alaric's forces overran some of the northern provinces, but Stilicho's delaying actions kept him in the north. During the winter Stilicho ordered forces from Gaul to Italy and did some personal recruiting among German tribes. The resulting army attacked Alaric's forces, which were besieging Milan. Alaric withdrew and marched south, looking for Stilicho's incompetent emperor, Honorius. After two difficult battles in March and April 402, Alaric asked for negotiations and agreed to leave Italy. Instead, Alaric marched for Gaul, which had been left unprotected. Stilicho learned of this maneuver and blocked him, defeating the Visigoths at Verona. Alaric again withdrew and Honorius moved the imperial capital to Ravenna, behind the marshy outskirts of which he felt safe from attack. Alaric decided to cooperate with Stilicho and was named master-general of Illyricum. When in 408 Honorius ordered Stilicho murdered, the general's followers appealed to Alaric to invade Italy. He did so gladly. After two attacks on Rome were

called off (owing to successful Roman bribery), Alaric marched his forces to Rome and on August 24, 410, Rome fell to foreign invaders for the first time in a thousand years. Alaric then marched south to invade Sicily but died on the way.

Under the leadership of Athaulf, the Visigoths invaded Gaul in 412—supposedly to recover it for Honorius. Athaulf accomplished the conquest by 414 and was rewarded with marriage to Honorius's half-sister. He then followed Honorius's direction to reconquer Spain, but died in the process in 415. His successor, Wallia, defeated a number of barbarian tribes in Spain. He was rewarded with a kingdom of his own in southern Gaul. From this point, the Visigoths settled into lands ranging from the Rhone River into Spain. The greatest king was Euric, who established a code of law based on a mixture of Roman and Germanic legal traditions. The one thing he could not do, however, was establish a hereditary line, because the nobility forbade it. The monarchy was elective and therefore subject to too much political infighting. The lack of unity laid the Visigothic kingdom open to outside pressure, and in 507 Clovis, the founder of the Merovingian dynasty of the Franks, defeated Alaric II and acquired much of the lands north of the Pyrenees. Although the Visigoths managed to maintain hold of Spain in the face of pressure from the Vandals, they ultimately fell to Muslim invasion. The last Visigothic king, Roderic, was defeated and killed in 711, and the remaining Visigothic tribe was confined to the province of Asturias.

The Visigoths played an important role in the fall of the Roman Empire in the west. They, like many of the barbarians that flooded the Empire, were converted to the Arian view of Christianity (which denied Christ's equality with God the Father), and thus often had troubles with the Roman Catholic Church, which viewed them as heretics. As soldiers, they proved themselves so talented that the Roman Army in the east, based in Constantinople, reconfigured itself to adapt to Gothic cavalry. The Goths had little effect on the course of European history after 500 CE, however, because they spread themselves too thinly—from the Balkans to Spain—and were finally defeated and absorbed by more powerful enemies.

Following their brothers, the Visigoths, through southeastern Europe, the Ostrogoths entered into an uneasy alliance with the Byzantine Empire. They occupied Pannonia in the Danube valley, and occasional forays took them to the gates of Constantinople. Finally tiring of dealing with them, the Byzantine emperor Leo agreed to pay the Ostrogoths large amounts of tribute in return for a hostage, the heir to the Ostrogothic throne, Theodoric. At age seven Theodoric went to the Byzantine court and became a favorite of Leo, although he did not absorb as much education as his mentor would have liked. He did, however, acquire some culture and the Byzantine lifestyle, which he could put to good use later in life.

Theodoric returned to his people in 471 CE after 10 years in the imperial Byzantine court. He became king of the Ostrogoths three years later and remained alternately a source of trouble and security on the Byzantine frontier. Finally, Emperor Zeno commissioned Theodoric to invade Italy and defeat the tyrant Odovacer, the self-styled king of that country and leader of a large number of Hunnish troops. The Ostrogothic invasion of Italy numbered the entire tribe, as many as 250,000 people. They entered Italy in August 489 and met

Odovacer's forces along the Isonzo River. It was not a one-battle war; the Ostrogoths fought Odovacer's men for four years, finally capturing his capital at Ravenna after a lengthy siege. Theodoric granted Odovacer exceedingly liberal terms of surrender, then killed him at a celebratory feast.

Having removed the leader of a barbarian force, and done so in a barbaric manner, Theodoric became a remarkably gifted and wise leader. He established his capital at Ravenna also, but was unable to get the Byzantine empire to recognize him as anything more than "King of the Goths." In actuality, he was virtually a new emperor in the west. Ostrogoths settled into Italy and Theodoric confiscated the lands of Odovacer's men, plus whatever was necessary to take from the Italians to accommodate the larger Ostrogothic population. Although not at first thrilled with their new overlords, the local population came to appreciate Gothic rule. Theodoric reigned from 493 until 526, and almost all of those 33 years were peaceful. Even the Byzantines had to admit that he was a capable ruler. He treated all male citizens equally, whether Roman, Gothic, or foreigner, and all received justice. Although the Goths were practitioners of the Arian sect of Christianity, there was no religious persecution in a country dominated by the Roman Catholic Church. Theodoric authorized reconstruction projects in Rome and encouraged intellectual pursuits.

Theodoric maintained the peace with a strong military, establishing garrisons in Sicily and Dalmatia. He also made good use of political marriages to pacify potential enemies. Theodoric himself married the sister of King Clovis of the Franks, and he married his own sister to the king of the Vandals and a daughter to the Burgundian king. When the Franks attacked the Visigoths in southern Gaul, Theodoric stepped in to save them and extend his own influence into their territory in the Iberian peninsula.

Theodoric's beneficent rule made the Byzantine emperors Justin and Justinian envious. Justinian longed to reestablish a united Roman empire under Eastern rule. His renewed persecution of the Arians in the east provoked Theodoric's wrath, and the final three years of the Ostrogoth king's rule were unpleasant. By threatening and ultimately causing the death of the pope in 526, Theodoric lost most of his public support. His death in that same year left an ambitious wife, Amalasuntha, attempting to rule by placing her and Theodoric's young son on the throne. This only succeeded in provoking the ire of Gothic nobles. A later attempt to rule through a cousin whom she married proved Amalasuntha's undoing, for he soon allowed rivals to murder her. The discontent resulting from these actions encouraged Justinian, who sent his talented general, Belisarius, to remove barbarian rule from Italy. This he succeeded in doing by breaking Gothic power during a siege at Rome and harrying the remaining Gothic forces northward. His capture of Ravenna sealed his victory, but it proved short-lived. When Belisarius returned to Constantinople, the Goths under their new leader Totila went about reconquering the peninsula. Between 541 and 543, most of Italy was once again in Gothic hands. Totila laid siege to Rome in 545 and was finally admitted to the city by disgruntled guards. He was obliged to reconquer it in 549, then fortified it and proceeded to conquer Corsica and Sardinia. By 550, he controlled more territory than had Theodoric.

Justinian had the last word, however. Dispatching a force under the 75-year-old Narses, the emperor was able to capture Ravenna and defeat the Gothic army. After a mopping-up campaign, the last few hundred Goths were allowed free passage out of Italy across the Alps, never to return. The removal of the "barbarians," however, did not bring better times to the Italian peninsula. The recurring wars had devastated the countryside and drained Constantinople's finances. There was no money to rebuild, so Italy remained little better than a wasteland in some areas. The Goths provided a short era of stability after the fall of the Roman Empire, and under Theodoric the peninsula had the least barbarian of overlords. Enlightened as Theodoric was, the indigenous population nevertheless viewed him and the Ostrogoths as outsiders and, to an extent, heretics. For this reason, little of Gothic rule had any lasting impact on the Italian peninsula other than to put an end to Roman rule. The Lombards soon moved into the power vacuum left by the Ostrogoths and later forced the Byzantines out, but they were defeated in their turn. Italy would not be unified again until the nineteenth century.

References: Burns, Thomas, *A History of the Ostrogoths* (Bloomington: University of Indiana Press, 1984); Heather, Peter, *Goths and Romans* (Oxford: Clarendon, 1991); Wolfram, Herwig, *History of the Goths* (Berkeley: University of California Press, 1988).

Goumiers

North African troops fighting under French command in World War II.

While the French held colonies in North Africa, they recruited local forces both for police work and as auxiliaries for the French troops. In Morocco, they organized the volunteers into units of approximately 200 men (called *goumiers*) in both infantry and cavalry roles. When World War II broke out, 126 goums were in existence. Some were used against the Italians along the Libyan-Tunisian border before France surrendered. After the Paris government signed surrender terms in June 1940, the local French administrator General Nogues was ordered to disband the goums. Instead, he secretly kept them trained and equipped. When the American forces landed in Morocco in 1942, the French forces, including the goumiers, joined with them against the Axis troops. The goumiers at that time were four regiments strong, organized as the *Groupement de Tabors Marocains*, or GTMs.

More men were recruited after the Axis forces were pushed out of North Africa, and the goums were organized into *tabors* (units of three goums, roughly 1,000 men). Three tabors made up a group. These Moroccan troops served with the American Seventh Army under George Patton in the campaign to capture Sicily in the summer of 1943, then accompanied the Allies into Italy. The First, Third, and Fourth GTMs served in Italy and made their greatest contribution in the final battle for Monte Cassino in central Italy in the spring of 1944. They were part of the French *Corps Expeditionnaire Francais* (CEF) commanded by General Alphonse Juin. On May 14, 1944, a shock force of 12,000 men of the Fourth Moroccan Mountain Division, of which many were goumiers, was placed under the command of General Guillame. They were assigned to infiltrate an extremely rugged section of the German defensive position, known as the Gustav Line. The area was lightly defended because the Germans were convinced that no one could possibly make their way through that difficult terrain. The goumiers, however, were born and raised in such country and could move both quickly and silently. The German soldiers they found they dispatched quickly with their preferred weapons, knives. By May 16, they had captured Monte Petrella, outflanking the Germans and forcing their withdrawal, easing considerably the advance of the British Eighth Army. That same day they captured Monte Revole and the next day were in possession of Monte Faggeto, which controlled the primary German supply line. To a great extent, the actions of the French Moroccans won the battle, for their quick action and appearance in the German rear obliged the Germans, who had held the Allies stalemated for months, to withdraw to other defensive lines farther north.

The goumiers made a reputation not only for their skill in mountain fighting, but also for their ruthlessness. The used their knives more than their rifles and often brought back German body parts as souvenirs. This, of course, produced great psychological effects. The goumiers reached the height of their fame in the battle for Monte Cassino, but other Moroccan tabors were involved in the capture of Corsica and Elba. The goumiers also were involved in the secondary landing on French soil in August 1944 along the Mediterranean coast. They fought in France and some went with the American armies into Germany. Other Moroccan troops remained in North Africa on garrison duty through the war.

References: Dear, E.D.S. and M.R.D. Foot, eds., *Oxford Companion to World War II* (Oxford: Oxford University Press, 1995); Ellis, John, *Cassino: The Hollow Victory* (New York:

McGraw-Hill, 1984); Majdalany, Fred, *The Battle of Cassino* (New York: Houghton Mifflin, 1957).

Grande Armée

The French army commanded by Napoleon that dominated Europe in the early nineteenth century.

The nature of armies and warfare changed after the French Revolution (1789–1793). After the Peace of Westphalia had ended the Thirty Years War in 1648, warfare in Europe was relatively limited in numbers and objectives. Kings fought each other with armies of professionals (often mercenaries) and a balance of power was maintained. No country was allowed to dominate the continent, and an ever-shifting series of alliances reflected the whims of monarchs hoping to gain a piece of land here or there to add to their country. When those European kings joined together in 1793 in an attempt to restore the French monarchy after Louis XVI's execution, they relied on their small professional forces. However, the army that met them was unlike any force Europe had ever seen. Encouraged by the equality granted them as a result of the Revolution, Frenchmen flocked to the colors to defend their nation and their new system of government. The French government introduced the *levée en masse*, conscription that drew from all classes of society and created a huge, but disorganized and amateur army. It was this disorganization, however, that was the new army's strength, for the French soldiers broke the rules of warfare not by marching in straight lines but by throwing themselves in massive waves over and around stunned and vastly outnumbered adversaries.

The French army beat back the European monarchs and kept the country independent, but internal squabbling, combined with the desire to spread their Revolution, caused political discord at home. As in ancient Rome, so it was in France: When a government is divided, generals can play important political roles. As the hero of campaigns in Italy and Egypt, Napoleon Bonaparte parlayed his military success into political power, overthrowing the weakened revolutionary government and installing himself as emperor of a new France. As a revolutionary himself, Napoleon promoted many of his political predecessors' goals, and many of the social and legal advances he implemented became permanent. But it was the spirit of the large and motivated army, coupled with his own genius and experience, that created the *Grande Armée*, or "Grand Army."

When Napoleon took control of the government in 1799, much of the revolutionary *élan* had faded among both the commissioned and noncommissioned officers. Rivalries arose within the army as the various forces, with different commanders and experiences, believed themselves superior to one another. Napoleon ended the discord in 1804 by combining all of these forces into the Grand Army, with himself as commander. Henceforward, the troops cooperated (for the most part) without petty bickering. Napoleon instead fostered regimental pride, giving each unit its own standard and variety of uniforms. The standard was to be carried into battle and protected at all costs. If a standard-bearer was killed in battle, another soldier would immediately take up the standard, so that the regiment could rally around its colors. The flag was carried in parades and decorated with mementoes of victories, hon-

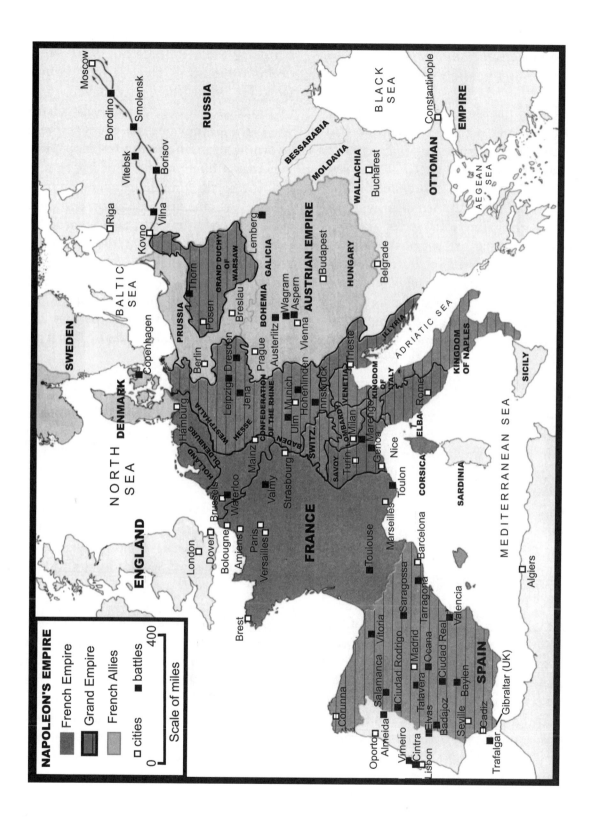

NAPOLEON'S EMPIRE

French Empire
Grand Empire
French Allies
□ cities ■ battles

Scale of miles
0   400

RUSSIA

BLACK SEA

OTTOMAN EMPIRE

Constantinople

BESSARABIA
MOLDAVIA
WALLACHIA

Bucharest

AEGEAN SEA

Belgrade

HUNGARY

□ Budapest

AUSTRIAN EMPIRE

GALICIA

□ Lemberg

Moscow

Borodino • Smolensk

Vitebsk
Borisov

□ Riga
Vilna

Kovno

BALTIC SEA

Thorn

GRAND DUCHY OF WARSAW

PRUSSIA

Posen
Breslau
BOHEMIA

Prague

SWEDEN

Copenhagen

DENMARK

NORTH SEA

Hamburg

Berlin
Leipzig
Dresden
Jena

WESTPHALIA
HESSE
OLDENBURG
HOLLAND

Brussels
Waterloo
Valmy

Mainz

Strasbourg

CONFEDERATION OF THE RHINE

BADEN
SWITZ.
SAVOY

Ulm
Munich
Hohenlinden
Innsbruck

Wagram
Aspern
Austerlitz
Vienna

ILLYRIA
Trieste

ADRIATIC SEA

VENETIA
LOMBARDY

Milan
Turin
Marengo
Genoa

KINGDOM OF ITALY

Rome

ELBA

KINGDOM OF NAPLES

SICILY

MEDITERRANEAN SEA

Nice

Toulon

Marseilles

CORSICA

SARDINIA

ENGLAND

London
Dover
Bolougne
Amiens
Paris
Versailles

Brest

FRANCE

Toulouse

Barcelona

Algiers

Corunna
Almeida
Vimeiro
Cintra
Lisbon

Oporto

Salamanca
Ciudad Rodrigo
Talavera
Elvas
Badajoz
Seville
Cadiz
Trafalgar

Vitoria
Madrid
Ocana
Ciudad Real
Baylen

Saragossa
Tarragona
Valencia

SPAIN

Gibraltar (UK)

ored in the headquarters, and retired to churches. Rather than petty rivalry, regimental pride created unit pride dedicated to doing the best possible job for emperor and country.

Napoleon's phenomenal victories in the first years of the nineteenth century had made attracting recruits easy. However, after 1809 when he began to suffer setbacks, Napoleon relied more heavily on the draft. Originally, all men who were 20 to 25 years of age were liable for military service (with some exceptions), but by 1812 Napoleon resorted to drafting younger men. He retained, however, the equality of opportunity that had characterized the revolutionary army. Although the Grand Army's top commanders, the marshals, tended to be from the upper classes, it was possible even for recruits from the lowest classes to rise through the ranks. After a battle, dead junior officers were immediately replaced by sergeants promoted almost on the spot.

The army drafted 1.5 million men between 1800 and 1815. About one-fourth of them were from countries occupied by, or allied with, Napoleon. He accepted deserters from other armies into his own and created multinational units. Even his personal Imperial Guard contained soldiers from Italy, Holland, and Hanover. Whether draftee or volunteer, the troops of the Grand Army received little formal training upon enlistment. Instead, they were given small increments of training daily while on the march. This way, they picked up valuable insights from veterans and learned what was actually vital for both survival and victory. This method, however, proved inadequate in later years, especially after Napoleon lost almost his entire army in Russia between 1812 and 1813. A new Grand Army, built virtually from scratch

in 1813, included veterans drawn from French combat forces in Spain and Italy, stiffening the new force but weakening the donor forces. Still, the recruits performed well, for while they may have lost their revolutionary ardor, Napoleon's charisma was often all they needed. He was liberal in awarding decorations to the troops, knowing that this fostered both loyalty and fighting spirit. Napoleon once commented that it was amazing what someone would do for "a bauble." He also awarded specially inscribed swords or muskets to commemorate outstanding acts of valor. Anyone of any rank or unit could be awarded the Legion of Honor: Of the 40,000 recipients of this award, only 25,000 survived through the Battle of Waterloo in 1815.

Those soldiers that particularly distinguished themselves in combat might be transferred to the Imperial Guard, Napoleon's personal reserve. This force was divided into three sections: The Old Guard was made up of soldiers with at least four years and two campaigns of experience. These were his favorites, and he liked to call them le grognards, the "grumblers." The Middle Guard was slightly less selective and contained some foreign units. The Young Guard was made up of the top recruits from each class of conscripts. The Imperial Guard was always better paid and better fed, which led to some envy, but its members often earned their pay. The sight of the Old Guard, always dressed for battle in parade uniforms, at times acted as both a spur to the French troops and an immediate visual threat to the enemy. Napoleon called upon them for the killing blow at battle's end. In his later years, however, he became more and more reluctant to commit the Old Guard, even when necessary. When the Imperial Guard, hastily re-formed after Napoleon's escape from Elba, broke at Waterloo, it was the signal for a general French collapse. The Imperial Guard did, however, cover the emperor's retreat. When caught by the British and told to lay down their arms, the Guard commander replied, "The Guard dies, but never surrenders" (Chandler, 1966). At its height, the Imperial Guard numbered 112,000 men.

The Grand Army was organized into a number of corps, each commanded by a marshal. The size of each corps varied, depending on the talent of its commander, the job it was assigned to do, or simply its ability to confuse enemy intelligence gathering. The marshals were appointed for their bravery and loyalty, and those officers that had served with Napoleon in his early campaigns in Italy or Egypt remained his favorites. The marshals, however, were not allowed much independence because Napoleon practiced a highly centralized form of command. He made all the decisions that mattered, and his staff existed not to advise him, but to follow his directives. Although this centralization accomplished its original purpose of uniting the army, it proved deleterious when Napoleon was obliged to detach units or create separate armies to operate in far-flung locales. Thus, his army in Spain, which was almost never under his direct command, suffered by being ignored. It can be said that wherever Napoleon was, success was assured; wherever he was not, disaster struck.

Although regarded as probably the greatest general of modern times, Napoleon had his shortcomings. In particular, his armies—and therefore his campaigns—suffered from inadequate supplies. In Italy, his relatively small army was easily able to live off the land, a practice Napoleon believed in. When the Grand Army grew, however, and campaigned in countries that were poor, food was often in short supply. Napoleon's strategy depended on speed to catch an enemy unprepared. On the one hand, this made maintaining his army almost impossible with traditional supply lines, which could not keep up. On the other hand, it can be argued that he moved so quickly in order to win and settle in, and to allow his supplies to reach him or local supply sources to be tapped. Even when Napoleon took supply problems into account, as in his invasion of Russia in 1812, the bases he established were too far apart and he still lacked sufficient transport to keep them or his troops fed. Thus, when the Russians instituted scorched earth tactics as they retreated, the French were unable to live off the land and suffered accordingly.

Napoleon was able to accomplish a long string of victories not only because of the quality of his army but because of his own brilliance. He developed the *batallion carrée*, whereby his army was divided into four separate corps travelling in an open square. Each corps was sufficiently independent to forage for itself, but close enough to respond quickly when the enemy was located. Once any of the corps engaged the enemy, the other three would respond immediately. For example, if the army were heading east (with corps located at the north, south, east, and west corners of the square), and the east corps met the enemy, they would engage. The north and south corners would come up to outflank the enemy position, while the west corps could draw up behind the east corps to act as a reserve. The Grand Army was therefore quickly in a position to attack the enemy's flanks, move around behind them on one flank or the other, or push the center with the reserve corps.

Napoleon was almost always able to sneak up on his enemies, for he kept the cavalry well in advance of his army to report enemy locations and give himself a screen behind which he could maneuver. Once in battle, Napoleon depended on massed artillery to weaken a section of the enemy line, then exploited that weakness with infantry. Once the line broke, French cavalry immediately turned the retreat into a rout.

Napoleon was almost able to control all of Europe using his Grand Army, but its innate logistical weaknesses and his inability to physically command on all fronts simultaneously seriously weakened it over time. Further, as the Imperial Guard expanded with veterans whom Napoleon increasingly hesitated to commit to battle, the line regiments had to make do with fewer experienced men. When the terrain proved daunting (as in Russia) or his enemies began to learn how to counter his moves (as at Leipzig and Waterloo), Napoleon's star set. When he was exiled to Elba in 1814, the Grand Army ceased to exist. When he escaped exile and reformed his army in 1815, he named it the Army of the North. At its height, however, Le Grande Armée was unbeatable.

References: Chandler, David, *The Campaigns of Napoleon* (New York: Macmillan, 1966); Paret, Peter, "Napoleon and the Revolution in War," in Peter Paret, *Makers of Modern Strategy* (Princeton: Princeton University Press, 1986); Rothenberg, *Gunther, The Art of Warfare in the Age of Napoleon* (Bloomington: University of Indiana Press, 1978).

Green Berets (Special Forces)

An elite unit of the modern U.S. Army.

The concept of special forces, units that operate outside the mainstream of the military organization, is not new in American history. From Roger's Rangers in the French and Indian War (1756–1760) through Mosby's Rangers in the Civil War, small guerrilla-type groups have been used to disrupt enemy operations away from a war's main battlefields. In World War II, the United States developed new ranger-type units. In Europe, Darby's Rangers were given special assignments to perform during the Normandy invasion in June 1944. The Devil's Brigade was a joint Canadian-American venture that operated first in the Italian theater, then in France. In the Pacific theater of operations, similar organizations were formed. Colonel Frank Merrill's Marauders operated against Japanese forces in Burma, while Lieutenant General Walter Krueger's Alamo Scouts in the Philippines harassed the Japanese in almost miraculous fashion.

Foundations for the Special Forces were laid during World War II. William Donovan's Office of Strategic Services (OSS) operated commando and intelligence-gathering units that penetrated occupied Europe, as well as organized Southeast Asian tribes into guerrilla units to fight the Japanese. These two functions, guerrilla operations and intelligence gathering, split into two separate organizations after the war. President Harry Truman disbanded the OSS, but created out of it the Central Intelligence Agency. The Special Forces took up guerrilla operations training, starting in June 1952.

Two men, Colonel Aaron Bank and Colonel Russell Volckman, OSS operatives from World War II, were the driving force in getting Army approval for the creation of the Special Forces. With the advent of the Cold War, secret operations behind enemy lines became an attractive option. Colonel Bank was given facilities at Fort Bragg, North Carolina, for establishing the Special Forces training center. He chose a location on base called Smoke Bomb Hill, and proceeded to fill the 2,300 personnel slots the Army had authorized him. He refused recruits, preferring veterans who had OSS, Ranger, or paratrooper experience, and took only volunteers looking for tough training and a challenge. All had to speak at least two languages and have parachute training, as well as hold at least sergeant's rank. They were also advised that their operations would usually take place behind enemy lines and sometimes in civilian clothes. Because this violated the rules of war, it would leave captured operatives to be tried and executed as spies, not soldiers. The training that Banks initiated was more rigorous than even these men had experienced. Paratroopers and Rangers had been used to acting quickly in advance of major attacks. The Special Forces, however, could be used for long operations in which they would have to sustain themselves in a hostile country with little to no outside support.

After a year and a half in training, the first overseas deployment took place when half the force, designated Tenth Special Forces Group, was sent to Bad Iz, West Germany, in November 1953. The half that stayed in Fort Bragg retained their original unit designation, but the forces in Germany were now assigned the title Seventy-seventh Special Forces Group. Special Forces from this point forward were incorporated into army strategic planning. In April 1956 the first Special Forces troops

were sent to Southeast Asia. These were not the first Special Forces in Asia, however, for a small group had operated secretly behind enemy lines in the Korean conflict, an operation that remained classified until the 1980s. The first Special Forces in Southeast Asia, however, were soon joined by other units to create the 8231st Army Special Operational Detachment, which was based on Okinawa. It is here that the Special Forces' basic unit of operation was developed: the A-Team. This 12-man unit contained two officers, two sergeants for operations and intelligence, two weapons sergeants, two communications sergeants, two medics, and two engineers. This organization allowed the team to divide into two six-man units, or Split A-Teams. Each man also had cross-training to take up the slack in case of casualties.

The coming of age of the Special Forces had a political aspect, for it was after recognition by President John Kennedy in 1961 that the organization really began to grow. With increasing tensions between the United States and communist regimes, Kennedy saw the potential for elite guerrilla-style units, and he ordered the army to expand the Special Forces. He also directed that the army allow the men to wear the green beret as a symbol of their separation from the regular army. This, he knew, would promote esprit de corps, and the term "Green Berets" came to be interchangeable with "Special Forces."

It was in Southeast Asia that the Special Forces reached the height of their fame, acting as advisors to the South Vietnamese Army in the 1950s and early 1960s. It was a Special Forces soldier, Captain Harry Cramer, Jr., of the Fourteenth Special Forces Operations Detachment, who was the first American killed in that conflict. During that time the Special Forces trained local soldiers and native tribes in guerrilla operations and counterinsurgency. In 1964 the Special Forces established their headquarters at Nha Trang, where it remained until their redeployment to Fort Bragg in 1971. By the end of their service in Vietnam, Special Forces personnel had received a total of 28,311 medals, including 16 Medals of Honor and 2,658 Purple Hearts.

Although Vietnam was their highest-profile mission, during the 1960s the Special Forces also conducted training and operations throughout Latin America, including the capture of Che Guevara. Still, Vietnam remained their major focus. There the Special Forces performed missions beyond just fighting. Some 254 separate posts were set up during the war, defended by Green Berets and local personnel they had trained. Montagnards, Nungs, Cao Dei, and other tribes provided manpower that became the 60,000-strong Civil Irregular Defense Group. Special Forces also provided engineering and medical aid to local villages, along with other noncombat projects designed to establish closer emotional and psychological ties between U.S. forces and the local population. Even though the bulk of the Special Forces were withdrawn in 1971, some remained to carry out missions behind enemy lines, operating out of Thailand into Cambodia and North Vietnam.

After the American involvement in Vietnam ended, the role of the Special Forces diminished rapidly as the army focused on potential major-force conflict in Europe. The Special Forces commanders convinced the army that the other, less combat-oriented tasks of the organization could be harnessed. Under the program called Special Proficiency at Rugged Training and Nation-building (SPARTAN), the men worked on engineering and medical projects in the United States on Indian reservations and in impoverished Appalachian areas, much as they had done with isolated Vietnamese populations. SPARTAN, however, was temporary, as the main goal of Special Forces was combat, and under President Ronald Reagan they got their chance to fight again. Like Kennedy, Reagan saw the need for counterinsurgency operations in hot spots around the world where large forces could not operate. In the early 1980s, Special Forces became an entirely separate branch within the army, and the training and entrance qualifications were toughened.

Special Forces troops saw action in Panama during Operation Just Cause, where they engaged the Panamanian Defense Forces attempting to capture a bridge leading to Ranger units. The Green Berets not only defeated the attackers, but also suffered no casualties in the action. Such actions brought the Special Forces back into favor, and by 1990, five Special Forces groups were on active duty status, based at Fort Bragg, Fort Carson (Colorado), Fort Lewis (Washington), Fort Campbell (Kentucky), and detached units in Germany and Okinawa, with reserves in the National Guard. The units continue to train for combat while aiding local populations in the United States and around the world.

References: Kelly, Ross, *Special Operations and National Purpose* (Lexington, MA: Lexington Books, 1989); Simmons, Anna, *The Company They Keep* (Free Press, 1997); Sullivan, *George, Elite Warriors* (New York: Facts on File, 1995).

Grenzschutzgruppe 9 (GSG-9)

Germany's counterterrorist team

During the 1972 summer Olympic games in Munich, Germany, the worst tragedy in the history of the games occurred. Black September, a Palestinian terrorist group, kidnapped 11 Israeli athletes and held them hostage at the Olympic village. Promised safe conduct to the airport and a plane to Egypt, the eight terrorists and nine of the hostages flew by helicopter to the airport, where they were to be intercepted by German police on board and scattered outside the airplane as snipers. The result was a disaster, as everything that could go wrong, did. When the smoke finally cleared, all nine of the hostages at the scene were dead, as were six of the eight kidnappers.

In the wake of this botched rescue operation, the German government decided it was well past time to create a counterterror unit. A number of terrorist groups operated within Germany, such as the Red Army Faction, but Germany had done nothing to train a specialized force to deal with such threats. Thus was born the Grenzschutzgruppe-9, better known simply as GSG-9. Fearful that an elite military force may bring negative comparisons to the Schutzstaffeln (SS) of Nazi days, the German government decided to place GSG-9 under the control of the Federal Border Police. Created and first commanded by Colonel Ulrich Wegener, the unit was declared operational by April 1973.

To join the unit one must already be a member of the Border Police. This makes the training somewhat different than similar units in other countries. The 22-week training course involves much more academic work than other, military-sponsored

Logo of the Grenzschutzgruppe 9 (GSG-9) Germany's counterterrorist team.

courses, since the applicant must know the details of German law enforcement regulations. The second half of the course gets into more specialized training. There are reports that a dropout/failure rate of 80 percent is common.

The organization is broken down into three units—GSG-9/1, 2, and 3. 1 and 2 each number approximately 100 members, while 3 totals about 50. Their tasks, respectively, are land, sea, and air operations. While their quarters and food have been described as Spartan, the government spares no expense in making sure the GSG-9 members have all the equipment they could ever want. Also different from similar units in other countries, the members are not rotated out but are encouraged to stay as long as they are interested and useful. This means that there is a much higher number of veterans to pass on the lessons learned from past operations.

GSG-9 first made its presence known during the 1974 World Cup matches in Germany, where an attack by the Baader-Meinhof gang, part of the leftist terrorist Red Army Faction (RAF), was supposedly planned. None occurred, and the unit also assisted both Canada and Austria during their 1976 Olympic Games. GSG-9 had an impressive first showing in 1977 when they staged a rescue operation against a hijacked airliner in Mogadishu, Somalia. Two male and two female terrorists took control of Lufthansa Flight 181, demanding the release of jailed Red Army Faction terrorists. Assisting in the operations were two members of Britain's Special Air Service, who provided the Germans with their newly developed "flash-bang" stun grenades. Forcing their way into the aircraft a few minutes after midnight on 18 October, they threw their stun grenades and quickly killed one of the female terrorists and wounded a second. While the passengers were quickly evacuated out the rear, the attackers focused on the two remaining terrorists in the cockpit. The hijackers attempted to fight their way out by using fragmentation grenades, but they inflicted no casualties and died themselves in the process. Final tally: three terrorists dead, one captured, no casualties among the GSG or the passengers, the entire operation over in a matter of minutes.

In the early 1980s, the GSG was involved in the arrests of most of the key Red Army Faction members still operating. Although this put a serious crimp in the RAF's ability to attack political targets, it did not finish them completely. In 1993, intelligence sources indicated that two remaining members, Birgit Hogefeld and Wolfgang Grams, were in the small town of Bad Kleinen. During the arrest, shooting started and a GSG-9 operative was killed, as was Grams. The official report was that Grams died during the shootout, but an eyewitness reported that he was murdered after surrendering. This severely hurt the unit's reputation, but it was salvaged somewhat when, just two months later, they successfully ended a hijacking in Düsseldorf with no casualties at all. A single terrorist had taken over a KLM flight from Tunis to Amsterdam and was demanding the release of Sheikh Omar Abdel Rahman, being held in connection with the first bombing of the New York World Trade Center in 1991.

The secretive nature of the GSG-9 unit means that the majority of its operations have not been made public. Official information releases claim it has been involved in hundreds of operations, including protection of sporting events, political meetings, high-ranking visitors, etc., as well as counterterror arrests.

References: "Germany–Grenzschutzgruppe 9," Special Operations.com, 22 September 2005, http://www.specialoperations.com/Foreign/Germany/GSG9.htm, 2 March 2006; "Germany's GSG-9," Specwarnet.net, 2001, http://www.specwarnet.net/europe/gsg9.htm, 2 March 2006; Kozlow, Christopher, *Counter-Terrorism* (London: Jane's, 1998).

Guerrillas

Specialists in nontraditional partisan warfare

The term *guerrilla* is Spanish for "little war." It came into common usage at the time the Spanish came into conflict with Napoleon's forces in the first decade of the nineteenth century. Although guerrilla war may have obtained its name in this conflict, its concept and practice date back many centuries, and it is probably impossible to find a record of its first use.

Guerrilla warfare is basically the harassing of a superior force by an inferior one. The key to guerrilla warfare—especially in its beginning stages—is to avoid direct contact with the stronger enemy at all cost. Thus, guerrillas seek to attack isolated outposts and units with quick assaults and temporarily superior numbers, then fade into the countryside before a response can be mounted.

One of the first recorded uses of such a type of warfare is in the Bible, in which David organized a small band to harass the incumbent King Saul. His group was regarded by the king as nothing but a band of robbers (which is mostly true, as they had to live off the land and the captured supplies of the king). David based his group in the wilderness where it was easy to hide and difficult for the king's army to surprise him. He also gained the foreign aid of the neighboring Philistines. By aiding the local poor, David's men gained public support. All of these elements have been repeated in guerrilla movements to this day. Later in the Old Testament, Judas Maccabeus led a guerrilla movement against the Greco-Syrian occupiers of Israel. His movement started out in the standard fashion, but as he gained more success his force grew to the point that he could challenge the foreign forces directly. This change from guerrilla war to conventional war is the ultimate goal of most such movements. At this point, the guerrilla forces may actually throw off their oppressors and implement their own policies for which they have been fighting, be they political, religious, social, or any combination of those.

This style of warfare seems not to have been utilized much before the Middle Ages, when strong armies attempted to occupy territories that were more technologically backward than theirs. The English found this type of resistance in Wales, Scotland, and Ireland, where, between the eleventh and fifteenth centuries, the inhabitants fought to maintain their independence. In Eastern Europe, similar struggles were fought, but there the primary goals were social or religious. Peasant uprisings were common and effective temporarily, usually when they were under the leader-

ship of a disaffected noble or someone else with some military experience. But peasant revolts rarely, if ever, reached the point of gaining sufficient strength to defeat the armies of the upper classes. Still, these wars did accomplish much toward the development of ethnic identity in the Balkans, because the hated upper classes tended to be invaders from elsewhere.

In the Western Hemisphere in the colonial period, one finds guerrilla conflicts as well. In North America, the native Indian population used their hunting skills to stalk English colonists or (with French support) to ambush columns of unsuspecting British troops. However, their inability to organize along intertribal lines doomed their attempts to failure. Also, the colonists themselves learned Indian methods and fought a counter-guerrilla war, which ultimately proved effective. In the Caribbean and South America, escaped slaves occasionally organized and fought guerrilla actions against their former owners. In Brazil, some former slave bands existed independently for years. In Haiti, such forces fought and defeated Napoleonic troops and gained the island's independence in 1803. In the Americas, the terrain proved advantageous to guerrilla movements, because the rugged and heavily wooded countryside allowed for easy ambush and escape.

In the seventeenth and eighteenth centuries, as European armies grew more nationalistic and professional, guerrilla tactics were still employed in some cases. Although the majority of battles were "set-piece," that is, units entering battle in formation, armies often recruited nonprofessional forces, which took the description "irregulars." The irregulars were often used for scouting and harassment of enemy supply lines, and sometimes to demoralize enemy civilians. In Africa and India, British and French colonial armies employed such troops widely where familiarity with local terrain was beyond most European officers' ken. The irregular forces were considered necessary for scouting purposes, but the troops themselves were often distrusted for their "irregular" discipline and loyalty. It was also difficult to control these irregular troops after or away from the battle, and pillaging and looting were common negative aspects of using such forces. Irregulars were also used to infiltrate enemy territory and foment local discontent.

In the American Revolution, the Indian-style fighting the colonists had learned often served them well when fighting the British regular army. The opening day of the conflict, 19 April 1775, proved this: At Lexington, a small group of militia stood to face a superior British force and suffered badly. Later that day, as that same British force retreated from Concord to Boston, colonial sniping and hit-and-run attacks inflicted three times as many casualties on the British as the American guerrillas suffered. A month later, a small force of men under the command of Ethan Allen surprised the isolated but strategic Fort Ticonderoga on Lake Champlain and captured it and some 100 cannon without a shot being fired. American commander George Washington spent the war creating a regular Continental Army, but often such commanders as Nathaniel Greene in the Carolinas exhausted the British sufficiently for Washington's regulars to take advantage of them. Greene commanded both regulars and militia, but he employed the standard guerrilla strategy of avoiding major battles while wearing down his enemy with skirmishing and harassment whenever possible.

It was during the Napoleonic Wars (1803–1815) that the strategy not only acquired its name of guerrilla warfare, but also saw some of its methods included in regular warfare. The French Revolution's *levée en masse* drafted huge numbers of peasants into the army. By this time, firearms were relatively common and easy to provide for large numbers of soldiers. However, the traditional fighting method of attacking in lines demanded more discipline than the peasants or their non-aristocratic officers were able to summon in the early days. Therefore, skirmishing and attacking by units rather than in a line became the normal practice. The fact that the peasant draftees were fighting for social and political rights similar to those pursued by peasant uprisings in previous centuries also increased their effectiveness. For a time, "irregular" was becoming "regular." Even these adaptations of guerrilla tactics to regular warfare, however, failed to defeat the traditional guerrilla combat the Spanish peasants engaged in when French forces invaded Iberia. Again, the rugged countryside, the ability of the guerrillas to mass at a single point for temporary numerical advantage and then dissipate quickly, and the constant harassment of supply lines and isolated outposts all proved too much for the French to overcome. In addition to this, the assistance of a foreign power (Great Britain) to provide direction and supplies contributed to the success of guerrilla warfare in Spain.

After the Napoleonic Wars, Europe did not see many guerrillas for the remainder of the century, except in France itself. Urban guerrillas made their appearance during the revolutions of 1830 and 1848, but their limited appeal outside the cities doomed their causes. They made another appearance in 1870–1871 during the Franco-Prussian War with some action against invading Prussian troops. It was here one sees the birth of the term *franc-tireur* (French terror), as much terrorist as freedom fighter. Still, the urban guerrilla did provoke government responses. The winding alleyways that were the urban version of the rural wilderness became the target of city planners in the nineteenth century, and wide straight avenues became the popular urban design. This made barricades more difficult to construct and opened up firing lanes for artillery.

Guerrilla warfare appeared more in colonial conflict in the nineteenth century. The French dealt with Muslim guerrillas fighting for their religion as much as independence in Algeria. The British fought the most difficult of guerrilla conflicts in South Africa, while the Spanish put down several revolts in Cuba culminating in serious guerrilla warfare on the part of the Cubans in the later 1890s. In all of these conflicts, the colonial powers were victorious because they had all developed counter-guerrilla strategies. The French in Algeria abandoned the fortress-based defense for the aggressive flying column strategy that took the war into the wilderness on the guerrillas' home territory. By using surprise, the French kept the Algerians on the move and thus denied them the ability to plan and gather supplies. The French administration also saw the need to implement political action to pacify the population by granting some of the concessions for which the guerrillas were fighting. Counterinsurgency thus took on as much of a political role as a military one.

In the United States, the regular army carried on offensives against Indian warriors in the Great Plains and the desert southwest. As the European powers had done against their guerrilla enemies in Africa and Cuba, the U.S. cavalry also took the war to the Indians, denying them supplies and forcing their surrender. The destruction of the buffalo on the Great Plains destroyed everything the Plains Indians needed for sustenance, and cavalry attacks on villages in the winter to steal their horses robbed the Indians of their only serious method of fighting. On foot they could not feed or fight, and the reservation became the only alternative. This, together with an inability of most tribes to cooperate with each other (a common guerrilla failing) and the overwhelming number of white soldiers and settlers pushing into their territories, meant that the Indians could not possibly win in the long run.

The Boers of South Africa at the end of the nineteenth century proved the most obstinate of guerrilla enemies for the British. Unlike native warriors who lacked modern weaponry, the Boers often had rifles and artillery equal to or better than whatever the British could put in the field. Their ability to live off the land, move about quickly on horseback, and also hold strong defensive positions when necessary made the Boers far superior to any guerrilla forces the British had faced. The British, however, followed the strategy implemented in Cuba by the Spanish: Deny the guerrillas their source of support, the local population. Local populations often provide supplies, information, and shelter to guerrilla armies. To prevent this, the British in South Africa and the Spanish in Cuba rounded up the population and concentrated them in camps, leaving anyone outside the camp by definition a "hostile." Although conditions in the camps at times proved deadly, owing to lack of fresh water, food, medicine, and sanitary facilities, the strategy was effective. With the local population incarcerated in the camps, there was no one to work the farms and the food supply for the guerrilla soldiers withered. In Cuba, the timely intervention of the United States in the spring of 1898 saved the guerrillas from imminent defeat. The Boers, on the other hand, could look to no outside savior, despite the fact that they received equipment and moral support from other countries. They were forced to sign surrender terms in 1902, although in the long run the Boers' political agenda—local autonomy—was accomplished through legal means.

Guerrilla warfare returned to Europe for a short time in the early twentieth century during the Balkan Wars of 1912–1913. The motivations for these conflicts were nationalistic as well as religious, but—like so many guerrilla movements—the Balkan guerrilla alliances could not withstand their own success. Once the Turks were sent packing by the victorious Balkan fighters, the rivalries within the guerrilla organization guaranteed that peace would not last.

Two very successful guerrilla operations took place during World War I, although not in Europe. In East Africa, Paul Emil von Lettow-Vorbeck used German soldiers and mobilized native troops to make life miserable for the British in one of the most successful campaigns of all time. His activities have come to be the model for irregular warfare. In a completely different climate, T. E. Lawrence mobilized Arab forces to attack the Turks in the Middle East during 1915–1918. Drawing on their Bedouin past, these horse- and camel-borne raiders greatly disrupted Turkish supply lines and outposts. Lawrence kept them supplied from British stores but (except for Lawrence himself) it was virtually a total Arab effort in terms of manpower. Promises of nationhood and free-

dom from Turkish domination motivated these men. By contrast, Lettow-Vorbeck's operation was conducted almost strictly for military purposes. As could the Boers, the Arabs were able to move quickly as light cavalry. However, owing to the introduction of automobiles and aircraft, this was to be about the last time such operations were feasible.

Guerrilla warfare and revolution came to be almost synonymous in the twentieth century as anticolonial forces grew in strength and popularity, especially after World War I. The great proponent of revolution was Karl Marx, who, together with Freidrich Engels, wrote the *Communist Manifesto* in 1848. Yet their vision of urban warfare of the workers against the owners rarely occurred. The Irish used urban guerrillas in their bid to create an independent Ireland during 1916–1921, but none there ever seriously embraced communism. It took other communist theorists to adapt revolution and guerrilla warfare into a cohesive whole and to seriously integrate the political aspects of revolution into the military strategy of guerrilla conflict. Although Vladimir Lenin in Russia made sure that political officers were in every unit of the Soviet military, it was Mao Tse-tung in China who became the leading theorist of national revolution among the agricultural rather than the industrial proletariat. His *On Guerrilla Warfare* (1937) became a text on national guerrilla uprisings.

Nationalist guerrilla warfare returned in World War II, most notably in the Soviet Union. The partisans who escaped Hitler's executioners were so successful in harassing German supply lines that ultimately almost half the German army was dedicated to rear areas, a fact that seriously affected the fighting at the front. Irregular warfare also showed itself in the formation of commando units that fought in all theaters, especially in North Africa and Southeast Asia.

Anti-colonial movements exploded after World War II as imperialism became an ever-less-popular political theme. Communism, however, became more popular and the United States, which had put down a guerrilla movement in the Philippines at the turn of the century and created special operations forces during World War II, became the primary anti-communist and anti-guerrilla combatant. In Latin America, communist guerrillas organized anti-government movements to remove dictators and implement social and economic reform. By embracing communism and receiving aid from the Soviet Union , these "freedom fighters" became the target of the United States' military attention. No guerrilla movement, however, drew so much attention as that directed by Ho Chi Minh in Vietnam. Although he was an avowed nationalist attempting to free his homeland from French colonial rule, Ho Chi Minh's Soviet training and the supplies he received from both the Soviet Union and Communist China guaranteed American political opposition.

The Vietnamese had fought a very successful guerrilla war against the French after World War II, moving from a purely harassing type of combat to a national army that beat the French on their own terms. When the United States supported a repressive anti-communist regime in the southern part of the country after 1956, Ho Chi Minh returned to his guerrilla tactics. Although the British had recently conducted a successful anti-guerrilla operation in Malaya, the Americans apparently did not learn from their example and attempted to defeat the Vietnamese com-

munists by conventional means. Although over time "special operations" forces became more widely used to fight an irregular war, the inability of the United States to offer a seriously attractive alternative political solution to the Vietnamese people almost guaranteed the victory of the communist forces.

As long as weaker forces find themselves unable to face stronger ones in head-to-head competition, guerrilla warfare will exist. However, only those movements that do not fragment, offer and promote a viable program that is acceptable to a majority of the population, and receive some form of outside assistance are likely to be successful, as shown by past experience. As long as the stronger forces have the adaptability to fight a guerrilla war of their own and beat the partisans at their own game, they can win a military victory. However, without having a viable program to offer the population (whether social, economic, political, religious, or any combination necessary), the military victory is likely to be short-lived.

This is a problem that continues to face the major military powers of the twenty-first century. The "new" guerrilla warfare is terrorism. Although used in many places at many times throughout history, the religious terrorism based in the Middle East has become the current pattern of warfare for the militarily weak population. The leading proponent is Al Qaeda, which translates from Arabic as "the Base." Using the most modern technology as well as major funding from radical individuals and governments, the stated goal of Al Qaeda is the "liberation" of the Middle East from Western (primarily American) "occupation" and the establishment of a fundamentalist Muslim caliphate. This would also entail overthrowing any current Muslim government seen by the group as too corrupt or westernized. With experience gained from fighting the Soviet army in Afghanistan in the 1980s, this fundamentalist Muslim organization has been able to inflict isolated though serious damage, including attacks on embassies in Africa, a United States Navy ship in harbor, Marine barracks in Saudi Arabia, and in its most horrific action, the crashing of hijacked airliners into the World Trade Towers in New York City and the Pentagon in Washington, DC. Although response against their bases in Afghanistan was rapid and deadly, Al Qaeda's founder Osama bin Laden is still at large as of this writing. The decentralized nature of Al Qaeda has made its destruction particularly difficult, and leaders of independent cells like Abu Musab al-Zarqawi in Iraq make a single decisive strike against the organization impossible. The ability to strike anywhere, for example, against public transport in Spain and London, make terrorists very effective from a psychological warfare point of view. With the potential to acquire biological, chemical, or nuclear weapons, and the demonstrated lack of scruples against using such weaponry against major civilian targets, terrorists are at this point probably the most dangerous guerrilla fighters in history.

References: Chaliand, Gerald, ed., *Guerrilla Strategies* (Berkeley: University of California Press, 1982); Gann, Lewis H., *Guerrillas in History* (Stanford: Hoover Institution Press, 1971); Mao Tse-tung, *On Guerrilla Warfare,* trans. by Samuel B. Griffith (New York: Praeger, 1961); Federation of American Scientists, "al-Qa'ida (The Base)" 12 October 2005, http://www.fas.org/irp/world/para/ladin.htm, 25 February 2006.

Gurkhas

Soldiers of Nepal fighting for the British army.

Gurkhas are the citizens of Nepal, descended from a mixture of Mongoloid races and Rajputs of India. Not surprisingly, they are an extremely hardy people, given the climate and terrain of their country, which features the Himalayas on its northern border. The Gurkhas present an unusual paradox: They are regarded as possibly the best fighters—man for man—of any army in the world, yet away from the battlefield they are also regarded as possibly the friendliest and most hospitable people. When in the early 1800s the king of Nepal decided to expand his borders, he pushed westward and southward toward Bengal and Oudh, both territories occupied or protected by the British East India Company. The result had long-term effects on both Nepal and Britain.

In November 1814, four British columns comprising some 34,000 men attacked Nepal, but only one column met any success. The generals were not prepared for the rough terrain of the country and the peculiar supply needs it entailed. During the second phase of the Gurkha war in 1815, the British fared better and pushed toward the capital of Kathmandu. In December 1815, representatives of the king negotiated a peace, the Treaty of Sagauli. The king, however, rejected the terms of the treaty and the British renewed their invasion. In March 1916, as British forces approached his capital, the king relented and the British decided not to impose more severe terms on him for his delay. By this time, the British were more than happy to stop fighting the Gurkhas because, even with their almost three-to-one advantage,

Subadar-Major Gurung Gurkha, 2nd King Edward's Own Gurkha Rifles (The Sirmoor Rifles), King Edward's last Indian orderly officer.

the campaign for them had been a near-run thing.

The two countries emerged from this war with a mutual respect for the other's fighting abilities, and soon the British army was recruiting Gurkha soldiers. Over time, the British recruited 10 Gurkha regiments, and the soldiers have proven to be among the best the British army has put in the field. They served in every British campaign in India after they began joining the army of the East India Company in 1816 and remained loyal during the Indian Mutiny of 1857. When the British Indian army began operations outside India, as they did in Burma and elsewhere in the late 1800s, the Gurkhas went with them when some other native troops balked. Even in World War I, Gurkhas joined Force A, which traveled to France, and for a year fought in the trenches against the Germans. There they fought alongside British soldiers of the Leicestershire Regiment and established a long relationship of mutual respect and trust. The Gurkhas adapted to the alien climate of France much sooner than the rest of the Indian army serving there, and in their 12 months of service, they earned three Victoria Crosses of the five awarded to Indian troops. The Gurkhas also served in an unfamiliar climate in Mesopotamia, where they fought the Turks in extreme desert heat and excelled in every battle. They also fought the Turks at the failed Gallipoli offensive of 1915. In both campaigns in the East the Gurkhas left behind a memorial. Near the beaches of Gallipoli south of Istanbul is a point of high ground that the Gurkhas held against tremendous Turkish assaults. To this day it is called Gurkha Bluff. in November 1915, while retreating from Ctesiphon, just outside Baghdad, 400 Gurkhas held a small hill against repeated attacks of an entire Turkish division. Gurkha Mound is still its name.

After World War I, the Gurkhas were, through no fault of their own, involved in one of the British Empire's most tragic and stupid events. In Armritsar, India, a large group of Indian nationalists rallied for independence in 1919. Meaning to "make a statement," General Dyer ordered his Gurkha troops to open fire on the crowd in an enclosed area, and they followed orders. Three hundred seventy-nine people were killed and over 1,200 wounded in the massacre, which became a focal point for rallying Indian opposition to British rule. In more traditional operations, Gurkhas also were involved in punitive expeditions against outlaws in Afghanistan and the Northwest Frontier region of India in the interwar years.

When World War II broke out, the Gurkhas were called on once again to aid the British Empire. Gurkha troops served in North Africa where they were able to operate in the hills of Tunisia and aid in driving German troops from well-entrenched positions. In Italy, they also had the chance to operate in mountainous terrain and again proved their worth. They were outstanding in patrolling and reconnaissance in Italy's mountains and often were able to sneak up on German machine gun positions and capture the crews without a shot being fired. In both North Africa and Italy, the Germans came to fear the Gurkhas, for when stealth failed, the Gurkhas were unmatched in hand-to-hand combat. The distinctive Gurkha weapon is the *kukri*, a knife with a blade some 14 inches long, curved slightly about a third of the way from the hilt. The rest of the blade is somewhat leaf-shaped and the blade is sharpened on the concave edge. In the heat of battle, many Germans were beheaded by these knives.

Gurkhas also fought in Southeast Asia during World War II. They were stationed in Singapore at the war's outbreak and were still attacking when the British commanders ordered surrender. Some Gurkhas refused and made their way into the jungle, fighting with guerrilla bands against the Japanese. Other Gurkhas fought with Orde Wingate's Chindit forces behind Japanese lines in Burma. When Field Marshall William Slim invaded Burma in 1944 to recover the country from the Japanese, the Gurkhas went with him. Slim made sure of that because he had served with a Gurkha unit since World War I and would not undertake an offensive without them.

Since World War II, the Gurkhas have kept units operating with the British army around the world, including fighting with them in the Falkland Islands in the 1980s. Gurkhas were some of the last British forces to be withdrawn from Hong Kong when the British turned the city over to mainland China in 1997. They are the inheritors of a tradition started in 1815 and the war against Nepal. To serve in the British forces is the height of honor in Nepal. Each year thousands of young men go to recruiting stations to apply for the few hundred positions available. Almost two hundred years of service and bravery keep the British recruiting there. No British officer who served with Gurkhas can help but admire them, and the stories of Gurkhas in combat are countless. For example, in the battle at Singapore before the British surrender in 1942, a Gurkha soldier was wounded in the arm. He asked a comrade to cut the arm off so he could continue fighting. When the comrade refused, the soldier cut off his own arm with his kukri, stuck the stump in creosote to cauterize it, and continued to fight for another 15 days before capture. Such stories are the rule rather than the exception. Crying *Ayo Gurkhali* ("Here come the Gurkhas"), these troops launched attacks few defenders could withstand. Even the Japanese, for whom surrender is the greatest dishonor, often fled from Gurkha attacks because the Gurkha code of conduct is no less strict than that of the Samurai. Their motto is, "Better to die than be a coward," and instances of Gurkha cowardice do not exist.

References: Bishop, Edward, *Better to Die* (London: New English Library, 1976); Farwell, Byron, *The Gurkhas* (New York: Norton, 1984); Tuker, Lt.-Gen. Sir Francis, *Gorkha: The Story of the Gurkhas of Nepal* (London: Constable, 1957).

H

Hessians

Mercenaries from Germanic states, best known for service with the British Army in the eighteenth century.

"Hessian" is the generic term used during the American Revolution to describe German mercenary troops employed by the British. The use of mercenaries in the eighteenth century was quite common because it allowed the employing countries to maintain smaller armies in peacetime while allowing the supplying countries to gain much-needed national income. Mercenaries in Europe first became widely used at the time of the condottieri in Italy in the 1400s. The first well-known mercenary troops came from the Swiss provinces. By the 1700s the German states were the source of most mercenaries. Germany at that time consisted of some 300 individual states of widely varying size, all ruled by a king, duke, prince, or other aristocrat who inherited his position. As many of them felt the need to outdo their neighbors in expenditures, the hiring out of local armies was a ready source of income.

During the American Revolution, the traditionally small British army needed supplementing. King George III was the first British-born monarch of the German house of Hanover, so there were close ties to German states. Six of the German states provided troops to King George, including Brunswick (5,700 men), Anspach-Beyreuth (2,300 men), Waldeck (1,200 men), Anhalt-Zerbst (1,100 men), Hesse-Cassel (17,000 men), and Hesse-Hanau (2,500 men). Owing to the predominance of troops from the last two related states, "Hessian" became the common description for any German soldier, although that was not appreciated by the other troops. Britain had hired German troops in the Seven Years War (1756–1763) and other conflicts, so the mixing of Anglo-German forces was hardly new. The employment contracts provided for the lion's share of the purchase price to go to the ruler, while the soldier received the standard low pay of all enlisted men of that era. For a price of some £4.5 million, the British army received the services of almost 30,000 troops.

The troops may have been regarded as mercenaries, but the average soldier probably was not serving for personal gain. Many of the troops were forced into service, and many more were not even citizens of the state for which they served, as methods up to and including kidnapping were not uncommon in order to put men in uniform. Traditional tactics, like promising wealth and adventure or taking advantage of drunks, brought in men, as did visits to prisons. Discipline was harsh, but effective enough to train troops that were as good as any at the time. The infantry was obtained in this manner, although the cavalry tended to come from the upper classes.

Surrender of Hessian troops to Gen. George Washington following the Battle of Trenton. Lithograph by Henry Toff, 1850. National Archives and Records Administration, Special Media Archives Services Division (NWCS-S), National Archives at College Park, 8601 Adelphi Road, College Park, MD. [Image 532880]

Officers were aristocrats with little care for the welfare of their men. On the voyage from Europe to America, conditions for the enlisted men often were little better than on slave ships, with cramped accommodations and poor food.

The first action the German troops saw in America was in August 1776 at the Battle of Long Island. There they fought well but gained a bad reputation for slaughtering prisoners. It was in the months following William Howe's capture of New York City, however, that the Hessian troops gained their first serious attention from the Americans. Howe ordered his army into winter quarters after defeating George Washington's army at White Plains in October 1776. Placed in a large arc around New York City, the regiments were ordered to quarter themselves in outlying towns and wait for the spring campaign. A Hessian regiment under Johann Rall was billeted in Trenton, New Jersey. Under the provisions of the Quartering Act passed by Parliament in 1774, the local population was obligated to provide housing and supplies for the occupying troops. This was an odious law to the colonists and one of the "Intolerable Acts" that had provoked the Revolution. Its implementation by mercenaries did nothing to assuage the colonists' ire. Washington, having just suffered three defeats, needed a victory to ensure recruits for the revolutionary army the following spring. He figured that beating the Hessians would rescue the population from a hated occupying force while restoring his flagging reputation for generalship at the same time.

Washington launched a surprise attack at dawn the day after Christmas 1776, and in a matter of minutes killed, wounded, captured, or scattered almost 1,500 men for a loss of but five of his own. This incident confirmed in the British a condescending attitude toward their allies, the Hessians, whom they thought overpaid and overrated. One British officer wrote to a friend that "these Hessians are the worst troops I ever saw. Government has been Cheated by their sending one half Militia, and the greatest part of the others Recruits, very few Viterons amongst them, they are voted British pay, which their Prince Cheats them out of one half, they are Exceedingly dissatisfied at this, so that to make it up they turn their whole thoughts upon plunder. It was their attention to this Plunder, that made them fall a sacrifice to the Rebels at Trenton" (Lowell, 1884).

Hessian troops seemed to fight quite well when part of a larger force, but the only other time they fought alone was also a disaster. In 1777, as John Burgoyne made his way south from Canada in an attempt to control New York, he sent a force of Hessians to obtain supplies and horses near the town of Bennington, Vermont. They met a force of local militia that outnumbered their own 800 troops and who used the terrain to its best advantage, outfighting and outmaneuvering the Hessians. Once beaten, they staged a fighting withdrawal toward Burgoyne's army and met with a 600-man relief force that had arrived

too late to assist in the earlier battle. Both Hessian units found themselves swamped by Vermonters. When it was all over, the Hessians had lost 900 killed or taken prisoner.

Other than these two defeats, the Hessians acquitted themselves fairly well in every major battle of the Revolution, up to and including the final battle at Yorktown in 1781. They remained in America until the signing of the peace treaty in 1783, but not all of them went home. The years they had spent in America affected many Hessians greatly, for they saw the American farmer working lush fields that were larger than many royal estates at home. The lure of good land, and the discovery of attractive and hard-working American women, convinced many Germans not to go home. The Duke of Brunswick encouraged many to stay in the new United States or in Canada. He could always raise more troops but did not want to pay transport for any more than necessary at that time. There was little reason to go home if one wanted to remain a mercenary, however, for their time was coming to an end. The American Revolution, soon followed by the revolution in France, began the creation of national armies using only citizen soldiers.

References: Hibbert, Christopher, *Redcoats and Rebels* (New York: Norton, 1990); Lowell, E.J., *The Hessians, and the German Auxiliaries of Great Britain in the Revolutionary War* (New York: Harper & Bros. 1884); Smith, Page, *A New Age Now Begins* (New York: McGraw-Hill, 1976).

Robert I, King of Scotland, usually known as Robert the Bruce.

Highlanders

A Scottish population known for its fighting spirit, both against and with the British army.

Highlanders has become a somewhat generic term for Scots, although such is not the case. The territory that makes up Scotland divides naturally into three parts: the borders, the lowlands, and the highlands. The borders, as the name implies, lie along the southern part of the region along the frontier with England to the south. The lowlands run east to west and then up the eastern coast toward Inverness. The highlands, then, occupy the region running mainly north and south between Loch Lomond and the Pentland Firth.

The Scots enter recorded history when the Romans encountered them in the first century CE. The Romans called the land Hibernia and nicknamed the inhabitants Picts. The first battle between Romans and Picts took place at Mons Grampius in 83 CE. The Romans were victorious but ventured no farther northward, instead erecting walls to keep the northerners at bay. The Picts remained between Hadrian's Wall and the Antonine Wall for some 200 years, although it was the Roman army more than the walls themselves that discouraged Pictish aggression.

Near the beginning of the sixth century, the Gaelic Celts in the highland west of Scotland established the first recognizable Scottish kingdom, which they called Dalraida, in the region of Argyll. In 843 the Scots and borderer Picts united under the leadership of Kenneth, the son of Alpin of Dalraida. After this time, the term "Pict" disappears into the generic term "Scot." In the eastern part of Scotland the population was of Norse, Danish, and Angle heritage. The Anglo-Roman borderers of the Strathclyde merged with the eastern Angles of Lothian under the rule of King Malcolm II between 1016 and 1018. All of these people were considered foreigners by the highlanders, although the highlanders' ethnic make-up includes all of them. The highlanders were, in turn, considered barbarians by the others. Unification came in 1034 under Malcolm II's grandson, Duncan, although the relations between highlander and lowlander remained fairly tense.

Society in Scotland at this time was based on the clan, although the number of clans is a matter of some dispute. As the word *clan* is Gaelic, it should therefore designate only highlanders. The number of clans varied somewhere between 35 and 50. The dispute often deals with the way in which the clans were grouped. What some consider clans, other researchers consider subclans of a more powerful chieftain. The basis of the clan was the chief, who was both patriarch and head of government. The chief ruled the clan but could not act without its cooperation, so tyrannic leaders were rare. Even the king had to deal with the possibly contrary nature of his subjects, and no leader would commit young men to war without widespread support within and among clans.

Malcolm III took advantage of the Norman invasion of England in 1066, seeing a golden opportunity to raid southward and extend Scottish dominion. Unfortunately, he did not succeed, and ultimately the new Norman king of England, William, forced the Scots to pay homage and deal with the feudal system and its interlocking hierarchy of loyalties. The Scottish king swore fealty, but the commoner in the north may or may not have recognized the king's action. In the twelfth century, Richard the Lionheart sold the Scots their freedom from their oath of fealty in return for funds to mount a crusade to the Holy Land. This suited the Scots well until 1286 when the royal lineage became tangled.

When several men claimed the throne in that year, the Scots went to another king in order to have an impartial judge among the claimants. Edward I of England gladly offered his services, but in exchange for the oath of loyalty necessary for his decision to be binding. He proceeded to name John Balliol as king of Scotland, but Balliol was now technically subservient to Edward. Edward proceeded to provoke Balliol and when rebellion ensued, Edward's victory gave him the Scottish estates, which the disloyal subjects thereby forfeited. Edward's forces occupied southern Scotland for 10 years while Balliol languished in the Tower of London. In Balliol's name, William Wallace raised a revolt with early

success, but eventually he was betrayed and executed.

Throughout all of this, the highland Scots remained aloof because their lands were too remote for Edward to occupy. In 1306 Robert Bruce claimed the throne, but his reign was short-lived. He was defeated by rival lowland factions under the Earl of Pembroke and forced to flee. Bruce ended up in the highlands where he promised wealth and power to those clans who would follow him. With the aid of the clan McKinnon, among others, Bruce achieved victory at Bannockburn in 1314. With this success, the highlanders were forever bound into the Scottish political scene. This also set the stage for the Arbroath Declaration in 1320, wherein the Scottish nobility swore that "so long as one hundred remained alive, the Scots would never submit to the English, 'for it is not for glory we fight, for riches or for honours, but for freedom alone, which no good man loses but with his life'" (MacKinnon, 1984). It was supposedly Robert Bruce himself who added a clause whereby any future Scottish king who submitted to England would be immediately dethroned.

Relations between England and Scotland were never cordial, but became closer through necessity in 1603 when Elizabeth I died without issue. The nearest relative was James Stuart, and he became at once James VI of Scotland and James I of England. This failed to bring about friendlier relations between the two countries, however, for James's Catholic heirs were not popular with England's predominantly Protestant population. As Scotland came to embrace Protestant Calvinism, the northern population often became split in their views of struggles in England. The English throne was contested by both Protestant and Catholic monarchs, as well as by Scottish and English monarchs. It was a Catholic Stuart's attempt to seize the English throne with French aid in 1745 that brought about a major change in Scottish-English relations. Some clans marched with Charles the Pretender, or Bonnie Prince Charlie as he was more popularly known, but many Protestant clans fought against him alongside the English. It was during this conflict that the British army commissioned the raising of a Scottish regiment to serve under English command: the famous Black Watch, which got its name from the dark color of its tartan and the fact that it was a unit originally detailed for national defense, that is, to watch the Scottish countryside. Although this unit fought against Charles at the battle of Culloden in 1745, the English government sought to punish those clans that had supported the Pretender. They did so by punishing almost all Scots: The wearing of tartans and the carrying of weapons, as well as the playing of the bagpipe, were all banned—unless one was a member of the army. Hence, those that could not bear to walk the street or countryside unarmed could and did join the British army. Scottish units were irregularly raised, however, and were often disbanded at war's end. Thus, many highlanders who fought in the regiments raised to serve in North America against the French in the Seven Years War were told that they would be civilians again when the Treaty of Paris was signed in 1763. Rather than face that alternative, the majority of them stayed in America.

William Pitt, the English leader responsible for raising the Scottish regiments to serve in America, praised their fighting ability to Parliament: "These men in the last war were brought to combat on your side; they served with fidelity as they fought with valour, and conquered for you in every part of the world" (MacKinnon, 1984). This was in contrast to his less widely quoted comment at the beginning of the war that sending the highlanders off to war would result in that much less trouble at home. Fifteen years later, more regiments were raised for North America, possibly to fight against their relatives during the American Revolution. In 1783 when the war ended, the majority of these were disbanded. Only three regiments were kept on the permanent rolls: the Black Watch, the Highland Light Infantry, and the Seaforth Highlanders. More regiments were raised again to fight in the Napoleonic Wars (1803–1815). This resulted in a few more permanent regiments: the Gordon Highlanders, the Queen's Own Cameron Highlanders, and the Argyll & Sutherland Highlanders. After the Cardwell Army Reforms in 1881, an alteration from one-battalion regiments to two-battalion regiments brought together other units into the above-named regiments. These, however, broke the tradition of pure Highland units, although the tartans, kilts, and bagpipes remained integral to their heritage.

Scottish units participated in virtually every war the British Empire fought in the nineteenth and twentieth centuries. Their bravery, hardiness, and discipline became legendary, but were nothing compared to the legends associated with the kilts and pipes. Enemies called the kilted Scots "Ladies from Hell," but by World War II the kilts were banned during combat, only to be worn on parade. Legends of the bagpipes' wail striking fear in the hearts of opposing troops come from virtually every conflict. One of the more famous comes from the battle at Gallipoli in World War I. British and ANZAC units had had little success against a stout Turkish defense, but at the sound of the pipes from advancing Scots, the Turks fled. Asked why they had fought so well up until that point, Turkish prisoners said any troops that could march, shoot, and slaughter hogs at the same time were too tough to face.

References: Brander, Michael, *The Scottish Highlanders and Their Regiments* (New York: Barnes & Noble, 1996); MacKinnon, Charles, *Scottish Highlanders* (London: Robert Hale, Ltd., 1984).

Hittites

An ancient population, dominant in Asia Minor between the nineteenth and twelfth centuries BCE, that rivaled the Egyptians.

Probably originating northeast of the Caucasus, the Hittites migrated into Asia Minor around 1900 BCE and began establishing a kingdom. They occupied the Anatolian plateau in modern-day Turkey and ultimately extended their influence toward Syria. It is possible that their migration pushed other populations southward, spurring the Hyksos' invasion of Egypt. The Hittites probably took their name from the Plain of Hatti that they occupied and upon which they imposed their culture and Indo-European language. Their first conquest was the town of Nesa (near modern Kayseri, Turkey), followed by the capture of Hattusha (near modern Bogazkoy).

Little is known of the Hittites until the seventeenth century BCE when Labarna (circa 1680–1650 BCE) established the Old Hittite Kingdom and set up his capital at Hattusha. He was the first major conqueror for the Hittites, spreading their control throughout Anatolia to the coast. Labarna's successors pushed their borders southward to Syria. Mursili (or Mushilish) raided deep into the Old Babylonian Empire,

captured Aleppo, and set the kingdom's southern boundary in Syria. This proved to be the extent of the Hittite conquest under Mursili, as they spent the next two centuries quelling internal disturbances and fighting the Mitanni of upper Mesopotamia.

The kingdom returned to some stability around 1500 BCE under the leadership of Telipinu, who laid down strict succession guidelines and possibly established a code of law. Some 50 years later, the New Hittite Kingdom was established. The Hittites had just suffered a defeat at the hands of the Egyptian pharaoh, Thutmosis III, and had begun paying the Egyptians tribute. One of the key figures in the New Kingdom was Suppiluliuma (Shubbiluliu), who seized power around 1380 BCE, reestablished Hittite authority in Anatolia, and defeated the Mitanni. He was unable to defeat the Egyptians, however, and the two powers remained rivals for the next century. During a time of Egyptian weakness under Akhenaton, the Hittites made gains in Lebanon at Egyptian expense. They also spread their power to the Aegean, Armenia, and upper Mesopotamia.

The key battle in the ongoing conflict with Egypt took place in 1294 BCE at Kadesh on the Orontes River. Pharaoh Rameses II led his army of Numidian mercenaries north to force his will on the Hittites once and for all. When two captured Hittite deserters informed the pharaoh that their army was still many days' march away, Rameses rode ahead of his army to set up camp near Kadesh. The two prisoners turned out to have been planted by the Hittite king, Muwatallis, and the Hittite army attacked the pharaoh without most of his troops. Rameses fought bravely until his army arrived, and their appearance forced a Hittite retreat into the city of

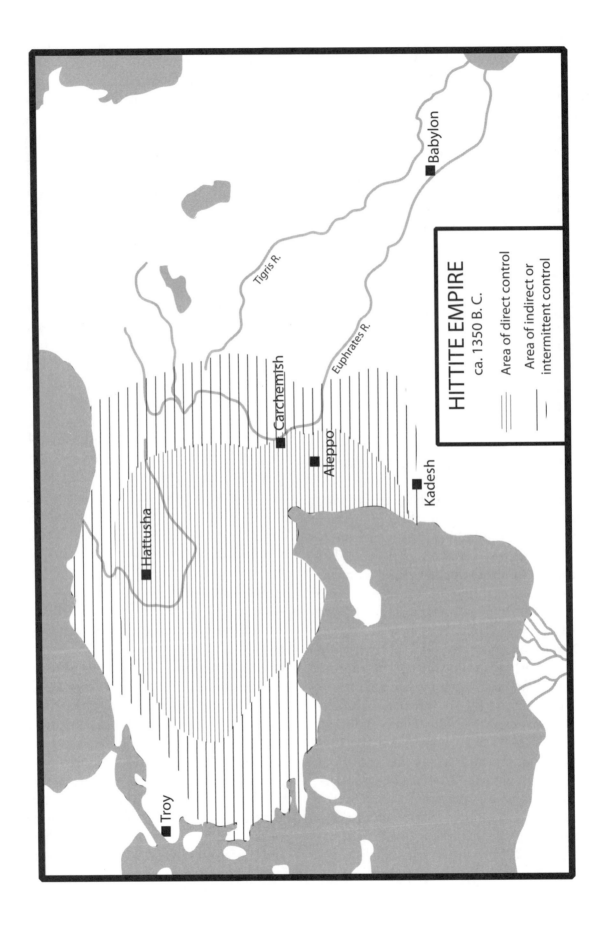

HITTITE EMPIRE
ca. 1350 B. C.

Area of direct control

Area of indirect or
intermittent control

Babylon

Tigris R.

Euphrates R.

Carchemish

Aleppo

Kadesh

Hattusha

Troy

Kadesh. Without siege equipment, Rameses could not force their surrender, so he withdrew. Shortly thereafter the two nations signed a peace agreement: The Egyptians recognized Hittite sovereignty in Syria in return for Hittite recognition of Egyptian dominance in Palestine. The alliance was sealed by a dynastic marriage. The two peoples remained at peace until the fall of the Hittite empire, which came at the hands of the "Peoples of the Sea" around 1200 BCE.

The secret of Hittite expansion and superiority lay in the fact that they were the first power to develop the process of smelting iron in large quantities, a method that was probably discovered about 1400 BCE. In a time when everyone used bronze for their weapons, iron weaponry gave its possessors a great advantage. Despite this advantage, however, the bulk of the Hittite army was made up of mounted troops and chariots, from which archers fought. Iron weaponry conferred less of an advantage on these troops, but the Hittite infantry carried iron swords and iron-tipped spears and fought in a phalanx formation. At the battle of Kadesh, the Hittite king was able to muster some 3,500 chariots, each with a driver and two archers. Probably half the Hittite army was in chariots, with between 8,000 and 9,000 infantry and archers recruited from Hittite vassals and allies.

The Hittite kingdom recognized a supreme ruler, but a strong aristocracy made absolute rule difficult. An early form of feudalism was the basic social and governmental structure, with the local lords being responsible for providing troops in times of emergency. The king maintained a standing army, however, especially as the empire expanded and garrisons were necessary to maintain control over subject populations. Further, the king maintained a personal guard of 1,200 (and possibly as many as 12,000) Elamites (from modern-day Iran), who were talented soldiers available for hire, and other mercenaries were employed as well. All of this lasted until the arrival of the Peoples of the Sea in the thirteenth and twelfth centuries BCE. The Hittite empire collapsed, but Hittite populations survived for several centuries in cities such as Carchemish, on the upper Euphrates, Sam'al (modern Zincirli), and Millid (modern Malatia).

In the Bible, Uriah the Hittite held a major position in King David's army but was unfortunately married to Bathsheba, and David's desire for her resulted in Uriah's being killed. The story illustrates the spread of the Hittite population and the respect for their military abilities throughout the ancient world.

The final blow for the Hittites came in the eighth century BCE when the power of Assyria absorbed everyone in the Middle East. The Assyrian king, Sargon, however, kept a strong contingent of Hittites in his army after their absorption into the Assyrian empire.

References: Ceram, C.W., *The Secret of the Hittites,* translated by Richard Winston and Clara Winston (New York: Alfred A. Knopf, 1956); Lehman, Johannes, *The Hittites: People of a Thousand Gods,* translated by J.M. Brownjohn (New York: Viking Press, 1977); Macqueen, J.G., *The Hittites and Their Contemporaries in Asia Minor* (London: Thames and Hudson, 1968).

Hood's Texas Brigade

An outstanding unit of the Confederate army during the American Civil War (1861–1865).

When troops of the newly created Confederate States of America fired on Union

General John Bell Hood, circa 1860. National Archives and Records Administration, Special Media Archives Services Division (NWCS-S), National Archives at College Park, 8601 Adelphi Road, College Park, MD. [Image 529378]

troops at Fort Sumter in the harbor of Charleston, South Carolina, on the morning of April 12, 1861, the American Civil War began. In southern states, from the Carolinas to Texas, men swarmed to recruiting stations to enlist. Texan enthusiasm matched that of any state in the Confederacy, and by the end of 1861, some 25,000 men had joined the Confederate army. Most Texan troops fought in the western theater of war, but a few regiments were ordered east to fight with the Army of Northern Virginia. The First, Fourth, and Fifth Texas Infantry Regiments marched to Virginia, which would be their home for most of the following four years and the site of many of their graves. Collectively, these three regiments, com-

bined with the Third Arkansas, made up of both Arkansans and Texans, became the First Texas Infantry Brigade. Their first commander was Louis T. Wigfall, but upon their arrival in Virginia and assignment to Thomas "Stonewall" Jackson's command, they were put under the leadership of a young Kentuckian, John Bell Hood. The Texans became "his" brigade even when he was promoted to divisional command, and they fought in almost every major battle in the eastern theater of war.

The Texans arrived too late to take part in the opening battle of the war at Bull Run, but they were on hand in early summer 1862 when Union troops under the command of George McClellan advanced on Richmond, Virginia, in what came to be called the Peninsular Campaign. The Texas Brigade made its debut at Eltham Landing, when it was assigned to skirmish and delay a Union landing. Whether through enthusiasm or ignorance, the troops overstepped their orders and launched a full assault on the Union lines, attacking so fiercely that the Union forces withdrew. It was a more costly attack than Confederate commander Joseph Johnston had anticipated, but it exceeded his expectations and set a standard for performance that the Texans lived up to for the remainder of the war.

When Johnston was wounded and replaced by Robert E. Lee, the Texans soon came to his attention as well. Well-entrenched Union forces at Gaines' Mill had repelled two Confederate attacks and were about to receive reinforcements. Lee feared that if those reinforcements arrived, the Union troops could turn the tide of battle and possibly regain the initiative toward Richmond. He called on Hood and asked if the Texans could break through the Union lines. Hood replied that they would try. The Texans advanced slowly under heavy fire through Boatswain's Swamp, not firing until they were within 10 yards of the Union lines. They then screamed a "rebel yell," fired a volley that cleared the front trenches, and attacked with bayonets. Union troops almost immediately broke, and Lee followed up with supporting attacks that drove McClellan's command back to their starting point at Yorktown. Although suffering heavy losses, the Texans had succeeded where two previous attacks had failed. Lee from this point came to depend on Hood's men.

The Texas Brigade distinguished itself again several weeks later at the second battle at Bull Run, where they first stopped the advance of a larger Union force, then participated in a flanking attack that crushed the Union line and forced its withdrawal from the field. Hood was promoted to the command of a division, and he gave credit for this to his Texans. On September 17, 1862, at the battle of Antietam Creek near Sharpsburg, Maryland, the Texas Brigade was engaged in the earliest fighting in a cornfield near the Dunker Church. Here the Brigade repulsed a Union corps and then pursued it. However, the Texans were obliged to withdraw, and the battle spread to other quarters, so this was the extent of the Texas Brigade's role in what proved to be the bloodiest day in American history. The Brigade played a small role in the next major battle at Fredericksburg, Virginia, on December 13, 1862, when the Confederates slaughtered Union troops in Ambrose Burnside's poorly conceived attack against strong Confederate entrenchments. The Texans also missed Lee's victory over Union General Joseph Hooker at Chancellorsville in May 1863 because they were detached from the main force on a foraging mission.

Hood's Brigade was in the thick of the fighting in the next battle, however, as Lee attempted to launch a final assault on Union territory. On the second day of the great battle at Gettysburg, Pennsylvania, on July 2, 1863, the Texans were ordered to assault the Union left flank anchored on the small rise called Little Round Top. The ground before the Little Round Top was a massive jumble of boulders called the Devil's Den, in which the Texans fought the most difficult battle of their lives. They once again gained ground against their Union foes, but were ordered to withdraw just as the Twentieth Maine Infantry Regiment launched a bayonet assault off of Little Round Top. The Texans were obliged to withdraw after sustaining heavy losses. Hood was wounded in the arm and so commanded his men during only part of the battle. He lost his arm and spent a few months recovering, months during which the Brigade was transferred west to Tennessee with General James Longstreet's corps. With Longstreet, the Texans fought at Chickamauga, where they displayed their vaunted élan in yet another daring charge on September 19–20, 1863. But again, they had to withdraw after more heavy losses in the face of far larger numbers. The following day they attacked again and, after early successes, were attacked in their flank. This produced the only pell-mell retreat the Texans suffered during the war. However, rallied by their newly returned leader Hood, they regained their composure and returned to the battle. Hood was again wounded, this time losing a leg.

Returned to the Army of Northern Virginia, the Texas Brigade served under Lee in the final campaign of the war. In

May 1864 General Ulysses Grant took command of Union forces and proceeded to pound Lee's army with a two-to-one numerical superiority. The opening battle in a heavily wooded area in northern Virginia, called the Wilderness, again showed Lee's confidence in the Texans. As Union troops threatened a breakthrough, Lee rode to the Texan position and called for their aid, crying "Hurrah for the Texans! The eyes of General Lee are on you. Texans, charge!" (Foote, 1958–1974). When Lee tried to lead the assault himself, the soldiers would have none of it. They swore not to attack unless Lee withdrew from the line of fire. When a Texan grabbed the reins of Lee's horse and pulled him to the rear, Lee rose in his stirrups, waved his hat and yelled "The Texans always move them!" (Foote, 1958–1974). Move them they did: The Union attack was blunted and Grant soon withdrew.

Grant continued to attempt to outflank Lee. Throughout May and June 1864, some of the most intense fighting of the war took place as the Confederates were slowly forced back to defensive positions around Richmond. At Spotsylvania and Cold Harbor, the Texans proved themselves again. The war settled into an extended siege around the city of Petersburg, south of Richmond, from June 1864 through the following April. As supplies grew increasingly difficult to obtain, Lee's forces began to melt away. The Texans vowed they would not dishonor themselves and made a written declaration of their intention to fight on. The Resolutions of the Texas Brigade vowed to "maintain, at all hazards, and to the last extremity, the rights and liberties which a merciful God has been pleased to bestow upon them. We seek a perpetual separation from the hated and despised foe, who have murdered our gray-haired fathers, insulted our women and children, and turned out thousands of helpless families to starve" (Simpson, 1995). When word came to the Texans of Lee's surrender on April 9, 1865, they destroyed their rifles rather than surrender them.

Of the 5,300 men that enlisted and fought in the Texas Brigade, only 617 remained to be paroled after the surrender. They marched home as a unit and received a hero's welcome in Houston on June 2, 1865. They had been present when Lee took command in June 1862, gained his favor for their determination in battle, and remained the troops upon which he depended most until the Southern cause was lost.

Steve Davis

References: Foote, Shelby, *The Civil War, A Narrative.* 3 vols. (New York: Random House, 1958–1974); Simpson, Harold, "Hood's Texas Brigade at Appomattox," in Wooster, Ralph, ed. *Lone Star Blue and Gray: Essays on Texas in the Civil War* (Austin: Texas State Historical Association, 1995).

Hoplites

Infantry troops utilized in ancient Macedonian and Greek warfare between the fifth and third centuries BCE.

The Greek citizen soldiers of Athens, Sparta, and the other Greek city-states were called hoplites (from *hoplon*, meaning "armor"), or heavily armored infantry. Their ancestors, like the heroes in epic poems such as the *Iliad*, fought as individuals, usually from chariots or cavalry. By contrast, the hoplites developed infantry tactics in which they advanced and fought en masse, shoulder to shoulder with shields overlapping to protect each other in the

An ancient Greek hoplite, from a map created by the Department of History, United States Military Academy

line. These formations were called phalanxes. Phalanxes were compact units of men, usually greater in length than in depth. As Greek colonies spread around the Mediterranean in the first millennium BCE, increased trade brought prosperity to the Greek mainland. This, in turn, allowed increasing numbers of the yeomen class (landowners not of the aristocracy) to afford the equipment of a hoplite, the bronze helmet, the long spear, the heavy breastplate, iron shield, and greaves (leg armor). Although military service was required for all able-bodied men in Greek city-states at the time, most Greeks agreed that each individual must take responsibility to sustain democracy and the survival of the state. Only citizens of the city-state could take their place in the battle lines.

The Greek phalanx was an ideal formation for a citizen army. It allowed a maximum efficiency of strength with a minimum of training (with the important exception of Sparta, where training was extensive). The strength of the phalanx rested in the mass cooperation of the hoplites, all bunched together, eight to 25 ranks deep, moving irresistibly forward. It

was not a permanent formation: Its dimensions and approach to attack varied according to each leader's tactics and the size of the army. As long as the soldiers remained together, their shields interlocking, they had relative safety. However, as a closed tactical formation, the phalanx was incapable of flexibility or operation on broken ground. The Persians never adopted it because archers drawn up in more than six ranks lose their effectiveness. The greatest weakness of the early phalanx was that on open ground heavy cavalry, such as that fielded by the Persians, could drive in its flanks or rear with relative ease. Notably, the Greek victories of Marathon and Plataea both took place on terrain where the flanks of the phalanxes were secured by hills or the sea.

As noted, each Greek provided his own equipment. Not every citizen could afford a horse so, as a result, cavalry played a very minor part in the Greek armies. Because there was always such a small number of Greek cavalry, it would have been foolish for them to try to oppose any enemy who possessed more numerous horsemen—such as the Persians—and apparently they never tried.

Early Greek armies also contained a number of archers, slingers, and javelin-armed skirmishers, called *peltasts*. These men, especially the archers and slingers, required far more training, in most cases starting in their youth, than did the hoplites. Many of the Greek archers wore the same body armor as the hoplites, although it appears that a majority were unarmored. It is possible that they were drawn from the less wealthy nobility, from families who could not afford a war horse but whose wealth could allow their sons sufficient free time to gain proficiency with the bow. It would appear that the best peltasts came from regions that specialized in such troops, such as archers from Crete, slingers from Rhodes, and javelineers from the half-Greek tribes of the Balkans.

In action, the peltasts usually advanced in front of the phalanx, showering the enemy with arrows, then falling back to protect the rear or flank of the hoplites once they had engaged. In retreat they could maintain a rear guard. After victories, the peltasts were often left to garrison the conquered lands. Their secondary role in military affairs ran in accordance to their social subordination at home. The phalanx was supreme, and the peltasts and cavalry remained very minor arms in the Greek system for many years. As long as the Greek armies retained their citizen-soldier nature, they were bound into a one-dimensional organization.

Citizen soldiers, aside from the men of Sparta, were almost by definition part-time warriors, training only as much as necessary to function adequately. However, with the spread of Greek cities around the Aegean, a new type of soldier appeared. Greek men who owned little or no land began to offer their full-time services for money. These mercenaries, who were constantly in service, could function together as highly skilled units or—dispersed among the ordinary hoplites—could raise the fighting abilities of all the Greek units considerably. Their professionalism allowed the phalanx to become a far more flexible formation. Smaller units of hoplites, along with the cavalry and the peltasts, were organized to protect their flanks from enemy cavalry. Some of these "beefed-up" hoplite units even became capable of dividing themselves into smaller units for special situations.

Another innovation in the use of hoplites is credited to Epaminondas of Thebes, who at the battle of Mantinea overcame the Spartans by strengthening his left flank with extra hoplites, cavalry, and light infantry, and by withholding his right flank from action. Epaminondas had noted that the phalanx had a natural tendency to move to its right in combat, and that two phalanxes locked in a melee pinwheeled counterclockwise. His stronger left flank checked the Spartan right flank and his cavalry and light infantry enveloped it on its sides and rear. The Spartan left flank never came into contact, and gave way when the right flank broke. Epaminondas had used the combined talents of the three branches of his army, along with a shrewd observation, to overcome the more traditional (and traditionally stronger) Spartans. This idea of combined arms remained to be developed to its fullest extent by Philip II of Macedonia and his son Alexander III.

The phalanx continued for many centuries to be the tactical master of the battlefield, until it was rendered obsolete by the much more mobile and flexible cohorts of Rome, which were manned by the most professional and perfectionist soldiers in the ancient world.

References: Keegan, John, *A History of Warfare* (New York: Random House, 1993); Parke, H.W., *Greek Mercenary Soldiers* (Chicago: Ares, 1981 [1933]); Sage, Michael, *Warfare in Ancient Greece* (London: Routledge, 1996).

Huns

An Asiatic population that devastated Europe in the fifth century CE.

The Huns were one of the myriad of tribes that rode out of central Asia, but little can be determined of their origin. Probably they were the Huing-nu, who failed in wars against the Chinese during the late

Stylized portrait of "Attila, Scourge of God". Anonymous. Uffizi, Florence, Italy. © SEF/Art Resource, NY

second century BCE and turned (or were forced) westward. Occasional early sources opine that they were the Nebroi mentioned by Herodotus as a semimythical people living on the fringes of territory controlled by the Scythians. Some of the earliest direct references come from clashes with the Goths around the area north of the Black Sea in the mid-fourth century CE. The first Hun conquest was of the Alans, who were then used in the vanguard of Hun attacks against the Goths or emigrated into the Roman Empire.

The Huns, like all the steppe peoples, were horsemen. They migrated westward across the Russian plains, constantly searching for new grazing lands. This meant that they were without material resources and, hence, totally reliant on what they could capture, steal, or bargain for. Thus, the metals needed for weaponry, saddlery, or decoration usually came as tribute from people unwilling or unable to resist the huge numbers of Huns. The Huns fought as light cavalry, using bows and arrows almost exclusively. These were compound bows made of horn and hide, as no wood existed on the steppes. Their arrows were also horn-tipped. The Huns used swords for infighting if necessary, although they also carried lassoes in order to immobilize their opponents. They moved as a mass, but subdivided into clans that foraged alone. When time came for battle, they easily formed up and launched mass attacks against outnumbered foes. They had no hesitation about retreating or avoiding combat if the enemy seemed too strong, for they did not fight for honor but for plunder. The Huns were completely unable to conduct sieges and the nature of central European terrain, with its forests and mountains, severely limited the ability of their wagon-borne families to maintain the pace set by the horsemen. In the end, it was the nature of the land in Europe that probably contributed to the Huns' defeat as much as any army.

In 376 the Huns began to harass the Caucasus lands controlled by the Ostrogoths. After fighting around the Crimea, the Ostrogoths were pushed back across the Dnieper to the Dniester River, where they began to pressure the Visigoths. The Visigoths had not fared too well against the armies of the Eastern Roman Empire, so their leader, Athanaric, had no wish to see his people defeated by a second enemy. Athanaric established his forces along the Dniester and sent a reconnaissance force east to keep touch with the advancing Huns. This force was easily destroyed, and the Huns were on Athanaric's army before his men could finish their defenses. The Visigoths vanished into the countryside and re-formed between the Pruth and Danube Rivers, where Athanaric ordered a wall to be built. Again the swift Hun army arrived and surprised the Visigoths, who once more scattered and retreated toward the Danube. The refugees, who numbered between 700,000 and one million, settled into the forests of Transylvania.

Pressed against the frontiers of the Roman Empire, the Visigoths in 376 begged the Emperor Valens for his protection. They were granted land along the Danube in return for military service, which they provided. The Ostrogoths who arrived later also begged imperial protection, but were denied it. They crossed the Danube anyway. Emperor Theodorus I, crowned in Constantinople in 379, led Roman campaigns against the Huns, who were rampaging through the Balkans, but he could not turn them back. The two Gothic peoples combined to fight against the eastern Romans, which left no strong force to oppose the slowly approaching Huns. The Huns settled into Pannonia along the Adriatic coast.

By 432 the Huns were well established and a force to be reckoned with. Emperor Theodosius II paid tribute to the Hun leader Ruas and gave him a general's commission. Ruas's sons Bleda and Atilla renewed the treaty and fought for Constantinople in campaigns against Persia, but Attila grew tired of doing another's fighting and made war against the eastern Romans. Between 441 and 443 he rampaged through the Balkans and defeated a Roman army outside Constantinople, but could not capture the city. He finally stopped upon receiving an increase in tribute. Attila killed his brother, Bleda, and in 447 renewed his war against the Romans. Although turned back from Constantinople again, Attila did manage to gain a threefold increase in tribute and cession of the eastern bank of the Danube. Theodosius's successor stopped paying the tribute in 450, by which time the Huns were looking westward.

Attila hoped to split the attention of the Western Roman Empire between himself and the Vandal leader Gaiseric, who was making trouble in north Africa. In addition, Attila was invited to aid a Frankish chieftain in a succession struggle against the chieftain's brother. Thus, there seemed to be plenty of reasons for Attila to march on Gaul. He crossed the Rhine north of modern-day Mainz with between 100,000 and 500,000 warriors, whose families followed, carrying supplies. The Huns, with a variety of auxiliaries, advanced along a 100-mile-wide front, destroying everything in their path but Paris. The Roman general Aetius formed an army of Franks, Germans, and Alans, but could muster no more than half Attila's strength. In mid-

June 451 the two armies fought at the site of modern-day Chalons, but Attila could not prevail. He retreated eastward, and western Europe was saved from Asian domination.

Attila turned instead and attacked south into Italy. He had demanded the hand of Honoria, the Western Roman Emperor's sister, and had been refused. The Huns ransacked northern Italy, and refugees fled to the marshlands, creating Venice. Aetius returned to face Attila, but the Huns were having problems. One of Attila's commanders had been defeated in Illyricum (northern Greece), and the Italian countryside proved to be disease-ridden and without supplies. Attila met with Pope Leo I outside Rome and, after an unrecorded discussion, turned the Huns northward and left Italy.

After Attila died in 453, his sons fought for his throne while subject tribes revolted. The remnants of the Huns retreated northeast of the Danube, leaving the rebellious tribes to their own devices. The last of the Huns, under Irnac, travelled as far as the Volga, but they were defeated and absorbed by the Avars. The Huns proved to be little more than plunderers, traveling from one ripe target to the next, never settling down or building any cities. They accomplished nothing more than mass destruction, gaining a reputation as the "scourge of God" punishing a sinful Roman Empire.

References: Brion, Marcel, *Attila: The Scourge of God* (New York: Robert McBride and Company, 1929); Bury, J.B., *The Invasion of Europe by the Barbarians* (New York: Russell and Russell, 1963); Thompson, E.A., *Romans and Barbarians* (Madison: University of Wisconsin Press, 1982).

Hussites

Protestant religious sect of Reformation Europe which fought for religious freedom and developed the first armored fighting vehicle.

Jan Hus, a rector at the University of Prague, was one of the first figures to speak out against the corrupt practices of the Catholic Church in the early fifteenth century. He was from Bohemia (corresponding roughly to the modern Czech Republic) and was a nationalist as well. He led worship services in Czech rather than Latin, dared to alter the order of worship, and announced that the only source of direction a Christian needed was the Bible: If the pope said something in contradiction of the Bible, then the papal pronouncement could and should be ignored. The Catholic Church was not disposed to let this man go unchallenged, and Hus's presence was demanded at the Council of Constance in 1414. Although guaranteed safe conduct, Hus was taken prisoner, condemned as a heretic, and executed. Many of the common people of Bohemia followed Hus, and they refused to stop following his teachings after his death. Rather than allow this defiance of the church to continue, a papal bull called for a crusade against the heretic Hussites.

These events coincided with political struggles within Bohemia, and between the country and its neighbors. King Wenceslaus IV (of "Good King Wenceslaus" fame) ruled Bohemia but faced opposition from Henry of Rosenburg, who had temporarily imprisoned Wenceslaus in 1395. The nobility and the common people migrated to one camp or the other, and for years Bohemia was the scene of guerrilla warfare between supporters of either Wenceslaus

or Henry. For a decade, roving bands of mercenaries looted the Bohemian countryside, pillaging in the name of their chosen faction. Those that followed Wenceslaus, the more nationalistic of the population, also followed Jan Hus. One soldier who followed both, and came to prominence at this time, was Jan Zizka.

Zizka was an officer in Wenceslaus's army and a leader of a band of guerrillas, known as *lapkas* ("burglars"). He was well known not only for his military prowess, but also for the fact that he had but one eye, the left eye having been lost sometime in childhood. He had previously served his king in conflicts against the Order of Teutonic Knights in Poland and took part in the Slavic victory over the Order at Tannenberg, or Grunwald, in 1410. He rose through the ranks to the position of royal gatekeeper and became quite wealthy. He was also an itinerant warrior who fought all over Europe, including service as a volunteer under Henry V's English army at Agincourt. After returning to Bohemia, Zizka joined the Hussite cause and was elected commander of their military forces when Sigismund of Hungary tried to take over the country. At Wenceslaus's death in 1419, Sigismund inherited the Bohemian throne, much to the anger of most of the population, because it had been Sigismund who had guaranteed Hus's safety in Constance.

The Hussites established headquarters at a town they called Tabor, in honor of the biblical Mount Tabor. Townspeople shared their property equally in a theocratic community. Zizka hoped to harness their religious ardor to military zeal. He instilled a military regimen as stringent as their religious practices, and he forged a disciplined force made up mainly of the lower classes. Zizka drew on both his experience as a guerrilla commander as well as his more formal military experience fighting against the Teutonic Knights. He raided Catholic strongholds for weapons and in order to give his men experience. He also took their farming implements and turned them into weapons. Most notable was the flail, which he had his men reinforce with iron bars and tip with nails. He also made use of the cannon and matchlock firearms that were coming into wide use in Europe.

Zizka's premier weapon, that which made him and the Hussites famous, was the war wagon. The Hussites reinforced ordinary peasant carts with strong planking on one side with gun slits cut into it. Each ten-by-six-foot cart could carry as many as 14 men, armed with matchlocks, pistols, crossbows, halberds, and flails. Some later carried cannon and howitzers. Each also carried equipment for digging and fortification construction. As Zizka could count on but few armored knights early in the Hussites' campaigns, he countered them with this early version of a tank. The war wagons could either draw into a circle and chain themselves together to withstand assaults, or act as mobile gun platforms for attacking the enemy. Each wagon's crew became an independent force, relying on each other to work as a team in combat.

Sigismund invaded Bohemia in 1420 to crush the Hussites and claim his throne. Zizka's forces met them at Sudomer in March, with the Bohemians outnumbered 2,000 to 400. Unable to successfully attack the circled wagons while on horseback, the knights dismounted and found themselves at a terrible disadvantage. The Hussites routed the invaders. This victory against five-to-one odds served to give Zizka's forces both experience and confidence. They would need both, for within three

months, Zizka was defending the capital city of Prague against Sigismund's army of 80,000. Zizka, with no more than 20,000, defended a prepared position on Vitkov Hill outside Prague. Knowing that capture meant torture and execution, the Hussites fought with a terrible ferocity. The charging knights attacked barricades on the hill that were defended by both men and women. Although the Hungarian attackers managed to capture one watchtower, Zizka's flanking attack drove them back down the hill. Although Sigismund's casualties were relatively light, he decided that taking the hill and the city would be too difficult. He retreated to the city of Hradcany, had himself crowned King of Bohemia, looted the city's treasury, and returned to Hungary.

Zizka continued the fight against Sigismund's allies. He attacked Rosenburg and forced a truce, then campaigned toward Plzen in early 1421. He soon controlled all of west and northwest Bohemia. His forces captured the Catholic stronghold of Kutna Hora, then took Hradcany and Bor Castle. In the last battle, Zizka was struck by an arrow just below his right eye, which soon led to loss of sight in that eye as well. Even completely blind, he was more than a match for his opponents. Riding among his troops carrying a mace shaped like a fist holding a spike, he inspired unquestioning loyalty and confidence.

In 1422 the Hussites offered the throne of Bohemia to Grand Duke Vytautus of Lithuania. This provoked Sigismund to reinvade with a force of 30,000. Zizka, with 10,000 men, waited for him just outside Kutna Hora. They beat back several Hungarian assaults from the circled wagons, but some horsemen slipped past their camp in darkness and, aided by some Germans inside Kutna Hora, took the city and slaughtered the Hussites inside. Zizka took the offensive the next day and broke the Hungarian lines, but Sigismund was now able to withdraw into the city for the winter. With reinforcements, Zizka attacked surrounding towns garrisoned by the Hungarians. Sigismund decided to abandon Kutna Hora and burn the city behind him, but Zizka's forces were so close that they were quickly able to put out the fires. Without stopping to celebrate, the Hussites charged after Sigismund and caught up to the Hungarians two days later at the village of Habry. There the demoralized Hungarians broke before the onrushing war wagons and fled across partially frozen rivers, where thousands fell through the ice and drowned.

In the wake of this success, Zizka had to deal with factionalism within the Hussite movement. The more religiously moderate Zizka opposed the more radical Taborite sect and withdrew his followers from Tabor to establish his own settlement at Orebovice in eastern Bohemia. His religious views in no way moderated his extremely strict military discipline, however, so he remained in command of an efficient fighting force. He provoked the wrath of the citizens of Prague, who allied themselves with some Catholics and attacked Zizka's camp. Zizka retreated before superior numbers, but made a stand near Kutna Hora, where he was once again victorious. This led to an armistice with the citizens of Prague and a reuniting of the Hussite factions. Zizka led his army to Moravia and along the way fell ill, probably with the plague. He died on October 11, 1424. Legend has it that he requested that his skin be tanned to make a drumhead, so he could lead his troops in battle after his death.

The Hussites remained a formidable force for another decade, beating back successive papist armies. Henry Beaufort of England led 1,000 English archers to Bohemia, where he met 150,000 German anti-Hussite crusaders in full flight. They had been besieging a Hussite stronghold but fled from the relieving force of 18,000; thus was the effectiveness of the war wagon's reputation. A fifth and final crusade was called in 1429, but it never reached Bohemia, instead joining with the English forces engaging the French under Joan of Arc. In the end, it was internal squabbling that destroyed the Hussites. The moderate Hussites and radical Taborites so divided the movement that the Catholics under Sigismund were able to defeat them and temporarily restore Catholic control in 1436.

References: Bartos, Frantisek, *The Hussite Revolution* (Boulder: East European Monographs, 1986); Kaminsky, Howard, *A History of the Hussite Revolution* (Berkeley: University of California Press, 1967); Oman, Charles, *A History of the Art of War in the Middle Ages* (Ithaca, NY: Cornell University Press, 1953 [1885])

Hyksos

An ancient population that conquered and dominated Egypt between the eighteenth and sixteenth centuries BCE.

Power slipped from the pharaohs of Egypt in the late Middle Kingdom, during the Thirteenth Dynasty (1786–1633 BCE), when they were conquered in a relatively easy victory by the Hikau-Khoswet people. The name Hikau-Khoswet originated from the Egyptian phrase meaning "rulers of foreign lands." An Asiatic group primarily composed of Semites, the Hikau-Khoswet, of Hyksos, reigned over Egypt for well over 100 years, beginning from about 1750–1700 BCE. and ending with the establishment of the New Kingdom in 1567 BCE. The main catalysts that enabled the Hyksos to conquer the Nile delta so easily were the internal dissent among the Egyptians themselves, a counterrevolt of the nobility, and a weakening of the power of the pharaohs.

The Hyksos were said to be well trained and well armed, and were credited with introducing the horse and chariot to Egypt. The Egyptian forces of the time were exclusively infantry armed with copper weapons. Assuming the Hyksos invaded with cavalry and chariots, scale armor, bronze weapons, and composite bows, the Egyptians would have been completely outclassed. Whether the Hyksos entered Egypt in one major invasion or through a gradual buildup of population (both theories are proposed), it is almost unthinkable that the Egyptians could have given them much serious military opposition. Moreover, if the Hyksos' forces included Arabs, then camel-borne troops would also have been used, which would have been a complete surprise to the defenders.

During the course of the Hyksos' invasion, towns and cities were burned, temples were damaged, and the native population was subjected to severe hardships and cruelties. Once the Hyksos gained control, they imposed heavy taxes as well as a strong military dominance on their subjects. Surprisingly, the majority of Egyptians accepted this style of leadership without much resistance.

The origin of the Hyksos is the subject of much debate, although they were probably a Canaanite tribe from the east coast of the Mediterranean, possibly Palestine. The third-century Egyptian historian Manetho describes the dynasties of the Hyksos'

occupation as Phoenician (XV Dynasty) and Syrian (XVI Dynasty). Most authorities agree that Canaanite culture introduced the chariot into Egypt. The Hyksos could well have been aided in their invasion, at least indirectly, by the Nubians. The Nubians were in conflict with Upper Egypt in the area of modern Sudan and through the region east of the Nile. It has been speculated that the Hyksos were to some extent allied with them. This may explain why the Hyksos remained concentrated in Lower Egypt, perhaps as the result of an agreement with the Nubians to divide the spoils of their conquests.

The Hyksos were not entirely preoccupied with military goals. According to William Hayes, "The Hyksos kings of the Fifteenth Dynasty brought about the construction of temples, production of statues, reliefs, scarabs, and other works of art and craftsmanship" (Hayes, 1959), some of which are regarded as the best examples of Egyptian literary and technical works of that time. Practical and useful inventions such as the well sweep, the vertical loom, and the composite bow were Hyksos legacies. Egypt until this time was behind other Mediterranean civilizations in technological advancements. Thanks to the Hyksos, they were now able to learn of bronze working, the potter's wheel, and the use of arsenic copper. The Hyksos also introduced hump-backed cattle and fruit crops, as well as new planting and harvesting skills. Evidence suggests that the Hyksos encouraged exercise through dance and expression through new musical instruments.

On the whole, the Hyksos seem to have been a powerful and influential people, but there were only a few rulers able to take credit for the advances. One of the six Hyksos rulers was Prince Salatis, a name that has been interpreted to mean "Sultan." During his rise to power, he banned the contemporary Egyptian rulers from the capital city of Memphis and extended his rule over most of Middle Egypt, eventually taking over Upper Egypt and Nubia as well. In the meantime, Hyksos rulers had moved the capital to Avaris, the location of which remains a mystery.

Although the Hyksos invaders were eventually overthrown by the Egyptians in the late 1560s BCE, they left behind the tools and knowledge that helped build Egypt's future empire.

References: Baines, J., and J. Malek, *Atlas of Ancient Egypt* (New York: Facts on File, Inc., 1980); Hayes, W., *The Scepter of Egypt* (Cambridge: Harvard University Press, 1959); Van Seeters, J., *The Hyksos* (New Haven: Yale University Press, 1966).

I

Immortals

Elite troops in the Persian army from 559 to 331 BCE.

When Cyrus the Great came to power over Persia in 559 BCE, he established the Achaemenid Dynasty, which would rule the Middle East from the Mediterranean to the Indian frontier for more than 200 years. He came to rule not long after the collapse of Assyria, which built and maintained its empire through terror. Cyrus proved his ability to conquer in a sufficient number of battles. However, his reputation for ruling with toleration and respect inspired the willing support of the countries he placed under his rule, which in the long run may have been more important for winning and maintaining his empire than his military prowess. In spite of this admiration of his subjects, Cyrus had to maintain an army sufficiently potent to protect his frontiers, and the army he built and his descendants wielded had few equals.

All subjects of the Persian empire were liable for military duty, but the people of the Persian homeland, the Persians and Medes, were the core of the military and the forces that the emperor could always count on to be well trained and motivated. Within this core of soldiery, Cyrus kept a standing force that acted both as a palace guard and as the elite troops in battle. These were termed the Immortals, for the size of the unit was not allowed to drop

below 10,000. In case of sickness or death, there was always another soldier prepared to step in and maintain the unit's constant size. Mostly Medes and Persians served in the Immortals, although there were also some Elamites from the area of modern Iraq.

Reliefs at the palace at Susa (modern-day Shush, Iran) give a glimpse of how the Immortals appeared. In those carvings the troops are Elamites, all dressed and armed alike. Their heads are bare and they wear elaborate robes that reach from neck to ankle, with leather shoes beneath. Each carries a spear with a silver blade and pomegranate (a metal ball attached to the butt of the spear). Each soldier holds a bow in his left arm with the quiver slung across the left shoulder. The symmetry of the scene breaks down in the personal touches of each soldier's attire. For example, the soldiers' quivers are decorated in different patterns, and their shoes and robes are often of different colors and studded with ornaments of various shapes and colors. Other carved reliefs at Susa of Persian or Medean Immortals show their heads covered with felt caps, and they often wear jackets and trousers rather than robes. Within the depicted unit is an even more elite grouping, the *hazarpat*, 1,000 soldiers whose spear pomegranates are gold.

Although they were the cream of the Persian army, the Immortals are mentioned in historical documents only once in any detail: when the Persians under Xerxes

Two life-size archers from the palace of Darius the Great, Susa, Iran. Louvre, Department des Antiquities Orientales, Paris, France. © Erich Lessing / Art Resource, NY

launched their invasion of Greece in 480 BCE. The Persian army marched around the edge of the Adriatic Sea with the Persian fleet pacing them. As the Persians marched through Thessaly, the navy was blocked from supporting them by a Greek fleet stationed between the Thessalian coast and the island of Euboea. Thus, when Xerxes' men found themselves blocked in a narrow pass at Thermopylae, the fleet was unavailable to land troops behind the force, which was commanded by Leonidas of Sparta. The Greek force of 7,000 was made up of mixed contingents from around Greece, but the Spartan force of 300 was the only professional unit among them. When Xerxes—who commanded more than 100,000 men—saw the small force, he waited for them to be overawed and flee. When they were not, he attacked.

In the narrow confines of the pass, the Persians could not employ the tactics of maneuver with which they normally fought, and the heavily armed infantry of the Greeks staged a stout defense. The Greek phalanx formation employed long spears with a greater length than anything the Persians carried, so the tightly packed Greek force stood their ground and kept the Persians at bay. Frustrated at the lack of progress, Xerxes ordered his Immortals to attack. They could not break the Greek line either, in spite of the fact that other Persians with whips drove them from behind. Thus, in the only extended description of Immortals in combat, they are defeated. Only by treachery did Xerxes outflank the Greeks and destroy the 300 Spartans who remained to cover the withdrawal of the rest of their forces.

The Persian army, though defeated in its attempt to invade Greece in the 400s BCE, remained a formidable fighting force that kept control over a huge empire for two centuries. Only with the arrival of Alexander the Great, antiquity's greatest general, did the Persian army meet its match.

References: Ferrill, Arther, *The Origins of War* (London: Thames and Hudson, 1985); Herodotus, trans. by Aubrey de Selincourt, *The Histories* (London: Penguin, 1954); Olmstead, A.T., *History of the Persian Empire* (Chicago: University of Chicago Press, 1948).

Irish Brigade

Part of the Union Army during the American Civil War, the Irish maintained the tradition of the "Wild Geese" by developing an outstanding reputation as an immigrant unit.

When President Abraham Lincoln called for volunteers to suppress rebellion after the April 12 Confederate cannonade on Fort Sumter in Charleston, South Carolina, states across the north began organizing regiments, usually far more quickly than they could be supplied. In New York, long an entry point for immigrants, a large number of Irish flocked to the colors, creating the Sixty-third, Sixty-ninth, and Eighty-eighth Regiments of New York Infantry. When they first began enlisting, there was some suspicion on the part of many New Yorkers, for the Irish had long been staunch Democrats, the party of the South. "Many Southerners assumed that the New York Irish would rise en masse rather than fight alongside those 'native' Americans whom they considered their enemies and exploiters." (Smith) Indeed, for all the discrimination the Irish suffered in the United States, it was somewhat surprising that so many enlisted.

After the Union defeat at First Bull Run (First Manassas) in July 1861, the three New York Irish regiments were joined

Lt. Col. James J. Smith and officers of the 69th New York Infantry, the Irish Brigade. Library of Congress, Prints and Photographs Division [reproduction number LC-B817-7642]

with the Twenty-eighth Massachusetts and the 116th Pennsylvania Infantry Regiments to form the Second Brigade, First Division, II Corps, Army of the Potomac. As the Pennsylvania and Massachusetts units were also predominantly Irish, the "Irish Brigade" was soon its nom de guerre. Its battle cry was " *Riamh Nar dhruid O sbairn lan*" ("Never retreat from the clash of spears"). The first and best-known of its commanders was Thomas Meagher, born in Ireland and involved in a number of independence movements there. He was exiled to Tasmania, but after a time managed to appear in New York City where he practiced a variety of professions. His oratorical skills won him attention among the Irish political factions.

The Brigade spent the winter in a forward position in Alexandria, Virginia, then was embarked for General George McClellan's sea-borne invasion of "the Peninsula" (between the James and York Rivers) in the

spring of 1862. The brigade fought in the battles of McClellan's advance and retreat: Fair Oaks, Gaines's Mill, Savage Station, and Malvern Hill. High numbers of casualties and sick brought more recruits from New York City. It was a foretaste of the numbers the brigade would lose over the course of the war.

The Irish Brigade was lucky enough to miss General John Pope's defeat in the Second Battle at Bull Run in mid-summer 1862, but were under McClellan's command in Maryland at the battle of Antietam (Sharpsburg) in September. Some of the worst fighting of the battle took place in the center of the Confederate line in the middle of the day, the infamous "Bloody Lane." Confederates stationed along a sunken road had a clear field of fire across the open field on which the Irish charged, reportedly chanting "Fág an bealach," or "clear the way." The brigade was finally relieved by another and retired to the rear, having suffered more than 500 men killed and wounded, including Meagher, who was carried off the field unconscious; two of the regiments suffered 60 percent casualties. Although it was his poor generalship that caused much of their losses, McClellan remained popular with the army, especially the Irish. When McClellan's dismissal was announced, many of the brigade's officers resigned their commissions in protest.

The best known of the Irish Brigade's battles was their assault on the entrenched Confederate positions at Fredericksburg, Virginia, in December 1862. The Confederates had dug into Marye's Heights just outside the town while the new commander of the Union Army, Ambrose Burnside, wasted almost a month building a pontoon bridge across the Rappahannock River. Once the bridge was completed, the Confederates offered only token resistance in the town but instead withdrew into virtually impregnable positions. Union forces had to attack across a wide-open field, cross a sunken road, then attack massed infantry behind stone walls, all under constant Confederate artillery fire. The Irish Brigade was only one unit of many shot to pieces that day. In one of the many ironies of the war, the Irish Brigade's target was a section of wall defended by the Twenty-fourth Georgia Infantry Regiment, also predominantly Irish. It has been supposed in many later accounts (primarily the film *Gods and Generals*) that there was a lot of uneasiness experienced by soldiers on both sides. Kelly O'Grady's book *Clear the Confederate Way* dismisses this story: "As the green flag came into clearer focus up the rise, [Twenty-fourth Regimental commander Colonel Robert] McMillan observed, 'That's Meagher's Brigade!' But shortly after, he gave the command to fire on that flag, crying out, 'Give it to them

now, boys! Now's the time! Give it to them!' He never wrote of any regret at that crucial moment." A gunner with the Washington Artillery of New Orleans wrote, "Of the 5,000 men led into action, 2,000 fell in the charge. With them were the Zouaves and the Irish Brigade of Meagher, bearing aloft the green flag with the golden harp of Ireland. The brave fellows came within five and twenty paces of the stone wall but encountered such a fire of shot, canister and musketry as no command was ever known to live through." (Eisenschiml and Newman)

With more than 40 percent casualties at Fredericksburg, the Irish Brigade was shrinking quickly. Although some of the men began questioning their cause, General Meagher was finally punished for his views. He had remained the fiery orator of his prewar days and was in contact with the Fenians, whose members in America and Canada were dedicated to expelling the English from Ireland. It has been suggested that Meagher was treating the brigade as his private army and the combat of the Civil War was a training ground for a future campaign with "his" brigade in Ireland when the American war was over. Not allowed to conduct any more recruiting, Meagher resigned his commission and went home.

The Irish Brigade, now at not much more than regimental strength, played a minor role at the battle of Chancellorsville in May 1863 and was with George Meade's army at Gettysburg in July. There they occupied the center of the Union line during the infamous Pickett's Charge on July 3, and the position they defended was Fredericksburg in reverse. Still, at the "High-Water Mark" of the Confederacy there was hand-to-hand combat, and the Irish were in the middle of it. Going into the battle numbering just 600, there were only half that many afterward.

In early 1864, the numbers once again began to increase; apparently recruiting was allowed now that Meagher was gone. Only 20 percent of the men were veterans when they marched south under Grant and fought in the Wilderness campaign and in the lines at Petersburg. During the nine-month siege, the Irish Brigade found themselves occupying trenches opposite Mahone's Division, also filled with Irish soldiers. Fraternization was common during the quiet times, but the fighting was as intense as ever during the battles. When the war finally came to an end at Appomattox Court House on April 9, 1865, some of the Irish Brigade were there.

Although the Irish Brigade was the largest collection of Irish immigrants in one unit, many smaller units had high numbers of Irish as well, and on both sides of the fighting. The Twenty-fourth Georgia Regiment has already been mentioned, but many of the Sixth Louisiana Brigade (Louisiana Tigers) in the Confederate division commanded by Jubal Early were Irish. Both they and the 40 percent Irish Tenth Louisiana lost heavily at Gettysburg, though against Union Irish.

Some question the larger number of Irish on the Union side. Certainly there was a higher Irish immigrant population in the North, but (as stated earlier) as Democrats, they were expected by many Southerners to be passive if not disruptive in Northern states. "The Irish traditionally favored the underdog and, in the beginning of the contest, many Irish favored the South as they saw the North attempting to act much as the English had in their native land of Ireland. However, when Britain began considering support for the Confederacy, many Irish threw their lot in with the North." (Mayers) Indeed, it has been suggested that the major cause of the Union victory in the war was the fact that the North had more Irish in their army.

References: Bilby, Joseph, *The Irish Brigade in the Civil War* (Conshohocken, PA: Combined Publishing, 1998); Eisenschiml, Otto and Ralph Newman, *The Civil War: An American Iliad* (New York: Mallard Press, 1991 [1947]); Mayer, Gerry, "America's Bloodiest Day: Slaughter along a Sunken Road—The Irish Brigade Enters the Fray," United States Civil War, 7 May 2003, www.us-civilwar.com/njrebel/picket29, 16 March 2006; McCormack, John F., "The Irish Brigade: Never Were Men so Brave," *Civil War Times*, 2005, www.thehistorynet.com/cwti/blneverweremensobrave, 16 March 2006; O'Grady, Kelley, *Clear the Confederate Way* (Cambridge, MA: da Capo Press, 1999); Smith, Page, *Trial by Fire* (New York: McGraw Hill, 1982).

Irish Legion

Mercenary/freedom fighter unit serving with Napoleon's army.

In 1803, the Emperor Napoleon, at war with England, anticipated an invasion of the British Isles by way of Ireland. His Adjutant General Bernard MacSheehy, a man of Irish birth, suggested the forming of a battalion of Irishmen to spearhead such an invasion. He reasoned there were be no shortage of Irish ready and willing to shoot Englishmen, if properly trained and supplied. The French Minister of War, Henri Clarke, himself of Irish descent, agreed wholeheartedly. Thus the "Legion Irlandaise" or Irish Legion came into being. Initially one battalion of five companies of 139 officers and men each was raised, but in time this increased to nine companies, which was the standard for all French battalions at the time. In March 1804, a second battalion was authorized (eventually there would be a third battalion as well), bringing the Irish Legion to regimental strength. Troops were raised from Irish and Scottish expatriates, from willing prisoners of war (Irish who served in the other armies of Europe), from Irish sailors who had been press-ganged into the British navy, and when these sources ran thin, from German and Polish recruits. The officers were to be Irish as much as possible, and although the official language of the unit was French, the officers and men spoke English among themselves.

The standard Irish Legion uniform was green (naturally) with yellow lapels, cuffs, turnbacks, and piping. The regimental flag bore the Irish gold harp on one side with the motto "L'Independence D'Irlande," while on the other side was "Napoleon Empereur des Francais a la Legion Irlandais." The unit was also granted an Eagle. Their equipment was that of standard light infantry in the Grande Armée.

After the defeat of the French navy at Trafalgar in September 1805, the invasion plans fell by the wayside. In 1807, the First Battalion of the Irish Legion was sent to Walchern Island to help defend the French naval base at Antwerp. Two years later, English forces attacked. The Irish Legion and the other French forces put up a desperate defense but were eventually forced to surrender. However, two Irish officers, Captain William Lawless and Lieutenant Terrence O'Reilly. managed to make an escape, bringing out the Regimental Eagle with them. Napoleon was so delighted with this exploit that he awarded both men the Legion of Honor and promoted Lawless to command the First Battalion, which was being re-formed.

The Second Battalion was sent to join Marshall Murat in Spain in 1807, where it put down local revolts, built fortifications,

patrolled, and fought Spanish guerrillas. In 1810, the battalion participated in the capture of Astorga, in which they fought bravely but every company suffered heavy casualties while carrying ladders to scale the walls of the town. The unit went on to participate honorably in the Siege of Almeida and the Battles of Bussaco, and Fuentes de Onor. Although the Legion was not totally engaged in every battle, they performed well; the men served with distinction, winning both acclaim and Legions of Honor. But it all took a terrific toll. When the battalion was ordered to leave Spain after nearly four years and sail for Holland in 1812, only 120 officers and men boarded the ships.

The Second Battalion was sent to Berg-op-Zoom to be rebuilt. The First Battalion garrisoned the islands of Goeree and Oveflanque. As part of the reorganization of the foreign regiments, a Third Battalion was raised and stationed in Willemstadt. By this time the actual number of Irishmen in the Irish Legion probably amounted to no more than 10 percent, not counting officers. Because of their refitting, the Irish Legion did not participate in the disastrous Russian Campaign of 1812. In 1813, the First and Second Battalions joined the rebuilt Grande Armée in Germany as part of the forces of Prince Eugene along the Elbe River. Under the command of their now Colonel William Lawless, the unit was in heavy action during May repulsing probes by the Russian army and capturing Seehousen. On May 21, the Irish Legion participated in the Battle of Bautzen, where for the first and only time, they were led by the Emperor Napoleon personally. The Legion performed brilliantly, driving the Allied forces back several miles. As a reward for their gallant service, the Irish Legion was allowed to stand guard for the

Emperor as he stayed at Lignitz until elements of the Imperial Guard could arrive.

In August the Legion saw action at the Battle of Lowenberg against the Army of Silesia, and later that month they fought at the Battle of Goldberg against the Prussians under Prince Carl von Mecklenburg. The Legion drove back successive attacks by Russian cavalry and infantry, losing 12 officers and over 300 men in a single day. On August 21, Colonel Lawless, while leading the Legion in an attack, was struck in the leg by a cannon ball. His men carried him on a door back to Napoleon's headquarters, where the Emperor's personal doctor tried to save his leg. In the end, it was necessary to amputate the limb, and Colonel Lawless' career came to an end, costing the Legion not only their most effective officer but their spiritual leader as well. For gallantry in action that month, 11 members of the Legion were awarded Legions of Honor, and several officers were promoted for their service.

However, at the end of the month, disaster struck. The Irish Legion, as part of General Puthod's Division, crossed the Bober River and was trapped by a superior allied force of Prussians and Russians. On August 29, in savage fighting and in what would prove to be the Legion's finest hour, the unit withstood successive attacks by Russian cavalry, then Prussian Hussars, and finally several bayonet charges by five Russian Jaeger battalions. They fought with the ferocity and doggedness for which the Irish were famous, but in the end, with their ammunition exhausted, the First and Second Battalions were wiped out; 20 officers were killed and almost all the enlisted men were killed or captured. The acting commander, Colonel Hugh Ware, swam back across the Bober River, carry-

ing with him the Regimental Eagle, but of the 2,000 men who had comprised the Irish Legion in January, only 117 were left. Of Puthod's Division, only 254 men escaped of the nearly 12,000 he had led across the river that morning.

The scant remnants of the Legion were reorganized with other foreign troops and slowly brought back up to regimental strength. In the fall the unit was sent to Antwerp where it again displayed admirable courage and élan in the gallant defense of that port. Upon Napoleon's abdication, Louis XVIII ordered a restructuring of the French Army that included disbanding the foreign units, including the Irish Legion, but also called for the reorganization of the Irish Legion as the Royal Irish Regiment. When Napoleon returned from exile, the unit swore allegiance to him, but there had not been sufficient time for the officers of the new Irish regiment to raise and refit the battalions, and the Irish saw no action during the Hundred Days leading up to the Battle of Waterloo. After Napoleon's defeat, the regiment swore allegiance to the French King, but to no avail. Louis XVIII ordered the unit disbanded on September 28, 1815. The officers were dismissed, and the enlisted men were incorporated into a Royal Foreign Regiment that was being organized. The flags and the Eagle of the Irish Legion were ordered burned. The days of the Irish fighting as a separate unit in French service were done.

David Beeson

References: Chandler, David, *The Campaigns of Napoleon*, MacMillan Co., 1966; Gallaher, John, *Napoleon's Irish Legion*, Southern Illinois University Press, 1993; Lochet, J., "The Irish Legion," *Empires, Eagles, and Lions*, no. 11, The Emperor's Press, NJ; McLaughlin, Mark, *The Wild Geese: The Irish Brigades of France and Spain*, Osprey, 1980; Medlen, Virginia Shaw,

"Legion Irlandaise (Napoleon's Irish Legion) 1803–1815" Military Heritage, 2006, www.militaryheritage.com/irish, 15 March 2006.

Iron Brigade

An outstanding unit of the Union army during the American Civil War (1861–1865).

In the course of American history, few events have been as momentous as the Civil War. In 1861 the great experiment in government by the people seemed to be failing, and a fledgling United States, not yet a century old, was divided with the inaugural blast at Fort Sumter on April 12. The call to arms was sounded on both sides, and boys soon became soldiers marching into epic battles. For the Union army, one brigade was to fight through the Civil War while distinguishing itself as the elite force in the Army of the Potomac. Respected by both comrade and enemy, it was known as the Iron Brigade.

The Iron Brigade was organized in the western states. One of the few completely "western" brigades in the eastern theater of the Civil War, the Iron Brigade took special pride in this distinction. Formed out of the Second, Sixth, and Seventh Wisconsin Infantry Regiments, and the Nineteenth Indiana Infantry, the brigade would later add the Twenty-fourth Michigan Infantry Regiment after the battle at Antietam in September 1862. Although the four initial regiments of the Iron Brigade were all formed at the beginning of the war, only the Second Wisconsin fought in the First Battle of Bull Run in July 1861, taking part in the assault on Henry House Hill. In the months following Bull Run, the Union army underwent drastic changes. The hierarchy of the Army was

Gen. Edward S. Bragg, Commander of the Iron Brigade. Library of Congress, Prints & Photographs Division, Civil War Photographs, [reproduction number, LC-BH831-728].

redesigned, and from this restructuring, Gibbon's Wisconsin Brigade was formed. It did not receive the honor of being labeled the Iron Brigade until after its second battle.

Brigadier General John Gibbon was a strict disciplinarian and he trained his green troops constantly. Wishing to instill some esprit de corps in his men, he ordered a distinguishing uniform to set his brigade apart. One piece of this new uniform was the felt "Hardee" hat (the type worn by the regular army) in black rather than the standard blue. The black hat would become the brigade's trademark.

Even with the training and the new uniforms, Gibbon's brigade was still untested in battle. The Brigade's initial baptism of fire did not happen until August 1862 at the Second Battle of Bull Run. While passing a small farm along the road to Manassas, where the rest of the army was massing, Gibbon's brigade was ambushed by veteran Confederate forces under "Stonewall" Jackson. Expecting an easy victory over the smaller and inexperienced Federal force, Jackson's veterans were stunned when the Union troops turned and charged headlong into the fight, firing organized massed volleys that dropped the front ranks of the Confederates.

The Battle at Brawner Farm had begun—and with it the Iron Brigade's legend. The 2,100 men of the brigade were facing 5,200 enemy troops, which were reinforced as the battle raged. For more than two hours they slammed away at each other, until Gibbon—in the face of overwhelming odds—decided to pull his troops back. After such a difficult battle, the Confederates were only too happy to let them go unmolested, but they would always remember those "damn black hat fellers"—as one Confederate soldier was heard to comment.

In this first fight, Gibbon's Wisconsin Brigade sustained a loss of 33 percent of its active strength while inflicting the same percentage of casualties on the larger enemy force. As impressive as this was, the fight did not end at Brawner Farm, for the next day found the brigade participating in Union General John Pope's ill-conceived attacks on the Confederate line. Throughout those attacks, the soldiers of the brigade fought bravely, once even turning their guns on their own comrades who were trying to run away and forcing them to get back in line to fight. The battle ended with the Confederates controlling the field and the Union Army in full retreat, but Gibbon's brigade had proved itself to the enemy and to its fellow troops.

The brigade got little rest, for less than a month later Confederate General Robert E. Lee launched his first invasion of the

North. At South Mountain in Maryland, the brigade was used in a daring assault on the Confederate line on September 14, 1862. While two other Union forces attacked the left and right flanks of the enemy line, Gibbon's brigade was sent up the center to break the Confederate middle. The brigade, assisted only by artillery, fought uphill against an entrenched enemy. From the start of the fighting, it was clear that this would be a terrific contest as each side fired mercilessly into the other. After a back-and-forth struggle, the brigade rallied at a stone wall near the Confederate line. As the Confederates launched an attack on its new position, the brigade met them with fixed bayonets and musket fire. The Confederates paid dearly for their assault. As night fell, the battle began to die down, but not before the two sides had taken grievous casualties. Through it all, the brigade held its line and forced the Confederates to pull back. Union General Joe Hooker witnessed the fight and, in a letter to General McClellan, he commented on the fighting skill of this "Iron Brigade," whose line seemingly could not be broken. The name stuck, and with it the honor of being among the Union army's most prized troops.

The celebration was brief, however. Lee's army began to concentrate around Sharpsburg, Maryland. McClellan was quick to react and the two armies faced each other along a little stream called Antietam Creek. So fierce was the ensuing battle at Antietam that September 17, 1862—the day of the battle—became the bloodiest single day in American history. The Iron Brigade took part in the opening assault on the Confederate left. Along with the rest of General Hooker's I Corps, the soldiers attacked Confederate forces under Stonewall Jackson. The objective of the

Federal assault was the small Dunker Church at the rear of the Confederate line. The battle raged through an open lot and a cornfield, with both sides clashing amidst stalks of corn and along rail fences. After two hours of incessant fighting, the Confederate line began to give way and the soldiers of the Iron Brigade and their comrades raced for the Dunker Church with victory on their minds. They were shocked to find, as they approached their objective, a gray line charging out of the fleeing rebels. The expected Union victory was quickly reversed as the famous Confederate force known as the Texas Brigade came roaring into the battle from its reserve position. Tired, wounded, and thrown off guard by the ferocity of this new attack, the members of the Iron Brigade and its companion forces quickly retreated back to their original positions until reinforcements were brought up to push back the Confederate assault. The Iron Brigade stayed on the defensive for the rest of the day. As night fell, it was apparent that Lee and his army had been defeated, but at a severe price.

With the victory came new changes for the Union army and for the Iron Brigade. The Army of the Potomac received a new commander in Major General Ambrose Burnside, and the Iron Brigade received a new regiment in the form of the Twenty-fourth Michigan Infantry. The members of the Twenty-fourth were well aware of their new brigade's fame and anxious to prove themselves worthy members and to win their black hats. They did not have to wait long, as General Burnside prepared to launch his famous ill-fated attack at Fredericksburg on December 13, 1862. The Iron Brigade's role in this battle was limited to the far left of the field away from the heaviest fighting, but it did see action.

Facing a line of Confederates posted in a wooded area, Gibbon ordered the Twenty-fourth Michigan to clear the woods and, in a manner to make their veteran comrades proud, the Twenty-fourth Michigan broke the enemy line. As the Confederates pulled back, the Iron Brigade was ordered to pursue with the Twenty-fourth Michigan in the lead. The new regiment took severe casualties but did not falter. By the end of the battle, however, the Union Army had suffered its worst defeat and was forced to retreat from Fredericksburg. But the Twenty-fourth Michigan earned something as valuable as a victory: They had earned their black hats and the right to call themselves a part of the Iron Brigade.

After so great a blunder, Burnside was replaced by Major General Joe Hooker as commander. With the arrival of spring, Hooker devised an attack to crush the rebel army. His plan called for a portion of the army to cross upstream of the main rebel force and attack Lee from his rear while the other force crossed at Fredericksburg and attacked his front. In order to cross the river, Hooker needed to secure one of the many river fords that was guarded by Confederate troops. For this task he turned to the Iron Brigade. As Union engineers began to set the bridge, the Iron Brigade, its soldiers lying down in boats to avoid Confederate rifle and cannon fire, surged across the river. Upon reaching the other shore, the troops leaped from their boats and charged the Confederate position. The assault was successful, and Hooker had his bridge, but the Iron Brigade had taken heavy losses. Due to its diminished strength, the brigade was held in reserve during the battle of Chancellorsville. At this battle, Lee and his forces decimated Hooker, and the Iron Brigade helped cover the retreat of the Union

Army back over the very bridge they had secured.

As the Union army suffered yet another humiliating defeat, Lee prepared his army to invade the North for a second time. This time the two armies met at the crossroads town of Gettysburg, Pennsylvania. The first day of the largest battle in the Civil War started with Union cavalry engaging a larger Confederate force. The Iron Brigade was called to reinforce the failing Union line. The Union generals on the scene recognized the need to hold the high ground until the rest of the army could be assembled. This task was left to I Corps with the Iron Brigade in the lead. Here, along McPherson's Ridge and the Chambersburg Pike, just northwest of Gettysburg, the Iron Brigade fought its most difficult battle. The larger Confederate force was slowly surrounding the Union force, but the Iron Brigade did not give an inch, making the Confederates pay for every step they took. The Sixth Wisconsin met the Second Mississippi in a fierce hand-to-hand contest over the regimental colors, with a young Wisconsin private capturing the rebel flag and later presenting it to his commanding general.

As I Corps finally began its withdrawal through Gettysburg and up to Cemetery Ridge, the Iron Brigade was ordered to retreat and head for the safety of the new Union line. In the presence of a superior force, the Iron Brigade could take pride in the fact that it gave no ground that it was not ordered to give. The Iron Brigade and its companion forces had accomplished their objective: They had saved the high ground and possibly the entire battle—but at an incredible cost. Of the 1,883 men of the Iron Brigade who marched up the Chambersburg Pike that morning, only 671 made it back to the Federal position on Cemetery Ridge that night. The Twenty-fourth Michigan alone lost 80 percent of its regiment. Most of the field officers had been killed, and in some instances entire companies had been reduced to one or two men. The brigade received the dubious honor of having the highest casualty percentage of any unit in the entire Civil War, North or South.

The Iron Brigade never recovered from these losses. After Gettysburg, the brigade was reorganized and supplemented with new regiments that effectively demolished its veteran ranks. The reconstituted Iron Brigade fought in the remaining battles of the Civil War, but the Iron Brigade of legend had fought its last battle at Gettysburg.

Steve Davis

References: Foote, Shelby. *The Civil War, A Narrative*, vol. 1 (New York: Vintage Books, 1958); Nolan, Alan T. *The Iron Brigade: A Military History* (Indianapolis: Indiana University Press, 1961).

J

Janissaries

Elite slave soldiers of the Ottoman Empire during the fourteenth through the nineteenth centuries.

First organized in the fourteenth century, the Janissaries of the Ottoman Empire became the first regular standing infantry force in medieval Eastern Europe. For four centuries, they formed the nucleus of the Ottoman armies who fought the wars of Allah and the Turkish Sultans. On a hundred battlefields they knew only victory or death, and their very presence was frequently enough to send their enemies fleeing in terror. The Janissaries' reputation for bravery and ferocity, coupled with their unmatched discipline and training, made them the most feared fighting unit of their era.

Ironically, in the beginning, none of the individuals who became Janissaries were Turks or even Muslims when they entered the service of the Sultans. The part of eastern Christian Europe under Turkish rule was required every four years to provide a tribute of around 3,000 boys between 12 and 20 years of age. Over the next decade, the boys underwent several stages of training, which involved living and working with farmers and tradesmen in Turkey, and learning the Turkish language and the Muslim religion. At around the age of 25, the best of these recruits were chosen for seven years of training by the Janissaries themselves in Constantinople. By the time a recruit was formally accepted into the corps, his indoctrination was so complete as to assure his total loyalty to the Sultan and to his fellows—unto death. He had become part of the "slave-family."

The clothing of a Janissary usually consisted of a long garment called a *spahi*, frequently made of brightly colored silk, and a cap with a distinctive long sleeve hanging down the back. Horsehair plumes and feather crests adorned this hat, and gave Janissary columns the appearance, said one witness, "of a moving forest." The weapons of a Janissary were the composite bow, later replaced by the harquebus (or matchlock musket), swords, and daggers. A Janissary wore very little armor, perhaps the occasional piece of chain mail, and did not use a shield or pavis. If categorized, he would have to be described as light infantry. The corps was exclusively infantry, although a few hundred might win promotion to the *Spahis of the Porte*, the Sultan's household cavalry. Handpicked archers could be assigned to the *Solaks*, the Sultan's bodyguards. Those 60 Janissaries deemed the finest warriors formed the *Peiks*, the personal guardians of the Sultan. They were distinguished by their caps of beaten gold, and their weapon: a two-handed axe.

After the first century and a half of the Janissaries' existence, the Sultan Suleiman the Magnificent increased the size of the Janissary corps to more than 20,000 men.

Palma Giovane (Jacopo Negretti). First attack on Constantinople in 1453 by the Turks. Palazzo Ducale, Venice, Italy. ©
Erich Lessing / Art Resource, NY

These were organized in messes of 10 men, of which 10 messes formed a company. Part of the Janissaries' solidarity was based on the practice of eating together, and each company's large copper soup cauldron was a symbol of the members' fraternity and unity. The loss of this cauldron to an enemy was equivalent in disgrace to the loss of an eagle standard for Napoleon's troops, while the overturning of cauldrons later in the history of the empire was a sign of dissension and perhaps insurrection against the Sultan.

When not on campaign, those Janissaries stationed outside of Constantinople garrisoned large towns throughout the empire. There they functioned as a sort of police force, maintaining law and order, punishing criminals, guarding the frontier, and enforcing the word of the Sultan. In combat, the Janissaries typically formed the center of the Ottoman horde, their flanks covered by wagon laagers chained together, with massed artillery to their front. When opposing other eastern armies, which were composed mostly of cavalry, the Ottomans always stood on the defensive, forcing their enemies into frontal attacks. In this manner, the Janissaries could deliver orderly and well-trained volleys of archery and harquebus fire on the enemy horses, while the Ottoman artillery, which frequently was chained together in large batteries, broke up the cavalry formations and slowed their charge. Against European armies, with their heavily armored knights, the Ottomans adopted deeper formations. Two and sometimes three lines of light and heavy cavalry, usually auxiliaries drawn from conquered provinces, fronted the chained artillery. Their purpose was to slow down the knights and dissipate their charge. Then, close-range artillery fire and the Janissaries' musketry would drive the Europeans away before they could close with the Ottoman infantry. Light cavalry waiting on the flanks would then swoop in to pursue and destroy the retreating knights.

Ottoman expansion westward into Europe and the Mediterranean called for attacks on walled cities and castles as much as battles in the fields. It was in siege work that the Janissaries perhaps performed their best. They led the final assaults at Constantinople in 1453 and at Rhodes in 1522. As snipers and sappers, they had no equals and, once fortification walls had been breached, their attacks were pushed forward with a fanaticism that ignored danger and death. With trumpets blaring, kettledrums and cymbals banging, they would

charge screaming and wailing over their own dead and dying. They boasted that "the body of a Janissary is only a stepping stone for his brethren into the breach." However, their lack of armor and their almost suicidal attacks soon thinned their ranks to an alarming degree. The quantity of training for a Janissary declined from seven years to sometimes as little as 18 months, and the quality of the recruits themselves declined. By the end of the reign of Suleiman the Magnificent, sons of Janissaries had the hereditary right to join the corps, and by 1600, any Turk or Muslim could apply.

Westward expansion brought the Ottomans into battle with pike- and harquebus-armed European armies that were, in many cases, as well trained as the Janissaries. While the Europeans made steady advancements in armor, weapons, and tactics, the Janissaries tended to remain stagnant, rooted in tradition. This lethargy resulted in the Ottoman expansion finally being halted at the great sea battle of Lepanto in 1571. There Christian Europeans, using harquebusses and muskets and protected by steel breastplates and helmets, killed 30,000 of the 60,000 Turks present, signaling the end of Ottoman power in the Mediterranean.

The Janissaries continued as a unique force for another century and a half, clinging to their traditions and privileges. More and more, they assumed a political role in the empire, supporting certain Sultans and bringing down others. In many ways they came to mirror the role that the Praetorian guard played in Imperial Roman politics. Any attempts by the Sultans to replace them with more modern infantry formations resulted in violent Janissary riots. The corps, the force on which the security of the Empire had so long depended, had itself become a threat. Worse, it was a toothless tiger, a worthless military force against its enemies in the nineteenth-century world.

Finally in 1826, after still another revolt, troops loyal to Sultan Mahmut II surrounded the Janissaries in their barracks and, when they refused to surrender, blasted them into submission with artillery. The survivors were hanged, and their soup caldrons, the symbols of their solidarity, were cast into the Adriatic. Four centuries after beginning in fidelity to religion and ruler, the march of the Janissaries across the history of Eastern Europe and the Middle East ended in dishonor and death.

References: Goodwin, Godfrey, *The Janissaries* (London: Saqi, 1994); Kinross, Patrick, *The Ottoman Centuries* (New York: Morrow, 1977); Shaw, Stanford, *The History of the Ottoman Empire and Modern Turkey*, 2 vols. (Cambridge: Cambridge University Press, 1976–1977).

K

Kamikazes

Suicide pilots of the Japanese air forces during World War II.

Japan's introduction of intentionally planned, government-sponsored suicide tactics in the final year of World War II was virtually unprecedented in all of warfare. Yet, considering the nature of Japanese society over the several centuries preceding the kamikaze, this development seems not only logical, but in some ways inevitable.

In the late 1200s, the island nation of Japan was under attack by Mongol forces from mainland China. Early assaults had been met and turned back on the beaches, but the arrival of Mongol reinforcements made the situation look dire for the defending Japanese. They were saved, however, by the timely arrival of a typhoon that destroyed the Mongol invasion fleet. The natural disaster seemed to the Japanese to be heaven sent, so the typhoon that saved Japan was called the *kamikaze*, or "divine wind." It was the recollection of that thirteenth-century salvation that inspired the creation of the twentieth-century kamikaze, to whom many Japanese looked for their salvation from a different foreign invasion almost seven centuries later.

In the intervening centuries, Japan was ruled by a military society under the direction of the *shogun*. He was the titular military advisor to the emperor but was in fact the real power in Japan until 1868. In that year, forced contact with the outside world initiated by the American naval officer Matthew Perry woke the Japanese up to the progress the world had made while they had strictly maintained their own isolation. Within 30 years, under the Meiji emperor, Japan staged a major leap forward to become an industrialized power. Japan army's remained organized along the lines of the Samurai warrior class that had dominated the country for hundreds of years. In addition, it created a modern navy that soon destroyed the Russian navy in 1905 and threatened the pre-eminence of the United States in the Pacific Ocean. Japanese success in wars against China in the 1890s and Russia in 1904–1905, along with its military occupation of Korea, reinforced the martial climate of the new Japan and gave encouragement to the more aggressive nationalists in the military and government. The well-trained and motivated army captured Manchuria in 1931–1932 and took over most of eastern China between 1937 and 1941.

Although this success encouraged many Japanese in positions of power to challenge the United States in the Pacific, some men in key positions counseled restraint. These included Admiral Isoroku Yamamoto, commander of the Imperial Japanese Navy Combined Fleet. He foresaw the potential for destruction latent in American culture, but the other militarists in the government

The Bunker Hill after being hit by two kamikazes in thirty seconds, May 11, 1945. National Archives and Records Adminitration, Special Media Archives Services Division (NWCS-S), National Archives at College Park, 8601 Adelphi Road, College Park, MD. [Image 520678]

pushed for war. For a war to be dominated by naval operations and their accompanying air maneuvers, the Japanese needed—but did not possess—numeric superiority in ships and aircraft. Thus, they were doomed from the start. But Japanese warriors have never been more prone to extreme actions than when faced with imminent defeat. The virtually inbred creed that no soldier surrenders, that death for one's country and emperor is far preferable to surrender or defeat, almost guaranteed that the Japanese would sooner or later engage in desperate measures.

The United States Marines have had throughout their existence a motto: Death before dishonor. It is somewhat fitting, therefore, that they were the first Americans to learn that the Japanese military took that phrase quite literally. In the first offensive ground combat on Guadalcanal, in the Solomon Islands northeast of Australia, Marines faced what came to be called banzai charges. *Banzai* (literally "10,000 years") was the cry that Japanese soldiers raised to their emperor, not only for his long life, but for his soldiers' commitment to die for him. It was screamed by attacking Japanese in assaults that seemed to the

Marines like human waves. These charges, coupled with the almost complete lack of captured Japanese prisoners, showed the Americans how determined the typical Japanese soldier was to win—or die trying.

The banzai charges were repeated in almost every battle fought by Japanese soldiers, and the Marines came to almost expect them as battles were winding down and the Japanese defenders were fewer in number. What came to be a common occurrence for Marines to witness was begun by Japanese pilots in 1944. The first recorded intentional suicide attack by a Japanese pilot was in May of that year off the coast of New Guinea. Prime Minister Tojo in the Japanese cabinet had already ordered preparations for "special attack units." The first serious call for self-sacrificial attacks, however, came from lower-ranking officers who felt the personal need to employ special measures to relieve the increasingly desperate straits of the Japanese army and navy, which faced superior American numbers in both aircraft and ships.

By the summer of 1944, when American forces landed in the Marianas Islands and came within bomber range of the home islands, the Japanese army and navy high commands began to listen more closely to the calls for suicide tactics. The Aerial Research Department of Tokyo's Imperial University began designing a rocket-propelled aircraft called *Ohka* ("cherry blossom") with a warhead in the nose. The pilots trained to fly these rocket-bombs were called Thunder Gods. The Ohka were not mass produced (only a few hundred were made), so the vast majority of airborne kamikaze attacks were made by regular aircraft, both bombers and fighters. These made their initial appearance during the American invasion of the Philippines in

October 1944. The Special Attack units in the Philippines were commanded by Vice Admiral Takijiro Onishi. The suicide attacks shocked the American forces, so much so that for six months the public in the United States was not informed of them. Although the attacks were occasionally successful, most of the effect was psychological. It was not enough of a psychological deterrent, however, to force a cancellation of the invasion as the Japanese had hoped.

The pilots who volunteered for kamikaze missions did so from a sense of duty and usually had a lot of time to think about their decision, for almost no one was sent off immediately upon volunteering. In some cases the pilot waited weeks or even months before his assignment came. Before his mission, the pilot donned a white head scarf (*hachimaki*) with the rising sun emblazoned in the center. Many times he also wore a ceremonial waist sash (*senninbari*), called "thousand-stitch belts," for which 1,000 women in Japan had sewn one stitch each in order to show the widespread support for the pilot. They were then served ritual cups of water or rice wine (*sake*). Often the pilots composed death poems, traditional for Samurai warriors prior to suicide.

Survivors of the kamikaze missions did exist. Although some sources tell of pilots who returned with mechanical difficulties being shunned by their compatriots, other sources report that, if no target was found, the pilot was instructed to return to base. This was how Saburo Sakai, Japan's highest-scoring fighter ace, managed to survive the war.

The results of the attacks in the Philippines were encouraging enough for the government to continue pushing the development of the Ohka. Furthermore, in

January 1945 the Japanese army and navy chiefs of staff submitted a plan to the emperor to require all the armed forces to engage in suicide tactics. The emperor disagreed. By February, the large number of early volunteers was beginning to dry up, and kamikaze pilots began being drafted. Only a few attacks took place during the Iwo Jima campaign in February and March 1945, but when American forces landed on Okinawa in April, the full force of the Special Attack units was felt. Fifteen ships were sunk and another 59 damaged, with a total loss of more than 48,000 Americans killed and wounded during the Okinawa campaign. The last major assault was in mid-May, after which time the shortage of pilots and aircraft was acute. The last American ship sunk by a kamikaze was on July 29, 1945. The last attack took place on August 13, only two days before the emperor announced Japan's surrender. Japanese navy pilots who died in the attacks numbered 2,525, with 1,388 army pilots also dead.

Although the aerial kamikazes were the best known of the suicide units, there were also midget submarines fitted out for one-way trips against American shipping. These were called *Kaiten*, or "heaven shifter," in the hopes that they could shift the fate of Japan's forces. Individual soldiers are reported to have laden themselves with explosives and jumped on tanks to disable them. Plans were also under way to encourage the civilian population of Japan to assume a suicidal role when the American invasion came. They were designated the *Ichioku Tokko*, or "hundred million as a special attack force." Many believe that only the shock of the two atomic bombs in August 1945 was sufficient to overcome the duty many of Japan's population were preparing to undertake.

References: Dower, John, *War Without Mercy* (New York: Pantheon, 1986); Inoguchi, Rikihei, Tadashi Nakajima, and Roger Pineau, *The Divine Wind* (Annapolis: United States Naval Institute Press, 1958); Naito, Hatsuho, *Thunder Gods* (New York: Kodansha International USA Ltd., 1989).

Knights

Armored troops dominant in warfare of the Middle Ages.

Of all the warriors of antiquity, none had a longer career or more of a social, cultural, and political influence on his society than did the European knight. For 700 years knights were the supreme projection of military power on whatever battlefields they appeared. Princes and kings attached themselves to the institution, conferred knighthood, and aspired to become knights themselves. Knights frequently were king makers, and sometimes even kings by their own hands. Undeniably, they were the kings of the battlefield, and for much of the Middle Ages most of the world trembled at their thundering approach.

First, foremost, and always, the knight was a soldier: in Latin *milles*, in French *chevalier*, in German *Ritter*, Italian *cavaliere*, Spanish *caballero*, and in Anglo-Saxon *cnicht*. As these terms imply, a knight was usually mounted, and because he wore as much armor as possible, he was in the simplest terms an armored cavalryman. The emergence of the medieval knight is clouded in the distant mists of the eighth century, for it was then that the first serious European cavalry arm came into being. In 702 CE, Muslim invaders came sweeping through Spain and into modern-day France. In order to meet their swift mounted tactics, it was necessary that the Frankish rulers Charles Martel and the

Three Soldiers with a ram forcing open the gate of fortification. From 'Four Books of Knightship'. Manuscript, 16th c. Dillingen Library, Dillingen, Germany. © Erich Lessing / Art Resource, NY

emperor Charlemagne develop a standing army with an aristocratic, armored, heavy cavalry core. The horses, equipment, and training necessary to support these warriors were very expensive. To meet these expenses, the Frankish emperors tended to seize church lands and either use the proceeds from those lands directly or grant them as estates to the mounted soldiers.

Thus, the knight was born in France as a military necessity to meet the dangers of marauding Muslims. At first, the knight was merely another specialized warrior—very expensive, but necessary. He could serve in the retinue or house of a great lord and receive wages with which he could equip himself, or he could receive land from a lord and use the income from that land to outfit himself for war. Either way, he was the vassal of a lord to whom he owed everything, and the beneficence of that lord (either protection or land) could be withdrawn if the knight's service faltered. As time passed, fewer and fewer knights served directly in the houses of great men, but instead occupied land granted to them for their use and showed up for service when called by their lord.

Soon, however, especially in England and then other countries, the land granted to a knight became a permanent possession of his family, passed down from father to son, and even to wives and daughters. The knight became a lord in his own small manor, and thus entered the lower ranks of the aristocracy. He could even pay money (called *scutage*, or "shield money") in lieu of actual service.

As a vassal, the knight owed his lord service, avenged his wrongs, protected his power, defended his dignity, and swore allegiance to him unto death. However, as much as he was a vassal, he was first and foremost a warrior, and war was his profession and his delight. A knight was highly trained and highly dangerous. His ability, equipment, and relationship with the great lords set him apart from the rest of society, and he could do pretty much as he wished, both above and beyond the established laws.

Like almost everyone in medieval times, the early knight was illiterate, brutish, and cruel by modern standards, rough in speech and manners, earning his living by violence, and unfettered by public justice. He lived by the sword and answered only to greater strength. Unarmed segments of society were bystanders, or worse, victims. Even on a holy crusade or pilgrimage, a knight could, in desperate circumstances, fall upon merchants and peasants and strip them bare, or kill them, with little or no regret. It appears from a distance that society had as much to fear from this warrior as to gain from him.

Then, about the eleventh century, knights and knighthood began to evolve. Part of this change came from the church, which taught forgiveness and gentleness, and tried to restrain these impetuous warriors with the papal pronouncements *Peace of God* (989 CE) and the *Truce of God* (1041 CE). The *Peace of God* sought to protect the clergy and church lands, and unarmed or poor men, merchants, or men going to or from church. The *Truce of God* restrained violence or the pleasure of war on Sundays and holy days (at that time, Thursdays, Fridays, and Saturdays).

Then the church promoted the Crusades, holy wars against the Muslims in the Holy Land. Knights who went were promised forgiveness for their sins, the possibility of estates in the conquered lands, and all the fighting they could stand. In a frenzy composed of equal parts of religious faith, adventure, and greed, thousands accepted the call. By the middle of the twelfth century, knighthood had become the bright sword of Christendom.

How successful these measures were in curbing the more violent natures of the medieval fighting men is debatable, but there is no doubt they did eventually affect the institution of knighthood by forcing knights to realize a responsibility to other segments of society. Eventually, the church broadened this to include a responsibility to protect those oppressed segments of society. Fraternities of knights arose from the Crusades, such as the Knights of the Temple, the Knights of the Hospital, the Knights of St. John, the Teutonic Military Order, and others. These orders achieved a measure of discipline, brotherhood, experience, and sense of duty and service that they managed to pass on to the remainder of knighthood. In all likelihood this was never more than a thin veneer for most, but out of it the code of living known as chivalry was born. With chivalry came the association of the knight with gentle birth, truly a *gentle*man, an aristocrat. Emperors and kings became knights. Excluding women, their entire courts consisted of knights. Their vassals—princes, dukes, and counts—were all knights, and those people in turn surrounded themselves with knights. The only other estate equally represented in medieval society was the clergy. Knighthood soon cut across national lines, forming an international fraternity.

The church then took the final step in gentling these warriors by becoming involved in the Ceremony of Investiture, thus sanctifying the status of knight. This probably began in the eleventh century with a simple ceremony blessing the sword, to dubbing in the twelfth century, to the final elaborate ceremony of knighting complete with fasting, prayer, and a

high mass in the thirteenth and fourteenth centuries. In this, the church did as it had often done before: It merely adopted a pagan rite or ritual (the acceptance of a male child into the fraternity of warriors of the tribe or clan) as its own, just as it had adopted so many previous holidays and traditions. In this way, over a few centuries the knight underwent a transformation from ordinary soldier, to kept retainer, to loose cannon, to soldier of Christ.

Originally, knights were no more than well-armed peasants—on the social scale anyway. But the granting of land set them apart, and the time necessary to become proficient with their weapons meant they could not labor like peasants. Soon the idea of a knight as the social equal of a peasant, or of falling to the level of a peasant, became unthinkable. He occupied a position of honor, and his family and the families of other retainers soon grouped around the king or great lord in close knit clans. They intermarried, and continued service to the great lord, and soon their rank became hereditary, as did their lands and their service. They had become lesser nobles.

Theoretically, knighthood was open to all brave or rich men, and any knight could raise a worthy person to membership in the fraternity. However, by the end of the twelfth century this had changed. Only the sons of knights, or those of noble or gentle birth, could aspire to knighthood. The fraternity had become either hereditary or highly exclusive, and both conditions prevented the lower orders from gaining admittance. Knights were now a social and professional class.

A knight's training was imparted individually: A father might train his own son, hire a man at arms to train him, or send his son to serve as a squire in the castle of a great lord where he trained in a group of other squires. Even then, training was as an individual. The candidate for knighthood practiced sword cuts on wooden poles and learned to use a spear on foot or on a wooden horse propelled by his fellows. He hunted stags and wild boars with a spear, either on foot or on horseback, and learned the art of controlling a horse under all conditions. He wrestled with others and fought with wooden weapons, all the while wearing the armor that was to become his second skin. All this training was aimed at making the youngster proficient in horsemanship and the use of arms, and at hardening him to physical pain and the strain of battle.

The chance to show off one's skills and to practice the arts of war came in those great shows called tournaments. The earliest such contests date to 842 CE. Originally, these were friendly competitions in which the participants used blunted weapons. By the twelfth century, they had become highly dangerous, causing various popes to ban tournaments in 1130, 1139, 1148, and 1179. Obviously, these bans were not successful. Tournaments were a means to win glory (under the admiring eyes of young women, who began to attend such affairs toward the end of the twelfth century) without the discomfort and expense of a long campaign. William Marshall, the Earl of Pembroke, gained great wealth from such affairs, acquiring ransoms, horses, and armor from over 500 knights during a lifetime of tournaments in the late twelfth and early thirteenth centuries.

Three technological advances combined to bring the knight into being: the nailed horseshoe, the stirrup, and the high-backed saddle. The nailed shoe transformed a knight's horse into a firm fighting platform that could take him into all but the most heavily wooded terrain. The stirrup traces back to fifth-century Korea. Nomads from the eastern steppes brought the stirrup into the Byzantine Empire, and from there its use spread into Europe. The stirrup allowed the rider a firmer seat on his mount; he could strike a blow and not unhorse himself. The high-backed saddle allowed the knight to transfer the energy of rider and mount into his weapon, to charge with couched lance and deliver a shattering impact. Without these things, there could be no knights as we know them, and these things were not present in Europe until 850 CE at the earliest.

In the tenth and eleventh centuries, the weapons of a knight were the lance and sword. The lance, which was a light spear with a broad leaf-shaped point, could be thrust like a spear or thrown like a javelin. Only at the end of this period did knights begin to charge with *couched* lances, that is, lances lowered to a horizontal position. By the thirteenth century, the lance had become longer, much heavier, and was used couched and only for charging.

The early broad-bladed sword for use in one hand was carried in a leather and wood scabbard. Sometimes a light-weight battle-axe with a single fan-shaped edge could be added. On occasion, a mace or iron-tipped club might be carried, especially if the knight had some church affiliation that forbade the shedding of blood. Knights did not use bows or crossbows in battle. By the thirteenth century, swords had increased in weight and length (with blades longer than 38 inches), becoming the "sword of war" with a two-handed grip. Short stabbing daggers became popular, as did heavy chopping swords called falchions. Danish-type axes with six-foot shafts became popular at this time, too.

For defense, a knight depended on his helmet, armor, and shield. The helmet was at first made of solid iron, with a conical or round shape, and an open face. A nasal guard, or bar, was added in the eleventh century. Later helmets were made of two joined pieces of metal, with a moveable visor covering the face. The visors could be decorated with ornate—even wildly grotesque—countenances.

Early armor consisted of a mail hauberk or coat handmade by a time-consuming process of winding metal wire around a rod and cutting the wire entirely down one side of the rod, producing dozens of open rings. These rings were then linked, overlapped, and the ends hammered shut and riveted. Such a mail coat usually reached to the knees, divided in front and back for riding, and had long sleeves. A hood of mail protected neck and chin, mail leggings protected lower extremities, and even mail gloves could be added to complete the ensemble. By the thirteenth and fourteenth centuries, plate armor had replaced mail among the richer knights, and weight became an important consideration. Some plate suits weighed over 90 pounds and required very large and strong (not to mention expensive) horses to carry such loads.

Around 1100, knights began to wear a loose-flowing linen garment or gown over their hauberks. At first these bore no designs, except possibly crosses, and offered little in the way of protection from rain or sun. Over time, these gowns became more elaborate and were emblazoned with the coat of arms of the wearer—an important feature because faces were hidden from view in battle and most knights were illiterate.

The typical tenth- and eleventh-century shield was made of wood covered with leather, concave or teardrop in shape (called kite shaped), round at the top and pointed at the bottom. It hung from around the neck by a strap and was held in the left hand by a shorter strap. Shields were usually painted with geometric designs, fantastic animals, and crosses. Originally, these designs had no purpose other than to indulge personal fancy and identify the bearer in battle or in tournaments. By 1150, however, a number of shield designs began to be passed on from father to son, thus initiating the system of heraldry. With the advent of plate armor, the shield became unnecessary. It was discarded, except in jousts.

The Hundred Years' War of 1333–1457 spelled the beginning of the end for knights on the battlefield. Dense infantry formations, based on the Swiss style and armed with long spears or pikes, could keep even the most determined knights at bay. Gunpowder weapons meant that even the heaviest armor could no longer protect knights from long-range death. Heavily armored cavalry quickly began to disappear from European warfare, replaced by more agile, and less expensive, horsemen. Knighthood became more an honorary title than a military one. Still, the romantic image of the knight has continued to flourish down through the generations. It lives today in the stories of King Arthur and his Round Table, and even in science fiction visions of the future made popular in films such as the *Star Wars* sagas.

References: Gies, Frances, *The Knight in History* (New York: Harper & Row, 1984); Oman, C.W.G., *The Art of War in the 16th Century* (New York: AMS Press, 1979 [1937]); Turnbull, Stephen, *The Book of the Medieval Knight* (New York: Crown, 1985).

Knights Hospitallers (Knights of St. John)

A religious order of knights created during the Crusades for the defense of pilgrims.

In the summer of 1099 CE, the Christian armies of the First Crusade captured the city of Jerusalem, which had been in Muslim hands since it was taken from the Byzantines by Caliph Omar in 638 CE. Within a few months, Baldwin I was crowned the first Christian King of Jerusalem. Baldwin quickly incorporated fiefdoms held by feudal warlords into one entity, known as the Latin Kingdom of Jerusalem.

The period after the First Crusade saw a large influx of European knights and soldiers to the newly established kingdom. Many had ties to feudal lords already established in the area. For these men there was already a strong feudal structure in place. Those without feudal ties were left to find a place for themselves in the new world. Into this void, the military orders were formed out of landless knights with no feudal overlord. Knights with wealth tended to gravitate toward the more prominent Sacred Order of the Knights Templar, while men without wealth gravitated toward smaller and less elite orders like the Order of Saint John of Jerusalem, also known as the Knights of St. John, or the Hospitaller Knights.

The order was founded on 15 February 1113 by Pope Paschal II. Its original charter was to protect caravan routes in the Holy Land, and run several hospitals that cared for sick pilgrims. The order had a reputation for being less militantly Christian than other orders, and not as harsh toward non-Christian inhabitants. The more popular orders like the Templars tended to attract more worldly men who were looking for riches and plunder, while the Hospitallers tended to attract those more interested in a monastic life of service. There was, of course, a military side to the Hospitallers. Within 50 years of being established, there was a clear split between brothers who cared for the sick and those who were strictly a military organization. The knights participated in every major military action fought in the Holy Land during the Crusader period, earning a reputation as a strong fighting force that was much more reliable than the fanatical Templars.

The fall of the city of Acre in 1291 ended Christian involvement in the Holy Land. The order moved to the island kingdom of Cyprus under the protection of its king. Unlike most who fled the Holy Land, the order was able to get away with riches intact, and quickly became a player in the politics of the eastern Mediterranean. The knights purchased and outfitted a small fleet of modern galleys, and quickly set their sights on the Byzantine island of Rhodes as their new home. After fighting several successful sea actions against the Byzantines, the Hospitallers took over the island on 15 August 1309. Rhodes would be the home base of the order for the next 200 years.

In 1312, the Knights Templar were disbanded, and most of their possessions were turned over to the Hospitallers. Within five years, the order's fleet dramatically expanded both in size and quality. The Hospitallers became a dominant Mediterranean sea power, able to sweep aside Barbary pirates who had plagued the eastern Mediterranean since the time of the Roman Empire. The order clashed almost continually with Muslim sea forces and, for a time, even considered expeditions to recover the Holy Land.

The powerful Ottoman Empire vowed to crush the Hospitallers and launched frequent attacks against their holdings, including two invasions of Rhodes. However, the order always seemed a step ahead. In 1444, they crushed a large Ottoman army, which was forced to withdraw from Rhodes. The order's fleet harassed the Ottomans all the way back to Egypt. This episode became a great embarrassment to the Ottomans. After the fall of Constantinople in 1453, Sultan Memhed II, decided he had had enough of the order, and started assembling an overwhelming military force with which to crush it. Memhed would not live long enough to see his dream come to fruition, but in 1522 Sultan Suleiman I attacked the order on Rhodes with a force of 200,000 men and over 400 warships. Against a force this large, the order's fleet was driven back into the safe harbor of Rhodes and the 15,000-man military settled in to defend the walls of the city. In past sieges, the Hospitallers' fleet was able to run the blockade and bring in needed supplies. In this siege, the Ottoman fleet was so large and the blockade so complete that no supplies were able to reach the city. The Ottomans, though, were not able to take the city by force. The small army of the order fought so fiercely that after seven months the Ottomans agreed to allow the remaining members of the order to leave the island with all their possessions.

In 1530, the Hospitallers were reestablished on the island of Malta by King Charles V of Spain. Within a year, they continued their naval attacks on the Barbary pirates, who were now a client state of the Ottomans in all but name. Over the next 10 years, the corsairs of the order,

with their Venetian mercenary crews, wrought havoc on the shipping of the eastern Mediterranean. Once again, this brought them into conflict with the powerful Ottomans. In 1565, a vast Ottoman fleet arrived at Malta, bringing an army of some 100,000 men. To oppose this, the order was able to field a very small but highly elite force of 400-500 knights, along with about 6,000 mercenaries. The defenders were deployed in some of the most impressive defensive fortifications seen to date, and after a year of intense fighting the Ottomans finally gave up the venture, losing close to 30,000 men.

The order's last organized military action was at the battle of Lepanto as part of the Christian fleet that opposed their old enemy, the Ottoman Empire. The boarding ability of the Hospitaller marines turned the tide on the left flank of the battle, allowing the Christian fleet to flank the Ottomans and carry the day. So complete was the Christian victory that the naval power of the Ottomans in the Mediterranean was broken forever.

From a tactical point of view, there is much to admire about the Knights Hospitallers. At a time when European wars were being won and lost based on outmoded tactics, the knights of the order were able to constantly change and adapt their military system to fit changing times. Throughout the Crusades, the order fielded an elite mounted strike force of heavily armed knights backed by lesser armed sergeants. These troops operated as mounted lancers, with the impact of the cavalry charge as their main strike weapon. The liberal treatment of local inhabitants allowed the order to bolster this mounted strike force with Christianized light cavalrymen armed with short lance and bow, who gave the order a decided edge in combat. Most Christian armies of the day relied on leading the battle with a charge of armored knights that was considered "the point of the lance," followed by mass attacks by infantry. Their Muslim enemies relied on masses of horse archers, used to soften up the enemy, who were then followed up by lightly armed lancer cavalry. The Hospitallers used the best parts of both tactics, creating an army that first attacked the enemy with mass missile fire from highly trained horse archers, and then followed this up with the irresistible charge of the mounted knights. Infantry was normally limited to lightly armed crossbowmen used to defend castles and hospitals.

Following the collapse of the Crusader kingdoms, the Hospitallers augmented their land armies by becoming a major naval power. In order to adapt to life on Rhodes, the order shifted its land army from a system based on mobile mounted warfare to an army primarily made up of large numbers of infantry militia, backed by heavily armored knights who often fought dismounted. Using knights to bolster the strength of the militia was a major innovation in this region. The wealth of the order allowed them to field the very latest equipment. A major factor in the successful defense of Rhodes was the vast stores of crossbow bolts available for battle.

The order also became adept at the art of fortification. The defenses on Rhodes were some of the most advanced of the day. The completely walled harbor gave the order's fleet a major advantage because it offered a safe harbor from which to launch operations against enemies. At sea, the order was one of the first naval powers to field large numbers of modern Venetian-style galleys. In the early years following the introduction of this type of vessel, the order became

the shipbuilder's biggest client. The speed of these ships gave the order supremacy over other Mediterranean naval powers. Another advantage was that the order was able to use rowing crews of free men on their ships, something that had not been seen on a large scale in the Mediterranean since the time of the Athenians. All of these innovations at sea allowed the order to deploy entire fleets of mobile ships with crews that could all be counted on to fight. This gave the ships of the order superiority in boarding actions. In a ship-to-ship boarding action, they would usually outnumber and out-armor any opponent.

On Malta, the order was again able to change land tactics. It no longer had the large militia structure in place that it had employed on Rhodes, so instead it fielded an army primarily of highly paid and specialized mercenaries from all over Europe. The foundation of the army was still the heavily armored knight who now fought primarily on foot with a heavy pole weapon. The wealth of the order allowed these knights to wear the most modern of armor, making them all but invulnerable in hand-to-hand combat. Venetian marines were recruited in large numbers, both to fight on the order's corsairs and as a land force to support the knights. These men were normally armed with heavy pole arms and crossbows. Large numbers of hand gunners and artillerymen from Spain were recruited along with light crossbowmen from France and Switzerland. There were even small longbow contingents from England who fought as mercenaries on Malta. Mercenaries were organized into fighting groups called Langes, based on language. This allowed orders to be transmitted quickly and efficiently.

As was the case on Rhodes, the order advanced the art of fortification building on Malta. Immediately after taking possession of Malta, the best master builders in Europe were hired to strengthen existing fortifications. Some of the advances were routine, like strengthening and heightening walls, while others were major innovations like dedicated structures designed to use as gunpowder artillery platforms. These platforms had self-contained powder and munitions magazines, which gave a rate of fire that the Ottoman attackers were not able to match. The knights of the order also used a long-existing siege technique in order to sally out against the enemy siege lines. This involved mass artillery at a small point, with dismounted, heavily armed knights moving out under the cover of smoke to rupture the enemy lines. This was to prove very dangerous to the Ottomans attacking Malta, who continually had their camps overrun, with great loss in materiel and munitions. By the time the relief army arrived from Sicily, the Ottomans had already lost most of their artillery to capture and counter-battery fire.

In the years following the battle of Lepanto, the order fell into the hands of men who were less interested in defending the faith and more concerned with turning a profit. Malta became a major slave trading port, and the ships of the order were manned by some of the most dangerous pirates in the Mediterranean. The Emperor Napoleon finally broke the power of the Hospitallers in 1798, when his forces captured the island of Malta.

The order exists today as a humanitarian organization named the Sovereign Military Order of Malta. Its members have participated as United Nations observers in Somalia, Angola and Liberia.

References: Alliott, E. A. *The Rhodes Missal*, London: Order of St. John,1980; Barber, M. C. *The Military Orders: Fighting for the Faith and Caring for the Sick*, Variorum, 1995; Bradford, E. *The Shield and the Sword: the Knights of St. John of Jerusalem, Rhodes and Malta*, New York, Penguin, 2002; Nicholson, Helen, D, *Knights Hospitaller*, Boydell & Brewer, 2006; Nicolle, David. *Knight Hospitaller: 1100–1306*, Osprey, 2001; Pickles, T. *Malta 1565* Praeger Publishers, 2005; Riley-Smith, J *Hospitallers: The History of the Order of St. John*, Hambledon & London Publishers, 2003; Riley-Smith, J. *The Knights of St. John in Jerusalem and Cyprus 1050-1310*, Hambledon & London, 1967.

Knights Templar

An organization of religious warriors in the Middle Ages.

The early twelfth century saw two major developments in European society: the Crusades to reclaim the Christian Holy Land from Muslim rule and the armored knight to do the fighting.

The knight was the cream of European feudal society. He swore loyalty to the aristocrat or king above him and received similar loyalty from vassals below him. A man with lands and income, the feudal knight was able to afford the necessary accoutrements for serious warfare and supplied himself with horse, armor, and weapons. These warriors, fighting as heavy cavalry, responded to the call of Pope Urban II in 1097 to march to the Holy Land and liberate it from the possession of the Muslims. The knights succeeded in establishing European control in Jerusalem and the area surrounding it, dominating the eastern Mediterranean coastal region from Turkey to the Red Sea. However, one of the main goals of the Crusades—the protection of Christian pilgrims to holy sites in the Middle East—was not accomplished. The Europeans controlled the major cities, but were too few in number to control the countryside. It was this need for protection of European pilgrims that brought the Knights Templar into existence.

In 1118, a French knight, Hugh de Payans, offered his services to the newly installed king of Jerusalem, Baldwin II, to organize a force to patrol and protect the countryside. Baldwin assigned de Payans quarters at the al-Aqsa Mosque, reputedly the site of Solomon's Temple, hence the name for de Payans's new organization—the Poor Fellow Soldiers of Christ and the Temple of Solomon. At a time when most European nobility were obsessed with gathering wealth any way they could (and many had profited in land and money during the Crusades), the knights who joined the Templars were as ascetic as monks. They wore second-hand clothing and lived by charity. Theirs was a poor existence without worldly diversions. Gambling, fraternizing with women, and hunting were banned. In 1128 the new hierarchy of the Catholic Church, riding a wave of reform, recognized the Templars as a force that could be controlled by them and that would swear no loyalty to king or aristocrat.

The result was basically a force of fighting monks. They trained in and mastered the martial skills of the age, but never had huge numbers. Rarely did Templars fight in groups of more than a few hundred, about 500 being the maximum on duty in the Holy Land, with some 2,000 support troops. They established a network of recruiters throughout Europe that maintained a steady supply of men to the ranks. Many of those who joined were not aristocrats, but outlaws or excommunicants. Nevertheless, as long as they swore to fight for God and their fellow Templars, they were accepted. The Templars' success spawned other, similar elite units dedicated

to fighting for God's kingdom on earth. These organizations sometimes fought among themselves, but always united in the face of the infidel threat.

The Templars started out fulfilling their role as protectors by building forts, patrolling the roads, and attacking Muslim bands or strongholds. They even forced tribute from the infamous order of the Assassins. All of this construction and military activity required funding, and the recruiting groups in Europe also raised money. In doing so, the order became fabulously wealthy and they became history's first international bankers. In order to pay for recruitment, training, and the needs of the knights in the Holy Land, the Templars had to have sufficient funds to pay for these things no matter where the necessity arose, so a promissory note from one Templar headquarters was payable at any other. Their annual income reached the equivalent of billions of dollars in today's terms. They received vast amounts of land, donated by nobles who did not go to the Holy Land but wanted to contribute, or by nobles who joined and pledged their wealth to the order. It is said that by 1250 the Templars controlled 9,000 manors throughout Europe and the Holy Lands.

The Knights Templar were organized into a hierarchy with the Grand Master at the top, followed by the Seneschal, Provincial Marshals, Commander of the Land and Realm of Jerusalem, and the commander of the fleet based at Acre. The Knights wore white mantles with a red cross emblazoned on front and back. Lower ranks had the red cross sewn onto brown or black clothing. The organization's banner was black on top and white beneath; black symbolizing their sternness toward their enemies and the white their devotion to Christianity.

After the end of the Crusades in the late thirteenth century, the Knights Templar were left without a military role. Instead, they turned to banking. Not just their wealth, but also their secretive ways, excited jealousy—even among kings. Eventually, Philip IV of France campaigned against the Knights Templar in an attempt to replenish his own coffers and acquire the Templars' lands. He accused them of a variety of heinous crimes, supported with confessions tortured out of captured Templars. Fifty-four knights were burned at the stake in 1310 and within two years the order was almost completely suppressed. Since that time, however, the Knights Templar have become almost mythical. Persecuted knights fled, taking their wealth and military knowledge to distant lands. The nature of the order's origins, based in what was supposedly Solomon's Temple, led to legendary attributions of mystical powers to the Knights Templar, which they allegedly gained by acquiring religious artifacts found there. Even into the modern day, superstitions about the ultimate fate of the Knights Templar abound: Recent books have claimed that the Templars possessed the Holy Grail and that Christ did not rise to Heaven after his resurrection but moved to France to wed and father children with Mary Magdalene— their descendants being in one way or another involved with a Templar/Masonic conspiracy. The truth is undoubtedly more prosaic: Like most of the orders of their time, the Knights Templar outlived their mission and usefulness with the end of the Crusades.

References: Campbell, George, *The Knights Templar, Their Rise and Fall* (New York: Robert McBride, 1937); Norman, A.V.B., *The Medieval Soldier* (New York: Thomas Y. Crowell, 1971); Partner, Peter, *The Murdered Magicians: The Templars and Their Myth* (New York: Oxford University Press, 1982).

L

Lafayette Escadrille (Escadrille Americaine)

American volunteer pilots fighting for France in World War I.

Well before the United States officially entered the First World War, American volunteers joined the French Air Service. They came to fight against Germany through a number of avenues, including the French Foreign Legion and the American Field Service of ambulance drivers. Some, stranded in France when war broke out, joined other Americans to offer their services. Few were pilots when they joined, but the lure of flying was much greater once they learned, firsthand or through reports, of life in the trenches.

A painting of the Nieuport 12, along with the insignia of the Lafayette Escadrille. Courtesy of Paul Davis.

The originator of the unit was the American Norman Prince. He was in France when the Germans invaded, vacationing there as he had done many times before. He wanted to assist France, so he returned home to Marblehead, Massachusetts, entered a flying school, and began looking for other volunteers. He fell in with Frazier Curtis, who also wanted to assist the Allies but thought he would rather join the British Royal Flying Corps. After receiving his pilot's license, Prince returned to France in March 1915 and joined the French army. Because of his flying ability, he was assigned to a French pilot training school, where he learned the rudiments of aerial combat. He also haunted the streets of Paris, seeking out other Americans to join him, and there he met two African-Americans, Bob Scanlon and Eugene Bullard. Bullard joined up, earned his wings, and flew for a while, but later lost interest in flying and ended the war fighting with the French army in the trenches. Scanlon also joined and became an observer, flying in the rear of two-seater scout aircraft.

The French authorities were skeptical of training an entire unit of volunteers, so Prince flew with a French bomber squadron for eight months before he got the opportunity to organize an all-American unit. He was rejoined by Frazier Curtis, who had decided against joining the Royal Flying Corps, and together they began to actively seek permission to form an all-American squadron. Curtis worked with an American doctor in Paris, Edmund Gros, who had connections in the French government and with important people in the United States. He gained the financial assistance of William Vanderbilt, a Francophile whose donations supported both the American Field Service and the attempt to organize a flying squadron. Prince and Curtis finally received approval of their plan in July 1915, but the paperwork was not completed and the unit not officially organized until April 20, 1916. Prince had in the meantime collected six more Americans who had fought with the French Army and were looking for a way out of the trenches: Bill Thaw, Victor Chapman, Kiffin Rockwell, James McConnell, Eliot Cowdin, and Bert Hall. Two French officers, Captain Georges Thennault and Lieutenant de Laage de Meux, were assigned to teach them combat flying and tactics and to serve as a liaison with the French government. They were given Nieuport 17s, the standard French fighter plane of the time. Later in the war they would be given SPADs, but the lighter, more maneuverable Nieuport remained their favorite.

Their first combat mission was in May of 1916, but it involved only an unsuccessful attack on three German scout planes and resulted in a number of holes in the Nieuport aircraft from antiaircraft fire. The experience showed that the Americans had more enthusiasm than self-control or discipline. The first victory in the air occurred on May 16 with Kiffin Rockwell receiving credit. In August, the squadron, called the Escadrille Americaine, received more pilots. Among them was Raoul Lufbery, a French-born naturalized American who would become the most famous member of the group and the leading ace, with 19 confirmed victories over German aircraft. By late summer, the Escadrille was becoming fairly well known, and the fact that the pilots were Americans brought diplomatic complaints from Germany. The group renamed their squadron the Lafayette Escadrille in an attempt to downplay their nationality, as the United States was still many months away from joining the conflict. In September 1916, the Escadrille suffered its first loss when Kiffin Rockwell was killed in combat. Norman Prince was killed in mid-October.

The Lafayette Escadrille's actual impact on the air war in France was certainly no greater than that of many other squadrons, but its existence provided a morale boost in many ways. The French civilians living near their airfields always went to great lengths to assist the pilots and provide for their needs and wants. The squadron responded by playing on its notoriety and enhancing it. The members followed the already established practice of creating a squadron insignia to be displayed on their aircraft. The pilots believed that because they were the first American pilots in France, the first Americans, the Indians, should provide the squadron's emblem. A screaming profile painted in bright colors was adapted from the logo of the Savage Arms Company. The pilots also advertised themselves by their choice of squadron mascot. Along with the usual collection of animals that congregate around airfields and military bases, four of the pilots on leave in Paris joined together to buy a four-month-old lion cub, which came to be called Whiskey. A year later they bought Whiskey a mate, which they named Soda. Such actions enhanced their public relations value both in France and the United States, but of course led to exaggerations by the press. There was also some exaggeration concerning the size of the organization. The Lafayette Escadrille, officially designated in the French Air Service as N.124 (later Spa.124), comprised only 38 Americans. Other Americans who flew for the French wanted a special designation in recognition of their status, so all American volunteer pilots were given membership in what came to be called the Lafayette Flying Corps. This semiofficial organization ultimately numbered more than 200 men, including the members of the Lafayette Escadrille.

When the United States declared war in April 1917, many in the Escadrille thought they would be transferred to the American Aviation Service. Colonel Billy Mitchell was sent to command such a service in France, but he was sent alone and without authority to bring Americans under arms from out of British or French service. For several months the French government continued to recruit American volunteers and train them as pilots. Thus, the men stayed under French command until February 1918 when the Lafayette Escadrille was incorporated into the United States Air Service (U.S.A.S.) as the 103d Pursuit Squadron. The pilots received commissions in the United States military, but remained attached to French units and operated from French airfields. Over time, the veterans were assigned to command newly arriving American squadrons in order to share their expertise.

References: Mason, Herbert Malloy, *The Lafayette Escadrille* (New York: Random House, 1964); Whitehouse, Arch, *Legion of the Lafayette* (New York: Doubleday, 1962); *The Years of the Sky Kings* (New York: Doubleday, 1964).

Lincoln Battalion

A unit of American volunteers that fought in the Spanish Civil War between 1936 and 1938.

In February 1936, the Spanish people elected, by an extremely slim majority, a coalition of representatives from the Popular Front to their government, the Cortes. This was a group of people of mixed political standing, favoring democracy, socialism, communism, and anarchy. Although the coalition was probably too disorganized to rule effectively, the conservatives in Spain were horrified and convinced that stable government was about to come to an end. This seemed to be confirmed as the government began to make friendly overtures to the Soviet Union. Many members of the army began to plot a coup, gathering around the leadership of General Francisco Franco. Referred to as Nationalists, Franco and his supporters were based in Spanish Morocco. However, with the assistance of Adolph Hitler, they were airlifted into Spain and in July 1936, the Spanish Civil War broke out. More than 30,000 soldiers in the regular army remained loyal to the government, but equal that number in Spain, reinforced by another 30,000 from Morocco, gave Franco a potent force. This potency was augmented by Hitler, who provided aircraft, and by Italy's dictator Benito Mussolini, who provided troops, aircraft, and heavy weapons.

Members of the elected Spanish government (who came to be called Republicans) sought aid from other countries, but few were willing to assist. Through the League of Nations, most said that the conflict in Spain was an internal matter and therefore not something with which the international community should become involved. Thus, while Franco received much military assistance, only the Soviet Union offered any aid to the Republicans—and the Soviets offered this at high prices. Any other aid that came to the Republicans was from volunteers, which included young intellectuals from around the world who saw the civil war as the first attempt to stop the spread of fascism. In North America and western Europe, volunteers joined Republican recruiters to go to Spain and fight for freedom and democracy. Almost all of the recruiters were communists, but they called for volunteers under a variety of names, mostly popular fronts of one stripe or another. In the United States, the primary recruiting bureau was the North American Committee to Aid Spanish Democracy. Although the organizers were communists, the number of volunteers who actually believed in Marxism is impossible to determine. However, it was almost certainly more than half.

Approximately 3,000 Americans responded to the call, of which about 600 were seamen and 500 were college students. Only about 100 of them had any military training. The oldest was 54, but most were in their twenties. They formed three units: the Washington Battalion, the Lincoln Battalion, and the American-Canadian Mackenzie-Papineau Battalion. Owing to high casualties, the Washington Battalion was absorbed into the Lincoln Battalion fairly early in the conflict. In order to give the impression of a larger American interest, the Spanish always referred to the unit as the Lincoln Brigade, but it was actually part of the Fifteenth International Brigade, made up of the three North American battalions joined with battalions from Britain, France, and Yugoslavia. The troops were commanded by a Yugoslav, Colonel Vladimir Copic.

Because both British and French governments had officially discouraged volunteers, neither country cared to have Americans pass through on their way to Spain. The French, although they occasionally arrested an American, for the most part turned a blind eye to the volunteers, who sneaked across the Franco-Spanish border and joined the Republicans at Tarazona, west of the Mediterranean coastal city of Valencia. There they received—at first, at any rate—only rudimentary training before being thrown into combat in Madrid. There, in February 1937, the International Brigade assisted in beating back a Nationalist attack on the capital.

Although the volunteers gained only slight experience during this battle, their divisional commander ordered the International Brigade to follow the Nationalists and dislodge them from a very strong position on Pingarron Hill in the Jarama River Valley. The Lincoln Battalion was given the key position in the attack, but the entire plan was faulty and the assault doomed. Promised air, armor, and artillery support never materialized, and the Americans (after a protest by their commander) attacked into a hail of Nationalist fire that inflicted 65 percent casualties. The brigade and divisional commanders should never have ordered this attack, but to the American survivors it was their own battalion commander, Robert Merriman, who received the blame for following orders he knew to be suicidal. The Battle of Jarama was the Lincoln Battalion's baptism of fire, and a costly one.

The Americans' second battle took place four months later. Franco's forces had kept up a steady artillery bombardment of Madrid, and the Republicans hoped a diversionary attack would ease the pressure on the capital. They sent 85,000 men, including the Americans, toward the village of Brunete, 20 miles west of Madrid. The Lincoln and Washington Battalions were to bypass the village and secure the high ground, the Mosquito Crest. This time, armor was there for support, but it was badly deployed. The tanks sped ahead of the infantry, and the Americans were easy targets for the Nationalists on the hilltop. The result was almost as bad as Jarama had been. The battalion's new commander, Oliver Law, was killed in the battle. Law was an African-American veteran of the U.S. Army. His place was taken by Commissar Steve Nelson, a Croatian-American communist from Pittsburgh. The commissar acted as second-in-command, as well as being the political, morale, and liaison officer. The battle ended in a stalemate, but as Franco diverted large numbers of his men to recapture Brunete, it did ease the Nationalist siege of Madrid.

The Republican cause scored a few successes, but they were always overturned by superior Nationalist fire power in Franco's counteroffensives. Meanwhile, the Republican cause was further harmed by political infighting between rival leaders in the Republican command structure. This went so far as to result in combat between anarchists and communists in Barcelona in May 1937. Political struggles within the American ranks have also been reported. Unconfirmed reports tell of executions not only for desertion, but also for spreading anti-Stalinist propaganda. Even if executions were rare and only for desertion, other reports claim that unpopular political statements often resulted in assignments to the most dangerous areas of the battle. Despite this, the major political arguments took place at the highest levels and the Americans did not seem to have been involved, or even to have taken much notice of them.

The Lincoln Battalion fought in the battles of Aragon and Teurel in late 1937 and early 1938. It performed well in the conquest of Zaragoza, the capital of Aragon, capturing the village of Quito and 1,000 Nationalist prisoners. Franco's counterattack, however, forced the Americans out. After Republican forces captured the town of Teurel around Christmas, the Lincoln Battalion was sent into defensive positions there. When Franco launched a massive offensive to retake the town in March 1938, the Lincoln Battalion was virtually wiped out. Pounded by air and artillery, they could do little but cower under what protection they could find. They finally split into two groups to attempt to return to Republican positions. The Americans found themselves behind Nationalist lines and spent weeks roaming the hills in small bands. When they finally returned to Republican lines on the Ebro River, they numbered no more than 100.

Although the few remaining men fought in a last battle along the Ebro in the summer of 1938, they were no longer a real unit. The International Brigade had by this time become predominantly Spanish owing to the large number of replacements brought in over the course of the war. In September 1938, Spanish Prime Minister Juan Negrin announced the withdrawal of all foreign soldiers fighting for the Republican cause. It has been argued that he did this on Stalin's orders, because the Soviet leader then had no more hope of shaming western democracies into action. It is also possible Negrin hoped that a public withdrawal of his foreign troops would pressure Franco to do the same. By that time, the Lincoln Battalion was made up of 200 Spaniards and 80 Americans. They marched through Barcelona in a farewell parade in October. Spanish communist leader Dolores Ibarruri told them: "You can go proudly. You are history. You are the heroic example of democracy's solidarity and universality. We shall not forget you, and, when the olive tree of peace puts forth its leaves again, mingled with the laurels of the Spanish Republic's victory—come back" (Meisler, 1995). Not until Franco died and his dictatorship came to an end in the 1970s were any of these veterans able to return.

The Americans who returned to their country in 1938 were for a time treated as heroes by the public, and many fought for the United States in World War II a few years later. However, in the anticommunist hysteria of the McCarthy era, these veterans were branded as communists. Some of their number were arrested under the Smith Act, which prohibited advocacy of the violent overthrow of the government. One of the arrested veterans, Alvah Bessie, was a member of the famous Hollywood Ten jailed for contempt of Congress in 1954. Many former volunteers in the Spanish Civil War fled the United States to escape political repression. How many of them were communists, either before or after the Spanish Civil War, is difficult to tell, but McCarthy's broad brush tarred them all. Communist or not, the members of the Lincoln Battalion did fight for a cause they believed in: to halt the spread of fascism. It was a cause much of the world was obliged to embrace not long after the members of the Lincoln Battalion did.

References: Eby, Cecil, *Between the Bullet and the Lie* (New York: Holt, Rinehart, & Winston, 1969); Lawson, Don, *The Abraham Lincoln Brigade* (New York: Thomas Crowell, 1989); Meisler, Stanley, "The Lincoln Battalion," in *Military History Quarterly*, vol. 8, no. 1 (Autumn, 1995); Rosenstone, Robert, *Crusade of the Left* (New York: Pegasus, 1969).

Lombards

A tribe from northern Germany that conquered and settled in Italy after the fall of the Roman Empire.

The Lombards first appear in recorded history in the fifth century, during the later stages of the Roman Empire. The Romans gave them their name, *langobard*, or "long beard." Although known to fight occasionally against either their neighbors or the Romans, the Lombards tended at first to be peaceful pastoral people. Throughout the fourth and fifth centuries they began to migrate southward into the Danube River region known as Pannonia, modern Austria. The Lombards fought for Byzantine Emperor Justinian in his campaigns against the Ostrogoths in the Italian peninsula and received favored status during his rule. His successors, however, favored the Gepids, a hostile tribe neighboring the Lombards. Fearing a war against the Gepids supported by the Byzantines, the Lombards under their king, Alboin, allied themselves with a tribe newly arrived from central Asia, the Avars. Together they were victorious and split the Gepids' lands between them.

In the middle of the sixth century, the Lombards established a new tribal organization based on an aristocratic hierarchy. Dukes and counts commanded clans organized into military units (*farae*), all serving under a king. It was with this new organization that the Lombards, now in fear of their former allies, the Avars, decided in the late 560s to migrate farther into the Italian peninsula. As the long-running war between the Ostrogoths and the Byzantine Empire had left a power vacuum in northern Italy, the Lombards were able to move in and take over fairly easily. By 572, under Alboin's leadership, they had conquered the entire northern peninsula to the Po River, and then, occasionally, districts in southern and eastern Italy.

Alboin was murdered shortly after the Lombards' arrival in Italy, and for the next few decades the tribe struggled internally while they exploited the indigenous people and countryside.

Within Lombard society, military service was required in times of emergency.

The nature of the soldiery depended on one's wealth and land possession. The largest landowners were each obliged to provide a horse, some armor, and a lance. The middle-class landowners had to supply a horse and a lance, while the small landowner brought a shield and bows and arrows. As in many earlier cultures, the wealthy, who could afford to raise and maintain horses, served as cavalry. Each man came to the colors as a member of his clan and followed his local lord, with provincial forces gathering under the leadership of a *dux*. Usually the nobility also brought warrior bands called *Gasindii*, full-time soldiers who swore personal loyalty to their lords. Also serving with the Lombards were mercenaries, whose makeup depended on shifting alliances, the relative power of neighbors, or the region of conflict. Magyars, Avars, Normans, Germans, and even Saracens served at one time or another in Lombard armies.

The Lombards established themselves as the dominant force in northern Italy, but they adapted readily to the existing agricultural framework in the area, believing that whatever the Romans had organized was the best format for agricultural production. The tribal dukes exercised the most power, with little or no central control. Only when threatened from outside, by the Franks, did the Lombards again form a united front. In 590 the Lombards elected the duke of Turin, Agiluf, to the kingship and, establishing a capital at Pavia, he reconsolidated Lombard power. King Rothari, who ruled in the mid-seventh century, issued a legal code for his people along the lines of that produced by Justinian in Constantinople. The leading Lombard king was Liutprand (712–744), who further focused on the internal needs of his kingdom. Later in his reign, he reinstituted the campaign against Byzantine power in Italy.

The Lombard incursion into Italy frightened the pope. At first the Lombards practiced Arian Christianity, which denied the equality of God and Jesus. Their military success, coupled with their heretical views, posed a threat to orthodox Catholicism. Even when they converted to orthodox views in the late seventh century, Lombard power remained a source of concern for the pope. When the Lombards under King Aistulf captured Ravenna in 751 and threatened Rome in 754, Pope Stephen II appealed to the Franks for deliverance. Pepin the Short, first of the Carolingian dynasty, marched to Italy and defeated the Lombards in 754 and 756. Pepin recaptured Ravenna and gave land to the church, creating the Papal States. In return, the pope anointed Pepin as King of the Franks and Defender of Rome.

Aistulf remained as king of the Lombards, but his successor Desiderus was defeated by another Frank, Pepin's grandson Charlemagne, in 773. Charlemagne made himself king of the Lombards and incorporated northern Italy into the Holy Roman Empire, thus bringing to an end the Lombards' independent existence.

Although their rule in Italy was often harsh, the Lombards did contribute to the country's heritage. Much of the legal system of the area descends from Lombard practice. King Rothri, who reigned in the mid-600s, issued a code of law patterned after that compiled by Justinian in Constantinople. One of the most important aspects of Rothri's code was the attempt to end the practice of *vendetta*, or personal revenge. Instead, the personal feud was to be replaced by monetary payment for damages. This was known as *guidrigild*, which appears in later Scandinavian cultures as *weregild*. The Lombards' greatest effect, however, was indirect, in that they removed Byzantine power in Italy once and for all. This ended any chance of Eastern Orthodoxy challenging papal authority in western Europe. In the eleventh century, Lombardy dominated the trade routes from the Mediterranean into the European continent. The resulting wealth gave the Lombards commercial and financial leadership, which later translated into political power when they formed the Lombard League, which resisted the invasion of Frederick Barbarossa of Germany in 1176.

References: Bona, Istvan, *The Dawn of the Dark Ages: The Gepids and the Lombards* (Budapest: Corvina Press, 1976); Hallenbeck, Jan, *Pavia and Rome: The Lombard Monarchy and the Papacy in the Eighth Century* (Philadelphia: American Philosophical Society, 1982); Paul the Deacon, tr. by W.D. Foulke, *History of the Langobards* (Philadelphia: University of Pennsylvania Press, 1974).

Long Range Desert Group

A British commando unit operating in North Africa during World War II.

In 1940, the British forces based in Egypt were isolated and outnumbered, with their primary threat being several divisions of the Italian army based in Libya. If the Italians were to attack the British base at Wadi Halfa on the Nile River, it would effectively sever contact between British forces in Cairo and in the Sudan at Khartoum. This would have been the only supply route available, had the Italian navy controlled the Red Sea. It also would have laid the dams at Aswan open to attack. The Italians could also strike southward toward French Equatorial Africa, dominating it before the French administration there could decide whether to support the Free French under de Gaulle. As the Italian positions were too far from Cairo or Alexandria for British aircraft to patrol, the only way to gain information on Italian actions or plans was on the ground.

In World War I, a small force of British troops had organized the Light Car Patrols, which scouted the deserts fairly successfully with modified Ford Model Ts. Between the wars, a small group of independent British officers had explored the deserts on their own, testing theories about operations in the desert. They learned lessons about food, water, fuel, and navigation. One of those officers was R. A. Bagnold, a major in the Royal Corps of Signals. When World War II broke out, he proposed an updated version of the Light Car Patrols, and in July 1940 British General Archibald Wavell granted him permission to organize such a unit. As everything was in short supply, the newly formed Long Range Desert Group had to scrounge for everything from weapons to vehicles. The vehicles they appropriated were one-and-a-half-ton Chevrolets bought in Cairo or begged from the Egyptian Army. These were modified with extra-strong springs, had the cabs and doors removed, and had condensers fitted to the radiators. The Group's first recruits were from the New Zealand Division, while later volunteers came from the British Brigade of Guards, the Yeomanry, and the Rhodesian army.

The Long Range Desert Group was ultimately organized into columns of five vehicles with one officer and 15 men. Each truck was fitted out with at least two machine guns and often with a 37-mm Bofors antitank gun in the bed or, later, captured Italian Breda 20-mm guns. The men learned to live in the field for weeks at

a time on six pints of water a day and with all their meals coming out of tin cans. They also learned to navigate in the desert, which is much like navigating at sea. A sun compass was used, because a magnetic compass often gave false readings from the trucks' magnetic fields. Using a compass and odometer, they drove to their targets by dead reckoning with amazing accuracy. They also developed techniques for driving through the Libyan desert, most notably the use of sections of steel track to get out of deep sand.

The Long Range Desert Group went into operation in August 1940. Its first bit of intelligence was that the Italians were planning none of the threatening operations that the British had feared. This meant that the Group could go on the offensive themselves, as well as keep up their primary task of reconnaissance. They began raiding Italian outposts and supply convoys, striking just often enough to keep the enemy unbalanced and looking over his shoulder. In January 1941 the Group sent 75 men in 25 trucks to assault the Italian fort at Murzuq, a journey of 1,500 miles from Cairo. They made the trip to the fort in 17 days, stopping just short of their destination to pick up five members of the Free French forces from Fort Lamy in Equatorial Africa (modern Chad), who had brought extra fuel supplies. The attack was a total surprise and destroyed the fort and three aircraft for the loss of two killed and three wounded. This success encouraged Free French forces under General Leclerc to attack and capture the major Italian post at Kufra on March 1, 1941. The Long Range Desert Group began using Kufra as an advanced base after this time. Over time, the Sudan Defense Force began to garrison Kufra and a much steadier flow of supplies started to arrive.

For the remainder of 1941, the Group constantly patrolled the Libyan desert, attacking Italian patrols and supply columns, as well as scouting potential routes for attack for the British army based in Egypt. In November 1941 the major British offensive, code named "Crusader," benefitted from the information that the Group obtained. Also in that month, the unit began operations with the Special Air Service (SAS), a commando organization formed by Major David Sterling. For several months, the Long Range Desert Group ferried the SAS troops to a point just short of their target, then evacuated them after their raids. This continued successfully until the SAS began to acquire its own vehicles. The Long Range Desert Group continued to raid and patrol until the final defeat of the German and Italian forces in the North African desert in May 1943. The Group's harassment of their supply lines was a major source of chagrin for Axis commanders and one they were rarely able to effectively combat.

References: Cowles, Virginia, *The Phantom Major* (New York: Harper & Bros., 1958); Kennedy Shaw, Major W.B., "Britain's Private Armies," in *History of the Second World War* (London: BBC Publishing, 1966); Swinson, Arthur, *The Raiders: Desert Strike Force* (New York: Ballantine, 1968)

Longbowmen, English

Specialist archers originating in Wales in medieval times

An old Scottish saying dictates that, "Every English archer carries on his belt 24 Scots." From the thirteenth until the sixteenth century, there was no question why the longbow held the Scots' respect, as it became the national weapon of the English military. It transformed the English army

Longbowmen in the Battle of Crecy during the Hundred Years' War. Source: http://www.english.upenn.edu/~jhsy/battle-crecy.html. From 15th century illuminated manuscript, Jean Froissart's Chronicles (Bib. Nat. Fr., FR 2643, fol. 165v).

into one of the most powerful military forces in the medieval world, surpassing even the might of its rival the French and their impetuous knights. In a relatively short period of some 300 years, the longbow conquered Wales and Scotland, and reached the pinnacle of efficiency when it was the deadly weapon of choice employed by Edward III and the Black Prince in their victories over the French during the Hundred Years' War.

The rise of the longbow begins in the Anglo-Norman invasion of Wales in the twelfth century, where Welsh archers using a unique type of bow exacted huge losses on the invaders. After the successful, but costly, campaign was over, the English were quick to realize the potential of such a devastating weapon. By the end of the century, Welsh archers were already being conscripted in large numbers as a supplementary force within the English army. The army, bolstered by the new mercenaries, proceeded to achieve decisive victories over the Scots and the French. A force that could not be ignored, the English stopped using mercenaries and mandated the creation and practice of the longbow among their non-noble regular troops. Royal decrees were issued concerning days of practice, conditions, even ranges: Henry VIII declared that no archer could practice at a distance under 220 yards, in order to increase his effectiveness.

The accessibility of the longbow among even the poor would prove the deciding factor in a number of battles, the two most significant being the Battle of Crécy and later, the Battle of Agincourt during the Hundred Years' War in the fourteenth century. Even at home, the English nobility was careful not to push the yeomen too far out of fear of the possible destructive results, as witnessed in the Peasants' Revolt of the late fourteenth century. The longbow single-handedly gave the peasant class of England a check on the gentry's power not seen on the mainland of Europe. Cheap and simple enough for even a peasant to own and master, the longbow possessed advantages apparent in its construction. A selfbow, that is, a bow made from one single piece of wood, the longbow involved relatively little labor and could be produced rapidly. Welsh yew was the wood of choice because of its high compressive strength, light weight, and resilience. It is said that at the height of production of longbows during the Hundred Years' War in the fourteenth century, an expert bowyer could shape a longbow out of a piece of yew in only about two hours. The "D" shape of the bow was the maximum threshold to which the elastic nature of the wood could stretch and still return to its natural straightness after an arrow was loosed. As tall as an average yeoman, the longbow stood anywhere from five to six feet upon its completion,

and had a supreme draw weight of between 80 and 90 pounds. Arrows were drawn back to the ear, as opposed to the breast with a normal bow, thus increasing range and striking power. Skeletal remains of archers from this period still bear the obvious signs of wear produced by the repetition of the weight of the drawstring, as shoulder muscles became disproportionately stronger, dramatically reshaping the bones and creating bone spurs in the joints of the arm. Such strength allowed English archers to achieve an average effective range of over 200 yards, an astonishing (and condemned by the French as decidedly unchivalrous) distance.

To protect the bows from moisture and the weather, a mixture of wax, resin, and tallow would be applied to them, and they would be stored in cases made of canvas or wool. Bow strings were made of hemp, fine flax, or even silk. Strings were attached to nocks on the end of the bow made of bone or horn. The typical English longbow arrow was known as the clothyard shaft; from 27 to perhaps even 36 inches in length. It was cheap and easy to mass-produce, made from either ash or birch. It is estimated that greater numbers of longbow shafts were produced than any other type of arrow in history.

Though longbows were accurate and could shoot the farthest of any bow in the Middle Ages, they could not usually do both effectively at the same time. Reports indicate that diminishing returns on targets kicked in when the target was about 80 yards away. However, when taking into account the fact that an expert archer could shoot up to 10–12 arrows per minute, a group of archers could create a virtual storm of arrows and still hit something (it is difficult to miss an army). With the development of arrows with massive bodkin points (a point with an elongated pyramid shape and a sharpened point), even plate armor could be pierced with a direct impact. No longer was it the rule that infantry could not stand up to a heavily armored cavalry unit. In order to increase the reload speed, archers would stick these bodkin tips point down into the ground in front of them; another more grisly result of this practice was to increase the chance of infection in the victim's wounds. The only way to remove such an arrow cleanly would be to tie a piece of cloth, soaked in boiling water or another sterilizing substance, to the end of it and push it through the victim's wound and out the other side. If bone was hit or broken, only specialist tools could extract the points in order to minimize the risk that the marrow would seep into the bloodstream.

Commanders developed their tactics to fully utilize the chaos the longbow could create. Starting in a line in front of the main body of the English army, a group of longbow men would shoot an opening skirmish volley, disrupting the enemy and forcing them to advance before they were ready. The main body of archers usually would take up positions on both flanks of the battle line in enfilade positions, then proceed to loose successive volleys at the closing enemy army. The ability of the English to take a defensive posture and force the enemy to expend their energy and much of their manpower just crossing the field of battle became their favorite and most effective tactic for three centuries. At the battle of Crécy, almost a third of the French nobility (fighting as mounted knights) were destroyed by infantry equipped with longbows before even coming into contact with the main body of the English army. The French force of some 30,000 men was decisively defeated by a relatively immobile army of 12,000 English consisting of little cavalry. During the 400-year period when it was employed widely, the longbow rewrote the rules of engagement, and crippled the utility of once-dominant cavalry forces. As a result, English longbow units were sought-after mercenaries in European conflicts, fighting at various times with the Swiss, the Teutonic Knights, the Portuguese, and with the famous mercenary White Company of Sir John Hawkwood in Italy.

Longbows continued in effective use until about the sixteenth century, when the development and weaponization of gunpowder became more common, and units such as arquebusers, musketeers, and grenadiers began appearing. Even though the longbow had faded out of military use by the seventeenth century, it left an indelible mark on English society. For four centuries, the peasant class had a weapon of their own, and stories like the legend of Robin Hood grew out of this consciousness and empowerment. The longbow allowed for the blossoming of English military power and the development of its place as a dominant world entity.

Clinton Chase Hamilton

References: Hardy, Robert, *Longbow* (Cambridge: Patrick Stevens, 1976); Kaiser, Robert E., *The Medieval English Longbow*, Journal of the Society of Archer-Antiquaries, volume 23, 1980; Norman, A.V.B. and Don Pottinger, *English Weapons & Warfare (449–1660)* (New York: Prentice Hall, 1982).

M

Macedonians

Southeastern European population that dominated Greece, Egypt, Persia, and India between the fourth and first centuries BCE.

When Philip II came to power in 359 BCE, Macedonia was basically an agrarian state with very little urban population. A majority of the people were farmers and shepherds, and were too poor to afford the equipment of a Greek hoplite, the standard infantryman of the time. Also, owing to the size of the country, the people were unable to gather easily into large groups in a single place. The nobility and landed gentry had developed into a military class that specialized in fighting on horseback, while the common folk fought as unarmored peltasts, or slingers. Together they formed a very weak military organization. Philip increased taxes and used the monies to create a standing army and to pay Greek mercenaries. His army engaged in the intensive training that only the mercenary forces had previously received. Philip merged the natural talents of his people with the accepted tactics of the Greeks and produced an army of truly combined skills. In essence, he elevated warfare to a new level, and the army he created made his son Alexander a legend.

Though Philip found the money to pay a standing army, he lacked the resources to equip each infantryman with hoplite armor. Instead he opted for offensive reach and mobility. The Greek hoplite spear was about seven feet in length and was intended to be held with the right hand while the left hand held the shield. Philip replaced the spear with a fourteen foot *sarissa* (pike), which doubled the reach of his men, often called *phalangites* ("those fighting in a phalanx"), and allowed them to strike the first blows against the hoplites. The sarissa required two hands to wield, so the phalangite's shield was made smaller, and it was attached to the upper left arm with straps. Finally, the entire phalanx was compacted and the formation deepened. The long reach of the sarissa gave an increased number of men the ability to fight on a given frontage. According to ancient accounts, the standard strength of a Macedonian phalanx was 1,500 men. These were probably arrayed in 15 ranks of 100 men each.

The lack of defensive armor allowed the phalangites to attain a degree of mobility that hoplites could never hope to match. They could execute intricate maneuvers at fast speeds and march long distances with little rest. By the second half of Philip's reign, he well could have afforded to equip his men with breastplates if he so desired, but by then it had become apparent that armor was no longer necessary to win victories. Alexander must have agreed with this, for he appears to have made no attempt to rearmor his phalangites.

Battle between Alexander the Great and King Darius, depicted in a mosaic from the House of the Faun, Pompeii. Museo Archeologico Nazionale, Naples, Italy. © Erich Lessing / Art Resource, NY

Philip created a second group of infantrymen, the foot guards, or *Hypaspists*. It appears that these men had the same equipment as the phalangites, fought in a similar phalanx, and were recruited from the same peasant stock. However, it seems that the Hypaspists were handpicked from the best of the phalangites, and served as a national unit, despite their local origins. In essence, they formed an elite infantry corps about 3,000 strong, which appears to have operated in three phalanxes of 1,000 men each. Alexander favored them over his other infantry, and had more confidence in their abilities. Whenever he had to make a long forced march, he took along the Hypaspists, and left the phalangites to follow at a slower pace. This is not to say that the phalangites did not fight as well as the Hypaspists but, as the king's personal troops, the guards had a discipline and esprit de corps that the phalangites could never match. Philip's army also included a large number of mercenary infantry, and this continued with Alexander, who reportedly had 5,000 mercenaries with him when he crossed into Asia. In addition, the League of Corinth had placed at his disposal a large force of Greek allied infantry, perhaps 7,000. These men may have assumed the arms of the phalangites or may have retained their hoplite equipment. They were primarily used for garrison and reserve line duties. Darius usually placed

200

his Greek mercenaries in the center of his army, and it is doubtful if Alexander wished to test the loyalty of his hoplites by asking them to fight against fellow Greeks. Macedonians, on the other hand, felt no qualms whatsoever about killing Greeks.

In Philip's and Alexander's armies, phalanxes formed the center and left of the main battle line: the unshakable core of the army. Their function was to advance upon the enemy center, pin it in place, and prevent it from reacting to the decisive thrust of the Macedonian heavy cavalry. The phalangites set the tempo of the battle, but never administered the winning blow. The Hypaspists' function was to occupy the right side of the battle line and maintain contact between the phalangites and the cavalry. If need be, each of the phalangite battalions (*taxis*), 1,500 strong, or the Hypaspists, could operate as independent units.

Philip and Alexander recruited the Macedonian cavalry from the nobility and the landed gentry of the country. They formed a body of heavy cavalry known as the *Hetairoi*, or Companions. The Companions wore metal breastplates, greaves, and helmets, and wielded spears, swords, and shields. However, Greeks and Macedonians had no knowledge of saddles or stirrups, and without firm seats it would be impossible to fully utilize the momentum of horses in charges. Spears were almost certainly used in an overhand thrusting manner. About 2,000 strong under Alexander, the Companions fought in tactical units of varying strengths called *ilai*. The strongest ilai became the royal squadron and numbered 300 picked men. The Companions usually attacked in wedge-shaped formations that could penetrate any opposing line of cavalry.

About 2,000 Thessalians reinforced Alexander's Macedonians. They also fought as heavy cavalry in small units and made use of the rhomboid or diamond formation, which functioned the same as the wedge. When forced to stand on the defensive, the Thessalians adopted a looser linear formation, more conducive to skirmishing.

In addition to the Thessalians, Alexander had the services of groups of Greek mercenary cavalry; Macedonian *Prodromo* (scouts); and Paeonian, Odrysian, and Greek allied cavalry, about 3,000 in all. They functioned as light cavalry. The Prodromoi and Paeonians carried the cavalry sarissa, and were known as *sarissaophorai* (lancers). The remainder of the light cavalry fought with javelin and shield.

Cavalry was the single most significant element in the Macedonian system. From a nonexistent force in the Greek armies, it grew to represent 20 percent of Alexander's total manpower, and its importance far outweighed its numbers. The Companions became the major offensive weapon of the Macedonian army. Their charge decided all of Alexander's battles against the Persians, and he always personally led them into combat. The Companions' position was on the right side of the battle line and the Thessalians' on the left. Alexander stationed the other cavalry units wherever they might be needed, but mostly they ended up on the right flank, to keep pressure off the Companions and allow them to make their climactic charges unimpeded.

The majority of the light infantry had to be recruited from outside Macedonia, one unit of archers being the only native troops of this type. The Agrianians, Triballians, Odysians, and Illyrians furnished men who were skilled in the use of the javelin. For generations Crete had provided units of archers to the Greek world. They were valued for their ability, if not for their tenacity. In all, Alexander had about 9,000 light infantry. These men did not resemble the peltasts of the Greek armies. They wore no armor and carried only light shields. They cushioned the flanks of the phalanx, fanned out in front of the army, and intercepted charging light cavalry, chariots, or elephants. They harassed the enemy and supported friendly charges with archery fire, and they diverted any pressure from the Companions. Finally, they operated in broken or wooded terrain where the phalangites or cavalry could not go.

The strength of the Macedonians lay in the combined use of all their armies' branches: phalanx, cavalry, and light troops. As the army moved into action, the phalanx advanced to engage the main strength of the enemy. The archers opened fire, usually on the enemy cavalry. The javelineers would move forward, just in advance of the main line, covering them from accurate enemy archery and seeking to disrupt enemy charges. The left flank under Alexander's subordinate Parmenion usually adopted a defensive posture, inclining back from the main battle line or pressing ahead, as the situation warranted. Parmenion fed units into the battle as needed to maintain his flank. The light cavalry units on the right would move out to intercept enemy flanking movements as the Hypaspists sought to maintain contact between the Companions and the phalanxes and ensure an unbroken line. The second line of infantry would stand ready to move up to reinforce faltering front-line units, to intercept any breakthroughs and reform the line, or to face about if the army became encircled. While this transpired, the Companions—with Alexander at their head—waited for a gap to appear in the enemy ranks. The javelineers sought to ward off any units that might impede their charge. Finally, at the decisive moment, Alexander would launch the Companions. Their wedges would pierce the enemy forces like arrows and explode laterally, rolling up the ranks in both directions. The following Companions would drive through the widening gap into the rear of the enemy army. The enemy center, attacked on its front, flank and rear, would give way and the battle would be over. This same pattern was repeated in each of Alexander's three great victories over the Persians, in the battles of Granicus, Issus, and Gaugamela, and in his other engagements for which accounts exist.

Each Macedonian unit knew what was expected of it. The objective of the entire army was to set up the enemy for the decisive thrust to be delivered by Alexander and the Companions. The divisions of the army did not have to win their particular engagements; rather, they had only to pin the enemy and prevent him from overwhelming them. Thus, in a rather selfless manner, the entire army existed to provide Alexander's 2,000 elite horsemen the opportunity to repeatedly cover themselves with glory. Of course, the alternative was defeat and quite possibly death, which also had to affect not only the soldiers' outlook but their performance as well.

The question might be raised as to what the Macedonians would have done if one of Alexander's charges had been repulsed. Quite simply, the task of achieving victory would fall to the Thessalians, or the phalangites, or the Hypaspists. Just because these units never won any of Alexander's large battles does not mean they were not capable of doing so. Each was a formidable fighting unit, as they proved time and again in independent actions, and each could, if necessary, deliver the telling strike themselves.

Further proof of this can be seen in the wars of Alexander's successors. The Macedonian system lived on with these men and the empires they founded. However, two armies of a similar nature knew what to expect from each other, and the chances for a decisive blow to be delivered by the heavy cavalry declined markedly. By 217 BCE, at the Battle of Raphia between the heirs of Ptolemy and Seleucus, 115,000 men took the field on both sides; only 11,000 were cavalry. This heralded the era of the Romans, when tactical mobility was further extended to the infantry while the horsemen entered a 400-year eclipse.

References: Adcock, Frank, *Greek and Macedonian Art of War* (Berkeley: University of California Press, 1974); Ashley, James, *The Macedonian Empire* (McFarland & Co., 1997); Ginouves, Rene, and Giannes Akamates, *Macedonia: From Philip II to the Roman Conquest* (Princeton: Princeton University Press, 1994).

Magyars

Asian peoples, related to the Huns, who invaded Europe in the ninth century and established the Hungarian population.

A fanciful legend traces the origins of the Magyars to Nimrod, a descendant of Noah's son Japheth, who left Babel after the ill-fated attempt to construct there the tower of biblical fame. Nimrod had two sons, Hunor and Magyar, who in turn begot the two great tribes of the Huns and the Magyars. The myth has it that the tribes followed a magical elk to the Caucasus where they lived in peace. As time passed and the tribes grew, the Magyars

remained in the Caucasus and the Huns began a nomadic life, which ultimately took them past the Volga into Europe. There, under the leadership of Attila, the Huns waged a campaign of terror and conquest. After Attila's defeat and death, his sons returned to the Caucasus and pleaded with the Magyars to return with them to Europe where they could find new lands and opportunity.

Though the legend is compelling, in reality the Magyars seem to have had Finno-Ugric origins with traces of Turco-Tartar elements. They had long practiced a nomadic lifestyle in central Asia and finally migrated westward past the Ural, Volga, Don, Dnieper, and at last, the Danube Rivers. In this movement, they successively fought and defeated other nomadic tribes, such as the Khazarsand Petchenegs. The pressure of the Petchenegs and Bulgars finally drove them into Europe. As the Magyars entered eastern Europe, they encountered the power of the Byzantine Empire, which hired them as mercenaries and introduced them to Christianity. Likewise, Germanic kings hired them to aid in fighting the Slavs.

By the ninth century CE, the Magyars had moved into central Europe under leadership of Arpad. Under his direction, they entered the Hungarian plain with some 150,000 men. They defeated the Slavs and Alans and settled in, using their new home as a base for further raids into German and Italian lands. The Magyars became the permanent occupants of this region and were as Hungarians. Magyar soldiers under Arpad ranged successfully into the Italian peninsula as far as Milan and Pavia in 899, leaving only upon receiving sufficient bribes.

The Magyars fought in much the same style as the Huns and were precursors to the Mongol invasion of Europe. Employing mostly light cavalry and archers, they avoided close contact with their enemies, harassing them into exhaustion and then exploiting any openings. The heavy cavalry developed in Europe at this time did not at first succeed against the Magyars, but over time the European defenders adopted some of the eastern tactics and began to have more success.

By 907 Magyar interest in German lands forced the Germanic rulers into cooperation with each other. Luitpold of Bavaria allied with Ditmar, the Archbishop of Salzburg. Nevertheless, their efforts proved futile and the Magyars defeated them at Presburg. In the 920s the Magyars raided as far as the Champagne region of France, into northern Italy again, and as far as the Pyrenees. The Magyars created as much terror in their campaigns as did the Vikings, who were pressing from the north, but the Germanic nobles soon began to prevail against them. Henry the Fowler defeated them in 933 at Merseburg, inflicting 36,000 Magyar casualties. He and his successors began fortifying the frontier, which lessened the frequency of the Magyar raids, while the Bavarians turned the tables and began to raid Magyar lands. Nevertheless, in 954 up to 100,000 Magyars attacked deep into Germany and France, taking advantage of the revolt of Lorraine against Otto the Great, Henry's son. They again made a huge pillaging sweep through France, into northern Italy, and back to the Danube valley. Otto finally defeated them the following year at Lechfeld, after which the Magyars were on the decline.

At home in Hungary, they settled down to a more stable and civilized lifestyle under the leadership of Duke Geyza in the 970s. Christianity replaced their Asiatic animistic and totemic beliefs, and they began showing a toleration and acceptance of other cultures. King Stephen (997–1038) defended his homeland from takeover by the Holy Roman Empire and acquired authority from the pope over a national church. Stephen oversaw the construction of monasteries and cathedrals and, for his efforts and example, was later canonized. The Magyar language became and remains the official language of Hungary: But for the battle at Lechfeld, it may have been the language of much of western Europe. For all their terrorism of the west, it was the Hungarians who ultimately defended western Europe from the Ottoman Turks as they fought to bring down the Byzantine Empire and expand the Muslim faith into Europe in the mid-fifteenth century.

References: Bartha, Antal, *Hungarian Society in the 9th and 10th Centuries,* translated by K. Baazs (Budapest: Akademiai Kiado, 1975); Macartney, C.A., *The Magyars in the Ninth Century (Cambridge: University Press, 1968); Vambery, Arminius, Hungary in Ancient, Medieval, and Modern Times* (Hallandale, FL: New World Books, 1972).

Mamluks

Muslim slave-soldiers who rose to power in Egypt during the Middle Ages.

The Koran states that the only legitimate sources of slaves are the children of slaves and prisoners of war. It was through the second route that most of the slaves who lived under early Islam came to their condition. Because slaves were used for every conceivable purpose, perhaps it is not surprising that the rulers of Egypt used them as soldiers, or *ghulams.* The Fatimid (909–1171) and Ayyubid (1171–1250) dynasties of Egypt built armies of slave-soldiers. As happened in other slave-holding societies, those most talented rose in power and influence, despite their official status as slaves. Just as trustworthy eunuchs rose to positions of political power as advisors to royalty, so did slave-soldiers rise to command armies under the caliphs and viziers.

The *mamluks* (from the Arabic word for "owned") were white slaves, acquired in raids conducted into Turkey and the Caucasus. Other slave-soldiers were called *Abid al-Shira* ("purchased slaves"), and they tended to be of Sudanese or Berber descent. A Mamluk was usually purchased and trained by his master, which in theory would ensure the slave's loyalty to the master. When they became trustworthy, they were often freed and awarded a piece of land called an *iqta'*. Ownership of the iqta' provided the Mamluk not only with produce from farming, but with enough of an estate to control his own slaves or peasant tenants. Thus, the iqta' roughly corresponded with the feudal system developing in Europe, whereby the master could call on his subordinates to provide troops for him when campaigning was necessary. The master who could provide Mamluks for war became known as the amir, and his rank varied according to the number of Mamluks he controlled. Thus, there were amirs of five, amirs of 10, and so forth—up to amirs of 100, although the actual number of Mamluks under an amir's command might vary wildly. Still, five was the minimum number in order to be given the title of amir. Under the control of the caliph, the core troops of the Fatimid dynasty were the Royal Mamluks, an organization that usually numbered 5,000 men (although it varied widely in later times). The Mamluks fought as fully armed cavalry, while the troops they procured from their own estates, as well as other auxiliaries recruited by the government,

operated as infantry armed with spears or bows.

The Mamluks fought well and bravely under their Muslim masters, but in the mid-thirteenth century, they took power for themselves. The final Ayyubid sultan, al-Salih, died in 1249, but his wife Shajar-al-Durr kept his death secret for a time and gave orders in his name. When she was discovered, rather than remove her, the Muslim leaders in Cairo paired her with the Mamluk general Aybak. After they married, Shajar-al-Durr continued to rule and had Aybak assassinated, but he is regarded as the first of the Mamluk dynasty. The dynasty lasted more than 265 years and saw occasionally brilliant leaders as well as a renaissance in the arts.

The first Mamluk leader to distinguish himself was al-Malik Baybars (ruled 1260–1277). He was born a slave rather than captured, and his training as well as innate talents took him to the heights of command in the Ayyubid army. He commanded the forces that defeated and captured French King Louis IX in 1250 at the battle of Masura, during Saint Louis's abortive crusade. He was second-in-command to Qutuz 10 years later at the battle of Ain-Julut, where the Mamluks defeated the Mongols and turned back the Asian tide flowing into the Middle East. During the army's return to Cairo after the great victory, Baybars killed Qutuz and named himself sultan. He spent his reign repeatedly defeating European Crusaders, a feat that gained him the highest respect in Muslim eyes. When not fighting, he was a judicious ruler who showed remarkable religious tolerance in his domain. The government organization he established served the Mamluk dynasty through to its end in 1517. He also oversaw the construction of numerous public works and built both a strong navy as well as a strong standing army.

The Mamluk army was divided into three main divisions: the Royal Mamluks, the Mamluks of the amirs, and the al-Halqa. Under Baybars the Royal Mamluks increased to as many as 16,000 men. From the ranks of the Royal Mamluks came the amirs. The amirs continued to provide and command other Mamluks, but they also commanded the al-Halqa, which first were organized in 1174 and served as cavalry. The soldiers serving in these units were Egyptians or the sons of freed Mamluks. Although by this time the term "Mamluk" was more historical than descriptive of soldier slaves, native Egyptians and Arabs still could not become Mamluks. Thus, they were relegated to serving in the al-Halqa contingents. Even the sons of Mamluks were segregated into this third contingent and treated as second class because they had not been born Turkish or raised as slaves. This is almost certainly the only time in history that one could attain a higher social and professional status by having been born or raised a slave than having been born free.

After 1381, a second ruling family rose to power from Mamluk descendants: the Burjis. The Burji dynasty, although it lasted another 136 years, was rocked by almost constant palace intrigue and assassinations. During this time the sultans spent lavishly and Cairo became the richest city in the Mediterranean world. However, the instability of the succession to power spelled the dynasty's doom. Selim I of the Ottoman Empire defeated the Mamluk armies in 1517, after which Egypt became a vassal state ruled by a Turkish governor. Still, the Mamluks retained some influence in government, serving under the Turkish pasha and still holding command positions in the army. When in 1798 Napoleon Bonaparte arrived to attempt the conquest of Egypt, a Mamluk army fought him. The Mamluks were defeated at the Battle of the Pyramids in 1798, but after the French withdrew, the Mamluks tried to regain the throne. The Turks defeated them in 1805 and again in 1811, breaking Mamluk power for good.

References: Glubb, John Bagot, *Soldiers of Fortune: The Story of the Mamlukes* (London: Stein & Day, 1957) Irwin, Robert, *The Middle East in the Middle Ages* (Carbondale: Southern Illinois University Press, 1986); Muir, William, *Mameluke, or Slave Dynasty of Egypt* (New York: AMS, 1973).

Marathas

An Indian ethnic group that resisted the British occupation of India.

The homeland of the Marathas, another of the martial races of India, is the Deccan, the plateau of central India south of the Narbudda River stretching to the west coast. This region was one of the final acquisitions of the Aryans in prehistoric times, and the inhabitants are descendants of both those invaders and the aboriginal tribes that lived there prior to conquest. The Marathas first displayed their warlike tendencies with the arrival of the Muslims in India. As Hindus, the Marathas fiercely resisted the imposition of Islam, especially under the Mogul dynasty. Their leader was Sivaji, called "the mountain rat," and his successes against the Moguls, including the kidnapping of an emperor, laid the groundwork for what became the Mahratta Confederacy. Prior to the arrival of the British in the 1700s, the only serious military opponents the Marathas had faced were the Afghans, who had defeated them along the

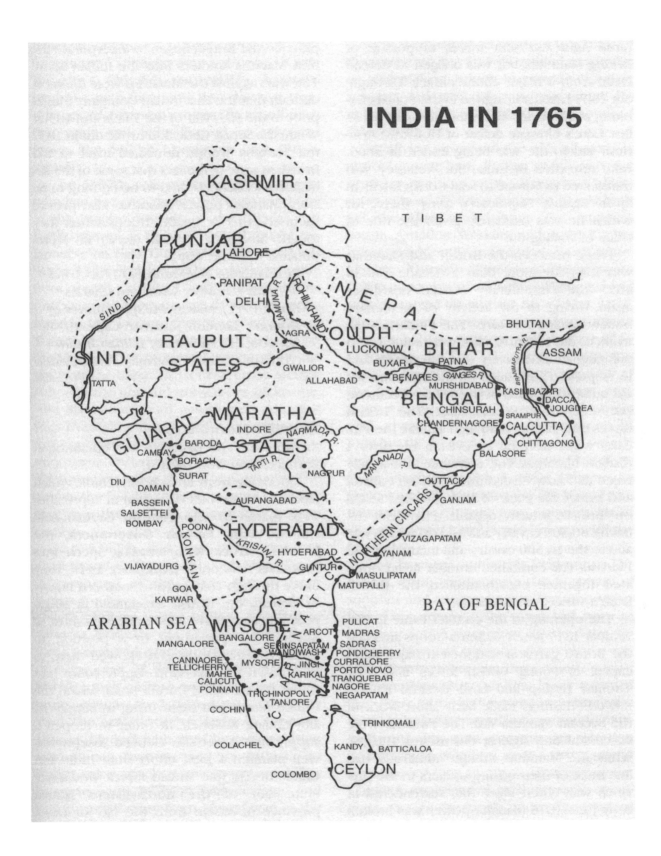

INDIA IN 1765

KASHMIR

TIBET

PUNJAB

• LAHORE

SIND R.

PANIPAT

DELHI

JAMUNA R.

ROHILKHAND

N E P A L

BHUTAN

AGRA

OUDH

LUCKNOW

BIHAR

ASSAM

RAJPUT
STATES

GWALIOR

BUXAR

PATNA

BRAHMAPUTRA R.

SIND

ALLAHABAD

BENARES

GANGES R.

MURSHIDABAD

KASIMBAZAR

DACCA

TATTA

JOUGDEA

BENGAL

CHINSURAH

SRAMPUR

CHANDERNAGORE

CALCUTTA

GUJARAT

MARATHA

INDORE

NARMADA R.

BARODA

STATES

CHITTAGONG

CAMBAY

BALASORE

BORACH

TAPTI R.

SURAT

NAGPUR

DIU

DAMAN

CUTTACK

MANANADI R.

BASSEIN

AURANGABAD

GANJAM

SALSETTEI

BOMBAY

POONA

HYDERABAD

NORTHERN CIRCARS

KONKAN

VIZAGAPATAM

KRISHNA R.

HYDERABAD

VIJAYADURG

GUNTUR

YANAM

MASULIPATAM

GOA

MATUPALLI

KARWAR

BAY OF BENGAL

ARABIAN SEA

MYSORE

ARCOT

PULICAT

MANGALORE

BANGALORE

MADRAS

SERINGAPATAM

SADRAS

WANDIWASH

PONDICHERRY

CANNAORE

MYSORE

JINGI

CURRALORE

TELLICHERRY

KARIKAL

PORTO NOVO

MAHE

TRANQUEBAR

CALICUT

NAGORE

PONNANI

TRICHINOPOLY

NEGAPATAM

TANJORE

COCHIN

TRINKOMALI

COLACHEL

KANDY

BATTICALOA

COLOMBO

CEYLON

border at Panipat in 1761. That defeat laid the foundation for internal disputes that brought about the two Maratha wars.

As long as Sivaji lived, the Marathas were united, but after his death the population broke into factions under rival princes who swore only nominal fealty to a central government under the rajah of Satara. The chief minister of the rajah was the peshwa, a hereditary position that exercised great influence. The princes collectively formed the Maratha Confederation, and for all their independent stances stood together when faced with outside threats. The confederation consisted of the princes Scindia, Holkar, and Bhonsla, along with the peshwa, and the European military advisors they employed at the opening of the nineteenth century, who were predominantly French refugees from the court of the recently deposed Tipoo Sultan of Mysore.

The Marathas staged two campaigns against the British. The first started in 1804 as the British were embroiled in European problems with Napoleon. Always on the alert to find some way to divert the British, Napoleon sent agents to India (where the French presence was coming to an end) to stir up trouble. Indian princes had long hired Europeans to train and command their armies, and the Marathas accepted the offer of French assistance against the growing power of Britain along the western coast of India. The forces comprising the Maratha army were neither citizen-soldiers nor patriots, but mercenaries and outlaws fighting for pay and to practice their chosen profession. Long a haven for raiders and bandits, British possessions around Bombay had suffered from decades-long harassment. As it was the British East India Company's view that law and order promoted profits, conflict between them and

the Marathas would certainly have broken out even without French aid.

It was the British defeat of Tipoo Sultan in 1798 that precipitated the conflict. The British had viewed Tipoo Sultan as a particularly despicable character who needed deposing, so they replaced him with a more cooperative ruler, who became the Nizam of Mysore. Upon disbanding the French forces, the Nizam was urged to accept a garrison of East India Company soldiers: four battalions from Madras and some artillery to defend the capital city of Hyderabad. These troops were necessary to defend Mysore from the bandit raids emanating from Maratha territory, while the British at the same time opened negotiations with the Marathas to end the banditry and cooperate against the threat of Afghan pressure. These negotiations, coupled with the death of Peshwa Madho Rao, led to internecine fighting among the Marathas. The new peshwa, Bajee Rao, broke ranks and allied himself with the British in return for East India Company troops and artillery. The Marathas responded by naming Bajee's brother, Amrut, to be peshwa, which led to an inevitable conflict between the confederacy on one side and the British, forces loyal to Bajee Rao, and the forces of the Nizam of Mysore on the other.

The army that took the field against the Maratha Confederacy was led by Arthur Wellesley in his first major combat command. In total, some 50,000 men were under his command, operating in a number of smaller columns. He quickly captured the supposedly impregnable fortress at Ahmadnagar, then found himself facing a huge challenge at the village of Assaye at the Jua and Kelna Rivers. On September 23, 1803, with only 4,500 men, Wellesley charged a force of 55,000 led by a number of French officers. In a few hours Wellesley drove them from the field at a cost of almost half the British force killed or wounded. He followed these successes with victories at Argaon in November and Gawilarh in December, while one of his subordinates captured the fort at Aseergurh.

While Wellesley consolidated his hold in the southern region of Maratha territory, a second army under General Lord Lake operated farther north in the vicinity of Delhi, where he rescued the Mogul emperor, Shah Alam, from his Mahratta captors. Lake's army operated against Holkar, one of the Maratha princes, while Wellesley had fought against princes ScIndia and Bhonsla. Lake soon captured Agra and sent forces in pursuit of fleeing Marathas, but was obliged to defend Delhi from a major counterattack. Throughout 1805, Lake campaigned in the Punjab, ferreting out Holkar's forces and those of his allies. Lake's ultimate defeat of Holkar at Armritsar led to the war's end in 1806. Lake remained in India, but Wellesley was transferred to Europe to lead British forces in Spain against Napoleon's army there, for which he was ultimately given the title of Duke of Wellington.

Peace between the British and Marathas was kept for more than a decade, but in 1817 the confederacy started hostilities again, owing to the activity of mercenary outlaws called *Pindaris*. The Pindaris, remnants of old Mogul armies, were raiding and pillaging so extensively that the British had to respond. They called on the Marathas for aid under the terms of the 1806 agreement, but received little assistance. The British forces thus had to campaign against the Pindaris while keeping an eye on the always restless Marathas. The erstwhile British ally Bajee Rao now chafed

under British control and, under the guise of raising troops to aid the British, actually organized an army totaling 86,500 cavalry and 66,000 infantry to add to the 16,500 cavalry and infantry of the Pindaris. The combined number never operated together, but threatened the British from a variety of directions.

The opening of the conflict came in November 1817 when Mahratta troops attacked the British garrison stationed at Bajee Rao's capital of Poona. British forces under Sir Thomas Hyslop and Lord General Francis Rawdon-Hastings made fairly short work of the Second Maratha War. The Pindaris were successful only against defenseless villages, while the Marathas, though numerous, had lost most of their quality soldiers in the previous war. When Bajee Rao surrendered in early June 1818, Maratha power was broken for good, and the East India Company attained dominance in the subcontinent. The British were obliged to interfere in a succession dispute in 1825–1826 but, as was their practice, the British began to incorporate the best Maratha soldiers into the Indian Army. The wars against the Marathas were the most difficult that the East India Company fought prior to the Sikh War of the 1840s and 1850s. When the Sepoy Rebellion broke out in 1857 the Maratha troops remained loyal to the British in spite of the fact that some of the Rebellion's leaders claimed to be fighting to restore Maratha power. Marathas also proved themselves to be quality troops when they fought alongside British forces in Meso-potamia in World War I.

References: MacMunn, G.F., *The Armies of India* (London: Adam and Charles Black, 1911); Mason, Philip, *A Matter of Honour* (London: Jonathan Cape, 1974); Roberts, P.E., *History of British India* (London: Oxford University Press, 1952).

Merrill's Marauders

An American special forces unit operating in Burma during World War II.

Operating from French Indochina, which Japanese forces had occupied in September 1940 thanks to help from the German-controlled Vichy French Government, the Japanese struck with amazing speed into Southeast Asia on December 8, 1941. They drove through Thailand and southern Burma to capture the British stronghold at Singapore and also drove west to occupy most of Burma. This put them in a position to threaten British India and allowed them to shut down the overland supply route into China, the so-called Burma Road, which the United States had been using to supply its ally, Chiang Kai-shek. In order to reopen a supply line, American General Joseph Stilwell planned a joint effort from India and China. British and Indian forces would operate out of the northeastern Indian province of Assam from the city of Ledo, while Chinese forces would attack out of Hunan toward the town of Bhamo, to which a road from Ledo would be built. The British found themselves quite busy dealing with Japanese offensives against India, but their long-range penetration group, Orde Wingate's Chindits, successfully harassed Japanese rear areas and tied down a large number of Japanese troops. To accomplish that same end, Stilwell used an American group, the 5307th Composite Unit (Provisional).

The 5307th was made up of volunteers who had had experience training or fighting in the jungle. Veterans of the Guadalcanal battle, as well as those who had fought the Japanese on New Guinea, formed two-thirds of the 3,000-man force. The remain-

Some of the men of Merrill's Marauders. The "international character of the 5307th is shown" in this image. Courtesy of the Merrill's Marauders Association (hhtp://www.marauder.org) image "Lt. Lubin #63/ MM #120.

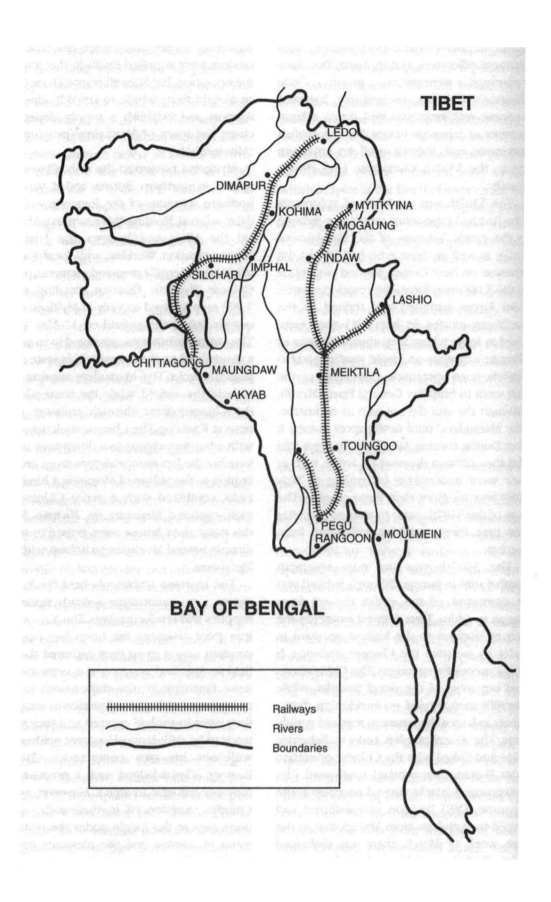

TIBET

LEDO

DIMAPUR

KOHIMA

MYITKYINA

MOGAUNG

INDAW

SILCHAR

IMPHAL

LASHIO

CHITTAGONG

MAUNGDAW

MEIKTILA

AKYAB

TOUNGOO

PEGU

RANGOON

MOULMEIN

BAY OF BENGAL

	Railways
	Rivers
	Boundaries

der came from forces stationed and trained in the Caribbean jungles. In late 1943 they organized in India, where they absorbed some of Wingate's theories on jungle warfare and behind-the-lines operations. Command of the unit went to Brigadier General Frank Merrill, although the unit did not gain its nickname, "the Marauders," until newspapers coined it later. During training, Merrill's men were told that the optimum duration for action such as they were undertaking (according to Wingate) was no more than three months. The men of the 5307th came to assume that after that time they would be withdrawn from combat.

The 5307th was the only American combat unit in Burma, although Stilwell was in command of the entire theater from Burma to China. Thus, Stilwell expected the unit to perform to the highest standard in order to motivate the Chinese divisions. It was a successful stratagem. The Chinese carried out most of the direct assaults, while Merrill's men carried on enveloping movements to harass the Japanese rear and supply lines. The Americans left Ledo in February 1944 and linked with the Chinese operating from Hunan, then worked southward. The two-pronged attacks proved successful: The Japanese XVIII Division was defeated and forced to withdraw from Maingkwan in the first week of March, then was dislodged from Shaduzup at the end of the month. Both times the Japanese were forced to withdraw hastily and under fire. The Marauders were supplied by air in this stage of the operation, but Stilwell wanted to acquire an airfield from which to provide close air support and establish a supply depot. He chose the town of Myitkyina (pronounced "Mitchinah").

Myitkyina possessed the only all-weather airfield in northern Burma, and it was the northern terminus of the Rangoon-to-Mandalay railroad. Holding this town would both aid the Allies and hamper the Japanese supply situation. Working with local Kachin tribesmen, Merrill's men and elements of the Chinese Thirtieth Division (totaling some 7,000 men) arrived secretly at Myitkyina and quickly seized the airfield on May 17, 1944. The Japanese, however, managed to maintain a strong hold on the town itself, in spite of repeated attacks. The Marauders' mission was to hold the airfield while the remainder of the Chinese drove through Japanese positions at Kamaing. The Chinese took the town with a bayonet charge in a downpour on June 16, but the Japanese withdrew in an orderly fashion to the village of Mogaung. Chindit attacks, combined with a major Chinese assault, captured Mogaung on June 26. From this point, the Chinese were poised to strike directly toward Myitkyina to link up with the Marauders.

The Japanese stubbornly held out in Myitkyina, even maintaining a steady stream of supplies and reinforcements. The Sino-American force attacking the town had been in constant action since they had captured the airfield in May and were on the verge of collapse. Furthermore, the three-month period of operations that the Americans assumed they were in for had expired, and they were ready to be withdrawn. However, neither Stilwell nor his area commander, Hayden Boatner, acknowledged such a promise and they needed men to attack. As the Chindits experienced in their early operations, though, men in the jungle under the constant strain of combat and the elements have a limit. Merrill's men had reached it. The rate of sickness swelled and men often fell asleep while fighting. The morale of the unit collapsed. Stilwell wanted them to stay because they were the only American unit operating. The Chinese were still fighting well, but their organization and supply system was much stronger than Merrill's.

The siege of Myitkyina ended on August 3 when a new Japanese commander deemed the delay to the American plans sufficient. He withdrew his men after an 11-week battle and the loss of approximately 3,000 dead. The Americans also suffered heavy losses. The 5307th consisted of 1,310 men out of the original 3,000 who had first arrived at Myitkyina. Half that number were evacuated to hospitals between their arrival on May 17 and June 1. When the last of the unit was pulled out on August 3, it consisted of only 200 Marauders. For their time in combat, the 5307th Composite Unit (Provisional) earned a Distinguished Unit Citation, summarized thus: "After a series of successful engagements in the Hukawng and Mogaung Valleys of North Burma, in March and April 1944 the unit was called on to lead a march over jungle trails through extremely difficult mountain terrain against stubborn resistance in a surprise attack on Myitkyina. The unit proved equal to the task and after a brilliant operation on 17 May 1944 seized the airfield at Myitkyina, an objective of great tactical importance in the campaign, and assisted in the capture of the town of Myitkyina on 3 August 1944" (Dupuy, 1966). Fifty-five men received the Bronze Star, 40 received the Silver Star, six were awarded the Distinguished Service Cross, and four received the Legion of Merit.

References: Bjorge, Gary, "Merrill's Marauders: Combined Operations in Northern Burma in 1944," in *Army History*, Spring/Summer 1995; Center of Military History, *Merrill's Marauders* (Washington, D.C.: Historical Division, War Department, 1945); Dupuy, Trevor N., "Burma: The Drive from the North," in *History of the Second World War*, vol. 71 (London: BBC Publications, 1966); Stilwell, Joseph W., The Stilwell Papers, ed. *Theodore H. White* (New York: William Sloane Associates, 1948)

Minutemen

Special militia units operating at the outbreak of the American Revolution.

The Minutemen of the American Revolution were formed some months before the outbreak of hostilities. In early September 1774, delegates from 12 of the 13 colonies assembled in Philadelphia to discuss a response to the Coercive (or Intolerable) Acts recently passed in London by Parliament. These were designed to punish the American colonies in general—and Massachusetts in particular—for the infamous Boston Tea Party, as well as other mischief and troublemaking that the colonists had perpetrated since the Boston Massacre of March 1770. The representatives in Philadelphia decided to implement an embargo on British goods, a tactic that had proved successful in the past, in order to pressure the British government. It was the adoption of the Suffolk resolves, however, that really made war inevitable.

The Suffolk Resolves were introduced by a delegation from Suffolk County, Massachusetts, where Boston is located. Adopted by the First Continental Congress toward the end of its September 1774 gathering, the Resolves called for Americans to ignore the Coercive Acts, to arrest a British officer in return for any American arrested, and to attack British facilities if the British moved troops to enforce order. The final resolves called for the removal of any militia officer not 100 percent trustworthy and for the inhabitants of every town to "use their utmost dili-

Minutemen firing upon British soldiers at the Battle of Lexington in an engraving by Cornelius Tiebout. Library of Congress, Prints and Photographs Division [reproduction number LC-DIG-ppmsca-05483]

gence to acquaint themselves with the art of war as soon as possible, and to, for that purpose, appear under arms at least once a week." These resolves, and the threat to attack the British directly unless the Coercive Acts were repealed, were made by an unauthorized body acting with only the limited support of the people, who had not elected them to speak for the country as a whole. When word of the Suffolk Resolves reached London, the British government had no choice in how to respond: King George ordered the dispatch of troops.

The colonies were racked with local political conflict. The colonies had a royally appointed governor who, along with the

popularly elected legislatures, exercised control over the militia. In Massachusetts particularly, and other colonies to a lesser extent, provincial congresses and committees of safety were forming that acted like governments and in many cases came to control the militias. "Disloyal" officers were removed and more "patriotic" officers were appointed. The traditional militia organization consisted of the volunteer militia and the common militia: The first traditionally were more ready to respond while the second were organized and prepared for duty. Militia units across the country (again, more commonly in Massachusetts where most of the revolutionary sentiment was centered) were told to appoint one man in three, or one in four, to be prepared for a quick response to back up the threat made through the Suffolk Resolves. These men quickly came to be regarded as "Minutemen," for their supposedly instant readiness.

Throughout the autumn and winter of 1774–1775, the Minutemen trained much more often than normal. Prior to this, the common militia had often gathered no more than once a year, and then often more for socializing than training. Still, the quality of the Minuteman units varied according to their leaders and the motivation of the rank and file. In those months after the Continental Congress met, tensions between British troops and colonials intensified, with incidents sometimes resulting in minor bloodshed. With the promised reinforcements on the way, however, British commander General Thomas Gage laid plans for seizing the rebel supplies of munitions stored at Concord, some 20 miles outside his headquarters of Boston. While he strove for secrecy in his planning, the colonials kept a constant vigil on British troop activities. When he ordered his men into action on the night of April 18, 1775, his troops were no sooner forming up than rebel messengers were already riding the countryside to alert the Minutemen. The most famous of these was Paul Revere, but he was hardly the only one to be spreading the word.

The first unit to gather on the night of April 18 met at Lexington, a town roughly halfway between Boston and Concord that was the site of their weekly drills. The men drifted in from their farms in the area and gathered inside a tavern to await the British arrival. The British appeared as the sun was coming up on April 19. Colonel John Parker assembled his 75 to 100 Minutemen

on Lexington Green. When some 700 British troops came marching into view, the Minutemen, who were mainly young farmers without combat experience, must have been having second thoughts about having volunteered. When ordered by a British officer, John Pitcairn, to disperse, Parker decided discretion would be the better part of valor and ordered his men to do so. As they were leaving, a shot was fired. Pitcairn reported later that some colonists, having jumped over a wall, fired four or five shots at his men, who had been ordered not to fire but to disarm the rebels. Although just who fired the first shot has been a source of debate since that morning, it was most likely one of the Minutemen. Hours of anxious waiting and the appearance of well-ordered troops by comparison with what the Minutemen could muster almost certainly conspired to produce an itchy trigger finger or a nervous accidental firing.

When the smoke cleared, eight Americans were dead and 10 were wounded. Although all the Americans were familiar with their weapons and had as a target a mass of soldiers in formation silhouetted against the rising sun, the Minutemen managed to wound only one British trooper and hit Pitcairn's horse. Brushing aside this feeble resistance, the British marched on to Concord, reaching the town late in the morning. Most of the rebels' stockpile of weapons had been removed by this time, so the British destroyed what they could find and turned to march back to Boston. As they approached the Sudbury River on the outskirts of Concord, they found another Minuteman force. After the experience at Lexington, they could not have been worried. However, these soldiers stood their ground and their firing was much more effective. The British regrouped and forced the Minutemen back across the Old North Bridge, but from that point on the British force was in serious trouble.

Word spread quickly about the dawn encounter, and angry colonists grabbed their muskets and made for the Concord-Boston road. Here the heritage of fighting Indians in North America proved itself valuable, for hundreds of colonists lined the road and, from the cover of trees and farmhouses, began to snipe at the British column. Hit-and-run guerrilla warfare, which was the common form of fighting in the colonies, proved deadly to the British. Although met by a relieving force of 1,200 at Lexington in mid-afternoon, the British had no better luck in fighting the harassing enemy. By the time the British returned to Boston, they had suffered some 270 dead and wounded, while the colonists had only 95 casualties.

Within a matter of weeks, 20,000 colonists were besieging Boston. The Revolution had begun in earnest, and many more than just the Minutemen were now bearing arms. Indeed, the need for Minutemen, a rapid response force, was no longer necessary. The volunteers who went to Boston to stand up for their rights or to avenge the deaths at Lexington included men who ultimately formed the core of the Continental Army under George Washington, but the militia would prove to be both the bane and boon of the war effort. They always outnumbered the force that Washington tried to mold into a regular army, but their training, discipline, and morale were always directly proportional to their success on the battlefield. The Minutemen, the cream of the militia units prior to the outbreak of the fighting, lost their special status after the first day of the Revolution.

References: Alden, John, *The American Revolution* (New York: Harper & Row, 1954); Fischer, David Hackett, *Paul Revere's Ride* (New York: Oxford University Press, 1995); Smith, Page, *A New Age Now Begins* (New York: McGraw-Hill, 1976).

Mongols

An Asiatic population that conquered from China to Europe between the thirteenth and fifteenth centuries.

The Mongols, one of the most feared of all warrior populations, were horsemen from the steppes of central Asia. Their reputation is almost completely attributable to one man, Genghis Khan. Born in the middle 1100s and named Temujin, this son of a dispossessed tribal leader endured captivity as a child to avenge his father's murder and reclaim leadership of his tribe in young manhood. From that point he built a nation, absorbing conquered peoples and incorporating them into his greater Mongol horde. Although without formal education, Genghis Khan showed an innate intelligence in psychology, strategy and tactics, and statecraft. Without his vision there almost certainly would never have been a great Mongol people.

A handful of Mongol tribes named Temujin Genghis Khan (roughly translated "all-encompassing leader" or "universal ruler") in 1206. He quickly set about expanding his domain by superior leadership and organization. Upon defeating an enemy tribe, he would force the survivors to swear personal loyalty to him, thus making the resulting society his own. Although ruthless in battle, he was open-minded in peace. He absorbed the technology and learning of conquered peoples and forced no one to practice any particular religion. He oversaw the compilation of

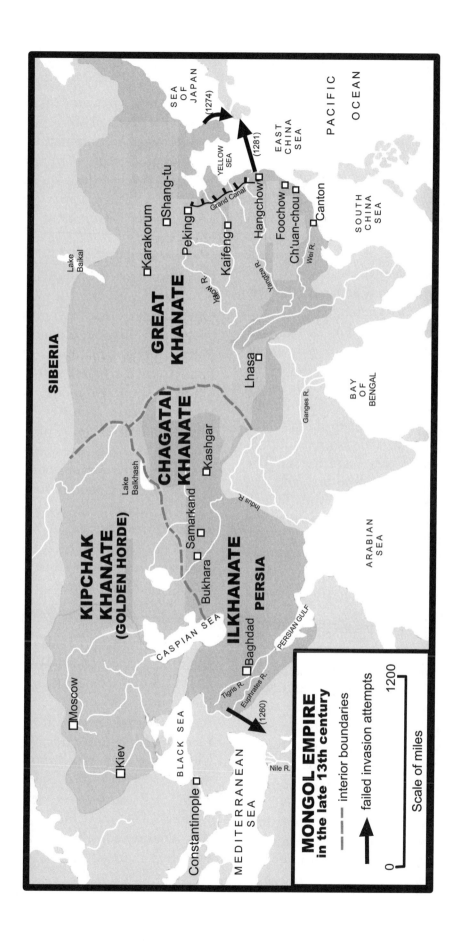

SEA OF JAPAN (1274)

(1281)

PACIFIC OCEAN

EAST CHINA SEA

YELLOW SEA

Karakorum

Shang-tu

SIBERIA

Lake Baikal

□Peking

Kaifeng

Grand Canal

Hangchow

Foochow

Ch'uan-chou

Canton

SOUTH CHINA SEA

GREAT KHANATE

Yellow R.

Yangtze R.

Wei R.

Lhasa

CHAGATAI KHANATE

Kashgar

Ganges R.

BAY OF BENGAL

Lake Balkhash

KIPCHAK KHANATE (GOLDEN HORDE)

Samarkand

Bukhara

ILKHANATE PERSIA

Indus R.

ARABIAN SEA

□Moscow

CASPIAN SEA

Baghdad

PERSIAN GULF

Tigris R.

Euphrates R.

(1260)

□Kiev

BLACK SEA

Constantinople

Nile R.

MEDITERRANEAN SEA

MONGOL EMPIRE
in the late 13th century

- - - interior boundaries

↑ failed invasion attempts

0   1200

Scale of miles

the Great Yasa, a code of laws that covered every part of Mongol life. Once the conquests came to an end, the resulting *Pax Mongolica* allowed for increased trade and a freer flow of ideas as people and goods began to pass back and forth from East to West. Upon his death in 1227, Genghis Khan had established such an effective organization that the expansion continued almost without hesitation after his funeral.

The innate toughness of the Mongol people, developed over generations of surviving on the relatively barren steppes, served them well in training, travel, and battle. The nomadic Mongols had always been horsemen, traveling in search of pasture for their animals and food for themselves. Genghis Khan took advantage of these traits and molded some of the finest light cavalry the world has ever known. Each man carried his own supplies on his back and on two spare horses. The spares were used as fresh mounts, and one of them was a mare to provide milk, which was often fermented into a drink the Mongols called *kumiss*. The soldiers carried two kinds of bows and three kinds of arrows, using different combinations for different types of targets. They also carried a lance, javelin, or scimitar.

The Mongols were organized into graduated groupings, starting at units of 10 men, then 100 men, 1,000 men, and finally 10,000-man units called *tumans*, the basic divisional structure. Twelve tumans comprised an army. The armies stayed in close contact through riders and signal flags, a system so effective that it provided for incredible coordination in attacks. In open battle the Mongols would converge on their enemies from all sides and pelt them with arrows from a long range, then close in on the disorganized and outnumbered foe with lance and sword. Genghis adopted

siege weaponry from conquered populations and used it effectively. Cities that opened their gates on demand were spared; those that resisted were put to the sword and torch. The reputation for brutality thus accomplished was often sufficient to cow city dwellers into surrender. Working with spies and turncoats also allowed the Mongols to bring about a swift end to most sieges.

Genghis Khan led his forces eastward past the Great Wall into China and westward almost to the Caspian Sea. His son Ogatai, teamed with Genghis's most talented general Subotai, extended the Mongol dominions as far as the northern edge of Arabia, northern India, Russia, and all of China as far as modern Vietnam and achieved great victories over European forces in Poland and Hungary. Only the recall of men to attend Ogatai's funeral stopped their further spread into Europe.

Genghis's grandson Batu Khan led the Golden Horde that established Mongol control over Russia, an occupation that lasted until the 1400s. Another grandson, Kubilai, occupied China and absorbed much of Chinese culture and learning. His only defeats came in two failed attempts to invade Japan in the 1270s and 1280s. Yet another grandson, Hulagu, invaded the Middle East and controlled territory as far as the borders of Egypt. In the later part of the fourteenth century, the destructive invader Tamurlane claimed descent from Genghis Khan and raided deep into India. The Mongols controlled the vast part of Asia for almost two centuries, but ultimately fell to the twin vices of greed and laziness. The good life of the civilizations they conquered seduced the warriors, and they lost their edge; it is a story repeated often in history.

References: Chambers, James, *The Devil's Horsemen* (New York: Atheneum, 1979); Curtin, Jeremiah, *The Mongols: A History* (Westport, CT: Greenwood Press, 1972); Kwanten, Luc, *Imperial Nomads* (Philadelphia: University of Pennsylvania Press, 1979).

Mosby's Rangers

A partisan cavalry unit of the Confederate army during the American Civil War.

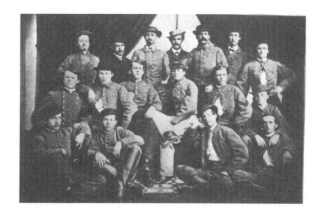

The men of Mosby's Rangers.

John Singleton Mosby was a lawyer practicing in far western Virginia in the years immediately preceding the Civil War. He was a staunch Unionist and made no attempt to hide his feelings, openly supporting Democrat Stephen A. Douglas for the presidency in 1860 against the wishes of the Southern wing of the party. He also spoke against secession when South Carolina started that process in December 1860. Like the most famous Virginian of the war, Robert E. Lee, Mosby found that when Virginia seceded from the Union, he had to remain loyal to his home state. Nothing in his first months as a soldier distinguished him—other than his quick temper, which had landed him in trouble and even in jail in his earlier life.

About the time of the opening battle of the war at Bull Run in July 1861, Mosby came to the attention of the man destined to command the Confederate cavalry arm, J. E. B. Stuart. Stuart saw in Mosby a man with enough intelligence to avoid recklessness but enough dash to act while others talked. Mosby served under Stuart and was active in Stuart's famous ride around the Union army prior to the Seven Days battles in the summer of 1862. Soon afterward, Mosby was given command of his own unit, although he was obliged to raise his own recruits. Mosby was captured while on a trip to visit Confederate General Thomas "Stonewall" Jackson to confer about recruiting. He was held only 10 days before being exchanged, but in that time he learned of the Union plans to abandon the thrust toward Richmond under George McClellan and focus on a second attack from the north under John Pope. This information convinced Lee to turn his back on McClellan and face the new threat, defeating Pope at the second battle at Bull Run in August 1862.

His ability to gather intelligence beyond doubt, Mosby acquired men and enhanced his reputation. Ordered to operate behind Union lines in the neighborhood of Washington, DC, he was eminently successful, stealing supplies, attacking camps, capturing enemy troops, and even kidnapping Union Brigadier General Edwin Stoughton out of his bed. Mosby received a promotion to major and was given command of the newly formed Company A of the Forty-third Battalion Partisan Rangers in June 1863. He soon proved his worth once again by slipping, with some of his officers, into the camp of Joseph Hooker's Army of the Potomac. The spies captured documents relating to Hooker's intentions, then made their way back through camp undiscovered.

After the Confederate setbacks at Gettysburg and Vicksburg in July 1863, the need to harass Union forces and tie them down was much greater. Mosby's Rangers spent the summer and fall of 1864 in the Shenandoah Valley looting the countryside and tying down General Philip Sheridan's command so completely that they were unable to aid Grant's siege of Petersburg. It was during this time that Mosby's enemies dubbed him the Gray Ghost. In October 1864 his men damaged a rail line near Martinsburg, West Virginia, and waited for the train to pass. When it derailed, the Rangers entered the wrecked train and looted Sheridan's payroll of $170,000. Although Mosby unknowingly missed an opportunity to stop a train upon which General Grant was traveling unescorted, he still was such a thorn in the Union side that a price was put on his head. The reward was still unclaimed (and still offered) when the war came to an end April 9, 1865. Indeed, Mosby's last raid took place the day after the surrender had been signed. Unwilling to give himself up for execution, he waited until the "Wanted Dead or Alive" order was rescinded more than two months after the war's end. He was therefore able to claim the status of being the last Confederate officer to surrender.

After the war, Mosby remained in the public eye, not as a war hero but for his almost immediate return to the Unionist stance he had held prior to the conflict. Mosby supported candidates often unpopular in the South, including Grant. When Grant ran for the presidency in 1868, Mosby saw in him an honest man who would work for reconciliation between the two regions. Mosby spoke with Grant, and the two became good friends. He became Grant's main advisor on southern issues after the election and lobbied for an in-crease in federal jobs in the southern states. Mosby served as U.S. consul in Hong Kong and as an assistant attorney in the Justice Department. His popularity in the South suffered for his political activity, but as the immediate fervor of the war passed, Mosby was once again embraced by his state. Before his death in 1916 at the age of 82, he received a medal from his alma mater, the University of Virginia.

References: Jones, Virgil Carrington, *Gray Ghosts and Confederate Raiders* (New York: Henry Holt & Co., 1956); Siepel, Kevin, *Rebel: The Life and Times of John Singleton Mosby* (New York: St. Martin's Press, 1983).

Mujahidin

Muslim fighters, primarily in Afghanistan, originally resisting Soviet control of their country.

Contrary to popular belief, the term *Mujahidin* does not refer to a specific group of warriors. Rather, it is one of many accepted spellings for an Arabic term that can be translated as "those who struggle for jihad" or "holy warriors." Afghan resistance fighters in the late 1970s and 1980s assumed this title to indicate that they were waging a just war, a jihad, against the Soviet Union and its puppet government in Afghanistan. In modern Afghanistan, the United States has allied with certain Mujahidin groups and battled others in its war against the Taliban and Al-Qaeda. The fractured, tribal, and devoutly religious Afghan countryside saw the Soviet invasion as a threat to their lives, culture, values, and religion, and hence gave birth to the Mujahidin. They did not expect to achieve battlefield victory, but were able to accept an asymmetry of casualties in order to drive the Soviets from their land. And while they never achieved any lasting form of political unity, the Mujahidin have become some of the toughest and most resilient guerilla groups in history.

Mujahidin resistance fighters belong to a wide variety of ethnic, political, and tribal groups, but are primarily recruited from the rural population of Afghanistan, which comprises about 75 percent of the country. Foreign fighters from Saudi Arabia, Pakistan, and other Middle Eastern nations also swelled the ranks of Mujahidin groups during the Soviet occupation and the current (2001–2006) conflict.

The harsh conditions in rural Afghanistan require that the Mujahidin be some of the most physically tough people on earth. They are extremely mobile over what is often nearly impassible terrain and can endure hardships that many modern soldiers would find unbearable. Before the Soviet invasion, the British in the nineteenth and twentieth centuries had witnessed the resolve, toughness, and skill of these fighters when they were engaged in constant conflict with them along the Afghan-Pakistani border. The proliferation of modern weaponry has enabled these fighters to become even more accomplished in guerrilla warfare.

Due to the tribal nature of Afghan society and the diverse nature of the groups involved in the resistance to the Soviet Union , the Taliban, and United States, the Mujahidin never developed as a strong political entity. In fact, they routinely engaged in armed conflict with one another before and after the Soviet-Afghan conflict. They created neither a formal command structure nor attempted to develop an advanced and diversified military presence. Their strategy has always been to attack, survive, then disperse in order to fight again another day. They emerged as a

determined, low-tech, and persistent insurgency that largely defied efforts to eliminate them.

Soviet forces occupied Afghanistan for approximately a decade during the Soviet-Afghan War which lasted from 1979 until February of 1989. During the occupation, the Soviets seized control of the major cities while the Mujahidin mounted attacks from the mountains and ambushed Soviet forces on the periphery. Apart from areas directly occupied by large Soviet forces, the rural areas of the country were effectively under Mujahidin control by 1981. However, the Mujahidin, armed with World War II-era rifles and virtually no heavy weaponry, enjoyed few major successes before the late 1980s. This is, however, the nature of guerilla warfare. The Mujahidin did not defeat the Soviets on the battlefield, yet despite heavy casualties they continued to attack and harass Soviet forces throughout the country.

Meanwhile, the Soviets increasingly focused their efforts on weakening the Mujahidin. Due to a difficulty in distinguishing between the holy warriors and the civilian population harboring them, the Soviets adopted an indiscriminate policy throughout the conflict. They engaged in a brutal policy that included attacks on civilian centers in the countryside in order to depopulate the rural areas the Mujahidin depended on for support. Their campaign was successful in that the Mujahidin sustained heavy casualties and did not register many successes in the first seven and a half years of the war (1979–1986). However, the Mujahidin did maintain the support of the Afghani people and the international community, and continued insurgent activities throughout the country.

In the last stage of the war, from 1987–1889, the Mujahidin became increasingly better armed and militarily improved due to support and training from the American Central Intelligence Agency. They relied on ambushes and quick raids against Soviet outposts, creating a large number of casualties without directly engaging Soviet forces. When faced with organized resistance, the Mujahidin would retreat and vanish into the local population. They were so successful that often the only traffic able to cross Afghani highways at night were jeeps laden with insurgents.

The stinger missile, along with mortars, other heavy weapons, and modern small arms, was supplied to the Mujahidin in larger and larger numbers by the CIA as the conflict dragged on; the firepower supplied by these weapons, especially the surface-to-air missiles, became important leveling factors in the late stages of the war. They dramatically expanded the capability of the Mujahidin by providing a relatively cheap, yet highly portable air defense, and a way to engage Soviet forces from a distance. Despite the additions of these more modern weapons, the Soviets still enjoyed an enormous technological advantage. However, due to the primitive conditions in Afghanistan and Soviet supply difficulties, these technological advantages did not translate into a strategic victory for Soviet forces in the long run.

The increased persistence and success of the Mujahidin, combined with a changing political situation in the Soviet Union, led to the withdrawal of Soviet forces in February of 1989. In spite of this, the rivalries and differences among Mujahidin groups led to a long and bloody civil war after the Soviet withdrawal that eventually culminated with the Taliban assuming control over much of the country, with the exception of the territory governed by the resistance movement deemed the Northern Alliance.

Because of their inherently fractured nature, the Mujahidin could never hope to achieve political unity. It was not a political movement, but a resistance movement, bred to fight an extremely powerful enemy with only limited technology, numbers, and resources. The Mujahidin made it impossible for the Soviet Union, one of the world's two most powerful states at that time, to control Afghanistan by mounting a determined guerilla movement, and they are now providing a significant challenge to American military might by using many of the same weapons and tactics.

Austin DeArmand

References: Ademac, Ludwig W. *Historical Dictionary of Afghanistan.* 2nd edition. (Lanham, Md: The Scarecrow Press, Inc.,1997). Giradet, Edward. *Afghanistan: the Soviet war.* (New York: St. Martin's Press: New York 1985). Goodson, Lary P. *Afghanistan's Endless War: state failure, regional politics and the rise of the Taliban* (Seattle: University of Washington Press, 2001). Jalali, Ali Ahmad and Lester W. Grau. *The Other Side of the Mountain: Mujahideen Tactics in the Soviet-Afghan War.* (Quantico, VA: The United States Marine Corps Studies and Analysis Division,1999). Shay, Shaul. *The Endless Jihad: The Mujahidin, the Taliban and Bin Laden.* (Herzliya, Israel: The International Policy Institute for Counter-Terrorism, 2002). *The Soviet-Afghan War: how a superpower fought and lost.* The Russian general Staff. Translated and edited by Lester W. Grau & Michael A. Gress. University Press of Kansas: Lawrence, Kansas, 2002.

N

Normans

A northeastern European population that conquered Great Britain and areas of the Mediterranean during the eleventh and twelfth centuries.

In the eleventh century, a remarkable people of purposeful drive and indomitable will appeared on the European stage. Their attitudes and practices changed their world and helped to shape ours. Feared, reviled, and ultimately rehabilitated in modern history, the Northmen, or Normans, were a catalyst for change in Europe.

The early years of the tenth century witnessed the last gasp of Viking expansion in Europe, an invasion of northern France by Hrolf the Ganger (also known as Rollo). Although successful in general terms, Hrolf found the exertions of his undertaking so debilitating—and the resistance of the degenerating Franks so effective—that a conciliatory offer from Charles the Simple proved irresistible. Viking opportunism and practicality could not pass up a deal like the Treaty of St. Clair-Sur-Epte: Rollo received the area around Rouen (and a royal daughter) to have and to hold in exchange for an agreement to be a faithful vassal and to keep friend and foe alike from pillaging the territory. While these particular Northmen were assimilated into Frankish culture and military practice with some speed, they were still only a generation or so removed from a Viking tradition that practiced peaceful trade and coexistence only with those who looked as though they could put up a good fight. Others were slain and sacked as a matter of course. Only one Norman relapse to these old raiding ways is reported: Shortly after the death of Charles the Simple, the Normans made an unsuccessful foray through western France and were defeated along with the Aquitanians by Rudolph at Limoges in 929. Thereafter, with increasing adaptation to Frankish culture, the Normans became boisterous yet faithful adherents to the French throne.

Duke Robert of Normandy demonstrated his support for the French King Henry I's cause by assisting in campaigns on Henry's behalf against rebellious nobles in northern France, including Champagne and Blois (about 1033). Henry returned the favor by helping Robert's illegitimate heir, William, in a fight against his own rebellious nobles, notably at Val-Les-Dunes (1047) where the rebellion was finally suppressed. Some Norman lords had objected to the circumstances of William's birth. Others simply used the excuse to make a grab for land and power. The Conqueror of 1066 was previously known as The Bastard, and at a tender age had to leave home at night in his socks when news of Duke Robert's death became common knowledge. Two years after Val-Les-Dunes, William and Henry were at war with one another, with William successfully repulsing a French invasion in 1049 and

The Norman army prepares to fight King Harold, as depicted in this scene from the Bayeux tapestry. Musee de la Tapisserie, Bayeux, France. © Erich Lessing / Art Resource, NY

fighting the prolonged and inconclusive war (1053–1058) that was typical of the era. Once firmly in control, William looked to his own interests and prerogatives.

The Normans had adopted the Frankish military system, which reflected the efforts of Charlemagne and his successors to emulate what fragments of Roman organization, tactics, and strategy remained extant. Javelin-armed heavy cavalry formed the core of the Frankish army, including mounted nobles and their retainers in an irregular approximation of late Roman *equites*. These horsemen, in their scale and chain mail armor (but still lacking stirrups), saw themselves as heirs to the Roman tradition and consciously imitated what they perceived to be the dress and style of their great precursors. True Roman drills, formations, and evolutions were unknown, but devotion and sufficient practice of established moves enabled the army to remain quite effective against the Franks' more barbarous enemies.

Frankish infantry retained the shield-wall, shoulder-to-shoulder tactics of other early Middle Age armies. In battle, they seem to have been effective enough, and in straitened circumstances would have been strengthened by dismounted cavalry—a practice unthinkable 100 years later, when the lofty concepts of chivalry had taken hold. Auxiliary troops included archers (reintroduced to western Europe by Charlemagne, but allowed to languish under later kings), javelin skirmishers, light cavalry from Gascony and Brittany (possibly descendants of Alans resettled by the Romans), and lighter infantry and cavalry recruited from defeated Slavs, Magyars, Vikings, and others. The wisdom and willingness to use a greater variety of troop types to cope with different battlefield situations originated with Charlemagne. It differentiated his armies from the monolithic masses of his enemies. However, the effectiveness of his system was not lost on Norman leaders in France, England, or in the Mediterranean.

Charlemagne bequeathed the Frankish armies a somewhat improved supply system that utilized frontier fortresses as advanced depots for operations along the frontiers. He also seems to have instituted the rudiments of intelligence and staff work, including the study of opponents' strengths and weaknesses and the considerations of more esoteric factors in the field of strategy than simply finding the enemy and having at him. To what degree these practices survived when Norman armies took the field in the eleventh century no one can say with certainty, but William's preparations for the invasion of England

and his apparent awareness of Anglo-Saxon moves and situations certainly support a tradition of attention to such details.

Norman armies evolved their own distinctions from their Frankish models. Missile troops, including archers and slingers, were used more extensively, and the first documented use of the crossbow occurred at the Battle of Hastings. Norman mercenaries fighting in Italy brought the stirrup and lance to western Europe (the partial transition from javelin thrust overhand to couched lance can be seen on the Bayeux Tapestry), and the result was a vastly improved cavalry charge. Stirrups allowed the mass and velocity of charging horse and rider to be concentrated on the point of the couched lance, a lesson learned from Byzantine cataphracts (heavily-armored cavalrymen) at Cannae in 1018. Stirrupless javelin cavalry could not withstand such a charge, nor could any but the most determined infantry. The lesson was not lost on practical Norman warriors, and by the 1070s the change to charging, lance-carrying cavalry seems to have been complete.

Breton allies and mercenaries retained the javelin throughout the period, however, and preferred skirmishing with thrown javelins until an opportunity to charge in with swords and sidearms was presented. A Breton tactic, the feigned flight was possibly a throwback to those Alans settled in Armorica (Brittany) by Romans in the chaotic fifth century. The tactic is recorded by the chronicler William of Poitiers as having been used successfully at Hastings, another instance of Norman willingness to adapt and innovate their style of warfare.

Another innovation of the time was the appearance of bodies of professional warriors, formed by enterprising nobles to hire out to other nobles, kings, and aspiring kings in order to flesh out, support, or supplant their regular standing forces. A substantial part of William the Conqueror's army at Hastings consisted of such troops. The practice of forming these professional troops also points, albeit distantly, to the permanent companies and ultimately regiments formed in this manner by contractors in the 1500s through 1700s.

When William of Normandy landed at Pevensey in the fall of 1066, he and his army had a number of distinct advantages working for them. In less than a month, the English/Saxon army had already dealt with a raid by Tostig Godwinson (English King Harold's renegade brother) and a more serious full-scale invasion by King Harald Hardraada of Norway (an authentic hero and man of the world who was single-minded and ruthless in a manner reminiscent of William of Normandy). The Battles of Gate Fulford and Stamford Bridge had depleted the northern English levies, and although King Harold surprised and destroyed the Norse army at Stamford Bridge, killing Tostig and Hardraada as well, the victory was a bloody one and cost Harold losses he could ill afford in the ranks of his housecarls. These household troops, or bodyguards, were first-rate warriors. Clad in mail and using large axes that required both hands to wield, the housecarls were the only professional troops available to King Harold. The loss of a third or more of their number was a far more serious blow to Harold's, and England's, fortunes than the decimation of the northern feudal levy.

Prodigious feats of organization, marching, and tough fighting had availed King Harold little. As he rested his foot-sore and wounded army at York, word reached him of William's arrival in the south. Less than a week had passed since the victory at

Stamford Bridge. It is a measure of Harold's resolve and abilities that he would cobble together an army and fight again, over 200 miles away, in less than two weeks.

That William of Normandy profited from the works of Tostig and Harald Hardraada is without question. He seems to have communicated with Tostig when the latter was in Flanders a year earlier. Any suggestion of collaboration or alliance with the renegade Godwinson or Hardraada, beyond obviously wishing them well, is very hard to determine.

In the south, William had moved from Pevensey along the coast to establish a base at the more defensible port of Hastings. Aware of what had transpired in the north, the duke no doubt played down Harold's victory and broadcast the more comforting truth: Harold's army was tired, bloodied, and far away. Norman morale was also surely bolstered by the knowledge that Pope Alexander II had sanctioned what amounted to a "holy" crusade to regain what was rightfully William's: the throne of England. It is beyond the scope of this account to explain the near-Byzantine maneuvers to position this or that person to inherit the English crown that were undertaken in the latter days of Kind Edward the Confessor—or to discuss the merits of each of their claims. Suffice it to say that William the Bastard of Normandy and a sufficient number of nobles and mercenaries (and a pope) believed that he had a valid claim.

In the middle of the night of October 13, King Harold encamped his exhausted army about seven miles north of Hastings. Prodigious marching and the housecarls' endurance had again succeeded in placing the English army in position to strike its foes. But the army that deployed on Senlac Hill the morning of October 14 was not the force that had prevailed at Stamford Bridge. The remaining housecarls formed the front rank of a massive phalanx-like formation. Supporting ranks were filled first by "Select Fyrd," fairly well-equipped landowners and freemen, and then by men of the "Great Fyrd": peasants, townspeople, and tenant farmers with a random assortment of simple, often ad hoc weapons. Except for the housecarls, the English army consisted of part-time troops with little training or organization. We know that the housecarls had few bowmen, and the southern feudal levies also seem to have contained fewer as well—a fact that, in the end, may have proved crucial. Certainly the command and control structure of this force was primitive. Harold believed he was outnumbered; he was certainly outclassed by the enemy army. He chose a defensive position that blocked the London road. On the slope of a hill, with both flanks anchored and the dependable housecarls in the front rank, King Harold prepared for the attack, which he thought would not be long in coming.

The Norman army has already been described in general terms. The force that took the field at the Battle of Hastings consisted of three divisions: a Breton force on the left, Normans in the center, and French and Flemish on the right. Each division deployed a line of light infantry archers in front, supported by a line of infantry men-at-arms, and followed by heavy cavalry. Estimates of numbers vary greatly. Any advantage in efficiency on the Norman part was offset by the strength of the English position. It is thus possible to say that the two armies were evenly matched.

The Battle of Hastings was an all-day affair during which William attempted to break the English shield wall with almost no success. He finally was able to break the English line by feigning retreat and drawing some of the less disciplined of Harold's troops down the hill after him. There, on open ground, his cavalry could operate. William continued a rotation of archery harassment and infantry and cavalry assaults on the English throughout the afternoon. He ordered his archers, unopposed by a like force on the English side, to utilize high-angle fire so that their projectiles would plunge down onto the defenders from above. The English, given no relief from continued Norman assaults and missile fire, were approaching the limit of their endurance. At about this time, an arrow struck King Harold in the eye and wounded him mortally.

Taking heart from this development, William and his army renewed their attacks with vigor. The English army began to come apart. The Fyrd fled from Senlac Hill. Harold's housecarls stood firmly by their dying king. Now completely surrounded, they could not hold together any longer. A few diehards fought on in retreat through the dark, but by nightfall the Normans held Senlac Hill. Shortly after the battle, William seized Dover, then marched on London. On Christmas Day of 1066, he was crowned William I, King of England.

The campaign to put William in that seat had amounted to a "national" effort by the Normans in planning, preparation, and ultimate conquest. A curious footnote to these endeavors is the unusual conquest of southern Italy and Sicily late in the eleventh century. Again the superiority of even small bodies of Norman troops, combined with resolute Norman leadership paid big dividends for those sufficiently daring.

Normans appear in the Mediterranean almost accidentally. Norman pilgrims returning from the Holy Land helped to defend Salerno against a Muslim attack. Fighting Muslims evidently seemed no harder than scrambling for inheritance and rewards back home, so before too long second (and subsequent) sons and a host of adventurers began showing up in Italy. Normans are subsequently mentioned in Italy as mercenaries for hire, and none too picky about who their employers were. A small Norman settlement appeared in Aversa under Rainulf in 1027 followed by expansion in Apulia and Calabria through the 1030s and 1050s.

George Maniakes's Byzantine army that invaded Sicily in 1038 included many Normans, as did many papal armies of the era. It is emblematic of the Norman experience in Italy that they fought for and against both the major players in the peninsula until their own position improved sufficiently to challenge their previous employers. These ruffians would soon prove to be a problem, as was illustrated in the Civitella campaign. A papal army of Pope Leo IX was trying to relieve the region of Apulia from Norman depredations. The brothers Humphrey and Robert Guiscard, with 3,000 men, totally routed the papal army's mixed bag of Italians and Germans, of whom only the Germans put up a fight and were cut down to a man. The pope was handed over to the victorious Normans by the citizens of the town, who had witnessed the battle and could see which way the wind was blowing. Leo IX caused no more trouble. In fact, a successor of Leo, Pope Nicholas II, wound up making a deal with Robert Guiscard: In exchange for help against German Emperor Henry IV, Robert was appointed Duke of Calabria and Apulia and authorized to conquer Sicily. Sicily was being held by the Muslims at the time and Nicholas wasn't too concerned with offending them. Dynasty-building seemed a Norman pastime. While conquering Sicily from the Muslims, Robert Guiscard and his associates also managed to pinch off Byzantine holdings in Italy—the last was Bari, taken in 1071. Not content with beating the Byzantines in Italy, Robert carried the fight to Greece in 1081. He won handily against Alexius Comnenus at Durazzo in 1082 and might have grabbed a large slice of Greece itself had he not been called back to Rome by the pope.

Because Pope Gregory VII had refused to recognize Henry IV as emperor, Henry besieged Rome in 1083. Hearing the pope's call for aid, Robert Guiscard collected an army of Normans, Muslims, and Lombards and marched north. Refusing to risk a battle, Henry withdrew. Robert's army then sacked Rome—whether as a warning to the pope or out of frustration is not really clear. A note of interest is the continued Norman use of foreign specialists and auxiliary troops in their armies. Lombard lancers, Muslim archers, and Italian infantry made up sizable portions of the Norman armies in Italy and Sicily. After squabbling with the papacy, the Byzantines, the Muslims, and one another, the Normans carved a kingdom out of southern Italy and Sicily from 1060 to 1300. As the Kingdom of the Two Sicilies, it would last for centuries, much longer than the Normans themselves.

Michael Forbes

References: Davis, Ralph H. C., *The Normans and Their Myth* (London: Thames and Hudson, 1976); Lindsay, Jack, *The Normans and Their World* (New York: St. Martin's Press, 1975); Loyn, H. R., *Anglo-Saxon England and the Norman Conquest* (New York: Longman, 1991).

P

Paratroopers

Specialized troops trained to enter battle by parachute.

The concept of transporting soldiers by air behind enemy lines is as old as piloted flight, which began with the Montgolfier brothers' balloon in the 1700s. Napoleon considered using balloons to transport soldiers across the English Channel. In World War I, observers in balloons were supplied with parachutes for emergencies, and visionary American General Billy Mitchell proposed dropping parachute troops behind German lines in 1919—had the war gone on that long. In 1922, the Russians began promoting private trials with parachutes and gliders. The first serious government paratrooper training began with the Italians, inspired by the air power theories of Giulio Douhet. In 1927, the best method of deploying the parachute was considered. The Italians chose the static cord method: A line connecting the parachute pack and the aircraft would pull the pack open and jerk the parachute out. Complete battalions were training by 1930, and the Italians organized two airborne divisions, but they never made a combat drop.

The United States Army toyed with parachuting in 1928, preferring the individual rip cord for deploying the chute. The use of paratroopers for sabotage was considered, but the army dropped any further development with the coming of the Great Depression. It was Germany that first realized the idea of airborne warfare. Hitler's government supported glider clubs as a method of training airplane pilots in contravention of the Treaty of Versailles. When he began to openly violate the treaty in 1935, gliders and pilots were developed and available. Because Germany was surrounded by countries with strong natural or man-made defenses, the concept of delivering troops behind those defenses appealed to Germany's military planners. In 1936 a paratrooper school was established at Stendal in Bavaria and, following Italian doctrine, the instructors chose the static line method of deployment. Command of the school fell to Major-General Oswalt Bassenge. No one knew exactly for what the paratroopers would be used or even which branch of the military would command the forces, but training went forward. These parachute forces were called in German *Fallschirmjaeger*.

Bassenge's school trained troops from the army, the Luftwaffe (air force), and the elite troops, Schutzstaffeln (SS), but there was no command coordination or organization. In 1938, when he was told to prepare for possible operations in Czechoslovakia, Bassenge informed the government and military that he could not possibly command a unit mixed with soldiers from various branches of the military and that some organization had to be created—both for training and combat operations.

Paratroopers

Dwight Eisenhower giving orders to American paratroopers in England, June 6, 1944. Library of Congress, Prints and Photographs Division [reproduction number LC-USZ62-25600]

In response, the Luftwaffe commander-in-chief, Hermann Goering, appointed Major-General Kurt Student, commander of a Luftwaffe division, to command the paratroops. Student at this point really became the father of the German airborne forces. He organized the Seventh Flieger (Flyer) Division of both parachute and glider troops made up of troops from the SA (*Sturmabteilung*, the paramilitary wing of the Nazi party), the army's Sixteenth Infantry Regiment, and the Luftwaffe's Hermann Goering Division. His division consisted of two parachute and seven glider battalions. The Seventh Flieger Division saw no combat in Czechoslovakia because diplomats did the work in September 1938. However, Student did stage an exercise in Moravia after Germany occupied the Czech Sudetenland. It was an impressive drop, but soon afterward his men were dispersed back to their original organizations and Student was left with only a skeleton force. He was given permission to build up the Seventh Flieger Division, and by the outbreak of war in September 1939, he had the parachutists trained. The army had guaranteed the Twenty-second Infantry Division would be available for transport to the battlefield by glider or transport aircraft.

The paratroopers were not used in combat when Germany invaded Poland in 1939, but Student was instructed to prepare for operations in Western Europe for the spring of 1940. Finally, in April of that year, the airborne forces saw action. The operation was to be in support of the Nazi invasions of Denmark and Norway. The paratroopers were to seize airfields and hold them undamaged for German aircraft to bring in manpower and supplies. The two Danish targets were captured with no trouble, but bad weather and alert enemy troops made operations in Norway more difficult. Still, despite incurring casualties, the paratroopers secured their targets and proved the viability of the concept. In Holland in May 1940, glider-borne troops were used more widely in seizing Dutch forts and bridges in the area around Rotterdam. The Dutch were more prepared for airborne operations, having learned from the Norwegian experience, but the Germans still had some notable successes. Although some of their landings around Rotterdam were disasters, others went off without a hitch. The most successful of these came near Maastricht and the Albert Canal. Bridges across the canal had to be captured if the Germans were to easily invade Belgium, but their construction, preset demolition charges, and the extremely strong Eban-Emael Fort defied conventional attack. Glider troops aided by paratroopers, however, seized two of the three bridges intact and quickly captured the surprised garrison in Eban-Emael.

Even more successful for the new airborne arm was the German invasion of Crete. The British army held strong positions on the island in the eastern Mediter-ranean and the Germans had no serious ability to mount an amphibious landing. Again, parachute and glider troops seized key airfields and allowed the Germans to funnel in troops and equipment. What was considered a virtually impregnable island fell in a matter of days with the help of these airborne forces. Successful as these operations were, however, they were the final major airborne operations Germany conducted. Although used again for air-field seizure in North Africa after the American landings, the paratrooper land-ing there was a small operation with limited effect. In the future, the paratroop-ers that had become elite forces were used strictly as infantry, fighting mostly in Italy.

British and American army commands were quick to grasp the potential of para-troopers, but only after the Germans proved the concept workable. The British committed a hastily trained battalion to combat in North Africa near the Algerian-Tunisian border. They were dropped in coordination with the American landings on the North African coast on November 8 ,1942, and seized airfields held by the French colonial forces. British and Ameri-can airborne forces took part in the Allied invasion of Sicily in summer 1943, and the results were tragic. Most of the Allied shipping lying off the coast had not been forewarned of the parachute drop and began firing at their own aircraft as the transports flew toward the drop zones. In addition, poor weather and an unnecessari-ly long and complicated flight plan caused some 60 percent of the gliders to crash into the sea rather than reach the island. In spite of the fiasco, those paratroopers and glider forces that did land did good work. British paratroopers seized a key bridge and held it long enough for amphibiously landed

forces to link up to them. American para-troopers, although scattered over 65 miles, still managed to collect enough men to hold the key position of Gela Ridge against two German armored and several infantry assaults. A second landing a few days later fared little better when these paratroopers, too, were recipients of deadly "friendly" fire.

The best airborne operation the Ameri-cans conducted was on the night of June 5–6, 1944, as Allied forces invaded the Normandy coast in the famous D-Day landings. The American Eighty-second and 101st Airborne Divisions landed behind German lines in order to capture bridges and control road junctions to delay any German reinforcements sent to the beach-head. Although hampered by bad weather, the two divisions dropped by parachute and glider accomplished almost all of their objectives. Their next major operation, however, was not so successful. In the autumn of 1944, British General Bernard Montgomery designed a three-stage air-borne operation to seize a set of bridges across rivers and canals in Holland. Once the bridges were in paratrooper possession, they were to hold them until armored columns linked up and relieved them. Poor planning and command decisions resulted in a fiasco, especially for the British First Airborne Division. That division held on to the bridge in Arnhem until overrun by a German counterattack, and the soldiers had to make their way individually and in small groups back to Allied lines. The American target bridges were captured and held, but as was observed after the opera-tion, Arnhem was a bridge too far. For the remainder of the war, American airborne troops, like their German counterparts, for the most part fought as infantry. The 101st Airborne Division gained its greatest fame in this role by being one of the units holding the road junction of Bastogne, Belgium, during the Germans' last major offensive through the Ardennes Forest in December 1944: the famous Battle of the Bulge.

Paratroopers fought in the Pacific theater of operations as well. A small Japanese force was successful in capturing its objectives in Indonesia in January 1942. American paratroopers landed in New Guinea, where the jungle terrain made flanking operations difficult for conventional ground forces. When American forces returned to the Philippines in 1944, American paratroopers saw action on the islands of Leyte and Luzon and were involved in the recapture of the stronghold on Corregidor. World War II also saw the first use of paratroopers for commando operations, the role for which they are most used today. British General Orde Wingate jumped with his "Chindit" guerrillas into Burma to harass Japanese rear areas with some success.

After World War II, airborne training altered a bit. The soldier who was trained to jump out of airplanes with a parachute was still considered a member of the elite forces. Warfare in underdeveloped countries with poor road networks, however, made the need for large-scale airborne operations necessary. The introduction of the helicopter revolutionized airborne warfare. Starting initially with the American experience in Vietnam in 1965, large-scale, helicopter-borne assaults almost came to be considered conventional warfare. For small-unit actions, long-range reconnaissance, and commando operations, helicopters became the primary method of delivery.

In modern armies, some airborne divisions still primarily depend on developing skills in parachute training, and special forces around the world (such as the Green Berets, French Foreign Legion, and the British Special Air Service) all have jump-trained soldiers. Paratrooper landings are still the preferred method of quiet insertion behind enemy lines, and for sabotage and other guerrilla operations, dropping by parachute will probably remain a necessary military skill.

References: Barker, Geoffrey, *A Concise History of the United States Airborne* (Brandon, FL: Anglo-American Publishing, 1989); Hickey, Michael, *Out of the Sky* (New York: Scribner, 1979); Weeks, John, *Assault from the Sky* (New York: Putnam, 1978).

Peoples of the Sea

A mysterious ancient population that brought about a Dark Age in ancient times, during the thirteenth and twelfth centuries BCE.

In the late thirteenth century BCE, the known world of the Middle East was fairly peaceful. The two major powers in the region, Egypt and the Hittites, had settled into spheres of influence, and the entire area was engaged in widespread trade. All of this was upset by the arrival of the Peoples of the Sea, or simply Sea Peoples. Whence they came has been the subject of debate since their first arrival more than 3,000 years ago. The primary contemporary accounts of these peoples are in Egyptian, with some few others from the eastern Mediterranean city-state of Ugarit. The Sea Peoples first appeared as invaders in 1218 or 1208 BCE, allied with the Libyan king Meryre. Meryre seems to have organized a coalition force of northern soldiers of fortune, but "northern" is an all-encompassing word in this case. The various peoples recruited included men of the Ekwesh, Lukka, Sherden, Shekelesh, and Teresh tribes. The Teresh have been identified (possibly) as Etruscan, the Shekelesh with the Sikels of Sicily, and the Ekwesh as Achaean Greeks. The Lukkans have been identified as pirates operating out of southwestern Anatolia, and the Sherdens seem to have given their name to Sardinia, although that may have been a later conquest. The Sherdens, however, were the first of the northerners to appear and, having been defeated by the Egyptians, began to fight alongside them, probably as mercenaries.

The introduction of the Sherdens to the Egyptian army could possibly signify a major change in military thinking at the time. For a few centuries, the dominant arm of the Middle Eastern armies were the chariots, so much so that by the late thirteenth century BCE, they were practically the sole arm, with infantry being used merely for policing, guard duty, and the occasional punitive expedition into rugged terrain where chariots could not go. Because chariots and the horses needed to pull them were expensive, the social elite became the military elite, while the masses remained unarmed and untrained for the most part. The Sherdens, however, introduced a new element to chariot warfare. Prior to this time, a support group of infantry, called runners, followed after the chariots in battle in order to finish off wounded enemy soldiers and gather loot. The Sherdens, using newly introduced long swords and hunting javelins, became light infantry that moved quickly through the battlefields, disabling enemy horses and attacking enemy charioteers and archers. This proved effective enough to mark the end of the chariot as a fighting machine.

When Meryre invaded Egypt with his Sea People allies in 1218 or 1208 BCE, they came on foot and with few chariots. The allies were dressed in light body armor with horned helmets, long swords, and round shields. They invaded in the early years of the reign of Rameses II's son, Merneptah. At that time, the chariots of Egypt prevailed and the Libyans lost 6,000 dead, the Ekwesh 2,200, and other northerners significant numbers as well. Nine thousand swords were captured, but only 12 Libyan chariots, indicating Meryre's determination to fight with infantry.

This was just the beginning of the Sea Peoples' invasion, however. They had probably already overtaken mainland Greece (possibly identified with the Dorians who brought about the Greek Dark Ages) and also destroyed Troy in an action that may have been mentioned in the *Iliad*. In Homer's story of the siege, the foot soldiers of the invaders overcame the chariot forces of the Trojans. The Hittite Empire was overcome at this time (the early twelfth century BCE), and invaders worked their way down the eastern Mediterranean coast, sacking Ugarit. As they approached the Egyptian frontier, Pharaoh Rameses III rallied his army to meet them. The two battles that ensued are memorialized on Rameses III's tomb at Medinet Habu. The inscription describes the successes of the invaders as they approached: "They laid their hands upon lands as far as the circuit of the earth, their hearts confident and trusting."

Apparently, Rameses III had learned from the failures of his neighbors, for when his army fought the Sea People invaders in 1175 BCE, he had abandoned most of his chariots and fought the first battle primarily with infantry. The second battle was a naval conflict. In both, the Egyptians were victorious, but the battles ultimately proved negatively decisive for

Rameses and his descendants. With the development of trained infantry as the new dominant arm of the military, the era of the social and military elite was doomed. Masses of infantry, well trained and armed, were vital for the new armies, and the social repercussions were immense. Egypt began a downward slide from this point onward, and was never again a major power.

The Sea Peoples, while unable to conquer Egypt, did not leave the region. Many of the populations along the eastern Mediterranean coast are believed to be their descendants, particularly the Philistines. Indeed, the settlement of the Middle East in the wake of the invasion casts a dark age over much of the area, for no major power arose again until the Assyrians almost 300 years later, between 1000 and 612 BCE. Whether the Sea Peoples were little more than professional soldiers of fortune who inflicted new weaponry and tactics on late Bronze Age societies, or whether they were mass populations engaged in migration more than conquest, is a question that may never be answered completely.

References: Drews, Robert, *The End of the Bronze Age* (Princeton, NJ: Princeton University Press, 1996); Sandars, N. K., "The Sea Peoples," in Cotterell, Arthur, *The Encyclopedia of Ancient Civilizations* (London: Rainbird Publishing, 1980); Silberman, Neil Asher, "The Coming of the Sea Peoples," in *Military History Quarterly*, vol. 10, no. 2 (Winter 1998).

Persians

Little is known of the military practices of the early Achmaenid Persians (559–331 BCE) before Xerxes' invasion of Greece in 480 BCE. The early Persians must have possessed a sophisticated concept of war, for they managed to conquer and hold quite a large empire. They were probably drawing upon the military traditions of the Assyrians and the Medes, whose empires they assimilated, and combining them with the tribal methods of warfare of the eastern nomads. Regardless of how they acquired their military expertise, the army that Xerxes led into Europe was an efficient fighting machine.

The heart of Xerxes' army was his heavy cavalry and an elite corps of infantry, the 10,000 Immortals (so-called because when one was killed another was supposedly waiting to take his place, thus maintaining their number). Around this unshakable core revolved the full panoply of the Persian horde: fighting men drawn from the far reaches of the empire, each contributing his own unique martial talents. Infantry comprised the majority of the army and this more than likely was by design. Xerxes knew he would be fighting in hilly and broken country, besieging cities, and maneuvering in conjunction with his fleet. It is understandable that in such circumstances he would recruit more foot than horse soldiers. He could just as easily have fielded a force predominantly composed of cavalry.

Three features of the Persian army of this time are worth noting. The first is a heavy dependence upon the bow. It would appear that a majority of Persian troops carried bows, sometimes in addition to their other weapons. Persian tactics revolved around showering the enemy army with arrows until it became disorganized, then closing with the Immortals and the heavy cavalry for the *coup de grace*. It is fairly safe to assume that all the Asian peoples against whom the Persians fought used basically these same tactics. As a result, the Persian army evolved into a force skilled in skirmish and maneuver,

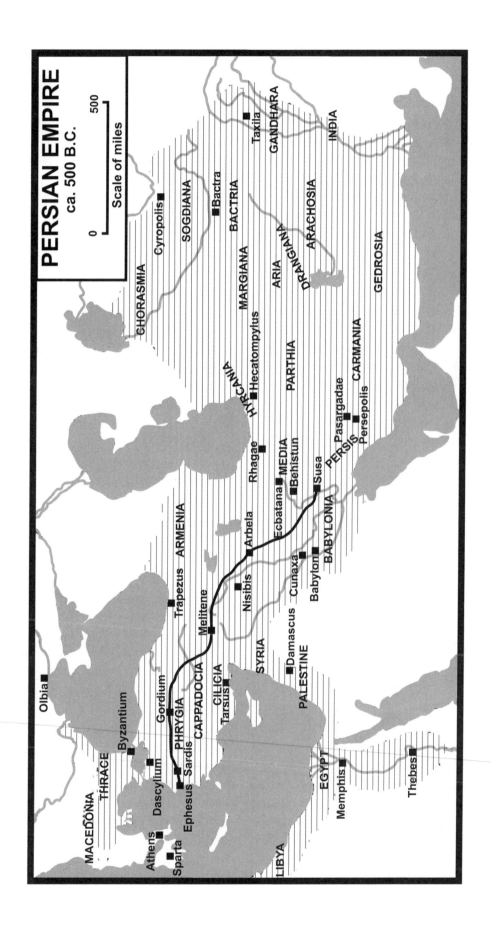

PERSIAN EMPIRE
ca. 500 B.C.

Scale of miles
0   500

MACEDONIA
THRACE
Athens
Sparta
Olbia
Byzantium
Dascylium
Ephesus
Sardis
Gordium
PHRYGIA
CAPPADOCIA
CILICIA
Tarsus
Trapezus
Melitene
ARMENIA
Nisibis
SYRIA
Damascus
PALESTINE
Cunaxa
Babylon
BABYLONIA
Arbela
Ecbatana
MEDIA
Behistun
Susa
PERSIS
Pasargadae
Persepolis
CARMANIA
Rhagae
HYRCANIA
Hecatompylus
PARTHIA
ARIA
DRANGIANA
ARACHOSIA
GEDROSIA
MARGIANA
BACTRIA
Bactra
SOGDIANA
Cyropolis
CHORASMIA
GANDHARA
Taxila
INDIA
LIBYA
EGYPT
Memphis
Thebes

able to withstand only short periods of hand-to-hand melee.

The second notable feature of the Persian army was a lack of body armor, aside from light chain mail for the Immortals and heavy cavalry. Because the troops stressed the skills of skirmish and maneuver, they had little need of personal body armor. A wicker shield and light mail provided about as much protection from an arrow as would a metal cuirass. One of the favorite tactics of the Immortals, for instance, was to form "mantelets" by standing their shields up with an attached prop, usually their rounded-end spear, and using this shield wall for cover while firing their bows. Also, because the Persian army bore the responsibility for the protection and control of the entire empire, troops were required to be able to march to any part of the country to repel invaders or put down rebellions. Mobility was vital to such a force, and the kings built military highways for that purpose. In an empire of such vast distances and often extreme temperatures, the disadvantages of armor, namely weight and heat, would not be offset by its protective advantages. Finally, armor was expensive and (aside from the Immortals and heavy cavalry) it appears there was no standing army. Troops levied from the subject races of the empire were responsible for their own equipment, and probably very few could afford costly chain mail.

The third important feature of the Persian army was its polyglot nature. Whenever the king assembled an army it would be slightly different. At least 20 different peoples fought alongside the Persians at one time or another. If this collection engendered no other problem than a language barrier, that alone would have been sufficient to cause great difficulties. But

other problems can readily be imagined, such as racial and tribal hatred, differing dietary requirements, and varying customs and traditions. The fact that the early Achmaenid rulers managed to mold such divergent groups into an effective fighting force, capable of defending the empire, capturing Athens, and nearly conquering Greece, is a credit to their expertise and efficiency. It has been suggested by some historians that religion, in this case the Revelation of Zarathustra, also may have exerted a unifying influence on the Persian hordes.

However, in the century and a half between Xerxes' invasion of Europe and Alexander's invasion of Asia Minor, the Persian military system changed. Xerxes' dreams ended with the Greek victory at Plataea in 479 BCE in what the poet Aeschylus labeled the "triumph of the spear over the bow." Though simply stated, this sums up the situation. The Persian infantry, even the Immortals, could not stand up to the bronze-encased phalanx of the Greeks. The Persian rulers were immensely impressed by the fighting qualities of the hoplite. The Peloponnesian Wars had produced a large number of Greeks who had no trade except war, and they were more than willing to hire themselves out to anyone who could pay. Rather than begin to train their own hoplites, the Persians found it easier and cheaper to hire large numbers of these Greek mercenaries.

The sheer power of the hoplite was demonstrated for all to see in 401 BCE, when 13,000 Greeks hired themselves to Cyrus the Younger for a war against his brother Artaxerxes. At the Battle of Cunaxa outside Babylon, the Greek phalanx was unstoppable, and Cyrus was well on his way to becoming king. Unfortunately, he had the ill luck to get himself killed, and the remainder of his army melted away, leaving only the Greeks as a viable unit. Despite treachery and all Artaxerxes and his satraps could do to stop them, the Greeks stalked majestically 1,500 miles back to Greece with the majority of their force intact. This deed, known to history as the *Anabasis*, or "March of the 10,000," clearly illustrated that nothing in the Persian empire could stand up to the hoplites.

Before too long, most satraps in the western empire had forces of mercenary Greeks. By the time of Darius III, the Persian heavy infantry had disappeared, and the main infantry force was made up of the mercenaries, perhaps as many as 20,000. The demise of the Immortals may be attributed first to expenses. Throughout history, elite troops have been costly to maintain, and the Immortals were no exception. The Persian kings found they could not afford to pay both the Immortals and the Greek mercenaries, and since the hoplites consistently outperformed the Persian heavy infantry in combat, they seemed to represent a better investment. They were supplemented by native levies, half-armed peasants of questionable enthusiasm, and hill tribesmen, who were brave but undisciplined warriors. The majority of these levies were light infantry who fought with the javelin or bow. At Issus, a force of young Persian recruits called *Cardaces* were put up against the Macedonians with disastrous results. The Cardaces probably represented an attempt by Darius to reconstitute an elite Persian unit, but they were squandered before their training was complete.

Another reason for the eclipse of the Persian infantry could have been the Persian land system. Aside from the Greek city-states along the coast, the entire empire was the king's land. He ruled it through satraps or through grants to large landowners. It was the duty of these men to provide fighting troops in return for their offices. By the time of Darius III, this had come to mean units of cavalry retainers instead of infantry. Horsemen were far more useful in governing the large Persian holdings. In this area, at least, the quality of the local forces had not declined. However, Persian cavalry were still armed with the bow and javelin.

The armies of Darius, like those of Xerxes, were polyglot in nature, but there the resemblance ends. The emphasis had shifted from fire power and maneuver to shock and melee. The proportion of cavalry was much higher in Darius's armies (by the time of Alexander the Great's victory at Gaugamela they probably constituted 40 percent of the total manpower), and the number of archers and bow-armed troops was lower. The Greek mercenaries had replaced native soldiers as the backbone of the Persian forces, and the hoplites' sole function was melee combat.

More importantly, the Persian army had lost the ability to work together in a combined fashion. The mercenaries were the only truly professional force left in the empire. The cavalry retainers and the subject tribes undoubtedly fought well at times, but they lacked the cohesion and tactical coordination that only a standing army could achieve. The entire thrust of Persian military thought had changed, partly as a result of the Persians' own neglect, and partly through exposure to the Greek world. Persian power became but a memory, and the Immortals marched only in the fading wall murals of crumbling palaces.

References: Aeschylus, *Persians*, trans. Edith Hall (Warminster: Aris & Phillips, 1996); Delbruck, Hans, *History of the Art of War* (Lincoln:

University of Nebraska Press, 1991); Fuller, J. F. C., *The Generalship of Alexander* (Westport, CT: Greenwood, 1981).

Philippine Scouts

Polished and trained and weeded out;
Pick of the best of the Philippines
Perfect precision fighting machines,
Polished and trained since nineteen-four
To be expended in four months war.

Abucay Withdrawal by Henry G. Lee

The situation seemed hopeless. The meager air defense of two lone P-40s had been gone for more than an hour. A Japanese division, estimated at 45,000 by Gen. Douglas MacArthur, was advancing with their sights set on Bataan. The only impediment to delay this onslaught was the Thirty-first American Infantry Regiment augmented by the Philippine Scout First Battalion's Twenty-third and Eighty-eighth Field Artillery. Although their 75 mm guns had splintered enemy units and hindered their progress, this advantage lasted only 30 minutes. For within that time, the Japanese army had emplaced their supporting artillery consisting of longer-range 75 mm and Model-4 150 mm howitzers. With this accomplished, a murderously accurate counterfire was unleashed. The first target to disintegrate in an explosion was the ammunition train. In the shower of shrapnel, seven of the eight artillery pieces of the Philippine Scout Twenty-third Field Artillery were destroyed. Some members of the American Thirty-first Infantry dropped their WWI vintage equipment and began to retreat to the hoped-for sanctuary that Bataan might provide. Left alone, the Philippine Scout Eighty-eighth Field Artillery knew it had to slow the Japanese juggernaut. This delay was crucial, as this was the last line of defense. Bataan needed to hastily collect its soldiers, gather provisions, and prepare defenses. Now enemy shells, accurately guided by uncontested aerial ranging, soon devastated the gun crews of Battery A of the Eighty-eighth Field Artillery.

Now, nothing opposed the Japanese Imperial troops from flanking that position save one man. This lone soldier, a mess sergeant from Battery B, located more than 100 yards away, was more than an average soldier: This man was Jose Calugas, Philippine Scout. Calugas, a 12-year veteran of the Philippine Scouts, knew what had to be done. Ripping off his apron, he began dipping and weaving across the battle-scarred terrain, finally thrusting himself into the protective trench atop two of the surviving gun crew. At the first lull in the fighting, Calugas leapt out of the trench and into action. Dragging the wounded to safety, he ordered the surviving gun crew members and other cooks to make ready the 75 mm gun. Within minutes, he and his makeshift crew were returning fire to the enemy, giving precious time to the army in retreat.

Although awarded a Medal of Honor for his actions, bravery, cunning, and focus on comrades rather than self, these qualities were all reflective of the elite military unit known as the Philippine Scouts. Born out of necessity, the growth of the unit came to reflect the pride and challenges of their motherland in her birthing process. Always ready to accomplish the seemingly impossible, the Scouts were central, if unsung, heroes of not only the Philippines, but also the Pacific theater as well.

The birth of the Philippine Scouts was beset by problems. America had opened a diplomatic/philosophical Pandora's box in regard to the territory taken during the

Spanish-American War. President McKinley announced to the world that America's occupying armies were only in place to "win the confidence, respect, and affection of the inhabitants of the Philippines," until the Philippines were ready for self-rule. The only problem was that since 1892, Philippine revolutionaries led by General Emilio Aguinaldo had been fighting against Spain for the very same right. So desperate was the rebels' desire that little reflection was taken before resorting to guerrilla tactics in 1897. With the peace treaty signed, the undermanned and under-equipped U.S. Army was to become guardians of the "Benevolent Imperialism" that prepared the Philippines for self-rule. Therefore, beyond their military duties of counterinsurgency, the Army was also mandated to perform civilian tasks such as the establishment of civil governments, infrastructure, and the accouterments of civility of a police and education system. All of this was to be accomplished in a strange land filled with mysterious natives who perplexed the American soldiers. Capt. Delphney T. E. Casteel reflected on the irritating situation: "One day we may be fighting with thousands of their people [and] the next day you can't find an enemy, they are all 'amigos.' They have hidden their rifles and may be working for you, for all you know."

Lt. Matthew A. Batson came up with a novel solution to assist in pacification. Batson recruited a company of Native Scouts from the town of Macabebe to assist his forces. Besides being the only Filipinos willing to serve, these Macabebe Scouts had likewise served with the Spanish. Also, they, unlike the Americans, held a thorough knowledge of the land. On September 10, 1899, the Macabebe Scouts were organized into a 100-man First Company, equipped with Krag carbines, and sent out to stop guerrilla forces. So effective were they in stifling activity that the military quickly expanded their numbers to a five-company battalion. Other areas of the Philippines also began to recruit natives, and units like the Ilocano Scouts and the Tagalog Scouts (armed with Springfield rifles) were created. Attached to American units, besides the search-and-destroy missions ferreting out guerrilla strongholds, they also kept order in municipalities, patrolled neighborhoods, and monitored traffic. Examples of their cunning and bravery abounded. One group of Macabebe Scouts, for example, disguised themselves as bull cart drivers to ambush a guerrilla band that was levying tolls on provincial roads. In September 1900, a small group of Ilocano boatmen and four Ilocano Scouts successfully repelled an attack of almost 100 guerrillas after their U.S. Army escort had fled.

Although the Scouts "served faithfully" and did "splendid work" in the words of Brig. Gen. Samuel B. M. Young, problems did began to appear. This was especially true with the Macabebe Scouts, nicknamed the Macs. Their ruthless policy toward the enemy began to generate the belief that they actually created more enemies than they killed. On March 23, 1900, the U.S. Army was horrified to learn that the Macs' 130 prisoners "were all killed in an attempt to escape." One commander, Lt. Col. Plummer, demanded the withdrawal of the Macs from his area after hearing of an alleged series of rapes and robberies. In less than a month, however, Plummer utilized the threat of the Macs' return if the people did not cooperate against the guerrillas. Yet other groups, such as the Ilocano Scouts, had proven themselves "entirely trustworthy, orderly, enthusiastic to learn, brave in action, and loyal to the United States"; the value of the Scouts was apparent. Indeed, it was through the subterfuge of Filipino Scouts pretending to surrender to rebel forces that the whereabouts of rebel leader Gen. Emilio Aguinaldo was learned. Aguinaldo's capture and subsequent recognition of American occupation in 1901 officially ended the Filipino-American war.

The end of the war brought about the official organization of the Philippines. In March 1901, despite the indifference of newly appointed Military Governor Arthur MacArthur, the Philippine Scouts were officially organized. Drawn from various ethnic groups, their primary duty was to suppress of the Muslim Moro rebels. With a fighting strength of only 5,000 men, the Scouts bravely defended the country in its infancy. By 1908, whole battalions of multilingual Scouts were authorized. In 1912, the rank of officer became open to the Filipinos when the first Filipino to graduate from West Point also became the first Filipino officer. Such advances came at a cost, however, as the Scouts lost 108 men killed in action, as well as 174 wounded in action from 1901–1915.

Following World War I, serious steps were taken to assist the Philippines in its process of nationhood. The Philippine Scouts were inducted into the Regular U.S. Army, with the Philippine Division holding two infantry regiments (the Forty-fifth and Fifty-seventh), two artillery regiments (the Ninety-first and Ninety-second), and the Twenty-sixth Cavalry Regiment. As recruits for this exceptional group of military elites, only the best and most disciplined were allowed. When the Philippines became a commonwealth in 1935, the Philippine Scouts were entrusted to train the new recruits and furnish the most able Filipino officers for the new Philippine

Army. As a sign of their passion for soldiering, retirement from the unit was rare, as was the need for courts-martial. New recruits usually came from the same families. However, if the offer was extended to an officer of the Philippine Army, he would eagerly have turned in his bars to become an enlisted man in the elite Scouts.

Indeed, things proceeded so well that only one thing stood in the way of the proposed independence of the Philippines in 1946: the Japanese. By the late 1930s, Japanese ambitions had caused nervous American planners to devise War Plan Orange. Under this plan, Manila Bay would be defended for up to six months by units garrisoned in Bataan and the island fortress of Corregidor. This would allow the United States Navy the time to arrive with the forces necessary to repel the offensive. Two problems arose with this plan, however. First, the plan was detailed in military colleges in the U.S., which were attended by some of the Japanese Imperial Navy officers. Secondly, Douglas MacArthur, newly appointed commander of the Armed Forces in the Philippines, felt that the plan was too passive. MacArthur instead favored Rainbow 5, an alternative plan designed to thwart Japanese ambitions to secure the oil fields and rubber plantations of the Malay Peninsula by establishing an island fortress. This would occur with massive shore batteries on the Philippine shoreline and allied action with the British in their Asian colonies. By relying on this plan, however, MacArthur overextended his ill-prepared and ill-supplied troops.

This defensive dream turned into a nightmare during December 1941. One day after wreaking havoc on the Pacific fleet with the surprise attack on Pearl Harbor, the Japanese Imperial Air Force destroyed

17 B-17s and 53 P-40s, more than half of the entire Far East Air Force. The pockets of 3-inch and 37 mm American anti-aircraft guns that were spread about the island offered little protection. Their range was too short to endanger the high-flying Japanese bombers. Air superiority gained, the Japanese then launched four successful invasions of the island of Luzon that met a vastly unprepared Thirty-first Infantry. This unit was barely at half-strength, overloaded with young ROTC officers and 12-month trainees from the States whose purpose had been not combat, but to be the instructors of the Philippine Army. As for the Philippine Army, not one division was fully mobilized or, for that matter, at full strength. Three divisions had to convert from artillery regiments to infantry regiments when the units failed to receive their guns. Needless to say, the Japanese inroads into the island were so quick that on December 23, MacArthur reverted to War Plan Orange and ordered all troops to make strategic retreats to Bataan. Protection during the retreat depended on the rear guard provided by the elite Twenty-sixth Cavalry Philippine Scouts.

By January 9, Japan began intensive attacks in an attempt to break the defensive lines. Time and time again the Philippine Scouts were called in to search the cane fields and disable enemy snipers who had managed to infiltrate the lines. Indeed, the Twenty-sixth Cavalry was so intent on holding its position that the fighters did not hear the order to withdraw, and only discovered the fact that they had been left behind enemy lines when an undecipherable code came over their radios an hour after they were abandoned. They could not decipher the code because it had been changed without their knowledge. In their attempt to reunite with the Thirty-first Infantry, the Japanese intercepted their convoy. Three of the four Scout cars were destroyed, two officers were killed, one captured, and 18 other Scouts lost their lives in the skirmish. The one Scout car that did make it through proceeded to regimental headquarters posthaste to announce that the road had been cut.

As the staggered retreat to Bataan continued, so did the Scouts' ferocity. During a heavy Japanese night attack, Scout Cpl. Narcisco Ortilano was working to unjam his rifle when a bayonet-wielding Japanese soldier charged him. Enraged, Ortilano grabbed the bayonet with his bare hands and ripped it out of his enemy's hands. Ignoring the pain caused by the fact that Ortilano had cut off his little finger, he turned the rifle on his enemy and bayoneted him to death. Before he could relax from this struggle, another enemy soldier leapt upon him, slashing and cutting him repeatedly before he was able to parry the attack and kill this second soldier with the same rifle. To combat against possible enemy infiltration, another Scout officer, Lt. Arthur Nineger, ordered his exhausted squad to stand down while he searched for the enemy. His only weapons were hand grenades and a .45 pistol. During the night, he disabled and eradicated numerous enemy positions despite receiving two wounds in the process. His third and fatal wound was received as he charged a Japanese automatic-weapon position. As the enemy bullets struck, he lobbed his hand grenade, killing the two-man gun crew and one officer. This was the story that his lifeless body told the Scout patrol that had left cover in an attempt to find him. On their return trek to the lines, the Scouts were able to eradicate more than a dozen of the enemy.

The counterattacks continued with great success. On February 2, 1942, units of the Scouts attacked and eliminated pockets of surviving Japanese forces. They were even able to turn back three attempted amphibious landings on Bataan. But for all these successes, the days of the "Battling Bastards of Bataan" were numbered. Full supplies and provisions that were supposed to sustain 50,000 men for six months, much less supplies for the 75,000 present, were never received. Men were on quarter rations, and were forced to slaughter the Cavalry's horses and pack mules for meat.

Meanwhile, the Japanese built up their forces and supplies and waited for the right moment to sweep in on their exhausted enemy. On Good Friday, April 3, 1942, a massive air assault followed by a coordinated tank and infantry attack broke through the defensive lines. The Philippine Scouts, with their stamina as well as supplies exhausted, could not forge an effective counterattack. The commander of the forces at Bataan surrendered and the prisoners taken were forced to undertake the grueling Bataan death march, a 65-mile march without medical care or food, and exposed to indiscriminate beating and bayoneting of 10,000 of the prisoners. With the fall of Corregidor after a month of bombardment, the Philippines fell into enemy hands. When the American forces returned in October 1944, only half of the original Scouts were still alive. With independence granted in 1946, the Philippine Scouts were dissolved, leaving a history of their resilience, bravery, and dogged determination.

Andy Galloway

References: Linn, Brian, *The US Army and Counterinsurgency in the Philippine War, 1899–1902*, (Chapel Hill: University of North Carolina Press, 1989); Wainwright, Jonathan, *General Wainwright's Story* (Garden City: Doubleday, 1949); Whitman, John W., *Bataan: Our Last Ditch* (New York, Hippocrene Books, 1990); Young, Donald J., *The Battle of Bataan: A History of the 90 Day Siege and Eventual Surrender of 75,000 Filipino and United States Troops to the Japanese in World War II* (Jefferson, NC: McFarland & Company, Inc., 1992)

Plains Indians

Numerous tribes of central North America, most notably the Sioux, Cheyenne, Crow, Kiowa, and Comanche.

Included among the greatest light cavalry the world has ever seen must be the native people of the North American plains. They hunted mastodons and caribou, and later the great herds of buffalo that covered the plains. Although game was abundant, these early Indians faced severe logistical problems because they hunted and traveled on foot. New World horses had become extinct, probably due to overhunting by the Indians themselves. Since the buffalo herds moved constantly, the Indians had to follow and could keep only those possessions that they could carry themselves. The old, sick, or injured would frequently have to be abandoned as the hunting band moved on. Their existence must have been very poor in terms of material wealth. Native Americans simply did not have the opportunity to transform their cultures and their lives the way the Mongols, Huns, and other great steppe horse peoples of Asia did.

In 1540 the Spanish conquistador Francisco Coronado explored north from Mexico City in search of the Seven Cities of Gold. He took with him more than 1,200 horses and mules. When the Plains Indians saw these Spanish ride by, their world

Start of a war party. Several Dakota men on horseback circle a tipi, circa 1907. Library of Congress, Prints & Photographs Division, Edward S. Curtis Collection [reproduction number LC-USZ62-46959]

changed in an instant. They proceeded to steal every Spanish horse available, and within half a century the horse had transformed the culture of the tribes living on the southern Great Plains, and through them eventually all the Plains tribes. No longer were they earthbound hunter-gatherers, but now they entered into history as the mounted and fearsome "Lords of the Plains."

From the northern to the southern Great Plains, an area stretching from modern-day Canada to Texas, the major Indian tribes were the Sioux, the CheyenneCheyenne, the Pawnee, the Crow, the Arapaho, the Kiowa, and the Comanche. Although each tribe had its own language and customs, they all had one overriding thing in common: their culture, their very way of life itself, was completely adapted to and dependent on the horse. The buffalo herds supplied the Indians with the necessities of life, such as food, shelter, and tools, but it was the horse that transformed that life. Mobility lent to them by the horse made the Plains Indians formidable foes, both strategically and tactically.

Strategically, the Indians presented no fixed targets at which their enemies could strike. Because they practiced no agricul-

ture, they were not tied to the land, and they roamed freely over thousands of square miles of open prairie. Although they belonged to distinct tribes, the Indians actually lived most of their lives in small individual hunting bands of anywhere from 50 to 400 people. These hunting bands would congregate as tribal units once every one or two years for a great celebration or religious festival (sometimes known as a sun dance), but would quickly break up again as their food supplies dwindled. Every man, woman, and child in the band was mounted, and all the accoutrements of their lives from tipis on down were designed to be transportable. A hunting band could easily travel 80 miles in a day, but if necessary could cover 200 miles in a 24-hour period. This mobility, combined with the vastness and emptiness of the land over which they roamed, made it almost impossible for slower-moving, European-influenced cavalry forces to even find the Indians, much less bring them to battle on favorable terms.

On a tactical level, the Indians held most of the advantages, too. All true Plains Indians fought only from horseback, armed with a short compound bow, long lance, and shield. Some Indians adopted firearms—especially repeating rifles—as they became available, but most tribesmen were indifferent marksmen at best. It was with the bow that they were most dangerous. At close range, this powerful weapon could propel an arrow completely through a buffalo. A typical plains warrior could fire an arrow more than 200 yards, renock and fire three or four more missiles before the first had reached its mark, and do all this while riding his horse at full speed, controlling it only with knee pressure. Not only did Indians ride excellent horses, but every warrior took the warpath with several horses in tow, as opposed to the single animals organized cavalry or civilian militia forces rode. This tremendous advantage in quality and number of mounts allowed the Indians to pick and choose their fights, to fall back in the face of superior odds, to ride down inferior forces, and to easily escape when a battle went against them. They always fought on their own terms, and almost never allowed their enemies, primarily the United States Cavalry, to bring superior weight in numbers or fire power to bear on them. For more than three centuries these warriors blocked the advances of Spain, then Mexico, and then the United States into their hunting grounds. Even the famous Texas Rangers did no better than to hold their own against these warrior peoples.

Every Plains Indian tribe possessed an intensely militaristic culture in which advancement in rank and prestige was based almost solely upon deeds in war and the hunt. Warriors sought to exceed each other in daring reckless exploits. For them, the greater the danger, the greater the honor gained. Among these peoples, warfare became as ritualized as among medieval knights, and warrior societies abounded. Every tribe had its elite fraternity, the best of the best. Among the CheyenneCheyenne, it was the Dog Soldiers, and among the Kiowas it was the *Koietsenko*, the Principal Dogs, both so-called to honor their faithful companions. Usually no more than 10 members would be allowed, and each had to earn his place by numerous recognized acts of bravery, called "counting coup," which could include being the first to touch an enemy in combat, or stealing a horse, or taking a scalp. Election to these societies brought not only great prestige and political power, but also great responsibility. Each member had to be

ready to lay down his life to protect the hunting band or tribe. Some wore a cloth or leather sash around their bodies, and in times of great danger would pin this sash to the ground with a knife or arrow, and there they would stay, in the path of the enemy, covering the retreat of their people until death. Only another member of their society could release them by unpinning the sash. These warrior elites set examples for all others to emulate, a pinnacle for which to strive.

At the end of the American Civil War, new U.S. Army leaders emerged, foremost among them William Tecumseh Sherman. During the Civil War, Sherman had been the leading proponent and practitioner of the concept known as "total war"—the idea that in war there are no noncombatants and no rules. In 1864 he had led an army across Confederate Georgia, burning everything in his path, and in the process had destroyed the will of Southerners to resist. By 1871 Sherman had become General of the Army, the highest ranking officer in the U.S. military, and he resolved to do the same thing to the Plains Indians that he had done to the Confederacy: Break the will of the enemy people to resist.

The first step in this process was to destroy the Indian's supply system. The buffalo herds appeared to be limitless, but they were not. At the urging of the U.S. government, tanning companies hired small armies of buffalo hunters (composed of men such as Buffalo Bill Cody) to harvest the buffalo for their hides. From 1872 to 1882 an estimated 20 million buffalo were slaughtered. Fewer than 1,200 animals were left by the end of the killing. This massive butchery shocked many, but General Philip Sheridan summed up the government's position when he said "Let them kill, skin, and exterminate the buffalo, as it is the only way for civilization to advance." Thus the Plains Indians' supply system, their principal means of sustaining life, was destroyed.

The second step in Sherman's plan was to strike directly at the Indians themselves. Sherman noted that the Indians' mobility was not complete. The horses they rode ate prairie grass, and during the dead of the winter there was no fodder for them. All the plains tribes passed the cold months in winter encampments, and during those months the Indians were nearly as immobile as the Confederate cities had been. The U.S. Army rode grain-fed horses and could carry fodder with their columns in wagons; they could even move infantry in wagons. In truth, the U.S. Army was not much slower in winter than they were in summer, so Sherman laid plans for a winter campaign on the southern plains in the fall and winter of 1874–1875. The purpose of this campaign was to sweep the plains with columns of cavalry and infantry, searching for the Indian encampments and, when discovered, attack them. The intention was not so much to kill Indians, although Indians certainly were killed. Instead, the intention was to destroy everything that supported the Indians' way of life. This operation, known as the Red River War, was grimly effective. The army maintained a relentless pressure on the Indians, attacking them at every opportunity, destroying their homes and food supplies, and pursuing the survivors across the frigid plains. One by one, the exhausted southern tribes came into the reservations the government had established in order to surrender. Their horses and weapons were seized, and their chiefs were arrested and sent to far-off prisons. In this manner, the power of the tribes of the southern plains was broken.

On the northern plains, the U.S. Army did not fare as well. In June 1876 Lt. Colonel George Armstrong Custer and more than 260 men of the Seventh Cavalry were wiped out at the Battle of the Little Big Horn River by Sioux and Cheyenne-Cheyenne warriors led by Chief Crazy Horse and Chief Sitting Bull. The Indian advantage was brief. Subjected to the full power of the U.S. Army, which utilized the same winter war tactics that had broken the southern tribes, the northern Indians were hounded from encampment to encampment, driven across the plains and even into Canada, before they too came to the reservations to surrender. By 1881 the last of the great nomadic warrior peoples in North America had finally submitted to overwhelming numbers and the power of modern civilization.

References: Hamilton, Allen, *Sentinel of the Southern Plains* (Fort Worth: TCU Press, 1987); Secoy, Frank, *Changing Military Patterns of the Great Plains Indians* (Lincoln: University of Nebraska Press, 1992); Utley, Robert, *Frontiersmen in Blue* (New York: Macmillan, 1967).

Polish Winged Hussars

An elite cavalry unit in Poland in the seventeenth century.

Traditionally, the term *hussar* is used to describe light cavalry. However, in Poland in the sixteenth and seventeenth centuries, special units of heavy cavalry dominated by Poland's nobility took the name hussar for their heavy cavalry units. The origin of the word probably derives from the Slavic word *gussar*, meaning "bandit," a term that described the harassing form of combat in which they engaged. In a time of heavily armored knights, lightly armored hussars were used mainly for scouting and pursuit.

Large numbers of foreign volunteers swelled the ranks of Poland's army in what was that country's heyday as a European power.

The hussars who were accepted from other countries brought with them their traditional uniforms, which were among the most aggressively fashionable cavalry attire ever worn. The Polish nobility saw a chance to flaunt their wealth and position while serving their king and country, so the flashy hussar uniform drew them in large numbers. The nobility, however, had been the armored knights and preferred the role of attacking to scouting, so they blended their traditional role with the more fashionable name and uniforms.

The uniform that they adopted started with the traditional tight-fitting pants, fur-lined jackets with braiding, and round fur hats with flat tops. For protection, the hussar wore a metal breastplate and a skirt of chain mail or heavy cloth. In battle the fur hat was replaced by a metal bowl-shaped helmet. In keeping with his need for expression, the hussar often wore a cape made of leopard skin and lined with silk. The horses were decorated as well, the rider painting them with dye, fitting the harness and livery with brass, and festooning the horse with feathered plumes. For dress parade, the traditional wing-shaped shield would sometimes be topped with stuffed animals, such as eagles.

The most distinctive accoutrement, however, was the addition of tall feathered wings attached to the saddle or the hussar's back. There is some debate as to the function of these wings: Some authorities say they were purely decorative, some say they were to foul lassoes used by steppe horsemen, while still others say that the feathers emitted a loud whistle when the horseman was at a gallop that enhanced the already fearsome visage of the onrushing cavalryman.

For weaponry, the Polish hussar had both a collection of personal arms and his steed itself. The type of horse necessary to bear an armored rider had long been bred in Europe, and the Poles mixed these with Arabian horses stolen or received as tribute from the Ottoman Empire. The strength, size, and endurance of the mixed breed made these horses among Europe's finest, and only the wealthiest could afford them. Each hussar charged the enemy with a lance that measured as long as 24 feet, easily outreaching the pikes held by the defending infantry. Not surprisingly, the lance was also brightly decorated and strung with a pennant designating the rider's unit. The hussar operated in a time when firearms were making their first major appearance in Europe, and he often carried wheel-lock pistols himself. His primary weapon, however, was a sword, either a straight-bladed sword for stabbing or the standard curved sabre for slashing. Some also carried a six-pound sledgehammer for throwing; it was tied to a lanyard fastened to the saddle for easier retrieval.

The hussars rode into battle organized in a unit called a *poczet* ("post"), consisting of a nobleman and two to five retainers, depending on how many the nobleman could afford to equip. Multiple poczets were organized into a *choragiew* ("banner") numbering up to 200 men. This was the basic operational formation, and could be joined to as many as 40 more into a *pulk*, which operated as an independent division. Their main tactic was relatively simple: Mass into a wedge formation and break the enemy line. The hole would then be exploited by following infantry or light cavalry units while the hussars wrought havoc in the enemy rear.

The first major victory in which the hussars fought was in September 1605 at Kircholm near the Lithuanian border. Seven hundred of the winged hussars attacked a formation of 8,300 of Charles IX's Swedish infantry and broke them. They also distinguished themselves against the Russians at the battle of Klushino in 1610 where 3,800 horsemen and 200 infantry defeated a force of 30,000, killing 15,000. Against the Swedes at the battle of Sztum in 1629, the hussars stood out in what was an inconclusive battle except for the serious wounding of the great Swedish king and general Gustavus Adolphus. Perhaps the hussars' greatest glory was achieved among the later victories. Serving in the army of the great Polish leader Jan Sobieski, they fought against the Turks and proved decisive in the battle of Chocim, where 30,000 Turkish soldiers were defeated and Poland was cleared of Turkish forces. The hussars were also prominent in Sobieski's 30,000-man force that defeated the Turks at Vienna in September 1683. There, on the right wing of the Polish-German force, they pierced the Turkish lines, found themselves surrounded, and hacked their way out. They then re-formed and charged again, breaking the Turkish line.

After the victory at Vienna, the hussars' days were numbered. By this time, armies were becoming increasingly dependent on firearms, and the heavy cavalry was a dying breed. As the Poles turned increasingly to the more traditional light cavalry for scouting and pursuit roles, the winged hussars faded away. They did, however, go out on a winning note, for they were never beaten in battle. Time and technology, not defeat, forced their demise.

Reference: Guttman, John, "Poland's Winged Warriors," *Military History*, vol. 10, no. 5 (December 1993).

Prussians

A population of a German state important in eighteenth- and nineteenth-century Europe, known for their military-dominated society.

The Treaty of Westphalia in 1648 ended the Thirty Years War. Perhaps in revulsion of the widespread devastation, warfare for the next one and a half centuries was more sedate. Professional armies fought only among themselves. Civilians were for the most part left out of the fighting, as governments now grasped the need for taxpayers and suppliers of food and material. European warfare settled almost into a great game, with alliances constantly shifting and no one country being allowed to dominate all others. In this atmosphere of increasing military professionalism, the most professional of European armies was born, created by Frederick William Hohenzollern, the great elector of Brandenburg (ruled 1640–1688).

In the seventeenth century, north central Europe was still a collection of duchies and principalities somewhat generically de-

Surrender of Napoleon III to Wilhelm I, King of Prussia, following the battle at Sedan—September 2, 1870. Library of Congress, Prints & Photographs Division [reproduction number LC-DIG-pga-02713]

scribed as German. When Frederick William died, he left behind a powerful, though medium-sized Germanic state with a population of 1.5 million people and an army of some 28,000 men. In 1701, the Kingdom of Prussia was created from Frederick William's territories. The army he created was enlarged and polished by two successors, Frederick William I (ruled 1713–1749) and his son Frederick II (ruled 1740–1786). Frederick I took Prussia, which looked politically and socially like almost every other small European state, and turned it into a war machine the like of which had not been seen in Europe since Sparta in the sixth to fourth centuries BCE. He did it not so much with national pride as with iron discipline, forcing men into the ranks and keeping them there by brute force. The lash was a constant form of punishment and hanging (even for minor infractions) was used only slightly less often. Frederick did, however, create an army that was obedient to the will of its officers and its king, and it set the standard for armies in Europe until the French revolutionary army under Napoleon. By the end of Frederick I's reign, the army numbered 80,000 men, the fourth-largest in Europe, and one that had one soldier for each 25 civilians.

However, it was under the rule of his son, Frederick II, that the Prussian army rose to its height in size and ability. Frederick II came to be called "the Great" for his military ability as well as his cultured court. Frederick the Great took his army into the War of the Austrian Succession in 1740 and soundly defeated the larger armies of his neighbors. In the Seven Years War (1756–1763) he successfully beat back almost continual invasions of Prussia by Austria, Russia, and France in possibly the most masterful use of

interior lines ever seen. Although protecting a relatively small state in terms of overall population, Frederick's army was in 1763 the second-largest in Europe at 162,000 men. He was also masterful in administering his government and keeping his country financially stable in spite of regular warfare, while larger states like France went bankrupt.

After Frederick the Great's death, however, the guiding hand was gone and sorely missed. The command structure, made up of Prussian aristocrats called Junkers, began to rest on its laurels. Although the previous monarchs had been innovators, the Prussian army at the end of the eighteenth century was secure in its traditional iron discipline and tested methods. It, like every other army in Europe, was completely unprepared for the French Revolution and the military transformation it brought about. With the overthrow of the aristocracy (the traditional breeding ground of officers throughout Europe), the French called on all equal male citizens to defend their rights and their country. This led to the *levee en masse*, the conscription of huge numbers of soldiers. They were almost completely untrained, and for a time that was their advantage. Rather than march in lines, they swarmed the battlefield, and invading generals were at a loss about how to respond. Smaller professional armies were swamped by vast numbers of Frenchmen, who quickly became veterans. When a professional harnessed the size and enthusiasm of the French army, it became a virtual juggernaut. Napoleon Bonaparte was that professional, a military mind that appears in history only occasionally. He proceeded to dominate all of Europe, and the professional soldiers of other countries were no match.

In 1806 Napoleon invaded Prussia and the proud Junkers, secure in their traditional power, marched to destruction. At Jena and Auerstadt they were virtually slaughtered, and Prussia was humbled. But Napoleon's conquests took with them the seeds of his destruction. Nationalism became the motivating factor in military service, and citizens of other countries rallied to their nation as had the French. In Prussia, a further modification took place, for here the army learned military as well as political and social lessons, and the result was the formation of the general staff concept. Prussians developed the concept of specializing various command necessities, such as planning, supply, intelligence gathering, recruiting, etc. They also developed a command for studying history and the military developments of other nations. After Napoleon's defeat, Prussian officers observed every war fought anywhere in order to learn from others' mistakes and advances. Observations were scrutinized and fine-tuned for inclusion in the Prussian army. Never again would an enemy's new strategies, tactics, or weaponry catch them unaware. Also in this time, military philosophy came into its own, and the Prussian Karl von Clausewitz's work *On War* became a bible for future soldiers and commanders.

In the 1860s the next major figure in Prussian history, Otto von Bismarck, began to exercise control. Bismarck was chancellor of the Prussian government under Kaiser Wilhelm I, and his dream of Prussian power took the state to its next level. Using the revitalized Prussian military, he embodied the Clausewitzian dictum that "war is an instrument of foreign policy by other means." He played his neighbors against each other and forged a shifting set of coalitions to consolidate Prussian political power in Shleswig-Holstein, south of Denmark. In 1866 he quickly crushed his recent ally Austria, then bound that country to him by means of a moderate peace treaty. In 1870 he trumped up an excuse to go to war with France and scored his greatest triumph. The French army, the largest of the time, was beaten in a rapid series of battles that not only destroyed the army but resulted in the capture of the French leader, Napoleon III. Paris held out for several months before finally surrendering in 1871. In the meantime, Bismarck had consolidated the remaining Germanic principalities into the nation of Germany.

Thus, after 1871 Prussia was the dominant state in a German nation. The general staff system that the Prussians had pioneered began to be copied by other nations. The military, which was born in the 1600s, had created the state of Germany more than two centuries later. However, the ambition of the German rulers, Wilhelm II in 1914 and Adolph Hitler in 1939, perverted that accomplishment by seeking not a stake in European politics, but world power.

References: Crankshaw, Edward, *Bismarck* (New York: Viking, 1981); Dupuy, Colonel Trevor N., A *Genius for War* (New York: Prentice-Hall, 1977).

R

Rangers

Elite commando units of the American colonial and United States armies.

The concept of rangers, or ranging units, developed during the wars between the colonists and the Indians in North America. They were first organized in 1670 and saw action in King Philip's War in Massachusetts from 1675 to 1676. They proved successful enough that when French colonists and their Indian allies began harassing the English colonial frontier in the 1750s, new units were organized. The best known of these was Rogers's Rangers, organized by Robert Rogers of New Hampshire, who founded nine such companies to fight with the British regular army that was dispatched to North America in the ensuing French and Indian War. They fought using Indian tactics and proved quite successful—so much so that the British army began training some of their own troops in ranger tactics. Rogers is regarded somewhat as the father of the ranger concept, for he developed and implemented a training program for this style of fighting during the war. Much of their success, however, was tempered by a lack of discipline, which sometimes worked against them.

When the colonies rebelled against England in 1776, Rogers formed a company of rangers to fight on the side of the British against the colonists in New York and Connecticut. The Americans, of course, had plenty of men with experience fighting Indians, so it was little trouble to form ranger units of their own. The Continental Congress called for 10 companies of expert riflemen to be raised. The accuracy of their rifles, in contrast to the commonly used musket of the time, proved valuable in many instances. Colonel Daniel Morgan's Riflemen played a key role in slowing General John Burgoyne's advance into New York by inflicting heavy losses at Freeman's Farm near Saratoga. In the south, Francis Marion's Partisans were all expert riflemen and horsemen who carried out numerous attacks on British supply bases in the Carolinas during Cornwallis's campaign in 1780–1781. Known as the Swamp Fox, Marion also intimidated area loyalists to ensure a lack of local intelligence for the British. Although Rogers fought for the British, his training and orders from the previous war were followed by Americans in the Revolution. The British again adopted ranger units themselves, as they had in the French and Indian War, mainly manned by American loyalists.

After the war, the American regular army shrank to almost nothing, and the primary fighting units in the new United States were militia raised by each state. They often fought Indians and thus maintained the necessary skills to implement ranger tactics when necessary. Twelve ranger companies were on the active rolls

World War II poster promoting the services of the United States Army Rangers. Office for Emergency Management. Office of War Information. Domestic Operations Branch. Bureau of Special Services 1943–1945. National Archives and Records Administration, Special Media Archives Services Division (NWCS-S), College Park, MD. [Image 514820]

during the War of 1812. One of the most famous of all ranger units, the Texas Rangers, was informally created in the Mexican province of Texas in the 1820s to fight Indians, then formalized as a unit in 1835 during the war for Texas independence. The Texas Rangers proved most effective in scouting and guerrilla operations during the ensuing Mexican-American War of 1846–1848.

In the American Civil War, partisan ranger units were employed by both sides, though more often by the Confederacy. Colonel John Mosby was probably the premier ranger commander of this war, although units under the command of John Hunt Morgan and Turner Ashby were also effective in behind-the-lines attacks to interdict Union supply lines. Morgan's Rangers carried out the deepest penetration of the Union by any Confederate unit when they attacked through Kentucky into Indiana and almost to Lake Erie before they were caught and captured near East Liverpool, Ohio, in 1863. This incursion so frightened Union commanders that men assigned to Tennessee for the upcoming battle at Chickamauga were withdrawn to protect rear areas.

After the Civil War, there were no formal ranger units, although some cavalry commanders employed Indian-style tactics in fighting the tribes of the Great Plains. Not until 1942 was a unit organized and again given the name "Rangers." At that time, 2,000 Americans were trained in Ireland by British commandos. The 500 that completed the training came to be the First Ranger Battalion under the command of Colonel William Darby. Some of these men took place in the abortive Dieppe raid on the coast of northern France in August 1942. They fought in Algeria when American forces landed there in November 1942 and received a presidential unit citation for their service in the battle of El Guettar in March 1943. Darby organized two more battalions of rangers in North Africa, and all three together became the Ranger Force, better known as Darby's Rangers. They served in the invasion of Sicily in the summer of 1943 and then took part in major operations in Italy, including holding the Chunzi Pass against eight German attacks in 18 days. They also played a key role in neutralizing beach defenses at Anzio on January 22, 1944. On February 1, 1944, the unit was destroyed almost to the last man while attempting to infiltrate the Italian town of Cisterna; the six survivors went back to the United States to join the Canadian-American Special Service Force, the so-called Devil's Brigade.

Colonel James Rudder commanded a new ranger unit formed at Camp Forrest in Tennessee in 1943. These men landed at Omaha Beach on the Normandy coast early in the morning of D-Day on June 6, 1944, and scaled cliffs at the heavily defended Pont du Hoc where German artillery was causing extreme casualties. As the Americans were pinned down by heavy German fire, Twenty-ninth Infantry Division commander Norman Cota ordered the Fifth Ranger Battalion, "Rangers, lead the way off this beach." The motto "Rangers lead the way" was born here.

Ranger units also operated in the Pacific theater, where they were known as Raider Battalions among the marines. One of the chief army units was under the command of Lieutenant Colonel Henry Mace. His Sixth Ranger Battalion went into the Philippines in September 1944 and carried out many missions behind Japanese lines. In January 1945, they liberated a prison camp at Cabanatuan, defeating 200 Japanese defenders for the loss of two killed and 10 wounded, while freeing 500 American and Filipino prisoners.

The ranger units were once again disbanded at war's end but were reborn in 1950 at Fort Benning, Georgia, under Colonel John Gibson van Houton. He was ordered to create a ranger headquarters and four airborne ranger companies. Most of the volunteers for the ranger school came from the Eighty-second Airborne Division. The men were taught infiltration techniques, sabotage, demolition, and familiarization with U.S. and foreign weapons. The first class was composed of eight

companies, each of which was assigned to an infantry division. They saw their first action in Korea, where they carried out scouting missions, ambushes, and long-range patrolling. One of their major successes was the destruction of the Twelfth North Korean Division Headquarters nine miles behind enemy lines. One of the companies, the Sixth, was transferred to Europe in the face of increasing communist activity. The final ranger company graduated from Fort Benning in October 1951.

In Vietnam, ranger tactics were once again introduced in the form of Long Range Reconnaissance Patrols (LRRPs). Thirteen LRRP companies assigned to various brigades and divisions maintained the ranger tradition of deep patrolling, ambush, and intelligence gathering. As the original rangers had done, the Vietnam-era soldiers fought in the style of the enemy and usually beat them at their own game. On June 1, 1969, the companies were banded together to create the Seventy-fifth Infantry Regiment (Ranger). It was deactivated after the war, as all previous ranger units had been. This pattern of creation during wartime and re-creation during the next war came to an end in 1973 when Army Chief of Staff Creighton Abrams called for a permanent ranger establishment. The First Ranger Battalion was stationed at Fort Stewart, Georgia, and the Second Ranger Battalion at Fort Lewis, Washington. A small detachment of rangers operated as security forces for the abortive Iran hostage rescue mission in 1980. The rangers were also among the first troops into Grenada on October 25, 1983, securing the airfield at Salines as well as the medical school campus where American students were located. The operation was marked by confusion, mainly on the part of the aircraft carrying the ranger units, which had little training in night flying operations. On October 27, they captured the Cuban barracks at Calivigny. The barracks were undefended, but a number of casualties were suffered in helicopter accidents.

A year later, the army activated the Third Ranger Battalion, followed by the formation of the Seventy-fifth Ranger Regimental Headquarters at Fort Benning in 1986. The unit strength was nearly 2,000 men, and all of them took part in the 1989 Operation Just Cause, the invasion of Panama. Again, their assignment was to capture and hold the main airfields. They also assisted in the capture of the headquarters of the Panamanian Defense Forces and guarded the Vatican embassy, where President Manuel Noriega took refuge before his surrender. Rangers also conducted raids during Desert Storm in 1991 and were deployed in Somalia in 1993. Here they engaged in a serious fire fight with the supporters of local warlord Mohammed Aidid and lost six dead and several wounded—more losses than they had suffered in the Desert Storm and Panama operations combined.

The ranger tradition established in the days of the American colonies remains active in today's rangers, who continue to train to fight by stealth and surprise in order to inflict as much psychological as physical damage on their enemies.

References: King, Michael, *Rangers* (Ft. Leavenworth: Combat Studies Institute, 1985); Payne, Chuck, "'Rangers Lead the Way': The History of the U.S. Army Rangers" (http://users.aol.com/armysof1/Ranger.html).

Red Shirts

Volunteer troops who followed Italian revolutionary Giuseppi Garibaldi, 1834–1867.

The Italian peninsula in the mid-nineteenth century was a hotbed of political intrigue. Ever since 1820, Italian nationalists inspired by French revolutionary ideals had attempted to unite the peninsula, but they had consistently been defeated by Austrian armies. In 1848–1849, Italian forces had better luck and succeeded in forcing some Austrian retreats, but they were unable to prevail over the talented Austrian General Radetzky who, with French reinforcements, besieged Rome from April to June 1849. When the city fell, Austria was once again master of most of Italy. But despite the variety of independent kingdoms within the peninsula and the direct or indirect control of Austria, a movement toward Italian unification persisted. The most likely leader of a unified Italy was Victor Emmanuel of the house of Savoy, king of the Piedmont. His able and Machiavellian prime minister was Count Camillo di Cavour, who wheeled and dealed with all the players in the Italian drama.

In 1859 Piedmont, aided by Emperor Napoleon III of France, fought a short war against Austria for control of the northern provinces. Although Austria lost all its battles, it kept its army intact and in Italy. Austrian Emperor Franz Josef and Napoleon negotiated a settlement without consulting Cavour or any other Italian, leaving an even more unsettled situation as Piedmont, the Papal States of central Italy, Austria, and France saw the war end with no final settlement distributing territory. In 1860 Cavour once again negotiated with Napoleon III, secretly promising him the

A memorial statue to Giuseppe Garibaldi in Perugia, Italy. Paul Davis

provinces of Nice and Savoy along the French border in return for a free hand and French support in Piedmont's acquisition of central Italy. That deal, made public in March 1860, infuriated Italy's premier revolutionary, Giuseppi Garibaldi.

Garibaldi, as a young Sardinian sailor, had been fighting for Italian unification and independence since 1834. Fleeing Austrian captivity that year, he moved to South America where he helped defend Montevideo, Uruguay, from Argentine aggression. His followers there, in need of uniforms, acquired the only consistent outfits they could: surplus red tunics manufactured for slaughterhouse workers. For the remainder of his career, Garibaldi's followers would be identified by their red shirts. He led a contingent of 5,000 in the defense of Rome in 1849 and made the French pay dearly for their capture of the city. He then fled to America, where he spent a number of years and even became a citizen, but he could not stay away from his troubled homeland. When he learned of Cavour's arrangement with Napoleon III, Garibaldi returned to action. He gave lip service to Victor Emmanuel and by doing so gained covert aid from Cavour's government. With Peidmontese weapons and financial aid, Garibaldi in 1860 went back to war.

Garibaldi, at heart a republican, seemed willing to accept a monarchy under Victor Emmanuel if it would unite Italy. As unification needed to start somewhere, Garibaldi took advantage of political strife in the southern Kingdom of the Two Sicilies. When the harsh government based in the capital city of Naples moved to suppress popular uprisings on the island of Sicily, Garibaldi and his nationalist followers invaded. "Garibaldi's Thousand" landed on April 4, 1860, at Marsala and rallied the Sicilian population. They defeated the

Neapolitan forces at Calatafimi in mid-May and captured Palermo on May 27, then defeated another Neapolitan force near Messina on July 20. With the aid of British naval vessels, Garibaldi's men crossed the Straits of Messina and marched on Naples, capturing the city against only slight opposition on September 7. The Neapolitan king, Francis II, withdrew the bulk of his force northward to the fortress of Gaeta, which Garibaldi soon besieged.

As Garibaldi was overthrowing the tyrannical Neapolitan government, Cavour maneuvered. While supplying Garibaldi with equipment and trained men, Cavour was obliged to publicly criticize the invasion in order to keep his involvement secret. He also directed his own General Manfredo Fanti to invade the Papal States in order to support "popular risings," which Cavour had secretly instigated. Napoleon III, who had a Catholic population to keep happy, guaranteed Pope Pius IX's safety. He had, of course, already ceded to Cavour the occupation of central Italy when he received Nice and Savoy earlier in the year. So, like Cavour in his public/private dichotomy over Garibaldi's offensive, Napoleon III had to play the same game concerning the Piedmontese advance toward Rome. As long as the city was not occupied, the pope was not harmed, and no French possessions were attacked, Cavour had Napoleon III's private permission to do what he liked. Napoleon also urged Cavour to protect Rome and the pope from Garibaldi.

The Red Shirts besieged Gaeta from November 3, 1860, through February 13, 1861. Garibaldi realized that, while his forces had plenty of revolutionary ardor, they did not have the patience to maintain a long siege. He therefore was obliged to request Cavour's assistance in capturing the fortress. Piedmontese ships bombarded Gaeta and forced its surrender. Shortly thereafter, an all-Italian parliament declared Victor Emmanuel king of all Italy. Cavour died shortly thereafter, but Garibaldi was intent on finishing the job of unification by including Rome and Venice, both of which remained independent. Victor Emmanuel covertly supported occasional attempts at besieging Rome, but the French had made a public promise to protect the pope and they stood by it. When Garibaldi returned from Sicily in late summer 1862 to march on Rome, the new Italian government could not allow this idealist to upset their close relations with Napoleon III's France. At the battle of Aspromonte, Italian forces defeated Garibaldi's army on August 29, 1862. Garibaldi was taken prisoner, but was released with all of his men shortly afterward.

Garibaldi was not yet finished. In May 1866 Italy concluded a mutual defense treaty with Prussia, and a month later declared war on Austria to coincide with Prussia's attack on that country. Garibaldi's charisma was such that 30,000 men flocked to his banner when he called for volunteers. Garibaldi hoped that an Austrian defeat would mean the liberation of Venice from Austrian control and Italian annexation of the city. Garibaldi's force gained some small successes in the Alps, but the poor performance of the Italian regular army, as well as the short duration of the war, kept him from gaining any territory for his country. However, the Austrians did give up Venice to France in return for French aid in negotiating with Prussia, and Napoleon III gave the city to Italy. All that was left to make a completely unified nation was to acquire the traditional capital city, Rome.

Garibaldi took it upon himself to wrest political control of Rome away from the pope. Victor Emmanuel again tacitly supported him. France, which had evacuated its defensive forces from Rome in December 1866, seemed to be abdicating its responsibility to Pope Pius. Garibaldi therefore organized yet another force of volunteers to annex Rome and invaded what was left of papal territory in January 1867. Napoleon III had to respond. Recently expelled from Mexico and fearful of the rising influence of Prussia, the French leader believed that France could not appear weak. In October 1867, Napoleon III sent 2,000 men to Rome. Combined with 3,000 papal troops, the French General de Failly met Garibaldi's 4,000 at Mentana, near Rome, on November 3. The French, armed with the new, rapid-firing *chassepot* rifle, mauled the Red Shirts in their final battle. Italian authorities arrested Garibaldi and his men, but again released them quickly. Garibaldi was forced to remain on the sidelines when in 1870 Italian forces finally captured Rome.

In spite of his long war against the French, Garibaldi and his two sons went to France in 1870 and fought against the Prussian invasion there. Afterward, he returned to his home on the island of Caprera. His fighting days done, he was elected to the Italian parliament in 1874, and he died in 1882.

References: Coppa, Frank, *The Origin of the Italian Wars of Independence* (New York: Longman, 1992); DePolnay, Peter, *Garibaldi, the Man and the Legend* (New York: T. Nelson, 1961); Hibbert, Christopher, *Garibaldi and His Enemies* (London: Longman, 1965).

Redcoats

British army soldiers from the seventeenth through nineteenth centuries.

Although the British army of the eighteenth and nineteenth centuries was one of the smallest European regular armies, it developed a reputation as one of the best. The soldiers were recognizable by the red coats of their uniforms, a bright color that seems incongruous for combat, considering the dull camouflage uniforms of modern armies. This was not mere affectation, for all the armies of the time wore distinctive colored uniforms. The color was not chosen just because it looked good while the troops marched and drilled, but because of the nature of the battles of the time. Massed musket fire at close range was necessary then because of the lack of range and accuracy of the weapon, and the smoke created by the black powder created a hazy view. The nearness of the forces at the time of firing meant that the troops, having fired, closed on each other quickly with bayonets. In the resulting melee, the chaos of the struggling bodies obscured by the massive amounts of smoke made it necessary for soldiers to immediately recognize

Death of General Wolfe during the siege of Quebec in 1759, painted by B. West and engraved by Wm. Woollett. Library of Congress, Prints & Photographs Division [reproduction number LC-DIG-pga-03074]

who was on their side and who was an enemy. Brightly colored uniforms were helpful in making this crucial determination.

The men recruited into the British army were hardly the elite, despite the high quality of the army in battle. Although most of the officer corps were of the upper classes, because commissions were available for purchase, the foot soldier was an English, Irish, or Scottish peasant. Usually they were recruited young, when the urge for adventure and an escape from the monotony of the farm was greatest. They were also recruited from the jails, especially in time of war when men were needed quickly. Young men on the run from a bad home life, an unexpectedly pregnant girlfriend, or through peer pressure joined the ranks, described at the time as "taking the King's shilling," the first payment upon joining.

Pay for the soldiers was small, and what they received was required for the purchase of daily rations. Money was held back from their wage to pay for the new uniforms they were to receive annually, as well as to pay for the replacement of sundries like socks, shirts, hats, etc. As the pay was distributed to the regimental commander for disbursement, anything he could save by issuing lower-quality goods meant extra money in his own pocket. All this meant that, while food, shelter, and clothing were provided more regularly in the army than some were used to as civilians, joining the army was no way for a young man to put money aside for his future. Moreover, when that future arrived was somewhat problematic. Usually recruits (especially the criminal types) were discharged after six months or at the end of a conflict. Because the British populace traditionally feared a large standing army as a potential tool of abuse by the king, regiments brought to full strength for wartime were cut to cadre strength or disbanded when the fighting stopped. If a soldier found that he liked the army life or had no reason to return to civilian life, opportunity for reenlistment in another unit was high.

For the first year of his enlistment (if in peacetime), the British recruit learned to march in close order drill and to handle his musket. Musket firing was rare, although the practice of loading and reloading was repeated over and over. Unless the country was at war, the government was hesitant to pay for large numbers of musket balls, so actual live firing may have been done once or twice a year, hardly enough to gain proficiency at marksmanship. This was one skill with limited usefulness in armies of the day, for the musket was a highly inaccurate weapon. Therefore, the need to load, aim, and fire by the numbers—that is, to volley fire—became more important than accuracy. The British platoons went into battle in three ranks: the first knelt, the second crouched, and the rear line stood, all according to directions laid out in the regulations written in 1728, which were taken almost directly from Humphrey Bland's 1727 *Treatise of Military Discipline*. In later modifications, the ranks also staggered themselves so that they shot between as well as over the soldiers in front of them. The ability of the redcoats to exercise discipline in firing volleys in combat was one of the factors that made them superior to most continental armies of the time. The soldiers also received slight instruction in the aggressive use of the bayonet, it being primarily viewed as a defensive weapon.

Incessant marching and countermarching drilled into the soldier the instant and unthinking response to orders. After several months or a year, the unit began weekly or semiweekly drills with other units, learning how brigades and ultimately armies moved in coordination on the battlefield. These drills proved vital to the performance of the soldiers in battle. Just as important to performance was the discipline a redcoat recruit received—not just the ability to follow orders—but the punishment that came from not doing so. In the British army punishment was detailed for a large variety of offenses, with the most common penalty being flogging. Up to 1,200 lashes could be imposed as a sentence, although they were usually not given all at once. Lesser offenses brought extra duty, while more serious offenses warranted execution. As the sentence was usually imposed and carried out by the sergeant, and only occasionally by officers, the soldiers came to fear their sergeant even more than the enemy. This also proved valuable on the battlefield.

The British proved themselves steady and disciplined in the series of continental wars fought through the first half of the eighteenth century. When they fought in North America, however, they began to adapt some of the frontier tactics of the colonists to their own forces. The rough terrain and guerrilla tactics employed by the Indians and their French allies in the American colonies obliged the British to respond in kind. Not only did they use colonial militia, but they also began organizing separate platoons and companies to fight in a more open style. Grenadier units served on the flanks of the regular battalions and regiments, and in the French and Indian War (1755–1760), light infantry units also were created to act as skirmishers and provide rapid response for flank protection or following up a retreating enemy.

Independent ranger units were created as well, operating away from the regular troops in scouting and ambush roles.

A new training manual was introduced in 1792, adapted from Colonel David Dundas's 1788 *Principles of Military Movements*. (A 1778 manual, introduced in the midst of the American Revolution, was never really used.) Having learned in North America that a few shots followed by a bayonet charge incurred fewer casualties, Dundas introduced this new method of combat in his work. The soldiers now formed two ranks when firing rather than three, but both ranks stood and locked themselves into a tightly packed mass with (theoretically) each man taking up 22 inches of space but in reality being jammed up against each other. This created a solid mass of fire, and the new regulations called for firing not by platoons but by battalions as a whole. This type of fire would create a massive hole in the enemy ranks, which hopefully a determined bayonet charge would then exploit. Dundas did not widely incorporate the use of light infantry tactics developed in America, however, although he did recognize them as an accepted part of every regiment. The light infantry again served as scouts and skirmishers, and more importantly (in the long run) were equipped not with muskets, but with rifles. With more accuracy, the riflemen were charged with sniping and harassment, something difficult to do with short-range muskets. Muskets, however, being easier and quicker to load, remained the primary weapon for the majority of the soldiers.

The redcoats did not fight the French directly for much of the Napoleonic Wars, but did engage them extensively in Spain between 1808 and 1814. Napoleon established authority over Spain early in his tenure as emperor of France and later installed his brother on the throne. England provided the army to assist the Spanish monarchy. Under the able command of Arthur Wellesley and with the assistance of Portuguese and Spanish troops and guerrillas, Spain became a major thorn in Napoleon's side. When Napoleon escaped his exile on the island of Elba in 1815, it was the British army (supported by the Prussians) that dealt him his final defeat. Wellesley, now the duke of Wellington, and his redcoats defeated Napoleon at Waterloo and gained both the duke's and the army's greatest fame.

The British army engaged in no more continental fighting for 40 years, but fought regularly against colonial forces around the world. The redcoats fought in Africa, India, Canada—anywhere the British Empire held sway. As long as the musket was the primary weapon, the "thin red line of heroes," as Kipling called them, were the mainstay of British land power. Over time, however, two things worked to change that. One was the increasing number of campaigns fought in rough terrain against guerrilla enemies, wherein red uniforms were easy targets for snipers. The second was the introduction of the rifle as the main weapon of almost every army in the world. With increased range and accuracy, close ranks of men were now too easy to hit from great distances, so more open formations and more subtle uniform coloration became necessities. The last major conflict in which the redcoats were prominent was the Crimean War of 1854–1856, but that was also the last major war with muskets. The American Civil War was fought primarily with rifles and rifled muskets, and the close formation (while still used) proved itself to be a recipe for disaster as defensive positions and massed artillery became primary tactics. The last

time the British went into combat with redcoats was in the first Boer War, in 1881. The Dutch South African farmers, however, were not only equipped with modern rifles, but they also were experienced with them. Although the red-coated troops had fought against the Zulus just a few years earlier, against modern weaponry this practice had become suicide. After this time, red uniforms were relegated strictly to the parade ground.

References: Chandler, David, and I. F. W. Beckett, *Oxford Illustrated History of the British Army* (London: Oxford University Press, 1994); Reid, Stuart, *British Redcoat, 1740–1793* (London: Reed International, 1996); Reid, Stuart, *British Redcoat, 1793–1815* (London: Reed International, 1997).

Romans

A population centered in present-day Italy that built the dominant empire of the European and Mediterranean world from the sixth century BCE to the fifth century CE.

The soldiers that laid the groundwork for the Roman Empire and the Pax Romana were the Bronze Age warriors of the Etruscan civilization. These men fought primarily with spears, or swords if they were wealthy enough. Those even wealthier who could afford horses fought as cavalry. They followed a king and fought, as did most of the ancient world, in the phalanx formation. The basic unit of the early army was the *century*, made up—not surprisingly—of 100 men. These centuries were grouped together as legions, probably numbering 4,000 men at full strength. When the century and legion were created, the ancient warriors became soldiers, fighting as a team rather than as individuals.

261

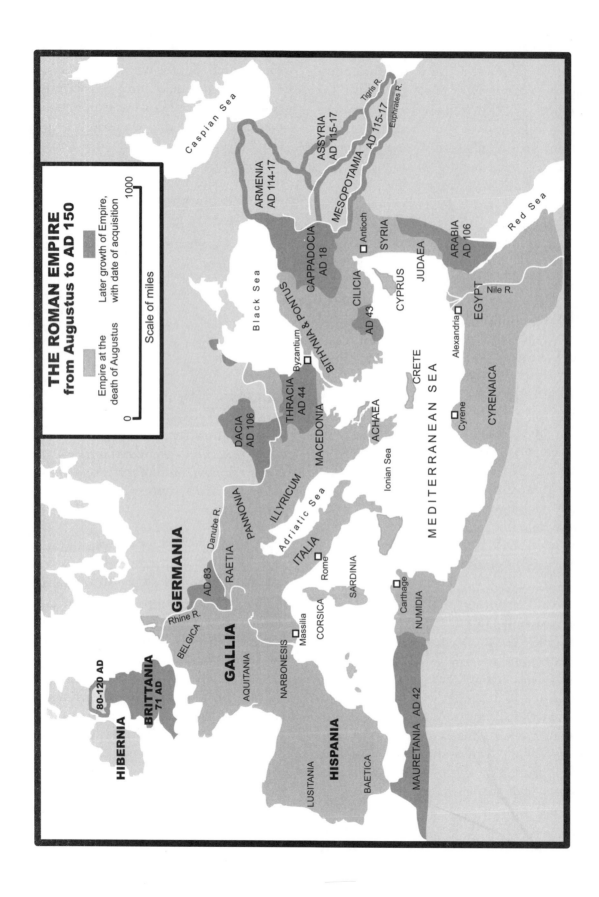

THE ROMAN EMPIRE
from Augustus to AD 150

Empire at the death of Augustus

Later growth of Empire, with date of acquisition

Scale of miles

0   1000

HIBERNIA

BRITTANIA
71 AD

80-120 AD

GERMANIA

AD 83

Rhine R.

BELGICA

GALLIA

AQUITANIA

NARBONESIS

Massilia

LUSITANIA

HISPANIA

BAETICA

MAURETANIA
AD 42

NUMIDIA

Carthage

CORSICA

SARDINIA

ITALIA

Rome

RAETIA

Danube R.

PANNONIA

ILLYRICUM

Adriatic Sea

Caspian Sea

DACIA
AD 106

THRACIA
AD 44

Byzantium

BITHYNIA & PONTUS

Black Sea

MACEDONIA

ACHAEA

Ionian Sea

CRETE

MEDITERRANEAN SEA

CYRENAICA

Cyrene

CYRENAICA

Alexandria

EGYPT

Nile R.

Red Sea

ARMENIA
AD 114-17

Tigris R.

ASSYRIA
AD 115-17

MESOPOTAMIA AD 115-17

Euphrates R.

CAPPADOCIA
AD 18

CILICIA
AD 43

Antioch

SYRIA

CYPRUS

JUDAEA

ARABIA
AD 106

The Etruscans of central Italy, the people who ultimately became Romans, were governed by monarchs until 509 BCE, the traditional date of the founding of the Roman Republic.

As Rome became a more organized society and expanded its borders, its increasing wealth meant that the army was better supplied and armed. Rome depended on citizen soldiers who spent the majority of their time farming but responded to the government's call in time of emergency. The aristocracy provided the officer corps and, as before, the better-armed soldiers. Because the independent farmers formed the bulk of the army, however, they could often influence—if not control—the military and its decision making. From the fifth through the third century BCE, the upper-class patricians and the lower-class plebians struggled for both military and political control in what was called the Struggle of the Orders. In this time Rome was regularly at war, so the patricians needed to keep the plebians content in order to ensure the necessary numbers on the battlefield. As the wars began to range farther afield, necessitating longer time away from the farms that provided the farmers' sole means of support, the government in the fifth century began appropriating money to pay its soldiers and to provide for more standardized equipment. Longer service began to be rewarded by rank and pay, and mid-level command gradually went to experienced veterans rather than well-born aristocrats. However, the wealthy dominated the government after the third century, and only the chief executives, known as consuls, had the authority to assume the top command.

As long as the Romans fought along the coastal plains, the phalanx formation served them well. However, when they fought enemies in the rugged terrain of central Italy, they found it necessary to alter their organization and tactics. The legion was the primary unit, although now expanded slightly to 4,200 at full strength. The new unit was the *maniple*, consisting of two centuries, although that term now designated a unit type rather than exactly 100 men. The army began to go into battle, not in the squares of the phalanx, but in lines. The first line was made up of 1,200 men, the youngest and least experienced soldiers, with gaps between the maniples. The second line, staggered so that its maniples matched the gaps in the first line, was made up of 1,200 men with greater age and experience. The third line, again staggered to match the gaps in the second line (thereby creating a checkerboard pattern) comprised 600 of the most experienced veterans. The remaining 1,200 men of the legion were used as light infantry, skirmishers, and scouts. Ten 80-man cavalry squadrons fought on the flanks. The infantry in the three lines were armored with helmet, chestplate, and greaves, and carried a large oval shield. The younger front-line soldiers carried the traditional thrusting spear, but the men in the second and third lines now carried a throwing spear, called a *pilum*. All the men carried a *gladius*, a short double-edged thrusting sword.

This improved weaponry called for better training, especially with the gladius. This, in turn, required more time spent away from the farm in order to master the weapons, and hence a greater need for longer-term soldiers. When war was frequent and close by, combat itself provided sufficient training for the soldiers. Campaigns began to take place farther and farther away, however, again pointing up the need for long-term professionals. So long as the government required some property ownership for membership in the army, farmers could not grow the necessary crops to feed the nation and fight foreign wars at the same time. As Rome and other cities grew, fewer people were left as farming property owners. After the destruction of much of the Italian countryside during 17 years of Carthaginian campaigning in the Second Punic War, even fewer farms existed. The urban population had to be included in the military. That meant soldiering would no longer be a civic duty, but a profession.

The leader that brought about this change was Marius. In the Roman wars against the African leader Jugurtha (111–106 BCE), Marius began recruiting the poverty-stricken city dwellers to his army. To pay them, he promised loot and pillage after battle, plus a cash bonus or a land grant at war's end. This solved the problem of manpower, but it also created what was, in effect, a private army raised by Marius, not the government. Although he was a consul and therefore the legal commander in chief, the army was still his personal organization. Marius also re-formed the legion in light of experience in northern campaigns against Germanic tribes. The legion was expanded to include 5,000 to 6,000 men, and the maniple was replaced by the *cohort*, a unit of six centuries. Marius also did away with the light infantry. He introduced rigorous training procedures that developed not only skill with weapons but also overall physical fitness. He made the army more mobile when he reduced its baggage train by loading up each soldier with 80 to 100 pounds of equipment. The legion was given a silver or gold eagle for its standard, promoting esprit de corps.

All this worked well, and Marius was successful in a number of foreign campaigns and in defending the Italian peninsula from invasion. However, when he began to use his army for political influence, the nature of Roman government and society began to change. For a long time, the average soldier remained loyal to the government, but when his commander provided his pay and bonuses, a soldier's loyalty could easily shift. In the early decades of the first century BCE, garnering an army command and its soldiers' loyalty became the most important path to political power. By mid-century, Julius Caesar had invaded Italy from Gaul, defeated other consular armies, and made himself consul for life. This violated the long-standing law of year-long terms for consuls and provoked Caesar's assassination. By that time, however, generals held the political power, and Caesar's nephew and successor, Octavian, became Rome's first emperor, forever abolishing the Republic.

Once in power, Octavian (who took the name Augustus) worked to remove the army from the political realm. He divided Rome's foreign holdings into imperial and senatorial provinces, with the army based in the imperial provinces. The senate controlled the nearer provinces, while Augustus appointed legates to command the legions along the frontiers. Thus, the commanders (and therefore their legions) remained loyal to Augustus. The officers were political appointees, as were the tribunes that made up their staffs. The army was in reality run by the centurions, who were experienced noncommissioned officers: the actual administrators of any decent military force in any time or place. Time of service was set at 20 years for citizens, 25 years for foreign auxiliaries, and the retirement bonus was guaranteed. For foreigners, Roman citizenship was also thrown in as a retirement perk. As more distant provinces ever farther from the capital became part of the empire, more and more people became Roman citizens. This kept the citizenship requirement from limiting the number of men in the army. It also—by the second century CE—meant that about 1 percent of the army was actually Roman. The legionaries remained heavy infantry while the foreigners provided light infantry and cavalry. Also, part of the legions were made up of engineers and technicians to build and operate catapults.

Augustus also reestablished the Praetorian Guard. Previous commanders had kept personal guards for their security, and Augustus created a force of 4,500 German infantry organized into nine cohorts along with 90 cavalry. This was an elite unit that had a shorter enlistment (16 years) and triple the pay of other units. It was not a crack combat unit, but was always kept in or near the capital and was first on the scene in case of any political trouble.

Most importantly, Augustus for the first time created an official standing army. Garrisons were needed to protect distant provinces from border raids and to maintain order. The army stood at 28 legions, roughly 150,000 men, with an equal number of auxiliaries. The garrisons were on the frontiers to act as staging points for offensives designed to beat back any invading forces. These garrisons became permanent, and in order to supply the soldiers' needs, towns grew up around them. Many of modern-day Europe's major cities started as Roman garrisons. Augustus's army was large enough to meet military attacks from any quarter, but because it was greatly reduced in size from the army that existed when he took power, it seemed a much smaller political threat. Still, the army remained the tool of the caesar more than of the government, and even when

Augustus's heirs proved incompetent or evil, the army for the most part remained loyal to them. When Augustus's line died out, the resulting struggle for power took Rome back to the days of commanders with private armies jockeying for power.

The second century CE saw some good caesars, and the army remained loyal to them, but with the rise and then the assassination of Commodus (ruled 180–192), the legions began pushing their own commanders as caesars. As the military became less Roman and more provincial, the caesars themselves began to come from the provinces. After Commodus, Severus rose to power and openly courted army support. Because the Praetorian Guard had become increasingly political, he disbanded it and then immediately recreated his own version, opening it to non-Romans who were loyal to him more than to the position of the caesar. He stationed a legion in Italy for the first time, breaking tradition but keeping more military power on hand in case of political emergency. He also gave the soldiers a major raise, the first in a century. He allowed the soldiers to marry and opened civil service positions to veterans, which made the army more attractive as a path to a lifelong career. Although the army remained effective, it began to attract employees rather than fighters.

After Severus and his line ended in 235 CE, a half century of anarchy rocked the empire. Almost any military commander with any legion support at all could and did make a run at political power. The army organization began to change as well. Not only was it becoming more political, but it also altered its form. Heavy infantry began to give way to cavalry in response to the Parthian and Sassanid Persian armies that the Romans faced in the Middle East.

Also, more barbarian raids occurred in northern Europe, and cavalry was necessary to provide a more rapid response, especially because the army was so busy engaging in politics. The Praetorian Guard also began to take on more cavalry as the emperor needed quicker response time in the ever-shifting political arena. The infantry arm grew smaller and smaller as fewer recruits joined and the government spent more money on domestic needs. The quality of training dropped off dramatically, and the frontier forces became more defensive in nature and more local in composition. The Germans became more aggressive, and the frontier receded in the north. With a less effective army, it was more difficult to maintain order in the provinces or carry on effective diplomacy with enemies. The period of anarchy took from the provinces the civilizing presence of Romans, which had always been the empire's strength.

The anarchy came to an end with the rise of Diocletian in 285. He divided the empire in eastern and western halves and created the tetrarchy, whereby the eastern and western caesars each had a junior colleague to aid in administration and to take over upon the caesar's death or retirement. That system lasted until Diocletian retired in 305, at which time the empire was once again rocked by civil wars. The army was now almost half a million strong, and divided into three types of soldiers. First were the *limitanei*, locally recruited and haphazardly trained defensive forces on the frontiers. The limitanei were primarily farmers who defended fortresses when foreigners attacked, a job that required much less training and competence with weapons. These were backed by the *comitatenses*, better trained and more mobile reserve forces that responded to attacks.

Finally, there were the *palatini*, the elite units within the mobile forces. Although the primary unit was still called a legion, it now comprised about 1,000 men on the frontier and 3,000 for the reserves. The discipline that had made the Roman army virtually unbreakable on the battlefield was gone, and combat was once again a free-for-all as it had been in the time of the Etruscans.

The Roman army was increasingly made up of "barbarians," as more and more men were recruited along the frontiers, especially the German frontier. The warlike Germanic tribes had always been worthy opponents, and by the fourth century they became worthy allies and soldiers. Constantine disbanded the Praetorian Guard during this time and replaced it with the *scholae palatinae*, an elite unit of Germans. Other circumstances forced the use of Germanic troops, like the major migrations from northern Europe in the fourth century. Goths, Vandals, and other populations spread south and west, pressuring the Roman frontiers and often breaking through. When the Goths defeated the eastern Roman army at Adrianople in 378, the Emperor Theodosius gave them land and titles in return for their becoming his army. In 395 the empire was formally divided into independent halves, and "Roman" became more descriptive of a political, rather than a geographical, entity.

The eastern Roman Empire based in Byzantium focused on Middle Eastern affairs for the most part and established itself as a major power for another thousand years. The western Roman Empire became little more than home for a succession of occupying populations until 800 when Charlemagne finally restored some political order, albeit in France rather than Italy. Thus, the Roman army came to an end, replaced by Byzantine armies in the east and multiple ethnic armies in the west. For a thousand years it had successively dominated central Italy, the entire peninsula, the western Mediterranean, then everything from Britain almost to Persia. The legionary was both soldier and civilizer, and the culture that spread with those armies affects Europe to this day.

References: Grant, Michael, *The Army of the Caesars* (New York: Scribner,1974); Luttwak, E. N., *The Grand Strategy of the Roman Empire* (Baltimore: Johns Hopkins University Press, 1977); Watson, G. R., *The Roman Soldier* (Ithaca: Cornell University Press, 1969).

Rough Riders

Volunteer cavalry serving with the United States Army during the Spanish-American War in 1898.

When the United States went to war against Spain in 1898, the U.S. Army was

Teddy's colts, at the top of the hill which they captured in the battle of San Juan. Colonel Theodore Roosevelt and his Rough Riders, 1898. Special Media Archives Services Division (NWCS-S), National Archives at College Park, 8601 Adelphi Road, College Park, MD. (Image 542082)

small. This was in keeping with the traditional American view against a large standing army, an attitude held since colonial times. Therefore, when war broke out in April, it was necessary to raise an army as quickly as possible. Americans did so in the same fashion they had always done, not through conscription but by raising volunteer units.

Although most of the units raised were infantry, some cavalry units were also formed. What came to be designated the First Volunteer Cavalry was officially under the command of Regular Army Colonel Leonard Wood. However, its highest profile member and the one responsible for its character was Theodore Roosevelt. Roosevelt had long advocated action against the Spanish over their actions in the Cuban Revolution, and now that war had come, he was not about to let others do all the fighting. Roosevelt believed that one should participate in the actions one advocates, so he quickly resigned his position as assistant secretary of the navy in order to join his friend Leonard Wood in San Antonio, Texas, where the First Volunteer Cavalry was forming in early May. Friends of Roosevelt flocked from across the country to join their comrade, and he attracted a mixed lot of recruits. Fellow polo players from Ivy League universities joined cowboys from the Dakotas with whom Roosevelt had worked in his younger days.

The unit's training in San Antonio was fairly informal. An unnamed Rough Rider described them as "twelve hundred as separate, varied, mixed, distinct, grotesque, and peculiar types of men as perhaps were ever assembled in one bunch in all the history of man. . .and one—possibly two—Democrats" (Millis, 1931). Roosevelt's extroverted character and almost childlike enthusiasm dominated their short tenure in

San Antonio. After just two weeks of training, the unit was ordered to Tampa, Florida, for transport to Cuba.

The scene in Tampa was one of utter chaos. Supplies piled up near the docks as men arrived from all over the country, with most of the infantry arriving from their training experience in Alabama. The U.S. Navy possessed virtually no transport vessels, for it had not conducted operations outside the United States since the invasion of Mexico in 1847. Thus, transport ships had to be leased, and those readily available had just returned from South Africa, where they had delivered horses for the British army. The still uncleaned ships sat in the Florida heat as increasing numbers of men and materiel arrived at the harbor, yet no one was in command to order any movement. Finally, when orders did arrive from Washington, the men scrambled aboard any handy ship and staked out what space was available for their unit—leaving all the supplies ashore. When the supplies were finally placed aboard ship, it was completely haphazard, for the science of loading was still far in the future. At this point, the number of ships available was sufficient only for men and materiel, which meant only essential animals could be taken along. Mules for hauling supply wagons and artillery, as well as officers' mounts, were taken aboard while the remainder were left behind. Thus, the First Volunteer Cavalry found itself without horses when the convoy sailed for Cuba.

Disorganized as the operation had been so far, it became worse when the force reached the south Cuban coast. Unable to land at the Spanish stronghold of Santiago, the convoy anchored offshore some five miles east of the city at the town of Daiquiri. As this town did not possess a harbor, the soldiers, supplies, and animals had to go ashore the best way they could. For the army and its supplies, that was by longboat; for the horses and mules, it was by swimming. Horses and mules were jumped overboard and then expected to swim for the beach, but hundreds drowned in the process. Only the total lack of resistance on the part of the Spaniards kept this landing from becoming a disaster.

Once ashore, the army faced toward Santiago. Between their position and the city lay a number of hills upon which the Spaniards had constructed defensive positions. It was in the assault on these hills that Roosevelt and the Rough Riders would enter American folklore. With their horses drowned, the Rough Riders were obliged to walk into combat. Roosevelt, who had two horses brought to Cuba on his yacht, was the only Rough Rider mounted. The other famous misconception about the Rough Riders' combat experience concerns the location of their attack. They did not charge up San Juan Hill, but rather Kettle Hill, next to it. The blockhouses on San Juan Hill were assaulted and captured by infantry units. Roosevelt led his men up Kettle Hill, so named because of a large vat on the top used for sugar refining. According to Roosevelt's account of the charge, there was a lot of shooting but not many casualties, at least not among the Americans. The Spanish artillery was more effective than their infantry, but a mixed formation of Rough Riders, the Tenth Cavalry, and regular army troops captured Kettle Hill and the one just past it, from which they could look down on the city of Santiago.

There was no real Battle of Santiago. Spanish troops stayed inside their defenses awaiting an American attack that never came, owing to the hesitation to assault strong entrenchments. The destruction of the Spanish fleet attempting to escape Santiago harbor, coupled with the realization that no aid was coming, convinced the Spanish authorities to surrender their forces in Cuba without major fighting. The besieging American force suffered greatly from disease, and many more Americans died from that enemy than from combat with the Spanish. Shortly after the Spanish surrender, diplomats in Paris began work on a peace treaty.

What made the Rough Riders so famous was not really their actions, but their publicity. Almost as soon as Roosevelt returned to the United States after the war, he began writing a book on his experience in Cuba, and *The Rough Riders* was an instant bestseller. It was during his campaign for national office (vice president in 1900, president in 1904) that Roosevelt called on his comrades from Cuba to speak for his cause. The press constantly asked him about the charge up San Juan Hill, and he finally got tired of correcting them and accepted the misinformation without contradiction. Thus, the highest profile unit in the war that brought the United States to international power became famous for something it never did: mount a cavalry charge up San Juan Hill.

References: Freidel, Frank, *The Splendid Little War* (Boston: Little, Brown and Company, 1958); Millis, Walter, *Martial Spirit* (New York: Houghton, Mifflin, 1931); Roosevelt, Theodore, *The Rough Riders* (New York: Charles Scribner's Sons, 1924 [1899]).

Royal Air Force (Battle of Britain)

The air force that defended Great Britain in 1940.

Few organizations in the twentieth century have garnered so much attention as "the few" immortalized by Winston Churchill during the Battle of Britain in the summer of 1940. With Adolph Hitler's Germany in control of almost all of continental Europe, Great Britain was the single nation able to hold out against the Nazi aggression. If Hitler had had his way, an invasion of Britain would have removed this last obstacle to European domination, and the Royal Air Force was the lone fighting group that could halt the proposed invasion. Hitler needed control of the skies for his air force to effectively keep the British navy at bay while his army crossed the English Channel. If the Royal Air Force (RAF) could be neutralized, nothing—it seemed—could halt Germany's conquest.

Hitler's *Luftwaffe* (air force) was twice the size of Britain's RAF, with some 2,000 fighter and bomber aircraft. The Battle of Britain was mainly a fighter's battle, and the two air forces were able to employ some of the finest fighter aircraft available anywhere. The *Luftwaffe's* main fighters were the Messerschmidt Bf-109 and Focke-Wulf FW-190, both fast and agile single-engine aircraft, but both with limited range. The Messerschmidt Bf-110 was a twin-engine aircraft for which the Germans held high hopes, but it proved inferior to the two primary British fighter planes and so was relegated to primarily escort and fighter-bomber roles. The RAF employed mainly the Hawker Hurricane and the Supermarine Spitfire, the former in greater numbers but the latter a superior fighter. When possible, the British attempted to employ the Hurricane to attack German bomber aircraft while the Spitfire was the preferred machine for dogfighting, as air-to-air combat was called.

Britain's major weapon, however, was more scientific than mechanical. Within the previous few months, British scientists had invented radar, which effectively precluded the Germans from launching surprise attacks. With advance knowledge of approaching German planes, the RAF could respond to particular threats and avoid the fuel- and time-consuming practice of constant patrols. Radar allowed the RAF to concentrate forces at the point of attack and, by conserving fuel, to give them more time in the air than the short-range German fighter aircraft had. Once the Germans learned this, the logical response was to focus their attacks on the radar sites. The construction of the radar antennae, however, made destroying them difficult.

They looked like nothing more than radio antennae, tall towers made up of structural steel; thus, there was more open space in the construction than steel, producing little effect from bomb fragments. The Germans possessed a dive bomber, the Junkers Ju-87 *Stuka*, which was incredibly accurate and capable of dropping bombs directly on the antennae, but the *Stuka* was quite slow and easy for British fighters to destroy. Extremely high dive-bomber losses suffered in late June and early July 1940 forced the Germans to formulate another strategy.

If the RAF had no airfields from which to operate, they reasoned, then the British

A painting of the Spitfires of the Royal Air Force. Courtesy of Paul Davis.

aircraft could be destroyed on the ground. The Germans proceeded to implement this plan with their force of medium bombers, made up of three different aircraft: the Junkers Ju-88, the Dornier Do-17, and the Heinkel He-111. All three of these were twin-engine bombers with independently manned machine guns for defensive armament. They were effective and accurate, and the aircrews were highly trained, with experience gained in earlier campaigns against Poland, Denmark, Norway, and France, as well as (in some cases) combat experience gained during the Spanish Civil War. The German attacks on the airfields were effective in damaging or destroying British hangar and repair facilities, but the airstrips themselves were, for the most part, dirt fields that were easily repaired. The German campaign limited, but did not eliminate, the RAF's ability to put fighters in the air and defend themselves.

By August the Germans realized that this second tactic was not working well enough. German strategy shifted to destroying British aircraft factories, reasoning that the RAF would then not be able to replace its losses, while German factories could continue to produce replacements for their aircraft lost in combat. This new strategy, coupled with the continued bombing of facilities at the airfields, began to bear fruit. Further, it was difficult for the RAF to replace their lost pilots in a timely fashion. By late August 1940, the Royal Air Force was rapidly dwindling as daily aerial duels took their toll. By mid-September, the crisis was desperate. Only an emotional decision by Adolph Hitler saved the RAF and Great Britain.

As the *it Luftwaffe was bombing British targets by day, RAF bombers attacked targets on the continent at night. In late August, a small British force attacked Germany's capital city, Berlin. Although the raid did little damage physically, it was a severe blow to German morale. Hitler was infuriated that Churchill would allow his air force to attack targets that were strictly civilian centers that had no military value. If that was Churchill's choice, Hitler reasoned, then he could and would respond in kind. He ordered his air force to stop bombing factories and start bombing cities. This reprieve for the aircraft factories allowed them to begin replacing the aircraft they had been unable to build during the German raids, and the immediate crisis passed. Most importantly, the RAF was still operational, though at the limits of its strength, when Hitler decided on September 15 to postpone his invasion of the British Isles until better weather the following spring. The postponement turned out to be permanent, however, when Hitler redirected his attention eastward and began preparations for an attack on the Soviet Union.

The Royal Air Force, by maintaining air superiority, thwarted Nazi invasion plans. The men who flew in the summer of 1940 were mainly young British pilots with only marginal experience. Among the pilots who became famous during this battle were Douglas Bader, equally well known for his aggressiveness and the fact that he lost one leg above and one leg below the knee in an accident before the war; Johnny Johnson, who went on to become the RAF's highest-scoring ace, credited with shooting down 38 enemy aircraft; and Alan Deere, a South African who answered the call for volunteers from across the British Empire. Also flying for the RAF were units incorporating Australian, New Zealand, and Canadian pilots; two squadrons of Polish pilots who escaped the conquest of their country by the Nazis; and the Eagle

Squadron made up of volunteer American pilots.

References: Hough, Richard, and Denis Richards, *The Battle of Britain* (New York: Norton, 1989); Macksey, Kenneth, *Invasion* (New York: Macmillan, 1969); Wood, Derek, and Derek Dempster, *The Narrow Margin* (New York: Coronet, 1969).

Royal Americans

A unit of troops made up of British colonists in North America who served with distinction in the wars against the French and Indians

As hostilities arose in the Americas during the French and Indian War, the British began to see that the Indians, who had the "home-field advantage," had a fighting style more conducive to the terrain of this area to which the British would need to adapt. One of the units best able to adapt, and because of this, succeed, was the Sixtieth Regiment of Foot, the Royal Americans. The Royal Americans were able to pioneer a new style of fighting and have been one of the most reliable units in the British army since they came into existence.

As with most units, the Sixtieth was organized out of necessity. The British, seeing the advancing French and Indian forces encroaching farther and farther into the British colonies, feared they could lose the colonies altogether. As a result, they added 11 regiments, one of which was the Sixty-second Regiment of Foot, whose number was soon lowered to Sixtieth. The Sixtieth's structure would contain four battalions, each of 1,000 men—an exceptionally large force for the time, but the British intended for this regiment to spread across North America and defend all parts of the frontier. Because of its size, the Sixtieth was difficult to man with enough officers, so the British actually recruited German and Swiss officers to join the regiment.

Once the leadership was assigned, these officers traveled to America and mustered their units with local colonists. The effectiveness of the units, which were actually armed with muskets "not fit for regular regiments," was ensured, however, by the First Battalion's second command, Lt. Col. Bouquet. He removed the unnecessary decorations from the uniform and made the jacket less constricting. The regiment would also later discard the standard red coats and replace them with green ones, which would provide camouflage on the heavily wooded frontier. In addition, Bouquet instituted a tactic that allowed his men to redeploy from column formation to line formation quickly. These changes greatly contributed to the unit's future success and would soon be adopted by other British units.

Recruiting went slowly, because the colonists who were being protected by this unit wanted little to do with the fighting itself, or assisting those in the fighting. Bouquet wrote, "They're extremely pleased to have Soldiers to protect their Plantations but will feel no inconveniences from them." After two years, the regiment was finally fully manned, and in 1757, the regiment deployed. The First Battalion was split in two, with one half marching south to defend South Carolina, and the other marching to fight at Fort Duquesne. The Third Battalion was left with the sick and unfit troops, while the Second and Fourth were deployed to Halifax in campaigns against the French in Canada. After attacks in New York, however, they were redeployed there, with the Second Battalion guarding the western front and the Fourth guarding the north.

The Royal Americans' first fighting came in 1758, when parts of the First and the entire Fourth Battalions invaded Canada across Lake Champlain. The rest of the First, along with the Second and Third, launched an offensive against the French in the Ohio Valley. In November 1758, the First Battalion was part of the force that secured Fort Duquesne for the British, and the Second and Third were the leading units in the assault against Cape Breton Island. On this raid, they wore their famous green jackets, a uniform which is still worn by the descendant of this unit today. The Fourth continued fighting on the New York frontier, participating in the capture of Fort Frontenac. Later in the war, the Second and Third Battalions would be in the force, commanded by Wolfe, that captured Quebec. In the French counterattack on Quebec, they earned their motto, "Celer et Audax," meaning "Swift and Brave."

After the French and Indian War, Royal American forces remained stationed in frontier forts. Part of the First Battalion, stationed at Fort Detroit, held off Indian attacks for all of the summer of 1763 during Pontiac's War, when most other British units were falling left and right. A force of Royal Americans, commanded by Bouquet, also won a great victory at Bushy Run. They were on their way to relieve the besieged British force at Fort Pitt, but were attacked by Pontiac at a creek about a day's march from the fort. Bouquet, almost completely surrounded, took a page out of the Spartan playbook and executed a feigned retreat, which drew the Indians into a charge. Bouquet's men fired volleys at them from the forest, and then charged the Indians with fixed bayonets. This forced the Indians to withdraw and relieved the siege of Fort Pitt.

Upon the completion of Pontiac's War, the Royal Americans were still stationed around the frontier until 1767, when they were recalled to Britain to fight on the continent there. After the American Revolution, they were renamed the King's Royal Rifle Corps, which served under Wellington in his campaigns against Napoleon. Wellington even had a battalion of the Ninety-fifth Rifles, as the King's Royal Rifle Corps was redesignated, lead his army's march into Paris. In 1926, the Rifle Corps continued in the pioneering spirit of its Royal American predecessors by becoming one of the first mechanized infantry units. The U.S. Army War College at Carlisle, Pennsylvania, on the frontier the Royal Americans once defended, has named the adjutant's building "Bouquet Hall" in honor of the great commander.

The Royal Americans served a vital role in the British army in one of its most critical fights. The French and Indian War's outcome was hanging in the balance when the Royal Americans entered the fight, and they then proceeded to be a major part of the British forces at the battles at Fort Duquesne, Lake Champlain, and Quebec. They also began the dissemination of Indian fighting tactics into European fighting. The Royal Americans took the best of European discipline and training, united it with the successful fighting style of the French and Indians, and produced an incredibly effective result for the British army. The great irony with the Royal Americans is that they are perhaps all but forgotten by the people they defended, the Americans, and are instead remembered more by the British army, who witnessed all that they had fought for slip away in the American Revolution.

Trent Melcher

References: Peckham, Howard H., *Pontiac and the Indian Uprising* (Detroit: Wayne State Press, 1994 [1947]); Stuart, Kenneth P., "The Fighting Royal Americans," *Military History*, April 2004.

Royal Marines

British forces created in the seventeenth century, from which the first commando forces of World War II were created.

Although serving aboard ship was their duty, the Royal Marines actually got their start as part of the Royal Army. Created by an Order in Council in 1664, they were originally given the designation "Duke of York and Albany's Maritime Regiment of Foot." As the Duke was at the time the Lord High Admiral of the Royal Navy, the unit became known as the Admiral's Regiment. Though they were officially part of the army, they served at sea and were paid by the Admiralty.

Their first major action came in 1704 during the War of the Spanish Succession. Nineteen hundred Marines, along with 400 Dutch Marines, fought at Gibraltar, first driving off Spanish reinforcements, then storming the fortress, capturing it, and holding it for nine months against Franco-Spanish attempts to retake it. This provided the first and only named battle honor for the Marines, which is part of their emblem today. (Most of the rest of the emblem depicts a globe, in recognition that they were involved in so many actions around the world that they cannot be individually named.) In 1755, "His Majesty's Marine Forces" (numbering 50 companies) transferred from the army to the Admiralty. They received the modern title of Royal Marines in 1802.

The Marines accompanied the Royal Navy as Britain spread its influence around the world: Australia in 1788, Trafalgar in 1805, Algiers in 1816, in the First Ashanti War in 1824, and Navarino in 1827. In 1831, the were sent to Ireland and Newcastle to quell civil disturbances.

Adjunct forces and reorganizations also brought change to the Marines over time. In 1804, the Royal Marine Artillery was created and the official name of the unit in 1855 was "Royal Marines, Light Infantry." Not until 1923 were all the parts finally melded into a single whole, the Corps of Royal Marines. In the meanwhile, they had performed a major role in World War I during the landings at Gallipoli in 1915 and the massive raid on the Dutch port of Zeebrugge in 1918.

During World War II, 80,000 men served in the Marines, but there was also a major change in some of its units. In 1942, the Admiralty created the Royal Marines Commando (at the urging of Prime Minister Winston Churchill) in the wake of the evacuation of Dunkirk in 1940. Churchill

Commandoes of the 41st Royal British Marines plant demolition charges along railroad tracks of enemy supply line, Songjin, Korea. April 1951. National Archives and Records Administration, Special Media Archives Services Division (NWCS-S), National Archives at College Park, 8601 Adelphi Road, College Park, MD. [Image 520790]

wanted to implement hit-and-run-style raids along the European coastline to keep the German occupation troops nervous. Royal Marine (RM) "A" Commando was officially created February 14, 1942 and had its baptism of fire during the abortive raid on Dieppe, France, in August of that year. Other commandos were also created and were joined together into brigade strength in 1943, when they took part in the Allied invasion of Sicily. They then fought alongside other allied forces up the Italian peninsula and also raided the Yugoslav coast. In 1943, a section designated 3 Special Service Brigade fought in India against the Japanese. Five RM Commando units landed at Normandy in June 1944 and were responsible (during the landings) of manning the majority of the landing craft. They fought across France and into the Netherlands by war's end.

During the war, army commando units were also created, but they were disbanded at the end of the war and commando units became the special purview of the Royal Marines. The Marines and the Commandos were not idle for long after the war, seeing action in Palestine, Aden, Brunei, Kuwait, and Tanganyika. Units were deployed to Korea in 1950–1951, where some of them (attached to the U.S. First Marine Division) were involved in the hard-fought retreat from the Chosin Reservoir. They soon went to entirely different climes when they were deployed in Malaya to suppress the guerrilla independence movement. In 1956, they attacked Port Said during the Suez Crisis, where Commando 40, 42, and 45 performed military history's first combat helicopter-borne assault. Other units were deployed to Borneo to aid Indonesian forces, and Marines and Commando units after 1969 often served in Northern Ireland during "the Troubles."

As seems to be the nature of Marines worldwide, they specialize in an extremely difficult basic training. Unlike most other Marines, however, the Royal Marines have no separate training facilities for enlisted men and officers—both undergo exactly the same training, though the officers are at times required to do things more quickly. For example, one of the major tests of basic training is a 30-mile march wearing "fighting order" (the standard 32 pounds of gear) across the damp grasslands of Dartmoor; recruits are required to complete the march in eight hours, but officers have to do it in seven. All Marines have to complete the Commando course (first established in and little changed since World War II) as part of basic training. This is a variety of timed marches and obstacle courses, all done in fighting order. With basic training completed, the Marine is awarded a green beret, but he must continue specialized training and (for the Commandos) be accepted by the members of a unit with which he has trained. Specialties include sniper training, mountain warfare, amphibious warfare, pilot training, or application for one of the elite units such as the Special Boat Service.

During the 1970s, Marines and Commandos were stationed on NATO's flanks, basing in Malta and also training in Norway. The most serious combat the Marines saw in the 1980s was in the Falklands War of 1982. "3 Commando Brigade, augmented by two battalions from the Parachute Regiment, . . .completed successful amphibious landings at San Carlos, and then fought throughout the six-week campaign, which resulted in the surrender of all Argentinean forces on the island." In 1990–1991, Royal Marines participated in Operations Desert Shield and Desert Storm, then had some of their units stay on extended duty protecting the Kurds in northern Iraq from Saddam Hussein. Between 1991 and 2000, Commando units served in Bosnia and Kosovo. In 1996, Commandos joined in the Joint Rapid Deployment Force, which sent troops into the Congo in 1998 and Sierra Leone in 2000.

The Royal Marines and Commandos' latest missions have been in Afghanistan and Iraq. Thanks to the introduction of the *HMS Ocean*, *HMS Albion*, and *HMS Bulwark* (all Landing Platform [Helicopter] or Landing Platform [Dock] ships), the Marines now have the capability to stay in a combat area for an extended period of time. This made it possible for them to extend their October 2001 exercise in Oman into a combat operation in Afghanistan, where they saw intense action against Taliban and Al Qaeda fighters. They also were the initial troops seeing combat in Operation Telic in 2003 when they staged an amphibious assault against Iraqi oil facilities at Al Faw and assisted in the drive that captured and subdued the key city of Basra.

References: "A Short History of the Royal Marines," Royal Marines; 1 February 2006, www.royal-navy.mod.uk/static/pages/2215; "Commandos–History," Royal Marines, 1 February 2006, www.royal-navy.mod.uk/static/pages/2276; "Royal Marines–Historical," The Royal Marines Regimental Site, 5 February 2006, www.royalmarinesregimental.co.uk/historical.

S

Sacred Band of Thebes

An elite fighting unit of ancient Greece in the fourth century BCE.

The Sacred Band of Thebes was founded in ancient Greece by the Theban leader Gorgidas, who probably first formed the unit as a guard for the city-state's citadel. It contained 300 men for whom Thebes provided training facilities and barracks. At first the Sacred Band did not distinguish itself in combat, possibly because Gorgidas placed its soldiers in the front ranks of the central Theban phalanx, where it was integrated with other soldiers. This did not allow the special training of the Band to be demonstrated, for other, less-talented soldiers "diluted" the Band's strength. The army, therefore, did not benefit from the striking power that the Band was supposed to provide.

Under the later leadership of Pelopidas, however, the Sacred Band came into its own. Pelopidas commanded the Sacred Band at the Battle of Leuctra in 371 BCE in which the Thebans fought the Spartan army, generally regarded as the best army in Greece. Epaminodas commanded the Theban army, and placed the Sacred Band in the key position on the left flank. Epaminodas's strategy was to form an oblique angle with his army in order to divide the Spartan army and isolate its right wing, its strongest part. The Spartans reacted quickly to the attack by turning their forces and attempting to encircle the Thebans. As their turning movement was just starting, the Sacred Band struck. The shock of the assault broke the Spartan ranks, resulting in "a rout and slaughter of the Spartans such as had never before been seen," according to Plutarch.

The Theban victory at Leuctra proved decisive, for it led to the decline of Sparta as the premier military power in Greece. The Thebans followed up the victory by expelling the Spartan government, which had been imposed on Thebes, then creating an army made up almost entirely of Theban citizens with very few mercenaries. Within the Theban army, the Sacred Band's decisive role in the Leuctra victory took its members to elite status and ensured that in the future no dilution of their strength would be allowed; they would always fight as a separate unit. Patriotism soared not only in Thebes but throughout Greece as the power of Sparta waned.

The Sacred Band derived its reputation for outstanding fighting ability not only from its training, but also from the makeup of the unit. The 300 soldiers were 150 homosexual couples. Homosexuality was not frowned upon in ancient Greece. The theory within this organization was that the desire to protect and impress one's lover would bring out the best fighting spirit in each soldier. Therefore, the unit would remain close-knit as each soldier acted not only for himself, but also for his partner, as well as for the unit and army as a whole.

The Band remained the elite of the Theban army until both unit and army were defeated in 338 BCE. Thebes and Athens that year formed an alliance against the rising power of Macedon under Philip II. They marched to meet the Macedonians at Cheronea but could not withstand the power of the Macedonian army and the brilliance of its leader. The Macedonian victory brought Philip to power in Greece while destroying the power of the city-states. After the battle, Philip walked the field. When he came to the area where the Sacred Band had fought and died to the last man, he is reported to have commented, "Perish any man who suspects that these men did or suffered anything that was base" (Plutarch, 1986).

The Sacred Band achieved its reputation by defeating the premier army of ancient Greece, the Spartans, but they could not match the new organization and tactics introduced by Philip, whose army—led by Philip's son Alexander—would conquer most of the known world. The Sacred Band existed for only a few decades and was never revived after its annihilation at Cheronea.

References: Plutarch, trans. by Ian Scott-Kilvert, *The Age of Alexander* (Middlesex: Penguin Books, 1986); Warry, John, *Warfare in the Classical World* (London: Salamander Books, 1980).

Samurai

The warrior class of feudal Japan between the thirteenth and nineteenth centuries.

The Samurai, the warrior class of ancient Japan, dominated that country's political

Illustration depicting Ronin, or masterless Samurai, leaning on his spear and grimacing fiercely. *Library of Congress, Prints & Photographs Division [reproduction number LC-USZC4-8657].*

and social structure for centuries. The Samurai came into existence in the early thirteenth century with the establishment of a feudal society in Japan. As in medieval Europe, the large landowners dominated the economy in an agricultural society and therefore had sufficient monetary resources to pay for the best in military supplies. Thus, as in Europe, the ability to own armor, horses, and superior weaponry brought one an exalted social status to be carefully maintained. Thus, the Samurai were dedicated to perfecting their martial skills and living by a strict code of honor that supported the feudal system. At the height of the Samurai's preeminence, loyalty to one's overlord and the ability to

278

defend his property and status, even to the detriment of one's own property and status, became the pinnacle of honor.

The original soldiers of Japan were called *bushi* ("warrior"), from the Japanese pronunciation of a Chinese character signifying a man of letters and/or arms. The rise of these warriors to the status of a special class began with an interclan struggle in the late 1100s. The Genji and Heike clans were maneuvering for influence in the imperial court, and the Heike managed to obtain the upper hand. In the fighting that ensued, the Genji clan was almost completely destroyed, but two sons managed to escape northward from the area of the capital city, Kyoto. When the elder son, Yoritomo, reached his majority, he rallied his remaining supporters and allied with the clans of northern Honshu that looked down on the imperial clans, which they considered weak and effete. Yoritomo's return renewed the fighting, and in the second struggle it was the Heike that were defeated.

In 1192 Yoritomo was named *shogun* (roughly "barbarian-defeating generalissimo"), the supreme military position as personal protector of the emperor. However, as the emperor had more figurative than literal power, the position of shogun came to wield real authority in Japan. What national unity Japan had ever attained, though, came through the population's belief in the emperor as the descendent of the gods that created the world. Therefore, the shogun could not seize the throne without alienating the people. The emperor could not rule, however, without the military power of the shogun to protect him and enforce the government's will. Thus, the shogun became the power behind the throne in a mutually dependent relationship.

Yoritomo and his descendants enjoyed a relatively brief ascendancy, but by the middle 1300s factional struggles broke out. For a time there were two rival emperors, each with his warrior supporters. In the latter half of the 1400s, the Ashikaga clan went through an internal power struggle before it took control of the country, though that control was often merely nominal during the century that they ruled. As the emperor and the central government exercised less control over time, the local landed gentry, or *daimyo*, came to prominence and wielded power in the countryside. By alliances and conquests, these feudal lords enhanced their economic, political, and military positions, until by the late 1500s, there was serious fighting among these leaders, and the emperor had no shogun to protect him or display his authority. It was in the 1500s that the Samurai came to be a true warrior class of professional, full-time soldiers, sworn to their daimyo overlords.

The Samurai tended to dominate the command positions as heavy cavalry, while the mass of soldiers became pikemen. All soldiers, no matter their status or function, carried a sword. For the Samurai warrior, the sword became a symbol of his position, and the Samurai were the only soldiers allowed by law to carry two swords. Anyone not of the Samurai class who carried two swords was liable to be executed. The two swords were the *katana*, or long sword (averaging about a three-foot blade), and the *wakizashi*, or short sword (with the blade normally 16–20 inches long). The finest swords became the property of the richest warriors, and being a swordsmith was the most highly respected craft. Both swords were slightly curved with one sharpened edge and a point; they were mainly slashing weapons, although they could be used for stabbing. The short sword in particular was a close-quarters stabbing weapon and also used in *seppuku*, the Samurai's ritual suicide. The blades were both strong and flexible, being crafted by hammering the steel thin, folding it over, and rehammering it, sometimes thousands of times. The sword and its expert use attained spiritual importance in the Samurai's life. The other main weapon in Japanese armies of the time was the *naginata*, a long-handled halberd used by the infantrymen. It consisted of a wide, curved blade sharpened on one edge and mounted on a long pole. By 1600 this had been largely replaced by the *yari*, more of a spear. Occasionally, unusual weapons were developed, such as folding fans with razor-sharp edges.

The Samurai wore elaborate suits of armor, made of strips of metal laced with leather. The finished product was lacquered and decorated to such an extent that it not only was weatherproof and resistant to cutting weapons, but it became almost as much a work of art as was a fine sword. Armor proved unable to stop musket balls, however, and became mainly ceremonial after 1600.

Japanese armies also had bowmen, although most archery was practiced from horseback and therefore in the province of the Samurai. By the end of the sixteenth century, however, Oda Nobunaga (1534–1582) became the first of the daimyo to effectively adopt firearms. European harquebuses had been introduced to Japan in the 1540s by shipwrecked Portuguese, and Japanese artisans began to copy the design. Nobunaga fielded 3,000 musketeers in a battle in 1575 with such positive effect that the other daimyo rushed to acquire as many of the weapons as possible. The technology advanced little in the following generations, however, owing to Japan's self-imposed exile from the rest of the world.

Nobunaga, starting with a relatively small landholding in central Japan, schemed and fought his way to become the strongest of the lords. In this time, the daimyo built huge castle/fortresses, equal to or better than anything built in Europe at the time. Nobunaga defeated many of the military religious sects on his way to dominance, but not surprisingly created a number of enemies, which allied and attacked his palace in 1582, burning it to the ground with him inside. Nobunaga was succeeded by Toyotomi Hideyoshi (1536–1598), one of his commanders, who almost succeeded in accomplishing Nobunaga's dream of unifying Japan under his rule. At his death in 1598 one of his vassals, Tokugawa Ieyasu, took control of half of Hideyoshi's forces and won the battle of Sekigahara. He was named shogun in 1603—the first to hold that position in years—and finished consolidating his power in 1615 with the capture of Osaka castle, where the last remnants of the defeated Hideyoshi faction held out.

The Tokugawa shogunate lasted until the middle 1800s, when it was dismantled during the Meiji Restoration. This movement returned real power to the emperor and abandoned the traditional feudal state that had kept Japan isolated and technologically backward for more than two and a half centuries. During the Tokugawa period, however, the Samurai both experienced their golden age and sowed the seeds of their own downfall. The Samurai came to hold the ruling administrative positions as well as exercising military functions. The Samurai warrior, who had over time blended the hardiness of the country warrior with the polish of the court, was the pinnacle of culture, learning, and power. The problem was that Tokugawa had succeeded too well, establishing a peace that lasted 250 years. Without the almost constant warfare that had preceded the Tokugawa era, the Samurai warrior had fewer and fewer chances to exercise his profession of arms. He became more of a bureaucrat, and therefore he could not be rewarded in combat or expand his holdings through warfare. The Samurai class increased in numbers, but not through "natural selection" in combat, and their larger numbers in a more and more bloated bureaucracy brought about their economic slide. The merchant class grew increasingly wealthy, while the Samurai upper class became impoverished. The tax burden required to operate the government fell on the peasants, who turned to shopkeeping rather than follow an unprofitable agricultural life. By the time the American Matthew Perry sailed into Tokyo Bay in 1854 and "opened" Japan to the outside world, the artisans and merchants were the only ones in a position to deal with the new reality, and the Samurai's status in society quickly dropped.

In spite of this setback, the martial attitude engendered by centuries of military rule never completely left the Japanese national psyche. The military became modernized with European weaponry, but the dedication to a martial spirit and professionalism remained strong in the new warrior class. In the 1920s and 1930s, the military came back into power and dominated the government, laying the groundwork for national expansionism to obtain the raw materials necessary to maintain and enlarge their military and industrial base. The cult of the Samurai, *bushido* (the "Way of the Warrior"), enjoyed a resurgence in the Japanese military. It showed itself in the brutal actions of the Japanese in their dealings with defeated enemies in China, Southeast Asia, and the Pacific, and in their dedication to death before dishonor in serving their emperor. The world saw firsthand the twentieth-century version of the Samurai in the extremely difficult fighting against Japanese soldiers during World War II and in the Japanese use of suicide tactics late in the war in an attempt to save their country from invasion and defeat. Japanese texts on Samurai philosophy and lifestyle, such as *Hagakure* and *The Five Rings*, still influence the views of the modern Japanese in their business practices.

References: King, Winston, *Zen and the Way of the Sword* (New York: Oxford University Press, 1993); Turnbull, Stephen, *Samurai Warriors* (New York: Sterling Publishing, 1991); Turnbull, Stephen, *The Samurai: A Military History* (New York: Macmillan, 1977).

San Patricio Battalion

A unit of the Mexican Army made up of Irish deserters from the U.S. Army during the Mexican-American War

Most Americans who know of the Mexican War, which lasted from April 25, 1846, until the signing of the treaty of Guadalupe Hidalgo on February 2, 1848, know only of the results of the war, namely the acquisition of a large tract of land that makes up several current U.S. states. They also may know that it was a relatively short war that was fought not only in present day Mexico, but also in New Mexico and California. What many fail to remember about the war, which the Mexicans still celebrate today, is the existence of an interesting band of soldiers that crossed over to the Mexican forces and fought

BATTLE OF BUENA VISTA.

Battle of Buena Vista, February 23, 1847, where the Battalion of St. Patrick was first employed. The battalion suffered its greatest losses at Churubusco, just outside Mexico City. Library of Congress, Prints & Photographs Division, Edward S. Curtis Collection [reproduction number LC-USZC4-2957]

against their own troops with ferocity and passion.

This band of about 260 American soldiers, who called themselves "The Battalion of St. Patrick," was led by John Riley, formerly of Company K, Fifth Infantry Regiment. Riley had obtained a pass to attend mass when his unit was near Matamoras in 1846 and never returned. It is believed that Riley had also deserted the British army when it was in Canada. He was known by his superiors in the U.S. Army to be a good soldier, and to have sought out and banded together captured American soldiers who were behind Mexican lines.

Nonetheless, Riley and a number of soldiers from the U.S. Army came to be a part of the Mexican forces. After assembling themselves, the Battalion saw their first battle as a Mexican force when they defended the fortified town of Monterrey after it was attacked on September 19, 1846. They then moved south to Saltillo, and then fought a major battle between American and Mexican forces in February of 1847 at Buena Vista. It was there that the Battalion was first organized into a functional unit. General Antonio Lopez de Santa Anna, the commander of the Mexican Army, had decided to attack the area just south of Buena Vista after he discovered that the American numbers there had been reduced. The Battalion fought with the Mexicans in what was, for a time, a certain victory for the Mexicans. They were overcome, however, and were forced to retreat. After their retreat from Buena Vista, a hiatus occurred for the group as a Battalion to regroup and reorganize, but it is also speculated that the Mexicans were not comfortable working with traitors and kept them out of battles.

The "San Patricios," as the Mexican army referred to them, were called back into action when General Winfield Scott of the American Army began to push into the area surrounding Mexico City in the summer of 1847. Santa Anna needed them as reinforcements, since the geography of the area had little in the way of natural defenses. They were not sent alone, however; two other groups, the *Independencia* and the *Bravo* regiments, were sent along to make sure that the San Patricios were not going to desert or wander off as they had in the American Army. The Mexicans would not be disappointed.

The battalion had been moved to a convent, San Pablo, in Churubusco, a suburb of Mexico City. It was here, on August 20, that the Battalion of St. Patrick, about 260 strong, fought like madmen to hold off the American army. (Some sources say the Battalion never numbered more than 204.) General Rincòn, the commander of the Mexican forces at Churubusco, attempted to raise a white flag to surrender the convent. Three times the San Patricios ripped it down and continued to fight. Many of the men fought hand to hand in what was by far the most difficult and deadly battle that the American forces faced in the entire war. The San Patricios' vigor in battle has been attributed not to Mexican nationalism, but rather terror of

what would happen to them if captured. At the end of the battle, only 65 men remained of the Battalion, including their leader John Riley, and they were taken into American captivity.

It was at this point that the stories of the remaining soldiers came out of the woodwork. They were detained for a short time in the Castle of Chapultepec as the last attacks on Mexico City were carried out. A few days after their capture, 29 of the men were tried for committing treason. Many argued that they had been captured by the Mexicans and had been forced to fight. Many Mexicans who were also captured by the U.S. discredited this claim, so all were condemned to death by hanging. General Scott, whose troops had fought the San Patricios at Churubusco, reviewed each of the cases. He commuted seven of the sentences to lashing and branding, including that of John Riley. This was based on a strict interpretation of the U.S. law, and because war had not officially been declared against Mexico when Riley and the other six had deserted, they were given lesser sentences. Two of the 29 were pardoned altogether for actually having been captured and for refusing to fight in the Battalion. The others were hanged on September 10, 1847. The soldiers who were not tried at that time were tried in separate courts, and were all ultimately sentenced to death. General Scott again stepped in, pardoned two, and sentenced four to the same lashing and branding given to Riley. The rest were all hanged on September 13, 1847.

The trials revealed interesting facts regarding the nature of the Battalion. Because they had the name "The Battalion of St. Patrick," many had assumed that they were a band of Irish Catholics who were being disloyal to the American people.

Even many Mexicans believed this fact, and a large part of the Mexican national defense plan had been to use the clergy to lure Catholic soldiers in the American Army into their own, a tactic which failed. On the contrary, it was discovered that, of the men tried for treason, only 24–27 appeared to be of Irish descent. Many were, in fact, Englishmen and Germans, and it was only their leader, John Riley, who impressed the Irish tradition onto the men. Furthermore, of the group hanged on September 10, only seven of them asked for last rites by a Catholic priest; the other nine made no such request.

When all were accounted for, only two of the convicted men stated that a priest was responsible for their desertion, and some claimed that conditions in the army were so poor that they fled because the Mexicans offered them clothing and money. The prevailing excuse, however (which came from about 30 of the men captured), was intoxication—they claimed that while drinking, they wandered off and were captured by Mexicans.

Because of their name, many historians wish to argue that it is a prevalent example of the rebelliousness of Irish Catholics in American history. Others still claim that they deserted based on religious conviction to help the Catholic Mexicans and prevent desecration of their churches. Neither is true, however, and there isn't a great deal of evidence to argue that the band as a whole deserted the American forces based on religious conviction or ethnic background. They were merely a band of soldiers who, for whatever reason, wandered away from the army and most likely only fought fiercely after realizing what awaited them if they were captured. Their involvement in the war resulted in a relatively small inconvenience for the American army, and their memory lives on only in the hearts of the Mexican people, who saw them as their only foreign ally in an uphill battle. The Mexicans remember them on St. Patrick's Day and on the days of their hangings as heroes, while Americans may always view them as traitors. Either way, their actions, while unnoticed by some, are an interesting point of controversy for all historians.

Tanya Alvarez

References: Hogan, Michael, *The Irish Soldiers of Mexico* (Guadalajara, Mexico: Fondo Editorial Universitario, 1997); Miller, Robert Ryal, *Shamrock and Sword* (Norman: Univ. of Oklahoma Press, 1997); Wallace, Edward, "The Battalion of San Patricio in the Mexican War," *Military Affairs*, vol. 14, no. 2 (April 1950); Wynn, Dennis J., *The San Patricio Soldiers: Mexico's Foreign Legion*, Southwestern Studies: Mono No. 74 (El Paso: Texas Western Press, 1984).

Scythians

From eighth to the second century BCE, the Scythians represented the most terrifying military power in Asia, defeating large armies and dominating substantial parts of what is now Russia, Azerbaijan, Ukraine, Kazakhstan, and the Eurasian plains. These warring nomads were well-known throughout the continent for their fierce bravery and innovative battlefield tactics. Yet because the Scythians had no written language, most of what is known about them comes from the fifth century BCE recordings of the Greek historian, Herodotus.* It is only through modern-day ar-

*It is important to note that the validity of many of Herodotus's claims still has yet to be proven. However, archeological discoveries have increasingly verified his observations.

chaeological finds that Herodotus's seemingly unbelievable claims of Scythian war practices are finally being verified.

Though the Scythians did not domesticate the horse, they were among the first to adapt their way of life around it. As a pastoral nomadic people, this allowed them to cover greater distances more quickly. From the Russian steppes, the Scythians are believed to have wandered as far as the borders of Egypt on horseback. During their travels, they met and defeated several different peoples, and eventually extended their territory over large parts of Eastern Europe and Central Asia.

According to common belief, the Scythians first appeared on the world map in 750 BCE as a pastoral nomadic group settled between the Carpathians and the Don River. However, the first real written record of Scythian activity is seen in Assyrian texts from the early seventh century, when Scythian King Partatua married an Assyrian princess in 674 following a Scythian victory over the Assyrians. Later, in 653, the Scythians invaded the Medean empire, where they continued to exert influence until 626, when the Medes defeated them. Yet, the Medes united with the Scythians in 612 to capture Nineveh and destroy the Assyrian empire before driving the Scythians north of the Caucasus in the late seventh century. The Scythians continued to grow stronger over time, even managing to repel the Persian army (the largest in the world at that time) under King Darius the Great when the Persians invaded in 514. Herodotus wrote about this outstanding Scythian victory when he observed them in the fifth century. Later, in 360, King Atheas united all the tribes and expanded their territory to the border with Macedonia. It was not much later, though, that Scythian power began to

decline after losing a war against Philip II of Macedonia in 339. However, the Scythians managed to continue wielding enough power to defeat both a general of Alexander the Great in 330 and the Caucasians in 310 BCE, before the Celts and the Sarmatians (who had long been encroaching on Scythian territory) destroyed the Scythians' kingdom in 225 BCE.

During their many campaigns, the Scythians earned a reputation as brutal and ferocious warriors. Their military prowess was proved time and again through innovative weapon use and battlefield tactics. The Scythians were primarily archers, and almost exclusively cavalrymen. They were horse archers at a time when other armies depended mostly on foot soldiers and chariots. In fact, the Scythians were often the first cavalry many soldiers had ever seen in combat. This, in combination with full body tattoos, gave the Scythians a fierce and frightening appearance that terrified the people of the lands they invaded. Even when the opposing force did not run away out of fear, the Scythians proved an intimidating force; they appeared and disappeared too quickly for any kind of successful infantry attack. The Scythians, for their part, took full advantage of their military resources.

The Scythians became masters of archery on horseback, even learning how to shoot backwards while on horseback. "Scythian tactics were to advance on an enemy shooting fusillades of arrows. They would plunge forward as if to attack, but at the last instant wheel away and launch a fresh volley of arrows over the rumps of their retreating horses, thus leaving the dust-enveloped enemy in disarray." (Kuzych) This sort of guerrilla warfare was very common with the Scythians. And as they were nomads, they had the advantage of combining scorched earth tactics with their guerrilla attacks in order to keep the enemy at a distance and sap his resources while the Scythians moved farther away. In fighting smaller armies, they could be much more directly aggressive, first disorganizing their opponents by attacking them with arrows, then launching javelins and darts before charging with a lance and hand-to-hand weapons as they enemy's lines began to break. Due to firm discipline and great skill, "the Scythian cavalry managed to retain its cohesion after breaking through the enemy lines; regrouped in the thick of the battle; and decided the day by a second charge in another direction at a second body of the enemy. Very few armies of antiquity were capable of that manoeuvre." (Cernenko 32)

The value of the composite bow used by the Scythians cannot be overemphasized. Its stiffness and power allowed arrows to reach a distance of up to 200 yards with remarkable accuracy. For this reason, the Scythians were able to effectively use archery in both hunting and war. Unfortunately, the materials used to make bows—wood, bone, and animal tendons—deteriorate easily, and so very few bow remains have been found. The arrows that accompanied them fared better, being made of bronze, iron, or bone, depending on the date. Warriors kept both the bow and up to 75 arrows in a treasured gorytos, or bow case, which was never far from their side.

However, as mentioned previously, bows and arrows were not the only weapons used by the Scythians. They employed spears, long two-edged swords, short swords known as akinakes, narrow-bladed battle-axes, war picks, daggers, maces, and heavy darts. Most of these could either be thrown or used in close combat with the enemy.

Scythian armor usually consisted of leather corselets covered with overlapping bronze or iron "fish-scales" which shielded the chest and shoulders. Scythians are also credited with the development of chain mail, but its use was not common among the warriors, being expensive and difficult to produce. Scythian helmets evolved from pointed leather caps to scale-covered leather caps to tightly fitting bronze helmets. As for leg coverings, the Scythians are credited with the invention of trousers as they are known today. For avid horse riders, tight-fitting trousers offered protection for the legs, since only the most rudimentary kind of saddles existed at the time. Metal-plated leg armor was also usually included, though it varied in style. The shields they carried were unique in style and decoration. Although ordinary warriors preferred light shields, the classic example of Scythian shields is seen in those carried by higher-ranking cavalrymen: a wooden base covered in iron scales. The iron scales could sometimes be replaced by a single circular iron plate. On top of the iron, it is common, mostly among noblemen, to see gold ornamentation.

The Scythians had access to gold through their kinfolk in the Altas Mountains. They used this gold as ornamentation for their clothes, horses, and weapons. It was often seen glittering as a cover for their gorytos, a hilt for their sword, and a handle for their battle-axe. Intricate carvings were etched in the gold plates that covered their most precious objects. Since the Scythians were nomads, their prized possessions—clothes, horses, and weapons—were transportable and elaborately decorated. The Scythians carved animal figures, but they also mixed fantasy with reality to create the "Scythian animal style" of artwork. Sometimes, the Scythians would even commission Greeks to do gold work for them. This usually resulted in the incredibly detailed recreation of whole battle scenes done entirely in gleaming gold.

Also, if the sight of fully tattooed warriors shining with gold as they rapidly advanced on horseback wasn't enough to send the enemy screaming in the opposite direction, there was always the Scythian reputation. Their war practice was well-known to all, and is best recorded in Herodotus's *Histories*. Herodotus first writes about his dislike for the Scythians' assured victory in war. He particularly questions "the contrivance whereby they make it impossible for the enemy who invades them to escape destruction, while they themselves are entirely out of his reach. . . how can they fail of being unconquerable, and unassailable even?" As for their customs in battle, Herodotus describes the Scythians as savage and bloodthirsty warriors. He writes that Scythian soldiers drank the blood of the first man they killed in battle. They then cut off all the heads of those they slew, and took them to the king. Next, they scalped the heads and cut the scalps clean of flesh, in order to use it as a napkin. A warrior would either hang the scalps from his horse's bridle or fashion a cloak out of them. Some would skin the arm of their enemy's corpse and make a covering for their quivers. Others would go so far as to skin the entire body of the corpse and take it with them wherever they rode. With regard to the corpses of their most detested foes (or kin with whom they have been feuding), the Scythians would often fashion their skulls into drinking cups and use them socially.

It is clear, then, that the Scythians were brutal warriors who represented a significant threat to the peoples of their time.

Their creative use of weapons and nontraditional battlefield tactics earned them both victories and reputations that would outlast time.

Colleen Elizabeth Garcia

References: Cernenko, E.V., *The Scythians: 700–300 BC.* (New York: Osprey Publishing, 2005); Dwyer. Bede, "Scythian-Style Bows Discovered in Xinjiang." Asian Traditional Archery Research Network, 19 March 2004, www.atarn.org/chinese/scythian_bows, 1 March 2006; Godolphin, Francis R. B., "From the Lands of the Scythians: Ancient Treasures from the Museums of the U.S.S.R. 3000 B.C.-100 B.C.," *The Metropolitan Museum of Art Bulletin*, New Series, Vol. 32, No. 5, (1973–1974), pp. 129–149. http://links.jstor.org/sici?sici=0026-1521%281973%2F1974%292%3A32%3A5%3C129%3AHOTS%3E2.0.CO%3B2-A; Herodotus, *The Histories*, trans. by Aubery de Sleincourt (New York: Penguin Classics reprint, 2003); Kuzych, Ingert. "Scythian legacies," *The Ukrainian Weekly*, 7 November 1999, No. 45, Vol. LXVII, http://www.ukrweekly.com/Archive/1999/459930.shtml, 2 March 2006; "The Legacy of the Horse." International Museum of the Horse, 2000, www.imh.org/imh/kyhpl1b, 1 March 2006.

SEALs

An elite unit in the U.S. Navy.

World War II was the first conflict in which amphibious landings took place with regularity, and the doctrine for such operations to a great extent developed during the landings themselves. From 7 August 1942, when American forces invaded the island of Guadalcanal in the Solomon Island chain northeast of Australia, the United States dominated amphibious warfare. Although used at first primarily by the United States Marines, amphibious tactics were adopted over time by the U.S. Army and the armies of other countries. Early difficulties with natural and enemy-

Insignia of the United States Navy SEALs.

built obstacles led to the formation of navy combat demolition units in May 1943 which were designed to locate and neutralize anything in the way of the landing craft. They operated not only as the immediate vanguards of landing forces, but also as scouting units far in advance of any major landing.

As the fighting in the Pacific progressed, more specialized units were formed to handle newly discovered aspects of amphibious operations. Combat swimmer reconnaissance units were formed to explore potential landing sites, and underwater demolition teams (UDTs) took part in landings on the islands of Kwajalein, Roinamur, Pelelieu, and Okinawa, opening holes in beach and offshore defenses through which troops could advance. Commander John Koehler led the development of UDT methods, creating courses in long-range and night reconnaissance, special weaponry, and small-unit tactics. This training continued after World War II, and when fighting broke out in Korea in the summer of 1950, UDTs were back in action. An early setback in a failed mission to destroy a bridge behind North Korean lines led to more fine-tuning of UDT training and doctrine. Leadership of this training during the Korean conflict was under the direction of Marine Corps Major Edward Dupras, who had served in guer-

rilla and raider units during World War II. He oversaw the short-lived Special Operations Group that secretly scouted the planned invasion route into the harbor of Inch'on in September 1950. UDTs continued to operate during the fighting in Korea, training Korean personnel and acting at times under the command of the newly created Central Intelligence Agency (CIA). During this time, it was discovered that once ashore, these units could and should be able to operate further inland, thus expanding the role of the UDTs. Therefore, the navy created special operations teams to do just that, laying the groundwork for the SEAL teams, so named because of their ability to operate by sea, air, and land. They were officially designated as such in January 1962 upon the directive of President John Kennedy, whose interest in covert operations also created the Green Berets. The SEALs from the start were a separate organization from the UDTs, which kept their operations limited to coastal and offshore demolition.

The mission statement developed for the SEALs contained five points: (1) carry out clandestine or covert operations against selected enemy targets, especially in harbors and along rivers; (2) serve as guides for agents operating behind enemy lines and facilitate their entry and removal from their missions; (3) perform short-range and long-range reconnaissance missions; (4) conduct counterinsurgency operations; and (5) act as advisors and trainers for U.S. allies. The first major operation in which the new organization found itself was Vietnam, where SEALs both saw action and trained South Vietnamese units in SEAL tactics. By 1966, the SEALs were active in two major areas in Vietnam—the Mekong Delta and the Rung Sat Special Zone—operating with the "Brown Water

Navy," light river craft patrolling Vietnamese waterways. They also continued to be used in occasional CIA operations. Vietnam proved to be the primary training ground for SEALs and their implementation of new tactics and ideas. The concept of teamwork was finely honed here and remains the basis of SEAL training. Although SEALs are expected to be able to operate and survive independently if necessary, the subordination of the individual to the team is paramount.

In order to become a SEAL, one has to go through Basic Underwater Demolition/ SEAL training (BUD/S) at the Naval Special Warfare Center at Coronado, California, a 35-week course divided into three phases. In Phase One, the recruit has two weeks of physical and mental testing to determine his basic fitness for the course. He then spends three weeks learning first aid, lifesaving, and handling small boats. At the end of his fifth week, the true test of the SEAL takes place, five days called Hell Week. Placed in a six- or seven-man team, the recruit is pushed to and past his physical limits and constantly challenged mentally and psychologically. Here, those unable to cooperate in teams are weeded out, as well as those physically or mentally unable to continue. There are also those who fail to finish owing to injury, but they are given second chances later. Having survived Hell Week, the recruit then can catch his breath while learning how to chart beaches.

In Phase Two, the recruit learns to handle weapons and explosives and receives training in intelligence gathering, handling prisoners, navigation on land and sea, and marksmanship. SEALs learn to handle a variety of firearms, as well as hand grenades and mines. Mock operations are conducted during this phase to implement the information just learned. The seven weeks of Phase Three of the training is focused on dive training. Once this is complete, BUD/S is over. However, SEAL Tactical Training continues for the six months after BUD/S, which is a probationary period. During this time, the SEAL also undergoes parachute training at the Army's Fort Benning, Georgia, jump school. At the end of that time, a review board is conducted and SEALs who meet the standards are awarded badges marking their acceptance into the organization. In the 1980s only 15–30 percent of those entering BUD/S graduated the course.

In the wake of the Vietnam War, special operations in the military suffered a reduction in emphasis and recruits, but the SEALs managed to maintain a high enlistment rate. The Navy Special Warfare Center continued to develop doctrine for covert amphibious operations. The SEAL teams came under the direction of the fleet commanders in chief, with Teams One, Three, and Five based at Coronado under the C-in-C (commander in chief) Pacific, while Teams Two, Four, and Six were based at Little Creek, Virginia, under the command of the C-in-C Atlantic. In addition, a special warfare unit was based in Europe and one in the Pacific, where they trained with similar units in allied military forces. Special delivery vehicle units and special boat unit teams support the SEALs as the transportation that delivers them to their mission site. All these teams are dedicated to the tasks of counterinsurgency, intelligence gathering, counter-terrorism, deception missions, as well as the traditional coastal and beach reconnaissance missions. In 1983, the UDTs were deactivated and incorporated into the SEAL command. By 1987, the size of the organization was expanded from 17 to more than 60 platoons, with a directive in place to expand a further 60 percent by 1991.

In 1980, a special counter-terror (CT) unit was created in the wake of the failed Iranian hostage rescue attempt. Although only two SEAL teams were in existence at the time, this unit took the name SEAL Team Six, possibly to confuse enemy intelligence concerning the actual number of teams. The founder of this unit was probably Richard Marcinko, although the government refuses to confirm any information on this organization and has actually sued Marcinko for making such claims. The team's designation changed in 1987 to Naval Warfare Special Operations Development Group, or DEVGRU. This team has developed into a Navy parallel of the Army's Delta Force.

SEAL operations since the Vietnam war have been focused primarily in the Middle East. From 1987–89 the SEALs engaged in Operation Earnest Will, patrolling the Straits of Hormuz leading into the Persian Gulf. Their aim was to stop Iranian ships from mining the straits and at one point captured a ship and its crew that they caught in the act. Other mine-clearing activities took place in the weeks prior to the Allied invasion of Kuwait (Operation Desert Storm) in 1991. They also engaged in reconnaissance operations behind Iraqi lines prior to the invasion. Additionally, they provided diversionary raids and took part in capturing Iraqi oil platforms in the Persian Gulf. After Desert Storm, SEALs stayed in Kuwait to assist in training commandos and maintaining the embargo on Iraq. During that part of their duty, they captured a Russian tanker smuggling out Iraqi oil. They were also involved in the U.S. operations in Somalia and in Bosnia, where they sought to capture war criminals.

Operations of the SEALs and DEVGRU are strictly confidential, but rumors and secondhand reports abound. In the wake of the Al Qaeda terror attacks of 11 September 2001, they have been involved in CT operations throughout the Middle East. It is generally accepted that they were some of the first U.S. troops in Afghanistan in October 2001 and were engaged in combat operations as well as in the search for Osama bin Laden. "In January of 2002, a planned, simple 12-hour intelligence-gathering mission turned into a nine-day bonanza of exploration and destruction. Nearly a million pounds of ammunition and equipment were found in an extensive network of 70 caves and tunnels in a narrow valley at Zhawar Kili in eastern Afghanistan, near the Pakistan border." A month later, SEALs paired with a Danish special forces team to capture a high-ranking Taliban official. In all of these actions, the teams showed that they are certainly not limited to sea-based operations.

In Operation Iraqi Freedom, SEALs went into Iraq (reportedly around Al Faw on the Persian Gulf) prior to the primary invasion in order to secure key positions like oil platforms and port facilities. Operating alongside Polish commandos, SEALs seized the Mukarayin Dam northwest of Baghdad and held it for five days before being relieved.

It is unknown when information on SEAL Team actions will be declassified, but they recruit regularly, and the brutal training regimen is widely advertised in order to keep out any but the most serious applicants. With the growing use of unconventional warfare tactics, the SEALs are hoping to expand their numbers but not lose quality in the process. In order to do so, a higher graduation rate (approximately 55 percent) from BUD/S is required, a requirement that older SEALs believe could decrease the quality of the graduate. The view of the navy, however, is that with the increased need for technical training that the earlier SEALs did not need, the higher number is necessary if the mission is to be fulfilled. Even with a higher graduation rate, the SEALs remain the elite unit of the United States Navy. They resent the motion-picture portrayal of the SEALs as mercenaries or loose cannons. One of its members described them thus: "A SEAL is a motivated, proud, highly skilled individual who can make split-second decisions that count. He's a military professional charged with the responsibility of carrying out his missions with success. SEALs are people who are special, and once you've become one, there's nothing else you can't do" (Walker, 1989).

References: Hoyt, Edwin, *SEALs at War* (New York: Bantam Doubleday Dell, 1993); Kelly, Orr, *Brave Men, Dark Waters* (Novato, CA: Presidio Press, 1992); "U.S. Navy SEALs", Special Operations.com, 12 January 2006, www.specialoperations.com/Navy/SEALs/default2.html; Walker, Greg, "Elite SEAL Units," in *International Combat Arms*, vol. 7, no. 6 (November 1989).

Seminoles

An American Indian tribe that fought for a homeland in Florida, defeating the United States Army and maintaining their independence.

The Seminole Indians of Florida have a heritage of independence that is reflected in their tribal name, which translates as "those who live apart." Although originally they were probably part of the Creek Indian Confederation, the Seminoles be-

Osceola, a Seminole leader, as drawn by J.T. Brown's lithographic establishment, circa 1842. Library of Congress, Prints & Photographs Division [reproduction number LC-USZC4-2380].

came a conglomeration of tribal mixtures that ultimately spoke a wide variety of dialects, called *Mikasuki*, derived from the Lower Creek Hitchiti language. By the early nineteenth century, they inhabited a number of villages scattered throughout Florida, each organized along the lines of an independent city-state after the Seminoles rejected the authority of the Creek Confederation. The Seminoles included in their society almost anyone who chose to live among them, including escaped slaves from the United States or Spanish holdings in Florida. They kept slaves themselves, after a fashion. Slaves given to them became more like tenant farmers, paying a portion of their crops or livestock to their "owners." It was their acceptance of escaped slaves, however, that brought them into conflict with American Southerners.

When parties of Southerners ventured into Spanish Florida to recover their slaves, they often brought back anyone with whom the slave happened to be. This sometimes included Seminole wives whom the slaves may have married and the children they had produced. The tribe resented this kidnapping of its members. Hence, they attacked slave catchers in their territory and mounted attacks into Georgia on plantations there. In 1817 the federal government looked the other way when Andrew Jackson, hero of the War of 1812, invaded Florida on punitive expeditions against the Seminoles. When foreign citizens were killed and the Spanish government protested, the American response was to buy Florida in 1819. The Spanish, who had little real interest in the land, realized they could either sell the territory or have it taken away. They chose to sell for $5 million. The new American administration assigned the Seminoles to a reservation in the central part of the peninsula, ending what was termed the First Seminole War (1816–1823). They also promised the Indians food, farming equipment, and money, none of which was forthcoming. When the Seminoles complained, the U.S. government in 1835 offered to pay them to leave Florida and relocate west of the Mississippi.

Upon receiving this offer, a Seminole chief showed the American negotiators at Payne's Landing what he thought of it. He drove his knife into the agreement, initiating the Second Seminole War. The chief at that time was Osceola, and he came to symbolize the fiercely independent nature of the Seminoles. He was to his tribe what

Geronimo would later be to the Apache, and Sitting Bull or Crazy Horse to the Sioux. Osceola was originally a Creek but was driven from the Mississippi Territory during the War of 1812. During the Second Seminole War, he mounted an extremely effective guerrilla campaign against the American army, beginning in December 1835 when his men ambushed a 112-man company of the Fourth Infantry Regiment. Only two soldiers escaped to tell the story of the massacre. Using the swamps as cover and refuge, the Seminoles attacked the soldiers sent into the region to capture them and sent them and their leaders back to the states in disgrace.

This guerrilla warfare was natural for the Seminoles, but the U.S. army had become lax in these tactics. The invading U.S. soldiers had no experience with swamps and were as afraid of the natural predators found there as of the Indians. Disease and heatstroke felled the majority of casualties. Still, the army's constant raids on Seminole villages and the destruction of the Seminoles' crops began to have some effect. In 1837 some of the tribe surrendered to General Thomas Jesup. He fed them and arranged for their transport to Tampa, whence they were to be transported west. While awaiting this move, Osceola sneaked into the camp and convinced his comrades to go with him. When he learned of the flight of his prisoners, Jesup asked Osceola for a parley. When Osceola appeared under a white flag, Jesup arrested him. Osceola, already sick with malaria, died after a short imprisonment in South Carolina in January 1838. Other leaders, including Abiaka, a prominent medicine man, kept up the fight.

Zachary Taylor, who assumed command from Jesup, was known as a "soldier's general," ready to undergo the same hardships as his men. He marched into Florida with 1,000 men, artillery, pack mules, and wagons. He ran into Chief Alligator near Lake Okeechobee on Christmas Day of 1837. Alligator placed his men on a rise almost surrounded by swamps, forcing Taylor to attack him head-on. The mire sucked under men and horses alike, making outflanking operations impossible. Seminole sharpshooters picked off officers and non-commissioned officers during the assault, but Taylor kept up the pressure and Alligator finally ordered his men to fade into the swamps, leaving behind their 13 dead and nine wounded. It was a victory, but a Pyrrhic one. Seminoles continued to harass soldiers and civilians alike. But by 1841, the continued destruction of their villages and farms forced many Seminoles to surrender. Chiefs came in one by one to give up their followers and be transported west. Some 4,000 had surrendered by 1842. However, several hundred never surrendered and continued to live deep in the Everglades where U.S. soldiers would not or could not go. The American government ultimately spent almost $20 million, the services of 30,000 men, and the deaths of almost 1,500, but no peace treaty was ever signed with the Seminoles. To this day the Florida Seminoles point with pride to the fact that they were the only undefeated tribe in the wars that the United States waged against the Native Americans.

References: Heidler, David Stephen, *Old Hickory's War* (Mechanicsburg, PA: Stackpole, 1996); Mulroy, Kevin, *Freedom on the Border* (Lubbock: Texas Tech University Press, 1993); Wright, J. Leitch, *Creeks and Seminoles* (Lincoln: University of Nebraska Press, 1996).

Shaolin Priests

Warrior priests in China who developed specialized martial arts from the fifth to nineteenth centuries.

Information on the Shaolin temple where the development of martial arts training began is sketchy and at times contradictory. The main Shaolin temple was located just outside the city of Zhengzhou, in Henan Province, in the Central Plains of China near the Songshan Mountains. One source states that the Shaolin order was founded in 497 CE by Ba Tuo, a Buddhist monk from India. Ba Tuo was interested in the Chinese martial art known as *wushu*, and his followers perfected their skills in this form of training. Other sources state that Bodhidharma (or Tamo in Chinese), another Buddhist monk from India, was the founder of the Shaolin religion in the mid-sixth century. He supposedly visited the Chinese emperor, who had sponsored a widespread translation of Indian Buddhist texts from Sanskrit to Chinese, in the hopes of making the faith more accessible to the public. Apparently, the emperor believed that undertaking this worthy project would lead him to Nirvana. Tamo disagreed, believing no one could achieve that exalted state through the work of others. Hence, the two parted company.

Tamo then traveled to a Buddhist monastery nearby, but was refused entrance because he was a foreigner. He withdrew to a nearby cave and engaged in intense meditation, a practice that convinced the nearby monks that he was, indeed, serious about entering their company. Once there, Tamo observed that the priests, engaged in translation all day, were in poor physical condition. Tamo believed that in order to perfect oneself, meditation was necessary, and intense meditation was physically challenging. He thus developed a series of exercises for his fellow monks to develop their physical strength and stamina and to enhance the flow of *chi*—the life force. Drawing on hatha and raja yoga, both developed in India in the second century BCE, Tamo developed movement exercises based on 18 animals from Indo-Chinese iconography. These exercises were not originally intended as a martial art, but nevertheless became the foundation of *kung fu* (or *gung fu*). It is possible that Tamo refined the practice of martial arts already existing since the time of Ba Tuo. Or, perhaps he was more instrumental in altering the teachings at the temple, for it is reported he developed what came to be the Chan Sect.

It was the particular blend of Buddhism and Taoism that became the basis of Shaolin, named after the temple where Tamo lived. The temple was constructed in a wooded area that had been deforested and only recently replanted. It was named *Shaolin*, which means "new forest" in Mandarin Chinese. Apparently, during the Sui dynasty (589–618), the Shaolin found favor with the emperor, who granted them 1,648 acres of land upon which they built extensive buildings and employed a large staff of attendants. The wealth of the temple attracted the attention of bandits, further motivating the monks to train for self-defense. The exercises they practiced blended into the Buddhist/Taoist creed of nonviolence by being strictly defensive, and in levels of intensity and lethality designed to reflect the aggressiveness of the attacker. Thus, the Shaolin priest was not to attack, only defend himself in direct relation to the intent of his attacker. This means, however, that an attacker intent on killing the priest would be met with equal force and intent.

The practice of kung fu that the priests developed was a variation on wushu martial arts and Luohan boxing. During the Song (or Sung) dynasty (960–1279), the Shaolin abbot Fu Ju invited wushu experts from around China to visit the temple to exchange knowledge and training techniques. After three years, a Shaolin boxing manual was created describing 280 exercise routines. The monks also developed techniques using a variety of weapons, most notably the cudgel. This choice was consistent with the original Buddhist teaching against the use of sharp or pointed weapons, although over time the Shaolin monks developed skill with those weapons as well. The four major weapons of the Shaolin priests came to be the cudgel, spear, sword, and broadsword, although small weapons hidden about the monk's person were also used.

Because of its relatively central location and the less restrictive rules (compared with other orders) laid down by the Chan Sect, the temple attracted retired generals, malcontents, and refugees from the law. The spreading fame of the Shaolin priests impressed the government, which alternately used their skills in wars against rebel peasants such as the Red Turbans or in conflicts with Japanese pirates, or persecuted them and attacked their temples. Occasionally, a priest would decide to support one political faction or another, bringing kung fu even more into public notice. These few politically or militarily active monks ultimately brought the wrath of the government down on the sect as a whole.

In the 1600s China came under the rule of the Manchu dynasty, who were invaders from the north. Elements supporting a return of the deposed Ming dynasty organized the Hung Society, which probably grew out of another secret society called the White Lotus. Although unsuccessful in their attempts to restore the Ming dynasty, members of the Hung Society inspired a similar rebel movement based at a Shaolin temple in Fukien. These monks answered the emperor's call for troops in 1672 to put down an invasion from western tribes, and succeeded in doing so. However, the government discovered that the Shaolin were merely positioning themselves for a rebellion. Their temple was destroyed. In what came to be famous in Chinese folklore, five escapees of that destruction hid under a bridge, where they were rescued by five brave men. They were soon joined by five more monks. These earned the titles of the Five Early Founding Fathers, Five Middle Founding Fathers, and Five Later Founding Fathers, and these 15 organized continued revolts against the Manchus. In 1674, these men swore to be fraternal brothers and fight to overthrow the Manchus, and their band came to be called the Heaven and Earth Society. How much of this story is true is debatable, but the burning of the temple has often been eulogized in Chinese literature and drama. As a movement, the Heaven and Earth Society spread to southern China and across to Formosa, then back to cover the whole of China, and the Heaven and Earth Society played a key role in later uprisings such as the Taiping Rebellion in the mid-1800s.

References: de Bary, William Theodore, et al., eds., *Sources of Chinese Tradition* (New York: Columbia University Press, 1960); Winderbaum, Larry, *The Martial Arts Encyclopedia* (Washington: Inscape Corp., 1977).

Sikhs

A religious sect that resisted the British occupation of India in the nineteenth century.

The Sikhs are one of what are called the martial races in India, in this case originating in the northwestern province of the Punjab. Sikhs are not truly a race, but rather a religious sect, so the title in their case is a misnomer. They are one of the groups upon which the British administration drew for soldiers in India during the nineteenth and twentieth centuries.

The term *Sikh* means "disciple." Sikhism is a form of Islam with Hindu aspects. The first Sikh *guru* was Baba Nanak, born in 1469. He developed the sect with a reformed Hinduism, including the principles of simplicity, purity, and brotherhood. The sect grew under the oppression of the ruling Moghul dynasty. Baba Nanak was

The Queen's Indian troops (Sikhs) on guard in the grounds of the summer palace near Peking, China, 1902. Library of Congress, Prints & Photographs Division [reproduction number LC-USZ62-68805]

295

succeeded by nine gurus. The tenth, named Govind, radically altered the nature of the faith. Apparently unwilling to passively accept persecution, he turned the Sikh faith into a powerful military sect that attracted lower-caste Hindus who had little or no future in their own social system. Some two-thirds of the Sikh converts came from the martial race of Jats, although many of that race retained their Muslim faith and thus split the Sikh community. Probably in order to instill some fighting spirit, Govind added the term *Singh*, or "lion," to the title of Sikh.

A person entering the Sikh faith does so not by birth but by baptism, initiated by the sprinkling of water from a two-edged dagger. Joining the faith requires a certain austerity, and thus many young men postpone the baptism. The British Indian Army, when recruiting from Sikh society in the Punjab, took those baptized and used to a tougher life. The holy life ordained originally by Nanak became a zealous one under Govind, dedicated to religious fervor. The hardiness of the Sikh soldiers comes also from their profession (mainly farming) and their heritage, for the Jats who make up so many of the Sikh faith are reputed to be descended from the Aryans, who conquered India from the north at the start of historic time. The military brotherhood established among the Sikhs, called the *Khalsa*, was the core of their army. Another branch of the Sikhs recruited by the British into the Indian army were inducted into the Pioneer, or engineer/construction regiments. Those Hindus of lower caste, obliged to sweep gutters and latrines for a living, gained status by joining the Sikh faith as well as the Indian army. The engineer/construction units, along with Sikh fighting units, served with distinction in the Indian army. However, before this distinguished service for the Crown could come about, the British first had to defeat the Sikhs in two wars.

The First Sikh War was fought in 1845–1846. The Sikhs had been molded into a first-rate fighting force by their leader, Ranjit Singh, in the first decades of the nineteenth century. As an ally of the British, he learned his training methods from the army of the British East India Company and by hiring European mercenaries. The war was actually started by a Sikh leader, Tej Singh, who was unable to gain the support of the army in his bid to replace Ranjit Singh after his death. Tej Singh provoked a war with the British hoping that victory would unite the nation behind him. The British found the Sikh army the most difficult force they had yet faced in India. In four battles between December 1845 and February 1846, the Sikhs showed their ability to prepare strong defensive positions and to use their artillery extremely well. The British won all four battles but took heavy losses in the process. The peace treaty forced on the Sikhs obliged them to cede the territory of Kashmir along with an indemnity of £1 million. They were also forced to reduce the size of their army. The British did not annex the Sikh homeland, fearing the cost and manpower it would take to hold it, but did assign a resident to oversee Anglo-Sikh relations.

In late 1848, Sikh nationalists masterminded an uprising against the British presence in their country. The uprising centered around the city of Multan. The capture of this city in early 1849 after a number of hard-fought battles marked the end of the Second Sikh War. In the wake of this conflict, Governor-General Dalhousie annexed all of the Punjab, expanding the borders of British-held India to the mountains of Afghanistan. The quality of the Sikh army had made a great impression on the British, and the British administration began to consider the incorporation of Sikh troops into the India army now that their country had been incorporated into British India. Indeed, two regiments had been formed after the First Sikh War and had served under British officers between conflicts. The leader of one of those units, Herbert Edwardes, was instrumental in building up the trust and mutual respect between soldiers of the two armies. Moreover, the reforms that the British instituted in the Punjab after they annexed the province did much to alleviate the oppression of many of the locals and earn their respect. When much of the Indian army mutinied in 1857, the Sikhs remained loyal and proved to be as fierce in combat alongside the British as they had been against them.

Sikhs served in the Indian army and incorporated into their ranks both Hindu and Muslim compatriots. They buried their differences and fought together alongside the British in campaigns up through World War II, but were unable to survive the independence of India in 1947. When India became free, and when Pakistan seceded to its own independence, regiments from the northwest had to go with one country or the other. Muslims went to Pakistan, Hindus and Sikhs went to India, and strong bonds built up over decades were destroyed in a matter of months.

References: Mason, Philip, *A Matter of Honour* (London: Jonathan Cape, 1974); Roberts, P.E., *History of British India* (London: Oxford University Press, 1952); Singh, Khushwant, *A History of the Sikhs*, 2 vols. (Princeton, NJ: Princeton University Press, 1963–1966).

Spartans

A Greek population known for its militaristic society between the sixth and fourth centuries BCE.

Of all the warrior populations of the ancient world, few are as well known as the Spartans. Unlike the Assyrians, who made aggressive warfare a national pastime, the Spartans built a society geared more toward martial training and values rather than pure aggression. They were probably the first society that dedicated itself to a martial lifestyle, much like the Mongols, Zulus, or Gurkhas in later centuries.

The country of Sparta lay on the Peloponnese, the peninsula extending southward from the main body of Greece. Like the rest of the region, Sparta was defeated by the Dorians, who invaded and occupied Greece around 1200 BCE. It seems, however, that the inhabitants of the Peloponnese had a more positive, relatively cooperative relationship with the invaders. The town of Sparta was founded around 900 BCE, and by the middle 800s BCE its inhabitants had conquered the surrounding area and established a *polis*, or city-state. The city-state was ruled by two kings, which were under the direction of a council of elders.

The traditional story of the establishment of the Spartan military society holds that the statesman Lycurgus laid the groundwork by establishing the nation's constitution in the ninth century BCE. In reality, the constitution was probably developed over time and in a manner that differed from most of Sparta's contemporary city-states. While other Greek polises reacted against the power of the aristocracy by revolution and the establishment of individual rulers, the Spartans developed a society in which there was no real aristocracy. All male citizens, called Equals, trained and fought together in the same fashion, and held land worked by helots, or serfs, who supported the Equals, all of whom were soldiers. A merchant and artisan class held rights somewhere between the two.

Toughness of mind and body were cultivated from birth, when a newborn male was subjected to inspection by the elders and a decision made as to its fitness for life. Those who failed were abandoned to nature. Those who passed were treated little better, for they were often forced to sleep outside. At age seven, the boy was taken from his home to start his education and training. In the barracks he was given his earliest training by the teenagers who had graduated from this first stage. The youth was often given short rations and told to steal if he wanted more. Those successful were praised; those caught were punished. This taught them to forage and prepared them for likely deprivations during campaigning. The boys were also given but one cloak, and were denied sandals in order to toughen their feet. As they grew older, certain boys were chosen to become assassins, practicing on helots who may have strayed from their dwellings.

Upon reaching adulthood, the young Spartan was expected to marry; indeed, bachelorhood was a crime punished by public taunting or beatings by groups of women. If unattached men or women reached an age at which it was unseemly for them to be single, they would be placed in a darkened room to pair off by touch. Many thought that mating in such a way was about as successful as arranged marriages or love matches. Once married, however, the man was obliged to live in his barracks with the group of comrades with whom he had grown up and trained. He could visit his wife but had to return to the barracks to spend the night. Only at age 30 could he start his own household. At this age, the Spartan male was accepted as an Equal and allowed voting rights.

The weaponry the Spartans employed was little different from that used by other Greek armies. Each infantryman was termed a *hoplite*, from the *hoplon*, or shield that each one carried. The hoplon was originally a wooden circle edged with brass, but the Spartans covered the entire shield, with brass. It was large enough to give protection to the bearer and to overlap with the soldier next to him, making a shield wall. Each man had body armor and a helmet, with additional armor, such as greaves or arm protection, as his wealth allowed. The hoplites marched and fought in the phalanx formation. This was a square of men several ranks deep and wide. In combat, the soldiers would tighten their ranks to create the shield wall, then advance with lowered spears. The spears were originally six to eight feet long, and when deployed, created a hedgehog effect. The phalanx was a shock formation that took little talent to employ, and the typical battle ended when one of the phalanxes broke and the soldiers fled. The Spartans, by creating a disciplined army, had a distinct advantage over those armies made up of conscripts or short-term volunteers. Ancillary forces of archers, cavalry, or lightly armed infantry rounded out the army, but these were mainly used in pursuit once the phalanx had done its job.

Sparta established its dominion over the southern Peloponnese by the middle 400s BCE, then extended its influence over most of the remainder of the peninsula through alliances. This Spartan-dominated group came to be called the Peloponnesian

League, and the members allowed Sparta to dictate their foreign policy and draw on their manpower in time of war. Nevertheless, Spartan policy did not advocate conquering for conquest's sake. Instead, the Spartans preferred staying in their own region to keep control over their land and their helots. When they did venture outside their own borders, they at first did so not for conquest but for defense.

In the 490s BCE, Persian King Darius crushed a revolt along the coast of Asia Minor by cities that had been supported by Greeks. He resolved to invade Greece to punish them for interfering in his affairs and to add the region to his empire. In 490 BCE the Persian army marched around the Aegean Sea into Greece. Darius's forces were defeated at Marathon by a Greek army dominated by Athenians; the Spartans were observing religious festivals and did not arrive at the battlefield until after the Athenian victory. The Spartans did get into the war 10 years later when Darius's successor, Xerxes, again attempted to impose Persia's will on Greece. This time, the first troops Xerxes' army met were part of a Spartan-led force at the coastal pass of Thermopylae. After repelling repeated Persian attacks with an army of 6,000, the Greeks under Spartan King Leonidas were outflanked by a Persian unit taking a mountain path. Leonidas had committed 1,000 men to protect that path, but they failed to do so for reasons that are unclear. About to be surrounded, Leonidas sent most of his troops away, forming a rear guard with his 300 Spartans, some Thespians, and 400 Thebans. The unit was slaughtered to the last man by Persian archers. It was the Spartans that brought the world the concept of "death before dishonor."

Spartan seamen participated a decade later in 480 BCE in the Greek naval victory over the Persian fleet at Salamis, then capped their performance with a leadership role in the victory over the Persians at Plataea in 479 BCE. These successes established Sparta as the preeminent military power in Greece, although Athens was the economic and naval power. Ultimately, the two city-states clashed in a decades-long conflict, the Peloponnesian War, lasting from 459 to 404 BCE. The war was fought in three phases. In the first, the Spartan army dominated the land warfare and bottled up the city of Athens. The Athenians dominated the seas and harassed the Spartan coastline, raising helot revolts. It has been described as the battle between the elephant and the whale: each the best in its element but unable to come to grips with each other. The opening phase ended in a draw.

Phase two was fought mainly in Sicily, the site of Athenian colonial interests. There, a Spartan general commanded troops for the city of Syracuse, which the Athenians besieged. Conflicting goals and orders brought about an Athenian defeat that cost them huge numbers of men and ships, weakening their naval power and prestige. This led to the third phase of the war, in which the Spartans enlarged their navy with assistance from Persia. Although the Athenian admirals managed to win victories, each successive battle further weakened their fleet. It could not be rebuilt as quickly as the Spartans received new ships from the Persians, and finally, in 405 BCE, the Athenian fleet was lost to the Spartans in the Dardanelles. Without the ability to supply their city by sea, the Athenians slowly starved under the Spartan siege. By 404 BCE the Athenians surrendered.

This proved to be the apogee of Spartan power, for Sparta proved unprepared and unable to rule all of Greece. The society Sparta had developed over the centuries was suited to a limited population and could not be forced on a large one. Sparta had spent too many citizens in too many wars to be able to impose its will on all of Greece. The Spartans began fighting their erstwhile allies, the Persians, who sent agents into Greece to sow dissension among the city-states. Spread too thin, the Spartans could not maintain their position. They could uphold their independence and dominance in the Peloponnese but in few other places. Sparta ultimately fell, as did all of Greece, to the rising power of Macedon in the mid-fourth century BCE.

References: Ferrill, Arther, *The Origins of War* (London: Thames and Hudson, 1985); Forrest, W. G., *A History of Sparta*, 950–192 BCE (New York: Hutchinson, 1968); Warry, John, *Warfare in the Classical World* (London: Salamander Books, 1980).

Special Air Service

An elite unit of the British army.

During Great Britain's war against Italian and German forces in North Africa in World War II, special operations forces were active in harassing Axis supply lines and creating confusion in their rear areas. The Long Range Desert Group (LRDG) was the first of these organizations, but the Special Air Service (SAS) came to be not only the more famous, but also the longer-lasting unit. The SAS was created in the summer of 1941 and was commanded by Major David Stirling, who had formerly served in the Scots Guards and No. 8 Commando. He was given the task of organizing the SAS by General Sir Claude Auchinleck, then in command of British forces in Egypt. The unit and its mission were Stirling's idea, but the possibility of inflicting serious damage on the Germans for the cost of training and equipping but a handful of men was attractive to the British high command. Stirling was ordered to recruit six officers and 60 men, to be designated "L" Detachment, Special Air Service.

Stirling's idea was to use small groups of men rather than the 200-man minimum advocated by most commando theorists. Stirling argued that because most commandos operated by sea, too many men were wasted in protecting the boats. Better, he argued, to insert half a dozen men who were all active and able to get in and out quickly without discovery. In November 1941, Stirling's men were in action with the Long Range Desert Group. The LRDG had been mapping and raiding across the Libyan desert and was assigned to provide the transport for the SAS. The SAS commandos parachuted into action on the night of November 16 against Gazala, but the weather so dispersed the aircraft and paratroopers that the operation was a complete failure. After that, the LRDG was the delivery team that took the SAS commandos to within walking distance of their target. From there, the SAS would slip into an enemy position, set explosives, and withdraw before the excitement started.

The SAS operated with increasing success for 15 months in 1941–1942, destroying German and Italian aircraft, vehicles, ammunition, and fuel depots, in addition to mining roads and attacking supply columns. This forced the German commander, Erwin Rommel, to divert badly needed troops from the front to cover his supply lines. Stirling, however, was cap-

Logo of the Special Air Service.

for guerrilla fighting in the light of Cold War combat necessities. The SAS operated in all the British postcolonial actions, in Malaya (1948–1960) and Africa (1952–1955) particularly. Its role grew from sabotage to intelligence gathering and reconnaissance, then to counterinsurgency and antiterrorist operations.

The SAS has evolved into Great Britain's elite unit, and inclusion in its ranks is as difficult to obtain as it is desirable. As part of NATO, British forces can be called upon to fight in a number of different climates, and those men accepted for SAS membership undergo the most rigorous training, including action in desert, tropical, mountain, and arctic conditions, extensive training with a large number of British and foreign weapons, amphibious and airborne operations, language training, as well as intense physical conditioning. In the past few years, the commandos have included in their repertoire high-technology weaponry and equipment as it is developed.

Two more recent high-profile operations brought the SAS into the public eye. The first was in May 1980 when terrorists took over the Iranian embassy in London. The SAS entered the building surreptitiously, then, using stun, flash, and gas grenades, rescued the hostages, killing four of the five terrorists with no losses to themselves. This was an impressive action, considering that the British government had only a few months prior expanded the SAS role to include antiterrorist operations. The SAS returned to its usual role of deep penetration and sabotage during the British war with Argentina over the Falkland Islands in the South Atlantic in 1982. Operating with the equally elite Special Boat Service, the SAS placed men secretly on the Falkland Islands prior to the main British

tured early in 1943. He managed to escape from Italian prison camps four times, but was finally transferred to the high-security German prison at Colditz. The SAS had grown by the time of his capture to include French and Greek squadrons. By the time of the Normandy invasion in June 1944 the SAS had grown to brigade size, with two British and two French regiments and a Belgian squadron. Stirling designed the unit's insignia, a winged sword with a banner bearing the motto: "Who Dares, Wins." Paddy Mayne commanded the unit for the remainder of the war.

After World War II, the SAS was disbanded, but when Winston Churchill was again elected prime minister in 1951, he ordered its revival. Like the American Special Forces, the SAS developed doctrine assault. They observed Argentine troop movements, observed and directed naval gunfire, captured (with 75 men) a 140-man Argentine garrison on San Carlos Island, destroyed an Argentine air base on Pebble Island, and cleared obstructions barring the landing of British regular forces.

The Special Air Service is kept small, maintaining only three 256-man regiments. The Twenty-second SAS Regiment is full-time, based at Hereford in England and operating the SAS training facilities. The Twenty-first and Twenty-third Regiments are territorial and reserve units. Each is made up of four squadrons of four troops, each troop containing 16 men, usually operating in four-man teams. There is some specialization within the Twenty-second, but for the most part all the men are trained in almost all specialties, to be prepared for action anywhere at any time, no matter which unit is currently on call. The commandos not only engage in constant training, they have been used regularly in Northern Ireland operating against the Irish Republican Army. They are also regularly called upon to travel to other countries to assist in organizing and training similar types of units for other governments. They assisted the Dutch in a hostage situation aboard a train in May 1977, and the Germans on a mission to rescue hostages aboard a Lufthansa airliner held in Somalia later that same year, among other similar events.

During the Soviet occupation of Afghanistan, SAS members aided Mujahadin resistance fighters with training and weaponry. When British forces cooperated in the liberation of Kuwait (1991), SAS units were there. During the conflict, SAS units were inserted well behind the front lines to locate and destroy Iraqi SCUD missiles which had been targeting Saudi Arabia and Israel. They have also been involved in rescue missions in Sierra Leone and Bosnia. Little is known as of this writing about SAS operations in Afghanistan and Iraq in the wake of the Al Qaeda attacks on the United States in 2001. It is reported that half a regiment fought in Afghanistan, where they captured a position doubling as an opium storage facility and an Al Qaeda headquarters. They are also known to be operating in Iraq since the coalition invasion of 2003, but details are sketchy. When terrorists set off bombs in London in 2005, SAS members were involved in the arrests of suspects in the city.

Special counterterrorism training has become part of the SAS routine. When a terrorist incident occurs, a Special Projects team goes into action. This is a temporary unit made up of the troops on alert when the trouble starts. This means that all the SAS members have to be trained in counterterrorism tactics via the Counter-Terrorism Warfare Squadron. Sniper training is especially emphasized in this mission. Much of the training takes place at the SAS facilities at Hereford in a special building called the Killing House. In an ever-changing interior, the men practice hostage rescues that demand the ability to decide in an instant who are the "bad guys." It is reported that high-ranking members of the British government are involved in these exercises.

The SAS remains one of the premiere special forces of the world, and is in almost constant exchange programs with similar units in the United States, Australia, New Zealand, France, Germany, Spain, and the Netherlands.

References: Cowles, Virginia, *The Phantom Major* (New York: Harper and Bros., 1958); Hunter, Thomas B., "Special Projects Team–22 Special Air Service", *Special Operations* (2000), http://www.specialoperations.com/Foreign/ United_Kingdom/SAS/CRW.htm, 25 February 2005; Kelly, Ross, *Special Operations and National Purpose* (Lexington, MA: Lexington Books, 1989).

Special Boat Service

An elite section of the Royal Marines.

One of the commando forces created by the British military in World War II, the Special Boat Service has undergone a number of unit designation changes since 1945, but has remained one of the best special forces and counterterrorist units in existence. They are not as well known as the Royal Army's Special Air Service (SAS), and they are content to keep it that way in order to enhance their mystique and their ability to undertake lower-profile missions.

Although many commando-type units were formed during World War II, many were disbanded at the end of the war since governments and military planners assumed there would be no need for them in an age of atomic weapons. The Tactical Investigation Committee at the War Office in London decided, however, to create a small sea-borne force for coastal reconnaissance, infiltration, and sabotage. During the war, the units had been known by a variety of names and given a variety of missions: the Special Boat Section (later a part of the SAS), Special Boat Service, Special Boat Squadron, Boom Patrol Detachment (for raids on shipping), Pilotage Parties (beach reconnaissance), Landing Craft Obstruction Clearance Units, Sea Reconnaissance Unit, etc. Members who remained in the service after the war and had experience in these units were gathered into the Combined Operations Beach and Boats Section, or COBBS, and stationed at

The logo of the Special Boat Service.

Eastney, Portsmouth. They were under the direction of the Royal Marines, with whom they undertook their first mission in 1948 under the designation Small Raids Wing. They operated in Haifa harbor in Palestine as the state of Israel was being created, where they were assigned to discover and remove mines placed by the Israelis.

Members of this unit came to be known as swimmer-canoeists, and "SC" remains their designation. They soon found themselves in a number of diverse locations, still with a variety of tasks. Some of them were stationed with the British Army of the Rhine during the Berlin crisis of 1948–1949, where they were assigned to be the last troops out in case of a Soviet invasion of Western Europe. They would stay behind, responsible for both gathering intelligence and destroying bridges, especially across the Rhine. Other members were with No. 41 Commando that served in Korea, attacking coastal installations and railways near the coast. Like other units of the Royal Marines and their commando forces, the SCs served throughout the 1950s in the Middle East, Mediterranean, and Malaya.

In 1958, consisting of six sections, the organization was once again given a new title, the Special Boat Company. At this time, they adopted their motto, "Not by Strength, by Guile," as well as their unofficial unit crest made up of crossed paddles, surmounted by a frog and parachute wings. A detachment became permanently stationed in Bahrain in 1961, when Iraq threatened an invasion. Another went to Singapore that same year with 3 Commando Brigade, whence they engaged in conflicts with Indonesia over Brunei in December 1962, where they supplied patrols and engaged in some cross-border reconnaissance into Malaysian-controlled Borneo. Others were stationed in Aden in 1967 as the British were withdrawing from the country, but were back in Oman in the early 1970s fighting communist-backed guerrillas trying to topple the pro-British sultan. It was in 1972 that they began their counterterrorist operations with an at-sea parachute drop into the North Atlantic to investigate the report of explosives aboard the *Queen Elizabeth II*. They also began to patrol in Ireland to intercept gun-runners and engaged in some narcotics-trafficking investigations in the Caribbean.

In 1975 the organization named changed again to the Special Boat Squadron (SBS). It began more intensive counterterror (CT) training when assigned to protect North Sea oil drilling platforms as part of the Royal Marines Commachio Company. Also during the 1970s, the SBS found themselves on a number of training missions, helping establish the Iranian Special Boat Service, the Australian Commando companies, and the Malaysian Special Service Regiment. They also engaged in a number of cooperative exercises with similar units from other countries in NATO and began training in Norway for combat in arctic and mountain terrains.

The Argentine invasion of the Falklands Islands in 1982 brought out the SBS along with every other aspect of the British military. SBS units arrived in the Falklands three weeks before the fleet, where they established observation posts and reconnoitered the beaches for the best landing sites. They were on-site to guide the commandos and paratroopers when they came ashore at San Carlo Bay and also acted as spotters for naval artillery. Once the main forces landed, SBS units operated behind Argentine lines, being inserted by helicopter, submarine, or in small boats from the Royal Navy ships. After the war, the SBS became more involved in CT operations. Along with Commachio Company, they began security operations for nuclear material production and transportation. In this role, an SBS team entered the Dounrey nuclear plant in Scotland in 1997 as a test of the facility's security. The SBS had the place under its control before the company police had any idea the plant was targeted—not a pleasant prospect in the modern world's problems with terrorism.

In 1987 the Special Boat Squadron finally came to be called by its present title, the Special Boat Service. The UK Special Forces Group was established that year, under the overall command of the Director of the SAS with a Royal Marine colonel as his deputy. The SBS, which prior to this time had numbered about 150 men, was expanded. It currently contains four squadrons, one of which (M Squadron) is specifically assigned to maritime counterterrorism operations.

Writings by SBS veterans claim that they have the most difficult entrance and training standards of any unit in NATO, or perhaps the entire world. Before applying, they have to have gone through Royal Marine training, then through commando training, and then (after three years as a commando) they can apply for SBS membership. As commandos, they would have had extra training in at least one specialty, such as demolition, sniping, languages, etc. The SBS training begins with a two-week aptitude test including combat fitness, swimming, canoe trials, and scuba diving. If they pass through this section, they proceed to the selection course. This includes three weeks of land navigation marches with full gear, two weeks of prejungle training, six weeks of jungle training in Brunei, one week of signals training, and one week of weapons training. They must then undergo the Army Combat Survival Instructor Course: two weeks of evasion, survival, escape, and extremely harsh training in techniques for resisting interrogation. Those who have survived thus far then go on to demolition training, observation post training, and a course in close-quarter battle. For eight weeks after that, they undergo specialized training and (for those not already qualified) parachute school. Another eight weeks follow of boating and diving training for underwater navigation and demolition. At this point, one becomes a Swimmer Canoeist Third Class. Even more courses are required for promotion to SC Second and First Class, which gives one the rank of corporal and sergeant, respectively. When one is not on an operational mission, an SC is training with new weapons, signals, counterterrorism tactics, underwater Swimmer Delivery Vehicle "driving," or learning a foreign language.

Since the 1987 reorganization, the Special Boat Service has been involved in Operations Desert Shield and Desert Storm, where they engaged in a deep-penetration mission to destroy communication links between Baghdad and SCUD missile launchers. They went into Bosnia with NATO forces in 1995 and served in East Timor during the rebel uprisings that same year. In 2000, the SBS was part of a contingent that deployed to Sierra Leone to protect and evacuate British citizens during a civil war. During the coalition invasion of Iraq in 2003, SBS units were involved in the initial landings at Al Faw peninsula to seize key oil facilities, while others were air-dropped into northern Iraq, around Mosul, for reconnaissance and sabotage missions.

References: Ladd, James, *SBS: The Invisible Raiders* (London: Arms and Armour, 1983); Parker, John, *SBS: The Inside Story of the Special Boat Service* (London: Headline, 1997); Paul, James and Martin Spirit, "The Special Boat Service" (2000), Britain's Small Wars, 2 February 2006, www.britains-smallwars.com/main/SBS; "Special Boat Service (SBS" (2000), Special Operations.com, 2 February 2006, www.specialoperations.com/Foreign/United_Kingdom/Royal Marines/SBS_Profile.

Spetznaz

Special forces units in the Soviet Union since the 1920s.

Just as the United States has special forces organizations like the Green Berets and the Rangers, and the British have the Special Air Service, so the Soviet Union's counterpart was the *Spetznaz*, a contraction of the Russian words for "special-purpose troops." These troops were expected to do a wide variety of jobs, which included spreading disinformation and training guerrillas, as well as fighting. They trace their heritage to similar units formed in the wake of the Russian Revolution of 1917 that performed in the Russian Civil War and against anticommunist guerrillas in the Ukraine and Central Asia during the 1920s and 1930s. During World War II, Spetznaz commandos trained the partisans that wrought havoc on the Nazi rear areas, then served in the postwar era in operations in Czechoslovakia and Afghanistan.

At the height of Soviet military strength in the 1980s, the Spetznaz forces numbered between 29,000 and 37,000. These were divided into 24 brigades, 41 long-range reconnaissance companies, three diversionary regiments, and 27 or more agent detachments. They also had detachments operating with the Soviet fleet and the GRU, the Soviet military intelligence organization. The three diversionary regiments served at theater-of-operations level where they were detailed for long-range reconnaissance and sabotage. Those serving with the navy had training in scuba and midget submarine operations. All units required parachute training.

The primary difference between the Soviet special forces and those of the United States or Great Britain was that the bulk of the troops were conscripts serving only the required two-year tour of duty. Actually, the troops themselves were only rarely aware that they were members of a special unit. Most knew only that they were receiving specialized training. Unlike the Green Berets, in which each man is required to have multiple specialties, the Spetznaz troops had only one per man because the two-year enlistment would not allow for any more varied training. The only training the Spetznaz troops had in common with their Western counterparts was an increased emphasis on unarmed combat, parachute qualification, and airborne/heliborne operations. The officers, being soldiers with longer tenure, received more specialized training, including in-

Spetznaz forces prepare for a mission in Afghanistan, 1988. Photo by Mikhail Evstafiev.

struction from the GRU Academy for senior officers.

As the Spetznaz training was only a more intense version of normal Soviet instruction, so were the commandos' weapons only slightly different from normal military issue. Weapons equipped with silencers were one such option, although the quality of that equipment tended to be inferior to Western counterparts. The Spetznaz forces were issued the best semiautomatic weapons, the AK-74 and AKSU, along with PKM general-purpose machine guns, RPG-7 and RPG-18 for antitank use, 30-mm and 40-mm grenade launchers, and occasionally Strela hand-held surface-to-air missiles. There are reports of small Spetznaz units operating in the early 1970s in Vietnam testing Dragunov sniper rifles. In Afghanistan it was reported that some Spetznaz were equipped with a spring-powered knife and most of the troops wore body armor. Their communications equipment was always the best available.

The Spetznaz forces in post-World War II Soviet doctrine were designed to neutralize critical targets behind enemy lines, such as nuclear launch sites, headquarters, or communications centers. Such deep penetration ability was proven in Czechoslovakia in 1968 and Afghanistan in 1979 as

Spetznaz troops seized key locations that paralyzed enemy reactions. Indeed, Soviet assassins killed Afghan leader Amin to facilitate the pro-Soviet coup. Reconnaissance troops (*Razvedchiki*) were contained within all Soviet army divisions. All these parachute-trained troops would have been used for deep penetration operations, although mainly in a scouting rather than a combat role. Raiders (*Raydoviki*) operated in company- and battalion-sized units for sabotage and guerrilla training, along the same lines as operations assigned to U.S. Army Ranger units. The *Vysotniki* troops acted like American Green Beret units. Operating in small units, their missions would be more specialized, secretive, and dangerous. These would have been trained in HALO (high altitude, low opening) parachute jumping.

More specialized units appeared during the Soviet operations in Afghanistan. Mountain troops were observed there in greater numbers than Western analysts predicted, with the special training and equipment such operations entail. Training facilities were also reported to have been planned in Afghanistan for mobile desert warfare operations that potentially could have been used farther south in Iran. The GRU-trained troops had even more specialized training for covert operations. These soldiers learned to act individually, in civilian clothes or enemy uniforms, for intelligence gathering, sabotage, and even assassination. All the Spetznaz units, especially those with the most delicate missions, would have been committed immediately upon commencement of hostilities, rather than beforehand, in order to try to make impossible any early warning of the enemy.

The fear of Spetznaz operations to commence at the outbreak of any hostilities was sufficient at the height of the Cold War for Western armies to hold large-scale exercises dealing with the threat. Special operations forces, such as the SAS or Green Berets, at the "aggressor" military bases in the United States, Great Britain, and throughout Europe, practiced identification procedures and base defense training. Spetznaz success in places like Afghanistan was sufficient rationale for such exercises. With the end of the Cold War, however, many such training operations have been downgraded. However, with terrorism still a problem overseas, base defense for American troops is still vital. Although the Spetznaz have officially been severely cut back since the collapse of the Soviet Union (as have all Soviet forces), their skills will almost certainly become available in Third World military markets just as other Soviet specialists and weaponry are.

References: Isby, David, *Ten Million Bayonets* (London: Arms and Armour Press, 1988); Kelly, Ross, *Special Operations and National Purpose* (Lexington, MA: Lexington Books, 1989).

Stonewall Brigade

Named for its commanding general, this unit served from the opening to the close of the American Civil War in Virginia.

The origins of the Stonewall Brigade lie in the nickname given to its first commander, Thomas Jackson. Jackson, a West Point graduate and veteran of the Mexican-American War, had retired from the military and for some years had been teaching at the Virginia Military Institute. When the Civil War broke out in April 1861, Jackson immediately offered his services to the newly formed Confederate States of America. Virginia Governor John Letcher gave him command of the First Brigade, Virginia Volunteers, formed at Harper's Ferry at the northern end of the Shenandoah Valley. The unit consisted of 2,611 men organized into five infantry regiments and an artillery battery.

The unit was originally part of the Confederate Army assigned to protect the Shenandoah Valley from invasion, but when the initial Union offensive came from Washington, DC, westward toward Manassas Junction on Bull Run, the Shenandoah units were transported by rail to aid the Confederates defending Manassas. Luckily for the Confederates, Union General Irwin McDowell failed to launch a timely attack against the defenders and the units from the west were able to arrive in time to place themselves on high ground west of Manassas. It was there that the bulk of the fighting took place.

From the time the fighting started around noon on July 21, the outcome of the battle was in doubt. At times, the Confederates had the upper hand on the high ground; at others, the Union forces made strong advances up the hill. At one point, under heavy pressure, Confederate units began to fall back. In their center, however, was Jackson's First Virginia Brigade. A man of amazing intensity and faith in what he perceived to be a divine cause, Jackson refused to allow his men to withdraw. General Bernard Bee called to the retreating to units to stop and see what Jackson's Brigade was doing: "Yonder stands Jackson like a stone wall; let's go to his assistance. Rally behind the Virginians!" That rally, plus Jackson's orders to charge rather than stay on the defensive, was the turning point of the battle and gave the day to the Confederates. "Stonewall"

General Thomas J. "Stonewall" Jackson. National Archives and Records Administration, Special Media Archives Services Division (NWCS-S), National Archives at College Park, 8601 Adelphi Road, College Park, MD. [Image 526067]

Jackson and the Stonewall Brigade both earned their nicknames.

Owing to his performance at the First Battle of Bull Run (First Manassas), Jackson was promoted to higher command, but the First Virginia Brigade stayed in his chain of command. Its next commander was Brigadier Richard B. Garnett. Still, it remained Jackson's favorite unit and he always felt a special fondness for it, a feeling which his men returned. It was definitely a relationship born in battle, for the campaign through which Jackson led his men in the winter and spring of 1861–1862 included some of the hardest marching and fighting of any units in the war.

Jackson's duty was to protect the Shenandoah Valley. The units of his command were born and raised in this region, as was Jackson, and they fought for it as anyone fights to protect one's home. One of Jackson's most baffling traits was to develop plans for operations without sharing them with his subordinates, who were told when to move and where to go but were never given a view of the "big picture." This frustrated his immediate subordinates, but forced them (as well as the rest of the army) to trust Jackson's views. Thus, his men marched back and forth through the Shenandoah Valley with no clear concept of their destination, other than when they reached it a Union force would be there. Jackson used his intimate knowledge of the region and interior lines to continually beat back Union forces attempting to join up and overwhelm him. Only the originator of the strategy of the central position, Napoleon Bonaparte, employed it so well. By marching his men long and rapidly, they beat Union forces again and again. His army during this campaign gained its second nickname, the Foot Cavalry, for the speed at which they marched. All this was done in miserable weather and with irregular supplies, but Jackson's uncanny ability to be in the right place at the right time produced victory after victory, and the men soon had complete faith in him. In this campaign the Stonewall Brigade suffered but one defeat, at Kernstown, which resulted in Jackson relieving Garnett of his command and replacing him with Brigadier General Charles Winder.

Jackson's force was transferred from the Valley to Richmond in the spring of 1862 to aid in the repulse of Union General George McClellan's attempt to reach the Confederate capital from the southeast. Jackson's reputation for speed and decisiveness failed him in the Seven Days' Battles, but he did develop a strong and lasting relationship with his senior commander, Robert E. Lee. The Stonewall Brigade, however, was key to Lee's victory at Gaine's Mill. In early August, taking a forward position in northern Virginia, Jackson fought a hard battle at Cedar Mountain. When General Winder was killed in action, Jackson himself took temporary command of the brigade and rallied them to victory. Their next commander was Colonel William Baylor. The Brigade was in the thick of the fighting at the Second Battle of Bull Run (Second Manassas), facing elements of the Iron Brigade. Colonel Baylor was killed in the fighting and replaced by Lieutenant Colonel Andrew Grigsby. Jackson's men faced and halted overwhelming numbers under the command of John Pope, holding on until Lee and his James Longstreet arrived to deliver a crushing blow. In the wake of that battle, Lee reorganized his army into two corps, with Jackson and Longstreet the commanders.

By August of 1862, the Confederates had been very successful in defending Virginia, but their government still lacked the foreign recognition necessary to establish legitimacy and acquire aid from overseas. In order to prove their abilities, Lee and Confederate President Jefferson Davis decided to launch an attack on the Union in order to show that the Confederate grand strategy of defense was followed by choice and not by necessity. Lee's march northward called for his army to divide and create as much havoc as possible to show its effectiveness to foreign powers and to give impetus to a nascent peace movement in the North. The Stonewall Brigade was instrumental in capturing Harpers Ferry, then moved east to join with Lee near Sharpsburg, Maryland. There, with the army still divided, Lee was confronted by McClellan's Army of the Potomac, whose 75,000 men more than doubled Lee's numbers. Again, luckily for the Confederates, the Union force did not attack quickly and employ its overwhelming force, and reinforcements were soon on their way. Before they could arrive, however, McClellan launched the first of his attacks on the Confederate position on September 17, 1862.

Jackson's corps was on the left flank when assaulted early in the morning. The Stonewall Brigade (along with Hood's Texas Brigade) bore the brunt of the initial fighting and took high casualties, but succeeded in repelling the attack. For reasons Jackson did not disclose, Grigsby was replaced after this by Brigadier General Elisha Paxton. Paxton commanded the Brigade at the next major battle, Fredericksburg, in December 1862, helping to anchor the right flank of Lee's impregnable position. In a year's fighting, the Brigade lost 1,200 men killed.

The Brigade last followed their commander in May 1863 at the Battle of Chancellorsville. The Army of the Potomac under Joseph Hooker had been repelled in its first assault against Lee's position west of Fredericksburg. In one of the most daring moves in all military history, Lee divided his outnumbered force and sent half of it with Jackson on a broad flanking movement which succeeded in striking the Union's extreme right flank and overwhelming it. Ever the aggressor, Jackson scouted ahead to find the weakest point in the collapsing Union position. Upon returning to his lines in the darkness, he and his staff were mistaken for Union cavalry. Jackson was shot and died several days later. Brigadier General Paxton was also killed in the fighting.

Jackson's death was a blow from which the Confederate Army never really recovered. Few generals on either side of the war had Jackson's vision and determination. Certainly his successor as corps commander did not. Lee followed his victory at Chancellorsville with another attack on the Union. In the initial stages of this campaign, the Stonewall Brigade (now commanded by Brigadier General James Walker) fought at Winchester and captured six Union regiments. They arrived at Gettysburg on the afternoon of July 1 (the first day of the battle). They were thus spared the embarrassment of being under the direct command of Jackson's replacement, General Richard Ewell, whose hesitation to press the retreating Union forces allowed them to dig in on high ground southeast of the town. It has been said almost since that day that if Jackson had been alive, the battle would have ended the first day and the decisive battle at Gettysburg would have been completely different. The Stonewall Brigade was involved in fighting along the northern end of the Gettysburg battlefield at Culp's Hill, which the Confederates failed to capture.

After the Confederate retreat from Gettysburg on July 4, 1863, little fighting took place on the Virginia front until the following May. New Union commander Ulysses Grant led the Army of the Potomac into Virginia, intending to "fight it out along this line if it takes all summer." One of the most intense of the battles of that Wilderness Campaign came at Spotsylvania Courthouse. The Stonewall Brigade was in the thick of the fight at the "Bloody Angle" and came out of the battle with a strength of only 200 men. At this point, the unit was so depleted that it lost its brigade status, and was combined with a number of other units to form a new brigade. Under the command of Jubal Early, they fought another Valley Campaign in 1864, but the overwhelming Union numbers meant they could not duplicate the masterful campaign of 1862. The unit was reassigned to Petersburg to engage in the nine-month-long siege south of Richmond.

At the beginning of April 1865, Union forces won the battle of Five Forks, and the remnants of Lee's army was forced to retreat west. General John B. Gordon wrote, "The old corps of Stonewall Jackson, which it was my privilege to command, was the last to abandon those mortar-battered lines around Petersburg. After all the other troops were safely on the march to the rear, we sadly withdrew." When Lee signed the terms of surrender at Appomattox Courthouse on April 9, 1865, the last 210 men of the Stonewall Brigade were present.

The legacy of the Stonewall Brigade was an example of determination to overcome both the elements and the enemy. The men also learned that Jackson's aggressiveness, while it cost them sleep as well as sore and bleeding feet, meant victory, and nothing else is as motivational in war.

The dedication of the men to their commander was revealed in 1891, when a statue to Jackson was raised in Lexington, Virginia, home of the Virginia Military Institute. Surviving veterans were there for the dedication on July 21, the thirtieth anniversary of Jackson and the Brigade earning their nickname. The citizens of Lexington wanted to honor the veterans by taking them into their homes for the night. "Near midnight the Brigade was found, huddled in blankets around Jackson's statue in the cemetery. Urged to leave the damp ground and partake of the town's

hospitality, none of the men stirred. Finally one said, 'Thank you, sirs, but we've slept around him many a night on the battlefield, and we want to bivouac once more with Old Jack.'"

Today, the 116th Infantry Regiment of the First ("Stonewall") Brigade of the Tweny-ninth Infantry Division (Light) of the Virginia National Guard claims ancestry from the Fifth Regiment of Thomas Jackson's Stonewall Brigade. They trace a lineage from colonial times through a variety of militia units which includes the Fifth Virginia Regiment.

References: John B. Gordon, quoted in Otto Eisenschiml and Ralph Newman, *The American Iliad*, (New York: Bobbs-Merrill, 1947); Green, Ralph, *Sidelights and Lighter Sides of the War Between the States*, Sons of Confederate Veterans, at "Stonewall in the Valley," stonewall.hut.ru/leaders/stonewall_brigade; "History of the Stonewall Brigade," www.stonewallbrigade.com/history; "116th Infantry Regiment (Stonewall Brigade) Lineage and Honors," www.staunton.com/116th/Lineage.html.

Storm Troops

Specialized soldiers operating with the German army in France in World War I.

World War I in France was fought in what was certainly the most futile way possible. The Industrial Revolution had produced weapons of mass destruction like the machine gun, tank, and poison gas, yet the generals throughout most of the war sent their troops into combat in the same fashion in which soldiers had attacked for more than 100 years: mass infantry assaults with soldiers rushing forward line abreast over open ground. The trench system that was developed soon after the war started made such attacks suicide, yet the generals

German Commander Field Marshall Ludendorff who planned and executed Operation Michael and Operation Georgette, successfully employing Germany's Storm Troops.

continued to send their men forward like this from 1914 through 1918. The "no man's land" between the trenches became a killing ground, while the trenches themselves became underground living quarters that only occasionally were lost or gained by combat. The only change in tactics was to precede each assault with massive amounts of artillery. This, however, gave the defenders plenty of warning as to when and where the infantry assault would be coming. As soon as the artillery stopped, the defenders came out of their underground shelters and mowed down the advancing troops. Millions of men died.

In 1918, with the war going badly for them, the Germans developed a new method of fighting in an attempt to break the stalemate of trench warfare. They learned a lesson from the Eastern front, where Russian general Brusilov had surprised an Austrian army after attacking with only minimal artillery fire. The Germans took this idea and honed it into the *Sturmtruppen*, the Storm Troops. Instead of attacking in mass waves, they reasoned, send in smaller units on the heels of shorter preliminary barrages. Give them objectives to reach behind the enemy lines, which would paralyze communications and reinforcement while sowing seeds of panic. Move quickly and do not worry about rear or flanks, for the main offensive would follow and clear those up. These rubrics did not represent a particularly new concept, for small parties of men had throughout the war infiltrated enemy positions in order to reconnoiter the lines or bring back prisoners. The Storm Troops, however, would do this on a much larger scale, operating from squad- to battalion-sized units.

The effectiveness of this new tactic was enhanced by the talents of two German officers. General Oskar von Hutier, commander of the German Eighteenth Army, had been the man who developed the new tactics and tested them against the Russians on the Eastern front. He commanded the forces that launched the new style of attack against the British in France. The other key figure was Colonel Georg Bruchmüller, who developed a new type of artillery barrage to assist in the Storm Troops' assaults. Instead of tearing up the ground with large amounts of high explosives, as had been done for the previous three years, he used more poison gas shells. Mustard gas was used on the flank areas of the assault, as its slow diffusion rate would hinder reinforcement from neighboring trench lines. Phosgene gas, which dissipated much more quickly, would be used on the areas of immediate attack to immobilize the troops defending them, as well as into the rear areas to neutralize British artillery positions.

Operation Michael was the code name for the first attempted use of Storm Troops tactics in France on March 21, 1918. It succeeded brilliantly. The British Fifth Army in the region around St. Quentin and Albert was caught unawares and soon fled in panic as Storm Troopers, using hand grenades and flame throwers, captured hundreds of prisoners and quickly made their way to rear areas. Here they found evidence of such hurried withdrawal that mess halls still had food cooking with no one in sight. The Germans fed themselves and pushed on toward their objectives of road junctions and British artillery positions. By the end of the day they had accomplished what had been dreamed of by every general since the war started: a hole in the enemy's lines that could be exploited, putting Germans in the Allied rear areas to start the long-hoped-for war of maneuver.

It was fortunate for the British, however, that they had fled so quickly, because the Germans were unable to keep pace. The British managed to establish another defensive position along the Somme River. This is not what stopped the Germans, however. Instead, they succumbed to exhaustion and began looting. The Germans had been on short rations and supplies for some months and, to them, the British rear areas were a paradise of food and equipment. In three days they had created a massive bulge in the Allied lines, capturing more territory in less time with fewer casualties than almost any operation of the war. However, three days of constant moving and fighting had worn the Storm Troops out, and the burden of their accumulated loot further slowed them down. German Commander Field Marshall Lu-

dendorff called the offensive a success and canceled further assaults for the time being.

Ludendorff followed up Operation Michael with Operation Georgette, a similar offensive against the British positions farther north around Armentieres. This was launched on April 9, 1918, and was just as successful for the Germans, although they failed to reach their intended goal of the rail junction at Hazebrouch. Had that fallen, it would have severed the supply line to the British army from the ports along the English Channel. Still, Operation Georgette caused another massive bulge in British lines as they were again mauled and pushed back. Once more, exhaustion on the part of the Storm Troops slowed their advance as time went by.

Buoyed by the huge gains made during these two offensives, Ludendorff prepared for a similar attack to the south in the area called the Chemin des Dames along the Aisne River. It was a quiet sector held by French units and British divisions that had been sent there for rest and refitting. It was more rugged than the area of Operation Michael, so the Germans added some mountain troops to the Storm Troop units. On May 28, 1918, the Germans once again threw the Allies into a panic. The French troops, already demoralized from earlier slaughter, broke and ran. Reinforcements found themselves overwhelmed by the rapid German advance. The Germans captured undamaged virtually every bridge across the Aisne River. The offensive moved inexorably toward Paris as reinforcements were pushed forward. At this point, a new player emerged: the United States. Although America had declared war on Germany more than a year earlier, it was still drafting and training men, most of whom were still at home. Some 120,000 Americans were in France, but they were half-trained and untested. They were also the only troops available. American General John Pershing temporarily lent the American Second, Third, and Forty-second Divisions to the French, and they stemmed the German tide.

From May 30 to June 17, 1918, American marines and infantry halted the Germans, at enormous cost, at Belleau Wood south of Soissons. The German advance stalled at what came to be called the Second Battle of the Marne River, but Ludendorff ordered more men into the push for Paris. Had he followed his original intent and attacked in Flanders far to the north, he may have collapsed the entire Allied line. Instead, the lure of Paris was too great—but the Allies were now reinforced and waiting. This time it was Allied artillery that did the most damage, and the follow-up attacks by American and French troops at Soissons and Chateau-Thierry marked the beginning of the end for the German war effort.

Through the summer and fall of 1918, the Allies pushed a broken and undersupplied German army out of France and to the borders of Germany itself before an armistice was signed in November. The German Storm Troops had succeeded in their tasks, but the introduction of their tactics was a case of too little, too late. The lesson learned by the Storm Troops was not forgotten, however. The Germans between the wars focused on the idea of mission-oriented attacks that did not worry about flanks. The problem of exhaustion was solved by the development between the wars of German armored forces. The theory of quick penetration and disruption of rear areas was reborn in 1939 in Poland with the blitzkrieg that almost took Adolph Hitler's armies to European domination.

References: Barnett, Correlli, *The Swordbearers* (New York: Morrow, 1964); Pitt, Barrie, *1918: The Last Act* (New York: Ballantine, 1963); Toland, John, *No Man's Land* (New York: Doubleday, 1980).

Submariners

Specialized sailors operating in underwater craft.

Going underwater is not a recent phenomenon. Aristotle reported that Alexander the Great's men used a type of diving barrel at the siege of Tyre in 332 BCE. English sailors used crude diving bells to recover valuable cannons after the British fleet defeated the Spanish Armada in 1588. Cornelis Drebbel, a Dutch engineer, attempted to travel under water about 1620. Drebbel built a wooden-framed submarine covered in leather and waterproofed with grease. Twelve oarsmen powered the craft that could submerge to 12 feet. Submarine designs became abundant by the 1700s, and England had 14 patents by 1727.

David Bushnell, an American inventor, is credited with building the first war submarine, used during the Revolutionary War. His vessel, called the *Turtle*, was made of wood with iron bands and covered in tar to stop leaks. It was a one-man vessel propelled by turning cranks attached to propellers. One propeller made the craft go forward or backward; the other lifted or lowered the craft—depending on which way the cranks were turned. The operator opened a valve letting water into a tank to submerge the craft. A hand pump was used to force the water out when the operator wanted to surface. The *Turtle* had enough air to stay under water for 30 minutes, and could dive to 20 feet. A glass tube with a floating cork told the depth, and a compass

Photograph of the crew of the USS Requin, a submarine at the U.S. Naval Base in Key West, Florida, standing at attention for an inspection by President Truman, 1948. National Archives and Records Administration, Harry S. Truman Library (NLHST), 500 West U.S. Highway 24, Independence, MO. [Image 200490]

reported direction. The instruments were painted with phosphorus to be seen while under water. The *Turtle* would approach an anchored ship to attach a timed charge to its hull, then move away. The first attack was in 1776 at New York against the British ship *HMS Eagle*, but the charge exploded harmlessly in the river.

The first effective submarine was the *CSS Hunley* designed by H. L. Hunley in 1863. It was powered by eight men cranking a shaft connected to the propeller. Catastrophe plagued this vessel: It sank twice in heavy seas, then failed to surface during a drill, killing Hunley and the crew he was training. The refloated sub finally achieved results by sinking the Union warship *USS Housatonic*, but the resulting wave also took the *Hunley* to its doom with all hands. This marked the first time a submarine sank an enemy ship.

The United States Navy commissioned the *USS Holland* in 1900. It was the first submarine to use a gasoline engine on the surface and electric power when submerged. It had a primitive periscope and

carried three torpedoes. This vessel validated the submarine as a legitimate weapon for war, and by World War I all major navies had submarines. Early use was limited to coastal operations, duties that included mine laying and supply. Germany, however, would begin using U-boats (*Unterseeboote*, literally "underseaboats") instead of surface vessels to attack shipping, and the British developed antisubmarine submarines to counter the threat. Thus, the submarine established its role as an effective weapon of war.

Submarines improved considerably in World War II. They had long range, could patrol for weeks at a time, and became very lethal. American submarines were assigned less than 2 percent of all navy personnel but accounted for 55 percent of enemy shipping destroyed in the Pacific Ocean. Submarines were also dangerous for the crews. Forty thousand German sailors served in submarines and 30,000 of them were lost. All submariners were considered special for these reasons. Promotions came quickly, and military procedures tended to be more relaxed for them. German submarine crews could grow beards with the captain's approval and wear nonuniform apparel; some sported bowler hats or ski caps. A German captain could paint insignias on the U-boat's conning tower. These insignias came from various sources: family crests, coats of arms, and good luck symbols like a horseshoe or black cat. The insignia had special meaning to the crew. To boost morale, U-boat crews also painted on the conning tower their total tonnage of shipping sunk.

Submarine life was demanding. A submarine might patrol as long as 90 days, and the crew had no contact with their families. The craft ran submerged in daytime and surfaced at night to recharge batteries, so the crew would see little daylight. Men stood lookout in all types of weather, and were always wet. American submarines were heated, but German submarines were not. Germans wore leather uniforms to stay warm. Food would spoil, so no fresh fruit or vegetables were available after a few weeks at sea. Americans had refrigerators for meat, and made bread daily. Germans, with no refrigerators, ate canned meat and carried many loaves of bread that soon grew moldy; the German submariners called this bread "white rabbit" when mold grew on the loaf. American submariners had saltwater showers, but Germans bathed only in sea spray when allowed on deck. Men shared the same bunks, due to lack of space, by alternating when changing watches. This procedure is called "hot bunking" because the mattress is still warm from the last occupant. Japanese submarines were even less accommodating than German subs, for they used no bunks at all and efficiency suffered greatly as a result.

The United States, Germany, and Japan were the main submarine powers in World War II. German submarines were very effective in the Atlantic Ocean due to strategy developed by Admiral Karl Doenitz (1891–1980). He invented the technique for U-boats known as the wolf pack. A U-boat would locate an enemy convoy and radio others to come and—like wolves—to join in the kill. The United States' main submarine campaign was in the Pacific Ocean attacking Japanese shipping. Japanese submarines were also formidable in the Pacific. The "I class" submarine could reach the United States coast, but heavy losses of men and equipment diminished their effectiveness. Japan resorted to human torpedoes (called *kyokoku heiki*, meaning "national salvation weapon," later called *kaiten*, or "heaven-shaker") in 1944,

but the end of the war came before they could influence the outcome.

The Japanese submariners were going to certain doom. American submariners also faced doom, but theirs was uncertain. This doom took the form of faulty torpedoes, which ran too deep, or worse, would fail to explode, leaving the submarine detected and vulnerable to counterattack. A new magnetic warhead, supposed to explode in close proximity to a ship's hull, was no better. Washington officials even blamed the crews for failing to use the torpedoes properly. The trouble was discovered in late 1943. Torpedoes were dropped from a crane onto a steel plate to simulate hitting a target. The investigation showed that firing pins were bending instead of striking the charge and exploding. The problem was rectified and the American subs became deadly hunters. It is a tribute to submarine crews that they carried out patrols with faulty torpedoes, knowing they may have been risking their lives in vain. This dedication to duty is what confers on these men a well-deserved place in history.

Many men contributed to the American submarine service, but one who stands out is Admiral Hyman G. Rickover (1900–1986). He helped develop the nuclear-powered submarine *USS Nautilus*, launched in 1954. Nuclear-powered submarines are specifically designed to travel under water at all times. The nuclear submarine, by leaving port and remaining submerged until returning to base, established new tactics in submarine warfare. Its mission is one of deterrence and prevention of nuclear war, and is an important factor in keeping the peace. A nuclear sub is able to deliver ballistic missiles on enemy targets anywhere in the world. The missiles can reach targets in less than 15 minutes because no location on land is far from an ocean. For these warriors, however, a successful mission is returning to base with no shots fired.

Nuclear submarine crew members are also different from their predecessors. Instead of hunting ships to sink, they patrol to locate and monitor the movement of other vessels, while keeping their submarine at full readiness. This highly complex craft requires fully one-half of the crew to be assigned to engineering and maintenance. This technical work requires much training because the entire crew may depend on one individiual doing the job correctly. A nuclear submarine dive alone requires more than 200 operational checks. The typical sailor goes through exhaustive physical and psychological screening and experiences a couple of years of training before being assigned to a nuclear sub. An officer must have a science or engineering degree and more than five years of training before being awarded supervisory duties. Once aboard the sub, all men have to pass their qualifications in order to earn their "Dolphins" pin, which is worn by all submariners who have completed training in their job categories. Officers are awarded gold and enlisted sailors wear silver dolphins. Men are rated in different areas and are qualified in many fields to be able to do several jobs if needed. School is conducted on the submarine while on patrol and training never stops. One rating, for example, is the ELT (Engineering Laboratory Technician). This sailor's duties require monitoring personnel for radiation and maintaining primary and secondary reactor chemistry. This person is trained in chemistry, radiology, and radiation. Another series of ratings held by an officer could be in sonar, propulsion, chemistry and radiation, and torpedo and fire control.

Routine aboard a nuclear submarine can be described as quiet. The term "Silent Service," denoting a submarine's underwater stealth, has new meaning in the electronic age. Detection by sound is a submarine's enemy. Listening devices can hear a sub miles away. Silence is so important that the hull is covered in rubber plates that absorb electronic signals, and acoustic sensors inside the sub report excessive internal noises to the crew. Submarines are now quieter than the surrounding ocean.

American submarines have two crews, called Blue and Gold, to reflect traditional navy colors. One crew is on shore duty while the other is at sea. They rotate every four months. Crews at sea work six hours on watch and 12 hours off watch. Off-watch crews train, do maintenance, or conduct drills. Sleeping is done in short periods and enlisted ranks, where required, use hot bunking. Food is the best the navy can offer; the traditional meal halfway through the cruise is steak and crab. Fresh eggs are available by putting wax on the shells for preservation. There are also soda and ice cream machines on board. Still, fresh fruit ranks high on a sailor's list upon returning to shore. Crew members each get a 40-word "familygram" each week, but send out no messages. The sub has a library, and videos are available on closed-circuit TV.

Submarines are an elite service with many hardships, but also many rewards. Besides constant schooling and having to maintain their ratings, submariners also go to battle, fight, and demonstrate courage as do other soldiers, and men who choose submarine duty seldom transfer.

John Stephen Drake

References: Clancy, Tom. *Submarine: A Guided Tour Inside a Nuclear Warship* (New York: Berkley Books, 1993); McKay, Ernest A., *Un-*

dersea Terror: U-Boat Wolf Packs in World War II (New York: Julian Messner, 1982); Weller, George Anthony, The Story of Submarines (New York: Random House, 1962).

Swedes of Gustavus Adolphus

The dominant army in the Thirty Years War (1618–1648) responsible for many military innovations, as well as establishing the first modern professional army.

Much of northern Europe went to war in 1619 for political and religious reasons. The Diet of Augsburg in 1555 had decreed that a prince could mandate a particular religion within the borders of his domain. This applied to Lutherans as well as Catholics. It did not, however, include Calvinists. As Calvinism grew in popularity with many in the lower classes, it also became more distasteful to many princes. In 1619 Ferdinand of Bohemia, a staunch Catholic, rose to the position of Holy Roman Emperor. Although placed in that position by the seven electors whose duty it was to choose the emperor, Ferdinand had but two days prior to his election been deposed by his Bohemian subjects in favor of a Calvinist ruler, Frederick V of the Palatinate. In order to regain his Bohemian throne and crush the Calvinists he despised, Ferdinand brought the power of the Holy Roman Empire to bear on Calvinists in his homeland and on Protestants in northern Europe in general. Thus began the Thirty Years War.

Throughout the 1620s, the Catholic imperial forces pillaged their way through Protestant territory, the armies led by Johann Tilly and Albrecht von Wallenstein. These two generals raised forces through force, principally by devastating a region so thoroughly that the only alternative for the survivors was to join the army and be paid in loot. With an army driven by blood lust more than principle, the Catholics defeated Frederick V and gave his homeland of the Palatinate to a Catholic monarch. They then defeated Danish forces raised by King Christian IV that entered the war in 1625. By 1628, however, the Catholic armies had stretched their forces too thin and ran into trouble when attempting to besiege the port city of Stralsund on the Baltic Sea.

A few days prior to the beginning of the siege, the city of Stralsund concluded a treaty with Swedish King Gustavus Adolphus. Gustavus's army was the best of its era and was molded completely by its commander. With this army, Gustavus acquired the provinces of Estonia and Latvia after defeating the forces of both Poland and Russia between 1604 and 1617. It was an army unlike any other of its day, and Gustavus embarked for Stralsund to both protect his newly acquired provinces and to fight for the Protestant cause.

The armies of Europe at that time were primarily mercenary. The core of the force typically consisted of professionals who hired out their services, while the rank and file would be whatever manpower could be obtained. Such an army was therefore lacking in discipline and cohesion, but if well led, could be devastating. Gustavus, however, created his army strictly from Swedes, and did so by mandating that every tenth man in each parish was liable for military service. This created a national army of citizen-soldiers such as had not been seen in Europe since the fall of Rome. It was also the first standing army since the Roman Empire, for Gustavus kept 20,000 men under arms at all times. Seventy percent of Sweden's budget was dedicated to this army, and it was one of the few armies of the age regularly and fairly paid. Gustavus instilled in his men a spirit that combined nationalism and religion, and it was an army that was motivated, disciplined, well prepared, and well equipped.

Although all the armies of the seventeenth century were equipped with firearms, Gustavus improved his weaponry with mobility in mind. The standard formations of the day were large squares based upon the system developed by the Spaniards some decades earlier. The standard square was made up of a mixture of pikemen and musketeers, who used a heavy wheel-lock musket. The Swedish musket was redesigned by Gustavus to lighten it from the standard 25 pounds to a more manageable 11 pounds. This made the standard forked support used by other armies unnecessary. He also created the cartridge, a paper package with a premeasured amount of gunpowder and a musket ball. This made for much quicker reloading, hence much greater firepower. The musketeers were deployed in ranks six deep, unlike the 10 ranks used in other armies. The front three would face the enemy with ranks successively kneeling, crouching, and standing. They would volley fire, then countermarch to the rear to reload while the other three ranks moved forward to deploy and fire. Although the standard formation of other armies called for a greater number of pikemen to act as defenders for the musketeers, the Swedes introduced a 150-man company that included 72 musketeers to only 54 pikemen. The smaller company could be used much more flexibly than the large square formation.

Gustavus also improved his artillery. Most guns of the time shot a 33-pound ball and were so heavy that they were arranged to stay in one place all day. The Swedish artillery was much lighter. Most fired only six- or 12-pound balls while the smallest (which could be easily moved by a single horse or three men) fired only a three-pound ball. Constant training that only a standing army could provide made Gustavus's artillerists able to fire their cannon eight times while the enemy musketeers could fire but six times in the same span. Again, this meant increased fire power for the Swedes. By quickly moving light field pieces around the battlefield and using smaller infantry units to outflank the bulky enemy squares, the Swedish rate of fire was designed to take advantage of the large target the enemy formations presented.

Finally, Gustavus remolded the cavalry. The standard European horseman was little more than a semimobile gun platform. He would ride to a position on the battlefield, usually on the flanks of the infantry squares, and deploy with the same large musket the men in the squares carried. The cavalry was trained to fight in much the same fashion as Gustavus's infantry, with a line of horsemen delivering a volley of pistol fire, then riding to the rear to reload as another line advanced. The Swedish cavalry was again more lightly armed, with carbines (shortened muskets) and pistols. In the early years of his reign, Gustavus's cavalry fought as dragoons, mounted infantry who dismounted to fight in order to capture positions before the arrival of the infantry. In later times they were equipped with sabres and fought from the saddle. The Swedish horsemen would charge the enemy cavalry, which had to maintain its formation in order to maintain its fire, and the speed and shock of the Swedish assault shattered whatever cohesion the enemy may have had. Then the close-range pistol fire, coupled with the cold steel of the sabres, proved more than most horsemen could withstand. The coordination necessary among cavalry, infantry, and artillery only came from the constant training that a regular standing army could provide.

All of this fire power and coordination needed direction, however, and Gustavus provided that as well. He proved himself in battle (which always endears men to their leader) but ruled his army with an iron hand. Unlike the pillaging and looting encouraged in the armies of Tilly and Wallenstein, the Swedish army was banned from any action against civilians. Hospitals, schools, and churches were strictly off-limits as targets. Anyone caught looting or harming a civilian was punished by death, the sentence for violating about a quarter of Gustavus's regulations. Gustavus apparently believed that if one fought for religious reasons, one should behave in a more religious manner.

Thus, it was a thoroughly professional army that Gustavus Adolphus brought to the continent to assist the city of Stralsund in 1628. Although he was forced to recruit replacements while on campaign, he tended to hire individuals and not mercenary units. This brought the new man into an already organized unit with an existing identity, and he became part of the Swedish army rather than remaining a part of a mercenary band. The Swedes arrived on the coast of Pomerania in 1630 but, rather than welcoming them, the hard-pressed Protestants viewed Gustavus's forces at first with suspicion. In the fall of 1631, Gustavus finally found an ally in the Elector of Saxony, and in September the allied force met and defeated Tilly's imperial force at Breitenfeld, near Leipzig. In three hours, the entire momentum of the war was reversed. Thirteen thousand of Tilly's 40,000 men were killed or wounded,

and the army of the Holy Roman Empire fled, abandoning all their artillery. This victory helped unite the Protestants into an army that numbered almost 80,000 by the end of the year.

The following spring, Gustavus defeated Tilly again, and the imperial commander died of wounds a few weeks later. The Protestant army liberated much of southern Germany, but in the process extended their supply lines too far. Wallenstein took advantage of this by moving a new army into Saxony, threatening Gustavus's rear. Wallenstein occupied a strongly fortified position at Alte Veste, which the Protestants failed to take after a two-day battle in September 1632. When Wallenstein dispersed his men into winter quarters in November, Gustavus seized his opportunity and attacked with 18,000 men against Wallenstein's 20,000 at Leuthen, about 20 miles from Breitenfeld. Again the forces of the empire were forced to retreat, but Gustavus was killed in the battle.

Command of the army fell to Prince Bernhard of Saxe-Weimar, who led it during the majority of the battle at Leuthen, but Gustavus was irreplaceable. Luckily for the Protestants, however, Wallenstein failed to follow up on the advantage of having killed Gustavus. Instead, he entered into a variety of political maChinations that ultimately lost him his job and then his life. With the deaths of Wallenstein and Tilly, the empire's armies were left without talented leadership. Nevertheless, the war dragged on until the Peace of Westphalia in 1648. The Protestants (including the Calvinists) won significant concessions in the peace treaty, and religious war came to an end in Europe for a long time. The reforms implemented by Gustavus had a great effect on the other armies of Europe. Professional standing armies became the norm, and civilians remained out of the way of the battlefield until the nineteenth century. Nationalism, which had been growing for 200 years, began to take serious root in Europe. Gustavus Adolphus's professional military was the standard by which others were created until the development of the completely nationalist armies engendered by the French Revolution.

References: Addington, Larry, *Patterns of War through the Eighteenth Century* (Bloomington: University of Indiana Press, 1990); Roberts, Michael, *Gustavus Adolphus: A History of Sweden*, 2 vols. (New York: Longman, 1953–1958); Wedgewood, C. V., *The Thirty Years War* (Gloucester, MA: P. Smith, 1969 [1938]).

T

Terry's Texas Rangers

A partisan unit operating as part of the Confederate army during the American Civil War (1861–1865).

One of the Confederacy's best-known cavalry units was informally created on board a stagecoach between Austin and Brenham, Texas, in March 1861. Benjamin F. Terry, Thomas Lubbock, and John Wharton, all representatives at Texas's secession convention, decided among themselves to organize a cavalry regiment for service in the war they were sure would not be long in coming. Terry was a wealthy planter from the Houston area, Lubbock was a Houston merchant and a veteran of the Texas revolution, and Wharton was a lawyer born in Tennessee but brought to Texas as an infant. These men, all financially secure and socially respectable, did what many Southerners did in early 1861: They voluntarily raised their own forces for service to their country.

The unit was not organized immediately, however. Confederate President Jefferson Davis, overwhelmed by pleas for command and rank, rejected the Texans' offer because he was sure the war would be short and that transportation of units from Texas would be unnecessary and costly. Terry and Lubbock, however, traveled to Virginia on their own and managed to wrangle assignments to General James Longstreet's staff for the battle at Bull Run in July 1861.

There they impressed influential people in the Confederate command and were granted permission to raise their unit. They quickly returned to Texas and advertised for volunteers. Each man was to bring his own horse and weapons, and the term of enlistment was for the duration of the war. Four thousand men arrived in Houston, and Terry was obliged to turn some of them away, finally accepting almost 1,200 men into his command. The men were immediately sworn into the Confederate army, but Terry delayed formally organizing the regiment until they arrived in Virginia. Although he was the unit's organizer, he refused to take any rank until elections were held by the men.

The Texans traveled to Beaumont, where Terry directed the horses to be sent back. The men marched through Louisiana to New Iberia, then floated down the Mississippi to New Orleans, arriving in September 1861. The experience was not pleasant, for the men were not prepared to march and the weather turned cold. It was a small foretaste of future misery. In New Orleans, the recruits were referred to as the Texas Rangers, the local population believing they were indeed that frontier organization. Although the Texas Rangers did not officially organize any forces during the war, the appellation stuck to Terry's command. Also, in New Orleans Terry received word from his old friend Albert Sydney Johnston, now commander of Confederate forces in the west. Johnston notified Terry that the cavalry were to travel to Kentucky and join his forces. Johnston promised the best horses Kentucky could provide and that the Texans would operate as an independent command as long as he was in charge. Serving under a Texan and being offered quality free horses was too good an offer to refuse, and in October 1861 the regiment boarded trains for Columbus, Kentucky.

In Tennessee, the population also believed the Texas Rangers had arrived, and the Texans either could not or would not convince them otherwise. Although they were welcomed by the citizens of Nashville, the Texans suffered their first casualties, not from combat, but from disease and sickness, including measles, various fevers, and respiratory infections. After 10 days in Nashville, the Texans were transferred to Bowling Green, Kentucky. Here the 10 companies were officially organized into a regiment and the Confederate government designated them the Eighth Texas Cavalry. Had Terry officially organized his regiment upon its creation, they almost certainly would have been designated the First Texas Cavalry. As it was, seven units had been organized before his. Not happy with the later number, the unit took to calling themselves what the civilians had: Terry's Texas Rangers. In Bowling Green, elections were held and Terry now officially became a colonel, with Lubbock his second in command. They were now a real regiment, but little else about them was regulation. There were no consistent uniforms or weapons, each man wearing and shooting whatever he brought with him. Pistols and shotguns were the preferred weapons, with Bowie knives chosen over sabres. Johnston provided the horses as promised.

In the field, the first few months of the regiment's existence were dreary. The weather was cold and damp, and the numbers of sick rose steadily. Outbreaks of measles and respiratory infections disabled and killed so many that by January 1862 only half the men were available for duty. Eighty-four men died that winter, but only five owing to enemy action. Still, the unit did see some action. On December 17, Terry led his men on reconnaissance to Woodsonville, Kentucky. There they engaged elements of the Thirty-second Indiana Regiment. It was a short and relatively inconsequential skirmish, but Terry was killed. A man widely respected by his command and potentially a great cavalry commander, Terry was struck down early in the war before he could prove himself. Lubbock took command, but he, too, was killed a month later. This established a pattern for command in the Rangers: The officers at all levels were regularly wounded or killed. Such is the fate of leaders who lead rather than direct. Command fell to the third inhabitant of that stagecoach almost two years earlier, John Wharton. The Rangers continued to operate patrols in Kentucky throughout February, but withdrew to Corinth, Mississippi, after the Union capture of Forts Henry and Donelson in northwestern Tennessee in mid-month.

The Rangers were involved in the battle at Shiloh in early April 1862, but most of their work came covering the Confederate retreat. Wharton was wounded in the battle and turned command over to Major Thomas Harrison, who was considered by the men to be something of a gun-shy martinet. He was to prove them wrong. Joined with Tennessee cavalry under the command of Nathan Bedford Forrest, the Rangers were detailed to slow the close Union forces pressing on the retreat. The Rangers led the attack and stunned the

Union with the ferocity of their charge. At close range, with buckshot-loaded shotguns, they dispersed the Union forces trying to stand against them. They then chased them all the way back to the main Union body, securing the retreat of the main Confederate army. The action cost the regiment three company commanders wounded.

After some raiding and scouting into central Tennessee in early summer 1862, the new Confederate commander, P. G. T. Beauregard, ordered Forrest to unite the cavalry commands into one unit under Forrest's direction. Under the command of one of the finest cavalry generals in all of history, the Texans shone. At Murfreesboro in mid-July they captured 1,200 Union troops, along with much-needed supplies, artillery, and horses. Forrest's brigade harassed Union supply lines throughout the summer and fall of 1862, creating havoc for Union General Buell. In September, Wharton returned to duty and was given command of the brigade. Forrest was ordered to create another similar unit. With Wharton's promotion, Thomas Harris was elevated to command of the Ranger regiment. The Texans continued to harass Union supply columns for the remainder of the year, developing a reputation with the Union as well as with their own forces. Regimental strength, however, now barely reached 700, although returning wounded and a dribble of recruits from home kept the Rangers stronger than many other Confederate regiments.

The Rangers again did good work around Murfreesboro in early January 1863 at the Battle of Stones River. After this battle, Harrison resigned his command to be replaced by L. N. Rayburn, who was soon succeeded by Gustave Cook. The spring and summer of 1863 brought more

scouting and harassment of Union supply lines in Tennessee, with a number of trains captured or destroyed. In July the Rangers were able to withdraw to Georgia and spend two months resting and refitting, but their numbers were now just over 400. At Chickamauga they covered a Confederate flank and captured 136 members of a cavalry brigade commanded by General Thomas Crook, who went on to fame after the war as an Indian fighter. In the autumn they were back to their raiding, destroying large numbers of Union supplies in eastern Tennessee, but the pro-Union population of that area, coupled with the constant riding and fighting, took its toll on the unit. By spring of 1864, Terry's Texas Rangers were back in Georgia, preparing for General William Sherman's offensive toward Atlanta. They fought Sherman's men, sometimes as cavalry and sometimes dismounted as infantry. They were detailed to an attack on Sherman's supply lines in late July, but strong Union forces in the rear lessened the effect of their raiding. Meanwhile, Sherman occupied Atlanta. The Rangers did what they could to harass Sherman's flanks as his army staged the infamous "March to the Sea" in November and December, but they could not do much to limit the destruction. After Savannah fell in December 1864, the Rangers continued to fight and harass Sherman's command as he marched into the Carolinas, and Sherman singled the Texans out as particularly bothersome to his progress.

The regiment made its last major charge at Bentonville, North Carolina, on March 19, 1865. Gustave Cook, in command for almost two years, was wounded and replaced by J. F. Matthews, who oversaw the surrender of the Rangers. In late April 1865, Matthews gave each company commander permission to do what he would with his company, withdraw or surrender. The regiment now numbered a mere 248 men. Like the rest of the Confederate army, they took their paroles and went home.

Melvin C. (Mel) Wheat

References: Cutrer, Thomas, ed., *Terry's Texas Rangers* (Austin: State House Press, 1996); Fitzhugh, Lester Newton, *Terry's Texas Rangers, unpublished memoirs* (Austin: Barker Center Archives); Fletcher, William, *Rebel Private, Front and Rear* (New York: Penguin, 1995).

Teutonic Knights

A religious and political group of knights operating in Eastern Europe and the Middle East during the thirteenth through sixteenth centuries.

Many crusades followed the first crusade of the western Christians against the Muslims in the Holy Land in the year 1095. Many of these campaigns, which spanned centuries, had nothing to do with the eastern Mediterranean shores and the Holy Land. Europe sought to correct aberrant Christian behavior in Bohemia against the Hussites, in southern France against the Albingensians, in England against the Lollards, and even in the Near East, when Christian crusaders in the Fourth Crusade attacked their fellow Christians of the Byzantine Empire and conquered Constantinople (Istanbul) in 1204. But, one of the last and longest crusades (1226–1525) was that conducted by The Order of the Hospital of the Blessed Virgin Mary of the German House of Jerusalem—more commonly known as the Order of the Teutonic Knights (in German *Deutsche Ritterorden*).

During this period of three centuries, the Teutonic Knights waged war in the name of Christ against the peoples of the southern shores of the Baltic, from what is now northeast Germany to northwest Russia. This land includes portions of the present countries of Germany, Poland, Lithuania, Latvia, Estonia, and Russia. Although many historians have made much of the theory that this was an aggressive and deliberate strategy on the part of the Knights, it would seem that the Knights' activities were motivated more by the personal interests of the leaders of the order than by religious or nationalistic reasons.

Maurice Keen, a historian of the warfare of the Middle Ages, discussed the role played by the Knights in the spectrum of both the Crusades specifically and medieval warfare in general: "In these wars, the Teutonic Knights relied heavily on the voluntary aid of visiting knights from other parts of Europe; and Prussia and Lithuania became, in consequence, a principal center of crusading activity for western knighthood in the fourteenth century" (Keen, 1984). Before the fourteenth century, as well as later in the fifteenth and early sixteenth centuries, the Knights not only relied heavily on support from "western Christianity" but eagerly sought such support by appeals to individual knights, and even negotiated alliances with various monarchs and noblemen in northeastern and central Europe.

In fact, the very presence of the Teutonic Knights in northeastern Europe was predicated on an invitation from one of the various dukes of Poland in the last quarter of the thirteenth century. Duke Konrad of Mazovia invited the Knights to help conquer and Christianize the pagan and unruly Prussians, who inhabited the lands north of Konrad's principality and blocked his access to the Baltic Sea. Actually, in the first quarter of the thirteenth century, the

Knights had already begun diversifying their crusading efforts into other geographic areas because of the deteriorating Christian situation in the Holy Land. In 1223, King Andrew II of Hungary expelled them because he had strong indications that they were attempting to create their own principality in Transylvania at his expense. Fortunately, Konrad's invitation had arrived as the Knights' tenure in both the Near East and Transylvania became strained.

To understand why the Knights emerged as a major aggressive force in northeastern Europe, an explanation of their origins is necessary. The Teutonic Knights first emerged in the Near East as an offshoot of a hospital confraternity composed of Germans (*Domus hospitalis sanctae Mariae Teutonicorum*), which had been formed in 1128 in the Latin Kingdom of Jerusalem. German knights, stranded by the death of Emperor Frederick I during the Third Crusade (1189–1192), had begun to affiliate with this confraternity, which had moved to Acre after Jerusalem fell in 1187. A large number of the German knights decided not to return home and, after copying the example of the Knights of the Hospital of St. John, were incorporated in 1198 as a military order. At that time the Teutonic Knights were recognized by Amalric, King of Jerusalem, and Pope Innocent III. Emperor Henry VI's chancellor, Conrad of Hildesheim, recognized the potential of this new knightly order, as did other German magnates, and helped them accrue large estates in areas of the Holy Roman Empire. These acquisitions provided them with substantial revenue that helped to finance many of their subsequent efforts, both in the Holy Land and in the Baltic.

The Knights reciprocated the favor bestowed on them by the most powerful political elements in Germany by serving as a vital support for German efforts after the Third Crusade, including accompanying German-led expeditions in the Holy Land. Beginning in Acre, they expanded their resources by accepting feudal lands and castles belonging to King Leo III of Armenia in Cilicia (present-day southern Turkey) in 1212 and by adding the castle of Montfort, near Tyre, in 1227. In the early years of the thirteenth century Hermann Bardt, the grand master (*Hochmeister*) and his successor, Hermann von Salza, were both mentioned prominently in the records of activities in the Holy Land. Von Salza (Hochmeister from 1210 to 1239) negotiated the acquisition of the Turkish castles, negotiated and planned the subsequent activities in Transylvania, accepted Konrad of Mazovia's invitation to establish the Knights on the Baltic shores, and united with the Livonian Knights in 1237. In fact, he was such a recognized force in the spectrum of German politics that Holy Roman Emperor Frederich II appointed him to the position of imperial chancellor and also made him a prince of the empire.

Von Salza's agenda for the Knights in Transylvania apparently was a prelude to later attitudes and strategies as they established themselves in northeastern Europe. King Andrew II of Hungary had requested their aid in his efforts to deal with the non-Christian Cumans in his eastern lands and also in his confrontations with the Byzantine Empire in 1211. Thirteen years later in 1223, he realized that the Knights he had called on for help were establishing an independent principality in his territory, so he expelled them. This pattern of styling themselves as the bulwark of Christianity in eastern and northeastern Europe while organizing de facto self-governing "colonies" of Knights was to repeat itself many times.

The Knights remained active in the Holy Land even while they began to develop opportunities for expansion into new lands. Several historians have labeled their efforts as a willingness to sell their services "to any ruler who was willing to pay them to fight *pagans and infidels*" (Keen, 1984). However, long after Lithuanians, Poles, Prussians, and Russians had been "Christianized," the Knights continued their aggression. After accepting Konrad of Mazovia's invitation to aid his efforts to open up Mazovia's access to the Baltic Sea, they continued assaults on Christians and non-Christians alike in the Baltic lands.

Despite their aggressiveness, the Teutonic Knights were not always noted for distinction in battle. In 1197, while assisting in the siege of the fortress of Toron in Galilee, the crusaders where informed that an army from Egypt had marched across the Sinai Peninsula and was nearing the fortress. The leaders of the crusaders and the various orders of the monastic knights (including the Teutonic Knights) fled Toron, deserting the helpless foot soldiers, who were left to their own destiny. During the Fifth Crusade, the Knights set fire to food and other supplies during a retreat and thereby alerted the Muslim forces who immediately attacked and decimated the crusading army. In 1242 the Teutonic Knights, together with their brethren the Livonian Knights and their momentary allies the Lithuanians, were defeated by Alexander Yaroslavski, Prince of Novgorod, at the battle of Lake Peipus. The mounted Knights had charged in full armor across the frozen surface of the lake and the ice could not bear their weight.

The most famous defeat of the Knights occurred in 1410 when a combined force of Poles, Lithuanians (together with their Tartar allies), Czechs, Hungarians, and Wallachians under the leadership of King Jogaila confronted them at Grunwald (Tannenberg). For that battle, the Hochmeister, Ulric von Jungingen, had summoned assistance from many Christian countries of western Europe. However, the Knights and their allies were outnumbered with 27,000 men to an estimated 39,000 men on the side of the confederated forces. In many respects, the Teutonic Knights never recovered from this defeat. The Hochmeister, grand marshall, grand commander, and half the Knights were killed. After the battle, the remnants of the defeated army retreated to Marienburg, their magnificent castle/headquarters in Gdansk where they were besieged for several months. The Teutonic Knights never again regained the initiative against the various peoples allied against them. From 1410 forward they were engaged in efforts merely to maintain their existence.

The Teutonic Knights carved out a feudal principality that included most of the Baltic coastline from Gdansk (Poland) to Riga (Latvia) and included portions of present-day Germany, Poland, Lithuania, Latvia, Estonia, and western Russia, where it is estimated that they founded over 1,400 villages and 93 towns. Several historians have noted that their strength resided in their tenacity. Most historians acknowledge that they were very effective—albeit ruthless—administrators and colonizers. Rather than referring to their efforts as a focused policy of "Drang nach Osten" (Drive to the East), some historians have described them as being similar to the less organized evolution of "Manifest Destiny" in the United States. The Knights moved inexorably east against various peoples they chose to consider as theologically unacceptable.

The chronology of the Knights' evolution in northeastern Europe is ultimately one of expediency. They were the products and exponents of feudalism, cloaked with the white robe and the red cross, patterned after that of the Knights Templar (who were thereby incensed). They later replaced the red cross with the black cross (the same iron cross adopted by a later German army), but otherwise did not emulate the Templars. Unlike the Templars, they created a feudal state, which became the inspiration for the Knights of the Hospital of St. John (Hospitallers or Knights of Rhodes/Malta), who created principalities in Rhodes and later in Malta. Civil and church authorities and conquerors were busily creating principalities in the thirteenth through the fifteenth centuries throughout Europe.

During the three centuries of the Knights' existence on the Baltic coast, they relied on the support of the Holy Roman Emperor, German magnates within the empire, aspirants to the imperial crown, the papacy, and the nobility of much of western and central Europe. They were also able to depend on their own substantial financial resources accrued over the years from bequests from the German nobility. In 1400 the Knights relied on their *Wehrpflichtige* (mobilized or conscripted forces), which included 426 knights, 3,200 serving men, 5,872 sergeants, 1,963 troops (conscripted from the towns they ruled), and some 1,500 additional levies from the abbeys in their principality. Hochmeisters represented several of the major ruling families of German principalities and the imperial families, including Habsburgs, Hohenzollerns, Wettins, and others. The Knights also attracted to their crusading efforts such knightly luminaries as Henry Grosmont, duke of Lancaster; Henry of Bolingbroke (later King Henry IV of England); Gaston-Phoebus of Foix; and Duke Albert III of Austria (a Habsburg).

From 1226 to 1525, the various grand masters of the order virtually ignored the subsequent Christianization of numerous Baltic peoples or the authority of vested rulers in the different lands they subjected, or sought to subject, to their authority. During these three centuries they also engaged in activities that were designed to defend or even expand their territories, fighting numerous battles with Poland and Lithuania. The Teutonic Knights approached the sixteenth century unalterably opposed to acknowledging any authority other than their own and continued to refuse to swear homage to Poland-Lithuania. In 1511 Albrecht von Hohenzollern-Ansbach, who was both grandson of Casimir IV of Poland and the elector of Brandenberg, became Hochmeister. In 1525 he acknowledged the sovereignty of the Kingdom of Poland-Lithuania in his new capacity as duke of Prussia. His descendants (the Hohenzollern family, who ultimately became kings of Prussia and then the Kaisers of Germany) were to continue to confront Poland for 250 years and eventually assume control of major portions of western and northern Poland in the eighteenth century.

Robert Burke

References: Halecki, O., *A History of Poland* (New York: David McKay Company, 1981); Johnson, Lonnie R., *Central Europe* (New York and Oxford: Oxford University Press, 1996); Keen, Maurice, *Chivalry* (New Haven and London: Yale University Press, 1984); Wandycz, Piotr, *The Price of Freedom: A History of East Central Europe from the Middle Ages to the Present* (London: Routledge, 1992).

Texas Rangers

Protectors of the American frontier, later serving as soldiers under the federal government, and finally becoming a law enforcement agency.

In the early 1820s, Mexico gained its independence from Spain. In need of citizens to protect the country should Spanish troops return, and in need of a buffer between Mexican citizens and hostile Plains Indians, the Mexican government advertised for settlers to move from the United States. Empresarios (basically immigrant brokers) contracted with the Mexican government to bring in Anglo settlers in return for large tracts of land. The first and most successful operation was that conducted by Stephen F. Austin, who oversaw the creation of the Rangers in May 1823. The Americans moving to the north-ern Mexican province of Texas settled along the Colorado and Brazos Rivers and stayed, for the most part, east of the lands dominated by the warlike Comanche tribe. But the frontier between Anglo and Indian lands was close enough to cause friction, and the Rangers were given the task not only of protecting the frontier from attack, but launching punitive expeditions as well.

The Rangers were largely a haphazard organization, but when the Texans broke away from Mexico in the autumn of 1835, the fledgling Texas provisional government officially gave them the title "Texas Rangers." At first, the Rangers provided their own horses and weapons, with ammunition and supplies furnished irregularly by the new government of the Republic of Texas after 1836. The Rangers spent the next nine years not only protecting the settlements from the Indians, but also taking reprisals against Mexican army ex-

Some members of the Frontier Battalion of the Texas Rangers, ca. 1885.

peditions sent to harass Texas. They had no more than a few hundred men in their ranks at any time. It was in this period of the Republic that the Rangers developed a fearsome reputation among the Indians and the Mexicans for determination, bravery, and marksmanship.

The first major battle they fought with the Comanches came in 1840. During a meeting in San Antonio in which some Comanche were discussing peace and returning hostages, the Indians were ambushed and slaughtered by local citizens. The Comanches came back for vengeance a few months later, raiding and pillaging almost to the Texas coast, where they burned every farmhouse they passed and stole every horse they found. Slowed by the 3,000 horses they had accumulated, the Comanches were caught by a Ranger unit under one of the organization's early legends, Ben McCulloch. At the battle of Plum Creek on August 11, 1840, the Rangers inflicted a severe defeat on the Comanches. This fight marked the first use of Colt repeating pistols, which proved so effective that the United States Army took notice and mandated those sidearms for their cavalry from that point forward. Indeed, the Rangers were the first organization to purchase revolvers and use them in combat.

When the United States annexed Texas in 1845, the Mexican government disputed the border the Texans had claimed: the Rio Grande River from mouth to source. When the United States recognized that border, the Mexicans threatened war. War came in April 1846 just north of the lower Rio Grande, where Mexican cavalry captured and killed some American dragoons in the force occupying the disputed territory. The army commander, General Zachary Taylor, called on the Texas government to provide him with volunteer forces, and the Texas Rangers were the first to respond. This unit, commanded by John Coffee Hays, served under Taylor's command when he invaded Mexico in September 1846 and fought with him at the capture of Monterrey and in the defeat of General Santa Anna's Mexican army at Buena Vista the following February. The Rangers transferred to General Winfield Scott's command for the assault on Vera Cruz and served as scouts and in antiguerrilla action during the cross-country march on Mexico City in 1847. The already-established reputation for ruthlessness among Mexicans was reinforced during this war, but there were reports of atrocities on the part of the Rangers. Most of these were later proven to be untrue, but the allegations did result in some damage to the Rangers' reputation. The Rangers' abilities in stealth and reconnaissance, however, proved invaluable for both Taylor and Scott.

Once the Mexican-American War was over and Texas was part of the United States, the Rangers' duties focused more on fighting Indians but also began to include more general law enforcement. The western half of Texas was inhabited largely by Indians and outlaws, and the Rangers learned to operate on their terms and beat them at their own games. It was at this time that the Texas Rangers developed their unofficial motto: "Ride like a Mexican, track like an Indian, shoot like a mountain man, fight like the devil." They did all of these much better than did their enemies. With each ranger armed with at least two pistols, a rifle, and a knife, they operated in small groups that could move quietly and strike quickly.

During the Civil War, Rangers did not join the Confederate army as complete units, as they had done in the Mexican-

American War, but virtually all of them served in the Confederate cause. One of the most respected of the Ranger captains, John "Rip" Ford, commanded a cavalry unit in South Texas made up of Texans too young or too old to join the army. His force of no more than 1,500 men almost never operated as a complete unit, but in small groups managed to clear the lower Rio Grande Valley of Union soldiers, capture Brownsville from a much larger force, and fight the last battle of the war at Palmito Ranch, a Confederate victory that came on May 12–13, 1865, four weeks after the war had ended at Appomattox Court House, Virginia. They lived off the land and outfought the Union troops at every turn, just as Ford had done in his fighting against the Indians.

The Rangers not only tracked down Indians and outlaws, but were called upon to maintain peace as range wars and ethnic conflicts broke out in the post-Civil War era. Often they quelled disturbances merely by their presence and reputation. "One riot, one Ranger" has become a modern slogan. In the twentieth century they have become strictly a law enforcement agency with high standards, but their methods are still controversial. At times criticized for possibly racist or sexist attitudes (although they now admit racial minorities and women to their ranks), the Texas Rangers are regarded nevertheless as an elite law enforcement organization, with a standard of conduct on the job that recalls the discipline and tenacity of the roughest days on the frontier.

References: Davis, John, *The Texas Rangers* (San Antonio: University of Texas Institute of Texan Cultures, 1975); Webb, Walter Prescott, *The Story of the Texas Rangers* (Austin: Encino Press, 1971); Wilkins, Frederick, *The Highly Irregular Irregulars: Texas Rangers in the Mexican War* (Austin: Eakin Press, 1990).

Tuskegee Airmen

A Unit of African-American pilots who excelled in combat during World War II

In the United States, African-American units were raised for the first time during the Civil War (1861–1865). Afterwards, two infantry units, the Twenty-fourth and Twenty-fifth infantry, and two cavalry regiments, the Ninth and Tenth (known as the Buffalo Soldiers) were retained in service. For eight decades, Black Americans were forced to serve in segregated units. An Army War College study conducted in 1925 concluded that African-Americans were not capable of serving in combat, and inherently not suited for the technically challenging jobs of flying and maintaining aircraft. As war in Europe broke out in 1939, the U.S. government started flight schools at various colleges around the nation, but none were established at any Black colleges. However, pressure and protests from Black leaders, the NAACP, and Eleanor Roosevelt herself caused the Army to rethink its position. On July 19, 1941, the Army Air Corps founded a flight school at Tuskegee University in Alabama.

Thirteen African-Americans formed the first class, including their Captain, Benjamin Davis, a 1936 West Point graduate who would later become the first Black General in United States Air Force history. These men and the 913 graduates who followed them were designated as the Ninety-ninth Pursuit Squadron, later expanded to form the 332nd Fighter Group. However, they would all became known in history as the "Tuskegee Airmen."

These intrepid pioneers were determined to succeed in one of the most daunting tasks faced by any World War II soldiers: becoming fighter pilots. Facing the same discrimination that African Americans had borne for 340 years, these men had to put up with, at least in the beginning, second-hand equipment, inferior facilities, and an expectation of failure on the part of the Army. Since the military at that time was completely segregated, only Black mechanics could service the planes, only Black armament technicians could arm them, and only Black radio operators could maintain the communications. However, as pilot losses mounted in Europe and North Africa, it became evident that no matter their color, the Tuskegee Airmen's turn in combat would come.

In May 1943, the Ninety-ninth Fighter Squadron began combat operations in Tunisia, flying P-40 War Hawks, and in June they began escort missions over Sicily. In September, the Ninety-ninth began fight-er-bomber missions in Italy, flying P-39 Airacobras, escorting bomber missions, and attacking railroad lines, bridges, and other targets of opportunity. In January, the unit was issued P-47 Thunderbolts, and on January 24, 1944, the Black pilots of the Ninety-ninth shot down five German planes, and four more the next day. In July 1944, the Ninety-ninth was joined with three other Black squadrons, all who trained at Tuskegee, to form the 332nd Fighter Group. At last the new group was issued state-of-the-art P-51 Mustangs, and they proudly proceeded to decorate their planes with bright red propeller spinners, red wing bands, and all-red tails surfaces. Almost overnight they became known to friend and foe alike as the "Red Tails." The Germans, out of respect for the airmen's superior performance, called them the " *Schwartze Vogelmenschen*" or the "Black Birdmen," but to U.S. bomber crews they

African American aviators in flight suits, Tuskegee Army Air Field, World War II. Credit line: Library of Congress, Prints & Photographs Division, Visual Materials from the NAACP Records [reproduction number LC-USZ62-35362].

were the "Red Tails" or the "Black Red Tail Angels."

As the nature of the air war over Germany entailed more and more daylight bombing, the missions flown by the "Red Tails" became almost totally bomber escorts, a task at which the Tuskegee Airmen excelled. Their new commanding officer, now Lt. Colonel Benjamin Davis, began to insist on one simple rule: If his pilots' main task was to be escorting the heavy B-24 bombers, then under absolutely no circumstances could his men abandon the B-24s and go chasing German fighters. The men had trained as fighter pilots, but they subjugated their personal interests and desires for glory to the good of the unit and for the protection of the bombers they escorted. Mostly because of this policy, there were no Tuskegee aces (pilots who had shot down at least five enemy planes), but to their credit, over the course of 2,000 escort missions, not one single bomber they protected was lost to enemy fighters—an astounding achievement. One bomber pilot reported that "the P-38s always stayed too far out. Some of the Mustang groups stayed in too close.... Other groups, we got the feeling that they just wanted to go and shoot down [Messerschmitt] 109s.... The Red Tails were always out there where we wanted them to be.... We had no idea they were Black; it was the Army's best-kept secret." Soon word spread among white U.S. bomber pilots about the skill and fighting ability of the 332nd, and many units began to request escort by the all-Black group.

Right up to the end of the war, the Airmen maintained their amazing record and iron discipline. They led the longest escort mission ever flown by the Fifteenth Air Force, a 1,600-mile round trip to the Daimler-Benz tank works in Berlin in March 1945. On this mission, the Airmen went up against German ME-262 jet fighters for the first time. Colonel Davis and his men shot down three of the jets, damaged six others, and most importantly, protected their bombers from any losses.

At the end of the war, after flying over 15,000 sorties, 66 Tuskegee Airmen had been killed in combat and 32 shot down and taken prisoner. The Airmen are credited with shooting down 111 enemy aircraft and destroying another 200 on the ground, demolishing 950 railroad cars, locomotives, and trucks, and even sinking a destroyer using only machine gun fire. The Airmen earned 150 Distinguished Flying Crosses, 744 Air Medals, 8 Purple Hearts, one Silver Star, 14 Bronze Stars, a Legion of Merit, the Red Star of Yugoslavia, and two Presidential Unit Citations. However, their finest achievement, one that no other flying unit in the war could make, is the unique claim that the "Red Tails" never lost a bomber to enemy aircraft.

Four years after the end of the war, partly as a testament to the abilities and courage of the Tuskegee Airmen, President Harry Truman, with Executive Order 9981, ended the practice of segregation in the U.S. military.

Clinton Chase Hamilton

References: Francis, Charles E., *Tuskegee Airmen: The Men Who Changed a Nation* (Boston: Branden Pub. Co.,1993); Rose, Robert A., *Lonely Eagles: the Story of America's Black Air Force in World War II* (Los Angeles: Tuskegee Airmen, Western Region, 1976); Sandler, Stanley, *Segregated Skies: All-Black Combat Squadrons of WW II* (Washington, D.C. : Smithsonian Institution Press, 1992).

U

United States Marines

Troops trained in amphibious warfare, known for intense pride of service.

The Marine Corps, like the navy and army, was created during the American Revolutionary War. The Marines were formed on 10 November 1775, seven months after the first shots were fired at Lexington and Concord, Massachusetts. For the first 20 years of their existence, they did what all marines did: served aboard ships in the equal role of enforcing discipline among the crews and engaging enemy marines in combat. After two ships would blast one another with artillery fire, one warship would often close in on the other and its

Seal of the US Marine Corps.

crew grapple onto the enemy ship. Marines acted both as snipers from the rigging and as members of the boarding parties, both to fight the enemy and to secure possession of the captured vessel.

American Marines had little to do after the Revolution, for the United States Navy did not exist. Merchant ship protection from pirates was the main role the Marines served. In the 1790s, conflict in Europe over the French Revolution had repercussions in America. In need of ships to enlarge their navy, the French began seizing American vessels. The British reacted to American privateers operating under French letters of marque by capturing and incorporating American ships into the Royal Navy. Without warships, the United States had no ability to respond to these indignities, so in 1794, Congress appropriated money for the construction of six warships. They came to service too late to keep the United States from being forced to sign a treaty paying tribute to pirates along North Africa's Barbary Coast. In 1798, Congress passed legislation enlarging the Marine Corps to 500 men and ordering their use aboard ships.

The early Marine Corps had no traditions or esprit de corps upon which to build, and the early recruits were not of the highest quality. They soon showed themselves to be excellent fighters, however. Within a matter of months in 1798, American ships and Marines were driving off French warships in the Caribbean as well as landing shore parties that attacked French coastal fortifications. The amphibious nature of the Marines was thus begun. The first major conflict in which they took part was the first serious international fighting U.S. forces had engaged in since the Revolution: an attack on the Barbary pirates. After Stephen Decatur rescued American hostages from North Africa in February 1804, a force of eight Marines, accompanied by about 500 European mercenaries and commanded by U.S. Army General William Eaton, landed in Egypt and marched 600 miles along the coast to attack the pirate stronghold at Derna, in modern Libya. On the morning of 27 April 1805, with support from American ships bombarding the fort, Eaton's force attacked. The Marines were under the command of Lieutenant Presley O'Bannon, and they not only captured the cannons defending the pirate fort, but also turned them on the commander's headquarters and forced his surrender after a two-hour cannonade. For a total loss of 13 dead, including two Marines, the fortress was seized and its garrison captured or scattered. O'Bannon received from the pirate commander a sword patterned after the style of that used by Egyptian Mameluke troops, and that sabre became the one upon which Marine dress swords have been patterned ever since.

During the War of 1812, the U.S. Navy began to show its abilities, and the Marines enhanced their reputation for mobility and fighting well under difficult conditions. They continued to fight enemy sailors and marines in ship-to-ship actions and were again landed on British-held Caribbean islands for attacks on shore facilities. In the decades that followed, the Marines were used in antislaving operations and piracy suppression. In 1847, they were involved in the American attack on Mexico City alongside forces of the U.S. Army. A force of Marines under command of Army Colonel Robert E. Lee was responsible for attacking and capturing a force of insurrectionists under the leadership of John Brown, who seized an arsenal at Harper's Ferry, Virginia, in 1859 and planned to provoke slave rebellions in the American South. As the American (Union) navy did little during the Civil War except blockade duty, the Marines did not see much action, but after the war, as the government severely reduced the size of both army and navy, the Marines became the instrument of American "force projection" abroad. They were used extensively in expeditions to Caribbean islands and Central American nations to maintain the peace or protect American interests and lives, as well as in the Philippines, suppressing the insurrection against the American occupation after the Spanish-American War of 1898–1901.

During World War I, Marines served under the control of the U.S. Army, as the traditionally small American military establishment needed trained soldiers to be committed to France as quickly as possible, and the Marines provided a ready-made contingent. One-fifth of the U.S. force in France in World War I were Marines. In the 1920s, the Marines saw a need to become amphibious. This was not only to be able to "project force" into an enemy country, but also to give the Marines a specialty no other branch of the military had, thus ensuring their continued funding and even their continued existence as an independent force. After the British disaster at Gallipoli in 1915–1916, many thought that amphibious warfare was impracticable, but the Marines spent the next two decades devising methods and doctrine. It was fortunate that they did, for it proved to be the only way to take the war to the Japanese in the Pacific during the Second World War.

It was during World War II that the Marines achieved their highest status. As an all-volunteer force, they had maintained strict recruitment standards that made them the most professional and highly trained force the United States possessed at the outset of hostilities. Thus, the Marines were the first American troops to engage enemy ground forces. On 7 August 1942, the United States took the offensive against Japan by landing Marines on the island of Guadalcanal in the Solomon Islands northeast of Australia. The First Marine Division learned how to fight the Japanese and deal with jungle warfare as the battle progressed. It was a learning experience for which prewar training had not equipped them, except in the ability to adapt and overcome. This was also the first large-scale amphibious operation the United States had ever undertaken. The Marines, and later the army, learned valuable lessons in jungle warfare that would serve them well on other South Pacific islands. Not all islands were covered with jungle, however, and the Marines fought on coral atolls with little cover, mountainous islands strewn with well-defended caves, or islands consisting of nothing but volcanic ash and sand. In all of these battles, the Marines fought entrenched Japanese forces that always were in superior numbers, and each island battle was an American victory.

During World War II, amphibious tactics was perfected as the Marines staged landing after landing on hostile beaches. Also developed at this time was the use of close air support, and the Marine Air Wing came into being. Neither of these were used to any great extent in the Marines' next major conflict in Korea, 1950–1953.

Only at Inch'on in September 1950 did an amphibious landing take place, but the Marines were in the thick of the fighting throughout the war. When the Communist Chinese staged their massive counteroffensive in November 1950, Marine units were surrounded and in some cases overwhelmed. The Marine Corps creed not to abandon anybody, living or dead, to the enemy, meant extremely difficult operations wherein the Marines had to fight not only a determined enemy but subfreezing temperatures as well. Chosin Reservoir became another battle added to the ever-growing list of Marine honors. This was the scene of the famous comment by one Marine commander, "Retreat, hell! We're just attacking in a different direction." Once again, as in World War I, Marines served as ground troops under overall army command.

That same duty fell to them again during the Vietnam War. No landings took place against hostile beaches, but the Marines were once again the first combat troops committed to action in March 1965. The professional, all-volunteer force reached a psychological low point in its existence, as did all branches of the American military, in a war with ever-changing goals that proved frustrating for all involved. Having to defend entrenched positions against attacking forces was an anathema to Marine doctrine, and the morale problems associated with the inability to successfully implement their training and dealing with a hostile populace at home and in Southeast Asia proved extremely demoralizing. After the American withdrawal, Marine recruiting suffered, to the point that organizations such as the Brookings Institution theorized disbanding the force.

However, the type of "small wars" that the Marines had fought so successfully throughout the nineteenth century reappeared and the need to project force kept the Marines not only in existence, but busy. Marines fought in American operations in Grenada, Panama, Somalia, and the Gulf War. In Somalia, the Marines were among the first United Nations forces deployed (1992) and the last to be withdrawn (1995). Other Marines performed a rescue mission of a downed U.S. Air Force pilot in Bosnia in 1995. When coalition forces went into Afghanistan in the wake of the 9/11 attacks, the Marines were the first conventional forces in-country, and they have been deployed there continuously ever since (as of this writing), engaging the remnants of the Taliban and Al Qaeda forces. Marines were also deployed in Iraq in the invasion of 2003 and spearheaded the occupation of the terrorist-controlled city of Fallujah.

The carefully-cultivated persona of the Marines has been used for psychological purposes. Their high-profile landings on Iraq's coast in Operation Desert Storm pinned down a large portion of the Iraqi army while the rest of the coalition forces engaged in their huge flanking movement. In the Iraq war begun in 2003, the Iraqi troops and rebels quickly learned to identify the difference between Marine helicopters and uniforms from those used by other troops. There are numerous reports of enemy forces in Marine areas of operation describing them as "devils," a designation which the Marines relish.

The new American doctrine of rapid response forces, able to move quickly anywhere in the world by sea or air, fit well into traditional Marine operational views. Currently, the Marines are part of the Fleet Marine Forces, which include the navy's transport and supply ships. The Marine contingent is made up of four

parts: (1) ground combat elements with infantry, armor, artillery, and engineers; (2) air support; (3) command and control for planning and directing operations; and (4) service support to maintain the necessary supplies. Although paratroopers can deploy more quickly than any other force, the Fleet Marine Forces are necessary to continue the missions that the airborne forces start.

On 1 November 2005, the U.S. Secretary of Defense announced the formation of a new unit, the Marine Special Operations Command (MARSOC) as part of the larger Special Operations Command (SOCOM). This will serve as a Marine version of the Army Rangers and the Navy SEALs, engaging in pre-invasion reconnaissance missions, long-range penetration for intelligence-gathering, and internal defense in foreign countries. Force Reconnaissance units have long existed in the Marines, and they have resisted being paired with other special forces units since SOCOM was created in 1986. Their view that the entire Corps is elite means that to single out any particular unit would be detrimental to the morale of the whole. The Defense Department emphasis on inter-service cooperation since 9/11 overcame the Marines' longstanding view on the matter.

Marines believe that their standard training is virtually the equivalent of that provided for special forces like the Green Berets and the SEALs. Basic training is a three-month affair. The first month is dedicated to physical conditioning, code of conduct, and history—an area to which the Marines believe they are the most dedicated of services. The second month comprises weapons training and outdoor survival. The final month finds the recruits engaged in more physical training as well as combat training. About 10 percent of the recruits do not make it to the end of basic training. Those who take the Officer Candidate Course find the same things they found in basic training, but even more intense. Almost half the officer candidates do not finish the course.

The final product is a soldier who believes he or she has become a part of the best and toughest branch of the American military. As one officer put it, "You aren't afraid of death or of getting wounded so much as the horror of letting the other Marines on your left and right down. It isn't the enemy so much as that 217-year-old tradition of the Corps. People expect a lot from us—and we expect more from each other. *That's* the difference between us and the other services" (Halberstadt, 1993). Those with Corps experience believe that there are no ex-Marines, only those no longer wearing the uniform.

References: Alexander, Joe, et.al., *A Fellowship of Valor* (New York: HarperCollins, 1997); Halberstadt, Hans, *US Marine Corps* (Osceola, WI: Motorbooks International, 1993); Millett, Allan, *Semper Fidelis* (New York: Macmillan, 1980).

Vandals

A northern European population that settled in North Africa during the decline of the Roman Empire.

The Vandals were one of the tribes that migrated from the area below the Baltic Sea during the late Roman Empire. They were of the same racial stock as the Goths but traveled across Germany more directly than did the Goths, who migrated at the same time but took a more southerly route before moving westward across Europe. Little is known of their early history, but the Vandals crossed into Germany about the time Rome was loosening its grip on the area in the mid-300s CE. The Vandals were actually the leaders of a group of tribes, and were themselves divided into two groups, the Asdings and the Silings. They conquered and incorporated the Sueves, another Germanic tribe, and the Alans, who were a non-Germanic people driven into Europe by the advance of the Huns.

The Vandal coalition moved across Germany as the western Goths (Visigoths) were occupying northern Italy and Dacia, and the two fought each other in the mid-fourth century. The Visigoths had the better of the encounter and the Vandals seemed to disappear for a time, but emerged again in 406 when they led their forces across the Rhine River. Their passage into western Europe was bloody as the Vandals pillaged through Gaul, areas covered by modern-day Belgium, Holland, and northern France, then turned south and cut a wide swath of destruction to the Pyrenees. This was all officially territory of the Roman Empire, and the emperor tried to convince his Visigothic allies/mercenaries to save Gaul, but by the time they turned to face the Vandal threat, the tribes had moved into northern Spain in 409.

The Vandals, like the Goths, were Arian Christians. The two peoples were of the same heritage and spoke a similar language. The Goths, however, had established themselves in Italy as occasional allies to what remained of the Roman Empire. They therefore went to Spain to regain control of the area for Rome and to carve out whatever good lands they could acquire for themselves, even if it meant making war against people much like themselves. The four Vandalic tribes had spread quickly over much of central and western Iberia, and the Goths operated out of the eastern part of the peninsula. After a failed attempt to cross over to North Africa, the Goths made war against the Vandalic tribes. After a few defeats, the Vandals appealed to Rome for protection. The emperor played one tribe against another by granting or denying favors. The imperial aid went mainly to the Asdings and the Suevians, so the Goths continued to fight the Silings and the Alans. The Silings were virtually exterminated and the

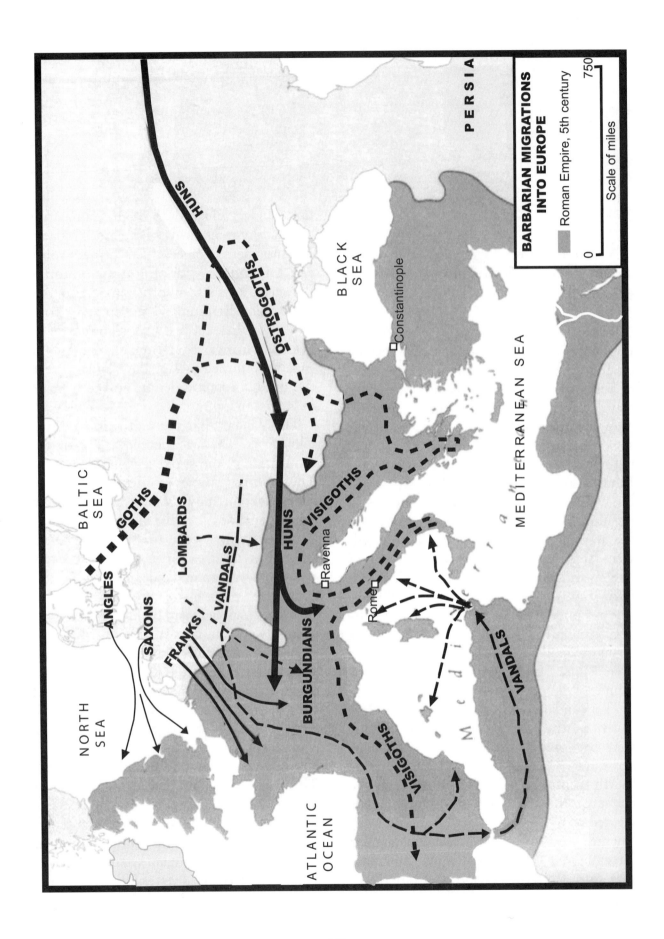

BARBARIAN MIGRATIONS
INTO EUROPE

Roman Empire, 5th century

0   Scale of miles   750

PERSIA

BLACK SEA

Constantinople

MEDITERRANEAN SEA

OSTROGOTHS

HUNS

VISIGOTHS

Ravenna

Rome

BALTIC SEA

GOTHS

ANGLES

SAXONS

LOMBARDS

VANDALS

FRANKS

NORTH SEA

BURGUNDIANS

VISIGOTHS

VANDALS

ATLANTIC OCEAN

M e d i t e r r a n e a n

Alans, after losing their king, retreated westward to join the Asdings. The ruler of this remainder came to be called "King of the Vandals and the Alans."

Once the Visigoths went about establishing their own claims, the remaining Vandals were left to themselves. An argument soon arose between the Vandals and the Sueves and, after a battle, they parted company. The Sueves stayed in northwest Iberia; the Vandals and Alans moved to the south. They fought and defeated a Roman force on their way south and established themselves in the province of Baetica. The Vandal king, Gunderic, raided into other areas of Spain and possibly across the Mediterranean into Mauritania. His brother and successor, Gaiseric, saw the potential of the farmland of North Africa, which had long been Rome's primary food source. He was leader of the Vandals when chance called them to Africa.

The general commanding Roman forces in Africa was Boniface, loyal to Rome and a strong Christian. He took a second wife, however, who was an Arian and that placed him in opposition to the Roman Catholic Church. He refused to return to Rome to answer to the government, and Boniface defeated the first army that came after him. The second one defeated him, however, and Boniface fled to the Vandals. He invited them to come to Africa and fight alongside him; in turn, he would reward them with land. Boniface provided shipping, and some 80,000 people crossed the Mediterranean, of which about 15,000 were fighting men.

The Vandals proved to be unmerciful in their treatment of the Mauritanian population. They killed people and looted towns and churches, caring nothing for Catholic shrines or priests. Gaiseric proved an able military leader and a cunning diplomat.

His treatment of Roman citizens encouraged other groups that disliked Rome to join in the fray: Moors and Egyptian Donatists attacked eastward along the Mediterranean shore, and other groups branded as heretics saw a chance to take some vengeance on their Roman oppressors. Attempts to negotiate with Gaiseric proved futile, and he not only fought the Roman armies sent against him, but he turned on Boniface as well and drove him back into Roman arms. In 430 the Vandals invaded Numidia and besieged the city of Hippo, home to St. Augustine, which held out for a year. When Boniface joined with an army sent from Constantinople in 431, Gaiseric defeated them, also, then turned back and captured Hippo.

In Rome, internal power struggles kept the government from any effective resistance to Gaiseric. Finally, the Visigoth general Aetius was able to speak for Rome and convince the Vandals to stop fighting. In 435 they were ceded the Mauritanian provinces and part of Numidia in return for acknowledging the overlordship of the Roman government. Gaiseric consolidated his hold on northwestern Africa but continued to consider his options. Basing himself in Carthage, Gaiseric built a fleet and began raiding at sea. His forces raided Italy and occupied Sicily and Sardinia. The Vandals did not long survive Gaiseric, however. Roman forces ultimately returned and reconquered the area, bringing the Vandal tribe to an end in 533.

Although the Vandals' power lasted about a century, they left behind little cultural heritage. Their time in Spain was sufficiently brief that they had no impact there, and even in North Africa they built and contributed little. The effect of the Vandal migrations and conquests was not small, however. By their very presence in

North Africa, controlling the grain-producing lands that had for centuries fed Italy, the declining power of Rome declined even faster. Without the logistical support of Africa, Roman forces could not aggressively respond to threats in Europe, mostly in Gaul. The advances of the Huns and the Ostrogoths, then of the Franks, came about more easily because Rome could not support enough troops in the field. Roman power fell more quickly, and German influence rose more rapidly in Europe because the Vandals, at Rome's back door, split the attention of the fading empire.

References: Bury, J.B., *The Invasion of Europe by the Barbarians* (New York: Russell and Russell, 1963); Isadore of Seville, *The History of the Goths, Vandals and Suevi,* trans. Guido Donini and Gordon Ford (Leiden: E.J. Brill, 1970); Thompson, E. A., *Romans and Barbarians: The Decline of the Western Empire* (Madison: University of Wisconsin Press, 1982).

Varangian Guard

An elite unit of household guards in the Byzantine Empire between the ninth and fourteenth centuries.

In the latter part of the tenth century, the Byzantine emperor Basil II recruited a number of Varangians, reputedly Norsemen from Russia, as a personal bodyguard. The term Varangian comes from the Norse *var*, meaning "pledge," and denotes one of a band of men who pledged themselves to work together for profit. Usually this meant in trade, but the oath of loyalty to each other certainly had more than commercial meaning, for they were bound to fight for each other's safety as members of a merchant band. The term also refers to men who hired themselves into the service of an overlord for a set period of time, as the Norsemen did for the lords of Novgorod and Kiev in Russia. Thus, the term *Varangian* does not necessarily mean "Viking" or "Scandinavian," although most of them were from that part of the world. Generally, however, it refers to the Scandinavian Russian empire led by the city-states of Kiev and Novgorod.

Varangians fought southward down the Volga toward territory under Byzantine control, raiding the area around Constantinople in 865. As the Byzantine emperors fought to protect their northern frontiers, they gained firsthand knowledge of the fighting abilities of these men. In 911 Prince Oleg of Russia concluded a trade agreement with Constantinople, and it was through these more peaceful contacts that Emperor Basil II began to hire Varangians for his personal guard, starting an organization that lasted until at least the 1300s. Basil made use of his new soldiers immediately, taking them with him on an expedition into Bulgaria, where the Varangians so distinguished themselves that Basil separated them from the remainder of the army in order to give them a larger share of the loot. They also served under his command in Anatolia and Georgia, continuing to fight ferociously and earn the emperor's respect. In the Balkans, the Varangians fought one of the most determined of Byzantine foes, the Pechenegs. The Pechenegs' defeat led to a peace treaty with Constantinople in 1055. After another defeat at Varangian hands in 1122, they served the emperor's army as light cavalry.

Although the Varangians served in the army that fought in Byzantine campaigns, their service as a palace guard was most important to the various emperors. They had three main functions. First, they guarded the safety of the emperor, standing at the entrance to his bedchamber and in the reception hall. Second, they occasionally were known to have guarded the imperial treasury, over the funds of which they apparently thought they exercised some control. Third, late in their tenure, they acted as prison guards and probably as torturers. The Varangian Guard was best known for its weaponry, for they carried axes, sometimes described as single-bladed and sometimes as double. "The imperial axe-bearers" is a common description of them.

The Varangian Guard's top commanders seem to have been Byzantine, although smaller units had foreign commanders. By the later stages of their service, larger numbers of Anglo-Saxons, especially from England, entered the Guard. One source refers to an "axe-bearing Keltikon," and Celt seems to have become a standard description of the Guard members by the late eleventh and early twelfth centuries, especially after the capture of England by William the Conqueror. Icelandic sagas tell of their natives serving in the Guard as well.

The primary characteristic of Guard members, apparently, was their loyalty. The Byzantine Empire was a virtual breeding ground of intrigue, and the emperors seemed always to be under threat of overthrow or assassination. By hiring foreign troops and paying them very well, the rulers hoped to avoid the problems of subversion and infiltration by local political factions. This was a successful strategy, but often put the Varangians themselves in difficulty. The generally accepted view of overthrow and assassination in the Byzantine Empire was a variation on the Chinese concept of the "Mandate of Heaven." If an individual came to the throne, it was through God's will. If he was removed,

violently or otherwise, that was also God's will. Thus, the Varangians had to accept an ever-changing political situation and be prepared to fight to the death for one emperor but immediately support his successor against whom they may have fought hours earlier. The record of the lavish gifts and bonuses given to the Varangian Guard upon the succession of a new emperor shows the Guard's ability to adapt to, and indeed profit from, this power shift.

The best known of the Varangians was Harald Sigurdson, also known as Harald Hardraada, who served in Constantinople as a young man before returning to his homeland and leading forces defeated by King Harold of England at Stamford Bridge in 1066. Harald fled his homeland at age 15 after his family, the ruling power of Norway, was defeated in battle. He served in the military in Russia, where he seems to have fallen in love with the daughter of an aristocrat, Yaroslav. She apparently was in the royal court in Constantinople, and he followed her there. Yaroslav wanted more than royal blood for his son-in-law, so he bade Harald make a name for himself before he could have the daughter's hand in marriage. Harald arrived in Constantinople in 1034 and entered into the service of the newly crowned Emperor Michael IV. The Icelandic saga penned by Snorri Sturluson tells Harald's tale and describes him as an outstanding military leader, determined and clever, and always able to end a battle with much plunder. Contemporary accounts written by Byzantine observers confirm his abilities in campaigns in Sicily and Bulgaria.

After the Byzantine defeat at the hands of the Turks at Manzikert in 1071, the Byzantine army became even more dependent on mercenaries, and the Varangians served as the loyal core of the military.

They were not always victorious, however. By 1082, the Guard was becoming increasingly Anglo-Saxon, and it was the descendants of the Norsemen, the Normans of France, who ironically were the instrument of a Guard disaster. The great Norman leader Robert Guiscard aspired to become the Byzantine emperor, so he led his forces out of Sicily across the Adriatic Sea. He laid siege to the city of Durazzo on the island of Corfu in 1081 but was forced to lift the siege upon the arrival of the Byzantine emperor, Alexius Comnenus, with 50,000 men. The Varangian Guard, some of whose members had fought the Normans at Hastings in 1066, couldn't wait for the bulk of the army to position itself. They flung themselves at the Norman position and succeeded in forcing a hasty retreat, but their pause to plunder the Norman base gave their enemy time to regroup and counterattack. Surrounded, the Guard fought to the last man.

The Guard also distinguished itself in a losing effort in 1204 when the Fourth Crusade attacked Constantinople instead of Muslim targets further inland. The Varangians defended the walls of the city for two days until Venetian ships flung incendiaries over the walls and set the city afire. In the ensuing melee, the Varangian Guard was virtually wiped out. The final references to Varangians in Constantinople occur in 1395 and 1400, when some appeared to have been serving in administrative, rather than military, capacities in the Byzantine government.

References: Bartusis, Mark C., *The Late Byzantine Army* (Philadelphia: University of Pennsylvania Press, 1992; Davidson, H. R. Ellis, *The Viking Road to Byzantium* (London: George Allen & Unwin, 1976).

Viet Minh

A guerrilla force resisting French colonization in Southeast Asia in the 1940s and 1950s.

Southeast Asia has long been a region dominated by foreign power. The Chinese Han dynasty imposed its will on the area in 208 BCE. They found, like every other power trying to occupy Vietnam, that the country might be occupied but the population would not be absorbed. The land that the Chinese called *Nam Viet* ("land of the southern Viets") was the eastern coastal region of Southeast Asia along the South China Sea, composed of three provinces: Tonkin in the north, Annam in the center, and Cochin China in the south. The people of these three provinces resisted Chinese authority constantly, staging revolts and dislodging the invaders, only to be reoccupied later. Still they fought on, and the Vietnamese people developed a warrior cult that worshipped military virtues and accomplishments. The leaders who fought the Chinese were national heroes above and beyond any other. Over time Chinese dynasties came and went, but they all tried to dominate Vietnam. The people accepted portions of Chinese governmental and social concepts, but continually rejected assimilation.

In the 1600s a power struggle within Vietnam broke out between two aristocratic families, the Nguyens and the Trinhs. The Trinhs won the power struggle and came to dominate Tonkin in the north, while the Nguyens retreated southward and established a power base in Cochin China and Annam. The two regions began to develop different personalities. The south, where the Mekong River provided periodic flooding for regular crops, developed into an easygoing society that could prosper without too much work. In the north, the Red River was too unpredictable to provide such a lifestyle, and the people needed a centralized governmental system to build dikes and wrest a living from the soil. The southerners also embraced Indian Buddhism, which taught of a future Nirvana achieved after life cycles of suffering. The northerners practiced Chinese Buddhism, which taught that anyone could achieve the status of a Buddha and live a peaceful and rewarding life in the present. The northerners created a society that depended on hard work and, at the same time, the ability to enjoy a life of personal satisfaction. The southerners had an easier physical life but without the immediate internal satisfaction. Thus, the north was more aggressive; the south, more accepting of what life had to offer.

In northern Annam, a region that seemed to embody elements of both northern and southern Vietnam, lay the province of Nghe An. The land provided scanty sustenance, but the people were intellectual, creative, and stubborn. The population of Nghe An produced the best poets and artists in Vietnam, but also the most discontented radicals. When France established a colonial presence in Southeast Asia in the middle 1800s, it was Nghe An that produced the first dissidents demanding independence. Just as the Vietnamese had spent centuries resisting Chinese rule, of which they were finally free in 938, they had not forgotten the stories of their military past and would just as tenaciously resist French rule. Into a family of anti-French agitators was born in 1890 Nguyen Sinh Cung. His sister became a well-known balladeer, singing songs protesting colonialism. His brother joined a conspiracy to poison French military officers. His

father, an employee of the ruling mandarin class through which the French ruled, was vehemently anti-French, a stance that ultimately got him fired from his civil service position. In such a family it is not surprising that Nguyen Sinh Cung became a revolutionary himself.

Unhappy with life in Vietnam, Nguyen left in 1912 aboard a French steamer on which he worked as a messboy. He sailed the world and saw the effects of colonialism everywhere: French Algeria and British South Africa in particular. He spent some time in the United States and was impressed with the democratic system and the ideas of the American forbears. He was working in a London restaurant when World War I broke out, and moved to Paris in 1918. There he found a large Vietnamese immigrant community, and he frequented their restaurants and became well known. His dormant political senses returned, and he joined the French Socialist Party. In 1919 as the Allies were meeting in Versailles to dictate the fate of Germany and much of the rest of the world, he composed a manifesto calling for the recognition of individual rights in Vietnam and the treatment of Vietnamese as equals within the French empire. He gained official notice, even if his demands did not. He turned away from the socialists and became one of the founding members of the French Communist Party. He had been given some of the writings of Vladimir Lenin, and he saw in them the path to Vietnamese liberation.

In Paris, Nguyen Sinh Cung began calling himself Nguyen *Ai Quoc*, or "Nguyen the Patriot." After traveling to the Soviet Union in 1923, he served as an advisor to the Soviet envoy to China in 1924. He met more Vietnamese immigrants, including exiles who had fled the

French after revolutionary activities at home got them in trouble. In Canton he organized a communist youth committee, then returned to Moscow. He traveled in communist circles in Europe, then in 1928 spent time in Bangkok organizing Vietnamese immigrants into communist organizations. In 1929 he went to Hong Kong, where he met two people who would assist him and Vietnam immensely over the next decades: Le Duc Tho and Vo Nguyen Giap. They were both from upper class families, but both had come to despise French rule.

In 1930, discontented peasants in Nghe An province marched to protest high taxes. The French government called in aircraft to strafe the column and killed some 175 people, then another 15 who later came to look for survivors among the bodies. This, more than any other incident, coalesced resistance to the French ruling elite. Although the mandarins through whom they had ruled had been abolished as a class, the French now governed through Vietnamese who embraced French culture by becoming Catholics and speaking French. They saw in a popular peasant rising the end of their preferential treatment, should the French be removed, and the French saw the potential for a mass movement that could lead to the loss of a colony. When the French began rounding up anyone with revolutionary tendencies, Nguyen Ai Quoc fled to Hong Kong. There, British authorities imprisoned him. He escaped in 1932 and spent five years in the Soviet Union before returning to China. He secretly entered his homeland in 1941 with Vo Nguyen Giap and established a headquarters in a cave in the north. Japan had succeeded the French as occupiers of his country, and he would fight them as well. In 1941 Nguyen Ai Quoc created the Viet Nam Doc Lap Dong Minh Hoi (League for Vietnamese Independence), or Viet Minh. He also changed his name yet again to the one for which he became world famous: *Ho Chi Minh*, or "He Who Enlightens."

He sought aid from Chiang Kai-shek in China, but was imprisoned for his trouble. Released in 1943 when the Chinese decided he may be of some assistance fighting the Japanese, he returned home to where Giap was organizing and fighting a guerrilla war against the Japanese and the French colonial infrastructure that still remained. Ho sought and obtained the support of the American Office of Strategic Services, receiving weapons in return for information on Japanese troop movements and aid in returning downed U.S. pilots. When Japan was defeated in 1945, Ho thought that all his work had paid off. The Japanese were gone and so were the French, but new troubles emerged. Chinese troops occupied territory in the north, and in order to remove them diplomatically rather than militarily, it was necessary to cooperate with France. That, however, brought the French colonial system back into Vietnam. Appeals to the United States for political assistance to convince France to grant Vietnamese independence gained sympathetic words but little else.

Ho Chi Minh went back to fighting his guerrilla war, now against the French. Giap proved to be an able military mind, and the hit-and-run tactics that had served them so well against the Japanese continued to work through the late 1940s and into the 1950s. French public opinion favored an end to colonialism in Vietnam, but the renewed interest of the United States, now dedicated to fighting communists anywhere, kept France in the country and in the fight. The Viet Minh over time not only continued to harm the French military, but gained continued popular support and a growing recruitment. In 1954, the Viet Minh did what every successful guerrilla campaign ultimately accomplishes: They built enough strength to beat the enemy at his own game, in a head-to-head pitched battle. In May 1954, the French base at Dien Bien Phu fell as French and Vietnamese negotiators in Geneva were discussing peace.

France promised to withdraw completely within two years, with national elections to be held in 1956 to elect a popular government. The United States, however, knew that Ho Chi Minh could not lose a popular election, so they unilaterally supported the creation of a government in the south based on the old French hierarchy and held it in place with American financial and military aid. The south, although socially different from the north, had always been part of a Vietnamese "nation," but after 1956 a distinct Republic of South Vietnam was created to formally separate the two regions. Ho Chi Minh and his followers, with their primary control and popular support among the northerners, responded by creating their own government. Most of the communists in the south (some 10,000) moved north, while those in the north with French connections fled south to avoid retribution. In reality, this exchange of populations ended the Viet Minh, for the military force under the control of Ho Chi Minh and Vo Nguyen Giap became the North Vietnamese army, a regular military force. The communists in the south came to be referred to as the Viet Cong, or Vietnamese Communists.

The southerners, who had lived longer under French rule but for the most part were more amenable to it, provided only some communist party strength. As the ruler of South Vietnam, Ngo Dinh Diem proved to be as oppressive as the pro-French Vietnamese had been during French rule. The communists began to gain recruits. What started as a nationalist attempt to free Vietnam from foreign rule became an ideological war between Ho Chi Minh's communist training and organization on the one hand and the anticommunist determination of the United States on the other. Although the United States threatened to abandon South Vietnam because of the oppressive policies Ngo Dinh Diem imposed on his people (mainly religious in nature), the administration of President Lyndon Johnson in the United States brought ideological concerns to military fruition. The guerrilla tactics that the Viet Minh had used against both French and Japanese worked just as well against the Americans, who brought massive logistical superiority and a colonial superiority complex. American Secretary of State Henry Kissinger once commented that he refused to believe the United States could be beaten by a group of farmers in black pajamas. That was much the same attitude held by the Chinese, French, and Japanese. It was also, ironically, the same attitude held by the British government when confronted with a group of farmers in the American colonies in the 1770s. Ho Chi Minh did not live to see the formation of an independent Vietnam, but it was created nonetheless. Communism no longer holds the sway it once did in the country, but the Vietnamese once again proved to be impossible for a foreign power to assimilate.

References: Davidson, Phillip, *Vietnam at War* (New York: Oxford University Press, 1988); Olson, James, and Randy Roberts, *Where the Domino Fell* (New York: St. Martin's Press, 1996); Short, Anthony, *The Origins of the Vietnam War* (New York: Longman, 1989).

Vikings

An aggressive Scandinavian population known for ruthlessness, raiding, commerce, and widespread settlement during the eighth through eleventh centuries.

The Vikings came out of Scandinavia in the later years of the eighth century to attack and plunder whatever source of wealth they could find. It was this raiding that possibly gave the Vikings their name, for *vikingr* translates as "sea-rover" or "pirate." It is also possible, however, that it denotes the region from which they originated, for the Vik is the stretch of water also known as the Skagerrak, the straits between the North and the Baltic seas. Whatever its origin, the name came to mean terror for residents of northern Europe, the British Isles, and even the Mediterranean.

The first Viking raid of consequence was at the Northumbrian abbey of Lindisfarne in 793. Abbeys, monasteries, and churches were regular Viking targets because they were defended lightly, if at all, and contained large amounts of wealth. What precipitated this onslaught into the European world is a matter of some debate. It probably had to do with growing population pressures in the Scandinavian countries, where farmland was at a premium. It also could have been aided by the defeat of the Frisians by Charlemagne in the late eighth century. The Frisians, living in modern Belgium/Holland, had dominated the waters of the North Sea. But now, with Frisian power broken, the Vikings were no longer bottled up in their homelands. In addition, raiding was easier and more profitable for some time in Britain, because Charlemagne and his son, Louis the Pious,

maintained a stout defense of continental Europe. When Louis' sons began a dynastic struggle for the Holy Roman Empire after Louis' death, the internal struggle diverted the military from the outside threat. It is also possible that Scandinavian mercenaries fought for Louis' son Lothar.

Whatever the reason, targets of opportunity were plentiful, and the Vikings took advantage of them all. Their raiding was so effective because of their transport, the Viking longship. Built with a shallow draft and a wide beam, these vessels were powered by both sail and oars. They were seaworthy, but with a shallow enough draft to allow them to land on any flat stretch of beach. Because harbors were unnecessary, the Vikings were able to arrive without warning, attack before a defense could be mounted, and withdraw before reinforcements could arrive. As pillage was their pay, it was the civilian population who suffered the most from these forays, and the prayer "God deliver us from the fury of the Northmen" was commonly spoken in the ninth and tenth centuries. Indeed, the only way to spare a town from pillage was by bribery, and *danegeld* (literally translated as "Danish money," but meaning bribes initially, and, later, legal fines or compensation for damages) was collected in huge amounts. Usually this totaled hundreds if not thousands of pounds of silver. This usually bought immediate, but temporary, protection, because other Viking bands could arrive within months.

The Vikings laid out spheres of influence, with the Swedes directing their attention eastward to the settlement of towns along the Volga, from which the nation of Russia ultimately formed. The Danes spent most of their energies in Britain and Ireland, while the Norse focused more on

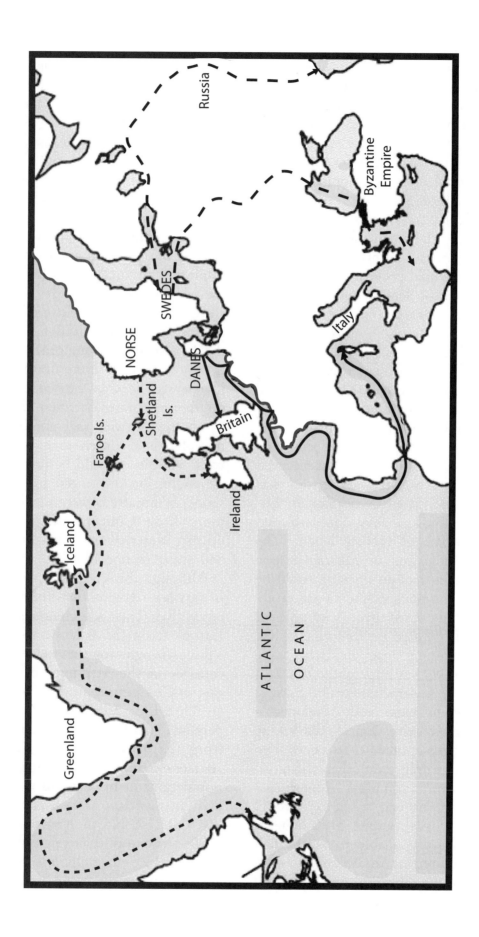

continental Europe. The Danes soon replaced raiding with conquest, for a time dominating northern England and most of Ireland. The Norse established settlements at the mouths of the major French rivers, from which they rowed upriver for attacks in the interior. Paris was a popular target, often attacked or held for the danegeld ransom. The Norse success was so great that land along the northeastern coast was offered to them as a permanent settlement if the settlers would prevent other Vikings from sailing up the Seine. Thus, the Norsemen became Normans; and Normandy, their home.

Most Vikings were armed alike, wearing a conical helmet (without horns or wings) and sometimes chain mail. They carried a sword or axe and a round wooden shield with a central metal boss to protect the hand. The axe could be either single or double bladed and usually bore carved decorations in the metal. The sword was on the Frankish pattern, common in Europe, being almost always double-bladed and fairly broad, of varying length. The sword fight consisted of hacking at one another's shield until an opening could be forced, with the point of the sword rarely used. They also carried spears with poles of ash that could be used for throwing or like a pike for fighting closer in. Bows were sometimes used, but apparently it was a weapon of the lower classes. The Vikings fought hand to hand and developed a reputation for ferocity. Among the Viking ranks were those called *berserkers* who would, through trance or other self-motivation, become unthinking killing machines until battle's end, when they would collapse from the output of adrenalin. When occasionally unable to reach their ships for rapid retreat, the Vikings showed themselves quite able to quickly build strong defensive positions that usually proved unassailable.

The Vikings followed their kings or other aristocrats, and the soldier was referred to as a *hird*, or *huscarl*. The king or *jarl* (earl) would call out his men for campaign, and the standard period of duty was four months per year. Mercenaries were also employed, and often the danegeld was collected to pay them, with the rest of the plunder going to the regular soldiers. The smallest unit in the army was the ship's crew, and the smallest ship allowed was 26 oars. Most ships tended to number between 32 and 50 oars, though the largest ships were probably used for transport nearer home rather than sea journeys. The ship carried the necessary number of soldier/oarsmen and additional troops up to twice that number, although one ship is recorded to have carried 574 men. The fleets could be just a few ships, depending on the target, but fleets in the scores or hundreds were much more common. King Cnut in the early eleventh century was reputed to have had a fleet of 850 ships in one flotilla.

Although the Vikings were also traders, it was as fighters that they made their reputation. Their settlements spread across Europe from the Atlantic to Russia, and Vikings fought for themselves or as mercenaries in the Mediterranean and as far east as Constantinople. There the Varangian Guard of Vikings was created as a personal guard for the Byzantine Emperor from the 900s until 1400. Other Viking settlers explored further west, establishing populations in Iceland and Greenland that exist to this day, as well as exploring the east coast of North America in the year 1000. The end of their reign of terror came in the 1100s through a combination of absorption by the conquered populations and a widespread conversion to Christianity from previously pagan beliefs.

References: Arbman, Olger, *The Vikings* (New York: Frederick Praeger, 1961); Jones, Gwyn, *A History of the Vikings* (New York: Oxford University Press, 1984 [1968]); Norman, A. V. B., *The Medieval Soldier* (New York: Thomas Crowell, 1971).

Waffen SS

An elite force operating in the Nazi army during World War II.

The *Schutzstaffeln* (Protection Squads), or SS, have an unusual reputation. They are regarded by many as outstanding soldiers who put forth the best performances of German soldiers in World War II. They are also hated as butchers and torturers of

"Volunteer for the Waffen-SS". A recruitment poster for the fighting unit of Hitler's Schutzstaffeln.

civilians, both in and out of concentration camps. As will be seen, the SS bears responsibility for many of the horrors of German actions in World War II, but the Waffen SS achieved positive reviews as a separate branch of the overall organization.

The SS had its roots in the early days of the Nazi Party with bodyguards chosen to drive and protect Adolph Hitler. This was a personal guard that was recruited in major cities where Hitler traveled and rarely numbered more than 20 in a local group and less than 300 in total nationwide. This group differed from the *Sturmabteilung* (Storm Troops), or SA, which were the paramilitary arm of the Nazi Party. Organized to protect party functions and attack the gathering of rival parties, the SA grew inordinately through the 1920s and became a fearsome group. Unfortunately for Hitler, they also came to be fearsome within the party. Under the leadership of Ernst Roehm, the SA was dominated by street thugs operating with some legitimacy within the Nazi organization. However, by the end of the decade they had grown too large and too independent. Their brutality, which had been effective in the early days when the Nazi Party was being established, now reflected badly on a party establishing itself as a major player in German politics. Hitler began depending more and more on the SS, under its director Heinrich Himmler.

Himmler received training in agriculture and attempted to raise chickens, but found

355

his experience in the Nazi Party more successful. Without an intimidating presence, he seemed an unlikely role model for a "protection" organization, but his subservient manner and utter devotion to Hitler filled the bill. Himmler viewed the SS as not just a bodyguard group, but as an adjunct to the army that would incorporate the best of German manhood. It would serve as an advertisement for Aryan supremacy by accepting only what Himmler considered to be perfect specimens of tall, blond, muscular young men with impeccable breeding—that is, having no Jewish or Slavic ancestry.

When Hitler rose to the position of chancellor of Germany in January 1933, the SA became a liability. Roehm's group continued to act like thugs and became less responsive to Hitler's will, so much so that Hitler feared Roehm's personal ambition to turn the SA into the new German army. The SA expanded from 300,000 in January 1933 to three million in early 1934, incorporating other nationalist paramilitary groups and unemployed men looking for authority and income. Himmler had meanwhile expanded the SS to about 50,000 and had convinced Hitler to make him head of the Berlin secret police. Himmler had already gained control of most of the police forces in major cities around Germany, so the number of men under his control was much greater than just the SS. Himmler was aided in this expansion by Reinhard Heydrich, who came to operate Himmler's *Sicherheitsdienst* (Security Service), or SD.

In talks with the army high command, Hitler was given an ultimatum: Get rid of the SA or lose the support of the army, one of Germany's most powerful and respected organizations. The SS received orders to assassinate Roehm and his inner circle of advisors. Starting on the night of June 30, 1934, the SS began the killing in what was called the Blood Purge or, later, the Night of the Long Knives. The total number of SA killed is unknown (estimates go as high as 2,000), but its leaders all died, along with some of Himmler's personal rivals. The SA was officially disbanded and the SS came to be the elite troops of the Third Reich. The army was glad to see the SA removed, but surprised that the SS had emerged as a more serious rival. The SS was loyal not to Germany, but to Hitler, for each member (especially of the *Leibstandarte Adolph Hitler*, Hitler's personal guard) swore this oath: "I swear to you, Adolph Hitler, as Führer and Reich Chancellor, loyalty and bravery. I vow to you, and to those you have named to command me, obedience unto death, so help me God."

The SS remained a political tool with military duties and was involved in Germany's reoccupation of the Rhineland in 1936 and the *Anschluss*, or joining, of Germany and Austria in March 1938. That same year, Hitler put control of Germany's armed forces under his direct command and, while stating that the SS would remain a political unit, ordered it armed and trained to assist the army in times of need. The SS participated in the occupation of Czechoslovakia in spring 1939, by which time its members were training with the army and dressed in the same field gray uniforms, although with their own collar tabs and other insignia. They were at division strength, with the addition of artillery, in September 1939 when World War II started in Poland.

Although their performance in the Polish invasion was not stellar, it was sufficiently good for Himmler to ask for, and receive, permission to expand the SS from one division to three. In order to build quickly and have men with some experience, Himmler drafted the policemen who had been under his control for some years. He also began to recruit among the *Volksdeutsch*, the Germans who lived in the newly acquired Polish and Slovakian territories. Through the months of winter 1939–1940, Himmler consolidated the training units, bodyguard, cadet schools, and reserves under the umbrella designation *Waffen* (Weapons) SS, which were the fighting units, as opposed to the concentration camp SS guards.

The new organization's first remarkable performance came in the campaign against France in spring 1940. The Waffen SS distinguished itself by driving 135 miles through Dutch resistance on the first day and was involved in the surrender of Rotterdam. Transferred south into France, the SS saw action in the attack on British forces around Dunkirk. Here, an SS company commander accepted the surrender of almost 100 British soldiers, then massacred them. Although not accepted policy, this was to be the first of many random acts of terror perpetrated by some SS commanders.

After the successful German campaigns against Holland, Belgium, Denmark, and Norway, Himmler began to recruit new soldiers from these occupied countries. Although not Germans, they were of acceptable Aryan stock and had already formed paramilitary right-wing organizations in the late 1930s. By summer 1941, SS strength stood at five divisions, divided among the three prongs of the Nazi advance into the Soviet Union in June. Because all were motorized divisions and had gained a reputation as good fighters motivated by their status and racial indoctrination, the SS units were often in the news. They became even better known

once the invasion was well under way, when the underground Russian partisan movement began harassing the German supply lines. Waffen SS units were detailed to engage in counterinsurgency and often did so with gusto, establishing their reputation for ruthlessness in their treatment of suspected partisans. It was also during the autumn of 1942 that SS divisions were withdrawn from the Eastern Front and relocated temporarily to France to receive and train with new equipment. The SS divisions became panzer grenadiers, not just motorized, but in tracked vehicles with newly added tank units.

More experience on the Eastern Front enhanced the SS divisions' reputations, and they were rewarded with the best and newest equipment. This was used to good effect in the counteroffensives around Stalingrad in February 1943, but in the summer of that year, the Waffen SS units were mauled along with the rest of the German forces at the massive tank battle at Kursk. From this point on, the SS and their compatriots were on the defensive. As the tide turned against the Germans, Himmler was obliged to abandon his ethnic views and recruit new SS units from other occupied countries, including what he considered "subhuman" Slavic populations. These foreign units consisted of troops from Hungary, the Caucasus, Bosnia-Herzegovina, Turkmenistan, and even captured Indian troops. Unlike their western European counterparts, they performed consistently badly for the Germans. The recruitment of troops from the Baltic states, Ukraine, and other provinces that disliked communism came too late to be of effective use.

On the Western Front, the SS were active in attempts to blunt Allied thrusts out of the Normandy region. The armored units performed well, outfighting their Allied counterparts, but were unable to overcome Allied air superiority and an ever-decreasing number of supplies from Germany. Although badly beaten in the fighting near Mortain in northern France in August 1944, SS tank units won a hard-fought victory a month later over British and American airborne forces attempting to establish a bridgehead over the Rhine at the Dutch town of Arnhem. In December, Hitler once again called on his SS forces, in which he had had the greatest faith through the years, to launch a surprise counteroffensive through British and American lines in Luxembourg. The Ardennes offensive, to break through the Allied positions and capture the huge number of supplies collecting in Antwerp, got off to a good start in the bad weather of mid-December, but once again the Germans could not stand up to Allied air superiority or a flanking attack by George Patton's Third Army cutting them off from the south. In this campaign, SS units again became notable for the execution of prisoners.

For the remainder of the war, SS units could do little better than other units in the German army. Hitler continued to order them to where the fighting was thickest, but their increasing lack of equipment and manpower spelled their ultimate doom. An SS guard was on hand at the end of April 1945 to carry Hitler's body to the surface above his bunker in Berlin and destroy it. The führer had died a suicide.

The SS leaders were brought up on war crimes charges after the war, and with justification. Some SS units actively engaged in activity well beyond the pale of decency—even in war, including the suppression of the Jewish uprising in Warsaw and the execution of partisans in the Soviet Union. There were also regular transfers of soldiers between front-line and concentration camp duties, where the worst of the crimes against humanity took place. Still, most of the Waffen SS performed well and honorably in combat, with a relative few engaging in war crimes. Because their creed from the beginning of their existence was racial purity, they drew upon themselves after the war a full measure of blame for the awful acts perpetrated upon concentration camp victims.

References: Höhne, Heinz, *The Order of the Death's Head,* trans. Richard Barry (London: Coward, McCann & Geoghegan, 1969); Keegan, John, *Waffen SS: The Asphalt Soldiers* (New York: Ballantine, 1970).

White Company

A unit of mercenaries operating in medieval Italy, 1361–1364.

Among the many groups of condottieri, the mercenary troops of Italy in the 1300s through the 1500s, one of the best known was the White Company. Its leader, John Hawkwood, was probably the best known of the captains-general of the era. The White Company got its name from the fact that the soldiers serving in it went to great lengths to make sure their armor was highly polished (often using goat bone marrow), so the Italians gave it the name *Compagnia Bianca.*

Hawkwood and most of the White Company were from the British Isles. They had served in the army of the English king during the Hundred Years War and found themselves unemployed when the Treaty of Bretigny brought the fighting, at least temporarily, to an end in 1360. Many of the knights had served both English and French monarchs in that conflict, but had no domains of their own to which they could return. Therefore, they banded together to continue their previous practice of living off the land. This naturally aroused the anger of the French king, who appealed to English King Edward III to rid his country of these "free companies." Edward had mixed success in complying with this request, but the free companies found that work could be had in the employ of Italian city-states. Most of Hawkwood's compatriots left France for Italy in 1361, but Hawkwood stayed behind for a few months. The White Company first organized itself under the leadership of a German knight, Albert Stertz, who spoke Italian and had served in Italy before. He got the group its first commission and led the members in their first combat as the White Company, but when Hawkwood joined the Company in 1362, the men voted him their new commander. Stertz became second-in-command and proved invaluable in negotiations in the early days before Hawkwood became fluent in Italian.

The White Company was made up predominantly of knights who, together with their squires and pages, formed the basic unit, called the "lance." In combat, however, these knights tended to fight on foot. While in the service of King Edward III, Hawkwood had learned firsthand the massive destruction that could be dealt by bowmen to heavily armored knights on horseback. Thus, in combat Hawkwood's men used their lances like pikes: Encountering this defense in a square, no charging cavalry could survive the pikes, while on offense the massive hedgehog formation recalled the Greek phalanx. This strategy was at variance with the normal condottieri units that relied on heavy cavalry. In Hawkwood's Company, horses were used for pursuit once the enemy had broken

(the page would come running with the knight's mount) or for retreat if the battle went badly. As auxiliaries, Hawkwood commanded a force of English archers. Their longbows had proven the key ingredient in English victories at Agincourt and Crécy, and their quickly shot arrows could penetrate armor. The Company also had slingers as well as men carrying flint, steel, and tinder for setting afire defensive positions and dwellings. Burning houses aided in the spread of panic among defenders.

The White Company's first action took place shortly after their entrance into Italy in 1361. As they marched out of the Piedmont area into Lombardy, the city of Milan sought to bribe them to keep peaceful. Stertz pretended to accept the offer to negotiate, then attacked the countryside around the city during New Year's Eve celebrations. His men grabbed all the loot they could and 600 nobles. As was customary at the time, the nobles were not harmed but held for ransom. The White Company made 100,000 gold florins for their night's work. Indeed, it was the ability to march and fight at night that distinguished not just the White Company but all English troops. Used to harsher weather conditions at home, the Italian nights bothered them little.

For all its fame, the life of the White Company was short. The word of the English escapade at Milan had reached Pisa, and Hawkwood's men were contracted to that city-state in its conflict with Florence when they went into action in February 1364. The campaign did not start well, as Florentine forces (mostly German mercenaries) bested Hawkwood's unit in a few skirmishes. In April, reinforced, Hawkwood led his Company and the remainder of forces under Pisan hire in an attack on Florence. They were blocked 12 miles from the city at the town of Prato. Hawkwood drew back and tried another route, negotiating rough terrain to secure the town of Fiesole, from whose heights he could look down on Florence. Hawkwood and his advisors decided the best time to attack would be May 1, hoping to take advantage of the city's May Day revelry as they had on New Year's Eve. The Pisan force successfully occupied the suburbs of Florence, but could make no headway against the city walls. Still, there was sufficient loot to justify their attack as well as enough destruction to please their employers. After a night of their own revelry back in Fiesole, they proceeded to harass and pillage the countryside, attacking Florence just often enough to keep the defenders from sallying out.

Unable to defeat Hawkwood's command by force, the Florentines tried bribery. It was successful. They convinced a portion of the attacking army to change sides, and the White Company took money to declare a five-month truce. When offered another large sum to abandon the Pisans for Florentine employment, Hawkwood refused. He stood by his bargain with Pisa, but a number of his men found the idea a good one. Many left the White Company, including Stertz, and Hawkwood was left with only 800 men. This effectively ended the attack on Florence.

Stertz re-formed some of those who had changed sides into a new unit, the Company of the Star, which soon was in the employ of Siena. Hawkwood later fought for Milan and was for a while employed by the Catholic Church. His final and longest-lasting employer was Florence, which he served faithfully until his death in 1394. He was given a public funeral and treated as a hero. Hawkwood had not only fought well for his employers, but he profited well, as did the men under his command. From his time in service with Pisa, Hawkwood had acquired the nickname Giovanni Acuto (John the Sharp), partly because of the difficulty in transcribing "Hawkwood" phonetically into Italian (which lacks the "h" and "w" sounds), but mainly because of his ability to drive a hard bargain. Hawkwood's service and reputation for loyalty, in a time and place in which fidelity was rare, made his reputation grander than any of the White Company with whom he had originally served.

References: Deiss, Joseph Jay, *Captains of Fortune* (New York: Thomas Crowell Company, 1967); Trease, Geoffrey, *The Condottieri* (New York: Holt, Rinehart and Winston, 1971).

Wild Geese

Irish exiles fighting with French and Spanish armies in the seventeenth and eighteenth centuries.

It seems as though the Irish and English have always been mutually antagonistic, certainly since the Norman conquest of Ireland in the late eleventh century. Resistance to English domination has been a regular facet of their relationship, and has shown itself in a number of ways. The Wild Geese were exiled from Ireland following the failed attempt by the Stuart dynasty to reclaim the throne of England and reestablish Catholic rule. James II led an uprising in Ireland in 1689 which was countered by English troops sent over by King William III. After his forces were defeated at the Boyne River in July 1690, James fled to France. A year later the rebellion was completely crushed. Although William proposed leniency for the Irish, including safe transport of their soldiers to France, the Protestant-dominated Irish Parliament instead adopted a harsh anti-Catholic penal code. These laws discriminated against the Irish in their own homeland, including denying them the ability to enlist in the British army. Although that may seem an option Irishmen would not have exercised anyway, inclusion of Irish troops could well have mitigated the flavor of foreign military rule on the island. Many Irishmen took the transport offer and went to France, hoping someday to return to their home victorious.

Through the first half of the eighteenth century, Irish soldiers settled in France, joining the army while marrying French women and having half-French children. They came to be called the Wild Geese, for they had flown far from home and seemed to be perpetually wandering. In 1745 they received an opportunity to fight the English once more. By this time, the men in command of the Irish regiments were second-generation Frenchmen, named Dillon, Lally, and Clare. James Dillon, called by the French Chevalier de Dillon, at age 46 commanded one of the regiments. At age 43, Arthur de Lally de Tollendal commanded a second. In command of a third, and in overall command of the brigade, was the sixth viscount Clare and ninth earl of Thomond, whose residence outside Ireland apparently meant little to him in claiming those titles. These men had relatives who had made their peace with the English and lived in Ireland, but these three had been raised by the brigade and knew no other home.

The latest Stuart pretender to the English throne, Prince Charles Edward, in 1745 again hoped that with French aid he could restore the Stuart dynasty. Europe was in the midst of the War of the Austrian Succession, wherein France and Bavaria

were aiding Frederick of Prussia against the empress of Austria, Maria Theresa, in her bid to inherit her father's throne. Supporting the empress were the German states of Saxony and Hanover (English King George II's homeland), the Spanish Netherlands, and England. With English troops on the continent, Irish troops in the service of French King Louis XV looked for the opportunity to draw some English blood.

Their time to shine came in May 1745 in Flanders at the battle of Fontenoy. The French General Maurice de Saxe, one of the most talented generals France has produced, laid siege to the Flemish town of Tournai. The duke of Cumberland, George II's son, led a combined Anglo-Dutch-Hanoverian force to relieve the city. Saxe left some 18,000 men to maintain the siege and placed the remaining 52,000 troops at the town of Fontenoy, on Cumberland's path. Saxe had his army dig a long line of entrenchments stretching from the Scheldt River on his right at the town of Anthoin, some two miles to the town of Fontenoy, then past that to Barri Wood. Between the towns and the woods he constructed three redoubts within which he placed most of his artillery. Cumberland would have to detour widely to bypass the French force, or attack it head-on. Saxe was banking on the latter choice, and Cumberland obliged. Saxe did have two conditions that hampered his performance, however. He was suffering from dropsy to such an extent that he had to have his swollen body hauled around the battleground in a cart. He also had King Louis XV in camp. Louis was little trouble, but his army of courtiers wore Saxe's nerves thin.

Cumberland's army numbered 50,000, of which 12,000 were British infantry and another 3,000 cavalry, 8,000 Hanoverians, and the remainder Dutch and Austrians in whom Cumberland had little faith. Although he realized the difficulty of attacking prepared positions in a frontal assault, he trusted his infantry. His redcoats were renowned for their discipline and tenacity, and both were sorely tested on May 10, 1745. After watching Dutch cavalry fruitlessly charge French positions on the flanks, then turn and flee the field, Cumberland massed his infantry in a huge square, British in the lead and Hanoverians covering the rear. His attack on the center of the French line allowed the French artillery in the redoubts on his flanks to continually rake his force, and both grapeshot and roundshot tore massive holes in the lines.

The British infantry closed ranks and pressed on, losing men at each step. When the British were within 50 yards of their entrenchments, the French infantry rose and loosed a massive volley that again wiped out ranks of redcoats. The British pressed on. At 30 yards away, they halted. Almost all firing on the field stopped. The British dressed their ranks, then Lieutenant Colonel Lord Charles Hay stepped in front of his men and faced the French. He took out a silver flask, toasted the French with an inflammatory remark about their poor performance in the last battle between the French and English, then saluted the French and returned to his men as they gave him three cheers. The French returned the salute and, as they were doing so, found themselves mowed down by the first volley of English musket fire. From that point on the redcoats stood and fired volley after volley, one rank firing as the next two reloaded, then took their place. Wave after wave of French soldiery died in repeated attempts to come to grips with the British, but the disciplined fire upon which Cumberland had depended proved its

worth. Panicked French cavalry, turned back by the awful fire, streamed to the rear past their king, who refused to evacuate.

Deadly as their fire was, the British and Hanoverians remained under constant French bombardment from the front and both flanks, and their numbers continued to dwindle. Then, Saxe sent in the Wild Geese. They had taken some casualties in the opening British volleys, but nothing like they took in this charge that broke the British assault. Although the first wave of Irish were mowed down, the second and successive waves closed and fought hand to hand with the redcoats. It was melee fighting at its worst and the Irish took the highest casualties of any unit in the French army that day. Unable to withstand the fury of the Irish and the pounding of the artillery, the British conducted an orderly withdrawal, firing and holding back any serious pursuit.

The Wild Geese lost 270 dead, including 13 officers, and another 400 wounded—one-sixth of their force. These were among the 7,200 reported French casualties. Their enemy had left behind at least 7,500 dead and wounded, and Cumberland had to withdraw from the field. Within weeks, Saxe had not only brought about the fall of Tournai, but had gone on to capture almost all of Flanders. Lally, the Irish brigade commander, was promoted for his efforts at Fontenoy, but was transferred to India to fight the British there in a losing cause that brought about his disgrace in the eyes of the French government. The French finally executed him after years of imprisonment. Such treatment of one of their heroes infuriated the Irish, who began to look at the French with a more jaundiced eye, especially in 1745, when the Stuart cause was crushed as the French monarchy stood idly by. Within a few months of Fontenoy, Prince Charles Edward failed in his bid to invade England. His defeat at Culloden marked the end of any hope of a restoration of Catholic rule. The British government, however, learned from this battle the quality of the Irish as fighting men and soon opened recruiting in Ireland. Although Anglo-Irish troubles remain, in times of emergency Irish troops have joined the British colors while both sides keep quiet about their differences for the duration of the conflict.

It has been suggested that while in French service, from 1691 to 1745, the Irish lost 450,000 dead. Although the Irish in French service were the best-known exile troops, Irish emigrés served across Europe. They were only occasionally in completely Irish units, however, more often being incorporated into existing organizations of the host country's army. Irish soldiers served in several regiments in the Spanish army, fighting alongside British forces under the Duke of Wellington against Napoleon's troops in Spain. One of those regiments later moved to Italy to serve the Kingdom of Naples as the Regimiento del Rey, or the King's Regiment. In possibly the best example of the freedom of movement of the Wild Geese, one regiment served alternately for the Duchy of Lorraine, Brandenburg-Anspach, Saxony-Poland, Brandenburg again, and finally in British imperial service.

References: Hennessey, Maurice, *The Wild Geese: The Irish Soldier in Exile* (London: Sidgwick & Jackson,1973); Smith, Robert Barr, *Men at War* (New York: Avon, 1997).

Z

Zealots

A radical Jewish sect resisting Roman occupation in the first century CE.

The Zealots were a revolutionary faction in Israel during the Roman occupation, active in the first century CE. Although the Romans rarely did anything to hamper the Jews of Israel in the practice of their religion, the Roman practice of their own religion offended many Jews. The affront they felt to their faith, coupled with a series of harsh Roman rulers, set off a revolt that had ruinous consequences for the Jewish people.

The first mention of a leader of resistors to Roman rule is that of Judas of Galilee in 6–7 CE. He preached resistance to the census ordered by the Romans, possibly the same one mentioned in the biblical Book of Luke. He was killed in this revolt, and his death gave rise to the Zealots. They were not only politically active against Roman rule, but were fundamentalist in their interpretation of Jewish law. They followed the teachings of Shammai, a member of the Sanhedrin, the semigoverning body of interpreters of Jewish law. Shammai took an extremely conservative view of Jewish law and objected to anyone converting to the faith who was not born a Jew, and any Israelite that cooperated with Rome became a target for his wrath. A small faction of the Zealots, the Sicarii (from *sica*, a dagger), became assassins, attacking not only Romans but Jews who cooperated with them. For a time the Zealots remained a religious faction, preaching their conservative values, but they came to the fore in 41 CE when the Romans attempted to place a statue of the emperor in the temple in Jerusalem. Later, a synagogue in the neighborhood was violated in the wake of an attack on a Roman patrol. Such incidents could well have been blown out of proportion and used to inflame the population. Nevertheless, the uprisings remained limited until the appointment of Gessius Florus as procurator for Israel in 67 CE.

Florus was unusually corrupt and made no attempt to take Jewish sensibilities into account in his actions. It is reported by Josephus (the only recorder of these incidents) that Florus provoked the Jews so he could bring in the troops and use the disturbances as an excuse for looting. Florus's high-handed activities, coupled with a division within the Jewish ranks over how to respond, led to violence. When the population of Jerusalem publicly jeered Florus, he let loose his legionaries to ransack the city. He then provoked the people further by demanding that they welcome two arriving Roman cohorts. When the Jews did so and their actions were not fully appreciated, they again vented their vocal ire on Florus. Again the troops were set loose and fighting took place throughout the city. The Romans occupied the temple and the Zealots began taking over the abandoned forts of Masada and Herodion, built decades earlier by King Herod and which still held sizable armories.

The leading citizens of Jerusalem saw the ultimate impossibility of defeating Rome and counseled moderation, but many of the Jewish religious leaders supported the rebellion. The area governor, Agrippa II, sent troops to Jerusalem, but they proved too few to recapture the city. To further seal their fate, the rebels massacred a Roman garrison granted safe passage out of the city. Throughout Israel, the Zealots and their supporters seized population centers, with only a few remaining in Roman control. The Roman legate in Syria, C. Cestius Gallus, marched to Israel with a legion and regained much of the countryside, but was not strong enough to besiege Jerusalem. He withdrew northward but was ambushed, and those Romans not killed fled, abandoning their weapons. Any hope of a negotiated peace was gone, but the Zealots could not capitalize on their early success. Instead, they quarreled among themselves to the point of combat, and did little to prepare themselves for a war. They were rebels, not soldiers, and the leadership and discipline necessary to train and prepare a real fighting force did not exist.

When word of the revolt reached Rome, Emperor Nero reinforced the military with troops under the command of Vespasian, a general who had proven his worth in campaigns in Britain. He again reestablished Roman control over the countryside but hesitated to attack Jerusalem, not only owing to its difficulty but because of the power struggle in Rome that followed Nero's death. Finally, Vespasian himself was named caesar and returned to Rome, leaving his son Titus in command of operations against the Zealots. In the months that Vespasian waited for news from Rome, the Zealots did not put the time to good use but continued to fight among themselves.

Titus laid siege to Jerusalem in the spring of 70 CE with four legions and auxiliary troops on hand. He weakened the city's defenses by allowing pilgrims to enter to celebrate Passover, then bottling them up inside to strain the food supply. In the face of the Roman enemy, the defenders buried their differences and held fast even though conditions in the city grew progressively desperate. With their experience in siege warfare, the Romans made steady progress against the successive walls the Jews defended, capturing them at the rate of one a month throughout the summer. In September, the last of the city fell to Roman soldiers and was almost completely razed.

The Zealots continued to hold out in the fortresses at Herodion, Macherus, and Masada. The task of capturing them fell to Governor Barrus, sent by Vespasian. Herodion fell immediately, but Macherus resisted until its commander, Eleazar, fell prisoner to the Romans. Barrus scourged Eleazar and made ready to crucify him in sight of the garrison, which offered its surrender in return for its leader's life. Barrus agreed, then proceeded to slaughter 1,700 men and boys among the surrendered garrison. The women and children he sold into slavery. At Masada, according to Josephus, the 1,000 Zealot defenders resisted to the very last and then committed mass suicide rather than give in to Roman captivity. This story has been challenged by some scholars, especially those that point out that the Zealots were fundamentalists, and one of the greatest of sins in the Jewish faith is suicide. Could such a conservative group act against one of its most strongly held beliefs? Certainly a siege took place there, for the siege ramp still exists, but the ultimate fate of those inside is recorded again only by Josephus, whose veracity is doubted on many points. Suicide or not, the Roman conquest was costly for the Jews, who suffered (according to both Josephus and Tacitus) 600,000 dead or as much as one-quarter of the population. Perhaps another quarter was sold into slavery.

The Zealot movement officially ended with the fall of Masada in 73 CE, but those who managed to escape earlier from Jerusalem or other battles spread their discontent to surrounding countries and fomented anti-Roman movements from Persia to Egypt. A last gasp of Zealot resistance was a movement in Cyrenaica (modern Libya) led by one Jonathan, who led a mass of the lower classes into the Libyan desert on the promise of divine deliverance. The Jewish authorities, by now afraid of Roman retribution, turned Jonathan over to the Romans. He was sent to Rome, scourged, and burned alive. Possibly one Zealot group escaped to Arabia and established a community at Medina, reportedly lasting until the seventh century.

References: Graetz, Heinrich, *History of the Jews*, vol. II (Philadelphia: The Jewish Publication Society of America, 1893); Soggin, J. Alberto, *A History of Ancient Israel*, trans. John Bowden (Philadelphia: Westminster Press, 1984); Yadin, Yigael, *Herod's Fortress and the Zealots's Last Stand* (New York: Random House, 1966).

Zouaves

Moroccan and Algerian troops fighting in French service in 1830–1891, and American units copying their uniform style.

The original Zouave troops were North African soldiers of the Zouaoua tribe recruited by the French during their campaigns in Algeria and Morocco in 1830. They developed a reputation not only as outstanding soldiers, but also for their attire. Most notable were the *serouels*, the baggy pants reminiscent of the Arabian Nights. These were combined with a short coat and a fez, creating a thoroughly Middle Eastern look. The French *Military Annual* of 1831 describes them as wearing "jacket with sleeves and waistcoat closed in front, in blue cloth. Moorish pants in wine-colored cloth. Turban and red riding breeches." Compared to the usual uniforms of the day, these were not really more colorful, although the cut was certainly distinctive.

The French formed local forces in North Africa into the *Armée d'Afrique*, not only because of the need for soldiers but because local recruiting created a bond (they hoped) between the population and the occupying power. The Zouaves were originally at a strength of two battalions, but because of their early success and their rapidly gained reputation for dash and courage, the unit was much in demand by commanding generals in Algeria. That, coupled with the strong desire of soldiers to join an elite and distinctive unit, led to the expansion of the Zouaves until they ultimately numbered 10 regiments that served not only in North Africa, but everywhere the French army fought. Although they attracted sufficient volunteers

Zouaves, 9th N.Y. Volunteer Infantry, circa 1860–1865. National Archives and Records Administration, Special Media Archives Services Division (NWCS-S), National Archives at College Park, 8601 Adelphi Road, College Park, MD. [Image 529972]

from the French army to fill the ranks of noncommissioned officers and officers, the rank and file remained Algerian. There was no lack of volunteers, and therefore no lack of replacements for the high number of casualties the units incurred. As once source states, "Most of the officers became generals; four died under fire or from overwork" (Detaille, 1992).

After meritorious service in North Africa, Zouave regiments served with the French expedition to Russia during the Crimean War in 1854. They suffered immense losses, as did most units in this war, not only from combat but from disease—notably cholera. The Zouaves distinguished themselves in every battle in which they took part, but the number of dead and wounded French officers was high. They also made a name for themselves in Russia as *bon vivants*. One Zouave hijacked a flock of sheep kept by the British commander, so that the French always had plenty of fresh meat; they did, however, share this with British troops, and stories

are told of French Zouaves and Scottish Highlanders sharing British mutton cooked by French soldiers. The Zouaves also became well known for their "theater." In the evenings, men would dance and sing music hall numbers, giving rise to the comment that the Zouaves were at the same time Parisian and Arab.

After the Crimean War, they returned to action in Africa, when the entire *Armée d'Afrique* fought with French forces in Italy in 1859. Some regiments fought in Syria, while others were sent along with Maximillian's ill-fated expedition to Mexico from 1863 to 1866. They also served in France during the Franco-Prussian War in 1870–1871. Although later troops were of lesser quality, the officer corps always remained first-rate, and the spirit of the regiments immediately infused those who transferred in. "A simple Zouave thought himself and knew himself to be an individual. With his *chechia* set back on his head, he surveyed from the heights of his grandeur everything that was not Zouave.... All those in the army who had the ambition and the fanaticism of his profession dreamed of joining the Zouaves. All dreamed of this but not everyone got there despite the fact that death harshly ravaged the chosen" (Detaille, 1992).

The reputation earned by the Zouaves in French service became well known in the United States in the 1850s. Most impressed was a New Yorker named Elmer Ellsworth, who had had a lifelong fascination with all things military. While attending law school in Chicago, he joined the Illinois state militia and formed his own unit called the United States Zouave Cadets. He drilled his men to perfection, ultimately taking them to the East Coast where they toured several cities, giving demonstrations of their marching skill that no other military unit could match. The intricacies of their maneuvering led to fanciful stories published in contemporary newspapers, and both the soldiers and their commander became popular public figures. Finally, however, the maintenance of the unit proved too expensive and the Zouave Cadets were disbanded in 1860. Ellsworth returned to Illinois where he entered into law practice with Abraham Lincoln. When Lincoln was elected president, he invited Ellsworth to Washington to work in the War Department.

When the Civil War broke out in April 1861, Ellsworth resigned his position and went to New York City. There he was determined to raise a new Zouave unit and went looking for recruits. He found them in the New York Fire Department. The firemen remembered his Cadets and embraced the idea of forming such a unit, so the New York Fire Zouaves were created, officially the Eleventh New York Regiment. Marching into Virginia in May 1861, Ellsworth entered a tavern in Alexandria to remove a Confederate flag. The tavern owner killed him. Thus, when the Zouaves went into combat at the first battle of Bull Run in June, they were under the command of Noah Farnham. Their performance in combat was no better or worse than most of the rest of the untrained Union army, although some individuals did distinguish themselves. The unit was disbanded a few months later.

The romance of the French Zouave troops and the exotic uniform motivated many units on both sides of the war to adopt the Zouave heritage. Most of the early units on the Union side were from New York, and many contained French immigrants, even some who had served in French Zouave units. Over time, the idea spread westward and Zouave units were formed in Ohio and Indiana. The most famous of the Indiana units was the Eleventh Indiana Volunteer Infantry, known as Wallace's Zouaves. Their commander was Lewis Wallace, the youngest Union soldier to hold the commission of major general, but more famous for his postwar accomplishment of writing *Ben-Hur*. The Eleventh started the war as mounted soldiers, unusual for Zouaves, and distinguished themselves in a sharp fight with Confederate cavalry at Romney, Virginia, when a detachment fought off a cavalry unit through an afternoon and evening and inflicted 28 casualties on the Confederates for a loss of but one of their own killed. Wallace, like Ellsworth, prided himself on having the best-drilled unit in Indiana, and they fought throughout the war in campaigns such as Fort Donelson, Shiloh, Champion's Hill, Vicksburg, and in the Shenandoah Valley.

The South had Zouave units as well, not surprisingly originating in Louisiana. The best known was Wheat's Tigers (First Special Battalion, Louisiana Infantry), named for their commander, Roberdeau Wheat. Wheat's Tigers made their debut at the first battle of Bull Run in 1861, where they fought well. They had a reputation for wildness that was only partially curbed when Wheat was temporarily replaced (due to a wound received at Bull Run). His second in command, Charles de Choiseul, sought to establish a more disciplined unit and executed two men for attacking an officer. Both the battalion and Wheat were subdued by this action. They fought with General Thomas "Stonewall" Jackson in the Shenandoah Valley campaign in the summer of 1862, making up his famous "foot cavalry" known for their rapid marches. The Zouaves' last great battle was in that summer at Gaines's Mill east of

Richmond, where Wheat was killed. His men were heartbroken at his death, and many stopped fighting immediately and left the battlefield. Some men went home, and the remainder were transferred to other units.

Another famous Louisiana unit was the First Battalion Louisiana Zouaves, commanded by wealthy New Orleans socialite George Auguste Gaston de Coppens. These Zouaves earned a reputation for wildness far outstripping that of Wheat's men. They terrorized every town through which their train traveled on its way to Richmond, Virginia, in the summer of 1861. That same ferocity showed itself during and after battles as well, as they engaged in widespread burning of buildings in the first town they captured. Called "the most rakish and devilish looking beings I ever saw" by one Confederate soldier, Coppens's Zouaves proved themselves in battle at Seven Pines in June 1862, then later at Gaines's Mill with Wheat's Zouaves. They suffered severe losses at the second battle at Bull Run in August, and their last major battle was Antietam in September 1862. Coppens was killed there, and the unit was so badly decimated it was withdrawn from combat for reorganization. It saw no serious fighting for the remainder of the war.

One other aspect of Zouave units should be mentioned, and that is the position of *vivandiere*, a mixed French and Latin word literally meaning "hospitality giver." The vivandiere was a woman, often the wife of one of the men in the unit, who acted as sort of an unofficial (and later official) commissary. She wore a skirted uniform, and marched with the men on campaign. She was responsible for acquiring "necessaries" such as tobacco, liquor, extra food, etc., for the troops. The vivandiere tradi-

tion started with the French Zouaves, and the women traveled to French battlefields in the Crimea, Italy, and Mexico. In some cases, women fought and were decorated for valor, although they usually stayed out of combat. Vivandieres also traveled with the American Zouave formations on both sides.

More than 50 regiments were formed in the American Civil War, and American Zouaves had uniforms that were variations on those worn by French Zouaves: Officers usually did not wear the baggy pants, but red and blue were the primary colors. The uniform coats were usually decorated with contrasting piping sewn into elaborate clover leaf designs and with *tambeaus*, or false pockets. The hats varied from fezzes to kepis to turbans to stocking caps. Wheat's Tigers wore baggy white pants with blue pinstripes, but most were either solid or trimmed red or blue. After the war, some militia units continued to wear the Zouave uniforms, but with the adoption of more subdued uniforms in armies worldwide, men in such elaborate and decorative garb never saw combat again.

References: Detaille, Edouard, *L'Armée Francaise,* trans. Maureen Reinertsen (New York: Waxtel & Hasenauer, 1992); McAfee, Michael, *Zouaves: The First and the Bravest* (Dallas: Thomas Publishing, 1994); Smith, Robin, *Zouaves of the American Civil War* (London: Stackpole, 1996).

Zulus

A tribe dominating southern Africa in the early nineteenth century, known for the toughness of their warriors.

The Zulu nation began in southeastern Africa as a vassal to the neighboring Mtetwa tribe. The Mtetwa first began to

Zulu Warriors, ca. 1870. Library of Congress, Prints & Photographs Division [reproduction number LC-DIG-ggbain-00042]

rise to prominence under the leadership of Dingiswayo, who became chief in 1795 at the age of 25. Dingiswayo began the practice of organizing his population along regimental lines, establishing a military framework for his tribe. After training them intensively, he went on campaign, beginning a series of wars called the Mfecane. Dingiswayo refused to allow his warriors to slaughter captives, preferring to unify the tribes through intermarriage. He defeated virtually every tribe in the region and made them tributaries. The subject tribes were incorporated into a confederation with the Mtetwa as the leaders. The one tribe that Dingiswayo failed to bring totally under his control was the

Ndwande, whose chief, Zwide, would prove to be Dingiswayo's undoing.

Dingiswayo took under his tutelage a young exile from the Zulu tribe who had escaped with his mother to the Mtetwa. The illegitimate son of the Zulu chief, this young man was Shaka, who had fled his homeland to escape persecution from his half-brothers. Shaka distinguished himself in combat, gained Dingiswayo's attention, and rose to the highest ranks. He became one of the tribe's leading figures through his fighting skill and his devotion to Dingiswayo. Shaka disagreed with his mentor on the appropriate policy for dealing with defeated enemies; rather than follow Dingiswayo's more peaceful meth-

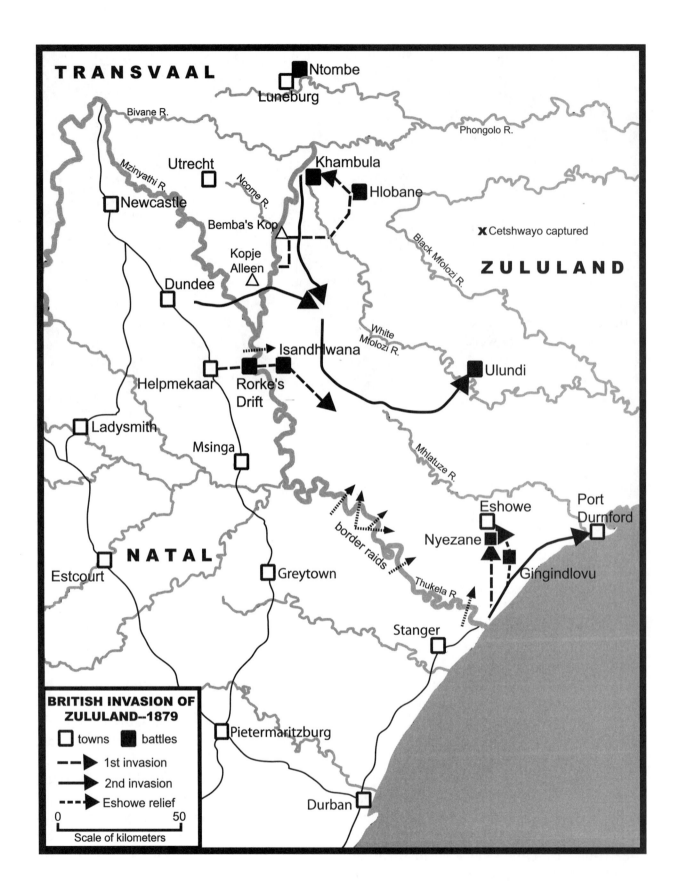

od, he believed the warriors should be killed and the remainder of the tribe forcibly integrated. As a subordinate, however, he continued to faithfully follow his chief's lead.

In 1810, Shaka learned that his father had died and had been succeeded by one of Shaka's half-brothers. Shaka wanted his father's position and arranged for the new chief's assassination. Dingiswayo then appointed Shaka to fill the position. Shaka thus came to lead his old tribe in 1816 at the age of 32. The Zulus remained vassals to the Mtetwa, and Shaka continued to fight under Dingiswayo's command. Three of these campaigns were fought against the Ndwande tribe, and the Mtetwa were victorious. The defeated Chief Zwide swore fealty to Dingiswayo, but secretly plotted against him. In 1818, Zwide captured Dingiswayo in battle and executed him. By this act, he hoped to succeed to overall command of the confederation, but the tribesmen recognized Shaka as the new chief instead.

Zwide led his Ndwande tribe against Shaka when, in April 1818, Zwide's army invaded Zululand. At the battle of Qokli Hill a force of some 4,300 Zulus defeated a force twice their size, but the retreating Ndwande stole a large number of Zulu cattle. A second invasion occurred 14 months later. This time Shaka ordered his people to hide all available supplies, then he withdrew his troops before an ill-supplied invading Ndwande army of some 18,000. After leading his enemies deep into Zululand and wearing them down, Shaka attacked. The Zulus scored a major victory and immediately advanced on Zwide's capital. Zwide escaped capture, but was never again to bother the new chief. Shaka proceeded to put down any other resistance to his rule while incorporating the tribes he inherited from Dingiswayo into the Zulu nation.

Shaka now became the leader of all the tribes of the Natal area of southeastern Africa. He built on Dingiswayo's idea of organizing his population along military lines and ultimately created one of the most powerful military forces in history. At its height, the Zulus numbered 600,000 men, and Shaka's empire covered 11,500 square miles. He established a training program second to none, whereby warriors were forbidden to wear sandals in order to toughen their feet. They developed the stamina to travel long distances at a run, covering as much as 50 miles a day, and then go straight into combat. He also developed a new weapon for his warriors, the *iklwa*, a stabbing spear with a blade about 10 inches long in a leaf shape, fastened on a three-foot-long shaft. The name comes from the sound the blade makes upon being removed from an enemy body. Another favorite weapon was the knobkerrie, or *iwisa*, a club made of ironwood. The shields they carried were of hardened cowhide in an oval shape 4.5 by 2.5 feet. Each shield was painted with the identifying marks of the warrior's unit. Each unit was also designated by a particular decorative piece of clothing, like an armband made of feathers. Necklaces were crafted to indicate the number of enemies killed in battle. When the Europeans arrived and became aggressive, the Zulus adopted firearms, but they were rarely very skilled with them and preferred the traditional melee style of fighting.

Shaka also developed the traditional formation employed by the Zulus, based upon the body of a bull. The army would form into four units, with three of the units forming up side by side. The central unit of the formation was the chest, which engaged the enemy head-on. Units to the right and left of the chest were regarded as the horns, and these were used to outflank the enemy force in a double-envelopment. Directly behind the chest unit was a reserve unit called the loins.

All Zulu males were raised from childhood to become warriors and learned to fight with Shaka's weapons and in his attack formation. Boys ages 13 through 18 were organized into military groups in which they served three years as cadets, practicing military skills while herding the cattle that were the major source of wealth and influence in the Zulu society, or working in the fields. When their training was over, they went to a regiment assigned to them by the king, where they would await his permission to marry. This would usually come around age 35, at which point a warrior could leave his regiment and begin a family.

The principal reason for war was cattle. Cattle played an important part of Zulu life by providing milk, food, and raw materials. All cattle captured in battle became the property of the king, who distributed them to men who had reached marrying age and proved themselves in battle. The importance of putting age restrictions on marriage is thus shown. Had there been no restrictions, there would not have been enough cattle available for all those who wanted to marry, and Zulu society would have broken down.

Ironically, It was this military and social system that was a key factor in bringing about the decline of Zulu power. When the Dutch settlers of South Africa began to move northward toward Zulu territory in the 1830s and 1840s, they often found themselves in bloody conflict with the Zulu population. As the British administration stretched into the region in the

1870s, they became arbitrators in Zulu-Boer disputes. The British governor, Sir Henry Bartle Frere, ran into a dilemma when a border commission ruled in favor of Zulu claims against the Boer state of the Transvaal. Already at odds with the Boers, Frere did not want to further anger them by enforcing the commission's decision. He also heard the taunts of other native tribes that the British had never fought the Zulus, inferring a British fear of them. Frere decided a war against the Zulus would impress the natives and appease the Boers. Frere provoked a conflict by demanding that the Zulu king dismantle his military and allow the adult males to marry when they pleased. He also demanded an immediate reply that would not give the tribe sufficient time to gather and discuss the ultimatum.

The Zulu King Cetshwayo could not comply. To allow men to marry early would deplete the cattle supply, while the inability to go to war would make it impossible to acquire sufficient new cattle. As Cetshwayo put it, he felt like a man "trying to ward off a falling tree." The British deadline passed on January 11, 1879, and British troops were almost immediately on the move. Lord Chelmsford, in command of British troops, invaded Zululand along a 200-mile front with his three columns directed to converge at the Zulu capital of Ulundi. Cetshwayo mobilized his army to defend his country, and his forces scored the initial victory at Ishandlwana on January 22. There, 20,000 Zulus overran a British camp defended by 1,300 British and native soldiers; all were slaughtered by the time-honored strategy of the Zulu bull formation. Overwhelming numbers and bravery had allowed the Zulu *iklwas* to overcome the British Martini-Henry rifles. Ishandlwana was the worst defeat the British ever suffered in one battle during their entire imperial experience. The small British outpost at Rorke's Drift was attacked that evening, but the 130-man contingent managed to survive a number of Zulu onslaughts.

After Ishandlwana, the Zulu fortunes began to turn. The disciplined defense at Rorke's Drift forced the withdrawal of their far larger force, while a defeat at the hands of another attacking British column at Inyezane River the same day began to shake Zulu morale. They thus refrained from directly attacking a British force at the mission at Eshowe, but surrounded it and attacked patrols and supply columns. The Zulus were badly defeated by a force marching to Eshowe, and the garrison was relieved in early April 1879 after more than two months under siege. The Zulus regained some momentum with victories over a supply column at Intombe River and a British unit at Hlobane Mountain, but after those battles the British gained the upper hand. On March 29 and April 2, the British dealt serious defeats to larger Zulu forces, then captured the capital at Ulundi on July 4. British forces by that time were under the command of Sir Garnet Wolseley, who oversaw the destruction of Zulu power and independence. Cetshwayo was captured a month after the battle at Ulundi and was sent to England, where he met with Queen Victoria. After two years there, he was returned to Zululand as king, but as little more than a figurehead. In 1897, Zululand was annexed into Natal Province. The Zulus made a final attempt to regain their freedom in 1906, but the rebellion was quickly crushed. The Zulus, who had once dominated southeastern Africa, became just another native tribe under British rule. They maintain to this day a strong tribal heritage. Although they played a significant role in the Republic of South Africa's first postapartheid elections in 1994, their trademark cowhide shields and short stabbing spears are now more tourist items than the weapons of war that temporarily shocked the British nation in 1879.

References: Farwell, Byron, *Queen Victoria's Little Wars* (New York: Harper and Row, 1972); Ritter, E.A., *Shaka Zulu; the Rise of the Zulu Empire* (London: Longman, 1960); Roberts, Brian, *The Zulu Kings* (New York: Scribner, 1974).

SECTION TWO: BIBLIOGRAPHY

Bibliography

Adamec, Ludwig. *Dictionary of Afghan Wars, Revolutions, and Insurgencies* (Lanham, MD: Scarecrow Press, 1996).

Adcock, Frank. *Greek and Macedonian Art of War* (Berkeley: University of California Press, 1974).

Addington, Larry. *Patterns of War through the Eighteenth Century* (Bloomington: University of Indiana Press, 1990).

Aeschylus. *Persians*, trans. Edith Hall (Warminster: Aris & Phillips, 1996).

Alden, John. *The American Revolution* (New York: Harper & Row, 1954).

Alexander, Joe, *et al. A Fellowship of Valor* (New York: HarperCollins, 1997).

Arbman, Olger. *The Vikings* (New York: Frederick Praeger, 1961).

Ashley, James. *The Macedonian Empire* (Jefferson, NC: McFarland & Co., 1997).

Baines, J., and J. Malek. *Atlas of Ancient Egypt* (New York: Facts on File, Inc., 1980).

Barker, Geoffrey. *A Concise History of the United States Airborne* (Brandon, FL: Anglo-American Publishing, 1989).

Barnett, Correlli. *The Desert Generals* (Bloomington: University of Indiana Press, 1982).

_____. *The Swordbearers* (New York: Morrow, 1964).

Bartha, Antal. *Hungarian Society in the 9th and 10th Centuries*, trans. K. Baazs (Budapest: Akademiai Kiado, 1975).

Bartos, Frantisek. *The Hussite Revolution* (Boulder, CO: East European Monographs, 1986).

Bartusis, Mark C. *The Late Byzantine Army* (Philadelphia: University of Pennsylvania Press, 1992).

Bary, William Theodore de, *et al.* eds . *Sources of Chinese Tradition* (New York: Columbia University Press, 1960).

Bianco, Richard. *Rommel, the Desert Warrior* (New York: Julian Messner, 1982).

Bickers, Richard Townshend. *Von Richthofen: The Legend Evaluated* (Annapolis, MD: Naval Institute Press, 1996).

Bidwell, Shelford. *The Chindit War* (New York: Macmillan, 1980).

Bilgrami, Ashgar. *Afghanistan and British India* (New Delhi: Sterling Press, 1972).

Bishop, Edward. *Better to Die* (London: New English Library, 1976).

Bjorge, Gary. "Merrill's Marauders: Combined Operations in Northern Burma in 1944," in *Army History*, Spring/Summer 1995.

Bona, Istvan. *The Dawn of the Dark Ages: The Gepids and the Lombards* (Budapest: Corvina Press, 1976).

Brander, Michael. *The Scottish Highlanders and Their Regiments* (New York: Barnes & Noble, 1996).

Brion, Marcel. *Attila: The Scourge of God* (New York: Robert McBride and Company, 1929).

Burns, Thomas. *A History of the Ostrogoths* (Bloomington: University of Indiana Press, 1984).

Bury, J. B. *The Invasion of Europe by the Barbarians* (New York: Russell and Russell, 1963).

Caidin, Martin. *The Ragged, Rugged Warriors* (New York: E. P. Dutton, 1966).

Campbell, George. *The Knights Templars, Their Rise and Fall* (New York: Robert McBride, 1937).

Carroll, John M. *The Black Military Experience in the American West* (New York: Liveright, 1971).

Center of Military History. *Merrill's Marauders* (Washington, D.C.: Historical Division, War Department, 1945).

Ceram, C. W. *The Secret of the Hittites*, trans. Richard Winston and Clara Winston (New York: Alfred A. Knopf, 1956).

Cervens, Thierry de. "The French Foreign Legion" (www.instantweb.com/l/legion).

Chaliand, Gerald, ed. *Guerrilla Strategies* (Berkeley: University of California Press, 1982).

Chambers, James. *The Devil's Horsemen* (New York: Atheneum, 1979).

Chandler, David. *The Campaigns of Napoleon* (New York: Macmillan, 1966).

Chandler, David, and I. F. W. Beckett. *Oxford Illustrated History of the British Army* (London: Oxford University Press, 1994).

Clancy, Tom. *Submarine: A Guided Tour inside a Nuclear Warship* (New York: Berkley Books, 1993).

Coppa, Frank. *The Origin of the Italian Wars of Independence* (New York: Longman, 1992).

Cowles, Virginia. *The Phantom Major* (New York: Harper and Bros. 1958).

Crankshaw, Edward. *Bismarck* (New York: Viking, 1981).

Cunliffe, Barry. *The Ancient Celts* (Oxford: Oxford University Press, 1997).

Curtin, Jeremiah. *The Mongols: A History* (Westport, CT: Greenwood Press, 1972).

Cutrer, Thomas, ed. *Terry's Texas Rangers* (Austin, TX: State House Press, 1996).

Davidson, H. R. Ellis. *The Viking Road to Byzantium* (London: George Allen & Unwin, 1976).

Davidson, Phillip. *Vietnam at War* (New York: Oxford University Press, 1988).

Davis, John. *The Texas Rangers* (San Antonio: University of Texas Institute of Texan Cultures, 1975).

Davis, Ralph H. C. *The Normans and Their Myth* (London: Thames and Hudson, 1976).

Dear, E. D. S., and M. R. D. Foot, eds. *Oxford Companion to World War II* (Oxford: Oxford University Press, 1995).

Deiss, Joseph Jay. *Captains of Fortune* (New York: Thomas Crowell Company, 1967).

Delbruck, Hans. *History of the Art of War* (Lincoln: University of Nebraska Press, 1991).

DePolnay, Peter. *Garibaldi, the Man and the Legend* (New York: T. Nelson, 1961).

Descola, Jean. *The Conquistadors, trans. Malcolm Barnes* (London: George Allen and Unwin, 1957).

Detaille, Edouard. *L'Armée Francaise, trans. Maureen Reinertsen* (New York: Waxtel & Hasenauer, 1992).

Diner, Helen. *Mothers and Amazons* (New York: The Julian Press, 1965).

Dower, John. *War Without Mercy* (New York: Pantheon, 1986).

Downey, Fairfax. *The Buffalo Soldiers in the Indian Wars* (New York: McGraw-Hill, 1969).

Drews, Robert. *The End of the Bronze Age* (Princeton, NJ: Princeton University Press, 1996).

Dudley, Donald. *The Romans* (New York: Alfred Knopf, 1970).

Dupuy, Colonel Trevor N. A *Genius for War* (New York: Prentice-Hall, 1977).

_____. "Burma: The Drive from the North," in *History of the Second World War*, vol. 71 (London: BBC Publications, 1966).

Durant, Will, and Ariel Durant. *Rousseau and Revolution* (New York: Simon and Schuster, 1967).

Eby, Cecil. *Between the Bullet and the Lie* (New York: Holt, Rinehart & Winston, 1969).

Edwards, I. E. S., ed. *The Cambridge Ancient History* (Cambridge: Cambridge University Press, 1980).

Ellis, John. *Cassino: The Hollow Victory* (New York: McGraw-Hill, 1984).

Erman, Adolf. *Life in Ancient Egypt*, trans. H. M. Tirard (New York: Dover Publications, 1971 [1894]).

Fabing, Howard D. "On Going Berserk: A Neurochemical Inquiry," in *Scientific Monthly*, vol. 83 (November 1956)

Fage, J. D. *A History of West Africa* (London: Cambridge University Press, 1969).

Farwell, Byron. The Gurkhas (New York: Norton, 1984).

_____. *Queen Victoria's Little Wars* (New York: Harper & Row, 1972).

Featherstone, Donald. *Colonial Small Wars* (Newton Abbot, Devon: David & Charles, 1973).

Ferrill, Arther. *The Origins of War* (London: Thames and Hudson, 1985).

Firkins, Peter. *The Australians in Nine Wars* (London: Robert Hale & Co., 1972).

Fischer, David Hackett. *Paul Revere's Ride* (New York: Oxford University Press, 1995).

Fitzhugh, Lester Newton. *Terry's Texas Rangers*, unpublished memoirs (Austin: Barker Center Archives).

Fletcher, William. *Rebel Private, Front and Rear* (New York: Penguin, 1995).

Foote, Shelby. *The Civil War, a Narrative*, 3 vols. (New York: Vintage Books, 1958–1972).

Ford, Daniel. *Flying Tigers: Claire Chennault and the American Volunteer Group* (Washington, DC: Smithsonian Institution Press, 1991).

Forrest, W. G. *A History of Sparta, 950–192 BCE* (New York: Hutchinson, 1968).

Freidel, Frank. *The Splendid Little War* (Boston: Little, Brown and Company, 1958).

Fuentes, Patricia de. *The Conquistadors: First Person Accounts of the Conquest of Mexico* (New York: Orion, 1963).

Fuller, J. F. C. *The Generalship of Alexander* (Westport, CT: Greenwood, 1981).

Gabriel, Richard. *From Sumer to Rome* (New York: Greenwood Press, 1991).

_____. *The Culture of War* (New York: Greenwood Press, 1990).

Gann, Lewis H. *Guerrillas in History* (Stanford, CA: Hoover Institution Press, 1971).

Gibbons, Floyd. *The Red Knight of Germany* (London: Cassell, 1932).

Gies, Frances. *The Knight in History* (New York: Harper & Row, 1984).

Ginouves, Rene, and Giannes Akamates. *Macedonia: From Philip II to the Roman Conquest* (Princeton: Princeton University Press, 1994).

Glubb, John Bagot. *Soldiers of Fortune: The Story of the Mamlukes* (London: Stein & Day, 1957).

Gokhale, Balkrishna. *Ancient India: History and Culture* (Bombay and New York: Asia Publishing House, 1959).

Goodwin, Godfrey. *The Janissaries* (London: Saqi, 1994).

Graetz, Heinrich. *History of the Jews*, vol. II (Philadelphia: The Jewish Publication Society of America, 1893).

Grant, Michael. *The Army of the Caesars* (New York: Scribner, 1974).

Gregory of Tours. *History of the Franks*, trans. Ernest Brehaut (New York: Norton, 1969).

Guttman, John, "Poland's Winged Warriors," in *Military History*, vol. 10, no. 5 (December 1993).

Hackett, General Sir John. *Warfare in the Ancient World* (London: Sidgwick & Jackson, 1989).

Halberstadt, Hans. *US Marine Corps* (Osceola, WI: Motorbooks International, 1993).

Halecki, O. *A History of Poland* (New York: David McKay Company, 1981).

Hallenbeck, Jan. *Pavia and Rome: The Lombard Monarchy and the Papacy in the Eighth Century* (Philadelphia: American Philosophical Society, 1982).

Hallett, Robin. *Africa to 1875* (Ann Arbor: University of Michigan Press, 1970).

Hamilton, Allen. *Sentinel of the Southern Plains* (Fort Worth, TX: TCU Press, 1987).

Hanson, Lawrence. *Chinese Gordon* (New York: Funk and Wagnalls, 1954).

Hassig, Ross. *Aztec Warfare: Imperial Expansion and Political Control* (Norman: University of Oklahoma Press, 1995).

Hayes, W. *The Scepter of Egypt* (Cambridge, MA: Harvard University Press, 1959).

Heather, Peter. *Goths and Romans* (Oxford: Clarendon, 1991).

Heidler, David Stephen. *Old Hickory's War* (Mechanicsburg, PA: Stackpole, 1996).

Heiferman, Ron. *Flying Tigers: Chennault in China* (New York: Ballantine, 1971).

Hennessey, Maurice. *The Wild Geese: The Irish Soldier in Exile* (London: Sidgwick & Jackson,1973).

Herodotus. *The Histories*, trans. Aubrey de Selincourt (Baltimore: Penguin, 1954).

Hibbert, Christopher. *Garibaldi and His Enemies* (London: Longman, 1965).

_____. *Redcoats and Rebels* (New York: Norton, 1990).

Hickey, Michael. *Out of the Sky* (New York: Scribner, 1979).

Höhne, Heinz. *The Order of the Death's Head*, trans. Richard Barry (London: Coward, McCann & Geoghegan, 1969).

Hough, Richard, and Denis Richards. *The Battle of Britain* (New York: Norton, 1989).

How, W. W. "Arms, Tactics, and Strategy in the Persian War," in *Journal of Hellenic Studies*, vol. LXIII.

Hoyt, Edwin. *SEALs at War* (New York: Bantam Doubleday Dell, 1993).

Innes, Hammond. *The Conquistadors* (New York: Knopf, 1969).

Inoguchi, Rikihei, Tadashi Nakajima, and Roger Pineau. *The Divine Wind* (Annapolis: United States Naval Institute Press, 1958).

Irwin, Robert. *The Middle East in the Middle Ages* (Carbondale: Southern Illinois University Press, 1986).

Isadore of Seville. *The History of the Goths, Vandals and Suevi*, trans. Guido Donini and Gordon Ford (Leiden: E. J. Brill, 1970).

Isby, David. *Ten Million Bayonets* (London: Arms and Armour Press, 1988).

Jimenez, Ramon. *Caesar against the Celts* (New York: Sarpedon Publishers, 1995).

Johnson, Lonnie R. *Central Europe* (New York and Oxford: Oxford University Press, 1996).

Jones, Gwyn. *A History of the Vikings* (New York: Oxford University Press, 1984 [1968]).

_____. *Eirik the Red and Other Icelandic Sagas* (New York: Oxford University Press, 1961).

Jones, Virgil Carrington. *Gray Ghosts and Confederate Raiders* (New York: Henry Holt & Co., 1956).

Kaminsky, Howard. *A History of the Hussite Revolution* (Berkeley: University of California Press, 1967).

Keegan, John. *A History of Warfare* (New York: Random House, 1993).

_____. "Ashanti," in *War Monthly*, no. 7, 1974.

_____. *Waffen SS: The Asphalt Soldiers* (New York: Ballantine, 1970).

Keen, Maurice. *Chivalry* (New Haven and London: Yale University Press, 1984).

Kelly, Orr. *Brave Men, Dark Waters* (Novato, CA: Presidio Press, 1992).

Kelly, Ross. *Special Operations and National Purpose* (Lexington, MA: Lexington Books, 1989).

Kennedy Shaw, Major W. B. "Britain's Private Armies," in *History of the Second World War*, vol. 28 (London: BBC Publishing, 1966).

Kenrick, John. *Ancient Egypt under the Pharaohs* (New York: John B. Alden, 1883).

King, Michael. *Rangers* (Ft. Leavenworth, KS: Combat Studies Institute, 1985).

King, Winston. *Zen and the Way of the Sword* (New York: Oxford University Press, 1993).

Kinross, Patrick. *The Ottoman Centuries* (New York: Morrow, 1977).

Kipling, Rudyard. "Fuzzy Wuzzy," from *The Complete Verse* (London: Kyle Cathie, 1995).

Kwanten, Luc. *Imperial Nomads* (Philadelphia: University of Pennsylvania Press, 1979).

Lasko, Peter. *The Kingdom of the Franks* (New York: McGraw-Hill, 1971).

Lawson, Don. *The Abraham Lincoln Brigade* (New York: Thomas Crowell, 1989).

Lehman, Johannes. *The Hittites: People of a Thousand Gods*, trans. J. M. Brownjohn (New York: Viking Press, 1977).

Lindsay, Jack. *The Normans and Their World* (New York: St. Martin's Press, 1975).

Longworth, Philip. *The Cossacks* (New York: Holt, Rinehart and Winston, 1970).

Lord, Walter. *The Good Years* (New York: Harper & Bros. 1960).

Lowell, E. J. *The Hessians and the German Auxiliaries of Great Britain in the Revolutionary War* (New York: Harper & Bros. 1884).

Loyn, H. R. *Anglo-Saxon England and the Norman Conquest* (New York: Longman, 1991).

Luttwak, E. N. *The Grand Strategy of the Roman Empire* (Baltimore: Johns Hopkins University Press, 1977).

Macartney, C. A. *The Magyars in the Ninth Century* (Cambridge: Cambridge University Press, 1968).

MacKinnon, Charles. *Scottish Highlanders* (London: Robert Hale, Ltd., 1984).

Macksey, Kenneth. *Invasion* (New York: Macmillan, 1969).

MacMunn, G. F. *The Armies of India* (London: Adam and Charles Black, 1911).

MacPherson, James. *Ordeal by Fire* (New York: McGraw-Hill, 1982).

Macqueen, J. G. *The Hittites and Their Contemporaries in Asia Minor* (London: Thames and Hudson, 1968).

Majdalany, Fred. *The Battle of Cassino* (New York: Houghton Mifflin, 1957).

Mao Tse-tung. *On Guerrilla Warfare*, trans. Samuel B. Griffith (New York: Praeger, 1961).

Mason, Herbert Malloy. *The Lafayette Escadrille* (New York: Random House, 1964).

Mason, Herbert Malloy. *The Rise of the Luftwaffe*, 1918–1940 (New York: Dial Press, 1973).

Mason, Philip. *A Matter of Honour* (London: Jonathan Cape, 1974).

McAfee, Michael. *Zouaves: The First and the Bravest* (Dallas: Thomas Publishing, 1994).

McCormick, T. J. *China Market: America's Quest for Informal Empire* (Chicago: Quadrangle Books, 1967).

McKay, Ernest A. *Undersea Terror: U-Boat Wolf Packs in World War II* (New York: Julian Messner, 1982).

McLeave, Hugh. *The Damned Die Hard* (New York: Saturday Review Press, 1973).

Millett, Allan. *Semper Fidelis* (New York: Macmillan, 1980).

Millis, Walter. *Martial Spirit* (New York: Houghton Mifflin, 1931).

Mitcham, Samuel. *Rommel's Desert War: The Life and Death of the Afrika Korps* (New York: Stein and Day, 1982).

Moorehead, Alan. *Gallipoli* (London: H. Hamilton, 1956).

Muir, William. *Mameluke, or Slave Dynasty of Egypt* (New York: AMS, 1973).

Mulroy, Kevin. *Freedom on the Border* (Lubbock, TX: Texas Tech University Press, 1993).

Naito, Hatsuho. *Thunder Gods* (New York: Kodansha International USA Ltd., 1989).

Nolan, Alan T. *The Iron Brigade: A Military History* (Indianapolis: Indiana University Press, 1961).

Norman, A. V. B. *The Medieval Soldier* (New York: Thomas Y. Crowell, 1971).

Nuttingham, Anthony. *Scramble for Africa: The Great Trek to the Boer War* (London: Constable, 1970).

Olmstead, A. T. *History of the Persian Empire* (Chicago: University of Chicago Press, 1948).

Olson, James, and Randy Roberts. *Where the Domino Fell* (New York: St. Martin's Press, 1996).

Oman, C. W. G. *The Art of War in the 16th Century* (New York: AMS Press, 1979 [1937]).

Oman, Charles. *A History of the Art of War in the Middle Ages* (Ithaca, NY: Cornell University Press, 1953 [1885]).

Pakenham, Thomas. *The Scramble for Africa: White Man's Conquest of the Dark Continent* (New York: Random House, 1991).

Paret, Peter. "Napoleon and the Revolution in War," in *Makers of Modern Strategy* (Princeton: Princeton University Press, 1986).

Parke, H. W. *Greek Mercenary Soldiers* (Chicago: Ares, 1981 [1933]).

Partner, Peter . *The Murdered Magicians: The Templars and Their Myth* (New York: Oxford University Press, 1982).

Paul the Deacon. *History of the Langobards*, trans. W. D. Foulke (Philadelphia: University of Pennsylvania Press, 1974).

Payne, Chuck. "'Rangers Lead the Way': The History of the U.S. Army Rangers" (http://users.aol.com/armysof1/Ranger.html).

Pitt, Barrie. *1918: The Last Act* (New York: Ballantine, 1963).

Plutarch. *The Age of Alexander, trans.* Ian Scott-Kilvert (Middlesex: Penguin Books, 1986).

Porch, Douglas. *The French Foreign Legion* (New York: HarperCollins, 1991).

Reid, Stuart. *British Redcoat, 1740–1793* (London: Reed International, 1996).

_____. *British Redcoat, 1793–1815* (London: Reed International, 1997).

Reitz, Deneys. *Commando: A Boer Journal of the Boer War* (London: Faber & Faber, 1929).

Richthofen, *Baron Manfred von, Der Rote Kampfflieger* (Berlin: Ullstein, 1917).

Ritter, E. A. *Shaka Zulu; the Rise of the Zulu Empire* (London: Longman, 1960).

Roberts, Brian. *The Zulu Kings* (New York: Scribner, 1974).

Roberts, Michael. *Gustavus Adolphus: A History of Sweden*, 2 vols. (New York: Longman, 1953–1958).

Roberts, P. E. *History of British India* (London: Oxford University Press, 1952).

Rooney, David. *Burma Victory* (London: Arms and Armour Press, 1992).

Roosevelt, Theodore. *The Rough Riders* (New York: Charles Scribner's Sons, 1924 [1899]).

Rosenstone, Robert. *Crusade of the Left* (New York: Pegasus, 1969).

Rothenberg, Gunther. *The Art of Warfare in the Age of Napoleon* (Bloomington, IN: University of Indiana Press, 1978).

Sage, Michael. *Warfare in Ancient Greece* (London: Routledge, 1996).

Sahagun, Bernardino de. *The War of Conquest, trans.* Arthur Anderson and Charles Dibble (Salt Lake City, UT: University of Utah Press, 1978).

Sandars, N. K. "The Sea Peoples," in Cotterell, Arthur. *The Encyclopedia of Ancient Civilizations* (London: Rainbird Publishing, 1980).

Seaton: Albert. *The Horsemen of the Steppes* (London: Hippocrene, 1985).

Secoy, Frank. *Changing Military Patterns of the Great Plains Indians* (Lincoln, NE: University of Nebraska Press, 1992).

Shaw, Stanford. *The History of the Ottoman Empire and Modern Turkey*, 2 vols. (Cambridge: Cambridge University Press, 1976–1977).

Short, Anthony. *The Origins of the Vietnam War* (New York: Longman, 1989).

Siepel, Kevin. *Rebel: The Life and Times of John Singleton Mosby* (New York: St. Martin's Press, 1983).

Silberman, Neil Asher. "The Coming of the Sea Peoples," in *Military History Quarterly*, vol. 10, no. 2 (Winter, 1998).

Simons, Anna. *The Company They Keep* (New York: Free Press, 1997).

Simpson, Harold. "Hood's Texas Brigade at Appomattox," in Wooster, Ralph, ed. *Lone Star Blue and Gray: Essays on Texas in the Civil War* (Austin: Texas State Historical Association, 1995).

Singh, Khushwant. *A History of the Sikhs*, 2 vols. (Princeton, NJ: Princeton University Press, 1963–1966).

Slim, Field Marshal William, *Defeat into Victory* (London: Cassell and Company, 1956).

Smith, Page, *A New Age Now Begins* (New York: McGraw-Hill. 1976).

Smith, Page. *Trial by Fire* (New York: McGraw-Hill, 1982).

Smith, Robert Barr. *Men at War* (New York: Avon, 1997).

Smith, Robin. *Zouaves of the American Civil War* (London: Stackpole, 1996).

Soggin, J. Alberto. *A History of Ancient Israel*, trans. John Bowden (Philadelphia: Westminster Press, 1984).

Starr, Chester. *A History of the Ancient World* (New York: Oxford University Press, 1965).

Stearns, Peter, *et al. World Civilizations* (New York: HarperCollins, 1992).

Stilwell, Joseph W. *The Stilwell Papers*, Theodore H. White, ed. (New York: William Sloane Associates, 1948).

Strabo. *Geography*, trans. Horace Leonard Jones (Cambridge: Harvard University Press, 1966).

Sullivan, George. *Elite Warriors* (New York: Facts on File, 1995).

Swinson, Arthur. *The Raiders: Desert Strike Force* (New York: Ballantine, 1968).

Thomas, Hugh. *The Spanish Civil War* (New York: Harper and Row, 1961).

Thompson, E. A. *Romans and Barbarians* (Madison, WI: University of Wisconsin Press, 1982).

Thomson, Alastair. *ANZAC Memories* (New York: Oxford University Press, 1994).

Time-Life series, *The Third Reich: Fists of Steel* (Alexandria, VA: Time-Life, 1988).

Toland, John. *No Man's Land* (New York: Doubleday, 1980).

Townsend, Richard. *The Aztecs* (London: Thames and Hudson, 1992).

Trease, Geoffrey. *The Condottieri* (New York: Holt, Rinehart, and Winston, 1971).

Trench, Charles Chenevix. *The Road to Khartoum* (New York: Norton, 1978).

Trimingham, J. S. *Islam in West Africa* (London: Oxford University Press, 1962).

Tuker, Lt.-Gen. Sir Francis. *Gorhka: The Story of the Gurkhas of Nepal* (London: Constable, 1957).

Turnbull, Stephen. *The Samurai: A Military History* (New York: Macmillan, 1977).

————. *The Book of the Medieval Knight* (New York: Crown, 1985).

————. *Samurai Warriors* (New York: Sterling Publishing, 1991).

Utley, Robert. *Frontiersmen in Blue* (New York: Macmillan, 1967).

Vambery, Arminius. *Hungary in Ancient, Medieval, and Modern Times* (Hallandale, FL: New World Books, 1972).

Van Seeters, J. *The Hyksos* (New Haven, CT: Yale University Press, 1966).

Walker, Greg. "Elite SEAL Units," in *International Combat Arms*, vol. 7, no. 6 (November 1989).

Wandycz, Piotr. *The Price of Freedom: A History of East Central Europe from the Middle Ages to the Present* (London: Routledge, 1992).

Ward, Christy. "Description of the Berserk," (www.realtime.com/$flsim $gunnora).

Warry, John. *Warfare in the Classical World* (London: Salamander Books, 1980).

Watson, G. R. *The Roman Soldier* (Ithaca, NY: Cornell University Press, 1969).

Webb, Walter Prescott. *The Story of the Texas Rangers* (Austin, TX: Encino Press, 1971).

Wedgewood, C. V. *The Thirty Years War* (Gloucester, MA: P. Smith, 1969 [1938]).

Weeks, John. *Assault from the Sky* (New York: Putnam, 1978).

Weller, George Anthony. *The Story of Submarines* (New York: Random House, 1962).

Wheeler, Radha. *Early India and Pakistan* (New York: Praeger, 1959).

Whitehouse, Arch. *Legion of the Lafayette* (New York: Doubleday, 1962).

_____. *The Years of the Sky Kings* (New York: Doubleday, 1964).

Wilkins, Frederick. *The Highly Irregular Irregulars: Texas Rangers in the Mexican War* (Austin, TX: Eakin Press, 1990).

Wilson, Andrew. *The Ever Victorious Army* (Edinburgh: Blackwood, 1868).

Winderbaum, Larry. *The Martial Arts Encyclopedia* (Washington, DC: Inscape Corp. 1977).

Wise, Terence. *Ancient Armies of the Middle East* (London: Osprey Publishing, 1981).

Wiseman, D. J. "The Assyrians," in *Warfare in the Ancient World*, John Hackett, ed. (London: Sidgwick and Jackson, 1989).

Wolfram, Herwig. *History of the Goths* (Berkeley: University of California Press, 1988).

Wolpert, Stanley. *India* (Englewood Cliffs, NJ: Prentice-Hall, 1965).

Wood, Derek, and Derek Dempster. *The Narrow Margin* (New York: Coronet, 1969).

Woolman, David. "The Day the Hadendowa Broke the British Square—or Did They?," in *Military History*, vol. 11, no. 2 (June, 1994).

Wright, J. Leitch. *Creeks and Seminoles* (Lincoln, NE: University of Nebraska Press, 1996).

Yadin, Yigael. *Herod's Fortress and the Zealots' Last Stand* (New York: Random House, 1966).

Young, John Robert. *French Foreign Legion* (New York: Thames and Hudson, 1984).

Young, Marilyn. *The Rhetoric of Empire: American China Policy, 1895–1901* (Cambridge: Harvard University Press, 1968).

SECTION THREE: READINGS

Introduction

What makes a good soldier? What makes a good battle commander? Why should we enter into service to our national military establishments at all? When and how should our armies go into battle? What creeds, mottos or beliefs should they fight for? What tactics provide soldiers the best opportunities for survival while achieving the greatest results? What training is more advantageous, and which weapons should be employed?

The following readings offer several historic and contemporary answers to such questions. From the ancient Egyptians to the modern U.S. Army, soldiering has almost always been an honorable profession that attracted men from many walks of life. Many great leaders, philosophers, politicians and common soldiers, have set their thoughts and beliefs down on paper, papyrus or in public speeches. Some speak of "esprit de corps" while others speak of opposition and resistance. Some offer recollections of successful tactics, and the science of war, while others discuss epic bravery and faith in the face of adversity or slim odds. The following readings offer words of patriotism, duty, respect and courage. Warriors and fighting groups refuse to be defined on battlefields or by their "operations" and missions, but instead by their lives, conduct, and codes.

Allen Hamilton, 2006

Letters Home from Roman Soldiers

2 CE

Reprinted with permission. From *Papyri, I, Private Documents (Agreements, Receipts, Wills, Letters, Memoranda, Accounts and Lists, and Others)* Translated by A. S. Hunt, C. C. Edgar. The Loeb Classical Library. Harvard University Press, 1932.

Letter of a Recruit: Apollinarius
Select Papyri I (1932) #111 (2 CE)

Apollinarius to Taesis, his mother and lady, many greetings!

Before all I pray for your health. I myself am well, and make supplication for you before the gods of this place. I wish you to know, mother, that I arrived in Rome in good health on the 20th of the month Pachon, and was posted to Misenum, though I have not yet learned the name of my company (kenturian); for I had not gone to Misenum at the time of writing this letter. I beg you then, mother, look after yourself and do not worry about me; for I have come to a fine place. Please write me a letter about your welfare and that of my brothers and of all your folk. And whenever I find a messenger I will write to you; never will I be slow to write. Many salutations to my brothers and Apollinarius and his children, and Karalas and his children. I salute Ptolemaeus and Ptolemais and her children and Heraclous and her children. I salute all who love you, each by name. I pray for your health.
[Address:] Deliver at Karanis to Taesis, from her son Apollinarius of Misenum.

Letter of a Recruit: Apion
Select Papyri I (1932) #112 (2 CE)

Apion to Epimachus, his father and lord, very many greetings.

Before all else I pray for your health and that you may always be well and prosperous, together with my sister and her daughter and my brother. I thank the Lord Serapis that when I was in danger at sea he straightway saved me. On arriving at Misenum, I received from Caesar three gold pieces for travelling expenses. And it is well with me. Now I ask you, my lord and father, write me a letter, telling me first of your welfare, secondly of my brother's and sister's, and enabling me thirdly to make obeisance before your handwriting, because you educated me well and I hope thereby to have quick advancement, if the gods so will. Give many salutations to Capiton and my brother and sister and Serenilla and my friends. I have sent you by Euctemon a portrait [eikonin] of myself. My name is Antonius Maximus, my company [kenturi(a)] is the Athenonica. I pray for your health.
[Postscript:] Serenus, son of Agathodaemon, salutes you, and . . . , and Turbo son of Gallonius, and . . . .
[Addressed:] To Philadelphia, to Epimachus from Apion his son.
[Additional address:] Deliver at the camp of the first cohort of the Apameni to Julianus, vice-secretary [antiliblario] this letter from Apion to be forwarded to his father Epimachus/

On Military Science from Libro XVI of the Noctes Atticae by Aulus Gellius

2nd Century CE

Reprinted with permission. From *Attic Nights, I, Books 1-5.* By Aulus Gellius. Translated by J. C. Rolfe. The Loeb Classical Library. Harvard University Press, 1927.

Also, in the fifth book of the same Cincius On Military Science we read the following: "When a levy was made in ancient times and soldiers were enrolled, the tribune of the soldiers compelled them to take an oath in the following words dictated by the magistrate:

In the army of the consuls Gaius Laelius, son of Gaius, and Lucius Cornelius, son of Publius, and for ten miles around it, you will not with malice aforethought commit a theft, either alone or with others, of more than the value of a silver sesterce in any one day. And except for one spear, a spear shaft, wood, fruit, fodder, a bladder, a purse, and a torch, if you find or carry off anything there which is not your own and is worth more than one silver sesterce, you will bring it to the consul Gaius Laelius, son of Gaius, or to the consul Lucius Cornelius, son of Publius, or to whomsoever either of them shall appoint, or you will make known within the next three days whatever you have found or wrongfully carried off; or you will restore it to him whom you suppose to be its rightful owner, as you wish to do what is right.'
Moreover, when soldiers had been enrolled, a day was appointed on which they should appear and should answer to the consul's summons; then an oath was taken, binding them to appear, with the addition of the following exceptions:
unless there be any of the following excuses: a funeral in his family or purification from a dead body (provided these were not appointed for that day in order that he might not appear on that day), a dangerous disease, or an omen which could not be passed by without expiatory rites, or an anniversary sacrifice, which could not be properly celebrated unless he himself were present on that day, violence or the attack of enemies, a stated and appointed day with a foreigner; if anyone shall have any of these excuses, then on the day following that on which he is excused for these reasons he shall come and render service to the one who held the levy in that district, village or town.'

The De Re Militari of Vegetius: A Classical Text in the Middle Ages
By Christopher Allmand

Volume: 54 Issue: 6
June 2004

The De Re Militari (also referred to as the Epitoma Rei Militaris) of the late-fourth-century writer, Flavius Vegetius Renatus, is today not as widely known or appreciated as it deserves to be. Probably written as a call for military reform in the dying years of the Roman empire, it is in no real sense the work of an original thinker. Yet the De Re Militari, respected as an example of practical Roman culture, greatly influenced the medieval world. It was frequently read, and its proposals eagerly studied, by men of many backgrounds in the Middle Ages. Even in quite recent times it has been used in the education of soldiers at military academies. Today, 226 manuscripts of the Latin text (a large number for a classical text) survive, while translations into several European languages considerably increase that figure

In Vegetius' view, an army generally owed its successes to the twin processes of good selection and sound training. The choice of suitable recruits was a task of weighty responsibility. As the first book states:

...the strength of the realm and the foundation of the Roman empire depend on the initial examination of the levy. Let it not be thought an unimportant duty, nor one which may be delegated to anyone, anywhere.

Once selected according to criteria which emphasized the recruit's moral and intellectual qualities, as well as his physical ones, the future soldier was put through a preliminary four-month period of intense training enabling him to learn skills that made him confident and ready to take part in war. Having passed a final assessment, he was tattooed and taken into service.

Vegetius was encouraged by his imperial master and patron (possibly Theodosius I) to write more. He obliged with a second book largely given over to the workings and administration of the ideal Roman army. Less directly relevant to later military practice, this book appealed rather less to a medieval readership in terms of what it taught. However, what it revealed regarding the day-to-day workings of the Roman army was appreciated by those interested in how the Roman empire had been won and defended. The book also contained practical advice that could be valuable:

Every recruit without exception should in the summer months learn the art of swimming, for rivers are not always crossed by bridges, and armies, both when advancing and retreating, are frequently forced to swim.

Likewise, they must learn to cross difficult terrain, to run 'so as to charge the enemy with greater impetus', and to jump with a heavy pack on their backs, 'for both mobility and strength are thought to be required of the [soldier]'. Most important was the public role that Vegetius envisaged for soldiers who, once trained, took an oath:

by God, Christ and the Holy Spirit … that they will strenuously do all that the Emperor may command, will never desert the service, nor refuse to die for the Roman State....

whose servants they became and whose remuneration they accepted.

Book III came to be regarded as the core of the work. It took as its basic premise the need to defeat the enemy, but to do this avoiding bloody battle as far as possible. Indeed, the duty of the general (the dux) was essentially to preserve 'the wealth of landowners, the protection of cities, the lives of soldiers and the glory of the State'. Not surprisingly, since Vegetius wrote when Rome was being attacked by exterior forces, he regarded war as being mainly defensive in aim and character. The famous statement that 'he who desires peace, let him prepare for war' derives from Vegetius. Yet the remainder of that statement is often ignored. It continues:

...he who wants victory, let him train soldiers diligently. He who wishes a successful outcome, let him fight with strategy, not at random. No one dares challenge or harm one whom he realizes will win if he fights. [III, Preface]

What was Vegetius saying here? The statement can be seen as an assertion of deterrent theory. Yet the existence of an army did not, in itself, deter an ambitious enemy or aggressor. What did was the likelihood, better still the virtual certainty, of defeat, a much more effective deterrent than numbers alone. So we come to a theme that touched Vegetius deeply: the quality of the army as a fighting force. Regular training was essential in making an army effective and successful. Training taught skills, and then honed them; it gave both the individual soldier and the army as a whole the necessary confidence to achieve victory. In addition, the army had to fight 'with strategy, not at random'. What Vegetius meant was that the army's approach to fighting must be planned, ordered and principled. In a series of chapters in Book III (beginning at chapter 14) Vegetius outlined the factors that he saw as crucial to victory. Granted that the army fought as a unit (although one of many parts) it must learn to advance, to wheel, even to retreat in an orderly way, 'not at random'. To be fully efficient each man must have proper space in which to move and to wield his weapon effectively. The placing of the army's units in different formations (depending upon the circumstances of the moment) was also given prominence, as was the position in which the dux should place himself in order to have an overview of the action, encourage his soldiers, and convey his orders through the system of signals that Vegetius described. This mixture of preparation and order, coupled with a strong element of adaptability, created an army whose power to deter few might wish to challenge, thus opening the way to peace.

Added to this was the importance Vegetius attributed to good generalship. The commander's qualities were essentially those of being prepared: he must inform himself in advance about the nature of the country through which he would be advancing; he must also try to discover the enemy's intentions, so that these could be countered effectively. Being properly prepared, the general would win the day by being one step ahead of the enemy, thus surprising him when he least expected it. Vegetius' commander had the good of his own men very much in mind. The picture was one of a dux who cared for the health (a matter of great practical importance) and well being of those under his command. Soldiers were men of flesh and blood, strengths and weaknesses, and should be treated as such. The dux should therefore consider the feelings of the warrior when faced with the proximity of the enemy and the likelihood of imminent action. A camp was not only a place to rest; it was constructed, and guarded, to be a place of safety. Regular training made a man familiar with his weapon, so that in changing situations a well prepared army reacted positively to the unfamiliar, a common cause of fear among soldiers. Vegetius therefore warned against leading hesitant soldiers into battle; they did neither themselves nor anyone else any good.

Just as he sought to encourage his own men, so the good dux should show himself aware of the advantages to be gained from playing upon the collective fears of the enemy and undermining the confidence of his men, using deceit if necessary. Everything should be done to secure an advantage, particularly a psychological advantage, over the enemy. Occupy the high ground, Vegetius urged 'for he who struggles uphill enters a double contest with the ground and with the enemy'; 'the glitter of arms strikes very great fear in the enemy'; surprise is a great demoralizer; above all, 'hunger is more savage than the sword'. We see here how anxious Vegetius was to ensure that victories should be won with minimum effort or cost of life. Much of what he taught was written to ensure that the enemy surrendered or withdrew before the battlefield became a place of slaughter.

The fourth book, divided into a fifth in a number of manuscripts, drew the attention of readers away from battles on land to sieges and to conflict at sea. In both cases the information provided was rather technical. For example, Vegetius described a wide array of siege engines available to the Roman army of his time; not all, however, would survive the centuries that followed. Moreover, as comments on manuscripts clearly indicate, the meanings of some technical terms were no longer fully understood. None the less the growing importance of siege warfare assured interest in the relevance of much of what the book contained. How sieges should be organized and resisted, what weaponry was needed to further the interests of both attacker and besieged, were matters considered by Vegetius, who had much to say about the use of mobile towers, and the various weapons that threw the missiles increasingly used in siege warfare. On the other hand, most of what Vegetius wrote regarding ships and naval warfare was of such a general nature that, lacking specifics, it largely failed to catch the attention of readers in the Middle Ages even though, by the end of the period, war at sea was coming to take on greater military significance.

Over a period of many centuries, from the ninth to the sixteenth, the Middle Ages would turn the De Re Militari into a sort of military bible. How influential it was before the twelfth century is difficult to say precisely. The work was not yet, in any meaningful sense of the term, the intellectual property of military men, although it was probably known to some, including Fulk Nerra, Count of Anjou in the first half of the eleventh century. One may doubt, however, whether at this time a book, in particular one written in Latin, would have superseded practical experience as the source of military knowledge, although the need to train young men in the ways and skills of the active military life, a basic message of the De Re Militari, would certainly have been recognized. Yet passages such as Vegetius' description of the semi-religious ceremony of acceptance of the recruit into the ranks of the army had something in common with the ritual dubbing of the knight. Here and there, in works of both literature and history, descriptions of military events suggest that aspects of Vegetius' teaching were to influence actual practice. How is such evidence to be interpreted? Does it reflect real knowledge and appreciation of what Vegetius had urged and a conscious attempt by commanders to put his ideas into practice? Or is the answer that certain well-read writers of chronicles, aware of what Vegetius had taught, retold the military events of the past using his language and his ideas irrespective of how things had actually been done? How deep did a knowledge of Vegetius' text actually go among the military elite of the twelfth century?

Some historians are skeptical about accepting at face value the chronicler's story that Geoffrey Plantagenet consulted a copy of the De Re Militari when faced with a practical problem at the siege of Montreuil-Bellay in 1150, not least, in this case, because he cited Vegetius as having proposed something which does not appear in his text. Was the chronicler engaged in a 'name-dropping' exercise to impress his readers? Few of the manuscripts that survive today were of a format which might have been taken to a siege or field of battle. The story also suggests that the De Re Militari was a kind of handbook providing solutions to practical problems. That is to misconstrue its nature entirely.

It would be some time, therefore, before the work became part of the intellectual property of military men. As a work written in Latin, it was largely 'owned' by the clergy, the main day-to-day guardians of the language since the days of late antiquity. Inspection of the manuscript tradition reveals that in the early days the work was copied more often than not for libraries attached to monasteries, cathedrals and other ecclesiastical establishments. Surviving library catalogues, most compiled in the thirteenth century or later, also underline the importance of the De Re Militari in clerical culture. The monk Bede, writing in the early eighth century, was one of the first to have cited Vegetius; for many centuries those who followed him were, with a few exceptions, mainly men of a religious rather than a military bent. The life of constant training and self-discipline encouraged by Vegetius will have appealed to the followers of the monastic rule. Furthermore, the Church looked upon the disciplined soldier as an instrument of social order and stability. Knighthood was originally a function whose aim was the achievement and maintenance of such an order.

The De Re Militari stressed that the soldier must carry out the orders of the ruler under whom he served. What that ruler should know about the practice of war was becoming a matter of increasing concern to those who felt that kings and princes should have access to the best advice on how to be good rulers. It was for this reason that, by the twelfth century at the latest, certain parts of Vegetius' text came to be incorporated into a new form of political literature, written in Latin by members of the clergy, giving guidance on how to rule. The nature of these works was essentially didactic; they served to instruct, as Vegetius had sought to instruct. From the England of Henry II and Thomas Becket (who had a copy of Vegetius at Canterbury) emerged what would become a 'best seller', the Policraticus of John of Salisbury, part of which, on the military education of the prince, depended unashamedly on the De Re Militari, which taught that a ruler's people could benefit greatly from his military skills, effectively linking these with the defense of the common good. A century later Giles of Rome, who became archbishop of Bourges and tutor to the future Philip IV of France, compiled his widely read De Regimine Principum (On the Rule of Princes) into which he, too, incorporated ideas from Vegetius, thus helping to disseminate these still further.

By the thirteenth century Vegetius' text was coming into the hands of a widening circle of readers causing it to be copied in increasing numbers. By then a growing number of readers must have been people with a practical interest in military matters. Surviving manuscripts show what attracted their attention. The practice of marking, often with a finger pointing from the margin to a particular passage, those parts of a work that had aroused a reader's interest, is useful for us today, as

a means of offering an insight into the minds and ideas of past readers.

Much appreciated, for example, was Vegetius' emphasis, found throughout his book, upon the need for an army to fight as a team; little room was left for the heroic action that earned its perpetrator fame and glory. Likewise, for some it was a novelty to discover what the Romans had regarded as an army, whom it was intended to serve, and what its 'social' purpose was. Vegetius drew attention to the army as an instrument, which, created by the ruler for the defense of a society, owed its loyalty to the prince (or king) from whom it took its orders. His discussion of these fundamental matters appears to have taken some by surprise. By the end of the Middle Ages, however, these ideas had won support in some states on the Italian peninsula, as well as in France, whose 'national', indeed 'statist' army, ultimately under the command of the king, was gradually developed, on this basis, in the fourteenth and fifteenth centuries.

Other aspects of Vegetius' ideas also encouraged later men's thinking. The process of selecting young men capable of forming an army (and, by implication, rejecting those deemed unsuitable) was in early times seen as a new departure. So the need first to train them to a high level of competence and then to keep them in a state of sustained preparation ('men who stopped fighting a long time ago should be treated as recruits') was often noted as something to be acted upon. The value of experience and what might be learned from consulting veterans, was emphasized in Book III:

...an important art and technique of a general is to call in persons from the entire army who are knowledgeable about war and aware of their own and the enemy's forces, and to hold frequent discussions with them in an atmosphere from which all flattery, which does so much harm, has been banished.

Annotations in many manuscripts strongly suggest that Vegetius' view was closely studied and appreciated. The management of the army on the march; the way it should be protected in camp; and, finally, the things that ought to be done in advance to bring about the enemy's defeat were all discussed.

The judgment of the Middle Ages that there was much to be learned from Vegetius' work accounts for its presence among the early translations into the developing vernacular languages commissioned from the mid-thirteenth century onwards. The first translation, into Anglo-Norman, was made in the 1260s, probably for the future Edward I. It would be followed some twenty years later by the first of a number made into French and, not long afterwards, by one into Italian. These were only the beginnings of a lengthy development which would see Vegetius rendered into seven languages, including German, Castilian, Catalan, English and, probably, Portuguese before 1450. About 1473-74 he would become the first of the classical authors on technical matters to be printed in Latin, while vernacular versions would also appear in print. At the same time manuscripts continued to be copied years after the appearance of the printed word. Old practices died hard.

By the fourteenth century, with the development of education, Vegetius' text was coming both to be known and, significantly, owned by an ever expanding range of readers. Some were men of great fame; the manuscript owned, read and annotated by Petrarch is today in the Vatican Library. Rulers would also come to possess their own copies: Alfonso V, king of Aragon and Naples, Louis XII of France and Richard III of England, whose copy of the English translation is in the British Library, were among those fifteenth-century kings who, along with members of great Italian families such as Malatesta, Medici and Visconti, owned manuscripts of Vegetius' work. Among lesser mortals who possessed a copy of the De Re Militari were administrators and lawyers, as well as scholars, men of education who had, particularly in Renaissance Italy, an interest in

texts that reflected the classical world, its ideas, practices and modes of expression.

Probably the factor that most attracted these readers to Vegetius' text was its mixture of the 'philosophical' and the 'practical'. In the long-term perspective the De Re Militari may be seen as a work which set out a reasoned approach to war, by relating its outcome closely to action founded upon foresight and experience. Vegetius and the author of the biblical Book of Maccabees were at one in saying that victories did not depend upon numbers alone. But they might not have agreed with what came to be the Christian view that the result of battle depended essentially on divine favor or intervention. In the age that witnessed the development of the theory of 'just war', God was seen as 'awarding' victory to the side with the better moral cause. While admitting that the outcome of battle was often unpredictable, Vegetius hinted at something else. Victory, he suggested, was achieved by (not given to) those whose armies consisted of well selected, properly trained 'professional' forces, led by men who did not wait for things to happen but themselves took initiatives, founded on good information and a reflective approach to the conflict. New and important attitudes were beginning to take over, as man was coming to assume more responsibility for his own destiny.

Further Reading:

Vegetius: Epitome of military science, trans. N. P. Milner, 2nd rev. edn (Liverpool University Press, 1996); The earliest English translation of Vegetius' De Re Militari, ed. G. Lester (Carl Winter Universitätsverlag, 1988); C. T. Allmand, 'The De Re Militari of Vegetius in the Middle Ages and Renaissance', in Writing war: Medieval literary responses to warfare, ed C. Saunders, F. Le Saux & N. Thomas (D.S. Brewer, 2004); C. T. Allmand, 'Fifteenth-century versions of Vegetius' De Re Militari', in Armies, chivalry and warfare in medieval Britain and France, ed M. Strickland (Paul Watkins, 1998). B. S. Bachrach, 'The practical use of Vegetius' De Re Militari during the early Middle Ages', Warfare and military

organization in pre-Crusade Europe (Ashgate
Publishing, 2002).

Epitoma Rei Militari
by Flavius Vegetius Renatus

390 CE

The Military Institutions of the Romans (De Re Militari). Translated from the Latin by Lieutenant John Clarke
Text written in 390 CE British translation published in 1767. Copyright Expired

Introduction
The most influential military treatise in the western world from Roman times to the 19th Century was Vegetius' DE RE MILITARI. Its impressions on our own traditions of discipline and organization are everywhere evident.

The Austrian Field Marshal, Prince de Ligne, as late as 1770, called it a golden book and wrote: "A God, said Vegetius, inspired the legion, but for myself, I find that a God inspired Vegetius." Richard Coeur de Lion carried DE RE MILITARI everywhere with him in his campaigns, as did his father, Henry II of England. Around 1000 A. D. Vegetius was the favorite author of Foulques the Black, the able and ferocious Count of Anjou. Numerous manuscript copies of Vegetius circulated in the time of Charlemagne and one of them was considered a necessity of life by his commanders. A manuscript Vegetius was listed in the will of Count Everard de Frejus, about 837 A. D., in the time of Ludwig the Just.

In his Memoirs, Montecuculli, the conqueror of the Turks at St. Gotthard, wrote: "However, there are spirits bold enough to believe themselves great captains as soon as they know how to handle a horse, carry a lance at charge in a tournament, or as soon as they have read the precepts of Vegetius." Such was the reputation of Vegetius for a thousand years.

Manuscript copies dating from the 10th to the 15th centuries are extant to the number of 150. DE RE MILITARI was translated into English, French, and Bulgarian before the invention of printing. The first printed edition was made in Utrecht in 1473. It was followed in quick succession by editions in Cologne, Paris and Rome. It was first published in English by Caxton, from an English manuscript copy, in 1489.

Flavius Vegetius Renatus was a Roman of high rank. In some manuscripts he is given the title of count. Raphael of Volterra calls him a Count of Constantinople. Little is known of his life. It is apparent from his book that he had not had extensive practical experience as a soldier.. He states quite frankly that his purpose was to collect and synthesize from ancient manuscripts and regulations the military customs and wisdom that made ancient Rome great. According to his statement, his principal sources were Cato the Elder, Cornelius Celsus, Paternus, Frontinus, and the regulations and ordinances of Augustus, Trajan and Hadrian.

The Emperor Valentinian, to whom the book is dedicated, is believed to be the second emperor of that name. He evidently was not Valentinian I since his successor, Gratian, is named in the book. Between the reign of Valentinian II and Valentinian III, Rome was taken and burned by Alaric, King of the Goths, an event that unquestionably would have been mentioned had it occurred before the book was written. Vegetius mentions the defeat of the Roman armies by the Goths, but probably refers to the battle of Adrianople where Valens, the colleague of Valentinian I, was killed.

It is a paradox that DE RE MILITARI, which was to become a military bible for innumerable generations of European soldiers, was little used by the Romans for whom it was written. The decay of the Roman armies had progressed too far to be arrested by Vegetius' pleas for a return to the virtues of discipline and courage of the ancients. At the same time Vegetius' hope for a revival of the ancient organization of the legion was impracticable. Cavalry had adopted the armor of the foot soldier and was just commencing to become the principal arm of the military forces. The heavy armed foot-soldier, formerly the backbone of the legion, was falling a victim of his own weight and immobility, and the light-armed infantry, unable to resist the shock of cavalry, was turning more and more to missile weapons. By one of the strange mutations of history, when later the cross-bow and gun-powder deprived cavalry of its shock-power, the tactics of Vegetius again became ideal for armies, as they had been in the times from which he drew his inspiration.

Vegetius unceasingly emphasized the importance of constant drill and severe discipline and this aspect of his work was very tiresome to the soldiers of the middle ages, the feudal system lending itself but poorly to discipline. "Victory in war," he states in his opening sentence, "does not depend entirely upon numbers or mere courage; only skill and discipline will insure it." His first book is devoted to the selection, training and discipline of recruits. He insists upon the utmost meticulousness in drill. "No part of drill is more essential in action than for soldiers to keep their ranks with the greatest exactness." His description of the many arms which the Roman soldier was required to become expert in reminds one of the almost innumerable duties of the present day infantryman. Recruits were to be hardened so as to be able to march twenty miles in half a summer's day at ordinary step and twenty-four miles at quick step. It was the ancient regulation that practice marches of this distance must be made three times a month.

The second book deals with the organization and officers of the legion, the ancient system of promotion, and how to

401

form the legion for battle. We find the Romans provided for soldier's deposits, just as is done in the American army today; that guard and duty rosters were kept in those days as now; and that the Roman system of guard duty is only slightly different from our manual for interior guard duty. The field music is described and is an ornamental progenitor of that in use in United States. The legion owed its success, according to Vegetius, to its arms and its machines, as well as to the bravery of its soldiers. The legion had fifty-five ballista for throwing darts and ten onagri, drawn by oxen, for throwing stones. Every legion carried its ponton equipment, "small boats hollowed out of a single piece of cimber, with long cables or chains to fasten them together." And in addition were "whatever is necessary for every kind of service, that the encampments may have all the strength and conveniences of a fortified city." Trains of workmen were provided to perform all the duties now performed by the various services in armies.

The third book deals with tactics and strategy and it was this portion of Vegetius that influenced war in the Middle Ages so greatly. He explains the use of reserves, attributing this invention to the Spartans, from whom the Romans adopted it. "It is much better to have several bodies of reserves than to extend your front too much" - an injunction as good today as when it was written. Encircling pursuit is described. The terrain is not overlooked. "The nature of the ground is often of more consequence than courage." The enemy should be estimated carefully. "It is essential to know the character of the enemy and of their principal officers-whether they be rash or cautious, enterprising or timid, whether they fight from careful calculation or from chance."

Vegetius' work is filled with maxims that have become a part of our everyday life. "He, therefore, who aspires to peace should prepare for war." "The ancients preferred discipline to numbers." "In the midst of peace, war is looked upon as an object too distant to merit consideration." "Few men are born brave; many become so through training and force of discipline."

Vegetius was a reformer who attempted to restore the degenerate Romans of the 4th Century to the military virtues of the ancients, whom he never ceases to laud. His little book was made short and easy to read, so as not to frighten, by a too arduous text, the readers whom he hoped to convince. He constantly gives the example of the " Ancients" to his contemporaries. The result is a sort of perfume of actuality, which had much to do with his success. It still is interesting reading and still is the subject of modern commentaries. No less than forty have appeared in Germany in the 19th and 20th centuries. Revue Mititare Generate (France) and our own Infantry Journal carried articles on Vegetius in 1938. Dankfried Schenk published an interesting article in Klio in 1930, which gives Vegetius the highest place among the writers of his time.

The present edition includes the first three books of Vegetius' work, omitting only repetitions. The fourth and fifth books, both very brief, deal with the attack and defense of fortified places and with naval operations. These are of interest only to military antiquarians and for that reason have not been included. The present translation was made by Lieutenant John Clarke and published in London in 1767. It is the best available in English and has been edited only to the minimum extent necessary to conform to modern usage.

An excellent discussion of Vegetius can be found in Warfare, by Spaulding, Nickerson and Wright, page 294, et sequens, Harcourt Brace & Co., 1925. Delpech, La Tactique au 13me Siecte, Paris, 1886, gives the best account of the influence of Vegetius on European military thought. Hans Delbruck's discussion of Vegetius in Geschichte der Kriegskunft, Vol. II, Berlin, 1921, although brief, is very acute

Book I
Preface to Book I

It has been an old custom for authors to offer to their Princes the fruits of their studies in belles letters, from a persuasion that no work can be published with propriety but under the auspices of the Emperor, and that the knowledge of a Prince should be more general, and of the most important kind, as its influence is felt so keenly by all his subjects. We have many instances of the favorable reception which Augustus and his illustrious successors conferred on the works presented to them; and this encouragement of the Sovereign made the sciences flourish. The consideration of Your Majesty's superior indulgence for attempts of this sort, induced me to follow this example, and makes me at the same time almost forget my own inability when compared with the ancient writers. One advantage, however, I derive from the nature of this work, as it requires no elegance of expression, or extraordinary share of genius, but only great care and fidelity in collecting and explaining, for public use, the instructions and observations of our old historians of military affairs, or those who wrote expressly concerning them.

My design in this treatise is to exhibit in some order the peculiar customs and usages of the ancients in the choice and discipline of their new levies. Nor do I presume to offer this work to Your

Majesty from a supposition that you are not acquainted with every part of its contents; but that you may see that the same salutary dispositions and regulations which your own wisdom prompts You to establish for the happiness of the Empire, were formerly observed by the founders thereof; and that Your Majesty may find with ease in this abridgement whatever is most useful on so necessary and important a subject.

THE ROMAN DISCIPLINE THE CAUSE OF THEIR GREATNESS

Victory in war does not depend entirely upon numbers or mere courage; only skill and discipline will insure it. We find that the Romans owed the conquest of the world to no other cause than continual military training, exact observance of discipline in their camps and unwearied cultivation of the other arts of war. Without these, what chance would the inconsiderable numbers of the Roman armies have had against the multitudes of the Gauls? Or with what success would their small size have been opposed to the prodigious stature of the Germans? The Spaniards surpassed us not only in numbers, but in physical strength. We were always inferior to the Africans in wealth and unequal to them in deception and stratagem. And the Greeks, indisputably, were far superior to us in skill in arts and all kinds of knowledge.

But to all these advantages the Romans opposed unusual care in the choice of their levies and in their military training. They thoroughly understood the importance of hardening them by continual practice, and of training them to every maneuver that might happen in the line and in action. Nor were they less strict in punishing idleness and sloth. The courage of a soldier is heightened by his knowledge of his profession, and he only wants an opportunity to execute what he is convinced he has been perfectly taught. A handful of men, inured to war, proceed to certain victory, while on the contrary numerous armies of raw and undisciplined troops are but multitudes of men dragged to slaughter.

THE SELECTION OF RECRUITS

To treat our subject with some method, we shall first examine what provinces or nations are to be preferred for supplying the armies with recruits. It is certain that every country produces both brave men and cowards; but it is equally as certain that some nations are naturally more warlike than others, and that courage, as well as strength of body, depends greatly upon the influence of the different climates.

We shall next examine whether the city or the country produces the best and most capable soldiers. No one, I imagine, can doubt that the peasants are the most fit to carry arms for they from their infancy have been exposed to all kinds of weather and have been brought up to the hardest labor. They are able to endure the greatest heat of the sun, are unacquainted with the use of baths, and are strangers to the other luxuries of life. They are simple, content with little, inured to all kinds of fatigue, and prepared in some measure for a military life by their continual employment in their country-work, in handling the spade, digging trenches and carrying burdens. In cases of necessity, however, they are sometimes obliged to make levies in the cities. And these men, as soon as enlisted, should be taught to work on entrenchments, to march in ranks, to carry heavy burdens, and to bear the sun and dust. Their meals should be coarse and moderate; they should be accustomed to lie sometimes in the open air and sometimes in tents. After this, they should be instructed in the use of their arms. And if any long expedition is planned, they should be encamped as far as possible from the temptations of the city. By these precautions their minds, as well as their bodies, will properly be prepared for the service.

I realize that in the first ages of the Republic, the Romans always raised their armies in the city itself, but this was at a time when there were no pleasures, no luxuries to enervate them. The Tiber was then their only bath, and in it they refreshed themselves after their exercises and fatigues in the field by swimming. In those days the same man was both soldier and farmer, but a farmer who, when occasion arose, laid aside his tools and put on the sword. The truth of this is confirmed by the instance of Quintius Cincinnatus, who was following the plow when they came to offer him the dictatorship. The chief strength of our armies, then, should be recruited from the country. For it is certain that the less a man is acquainted with the sweets of life, the less reason he has to be afraid of death.

THE PROPER AGE FOR RECRUITS

If we follow the ancient practice, the proper time for enlisting youth into the army is at their entrance into the age of puberty. At this time instructions of every kind are more quickly imbibed and more lastingly imprinted on the mind. Besides this, the indispensable military exercises of running and leaping must be acquired before the limbs are too much stiffened by age. For it is activity, improved by continual practice, which forms the useful and good soldier. Formerly, says Sallust, the Roman youth, as soon as they were of an age to carry arms, were trained in the Strictest manner in their camps to all the fatigues and exercises of war. For it is certainly better that a soldier, perfectly disciplined, should, through emulation, repine at his not being yet arrived at a proper age for action, than have the mortification of knowing it is past. A sufficient time is also required for his instruction in the different branches of the service. It is no easy matter to train the horse or foot archer, or to form the legionary soldier to every part of the drill, to teach him not to quit his post, to keep ranks, to take a proper aim and throw his missile weapons with force, to dig trenches, to plant palisades, how to manage his shield, glance off the blows of the enemy, and how to parry a stroke with dexterity. A soldier, thus perfect in his business, so far from showing any backwardness to engage, will be eager for an opportunity of signaling himself.

THEIR SIZE

We find the ancients very fond of procuring the tallest men they could for the service, since the standard for the cavalry of the wings and for the infantry of the first legionary cohorts was fixed at six feet, or at least five feet ten inches. These requirements might easily be kept up in those times when such numbers followed the profession of arms and before it was the fashion for the flower of Roman youth to devote themselves to the civil offices of state. But when necessity requires it, the height of a man is not to be regarded so much as his strength; and for this we have the authority of Homer, who tells us that the deficiency of stature in Tydeus was amply compensated by his vigor and courage.

SIGNS OF DESIRABLE QUALITIES

Those employed to superintend new levies should be particularly careful in examining the features of their faces, their eyes, and the make of their limbs, to enable them to form a true judgment and choose such as are most likely to prove good soldiers. For experience assures us that there are in men, as well as in horses and dogs, certain signs by which their virtues may be discovered. The young soldier, therefore, ought to have a lively eye, should carry his head erect, his chest should be broad, his shoulders muscular and brawny, his fingers long, his arms strong, his waist small, his shape easy, his legs and feet rather nervous than fleshy. When all these marks are found in a recruit, a little height may be dispensed with, since it is of much more importance that a soldier should be strong than tall.

TRADES PROPER FOR NEW LEVIES

In choosing recruits regard should be given to their trade. Fishermen, fowlers, confectioners, weavers, and in general all whose professions more properly belong to women should, in my opinion, by no means be admitted into the service. On the contrary, smiths, carpenters, butchers, and huntsmen are the most proper to be taken into it. On the careful choice of soldiers depends the welfare of the Republic, and the very essence of the Roman Empire and its power is so inseparably connected with this charge, that it is of the highest importance not to be entrusted indiscriminately, but only to persons whose fidelity can be relied on. The ancients considered Sertorius' care in this point as one of the most eminent of his military qualifications. The soldiery to whom the defense of the Empire is consigned and in whose hands is the fortune of war, should, if possible, be of reputable families and unexceptionable in their manners. Such sentiments as may be expected in these men will make good soldiers. A sense of honor, by preventing them from behaving ill, will make them victorious.

But what good can be expected from a man by nature a coward, though ever so well disciplined or though he has served ever so many campaigns? An army raised without proper regard to the choice of its recruits was never yet made good by length of time; and we are now convinced by fatal experience that this is the source of all our misfortunes. So many defeats can only be imputed to the effects of a long peace which has made us negligent and careless in the choice of our levies and to the inclination so prevalent among the better sort in preferring the civil posts of the government to the profession of arms and to the shameful conduct of the superintendents, who, through interest or connivance, accept many men which those who are obliged to furnish substitutes for the army choose to send, and admit such men into the service as the masters themselves would not even keep for servants. Thus it appears that a trust of such importance should be committed to none but men of merit and integrity.

THE MILITARY MARK

The recruit, however, should not receive the military mark* as soon as enlisted. He must first be tried if fit for service; whether he has sufficient activity and strength; if he has capacity to learn his duty; and whether he has the proper degree of military courage. For many, though promising enough in appearance, are found very unfit upon trial. These are to be rejected and replaced by better men; for it is not numbers, but bravery which carries the day.

After their examination, the recruits should then receive the military mark, and be taught the use of their arms by constant and daily exercise. But this essential custom has been abolished by the relaxation introduced by a long peace. We cannot now expect to find a man to teach what he never learned himself. The only method, therefore, that remains of recovering the ancient customs is by books, and by consulting the old historians. But they are of little service to us in this respect, as they only relate the exploits and events of wars, and take no notice of the objects of our present enquiries, which they considered as universally known.

INITIAL TRAINING

The first thing the soldiers are to be taught is the military step, which can only be acquired by constant practice of marching quick and together. Nor is anything of more consequence either on the march or in the line than that they should keep their ranks with the greatest exactness. For troops who march in an irregular and disorderly manner are always in great danger of being defeated. They should march with the common military step twenty miles in five summer-hours, and with the full step, which is quicker, twenty-four miles in the same number of hours. If they exceed this pace, they no longer march but run, and no certain rate can be assigned.

But the young recruits in particular must be exercised in running, in order to charge the enemy with great vigor; occupy, on occasion, an advantageous post with greater expedition, and prevent the enemy in their designs upon the same; that they may, when sent to reconnoiter, advance with speed, return with greater celerity and more easily come up with the enemy in a pursuit.

Leaping is another very necessary exercise, to enable them to pass ditches or embarrassing eminences of any kind without trouble or difficulty. There is also another very material advantage to be derived from these exercises in time of action; for a soldier who advances with his javelin, running and leaping, dazzles the eyes of his adversary, strikes him with terror, and gives him the fatal stroke before he has time to put himself on his defense. Sallust, speaking of the excellence of Pompey the Great in these particulars, tells us that he disputed the superiority in leaping with the most active, in running with the most swift, and in exercises of strength with the most robust. Nor would he ever have been able to have opposed Serrorius with success, if he had not prepared both himself and his soldiers for action by continual exercises of this sort.

TO LEARN TO SWIM

Every young soldier, without exception, should in the summer months be taught to swim; for it is sometimes impossible to pass rivers on bridges, but the flying and pursuing army both are often obliged to swim over them. A sudden melting of snow or fall of rain often makes them overflow their banks, and in such a situation, the danger is as great from ignorance in swimming as from the enemy. The ancient Romans, therefore, perfected in every branch of the military art by a continued series of wars and perils, chose the Field of Mars as the most commodious for their exercises on account of its vicinity to the Tiber, that the youth might therein wash off the sweat and dust, and refresh themselves after their fatigues by swimming. The cavalry also as well as the infantry, and even the horses and the servants of the army should be accustomed to this exercise, as they are all equally liable to the same accidents.

THE POST EXERCISE

We are informed by the writings of the ancients that, among their other exercises, they had that of the post. They gave their recruits round bucklers woven with willows, twice as heavy as those used on real service, and wooden swords double the weight of the common ones. They exercised them with these at the post both morning and afternoon.

This is an invention of the greatest use, not only to soldiers, but also to gladiators. No man of either profession ever distinguished himself in the circus or field of battle, who was not perfect in this kind of exercise. Every soldier, therefore, fixed a post firmly in the ground, about the height of six feet. Against this, as against a real enemy, the recruit was exercised with the above mentioned arms, as it were with the common shield and sword, sometimes aiming At the head or face, sometimes at the sides, at others endeavoring to strike at the thighs or legs. He was instructed in what manner to advance and retire, and in short how to take every advantage of his adversary; but was thus above all particularly cautioned not to lay himself open to his antagonist while aiming his stroke at him.

NOT TO CUT, BUT TO THRUST WITH THE SWORD

They were likewise taught not to cut but to thrust with their swords. For the Romans not only made a jest of those who fought with the edge of that weapon, but always found them an easy conquest. A stroke with the edges, though made with ever so much force, seldom kills, as the vital parts of the body are defended both by the bones and armor. On the contrary, a stab, though it penetrates but two inches, is generally fatal. Besides in the attitude of striking, it is impossible to avoid exposing the right arm and side; but on the other hand, the body is covered while a thrust is given, and the adversary receives the point before he sees the sword. This was the method of fighting principally used by the Romans, and their reason for exercising recruits with arms of such a weight at first was, that when they came to carry the common ones so much lighter, the greater difference might enable them to act with greater security and alacrity in time of action.

THE DRILL CALLED ARMATURA

The new levies also should be taught by the masters at arms the system of drill called armatura, as it is still partly kept up among us. Experience even at this time convinces us that soldiers, perfect therein, are of the most service in engagements. And they afford certain proofs of the importance and effects of discipline in the difference we see between those properly trained in this branch of drill and the other troops. The old Romans were so conscious of its usefulness that they rewarded the masters at arms with a double allowance of provision. The soldiers who were backward in this drill were punished by having their allowance in barley. Nor did they receive it as usual, in wheat, until they had, in the presence of the prefect, tribunes, or other principal officers of the legion, showed sufficient proofs of their knowledge of every part of their study.

No state can either be happy or secure that is remiss and negligent in the discipline of its troops. For it is not profusion of riches or excess of luxury that can influence our enemies to court or respect us. This can only be effected by the terror of our arms. It is an observation of Cato that. misconduct in the common affairs of life may be retrieved, but that it is quite otherwise in war, where errors are fatal and without remedy, and are followed by immediate punishment. For the consequences of engaging an enemy, without skill or courage, is that part of the army is left on the field of battle, and those who remain receive such an impression from their defeat that they dare not afterwards look the enemy in the face.

THE USE OF MISSILE WEAPONS

Besides the aforementioned exercise of the recruits at the post, they were furnished with javelins of greater weight than common, which they were taught to throw at the same post. And the masters at arms were very careful to instruct them how to cast them with a proper aim and force. This practice strengthens the arm and makes the soldier a good marksman.

THE USE OF THE BOW

A third or fourth of the youngest and fittest soldiers should also be exercised at the post with bows and arrows made for that purpose only. The masters for this branch must be chosen with care and must apply themselves diligently to teach the men to hold the bow in a proper position, to bend it with strength, to keep the left hand steady. to draw the right with skill, to direct both the attention and the eye to the object, and to take their aim with equal certainty either on foot or on horseback. But this is not to be acquired without great application, nor to be retained without daily exercise and practice.

The utility of good archers in action is evidently demonstrated by Cato in his treatise on military discipline. To the institution of a body of troops of this sort Claudius owed his victory over an enemy who, till that time, had constantly been superior to him. Scipio Africanus, before his battle with the Numantines, who had made a Roman army ignominiously pass under the yoke, thought he could have no likelihood of success except by mingling a number of select archers with every century.

THE SLING

Recruits are to be taught the art of throwing stones both with the hand and sling. The inhabitants of the Balearic Islands are said to have been the inventors of slings, and to have managed them with surprising dexterity, owing to the manner of bringing up their children. The children were not allowed to have their food by their mothers till they had first struck it with their sling. Soldiers, notwithstanding their defensive armor, are often more annoyed by the round stones from the sling than by all the arrows of the enemy. Stones kill without mangling the body, and the contusion is mortal without loss of blood. It is universally known the ancients employed slingers in all their engagements. There is the greater reason for instructing all troops, without exception, in this exercise, as the sling cannot be reckoned any encumbrance, and often is of the greatest service, especially when they are obliged to engage in stony places, to defend a mountain or an eminence, or to repulse an enemy at the attack of a castle or city.

THE LOADED JAVELIN

The exercise of the loaded javelins, called martiobarbuli, must not be omitted. We formerly had two legions in Illyricum, consisting of six thousand men each, which from their extraordinary dexterity and skill in the use of these weapons were distinguished by the same appellation. They supported for a long time the weight of all the wars and distinguished themselves so remarkably that the Emperors Diocletian and Maximian on their accession honored them with the titles of Jovian and Herculean and preferred them before all the other legions. Every soldier carries five of these javelins in the hollow of his shield. And thus the legionary soldiers seem to supply the place of archers, for they wound both the men and horses of the enemy before they come within reach of the common missile weapons.

TO BE TAUGHT TO VAULT

The ancients strictly obliged both the veteran soldiers and recruits to a constant practice of vaulting. It has indeed reached our cimes, although little regard is paid to it at present. They had wooden horses for that purpose placed in winter under cover and in summer in the field. The young soldiers were taught to vault on them at first without arms, afterwards completely armed. And such was their attention to this exercise that they were accustomed to mount and dismount on either side indifferently, with their drawn swords or lances in their hands. By assiduous practice in the leisure of peace, their cavalry was brought to such perfection of discipline that they mounted their horses in an instant even amidst the confusion of sudden and unexpected alarms.

AND TO CARRY BURDENS

To accustom soldiers to carry burdens is also an essential part of discipline. Recruits in particular should be obliged frequently to carry a weight of not less than sixty pounds (exclusive of their arms), and to march with it in the ranks. This is because on difficult expeditions they often find themselves under the necessity of carrying their provisions as well as their arms. Nor will they find this troublesome when inured to it by custom, which makes everything easy. Our troops in ancient times were a proof of this, and Virgil has remarked it in the following lines:

The Roman soldiers, bred in war's alarms,
Bending with unjust loads and heavy arms,
Cheerful their toilsome marches undergo, And
pitch their sudden camp before the foe.

THE ARMS OF THE ANCIENTS

The manner of arming the troops comes next under consideration. But the method of the ancients no longer is followed. For though after the example of the Goths, the Alans and the Huns, we have made some improvements in the arms of the cavalry, yet it is plain the infantry are entirely defenseless. From the foundation of the city till the reign of the Emperor Gratian, the foot wore cuirasses and helmets. But negligence and sloth having by degrees introduced a total relaxation of discipline, the soldiers began to think their armor too heavy, as they seldom put it on. They first requested leave from the Emperor to lay aside the cuirass and afterwards the helmet. In consequence of this, our troops in their engagements with the Goths were often overwhelmed with their showers of arrows. Nor was the necessity of obliging the infantry to resume

their cuirasses and helmets discovered, notwithstanding such repeated defeats, which brought on the destruction of so many great cities.

Troops, defenseless and exposed to all the weapons of the enemy, are more disposed to fly than fight. What can be expected from a foot-archer without cuirass or helmet, who cannot hold at once his bow and shield; or from the ensigns whose bodies are naked, and who cannot at the same time carry a shield and the colors? The foot soldier finds the weight of a cuirass and even of a helmet intolerable. This is because he is so seldom exercised and rarely puts them on.

But the case would be quite different, were they even heavier than they are, if by constant practice he had been accustomed to wear them. But it seems these very men, who cannot support the weight of the ancient armor, think nothing of exposing themselves without defense to wounds and death, or, which is worse, to the shame of being made prisoners, or of betraying their country by flight; and thus to avoid an inconsiderable share of exercise and fatigue, suffer themselves ignominiously to be cut in pieces. With what propriety could the ancients call the infantry a wall, but that in some measure they resembled it by the complete armor of the legionary soldiers who had shields, helmets, cuirasses, and greaves of iron on the right leg; and the archers who had gauntlets on the left arm. These were the defensive arms of the legionary soldiers. Those who fought in the first line of their respective legions were called principes, in the second hastati, and in third triarii.

The triarii, according to their method of discipline, rested in time of action on one knee, under cover of their shields, so that in this position they might be less exposed to the darts of the enemy than if they stood upright; and also, when there was a necessity for bringing them up, that they might be fresh, in full vigor and charge with the greater impetuosity. There have been many instances of their gaining a complete victory after the entire defeat of both the principes and hastati.

The ancients had likewise a body of light infantry, slingers, and ferentarii (the light troops), who were generally posted on the wings and began the engagement. The most active and best disciplined men were selected for this service; and as their number was not very great, they easily retired in case of a repulse through the intervals of the legion, without thus occasioning the least disorder in the line.

The Pamonian leather caps worn by our soldiers were formerly introduced with a different design. The ancients obliged the men to wear them at all times so that being constantly accustomed to have the head covered they might be less sensible of the weight of the helmet.

As to the missile weapons of the infantry, they were javelins headed with a triangular sharp iron, eleven inches or a foot long, and were called piles. When once fixed in the shield it was impossible to draw them out, and when thrown with force and skill, they penetrated the cuirass without difficulty. At present they are seldom used by us, but are the principal weapon of the barbarian heavy-armed foot. They are called bebrae, and every man carries two or three of them to battle.

It must be observed that when the soldiers engage with the javelin, the left foot should be advanced, for, by this attitude the force required to throw it is considerably increased. On the contrary, when they are close enough to use their piles and swords, the right foot should be advanced, so that the body may present less aim to the enemy, and the right arm be nearer and in a more advantageous position for striking. Hence it appears that it is as necessary to provide soldiers with defensive arms of every kind as to instruct them in the use of offensive ones. For it is certain a man will fight with greater courage and confidence when he finds himself properly armed for defense.

ENTRENCHED CAMPS
Recruits are to be instructed in the manner of entrenching camps, there being no part of discipline so necessary and useful as this. For in a camp, well chosen and entrenched, the troops both day and night lie secure within their works, even though in view of the enemy. It seems to resemble a fortified city which they can build for their safety wherever they please. But this valuable art is now entirely lost, for it is long since any of

our camps have been fortified either with trenches or palisades. By this neglect our forces have been often surprised by day and night by the enemy's cavalry and suffered very severe losses. The importance of this custom appears not only from the danger to which troops are perpetually exposed who encamp without such precautions, but from the distressful situation of an army that, after receiving a check in the field, finds itself without retreat and consequently at the mercy of the enemy. A camp, especially in the neighborhood of an enemy, must be chosen with great care. Its situation should be strong by nature, and there should be plenty of wood, forage and water. If the army is to continue in it any considerable time, attention must be had to the salubrity of the place. The camp must not be commanded by any higher grounds from whence it might be insulted or annoyed by the enemy, nor must the location be liable to floods which would expose the army to great danger. The dimensions of the camps must be determined by the number of troops and quantity of baggage, that a large army may have room enough, and that a small one may not be obliged to extend itself beyond its proper ground. The form of the camps must be determined by the site of the country, in conformity to which they must be square, triangular or oval. The Praetorian gate should either front the east or the enemy. In a temporary camp it should face the route by which the army is to march. Within this gate the tents of the first centuries or cohorts are pitched, and the dragons* and other ensigns planted.

The Decumane gate is directly opposite to the Praetorian in the rear of the camp, and through this the soldiers are conducted to the place appointed for punishment or execution.

There are two methods of entrenching a camp. When the danger is not imminent, they carry a slight ditch round the whole circuit, only nine feet broad and seven deep. With the turf taken from this they make a kind of wall or breastwork three feet high on the inner side of the ditch. But where there is reason to be apprehensive of attempts of the enemy, the camp must be surrounded with a regular ditch twelve feet broad and nine feet deep perpendicular from the surface of the ground. A parapet is then raised on the side next the camp, of the height of four feet, with hurdles and fascines properly covered and secured by the earth taken out of the ditch. From these dimensions the interior height of the entrenchment will be found to be thirteen feet, and the breadth of the ditch twelve. On the top of the whole are planted strong palisades which the soldiers carry constantly with them for this purpose. A sufficient number of spades, pickaxes, wicker baskets and tools of all kinds are to be provided for these works.   There is no difficulty in carrying on the fortifications of a camp when no enemy is in sight. But if the enemy is near, all the cavalry and half the infantry are to be drawn up in order of battle to cover the rest of the troops at work on the entrenchments and be ready to receive the enemy if they offer to attack. The centuries are employed by turns on the work and are regularly called to the relief by a crier till the whole is completed. It is then inspected and measured by the centurions, who punish such as have been indolent or negligent. This is a very important point in the discipline of young soldiers, who when properly trained to it will be able in an emergency to fortify their camp with skill and expedition.

EVOLUTIONS

No part of drill is more essential in action than for soldiers to keep their ranks with the greatest exactness, without opening or closing too much. Troops too much crowded can never fight as they ought, and only embarrass one another. If their order is too open and loose, they give the enemy an opportunity of penetrating. Whenever this happens and they are attacked in the rear, universal disorder and confusion are inevitable. Recruits should therefore be constantly in the field, drawn up by the roll and formed at first into a single rank. They should learn to dress in a straight line and to keep an equal and just distance between man and man. They must then be ordered to double the rank, which they must perform very quickly, and instantly cover their file leaders. In the next place, they are to double again and form four deep. And then the triangle or, as it is commonly called, the wedge, a disposition found

very serviceable in action. They must be taught to form the circle or orb; for well-disciplined troops, after being broken by the enemy, have thrown themselves into this position and have thereby prevented the total rout of the army. These evolutions, often practiced in the field of exercise, will be found easy in execution on actual service.

MONTHLY MARCHES

It was a constant custom among the old Romans, confirmed by the Ordinances of Augustus and Hadrian, to exercise both cavalry and infantry three times in a month by marches of a certain length. The foot were obliged to march completely armed the distance of ten miles from the camp and return, in the most exact order and with the military step which they changed and quickened on some part of the march. Their cavalry likewise, in troops and properly armed, performed the same marches and were exercised at the same time in their peculiar movement and evolutions; sometimes, as if pursuing the enemy, sometimes retreating and returning again with greater impetuosity to the charge. They made these marches not in plain and even ground only, but both cavalry and infantry were ordered into difficult and uneven places and to ascend or descend mountains, to prepare them for all kinds of accidents and familiarize them with the different maneuvers that the various situations of a country may require.

CONCLUSION

These military maxims and instructions, invincible Emperor, as a proof of my devotion and zeal for your service, I have carefully collected from the works of all the ancient authors on the subject. My design herein is to point out the certain method of forming good and serviceable armies, which can only be accomplished by an exact imitation of the ancients in their care in the choice and discipline of their levies. Men are not degenerated in point of courage, nor are the countries that produced the Lacedaemonians, the Athenians, the Marsians, the Samnites, the Peligni and even the Romans themselves, yet exhausted. Did not the Epirots acquire in former times a great reputation in war?

Did not the Macedonians and Thessalians, after conquering the Persians, penetrate even into India? And it is well known that the warlike dispositions of the Dacians, Moesians and Thracians gave rise to the fable that Mars was born among them.

To pretend to enumerate the different nations so formidable of old, all which now are subject to the Romans, would be tedious. But the security established by long peace has altered their dispositions, drawn them off from military to civil pursuits and infused into them a love of idleness and ease. Hence a relaxation of military discipline insensibly ensued, then a neglect of it, and it sunk at last into entire oblivion. Now will it appear surprising that this alteration should have happened in latter times, if we consider that the peace, which lasted about twenty years or somewhat more after the first Punic war, enervated the Romans, before everywhere victorious, by idleness and neglect of discipline to such a degree, that in the second Punic war they were not able to keep the field against Hannibal. At last, after the defeat of many consuls and the loss of many officers and armies, they were convinced that the revival of discipline was the only road to victory and thereby recovered their superiority. The necessity, therefore, of discipline cannot be too often inculcated, as well as the strict attention requisite in the choice and training of new levies. It is also certain that it is a much less expense to a State to train its own subjects to arms than to take foreigners into its pay.

* This mark was imprinted on the hands of the soldiers, either with a hot iron, or in some other manner. It was indelible.

* The dragon was the particular ensign of each cohort.

Preface to Book II
To the Emperor Valentinian
Such a continued series of victories and triumphs proved incontestably Your Majesty's full and perfect knowledge of the military discipline of the ancients. Success in any profession is the most certain mark of skill in it. By a greatness of mind.

above human comprehension Your Majesty condescends to seek instruction from the ancients, notwithstanding your own recent exploits surpass antiquity itself. On receiving Your Majesty's orders to continue this abridgement, not so much for your instruction as convenience, I knew not how to reconcile my devotion to Your commands with the respect due to Your Majesty. Would it not be the greatest height of presumption to pretend to mention the art of war to the Lord and Master of the world and the Conqueror of all the barbarous nations, unless it were to describe his own actions? But disobedience to the will of so great a Prince would be both highly criminal and dangerous. My obedience, therefore, made me presumptuous, from the apprehensions of appearing more so by a contrary conduct. And in this I was not a little encouraged by the late instance of Your Majesty's indulgence. My treatise on the choice and discipline of new levies met with a favorable reception from Your Majesty, and since a work succeeded so well, composed of my own accord, I can have no fears for one undertaken by your own express commands.

Book II: The Organization of the Legion
THE MILITARY ESTABLISHMENT
The military establishment consists of three parts, the cavalry, infantry and marine. The wings of cavalry were so called from their similitude to wings in their extension on both sides of the main body for its protection. They are now called vexillations from the kind of standards peculiar to them. The legionary horse are bodies particularly annexed to each legion, and of a different kind; and on their model were organized the cavalry called Ocreati, from the light boots they wear. The fleet consists of two divisions, the one of men of war called Liburnae, and the other of armed sloops. The cavalry are designed for plains. Fleets are employed for the protection of seas and rivers. The infantry are proper for the defense of eminences, for the garrisons of cities and are equally serviceable in plain and in uneven ground. The latter, therefore, from their facility of acting everywhere, are certainly the most useful and necessary troops to a state exclusively of the consideration of their being maintained at a less

411

expense. The infantry are divided into two corps, the legions and auxiliaries, the latter of which are furnished by allies or confederates. The peculiar strength of the Romans always consisted in the excellent organization of their legions. They were so denominated ab eligendo, from the care and exactness used in the choice of the soldiers. The number of legionary troops in an army is generally much more considerable than that of the auxiliaries.

DIFFERENCE BETWEEN THE LEGIONS AND AUXILIARIES

The Macedonians, the Greeks and the Dardanians formed their troops into phalanxes of eight thousand men each. The Gauls, Celtiberians and many other barbarous nations divided their armies into bodies of six thousand each. The Romans have their legions usually six thousand strong, sometimes more.

We shall now explain the difference between the legions and the auxiliaries. The latter are hired corps of foreigners assembled from different parts of the Empire, made up of different numbers, without knowledge of one another or any tie of affection. Each nation has its own peculiar discipline, customs and manner of fighting. Little can be expected from forces so dissimilar in every respect, since it is one of the most essential points in military undertakings that the whole army should be put in motion and governed by one and the same order. But it is almost impossible for men to act in concert under such varying and unsettled circumstances. They are, however, when properly trained and disciplined, of material service and are always joined as light troops with the legions in the line. And though the legions do not place their principal dependence on them, yet they look on them as a very considerable addition to their strength.

But the complete Roman legion, in its own peculiar cohorts, contains within itself the heavy-armed foot, that is: the principes, hastati, triarii, and antefignani, the lightarmed foot, consisting of the ferentarii, archers, slingers, and balistarii, together with the legionary cavalry incorporated

with it. These bodies, all actuated with the same spirit, are united inseparably in their various dispositions for forming, encamping and fighting. Thus the legion is compact and perfect in all its parts and, without any foreign assistance, has always been superior to any force that could be brought against it. The Roman greatness is a proof of the excellence of their legions, for with them they always defeated whatever numbers of the enemy they thought fit, or their circumstances gave them an opportunity to engage.

CAUSES OF DECAY OF THE LEGION

The name of the legion remains indeed to this day in our armies, but its strength and substance are gone, since by the neglect of our predecessors, honors and preferments, which were formerly the recompenses of merit and long services, were to be attained only by interest and favor. Care is no longer taken to replace the soldiers, who after serving their full time, have received their discharges. The vacancies continually happening by sickness, discharges, desertion and various other casualties, if not supplied every year or even every month, must in time disable the most numerous army. Another cause of the weakness of our legions is that in them the soldiers find the duty hard, the arms heavy, the rewards distant and the discipline severe. To avoid these inconveniences, the young men enlist in the auxiliaries, where the service is less laborious and they have reason to expect more speedy recompenses.

Cato the Elder, who was often Consul and always victorious at the head of the armies, believed he should do his country more essential service by writing on military affairs, than by all his exploits in the field. For the consequences of brave actions are only temporary, while whatever is committed to writing for public good is of lasting benefit. Several others have followed his example, particularly Frontinus, whose elaborate works on this subject were so well received by the Emperor Trajan. These are the authors whose maxims and institutions I have undertaken to abridge in the most faithful and concise manner.

The expense of keeping up good or bad troops is the same; but it depends wholly on You, most August Emperor, to recover the excellent discipline of the ancients and to correct the abuses of later times. This is a reformation the advantages of which will be equally felt by ourselves and our posterity.

THE ORGANIZATION OF THE LEGION

All our writers agree that never more than two legions, besides auxiliaries, were sent under the command of each consul against the most numerous armies of the enemies. Such was the dependence on their discipline and resolution that this number was thought sufficient for any war they were engaged in. I shall therefore explain the organization of the ancient legion according to the military constitution. But if the description appear obscure or imperfect, it is not to be imputed to me, but to the difficulty of the subject itself, which is therefore to be examined with the greater attention. A prince, skilled himself in military affairs, has it in his power to make himself invincible by keeping up whatever number of well disciplined forces he thinks proper.

The recruits having thus been carefully chosen with proper attention to their persons and dispositions, and having been daily exercised for the space of four months at least, the legion is formed by the command and under the auspices of the Emperor. The military mark, which is indelible, is first imprinted on the hands of the new levies, and as their names are inserted in the roll of the legions they take the usual oath, called the military oath. They swear by God, by Christ and by the Holy Ghost; and by the Majesty of the Emperor who, after God, should be the chief object of the love and veneration of mankind. For when he has once received the title of August, his subjects are bound to pay him the most sincere devotion and homage, as the representative of God on earth. And every man, whether in a private or military station, serves God in serving him faithfully who reigns by His authority. The soldiers, therefore, swear they will obey the Emperor willingly and implicitly in all his commands, that they will never desert and will always be ready to sacrifice their lives for the Roman Empire.

The legion should consist of ten cohorts, the first of which exceeds the others both in number and quality of its soldiers, who are selected to serve in it as men of some family and education. This cohort has the care of the eagle, the chief ensign in the Roman armies and the standard of the whole legion, as well as of the images of the emperors which are always considered as sacred. It consists of eleven hundred and five foot and one hundred and thirty-two horse cuirassiers, and is distinguished by the name of the Millarian Cohort. It is the head of the legion and is always first formed on the right of the first line when the legion draws up in order of battle.

The second cohort contains five hundred and fifty-five foot and sixty-six horse, and is called the Quingentarian Cohort. The third is composed of five hundred and fifty-five foot and sixty-six horse, generally chosen men, on account of its situation in the center of the first line. The fourth consists of the same number of five hundred and fifty-five foot and sixty-six horse. The fifth has likewise five hundred and fifty-five foot and sixty-six horse, which should be some of the best men, being posted on the left flank as the first cohort is on the right. These five cohorts compose the first line.

The sixth includes five hundred and fifty-five foot and sixty-six horse, which should be the flower of the young soldiers as it draws up in the rear of the eagle and the images of the emperors, and on the right of the second line. The seventh contains five hundred and fifty-five foot and sixty-six horse. The eighth is composed of five hundred and fifty-five foot and sixty-six horse, all selected troops, as it occupies the center of the second line. The ninth has five hundred and fifty-five foot and sixty-six horse. The tenth consists of the same number of five hundred and fifty-five foot and sixty-six horse and requires good men, as it closes the left flank of the second line. These ten cohorts form the complete legions, consisting in the whole of six thousand one hundred foot and seven hundred and twenty-six horses. A legion should never be composed of a less number of men, but it is sometimes stronger by the addition of other Millarian Cohorts.

THE OFFICERS OF THE LEGION

Having shown the ancient establishment of the legion, we shall now explain the names of the principal soldiers or, to use the proper term, the officers, and their ranks according to the present rolls of the legions. The first tribune is appointed by the express commission and choice of the Emperor. The second tribune rises to that rank by length of service. The tribunes are so called from their command over the soldiers, who were at first levied by Romulus out of the different tribes. The officers who in action commanded the orders or divisions are called Ordinarii. The Augustales were added by Augustus to the Ordinarii; and the Flaviales were appointed by Flavius Vespasian to double the number of the Augustales. The eagle-bearers and the image-bearers are those who carry the eagles and images of the Emperors. The Optiones are subaltern officers, so denominated from their being selected by the option of their superior officers, to do their duty as their substitutes or lieutenants in case of sickness or other accident. The ensign-bearers carry the ensigns and are called Draconarii. The Tesserarii deliver the parole and the orders of the general to the different messes of the soldiers. The Campignei or Antefignani are those whose duty it is to keep the proper exercises and discipline among the troops. The Metatores are ordered before the army to fix on the ground for its encampments. The Beneficiarii are so named from their owing their promotion to the benefit or interest of the Tribunes. The Librarii keep the legionary accounts. The Tubicines, Cornicines, and Buccinatores derive their appellations from blowing the trumpet, cornet, and buccina. Those who, expert in their exercises, receive a double allowance of provisions, are called Armaturae Duplares, and those who have but a single portion, Simplares. The Mensores mark out the ground by measure for the tents in an encampment, and assign the troops their respective quarters in garrison. The Torquati, so denominated from the gold collars given them in reward for their bravery,

had besides this honor different allowances. Those who received double were called Torquati Duplares, and those who had only single, Simplares. There were, for the same reason, Candidatii Duplares, and Candidatii Simplares. These are the principal soldiers or officers distinguished by their rank and privileges thereto annexed. The rest are called Munifices, or working soldiers, from their being obliged to every kind of military work without exception. Formerly it was the rule that the first Princeps of the legion should be promoted regularly to the rank of Centurion of the Primiple. He not only was entrusted with the eagle but commanded four centuries, that is, four hundred men in the first line. As head of the legion he had appointments of great honor and profit. The first Hastatus had the command of two centuries or two hundred men in the second line, and is now called Ducenarius. The Princeps of the first cohort commanded a century and a half, that is, one hundred and fifty men, and kept in a great measure the general detail of the legion. The second Hastatus had likewise a century and a half, or one hundred and fifty men. The first Triarius had the command of one hundred men. Thus the ten centuries of the first cohort were commanded by five Ordinarii, who by the ancient establishment enjoyed great honors and emoluments that were annexed to this rank in order to inspire the soldiers of the legions with emulation to attain such ample and considerable rewards. They had also Centurions appointed to each century, now called Centenarii and Decani, who commanded ten men, now called heads of messes. The second cohort had five Centurions; and all the rest to the tenth inclusively the same number. In the whole legion there were fifty-five.

Lieutenants of consular dignity were formerly sent to command in the armies under the general, and their authority extended over both the legions and auxiliaries in peace and war. Instead of these officers, persons of high rank are now substituted with the title of Masters of the Forces. They are not limited to the command of two legions only, but have often a greater number. But the peculiar officer of the legion was the Praefect, who was always a count of the first order.

On him the chief command devolved in the absence of the lieutenant. The Tribunes, Centurions, and all the soldiers in general were under his orders: He gave out the parole and order for the march and for the guards. And if a soldier committed a crime, by his authority the Tribune adjudged him to punishment. He had charge of the arms, horses, clothing and provisions. It was also his duty to keep both the legionary horse and foot in daily exercise and to maintain the strictest discipline. He ought to be a careful and diligent officer, as the sole charge of forming the legion to regularity and obedience depended on him and the excellence of the soldiers redounded entirely to his own honor and credit.

The Praefect of the camp, though inferior in rank to the former, had a post of no small importance. The position of the camp, the direction of the entrenchments, the inspection of the tents or huts of the soldiers and the baggage were comprehended in his province. His authority extended over the sick, and the physicians who had the care of them; and he regulated the expenses relative thereto. He had the charge of providing carriages, bathorses and the proper tools for sawing and cutting wood, digging trenches, raising parapets, sinking wells and bringing water into the camp. He likewise had the care of furnishing the troops with wood and straw, as well as the rams, onagri, balistae and all the other engines of war under his direction. This post was always conferred on an officer of great skill, experience and long service, and who consequently was capable of instructing others in those branches of the profession in which he had distinguished himself.

THE PRAEFECT OF THE WORKMEN

The legion had a train of joiners, masons, carpenters, smiths, painters, and workmen of every kind for the construction of barracks in the winter-camps and for making or repairing the wooden towers, arms, carriages and the various sorts of machines and engines for the attack or defense of places. They had also traveling workshops in which they made shields, cuirasses, helmets, bows, arrows, javelins and offensive and defensive arms of all kinds. The ancients made it their chief care to have every thing for the service of the army within the camp. They even had a body of miners who, by working under ground and piercing the foundations of walls, according to the practice of the Beffi, penetrated into the body of a place. All these were under the direction of the officer called the praefect of the workmen.

THE TRIBUNE OF THE SOLDIERS

We have observed that the legions had ten cohorts, the first of which, called the Millarian Cohort, was composed of men selected on account of their circumstances, birth, education, person and bravery. The tribune who commanded them was likewise distinguished for his skill in his exercises, for the advantages of his person and the integrity of his manners. The other cohorts were commanded, according to the Emperor's pleasure, either by tribunes or other officers commissioned for that purpose. In former times the discipline was so strict that the tribunes or officers abovementioned not only caused the troops under their command to be exercised daily in their presence, but were themselves so perfect in their military exercises as to set them the example. Nothing does so much honor to the abilities or application of the tribune as the appearance and discipline of the soldiers, when their apparel is neat and clean, their arms bright and in good order and when they perform their exercises and evolutions with dexterity.

CENTURIES AND ENSIGNS OF THE FOOT

The chief ensign of the whole legion is the eagle and is carried by the eagle-bearer. Each cohort has also its own peculiar ensign, the Dragon, carried by the Draconarius. The ancients, knowing the ranks were easily disordered in the confusion of action, divided the cohorts into centuries and gave each century an ensign inscribed with the number both of the cohort and century so that the men keeping it in sight might be prevented from separating from their comrades in the greatest tumults. Besides the centurions, now called centenarii, were distinguished by different crests on their helmets, to be more easily known by the soldiers of their respective centuries. These precautions prevented any mistake, as every century was guided not only by its own ensign but likewise by the peculiar form of the helmet of its commanding officers. The centuries were also subdivided into messes of ten men each who lay in the same tent and were under orders and inspection of a Decanus or head of the mess. These messes were also called Maniples from their constant custom of fighting together in the same company or division.

LEGIONARY TROOPS OF HORSE

As the divisions of the infantry are called centuries, so those of the cavalry are called troops. A troop consists of thirty-two men and is commanded by a Decurion. Every century has its ensign and every troop its Standard. The centurion in the infantry is chosen for his size, strength and dexterity in throwing his missile weapons and for his skill in the use of his sword and shield; in short for his expertness in all the exercises. He is to be vigilant, temperate, active and readier to execute the orders he receives than to talk; Strict in exercising and keeping up proper discipline among his soldiers, in obliging them to appear clean and well-dressed and to have their arms constantly rubbed and bright. In like manner the Decurion is to be preferred to the command of a troop for his activity and address in mounting his horse completely armed; for his skill in riding and in the use of the lance and bow; for his attention in forming his men to all the evolutions of the cavalry; and for his care in obliging them to keep their cuirasses, lances and helmets always bright and in good order. The splendor of the arms has no inconsiderable effect in striking terror into an enemy. Can that man be reckoned a good soldier who through negligence suffers his arms to be spoiled by dirt and rust? In short, it is the duty of the Decurion to be attentive to whatever concerns the health or discipline of the men or horses in his troop.

DRAWING UP A LEGION IN ORDER OF BATTLE

We shall exemplify the manner of drawing up an army in order of battle in the instance of one legion, which may serve for any number. The cavalry are posted on the wings. The infantry begin to form on a line with the first cohort on the right. The second cohort draws up on the left of the first; the third occupies the center; the fourth is posted next; and the fifth closes the left flank. The ordinarii, the other officers and the soldiers of the first line, ranged before and round the ensigns, were called the principes. They were all heavy armed troops and had helmets, cuirasses, greaves, and shields. Their offensive weapons were large swords, called spathae, and smaller ones called semispathae together with five loaded javelins in the concavity of the shield, which they threw at the first charge. They had likewise two other javelins, the largest of which was composed of a staff five feet and a half long and a triangular head of iron nine inches long. This was formerly called the pilum, but now it is known by the name of spiculum. The soldiers were particularly exercised in the use of this weapon, because when thrown with force and skill it often penetrated the shields of the foot and the cuirasses of the horse. The other javelin was of smaller size; its triangular point was only five inches long and the staff three feet and one half. It was anciently called verriculum but now verutum.

The first line, as I said before, was composed of the principes; the hastati formed the second and were armed in the same manner. In the second line the sixth cohort was posted on the right flank, with the seventh on its left; the eighth drew up in the center; the ninth was the next; and the tenth always closed the left flank. In the rear of these two lines were the ferentarii, light infantry and the troops armed with shields, loaded javelins, swords and common missile weapons, much in the same manner as our modern soldiers. This was also the post of the archers who had helmets, cuirasses, swords, bows and arrows; of the slingers who threw stones with the common sling or with the fustibalus; and of the tragularii who annoyed the enemy with arrows from the manubalistae or arcubalistae.

In the rear of all the lines, the triarii, completely armed, were drawn up. They had shields, cuirasses, helmets, greaves, swords, daggers, loaded javelins, and two of the common missile weapons. They rested during the acnon on one knee, so that if the first lines were obliged to give way, they might be fresh when brought up to the charge, and thereby retrieve what was lost and recover the victory. All the ensigns though, of the infantry, wore cuirasses of a smaller sort and covered their helmets with the shaggy skins of beasts to make themselves appear more terrible to the enemy. But the centurions had complete cuirasses, shields, and helmets of iron, the crest of which, placed transversely thereon, were ornamented with silver that they might be more easily distinguished by their respective soldiers.

The following disposition deserves the greatest attention. In the beginning of an engagement, the first and second lines remained immovable on their ground, and the trairii in their usual positions. The light-armed troops, composed as above mentioned, advanced in the front of the line, and attacked the enemy. If they could make them give way, they pursued them; but if they were repulsed by superior bravery or numbers, they retired behind their own heavy armed infantry, which appeared like a wall of iron and renewed the action, at first with their missile weapons, then sword in hand. If they broke the enemy they never pursued them, least they should break their ranks or throw the line into confusion, and lest the enemy, taking advantage of their disorder, should return to the attack and destroy them without difficulty. The pursuit therefore was entirely left to the light-armed troops and the cavalry. By these precautions and dispositions the legion was victorious without danger, or if the contrary happened, was preserved without any considerable loss, for as it is not calculated for pursuit, it is likewise not easily thrown into disorder.

NAMES OF SOLDIERS INSCRIBED ON THEIR SHIELDS

Lest the soldiers in the confusion of battle should be separated from their comrades, every cohort had its shields painted in a manner peculiar to itself. The name of each soldier was also written on his shield, together with the number of the cohort and century to which he belonged. From this description we may compare the legion, when in proper order, to a well fortified city as containing within itself every thing requisite in war, wherever it moved. It was secure from any sudden attempt or surprise of an enemy by its expeditious method of entrenching its camp even in the open plains and it was always provided with troops and arms of every kind. To be victorious, therefore, over our enemies in the field, we must unanimously supplicate heaven to dispose the Emperor to reform the abuses in raising our levies and to recruit our legions after the method of the ancients. The same care in choosing and instructing our young soldiers in all military exercises and drills will soon make them equal to the old Roman troops who subdued the whole world. Nor let this alteration and loss of ancient discipline in any way affect Your Majesty, since it is a happiness reserved for You alone both to restore the ancient ordinances and establish new ones for the public welfare. Every work before the attempt carries in it an appearance of difficulty; but in this case, if the levies are made by careful and experienced officers, an army may be raised, disciplined and rendered fit for service in a very short time; for the necessary expenses once provided, diligence soon effects whatever it undertakes.

RECORDS AND ACCOUNTS

Several posts in the legion requiring men of some education, the superintendents of the levies should select some recruits for their skill in writing and accounts, besides the qualification to be attended to in general, such as size, strength and proper disposition for the service. For the whole detail of the legion, including the lists of the soldiers exempted from duty on private accounts, the rosters for their tour of military duties and their pay lists, is daily entered in the legionary books and kept we may almost say, with greater exactness than the regulations of provisions or other civil matters in the registers of the police. The daily guards in time of peace, the advanced guards and outposts in time of war, which are mounted regularly by the centuries and messes in their turns, are likewise punctually kept in rolls for that purpose, with the name of each soldier whose tour is past, that no one may have injustice done him or be excused from his duty by favor.

They are also exact in entering the time and limitation of furloughs, which formerly were never granted without difficulty and only on real and urgent business. They then never suffered the soldiers to attend on any private person or to concern themselves in private occupations, thinking it absurd and improper that the Emperor's soldiers, clothed and subsisted at the public expense, should follow any other profession. Some soldiers, however, were allowed for the service of the praefects, tribunes and even of the other officers, our of the number of the accensi or such as were raised after the legion was complete. These latter are now called supernumeraries. The regular troops were obliged to carry their wood, hay, water and straw into the camp themselves. From such kind of services they were called munifices.

SOLDIER'S DEPOSITS

The institution of the ancients which obliged the soldiers to deposit half of every donative they received at the colors was wise and judicious; the intent was to preserve it for their use so that they might not squander it in extravagance or idle expense. For most men, particularly the poorer sort, soon spend whatever they can get. A reserve of this kind therefore is evidently of the greatest service to the soldiers themselves; since they are maintained at the public expense, their military stock by this method is continually increasing. The soldier who knows all his fortune is deposited at his colors, entertains no thoughts of desertion, conceives a greater affection for them and fights with greater intrepidity in their defense. He is also prompted thereto by interest, the most prevailing consideration among men. This money was contained in ten bags, one for each cohort. There was an eleventh bag also for a small contribution from the whole legion, as a common fund to defray the expense of burial of any of their deceased comrades. These collections were kept in baskets in the custody of the ensigns, chosen for their integrity and capacity, and answerable for the trust and obliged to account with every man for his own proportion.

PROMOTION IN THE LEGION

Heaven certainly inspired the Romans with the organization of the legion, so superior does it seem to human invention. Such is the arrangement and disposition of the ten cohorts that compose it, as to appear one perfect body and form one complete whole. A soldier, as he advances in rank, proceeds as it were by rotation through the different degrees of the several cohorts in such a manner that one who is promoted passes from the first cohort to the tenth, and returns again regularly through all the others with a continual increase of rank and pay to the first. Thus the centurion of the primiple, after having commanded in the different ranks of every cohort, attains that great dignity in the first with infinite advantages from the whole legion. The chief praefect of the Praetorian Guards rises by the same method of rotation to that lucrative and honorable rank. Thus the legionary horse contract an affection for the foot of their own cohorts, notwithstanding the natural antipathy existing between the two corps. And this connection establishes a reciprocal attachment and union between all the cohorts and the cavalry and infantry of the legion.

LEGIONARY MUSIC

The music of the legion consists of trumpets, cornets and buccinae. The trumpet sounds the charge and the retreat. The cornets are used only to regulate the motions of the colors; the trumpets serve when the soldiers are ordered out to any work without the colors; but in time of action, the trumpets and cornets sound together. The classicum, which is a particular sound of the buccina or horn, is appropriated to the commander-in-chief and is used in the presence of the general, or at the execution of a soldier, as a mark of its being done by his authority. The ordinary guards and outposts are always mounted and relieved by the sound of trumpet, which also directs the motions of the soldiers on working parties and on field days. The cornets sound whenever the colors are to be struck or planted. These rules must be punctually observed in all exercises and reviews so that the soldiers may be ready to obey them in action without hesitation according to the general's orders either to charge or halt, to pursue the enemy or to retire. F or reason will convince us that what is necessary to be performed in the heat of action should constantly be practiced in the leisure of peace.

THE DRILLING OF THE TROOPS

The organization of the legion being thus explained, let us return to the drills. The younger soldiers and recruits went through their drills of every kind every morning and afternoon and the veterans and most expert regularly once a day. Length of service or age alone will never form a military man, for after serving many years an undisciplined soldier is still a novice in his profession. Not only those under the masters at arms, but all the soldiers in general, were formerly trained incessantly in those drills which now are only exhibited as shows in the circus for particular solemnities. By practice only can be acquired agility of body and the skill requisite to engage an enemy with advantage, especially in close fight. But the most essential point of all is to teach soldiers to keep their ranks and never abandon their colors in the most difficult evolutions. Men thus trained are never at a loss amidst the greatest confusion of numbers.

The recruits likewise are to be exercised with wooden swords at the post, to be taught to attack this imaginary antagonist on all sides and to aim at the sides, feet or head, both with the point and edge of the sword. They must be instructed how to spring forward to give the blow, to rise with a bound above the shield and then to sink down and shelter themselves under cover of it, and how to advance and retire. They must also throw their javelins at the post from a considerable distance in order to acquire a good aim and strengthen the arm.

The archers and slingers set up bundles of twigs or straw for marks, and generally strike them with arrows and with stones from the fustiablus at the distance of six hundred feet. They acquired coolness and exactness in acnon from familiar custom and exercise in the field. The slingers should be taught to whirl the sling but once about the head before they cast the stone. Formerlyall soldiers were trained to the practice of throwing stones of a pound weight with the hand, as this

was thought a readier method since it did not require a sling. The use of the common missile weapons and loaded javelins was another part of the drill strictly attended to.

To continue this drill without interruption during the winter, they erected for the cavalry porticos or riding halls covered with tiles or shingles, and if they were not to be procured, with reeds, rushes or thatch. Large open halls were likewise constructed in the same manner for the use of the infantry. By these means the troops were provided with places of drill sheltered from bad weather. But even in winter, if it did not rain or snow, they were obliged to perform their drills in the field, lest an intermission of discipline should affect both the courage and constitution of the soldier. In short, both legionary and auxiliary troops should continually be drilled in cutting wood, carrying burdens, passing ditches, swimming in the sea or in rivers, marching in the full step and even running with their arms and baggage, so that, inured to labor in peace, they may find no difficulty in war. For, as the well trained soldier is eager for action, so does the untaught fear it. In war discipline is superior to strength; but if that discipline is neglected, there is no longer any difference between the soldier and the peasant. The old maxim is certain that the very essence of an art consists in constant practice.

MACHINES AND TOOLS OF THE LEGION

The legion owes its success to its arms and machines, as well as to the number and bravery of its soldiers. In the first place every century has a balista mounted on a carriage drawn by mules and served by a mess, that is by ten men from the century to which it belongs. The larger these engines are, the greater distance they carry and with the greater force. They are used not only to defend the entrenchments of camps, but are also placed in the field in the rear of the heavy armed infantry. And such is the violence with which they throw the darts that neither the cuirasses of the horse nor shields of the foot can resist them. The number of these engines in a legion is fifty-five. Besides these are ten onagri, one for each cohort; they are drawn ready armed on carriages by oxen;

in case of an attack, they defend the works of the camp by throwing stones as the balistae do darts.

The legion carries with it a number of small boats, each hollowed out of a single piece of timber, with long cables and sometimes iron chains to fasten them together. These boats, joined and covered with planks, serve as bridges over unfordable rivers, on which both cavalry and infantry pass without danger. The legion is provided with iron hooks, called wolves, and iron scythes fixed to the ends of long poles; and with forks, spades, shovels, pickaxes, wheelbarrows and baskets for digging and transporting earth; together with hatchets, axes and saws for cutting wood. Besides which, a train of workmen attend on it furnished with all instruments necessary for the construction of tortoises, musculi, rams, vines, moving towers and other machines for the attack of places. As the enumeration of all the particulars of this sort would be too tedious, I shall only observe that the legion should carry with it wherever it moves, whatever is necessary for every kind of service so that the encampments may have all the strength and conveniences of a fortified city.

Preface to Book III
To the Emperor Valentinian
The Athenians and Lacedaemonians were masters of Greece before the Macedonians, as history informs us. The Athenians excelled not only in war but in other arts and sciences. The Lacedaemonians made war their chief study. They are affirmed to be the first who reasoned on the events of battles and committed their observations thereon to writing with such success as to reduce the military art, before considered as totally dependent on courage or fortune, to certain rules and fixed principles. As a consequence they established schools of tactics for the instruction of youth in all the maneuvers of war. How worthy of admiration are these people for particularly applying themselves to the study of an art, without which no other art can possibly exist. The Romans followed their example, and both practiced their institutions in their armies and preserved them in their writings. These are the maxims and

instructions dispersed through the works of different authors, which Your Majesty has ordered me to abridge, since the perusal of the whole would be too tedious, and the authority of only a part unsatisfactory. The effect of the Lacedaemonian skill in dispositions for general actions appears evidently in the single instance of Xantippus, who assisted the Carthaginians after the repeated ruin of their armies. And merely superior skill and conduct defeated Attilius Regulus at the head of a Roman army, till that time always victorious. Xantippus took him prisoner and thus terminated the war by a single action. Hannibal, also, before he set out on his expedition into Italy, chose a Lacedaemonian for his counselor in military operations; and by his advice, though inferior to the Romans both in number and strength, overthrew so many consuls and such mighty legions. He, therefore, who desires peace, should prepare for war. He who aspires to victory, should spare no pains to form his soldiers. And he who hopes for success, should fight on principle, not chance. No one dares to offend or insult a power of known superiority in action.

Book III: Dispositions for Action
THE NUMBER WHICH SHOULD COMPOSE AN ARMY
The first book treats of the choice and exercises of new levies; the second explains the establishment of the legion and the method of discipline; and the third contains the dispositions for action. By this methodical progression, the following instructions on general actions and means of victory will be better understood and of greater use. By an army is meant a number of troops, legions and auxiliaries, cavalry and infantry, assembled to make war. This number is limited by judges of the profession. The defeats of Xerxes, Darius, Mithridates and other monarchs who brought innumerable multitudes into the field, plainly show that the destruction of such prodigious armies is owing more to their own numbers than to the bravery of their enemies. An army too numerous is subject to many dangers and inconveniences. Its bulk makes it slow and unwieldy in its motions; and as it is obliged to

march in columns of great length, it is exposed to the risk of being continually harassed and insulted by inconsiderable parties of the enemy. The encumbrance of the baggage is often an occasion of its being surprised in its passage through difficult places or over rivers. The difficulty of providing forage for such numbers of horses and other beasts of burden is very great. Besides, scarcity of provisions, which is to be carefully guarded against in all expeditions, soon ruins such large armies where the consumption is so prodigious, that notwithstanding the greatest care in filling the magazines they must begin to fail in a short time. And sometimes they unavoidably will be distressed for want of water. But, if unfortunately this immense army should be defeated, the numbers lost must necessarily be very great, and the remainder, who save themselves by flight, too much dispirited to be brought again to action.

The ancients, taught by experience, preferred discipline to numbers. In wars of lesser importance they thought one legion with auxiliaries, that is, ten thousand foot and two thousand horse, sufficient. And they often gave the command to a praeter as to a general of the second rank. When the preparations of the enemy were formidable, they sent a general of consular dignity with twenty thousand foot and four thousand horse. In our times this command was given to a count of the first order. But when there happened any dangerous insurrection supported by infinite multitudes of fierce and barbarous nations, on such emergencies they took the field with two armies under two consuls, who were charged, both singly and jointly, to take care to preserve the Republic from danger. In short, by this management, the Romans, almost continually engaged in war with different nations in different parts of the world, found themselves able to oppose them in every quarter. The excellence of their discipline made their small armies sufficient to encounter all their enemies with success. But it was an invariable rule in their armies that the number of allies or auxiliaries should never exceed that of the Roman citizens.

MEANS OF PRESERVING IT IN HEALTH

The next article is of the greatest importance: the means of preserving the health of the troops. This depends on the choice of situation and water, on the season of the year, medicine, and exercise. As to the situation, the army should never continue in the neighborhood of unwholesome marshes any length of time, or on dry plains or eminences without some sort of shade or shelter. In the summer, the troops should never encamp without tents. And their marches, in that season of the year when the heat is excessive, should begin by break of day so that they may arrive at the place of destination in good time. Otherwise they will contract diseases from the heat of the weather and the fatigue of the march. In severe winter they should never march in the night in frost and snow, or be exposed to want of wood or clothes. A soldier, starved with cold, can neither be healthy nor fit for service. The water must be wholesome and not marshy. Bad water is a kind of poison and the cause of epidemic distempers.

It is the duty of the officers of the legion, of the tribunes, and even of the commander-in-chief himself, to take care that the sick soldiers are supplied with proper diet and diligently attended by the physicians. For little can be expected from men who have both the enemy and diseases to struggle with. However, the best judges of the service have always been of the opinion that daily practice of the military exercises is much more efficacious towards the health of an army than all the art of medicine. For this reason they exercised their infantry without intermission. If it rained or snowed, they performed under cover; and ill fine weather, in the field. They also were assiduous in exercising their cavalry, not only in plains, but also on uneven ground, broken and cut with ditches. The horses as well as the men were thus trained, both on the above mentioned account and to prepare them for action. Hence we may perceive the importance and necessity of a strict observance of the military exercises in an army, since health in the camp and victory in the field depend on them. If a numerous army continues long in one place in the summer or in the autumn, the waters become corrupt and the air infected. Malignant and fatal distempers proceed from this and can be avoided only by frequent changes of encampments.

CARE TO PROVIDE FORAGE AND PROVISIONS

Famine makes greater havoc in an army than the enemy, and is more terrible than the sword. Time and opportunity may help to retrieve other misfortunes, but where forage and provisions have not been carefully provided, the evil is without remedy. The main and principal point in war is to secure plenty of provisions and to destroy the enemy by famine. An exact calculation must therefore be made before the commencement of the war as to the number of troops and the expenses incident thereto, so that the provinces may in plenty of time furnish the forage, corn, and all other kinds of provisions demanded of them to be transported. They must be in more than sufficient quantity, and gathered into the strongest and most convenient cities before the opening of the campaign. If the provinces cannot raise their quotas in kind, they must commute for them in money to be employed in procuring all things requisite for the service. For the possessions of the subjects cannot be kept secure otherwise than by the defense of arms.

These precautions often become doubly necessary as a siege is sometimes protracted beyond expectation, the besiegers resolving to suffer themselves all the inconveniences of want sooner than raise the siege, if they have any hopes of reducing the place by famine. Edicts should be issued out requiring the country people to convey their cattle, grain, wine and all kinds of provisions that may be of service to the enemy, into garrisoned fortresses or into the safest cities. And if they do not comply with the order, proper officers are to appointed to compel them to do it. The inhabitants of the province must likewise be obliged to retire with their effects into some fortified place before the irruption of the enemy. The fortifications and all the machines of different kinds must also be examined and repaired in time. For if you are once surprised by the enemy before you are in a proper posture of defense, you are thrown into irrecoverable confusion, and you can no longer draw any assistance from the neighboring places, all communication with them being cut off. But a faithful management of the magazines and a frugal distribution of the provisions, with proper precautions taken at first, will insure sufficient plenty. When provisions once begin to fail, parsimony is ill-timed and comes too late.

On difficult expeditions the ancients distributed the provisions at a fixed allowance to each man without distinction of rank; and when the emergency was past, the government accounted for the full proportions. The troops should never want wood and forage in winter or water in summer. They should have corn, wine, vinegar, and even salt, in plenty at all times. Cities and fortresses are garrisoned by such men as are least fit for the service of the field. They are provided with all sorts of arms, arrows, fustibali, slings, stones, onagri and balistae for their defense. Great caution is requisite that the unsuspecting simplicity of the inhabitants be not imposed on by the treachery or perjury of the enemy, for pretended conferences and deceitful appearance of truces have often been more fatal than force. By observing the foregoing precautions, the besieged may have it in their power to ruin the enemy by famine, if he keeps his troops together, and if he divides them, by frequent sallies and surprises.

METHODS TO PREVENT MUTINY IN AN ARMY

An army drawn together from different parts sometimes is disposed to mutiny. And the troops, though not inclined to fight, pretend to be angry at not being led against the enemy. Such seditious dispositions principally show themselves in those who have lived in their quarters in idleness and effeminacy. These men, unaccustomed to the necessary fatigue of the field, are disgusted at its severity. Their ignorance of discipline makes them afraid of action and inspires them with insolence.

There are several remedies for this evil. While the troops are yet separated and each corps continues in its respective quarters, let the tribunes, their lieutenants and the officers in general make it their business to keep up so strict a discipline as to leave them no room to harbor any thoughts but of submission and obedience. Let them be constantly employed either in field days or in the inspection of their arms. They should not be allowed to be absent on furlough. They should be frequently called by roll and trained to be exact in the observance of every signal. Let them be exercised in the use of the bow, in throwing missile weapons and stones, both with the hand and sling, and with the wooden sword at the post; let all this be continually repeated and let them be often kept under arms till they are tired. Let them be exercised in running and leaping to facilitate the passing of ditches. And if their quarters are near the sea or a river, let them all, without exception, be obliged in the summer to have the frequent practice of swimming. Let them be accustomed to march through thickets, enclosures and broken grounds, to fell trees and cut out timber, to break ground and to defend a post against their comrades who are to endeavor to dispossess them; and in the encounter each party should use their shields to dislodge and bear down their antagonists. All the different kinds of troops thus trained and exercised in their quarters will find themselves inspired with emulation for glory and eagerness for action when they come to take the field. In short, a soldier who has proper confidence in his own skill and strength, entertains no thought of mutiny.

A general should be attentive to discover the turbulent and seditious soldiers in the army, legions or auxiliaries, cavalry or infantry. He should endeavor to procure his intelligence not from informers, but from the tribunes, their lieutenants and other officers of undoubted veracity. It would then be prudent in him to separate them from the rest under pretence of some service agreeable to them, or detach them to garrison cities or castles, but with such address that though he wants to get rid of them, they may think themselves employed by preference and favor. A multitude never broke out into open sedition at once and with unanimous consent. They are prepared and excited by some few mutineers, who hope to secure impunity for their crimes by the number of their associates. But if the height of the mutiny requires violent remedies, it will be most advisable, after the manner of the ancients, to punish the ringleaders only in order that, though few suffer, all may be terrified by the example. But it is much more to the credit of a general to form his troops to submission and obedience by habit and discipline than to be obliged to force them to their duty by the terror of punishment.

MARCHES IN THE NEIGHBORHOOD OF THE ENEMY

It is asserted by those who have made the profession their study that an army is exposed to more danger on marches than in battles. In an engagement the men are properly armed, they see their enemies before them and come prepared to fight. But on a march the soldier is less on his guard, has not his arms always ready and is thrown into disorder by a sudden attack or ambuscade. A general, therefore, cannot be too careful and diligent in taking necessary precautions to prevent a surprise on the march and in making proper dispositions to repulse the enemy, in case of such accident, without loss.

In the first place, he should have an exact description of the country that is. the seat of war, in which the distances of places specified by the number of miles, the nature of the roads, the shortest routes, by-roads, mountains and rivers, should be correctly inserted. We are told that the greatest generals have carried their precautions on this head so far that, not satisfied with the simple description of the country wherein they were engaged, they caused plans to be taken of it on the spot, that they might regulate their marches by the eye with greater safety. A general should also inform himself of all these particulars from persons of sense and reputation well acquainted with the country by examining them separately at first, and then comparing their accounts in order to come at the truth with certainty.

If any difficulty arises about the choice of roads, he should procure proper and skillful guides. He should put them under a guard and spare neither promises nor threat to induce them to be faithful. They will acquit themselves well when they know it is impossible to escape and are certain of being rewarded for their fidelity or punished for their perfidy. He must be sure of their capacity and experience, that the whole army be not brought into danger by the errors of two or three persons. For sometimes the common sort of people imagine they know what they really do not, and through ignorance promise more than they can perform.

But of all precautions the most important is to keep entirely secret which way or by what route the army is to march. For the security of an expedition depends on the concealment of all motions from the enemy. The figure of the Minotaur was anciently among the legionary ensigns, signifying that this monster, according to the fable, was concealed in the most secret recesses and windings of the labyrinth, just as the designs of a general should always be impenetrable. When the enemy has no intimation of a march, it is made with security; but as sometimes the scouts either suspect or discover the decampment, or traitors or deserters give intelligence thereof, it will be proper to mention the method of acting in case of an attack on the march.

The general, before he puts his troops in motion, should send out detachments of trusty and experienced soldiers well mounted, to reconnoiter the places through which he is to march, in front, in rear, and on the right and left, lest he should fall into ambuscades. The night is safer and more advantageous for your spies to do their business in than day, for if they are taken prisoners, you have, as it were, betrayed yourself. After this, the cavalry should march off first, then the infantry; the baggage, bat horses, servants and carriages follow in the center; and part of the best cavalry and infantry come in the rear, since it is oftener attacked on a march than the front. The flanks of the baggage, exposed to frequent ambuscades, must also be covered with a sufficient guard to secure them. But above all, the part where the enemy is most expected must be reinforced with some of the best cavalry, light infantry and foot archers.

If surrounded on all sides by the enemy, you must make dispositions to receive them wherever they come, and the soldiers should be cautioned beforehand to keep their arms in their hands, and to be ready in order to prevent the bad

effects of a sudden attack. Men are frightened and thrown into disorder by sudden accidents and surprises of no consequence when foreseen. The ancients were very careful that the servants or followers of the army, if wounded or frightened by the noise of the action, might not disorder the troops while engaged, and also to prevent their either straggling or crowding one another too much, which might incommode their own men and give advantage to the enemy. They ranged the baggage, therefore, in the same manner as the regular troops under particular ensigns. They selected from among the servants the most proper and experienced and gave them the command of a number of servants and boys, not exceeding two hundred, and their ensigns directed them where to assemble the baggage. Proper intervals should always be kept between the baggage and the troops, that the latter may not be embarrassed for want of room in case of an attack during the march. The manner and disposition of defense must be varied according to the difference of ground. In an open country you are more liable to be attacked by horse than foot. But in a woody, mountainous or marshy situation, the danger to be apprehended is from foot. Some of the divisions being apt through negligence to move too fast, and others too slow, great care is to be taken to prevent the army from being broken or from running into too great a length, as the enemy would instantly take advantage of the neglect and penetrate without difficulty.

The tribunes, their lieutenants or the masters at arms of most experience, must therefore be posted at proper distances, in order to halt those who advance too fast and quicken such as move too slow. The men at too great a distance in the front, on the appearance of an enemy, are more disposed to fly than to join their comrades. And those too far behind, destitute of assistance, fall a sacrifice to the enemy and their own despair. The enemy, it may be concluded, will either plant ambuscades or make his attack by open force, according to the advantage of the ground. Circumspection in examining every place will be a security against concealed danger; and an ambuscade, if discovered and promptly surrounded, will return the intended mischief with interest.

If the enemy prepare to fall upon you by open force in a mountainous country, detachments must be sent forward to occupy the highest eminences, so that on their arrival they may not dare to attack you under such a disadvantage of ground, your troops being posted so much above their and presenting a front ready for their reception. It is better to send men forward with hatchets and other tools in order to open ways that are narrow but safe, without regard to the labor, rather than to run any risk in the finest roads. It is necessary to be well acquainted whether the enemy usually make their attempts in the night, at break of day or in the hours of refreshment or rest; and by knowledge of their customs to guard against what we find their general practice. We must also inform ourselves whether they are strongest in infantry or cavalry; whether their cavalry is chiefly armed with lances or with bows; and whether their principal strength consists in their numbers or the excellence of their arms. All of this will enable us to take the most proper measures to distress them and for our advantage. When we have a design in view, we must consider whether it will be most advisable to begin the march by day or by night; we must calculate the distance of the places we want to reach; and take such precautions that in summer the troops may not suffer for want of water on their march, nor be obstructed in winter by impassable morasses or torrents, as these would expose the army to great danger before it could arrive at the place of its destination. As it highly concerns us to guard against these inconveniences with prudence, so it would be inexcusable not to take advantage of an enemy that fell into them through ignorance or negligence. Our spies should be constantly abroad; we should spare no pains in tampering with their men, and give all manner of encouragement to deserters. By these means we may get intelligence of their present or future designs. And we should constantly keep in readiness some detachments of cavalry and light infantry, to fall upon them when they least expect it, either on the march, or when foraging or marauding.

PASSAGES OF RIVERS

The passages of rivers are very dangerous without great precaution. In crossing broad or rapid streams, the baggage, servants, and sometimes the most indolent soldiers are in danger of being lost. Having first sounded the ford, two lines of the best mounted cavalry are ranged at a convenient distance entirely across the river, so that the infantry and baggage may pass between them. The line above the ford breaks the violence of the stream, and the line below recovers and transports the men carried away by the current. When the river is too deep to be forded either by the cavalry or infantry, the water is drawn off, if it runs in a plain, by cutting a great number of trenches, and thus it is passed with ease.

Navigable rivers are passed by means of piles driven into the bottom and floored with planks; or in a sudden emergency by fastening together a number of empty casks and covering them with boards. The cavalry, throwing off their accoutrements, make small floats of dry reeds or rushes on which they lay their rams and cuirasses to preserve them from being wet. They themselves swim their horses across the river and draw the floats after them by a leather thong.

But the most commodious invention is that of the small boats hollowed out of one piece of timber and very light both by their make and the quality of the wood. The army always has a number of these boats upon carriages, together with a sufficient quantity of planks and iron nails. Thus with the help of cables to lash the boats together, a bridge is instantly constructed, which for the time has the solidity of a bridge of stone.

As the enemy generally endeavor to fall upon an army at the passage of a river either by surprise or ambuscade, it is necessary to secure both sides thereof by strong detachments so that the troops may not be attacked and defeated while separated by the channel of the river. But it is still safer to palisade both the posts, since this will enable you to sustain any attempt without much loss. If the bridge is wanted, not only for the present transportation of the troops but also for their return and for convoys, it will be proper to throw up works with large ditches to cover each head of the bridge, with a sufficient number of men to defend them as long as the circumstances of affairs require.

RULES FOR ENCAMPING AN ARMY

An army on the march cannot expect always to find walled cities for quarters, and it is very imprudent and dangerous to encamp in a straggling manner without some sort of entrenchment. It is an easy matter to surprise troops while refreshing themselves or dispersed in the different occupations of the service. The darkness of night, the necessity of sleep and the dispersion of the horses at pasture afford opportunities of surprise. A good situation for a camp is not sufficient; we must choose the very best that can be found lest, having failed to occupy a more advantageous post the enemy should get possession of it to our great detriment.

An army should not encamp in summer near bad waters or far from good ones, nor in winter in a situation without plenty of forage and wood. The camp should not be liable to sudden inundations. The avenues should not be too steep and narrow lest, if invested, the troops should find it difficult to make their retreat; nor should it be commanded by any eminences from which it may be annoyed by the enemy's weapons. After these precautions, the camp is formed square, round, triangular or oblong, according to the nature of the ground. For the form of a camp does not constitute its goodness. Those camps, however, are thought best where the length is one third more than the depth. The dimensions must be exactly computed by the engineers, so that the size of the camp may be proportioned to the number of troops. A camp which is too confined will not permit the troops to perform their movements with freedom, and one which is too extensive divides them too much. There are three methods of entrenching a camp. The first is for the case when the army is on the march and will continue in the camp for only one night. They then throw up a slight parapet of turf and plant it with a row of palisades or caltrops of wood. The sods are cut with iron instruments. If the earth is held strongly together by the roots of the grass, they are cut in

the form of a brick a foot and one half high, a foot broad and a foot and one half long. If the earth is so loose that the turf cannot be cut in this form, they run a slight trench round the camp, five feet broad and three feet deep. The earth taken from the trench forms a parapet on the inside and this secures the army from danger. This is the second method.

But permanent camps, either for summer or winter, in the neighborhood of an enemy, are fortified with greater care and regularity. After the ground is marked out by the proper officers, each century receives a certain number of feet to entrench. They then range their shields and baggage in a circle about their own colors and, with. out other arms than their swords, open a trench nine, eleven or thirteen feet broad. Or, if they are under great apprehensions of the enemy, they enlarge it to seventeen feet (it being a general rule to observe odd numbers). Within this they construct a rampart with fascines or branches of trees well fastened together with pickets, so that the earth may be better supported. Upon this rampart they raise a parapet with battlements as in the fortifications of a city. The centurions measure the work with rods ten feet long and examine whether every one has properly completed the proportion assigned to him. The tribunes likewise inspect the work and should not leave the place till the whole is finished. And that the workmen may not be suddenly interrupted by the enemy, all the cavalry and that part of the infantry exempted by the privilege of their rank from working, remain in order of battle before the entrenchment to be ready to repel any assault.

The first thing to be done after entrenching the camp, is to plant the ensigns, held by the soldiers in the highest veneration and respect, in their proper places. After this the praetorium is prepared for the general and his lieutenants, and the tents pitched for the tribunes, who have soldiers particularly appointed for that service and to fetch their water, wood, and forage. Then the legions and auxiliaries, cavalry and infantry, have the ground distributed to them to pitch their tents according to the rank of the several corps. Four foot-soldiers of each century and four troopers of each troop are on guard every night. As it seemed impossible for a sentinel to remain a whole night on his post, the watches were divided by the hourglass into four parts, that each man might stand only three hours. All guards are mounted by the sound of trumpet and relieved by the sound of cornet. The tribunes choose proper and trusty men to visit the different posts and report to them whatever they find amiss. This is now a military office and the persons appointed to it are called officers of the rounds.

The cavalry furnish the grand guards at night and the outposts by day. They are relieved every morning and afternoon because of the fatigue of the men and horses. It is particularly incumbent upon the general to provide for the protection of the pastures and of the convoys of grain and other provisions either in camp or garrison, and to secure wood, water and forage against the incursions of the enemy. This can only be effected by posting detachments advantageously in the cines or walled castles on the roads along which the convoys advance. And if no ancient fortifications are to be met with, small forts must be built in proper situations, surrounded with large ditches, for the reception of detachments of horse and foot, so that the convoys will be effectually protected. For an enemy will hardly venture far into a country where he knows his adversary's troops are so disposed as to be ready to encompass him on all sides.

MOTIVES FOR THE PLAN OF OPERATIONS OF A CAMPAIGN

Readers of this military abridgement will perhaps be impatient for instructions relative to general engagements. But they should consider that a battle is commonly decided in two or three hours, after which no further hopes are left for the worsted army. Every plan, therefore, is to be considered, every expedient tried and every method taken before matters are brought to this last extremity. Good officers decline general engagements where the danger is common, and prefer the employment of stratagem and finesse to destroy the enemy as much as possible in detail and intimidate them without exposing our own forces.

I shall insert some necessary instructions on this head collected from the ancients. It is the duty and interest of the general frequently to assemble the most prudent and experienced officers of the different corps of. the army and consult with them on the state both of his own and the enemy's forces. All overconfidence, as most pernicious in its consequences, must be banished from the deliberations. He must examine which has the superiority in numbers, whether his or the adversary's troops are best armed, which are in the best condition, best disciplined and most resolute in emergencies. The state of the cavalry of both armies must be inquired into, but more especially that of the infantry, for the main strength of an army consists of the latter. With respect to the cavalry, he must endeavor to find out in which are the greatest numbers of archers or of troopers armed with lances, which has the most cuirassiers and which the best horses. Lastly he must consider the field of battle and to judge whether the ground is more advantageous for him or his enemy. If strongest in cavalry, we should prefer plains and open ground; if superior in infantry, we should choose a situation full of enclosures, ditches, morasses and woods, and sometimes mountainous. Plenty or scarcity in either army are considerations of no small importance, for famine, according to the common proverb, is an internal enemy that makes more havoc than the sword. But the most material article is to determine whether it is most proper to temporize or to bring the affair to a speedy decision by action. The enemy sometimes expect an expedition will soon be over; and if it is protracted to any length, his troops are either consumed by want,. induced to return home by the desire of seeing their families or, having done nothing considerable in the field, disperse themselves from despair of success. Thus numbers, tired out with fatigue and disgusted with the service, desert, others betray them and many surrender themselves. Fidelity is seldom found in troops disheartened by misfortunes. And in such case an army which was numerous on taking the field insensibly dwindles away to nothing.

It is essential to know the character of the enemy and of their principal officers-whether they be. rash or cautious, enterprising or timid, whether they fight on principle or from chance and whether the nations they have been engaged with were brave or cowardly.

We must know how far to depend upon the fidelity and strength of auxiliaries, how the enemy's troops and our own are affected and which appear most confident of success, a consideration of great effect in raising or depressing the courage of an army. A harangue from the general, especially if he seems under no apprehension himself, may reanimate the soldiers if dejected. Their spirits revive if any considerable advantage is gained either by stratagem or otherwise, if the fortune of the enemy begins to change or if you can contrive to beat some of their weak or poorly-armed detachments.

But you must by no means venture to lead an irresolute or diffident army to a general engagement. The difference is great whether your troops are raw or veterans, whether inured to war by recent service or for some years unemployed. For soldiers unused to fighting for a length of time must be considered in the same light as recruits. As soon as the legions, auxiliaries and cavalry are assembled from their several quarters, it is the duty of a good general to have every corps instructed separately in every part of the drill by tribunes of known capacity chosen for that purpose. He should afterwards form them into one body and train them in all the maneuvers of the line as for a general action. He must frequently drill them himself to try their skill and strength, and to see whether they perform their evolutions with proper regularity and are sufficiently attentive to the sound of the trumpets, the motions of the colors and to his own orders and signals. If deficient in any of these particulars, they must be instructed and exercised till perfect.

But though thoroughly disciplined and complete in their field exercises, in the use of the bow and javelin, and in the evolutions of the line, it is not advisable to lead them rashly or immediately to battle. A favorable opportunity must be watched for, and they must first be prepared by frequent skirmishes and slight encounters. Thus a vigilant and prudent general

will carefully weigh in his council the state of his own forces and of those of the enemy, just as a civil magistrate judging between two contending parties. If he finds himself in many respects superior to his adversary, he must by no means defer bringing on an engagement. But if he knows himself inferior, he must avoid general actions and endeavor to succeed by surprises, ambuscades and stratagems. These, when skillfully managed by good generals, have often given them the victory over enemies superior both in numbers and strength.

HOW TO MANAGE RAW AND UNDISCIPLINED TROOPS

All arts and trades whatever are brought to perfection by continual practice. How much more should this maxim, true in inconsiderable matters, be observed in affairs of importance! And how much superior to all others is the art of war, by which our liberties are preserved, our dignities perpetuated and the provinces and the whole Empire itself exist. The Lacedaemonians, and after them the Romans, were so aware of this truth that to this science they sacrificed all others. And the barbarous nations even at this day think only this art worth attention, believing it includes or confers everything else. In short, it is indispensably necessary for those engaged in war not only to instruct them in the means of preserving their own lives, but how to gain the victory over their enemies.

A commander-in-chief therefore, whose power and dignity are so great and to whose fidelity and bravery the fortunes of his countrymen, the defense of their cities, the lives of the soldiers, and the glory of the state, are entrusted, should not only consult the good of the army in general, but extend his care to every private soldier in it. For when any misfortunes happen to those under his command, they are considered as public losses and imputed entirely to his misconduct. If therefore he finds his army composed of raw troops or if they have long been unaccustomed to fighting, he must carefully study the strength, the spirit, the manners of each particular legion, and of each body of auxiliaries, cavalry and infantry. He must know, if possible, the name and capacity of every count, tribune, subaltern and soldier. He must assume the most respectable authority and maintain it by severity. He must punish all military crimes with the greatest rigor of the laws. He must have the character of being inexorable towards offenders and endeavor to give public examples thereof in different places and on different occasions.

Having once firmly established these regulations, he must watch the opportunity when the enemy, dispersed in search of plunder, think themselves in security, and attack them with detachments of tried cavalry or infantry, intermingled with young soldiers, or such as are under the military age. The veterans will acquire fresh experience and the others will be inspired with courage by the advantages such opportunities will give him. He should form ambuscades with the greatest secrecy to surprise the enemy at the passages of rivers, in the rugged passes of mountains, in defiles in woods and when embarrassed by morasses or difficult roads. He should regulate his march so as to fall upon them while taking their refreshments or sleeping, or at a time when they suspect no dangers and are dispersed, unarmed and their horses unsaddled. He should continue these kinds of encounters till his soldiers have imbibed a proper confidence in themselves. For troops that have never been in action or have not for some time been used to such spectacles, are greatly shocked at the sight of the wounded and dying; and the impressions of fear they receive dispose them rather to fly than fight.

If the enemy makes excursions or expeditions, the general should attack him after the fatigue of a long march, fall upon him unexpectedly, or harass his rear. He should detach parties to endeavor to carry off by surprise any quarters established at a distance from the hostile army for the convenience of forage or provisions. F or such measures should be pursued at first as can produce no very bad effects if they should happen to miscarry, but would be of great advantage if attended with success. A prudent general will also try to sow dissention among his adversaries, for no nation, though ever so weak in itself can be

completely ruined by its enemies unless its fall be facilitated by its own distraction. In civil dissensions men are so intent on the destruction of their private enemies that they are entirely regardless of the public safety.

One maxim must be remembered throughout this work: that no one should ever despair of effecting what has been already performed. It may be said that our troops for many years past have not even fortified their permanent camps with ditches, ramparts or palisades. The answer is plain. If those precautions had been taken, our armies would never have suffered by surprises of the enemy both by day and night. The Persians, after the example of the old Romans, surround their camps with ditches and, as the ground in their country is generally sandy, they always carry with them empty bags to fill with the sand taken out of the trenches and raise a parapet by piling them one on the other. All the barbarous nations range their carriages round them in a circle, a method which bears some resemblance to a fortified camp. They thus pass their nights secure from surprise.

Are we afraid of not being able to learn from others what they before have learned from us? At present all this is to be found in books only, although formerly constantly practiced. Inquiries are now no longer made about customs that have been so long neglected, because in the midst of peace, war is looked upon as an object too distant to merit consideration. But former instances will convince us that the reestablishment of ancient discipline is by no means impossible, although now so totally lost.

In former ages the art of war, often neglected and forgotten, was as often recovered from books and reestablished by the authority and attention of our generals. Our armies in Spain, when Scipio Africanus took the command, were in bad order and had often been beaten under preceding generals. He soon reformed them by severe discipline and obliged them to undergo the greatest fatigue in the different military works, reproaching them that since they would not wet their hands with the blood of their enemies, they should soil them with the mud of the trenches. In short, with these very troops he afterwards took the city of Numantia and burned it to the ground with such destruction of its inhabitants that not one escaped. In Africa an army, which under the command of Albinus had been forced to pass under the yoke, was by Metellus brought into such order and discipline, by forming it on the ancient model, that they afterwards vanquished those very enemies who had subjected them to that ignominious treatment. The Cimbri defeated the legions of Caepio, Manilus and Silanus in Gaul, but Marius collected their shattered remnants and disciplined them so effectually that he destroyed an innumerable multitude of the Cimbri, Teutones and Ambrones in one general engagement. Nevertheless it is easier to form young soldiers and inspire them with proper notions of honor than to reanimate troops who have been once disheartened.

PREPARATIONS FOR A GENERAL ENGAGEMENT

Having explained the less considerable branches of the art of war, the order of military affairs naturally leads us to the general engagement. This is a conjuncture full of uncertainty and fatal to kingdoms and nations, for in the decision of a pitched battle consists the fullness of victory. This eventuality above all others requires the exertion of all the abilities of a general, as his good conduct on such an occasion gains him greater glory, or his dangers expose him to greater danger and disgrace. This is the moment in which his talents, skill and experience show themselves in their fullest extent.

Formerly to enable the soldiers to charge with greater vigor, it was customary to order them a moderate refreshment of food before an engagement, so that their strength might be the better supported during a long conflict. When the army is to march out of a camp or city in the presence of their enemies drawn up and ready for action, great precaution must be observed lest they should be attacked as they defile from the gates and be cut to pieces in detail. Proper measures must therefore be taken so that the whole army may be clear of the gates and form in order of battle before the enemy's approach. If they are ready before you can have quitted the place, your

design of marching out must either be deferred till another opportunity or at least dissembled, so that when they begin to insult you on the supposition that you dare not appear, or think of nothing but plundering or returning and no longer keep their ranks, you may sally out and fall upon them while in confusion and surprise. Troops must never be engaged in a general action immediately after a long march, when the men are fatigued and the horses tired. The strength required for action is spent in the toil of the march. What can a soldier do who charges when out of breath? The ancients carefully avoided this inconvenience, but in later times some of our Roman generals, to say nothing more, have lost their armies by unskillfully neglecting this precaution. Two armies, one tired and spent, the other fresh and in full vigor, are by no means an equal match.

THE SENTIMENTS OF THE TROOPS SHOULD BE DETERMINED BEFORE BATTLE

It is necessary to know the sentiments of the soldiers on the day of an engagement. Their confidence or apprehensions are easily discovered by their looks, their words, their actions and their motions. No great dependence is to be placed on the eagerness of young soldiers for action, for fighting has something agreeable in the idea to those who are strangers to it. On the other hand, it would be wrong to hazard an engagement, if the old experienced soldiers testify to a disinclination to fight. A general, however, may encourage and animate his troops by proper exhortations and harangues, especially if by his account of the approaching action he can persuade them into the belief of an easy victory. With this view, he should lay before them the cowardice or unskillfulness of their enemies and remind them of any former advantages they may have gained over them. He should employ every argument capable of exciting rage, hatred and indignation against the adversaries in the minds of his soldiers.

It is natural for men in general to be affected with some sensations of fear at the beginning of an engagement, but there are without doubt some of a more timorous disposition who are disordered by the very sight of the enemy. To diminish these apprehensions before you venture on action, draw up your army frequently in order of battle in some safe situation, so that your men may be accustomed to the sight and appearance of the enemy. When opportunity offers, they should be sent to fall upon them and endeavor to put them to flight or kill some of their men. Thus they will become acquainted with their customs, arms and horses. And the objects with which we are once familiarized are no longer capable of inspiring us with terror.

CHOICE OF THE FIELD OF BATTLE

Good generals are acutely aware that victory depends much on the nature of the field of battle. When you intend therefore to engage, endeavor to draw the chief advantage from your situation. The highest ground is reckoned the best. Weapons thrown from a height strike with greater force; and the party above their antagonists can repulse and bear them down with greater impetuosity, while they who struggle with the ascent have both the ground and the enemy to contend with. There is, however, this difference with regard to place: if you depend on your foot against the enemy's horse, you must choose a rough, unequal and mountainous situation. But if, on the contrary, you expect your cavalry to act with advantage against the enemy's infantry, your ground must indeed be higher, but plain and open, without any obstructions of woods or morasses.

ORDER OF BATTLE

In drawing up an army in order of battle, three things are to be considered: the sun, the dust and the wind. The sun in your face dazzles the sight: if the wind is against you, it turns aside and blunts the force of your weapons, while it assists those of your adversary; and the dust driving in your front fills the eyes of your men and blinds them. Even the most unskillful endeavor to avoid these inconveniences in the moment of making their dispositions; but a prudent general should extend his views beyond the present; he should take such measures as not to be incommoded in the course of the day by different aspects of the sun or by contrary winds which often rise at a certain hour

and might be detrimental during action. Our troops should be so disposed as to have these inconveniences behind them, while they are directly in the enemy's front.

PROPER DISTANCES AND INTERVALS

Having explained the general disposition of the lines, we now come to the distances and dimensions. One thousand paces contain a single rank of one thousand six hundred and fifty-six foot soldiers, each man being allowed three feet. Six ranks drawn up on the same extent of ground will require nine thousand nine hundred and ninety-six men. To form only three ranks of the same number will take up two thousand paces, but it is much better to increase the number of ranks than to make your front too extensive. We have before observed the distance between each rank should be six feet, one foot of which is taken up by the men. Thus if you form a body of ten thousand men into six ranks they will occupy thirty-six feet. in depth and a thousand paces in front. By this calculation it is easy to compute the extent of ground required for twenty or thirty thousand men to form upon. Nor can a general be mistaken when thus he knows the proportion of ground for any fixed number of men.

But if the field of battle is not spacious enough or your troops are very numerous, you may form them into nine ranks or even more, for it is more advantageous to engage in close order that to extend your line too much. An army that takes up too much ground in front and too little in depth, is quickly penetrated by the enemy's first onset. After this there is no remedy. As to the post of the different corps in the right or left wing or in the center, it is the general rule to draw them up according to their respective ranks or to distribute them as circumstances or the dispositions of the enemy may require.

DISPOSITION OF THE CAVALRY

The line of infantry being formed, the cavalry are drawn up in the wings. The heavy horse, that is, the cuirassiers and troopers armed with lances, should join the infantry. The light cavalry, consisting of the archers and those who have no cuirasses, should be placed at a greater distance.

The best and heaviest horse are to cover the flanks of the foot, and the light horse are posted as abovementioned to surround and disorder the enemy's wings. A general should know what part of his own cavalry is most proper to oppose any particular squadrons or troops of the enemy. For from some causes not to be accounted for some particular corps fight better against others, and those who have defeated superior enemies are often overcome by an inferior force.

If your cavalry is not equal to the enemy's it is proper, after the ancient custom, to intermingle it with light infantry armed with small shields and trained to this kind of service. By observing this method, even though the flower of the enemy's cavalry should attack you, they will never be able to cope with this mixed disposition. This was the only resource of the old generals to supply the defects of their cavalry, and they intermingled the men, used to running and armed for this purpose with light shields, swords and darts, among the horse, placing one of them between two troopers.

RESERVES

The method of having bodies of reserves in rear of the army, composed of choice infantry and cavalry, commanded by the supernumerary lieutenant generals, counts and tribunes, is very judicious and of great consequence towards the gaining of a battle. Some should be posted in rear of the wings and some near the center, to be ready to fly immediately to the assistance of any part of the line which is hard pressed, to prevent its being pierced, to supply the vacancies made therein during the action and thereby to keep up the courage of their fellow soldiers and check the impetuosity of the enemy. This was an invention of the Lacedaemonians, in which they were imitated by the Carthaginians. The Romans have since observed it, and indeed no better disposition can be found.

The line is solely designed to repulse, or if possible, break the enemy. If it is necessary to form the wedge or the pincers, it must be done by the supernumerary troops stationed in the rear for that purpose. If the saw is to be formed, it must also be done from the reserves, for if once you begin to draw off men from the line you throw all into confusion. If any flying platoon of the enemy should fall upon your wing or any other part of your army, and you have no supernumerary troops to oppose it or if you pretend to detach either horse or foot from your line for that service by endeavoring to protect one part, you will expose the other to greater danger. In armies not very numerous, it is much better to contract the front, and to have strong reserves. In short, you must have a reserve of good and well-armed infantry near the center to form the wedge and thereby pierce the enemy's line; and also bodies of cavalry armed with lances and cuirasses, with light infantry, near the wings, to surround the flanks of the enemy.

THE POST OF THE GENERAL AND OF THE SECOND AND THIRD IN COMMAND

The post of the commander-in-chief is generally on the right between the cavalry and infantry. For from this place he can best direct the motions of the whole army and move elements with the greatest ease wherever he finds it necessary. It is also the most convenient spot to give his orders to both horse and foot and to animate them equally by his presence. It is his duty to surround the enemy's left wing opposed to him with his reserve of horse and light infantry, and attack it in the flank and rear. The second in command is posted in the center of the infantry to encourage and support them. A reserve of good and well-armed infantry is near him and under his orders. With this reserve he either forms the wedge to pierce the enemy's line or, if they form the wedge first, prepares the pincers for its reception. The post of the third in command is on the left. He should be a careful and intrepid officer, this part of the army being difficult to manage and defective, as it were, from its situation in the line. He should therefore have a reserve of good cavalry and active infantry to enable him always to extend his left in such a manner as to prevent its being surrounded.

The war shout should not be begun till both armies have joined, for it is a mark of ignorance or cowardice to give it at a distance.

The effect is much greater on the enemy when they find themselves struck at the same instant with the horror of the noise and the points of the weapons.

You must always endeavor to get the start of your enemy in drawing up in order of battle, as you will then have it in your power to make your proper dispositions without obstruction. This will increase the courage of your own troops and intimidate your adversaries. For a superiority of courage seems to be implied on the side of an army that offers battle, whereas troops begin to be fearful who see their enemies ready to attack them. You will also secure another great advantage, that of marching up in order and falling upon them while forming and still in confusion. For part of the victory consists in throwing the enemy into disorder before you engage them.

MANEUVERS IN ACTION

An able general never loses a favorable opportunity of surprising the enemy either when tired on the march, divided in the passage of a river, embarrassed in morasses, struggling with the declivities of mountains, when dispersed over the country they think themselves in security or are sleeping in their quarters. In all these cases the adversaries are surprised and destroyed before they have time to put themselves on their guard. But if they are too cautious to give you an opportunity of surprising or ensnaring them, you are then obliged to engage openly and on equal terms. This at present is foreign to the subject. However military skill is no less necessary in general actions than in carrying on war by subtlety and stratagem.

Your first care is to secure your left wing from being surrounded by the enemy's numbers or attacked in flank or rear by flying platoons, a misfortune that often happens. Nor is your right to be neglected, though less frequently in danger. There is only one remedy for this: to wheel back your wing and throw it into a circular position. By this evolution your soldiers meet the enemy on the quarter attacked and defend the rear of their comrades. But your best men should be posted on the angles of the flanks, since it is against them the enemy make their principal efforts.

There is also a method of resisting the wedge when formed by the enemy. The wedge is a disposition of a body of infantry widening gradually towards the base and terminating in a point towards the front. It pierces the enemy's line by a multitude of darts directed to one particular place. The soldiers call it the swine's head. To oppose this disposition, they make use of another called the pincers, resembling the letter V, composed of a body of men in close order. It receives the wedge, inclosing it on both sides, and thereby prevents it from penetrating the line.

The saw is another disposition formed of resolute soldiers drawn up in a straight line advanced into the front against the enemy, to repair any disorder. The platoon is a body of men separated from the line, to hover on every side and attack the enemy wherever they find opportunity. And against this is to be detached a stronger and more numerous platoon.

Above all, a general must never attempt to alter his dispositions or break his order of battle during the time of action, for such an alteration would immediately Occasion disorder and confusion which the enemy would not fail to improve to their advantage.

VARIOUS FORMATIONS FOR BATTLE

An army may be drawn up for a general engagement in seven different formations. The first formation is an oblong square of a large front, of common use both in ancient and modern times, although not thought the best by various judges of the service, because an even and level plain of an extent sufficient to contain its front cannot always be found, and if there should be any irregularity or hollow in the line, it is often pierced in that part. Besides, an enemy superior in number may surround either your right or left wing, the consequence of which will be dangerous, unless you have a reserve ready to advance and sustain his attack. A general should make use of this disposition only when his forces are better and more numerous than the enemy's, it being thereby in his power to attack both the flanks and surround them on every side.

The second and best disposition is the oblique. For although your army consists of few

433

troops, yet good and advantageously posted, it will greatly contribute to your obtaining the victory, notwithstanding the numbers and bravery of the enemy. It is as follows: as the armies are marching up to the attack, your left wing must be kept back at such a distance from the enemy's right as to be out of reach of their darts and arrows. Your right wing must advance obliquely upon the enemy's left, and begin the engagement. And you must endeavor with your best cavalry and infantry to surround the wing with which you are engaged, make it give way and fall upon the enemy in the rear. If they once give ground and the attack is properly seconded, you will undoubtedly gain the victory, while your left wing, which continued at a distance, will remain untouched. An army drawn up in this manner bears some resemblance to the letter A or a mason's level. If the enemy should be beforehand with you in this evolution, recourse must be had to the supernumerary horse and foot posted as a reserve in the rear, as I mentioned before. They must be ordered to support your left wing. This will enable you to make a vigorous resistance against the artifice of the enemy.

The third formation is like the second, but not so good, as it obliges you to begin the attack with your left wing on the enemy's right. The efforts of soldiers on the left are weak and imperfect from their exposed and defective situation in the line. I will explain this formation more clearly. Although your left wing should be much better than your right, yet it must be reinforced with some of the best horse and foot and ordered to commence the acnon with the enemy's right in order to disorder and surround it as expeditiously as possible. And the other part of your army, composed of the worst troops, should remain at such a distance from the enemy's left as not to be annoyed by their darts or in danger of being attacked sword in hand. In this oblique formation care must be taken to prevent the line being penetrated by the wedges of the enemy, and it is to be employed only when the enemy's right wing is weak and your greatest strength is on your left.

The fourth formation is this: as your army is marching to the attack in order of battle and you come within four or five hundred paces of the enemy, both your wings must be ordered unexpectedly to quicken their pace and advance with celerity upon them. When they find themselves attacked on both wings at the same time, the sudden surprise may so disconcert them as to give you an easy victory. But although this method, if your troops are very resolute and expert, may ruin the enemy at once, yet it is hazardous. The general who attempts it is obliged to abandon and expose his center and to divide his army into three parts. If the enemy are not routed at the first charge, they have a fair opportunity of attacking the wings which are separated from each other and the center which is destitute of assistance.

The fifth formation resembles the fourth but with this addition: the light infantry and the archers are formed before the center to cover it from the attempts of the enemy. With this precaution the general may safely follow the above mentioned method and attack the enemy's left wing with his right, and their right with his left. If he puts them to flight, he gains an immediate victory, and if he fails of success his center is in no danger, being protected by the light infantry and archers.

The sixth formation is very good and almost like the second. It is used when the general cannot depend either on the number or courage of his troops. If made with judgment, notwithstanding his inferiority, he has often a good chance for victory. As your line approaches the enemy, advance your right wing against their left and begin the attack with your best cavalry and infantry. At the same time keep the rest of the army at a great distance from the enemy's right, extended in a direct line like a javelin. Thus if you can surround their left and attack it in flank and rear, you must inevitably defeat them. It is impossible for the enemy to draw off reinforcements from their right or from their center to sustain their left in this emergency, since the remaining part of your army is extended and at a great distance from them in the form of the letter L. It is a formation often used in an action on a march.

The seventh formation owes its advantages to the nature of the ground and will enable you to oppose an enemy with an army inferior both in numbers and goodness, provided one of your flanks can be covered either with an eminence, the sea, a river, a lake, a city, a morass or broken ground inaccessible to the enemy. The rest of the army must be formed, as usual, in a straight line and the unsecured flank must be protected by your light troops and all your cavalry. Sufficiently defended on one side by the nature of the ground and on the other by a double support of cavalry, you may then safely venture on action.

One excellent and general rule must be observed. If you intend to engage with your right wing only, it must be composed of your best troops. And the same method must be taken with respect to the left. Or if you intend to penetrate the enemy's line, the wedges which you form for that purpose before your center, must consist of the best disciplined soldiers. Victory in general is gained by a small number of men. Therefore the wisdom of a general appears in nothing more than in such choice of disposition of his men as is most consonant with reason and service.

THE FLIGHT OF AN ENEMY SHOULD NOT BE PREVENTED, BUT FACILITATED

Generals unskilled in war think a victory incomplete unless the enemy are so straightened in their ground or so entirely surrounded by numbers as to have no possibility of escape. But in such situation, where no hopes remain, fear itself will arm an enemy and despair inspires courage. When men find they must inevitably perish, they willingly resolve to die with their comrades and with their arms in their hands. The maxim of Scipio, that a golden bridge should be made for a flying enemy, has much been commended. For when they have free room to escape they think of nothing but how to save themselves by flight, and the confusion becoming general, great numbers are cut to pieces. The pursuers can be in no danger when the vanquished have thrown away their arms for greater haste. In this case the greater the number of the flying army, the greater the slaughter. Numbers are of no signification where troops once thrown into consternation are equally terrified at the sight of the enemy as at their weapons. But on the contrary, men when shut up, although weak and few in number, become a match for the enemy from this very reflection, that they have no resource but in despair.

"The conquer'd's safety is, to hope for none."

MANNER OF CONDUCTING A RETREAT

Having gone through the various particulars relative to general actions, it remains at present to explain the manner of retreating in presence of the enemy. This is an operation, which, in the judgment of men of greatest skill and experience, is attended with the utmost hazard. A general certainly discourages his own troops and animates his enemies by retiring out of the field without fighting. Yet as this must sometimes necessarily happen, it will be proper to consider how to perform it with safety.

In the first place your men must not imagine that you retire to decline an action, but believe your retreat an artifice to draw the enemy into an ambuscade or more advantageous position where you may easier defeat them in case they follow you. For troops who perceive their general despairs of success are prone to flight. You must be cautious lest the enemy should discover your retreat and immediately fall upon you. To avoid this danger the cavalry are generally posted in the front of the infantry to conceal their motions and retreat from the enemy. The first divisions are drawn off first, the others following in their turns. The last maintain their ground till the rest have marched off, and then file off themselves and join them in a leisurely and regular succession. Some generals have judged it best to make their retreat in the night after reconnoitering their routes, and thus gain so much ground that the enemy, not discovering their departure till daybreak, were not able to come up with them. The light infantry was also sent forward to possess the eminences under which the army might instantly retire with safety; and the enemy, in case they pursued, be exposed to the light infantry, masters of the heights, seconded by the cavalry.

A rash and inconsiderate pursuit exposes an army to the greatest danger possible, that of falling into ambuscades and the hands of troops ready for their reception. For as the temerity of an army is increased and their caution lessened by the pursuit of a flying enemy, this is the most favorable opportunity for such snares. The greater the security, the greater the danger. Troops, when unprepared, at their meals, fatigued after a march, when their horses are feeding, and in short, when they believe themselves most secure, are generally most liable to a surprise. All risks of this sort are to be carefully avoided and all opportunities taken of distressing the enemy by such methods. Neither numbers nor courage avail in misfortunes of this nature.

A general who has been defeated in a pitched battle, although skill and conduct have the greatest share in the decision, may in his defense throw the blame on fortune. But if he has suffered himself to be surprised or drawn into the snares of his enemy, he has no excuse for his fault, because he might have avoided such a misfortune by taking proper precautions and employing spies on whose intelligence he could depend.

When the enemy pursue a retreating foe, the following snare is usually laid. A small body of cavalry is ordered to pursue them on the direct road. At the same time a strong detachment is secretly sent another way to conceal itself on their route. When the cavalry have overtaken the enemy, they make some feint attacks and retire. The enemy, imagining the danger past, and that they have escaped the snare, neglect their order and march without regularity. Then the detachment sent to intercept them, seizing the opportunity, falls upon them unexpectedly and destroys them with ease.

Many generals when obliged to retreat through woods send forward parties to seize the defiles and difficult passes, to avoid ambuscades and block the roads with barricades of felled trees to secure themselves from being pursued and attacked in the rear. In short both sides have equal opportunities of surprising or laying ambuscades on th1e march. The army which retreats leaves troops behind for that purpose posted in convenient valleys or mountains covered with woods, and if the enemy falls into the snare, it returns immediately to their assistance. The army that

pursues detaches different parties of light troops to march ahead through by-roads and intercepts the enemy, who are thus surrounded and attacked at once in front and rear. The flying army may return and fall on the enemy while asleep in the night. And the pursuing army may, even though the distance is great, surprise the adversary by forced marches. The former endeavor may be at the crossing of a river in order to destroy such part of the enemy's army as has already crossed. The pursuers hasten their march to fall upon those bodies of the enemy that have not yet crossed.

ARMED CHARIOTS AND ELEPHANTS

The armed chariots used in war by Antiochus and Mithridates at first terrified the Romans, but they afterwards made a jest of them. As a chariot of this sort does not always meet with plain and level ground, the least obstruction stops it. And if one of the horses be either killed or wounded, it falls into the enemy's hands. The Roman soldiers rendered them useless chiefly by the following contrivance: at the instant the engagement began, they strewed the field of battle with caltrops, and the horses that drew the chariots, running full speed on them, were infallibly destroyed. A caltrop is a machine composed of four spikes or points arranged so that in whatever manner it is thrown on the ground, it rests on three and presents the fourth upright.

Elephants by their vast size, horrible noise and the novelty of their form are at first very terrible both to men and horses. Pyrrhus first used them against the Romans in Lucania. And afterwards Hannibal brought them into the field in Africa. Antiochus in the east and Jugurtha in Numidia had great numbers. Many expedients have been used against them. In Lucania a centurion cut off the trunk of one with his sword. Two soldiers armed from head to foot in a chariot drawn by two horses, also covered with armor, attacked these beasts with lances of great length. They were secured by their armor from the archers on the elephants and avoided the fury of the animals by the swiftness of their horses. Foot soldiers completely armored, with the addition of long iron spikes fixed on their arms, shoulders and helmets, to prevent the elephant from seizing them with his trunk, were also employed against them.

But among the ancients, the velites usually engaged them. They were young soldiers, lightly armed, active and very expert in throwing their missile weapons on horseback. These troops kept hovering round the elephants continually and killed them with large lances and javelins. Afterwards, the soldiers, as their apprehensions decreased, attacked them in a body and, throwing their javelins together, destroyed them by the multitude of wounds. Slingers with round stones from the fustibalus and sling killed both the men who guided the elephants and the soldiers who fought in the towers on their backs. This was found by experience to be the best and safest expedient. At other times on the approach of these beasts, the soldiers opened their ranks and let them pass through. When they got into the midst of the troops, who surrounded them on all sides, they were captured with their guards unhurt.

Large balistae, drawn on carriages by two horses or mules, should be placed in the rear of the line, so that when the elephants come within reach they may be transfixed with the darts. The balistae should be larger and the heads of the darts stronger and broader than usual, so that the darts may be thrown farther, with greater force and the wounds be proportioned to the bodies of the beasts. It was proper to describe these several methods and contrivances employed against elephants, so that it may be known on occasion in what manner to oppose those prodigious animals.

RESOURCES IN CASE OF DEFEAT

If while one part of your army is victorious the other should be defeated, you are by no means to despair, since even in this extremity the constancy and resolution of a general may recover a complete victory. There are innumerable instances where the party that gave least way to despair was esteemed the conqueror. For where losses and advantages seem nearly equal, he is reputed to have the superiority who bears up against his misfortunes with greatest resolution. He is therefore to be first, if possible, to seize the spoils of the slain and to make rejoicings for the victory.

Such marks of confidence dispirit the enemy and redouble your own courage.

Yet notwithstanding an entire defeat, all possible remedies must be attempted, since many generals have been fortunate enough to repair such a loss. A prudent officer will never risk a general action without taking such precautions as will secure him from any considerable loss in case of a defeat, for the uncertainty of war and the nature of things may render such a misfortune unavoidable. The neighborhood of a mountain, a fortified post in the rear or a resolute stand made by a good body of troops to cover the retreat, may be the means of saving the army.

An army after a defeat has sometimes rallied, returned on the enemy, dispersed him by pursuing in order and destroyed him without difficulty. Nor can men be in a more dangerous situation than, when in the midst of joy after victory, their exultation is suddenly converted into terror. Whatever be the event, the remains of the army must be immediately assembled, reanimated by suitable exhortations and furnished with fresh supplies of arms. New levies should immediately be made and new reinforcements provided. And it is of much the greatest consequence that proper opportunities should be taken to surprise the victorious enemies, to draw them into snares and ambuscades and by this means to recover the drooping spirits of your men. Nor will it be difficult to meet with such opportunities, as the nature of the human mind is apt to be too much elated and to act with too little caution in prosperity. If anyone should imagine no resource is left after the loss of a battle, let him reflect on what has happened in similar cases and he will find that they who were victorious in the end were often unsuccessful in the beginning.

GENERAL MAXIMS

It is the nature of war that what is beneficial to you is detrimental to the enemy and what is of service to him always hurts you. It is therefore a maxim never to do, or to omit doing, anything as a consequence of his actions, but to consult invariably your own interest only. And you depart from this interest whenever you imitate such measures as he pursues for his benefit. For the same reason it would be wrong for him to follow such steps as you take for your advantage.

The more your troops have been accustomed to camp duties on frontier stations and the more carefully they have been disciplined, the less danger they will be exposed to in the field.

Men must be sufficiently tried before they are led against the enemy.

It is much better to overcome the enemy by famine, surprise or terror than by general actions, for in the latter instance fortune has often a greater share than valor. Those designs are best which the enemy are entirely ignorant of till the moment of execution. Opportunity in war is often more to be depended on than courage.

To debauch the enemy's soldiers and encourage them when sincere in surrendering themselves, is of especial service, for an adversary is more hurt by desertion than by slaughter.

It is better to have several bodies of reserves than to extend your front too much.

A general is not easily overcome who can form a true judgment of his own and the enemy's forces.

Valor is superior to numbers.

The nature of the ground is often of no more consequence than courage.

Few men are born brave; many become so through care and force of discipline.

An army is strengthened by labor and enervated by idleness.

Troops are not to be led to battle unless confident of success.

Novelty and surprise throw an enemy into consternation; but common incidents have no effect.

He who rashly pursues a flying enemy with troops in disorder, seems inclined to resign that victory which he had before obtained.

An army unsupplied with grain and other necessary provisions will be vanquished without striking a blow.

A general whose troops are superior both in number and bravery should engage in the oblong square, which is the first formation.

He who judges himself inferior should advance his right wing obliquely against the enemy's left. This is the second formation.

If your left wing is strongest, you must attack the enemy's right according to the third formation.

The general who can depend on the discipline of his men should begin the engagement by attacking both the enemy's wings at once, the fourth formation.

He whose light infantry is good should cover his center by forming them in its front and charge both the enemy's wings at once. This is the fifth formation.

He who cannot depend either on the number or courage of his troops, if obliged to engage, should begin the action with his right and endeavor to break the enemy's left, the rest of his army remaining formed in a line perpendicular to the front and extended to the rear like a javelin. This is the sixth formation.

If your forces are few and weak in comparison to the enemy, you must make use of the seventh formation and cover one of your flanks either with an eminence, a city, the sea, a river or some protection of that kind.

A general who trusts to his cavalry should choose the proper ground for them and employ them principally in the action.

He who depends on his infantry should choose a situation most proper for them and make most use of their service.

When an enemy's spy lurks in the camp, order all your soldiers in the day time to their tents, and he will instantly be apprehended.

On finding the enemy has notice of your designs, you must immediately alter your plan of operations.

Consult with many on proper measures to be taken, but communicate the plans you intend to put in execution to few, and those only of the most assured fidelity; or rather trust no one but yourself.

Punishment, and fear thereof, are necessary to keep soldiers in order in quarters; but in the field they are more influenced by hope and rewards.

Good officers never engage in general actions unless induced by opportunity or obliged by necessity.

To distress the enemy more by famine than the sword is a mark of consummate skill.

Many instructions might be given with regard to the cavalry. But as this branch of the service has been brought to perfection since the ancient writers and considerable improvements have been made in their drills and maneuvers, their arms, and the quality and management of their horses, nothing can be collected from their works. Our present mode of discipline is sufficient.

Dispositions for action must be carefully concealed from the enemy, lest they should counteract them and defeat your plans by proper expedients.

This abridgment of the most eminent military writers, invincible Emperor, contains the maxims and instructions they have left us, approved by different ages and confirmed by repeated experience. The Persians admire your skill in archery; the Huns and Alans endeavor in vain to imitate your dexterity in horsemanship; the Saracens and Indians cannot equal your activity in the hunt; and even the masters at arms pique themselves on only part of that knowledge and expertness of which you give so many instances in their own profession. How glorious it is therefore for Your Majesty with all these qualifications to unite the science of war and the art of conquest, and to convince the world that by Your conduct and courage You are equally capable of performing the duties of the soldier and the general!

Samurai Creed

5th Century CE

I have no parents; I make the Heavens and the Earth my parents.

I have no home; I make the Tan T'ien my home.

I have no divine power; I make honesty my Divine Power.

I have no means; I make Docility my means.

I have no magic power; I make personality my Magic Power.

I have neither life nor death; I make A Um my Life and Death.

I have no body; I make Stoicism my Body.

I have no eyes; I make The Flash of Lightning my eyes.

I have no ears; I make Sensibility my Ears.

I have no limbs; I make Promptitude my Limbs.

I have no laws; I make Self-Protection my Laws.

I have no strategy; I make the Right to Kill and the Right to Restore Life my Strategy.

I have no designs; I make Seizing the Opportunity by the Forelock my Designs.

I have no miracles; I make Righteous Laws my Miracle.

I have no principles; I make Adaptability to all circumstances my Principle.

I have no tactics; I make Emptiness and Fullness my Tactics.

I have no talent; I make Ready Wit my Talent.

I have no friends; I make my Mind my Friend.

I have no enemy; I make Incautiousness my Enemy.

I have no armor; I make Benevolence my Armor.

I have no castle; I make Immovable Mind my Castle.

I have no sword; I make No Mind my Sword

Thucydides on *The History of the Peloponnesian War*

5th Century CE

It follows that it was not a very wonderful action, or contrary to the common practice of mankind, if we did accept an empire that was offered to us, and refused to give it up under the pressure of three of the strongest motives, fear, honor, and interest. And it was not we who set the example, for it has always been law that the weaker should be subject to the stronger. Besides, we believed ourselves to be worthy of our position, and so you thought us till now, when calculations of interest have made you take up the cry of justice- a consideration which no one ever yet brought forward to hinder his ambition when he had a chance of gaining anything by might. And praise is due to all who, if not so superior to human nature as to refuse dominion, yet respect justice more than their position compels them to do.

Truce of God - Bishopric of Terouanne

1063

from Oliver J. Thatcher, and Edgar Holmes McNeal, eds., *A Source Book for Medieval History*, (New York: Scribners, 1905), pp. 417-418

Drogo, bishop of Terouanne, and count Baldwin [of Hainault] have established this peace with the cooperation of the clergy and people of the land. Dearest brothers in the Lord, these are the conditions which you must observe during the time of the peace which is commonly called the truce of God, and which begins with sunset on Wednesday and lasts until sunrise on Monday.

1. During those four days and five nights no man or woman shall assault, wound, or slay another, or attack, seize, or destroy a castle, burg, or villa, by craft or by violence.

2. If anyone violates this peace and disobeys these commands of ours, he shall be exiled for thirty years as a penance, and before he leaves the bishopric he shall make compensation for the injury which he committed. Otherwise he shall be excommunicated by the Lord God and excluded from all Christian fellowship.

3. All who associate with him in any way, who give him advice or aid, or hold converse with him, unless it be to advise him to do penance and to leave the bishopric, shall be under excommunication until they have made satisfaction.

4. If any violator of the peace shall fall sick and die before he completes his penance, no Christian shall visit him or move his body from the place where it lay, or receive any of his possessions.

5. In addition, brethren, you should observe the peace in regard to lands and animals and all things that can be possessed. If anyone takes from another an animal, a coin, or a garment, during the days of the truce, he shall be excommunicated unless he makes satisfaction. If he desires to make satisfaction for his crime he shall first restore the thing which he stole or its value in money, and shall do penance for seven years within the bishopric. If he should die before he makes satisfaction and completes his penance, his body shall not be buried or removed from the place where it lay, unless his family shall make satisfaction for him to the person whom he injured.

6. During the days of the peace, no one shall make a hostile expedition on horseback, except when summoned by the count; and all who go with the count shall take for their support only as much as is necessary for themselves and their horses.

7. All merchants and other men who pass through your territory from other lands shall have peace from you.

8. You shall also keep this peace every day of the week from the beginning of Advent to the octave of Epiphany and from the beginning of Lent to the octave of Easter, and from the feast of Rogations [the Monday before Ascension Day] to the octave of Pentecost.

9. We command all priests on feast days and Sundays to pray for all who keep the peace, and to curse all who violate it or support its violators.

10. If anyone has been accused of violating the peace and denies the charge, he shall take the communion and undergo the ordeal of hot iron. If he is found guilty, he shall do penance within the bishopric for seven years

Give Me Liberty or Give Me Death
By Patrick Henry

March 23, 1775

No man thinks more highly than I do of the patriotism, as well as abilities, of the very worthy gentlemen who have just addressed the House. But different men often see the same subject in different lights; and, therefore, I hope it will not be thought disrespectful to those gentlemen if, entertaining as I do opinions of a character very opposite to theirs, I shall speak forth my sentiments freely and without reserve. This is no time for ceremony. The questing before the House is one of awful moment to this country. For my own part, I consider it as nothing less than a question of freedom or slavery; and in proportion to the magnitude of the subject ought to be the freedom of the debate. It is only in this way that we can hope to arrive at truth, and fulfill the great responsibility which we hold to God and our country. Should I keep back my opinions at such a time, through fear of giving offense, I should consider myself as guilty of treason towards my country, and of an act of disloyalty toward the Majesty of Heaven, which I revere above all earthly kings.

Mr. President, it is natural to man to indulge in the illusions of hope. We are apt to shut our eyes against a painful truth, and listen to the song of that siren till she transforms us into beasts. Is this the part of wise men, engaged in a great and arduous struggle for liberty? Are we disposed to be of the number of those who, having eyes, see not, and, having ears, hear not, the things which so nearly concern their temporal salvation? For my part, whatever anguish of spirit it may cost, I am willing to know the whole truth; to know the worst, and to provide for it.

I have but one lamp by which my feet are guided, and that is the lamp of experience. I know of no way of judging of the future but by the past. And judging by the past, I wish to know what there has been in the conduct of the British ministry for the last ten years to justify those hopes with which gentlemen have been pleased to solace themselves and the House. Is it that insidious smile with which our petition has been lately received? Trust it not, sir; it will prove a snare to your feet. Suffer not yourselves to be betrayed with a kiss. Ask yourselves how this gracious reception of our petition comports with those warlike preparations which cover our waters and darken our land. Are fleets and armies necessary to a work of love and reconciliation? Have we shown ourselves so unwilling to be reconciled that force must be called in to win back our love? Let us not deceive ourselves, sir. These are the implements of war and subjugation; the last arguments to which kings resort. I ask gentlemen, sir, what means this martial array, if its purpose be not to force us to submission? Can gentlemen assign any other possible motive for it? Has Great Britain any enemy, in this quarter of the world, to call for all this accumulation of navies and armies? No, sir, she has none. They are meant for us: they can be meant for no other. They are sent over to bind and rivet upon us those chains which the British ministry have been so long forging. And what have we to oppose to them? Shall we try argument? Sir, we have been trying that for the last ten years. Have we anything new to offer upon the subject? Nothing. We have held the subject up in every light of which it is capable; but it has been all in vain. Shall we resort to entreaty and humble supplication? What terms shall we find which have not been already exhausted? Let us not, I beseech you, sir, deceive ourselves. Sir, we have done everything that could be done to avert the storm which is now coming on. We have petitioned; we have remonstrated; we have supplicated; we have prostrated ourselves before the throne, and have implored its interposition to arrest the tyrannical hands of the ministry and Parliament. Our petitions have been slighted; our remonstrances have produced additional violence and insult; our supplications have been disregarded; and we have been spurned, with contempt, from the foot of the throne! In vain, after these things, may we indulge the fond hope of peace and reconciliation. There is no longer any room for hope. If we wish to be free—if we mean to preserve inviolate those inestimable privileges for which we have been so long contending—if we mean not basely to abandon the noble struggle in which we have been so long engaged, and which we have pledged ourselves never to abandon until the glorious object of our contest shall be obtained—we must fight! I repeat it, sir, we must fight! An appeal to arms and to the God of hosts is all that is left us!

They tell us, sir, that we are weak; unable to cope with so formidable an adversary. But when shall we be stronger? Will it be the next week, or the next year? Will it be when we are totally disarmed, and when a British guard shall be stationed in every house? Shall we gather strength but irresolution and inaction? Shall we acquire the means of effectual resistance by lying supinely on our backs and hugging the delusive phantom of hope, until our enemies shall have bound us hand and foot? Sir, we are not weak if we make a proper use of those means which the God of nature hath placed in our power. The millions of people, armed in the holy cause of liberty, and in such a country as that which we possess, are invincible by any force which our enemy can send against us. Besides, sir, we shall not fight our battles alone. There is a just God who presides over the destinies of nations, and who will raise up friends to fight our battles for us. The battle, sir, is not to the strong alone; it is to the vigilant, the active, the brave. Besides, sir, we have no election. If we were base enough to desire it, it is now too late to retire from the contest. There is no retreat but in submission and slavery! Our chains are forged! Their clanking may be heard on the plains of Boston! The war is inevitable—and let it come! I repeat it, sir, let it come.

It is in vain, sir, to extenuate the matter. Gentlemen may cry, Peace, Peace—but there is no peace. The war is actually begun! The next gale that sweeps from the north will bring to our ears the clash of resounding arms! Our brethren are already in the field! Why stand we here idle? What is it that gentlemen wish? What would they have? Is life so dear, or peace so sweet, as to be purchased at the price of chains and slavery?

Forbid it, Almighty God! I know not what course others may take; but as for me, give me liberty or give me death!

FREDERICK THE GREAT'S *"MILITARY INSTRUCTIONS"*

1797

The King of Prussia's Military Instruction to His Generals

ARTICLE I.
Of Prussian Troops, their Excellencies and their Defects.
The strictest care and the most unremitting attention are required of commanding officers in the formation of my troops. The most exact discipline is ever to be maintained, and the greatest regard paid to their welfare; they ought also to be better fed than almost any troops in Europe.

Our regiments are composed of half our own people and half foreigners who enlist for money: the latter only wait for a favorable opportunity to quit a service to which they have no particular attachment. The prevention of desertion therefore becomes an object of importance.

Many of our generals regard one man as good in effect as another, and imagine that if the vacancy be filled up, this man has no influence on the whole; but one does not know how on this subject to make a proper application of other armies to our own.

If a deserter be replaced by a man as well trained and disciplined as himself, it is a matter of no consequence; but if a soldier, who for two years has been accustomed to arms and military exercise, should desert, and be replaced by a bad subject, or perhaps none at all, the consequence must prove eventually very material.

It has happened from the negligence of officers in this particular, that regiments have not only been lessened in number, but that they have also lost their reputation.

By accidents of this kind, the army becomes weakened at the very period when its completion is most essentially necessary, and unless the greatest attention is paid to the circumstance, you will lose the best of your forces and never be able to recover yourself.

Though my country be well peopled, it is doubtful if many men are to be met with of the height of my soldiers: and supposing ever that there was no want of them, could they be disciplined in an instant? It therefore becomes one of the most essential duties of generals who command armies or detachments, to prevent desertion. This is to be effected,

1st. By not encamping too near a wood or forest, unless sufficient reason require it.

2dly. By calling the roll frequently every day.

3dly. By often sending out patrols of hussars, to scour the country round about the camp.

4thly. By placing chasseurs in the corn by night, and doubling the cavalry posts at dusk to strengthen the chain.

5thly. By not allowing the soldiers to wander about, and taking care that each troop be led regularly to water and forage by an officer.

6thly. By punishing all marauding with severity, as it gives rise to every species of disorder and irregularity.

7thly. By not drawing in the guards, who are placed in the villages on marching days, until the troops are under arms.

8thly By forbidding, under the strictest injunctions, that any soldier on a march quit his rank or his division.

9thly. By avoiding night-marches, unless obliged by necessity.

10thly. By pushing forward patrols of hussars to the right and left, whilst the infantry are passing through a wood.

11thly. By placing officers at each end of a defile, to oblige the soldiers to fall into their proper places.

12thly. By concealing from the soldier any retrograde movement which you may be obliged to make, or giving some specious flattering pretext for doing so.

13thly. By paying great attention to the regular issue of necessary subsistence, and taking care that the troops be furnished with bread, flesh, beer, brandy, &c.

14thly. By searching for the cause of the evil, when desertion shall have crept into a regiment or company: enquiring if the soldier has received his bounty and other customary indulgencies, and if there has been no misconduct on the part of the captain. No relaxation of discipline is however on any account to be permitted. It may be said, that the colonel will take care of this business, but his efforts alone cannot be sufficient; for in an army, every individual part of it should aim at perfection, to make it appear to be the work of only one man.

An army is composed for the most part of idle and inactive men and unless the general has a constant eye upon them, and obliges them to do their duty, this artificial machine, which with the greatest care cannot be made perfect, will very soon fall to pieces, and nothing but the bare idea of a disciplined army will remain.

Constant employment for the troops is therefore indispensably necessary: the experience of officers who adopt such plan will convince them of its good effects, and they will also perceive that there are daily abuses to be corrected, which pass unobserved by those who are too indolent to endeavor to discover them.

This constant and painful attention may appear at first sight as rather a hardship on the general, but its consequences will make him ample amends. With troops so fine, so brave, and so well disciplined, what advantage can he not obtain? A general, who with other nations would be regarded as being rash or half mad, would with us be only acting by established rules. Any enterprise which

man is capable of executing, may be undertaken by him. Besides this, the soldiers will not suffer a man to remain amongst them who has betrayed any symptoms of shyness, which would certainly not be regarded in other armies.

I have been an eye-witness to the conduct both of officers and private soldiers, who could not be prevailed on, though dangerously wounded, to quit their post, or fall into the rear to get themselves dressed. With troops like these the world itself might be subdued, if conquests were not as fatal to the victors as to the vanquished. Let them be but well supplied with provisions, and you may attempt any thing with them. On a march you prevent the enemy by speed; at an attack of a wood, you will force them; if you make them climb a mountain, you will soon disperse those who make any resistance, and it then becomes an absolute massacre. If you put your cavalry into action, they will charge through the enemy at the sword's point and demolish them.

But as it is not alone sufficient that the troops be good, and as the ignorance of a general may be the means of losing every advantage, I shall proceed to speak of the qualities which a general ought to possess, and lay down such rules as I have either learned from well-informed generals, or purchased dearly by my own experience.

ARTICLE II.
Of the Subsistence of Troops, and of Provisions.
It has been said by a certain general, that the first object in the establishment of an army ought to be making provision for the belly, that being the basis and foundation of all operations. I shall divide this subject into two parts: in the first I shall explain how and where magazines ought to be established, and in the latter, the method of employing, and transporting them.

The first rule is to establish the large magazines invariably in the rear of the army, and, if possible, in a place that is well secured. During the wars in Silesia and Bohemia, our grand magazine was at Breslau, on account of the advantage of being able to replenish it by means of the Oder. When magazines are formed at the head of an army, the first check may oblige you to abandon them, and you may be left without resource; whereas, if they Are established in the rear of each other, the war will be prudently carried on, and one small disaster will not complete your ruin.

Spandau and Magdebourg should be the chosen situations for magazines in the frontier of the Electorate. Magdebourg, on account of the Elbe, will be particularly serviceable in an offensive war against Saxony, and Schweidenitz against Bohemia.

You cannot be too cautious in the choice of commissaries and their deputies, for if they prove dishonest, the state will be materially injured. With this view, men of strict honor should be appointed as superiors, who must personally, frequently, and minutely examine and control the accounts.

There are two ways of forming magazines, either by ordering the nobility and peasants to bring their grain to the depot, and paying them for it according to the rate laid down by the chamber of finance, or by taking a certain quantity from them by requisition. It is the business of the commissary to settle and to sign all these agreements.

Vessels of a particular construction are built for the purpose of conveying corn and forage along the canals and rivers.

Purveyors are never to be employed by in cases of the last necessity, for even Jews [sic] are less exorbitant in their demands: they increase the price of provisions, and sell them out again at a most extravagant profit.

The magazines should be established at a very early period, that no kind of necessary may be wanting when the army leaves its quarters to being a campaign: if they be too long neglected, the frost will put a stop to water-carriage, or the roads will become so excessively deep and heavy, that their formation will be a business of the utmost difficulty.

Besides the regimental covered wagons which carry bread for eight days, the commissary is provided with conveniences for carrying provisions for a month.

The advantage of navigation is, however, never to be neglected, for without this convenience, no army can ever be abundantly supplied.

The wagons should be drawn by horses: trial has been made of oxen, but they do not answer the purpose.

The wagon-masters must be exceedingly careful that due attention be paid to their cattle. The general of an army must also have an eye to this circumstance, for the loss of horses will necessarily occasion a diminution of wagons, and consequently of provisions.

Moreover, unless they receive a proper quantity of good food, these horses will be unable to undergo the necessary fatigue. On a march, therefore, not only the horses will be lost, but also the wagons and their contents. The best concerted measures may be ruined by a repetition of such disasters. the general, therefore, must not neglect any of these circumstances, which are so materially important in all his operations.

In order to facilitate the carriage of provisions in a war against Saxony, advantage must be taken of the Elbe, and in Silesia of the Oder. The sea affords you this assistance in Prussia , but in Bohemia and Moravia, your only dependence is on carriages. It sometimes happens, that three or four depots of provisions are formed on the same line, as was the case with us in Bohemia in the year 1742. There was a magazine at Pardubitz, at Nienbourg, at Podjebrod, and at Brandies, to enable us to keep pace with the enemy, and follow him to Prague, if he had thought proper to have gone thither.

During the last campaign in Bohemia, Breslau furnished Schweidenitz, Schweidenitz supplied Jaromirez, and from thence provisions were carried to the army.

Besides the covered wagons which carry provisions, iron ovens always travel with the army, (the number of which has of late been very much augmented), and, on every halting day they are set to bake bread. On all expeditions, you should be supplied with bread or biscuit for ten days. Biscuits is a very good article, but our soldiers like it only in soup, nor do they know how to employ it to the best advantage.

On a march through an enemy's country, the depot of meal should ever be in a garrisoned town near the army. During the campaign of 1745, our depot was first at Neustadt, then at Jaromirez, and last at Trautenau. Had we been farther advanced, we could not have had a depot in security nearer than that at Pardubitz.

I have provided hand-mills for each company, which are found to be exceedingly useful, as they are worked by the soldiers, who carry the meal to the depot, and receive bread in return. With this meal, you are enabled to husband your magazines, and have it in your power to remain much longer in camp than you could without such supply. Moreover, fewer escorts, and a smaller number of convoys will also be found sufficient.

On the subject of convoys, I must enlarge a little. The strength of escorts depends on the fear which you entertain of the enemy. Detachments of infantry are sent into the towns through which the convoy will pass, to afford then a point of support. Large detachments to cover them are sometimes sent out, as was the case in Bohemia.

In all chequered countries, convoys should be escorted by the infantry, to which a few hussars may be added, in order to keep a lookout on the march, and inform themselves of all situations where the enemy may lie concealed.

My escorts have been formed of infantry in preference to cavalry even in a plain country, and in my own opinion, with very much advantage.

For what regards the minutiae of escorts, I refer you to my military regulation. The general of an army cannot be too anxious about the security of his convoys.

One good rule to attain this end is, to send troops forward for the purpose of occupying the defiles through which the convoy is to pass, and to push the escort a league in front towards the enemy. By this maneuver the convoys are masked, and arrive in security.

ARTICLE III.
Of Sutlers, Beer, and Brandy.
When you have it in contemplation to make any enterprise on the enemy, the commissary must be ordered to get together all the beer and brandy that he can lay his hands on, that the army may

not want these articles, at least for the first days. As soon as the army enters an enemy's country, all the brewers and distillers who are in the neighborhood must immediately be put in requisition: the distillers, in particular, must be instantly set to work, that the soldier may not lose his dram, which he can very badly spare.

Protection must be afforded to the sutlers, especially in a country whose inhabitants are fled, and where provisions cannot be had for money. At such a time we are justified in not being over nice with respect to the peasantry.

The sutlers and women must be sent out in search of vegetables and cattle. The price of provisions is however, a matter that requires much attention, as the soldier ought to be allowed to purchase at a reasonable price, and at the same time the sutler should derive an honest profit.

It may here be added, that the soldier receives gratis during a campaign two pounds of bread per day, and two pounds of flesh per week. It is an indulgence which the poor fellows richly deserve, especially in Bohemia, where the country is but little better than a desert.

Convoys for the army should ever be followed by herds of cattle, for the support and nourishment of the soldier.

ARTICLE IV.
Of Dry and Green Forage.
Oats, barley, hay, chopped straw, &c. compose what is called dry forage,. and are carried to the magazine. If the oats be either fusty or moldy, the horses will contract the mange and farcy, and be so weakened as to be unserviceable even at the beginning of a campaign. Chopped straw is given because it is the custom, though it serves but barely to fill the belly.

The first object in collecting forage and carrying it to the magazine is, either to get the start of the enemy at the opening of a campaign, or to be prepared for some distant enterprise. But an army can seldom venture to move far from its magazines, as long as the horses are obliged to live on dry forage, on account of the inconvenience of moving it, as a whole province is sometimes unable to furnish a sufficient number of carriages. And in general, these are not the methods that we employ in an offensive war, unless there are no rivers, by means of which the forage can be transported.

During the campaign in Silesia, all my cavalry lived on dry forage, but we only marched from Strehla to Schwiednitz (where there was a magazine,) and from thence to Cracau, where we were in the neighborhood of the Brieg and the Oder.

When any enterprise is about to take place in the winter, the cavalry should carry with then forage for five days,. well bound together on their horses. If Bohemia or Moravia are to be the scene of action, unless you mean to destroy all your cavalry. We forage in the fields for corn and vegetables as long as any remain there, and after the harvest in the villages.

When we encamp on a spot where we mean to make some stay, an account should be taken of the forage; and when its quantity be ascertained, a regular distribution of it should be made according to the number of days which we intend to remain.

All large foraging parties are escorted by a body of cavalry, the strength of which is proportioned to the vicinity of the enemy, and the fear which you entertain of him. Foraging is sometimes carried on by the wings, or even the whole of an army.

The foragers always assemble on the road which they intend taking, either on the wings, in front, or in the rear of the army.

The advanced guard is composed of hussars, who are followed by the cavalry in a plain country, but in irregular situations, the infantry go before them. The advanced guard is to precede the march of about a fourth part of the foragers, who are to be followed by a detachment of the escort, partly horse and partly foot; then another party of foragers, followed by a detachment of troops, and after them the remainder in the same order. the march of the rear guard so to be closed by a troop of hussars, who will form the rear of the whole column.

It is to be remembered, that in all escorts the infantry take their cannon with them, and the foragers their swords and carbines.

When arrived at the spot where they intend foraging, a chain is to be formed, and the infantry posted near the villages, behind the hedges, and in the hollow ways. Troops of cavalry joined with infantry should be formed into a reserve, and placed in the centre to be ready to support any point where the enemy may endeavor to make an impression. The hussars are to skirmish with the enemy, in order to amuse them and draw them off from the forage. As soon as the enclosure is complete, the foragers divide the ground by regiments. Great care must be taken by the officers commanding, that the trusses be made very large, and bound well together.

When the horses are laden, the foragers are to return to camp by troops, protected by small escorts, and as soon as they have all left the ground, the troops of the chain are to assemble and form the rear guard, followed by the hussars.

The method of foraging in villages differs from the foregoing only in this instance, viz. the infantry are posted round the village, and the cavalry behind them in a situation where they may be able to act. Villages are to be foraged one by one, to prevent the troops of the chain from being too much dispersed.

In mountainous countries, foraging becomes an arduous business, and on such occasions the greatest part of the escorts must be composed of infantry and hussars.

When we are encamped near the enemy, and intend remaining there some time, we must endeavor to secure the forage which is between the two camps. After that, we are to forage for two leagues round, beginning with the most distant fields, and preserving those that are near home till the last. If no stay be intended, we forage in the camp and in the neighborhood.

When it becomes an object to secure a large quantity of green forage, I would rather send the parties out twice, than occupy too great an extent of country at once. By this means you will preserve your chain more snug and compact, and the foragers will be in much greater security: whereas if too great a space be occupied, the chain must consequently be weakened and rendered liable to be forced.

449

ARTICLE V.
Of the Knowledge of a Country.

The knowledge of a country is to be attained in two ways; the first (and that with which we ought to begin) is, by a careful and studious examination of a map of the country which is intended to be the scene of war, and by marking on it very distinctly the names of all the rivers, towns, and mountains that are of any consequence.

Having by this means gained a general idea of the country, we must proceed to a more particular and minute examination of it, to inform ourselves of the directions of the high roads, the situation of the towns, whether by a little trouble they can be made tenable, on what side to attack them if they are possessed by the enemy, and what number of troops are necessary for their defense.

We should also be provided with plans of the fortified towns, that we may be acquainted with their strength, and what are their most assailable parts. The course and depth of the large rivers should also be ascertained, how far they are navigable, and if shallow enough at any points to allow of being forded. It should also be known, what rivers are impassible in spring and dry in summer. This sort of enquiry must extend likewise to the marshes of any consequence that may be in the country.

In a flat, smooth country, the fertile parts should be distinguished from those that are not so, and we must be well acquainted with all the marches that either the enemy or ourselves can undertake, to pass from one great city or river to another. It will be necessary also to break up those camps, which are liable to be taken on that route.

A flat, open country can be reconnoitered presently, but the view is so confined in that which is woody and mountainous, that it becomes a business of much difficulty.

In order, therefore, to procure intelligence so highly important, we must ascend the heights, taking the map with us, and also some of the elders of the neighboring villages, such as huntsmen and shepherds. If there be one mountain higher than another, that must be ascended, to gain an idea of a country which we wish to discover.

We must gain a knowledge of the roads, not only to be satisfied in how many columns we may march, but also that we may be enabled to plan a variety of projects, and be informed how we may reach the enemy's camp and force it, should any be established in the neighborhood, or how place ourselves on his flank, should he alter his position.

One of the most material objects is, to reconnoiter situations that, in case of necessity, may serve as camps of defense, as well as a field of battle, and the posts that may be occupied by the enemy.

A just idea must be formed of all these matters of intelligence, as well as of the most considerable posts, the vallies, chief defiles, and all the advantageous situations which the country affords: and we must seriously reflect on every operation that may take place, so that by being prepared beforehand with a plan of arrangements, we may not be embarrassed when called into action. These reflections should be well connected, and maturely digested, with all the care and patience that an object of so much consequence requires; and unless we can arrange the matter to our satisfaction the first time, we must try it over again and again till we have got it perfect.

It is a general rule in the choice of all camps, whether for offence or defense, that both wood and water be near at hand, that the front be close and well covered, and the rear perfectly open.

If circumstances forbid the examination of a country in the manner laid down, clever, intelligent officers should be sent thither under any kind of excuse, or even in disguise if necessary. They are to be well informed of the nature of the observations which they are to make, and at their return, the remarks which they have made on the camps and different situations are to be noted on a map: but when we can make use of our own eyes, we ought never to trust to those of other people.

ARTICLE VI.
Of the Coup D'Oeil.

The coup d'oeil may be reduced, properly speaking, to two points; the first of which is the having abilities to judge how many troops a certain extent of country can contain. This talent can only be acquired by practice, for after having laid out several camps, the eye will gain so exact an idea of space, that you will seldom make any material mistake in your calculations.

The other, and by far the most material point, is to be most material point, is to be able to distinguish at first sight all the advantages of which any given space of ground is capable. This art is to be acquired and even brought to perfection, though a man be not absolutely born with a military genius.

Fortification, as it possesses rules that are applicable to all situations of an army, is undoubtedly the basis and foundation of this coup d'oeil. Every defile, marsh, hollow way, and even the smallest eminence, will be converted by a skilful general, to some advantage.

Two hundred different positions may sometimes be taken up in the space of two square leagues, of which an intelligent general knows how to select that which is the most advantageous. In the first place, he will ascend even the smallest eminences to discover and reconnoiter the ground; and assisted by the same rules of fortification, he will be enabled to find out the weak part of the enemy's order of battle. If time permit, the general would do well to pace over the ground, when he has determined on his general position.

Many other advantages may also be derived from the same rules of fortification, such as, the manner of occupying heights, and how to choose them, that they may not be commanded by others; in what manner the wings are to be supported, that the flanks may be well covered; how to take up positions that may be defended, and avoid those which a man of reputation cannot, without great risk, maintain. These rules will also enable him to discover where the enemy is weakest, either by having taken an unfavorable position, distributed his force without judgment, or from the slender means of defense which he derives from his situation. I am led by these reflections to explain in what manner troops ought to be distributed so as to make the most of their ground.

ARTICLE VII.
Of the Distribution of Troops.
Though the knowledge and choice of ground are very essential points, it is of no less importance that we know how to profit by such advantages, so that the troops may be placed in situations that are proper and convenient for them.

Our cavalry, being designed to act with velocity, can only be made use of on a plain, whereas the infantry may be employed in every possible variety of ground. Their fire is for defense, and their bayonet for attack. We always begin by the defensive, as much caution is necessary for the security of a camp, where the vicinity of the enemy may at any moment bring on an engagement.

The greater part of the orders of battle now existing are of ancient date: we tread in the steps of our ancestors without regulating matters according to the nature of the ground, and hence it is that a false and erroneous application so often takes place.

The whole of an army should be placed in order of battle agreeably to the nature of ground which every particular part of it requires. The plain is chosen for the cavalry, but this is not all which regards them; for if the plain be only a thousand yards in front, and bounded by a wood in which we suppose the enemy to have thrown some infantry, under whose fire their cavalry can rally, it will then become necessary to change the disposition, and place them at the extremities of the wings of the infantry, that they may receive the benefit of their support.

The whole of the cavalry is sometimes placed on one of the wings, or in the second line; at other times, their wings are closed by one or two brigades of infantry.

Eminences, church-yards, hollow ways, and wide ditches are the most advantageous situations for an army. If, in the disposition of our troops, we know how to take advantage of these circumstances, we never need to fear being attacked.

If your cavalry be posted with a morass in it's front, it is impossible that it can render you any service: and if it be placed too near a wood, the enemy may have troops there, who may throw them into disorder and pick them off with their muskets, whilst they are deprived of every possible means of defense. Your infantry will be exposed to the same inconveniencies if they are advanced too far on a plain with their flanks not secured, for the enemy will certainly take advantage of such error, and make their attack on that side where they are unprotected.

The nature of the ground must invariably be our rule of direction. In a mountainous country I should place my cavalry in the second line, and never use them in the first line except they could act to advantage, unless it be a few squadrons to fall on the flank of the enemy's infantry who may be advancing to attack me.

It is a general rule in all well-disciplined armies, that a reserve of cavalry be formed if we are on a plain, but where the country is chequered and intersected, this reserve is formed of infantry, with the addition of some hussars and dragoons.

The great art of distributing troops on the field is, so to place them, that all have room to act and be uniformly useful. Villeroi, who perhaps was not well acquainted with this rule, deprived himself of the assistance of the whole of his left wing on the plain of Ramillies, by having posted them behind a morass, where it was morally impossible that they could maneuver, or render and sort of support to his right wing.

ARTICLE VIII.
Of Camps.
To be convinced that your camp be well chosen, you must discover, whether a trifling movement of your's will oblige the enemy to make one of greater consequence, or if after one march, he be under the necessity of making others. They who have the least occasion to move, are certainly the best situated.

The choice of situation for a camp should rest entirely with the general of an army, as it often becomes the field of battle, and the success of his enterprises so materially depends upon it.

As there are many observations to be made on this subject, I shall enter into it very

particularly, saying nothing with respect to the method of placing troops in camp, but referring you on that head to my military regulation.

I now proceed to speak only of affairs of consequence, and of matters that more immediately concern the general himself.

All camps are designed to answer two purposes, defense and attack. The first class consists of those camps in which an army assembles where the sole object is the convenience and accommodation of the troops. They ought to be encamped in small bodies near the magazine, but so situate that they may readily be assembled in order of battle.

Camps of this kind are generally formed at such distance from the enemy as to be free from all alarm. the king of England, who neglected this caution, and imprudently encamped himself on the bank of the Mein opposite the French army, ran a very great risk of being defeated at Dettinghen.

The first rule to be observed in the marking out a camp is, that both wood and water be at no great distance.

It is our custom to entrench camps, in the manner of the Romans, not only to secure ourselves against any enterprise which the numerous light troops of the enemy may attempt against us, but also to prevent desertion.

I have constantly observed, that fewer men have left us when the redans were joined by two lines that extended all round the camp, than when this caution has been neglected. This is a serious fact, however ridiculous or trifling it may appear.

Camps of repose are those, where we expect forage; on some occasions that are designed to watch the enemy, who have as yet made no movements, that we may be regulated by their maneuvers. As relaxation is the only object in camps of this nature, they should be rendered secure by being in the rear of a large river or morass, or in short by any means that will render their front inaccessible. Of this description was our camp at Strehla.

If the brooks and rivers in front of the camp are too shallow, dams must be employed in order to deepen them.

Though there be no dread of the enemy to annoy us in camps of this kind, the general of an army must nevertheless on no account be idle. The leisure which he now has must be employed in paying attention to the troops, and re-establishing the usual discipline. He must examine if the service be carried on in strict conformity to order, if the officers on guard are attentive and well informed of the duties of their situation, and if the rules which I have laid down for the posting of cavalry and infantry guards be properly and strictly observed.

The infantry should go through their exercise three times a week, and the recruits once every day,: on some occasions also entire corps may perform their maneuvers together. The cavalry must likewise go through their evolutions, unless they are employed in foraging; and the general, knowing the exact strength of each corps, should take particular care that the recruits and young horses be well drilled. He must also frequently visit the lines, commending those officers who pay attention to their troops, and severely rebuking those who appear to have neglected them, for it is not to be supposed that a large army can be self-animated. It will ever abound with idlers and malingerers, who require the general's attention to be put in motion and be obliged to do their duty.

Very great utility will be derived from camps of this sort, if they be employed in the manner which I have recommended, and the succeeding campaign will prove the good effects of their discipline and order.

We form our encampment, or we forage, near to the enemy, or at a considerable distance from him—I shall only speak of the former, where it is necessary that we make choice of the most fertile spots, and encamp in a situation which art or nature has rendered formidable.

When foraging camps are situate near the enemy, they should be very difficult of access, as foraging parties are regarded as detachments sent out against the enemy.

These parties may consist of a sixth part, or even half of an army. It would afford fine amusement to the enemy, if they were able on these occasions to attack us to our disadvantage,

and it would certainly happen, but for the well-chosen situation of our camp.

But though the position be very good, and apparently there be nothing to fear from the enemy, there are, notwithstanding, other cautions which are by no means to be neglected. the most rigid secrecy must be observed both in regard to the time and place of foraging, nor should even the general who is to command on the occasion be acquainted with these circumstances till a late hour in the preceding evening.

We should send out as many detached parties as possible, to be more certainly informed of any movements which the enemy may make: and unless prevented by reasons that are very material, we may, to save trouble, forage on the same day that they do. We are not, however, to place too much confidence in this circumstance, as the enemy, by being apprized of our design, may countermand the order for foraging, and attack the main body.

The camp of Prince Charles of Lorraine under Koninginggraetz was inaccessible by nature, and extremely convenient for the purposes of foraging. That which we occupied at Cholm was made strong by art, viz. by the abbatis which I ordered to be thrown up on our right wing and the redoubts which were in front of the infantry camp.

We entrenched a camp, when it is our intention to lay siege to a place, to defend a difficult pass, and supply the defects of the situation by throwing up works so as to be secure from every insult on the part of the enemy.

The rules which a general has to observe in the formation of all entrenchments are, to take advantage of every marsh, river, inundation, and abbatis which may serve to render the extent of his entrenchments more difficult. They had better be too small than too large, for the progress of the enemy is not checked by the entrenchments themselves, but by the troops who defend them.

I would not wish to make entrenchments, unless I could line them with a chain of battalions, and had also at my disposal a reserve of infantry that could be moved to any point as occasion might require. Abbatis are no longer of service than whilst they are defended by infantry.

The chief attention should be paid to the proper support of the lines of countervallation, which generally end in a river; and in such case the fosse should be carried some length into the river, and be so deepened as not to allow if being forded. If this precaution be neglected, you run the hazard of having your flank turned. It is necessary that you be abundantly supplied with provisions before you sit down behind the lines to besiege any place.

The flanks of entrenchments should be particularly strong, nor should there be a single point which the enemy might attack without being exposed to four or five cross fires. Infinite care and caution are required in the formation of entrenchments which are designed to defend the passes and defiles of mountains. The support of the flanks is here most essentially necessary, to accomplish which, redoubts are formed on the two wings: sometimes the whole entrenchment itself is made up of redoubts, so that the troops who defend it are in no danger of being turned.

Intelligent generals are well informed how to oblige the enemy to attack those points where the work is made strongest by the ditch being widened, deepened, and lined with pallisadoes, chevaux de frize placed at the entrances, the parapet made cannon-proof, and pits dug in the places that are most exposed.

But for the covering of a siege, I would always prefer an army of observation to an entrenched camp, and for this plain reason, because we are taught by experience that the old method is not to be depended on.

The Prince of Conde saw his entrenchment which was before Arras forced by Turenne, and Conde (if I am not mistaking) forced that which Turenne had formed before Valenciennes—since that period, neither of these great masters in the military art have made any use of them, but, to cover a siege, have always employed armies of observation.

I shall now treat of defensive camps, which are only strong by situation, and intended solely to be secure from the attacks of the enemy.

To render these situations equal to the purposes for which they are designed, it is necessary, that the front and both flanks be of equal strength, and the rear perfectly free and open. Of such nature are those heights, whose front is very extensive, and whose flanks are covered by marshes, as was the camp of Prince Charles of Lorraine at Marschwitz, where the front was covered by a marshy river, and the flanks by lakes; or like that which we occupied at Konopist in the year 1744.

We may also shelter ourselves under the protection of some fortified place, as was done by the Marshal de Neipperg, who after being defeated at Mollwitz, took up an excellent position under the walls of Neiss. As long as a general can maintain his post in camps of this kind, he will be secure from attack; but as soon as the enemy is in motion with a view of turning him, he will no longer be able to remain. His arrangements should therefore be so settled before-hand, that if the enemy succeed in their attempt to turn him, he may have nothing to do but fall back, and take up another strong position in the rear.

Bohemia abounds in camps of this description, and as the country is so chequered by nature, we are often obliged to occupy some of them against our inclination.

I must again repeat how necessary it is for a general to be on his guard, lest he be led, by a bad choice of posts, into errors that cannot be remedied, or in a situation from which he has no means of escaping but by a narrow defile. For if he have a clever enemy to deal with, he will be so closely pent up, and so completely prevented from fighting by the nature of the ground, as to be obliged to submit to the greatest indignity which a soldier can suffer, that of laying down his arms without the power of defending himself.

In camps that are intended to cover a country, the strength of the place itself is not the object of attention, but those points which are liable to attack, and by means of which the enemy may penetrate. These should all be surrounded by the camp. Not that is necessary to occupy every opening by which the enemy may advance upon us, but that one only which would lead to his desired point, and that situation which affords us security, and from which we have it in our power to alarm him. In short, we should occupy that post, which will oblige the enemy to take circuitous routes, and enable us, by small movements, to disconcert his projects.

The camp at Newstadt defends the whole of the Lower Silesia against the attacks of an army that may be in Moravia. The proper position to take up, is to have the city of Neustadt and the river in front, and if the enemy shew a design to pass between Ottmachau and Glatz, we have only to move between Neiss and Ziegenhals, and there take up an advantageous camp which will cut them off from Moravia.

For the same reason the enemy will not dare to stir on the side of Cosel, for by placing myself between Troppau and Jaegerndorff (where there are many very excellent positions,) I cut him off from his convoys.

There is another camp of equal importance between Liebau and Schaemberg, which secures all Lower Silesia against Bohemia.

In all these positions, the rules which I have laid down ought to be observed, as far as circumstances will allow. I must yet add one more, which is, that when you have a river in front, you never allow tents to be pitched on the ground which you intend for the field of battle at a greater distance than half musket-shot from the front of the camp.

The frontier of the electorate of Brandenberg is a country which no camp can cover, as it has six leagues of plain ground which is open the whole way. To defend it against Saxony, it is necessary to be possessed of Wittenberg, and either encamp there or adopt the plan of the expedition which took place there in the winter of the year 1745. The camp at Werben covers and defends all that part which is on the side of the country of Hanover.

The front and flanks of a camp for offence must be always closed; for unless the flanks, which are the weakest part of an army, are well closed, you have nothing to expect form your troops. This was the fault of our camp at Czaslaw, before the battle of the year 1742.

The village houses which are on the wings, or in the front of our camp, are always occupied by troops, except on fighting days, when they are called in, lest by the enemy's setting fire to such badly-constructed wooden buildings (as our own cottages and those of our neighbors generally are) the men may also be destroyed. There may, however, be an exception to this general rules, when any stone houses are in the villages, or any church-yards which do not communicate with wooden buildings.

But as it is our constant principle to attack, and not act on the defensive, this kind of post should never be occupied except it be at the head of the army, or in front of it's wings; in such situations it will afford much protection to our troops in the attack, and prove of great annoyance to the enemy during the action.

It is also a circumstance of material import, that the depth of the small rivers or marshes which are in front or on the flanks of our camp be well ascertained, lest by the rivers being fordable, or the marshes practicable, you discover too late that you have trusted to a false point of defense.

Villars was beaten at Malplaquet by conceiving that the marsh on his right was impracticable, which proved to be only a dry meadow, which our troops passed to take him in the flank. Every thing should be examined by our own eyes, and no attentions of this nature treated on any account as matters of indifference.

ARTICLE IX.
How to secure a Camp.
The front of the first line must be defended by the regiments of infantry, and if a river be there, piquets must be posted on it's banks. The rear of the camp is to be guarded by piquets from the second line. These piquets are to be covered by redans, joined by slight entrenchments, by means of which the camp will be entrenched after the manner of the Romans. We must occupy the villages which are on the wings, or even to the distance of half a league from thence, if they serve to defend any other passages.

The cavalry guards are to be posted agreeably to the rules laid down in my military regulation. We seldom had more than 300 maitres de garde amongst 80 squadrons, unless we were very near to the enemy, as when we marched to Schweidenitz between the battle of Hohen-

Freidberg, and again when we marched into Lusatia in order to go to Naumbourg. These advanced guards should be composed of all sorts of troops, for example, 2000 hussars, 1500 dragoons, and 2000 grenadiers. The general who has the command of bodies of men that are advanced, should be a man of sound understanding, and as it is his object to gain intelligence, not expose himself to action, his camps should be chosen with judgment, having in their front either woods or defiles with which he is well acquainted. He must also send out frequent patrols for the purpose of gaining information, that he may know at every instant what is going forward in the camp of the enemy.

If in the mean time you employ the hussars who remain with you to patrol in the rear and on the wings of the camp, you have taken all possible precautions to be guarded against any hostile enterprises.

Should a considerable body of troops endeavor to slide in between you and your rear guard, you may be assured that they have formed some design against it, and you are therefore to hasten to it's support.

To conclude all that I have to say on this subject, it must be added, that if those generals who canton their troops wish to be free from danger and alarm, they should only occupy those villages which are between the two lines.

ARTICLE X.
In what Manner and for what Reason we are to send out Detachments.
It is only repeating an ancient maxim in war to say, "That he who divides his force will be beaten in detail." If you are about to give battle, strain every nerve to get together as many troops as you possibly can, for they never can be employed to better purpose. Almost every general who has neglected this rule, has found ample reason to repent of it.

Albemarle's detachment, which was beaten at Oudenarde, lost the great Eugene the whole campaign; and Gen. Stahrenberg was beaten at the battle of Villa Viciosa in Spain, by being separated from the English troops.

Detachments have also proved very fatal to the Austrians in the latter campaigns that they have made in Hungary. The Prince of Hildbourghausen was defeated at Banjaluka, and General Wallis suffered a check on the banks of the Timok. The Saxons also were beaten at Kesseldorf, for want of having joined Prince Charles, as they could have done. I should have been defeated at Sohr, and deservedly too, if presence of mind in my generals, and valor in my troops, had not rescued me from such misfortune. It may be asked, are we then never to send out detachments? My reply is, that it is a business of so delicate a nature, as never to be hazarded but on the most pressing necessity, and for reasons of the utmost importance.

When you are acting offensively, detachments ought never to be employed, and even though you are in an open country, and have some places in your possession, no more troops are to be spared than are barely sufficient to secure your convoys.

Whenever war in made in Bohemia or Moravia, necessity requires that troops be sent out to insure the arrival of provisions. Encampments must be formed on the chain of mountains which the convoys are obliged to pass, and remain there till you have collected provisions for some months, and are possessed of some strong place in the enemy's country that with serve as a depot.

Whilst these troops are absent on detachments, you are to occupy advantageous camps, and wait for their return.

The advanced guard is not reckoned as a detachment, because it should ever be near the army, and not ventured on any account too near the enemy.

It sometimes happens, that when we are acting on the defensive, we are forced to make detachments. Those which I had in Upper Silesia were in perfect safety by confining themselves, as I have already observed, to the neighborhood of fortified places.

Officers who have the command of detachments, should be men of prudence and resolution, for though they receive general instructions from their chief, it remains for themselves to consult on the propriety of advancing or retreating, as occasion may require.

When the force of the opponents is too strong, they should fall back, but on the other hand, they should well know how to take advantage, if the superiority happen to be on their own sides.

If the enemy approach by night, they will sometimes retire, and whilst they are supposed to be put to flight, return briskly to the charge and defeat them.

No regard whatever is to be paid to the light troops.

The first thing to be attended to by an officer who commands a detachment, is his own safety, and when that is secured, he is at liberty to form schemes against the enemy. To ensure rest to himself, he must keep his adversary constantly awake, by continually contriving plans against him, and if he succeed in two or three instances, the enemy will be obliged to keep on the defensive.

If these detachments be near the army, they will establish a communication with it by means of some town or neighboring wood.

In a war of defense, we are naturally induced to make detachments. Generals of little experience are anxious to preserve every thing, whilst the man of intelligence and enterprise regards only the grand point, in hopes of being able to strike some great stroke, and suffers patiently a small evil that may secure him against one of more material consequence.

The army of the enemy should be the chief object of our attention, it's designs must be discovered, and opposed as vigorously as possible. In the year 1745 we abandoned Upper Silesia to the ravages of the Hungarians, that we might be better enabled to thwart the intentions of Prince Charles of Lorraine, and we made no detachments until we had defeated his army. When that was done, General Nassau in fifteen days cleared the whole of Upper Silesia of the Hungarians.

It is a custom with some generals to detach troops when they are about to make an attack, to take the enemy in the rear during the action, but much danger attends a movement of this kind, as the detachments generally lose their road, and

arrive either too early or too late. The detachment which Charles XII. sent out on the evening before the battle of Pultawa lost it's way, and was the cause of the army's being beaten. Prince Eugene's design of surprising Cremona failed also from the too late arrival of the detachment of the Prince of Vaudemont, which was intended to attack the gate of Po.

Detachments should never take place on the day of battle, unless it be in the manner of Turenne near Colmar, where he presented his first line to the army of the Elector Frederick William, whilst the second line passing through defiles attacked him in flank and routed him. Or we may copy the example of the Marshal de Luxembourg at the battle of Fleury, in the year 1690, who posted a body of infantry in some high corn on the Prince of Waldeck's flank, and by that maneuver gained the battle.

After a victory, but never till then, troops may be detached for the protection of convoys, but even in this case they should not proceed a greater length than half a league from the army.

I shall conclude this article by saying, that detachments which weaken the army one half, or even a third part, are excessively dangerous, and strongly to be disapproved.

ARTICLE XI.
Of the Tricks and Stratagems of War.
In War, the skin of a fox is at times as necessary as that of the lion, for cunning may succeed when force fails. Since, therefore, force may at one time be repelled by force, and at another be obliged to yield to stratagem, we ought to be well acquainted with the use of both, that we may on occasion adopt either.

I have no wish to recite here the almost infinite list of stratagems, for they have all the same end in view, which is, to oblige the enemy to make unnecessary marches in favor of our own designs. Our real intentions are to be studiously concealed, and the enemy misled by our affecting plans which we have no wish to execute.

When our troops are on the point of assembling, we countermarch them in a variety of ways, to alarm the enemy, and conceal from him the spot where we really wish to assemble and force a passage.

If there be fortresses in the country, we choose to encamp in a situation that threatens three or four places at the same time. Should the enemy think proper to throw troops into all these places, the consequence will be, that his force will be so weakened, that we shall have a good opportunity of falling on him: but if one point only has been the object of his attention, we lay siege to that which is the most defenseless.

If the object be to pass a river, or be possessed of some post of importance, you must withdraw to a great distance both from the post and from the spot where you mean to pass, in order to entice the enemy after you. And when every thing is arranged and your march concealed, you are to betake yourself suddenly to the settled point and possess yourself of it.

If you wish to come to an action, and the enemy seems disposed to avoid it, you must appear to be in dread of the force which is opposed to you, or spread a report that your army is much weakened. We played this game before the battle of Hohen-Friedburg. I caused all the roads to be repaired as if I meant, at the approach of Prince Charles, to march to Breslau in four columns: his self-confidence seconding my design, he followed me into the plain, and was defeated.

Sometimes we contract the dimensions of the camp, to give it the appearance of weakness, and send out small detachments, (that we affect to be of great consequence,) in order that the enemy may hold us cheap, and neglect an opportunity which he might improve. In the campaign of 1745, if it had been my intention to take Konigingraetz and Pardubitz, I had only to make two marches through the country of Glatz on the side of Moravia, as that would certainly have alarmed Prince Charles and brought him thither, to defend the place from which, after leaving Bohemia, he drew all his provisions. You will be sure of creating jealousy in the enemy, if you threaten places that either communicate with the capitol or serve as depots for his provisions.

If we have no inclination to fight, we put a bold face upon the business, and give out that we are much stronger than we really are. Austria is a famous school for this sort of maneuver, for with them the art is brought to it's greatest perfection.

By keeping up a bold and determined appearance, you give the idea of wishing to engage, and occasion a report to be circulated that you are meditating some very bold and daring enterprise: by means of which the enemy, in dread of the consequences of an attack, will frequently remain on the defensive.

It is an essential object in a war of defense, to know how to make a good choice of posts, and to maintain them to the last extremity: when forced to retire, the second line begins to move, followed insensibly by the first, and as you have defiles in your front, the enemy will not be able to take advantage of you in the retreat.

Even during the retreat, the positions that are taken up should be so oblique as to keep the enemy as much as possible in the dark. The more he endeavors to discover your designs, the more he will be alarmed, whilst you indirectly obtain the object of your wishes.

Another stratagem of war is, to shew to the enemy a front of very great extent, and if he mistake a false attack for a real one, he will inevitably be defeated.

By means of tricks also, we oblige the enemy to send out detachments, and when they are marched, take the opportunity of falling on him.

The best stratagem is, to lull the enemy into security at the time when the troops are about to disperse and go into winter quarters, so that by retiring, you may be enabled to advance on them to some good purpose. With the view, the troops should be so distributed, as to assemble again very readily, in order to force the enemy's quarters. If this measure succeed, you may recover in a fortnight the misfortunes of a whole campaign.

Peruse with attention the two last campaigns of Turenne, for they are the chefs d'oeuvres of the stratagems of this age.

The schemes which our ancestors employed in war are now only in use amongst the light troops, whose practice it is to form ambuscades, and endeavor by a pretended flight to draw the enemy into a defile, that they may cut them in pieces. The generals of the present day seldom manage their matters so badly as to be taken in by such contrivances. Nevertheless, Charles XII. was betrayed at Pultawa through the treachery of one of the Cossac chiefs. The same accident also befell Peter I. on the Pruth, owing to the misconduct of a prince of that country. Both these men had promised a supply of provisions which it was not in their power to furnish.

As the method of making war by parties and detachments is fully laid down in my Military Regulation, I refer to that work all those who wish to refresh their memories, as it is a subject on which I have nothing farther to advance.

To be informed of the method to oblige the enemy to make detachments, we have only to read over the glorious campaign of 1690, made by the Marshal de Luxembourg against the King of England, which concluded with the battle of Neerwinde.

ARTICLE XII.

Of Spies, how they are to be employed on every Occasion,
and in what Manner we are to learn Intelligence of the enemy.

If we were acquainted beforehand with the intentions of the enemy, we should always be more than a match for him even with an inferior force. It is an advantage which all generals are anxious to procure, but very few obtain.

Spies may be divided into several classes: 1st, common people who choose to be employed in such concern; 2dly, double spies; 3dly, spies of consequence; 4thly, those who are compelled to take up the unpleasant business.

The common gentry, viz. peasants, mechanics, priests, &c. which are sent into the camp, can only be employed to discover where the enemy is: and their reports are generally so incongruous and obscure, as rather to increase our uncertainties than lessen them.

The intelligence of deserters is, for the most part, not much more to be depended on. A soldier knows very well what is going forward in his own regiment, but nothing farther. The hussars being detached in front, and absent the greatest part of their time from the army, are often ignorant on which side it is encamped. Nevertheless, their reports must be committed to paper, as the only means of turning them to any advantage.

Double spies are used to convey false intelligence to the enemy. There was an Italian at Schmiedeberg, who acted as a spy to the Austrians, and being told by us, that when the enemy approached we should retire to Breslau, he posted with the intelligence to Prince Charles of Lorraine, who narrowly escaped being taken in by it.

The post-master at Versailles was a long time in the pay of Prince Eugene. This unfortunate fellow opened the letters and orders which were sent from the court to the generals, and transmitted a copy of them to Prince Eugene, who generally received them much earlier than the commanders of the French army.

Luxembourg had gained over to his interest a secretary of the King of England, who informed him of all that passed. The king discovered it, and derived every advantage from it that could be expected in an affair of such delicacy: he obliged the traitor to write to Luxembourg, informing him that the allied army would be out the day following on a large foraging party. The consequence was that the French very narrowly escaped being surprised at Steinquerque, and would have been cut to pieces if they had not defended themselves with extraordinary valor. It would be very difficult to obtain such spies in a war against Austria: not that the Austrians are less alive to bribery than other people, but because their army is surrounded by such a cloud of light troops, who suffer no creature to pass without being well searched. This circumstance suggested to me the idea of bringing over some of their hussar officers, by means of whom a correspondence might be carried on in the following manner. It is a custom with hussars, when opposed to each other as skirmishing parties, to agree every now and then to a suspension of arms, which opportunity might be employed in conveying letters.

When we wish to gain intelligence of the enemy, or give him a false impression of our situation and circumstances, we employ a trusty soldier to go from our camp to that of the enemy, and report what we wish to have believed. He may also be made the bearer of hand-bills calculated to encourage desertion. Having completed his business, he may take a circuitous march and return to camp.

There is yet another way to gain intelligence of the enemy when milder methods fail, though I confess it to be a harsh and cruel practice. We find out a rich citizen who has a large family and good estate, and allow him a man who understands the language of the country dressed as a servant, whom we force him to take along with him into the enemy's camp, as his valet or coachman, under pretence of complaining of some injuries which he has received; he is to be threatened also at the same time, that if he does not return after a certain period, and bring the man with him, that his houses shall be burned, and his wife and children hacked in pieces. I was obliged to have recourse to this scheme at . . . and it succeeded to my wish.

I must farther add, that in the payment of spies we ought to be generous, even to a degree of extravagance. That man certainly deserves to be well rewarded, who risks his neck to do your service.

ARTICLE XIII.
Of certain Marks, by which the Intentions of the Enemy are to be discovered.

The knowledge of the spot which the enemy has chosen as a depot for his provisions is the surest means of discovering his intentions before the campaign opens. For example, if the Austrians establish their magazines at Olmutz, we may be assured that they mean to attack Upper Silesia: if at Konigingraetz, we may be convinced that part of Schweidenitz is threatened. When it was the wish of the Saxons to invade the frontier of the Electorate, their magazines marked their intended route, for they were established at Zittau, Goerlitz, and at Guben, which are on the road leading to Crossen.

The first object of intelligence should be, on what side and in what situations the enemy means to fix his magazines.

The French played a double game, by forming depots on the Meuse and on the Scheld, in order to conceal their intentions.

When the Austrians are encamped, it is easy to discover when they intend moving, by their custom of cooking on the days of march. If, therefore, much smoke be perceived in their camp at five or six o'clock in the morning, you may take it for granted on that day they mean to move.

Whenever the Austrians intend fighting, all their strong detachments of light troops are called in; and when you have observed this, it behooves you to be very well upon your guard.

If you attack a post which is defended by their Hungarian troops, without being able to make any impression on it, you may be satisfied that the army is near at hand to support them.

If their light troops endeavor to post themselves between your army and the body of men which you have detached, you may be assured that the enemy has a design on that detachment, and your measures must be taken accordingly. It must be added, that if the same general be always opposed to you, his designs will be readily discovered, and his plan of conduct very soon become familiar.

After mature reflection on the nature of the country which is the scene of war, the state of the army which you command, the safety of the magazines, the strength of the fortified places, the means which the enemy may be able to employ in order to gain possession of them, the mischief which the light troops may do by posting themselves on your flanks, rear, and other parts, or if the enemy should employ them to make a diversion; I say, after having well deliberated on all these points, you may conclude that an intelligent enemy will attempt that enterprise which is likely to give you the greatest annoyance, at least that such will be his intention, to frustrate which your every effort must be exerted.

ARTICLE XIV.
Of our own Country, and that which is either neutral or hostile; of the
Variety of Religions, and of the different Conduct which such Circumstances require.

War may be carried on in three different kinds of country: either in our own territories, those belonging to neutral powers, or in the country of an enemy.

If glory were my only object, I would never make war but in my own country, by reason of it's manifold advantages, as every man there acts as a spy, nor can the enemy stir a foot without being betrayed.

Detachments of any strength may boldly be sent out, and may practice in safety all the maneuvers of which war is capable.

If the enemy have the advantage, every peasant turns soldier and lends a hand to annoy him, as was experienced by the Elector Frederick William after the battle of Fehrbelin, where a greater number of Swedes was destroyed by the peasants than fell in the engagement. After the battle of Hohen-Friedberg, also, I observed that the mountaineers in Silesia brought into us the runaway Austrians in great abundance.

When war is carried on in a neutral country, the advantage seems to be equal, and the object of attention then is, to rival the enemy in the confidence and friendship of the inhabitants. To attain this end, the most exact discipline must be observed, marauding and every kind of plunder strictly forbidden, and it's commission punished with exemplary severity. It may not be amiss also, to accuse the enemy of harboring some pernicious designs against the country.

If we are in a protestant country, we wear the mask of protector of the Lutheran religion, and endeavor to make fanatics of the lower order of people, whose simplicity is not proof against our artifice.

In a catholic country, we preach up toleration and moderation, constantly abusing the priests as the cause of all the animosity that exists between the different sectaries, although, in spite of their disputes, they all agree upon material points of faith.

The strength of the parties you may be required to send out, must depend on the confidence that can be placed in the inhabitants of the country. In our country you may run every risk, but more caution and circumspection are necessary in a neutral country, at least till you are convinced of the friendly disposition of the whole, or the greatest part of the peasantry.

In a country that is entirely hostile, as Bohemia and Moravia, you are to hazard nothing, and never send out parties, for the reasons already mentioned, as the people there are not to be trusted any farther than you can see them. The greater part of the light troops are to be employed in guarding the convoys, for you are never to expect to gain the affection of the inhabitants of this country. The Hussites in the circle of Konigingraetz are the only people that can be induced to render us any sort of service. The men of consequence there, though seemingly well disposed towards us, are arrant traitors, nor are the priests or magistrates at all better. As their interest is attached to that of the house of Austria, whose views do not altogether clash with ours , we neither can nor ought to repose any sort of confidence in them.

All that now remains for our management is fanaticism, to know how to inspire a nation with zeal for the liberty of religion, and hint to them in a guarded manner, how much they are oppressed by their great men and priests. This may be said to be moving heaven and hell for one's interest.

Since these notes have been put together, the empress queen has materially increased the taxes in Bohemia and Moravia: advantage may be taken of this circumstance to gain the good-will of the people, especially if we flatter them that they shall be better treated if we become masters of the country.

ARTICLE XV.
Of every Kind of March, which it can be necessary for an Army to make.
An army moves for the purposes of advancing in an enemy's country, to take possession of an advantageous camp, join a reinforcement, give battle, or retire before the enemy.

When the camp is properly secured, the next object is, to reconnoiter the whole neighborhood and every road that leads from it to camp, that we may be enabled to make the necessary arrangements, as a variety of circumstances may require.

461

With this view, and under various pretences we send out large detachments, accompanied by some engineers and quartermasters, who are to pry into every place that is capable of being occupied by troops. They are also to take up the situation of the country, and reconnoiter the roads by which the troops can march. A certain number of chasseurs should follow them, who are to observe the roads very attentively, that they may be able to lead the columns, provided that the general marches thither.

On their return, the aforesaid officers are to make their report concerning the situation of the camp, the roads that lead to it, the nature of the soil, the woods, mountains, and rivers that are situate thereabouts; and the general, being well informed of all these particulars will make his dispositions accordingly. When the camp is not too near the enemy, the following arrangement may take place:

I suppose that the camp may be approached in four different ways. The advanced guard, composed of six battalions of grenadiers, one regiment of infantry, two of dragoons, (consisting of five squadrons each,) and two regiments of hussars, under the command of Mr. N. N. will depart at eight o'clock this evening. All the encampments of the army are to follow this advanced guard, which is to take their tents only with them, leaving their heavy baggage with the army.

These troops are to march four leagues in front and occupy the defile, river, height, town, village, &c. which may be objects of attention, and wait there the arrival of the army, after which they are to enter into the camp which has been already marked out.

On the following morning the army, marching in four columns, is to move forward after the advanced guard: those men who have been posted as guards in the villages, falling in with their respective regiments. The cavalry of the two lines of the right wing, marching by it's right, will form the first column: the infantry of the two lines of the right wing, marching by it's right, will form the second: the infantry of the two lines of the left wing, filing by it's right, will form the third; and the cavalry of the left wing, filing by it's right, will form the fourth column. The infantry regiments N. N. of the second line, and the three regiments of hussars under the command of General N. N. will escort the baggage, which is to march in the rear of the two columns of infantry.

Four aides-du-camp are to command this party, who are to take particular care that the carriages follow each other in order, allowing as little interval as possible.

If the general commanding the rear guard should be in want of support, he is immediately to apply to the commander in chief.

The chasseurs who have reconnoitered the roads, are to conduct the four columns.

A detachment of carpenters, with wagons laden with beams, joists, and planks, should precede each column, to throw bridges over the small rivers.

The heads of columns must be careful not to go before each other without allowing any intervals. Officers commanding divisions must be attentive in observing their distances.

When you have to pass a defile, the heads of columns must march very slowly, or halt now and then to allow the rear to recover it's situation.

It is thus that the order of march is to be conducted.

When mountains, woods, or defiles, are met with on the march, the columns are to be divided, and the head, which consists of the infantry, is to be followed by the cavalry, who will close the march.

If there be a plain in the center, it is to be assigned to the cavalry, and the infantry formed into columns on the two extremities, are to traverse the wood; but this is only to be understood of a march which is made not too near the enemy. In that situation, we are content to place some battalions of grenadiers at the head of each column of cavalry, that they may preserve the order of battle.

The most certain way to insure the safe arrival of a reinforcement is, to march through a difficult road to meet it, and to retire from the enemy to avoid an engagement. By means of the superiority which you gain by the arrival of this succor, you will soon recover that ground, which you have, as it were, only lent to the enemy.

When we are obliged to march parallel to the enemy, it must be done in two lines, either by the right or by the left, and each line must form a column, with an advanced guard in front. In other respects, those rules which I have just laid down, may also here be employed.

All the marches which we made from Frankenberg to Hohen-Friedberg were directed in this manner, marching to the right.

I prefer these dispositions to any others, because the army can be formed in order of battle by one to the right or one to the left, which is much the readiest way of collecting them, and I would ever practice this method, if I had my choice in attacking the enemy, though I lost the advantage of it at Sohr and at Hohen-Friedberg. In this sort of march, care is to be taken that the flank be never shown to the enemy.

When the enemy begins a march in preparation for an action, you are to disencumber yourself of all your heavy baggage, and send it under escort to the nearest town. The advanced guard is then to be formed, and pushed forward to the distance of a short half league.

When the army marches in front against the enemy, care must be taken not only that the columns do not go before each other, but also that when they draw near to the field of battle, they extend themselves in such a manner, that the troops do not take up more or less ground than they will occupy when they are formed. This is a business of much difficulty, as some battalions are generally too much crowded, and others have too much ground allotted them.

Marching by lines is attended with no sort of inconvenience, and on that account has by me ever been preferred.

When we expect to be engaged upon a march, great precaution is required, and it is necessary that the general be very much upon his guard. He should reconnoiter the ground, without exposing himself, from point to point, so as to have an idea of different positions, if the enemy should come to attack him.

Steeples and heights are to be made use of in order to reconnoiter the ground, and the road which leads to them is to be cleared by light troops, detached from the advanced guard.

Retreats are generally conducted in the following manner: A day or two before we depart, the heavy baggage is got together, and sent away under a strong escort.

The number of columns is then to be determined by the number of roads that can be made use of, and the march of the troops regulated by the nature of the ground. In a plain, the advanced guard is formed by the cavalry; if it be a chequered country, that post belongs to the infantry. in a plain country, the army will march in four columns.

The infantry of the second line of the right wing, filing by it's right, and followed by the second line of the cavalry of the same wing, will form the fourth column. The infantry of the first line of the right wing, filing by it's right, will be followed by the first line of cavalry of that wing, and form the third column.

The infantry of the second line of the left wing, followed by the cavalry of that same line, will form the second column. The infantry of the first line of the left wing will be followed by the cavalry of that same line, forming together the first column.

In this manner the rear guard will be formed by the whole of the cavalry, which may be supported, for security sake by the hussars of the army.

If, during the retreat, it be necessary to pass any defiles, the infantry must occupy them the evening before we depart, and be so posted as to cover the troops, in order that the passage of the defile may remain open.

Supposing that the army marches in two columns, the cavalry of the right will file by it's left, the second line moving first, and taking the lead of the second column: the infantry of the second line, followed by the first, will place itself in the rear and follow this cavalry.

The cavalry of the left wing will file by it's left, the second line moving first, and heading the first column. This will be joined by the infantry of the left wing, (whose second line will also move before the first,) and thus the first column will be formed.

Six battalions of the rear of the first line, supported by ten squadrons of hussars will form the rear guard. These six battalions are to place themselves in order of battle in front of the defile in two lines, as the checquered disposition.

Whilst the army is passing the defile, the troops that are posted in front must cover and protect by their fire those which still remain on the other side of it.

When the whole army shall have come up, the first line of the advanced guard is to throw itself into the defile, having passed through the intervals of the second line; and when it is gone on, the second line will follow in the same manner, under cover of the fire of those who are posted on the other side, who are to follow last, and will form the rear guard.

The most difficult of all maneuvers is, that of passing a river during a retreat in presence of the enemy. On this subject I cannot quote a better example that our repassing the Elbe at Kolin in the retreat of 1744.

But as towns are not always in the neighborhood of such situations, I will suppose that your only resource is in two bridges. In such a case a large entrenchment is to be thrown up which will include both bridges, leaving a small opening at the head of each of them.

This being done, we are to send across the river several pieces of cannon with a certain number of troops, and post them on the opposite bank, which should on no account be too steep, but sufficiently elevated to command that which is on the other side. The large entrenchment is then to be lined with infantry, and after such a disposition, the infantry are to be the first to pass over, whilst the cavalry, forming the rear guard, retire in a chequered way through the entrenchment.

When all are passed, the two small heads of the bridge are to be skirted by the infantry, whilst those who are in the entrenchment leave it, in order to retire.

If the enemy have any inclination for a pursuit, he will be exposed to the fire from both heads of the bridge, and from the troops who are posted on the other side of the river.

The infantry who were placed in the entrenchment having passed the river, the bridge is to be destroyed, and the troops who defended the heads of the bridge, are to pass over in boats, under cover of those who are posted on the other side of the river, whose duty it is to advance in order to support them.

When the pontoons are placed on the carriages, the last troops put themselves in motion.

Fougasses* may also be formed at the angles of the entrenchments, which may be set on fire by the last grenadiers at the moment that they have passed the river.

ARTICLE XVI.

On the Precautions necessary to be taken in a Retreat against Hussars and Pandours.

The hussars and pandours are dreadful only to those who do not know them. They are never brave but when animated by the hope of plunder, or when they can annoy others without exposing themselves. The first species of their bravery they exercise against convoys and baggage, and the other against troops who are obliged to retire, whom they endeavor to tease in their retreat.

Our troops have nothing serious to dread from them, but as a march is often retarded by their manner of skirmishing, and as some men will unavoidably be lost, and that too at a very inconvenient season, I shall explain the best method that I am acquainted with of getting rid of these gentry.

When we retreat through plains, the hussars are to be driven away by a few discharges of cannon, and the pandours by means of the dragoons and hussars, of whom they are in a very great dread. The most difficult retreats, and those in which the pandours have it in their power to do the greatest mischief are those where we have to pass woods, defiles, and mountains. In such cases, the loss of some men is almost inevitable.

In these situations, then, the heights should be occupied by the advanced guard with their front towards the enemy, and at the same time troops are to be detached on the flank of the line of march, who keeping along on the side of the army will always pass over the heights or through the woods. Some squadrons should also be at hand to be employed where the ground will allow of it.

On these occasions, we are never to halt, but keep constantly moving, for halting would certainly be an unseasonable sacrifice of some of your men.

The pandours fire as they lie down, and by that means keep themselves concealed; and when the marching of the army makes it necessary for the rear guard and the small parties that were detached to quit the heights and follow the main body, they then possess themselves of those situations, and being under cover, pick off those who are retreating. Neither musketry or cannon loaded with cartridge can do them much mischief, as they are scattered and concealed behind the heights and trees.

I made two retreats of this kind in the year 1745; one by the valley of Liebenthal, when marching to Staudenitz, and the other from Trautenau to Schatzlar. Notwithstanding every possible precaution, we lost sixty men killed and wounded in the first retreat, and more than two hundred in the second.

When we have to retreat through difficult ways, our marches should be very short, that we may be the more readily and perfectly on our guard. the longest march should not exceed two leagues, or one German mile, and as then we are not hurried, we are sometimes able to force the pandours, especially if they are imprudent enough to take shelter in a wood, which it is in our power to turn.

ARTICLE XVII.
Of the Method in which the Light Prussian Troops conduct
themselves when engaged with the Hussars and Pandours.
Our plan in forcing a post which is occupied by the enemy's light troops is, to attack it hastily, for as they disperse in their mode of fighting, they cannot stand against the attack of our regular troops, who are never to mince the matter with them.

We have only to detach a few troops to cover the flanks of the party which marches against them, and then attack them with spirit, to insure their running away.

Our dragoons and hussars attack them closely formed and sword in hand, and as this is a sort of rencontre which they cannot endure, it has always happened that we have beaten them, without paying any regard to the superiority of their numbers.

ARTICLE XVIII.
By what Movements on our Side the Enemy may also be obliged to move.
We are egregiously mistaking, if we suppose that the mere movement of an army will oblige the enemy also to put himself in motion. This is to be effected not simply by moving, but by the manner in which it is conducted. An intelligent enemy will not be induced to stir on account of any specious maneuvers which you may think proper to practice: settled positions must be taken up that will oblige him to reflect, and reduce him to the necessity of decamping.

For this reason we should be well informed of the nature of the country, the abilities of the general to whom we are opposed, the situation of his magazines, the towns that are most convenient to him, and those from which he draws his forage, and when these various circumstances are well combined together, the plan is to be formed and maturely digested.

That general who has the most fertile imagination, and attempts the most frequently to distress his enemy, will eventually rival his antagonist in glory.

He who at the opening of a campaign is the most alert in the assembling his troops, and marches forward to attack a town or occupy a post, will oblige his adversary to be regulated by his motions, and remain on the defensive.

You must always be possessed of very good reasons for wishing to oblige the enemy to move during a campaign: whether with a view of taking a town near where he is encamped, driving him to a barren country where he will hardly be able to exist, or with the hope of bringing on an engagement which will prove of material advantage. Induced by reasons of this nature, you set about arranging your plan, taking care that the marches which you are to make, and the camps which you are to occupy, do not lead you into greater inconveniencies than the enemy will suffer, by drawing you away from your depot, which may be in a place but badly fortified, and liable to be plundered by the light troops during your absence; by taking up a position where you may be cut off from all communications with your own country, or by occupying a situation which you will soon be obliged to abandon for want of subsistence.

After serious deliberation on these objects, and after having calculated the chances of enterprise on the part of the enemy, your plan is to be arranged, either for the purpose of encamping on one of his flanks, approaching the provinces whence he draws his subsistence, cutting him off from his capitol, threatening his depots, or in short, taking up any position by which you deprive him of his provisions.

To give an instance with which the greatest part of my officers are well acquainted-I had formed a plan by which I had reason to hope that I should oblige Prince Charles of Lorraine to abandon Konigingraetz and Pardubitz in the year 1745.

When we quitted the camp at Dubletz, we ought to have gone to the left, passed along by the country of Glatz, and marched near Hohenmauth. By this maneuver we should have forced the Austrians, whose magazines were at Teutschbrod, and whose provisions were, for the most part, drawn from Moravia, to have marched to Landscron, leaving to us Konigingraetz and Pardubitz. The Saxons, being cut off from their home, would have been obliged to quit the Austrians, in order to cover their own country.

What prevented my making this maneuver at that period was, that I should have profited nothing if I had gained Koenigingraetz, as I must have sent detachments to the support of the Prince of Anhalt, in case that the Saxons had returned home. Besides this circumstance, the magazines at Glatz were not equal to the subsistence of my army during the whole of the campaign.

The diversions that are made by detaching troops, will also sometimes oblige the enemy to decamp, for generally speaking, every kind of enterprise that comes on him unawares will have the effect of deranging him, and obliging him to quit his position.

Of such nature are the passing of mountains which the enemy deems impassible, and the crossing of rivers without his knowledge.

Sufficient information is to be gained on this head by reading the campaign of Prince Eugene in the year 1701. The confusion of the French army when it was surprised by Prince Charles of Lorraine; who had crossed the Rhine, is a matter sufficiently well understood.

I shall conclude by saying, that the execution of enterprises of this nature should always correspond with the design, and as long as the general's dispositions are wise and founded on solid principles, so long will he have it in his power to give the law to his enemy, and oblige him to keep on the defensive.

ARTICLE XIX.
Of the Crossing of Rivers.

As long as the enemy remains on the other side of a river which you wish to cross, all force is useless, and recourse must be made to stratagem. To be informed how we are to pass a large river, we have only to consult Caesar's passage of the Rhine, that of the Po by Prince Eugene, or of the Rhine by Prince Charles of Lorraine. These generals sent out detachments to impose upon the enemy, and conceal the spot where they intended to pass. They made every preparation for the building of bridges in places where they had no idea of employing them, whilst the main body of the army, by a night march, gained a considerable distance from the enemy, and had time to pass the river before the troop, who were to dispute their passage, could be put in order to prevent them.

We generally choose to cross rivers at those parts where there are some small islands, as they forward the business very materially. We wish also to meet on the other side with woods or other obstacles, that may prevent the enemy from attacking us before we have had time to get into proper order.

The most prudent measures and the most particular attention are required in enterprises of this nature. The boats or pontoons with every other article of necessary apparatus must be at the rendezvous by the appointed hour, and every boatman well instructed what generally attends expeditions by night. Everything being arranged, the troops are to pass over and establish themselves on the other side of the river.

Whenever rivers are to be crossed, care should be taken that the two heads of the bridge be entrenched, and well furnished with troops. The islands which are in the neighborhood should be fortified, in order to support the entrenchments, and prevent the enemy, during your operations, from seizing or destroying the bridges.

If the rivers be narrow, we choose our passage at those parts where they form angles, and where the bank, by being a little more elevated, commands that on the opposite side.

On this spot we place as many cannon, with a proportionate number of troops, as the ground will allow, under the protection of which the bridges are to be built; and as the ground grows narrower on account of the angle, we are to advance but very little, and insensibly gain ground as the troops pass.

If there be any fords, we slope the ground leading to them, to enable the cavalry to pass.

ARTICLE XX.
Of the Manner in which the Passage of Rivers is to be defended.
Nothing is more difficult, not to say impossible, than to defend the passage of a river, especially when the front of attack be of too great an extent. I would never undertake a commission of this kind, if the ground which I had to defend was more than eight German miles in front, and unless there were two or three redoubts established on the bank of the river within this distance; neither should any other part of the river be fordable.

But supposing the situation to be exactly as I have stated, time must always be required to make the necessary preparations against the enterprises of the enemy, the disposition of which should be nearly as follows:

All the boats and barks which can be found upon the river should be got together and conveyed to the two redoubts, that the enemy may not have it in his power to make use of them.

Both the banks of the river are to be reconnoitered, that you may discover and destroy those parts of them where it would be possible to pass.

The ground which might protect the passage of the enemy is to be particularly attended to, and your plans of attack must be regulated by the nature and situation of each part of it.

Roads sufficiently wide to admit of many columns are to be made along the whole front of the river which you are to defend, that you may march against the enemy free of every impediment.

These precautions being taken, the army is to be encamped in the center of the line of defense, that you may have but four miles to march to either extremity. Sixteen small detachments are then to be formed, and commanded by the most active, intelligent officers of dragoons and hussars; eight of which, under the orders of a general officer, are to have charge of the front of attack on the right, whilst the other eight, commanded in like manner, take care of the left.

These detachments will be designed to give information of the enemy's movements, and of the spot where it will be his intention to pass.

During the day, guards are to be posted to discover what is going forward, and by night patrols are to go out every quarter of an hour near to the river, and not retire till they have distinctly seen that the enemy has made a bridge, and that the head has passed.

The aforesaid generals and commanding officers of redoubts are to send their reports to the commander in chief four times a day.

Fresh horses should be stationed between them and the army, in order to hasten the arrival of their dispatches, and inform the general as immediately as possible when the enemy is about to pass. As it is the duty of the general to repair thither at a moment's warning, his baggage should be sent away beforehand, that he may be ready for every event.

The different dispositions for each part of the ground being already made, the generals are appointed by the commander in chief to those which regard the points of attack. No time is to be lost in marching, (the infantry taking the lead of the columns,) as you are to suppose that the enemy are entrenching themselves. When arrived, the attack is to be made instantly and with great spirit, as the only means of promising to yourself brilliant success.

The passages of small rivers are still more difficult to defend; their fords are to be rendered impassible, if possible, by throwing in of trees. But if the enemy's bank commands your's it is vain to attempt resistance.

ARTICLE XXI.
Of the Surprise of Towns.

A town must be badly guarded and weakly fortified that suffers a surprise; and if it's ditches be filled with water, the success of such enterprises must depend on a wintry season and hard frost.

Towns may be surprised by a whole army, as was the case at Prague in the year 1741, or the accident may happen from the garrison having been lulled into security by a long continued blockade, as was effected by Prince Leopold d'Anhalt at Glogau. Detachments also sometimes have the desired effect, as was attempted by Prince Eugene at Cremona, and as succeeded with the Austrians at Cosel.

The principal rule in making dispositions for surprise is, to be well informed of the nature of the fortifications and of the interiors of the place, so as to direct your attack to any particular spot.

The surprise of Glogau was a chef d'oeuvre, and is well worth the imitation of those who attempt such enterprises. There was nothing so extraordinary in the surprise of Prague, as it was impossible by such a variety of attacks must carry a place, where the garrison had so great an extent to defend. Cosel and Cremona were betrayed; the first by an officer who deserted and informed the Austrians that the excavation of the ditch was not quite completed, by which means they got over, and the place was carried.

If we wish to take small places, we batter some of the gates with mortars, whilst detachments are sent to the others to prevent the garrison from saving themselves.

If cannon are to be employed, they must be so placed that the artillerymen be not exposed to the fire of the musquetry; otherwise the guns will be in danger of being lost.

ARTICLE XXII.
Of Combats and Battles.

The Austrian camp is surrounded by such a number of light troops, as to render a surprise a work of very great difficulty.

If two armies keep near to each other, the business will very soon be decided, unless one of them occupies an inaccessible post that will secure it from surprises; a circumstance which seldom takes place between armies, though it be nothing uncommon between detachments.

To have it in our power to surprise an enemy in his camp, it is necessary that he relies entirely either on the superiority of his troops, the advantageous situation of his post, the reports of his emissaries, or lastly, on the vigilance of his light troops.

The nature of the country and the position of the enemy should be perfectly well understood prior to the formation of any plan.

The roads leading to camp must be well examined, and the general disposition of things formed from thence, being regulated in every point by the particular and exact knowledge of all attendant circumstances.

The most intelligent chasseurs, who are best acquainted with the roads, should be appointed to conduct the columns.

Be particularly careful to conceal your design, for secrecy is the soul of all enterprises.

The light troops should take the lead on the march, for which regulation various reasons may be assigned, though the real one be to prevent any scoundrel of a deserter from betraying you. They will also be of service by preventing the enemy's patrols from approaching too nearly and discovering your movements.

The generals who are under your orders must be well instructed of all events that may happen, and how to act when any accident occurs.

If the enemy's camp be situate in a plain, an advanced guard may be formed of dragoons, who, being joined by the hussars, will enter the enemy's camp on full speed, throw it into confusion, and cut down whatever comes in their way.

The whole army should support these dragoons, and the infantry being at the head of it, should be particularly employed in attacking the wings of the enemy's cavalry.

The advanced guard should begin the attack half an hour before day, but the army should not be more than eight hundred yards in it's rear.

During the march the most profound silence is to be observed, and the soldiers must be forbidden to smoke tobacco.

When the attack has commenced and the day appears, the infantry, formed into four or six columns, must march straight forward to the camp, in order to support it's advanced guard.

No firing is to be allowed before day-light, as it might prove the means of destroying our own people: but as soon as the day is broke, we should fire on all those places into which the advanced guard has not penetrated, especially on the wings of the cavalry, that we may oblige the troopers, who have not time to accoutre their horses, to abandon them and fly.

The enemy are to be followed even out of their camp, and the whole of the cavalry should be let loose after them to take advantage of their disorder and confusion.

If the enemy have abandoned their arms, a strong detachment must be left in charge of the camp, whilst the remainder of the army, instead of amusing themselves with plunder, pursue the enemy with all possible ardor; the more so, as a like opportunity of entirely routing them, may not soon present itself, and we may, by so doing, have the upper hand during the whole campaign, and be able to act just as we think proper.

Fortune intended to favor me with an opportunity of this kind before the battle of Mollwitz: we approached the army of the Marshal de Neuperg without being perceived, as they were cantoned in three villages; but at that time I wanted information how to profit by such circumstance.

My business then was, to have surrounded the village of Mollwitz by two columns, and to have attacked it. At the same moment I should have detached some dragoons to the other two villages where the Austrian cavalry lay, in order to throw them into confusion, whilst the infantry who followed them would have prevented the cavalry from mounting. By this method I am persuaded the whole army would have been destroyed.

I have already shewn the necessary cautions that respect our camp, and the manner in which it is to be protected: but if in spite of all our care, the enemy should approach the army, I would advise that the troops be formed in order of battle on the ground which is allotted to them, and that the cavalry remain firm on their posts, firing by platoons till daybreak. The generals are then to examine whether it be advisable to advance, if the cavalry has been victorious or suffered a repulse, and what farther methods are to be pursued.

On such occasions, each general should know how to act independently, without being obliged to wait for the instructions of the commander in chief.

For my own part, I am determined never to attack by night, on account of the confusion which darkness necessarily occasions, and because the major part of the soldiery require the eye of their officers, and the fear of punishments, to induce them to do their duty.

Charles XII. in the year 1715, attacked the Prince of Anhalt in the night, though he was but just disembarked on the island of Rugen. The King of Sweden had reason for so doing, as day-light would have discovered the weakness of his army. He came with four thousand men to attack five times the number, and of course was defeated.

It is an invariable axiom of war, to secure your flanks and rear, and endeavor to turn those of your enemy. This may be done in different ways, though they all depend on the same principle.

When you are obliged to attack an entrenched enemy, it should be done instantly, without allowing him time to finish his works. What would be of advantage to-day, may not be so to-morrow.

But before you set about making the attack, the enemy's position must be well reconnoitered with your own eyes, and your first dispositions of attack will convince you whether your scheme will be easily put into execution, or become a work of labor and difficulty.

The want of sufficient support is the chief reason that entrenchments are taken. The entrenchment of Turenne was carried, as was also that of . . . because there was sufficient ground to enable the Prince of Anhalt to turn it. That of Malplaquet was turned by the wood which was on the Marshal Villers' left. Had the allies been aware of this circumstance at the beginning of the battle, it would have saved their army fifteen thousand men.

If a fordable river support the entrenchment, it must be attacked on that side. The work at Stralsund, conducted by the Swedes, was carried because the attack was made on the sea-side, where it happened to be fordable.

If the enemy's entrenchments are of too great an extent, so that the troops are obliged to occupy more ground than they can well defend, we attack at several points, and provided we can keep our designs secret from the enemy, (which will prevent his meeting us with a sufficient force), we shall certainly get possession of the works.

Plate 6 (plate not reprinted in this volume) will explain the following dispositions of an attack on an entrenchment, where I shall form the line with thirty battalions, and strengthen the left wing by the river N. N. The attack on the left, where I wish to penetrate, shall be made by twelve battalions, and that on the right by eight. The troops destined for the attack are to be formed in a chequered way, with the allowance of proper intervals. The remainder of the infantry are to throw themselves into the third line, and behind them, at the distance of four hundred yards, the

cavalry should be posted. By this means my infantry will keep the enemy in check, and be ready to take advantage of any false movement which he may make.

Care must be taken that each of these attacks be followed closely by a number of pioneers with shovels, pick-axes, and fascines to fill up the ditch, and make a road for the cavalry, when the entrenchment shall have been forced.

The infantry who form the attack are not to fire till the work is carried, and they are drawn up in order of battle on the parapet.

The cavalry are to enter through the openings made by the pioneers, and attack the enemy as soon as they find themselves of sufficient force. If the cavalry be repulsed, they must rally under the cover of the infantry's fire until the whole army has got in, and the enemy are entirely routed.

I must here repeat, that I would never entrench my army unless I had a siege in contemplation; and I am not decided, whether it be not the best plan to go on before the army that comes to relieve a place.

But supposing for a moment, that we have an inclination to entrench ourselves; to execute such intention, the following method appears to me the most advantageous.

We contrive to have two or three large reserves, which are to be sent out during the attack to those points where the enemy is making his greatest efforts.

The parapet is to be lined by battalions, and a reserve placed behind them, to be at hand in case of necessity. The cavalry should be ranged in one line behind these reserves.

The entrenchments should be very well supported, and if it be joined by a river, the ditch should be carried some distance into it, to prevent it's being turned.

If it be strengthened by a wood, it should be closed at that end by a redoubt, and a large abbatis of trees should also be made in the wood.

Particular regard must be paid to the flanking of the redans.

The ditch should be very deep and wide, and the entrenchments must be improved every day, either by strengthening the parapet, placing palisades at the entrance of the barriers, digging of pits, or furnishing the whole of the camp with chevaux de frize.

The greatest advantage you have is, in the choice of your work, and in the observance of certain rules of fortification which will oblige the enemy to attack you on a small front, and that only in the principle points of your entrenchment.

Plate 7th (plate not reprinted in this volume) will give you a more exact idea of this business. The army, which is there placed at the head of the entrenchment. is thrown back on one side by the river, so that you present a projecting front to the enemy who comes to attack you. Your right is safe from attack by means of the batteries placed at the extremities of that wing, which would play upon the enemy's flank, whilst the centre redoubt would take him in the rear. The only point liable to attack therefore is the center redoubt, and even here he will be obliged to cut his way through the abbatis.

In your preparations for this attack it behooves you therefore to strengthen the fortifications of this redoubt, and as you have but one point which demands your particular attention, that one will consequently be more perfect and complete.

Plate 8th (plate not reprinted in this volume) exhibits entrenchments of a different kind, which are composed of projecting and receding redoubts, which cross each other, and are connected by entrenchments.

By this method of fortification, those that project from the point of attack, and as they are but few of them, much less time is required in completing them, than if the whole front was to be equally well fortified.

In these projecting redoubts, the fire of the musquetry must always cross each other, and for this reason they should never be more than six hundred yards apart.

Our infantry defend an entrenchment by the fire of entire battalions, and every soldier should be provided with one hundred rounds. This, however, is not to prevent the placing as many cannon as we can between the battalions and the projecting redoubts.

Whilst the enemy are at a distance, we fire shot, but when they approach within four hundred yards, we have recourse to cartridges.

If, notwithstanding the strength of your entrenchment, and the smartness of your fire, the enemy should make any impression, the reserve of infantry must march forward to repel him, and if they also be obliged to fall back, your last effort to put him to the route must depend upon your cavalry.

The principal reasons why entrenchments are carried are these, the want of attention to proper rules in their construction, or the troops being turned or panic struck: the superior freedom and boldness with which the attackers are able to conduct themselves, gives them this advantage.

Examples have already shewn, that when an entrenchment is forced, the whole army is discouraged and put to flight: I have a better opinion of my troops, and am persuaded that they would repel the enemy; but what end would this answer, if the entrenchments prevent their profiting by such advantages?

As there are so many inconveniencies attending entrenchments, it naturally follows that lines are still more useless. The fashion of our day is that which was practiced by Prince Louis de Baden, whose first lines were made on the side of Briel. The French also employed them after that in Flanders. I maintain that they are of no service whatever, since they compass more ground than the troops can possibly defend; they allow of a variety of attacks being made on them, and tempt the enemy to force a passage. On this account they do not cover the country, but, on the contrary, ensure the loss of reputation to the troops who have to defend them.

Although a Prussian army should be inferior to that which is opposed to them, they are not to despair of success, as the general's management will supply the want of numbers.

An army that is weak should always make choice of a difficult, mountainous country, where the ground narrows, so that the superior number of the enemy, not being able to pass their wings, becomes useless, and often an encumbrance to them.

It may here be added, that in a country which is close and hilly, the wings can better be supported than when we are on a plain. We should not have gained the battle of Sohr but for the advantage of the ground, for though the Austrian army doubled ours, they were not able to break through our wings, as the ground rendered both the armies nearly equal.

The choice of ground is my first object, and my second the disposition of the battle itself; it is here that my oblique order of battle may be employed to advantage, for you to refuse one wing to the enemy, whilst you strengthen that which ought to make the attack. By this means you turn all your force on that wing of the enemy which you wish to take in flank.

An army of ten thousand men, if it's flanks are turned, will very soon be defeated. Every thing is done by my right wing. A body of infantry will move by degrees into the wood, to attack the flanks of the enemy's cavalry, and protect the onset of our own: some regiments of hussars should be ordered to take the enemy in the rear whilst the army advances, and when their cavalry are routed, the infantry who are in the wood must take the enemy's infantry in flank, whilst the remainder are attacking them in front.

My left wing will not stir till the enemy's left wing is entirely defeated.

By this disposition you will gain the following advantages: 1st, that of making head with a small force against a much superior number; 2dly, of attacking the enemy at a point which will decide the business; 3dly, if your wing should chance to be beaten, as only a small part of your army has been engaged, three fourths of your troops, who are fresh, will be ready to support you in your retreat.

If you wish to attack an enemy that is advantageously posted, you must carefully examine both his strong and weak side before you make your dispositions for attack, and always choose that point where you expect to meet with the least resistance.

So many men are lost in the attacks on villages, that I have vowed never to undertake them, unless obliged by absolute necessity, for you run the hazard of losing the flower of your infantry.

It is said by some generals, that the most proper point of attack is the center of a post. Plate 10th (plate not reprinted in this volume) will represent the situation of such a post, where I suppose the enemy to have two large towns and two villages on it's wings. The wings must certainly be lost, when you have forced the center, and by similar attacks, the most complete victories may be obtained.

If must be added to the plan which I here lay down, that you must double your attack when you have once made an impression, in order to force the enemy to fall back both on his right and upon his left.

Nothing is so formidable in the attack of a post, as the discharge of cartridges from the batteries, which made a terrible havoc amongst the battalions. I witnessed the attacks on the batteries of Sohr and Kesseldorf, and shall here communicate the idea suggested by my reflections on that business, supposing that we wish to be possessed of a battery mounted with fifteen pieces of cannon, which it is not in our power to turn.

I have remarked, that the fire of cannon and of infantry who defend a battery render it inaccessible. We cannot make ourselves masters of the enemy's batteries but through their own fault: finding our infantry who attacked half destroyed and giving way, the infantry of the enemy quit their post to follow them, and being by this movement deprived of the use of their cannon, when they return to their batteries, our people enter with them and take possession.

The experience of those two battles gave me the idea, that in similar cases we should copy the example of our troops on this occasion, viz. to form the attack in two lines in a chequered way, and to be supported in the third line by some squadrons of dragoons.

The first line should be ordered to attack but faintly, and fall back through the intervals of the second, so that the enemy, deceived by this sham retreat, may abandon his post in order to pursue us.

This movement of theirs is to be our signal to advance and make a vigorous attack.

The disposition of this maneuver.

It is my principle, never to place my whole confidence in one post, unless it can be physically proved to be safe from any attack.

The great dependence of our troops is in attacking, and we should act very foolish part to give up this point without good reason.

But if it be necessary that posts should be occupied, we remember to get possession of the heights, and make our wings sufficiently strong.

I would burn every village which is at the head or on the wings of the army, if the wind did not drive the smoke into the camp.

If there were any strong stone houses in front, I would defend them by the infantry, in order to annoy the enemy during the action.

Great care should be taken, not to place troops on ground where they cannot act; it was this which made our position at Grotkau in the year 1741 worth nothing, for the center and left wing were posted behind impassible bogs. The only ground that would admit of being maneuvered on, was that which was occupied by a part of the right wing.

Villeroy was beaten at Ramillies for the very reason that I have just mentioned, as his right wing was rendered entirely useless, and the enemy crowded all it's force against the right wing of the French which could make no resistance.

I allow the Prussian troops to take possession of advantageous posts as well as other troops, and to make use of them in favor of any movement, or to take advantage of their artillery; but they must quit this post instantly to march against the enemy, who instead of being allowed to begin the attack, is attacked himself, and sees all his projects miscarry. Every movement which we make in presence of the enemy without his expecting it, will certainly produce a good effect.

We must rank battles of this kind amongst the best, always remembering to attack the weakest point.

On these occasions, I would not permit the infantry to fire, for it only retards their march, and the victory is not decided be the number of slain, but by the extent of territory which you have gained.

The most certain way of insuring victory is, to march briskly and in good order against the enemy, always endeavoring to gain ground. It is the custom to allow fifteen yards of interval between squadrons in a difficult, intersected country, but where the ground is good and even, they form in a line entire.

No greater interval is to be allowed between the infantry than is sufficient for the cannon. It is only in attacks of entrenchment, batteries, and villages, and in the formation of the rear guard in a retreat, that the cavalry and infantry are placed in a chequered way, in order to give an immediate support to the first line by making the second fall into it's intervals, so that the troops may retire without disorder, and be a mutual support to each other. This is a rule never to be neglected.

An opportunity offers itself here of giving you some principle rules on what you are to observe when you range the army in order of battle, whatever the ground may happen to be. The first is, to take up points of view for the wings; the right wing, for example, will align itself by the steeple N. N.

The general must be particularly careful that he does not suffer the troops to take up a wrong position.

It is not always necessary to defer the attack till the whole army can engage, as opportunity may present advantages which would be lost by a little delay.

A great part of the army, however, ought to be engaged, and the first line should be the chief object in the regulation of the order of battle. If all the regiments of that line are not present, they should be replaced by the same number of the second.

The wings should always be well supported, especially those which are expected to make the greatest exertions.

In an open country, the order of battle should be equally strong throughout, for as the enemy's movements are unconfined, he may have reserved a part of his army which he may make use of to cut you out a little employment.

In case that one of the two wings should not be properly supported, the general who commands the second line should send some dragoons thither, (without waiting for an order on the occasion) to extend the first line, and the hussars taken from the third line should replace the dragoons.

The reason for so doing, is, that if the enemy make a movement to take the cavalry of the first line in flank, your dragoons and hussars may be able in turn to repay the compliment.

You will see that I place three battalions in the interval between the two lines of the left wing, the better to support it: for supposing your cavalry to be beaten, these battalions will always prevent the enemy from falling foul on the infantry, an instance of which we witnessed at Mollwitz.

The general commanding the second line must preserve a distance of three hundred paces from the first, and if he perceive any intervals in the first line, he is to fill them up with battalions from the second.

In a plain, a reserve of cavalry should always be placed in the rear of the center of the battalions, and be commanded by an officer of address, as he is to act from himself, either in support of a wing that he sees hardly pressed, or by flanking the enemy who are in pursuit of the wing that is thrown into disorder, that the cavalry may in the mean time have an opportunity of rallying.

The affair should be begun by the cavalry on full gallop, and the infantry also should march on briskly towards the enemy. Commanding officers are to take care that their troops penetrate and entirely break through the enemy, and that they make no use of their fire arms till their backs are turned.

If the soldiers fire without the word of command, they are to be ordered to shoulder arms, and proceed without any halting.

When the enemy begins to give way, we fire, by battalions, and a battle conducted in this manner will very soon be decided.

A new order of battle which differs from the others in having bodies of infantry placed at the extremities of the wings of the cavalry. The battalions are intended to support the cavalry, by

playing with their own cannon and those belonging to the wings of the cavalry, on the enemy's cavalry, at the beginning of the affair, that our own may have a better game to play during the attack. Another reason is, that supposing your wings to be beaten, the enemy dare not pursue, for fear of being between two fires.

When your cavalry, to all appearance, has been victorious, this infantry is to approach that of the enemy, and the battalions which are in the intervals must make a quarter-wheel and place themselves on your wings, to take the enemy's infantry in flank and rear, and enable you to make a handsome business of it.

The conquering wing of your cavalry must not allow the enemy's cavalry to rally, but pursue them in good order, and endeavor to cut them off from the infantry. When the confusion becomes general, the commanding officer should detach the hussars after them, who are to be supported by the cavalry. At the same time some dragoons should be sent to the roads which the infantry have taken, in order to pick them up, and by cutting off their retreat, make a great number of them prisoners.

There is another difference in this order of battle, which is , that the squadrons of dragoons are mixed with the infantry of the second line: this is done, because I have remarked in all the affairs which we have had with the Austrians, that after the fire of their musquetry has continued for about a quarter of an hour, they get together round their colors; at Hohen Friedburg our cavalry charged many of these round-about parties, and made a great number of them prisoners. the dragoons, being near at hand, are to be let loose instantly, and they never fail to give a very good account of them.

It will be said, that I never employ my small arms, but that it is my wish in all these dispositions to make use of may artillery only: to this I answer, that one of the two accidents which I suppose will unavoidably happen, either that my infantry fire in spite of my orders to the contrary, or that they obey my commands, and the enemy begins to give way. In either case, as soon as you perceive any confusion amongst their troops, you are to detach the cavalry after them, and when they find themselves attacked in flank on one side, charged in front, and their second line of cavalry cut off by the rear, the greatest part of them will be sure to fall into your hands.

It then cannot be called a battle, but an entire destruction of your enemies, especially if there be no defile in the neighborhood to protect their flight.

I shall close this article with a single reflection, viz. if you march to battle in column, whether by the right or by the left, the battalions or divisions must follow each other closely, that when you begin to deploy, you may have it in your power readily to engage. But if you march in front, the distances of the battalions must be well attended to, that they be not too close or too far from each other.

I make a distinction between the heavy cannon and the field pieces attached to the battalions, as the former should be planted on the heights, and the latter fifty paces in front of the battalions. Both the one and the other should be well pointed and well fired.

When we are within five hundred yards of the enemy, the field pieces should be drawn by men, that they may fire without intermission as we advance.

If the enemy begin to fly, the heavy cannon are to move forward and fire a few rounds, by way of wishing them a good journey.

Six gunners and three regimental carpenters should be attached to every piece in the first line.

I had omitted saying, that at the distance of three hundred and fifty yards, the cannon should begin to fire cartridges.

But to what end serves the art of conquest, if we are ignorant how to profit by our advantage? To shed the blood of soldiers when there is no occasion for it, is to lead them inhumanly to the slaughter; and not to pursue the enemy on certain occasions, to increase their fear and the number of our prisoners, is leaving an affair to future chance which might be determined at the present moment. Nevertheless, you may sometimes be prevented from pursuing your conquest by a want of provisions, or the troops being too much fatigued.

It is always the fault of the general in chief if an army want provisions. When he gives battle, he has a design in so doing: and if he has a design, it is his duty to be provided with every thing necessary for the execution of it, and of course he ought to be supplied with bread or biscuit for eight or ten days.

With respect to fatigues, if they had not been too excessive, they must not be regarded, as on extraordinary occasions extraordinary feats should be performed.

When victory is perfectly decided, I would recommend a detachment to be made of those regiments who have been the greatest sufferers, to take care of the wounded, and convey them to the hospitals, which ought to be already established. Though our own wounded are to be the first objects of our attention, we are not to forget our duty to the enemy.

In the mean time the army is to pursue the enemy to the nearest defile, which in the first transport of their alarm they will not tarry to keep possession of, if you take care not to allow them sufficient time to recover their wind.

When you have attended to all these circumstances, the camp is to be marked out, paying strict regard to the established rules, and not allowing yourself to be lulled with too great an idea of security.

If the victory have been complete, we may send out detachments either to cut off the enemy's retreat, seize his magazines, or lay siege to three or four towns at the same time.

On this article, general rules only can be given, as a great deal must depend on fortuitous circumstances. You are never to imagine that every thing is done as long as any thing remains undone; nor are you to suppose but that a cunning enemy, though he may have been beaten, will keep a sharp look-out to take advantage of your negligence or errors.

I pray to heaven, that the Prussians never may be beaten, and dare affirm that such an accident never will happen if they are well led on and well disciplined.

But should they meet with a disaster of such a nature, the following rules are to be observed in order to recover the misfortune. When you see that the battle is inevitably lost, and that it is not in your power to oppose the enemy's movements, or even resist them much longer, you are to send the second line of infantry to any defile that may be near, and place them in it agreeably to the disposition which I have given under the article of retreats, sending thither at the same time as many cannon as you can spare.

If there be no defile in the neighborhood, the first line must retire through the interval of the second, and place itself in order of battle three hundred yards behind them.

All the remains of your cavalry must be got together, and if you choose it, they may be formed into a square to protect your retreat.

History furnishes us with accounts of two remarkable squares: one that was formed by General Schullembourg after the battle of Frauenstadt, by means of which he retired across the Oder without being forced by Charles XII.; the other by the Prince of Anhalt when General Stirum lost the first battle of Hochstaedt. This Prince traversed a plain of two leagues, and the French cavalry did not dare to molest him.

I shall conclude with saying, that though we are defeated, there is no occasion for running away forty leagues, but that we are to halt at the first advantageous post, and put a bold face upon the business, in order to collect the scattered army, and encourage those who are dispirited.

ARTICLE XXIII.
Of the Reasons which should induce us to give Battle, and in what Manner it is to be conducted. Battles determine the fate of nations. It is necessary that actions should be decisive, either to free ourselves from the inconveniencies of a state of warfare, to place our enemy in that unpleasant situation, or to settle a quarrel which otherwise perhaps would never be finished. A man that is wise will make no sort of movement without good reason; and a general of an army should never be engaged without some design of consequence. If he be forced into an engagement by his adversary, his former errors must have reduced him to that situation, and given his enemy the power of dictating the law to him.

On the present occasion it will be seen, that I am not writing my own panegyric: for out of five battles which my troops have given to the enemy, three of them only were premeditated, and I was forced by the enemy into the other two. At the affair of Mollwitz the Austrians had posted themselves between my army and Wohlau, where I kept my provisions and artillery. At that of the Sohr, the enemy had cut me off from the road to Trautenau, so that I was obliged to fight, or run the risk of losing my whole army. But how great is the difference between forced and premeditated battles! How brilliant was our success at Hohen-Friedberg, at Kesseldorf, and also at Czaslau, which last engagement was the means of procuring us peace!

Though I am here laying down rules for battles, I do not pretend to deny that I have often erred through inadvertence; my officers, however, are expected to profit by my mistakes, and they may be assured, that I shall apply myself with all diligence to correct them.

It sometimes happens that both the armies wish to engage, and then the business is very soon settled.

Those battles are the best into which we force the enemy, for it is an established maxim, to oblige him to do that for which he has no sort of inclination, and as your interest and his are so diametrically opposite, it cannot be supposed that you are both wishing for the same event.

Many are the reasons that may induce us to give battle, such as, a desire to oblige the enemy to raise the siege of any place that may prove of convenience to yourself, to drive him out of a province which he possess, penetrate his country, enable yourself to lay a siege, correct him for his stubbornness if he refuse to make peace, or make him suffer for some error that he has committed.

You will also oblige the enemy to come to action when, by a forced march, you fall upon his rear and cut off his communications, or by threatening a town which it is his interest to preserve.

But in this sort of maneuver great care is to be taken that you do not get into the same embarrassed situation, or take up a position which enables the enemy to cut you off from your magazines.

The affairs which are undertaken against rear guards are attended with the least danger.

If you entertain a design of this nature, you are to encamp near the enemy, and when he wishes to retire and pass the defiles in your presence, make an attack upon his rear. Much advantage is often gained by engagements of this kind.

It is also a custom to tease and tire the enemy, in order to prevent different bodies from forming a junction. The object in view sufficiently warrants such attempt, but a skilful enemy will have the address to get out of your way by a forced march, or escape the accident by taking up an advantageous position.

Sometimes when you have no inclination to fight, we are induced to it by the misconduct of the enemy, who should always be punished for his faults, if we can profit by so doing.

It must be urged, in addition to all these maxims, that our wars should ever be of short duration, and conducted with spirit, for it must always be against our interest to be engaged in a tedious affair. A long war must tend insensibly to relax our admirable discipline, depopulate our country, and exhaust it's resources.

For this reason, generals commanding Prussian armies should endeavor, notwithstanding their success, to terminate every business prudently and quickly. They must not argue, as the Marshal de Luxembourg did in the Flanders wars, who when he was told by his son, "Father, it appears to me, that we could still take another town," replied, "Hold your tongue, you little fool! Would you have us go home to plant cabbages?" In a word, on the subject of battles, we ought to be guided by the maxim of Sannerib of the Hebrews, "that it is better one man perish than a whole people."

With regard to punishing an enemy for his fault, we should consult the relation of the battle of Senef, where the Prince of Conde brought on an affair of the rear guard against the Prince of Orange or the Prince of Waldeck, who had neglected to occupy the head of a defile, in order to facilitate his retreat.

The accounts of the battle of . . . ., gained by the Marshal de Luxembourg, and that of Raucoux, will also furnish you with other examples.

ARTICLE XXIV.
Of the Hazards and unforeseen Accidents which happen in War.

This article would be of a melancholy length, if it was my intention to treat of all the accidents which might happen to a general in war. I shall cut the matter short by saying, that it is necessary a man should have both address and good fortune.

Generals are much more to be pitied than is generally imagined. All the world condemns them unheard. They are exposed in the gazette to the judgment of the meanest plebeian, whilst amongst many thousand readers there is not one perhaps who knows how to conduct the smallest detachment.

I shall not pretend to excuse those generals who have been in fault; I shall even give up my own campaign of 1744, but I must add, that though I have many times erred, I have made some good expeditions; for example, the siege of Prague, the defense and the retreat of Koelin, and again the retreat in Silesia. I shall not enter farther into these actions, but must observe, that there are accidents which neither the most mature reflection or keenest human foresight can possibly prevent.

As I write at present solely for my own generals, I shall not quote other examples than what have occurred to myself. When we were at Reichenbach, I intended to have reached the river Neiss by a forced march, and to have posted myself between the town of that name and the army of General de Neuperg, in order to cut off his communication. All the necessary dispositions were arranged for such operation, but a heavy fall of rain came on which made the roads so very bad, that our advanced guard with the pontoons were unable to proceed. During the march of the army also so thick a fog arose, that the troops who were posted as guards in the villages wandered about without being able to join their respective regiments. In short, every thing turned out so ill, that instead of arriving at four o'clock A.M. as I had intended, we did not get there till midnight. The advantages to be derived from a forced march, were then out of the question, the enemy had the start of us, and defeated our project.

If, during your operations, disease should break out amongst your troops, you will be obliged to act on the defensive, which was the case with us in Bohemia in the year 1741, on account of the badness of the provisions with which the troops were furnished.

At the battle of Hohen-Friedberg, I ordered one of my aids du camp (flugel-adjutants) to go to Margrave Charles, and tell him to place himself, as eldest general, at the head of my second line, because General Kalckstein had been detached to the command of the right wing against the Saxons: this aid du camp mistook the business entirely, and ordered the margrave to form the first line into the second. By great good fortune I discovered the mistake, and had time to remedy it.

Hence we see the necessity of being always on our guard, and of bearing in mind, that a commission badly executed may disconcert all our intentions.

If a general fall sick, or be killed, at the head of a detachment of any importance, many of your measures must consequently suffer a very material derangement. To act offensively, requires generals of sound understanding and genuine valor, the number of which is but very small: I have at the most but three or four such in my whole army.

If, in spite of every precaution, the enemy should succeed in depriving you of some convoy, your plans will again be disconcerted, and your project either suspended or entirely overset.

Should circumstances oblige the army to fall back, the troops will be very much discouraged.

I have never been so unhappy as to experience a situation of this sort with my whole army, but I remarked at the battle of Mollwitz, that it required a length of time to reanimate troops who had been disheartened. At that time my cavalry was so weakened, that they looked on themselves as merely led to the slaughter, which induced me to send out small detachments to give them spirits, and bring them forward to action. It is only since the battle of Hohen-Friedberg, that my cavalry are become what they ever ought to be, and what they are at present.

If the enemy should discover a spy of any consequence in their camp, the compass is lost which was to have directed you, and you are unable to learn any thing of the enemy's movements but from your own eyes.

The negligence of officers who are detached to reconnoiter may render your situation very distressed and embarrassing. It was in this way that Marshal de Neuperg was surprised; the hussar officer who was sent forward on the look-out, had neglected his duty, and we were close upon him before he had the least suspicion of it. It was also owing to the carelessness of an officer of the regiment of Ziethen in making his patrol by night, that the enemy built his bridges at Selmitz, and surprised the baggage.

Hence will appear the truth of my assertion that the safety of a whole army should never be entrusted to the vigilance of an individual officer. No one man or subaltern officer should be charged with a commission of such material consequence. Treasure up, therefore, carefully in your mind what I have said on this subject under the article, "Of the Defense of Rivers."

Too much confidence must not be reposed in patrols and reconnoitering parties, but in measures of more surety and solidity.

The greatest possible misfortune that can attend an army is treason. Prince Eugene was betrayed in the year 1733 by General St. . . . who had been corrupted by the French. I lost Cosel through the treachery of an officer of the garrison who deserted and conducted the enemy thither. Hence we are taught, that even in the height of our prosperity, it is not safe to trust to good fortune, or wise to be too much elevated with success; we should rather recollect, that the slender portion of genius and foresight which we may possess is at best but a game of hazard and unforeseen accidents, by which it pleases, I know not what destiny, to humble the pride of presumptuous man.

ARTICLE XXV.
If it be absolutely necessary that the General of an Army should hold a Council of War.
It was a saying of Prince Eugene, "that if a general did not wish to fight, he had nothing more to do than hold a council of war;" and his assertion is proved, by the general voice of councils of war being against engaging. Secrecy, so necessary in war, can here be no longer observed.

A general, to whom his sovereign has entrusted his troops, should act for himself, and the confidence placed in him by his king is a sufficient warrant for such conduct.

Nevertheless, I am persuaded that a general ought not to be inattentive to the advice of even a subaltern officer, as it is the duty of a good citizen to forget himself when the welfare of his country is at stake, and not regard who furnishes the advice that may be productive of happy, wished-for consequences.

ARTICLE XXVI.
Of the Maneuvers of an Army.
It will be seen by the maxims which I have laid down in this work, on what the theory turns of those evolutions which I have introduced amongst my troops. The object of these maneuvers is to gain time on every occasion, and decide an affair more quickly than has heretofore been the custom; and, in short, to overset the enemy by the furious shocks of our cavalry. By means of this impetuosity, the coward is hurried away, and obliged to do his duty as well as the bravest; no single trooper can be useless. The whole depends on the spirit of the attack.

I therefore flatter myself that every general, convinced of the necessity and advantage of discipline, will do every thing in his power to preserve and improve it, both in time of war and of peace.

The enthusiastic speech made by Vegece respecting the Romans, will never leave my memory: "And at length," says he, "the Roman discipline triumphed over the hordes of Germans,

the force of the Gauls, the German cunning, the barbarian swarm, and subdued the whole universe." So much does the prosperity of a state depend on the discipline of it's army.

ARTICLE XXVII.
Of Winter Quarters.
When a campaign is ended, we think of winter quarters, which must be arranged according to the circumstances in which we find ourselves.

The first thing to be done is, the forming the chain of troops who are to cover these quarters, which may be effected in three different ways, either behind a river, taking advantage of posts that are defended by mountains, or under the protection of some fortified towns.

In the year 1741-2, my troops who wintered in Bohemia, took up their position behind the Elbe. The chain which covered them began at Brandeis, and extending along by Nienbourg, Koelin, Pojebrod, and Pardubitz, ended at Konigingraetz.

I must add here, that rivers must not be too much confided in, as when frozen they can be crossed at any point. Care should be taken to post hussars in every part of the chain to watch the enemy's movements, for which purpose, they should patrol frequently in front to observe if all be quiet, or if the enemy be assembling troops.

Besides the chain of infantry, there should be placed also brigades of cavalry and infantry here and there, to be in readiness to lend assistance wherever it might be wanted.

In the winter of 1744-5, the chain of quarters was formed the whole length of those mountains which separate Silesia from Bohemia, and we guarded very particularly the frontiers of our quarters, that we might remain in quiet.

Lieutenant-General de Trusches had to take charge of the front of Lusatia as far as the country of Glatz, the town of Sagan, and the posts from Schmiedberg to Friedland, which last place was fortified by redoubts. There were also some other small entrenched posts on the roads of Schatzlar, Liebau, and Silberberg. The general had likewise contrived a reserve to support that post which might be first insulted by the enemy. All these detachments were covered by abbatis made in the woods, and all the roads leading into Bohemia were rendered impassible. Every post was also supplied with hussars, for the purpose of reconnoitering.

General Lehwald covered the country of Glatz with a detachment of the same nature, and with the same prudent cautions. These two generals lent each other assistance in such a way, that if the Austrians had marched against General Trusches, General Lehwald would have entered Bohemia to take the enemy in the rear, and Trusches would have returned the favor had Lehwald been attacked.

The towns of Tropau and Jagerndorf were our biggest points in Upper Silesia, and the communication was by way of Zeigenhals and Patchskau to Glatz, and by Neustadt to Neiss.

It must be observed here, that we are not to trust too much to the security of mountains, but remember the proverb, "that wherever a goat can pass a soldier can."

With regard to the chains of quarters that are supported by fortresses, I refer you to the winter quarters of Marshal Saxe. They are the best, but it is not in our power to choose, as the chain must be made according to the nature of the ground which we occupy.

I shall lay it down here as a maxim, that we are never to fancy ourselves perfectly secure from the enemy's annoyance in any one town or post, but that our attention must be constantly alive to the keeping of winter quarters quiet.

Another maxim to be observed in winter quarters is, to distribute the regiments by brigades, that they may be always under the eyes of the generals.

Our service also requires, that the generals should, if possible be with their own regiments: but there may be exceptions to this rule, of which the general commanding the army will be the best judge.

Here follow the rules that are to be observed respecting the maintenance of troops in winter quarters.

If circumstances absolutely require that we take up winter quarters in our own country, the captains and subaltern officers are to receive a gratuity proportionate to the common allowance which they receive in winter quarters. This is to be furnished with his bread and meat at free cost.

But if the winter quarters are in an enemy's country, the general in chief of the troops shall receive 15,000 florins, the generals of the cavalry and infantry 10,000 each, lieutenant-generals 7000, major-generals (camp marshals) 5000, captains of cavalry 2000, of infantry 1800, and the subaltern officers 1000 ducats or from 4 to 500 florins. The country is to supply the soldier with bread, flesh, and beer gratis, but he is to have no money, as that only tends to favor desertion.

The general in chief is to take care that this business be properly arranged, and that no pillaging be allowed, but he is not to be too strict with an officer who has it in his power to make any trifling, fair advantage.

If the army be quartered in an enemy's country, it is the duty of the general commanding to see that the necessary number of recruits be furnished: (such distribution should obtain in the circles, that three regiments, for example, should be assigned to one, and four to the other.) Each circle should also be subdivided into regiments, as is done in the enrolling cantonments.

If the recruits are furnished voluntarily by the states of the country, so much the better; if not, compulsive methods must be used. They ought to arrive very early, that the officer may have time to drill them and make them fit for duty the following spring. This, however, is not to prevent the captain from sending out recruiting parties.

As the general in chief ought to interest himself in the whole of this economy, he should be particularly careful that the artillery horses and the provisions, which are a tribute of the country, are furnished in kind or in hard cash.

All the baggage wagons, and in short, the whole apparatus of an army, is also to be repaired at the enemy's cost.

Minute attention must be paid by the general that the cavalry officers repair their saddles, bridles, stirrups, and boots, and that the officers of infantry provide their men with shoes, stockings, shirts, and gaiters for the ensuing campaign. The soldier's blankets and tent should also be repaired, the cavalry swords filed, and the arms of the infantry put in good condition. The artillery, likewise, must prepare the necessary quantity of cartridges for the infantry.

It still remains to be seen by the general, that the troops which form the chain are well provided with powder and ball, and in short, that nothing be wanting in the whole army.

If time allows, the general would do well to visit some of his quarters, to examine into the state of the troops, and satisfy himself that the officers attend to the exercising of their men, as well as to every other part of their duty; for it is necessary that the old soldiers should be employed in this way as well as the recruits, in order to keep them in practice.

At the beginning of a campaign, we change the cantoning quarters, and distribute them according to the order of battle, viz. the cavalry on the wings, and the infantry in the center. These cantonments generally extend nine or ten leagues (from four to five miles) in front, to four (two) in depth, and when the time of encamping draws near, they are to be contracted a little.

I find it very convenient in cantonments to distribute the troops under the orders of the six eldest generals: one , for example, shall command all the cavalry of the right wing, and another that of the left, in the first line, whilst two others shall command that of the second. In this method, all orders will more quickly be executed, and the troops be more easily formed into columns to go to camp.

On the subject of winter quarters, I must again advise you to be very careful of not going into them before you are well convinced that the enemy's army is entirely separated. Keep always in your recollection the misfortune which befell the Elector Frederick William, when he was surprised by the Marshal de Turenne in his quarters at Alsace.

ARTICLE XXVIII.
Of Winter Campaigns in particular.
Winter campaigns ruin the troops, both on account of the diseases which they occasion, and by obliging them to be constantly in motion, which prevents their being well clothed or recruited. The same inconvenience attends the carriage of ammunition and provisions. It is certain, that the best army in the world cannot long support campaigns of this kind, for which reason they ought ever to be avoided, as being, of all expeditions, the most to be condemned. Accidents, however, may occur, which will oblige a general to undertake them.

I believe that I have made more winter campaigns than any general of this age, and that I shall do right to explain the motives which induced me to such undertakings.

At the death of the Emperor Charles VI. in the year 1740, there were but two Austrian regiments in all Silesia. Having determined to make good the claims of my house on that duchy, I was obliged to make war in winter, that I might profit by every favorable circumstance, and carry the theatre of war to the Neiss.

If I had delayed my project till the spring, the war would have been established between Crossen and Glogau, and it would have required three or four hard campaigns to effect that which we accomplished by one simple march. This reason appeared to me sufficiently cogent.

If I did not succeed in the winter campaign which I made in the year 1742 to relieve the country from the Elector of Bavaria, it was because the French behaved like fools, and the Saxons like traitors.

My third winter campaign in the year 1741-2 was forced upon me, as I was obliged to drive the Austrians from Silesia, which they had invaded.

From the beginning of the winter 1745-6, the Austrians and Saxons wished to introduce themselves into my hereditary dominions, that they might put every thing to fire and sword. I acted according to my usual principle, and got the start of them by making war in the middle of winter in the very heart of their own country.

Should similar circumstances occur, I should not hesitate to pursue the same plan, and shall applaud the conduct of my generals who shall follow my example. But I must ever blame those who, without the concurrence of such reasons, shall undertake a war at that season of the year.

In regard to the detail of winter campaign, the troops are always to be as close to each other as possible in their cantonments, and two or three regiments of cavalry, mixed with infantry, should be lodged in one village, if it be large enough to hold them. Sometimes all the infantry are quartered in one town, as the Prince of Anhalt did at Torgau, Eilenbourg, Meissen, and two or three other small towns (whose names I forget) in Saxony, after which he encamped himself.

When we come near the enemy, a rendezvous is to be appointed to the troops, who are to continue marching as before in several columns; and when about to make any decisive movement, such as, storming the enemy's quarters, or marching against him to engage, we arrange ourselves in order of battle, remaining under the canopy of heaven, each company kindling a large fire, by which to pass away the night. But as such fatigues are too distressing to be long endured, all possible dispatch should be employed in enterprises of this nature. We must not stand contemplating our danger or hesitating about it, but form our resolution with spirit and execute it with firmness.

Be careful of undertaking a winter campaign in a country which is crowded with fortified places, for the season will prevent your setting down seriously before a place which you cannot carry by surprise. We may be assured beforehand that such project will miscarry, as it is morally impossible it should be otherwise.

If it be left to our choice, the troops should have as much rest during the winter as possible, and the time should be employed to the best advantage in recovering the army, that at the opening of the campaign they may get the start of their adversaries.

These are nearly the principal rules of the grand maneuvers of war, the particulars of which have been explained as much as was in my power. I have taken particular care that what I have said should be clear and intelligible, but if any parts should, in your idea, still remain obscure, I shall be favored by your communicating them, that I may either explain myself more fully, or subscribe to your opinion, if it prove better than mine own.

The small experience of war which has fallen to my share, convinces me, that it is an art never to be exhausted, but that something new will ever reward his labor who studies it with serious application.

I shall not think my moments misemployed, if what I have said should stimulate my officers to the study of that science, which will afford them the most certain opportunity of acquiring glory, rescuing their names from the rust of oblivion, and securing by their brilliant actions a glorious and immortal fame.

End

Excerpts from "The Fifteen Decisive Battles of The World: From Marathon to Waterloo" by Sir Edward Creasy, M.A.

1851

PREFACE

It is an honorable characteristic of the Spirit of this Age, that projects of violence and warfare are regarded among civilized states with gradually increasing aversion. The Universal Peace Society certainly does not, and probably never will, enroll the majority of statesmen among its members. But even those who look upon the Appeal of Battle as occasionally unavoidable in international controversies, concur in thinking it a deplorable necessity, only to be resorted to when all peaceful modes of arrangement have been vainly tried; and when the law of self-defense justifies a State, like an individual, in using force to protect itself from imminent and serious injury. For a writer, therefore, of the present day to choose battles for his favorite topic, merely because they were battles, merely because so many myriads of troops were arrayed in them, and so many hundreds or thousands of human beings stabbed, hewed, or shot each other to death during them, would argue strange weakness or depravity of mind. Yet it cannot be denied that a fearful and wonderful interest is attached to these scenes of carnage. There is undeniable greatness in the disciplined courage, and in the love of honor, which make the combatants confront agony and destruction. And the powers of the human intellect are rarely more strongly displayed than they are in the Commander, who regulates, arrays, and wields at his will these masses of armed disputants; who, cool yet daring, in the midst of peril reflects on all, and provides for all, ever ready with fresh resources and designs, as the vicissitudes of the storm of slaughter require. But these qualities, however high they may appear, are to be found in the basest as well as in the noblest of mankind. Catiline was as brave a soldier as Leonidas, and a much better officer. Alva surpassed the Prince of Orange in the field; and Suwarrow was the military superior of Kosciusko. To adopt the emphatic words of Byron:
"'Tis the Cause makes all, Degrades or hallows courage in its fall."

There are some battles, also, which claim our attention, independently of the moral worth of the combatants, on account of their enduring importance, and by reason of the practical influence on our own social and political condition, which we can trace up to the results of those engagements. They have for us an abiding and actual interest, both while we investigate the chain of causes and effects, by which they have helped to make us what we are; and also while we speculate on what we probably should have been, if any one of those battles had come to a different termination. Hallam has admirably expressed this in his remarks on the victory gained by Charles Martel, between Tours and Poitiers, over the invading Saracens.

He says of it, that "it may justly be reckoned among those few battles of which a contrary event would have essentially varied the drama of the world in all its subsequent scenes: with Marathon, Arbela, the Metaurus, Chalons, and Leipsic." It was the perusal of this note of Hallam's that first led me to the consideration of my present subject. I certainly differ from that great historian as to the comparative importance of some of the battles which he thus enumerates, and also of some which he omits. It is probable, indeed, that no two historical inquirers would entirely agree in their lists of the Decisive Battles of the World. Different minds will naturally vary in the impressions which particular events make on them; and in the degree of interest with which they watch the career, and reflect on the importance, of different historical personages. But our concurrence in our catalogues is of little moment, provided we learn to look on these great historical events in the spirit which Hallam's observations indicate. Those remarks should teach us to watch how the interests of many states are often involved in the collisions between a few; and how the effect of those collisions is not limited to a single age, but may give an impulse which will sway the fortunes of successive generations of mankind. Most valuable also is the mental

483

discipline which is thus acquired, and by which we are trained not only to observe what has been, and what is, but also to ponder on what might have been. [See Bolingbroke, On the Study and Use of History, vol. ii. p. 497 of his collected works.]

We thus learn not to judge of the wisdom of measures too exclusively by the results. We learn to apply the juster standard of seeing what the circumstances and the probabilities were that surrounded a statesman or a general at the time when he decided on his plan: we value him not by his fortune, but by his PROAIRESIZ, to adopt the expressive Greek word, for which our language gives no equivalent.

The reasons why each of the following Fifteen Battles has been selected will, I trust, appear when it is described. But it may be well to premise a few remarks on the negative tests which have led me to reject others, which at first sight may appear equal in magnitude and importance to the chosen Fifteen.

I need hardly remark that it is not the number of killed and wounded in a battle that determines its general historical importance. It is not because only a few hundreds fell in the battle by which Joan of Arc captured the Tourelles and raised the siege of Orleans, that the effect of that crisis is to be judged: nor would a full belief in the largest number which Eastern historians state to have been slaughtered in any of the numerous conflicts between Asiatic rulers, make me regard the engagement in which they fell as one of paramount importance to mankind. But, besides battles of this kind, there are many of great consequence, and attended with circumstances which powerfully excite our feelings, and rivet our attention, and yet which appear to me of mere secondary rank, inasmuch as either their effects were limited in area, or they themselves merely confirmed some great tendency or bias which an earlier battle had originated. For example, the encounters between the Greeks and Persians, which followed Marathon, seem to me not to have been phenomena of primary impulse. Greek superiority had been already asserted, Asiatic ambition had already been checked, before Salamis and Platea confirmed the superiority of

European free states over Oriental despotism. So, Aegos-Potamos, which finally crushed the maritime power of Athens, seems to me inferior in interest to the defeat before Syracuse, where Athens received her first fatal check, and after which she only struggled to retard her downfall. I think similarly of Zama with respect to Carthage, as compared with the Metaurus: and, on the same principle, the subsequent great battles of the Revolutionary war appear to me inferior in their importance to Valmy, which first determined the military character and career of the French Revolution.

I am aware that a little activity of imagination, and a slight exercise of metaphysical ingenuity, may amuse us, by showing how the chain of circumstances is so linked together, that the smallest skirmish, or the slightest occurrence of any kind, that ever occurred, may be said to have been essential, in its actual termination, to the whole order of subsequent events. But when I speak of Causes and Effects, I speak of the obvious and important agency of one fact upon another, and not of remote and fancifully infinitesimal influences. I am aware that, on the other hand, the reproach of Fatalism is justly incurred by those, who, like the writers of a certain school in a neighboring country, recognize in history nothing more than a series of necessary phenomena, which follow inevitably one upon the other. But when, in this work, I speak of probabilities, I speak of human probabilities only. When I speak of Cause and Effect, I speak of those general laws only, by which we perceive the sequence of human affairs to be usually regulated; and in which we recognize emphatically the wisdom and power of the Supreme Lawgiver, the design of The Designer.

MITRE COURT CHAMBERS, TEMPLE, June 26, 1851.

CHAPTER I.
THE BATTLE OF MARATHON.

"Quibus actus uterque Europae atque Asiae fatis concurrerit orbis."

…a council of Athenian officers was summoned on the slope of one of the mountains that look over the plain of Marathon, on the eastern coast of Attica. The immediate subject of their meeting was to consider whether they should give battle to an enemy that lay encamped on the shore beneath them; but on the result of their deliberations depended not merely the fate of two armies, but the whole future progress of human civilization.

There were eleven members of that council of war. Ten were the generals, who were then annually elected at Athens, one for each of the local tribes into which the Athenians were divided. Each general led the men of his own tribe, and each was invested with equal military authority. One also of the Archons was associated with them in the joint command of the collective force. This magistrate was termed the Polemarch or War-Ruler: he had the privilege of leading the right wing of the army in battle, and of taking part in all councils of war. A noble Athenian, named Callimachus, was the War-Ruler of this year; and as such, stood listening to the earnest discussion of the ten generals. They had, indeed, deep matter for anxiety, though little aware how momentous to mankind were the votes they were about to give, or how the generations to come would read with interest that record of their debate. They saw before them the invading forces of a mighty empire, which had in the last fifty years shattered and enslaved nearly all the kingdoms and principalities of the then known world. They knew that all the resources of their own country were comprised in the little army entrusted to their guidance. They saw before them a chosen host of the Great King sent to wreak his special wrath on that country, and on the other insolent little Greek community, which had dared to aid his rebels and burn the capital of one of his provinces. That victorious host had already fulfilled half its mission of vengeance. Eretria, the confederate of Athens in the bold march against Sardis nine years before, had fallen in the last few days; and the Athenian generals could discern from the heights the island of Aegilia, in which the Persians had deposited their Eretrian prisoners, whom they had reserved to be led away captives into Upper Asia, there to hear their doom from

the lips of King Darius himself. Moreover, the men of Athens knew that in the camp before them was their own banished tyrant, Hippias, who was seeking to be reinstated by foreign scimitars in despotic sway over any remnant of his countrymen that might survive the sack of their town, and might be left behind as too worthless for leading away into Median bondage.

The numerical disparity between the force which the Athenian commanders had under them, and that which they were called on to encounter, was fearfully apparent to some of the council…Every free Greek was trained to military duty: and, from the incessant border wars between the different states, few Greeks reached the age of manhood without having seen some service. But the muster-roll of free Athenian citizens of an age fit for military duty never exceeded thirty thousand, and at this epoch probably did not amount to two-thirds of that number. Moreover, the poorer portion of these were unprovided with the equipments, and untrained to the operations of the regular infantry. Some detachments of the best armed troops would be required to garrison the city itself, and man the various fortified posts in the territory; so that it is impossible to reckon the fully equipped force that marched from Athens to Marathon, when the news of the Persian landing arrived, at higher than ten thousand men…With one exception, the other Greeks held back from aiding them. Sparta had promised assistance; but the Persians had landed on the sixth day of the moon, and a religious scruple delayed the march of Spartan troops till the moon should have reached its full. From one quarter only, and that a most unexpected one, did Athens receive aid at the moment of her great peril…the brave Plataeans, unsolicited, marched with their whole force to assist in the defense, and to share the fortunes of their benefactors. The general levy of the Plataeans only amounted to a thousand men: and this little column, marching from their city along the southern ridge of Mount Cithaeron, and thence across the Attic territory, joined the Athenian forces above Marathon almost immediately before the battle. The reinforcement was numerically small; but the gallant spirit of the men who composed it must have made it of tenfold value to the Athenians: and its presence must have gone far to dispel the cheerless feeling of being deserted and friendless, which the delay of the Spartan succors was calculated to create among the Athenian ranks.

This generous daring of their weak but true-hearted ally was never forgotten at Athens. The Plataeans were made the fellow- countrymen of the Athenians, except the right of exercising certain political functions; and from that time forth in the solemn sacrifices at Athens, the public prayers were offered up for a joint blessing from Heaven upon the Athenians, and the Plataeans also. [Mr. Grote observes (vol. iv. p. 484), that "this volunteer march of the whole Plataean force to Marathon is one of the most affecting incidents of all Grecian history." In truth, the whole career of Plataea, and the friendship, strong even unto death, between her and Athens, form one of the most affecting episodes in the history of antiquity. In the Peloponnesian War the Plataeans again were true to the Athenians against all risks and all calculation of self-interest; and the destruction of Plataea was the consequence. There are few nobler passages in the classics than the speech in which the Plataean prisoners of war, after the memorable siege of their city, justify before their Spartan executioners their loyal adherence to Athens. (See Thucydides, lib. iii. secs. 53-60.)]

After the junction of the column from Plataea, the Athenians commanders must have had under them about eleven thousand fully-armed and disciplined infantry, and probably a larger number of irregular light-armed troops; as, besides the poorer citizens who went to the field armed with javelins, cutlasses, and targets, each regular heavy-armed soldier was attended in the camp by one or more slaves, who were armed like the inferior freemen. [At the battle of Plataea, eleven years after Marathon, each of the eight thousand Athenian regular infantry who served there, was attended by a light-armed slave. (Herod. lib. viii. c. 28,29.)] Cavalry or archers the Athenians (on this occasion) had none: and the use in the field of military engines was not at that period introduced into ancient warfare.

Contrasted with their own scanty forces, the Greek commanders saw stretched before them, along the shores of the winding bay, the tents and shipping of the varied nations that marched to do the bidding of the King of the Eastern world. The difficulty of finding transports and of securing provisions would form the only limit to the numbers of a Persian army…fearful odds against the national levies of the Athenians. Nor could Greek generals then feel that confidence in the superior quality of their troops which ever since the battle of Marathon has animated Europeans in conflicts with Asiatics…On the contrary, up to the day of Marathon the Medes and Persians were reputed invincible. They had more than once met Greek troops in Asia Minor, in Cyprus, in Egypt, and had invariably beaten them. Nothing can be stronger than the expressions used by the early Greek writers respecting the terror which the name of the Medes inspired, and the prostration of men's spirits before the apparently resistless career of the Persian arms. It is therefore, little to be wondered at, that five of the ten Athenian generals shrank from the prospect of fighting a pitched battle against an enemy so superior in numbers, and so formidable in military renown. Their own position on the heights was strong, and offered great advantages to a small defending force against assailing masses. They deemed it mere foolhardiness to descend into the plain to be trampled down by the Asiatic horse, overwhelmed with the archery, or cut to pieces by the invincible veterans of Cambyses and Cyrus. Moreover, Sparta, the great war-state of Greece, had been applied to, and had promised succor to Athens, though the religious observance which the Dorians paid to certain times and seasons had for the present delayed their march. Was it not wise, at any rate, to wait till the Spartans came up, and to have the help of the best troops in Greece, before they exposed themselves to the shock of the dreaded Medes?

Specious as these reasons might appear, the other five generals were for speedier and bolder operations. And, fortunately for Athens and for the world, one of them was a man, not only of the highest military genius, but also of that energetic character which impresses its own type and ideas upon spirits feebler in conception.

…When the Persian power was extended to the Hellespont and its neighborhood, Miltiades…prince of the Chersonese, submitted to King Darius; and he was one of the numerous tributary rulers who led their contingents of men to serve in the Persian army in the expedition against Scythia.

…Two other men of signal eminence in history, though their renown was achieved at a later period than that of Miltiades, were also among the ten Athenian generals at Marathon. One was Themistocles, the future founder of the Athenian navy and the destined victor of Salamis: the other was Aristides, who afterwards led the Athenian troops at Plataea, and whose integrity and just popularity acquired for his country, when the Persians had finally been repulsed, the advantageous pre-eminence of being acknowledged by half of the Greeks as their impartial leader and protector.

Miltiades felt no hesitation as to the course which the Athenian army ought to pursue: and earnestly did he press his opinion on his brother-generals. Practically acquainted with the organization of the Persian armies, Miltiades was convinced of the superiority of the Greek troops, if properly handled: he saw with the military eye of a great general the advantage which the position of the forces gave him for a sudden attack, and as a profound politician he felt the perils of remaining inactive, and of giving treachery time to ruin the Athenian cause.

One officer in the council of war had not yet voted. This was Callimachus, the War-Ruler. The votes of the generals were five and five, so that the voice of Callimachus would be decisive.

On that vote, in all human probability, the destiny of all the nations of the world depended. Miltiades turned to him, and in simple soldierly eloquence, the substance of which we may read faithfully reported in Herodotus, who had conversed with the veterans of Marathon, the great Athenian thus adjured his countryman to vote for giving battle:

"It now rests with you, Callimachus, either to enslave Athens, or, by assuring her freedom, to win yourself an immortality of fame, such as not even Harmodius and Aristogeiton have acquired. For never, since the Athenians were a people, were they in such danger as they are in at this moment. If they bow the knee to these Medes, they are to be given up to Hippias, and you know what they then will have to suffer. But if Athens comes victorious out of this contest, she has it in her to become the first city of Greece. Your vote is to decide whether we are to join battle or not. If we do not bring on a battle presently, some factious intrigue will disunite the Athenians, and the city will be betrayed to the Medes. But if we fight, before there is anything rotten in the state of Athens, I believe that, provided the Gods will give fair play and no favor, we are able to get the best of it in the engagement."

…The vote of the brave War-Ruler was gained; the council determined to give battle; and such was the ascendancy and military eminence of Miltiades, that his brother-generals, one and all, gave up their days of command to him, and cheerfully acted under his orders. Fearful, however, of creating any jealousy, and of so failing to obtain the co-operation of all parts of his small army, Miltiades waited till the day when the chief command would have come round to him in regular rotation, before he led the troops against the enemy.

The inaction of the Asiatic commanders, during this interval, appears strange at first sight; but Hippias was with them, and they and he were aware of their chance of a bloodless conquest through the machinations of his partisans among the Athenians. The nature of the ground also explains, in many points, the tactics of the opposite generals before the battle, as well as the operations of the troops during the engagement.

The plain of Marathon, which is about twenty-two miles distant from Athens, lies along the bay of the same name on the northeastern coast of Attica. The plain is nearly in the form of a crescent, and about six miles in length. It is about two miles broad in the centre, where the space between the mountains and the sea is greatest, but it narrows towards either extremity, the mountains coming close down to the water at the horns of the bay. There is a valley trending inwards from the middle of the plain, and a ravine comes down to it to the southward. Elsewhere it, is closely girt round on the land side by rugged limestone mountains, which are thickly studded with pines, olive-trees, and cedars, and overgrown with the myrtle, arbutus, and the other low odoriferous shrubs that everywhere perfume the Attic air. The level of the ground is now varied by the mound raised over those who fell in the battle, but it was an unbroken plain when the Persians encamped on it. There are marshes at each end, which are dry in spring and summer, and then offer no obstruction to the horseman, but are commonly flooded with rain, and so rendered impracticable for cavalry, in the autumn, the time of year at which the action took place.

The Greeks, lying encamped on the mountains, could watch every movement of the Persians on the plain below, while they were enabled completely to mask their own. Miltiades also had, from his position, the power of giving battle whenever he pleased, or of delaying it at his discretion, unless Datis were to attempt the perilous operation of storming the heights.

If we turn to the map of the old world, to test the comparative territorial resources of the two states whose armies were now about to come into conflict, the immense preponderance of the material power of the Persian king over that of the Athenian republic is more striking than any similar contrast which history can supply. It has been truly remarked, that, in estimating mere areas, Attica,

containing on its whole surface only seven hundred square miles, shrinks into insignificance if compared with many a baronial fief of the Middle Ages, or many a colonial allotment of modern times.

…Nor could a European, in the beginning of the fifth century before our era, look upon this huge accumulation of power beneath the scepter of a single Asiatic ruler, with the indifference with which we now observe on the map the extensive dominions of modern Oriental sovereigns. For, as has been already remarked, before Marathon was fought, the prestige of success and of supposed superiority of race was on the side of the Asiatic against the European. Asia was the original seat of human societies and long before any trace can be found of the inhabitants of the rest of the world having emerged from the rudest barbarism, we can perceive that mighty and brilliant empires flourished in the Asiatic continent. They appear before us through the twilight of primeval history, dim and indistinct, but massive and majestic, like mountains in the early dawn…we are thus better enabled to appreciate the repulse which Greece gave to the arms of the East, and to judge of the probable consequences to human civilization, if the Persians had succeeded in bringing Europe under their yoke, as they had already subjugated the fairest portions of the rest of the then known world.

The Greeks, from their geographical position, formed the natural vanguard of European liberty against Persian ambition…in their governments they lived long under hereditary kings, but never endured the permanent establishment of absolute monarchy. Their early kings were constitutional rulers, governing with defined prerogatives. And long before the Persian invasion the kingly form of government had given way in almost all the Greek states to republican institutions, presenting infinite varieties of the balancing or the alternate predominance of the oligarchical and democratical principles.

…This spirit of activity and daring, joined to a generous sympathy for the fate of their fellow-Greeks in Asia, had led them to join in the last Ionian war; and now, mingling with their abhorrence of the usurping family of their own citizens, which for a period had forcibly seized on and exercised despotic power at Athens, it nerved them to defy the wrath of King Darius, and to refuse to receive back at his bidding the tyrant whom they had some years before driven from their land…all the great kingdoms which we know to have existed in Ancient Asia, were, in Darius's time, blended with the Persian. The northern Indians, the Assyrians, the Syrians, the Babylonians, the Chaldees, the Phoenicians, the nations of Palestine, the Armenians, the Bactrians, the Lydians, the Phrygians, the Parthians, and the Medes, all obeyed the scepter of the Great King: the Medes standing next to the native Persians in honor, and the empire being frequently spoken of as that of the Medes, or as that of the Medes and Persians. Egypt and Cyrene were Persian provinces; the Greek colonists in Asia Minor and the islands of the Aegean were Darius's subjects; and their gallant but unsuccessful attempts to throw off the Persian yoke had only served to rivet it more strongly, and to increase the general belief: that the Greeks could not stand before the Persians in a field of battle. Darius's Scythian war, though unsuccessful in its immediate object, had brought about the subjugation of Thrace and the submission of Macedonia. From the Indus to the Peneus, all was his.

We may imagine the wrath with which the lord of so many nations must have heard, nine years before the battle of Marathon, that a strange nation towards the setting sun, called the Athenians, had dared to help his rebels in Ionia against him, and that they had plundered and burnt the capital of one of his provinces. Before the burning of Sardis, Darius seems never to have heard of the existence of Athens; but his satraps in Asia Minor had for some time seen Athenian refugees at their provincial courts imploring assistance against their fellow-countrymen. When Hippias was driven away from Athens, and the tyrannic dynasty of the Pisistratidae finally overthrown in 510 B.C., the banished tyrant and his adherents, after vainly seeking to be restored by Spartan intervention, had betaken themselves to Sardis, the capital city of the satrapy of Artaphernes. There Hippias (in the expressive words of Herodotus) [Herod. lib. v. c. 96.] began every kind of agitation, slandering the Athenians before Artaphernes, and doing all he could to induce the satrap to place Athens in subjection to him, as the tributary vassal of King Darius. When the Athenians heard of his practices, they sent envoys to Sardis to remonstrate with the Persians against taking up the quarrel of the Athenian refugees. But Artaphernes gave them in reply a menacing command to receive Hippias back again if they looked for safety. The Athenians were resolved not to purchase safety at such a price; and after rejecting the satrap's terms, they considered that they and the Persians were declared enemies. At this very crisis the Ionian Greeks implored the assistance of their European brethren, to enable them to recover their independence from Persia. Athens, and the city of Eretria in Euboea, alone consented. Twenty Athenian galleys, and five Eretrian, crossed the Aegean Sea; and by a bold and sudden march upon Sardis the Athenians and their allies succeeded in capturing the capital city of the haughty satrap, who had recently menaced them with servitude or destruction. The Persian forces were soon rallied, and the Greeks were compelled to retire. They were pursued, and defeated on their return to the coast, and Athens took no further part in the Ionian war. But the insult that she had put upon the Persian power was speedily made known throughout that empire, and was never to be forgiven or forgotten. In the emphatic simplicity of the narrative of Herodotus, the wrath of the Great King is thus described: "Now when it was told to King Darius that Sardis had been taken and burnt by the Athenians and Ionians, he took small heed of the Ionians, well knowing who they were, and that their revolt would soon be put down: but he asked who, and what manner of men, the Athenians were. And when he had been told, he called for his bow; and, having taken it, and placed an arrow on the string, he let the arrow fly towards heaven; and as he shot it into the air, he said, 'O Supreme God! grant me that I may avenge myself on the Athenians.' And when he had said this, he appointed one of his servants to say to him every day as he sat at meat, 'Sire, remember the Athenians.'"

Some years were occupied in the complete reduction of Ionia. But when this was effected, Darius ordered his victorious forces to proceed to punish Athens and Eretria, and to conquer European Greece. The first armament sent for this purpose was shattered by shipwreck, and nearly destroyed off Mount Athos, But the purpose of King Darius was not easily shaken. A larger army was ordered to be collected in Cilicia; and requisitions were sent to all the maritime cities of the Persian empire for ships of war, and for transports of sufficient size for carrying cavalry as well as infantry across the Aegean. While these preparations were being made, Darius sent heralds round to the Grecian cities demanding their submission to Persia. It was proclaimed in the market-place of each little Hellenic state (some with territories not larger than the Isle of Wight), that King Darius, the lord of all men, from the rising to the setting sun, required earth and water to be delivered to his heralds, as a symbolical acknowledgment that he was head and master of the country…Terror-stricken at the power of Persia and at the severe punishment that had recently been inflicted on the refractory Ionians, many of the continental Greeks and nearly all the islanders submitted, and gave the required tokens of vassalage. At Sparta and Athens an indignant refusal was returned: a refusal which was disgraced by outrage and violence against the persons of the Asiatic heralds.

Fresh fuel was thus added to the anger of Darius against Athens, and the Persian preparations went on with renewed vigor. In the summer of 490 B.C., the army destined for the invasion was assembled in the Aleian plain of Cilicia, near the sea. A fleet of six hundred galleys and numerous transports was collected on the coast for the embarkation of troops, horse as well as foot. A Median general named Datis, and Artaphernes, the son of the satrap of Sardis, and who was also nephew of

Darius, were placed in titular joint command of the expedition. That the real supreme authority was given to Datis alone is probable, from the way in which the Greek writers speak of him. We know no details of the previous career of this officer; but there is every reason to believe that his abilities and bravery had been proved by experience, or his Median birth would have prevented his being placed in high command by Darius. He appears to have been the first Mede who was thus trusted by the Persian kings after the overthrow of the conspiracy of the Median Magi against the Persians immediately before Darius obtained the throne. Datis received instructions to complete the subjugation of Greece, and especial orders were given him with regard to Eretria and Athens. He was to take these two cities; and he was to lead the inhabitants away captive, and bring them as slaves into the presence of the Great King.

Datis embarked his forces in the fleet that awaited them; and coasting along the shores of Asia Minor till he was off Samos, he thence sailed due westward through the Aegean Sea for Greece, taking the islands in his way. The Naxians had, ten years before, successfully stood a siege against a Persian armament, but they now were too terrified to offer any resistance, and fled to the mountain-tops, while the enemy burnt their town and laid waste their lands. Thence Datis, compelling the Greek islanders to join him with their ships and men, sailed onward to the coast of Euboea. The little town of Carystus essayed resistance, but was quickly overpowered. He next attacked Eretria. The Athenians sent four thousand men to its aid. But treachery was at work among the Eretrians; and the Athenian force received timely warning from one of the leading men of the city to retire to aid in saving their own country, instead of remaining to share in the inevitable destruction of Eretria. Left to themselves, the Eretrians repulsed the assaults of the Persians against their walls for six days; on the seventh day they were betrayed by two of their chiefs and the Persians occupied the city. The temples were burnt in revenge for the burning of Sardis, and the inhabitants were bound and placed as prisoners in the neighboring islet of Aegylia, to wait there till Datis should bring the Athenians to join them in captivity, when both populations were to be led into Upper Asia, there to learn their doom from the lips of King Darius himself.

Flushed with success, and with half his mission thus accomplished, Datis reembarked his troops, and crossing the little channel that separates Euboea from the mainland, he encamped his troops on the Attic coast at Marathon, drawing up his galleys on the shelving beach, as was the custom with the navies of antiquity. The conquered islands behind him served as places of deposit for his provisions and military stores. His position at Marathon seemed to him in every respect advantageous; and the level nature of the ground on which he camped was favorable for the employment of his cavalry, if the Athenians should venture to engage him. Hippias, who accompanied him, and acted as the guide of the invaders, had pointed out Marathon as the best place for a landing, for this very reason…But though "the fierce democracy" of Athens was zealous and true against foreign invader and domestic tyrant, a faction existed in Athens, as at Eretria, of men willing to purchase a party triumph over their fellow-citizens at the price of their country's ruin. Communications were opened between these men and the Persian camp, which would have led to a catastrophe like that of Eretria, if Miltiades had not resolved, and had not persuaded his colleagues to resolve, on fighting at all hazards.

When Miltiades arrayed his men for action, he staked on the arbitrement of one battle not only the fate of Athens, but that of all Greece; for if Athens had fallen, no other Greek state, except Lacedaemon, would have had the courage to resist; and the Lacedaemonians, though they would probably have died in their ranks to the last man, never could have successfully resisted the victorious Persians, and the numerous Greek troops, which would have soon marched under the Persian satraps, had they prevailed over Athens.

Nor was there any power to the westward of Greece that could have offered an effectual

opposition to Persia, had she once conquered Greece, and made that country a basis for future military operations…Had Persia beaten Athens at Marathon, she could have found no obstacle to prevent Darius, the chosen servant of Ormuzd, from advancing his sway over all the known Western races of mankind. The infant energies of Europe would have been trodden out beneath universal conquest; and the history of the world, like the history of Asia, would have become a mere record of the rise and fall of despotic dynasties, of the incursions of barbarous hordes, and of the mental and political prostration of millions beneath the diadem, the tiara, and the sword.

Great as the preponderance of the Persian over the Athenian power at that crisis seems to have been, it would be unjust to impute wild rashness to the policy of Miltiades, and those who voted with him in the Athenian council of war, or to look on the after- current of events as the mere result of successful indiscretion. as before has been remarked, Miltiades, whilst prince of the Chersonese, had seen service in the Persian armies; and he knew by personal observation how many elements of weakness lurked beneath their imposing aspect of strength. He knew that the bulk of their troops no longer consisted of the hardy shepherds and mountaineers from Persia Proper and Kurdistan, who won Cyrus's battles: but that unwilling contingents from conquered nations now largely filled up the Persian muster rolls, fighting more from compulsion than from any zeal in the cause of their masters. He had also the sagacity and the spirit to appreciate the superiority of the Greek armor and organization over the Asiatic, notwithstanding former reverses. Above all, he felt and worthily trusted the enthusiasm of the men under his command.

The Athenians, whom he led, had proved by their new-born valor in recent wars against the neighboring states, that "Liberty and Equality of civic rights are brave spirit-stirring things: and they who, while under the yoke of a despot, had been no better men of war than any of their neighbors, as soon as they were free, became the foremost men of all; for each felt that in fighting for a free commonwealth, he fought for himself, and, whatever he took in hand, he was zealous to do the work thoroughly." So the nearly contemporaneous historian describes the change of spirit that was seen in the Athenians after their tyrants were expelled; [Herod. lib. v. c. 87.] and Miltiades knew that in leading them against the invading army, where they had Hippias, the foe they most hated, before them, he was bringing into battle no ordinary men, and could calculate on no ordinary heroism. As for traitors, he was sure, that whatever treachery might lurk among some of the higher-born and wealthier Athenians, the rank and file whom he commanded were ready to do their utmost in his and their own cause. With regard to future attacks from Asia, he might reasonably hope that one victory would inspirit all Greece to combine against common foe; and that the latent seeds of revolt and disunion in the Persian empire would soon burst forth and paralyze its energies, so as to leave Greek independence secure.

With these hopes and risks, Miltiades, on the afternoon of a September day, 490 B.C., gave the word for the Athenian army to prepare for battle. There were many local associations connected with those mountain heights, which were calculated powerfully to excite the spirits of the men, and of which the commanders well knew how to avail themselves in their exhortations to their troops before the encounter. Marathon itself was a region sacred to Hercules. Close to them was the fountain of Macaria, who had in days of yore devoted herself to death for the liberty of her people. The very plain on which they were to fight was the scene of the exploits of their national hero, Theseus; and there, too, as old legends told, the Athenians and the Heraclidae had routed the invader, Eurystheus. These traditions were not mere cloudy myths, or idle fictions, but matters of implicit earnest faith to the men of that day: and many a fervent prayer arose from the Athenian ranks to the heroic spirits who while on earth had striven and suffered on that very spot, and who were believed to be now heavenly powers, looking down with interest on their still beloved country,

and capable of interposing with superhuman aid in its behalf.

According to old national custom, the warriors of each tribe were arrayed together; neighbor thus fighting by the side of neighbor, friend by friend, and the spirit of emulation and the consciousness of responsibility excited to the very utmost…The line consisted of the heavy-armed spearmen only. For the Greeks (until the time of Iphicrates) took little or no account of light-armed soldiers in a pitched battle, using them only in skirmishes or for the pursuit of a defeated enemy. The panoply of the regular infantry consisted of a long spear, of a shield, helmet, breast-plate, greaves, and short sword. Thus equipped, they usually advanced slowly and steadily into action in an uniform phalanx of about eight spears deep. But the military genius of Miltiades led him to deviate on this occasion from the commonplace tactics of his countrymen. It was essential for him to extend his line so as to cover all the practicable ground, and to secure himself from being outflanked and charged in the rear by the Persian horse. This extension involved the weakening of his line. Instead of an uniform reduction of its strength, he determined on detaching principally from his centre, which, from the nature of the ground, would have the best opportunities for rallying if broken; and on strengthening his wings, so as to insure advantage at those points; and he trusted to his own skill, and to his soldiers' discipline, for the improvement of that advantage into decisive victory.

[It is remarkable that there is no other instance of a Greek general deviating from the ordinary mode of bringing a phalanx of spearmen into action, until the battles of Leuctra and Mantineia, more than a century after Marathon, when Epaminondas introduced the tactics (which Alexander the Great in ancient times, and Frederic the Great in modern times, made so famous) of concentrating an overpowering force on some decisive point of the enemy's line, while he kept back, or, in military phrase, refused the weaker part of his own.]

In this order, and availing himself probably of the inequalities of the ground, so as to conceal his preparations from the enemy till the last possible moment, Miltiades drew up the eleven thousand infantry whose spears were to decide this crisis in the struggle between the European and the Asiatic worlds. The sacrifices, by which the favor of Heaven was sought, and its will consulted, were announced to show propitious omens. The trumpet sounded for action, and, chanting the hymn of battle, the little army bore down upon the host of the foe. Then, too, along the mountain slopes of Marathon must have resounded the mutual exhortation which Aeschylus, who fought in both battles, tells us was afterwards heard over the waves of Salamis, "On, sons of the Greeks! Strike for the freedom of your country! strike for the freedom of your children and of your wives—for the shrines of your fathers' gods, and for the sepulchers of your sires. All—all are now staked upon the strife!"

Instead of advancing at the usual slow pace of the phalanx, Miltiades brought his men on at a run. They were all trained in the exercises of the palaestra, so that there was no fear of their ending the charge in breathless exhaustion: and it was of the deepest importance for him to traverse as rapidly as possible the space of about a mile of level ground, that lay between the mountain foot and the Persian outposts, and so to get his troops into close action before the Asiatic cavalry could mount, form, and maneuver against him, or their archers keep him long under bow-shot, and before the enemy's generals could fairly deploy their masses.

"When the Persians," says Herodotus, "saw the Athenians running down on them, without horse or bowmen, and scanty in numbers, they thought them a set of madmen rushing upon certain destruction." They began, however, to prepare to receive them and the Eastern chiefs arrayed, as quickly as time and place allowed, the varied races who served in their motley ranks…But no national cause inspired them, except the division of native Persians; and in the large host there was no uniformity of language, creed, race, or military system. Still, among them there were many gallant men, under a veteran general; they were familiarized with victory; and in contemptuous confidence their infantry, which alone had time to form, awaited the Athenian charge. On came the Greeks, with one unwavering line of leveled spears, against which the light targets, the short lances and scimitars of the Orientals offered weak defense. The front rank of the Asiatics must have gone down to a man at the first shock. Still they recoiled not, but strove by individual gallantry, and by the weight of numbers, to make up for the disadvantages of weapons and tactics, and to bear back the shallow line of the Europeans. In the centre, where the native Persians and the Sacae fought, they succeeded in breaking through the weaker part of the Athenian phalanx; and the tribes led by Aristides and Themistocles were, after a brave resistance, driven back over the plain, and chased by the Persians up the valley towards the inner country. There the nature of the ground gave the opportunity of rallying and renewing the struggle: and meanwhile, the Greek wings, where Miltiades had concentrated his chief strength, had routed the Asiatics opposed to them; and the Athenian and Plataean officers, instead of pursuing the fugitives, kept their troops well in hand, and wheeling round they formed the two wings together. Miltiades instantly led them against the Persian centre, which had hitherto been triumphant, but which now fell back, and prepared to encounter these new and unexpected assailants. Aristides and Themistocles renewed the fight with their re-organized troops, and the full force of the Greeks was brought into close action with the Persian and Sacian divisions of the enemy. Datis's veterans strove hard to keep their ground, and evening [ARISTOPH. Vesvoe 1085.] was approaching before the stern encounter was decided.

But the Persians, with their slight wicker shields, destitute of body-armor, and never taught by training to keep the even front and act with the regular movement of the Greek infantry, fought at grievous disadvantage with their shorter and feebler weapons against the compact array of well-armed Athenian and Plataean spearmen, all perfectly drilled to perform each necessary evolution in concert, and to preserve an uniform and unwavering line in battle. In personal courage and in bodily activity the Persians were not inferior to their adversaries. Their spirits were not yet cowed by the recollection of former defeats; and they lavished their lives freely, rather than forfeit the fame which they had won by so many victories. While their rear ranks poured an incessant shower of arrows over the heads of their comrades, the foremost Persians kept rushing forward, sometimes singly, sometimes in desperate groups of twelve or ten upon the projecting spears of the Greeks, striving to force a lane into the phalanx, and to bring their scimitars and daggers into play. But the Greeks felt their superiority, and though the fatigue of the long-continued action told heavily on their inferior numbers, the sight of the carnage that they dealt amongst their assailants nerved them to fight still more fiercely on…At last the previously unvanquished lords of Asia turned their backs and fled, and the Greeks followed, striking them down, to the water's edge, where the invaders were now hastily launching their galleys, and seeking to embark and fly. Flushed with success, the Athenians dashed at the fleet…"Bring fire, bring fire," was their cry; and they began to lay hold of the ships. But here the Asiatics resisted desperately, and the principal loss sustained by the Greeks was in the assault on the fleet…Seven galleys were captured; but the Persians succeeded in saving the rest. They pushed off from the fatal shore: but even here the skill of Datis did not desert him, and he sailed round to the western coast of Attica, in hopes to find the city unprotected, and to gain possession of it from some of the partisans of Hippias. Miltiades, however, saw and counteracted his maneuver. Leaving Aristides, and the troops of his tribe, to guard the spoil and the slain, the Athenian commander led his conquering army by a rapid night-march back across the country to Athens. And when the Persian fleet had doubled the Cape of Sunium and sailed up to the Athenian harbor in the morning, Datis saw arrayed on the heights above the city the troops before whom his men

had fled on the preceding evening. All hope of further conquest in Europe for the time was abandoned, and the baffled armada returned to the Asiatic coasts.

…The number of the Persian dead was six thousand four hundred; of the Athenians, a hundred and ninety-two. The number of Plataeans who fell is not mentioned, but as they fought in the part of the army which was not broken, it cannot have been large.

The apparent disproportion between the losses of the two armies is not surprising, when we remember the armor of the Greek spearmen, and the impossibility of heavy slaughter being inflicted by sword or lance on troops so armed, as long as they kept firm in their ranks…The Athenian slain were buried on the field of battle. This was contrary to the usual custom, according to which the bones of all who fell fighting for their country in each year were deposited in a public sepulcher in the suburb of Athens called the Cerameicus. But it was felt that a distinction ought to be made in the funeral honors paid to the men of Marathon, even as their merit had been distinguished over that of all other Athenians. A lofty mound was raised on the plain of Marathon, beneath which the remains of the men of Athens who fell in the battle were deposited. Ten columns were erected on the spot, one for each of the Athenian tribes; and on the monumental column of each tribe were graven the names of those of its members whose glory it was to have fallen in the great battle of liberation…The columns have long perished, but the mound still marks the spot where the noblest heroes of antiquity, the MARATHONOMAKHOI repose…There was also a distinct sepulchral monument to the general to whose genius the victory was mainly due. Miltiades did not live long after his achievement at Marathon…These and other memorials of Marathon were the produce of the meridian age of Athenian intellectual splendor—of the age of Phidias and Pericles. For it was not merely by the generation of men whom the battle liberated from Hippias and the Medes, that the transcendent importance of their victory was gratefully recognized. Through the whole epoch of her prosperity, through the long Olympiads of her decay, through centuries after her fall, Athens looked back on the day of Marathon as the brightest of her national existence.

By a natural blending of patriotic pride with grateful piety, the very spirits of the Athenians who fell at Marathon were deified by their countrymen. The inhabitants of the districts of Marathon paid religious rites to them; and orators solemnly invoked them in their most impassioned adjurations before the assembled men of Athens. "Nothing was omitted that could keep alive the remembrance of a deed which had first taught the Athenian people to know its own strength, by measuring it with the power which had subdued the greater part of the known world. The consciousness thus awakened fixed its character, its station, and its destiny; it was the spring of its later great actions and ambitious enterprises. [Thirlwall.]

…EXPLANATORY REMARKS ON SOME OF THE CIRCUMSTANCES OF THE BATTLE OF MARATHON.

Nothing is said by Herodotus of the Persian cavalry taking any part in the battle, although he mentions that Hippias recommended the Persians to land at Marathon, because the plain was favorable for cavalry evolutions. In the life of Miltiades, which is usually cited as the production of Cornelius Nepos, but which I believe to be of no authority whatever, it is said that Miltiades protected his flanks from the enemy's horse by an abattis of felled trees. While he was on the high ground he would not have required this defense; and it is not likely that the Persians would have allowed him to erect it on the plain.

Bishop Thirlwall calls our attention to a passage in Suidas, where the proverb KHORIS HIPPEIS is said to have originated from some Ionian Greeks, who were serving compulsorily in the army of Datis, contriving to inform Miltiades that the Persian cavalry had gone away, whereupon

Miltiades immediately joined battle and gained the victory. There may probably be a gleam of truth in this legend. If Datis's cavalry was numerous, as the abundant pastures of Euboea were close at hand, the Persian general, when he thought, from the inaction of his enemy, that they did not mean to come down from the heights and give battle, might naturally send the larger part of his horse back across the channel to the neighborhood of Eretria, where he had already left a detachment, and where his military stores must have been deposited. The knowledge of such a movement would of course confirm Miltiades in his resolution to bring on a speedy engagement.

But, in truth, whatever amount of cavalry we suppose Datis to have had with him on the day of Marathon, their inaction in the battle is intelligible, if we believe the attack of the Athenian spearmen to have been as sudden as it was rapid. The Persian horse-soldier, on an alarm being given, had to take the shackles off his horse, to strap the saddle on, and bridle him, besides equipping himself (see Xenoph. Anab. lib.iii c.4); and when each individual horseman was ready, the line had to be formed; and the time that it takes to form the Oriental cavalry in line for a charge, has, in all ages, been observed by Europeans.

The wet state of the marshes at each end of the plain, in the time of year when the battle was fought, has been adverted to by Mr. Wordsworth; and this would hinder the Persian general from arranging and employing his horsemen on his extreme wings, while it also enabled the Greeks, as they came forward, to occupy the whole breadth of the practicable ground with an unbroken line of leveled spears, against which, if any Persian horse advanced they would be driven back in confusion upon their own foot.

Even numerous and fully-arrayed bodies of cavalry have been repeatedly broken, both in ancient and modern warfare, by resolute charges of infantry. For instance, it was by an attack of some picked cohorts that Caesar routed the Pompeian cavalry, which had previously defeated his own at Pharsalia.

I have represented the battle of Marathon as beginning in the afternoon, and ending towards evening. If it had lasted all day, Herodotus would have probably mentioned that fact. That it ended towards evening is, I think, proved by the line from the "Vespae" which I have already quoted, and to which my attention was called by Sir Edward Bulwer Lytton's account of the battle. I think that the succeeding lines in Aristophanes, also already quoted, justify the description which I have given of the rear-ranks of the Persians keeping up a flight of arrows over the heads of their comrades against the Greeks.

SYNOPSIS OF EVENTS BETWEEN THE BATTLE OF MARATHON, B.C. 490, AND THE DEFEAT OF THE ATHENIANS AT SYRACUSE, B.C. 413.

B.C. 490 to 487. All Asia is filled with the preparations made by King Darius for a new expedition against Greece. Themistocles persuades the Athenians to leave off dividing the proceeds of their silver mines among themselves, and to employ the money in strengthening their navy.

487. Egypt revolts from the Persians, and delays the expedition against Greece.

485. Darius dies, and Xerxes his son becomes King of Persia in his stead.

484 The Persians recover Egypt.

480 Xerxes invades Greece. Indecisive actions between the Persian and Greek fleets at Artemisium. Destruction of the three hundred Spartans at Thermopyae. The Athenians abandon Attica and go on shipboard. Great naval victory of the Greeks at Salamis. Xerxes returns to Asia, leaving a chosen army under Mardonius, to carry on the war against the Greeks.

478. Mardonius and his army destroyed by the Greeks at Plataea The Greeks land in Asia Minor, and defeat a Persian force at Mycale. In this and the following years the Persians lose all their conquests in Europe, and many on the coast of Asia.

477. Many of the Greek maritime states take Athens as their leader, instead of Sparta.

466. Victories of Cimon over the Persians at the Eurymedon.

464. Revolt of the Helots against Sparta. Third Messenian war.

460. Egypt again revolts against Persia. The Athenians send a powerful armament to aid the Egyptians, which, after gaining some successes, is destroyed, and Egypt submits. This war lasted six years.

457. Wars in Greece between the Athenian and several Peloponnesian states.

455. A thirty years' truce concluded between Athens and Lacedaemon.

440. The Samians endeavor to throw off the supremacy of Athens. Samos completely reduced to subjection. Pericles is now sole director of the Athenian councils.

431. Commencement of the great Peloponnesian war, in which Sparta, at the head of nearly all the Peloponnesian states, and aided by the Boeotians and some of the other Greeks beyond the Isthmus, endeavors to reduce the power of Athens, and to restore independence to the Greek maritime states who were the subject allies of Athens. At the commencement of the war the Peloponnesian armies repeatedly invade and ravage Attica, but Athens herself is impregnable, and her fleets secure her the dominion of the sea.

430. Athens visited by a pestilence, which sweeps off large numbers of her population.

426. The Athenians gain great advantages over the Spartans at Sphacteria, and by occupying Cythera; but they suffer a severe defeat in Boeotia, and the Spartan general Brasidas, leads an expedition to the Thracian coasts, and conquers many of the most valuable Athenian possessions in those regions.

421. Nominal truce for thirty years between Athens and Sparta, but hostilities continue on the Thracian coast and in other quarters.

415. The Athenians send an expedition to conquer Sicily.

CHAPTER II.
DEFEAT OF THE ATHENIANS AT SYRACUSE, B.C.413.

"The Romans knew not, and could not know, how deeply the greatness of their own posterity, and the fate of the whole Western world, were involved in the destruction of the fleet of Athens in the harbor of Syracuse. Had that great expedition proved victorious, the energies of Greece during the next eventful century would have found their field in the West no less than in the East; Greece, and not Rome, might have conquered Carthage; Greek instead of Latin might have been at this day the principal element of the language of Spain, of France, and of Italy; and the laws of Athens, rather than of Rome, might be the foundation of the law of the civilized world."—ARNOLD. "The great expedition to Sicily, one of the most decisive events in the history of the world."—NIEBUHR.

Few cities have undergone more memorable sieges during ancient and mediaeval times, than has the city of Syracuse. Athenian, Carthaginian, Roman, Vandal, Byzantine, Saracen, and Norman, have in turns beleaguered her walls; and the resistance which she successfully opposed to some of her early assailants was of the deepest importance, not only to the fortunes of the generations then in being, but to all the subsequent current of human events. To adopt the eloquent expressions of Arnold respecting the check which she gave to the Carthaginian arms, "Syracuse was a breakwater, which God's providence raised up to protect the yet immature strength of Rome." And her triumphant repulse of the great Athenian expedition against her was of even more wide-spread and enduring importance. It forms a decisive epoch in the strife for universal empire, in which all the great states of antiquity successively engaged and failed.

The present city of Syracuse is a place of little or no military strength, as the fire of artillery from the neighboring heights would almost completely command it. But in ancient warfare its position, and the care bestowed on its walls, rendered it formidably strong against the means of offence which then were employed by besieging armies.

The ancient city, in the time of the Peloponnesian war, was chiefly built on the knob of land which projects into the sea on the eastern coast of Sicily, between two bays; one of which, to the north, was called the bay of Thapsus, while the southern one formed the great harbor of the city of Syracuse itself. A small island, or peninsula (for such it soon was rendered), lies at the south-eastern extremity of this knob of land, stretching almost entirely across the mouth of the great harbor, and rendering it nearly land-locked. This island comprised the original settlement of the first Greek colonists from Corinth…and the modern city has shrunk again into these primary limits. But, in the fifth century before our era, the growing wealth and population of the Syracusans had led them to occupy and include within their city walls portion after portion of the mainland lying next to the little isle; so that at the time of the Athenian expedition the seaward part of the land between the two bays already spoken of was built over, and fortified from bay to bay; constituting the larger part of Syracuse.

The landward wall, therefore, of the city traversed this knob of land, which continues to slope upwards from the sea, and which to the west of the old fortifications (that is, towards the interior of Sicily) rises rapidly for a mile or two, but diminishes in width, and finally terminates in a long narrow ridge, between which and Mount

Hybla a succession of chasms and uneven low ground extend. On each flank of this ridge the descent is steep and precipitous from its summits to the strips of level land that lie immediately below it, both to the south-west and north-west.

The usual mode of assailing fortified towns in the time of the Peloponnesian war, was to build a double wall round them, sufficiently strong to check any sally of the garrison from within, or any attack of a relieving force from without. The interval within the two walls of the circumvallation was roofed over, and formed barracks, in which the besiegers posted themselves, and awaited the effects of want or treachery among the besieged in producing a surrender. And, in every Greek city of those days, as in every Italian republic of the middle ages, the rage of domestic sedition between aristocrats and democrats ran high. Rancorous refugees swarmed in the camp of every invading enemy; and every blockaded city was sure to contain within its walls a body of intriguing malcontents, who were eager to purchase a party-triumph at the expense of a national disaster. Famine and faction were the allies on whom besiegers relied. The generals of that time trusted to the operation of these sure confederates as soon as they could establish a complete blockade. They rarely ventured on the attempt to storm any fortified post. For the military engines of antiquity were feeble in breaching masonry…and the lives of spearmen the boldest and most highly-trained would, of course, have been idly spent in charges against unshattered walls.

A city built, close to the sea, like Syracuse, was impregnable, save by the combined operations of a superior hostile fleet and a superior hostile army. And Syracuse, from her size, her population, and her military and naval resources, not unnaturally thought herself secure from finding in another Greek city a foe capable of sending a sufficient armament to menace her with capture and subjection. But in the spring of 414 B.C. the Athenian navy was mistress of her harbor and the adjacent seas; an Athenian army had defeated her

troops, and cooped them within the town; and from bay to bay a blockading wall was being rapidly carried across the strips of level ground and the high ridge outside the city (then termed Epipolae), which, if completed, would have cut the Syracusans off from all succor from the interior of Sicily, and have left them at the mercy of the Athenian generals. The besiegers' works were, indeed, unfinished; but every day the unfortified interval in their lines grew narrower, and with it diminished all apparent hope of safety for the beleaguered town.

Athens was now staking the flower of her forces, and the accumulated fruits of seventy years of glory, on one bold throw for the dominion of the Western world. As Napoleon from Mount Coeur de Lion pointed to St. Jean d'Acre, and told his staff that the capture of that town would decide his destiny, and would change the face of the world; so the Athenian officers, from the heights of Epipolae, must have looked on Syracuse, and felt that with its fall all the known powers of the earth would fall beneath them. They must have felt also that Athens, if repulsed there, must pause for ever in her career of conquest, and sink from an imperial republic into a ruined and subservient community.

At Marathon, the first in date of the Great Battles of the World, we beheld Athens struggling for self-preservation against the invading armies of the East. At Syracuse she appears as the ambitious and oppressive invader of others. In her, as in other republics of old and of modern times, the same energy that had inspired the most heroic efforts in defense of the national independence, soon learned to employ itself in daring and unscrupulous schemes of self-aggrandizement at the expense of neighboring nations. In the interval between the Persian and Peloponnesian wars she had rapidly grown into a conquering and dominant state, the chief of a thousand tributary cities, and the mistress of the largest and best-manned navy that the Mediterranean had yet beheld…All republics that acquire supremacy over other nations, rule them selfishly and oppressively.

There is no exception to this in either ancient or modern times. Carthage, Rome, Venice, Genoa, Florence, Pisa, Holland, and Republican France, all tyrannized over every province and subject state where they gained authority. But none of them openly avowed their system of doing so upon principle, with the candor which the Athenian republicans displayed, when any remonstrance was made against the severe exactions which they imposed upon their vassal allies. They avowed that their empire was a tyranny, and frankly stated that they solely trusted to force and terror to uphold it. They appealed to what they called "the eternal law of nature, that the weak should be coerced by the strong." [THUC. i. 77.] Sometimes they stated, and not without some truth, that the unjust hatred of Sparta against themselves forced them to be unjust to others in self-defense. To be safe they must be powerful; and to be powerful they must plunder and coerce their neighbors. They never dreamed of communicating any franchise, or share in office, to their dependents; but jealously monopolized every post of command, and all political and judicial power; exposing themselves to every risk with unflinching gallantry; enduring cheerfully the laborious training and severe discipline which their sea-service required; venturing readily on every ambitious scheme; and never suffering difficulty or disaster to shake their tenacity of purpose. Their hope was to acquire unbounded empire for their country, and the means of maintaining each of the thirty thousand citizens who made up the sovereign republic, in exclusive devotion to military occupations, and to those brilliant sciences and arts in which Athens already had reached the meridian of intellectual splendor.

…the number of the dependencies of Athens, at the time when the Peloponnesian confederacy attacked her, was undoubtedly very great. With a few trifling exceptions, all the islands of the Aegean, and all the Greek cities, which in that age fringed the coasts of Asia Minor, the Hellespont, and Thrace paid tribute to Athens, and implicitly obeyed her orders. The Aegean Sea was an Attic lake…her strong fortifications, by which she was girt and linked to her principal haven, gave her, in

those ages, almost all the advantages of an insular position. Pericles had made her trust to her empire of the seas. Every Athenian in those days was a practiced seaman. A state indeed whose members, of an age fit for service, at no time exceeded thirty thousand, and whose territorial extent did not equal half Sussex, could only have acquired such a naval dominion as Athens once held, by devoting, and zealously training, all its sons to service in its fleets. In order to man the numerous galleys which she sent out, she necessarily employed also large numbers of hired mariners and slaves at the oar; but the staple of her crews was Athenian, and all posts of command were held by native citizens. It was by reminding them of this, of their long practice in seamanship, and the certain superiority which their discipline gave them over the enemy's marine, that their great minister mainly encouraged them to resist the combined power of Lacedaemon and her allies. He taught them that Athens might thus reap the fruit of her zealous devotion to maritime affairs ever since the invasion of the Medes; "she had not, indeed, perfected herself; but the reward of her superior training was the rule of the sea—a mighty dominion, for it gave her the rule of much fair land beyond its waves, safe from the idle ravages with which the Lacedaemonians might harass Attica, but never could subdue Athens." [THUC. lib. i. sec. 144.]

Athens accepted the war with which her enemies threatened her, rather than descend from her pride of place…Both sides at length grew weary of the war; and in 421 B.C. a truce of fifty years was concluded, which, though ill kept, and though many of the confederates of Sparta refused to recognize it, and hostilities still continued in many parts of Greece, protected the Athenian territory from the ravages of enemies, and enabled Athens to accumulate large sums out of the proceeds of her annual revenues. So also, as a few years passed by, the havoc which the pestilence and the sword had made in her population was repaired; and in 415 B.C. Athens was full of bold and restless spirits, who longed for some field of distant enterprise, wherein they might signalize themselves, and aggrandize the state; and who looked on the alarm of Spartan hostility as a mere old woman's tale. When Sparta had wasted their territory she had done her worst; and the fact of its always being in her power to do so, seemed a strong reason for seeking to increase the transmarine dominion of Athens.

The West was now the quarter towards which the thoughts of every aspiring Athenian were directed…With the capture of Syracuse all Sicily, it was hoped, would be secured. Carthage and Italy were next to be assailed. With large levies of Iberian mercenaries she then meant to overwhelm her Peloponnesian enemies. The Persian monarchy lay in hopeless imbecility, inviting Greek invasion; nor did the known world contain the power that seemed capable of checking the growing might of Athens, if Syracuse once could be hers.… The armament which the Athenians equipped against Syracuse was in every way worthy of the state which formed such projects of universal empire; and it has been truly termed "the noblest that ever yet had been sent forth by a free and civilized commonwealth." [Arnold's History of Rome.] The fleet consisted of one hundred and thirty-four war galleys, with a multitude of store ships. A powerful force of the best heavy-armed infantry that Athens and her allies could furnish was sent on board, together with a smaller number of slingers and bowmen. The quality of the forces was even more remarkable than the number. The zeal of individuals vied with that of the republic in giving every galley the best possible crew, and every troop the most perfect accoutrements. And with private as well as public wealth eagerly lavished on all that could give splendor as well as efficiency to the expedition, the fated fleet began its voyage for the Sicilian shores in the summer of 415 B.C.

The Syracusans themselves, at the time of the Peloponnesian war, were a bold and turbulent democracy, tyrannizing over the weaker Greek cities in Sicily, and trying to gain in that island the same arbitrary supremacy which Athens maintained along the eastern coast of the Mediterranean. In numbers and in spirit they were fully equal to the Athenians, but far inferior to them in military and naval discipline. When the probability of an Athenian invasion was first publicly discussed at Syracuse, and efforts were made by some of the wiser citizens to improve the state of the national defenses, and prepare for the impending danger, the rumors of coming war and the proposals for preparation were received by the mass of the Syracusans with scornful incredulity…[A] Syracusan orator told his countrymen to dismiss with scorn the visionary terrors which a set of designing men among themselves strove to excite, in order to get power and influence thrown into their own hands. He told them that Athens knew her own interest too well to think of wantonly provoking their hostility: "*even if the enemies were to come,*" said he, "*so distant from their resources, and opposed to such a power as ours, their destruction would be easy and inevitable. Their ships will have enough to do to get to our island at all, and to carry such stores of all sorts as will be needed. They cannot therefore carry, besides, an army large enough to cope with such a population as ours. They will have no fortified place from which to commence their operations; but must rest them on no better base than a set of wretched tents, and such means as the necessities of the moment will allow them. But in truth i do not believe that they would even be able to effect a disembarkation. Let us, therefore, set at nought these reports as altogether of home manufacture; and be sure that if any enemy does come, the state will know how to defend itself in a manner worthy of the national honor.*"

Such assertions pleased the Syracusan assembly…But the invaders of Syracuse came; made good their landing in Sicily; and, if they had promptly attacked the city itself, instead of wasting nearly a year in desultory operations in other parts of the island, the Syracusans must have paid the penalty of their self-sufficient carelessness in submission to the Athenian yoke. But, of the three generals who led the Athenian expedition, two only were men of ability, and one was most weak and incompetent. Fortunately for Syracuse, Alcibiades, the most skilful of the three, was soon deposed from his command by a factious and fanatic vote of his fellow-countrymen, and the other competent one, Lamachus, fell early in a skirmish: while, more fortunately still for her, the feeble and vacillating Nicias remained unrecalled and unhurt, to assume the undivided leadership of the Athenian army and fleet, and to mar, by alternate over-caution and over-carelessness, every chance of success which the early part of the operations offered. Still, even under him, the Athenians nearly won the town. They defeated the raw levies of the Syracusans, cooped them within the walls, and, as before mentioned, almost effected a continuous fortification from bay to bay over Epipolae, the completion of which would certainly have been followed by capitulation.

Alcibiades, the most complete example of genius without principle that history produces, the Bolingbroke of antiquity, but with high military talents superadded to diplomatic and oratorical powers, on being summoned home from his command in Sicily to take his trial before the Athenian tribunal had escaped to Sparta; and he exerted himself there with all the selfish rancor of a renegade to renew the war with Athens, and to send instant assistance to Syracuse…The Spartans resolved to act on his advice

…So nearly, indeed, had Nicias completed his beleaguering lines, and so utterly desperate had the state of Syracuse seemingly become, that an assembly of the Syracusans was actually convened, and they were discussing the terms on which they should offer to capitulate, when a galley was seen dashing into the great harbor, and making her way towards the town with all the speed that her rowers could supply. From her shunning the part of the harbor where the Athenian fleet lay, and making straight for the Syracusan side, it was clear that she was a friend; the enemy's cruisers, careless through confidence of success, made no attempt to cut her off; she touched the beach, and a Corinthian captain springing on shore from her, was eagerly conducted to the assembly of the Syracusan people, just in time to prevent the fatal vote being put for a surrender.

Providentially for Syracuse, Gongylus, the commander of the galley, had been prevented by an Athenian squadron from following Gylippus to South Italy, and he had been obliged to push direct for Syracuse from Greece.

The sight of actual succor, and the promise of more, revived the drooping spirits of the Syracusans. They felt that they were not left desolate to perish; and the tidings that a Spartan was coming to command them confirmed their resolution to continue their resistance. Gylippus was already near the city. He had learned at Locri that the first report which had reached him of the state of Syracuse was exaggerated; and that there was an unfinished space in the besiegers' lines through which it was barely possible to introduce reinforcements into the town. Crossing the straits of Messina, which the culpable negligence of Nicias had left unguarded, Gylippus landed on the northern coast of Sicily, and there began to collect from the Greek cities an army, of which the regular troops that he brought from Peloponnesus formed the nucleus. Such was the influence of the name of Sparta…and such were his own abilities and activity, that he succeeded in raising a force of about two thousand fully armed infantry, with a larger number of irregular troops. Nicias, as if infatuated, made no attempt to counteract his operations; nor, when Gylippus marched his little army towards Syracuse, did the Athenian commander endeavor to check him. The Syracusans marched out to meet him: and while the Athenians were solely intent on completing their fortifications on the southern side towards the harbor, Gylippus turned their position by occupying the high ground in the extreme rear of Epipolae. He then marched through the unfortified interval of Nicias's lines into the besieged town; and, joining his troops with the Syracusan forces, after some engagements with varying success, gained the mastery over Nicias, drove the Athenians from Epipolae, and hemmed them into a disadvantageous position in the low grounds near the great harbor.

The attention of all Greece was now fixed on Syracuse; and every enemy of Athens felt the importance of the opportunity now offered of checking her ambition, and, perhaps, of striking a deadly blow at her power. Large reinforcements from Corinth, Thebes, and other cities, now reached the Syracusans; while the baffled and dispirited Athenian general earnestly besought his countrymen to recall him, and represented the further prosecution of the siege as hopeless.

But Athens had made it a maxim never to let difficulty or disaster drive her back from any enterprise once undertaken, so long as she possessed the means of making any effort, however desperate, for its accomplishment. With indomitable pertinacity she now decreed, instead of recalling her first armament from before Syracuse, to send out a second, though her enemies near home had now renewed open warfare against her, and by occupying a permanent fortification in her territory, had severely distressed her population, and were pressing her with almost all the hardships of an actual siege. She still was mistress of the sea, and she sent forth another fleet of seventy galleys, and another army, which seemed to drain the very last reserves of her military population, to try if Syracuse could not yet be won, and the honor of the Athenian arms be preserved from the stigma of a retreat. Hers was, indeed, a spirit that might be broken, but never would bend. At the head of this second expedition she wisely placed her best general Demosthenes, one of the most distinguished officers whom the long Peloponnesian war had produced, and who, if he had originally held the Sicilian command, would soon have brought Syracuse to submission…His arrival was critically timed; for Gylippus had encouraged the Syracusans to attack the Athenians under Nicias by sea as well as by land, and by an able stratagem of Ariston, one of the admirals of the Corinthian auxiliary squadron, the Syracusans and their confederates had inflicted on the fleet of Nicias the first defeat that the Athenian navy had ever sustained from a numerically inferior foe. Gylippus was preparing to follow up his advantage by fresh attacks on the Athenians on both elements, when the arrival of Demosthenes completely changed the aspect of

affairs, and restored the superiority to the invaders. With seventy-three war-galleys in the highest state of efficiency, and brilliantly equipped, with a force of five thousand picked men of the regular infantry of Athens and her allies, and a still larger number of bowmen, javelin-men, and slingers on board, Demosthenes rowed round the great harbor with loud cheers and martial music, as if in defiance of the Syracusans and their confederates. His arrival had indeed changed their newly-born hopes into the deepest consternation. The resources of Athens seemed inexhaustible, and resistance to her hopeless. They had been told that she was reduced to the last extremities, and that her territory was occupied by an enemy; and yet, here they saw her, as if in prodigality of power, sending forth, to make foreign conquests, a second armament, not inferior to that with which Nicias had first landed on the Sicilian shores.

With the intuitive decision of a great commander, Demosthenes at once saw that the possession of Epipolae was the key to the possession of Syracuse, and he resolved to make a prompt and vigorous attempt to recover that position, while his force was unimpaired, and the consternation which its arrival had produced among the besieged remained unabated. The Syracusans and their allies had run out an outwork along Epipolae from the city walls, intersecting the fortified lines of circumvallation which Nicias had commenced, but from which they had been driven by Gylippus. Could Demosthenes succeed in storming this outwork, and in re-establishing the Athenian troops on the high ground, he might fairly hope to be able to resume the circumvallation of the city, and become the conqueror of Syracuse: for, when once the besiegers' lines were completed, the number of the troops with which Gylippus had garrisoned the place would only tend to exhaust the stores of provisions, and accelerate its downfall.

An easily-repelled attack was first made on the outwork in the day-time, probably more with the view of blinding the besieged to the nature of the main operations than with any expectation of succeeding in an open assault, with every disadvantage of the ground to contend against. But, when the darkness had set in, Demosthenes formed his men in columns, each soldier taking with him five days' provisions, and the engineers and workmen of the camp following the troops with their tools, and all portable implements of fortification, so as at once to secure any advantage of ground that the army might gain. Thus equipped and prepared, he led his men along by the foot of the southern flank of Epipolae, in a direction towards the interior of the island, till he came immediately below the narrow ridge that forms the extremity of the high ground looking westward. He then wheeled his vanguard to the right, sent them rapidly up the paths that wind along the face of the cliff, and succeeded in completely surprising the Syracusan outposts, and in placing his troops fairly on the extreme summit of the all-important Epipolae. Thence the Athenians marched eagerly down the slope towards the town, routing some Syracusan detachments that were quartered in their way, and vigorously assailing the unprotected part of the outwork. All at first favored them. The outwork was abandoned by its garrison, and the Athenian engineers began to dismantle it. In vain Gylippus brought up fresh troops to check the assault: the Athenians broke and drove them back, and continued to press hotly forward, in the full confidence of victory. But, amid the general consternation of the Syracusans and their confederates, one body of infantry stood firm. This was a brigade of their Boeotian allies, which was posted low down the slope of Epipolae, outside the city walls. Coolly and steadily the Boeotian infantry formed their line, and, undismayed by the current of flight around them, advanced against the advancing Athenians. This was the crisis of the battle. But the Athenian van was disorganized by its own previous successes; and, yielding to the unexpected charge thus made on it by troops in perfect order, and of the most obstinate courage, it was driven back in confusion upon the other divisions of the army that still continued to press forward. When once the tide was thus turned, the Syracusans passed rapidly from the extreme of panic to the extreme of vengeful daring, and with all their forces they now fiercely assailed the

embarrassed and receding Athenians. In vain did the officers of the latter strive to re-form their line. Amid the din and the shouting of the fight, and the confusion inseparable upon a night engagement, especially one where many thousand combatants were pent and whirled together in a narrow and uneven area, the necessary maneuvers were impracticable; and though many companies still fought on desperately, wherever the moonlight showed them the semblance of a foe…they fought without concert or subordination; and not unfrequently, amid the deadly chaos, Athenian troops assailed each other. Keeping their ranks close, the Syracusans and their allies pressed on against the disorganized masses of the besiegers; and at length drove them, with heavy slaughter, over the cliffs, which, scarce an hour before, they had scaled full of hope, and apparently certain of success.

This defeat was decisive of the event of the siege. The Athenians afterwards struggled only to protect themselves from the vengeance which the Syracusans sought to wreak in the complete destruction of their invaders. Never, however, was vengeance more complete and terrible. A series of sea-fights followed, in which the Athenian galleys were utterly destroyed or captured. The mariners and soldiers who escaped death in disastrous engagements, and in a vain attempt to force a retreat into the interior of the island, became prisoners of war. Nicias and Demosthenes were put to death in cold blood; and their men either perished miserably in the Syracusan dungeons, or were sold into slavery to the very persons whom, in their pride of power, they had crossed the seas to enslave.

All danger from Athens to the independent nations of the West was now for ever at an end. She, indeed, continued to struggle against her combined enemies and revolted allies with unparalleled gallantry; and many more years of varying warfare passed away before she surrendered to their arms. But no success in subsequent conquests could ever have restored her to the pre-eminence in enterprise, resources, and maritime skill which she had acquired before her fatal reverses in Sicily. Nor among the rival Greek republics, whom her own rashness aided to crush her, was there any capable of reorganizing her empire, or resuming her schemes of conquest. The dominion of Western Europe was left for Rome and Carthage to dispute two centuries later, in conflicts still more terrible, and with even higher displays of military daring and genius, than Athens had witnessed either in her rise, her meridian, or her fall.

SYNOPSIS OF THE EVENTS BETWEEN THE DEFEAT OF THE ATHENIANS AT SYRACUSE, AND THE BATTLE OF ARBELA.

412 B.C. Many of the subject allies of Athens revolt from her, on her disasters before Syracuse being known; the seat of war is transferred to the Hellespont and eastern side of the Aegean.

410. The Carthaginians attempt to make conquests in Sicily.

407. Cyrus the Younger is sent by the king of Persia to take the government of all the maritime parts of Asia Minor, and with orders to help the Lacedaemonian fleet against the Athenian.

406. Agrigentum taken by the Carthaginians.

405. The last Athenian fleet destroyed by Lysander at Aegospotamos. Athens closely besieged. Rise of the power of Dionysius at Syracuse.

404. Athens surrenders. End of the Peloponnesian war. The ascendancy of Sparta complete throughout Greece.

403. Thrasybulus, aided by the Thebans and with the connivance of one of the Spartan kings, liberates Athens from the Thirty Tyrants, and restores the democracy.

401. Cyrus the Younger commences his expedition into Upper Asia to dethrone his brother Artaxerxes Mnemon. He takes with him an auxiliary force of ten thousand Greeks. He in killed in battle at Cunaxa; and the ten thousand, led by Xenophon, effect their retreat in spite of the Persian armies and the natural obstacles of their march.

399. In this, and the five following years, the Lacedaemonians under Agesilaus and other commanders, carry on war against the Persian satraps in Asia Minor.

396. Syracuse is besieged by the Carthaginians, and successfully defended by Dionysius.

394. Rome makes her first great stride in the career of conquest by the capture of Veii.

393. The Athenian admiral Conon, in conjunction with the Persian satrap Pharnabazus, defeats the Lacedaemonian fleet off Cnidus, and restores the fortifications of Athens. Several of the former allies of Sparta in Greece carry on hostilities against her.

388. The nations of Northern Europe now first appear in authentic history. The Gauls overrun great part of Italy, and burn Rome. Rome recovers from the blow, but her old enemies, the Aequians and Volscians, are left completely crushed by the Gallic invaders.

387. The peace of Antalcidas is concluded among the Greeks by the mediation, and under the sanction, of the Persian king.

378 to 361. Fresh wars in Greece. Epaminondas raises Thebes to be the leading state of Greece, and the supremacy of Sparta is destroyed at the battle of Leuctra. Epaminondas is killed in gaining the victory of Mantinea, and the power of Thebes falls with him. The Athenians attempt a balancing system between Sparta and Thebes.

359. Philip becomes king of Macedon.

357. The Social War breaks out in Greece, and lasts three years. Its result checks the attempt of Athens to regain her old maritime empire.

356. Alexander the Great is born.

343. Rome begins her wars with the Samnites: they extend over a period of fifty years. The result of this obstinate contest is to secure for her the dominion of Italy.

340. Fresh attempts of the Carthaginians upon Syracuse. Timoleon defeats them with great slaughter.

338. Philip defeats the confederate armies of Athens and Thebes at Chaeronea, and the Macedonian supremacy over Greece is firmly established.

336. Philip is assassinated, and Alexander the Great becomes king of Macedon. He gains several victories over the northern barbarians who had attacked Macedonia, and destroys Thebes, which, in conjunction with Athens, had taken up arms against the Macedonians.

334. Alexander passes the Hellespont.

CHAPTER III.
THE BATTLE OF ARBELA, B.C. 331.

"Alexander deserves the glory which he has enjoyed for so many centuries and among all nations; but what if he had been beaten at Arbela having the Euphrates, the Tigris, and the deserts in his rear, without any strong places of refuge, nine hundred leagues from Macedonia?"—NAPOLEON.

Asia beheld with astonishment and awe the uninterrupted progress of a hero, the sweep of whose conquests was as wide and rapid as that of her own barbaric kings, or the Scythian or Chaldaean hordes; but, far unlike the transient whirlwinds of Asiatic warfare, the advance of the Macedonian leader was no less deliberate than rapid; at every step the Greek power took root,

and the language and the civilization of Greece were planted from the shores of the Aegean to the banks of the Indus, from the Caspian and the great Hyrcanian plain to the cataracts of the Nile; to exist actually for nearly a thousand years, and in their effects to endure for ever."—ARNOLD.

…the rapidity and extent of Alexander's conquests have through all ages challenged admiration and amazement, the grandeur of genius which he displayed in his schemes of commerce, civilization, and of comprehensive union and unity amongst nations, has, until lately, been comparatively unhonored. This long-continued depreciation was of early date. The ancient rhetoricians—a class of babblers, a school for lies and scandal, as Niebuhr justly termed them—chose among the stock themes for their commonplaces, the character and exploits of Alexander…Arrian, who wrote his history of Alexander when Hadrian was emperor of the Roman world, and when the spirit of declamation and dogmatism was at its full height, but who was himself, unlike the dreaming pedants of the schools, a statesman and a soldier of practical and proved ability, well rebuked the malevolent aspersions which he heard continually thrown upon the memory of the great conqueror of the East. He truly says, "Let the man who speaks evil of Alexander not merely bring forward those passages of Alexander's life which were really evil, but let him collect and review all the actions of Alexander, and then let him thoroughly consider first who and what manner of man he himself is, and what has been his own career; and then let him consider who and what manner of man Alexander was, and to what an eminence of human grandeur HE arrived. Let him consider that Alexander was a king, and the undisputed lord of the two continents; and that his name is renowned throughout the whole earth. Let the evil-speaker against Alexander bear all this in mind, and then let him reflect on his own insignificance, the pettiness of his own circumstances and affairs, and the blunders that he makes about these, paltry and trifling as they are. Let him then ask himself whether he is a fit person to censure and revile such a man as Alexander. I believe that there was in his time no nation of men, no city, nay, no single individual, with whom Alexander's name had not become a familiar word. I therefore hold that such a man, who was like no ordinary mortal was not born into the world without some special providence." [Arrian, lib. vii. AD FINEM.]

…Napoleon selected Alexander as one of the seven greatest generals whose noble deeds history has handed down to us, and from the study of whose campaigns the principles of war are to be learned. The critique of the greatest conqueror of modern times on the military career of the great conqueror of the old world, is no less graphic than true…The enduring importance of Alexander's conquests is to be estimated not by the duration of his own life and empire, or even by the duration of the kingdoms which his generals after his death formed out of the fragments of that mighty dominion. In every region of the world that he traversed, Alexander planted Greek settlements, and founded cities, in the populations of which the Greek element at once asserted its predominance. Among his successors, the Seleucids and the Ptolemies imitated their great captain in blending schemes of civilization, of commercial intercourse, and of literary and scientific research with all their enterprises of military aggrandizement, and with all their systems of civil administration…These considerations invest the Macedonian triumphs in the East with never-dying interest, such as the most showy and sanguinary successes of mere "low ambition and the pride of kings," however they may dazzle for a moment, can never retain with posterity…Alexander's victory at Arbela…broke the monotony, of the Eastern world by the impression of Western energy and superior civilization…

…Arbela, the city which has furnished its name to the decisive battle that gave Asia to Alexander, lies more than twenty miles from the actual scene of conflict. The little village then named Gaugamela is close to the spot where the armies met, but has ceded the honor of naming the battle to its more euphonious neighbor. Gaugamela is situated in one of the wide plains that lie between the Tigris and the mountains of Kurdistan. A few undulating hillocks diversify the surface of this sandy track; but the ground is generally level, and admirably qualified for the evolutions of cavalry, and also calculated to give the larger of two armies the full advantage of numerical superiority. The Persian King (who before he came to the throne, had proved his personal valor as a soldier, and his skill as a general) had wisely selected this region for the third and decisive encounter between his forces and the invaders. The previous defeats of his troops, however severe they had been, were not looked on as irreparable. The Granicus had been fought by his generals rashly and without mutual concert. And, though Darius himself had commanded and been beaten at Issus, that defeat might be attributed to the disadvantageous nature of the ground; where, cooped up between the mountains, the river, and the sea, the numbers of the Persians confused and clogged alike the general's skill and the soldiers' prowess, so that their very strength became their weakness. Here, on the broad plains of Kurdistan, there was scope for Asia's largest host to array its lines, to wheel, to skirmish, to condense or expand its squadrons, to maneuver, and to charge at will. Should Alexander and his scanty band dare to plunge into that living sea of war, their destruction seemed inevitable.

Darius felt, however, the critical nature to himself as well as to his adversary of the coming encounter. He could not hope to retrieve the consequences of a third overthrow. The great cities of Mesopotamia and Upper Asia, the central provinces of the Persian empire, were certain to be at the mercy of the victor. Darius knew also the Asiatic character well enough to be aware how it yields to the prestige of success, and the apparent career of destiny. He felt that the diadem was now either to be firmly replaced on his own brow, or to be irrevocably transferred to the head of his European conqueror. He, therefore, during the long interval left him after the battle of Issus, while Alexander was subjugating Syria and Egypt, assiduously busied himself in selecting the best troops which his vast empire supplied, and in training his varied forces to act together with some uniformity of discipline and system…Besides these picked troops, contingents also came in from the numerous other provinces that yet obeyed the Great King. Altogether, the horse are said to have been forty thousand, the scythe-bearing chariots two hundred, and the armed elephants fifteen in number. The amount of the infantry is uncertain; but the knowledge which both ancient and modern times supply of the usual character of Oriental armies, and of their populations of camp-followers, may warrant us in believing that many myriads were prepared to fight, or to encumber those who fought, for the last Darius.

The position of the Persian king near Mesopotamia was chosen with great military skill…Marching eastward from Syria, Alexander would, on crossing the Euphrates, arrive at the vast Mesopotamian plains. The wealthy capitals of the empire, Babylon, Susa, and Persepolis, would then lie to his south; and if he marched down through Mesopotamia to attack them, Darius might reasonably hope to follow the Macedonians with his immense force of cavalry, and, without even risking a pitched battle, to harass and finally overwhelm them…If, on the contrary, Alexander should defer his march against Babylon, and first seek an encounter with the Persian army, the country on each side of the Tigris in this latitude was highly advantageous for such an army as Darius commanded; and he had close in his rear the mountainous districts of Northern Media, where he himself had in early life been satrap, where he had acquired reputation as a soldier and a general, and where he justly expected to find loyalty to his person, and a safe refuge in case of defeat…His great antagonist came on across the Euphrates against him, at the head of an army which…consisted of forty thousand foot, and seven thousand horse. In studying the campaigns of Alexander, we possess the peculiar advantage of deriving our information from two of Alexander's generals of division, who bore an important part in all his enterprises. Aristobulus and Ptolemy (who afterwards became king of Egypt) kept regular journals of the military events which they witnessed…

…the strength of Alexander's army, seems reasonable when we take into account both the losses which he had sustained, and the reinforcements which he had received since he left Europe…The army which Alexander now led was wholly composed of veteran troops in the highest possible state of equipment and discipline, enthusiastically devoted to their leader, and full of confidence in his military genius and his victorious destiny.

The celebrated Macedonian phalanx formed the main strength of his infantry. This force had been raised and organized by his father Philip, who on his accession to the Macedonian throne needed a numerous and quickly-formed army, and who, by lengthening the spear of the ordinary Greek phalanx, and increasing the depth of the files, brought the tactic of armed masses to the greatest efficiency of which it was capable with such materials as he possessed. [See Niebuhr's Hist. of Rome, iii. 488.] He formed his men sixteen deep, and placed in their grasp the sarissa, as the Macedonian pike was called, which was four-and-twenty feet in length, and when couched for action, reached eighteen feet in front of the soldier: so that, as a space of about two feet was allowed between the ranks, the spears of the five files behind him projected in advance of each front-rank man. The phalangite soldier was fully equipped in the defensive armor of the regular Greek infantry. And thus the phalanx presented a ponderous and bristling mass, which as long as its order was kept compact, was sure to bear down all opposition. The defects of such an organization are obvious, and were proved in after years, when the Macedonians were opposed to the Roman legions. But it is clear that, under Alexander, the phalanx was not the cumbrous unwieldy body which it was at Cynoscephalae and Pydna. His men were veterans; and he could obtain from them an accuracy of movement and steadiness of evolution, such as probably the recruits of his father would only have floundered in attempting, and such as certainly were impracticable in the phalanx when handled by his successors: especially as under them it ceased to be a standing force, and became only a

Readings

militia. [See Niebuhr.] Under Alexander the phalanx consisted of an aggregate of eighteen thousand men, who were divided into six brigades of three thousand each. These were again subdivided into regiments and companies; and the men were carefully trained to wheel, to face about, to take more ground, or to close up, as the emergencies of the battle required. Alexander also arrayed in the intervals of the regiments of his phalangites, troops armed in a different manner, which could prevent their line from being pierced, and their companies taken in flank, when the nature of the ground prevented a close formation; and which could be withdrawn, when a favorable opportunity arrived for closing up the phalanx or any of its brigades for a charge, or when it was necessary to prepare to receive cavalry.

Besides the phalanx, Alexander had a considerable force of infantry who were called shield-bearers: they were not so heavily armed as the phalangites, or as was the case with the Greek regular infantry in general; but they were equipped for close fight, as well as for skirmishing, and were far superior to the ordinary irregular troops of Greek warfare. They were about six thousand strong. Besides these, he had several bodies of Greek regular infantry; and he had archers, slingers, and javelin-men, who fought also with broadsword and target. These were principally supplied to him by the highlanders of Illyria and Thracia. The main strength of his cavalry consisted in two chosen corps of cuirassiers, one Macedonian, and one Thessalian each of which was about fifteen hundred strong. They were provided with long lances and heavy swords, and horse as well as man was fully equipped with defensive armor. Other regiments of regular cavalry were less heavily armed, and there were several bodies of light horsemen, whom Alexander's conquests in Egypt and Syria had enabled him to mount superbly. A little before the end of August, Alexander crossed the Euphrates at Thapsacus, a small corps of Persian cavalry under Mazaeus retiring before him. Alexander was too prudent to march down through the Mesopotamian deserts, and continued to advance eastward with the intention of passing

the Tigris, and then, if he was unable to find Darius and bring him to action, of marching southward on the left side of that river along the skirts of a mountainous district where his men would suffer less from heat and thirst, and where provisions would be more abundant.

Darius, finding that his adversary was not to be enticed into the march through Mesopotamia against his capital, determined to remain on the battle-ground which he had chosen on the left of the Tigris; where, if his enemy met a defeat or a check, the destruction of the invaders would be certain with two such rivers as the Euphrates and the Tigris in their rear. The Persian king availed himself to the utmost of every advantage in his power. He caused a large space of ground to be carefully leveled for the operation of his scythe-armed chariots; and he deposited his military stores in the strong town of Arbela, about twenty miles in his rear...

On learning that Darius was with a large army on the left of the Tigris, Alexander hurried forward and crossed that river without opposition. He was at first unable to procure any certain intelligence of the precise position of the enemy, and after giving his army a short interval of rest, he marched for four days down the left bank of the river...On the fourth day of Alexander's southward march, his advanced guard reported that a body of the enemy's cavalry was in sight. He instantly formed his army in order for battle, and directing them to advance steadily, he rode forward at the head of some squadrons of cavalry, and charged the Persian horse whom he found before him. This was a mere reconnoitering party, and they broke and fled immediately; but the Macedonians made some prisoners, and from them Alexander found that Darius was posted only a few miles off and learned the strength of the army that he had with him. On receiving this news, Alexander halted, and gave his men repose for four days, so that they should go into action fresh and vigorous. He also fortified his camp, and deposited in it all his military stores, and all his sick and disabled soldiers; intending to advance upon the enemy with the serviceable part

508

of his army perfectly unencumbered. After this halt, he moved forward, while it was yet dark, with the intention of reaching the enemy, and attacking them at break of day. About half-way between the camps there were some undulations of the ground, which concealed the two armies from each other's view. But, on Alexander arriving at their summit, he saw by the early light the Persian host arrayed before him; and he probably also observed traces of some engineering operation having been carried on along part of the ground in front of them. Not knowing that these marks had been caused by the Persians having leveled the ground for the free use of their war-chariots, Alexander suspected that hidden pitfalls had been prepared with a view of disordering the approach of his cavalry. He summoned a council of war forthwith, some of the officers were for attacking instantly at all hazards, but the more prudent opinion of Parmenio prevailed, and it was determined not to advance farther till the battle-ground had been carefully surveyed.

Alexander halted his army on the heights; and taking with him some light-armed infantry and some cavalry, he passed part of the day in reconnoitering the enemy, and observing the nature of the ground which he had to fight on. Darius wisely refrained from moving from his position to attack the Macedonians on eminences which they occupied, and the two armies remained until night without molesting each other. On Alexander's return to his headquarters, he summoned his generals and superior officers together, and telling them that he well knew that their zeal wanted no exhortation, he besought them to do their utmost in encouraging and instructing those whom each commanded, to do their best in the next day's battle. They were to remind them that they were now not going to fight for a province, as they had hitherto fought, but they were about to decide by their swords the dominion of all Asia. Each officer ought to impress this upon his subalterns and they should urge it on their men. Their natural courage required no long words to excite its ardor: but they should be reminded of the paramount importance of steadiness in action. The silence in the ranks must

be unbroken as long as silence was proper; but when the time came for the charge, the shout and the cheer must be full of terror for the foe. The officers were to be alert in receiving and communicating orders; and every one was to act as if he felt that the whole result of the battle depended on his own single good conduct.

Having thus briefly instructed his generals, Alexander ordered that the army should sup, and take their rest for the night.

Darkness had closed over the tents of the Macedonians, when Alexander's veteran general, Parmenio, came to him, and proposed that they should make a night attack on the Persians. The King is said to have answered, that he scorned to such a victory, and that Alexander must conquer openly and fairly.... Besides the confusion and uncertainty which are inseparable from night engagements, the value of Alexander's victory would have been impaired, if gained under circumstances which might supply the enemy with any excuse for his defeat, and encourage him to renew the contest. It was necessary for Alexander not only to beat Darius, but to gain such a victory as should leave his rival without apology for defeat, and without hope of recovery.

The Persians, in fact, expected, and were prepared to meet a night attack. Such was the apprehension that Darius entertained of it, that he formed his troops at evening in order of battle, and kept them under arms all night. The effect of this was, that the morning found them jaded and dispirited, while it brought their adversaries all fresh and vigorous against them…the great host of King Darius passed the night, that to many thousands of them was the last of their existence. The morning…dawned slowly to their wearied watching, and they could hear the note of the Macedonian trumpet sounding to arms, and could see King Alexander's forces descend from their tents on the heights, and form in order of battle on the plain…

There was deep need of skill, as well as of valor, on Alexander's side; and few battlefields have witnessed more consummate generalship than was now displayed by the Macedonian king. There were no natural barriers by which he could protect his flanks; and not only was he certain to be overlapped on either wing by the vast lines of the Persian army, but there was imminent risk of their circling round him and charging him in the rear, while he advanced against their centre. He formed, therefore, a second or reserve line, which was to wheel round, if required, or to detach troops to either flank; as the enemy's movements might necessitate: and thus, with their whole army ready at any moment to be thrown into one vast hollow square, the Macedonians advanced in two lines against the enemy, Alexander himself leading on the right wing, and the renowned phalanx forming the centre, while Parmenio commanded on the left.

Such was the general nature of the disposition which Alexander made of his army…The eight troops of the royal horse-guards formed the right of Alexander's line…Then came the shield-bearing infantry…Then came the phalanx, in six brigades…Then came the infantry of the left wing, under the command of Craterus. Next to Craterus's infantry were placed the cavalry regiments of the …The Messalian cavalry, commanded by Philippus, were next, and held the extreme left of the whole army. The whole left wing was entrusted to the command of Parmenio, who had round his person the Pharsalian troop of cavalry, which was the strongest and best amid all the Thessalian horse-regiments.

The centre of the second line was occupied by a body of phalangite infantry, formed of companies, which were drafted for this purpose from each of the brigades of their phalanx. The officers in command of this corps were ordered to be ready to face about, if the enemy should succeed in gaining the rear of the army. On the right of this reserve of infantry, in the second line, and behind the royal horse-guards, Alexander placed half the Agrian light-armed infantry under Attalus, and with them Brison's body of Macedonian archers, and Cleander's regiment of foot. He also placed in this

part of his army Menidas's squadron of cavalry, and Aretes's and Ariston's light horse. Menidas was ordered to watch if the enemy's cavalry tried to turn the flank, and if they did so, to charge them before they wheeled completely round, and so take them in flank themselves. A similar force was arranged on the left of the second line for the same purpose. The Thracian infantry of Sitalces was placed there, and Coeranus's regiment of the cavalry of the Greek allies, and Agathon's troops of the Odrysian irregular horse. The extreme left of the second line in this quarter was held by Andromachus's cavalry. A division of Thracian infantry was left in guard of the camp. In advance of the right wing and centre was scattered a number of light-armed troops, of javelin-men and bowmen, with the intention of warding off the charge of the armed chariots…Conspicuous by the brilliancy of his armor, and by the chosen band of officers who were round his person, Alexander took his own station, as his custom was, in the right wing, at the head of his cavalry: and when all the arrangements for the battle were complete, and his generals were fully instructed how to act in each probable emergency, he began to lead his men towards the enemy.

It was ever his custom to expose his life freely in battle, and to emulate the personal prowess of his great ancestor, Achilles. Perhaps in the bold enterprise of conquering Persia, it was politic for Alexander to raise his army's daring to the utmost by the example of his own heroic valor: and, in his subsequent campaigns, the love of the excitement, of "the rapture of the strife," may have made him, like Murat, continue from choice a custom which he commenced from duty. But he never suffered the ardor of the soldier to make him lose the coolness of the general; and at Arbela, in particular, he showed that he could act up to his favorite Homeric maxim.

Great reliance had been placed by the Persian king on the effects of the scythe-bearing chariots. It was designed to launch these against the Macedonian phalanx, and to follow them up by a heavy charge of cavalry, which it was hoped would find the ranks of the spearmen disordered by the rush of the chariots, and easily destroy this most formidable part of Alexander's force. In front, therefore, of the Persian centre, where Darius took his station, and which it was supposed the phalanx would attack, the ground had been carefully leveled and smoothed, so as to allow the chariots to charge over it with their full sweep and speed. As the Macedonian army approached the Persian, Alexander found that the front of his whole line barely equaled the front of the Persian centre, so that he was outflanked on his right by the entire left-wing of the enemy, and by their entire right-wing on his left. His tactics were to assail some one point of the hostile army, and gain a decisive advantage; while he refused, as far as possible, the encounter along the rest of the line. He therefore inclined his order of march to the right so as to enable his right wing and centre to come into collision with the enemy on as favorable terms as possible though the maneuver might in some respects compromise his left.

The effect of this oblique movement was to bring the phalanx and his own wing nearly beyond the limits of the ground which the Persians had prepared for the operations of the chariots; and Darius, fearing to lose the benefit of this arm against the most important parts of the Macedonian force, ordered the Scythian and Bactrian cavalry, who were drawn up on his extreme left, to charge round upon Alexander's right wing, and check its further lateral progress. Against these assailants Alexander sent from his second line Menidas's cavalry. As these proved too few to make head against the enemy, he ordered Ariston also from the second line with his light horse, and Cleander with his foot, in support of Menidas. The Bactrians and Scythians now began to give way, but Darius reinforced them by the mass of Bactrian cavalry from his main line, and an obstinate cavalry fight now took place. The Bactrians and Scythians were numerous, and were better armed than the horsemen under Menidas and Ariston; and the loss at first was heaviest on the Macedonian side. But still the European cavalry stood the charge of the Asiatics, and at last, by their superior discipline, and by acting in

squadrons that supported each other, instead of fighting in a confused mass like the barbarians, the Macedonians broke their adversaries, and drove them off the field...Darius, now directed the scythe-armed chariots to be driven against Alexander's horse-guards and the phalanx; and these formidable vehicles were accordingly sent rattling across the plain, against the Macedonian line...The object of the chariots was to create unsteadiness in the ranks against which they were driven, and squadrons of cavalry followed close upon them, to profit by such disorder. But the Asiatic chariots were rendered ineffective at Arbela by the light-armed troops whom Alexander had specially appointed for the service, and who, wounding the horses and drivers with their missile weapons, and running alongside so as to cut the traces or seize the reins, marred the intended charge; and the few chariots that reached the phalanx passed harmlessly through the intervals which the spearmen opened for them, and were easily captured in the rear.

A mass of the Asiatic cavalry was now, for the second time, collected against Alexander's extreme right, and moved round it, with the view of gaining the flank of his army. At the critical moment, Aretes, with his horsemen from Alexander's second line, dashed on the Persian squadrons when their own flanks were exposed by this evolution. While Alexander thus met and baffled all the flanking attacks of the enemy with troops brought up from his second line, he kept his own horse-guards and the rest of the front line of his wing fresh, and ready to take advantage of the first opportunity for striking a decisive blow. This soon came. A large body of horse, who were posted on the Persian left wing nearest to the centre, quitted their station, and rode off to help their comrades in the cavalry fight that still was going on at the extreme right of Alexander's wing against the detachments from his second line. This made a huge gap in the Persian array, and into this space Alexander instantly dashed with his guard; and then pressing towards his left, he soon began to make havoc in the left flank of the Persian centre. The shield-bearing infantry now charged also among the reeling masses of the Asiatics; and five of the brigades of the phalanx, with the irresistible might of their sarissas, bore down the Greek mercenaries of Darius, and dug their way through the Persian centre. In the early part of the battle, Darius had showed skill and energy; and he now for some time encouraged his men, by voice and example, to keep firm. But the lances of Alexander's cavalry, and the pikes of the phalanx now gleamed nearer and nearer to him. His charioteer was struck down by a javelin at his side; and at last Darius's nerve failed him; and, descending from his chariot, he mounted on a fleet horse and galloped from the plain, regardless of the state of the battle in other parts of the field, where matters were going on much more favorably for his cause, and where his presence might have done much towards gaining a victory.

Alexander's operations with his right and centre had exposed his left to an immensely preponderating force of the enemy. Parmenio kept out of action as long as possible; but Mazaeus, who commanded the Persian right wing, advanced against him, completely outflanked him, and pressed him severely with reiterated charges by superior numbers. Seeing the distress of Parmenio's wing, Simmias, who commanded the sixth brigade of the phalanx, which was next to the left wing, did not advance with the other brigades in the great charge upon the Persian centre, but kept back to cover Parmenio's troops on their right flank; as otherwise they would have been completely surrounded and cut off from the rest of the Macedonian army. By so doing, Simmias had unavoidably opened a gap in the Macedonian left centre; and a large column of Indian and Persian horse, from the Persian right centre, had galloped forward through this interval, and right through the troops of the Macedonian second line. Instead of then wheeling round upon Sarmenio, or upon the rear of Alexander's conquering wing, the Indian and Persian cavalry rode straight on to the Macedonian camp, overpowered the Thracians who were left in charge of it, and began to plunder. This was stopped by the phalangite troops of the second line, who, after the enemy's horsemen had rushed by them, faced about,

countermarched upon the camp, killed many of the Indians and Persians in the act of plundering, and forced the rest to ride off again. Just at this crisis, Alexander had been recalled from his pursuit of Darius, by tidings of the distress of Parmenio, and of his inability to bear up any longer against the hot attacks of Mazaeus. Taking his horse-guards with him, Alexander rode towards the part of the field where his left wing was fighting; but on his way thither he encountered the Persian and Indian cavalry, on their return from his camp.

These men now saw that their only chance of safety was to cut their way through; and in one huge column they charged desperately upon the Macedonians. There was here a close hand-to-hand fight, which lasted some time, and sixty of the royal horse-guards fell, and three generals, who fought close to Alexander's side, were wounded. At length the Macedonian, discipline and valor again prevailed, and a large number of the Persian and Indian horsemen were cut down; some few only succeeded in breaking through and riding away. Relieved of these obstinate enemies, Alexander again formed his horse-guards, and led them towards Parmenio; but by this time that general also was victorious. Probably the news of Darius's flight had reached Mazaeus, and had damped the ardor of the Persian right wing; while the tidings of their comrades' success must have proportionally encouraged the Macedonian forces under Parmenio. His Thessalian cavalry particularly distinguished themselves by their gallantry and persevering good conduct; and by the time that Alexander had ridden up to Parmenio, the whole Persian army was in full flight from the field.

It was of the deepest importance to Alexander to secure the person of Darius, and he now urged on the pursuit. The river Lycus was between the field of battle and the city of Arbela, whither the fugitives directed their course, and the passage of this river was even more destructive to the Persians than the swords and spears of the Macedonians had been in the engagement…The narrow bridge was soon choked up by the flying thousands who rushed towards it, and vast numbers of the Persians threw themselves, or were hurried by others, into the rapid stream, and perished in its waters. Darius had crossed it, and had ridden on through Arbela without halting. Alexander reached that city on the next day, and made himself master of all Darius's treasure and stores; but the Persian king unfortunately for himself, had fled too fast for his conqueror: he had only escaped to perish by the treachery of his Bactrian satrap, Bessus.

A few days after the battle Alexander entered Babylon, "the oldest seat of earthly empire" then in existence, as its acknowledged lord and master. There were yet some campaigns of his brief and bright career to be accomplished. Central Asia was yet to witness the march of his phalanx. He was yet to effect that conquest of Afghanistan… His generalship, as well as his valor, were yet to be signalized on the banks of the Hydaspes, and the field of Chillianwallah…annexing the Punjab …. But the crisis of his career was reached; the great object of his mission was accomplished; and the ancient Persian empire, which once menaced all the nations of the earth with subjection, was irreparably crushed, when Alexander had won his crowning victory at Arbela.

SYNOPSIS OF EVENTS BETWEEN THE BATTLE OF ARBELA AND THE BATTLE OF THE METAURUS.

B.C. 330. The Lacedaemonians endeavor to create a rising in Greece against the Macedonian power; they are defeated by Antipater, Alexander's viceroy; and their king, Agis, falls in the battle.

330 to 327. Alexander's campaigns in Upper Asia.

327, 326. Alexander marches through, Afghanistan to the Punjab. He defeats Porus. His troops refuse to march towards the Ganges, and he commences the descent of the Indus. On his march he attacks and subdues several Indian tribes, among others the Malli; in the storming of whose capital (Mooltan), he is severely wounded.

He directs his admiral, Nearchus, to sail round from the Indus to the Persian Gulf; and leads the army back across Scinde and Beloochistan.

324. Alexander returns to Babylon.

323. Alexander dies at Babylon. On his death being known at Greece, the Athenians, and others of the southern states, take up arms to shake off the domination of Macedon. They are at first successful; but the return of some of Alexander's veterans from Asia enables Antipater to prevail over them.

317 to 289. Agathocles is tyrant of Syracuse; and carries on repeated wars with the Carthaginians; in the course of which (311) he invades Africa, and reduces the Carthaginians to great distress.

306. After a long series of wars with each other, and after all the heirs of Alexander had been murdered, his principal surviving generals assume the title of king, each over the provinces which he has occupied. The four chief among them were Antigonus, Ptolemy, Lysimachus, and Seleucus. Antipater was now dead, but his son Cassander succeeded to his power in Macedonia and Greece.

301. Seleucus and Lysimachus defeat Antigonus at Ipsus. Antigonus is killed in the battle.

280. Seleucus, the last of Alexander's captains, is assassinated. Of all Alexander's successors, Seleucus had formed the most powerful empire. He had acquired all the provinces between Phrygia and the Indus. He extended his dominion in India beyond the limits reached by Alexander. Seleucus had some sparks of his great master's genius in promoting civilization and commerce, as well as in gaining victories. Under his successors, the Seleucidae, this vast empire rapidly diminished; Bactria became independent, and a separate dynasty of Greek kings ruled there in the year 125, when it was overthrown by the Scythian tribes. Parthia threw off its allegiance to the Seleucidae in 250 B.C., and the powerful Parthian kingdom, which afterwards proved so formidable a foe to Rome, absorbed nearly all the provinces west of

the Euphrates, that had obeyed the first Seleucus. Before the battle of Ipsus, Mithridates, a Persian prince of the blood-royal of the Achaemenidae, had escaped to Pontus, and founded there the kingdom of that name.

Besides the kingdom of Seleucus, which, when limited to Syria, Palestine, and parts of Asia Minor, long survived; the most important kingdom formed by a general of Alexander was that of the Ptolemies in Egypt. The throne of Macedonia was long and obstinately contended for by Cassander, Polysperchon, Lysimachus, Pyrrhus, Antigonus, and others; but at last was secured by the dynasty of Antigonus Gonatas. The old republics of southern Greece suffered severely during these tumults, and the only Greek states that showed any strength and spirit were the cities of the Achaean league, the Aetolians, and the islanders of Rhodes.

290. Rome had now thoroughly subdued the Samnites and the Etruscans, and had gained numerous victories over the Cisalpine Gauls. Wishing to confirm her dominion in Lower Italy, she became entangled in a war with Pyrrhus, fourth king of Epirus, who was called over by the Tarentines to aid them. Pyrrhus was at first victorious, but in the year 275 was defeated by the Roman legions in a pitched battle…

264. The first Punic war begins. Its primary cause was the desire of both the Romans and the Carthaginians to possess themselves of Sicily. The Romans form a fleet, and successfully compete with the marine of Carthage…During the latter half of the war, the military genius of Hamilcar Barca sustains the Carthaginian cause in Sicily. At the end of twenty- four years, the Carthaginians sue for peace, though their aggregate loss in ships and men had been less than that sustained by the Romans since the beginning of the war. Sicily becomes a Roman province.

240 to 218. The Carthaginian mercenaries who had been brought back from Sicily to Africa, mutiny against Carthage, and nearly succeed in destroying her. After a sanguinary and desperate struggle, Hamilcar Barca crushes them. During this season of weakness to Carthage, Rome takes from her the island of Sardinia. Hamilcar Barca forms the project of obtaining compensation by conquests in Spain, and thus enabling Carthage to renew the struggle with Rome. He takes Hannibal (then a child) to Spain with him. He and, after his death, his brother, win great part of southern Spain to the Carthaginian interest. Hannibal obtains the command of the Carthaginian armies in Spain, 221 B.C., being then twenty-six years old. He attacks Saguntum, a city on the Ebro in alliance with Rome, which is the immediate pretext for the second Punic war.

During this interval Rome had to sustain a storm from the north. The Cisalpine Gauls, in 226, formed an alliance with one of the fiercest tribes of their brethren north of the Alps, and began a furious war against the Romans, which lasted six years. The Romans gave them several severe defeats, and took from them part of their territories near the Po. It was on this occasion that the Roman colonies of Cremona and Placentia were founded, the latter of which did such essential service to Rome in the second Punic war, by the resistance which it made to the army of Hasdrubal. A muster-roll was made in this war of the effective military force of the Romans themselves, and of those Italian states that were subject to them. The return showed a force of seven hundred thousand foot, and seventy thousand horse. Polybius mentions this muster.

228. Hannibal crosses the Alps and invades Italy.

CHAPTER IV.
THE BATTLE OF THE METAURUS, B.C. 207.

". . . The consul Nero, who made the unequalled march which deceived Hannibal, and defeated Hasdrubal, thereby accomplishing an achievement almost unrivalled in military annals. The first intelligence of his return, to Hannibal, was the sight of Hasdrubal's head thrown into his camp. When Hannibal saw this, he exclaimed with a sigh, that 'Rome would now be the mistress of the world.' To this victory of Nero's it might be owing that his imperial namesake reigned at all. But the infamy of the one has eclipsed the glory of the other. When the name of Nero is heard, who thinks of the consul! But such are human things."—BYRON.

About midway between Rimini and Ancona a little river falls into the Adriatic…That stream is still called the Metauro; and wakens by its name recollections of the resolute daring of ancient Rome, and of the slaughter that stained its current … when the combined consular armies of Livius and Nero encountered and crushed near its banks the varied hosts which Hannibal's brother was leading from the Pyrenees, the Rhone, the Alps, and the Po, to aid the great Carthaginian in his stern struggle to annihilate the growing might of the Roman Republic, and make the Punic power supreme over all the nations of the world.

…When the Metaurus witnessed the defeat and death of Hasdrubal, it witnessed the ruin of the scheme by which alone Carthage could hope to organize decisive success, the scheme of enveloping Rome at once from the north and the south of Italy by chosen armies, led by two sons of Hamilcar. [See Arnold, vol. iii, p. 387.] That battle was the determining crisis of the contest, not merely between Rome and Carthage, but between the two great families of the world, which then made Italy the arena of their oft-renewed contest for pre-eminence.

…It is difficult amid the glimmering light supplied by the allusions of the classical writers to gain a full idea of the character and institutions of Rome's great rival. But we can perceive how inferior Carthage was to her competitor in military resources; and how far less fitted than Rome she was to become the founder of centralized and centralizing dominion, that should endure for centuries, and fuse into imperial unity the narrow nationalities of the ancient races that dwelt around and near the shores of the Mediterranean Sea.

Carthage was originally neither the most ancient nor the most powerful of the numerous colonies which the Phoenicians planted on the coast of Northern Africa. But her advantageous position, the excellence of her…and the commercial and political energy of her citizens, gave her the ascendancy over Hippo, Utica, Leptis, and her other sister Phoenician cities in those regions; and she finally seduced them to a condition of dependency, similar to that which the subject allies of Athens occupied relatively to that once imperial city.… The Carthaginians did not seek to compete with the Greeks on the northeastern shores of the Mediterranean, or in the three inland seas which are connected with it; but they maintained an active intercourse with the Phoenicians, and through them with lower and Central Asia; and they, and they alone, after the decline and fall of Tyre, navigated the waters of the Atlantic. They had the monopoly of all the commerce of the world that was carried on beyond the Straits of Gibraltar.… It is indeed certain that the Carthaginians frequented the Cornish coast (as the Phoenicians had done before them) for the purpose of procuring tin; and there is every reason to believe that they sailed as far as the coasts of the Baltic for amber. When it is remembered that the mariner's compass was unknown in those ages, the boldness and skill of the seamen of Carthage, and the enterprise of her merchants, may be paralleled with any achievements that the history of modern navigation and commerce can supply.

…The Carthaginians abandoned the Aegean and the Pontus to the Greeks, but they were by no means disposed to relinquish to those rivals the commerce and the dominion of the coasts of the Mediterranean westward of Italy. For centuries the Carthaginians strove to make themselves masters of the islands that lie between Italy and Spain.

…With so many elements of success, with almost unbounded wealth with commercial and maritime activity, with a fertile territory, with a capital city of almost impregnable strength, with a constitution that ensured for centuries the blessings of, social order, with an aristocracy singularly fertile in men of the highest genius,

Carthage yet failed signally and calamitously in her contest for power with Rome.

…[There existed a] spirit of faction among their leading men, which prevented Hannibal in the second war from being properly reinforced and supported. But there were also more general causes why Carthage proved inferior to Rome. These were her position relatively to the mass of the inhabitants of the country which she ruled, and her habit of trusting to mercenary armies in her wars.

Our clearest information as to the different races of men in and about Carthage is derived from Diodorus Siculus. [Vol. ii. p. 447, Wesseling's ed.] That historian enumerates four different races: first, he mentions the Phoenicians who dwelt in Carthage: next, he speaks of the Liby-Phoenicians; these, he tells us, dwelt in many of the maritime cities, and were connected by intermarriages with the Phoenicians, which was the cause of their compound name: thirdly, he mentions the Libyans, the bulk and the most ancient part of the population, hating the Carthaginians intensely, on account of the oppressiveness of their domination: lastly, he names the Numidians, the nomad tribes of the frontier.

It is evident, from this description, that the native Libyans were a subject class, without franchise or political rights; and, accordingly, we find no instance specified in history of a Libyan holding political office or military command. The half-castes, the Liby-Phoenicians, seem to have been sometimes sent out as colonists; [See the "Periplus" of Hanno.] but it may be inferred, from what Diodorus says of their residence, that they had not the right of the citizenship of Carthage: and only a solitary case occurs of one of this race being entrusted with authority, and that, too, not emanating from the home government. This is the instance of the officer sent by Hannibal to Sicily, after the fall of Syracuse…and it is expressly mentioned what indignation was felt by the Carthaginian commanders in the island that this half-caste should control their operations.

With respect to the composition of their armies, it is observable that, though thirsting for extended empire, and though some of the leading men became generals of the highest order, the Carthaginians, as a people, were anything but personally warlike. As long as they could hire mercenaries to fight for them, they had little appetite for the irksome training, and they grudged the loss of valuable time, which military service would have entailed on themselves.

As Michelet remarks, "The life of an industrious merchant, of a Carthaginian, was too precious to be risked, as long as it was possible to substitute advantageously for it that of a barbarian from Spain or Gaul. Carthage knew, and could tell to a drachma, what the life of a man of each nation came to. A Greek was worth more than a Campanian, a Campanian worth more than a Gaul or a Spaniard. When once this tariff of blood was correctly made out, Carthage began a war as a mercantile speculation. She tried to make conquests in the hope of getting new mines to work, or to open fresh markets for her exports. In one venture she could afford to spend fifty thousand mercenaries, in another, rather more. If the returns were good, there was no regret felt for the capital that had been lavished in the investment; more money got more men, and all went on well." [Histoire Romaine, vol. ii. p. 40.]

Armies composed of foreign mercenaries have, in all ages, been as formidable to their employers as to the enemy against whom they were directed…. And even when we consider her armies with reference only to their efficiency in warfare, we perceive at once the inferiority of such bands of condottieri, brought together without any common bond of origin, tactics, or cause, to the legions of Rome, which at the time of the Punic wars were raised from the very flower of a hardy agricultural population trained in the strictest discipline, habituated to victory, and animated by the most resolute patriotism. And this shows also the transcendency of the genius of Hannibal, which could form such discordant materials into a compact organized force, and inspire them with the spirit of patient discipline and loyalty to their chief; so that they were true to him in his adverse as well as in his prosperous fortunes; and throughout the chequered series of his campaigns no panic rout ever disgraced a division under his command; no mutiny, or even attempt at mutiny, was ever known in his camp; and, finally, after fifteen years of Italian warfare, his men followed their old leader to Zama, "with no fear and little hope;"...and there, on that disastrous field, stood firm around him, his Old Guard, till Scipio's Numidian allies came up on their flank; when at last, surrounded and overpowered, the veteran battalions sealed their devotion to their general with their blood..."

It was in the spring of 207 B.C. that Hasdrubal, after skillfully disentangling himself from the Roman forces in Spain, and, after a march conducted with great judgment and little loss, through the interior of Gaul and the passes of the Alps, appeared in the country that now is the north of Lombardy, at the head of troops which he had partly brought out of Spain, and partly levied among the Gauls and Ligurians on his way. At this time Hannibal with his unconquered, and seemingly unconquerable army, had been eleven years in Italy, executing with strenuous ferocity the vow of hatred to Rome which had been sworn by him while yet a child at the bidding of his father, Hamilcar; who, as he boasted, had trained up his three sons, Hannibal, Hasdrubal, and Mago, like three lion's whelps, to prey upon the Romans. But Hannibal's latter campaigns had not been signalized by any such great victories as marked the first years of his invasion of Italy. The stern spirit of Roman resolution, ever highest in disaster and danger, had neither bent nor despaired beneath the merciless blows which "the dire African" dealt her in rapid succession at Trebia, at Thrasymene, and at Cannae. Her population was thinned by repeated slaughter in the field; poverty and actual scarcity wore down the survivors, through the fearful ravages which Hannibal's cavalry spread through their corn-fields, their pasture-lands, and their vineyards; many of her allies went over to the invader's side; and new

clouds of foreign war threatened her from Macedonia and Gaul. But Rome receded not. Rich and poor among her citizens vied with each other in devotion to their country. The wealthy placed their stores, and all placed their lives at the state's disposal. And though Hannibal could not be driven out of Italy, though every year brought its sufferings and sacrifices, Rome felt that her constancy had not been exerted in vain. If she was weakened by the continual strife, so was Hannibal also; and it was clear that the unaided resources of his army were unequal to the task of her destruction...

Hasdrubal had commanded the Carthaginian armies in Spain for some time, with varying but generally unpropitious fortune. He had not the full authority over the Punic forces in that country which his brother and his father had previously exercised. The faction at Carthage, which was at feud with his family, succeeded in fettering and interfering with his power; and other generals were from time to time sent into Spain, whose errors and misconduct caused the reverses that Hasdrubal met with...It is clear that in the year 208 B.C., at least, Hasdrubal outmaneuvered Publius Scipio, who held the command of the Roman forces in Spain; and whose object was to prevent him from passing the Pyrenees and marching upon Italy. Scipio expected that Hasdrubal would attempt the nearest route, along the coast of the Mediterranean; and he therefore carefully fortified and guarded the passes of the eastern Pyrenees. But Hasdrubal passed these mountains near their western extremity; and then, with a considerable force of Spanish infantry, with a small number of African troops, with some elephants and much treasure, he marched, not directly towards the coast of the Mediterranean, but in a north-eastern line towards the centre of Gaul. He halted for the winter in the territory of the Arverni, the modern Auvergne; and conciliated or purchased the good-will of the Gauls in that region so far, that he not only found friendly winter quarters among them, but great numbers of them enlisted under him, and on the approach of spring marched with him to invade Italy.

By thus entering Gaul at the southwest, and avoiding its southern maritime districts, Hasdrubal kept the Romans in complete ignorance of his precise operations and movements in that country; all that they knew was that Hasdrubal had baffled Scipio's attempts to detain him in Spain; that he had crossed the Pyrenees with soldiers, elephants, and money, and that he was raising fresh forces among the Gauls. The spring was sure to bring him into Italy; and then would come the real tempest of the war, when from the north and from the south the two Carthaginian armies, each under a son of the Thunderbolt, were to gather together around the seven hills of Rome. [Hamilcar was surnamed Barca, which means the Thunderbolt. Sultan Bajazet had the similar surname of Yilderim.]

In this emergency the Romans looked among themselves earnestly and anxiously for leaders fit to meet the perils of the coming campaign.

The senate recommended the people to elect, as one of their consuls, Caius Claudius Nero, a patrician of one of the families of the great Claudian house. Nero had served during the preceding years of the war, both against Hannibal in Italy, and against Hasdrubal in Spain; but it is remarkable that the histories, which we possess, record no successes as having been achieved by him either before or after his great campaign of the Metaurus. It proves much for the sagacity of the leading men of the senate, that they recognized in Nero the energy and spirit which were required at this crisis, and it is equally creditable to the patriotism of the people, that they followed the advice of the senate by electing a general who had no showy exploits to recommend him to their choice.

…The senators resolved that Livius should be put in nomination as consul with Nero…A quarrel had long existed between the two consuls, and the senators strove to effect a reconciliation between them before the campaign. Here again Livius for a long time obstinately resisted the wish of his fellow-senators. He said it was best for the state that he and Nero should continue to hate one another. Each would do his duty better, when he knew that he was watched by an enemy in the person of his own colleague. At last the entreaties of the senators prevailed, and Livius consented to forego the feud, and to co-operate with Nero in preparing for the coming struggle.

As soon as the winter snows were thawed, Hasdrubal commenced his march from Auvergne to the Alps. He experienced none of the difficulties which his brother had met with from the mountain tribes…They not only opposed no resistance to the passage of Hasdrubal, but many of them, out of the love of enterprise and plunder, or allured by the high pay that he offered, took service with him; and thus he advanced upon Italy with an army that gathered strength at every league. It is said, also, that some of the most important engineering works which Hannibal had constructed, were found by Hasdrubal still in existence, and materially favored the speed of his advance. He thus emerged into Italy from the Alpine valleys much sooner than had been anticipated. Many warriors of the Ligurian tribes joined him; and, crossing the river Po, he marched down its southern bank to the city of Placentia, which he wished to secure as a base for his future operations. Placentia resisted him as bravely as it had resisted Hannibal eleven years before; and for some time Hasdrubal was occupied with a fruitless siege before its walls.

Six armies were levied for the defense of Italy when the long- dreaded approach of Hasdrubal was announced…These numbers are fearfully emphatic of the extremity to which Rome was reduced, and of her gigantic efforts in that great agony of her fate. Not merely men, but money and military stores, were drained to the utmost; and if the armies of that year should be swept off by a repetition of the slaughters of Thrasymene and Cannae, all felt that Rome would cease to exist. Even if the campaign were to be marked by no decisive success on either side, her ruin seemed certain. In South Italy Hannibal had either detached Rome's allies from her, or had impoverished them by the ravages of his army. If Hasdrubal could have done the same in Upper Italy; if Etruria, Umbria, and Northern Latium had either revolted or been laid waste, Rome must have sunk beneath sheer starvation; for the hostile or desolated territory would have yielded no supplies of corn for her population; and money, to purchase it from abroad, there was none. Instant victory was a matter of life and death. Three of her six armies were ordered to the north, but the first of these was required to overawe the disaffected Etruscans. The second army of the north was pushed forward, under Porcius, the praetor, to meet and keep in, check the advanced troops of Hasdrubal; while the third, the grand army of the north, which was to be under the immediate command of the consul Livius, who had the chief command in all North Italy, advanced more slowly in its support. There were similarly three armies in the south, under the orders of the other consul Claudius Nero.

The lot had decided that Livius was to be opposed to Hasdrubal, and that Nero should face Hannibal. And "when all was ordered as themselves thought best, the two consuls went forth of the city; each his several way…"

Hannibal at this period occupied with his veteran but much reduced forces the extreme south of Italy. It had not been expected either by friend or foe, that Hasdrubal would effect his passage of the Alps so early in the year as actually occurred. And even when Hannibal learned that his brother was in Italy, and had advanced as far as Placentia, he was obliged to pause for further intelligence, before he himself commenced active operations, as he could not tell whether his brother might not be invited into Etruria, to aid the party there that was disaffected to Rome or whether he would march down by the Adriatic Sea. Hannibal led his troops out of their winter quarters in Bruttium, and marched northward as far as Canusium. Nero had his headquarters near Venusia, with an army which he had increased to forty thousand foot and two thousand five hundred horse, by incorporating under his own command some of the legions

which had been intended to set under other generals in the south. There was another Roman army twenty thousand strong, south of Hannibal, at Tarentum. The strength of that city secured this Roman force from any attack by Hannibal, and it was a serious matter to march northward and leave it in his rear, free to act against all his depots and allies in the friendly part of Italy, which for the last two or three campaigns had served him for a base of his operations. Moreover, Nero's army was so strong that Hannibal could not concentrate troops enough to assume the offensive against it without weakening his garrisons, and relinquishing, at least for a time, his grasp upon the southern provinces. To do this before he was certainly informed of his brother's operations would have been a useless sacrifice; as Nero could retreat before him upon the other Roman armies near the capital, and Hannibal knew by experience that a mere advance of his army upon the walls of Rome would have no effect on the fortunes of the war. In the hope, probably, of inducing Nero to follow him, and of gaining an opportunity of outmaneuvering the Roman consul and attacking him on his march, Hannibal moved into Lucania, and then back into Apulis; he again marched down into Bruttium, and strengthened his army by a levy of recruits in that district. Nero followed him, but gave him no chance of assailing him at a disadvantage…Hannibal returned to his former headquarters at Canusium, and halted there in expectation of further tidings of his brother's movements. Nero also resumed his former position in observation of the Carthaginian army.

…Meanwhile, Hasdrubal had raised the siege of Placentia, and was advancing towards Ariminum on the Adriatic, and driving before him the Roman army under Porcina…The Romans still fell back before Hasdrubal, beyond Ariminum, beyond the Metaurus, and as far as the little town of Sena, to the southeast of that river. Hasdrubal was not unmindful of the necessity of acting in concert with his brother. He sent messengers to Hannibal to announce his own line of march and to propose that they should unite their armies in South Umbria, and then wheel round against Rome. Those messengers traversed the greater part of

Italy in safety; but, when close to the object of their mission, were captured by a Roman detachment; and Hasdrubal's letter, detailing his whole plan of the campaign, was laid, not in his brother's hands, but in those of the commander of the Roman armies of the south. Nero saw at once the full importance of the crisis. The two sons of Hamilcar were now within two hundred miles of each other, and if Rome were to be saved, the brothers must never meet alive. Nero instantly ordered seven thousand picked men, a thousand being cavalry, to hold themselves in readiness for a secret expedition against one of Hannibal's garrisons; and as soon as night had set in, he hurried forward on his bold enterprise: but he quickly left the southern road towards Lucania, and wheeling round, pressed northward with the utmost rapidity towards Picenum. He had, during the preceding afternoon, sent messengers to Rome, who were to lay Hasdrubal's letters before the senate. There was a law forbidding a consul to make war or to march his army beyond the limits of the province assigned to him; but in such an emergency Nero did not wait for the permission of the senate to execute his project, but informed them that he was already on his march to join Livius against Hasdrubal. He advised them to send the two legions which formed the home garrison, on to Narnia, so as to defend that pass of the Flaminian road against Hasdrubal, in case he should march upon Rome before the consular armies could attack him. They were to supply the place of those two legions at Rome by a levy EN MASSE in the city, and by ordering up the reserve legion from Capua. These were his communications to the senate. He also sent horseman forward along his line of march, with orders to the local authorities to bring stores of provisions and refreshments of every kind to the roadside, and to have relays of carriages ready for the conveyance of the wearied soldiers. Such were the precautions which he took for accelerating his march; and when he had advanced some little distance from his camp, he briefly informed his soldiers of the real object of their expedition. He told them that there never was a design more seemingly audacious, and more really safe. He said

he was leading them to a certain victory, for his colleague had an army large enough to balance the enemy already, so that THEIR swords would decisively turn the scale. The very rumor that a fresh consul and a fresh army had come up, when heard on the battlefield (and he would take care that they should not be heard of before they were seen and felt) would settle the campaign. They would have all the credit of the victory, and of having dealt the final decisive blow, he appealed to the enthusiastic reception which they already met with on their line of march as a proof and an omen of their good fortune. [Livy. lib. xxvii. c. 45.] And, indeed, their whole path was amidst the vows and prayers and praises of their countrymen. The entire population of the districts through which they passed, flocked to the roadside to see and bless the deliverers of their country. Food, drink, and refreshments of every kind were eagerly pressed on their acceptance. Each peasant thought a favor was conferred on him, if one of Nero's chosen band would accept aught at his hands. The soldiers caught the full spirit of their leader. Night and day they marched forwards, taking their hurried meals in the ranks and resting by relays in the wagons which the zeal of the country-people provided, and which followed in the rear of the column.

…Nero had sent couriers forward to apprise his colleague of his project and of his approach; and by the advice of Livius, Nero so timed his final march as to reach the camp at Sena by night. According to a previous arrangement, Nero's men were received silently into the tents of their comrades, each according to his rank. By these means there was no enlargement of the camp that could betray to Hasdrubal the accession of force which the Romans had received. This was considerable; as Nero's numbers had been increased on the march by the volunteers, who offered themselves in crowds, and from whom he selected the most promising men, and especially the veterans of former campaigns. A council of war was held on the morning after his arrival, in which some advised that time should be given for Nero's men to refresh themselves, after the fatigue of such a march. But Nero vehemently opposed all delay…Nero's advice prevailed. It was resolved to fight directly; and before the consuls and praetor left the tent of Livius, the red ensign, which was the signal to prepare for immediate action, was hoisted, and the Romans forthwith drew up in battle array outside the camp.

Hasdrubal had been anxious to bring Livius and Porcius to battle, though he had not judged it expedient to attack them in their lines. And now, on hearing that the Romans offered battle, he also drew up his men, and advanced towards them. No spy or deserter had informed him of Nero's arrival; nor had he received any direct information that he had more than his old enemies to deal with. But as he rode forward to reconnoiter the Roman lines, he thought that their numbers seemed to have increased, and that the armor of some of them was unusually dull and stained. He noticed also that the horses of some of the cavalry appeared to be rough and out of condition, as if they had just come from a succession of forced marches. So also, though, owing to the precaution of Livius, the Roman camp showed no change of size, it had not escaped the quick ear of the Carthaginian general that the trumpet, which gave the signal to the Roman legions, sounded that morning once oftener than usual, as if directing the troops of some additional superior officer. Hasdrubal, from his Spanish campaigns, was well acquainted with all the sounds and signals of Roman war; and from all that he heard and saw, he felt convinced that both the Roman consuls were before him. In doubt and difficulty as to what might have taken place between the armies of the south, and probably hoping that Hannibal also was approaching, Hasdrubal determined to avoid an encounter with the combined Roman forces, and to endeavor to retreat upon Insubrian Gaul, where he would be in a friendly country, and could endeavor to re-open his communications with his brother. He therefore led his troops back into their camp; and, as the Romans did not venture on an assault upon his entrenchments, and Hasdrubal did not choose to commence his retreat in their sight, the day passed away in inaction. At the first watch of the night, Hasdrubal led his men silently out of their camp,

and moved northwards towards the Metaurus, in the hope of placing that river between himself and the Romans before his retreat was discovered. His guides betrayed him; and having purposely led him away from the part of the river that was fordable, they made their escape in the dark, and left Hasdrubal and his army wandering in confusion along the steep bank, and seeking in vain for a spot where the stream could be safely crossed. At last they halted; and when day dawned on them, Hasdrubal found that great numbers of his men, in their fatigue and impatience, had lost all discipline and subordination, and that many of his Gallic auxiliaries had got drunk, and were lying helpless in their quarters. The Roman cavalry was soon seen coming up in pursuit, followed at no great distance by the legions, which marched in readiness for an instant engagement. It was hopeless for Hasdrubal to think of continuing his retreat before them. The prospect of immediate battle might recall the disordered part of his troops to a sense of duty, and revive the instinct of discipline. He therefore ordered his men to prepare for action instantly, and made the best arrangement of them that the nature of the ground would permit.

…He seems to have been especially deficient in cavalry, and he had few African troops, though some Carthaginians of high rank were with him. His veteran Spanish infantry, armed with helmets and shields, and short cut-and-thrust swords, were the best part of his army. These, and his few Africans, he drew up on his right wing, under his own personal command. In the centre, he placed his Ligurian infantry, and on the left wing he placed or retained the Gauls, who were armed with long javelins and with huge broadswords and targets. The rugged nature of the ground in front and on the flank of this part of his line, made him hope that the Roman right wing would be unable to come to close quarters with these unserviceable barbarians, before he could make some impression with his Spanish veterans on the Roman left. This was the only chance that he had of victory or safety, and he seems to have done everything that good generalship could do to secure it. He placed his elephants in advance of his centre and right wing. He had caused the driver of each of them to be provided with a sharp iron spike and a mallet; and had given orders that every beast that became unmanageable, and ran back upon his own ranks, should be instantly killed, by driving the spike into the vertebra at the junction of the head and the spine. Hasdrubal's elephants were ten in number. We have no trustworthy information as to the amount of his infantry, but it is quite clear that he was greatly outnumbered by the combined Roman forces.

…of the forces that advanced on the Roman side to the battle of the Metaurus, Nero commanded the right wing, Livius the left, and the praetor Porcius had the command of the centre. "Both Romans and Carthaginians well understood how much depended upon the fortune of this day, and how little hope of safety there was for the vanquished. Only the Romans herein seemed to have had the better in conceit and opinion, that they were to fight with men desirous to have fled from them. And according to this presumption came Livius the consul, with a proud bravery, to give charge on the Spaniards and Africans, by whom he was so sharply entertained that victory seemed very doubtful. The Africans and Spaniards were stout soldiers, and well acquainted with the manner of the Roman fight. The Ligurians, also, were a hardy nation, and not accustomed to give ground; which they needed the less, or were able now to do, being placed in the midst. Livius, therefore, and Porcius found great opposition; and, with great slaughter on both sides, prevailed little or nothing. Besides other difficulties, they were exceedingly troubled by the elephants, that brake their first ranks, and put them in such disorder, as the Roman ensigns were driven to fall back; all this while Claudius Nero, laboring in vain against a steep hill, was unable to come to blows with the Gauls that stood opposite him, but out of danger. This made Hasdrubal the more confident, who, seeing his own left wing safe, did the more boldly and fiercely make impression on the other side upon the left wing of the Romans." ["Historie of the World," by Sir Walter Raleigh, p. 946.]

But at last Nero, who found that Hasdrubal refused his left wing, and who could not overcome the difficulties of the ground in the quarter assigned to him, decided the battle by another stroke of that military genius which had inspired his march. Wheeling a brigade of his best men round the rear of the rest of the Roman army, Nero fiercely charged the flank of the Spaniards and Africans. The charge was as successful as it was sudden. Rolled back in disorder upon each other, and overwhelmed by numbers, the Spaniards and Ligurians died, fighting gallantly to the last. The Gauls, who had taken little or no part in the strife of the day, were then surrounded, and butchered almost without resistance. Hasdrubal, after having, by the confession of his enemies, done all that a general could do, when he saw that the victory was irreparably lost, scorning to survive the gallant; host which he had led, and to gratify, as a captive, Roman cruelty and pride, spurred his horse into the midst of a Roman cohort; where, sword in hand, he met the death that was worthy of the son of Hamilcar and the brother of Hannibal.

Success the most complete had crowned Nero's enterprise. Returning as rapidly as he had advanced, he was again facing the inactive enemies in the south, before they even knew of his march. But he brought with him a ghastly trophy of what he had done. In the true spirit of that savage brutality which deformed the Roman national character, Nero ordered Hasdrubal's head to be flung into his brother's camp. Eleven years had passed since Hannibal had last gazed on those features. The sons of Hamilcar had then planned their system of warfare against Rome, which they had so nearly brought to successful accomplishment. Year after year had Hannibal been struggling in Italy, in the hope of one day hailing the arrival of him whom he had left in Spain; and of seeing his brother's eye flash with affection and pride at the junction of their irresistible hosts. He now saw that eye glazed in death and, in the agony of his heart, the great Carthaginian groaned aloud that he recognized his country's destiny…

SYNOPSIS OF EVENTS BETWEEN THE BATTLE OF THE METAURUS, B.C. 207, AND ARMININIUS'S VICTORY OVER THE ROMAN LEGIONS UNDER VARUS, A.D. 9.

B.C. 205 to 201. Scipio is made consul, and carries the war into Africa. He gains several victories there, and the Carthaginians recall Hannibal from Italy to oppose him. Battle of Zama in 201: Hannibal is defeated, and Carthage sues for peace. End of the second Punic war, leaving Rome confirmed in the dominion of Italy, Sicily, Sardinia, and Corsica, and also mistress of great part of Spain, and virtually predominant in North Africa.

200. Rome makes war upon Philip, king of Macedonia. She pretends to take the Greek cities of the Achaean league and the Aetolians under her protection as allies. Philip is defeated by the proconsul Flaminius at Cynocephalae, 198; and begs for peace. The Macedonian influence is now completely destroyed in Greece, and the Roman established in its stead, though Rome nominally acknowledged the independence of the Greek cities.

194. Rome makes war upon Antiochus, king of Syria. He is completely defeated at the battle of Magnesia, 192, and is glad to accept peace on conditions which leave him dependent upon Rome.

200-190. "Thus, within the short; space of ten years, was laid the foundation of the Roman authority in the East, and the general state of affairs entirely changed. If Rome was not yet the ruler, she was at least the arbitress of the world from the Atlantic to the Euphrates. The power of the three principal states was so completely humbled, that they durst not, without the permission of Rome, begin any new war; the fourth, Egypt, had already, in the year 201, placed herself under the guardianship of Rome; and the lesser powers followed of themselves: esteeming it an honor to be called the allies of Rome. With this name the nations were lulled into security, and brought under the Roman yoke; the new political

system of Rome was founded and strengthened partly by exciting and supporting the weaker states against the stronger, however unjust the cause of the former might be, and partly by factions which she found means to raise in every state, even the smallest."—(HEEREN.)

172. War renewed between Macedon and Rome. Decisive defeat of Perses, the Macedonian king, by Paulus Aemilius at Pydna, 168, Destruction of the Macedonian monarchy.

150. Rome oppresses the Carthaginians till they are driven to take up arms, and the third Punic war begins, Carthage is taken and destroyed by Scipio Aemilianus, 146, and the Carthaginian territory is made a Roman province.

146. In the same year in which Carthage falls, Corinth is stormed by the Roman army under Mummius. The Achaean league had been goaded into hostilities with Rome, by means similar to those employed against Carthage. The greater part of Southern Greece is made a Roman province, under the name of Achaia.

133. Numantium is destroyed by Scipio Aemilianus.

134. Commencement of the revolutionary century at Rome, I.E. from the time of the excitement produced by the attempts made by the Gracchi to reform the commonwealth, to the battle of Actium (B.C. 31), which established Octavianus Caesar as sole master of the Roman world. Throughout this period Rome was engaged in important foreign wars, most of which procured large accessions to her territory.

118-106. The Jugurthine war. Numidia is conquered, and made a Roman province.

113-101. The great and terrible war of the Cimbri and Teutones against Rome. These nations of northern warriors slaughter several Roman armies in Gaul, and in 102 attempt to penetrate into Italy. The military genius of Marius here saves his country; he defeats the Teutones near Aix, in

Provence; and in the following year he destroys the army of the Cimbri, who had passed the Alps, near Vercellae.

91-88. The war of the Italian allies against Rome. This was caused by the refusal of Rome to concede to them the rights of Roman citizenship. After a sanguine struggle, Rome gradually grants it.

89-86. First war of the Romans against Mithridates the Great, king of Pontus, who had overrun Asia Minor, Macedonia, and Greece. Sylla defeats his armies, and forces him to withdraw his forces from Europe. Sylla returns to Rome to carry on the civil war against the son and partisans of Marius. He makes himself Dictator.

74-64. The last Mithridatic wars. Lucullus, and after him Pompeius, command against the great King of Pontus, who at last is poisoned by his son, while designing to raise the warlike tribes of the Danube against Rome, and to invade Italy from the northeast. Great Asiatic conquests of the Romans. Besides the ancient province of Pergamus, the maritime countries of Bithynia, and nearly all Paphlagonia and Pontus, are formed into a Roman province, under the name of Bithynia; while on the southern coast Cilicia and Pamphylia form another, under the name of Cilicia; Phoenicia and Syria compose a third, under the name of Syria. On the other hand, Great Armenia is left to Tigranes; Cappodocia to Ariobarzanes; the Bosporus to Pharnaces; Judaea to Hyrcanus; and some other small states are also given to petty princes, all of whom remain dependent on Rome.

58-50. Caesar conquers Gaul.

54. Crassus attacks the Parthians with a Roman army, but is overthrown and killed at Carrhae in Mesopotamia. His lieutenant Cassius collects the wrecks of the army, and prevents the Parthians from conquering Syria.

49-45. The civil war between Caesar and the Pompeian party. Caesar drives Pompeius out of Italy, conquers his enemy's forces in Spain, and then passes into Greece, where Pompeius and the other aristocratic chiefs had assembled a large army. Caesar gives them a decisive defeat at the great battle of Pharsalia. Pompeius flies for refuge to Alexandria, where he is assassinated. Caesar, who had followed him thither, is involved in a war with the Egyptians, in which he is finally victorious. The celebrated Cleopatra is made Queen of Egypt. Caesar next marches into Pontus, and defeats the son of Mithridates, who had taken part in the war against him. He then proceeds to the Roman province of Africa, where some of the Pompeian chiefs had established themselves, aided by Juba, a native prince. He over throws them at the battle of Thapsus. He is again obliged to lead an army into Spain, where the sons of Pompeius had collected the wrecks of their father's party. He crushes the last of his enemies at the battle of Munda. Under the title of Dictator, he is the sole master of the Roman world.

44. Caesar is killed in the Senate-house; the Civil wars are soon renewed, Brutus and Cassius being at the head of the aristocratic party, and the party of Caesar being led by Mark Antony and Octavianus Caesar, afterwards Augustus.

42. Defeat and death of Brutus and Cassius at Philippi. Dissensions soon break out between Octavianus Caesar and Antony.

31. Antony is completely defeated by Octavianus Caesar at Actium. He flies to Egypt with Cleopatra. Octavianus pursues him. Antony and Cleopatra kill themselves. Egypt becomes a Roman province, and Octavianus Caesar is left undisputed master of Rome, and all that is Rome's…

CHAPTER V.
VICTORY OF ARMINIUS OVER THE
ROMAN LEGIONS UNDER VARUS, A.D. 9.

…Dark and disheartening, even to heroic spirits, must have seemed the prospects of Germany when Arminius planned the general rising of his countrymen against Rome. Half the land was occupied by Roman garrisons; and, what was worse, many of the Germans seemed patiently acquiescent in their state of bondage. The braver portion, whose patriotism could be relied on, was ill-armed and undisciplined; while the enemy's troops consisted of veterans in the highest state of equipment and training, familiarized with victory, and commanded by officers of proved skill and valor. The resources of Rome seemed boundless; her tenacity of purpose was believed to be invincible. There was no hope of foreign sympathy or aid; for "the self-governing powers that had filled the old world, had bent one after another before the rising power of Rome, and had vanished. The earth seemed left void of independent nations." [Ranke.]

The (German) chieftain knew well the gigantic power of the oppressor. Arminius was no rude savage, fighting out of mere animal instinct, or in ignorance of the might of his adversary. He was familiar with the Roman language and civilization; he had served in the Roman armies; he had been admitted to the Roman citizenship, and raised to the dignity of the equestrian order. It was part of the subtle policy of Rome to confer rank and privileges on the youth of the leading families in the nations which she wished to enslave. Among other young German chieftains, Arminius and his brother, who were the heads of the noblest house in the tribe of the Cherusci, had been selected as fit objects for the exercise of this insidious system. Roman refinements and dignities succeeded in denationalizing the brother, who assumed the Roman name of Flavius, and adhered to Rome throughout all her wars against his country. Arminius remained unbought by honors or wealth, uncorrupted by refinement or luxury…Often must the young chieftain, while meditating the exploit which has thus immortalized him, have anxiously revolved in his mind the fate of the many great men who had been crushed in the attempt which he was about to renew, the attempt to stay the chariot-wheels of triumphant Rome. Could he hope to succeed where Hannibal and Mithridates had perished?.... It was true that Rome was no longer the great military republic which for so many ages had shattered the kingdoms of the world. Her system of government was changed;

and, after a century of revolution and civil war, she had placed herself under the despotism of a single ruler. But the discipline of her troops was yet unimpaired, and her warlike spirit seemed unabated.

…While the progress of the Roman arms thus pressed the Germans from the south, still more formidable inroads had been made by the Imperial legions in the west. Roman armies, moving from the province of Gaul, established a chain of fortresses along the right as well as the left bank of the Rhine, and, in a series of victorious campaigns, advanced their eagles as far as the Elbe; which now seemed added to the list of vassal rivers, to the Nile, the Rhine, the Rhone, the Danube, the Tagus, the Seine, and many more, that acknowledged the supremacy of the Tiber. Roman fleets also, sailing from the harbors of Gaul along the German coasts, and up the estuaries, co-operated with the land-forces of the empire; and seemed to display, even more decisively than her armies, her overwhelming superiority over the rude Germanic tribes. Throughout the territory thus invaded, the Romans had, with their usual military skill, established chains of fortified posts; and a powerful army of occupation was kept on foot, ready to move instantly on any spot where a popular outbreak might be attempted.

Vast however, and admirably organized as the fabric of Roman power appeared on the frontiers and in the provinces, there was rottenness at the core. In Rome's unceasing hostilities with foreign foes, and, still more, in her long series of desolating civil wars, the free middle classes of Italy had almost wholly disappeared. Above the position which they had occupied, an oligarchy of wealth had reared itself: beneath that position a degraded mass of poverty and misery was fermenting. Slaves, the chance sweepings of every conquered country, shoals of Africans, Sardinians, Asiatics, Illyrians, and others, made up the bulk of the population of the Italian peninsula. The foulest profligacy of manners was general in all ranks. In universal weariness of revolution and civil war, and in consciousness of being too debased for self-government, the nation had submitted itself to the absolute authority of Augustus. Adulation was now the chief function of the senate: and the gifts of genius and accomplishments of art were devoted to the elaboration of eloquently false panegyrics [expressions of praise] upon the prince and his favorite courtiers. With bitter indignation must the German chieftain have beheld all this, and contrasted with it the rough worth of his own countrymen; their bravery, their fidelity to their word, their manly independence of spirit, their love of their national free institutions, and their loathing of every pollution and meanness. Above all, he must have thought of the domestic virtues that hallowed a German home; of the respect there shown to the female character, and of the pure affection by which that respect was repaid. His soul must have burned within him at the contemplation of such a race yielding to these debased Italians.

Still, to persuade the Germans to combine, in spite of their frequent feuds among themselves, in one sudden outbreak against Rome; to keep the scheme concealed from the Romans until the hour for action had arrived; and then, without possessing a single walled town, without military stores, without training, to teach his insurgent countrymen to defeat veteran armies, and storm fortifications, seemed so perilous an enterprise, that probably Arminius would have receded from it, had not a stronger feeling even than patriotism urged him on. Among the Germans of high rank who had most readily submitted to the invaders, and become zealous partisans of Roman authority, was a chieftain named Segestes. His daughter, Thusnelda, was pre-eminent among the noble maidens of Germany. Arminius had sought her hand in marriage; but Segestes, who probably discerned the young chief's disaffection to Rome, forbade his suit, and strove to preclude all communication between him and his daughter. Thusnelda, however, sympathized far more with the heroic spirit of her lover, than with the time serving policy of her father. An elopement baffled the precautions of Segestes; who, disappointed in his hope of preventing the marriage, accused Arminius, before the Roman governor, of having

carried off his daughter, and of planning treason against Rome. Thus assailed, and dreading to see his bride torn from him by the officials of the foreign oppressor, Arminius delayed no longer, but bent all his energies to organize and execute a general insurrection of the great mass of his countrymen, who hitherto had submitted in sullen inertness to the Roman dominion.

A change of governors had recently taken place, which, while it materially favored the ultimate success of the insurgents, served, by the immediate aggravation of the Roman oppressions which it produced, to make the native population more universally eager to take arms. Tiberius, who was afterwards emperor, had lately been recalled from the command in Germany, and sent into Pannonia to put down a dangerous revolt which had broken out against the Romans in that province. The German patriots were thus delivered from the stern supervision of one of the most auspicious of mankind, and were also relieved from having to contend against the high military talents of a veteran commander, who thoroughly understood their national character, and the nature of the country, which he himself had principally subdued. In the room of Tiberius, Augustus sent into Germany Quintilius Varus, who had lately returned from the proconsulate of Syria. Varus was a true representative of the higher classes of the Romans; among whom a general taste for literature, a keen susceptibility to all intellectual gratifications, a minute acquaintance with the principles and practice of their own national jurisprudence, a careful training in the schools of the rhetoricians, and a fondness for either partaking in or watching the intellectual strife of forensic oratory, had become generally diffused; without, however, having humanized the old Roman spirit of cruel indifference for human feelings and human sufferings, and without acting as the least check on unprincipled avarice and ambition, or on habitual and gross profligacy.... The Romans now habitually indulged in those violations of the sanctity of the domestic shrine …Arminius found among the other German chiefs many who sympathized with him in his indignation at their country's debasement, and many whom private wrongs had stung yet more deeply. There was little difficulty in collecting bold leaders for an attack on the oppressors, and little fear of the population not rising readily at those leaders' call. But to declare open war against Rome, and to encounter Varus's army in a pitched battle, would have been merely rushing upon certain destruction. Varus had three legions under him, a force which, after allowing for detachments, cannot be estimated at less than fourteen thousand Roman infantry. He had also eight or nine hundred Roman cavalry, and at least an equal number of horse and foot sent from the allied states, or raised among those provincials who had not received the Roman franchise.

It was not merely the number, but the quality of this force that made it formidable; and however contemptible Varus might be as a general, Arminius well knew how admirably the Roman armies were organized and officered, and how perfectly the legionaries understood every maneuver and every duty which the varying emergencies of a stricken field might require. Stratagem was, therefore, indispensable; and it was necessary to blind Varus to his schemes until a favorable opportunity should arrive for striking a decisive blow.

For this purpose the German confederates frequented the headquarters of Varus, which seem to have been near the centre of the modern country of Westphalia, where the Roman general conducted himself with all the arrogant security of the governor of a perfectly submissive province…Varus trusted implicitly to the respect which the Germans pretended to pay to his abilities as a judge, and to the interest which they affected to take in the forensic eloquence of their conquerors. Meanwhile a succession of heavy rains rendered the country more difficult for the operations of regular troops; and Arminius, seeing that the infatuation of Varus was complete, secretly directed the tribes near the Weser and the Ems to take up arms in open revolt against the Romans. This was represented to Varus as an occasion which required his prompt attendance at

the spot; but he was kept in studied ignorance of its being part of a concerted national rising; and he still looked on Arminius as his submissive vassal, whose aid he might rely on in facilitating the march of his troops against the rebels, and in extinguishing the local disturbance. He therefore set his army in motion, and marched eastward in a line parallel to the course of the Lippe. For some distance his route lay along a level plain; but on arriving at the tract between the curve of the upper part of that stream and the sources of the Ems, the country assumes a very different character; and here, in the territory of the modern little principality of Lippe, it was that Arminius had fixed the scene of his enterprise.

A woody and hilly region intervenes between the heads of the two rivers, and forms the water-shed of their streams. This region still retains the name (Teutoberger wald—Teutobergiensis saltus) which it bore in the days of Arminius. The nature of the ground has probably also remained unaltered. The eastern part of it, round Detmoldt, the present capital of the principality of Lippe, is described by a modern German scholar, Dr. Plate, as being "a table-land intersected by numerous deep and narrow valleys, which in some places form small plains, surrounded by steep mountains and rocks, and only accessible by narrow defiles. All the valleys are traversed by rapid streams, shallow in the dry season, but subject to sudden swellings in autumn and winter. The vast forests which cover the summits and slopes of the hills consist chiefly of oak; there is little underwood, and both men and horse would move with ease in the forests if the ground were not broken by gulleys, or rendered impracticable by fallen trees." This is the district to which Varus is supposed to have marched…Contrary to the usual strict principles of Roman discipline, Varus had suffered his army to be accompanied and impeded by an immense train of baggage-wagons, and by a rabble of camp followers; as if his troops had been merely changing their quarters in a friendly country. When the long array quitted the firm level ground, and began to wind its way among the woods, the marshes, and the ravines, the difficulties of the march, even without the intervention of an armed foe, became fearfully apparent. In many places the soil, sodden with rain, was impracticable for cavalry and even for infantry, until trees had been felled, and a rude causeway formed through the morass.

The duties of the engineer were familiar to all who served in the Roman armies. But the crowd and confusion of the columns embarrassed the working parties of the soldiery, and in the midst of their toil and disorder the word was suddenly passed through their ranks that the rear-guard was attacked by the barbarians. Varus resolved on pressing forward; but a heavy discharge of missiles from the woods on either flank taught him how serious was the peril, and he saw the best men falling round him without the opportunity of retaliation; for his light-armed auxiliaries, who were principally of Germanic race, now rapidly deserted, and it was impossible to deploy the legionaries on such broken ground for a charge against the enemy. Choosing one of the most open and firm spots which they could force their way to, the Romans halted for the night; and, faithful to their national discipline and tactics, formed their camp amid the harassing attacks of the rapidly thronging foes…On the morrow the Romans renewed their march; the veteran officers who served under Varus now probably directing the operations, and hoping to find the Germans drawn up to meet them; in which case they relied on their own superior discipline and tactics for such a victory as should reassure the supremacy of Rome. But Arminius was far too sage a commander to lead on his followers, with their unwieldy broadswords and inefficient defensive armor, against the Roman legionaries, fully armed with helmet, cuirass, greaves, and shield; who were skilled to commence the conflict with a murderous volley of heavy javelins, hurled upon the foe when a few yards distant, and then, with their short cut-and-thrust swords, to hew their way through all opposition; preserving the utmost steadiness and coolness, and obeying each word of command…Arminius suffered the Romans to march out from their camp, to form first in line for action, and then in column for marching, without

the show of opposition. For some distance Varus was allowed to move on, only harassed by slight skirmishes, but struggling with difficulty through the broken ground; the toil and distress of his men being aggravated by heavy torrents of rain, which burst upon the devoted legions as if the angry gods of Germany were pouring out the vials of their wrath upon the invaders. After some little time their van approached a ridge of high woody ground, which is one of the off-shoots of the great Hercynian forest, and is situated between the modern villages of Driburg and Bielefeld. Arminius had caused barricades of hewn trees to be formed here, so as to add to the natural difficulties of the passage. Fatigue and discouragement now began to betray themselves in the Roman ranks. Their line became less steady; baggage-wagons were abandoned from the impossibility of forcing them along; and, as this happened, many soldiers left their ranks and crowded round the wagons to secure the most valuable portions of their property; each was busy about his own affairs, and purposely slow in hearing the word of command from his officers. Arminius now gave the signal for a general attack. The fierce shouts of the Germans pealed through the gloom of the forests, and in thronging multitudes they assailed the flanks of the invaders, pouring in clouds of darts on the encumbered legionaries, as they struggled up the glens or floundered in the morasses, and watching every opportunity of charging through the intervals of the disjointed column, and so cutting off the communication between its several brigades. Arminius, with a chosen band of personal retainers round him, cheered on his countrymen by voice and example. He and his men aimed their weapons particularly at the horses of the Roman cavalry. The wounded animals, slipping about in the mire and their own blood, threw their riders, and plunged among the ranks of the legions, disordering all round them. Varus now ordered the troops to be countermarched, in the hope of reaching the nearest Roman garrison on the Lippe…But retreat now was as impracticable as advance; and the falling back of the Romans only augmented the courage of their assailants, and caused fiercer and more frequent charges on the flanks of the disheartened army. The Roman officer who commanded the cavalry, Numonius Vala, rode off with his squadrons, in the vain hope of escaping by thus abandoning his comrades. Unable to keep together, or force their way across the woods and swamps, the horsemen were overpowered in detail and slaughtered to the last man. The Roman infantry still held together and resisted, but more through the instinct of discipline and bravery than from any hope of success or escape. Varus, after being severely wounded in a charge of the Germans against his part of the column, committed suicide to avoid falling into the hands of those whom he had exasperated by his oppressions. One of the lieutenant-generals of the army fell fighting; the other surrendered to the enemy. But mercy to a fallen foe had never been a Roman virtue, and those among her legions who now laid down their arms in hope of quarter, drank deep of the cup of suffering which Rome had held to the lips of many a brave but unfortunate enemy. The infuriated Germans slaughtered their oppressors with deliberate ferocity; and those prisoners who were not hewn to pieces on the spot, were only preserved to perish by a more cruel death in cold blood.

The bulk of the Roman army fought steadily and stubbornly, frequently repelling the masses of the assailants, but gradually losing the compactness of their array, and becoming weaker and weaker beneath the incessant shower of darts and the reiterated assaults of the vigorous and unencumbered Germans. At last, in a series of desperate attacks the column was pierced through and through, two of the eagles captured, and the Roman host, which on the yester morning had marched forth in such pride and might, now broken up into confused fragments, either fell fighting beneath the overpowering numbers of the enemy, or perished in the swamps and woods in unavailing efforts at flight. Few, very few, ever saw again the left bank of the Rhine…

…Never was victory more decisive, never was the liberation of an oppressed people more instantaneous and complete. Throughout Germany the Roman garrisons were assailed and cut off; and, within a few weeks after Varus had fallen, the German soil was freed from the foot of an invader.

At Rome, the tidings of the battle was received with an agony of terror…how great was the awe which the Romans felt of the prowess of the Germans, if their various tribes could be brought to reunite for a common purpose…how weakened and debased the population of Italy had become…"Then Augustus, when he heard the calamity of Varus, rent his garments, and was in great affliction for the troops he had lost, and for terror respecting the Germans and the Gauls. And his chief alarm was, that he expected them to push on against Italy and Rome: and there remained no Roman youth fit for military duty, that were worth speaking of, and the allied populations that were at all serviceable had been wasted away. Yet he prepared for the emergency as well as his means allowed; and when none of the citizens of military age were willing to enlist he made them cast lots, and punished by confiscation of goods and disfranchisement every fifth man among those under thirty-five, and every tenth man of those above that age. At last, when he found that not even thus; could he make many come forward, he put some of them to death. So he made a conscription of discharged veterans and emancipated slaves, and collecting as large a force as he could, sent it, under Tiberius, with all speed into Germany."

…The Germans did not pursue their victory beyond their own territory. But that victory secured at once and for ever the independence of the Teutonic race. Rome sent, indeed, her legions again into Germany, to parade a temporary superiority; but all hopes of permanent conquest were abandoned by Augustus and his successors.

The blow which Arminius had struck never was forgotten, Roman fear disguised itself under the specious title of moderation; and the Rhine became the acknowledged boundary of the two nations until the fifth century of our era, when the Germans became the assailants, and carved with their conquering swords the provinces of Imperial Rome into the kingdoms of modern Europe.

...SYNOPSIS OF EVENTS BETWEEN ARMINIUS'S VICTORY OVER VARUS, AND THE BATTLE OF CHALONS.

A.D. 43. The Romans commence the conquest of Britain, Claudius being then Emperor of Rome. The population of this island was then Celtic. In about forty years all the tribes south of the Clyde were subdued, and their land made a Roman province.

68-60. Successful campaigns of the Roman general Corbulo against the Parthians.

64. First persecution of the Christians at Rome under Nero.

68-70. Civil wars in the Roman World. The emperors Nero, Galba, Otho, and Vitellius, cut off successively by violent deaths. Vespasian becomes emperor.

70. Jerusalem destroyed by the Romans under Titus.

83. Futile attack of Domitian on the Germans.

86. Beginning of the wars between the Romans and the Dacians.

98-117. Trajan, emperor of Rome. Under him the empire acquires its greatest territorial extent by his conquests in Dacia and in the East. His successor, Hadrian, abandons the provinces beyond the Euphrates, which Trajan had conquered.

138-180. Era of the Antonines.

167-176. A long and desperate war between Rome and a great confederacy of the German nations. Marcus Antoninus at last succeeds in repelling them.

192-197. Civil Wars throughout the Roman world. Severus becomes emperor. He relaxes the discipline of the soldiers. After his death in 211, the series of military insurrections, civil wars, and murders of emperors recommences.

226. Artaxerxes (Ardisheer) overthrows the Parthian, and restores the Persian kingdom in Asia. He attacks the Roman possessions in the East. 260. The Goths invade the Roman provinces. The emperor Decius is defeated and slain by them.

253-260. The Franks and Alemanni invade Gaul, Spain, and Africa. The Goths attack Asia Minor and Greece. The Persians conquer Armenia. Their king, Sapor, defeats the Roman emperor Valerian, and takes him prisoner. General distress of the Roman empire.

268-283. The emperors Claudius, Aurelian, Tacitus, Probus, and Carus defeat the various enemies of Rome, and restore order in the Roman state.

285. Diocletian divides and reorganizes the Roman empire. After his abdication in 305 a fresh series of civil wars and confusion ensues. Constantine, the first Christian emperor, reunites the empire in 324.

330. Constantine makes Constantinople the seat of empire instead of Rome.

363. The emperor Julian is killed in action against the Persians.

364-375. The empire is again divided, Valentinian being emperor of the West, and Valens of the East. Valentinian repulses the Alemanni, and other German invaders from Gaul. Splendor of the Gothic kingdom under Hermanric, north of the Danube.

376-395. The Huns attack the Goths, who implore the protection of the Roman emperor of the East. The Goths are allowed to pass the Danube, and to settle in the Roman provinces. A war soon breaks out between them and the Romans, and the emperor Valens and his army are destroyed by them. They ravage the Roman territories. The emperor Theodosius reduces them to submission. They retain settlements in Thrace and Asia Minor.

395. Final division of the Roman empire between Arcadius and Honorius, the two sons of Theodosius. The Goths revolt, and under Alaric attack various parts of both the Roman empires.

410. Alaric takes the city of Rome.

412. The Goths march into Gaul, and in 414 into Spain, which had been already invaded by hosts of Vandals, Suevi, Alani, and other Germanic nations. Britain is formally abandoned by the Roman emperor of the West.

428. Genseric, king of the Vandals, conquers the Roman province of North Africa.

441. The Huns attack the Eastern empire.

CHAPTER VI
THE BATTLE OF CHALONS, A.D. 451.

…A broad expanse of plains, the Campi Catalaunici of the ancients, spreads far and wide around the city of Chalons, in the northeast of France. The long rows of poplars, through which the river Marne winds its way, and a few thinly-scattered villages, are almost the only objects that vary the monotonous aspect of the greater part of this region. But about five miles from Chalons, near the little hamlets of Chaps and Cuperly, the ground is indented and heaped up in ranges of grassy mounds and trenches, which attest the work of man's hand in ages past; and which, to the practiced eye, demonstrate that this quiet spot has once been the fortified position of a huge military host.

Local tradition gives to these ancient earthworks the name of Attila's Camp. Nor is there any reason to question the correctness of the title, or to doubt that behind these very ramparts it was that…the

most powerful heathen king that ever ruled in Europe mustered the remnants of his vast army, which had striven on these plains against the Christian soldiery of Thoulouse and Rome. Here it was that Attila prepared to resist to the death his victors in the field; and here he heaped up the treasures of his camp in one vast pile, which was to be his funeral pyre should his camp be stormed…

…By the middle of the fifth century, Germanic nations had settled themselves in many of the fairest regions of the Roman empire, had imposed their yoke on the provincials, and had undergone, to a considerable extent, that moral conquest which the arts and refinements of the vanquished in arms have so often achieved over the rough victor. The Visigoths held the north of Spain and Gaul south of the Loire. Franks, Alemanni, Alans, and Burgundians had established themselves in other Gallic provinces, and the Suevi were masters of a large southern portion of the Spanish peninsula. A king of the Vandals reigned in North Africa, and the Ostrogoths had firmly planted themselves in the provinces north of Italy. Of these powers and principalities, that of the Visigoths, under their king Theodoric, son of Alaric, was by far the first in power and in civilization.

The pressure of the Huns upon Europe had first been felt in the fourth century of our era…tribe after tribe of savage warriors broke in upon the barriers of civilized Europe, "velut unda supervenit undam." The Huns crossed the Tanais into Europe in 375, and rapidly reduced to subjection the Alans, the Ostrogoths, and other tribes that were then dwelling along the course of the Danube. The armies of the Roman emperor that tried to check their progress were cut to pieces by them; and Panonia and other provinces south of the Danube were speedily occupied by the victorious cavalry of these new invaders. Not merely the degenerate Romans, but the bold and hardy warriors of Germany and Scandinavia were appalled at the numbers, the ferocity, the ghastly appearance, and the lightning-like rapidity of the Huns…Tribe after tribe, and city after city, fell before them. Then came a pause in their career of conquest in Southwestern Europe, caused probably by dissensions among their chiefs, and also by their arms being employed in attack upon the Scandinavian nations. But when Attila (or Atzel, as he is called in the Hungarian language) became their ruler, the torrent of their arms was directed with augmented terrors upon the west and the south; and their myriads marched beneath the guidance of one master-mind to the overthrow both of the new and the old powers of the earth.

…Attila's fame has not come down to us through the partial and suspicious medium of chroniclers and poets of his own race. It is not from Hunnish authorities that we learn the extent of his might: It is from his enemies, from the literature and the legends of the nations whom he afflicted with his arms, that we draw the unquestionable evidence of his greatness. Besides the express narratives of Byzantine, Latin, and Gothic writers, we have the strongest proof of the stern reality of Attila's conquests in the extent to which he and his Huns have been the themes of the earliest German and Scandinavian lays. Wild as many of these legends are, they bear concurrent and certain testimony to the awe with which the memory of Attila was regarded by the bold warriors who composed and delighted in them. Attila's exploits, and the wonders of his unearthly steed and magic sword, repeatedly occur in the Sagas of Norway and Iceland; and the celebrated Niebelungen Lied, the most ancient of Germanic poetry, is full of them…When we turn from the legendary to the historic Attila, we see clearly that he was not one of the vulgar herd of barbaric conquerors. Consummate military skill may be traced in his campaigns; and he relied far less on the brute force of armies for the aggrandizement of his empire, than on the unbounded influence over the affections of friends and the fears of foes which his genius enabled him to acquire. Austerely sober in his private life, severely just on the judgment-seat, conspicuous among a nation of warriors for hardihood, strength, and skill in every martial exercise, grave and deliberate in counsel, but rapid and remorseless in execution, he gave safety and security to all who were under his dominion, while

he waged a warfare of extermination against all who opposed or sought to escape from it. He matched the national passions, the prejudices, the creeds, and the superstitions of the varied nations over which he ruled, and of those which he sought to reduce beneath his sway: and these feelings he had the skill to turn to his own account. His own warriors believed him to be the inspired favorite of their deities, and followed him with fanatic zeal: his enemies looked on him as the pre-appointed minister of Heaven's wrath against themselves; and, though they believed not in his creed, their own made them tremble before him.

…The extensive territory north of the Danube and Black sea, and eastward of Caucasus, over which Attila ruled, first in conjunction with his brother Bleda, and afterwards alone, cannot be very accurately defined; but it must have comprised within it, besides the Huns, many nations of Slavic, Gothic, Teutonic, and Finnish origin. South also of the Danube, the country from the river Sau as far as Novi in Thrace was a Hunnish province. Such was the empire of the Huns in A.D. 445; a memorable year, in which Attila founded Buda on the Danube as his capital city; and ridded himself of his brother by a crime, which seems to have been prompted not only by selfish ambition, but also by a desire of turning to his purpose the legends and forebodings which then were universally spread throughout the Roman empire, and must have been well known to the watchful and ruthless Hun.

The year 445 of our era completed the twelfth century from the foundation of Rome, according to the best chronologers…An attempt to assassinate Attila, made, or supposed to have been made, at the instigation of Theodosius the Younger, the Emperor of Constantinople, drew the Hunnish armies, in 445, upon the Eastern empire, and delayed for a time the destined blow against Rome. Probably a more important cause of delay was the revolt of some of the Hunnish tribes to the north of the Black Sea against Attila, which broke out about this period, and is cursorily mentioned by the Byzantine writers. Attila quelled this revolt;

and having thus consolidated his power, and having punished the presumption of the Eastern Roman emperor by fearful ravages of his fairest provinces, Attila, A.D. 450, prepared to set his vast forces in motion for the conquest of Western Europe. He sought unsuccessfully by diplomatic intrigues to detach the King of the Visigoths from his alliance with Rome, and he resolved first to crush the power of Theodoric, and then to advance with overwhelming power to trample out the last sparks of the doomed Roman empire.

A strong invitation from a Roman princess gave him a pretext for the war, and threw an air of chivalric enterprise over his invasion. Honoria, sister of Valentinian III., the Emperor of the West, had sent to Attila to offer him her hand, and her supposed right to share in the imperial power. This had been discovered by Romans, and Honoria had been forthwith closely imprisoned, Attila now pretended to take up arms in behalf of his self-promised bride, and proclaimed that he was about to march to Rome to redress Honoria's wrongs…Two chiefs of the Franks, who were then settled on the lower Rhine, were at this period engaged in a feud with each other: and while one of them appealed to the Romans for aid, the other invoked the assistance and protection of the Huns. Attila thus obtained an ally whose co-operation secured for him the passage of the Rhine; and it was this circumstance which caused him to take a northward route from Hungary for his attack upon Gaul. The muster of the Hunnish hosts was swollen by warriors of every tribe that they had subjugated; nor is there any reason to suspect the old chroniclers of willful exaggeration in estimating Attila's army at seven hundred thousand strong. Having crossed the Rhine, probably a little below Coblentz, he defeated the King of the Burgundians, who endeavored to bar his progress. He then divided his vast forces into two armies, one of which marched northwest upon Tongres and Arras, and the other cities of that part of France; while the main body, under Attila himself marched up the Moselle, and destroyed Besancon, and other towns in the country of the Burgundians…It was not until the year 451 that the Huns commenced the siege of Orleans; and

during their campaign in Eastern Gaul, the Roman general Aetius had strenuously exerted himself in collecting and organizing such an army as might, when united to the soldiery of the Visigoths, be fit to face the Huns in the field. He enlisted every subject of the Roman empire whom patriotism, courage, or compulsion could collect beneath the standards; and round these troops, which assumed the once proud title of the legions of Rome, he arrayed the large forces of barbaric auxiliaries whom pay, persuasion, or the general hate and dread of the Huns, brought to the camp of the last of the Roman generals. King Theodoric exerted himself with equal energy, Orleans resisted her besiegers bravely as in after times. The passage of the Loire was skillfully defended against the Huns; and Aetius and Theodoric, after much maneuvering and difficulty, effected a junction of their armies to the south of that important river.

On the advance of the allies upon Orleans, Attila instantly broke up the siege of that city, and retreated towards the Marne. He did not choose to risk a decisive battle with only the central corps of his army against the combined power of his enemies; and he therefore fell back upon his base of operations; calling in his wings from Arras and Besancon, and concentrating the whole of the Hunnish forces on the vast plains of Chalons-sur-Marne. A glance at the map will show how scientifically this place was chosen by the Hunnish general, as the point for his scattered forces to converge upon; and the nature of the ground was eminently favorable for the operations of cavalry, the arm in which Attila's strength peculiarly lay.

It was during the retreat from Orleans that a Christian is reported to have approached the Hunnish king, and said to him, "Thou art the Scourge of God for the chastisement of Christians." Attila instantly assumed this new title of terror, which thenceforth became the appellation by which he was most widely and most fearfully known.

The confederate armies of Romans and Visigoths at last met their great adversary, face to face, on the ample battle-ground of the Chalons plains.

Readings

Aetius commanded on the right of the allies; King Theodoric on the left; and Sangipan, king of the Alans, whose fidelity was suspected, was placed purposely in the centre and in the very front of the battle. Attila commanded his centre in person, at the head of his own countrymen, while the Ostrogoths, the Gepidae, and the other subject allies of the Huns, were drawn up on the wings. Some maneuvering appears to have occurred before the engagement, in which Attila had the advantage, inasmuch as he succeeded in occupying a sloping hill, which commanded the left flank of the Huns. Attila saw the importance of the position taken by Aetius on the high ground, and commenced the battle by a furious attack on this part of the Roman line, in which he seems to have detached some of his best troops from his centre to aid his left. The Romans having the advantage of the ground, repulsed the Huns, and while the allies gained this advantage on their right, their left, under King Theodoric, assailed the Ostrogoths, who formed the right of Attila's army. The gallant king was himself struck down by a javelin, as he rode onward at the head of his men, and his own cavalry charging over him trampled him to death in the confusion. But the Visigoths, infuriated, not dispirited, by their monarch's fall, routed the enemies opposed to them, and then wheeled upon the flank of the Hunnish centre, which had been engaged in a sanguinary and indecisive contest with the Alans.

In this peril Attila made his centre fall back upon his camp; and when the shelter of its entrenchments and wagons had once been gained, the Hunnish archers repulsed, without difficulty, the charges of the vengeful Gothic cavalry. Aetius had not pressed the advantage which he gained on his side of the field, and when night fell over the wild scene of havoc, Attila's left was still unbroken, but his right had been routed, and his centre forced back upon his camp.

Expecting an assault on the morrow, Attila stationed his best archers in front of the cars and wagons, which were drawn up as a fortification along his lines, and made every preparation for a desperate resistance. But the "Scourge of God" resolved that no man should boast of the honor of having either captured or slain him; and he caused to be raised in the centre of his encampment a huge pyramid of the wooden saddles of his cavalry: round it he heaped the spoils and the wealth that he had won; on it he stationed his wives who had accompanied him in the campaign; and on the summit he placed himself, ready to perish in the flames, and baulk the victorious foe of their choicest booty, should they succeed in storming his defenses.

But when the morning broke, and revealed the extent of the carnage, with which the plains were heaped for miles, the successful allies saw also and respected the resolute attitude of their antagonist. Neither were any measures taken to blockade him in his camp, and so to extort by famine that submission which it was too plainly perilous to enforce with the sword. Attila was allowed to march back the remnants of his army without molestation, and even with the semblance of success.

…Attila's attacks on the Western, empire were soon renewed; but never with such peril to the civilized world as had menaced it before his defeat at Chalons. And on his death, two years after that battle, the vast empire which his genius had founded was soon dissevered by the successful revolts of the subject nations. The name of the Huns ceased for some centuries to inspire terror in Western Europe, and their ascendancy passed away with the life of the great king by whom it had been so fearfully augmented. [If I seem to have given fewer of the details of the battle itself than its importance would warrant, my excuse must be, that Gibbon has enriched our language with a description of it, too long for quotation and too splendid for rivalry. I have not, however, taken altogether the same view of it that he has. The notes to Mr. Herbert's poem of "Attila" bring together nearly all the authorities on the subject.]

534

SYNOPSIS OF EVENTS BETWEEN THE BATTLE OF CHALONS, A.D. 451, AND THE BATTLE OF TOURS, 732.

A.D. 476. The Roman Empire of the West extinguished by Odoacer.

482. Establishment of the French monarchy in Gaul by Clovis.

455-482. The Saxons, Angles, and Frisians conquer Britain except the northern parts, and the districts along the west coast. The German conquerors found eight independent kingdoms.

533-568. The generals of Justinian, the Emperor of Constantinople, conquer Italy and North Africa; and these countries are for a short time annexed to the Roman Empire of the East.

568-570. The Lombards conquer great part of Italy.

570-627. The wars between the Emperors of Constantinople and the Kings of Persia are actively continued.

622. The Mahometan era of the Hegira. Mahomet is driven from Mecca, and is received as prince of Medina.

629-632. Mahomet conquers Arabia.

632-651. The Mahometan Arabs invade and conquer Persia.

632-709. They attack the Roman Empire of the East. They conquer Syria, Egypt, and Africa.

709-713. They cross the straits of Gibraltar, and invade and conquer Spain…

CHAPTER VII.
THE BATTLE OF TOURS, A.D. 732,

…The broad tract of champaign country which intervenes between the cities of Poitiers and Tours is principally composed of a succession of rich originally a confederation of the Teutonic tribes that dwelt between the Rhine, the Maine, and the Weser) established a decided superiority over the other conquerors of the province, as well as over the conquered provincials, the country long remained a chaos of uncombined and shifting elements. The early princes of the Merovingian dynasty were generally occupied in wars against other princes of their house, occasioned by the frequent subdivisions of the Frank monarchy: and the ablest and best of them had found all their energies tasked to the utmost to defend the barrier of the Rhine against the Pagan Germans, who strove to pass that river and gather their share of the spoils of the empire.

The conquests which the Saracens effected over the southern and eastern provinces of Rome were far more rapid than those achieved by the Germans in the north; and the new organizations of society which the Moslems introduced were summarily and uniformly enforced. Exactly a century passed between the death of Mohammed and the date of the battle of Tours. During that century the followers of the Prophet had torn away half the Roman empire; and besides their conquests over Persia, the Saracens had overrun Syria, Egypt, Africa, and Spain, in an unchequered and apparently irresistible career of victory. Nor, at the commencement of the eighth century of our era, was the Mohammedan world divided against itself, as it subsequently became. All these vast regions obeyed the Caliph; throughout them all, from the Pyrenees to the Oxus, the name of Mohammed was invoked in prayer, and the Koran revered as the book of the law.

It was under one of their ablest and most renowned commanders, with a veteran army, and with every apparent advantage of time, place, and circumstance, that the Arabs made their great effort at the conquest of Europe north of the Pyrenees. The victorious Moslem soldiery in Spain,

"A countless multitude; Syrian, Moor, Saracen, Greek renegade, Persian, and Copt, and Tartar, in

one bond offering faith conjoined—strong in the youth And heat of zeal—a dreadful brotherhood,"

were eager for the plunder of more Christian cities and shrines, and full of fanatic confidence in the invincibility of their arms…

…these feelings of ambition and arrogance are attributed to the Moslems, who had overthrown the Visigoth power in Spain. And their eager expectations of new wars were excited to the utmost on the re-appointment by the Caliph of Abderrahman Ibn Abdillah Alghafeki to the government of that country, A.D. 729, which restored them a general who had signalized his skill and prowess during the conquests of Africa and Spain, whose ready valor and generosity had made him the idol of the troops, who had already been engaged in several expeditions into Gaul, so as to be well acquainted with the national character and tactics of the Franks…In addition to his cardinal military virtues, Abderrahman is described by the Arab writers as a model of integrity and justice. The first two years of his second administration in Spain were occupied in severe reforms of the abuses which under his predecessors had crept into the system of government, and in extensive preparations for his intended conquest of Gaul. Besides the troops which he collected from his province, he obtained from Africa a large body of chosen Barber cavalry, officered by Arabs of proved skill and valor: and in the summer of 732 he crossed the Pyrenees at the head of an army…

The Merovingian kings had sunk into absolute insignificance, and had become mere puppets of royalty before the eighth century. Charles Martel like his father, Pepin Heristal, was Duke of the Austrasian Franks, the bravest and most thoroughly Germanic part of the nation: and exercised, in the name of the titular king, what little paramount authority the turbulent minor rulers of districts and towns could be persuaded or compelled to acknowledge. Engaged with his national competitors in perpetual conflicts for power, engaged also in more serious struggles for safety against the fierce tribes of the unconverted Frisians, Bavarians, Saxons, and Thuringians, who at that epoch assailed with peculiar ferocity the Christianized Germans on the left bank of the Rhine, Charles Martel added experienced skill to his natural courage, and he had also formed a militia of veterans among the Franks.... Charles had no standing army, and the independent spirit of the Frank warriors who followed his standard, it seems most probable that it was not in his power to adopt the cautious policy of watching the invaders, and wearing out their strength by delay. So dreadful and so wide-spread were the ravages of the Saracenic light cavalry throughout Gaul that it must have been impossible to restrain for any length of time the indignant ardor of the Franks. And, even if Charles could have persuaded his men to look tamely on while the Arabs stormed more towns and desolated more districts, he could not have kept an army together when the usual period of a military expedition had expired. If, indeed, the Arab account of the disorganization of the Moslem forces be correct, the battle was as well-timed on the part of Charles as it was beyond all question, well-fought.

The monkish chroniclers, from whom we are obliged to glean a narrative of this memorable campaign, bear full evidence to the terror which the Saracen invasion inspired, and to the agony of that; great struggle. The Saracens, say they, and their king, who was called Abdirames, came out of Spain, with all their wives, and their children, and their substance, in such great multitudes that no man could reckon or estimate them. They brought with them all their armor, and whatever they had, as if they were thence forth always to dwell in France…"Then Abderrahman, seeing the land filled with the multitude of his army, pierces through the mountains, tramples over rough and level ground plunders far into the country of the Franks, and smites all with the sword, insomuch that when Eudo came to battle with him at the river Garonne, and fled before him, God alone knows the number of the slain. Then Abderrahman pursued after Count Eudo, and while he strives to spoil and burn the holy shrine at Tours, he encounters the chief of the

Austrasian Franks, Charles, a man of war from his youth up, to whom Eudo had sent warning. There for nearly seven days they strive intensely, and at last they set themselves in battle array; and the nations of the north standing firm as a wall, and impenetrable as a zone of ice, utterly slay the Arabs with the edge of the sword." ["Tunc Abdirrahman, multitudine sui exercitus repletam prospiciane terram," &c.—SCRIPT. GEST. FRANC. p. 785.]

The European writers all concur in speaking of the fall of Abderrahman as one of the principal causes of the defeat of the Arabs; who, according to one writer, after finding that their leader was slain, dispersed in the night, to the agreeable surprise of the Christians, who expected the next morning to see them issue from their tents, and renew the combat…but it is impossible to collect from them anything like a full or authentic description of the great battle itself, or of the operations which preceded or followed it.

…The Arabian writers who recorded the conquests and wars of their countrymen in Spain, have narrated also the expedition into Gaul of their great Emir, and his defeat and death near Tours in battle with the host of the Franks under King Caldus, the name into which they metamorphose Charles…They tell us how there was war between the count of the Frankish frontier and the Moslems, and how the count gathered together all his people, and fought for a time with doubtful success. "But," say the Arabian chroniclers, "Abderrahman drove them back; and the men of Abderrahman were puffed up in spirit by their repeated successes, and they were full of trust in the valor and the practice in war of their Emir. So the Moslems smote their enemies, and passed the river Garonne, and laid waste the country, and took captives without number. And that army went through all places like a desolating storm. Prosperity made those warriors insatiable. At the passage of the river, Abderrahman overthrew the count, and the count retired into his stronghold, but the Moslems fought against it, and entered it by force, and slew the count; for everything gave way to their scimitars, which were the robbers of lives. All the nations of the Franks trembled at that terrible army, and they betook them to their king Caldus, and told him of the havoc made by the Moslem horsemen, and how they rode at their will through all the land of Narbonne Toulouse, and Bordeaux, and they told the king of the death of their count. Then the king bade them be of good cheer, and offered to aid them. And in the 114th year [Of the Hegira.] he mounted his home, and he took with him a host that could not be numbered, and went against the Moslems. And he came upon them at the great city of Tours. And Abderrahman and other prudent cavaliers saw the disorder of the Moslem troops, who were loaded with spoil; but they did not venture to displease the soldiers by ordering them to abandon everything except their arms and war-horses. And Abderrahman trusted in the valor of his soldiers, and in the good fortune which had ever attended him. But (the Arab writer remarks) such defect of discipline always is fatal to armies. So Abderrahman and his host attacked Tours to gain still more spoil, and they fought against it so fiercely that they stormed the city almost before the eyes of the army that came to save it; and the fury and the cruelty of the Moslems towards the inhabitants of the city were like the fury and cruelty of raging tigers. It was manifest," adds the Arab, "that God's chastisement was sure to follow such excesses; and fortune thereupon turned her back upon the Moslems.

"Near the river Owar, [Probably the Loire.] the two great hosts of the two languages and the two creeds were set in array against each other. The hearts of Abderrahman, his captains, and his men were filled with wrath and pride, and they were the first to begin the fight. The Moslem horseman dashed fierce and frequent forward against the battalions of the Franks, who resisted manfully, and many fell dead on either side, until the going down of the sun. Night parted the two armies: but in the grey of the morning the Moslems returned to the battle. Their cavaliers had soon hewn their way into the centre of the Christian host. But many of the Moslems were fearful for the safety of the spoil which they had stored in their tents, and

a false cry arose in their ranks that some of the enemy were plundering the camp; whereupon several squadrons of the Moslem horseman rode off to protect their tents. But it seemed as if they fled; and all the host was troubled. And while Abderrahman strove to check their tumult, and to lead them back to battle, the warriors of the Franks came around him, and he was pierced through with many spears, so that he died. Then all the host fled before the enemy, and many died in the flight. This deadly defeat of the Moslems, and the loss of the great leader and good cavalier Abderrahman, took place in the hundred and fifteenth year.

It would be difficult to expect from an adversary a more explicit confession of having been thoroughly vanquished, than the Arabs here accord to the Europeans. The points on which their narrative differs from those of the Christians, as to how many days the conflict lasted, whether the assailed city was actually rescued or not, and the like, are of little moment compared with the admitted great fact that there was a decisive trial of strength between Frank and Saracen, in which the former conquered. The enduring importance of the battle of Tours in the eyes of the Moslems, is attested not only by the expressions of "the deadly battle," and "the disgraceful overthrow," which their writers constantly employ when referring to it, but also by the fact that no further serious attempts at conquest beyond the Pyrenees were made by the Saracens. Charles Martel, and his son and grandson, were left at leisure to consolidate and extend their power forth....

SYNOPSIS OF EVENTS BETWEEN THE BATTLE OF TOURS, A.D. 732, AND THE BATTLE OF HASTINGS, 1066.

A.D. 768-814. Reign of Charlemagne.

814-888. Repeated partitions of the empire and civil wars between Charlemagne's descendants. Ultimately, the kingdom of France is finally separated from Germany and Italy. In 982, Otho the Great, of Germany, revives the imperial dignity.

827. Egbert, king of Wessex, acquires the supremacy over the Anglo-Saxon kingdoms.

832. The first Danish squadron attacks part of the English coast. The Danes, or Northmen, had begun their ravages in France a few years earlier. For two centuries Scandinavia sends out fleet after fleet of sea-rovers, who desolate all the western kingdoms of Europe, and in many cases effect permanent conquests.

871-900. Reign of Alfred in England. After a long and varied struggle, he rescues England from the Danish invaders.

911, The French king cedes Neustria to Hrolf the Northman. Hrolf (or Duke Rollo, as he thenceforth was termed) and his army of Scandinavian warriors, become the ruling class of the population of the province, which is called after them Normandy.

1016. Four knights from Normandy, who had been on a pilgrimage to the Holy Land, while returning through Italy, head the people of Salerno in repelling an attack of a band of Saracen corsairs. In the next year many adventurers from Normandy settle in Italy, where they conquer Apulia (1040), and afterwards (1060) Sicily.

1017. Canute, king of Denmark, becomes king of England. On the death of the last of his sons, in 1041, the Saxon line is restored, and Edward the Confessor (who had been bred in the court of the Duke of Normandy), is called by the English to the throne of this island, as the representative of the House of Cerdic.

1035. Duke Robert of Normandy dies on his return from a pilgrimage to the Holy Land, and his son William (afterwards the conqueror of England) succeeds to the dukedom of Normandy.

CHAPTER VIII.
THE BATTLE OF HASTINGS, 1066.

…The interest of this eventful struggle, by which William of Normandy became King of England, is materially enhanced by the high personal characters of the competitors for our crown. They were three in number. One was a foreign prince from the North. One was a foreign prince from the South: and one was a native hero of the land. Harald Hardrada, the strongest and the most chivalric of the kings of Norway, was the first; [See in Snerre the Saga of Harald Hardrada.] Duke William of Normandy was the second; and the Saxon Harold, the son of Earl Godwin, was the third. Never was a nobler prize sought by nobler champions, or striven for more gallantly. The Saxon triumphed over the Norwegian, and the Norman triumphed over the Saxon: but Norse valor was never more conspicuous than when Harald Hardrada and his host fought and fell at Stamford Bridge; nor did Saxons ever face their foes more bravely than our Harold and his men on the fatal day of Hastings.

During the reign of King Edward the Confessor over this land, the claims of the Norwegian king to our Crown were little thought of; and though Hardrada's predecessor, King Magnus of Norway had on one occasion asserted that, by virtue of a compact with our former king, Hardicanute, he was entitled to the English throne, no serious attempt had been made to enforce his pretensions. But the rivalry of the Saxon Harold and the Norman William was foreseen and bewailed by the Confessor, who was believed to have predicted on his death-bed the calamities that were pending over England. Duke William was King Edward's kinsman. Harold was the head of the most powerful noble house, next to the royal blood, in England; and personally, he was the bravest and most popular chieftain in the land. King Edward was childless, and the nearest collateral heir was a puny unpromising boy. England had suffered too severely during royal minorities, to make the accession of Edgar Atheling desirable; and long before King Edward's death, Earl Harold was the destined king of the nation's choice, though the favor of the Confessor was believed to lean towards the Norman duke.

A little time before the death of King Edward, Harold was in Normandy. The causes of the voyage of the Saxon earl to the continent are doubtful; but the fact of his having been, in 1065, at the ducal court, and in the power of his rival, is indisputable. William made skilful and unscrupulous use of the opportunity. Though Harold was treated with outward courtesy and friendship, he was made fully aware that his liberty and life depended on his compliance with the Duke's requests. William said to him, in apparent confidence and cordiality, "When King Edward and I once lived like brothers under the same roof, he promised that if ever be became King of England, he would make me heir to his throne. Harold, I wish that thou wouldst assist me to realize this promise." Harold replied with expressions of assent: and further agreed, at William's request, to marry William's daughter Adela, and to send over his own sister to be married to one of William's barons. The crafty Norman was not content with this extorted promise; he determined to bind Harold by a more solemn pledge, which if broken, would be a weight on the spirit of the gallant Saxon, and a discouragement to others from adopting his cause. Before a full assembly of the Norman barons, Harold was required to do homage to Duke William, as the heir-apparent of the English crown. Kneeling down, Harold placed his hands between those of the Duke, and repeated the solemn form, by which he acknowledged the Duke as his lord, and promised to him fealty and true service…Harold was soon, after this permitted to return to England; and, after a short interval, during which he distinguished himself by the wisdom and humanity with which he pacified some formidable tumults of the Anglo-Danes in Northumbria, he found himself called on to decide whether he would keep the oath which the Norman had obtained from him, or mount the vacant throne of England in compliance with the nation's choice. King Edward the Confessor died on the 5th of January, 1066, and on the following day an assembly of the thanes and prelates present in London, and of the citizens of-the metropolis,

declared that Harold should be their king. It was reported that the dying Edward had nominated him as his successor; but the sense which his countrymen entertained of his pre-eminent merit was the true foundation of his title to the crown. Harold resolved to disregard the oath which he made in Normandy, as violent and void, and on the 7th day of that January he was anointed King of England, and received from the archbishop's hands the golden crown and scepter of England, and also an ancient national symbol, a weighty battle- axe. He had deep and speedy need of this significant part of the insignia of Saxon royalty.

A messenger from Normandy soon arrived to remind Harold of the oath which he had sworn to the…William sent another…and then the Duke published far and wide through Christendom what he termed the perjury and bad faith of his rival; and proclaimed his intention of asserting his rights by the sword before the year should expire, and of pursuing and punishing the perjurer even in those places where he thought he stood most strongly and most securely.

Before, however, he commenced hostilities, William, with deep laid policy submitted his claims to the decision of the Pope. Harold refused to acknowledge this tribunal, or to answer before an Italian priest for his title as an English king. After a formal examination of William's complaints by the Pope and the cardinals, it was solemnly adjudged at Rome that England belonged to the Norman duke; and a banner was sent to William from the holy see, which the Pope himself had consecrated and blessed for the invasion of this island. The clergy throughout the continent were now assiduous and energetic in preaching up William's enterprise as undertaken in the cause of God. Besides these spiritual…the Norman duke applied all the energies of his mind and body, all the resources of his duchy, and all the influence he possessed among vassals or allies, to the collection of "the most remarkable and formidable armament which the Western nations had witnessed." [Sir James Mackintosh's History of England, vol. i. p. 97.] All the adventurous spirits of Christendom flocked to the holy banner, under which Duke William, the most renowned knight and sagest general of the age, promised to lead them to glory and wealth in the fair domains of England. His army was filled with the chivalry of continental Europe, all eager to save their souls by fighting at the Pope's bidding, ardent to signalize their valor in so great an enterprise, and longing also for the pay and the plunder which William liberally promised. But the Normans themselves were the pith and the flower of the army; and William himself was the strongest, the sagest, and fiercest spirit of them all.

Throughout the spring and summer of 1066, all the seaports of Normandy, Picardy, and Brittany rang with the busy sound of preparation. On the opposite side of the Channel, King Harold collected the army and the fleet with which he hoped to crush the southern invaders. But the unexpected attack of King Harald Hardrada of Norway upon another part of England, disconcerted the skilful measures which the Saxon had taken against the menacing armada of Duke William.

Harold's renegade brother, Earl Tostig, had excited the Norse king to this enterprise, the importance of which has naturally been eclipsed by the superior interest attached to the victorious expedition of Duke William, but which was on a scale of grandeur which the Scandinavian ports had rarely, if ever, before witnessed. Hardrada's fleet consisted of two hundred war-ships, and three hundred other vessels, and all the best warriors of Norway were in his host. He sailed first to the Orkneys, where many of the islanders joined him, and then to Yorkshire. After a severe conflict near York, he completely routed Earls Edwin and Morcar, the governors of Northumbria. The city of York opened its gates, and all the country, from the Tyne to the Humber, submitted to him. The tidings of the defeat of Edwin and Morcar compelled Harold to leave his position on the southern coast, and move instantly against the Norwegians. By a remarkably rapid, march, he reached Yorkshire in four days, and took the Norse king and his confederates by surprise.

Nevertheless, the battle which ensued, and which was fought near Stamford Bridge, was desperate, and was long doubtful. Unable to break the ranks of the Norwegian phalanx by force, Harold at length tempted them to quit their close order by a pretended flight. Then the English columns burst in among them, and a carnage ensued, the extent of which may be judged of by the exhaustion and inactivity of Norway for a quarter of a century afterwards. King Harald Hardrada, and all the flower of his nobility, perished on the 25th of September, 1066, at Stamford Bridge…Harold's victory was splendid; but he had bought it dearly by the fall of many of his best officers and men; and still more dearly by the opportunity which Duke William had gained of effecting an unopposed landing on the Sussex coast. The whole of William's shipping had assembled at the mouth of the Dive, a little river between the Seine and the Orme, as early as the middle of August. The army which he had collected, amounted to fifty thousand knights, and ten thousand soldiers of inferior degree. Many of the knights were mounted, but many must have served on foot; as it is hardly possible to believe that William could have found transports for the conveyance of fifty thousand war-horses across the Channel. For a long time the winds were adverse; and the Duke employed the interval that passed before he could set sail in completing the organization and in improving the discipline of his army…It was not till the approach of the equinox that the wind veered from the north-east to the west, and gave the Normans an opportunity of quitting the weary shores of the Dive. They eagerly embarked, and set sail; but the wind soon freshened to a gale, and drove them along the French coast to St. Valery, where the greater part of them found shelter; but many of their vessels were wrecked and the whole coast of Normandy was strewn with the bodies of the drowned. William's army began to grow discouraged and averse to the enterprise, which the very elements thus seemed to fight against; though in reality the northeast wind which had cooped them so long at the mouth of the Dive, and the western gale which had forced them into St. Valery, were the best possible friends to the invaders. They prevented the Normans from crossing the Channel until the Saxon king and his army of defense had been called away from the Sussex coast to encounter Harald Hardrada in Yorkshire: and also until a formidable English fleet, which by King Harold's orders had been cruising in the Channel to intercept the Normans, had been obliged to disperse temporarily for the purpose of refitting and taking in fresh stores of provisions...the wind veered, and enabled the mediaeval Agamemnon to quit his Aulia.

With full sails, and a following southern breeze, the Norman armada left the French shores and steered for England. The invaders crossed an undefended sea, and found an undefended coast. It was in Pevensey Bay in Sussex, at Bulverhithe, between the castle of Pevensey and Hastings, that the last conquerors of this island landed, on the 29th of September, 1066.

Harold was at York, rejoicing over his recent victory, which had delivered England from her ancient Scandinavian foes, and resettling the government of the counties which Harald Hardrada had overrun, when the tidings reached him that Duke William of Normandy and his host had landed on the Sussex shore. Harold instantly hurried southward to meet this long-expected enemy. The severe loss which his army had sustained in the battle with the Norwegians must have made it impossible for any large number of veteran troops to accompany him in his forced march to London, and thence to Sussex. He halted at the capital only six days; and during that time gave orders for collecting forces from his southern and midland counties, and also directed his fleet to reassemble off the Sussex coast. Harold was well received in London, and his summons to arms was promptly obeyed by citizen, by thane, by sokman, and by ceorl; for he had shown himself during his brief reign a just and wise king, affable to all men, active for the good of his country, and (in the words of the old historian) sparing himself from no fatigue by land or sea. [See Roger de Hoveden and William of Malmesbury, cited in Thierry, book iii.] He might have gathered a much more numerous force than that of William, but his

recent victory had made, him over-confident, and he was irritated by the reports of the country being ravaged by the invaders. As soon therefore, as he had collected a small army in London, he marched off towards the coast: pressing forward as rapidly as his men could traverse Surrey and Sussex in the hope of taking the Normans unawares, as he had recently by a similar forced march succeeded in surprising the Norwegians. But he had now to deal with a foe equally brave with Harald Hardrada, and far more skilful and wary.

...Duke William's own ship was the first of the Norman fleet. "It was called the Mora, and was the gift of his duchess, Matilda. On the head of the ship in the front, which mariners call the prow, there was a brazen child bearing an arrow with a bended bow. His face was turned towards England, and thither he looked, as though he was about to shoot. The breeze became soft and sweet, and the sea was smooth for their landing. The ships ran on dry land, and each ranged by the other's side. There you might see the good sailors, the sergeants, and squires sally forth and unload the ships; cast the anchors, haul the ropes, bear out shields and saddles, and land the war-horses and palfreys. The archers came forth, and touched land the first, each with his bow strong and with his quiver full of arrows, slung at his side. All were shaven and shorn; and all clad in short garments, ready to attack, to shoot, to wheel about and skirmish. All stood well equipped, and of good courage for the fight; and they scoured the whole shore, but found not an armed man there. After the archers had thus gone forth, the knights landed all armed, with their hauberks on, their shields slung at their necks, and their helmets laced. They formed together on the shore, each armed, and mounted on his war-horse: all had their swords girded on, and rode forward into the country with their lances raised. Then the carpenters landed, who had great axes in their hands, and planes and adzes hung at their sides. They took counsel together, and sought for a good spot to place a castle on. They had brought with them in the fleet, three wooden castles from Normandy, in pieces, all ready for framing together, and they took the materials of one of these out of the ships, all shaped and pierced to receive the pins which they had brought cut and ready in large barrels; and before evening had set in, they had finished a good fort on the English ground, and there they placed their stores. All then ate and drank enough, and were right glad that they were ashore.

"When Duke William himself landed, as he stepped on the shore, he slipped and fell forward upon his two hands. Forthwith all raised a loud cry of distress. 'An evil sign,' said they, 'is here.' But he cried out lustily, 'See, my lords! by the splendor of God, [William's customary oath.] I have taken possession of England with both my hands. It is now mine; and what is mine is yours.'

"The next day they marched along the sea-shore to Hastings. Near that place the Duke fortified a camp, and set up the two other wooden castles. The foragers, and those who looked out for booty, seized all the clothing and provisions they could find, lest what had been brought by the ships should fail them. And the English were to be seen fleeing before them, driving off their cattle, and quitting their houses. Many took shelter in burying-places, and even there they were in grievous alarm."

Besides the marauders from the Norman camp, strong bodies of cavalry were detached by William into the country, and these, when Harold and his army made their rapid march from London southward, fell, back in good order upon the main body of the Normans, and reported that the Saxon king was rushing on like a madman. But Harold, when he found that his hopes of surprising his adversary were vain changed his tactics, and halted about seven miles from the Norman lines. He sent some spies, who spoke the French language, to examine the number and preparations of the enemy, who, on their return, related with astonishment that there were more priests in William's camp than there were fighting men in the English army. They had mistaken for priests all the Norman soldiers who had short hair and shaven chins; for the English layman were then accustomed to wear long hair and mustachios, Harold, who knew the Norman usages, smiled at their words and said, "Those whom you have seen in such numbers are not priests, but stout soldiers, as they will soon make us feel."

Harold's army was far inferior in number to that of the Normans, and some of his captains advised him to retreat upon London, and lay waste the country, so as to starve down the strength, of the invaders. The policy thus recommended was unquestionably the wisest; for the Saxon fleet had now reassembled, and intercepted all William's communications with Normandy; so that as soon as his stores of provisions were exhausted he must have moved forward upon London; where Harold, at the head of the full military strength of the kingdom, could have defied his assault, and probably might have witnessed his rival's destruction by famine and disease, without having to strike a single blow. But Harold's bold blood was up, and his kindly heart could not endure to inflict on his South Saxon subjects even the temporary misery of wasting the country. "He would not burn houses and villages, neither would he take away the substance of his people."

Harold's brothers, Gurth and Leofwine, were with him in the camp, and Gurth endeavored to persuade him to absent himself from the battle…Harold replied that he would not look on while others risked their lives for him. Men would hold him a coward, and blame him for sending his best friends where he dared not go himself. He resolved, therefore, to fight, and to fight in person: but he was still too good a general to be the assailant in the action. He strengthened his position on the hill where he had halted, by a palisade of stakes interlaced with osier hurdles, and there, he said, he would defend himself against whoever should seek him.

…When it was known in the invaders' camp at Hastings that King Harold had marched southward with his power, but a brief interval ensued before the two hosts met in decisive encounter.

William's only chance of safety lay in bringing on a general engagement; and he joyfully advanced his army from their camp on the hill over Hastings, nearer to the Saxon position. But he neglected no means of weakening his opponent, and renewed his summonses and demands on Harold with an ostentatious air of sanctity and moderation.

"A monk named Hugues Maigrot came in William's name to call upon the Saxon king to do one of three things—either to resign his royalty in favor of William, or to refer it to the arbitration of the Pope to decide which of the two ought to be king, or to let it be determined by the issue of a single combat. Harold abruptly replied, 'I will not resign my title, I will not refer it to the Pope, nor will I accept the single combat.' He was far from being deficient in bravery; but he was no more at liberty to stake the crown which he had received from a whole people on the chance of a duel, than to deposit it in the hands of an Italian priest. William was not at all ruffled by the Saxon's refusal, but steadily pursuing the course of his calculated measures, sent the Norman monk again, after giving him these instructions: 'Go and tell Harold, that if he will keep his former compact with me, I will leave to him all the country which is beyond the Humber, and will give his brother Gurth all the lands which Godwin held. If he still persist in refusing my offers, then thou shalt tell him, before all his people, that he is a perjurer and a liar; that he, and all who shall support him, are excommunicated by the mouth of the Pope; and that the bull to that effect is in my hands.'

"Hugues Maigrot delivered this message in a solemn tone; and the Norman chronicle says that at the word EXCOMMUNICATION, the English chiefs looked at one another as if some great danger were impending. One of them then spoke as follows: 'We must fight, whatever may be the danger to us; for what we have to consider is not whether we shall accept and receive a new lord as if our king were dead: the case is quite otherwise. The Norman has given our lands to his captains, to his knights, to all his people, the greater part of whom have already done homage to him for them;

they will all look for their gift, if their Duke become our king; and he himself is bound to deliver up to them our goods, our wives, and our daughters: all is promised to them beforehand. They come, not only to ruin us, but to ruin our descendants also, and to take from us the country of our ancestors and what shall we do—whither shall we go—when we have no longer a country?' The English promised by a unanimous oath, to make neither peace, nor truce nor treaty, with the invader, but to die, or drive away the Normans." [Thierry.]

The 13th of October was occupied in these negotiations; and at night the Duke announced to his men that the next day would, be the day of battle. That night is said to have been passed by the two armies in very different manners. The Saxon soldiers spent it in joviality, singing their national songs, and draining huge horns of ale and wine round their camp-fires. The Normans, when they had looked to their arms and horses, confessed themselves to the priests, with whom their camp was thronged, and received the sacrament by thousands at a time.

On Saturday, the 14th of October, was fought the great battle.

…Let us therefore…transport our imaginations to the fair Sussex scenery, northwest of Hastings, with its breezy uplands, its grassy slopes, and ridges of open down swelling inland from the sparkling sea, its scattered copses, and its denser glades of intervening forests, clad in all the varied tints of autumn, as they appeared on the morning of the fourteenth of October, seven hundred and eighty-five years ago. The Norman host is pouring forth from its tents; and each troop, and each company, is forming fast under the banner of its leader. The masses have been sung, which were finished betimes in the morning; the barons have all assembled round Duke William; and the Duke has ordered that the army shall be formed in three divisions, so as to make the attack upon the Saxon position in three places. The Duke stood on a hill where he could best see his men; the barons surrounded him, and he spake to them proudly. He told them how he trusted them, and how all that he gained should be theirs; and how sure he felt of conquest, for in all the world there was not so brave an army or such good men and true as were then forming around him. Then they cheered him in turn, and cried out, "'You will not see one coward; none here will fear to die for love of you, if need be.' ...Then the Duke called for his good horse—a better could not be found. It had been sent him by a king of Spain, out of very great friendship. Neither arms nor the press of fighting men did it fear, if its lord spurred it on. Walter Giffard brought it. The Duke stretched out his hand, took the reins, put foot in stirrup, and mounted; and the good horse pawed, pranced, reared himself up, and curveted. The Viscount of Toarz saw how the Duke bore himself in arms, and said to his people that were around him, 'Never have I seen a man so fairly armed, nor one who rods so gallantly, or bore his arms or became his hauberk so well; neither any one who bore his lance so gracefully, or sat his horse and managed him so nobly. There is no such knight under heaven! a fair count he is, and fair king he will be. Let him fight, and he shall overcome: shame be to the man who shall fail him.'

..."The barons, and knights, and men-at-arms were all now armed; the foot-soldiers were well equipped, each bearing bow and sword; on their heads were caps, and to their feet were bound buskins. Some had good hides which they had bound round their bodies; and many were clad in frocks, and had quivers and bows hung to their girdles. The knights had hauberks and swords, boots of steel and shining helmets; shields at their necks, and in their hands lances. And all had their cognizances, so that each might know his fellow, and Norman might not strike Norman, nor Frenchman kill his countryman by mistake. Those on foot led the way, with serried ranks, bearing their bows. The knights rode next, supporting the archers from behind. Thus both horse and foot kept their course and order of march as they began; in close ranks at a gentle pace, that the one might not pass or separate from the other. All

went firmly and compactly, bearing themselves gallantly.

"Harold had summoned his men, earls, barons, and vavassours, from, the castles and the cities; from the ports, the villages, and boroughs. The peasants were also called together from the villages, bearing such arms as they found; clubs and great picks, iron forge and stages. The English had enclosed the place where Harold was, with his friends and the barons of the country whom he had summoned and called together...There came also from the west all, who heard the summons...All who could bear arms, and had learnt the news of the Duke's arrival, came to defend the land. But none came from beyond Humbre, for they had other business upon their hands; the Danes and Tosti having much damaged and weakened them.

"Harold knew that the Normans would come and attack him hand to hand; so he had early enclosed the field in which he placed his men. He made them arm early, and range themselves for the battle; he himself having put on arms and equipments that became such a lord. The Duke, he said, ought to seek him, as he wanted to conquer England; and it became him to abide the attack who had to defend the land. He commanded the people, and counseled his barons to keep themselves altogether, and defend themselves in a body; for if they once separated, they would with difficulty recover themselves. 'The Normans,' he said, 'are good vassals, valiant on foot and on horseback; good knights are they on horseback, and well used to battle; all is lost if they once penetrate our ranks. They have brought long lances and swords, but you have pointed lances and keen-edged bills; and I do not expect that their arms can stand against yours. Cleave wherever you can; it will be ill done if you spare aught.'

"The English had built up a fence before them with their shields, and with ash and other wood; and had well joined and wattled in the whole work, so as not to leave even a crevice; and thus they had a barricade in their front, through which any Norman who would attack them must first pass. Being covered in this way by their shields and barricades, their aim was to defend themselves: and if they had remained steady for that purpose, they would not have been conquered that day; for every Norman who made his way in, lost his life, either by hatchet, or bill, by club, or other weapons. They wore short and close hauberks, and helmets that hung over their garments. King Harold issued orders and made proclamation round, that all should be ranged with their faces towards the enemy; and that no one should move from where he was; so that, whoever came, might find them ready; and that whatever any one, be he Norman or other, should do, each should do his best to defend his own place. Then he ordered the men of Kent to go where the Normans were likely to make the attack; for they say that the men of Kent are entitled to strike first; and that whenever the king goes to battle, the first blow belongs to them. The right of the men of London is to guard the king's body, to place themselves around him, and to guard his standard; and they were accordingly placed by the standard to watch and defend it…

"Meanwhile the Normans appeared advancing over the ridge of a rising ground; and the first division of their troops moved onwards along the hill and across a valley. And presently another division, still larger, came in sight, close following upon the first, and they were led towards another part of the field, forming together as the first body had done. And while Harold saw and examined them, and was pointing them out to Gurth, a fresh company came in sight, covering all the plain; and in the midst of them was raised the standard that came from Rome. Near it was the Duke, and the best men and greatest strength of the army were there. The good knights, the good vassals, and brave warriors were there; and there were gathered together the gentle barons, the good archers, and the men-at-arms, whose duty it was to guard the Duke, and range themselves around him. The youths and common herd of the camp, whose business was not to join in the battle, but to take care of the harness and stores, moved on towards a rising ground. The priests and the clerks also

ascended a hill, there to offer up prayers to God, and watch the event of the battle.

"The English stood firm on foot in close ranks, and carried themselves right boldly…The Normans brought on the three divisions of their army to attack at different places. They set out in three companies, and in three companies did they fight. The first and second had come up, and then advanced the third, which was the greatest; with that came the Duke with his own men, and all moved boldly forward.

"As soon as the two armies were in full view of each other, great noise and tumult arose. You might hear the sound of many trumpets, of bugles, and of horns: and then you might see men ranging themselves in line, lifting their shields, raising their lances, bending their bows, handling their arrows, ready for assault and defense.

"The English stood ready to their post, the Normans still moved on; and when they drew near, the English were to be seen stirring to and fro; were going and coming; troops ranging themselves in order; some with their color rising, others turning pale; some making ready their arms, others raising their shields; the brave man rousing himself to fight, the coward trembling at the approach of danger…Forthwith arose the noise and cry of war, and on either side the people put themselves in motion.

"The Normans moved on to the assault, and the English defended themselves well. Some were striking, others urging onwards; all were bold, and cast aside fear…Loud and far resounded the bray of the horns; and the shocks of the lances, the mighty strokes of maces, and the quick clashing of swords…Then came the cunning maneuvers, the rude shocks and strokes of the lance and blows of the swords, among the sergeants and soldiers, both English and Norman…In the plain was a fosse, which the Normans had now behind them, having passed it in the fight without regarding it. But the English charged, and drove the Normans before them till they made them fall back upon this fosse, overthrowing into it horses and men. Many were to be seen falling therein, rolling one over the other, with their faces to the earth, and unable to rise. Many of the English, also, whom the Normans drew down along with them, died there. At no time during the day's battle did so many Normans die as perished in that fosse. So those said who saw the dead…From nine o'clock in the morning, when the combat began, till three o'clock came, the battle was up and down, this way and that, and no one knew who would conquer and win the land. Both sides stood so firm and fought so well, that no one could guess which would prevail. The Norman archers with their bows shot thickly upon the English; but they covered themselves with their shields, so that the arrows could not reach their bodies, nor do any mischief, how true soever was their aim, or however well they shot. Then the Normans determined to shoot their arrows upwards into the air, so that they might fall on their enemies' heads, and strike their faces. The archers adopted this scheme, and shot up into the air towards the English; and the arrows in falling struck their heads and faces, and put out the eyes of many; and all feared to open their eyes, or leave their faces unguarded.

"The arrows now flew thicker than rain before the wind; fast sped the shafts that the English called 'wibetes.' Then it was that an arrow, that had been thus shot upwards, struck Harold above his right eye and put it out. In his agony he drew the arrow and threw it away, breaking it with his hands; and the pain to his head was so great, that he leaned upon his shield. So the English were wont to say, and still say to the French, that the arrow was well shot which was so sent up against their king; and that the archer won them great glory, who thus put out Harold's eye.

"The Normans saw that the English defended themselves well, and were so strong in their position that they could do little against them. So they consulted together privily, and arranged to draw off, and pretend to flee, till the English should pursue and scatter themselves over the field; for they saw that if they could once get their enemies to break: their ranks, they might be attacked and discomfited much more easily. As they had said, so they did. The Normans by little and little fled, the English following them. As the one fell back, the other pressed after; and when the Frenchmen retreated, the English thought and cried out that the men of France fled, and would never return.

"Thus they were deceived by the pretended flight, and great mischief thereby befell them; for if they had not moved from their position, it is not likely that they would have been conquered at all; but like fools they broke their lines and pursued…Then the Normans resumed their former position, turning their faces towards the enemy; and their men were to be seen facing round and rushing onwards to a fresh MELEE; the one party assaulting the other; this man striking, another pressing onwards. One hits, another misses; one flies, another pursues; one is aiming a stroke, while another discharges his blow. Norman strives with Englishman again, and aims his blows afresh. One flies, another pursues swiftly: the combatants are many, the plain wide, the battle and the MELEE fierce. On every hand they fight hard, the blows are heavy, and the struggle becomes fierce…And now might be heard the loud clang and cry of battle, and the clashing of lances. The English stood firm in their barricades, and shivered the lances, beating them into pieces with their bills and maces. The Normans drew their swords, and hewed down the barricades, and the English in great trouble fell back upon their standard, where were collected the maimed and wounded…Duke William pressed close upon the English with his lance; striving hard to reach the standard with the great troop he led; and seeking earnestly for Harold, on whose account the whole war was. The Normans follow their lord, and press around him; they ply their blows upon the English; and these defend themselves stoutly, striving hard with their enemies, returning blow for blow…Then those who kept close guard by him and rode where he rode, being about a thousand armed men, came and rushed with closed ranks upon the English; and with the weight of their good horses, and the blows the knights gave, broke the press of the enemy, and scattered the crowd before them, the good Duke leading them on in front. Many pursued and many fled; many were the Englishmen who fell around, and were trampled under the horses, crawling upon the earth, and not able to rise. Many of the richest and noblest men fell in that rout, but the English still rallied in places; smote down those whom they reached, and maintained the combat the best they could; beating down the men and killing the horses…The living marched over the heaps of dead, and each side was weary of striking…And now the Normans pressed on so far, that at last they had reached the standard. There Harold had remained, defending himself to the utmost; but he was sorely wounded in his eye by the arrow, and suffered grievous pain from the blow. An armed man came in the throng of the battle, and struck him on the ventaille of his helmet, and beat him to the ground; and as he sought to recover himself, a knight beat him down again, striking him on the thick of his thigh, down to the bone.

"Gurth saw the English falling around, and that there was no remedy. He saw his race hastening to ruin, and despaired of any aid; he would have fled but could not, for the throng continually increased and the Duke pushed on till he reached him, and struck him with great force…The standard was beaten down, the golden standard was taken, and Harold and the best of his friends were slain…The English were in great trouble at having lost their king, and at the Duke's having conquered and beat down the standard; but they still fought on, and defended themselves long, and in fact till the day drew to a close. Then it clearly appeared to all that the standard was lost, and the news had spread throughout the army that Harold for certain was dead; and all saw that there was no longer any hope, so they left the field, and those fled who could.

"William fought well; many an assault did he lead, many a blow did he give, and many receive, and many fell dead under his hand. Two horses were killed under him, and he took a third at time of need, so that he fell not to the ground; and he lost not a drop of blood. But whatever any one did, and whoever lived or died, this is certain, that William conquered, and that many of the English fled from the field, and many died on the spot. Then he returned thanks to God, and in his pride ordered his standard to be brought and set up on high where the English standard had stood; and that was the signal of his having conquered and beaten down the foe. And he ordered his tent to be raised on the spot among the dead, and had his meat brought thither, and his supper prepared there…King Harold was carried and buried at Varham…

…The king's mother now sought the victorious Norman, and begged the dead body of her son. But William at first answered in his wrath, and in the hardness of his heart, that a man who had been false to his word and his religion should have no other sepulcher than the sand of the shore. He added, with a sneer, "Harold mounted guard on the coast while he was alive; he may continue his guard now he is dead." The taunt was an unintentional eulogy; and a grave washed by the spray of the Sussex waves would have been the noblest burial-place for the martyr of Saxon freedom. But Harold's mother was urgent in her lamentations and her prayers: the Conqueror relented: like Achilles, he gave up the dead body of his fallen foe to a parent's supplications; and the remains of King Harold were deposited with regal honors in Waltham Abbey.

On Christmas day of the same year, William the Conqueror was crowned at London, King of England.

SYNOPSIS OF EVENTS BETWEEN THE BATTLE OF HASTINGS, A.D. 1066, AND JOAN OF ARC'S VICTORY AT ORLEANS, 1429.

A.D. 1066-1087. Reign of William the Conqueror. Frequent risings of the English against him, which are quelled with merciless rigor.

1096. The first Crusade.

1112. Commencement of the disputes about investitures between the emperors and the popes.

1140. Foundation of the city of Lubeck, whence originated the Hanseatic League. Commencement of the feuds in Italy between the Guelphs and Ghibellines.

1146. The second Crusade.

1154. Henry II. becomes King of England. Under him Thomas a Becket is made Archbishop of Canterbury: the first instance of any man of the Saxon race being raised to high office in Church or State since the Conquest.

1170. Strongbow, earl of Pembroke, lands with an English army in Ireland.

1189. Richard Coeur de Lion becomes King of England. He and King Philip Augustus of France join in the third Crusade.

1199-1204. On the death of King Richard, his brother John claims and makes himself master of England and Normandy and the other large continental possessions of the early Plantagenet princes. Philip Augustus asserts the cause of Prince Arthur, John's nephew, against him. Arthur is murdered, but the French king continues the war against John, and conquers from him Normandy, Brittany, Anjou, Maine, Touraine, and Poitiers.

1216. The barons, the freeholders, the citizens, and the yeomen of England rise against the tyranny of John and his foreign favorites. They compel him to sign Magna Charta.

1273. Rudolph of Hapsburg chosen Emperor of Germany.

1283. Edward I. conquers Wales.

1346. Edward III. invades France, and gains the battle of Cressy.

1356. Battle of Poitiers.

1360. Treaty of Bretigny between England and France. By it Edward III. renounces his pretensions to the French crown. The treaty is ill kept, and indecisive hostilities continue between the forces of the two countries.

1414. Henry V. of England claims the crown of France, and resolves to invade and conquer that kingdom.

1415. Henry invades France, takes Harfleur, and wins the great battle of Agincourt.

1417-1419. Henry conquers Normandy. The French Dauphin assassinates the Duke of Burgundy, the most powerful of the French nobles, at Montereau. The successor of the murdered duke becomes the active ally of the English.

1420. The Treaty of Troyes is concluded between Henry V. of England and Charles VI. of France, and Philip, duke of Burgundy. By this treaty it was stipulated that Henry should marry the Princess Catherine of France; that King Charles, during his lifetime, should keep the title and dignity of King of France, but that Henry should succeed him, and should at once be entrusted with the administration of the government, and that the French crown should descend to Henry's heirs; that France and England should for ever be united under one king, but should still retain their several usages, customs, and privileges; that all the princes, peers, vassals, and communities of France should swear allegiance to Henry as their future king, and should pay him present obedience as regent; that Henry should unite his arms to those of King Charles and the Duke of Burgundy, in order to subdue the adherents of Charles, the pretended dauphin; and that these three princes should make no truce or peace with the Dauphin, but by the common consent of all three.

1421. Henry V. gains several victories over the French, who refuse to acknowledge the treaty of Troyes. His son, afterwards Henry VI., is born.

1422. Henry V. and Charles VI. of France die. Henry VI. is proclaimed at Paris, King of England

and France. The followers of the French Dauphin proclaim him Charles VII., King of France. The Duke of Bedford, the English Regent in France, defeats the army of the Dauphin at Crevant.

1424. The Duke of Bedford gains the great victory of Verneuil over the French partisans of the Dauphin, and their Scotch auxiliaries.

1428. The English begin the siege of Orleans.

CHAPTER IX.
JOAN OF ARC'S VICTORY OVER THE ENGLISH AT ORLEANS, A.D. 1429.

…Seldom has the extinction of a nation's independence appeared more inevitable than was the case in France, when the English invaders completed their lines round Orleans…. A series of dreadful defeats had thinned the chivalry of France, and daunted the spirits of her soldiers. A foreign King had been proclaimed in her capital; and foreign armies of the bravest veterans, and led by the ablest captains then known in the world, occupied the fairest portions of her territory. Worse to her even than the fierceness and the strength of her foes were the factions, the vices, and the crimes of her own children. Her native prince was a dissolute trifler, stained with the assassination of the most powerful noble of the land, whose son, in revenge, had leagued himself with the enemy. Many more of her nobility, many of her prelates, her magistrates, and rulers, had sworn fealty to the English king. The condition of the peasantry amid the general prevalence of anarchy and brigandage, which were added to the customary devastations of contending armies, was wretched beyond the power of language to describe. The sense of terror and suffering seemed to have extended itself even to the brute creation.

…In the autumn of 1428, the English, who were already masters of all France north of the Loire, prepared their forces for the conquest of the southern provinces, which yet adhered to the cause of the Dauphin. The city of Orleans, on the banks of that river, was looked upon as the last

stronghold of the French national party. If the English could once obtain possession of it, their victorious progress through the residue of the kingdom seemed free from any serious obstacle. Accordingly, the Earl of Salisbury, one of the bravest and most experienced of the English generals, who had been trained under Henry V., marched to the attack of the all-important city; and, after reducing several places of inferior consequence in the neighborhood, appeared with his army before its walls on the 12th of October, 1428.

The city of Orleans itself was on the north side of the Loire, but its suburbs extended far on the southern side, and a strong bridge connected them with the town. A fortification which in modern military phrase would be termed a tete-du-pont, defended the bridgehead on the southern side, and two towers, called the Tourelles, were built on the bridge itself, where it rested on an island at a little distance from the tete-du-pont. Indeed, the solid masonry of the bridge terminated at the Tourelles; and the communication thence with the tete-du-pont on the southern shore was by means of a drawbridge. The Tourelles and the tete-du-pont formed together a strong fortified post, capable of containing a garrison of considerable strength; and so long as this was in possession of the Orleannais, they could communicate freely with the southern provinces, the inhabitants of which, like the Orleannais themselves, supported the cause of their Dauphin against the foreigners. Lord Salisbury rightly judged the capture of the Tourelles to be the most material step towards the reduction of the city itself. Accordingly he directed his principal operations against this post, and after some severe repulses, he carried the Tourelles by storm, on the 23d of October. The French, however, broke down the part of the bridge which was nearest to the north bank and thus rendered a direct assault from the Tourelles upon the city impossible. But the possession of this post enabled the English to distress the town greatly by a battery of cannon which they planted there, and which commanded some of the principal streets.

It has been observed by Hume, that this is the first siege in which any important use appears to have been made of artillery. And even at Orleans both besiegers and besieged seem to have employed their cannons more as instruments of destruction against their enemy's men, than as engines of demolition against their enemy's walls and works. The efficacy of cannon in breaching solid masonry was taught Europe by the Turks, a few years afterwards, at the memorable siege of Constantinople…famine was looked on as the surest weapon to compel the submission of a well-walled town and the great object of the besiegers was to effect a complete circumvallation. The great ambit of the walls of Orleans, and the facilities which the river gave for obtaining succor and supplies, rendered the capture of the place by this process a matter of great difficulty. Nevertheless, Lord Salisbury, and Lord Suffolk, who succeeded him in command of the English after his death by a cannon-ball, carried on the necessary works with great skill and resolution. Six strongly fortified posts, called bastillos, were formed at certain intervals round the town and the purpose of the English engineers was to draw strong lines between them. During the winter little progress was made with the entrenchments, but when the spring of 1429 came, the English resumed their works with activity; the communications between the city and the country became more difficult, and the approach of want began already to be felt in Orleans.

The besieging force also fared hardly for stores and provisions, until relieved by the effects of a brilliant victory which Sir John Fastolfe, one of the best English generals, gained at Rouvrai, near Orleans, a few days after Ash Wednesday, 1429. With only sixteen hundred fighting men, Sir John completely defeated an army of French and Scots, four thousand strong, which had been collected for the purpose of aiding the Orleannais, and harassing the besiegers. After this encounter, which seemed decisively to confirm the superiority of the English in battle over their adversaries, Fastolfe escorted large supplies of stores and food to Suffolk's camp, and the spirits of the English rose to the highest pitch at the prospect of the speedy capture of the city before them, and the consequent subjection of all France beneath their arms.

The Orleannais now in their distress offered to surrender the city into the hands of the Duke of Burgundy, who, though the ally of the English, was yet one of their native princes. The Regent Bedford refused these terms, and the speedy submission of the city to the English seemed inevitable. The Dauphin Charles, who was now at Chinon with his remnant of a court, despaired of maintaining any longer the struggle for his crown; and was only prevented from abandoning the country by the more masculine spirits of his mistress and his queen. Yet neither they, nor the boldest of Charles's captains, could have shown him where to find resources for prolonging the war; and least of all could any human skill have predicted the quarter whence rescue was to come to Orleans and to France.

In the village of Domremy, on the borders of Lorraine, there was a poor peasant of the name of Jacques d'Arc, respected in his station of life, and who had reared a family in virtuous habits and in the practice of the strictest devotion. His eldest daughter was named by her parents Jeannette, but she was called Jeanne by the French, which was Latinized into Johanna, and anglicized into Joan…At the time when Joan first attracted attention, she was about eighteen years of age. She was naturally of a susceptible disposition, which diligent attention to the legends of saints, and tales of fairies, aided by the dreamy loneliness of her life while tending her father's flocks, had made peculiarly prone to enthusiastic fervor. At the same time she was eminent for piety and purity of soul, and for her compassionate gentleness to the sick and the distressed…The district where she dwelt had escaped comparatively free from the ravages of war, but the approach of roving bands of Burgundian or English troops frequently spread terror through Domremy. Once the village had been plundered by some of these marauders, and Joan and her family had been driven from their home, and forced to seek refuge for a time at Neufchateau…from infancy to girlhood Joan had heard continually of the woes of the war, and she had herself witnessed some of the wretchedness that it caused. A feeling of intense patriotism grew in her with her growth. The deliverance of France from the English was the subject of her reveries by day and her dreams by night. Blended with these aspirations were recollections of the miraculous interpositions of Heaven in favor of the oppressed, which she had learned from the legends of her Church. Her faith was undoubting; her prayers were fervent. "She feared no danger, for she felt no sin;" and at length she believed herself to have received the supernatural inspiration which she sought.

According to her own narrative, delivered by her to her merciless inquisitors in the time of her captivity and approaching death, she was about thirteen years old when her revelations commenced. Her own words describe them best: [Proces de Jeanne d'Arc, vol. i. p. 52.] "At the age of thirteen, a voice from God came near to her to help her in ruling herself, and that voice came to her about the hour of noon, in summer time, while she was in her father's garden. And she had fasted the day before. And she heard the voice on her right, in the direction of the church; and when she heard the voice she also saw a bright light. Afterwards, St. Michael and St. Margaret and St. Catherine appeared to her. They were always in a halo of glory; she could see that their heads were crowned with jewels: and she heard their voices, which were sweet and mild. She did not distinguish their arms or limbs. She heard them more frequently than she saw them; and the usual time when she heard them was when the church bells were sounding for prayer. And if she was in the woods when she heard them, she could plainly distinguish their voices drawing near to her. When she thought that she discerned the Heavenly Voices, she knelt down, and bowed herself to the ground. Their presence gladdened her even to tears; and after they departed she wept because they had not taken her with them back to Paradise. They always spoke soothingly to her. They told her that France would be saved, and that she was to save it." Such were the visions and

the Voices that moved the spirit of the girl of thirteen; and as she grew older they became more frequent and more clear. At last the tidings of the siege of Orleans reached Domremy, Joan heard her parents and neighbors talk of the sufferings of its population, of the ruin which its capture would bring on their lawful sovereign, and of the distress of the Dauphin and his court. Joan's heart was sorely troubled at the thought of the fate of Orleans; and her Voices now ordered her to leave her home; and warned her that she was the instrument chosen by Heaven for driving away the English from that city, and for taking the Dauphin to be anointed king at Rheims. At length she informed her parents of her divine mission, and told them that she must go to the Sire de Baudricourt, who commanded at Vaucouleurs, and who was the appointed person to bring her into the presence of the king, whom she was to save. Neither the anger nor the grief of her parents, who said that they would rather see her drowned than exposed to the contamination of the camp, could move her from her purpose. One of her uncles consented to take her to Vaucouleurs, where De Baudricourt at first thought her mad, and derided her; but by degrees was led to believe, if not in her inspiration, at least in her enthusiasm and in its possible utility to the Dauphin's cause.

The inhabitants of Vaucouleurs were completely won over to her side, by the piety and devoutness which she displayed and by her firm assurance in the truth of her mission. She told them that it was God's will that she should go to the King, and that no one but her could save the kingdom of France. She said that she herself would rather remain with her poor mother and spin; but the Lord had ordered her forth. The fame of "The Maid," as she was termed, the renown of her holiness, and of her mission, spread far and wide. Baudricourt sent her with an escort to Chinon, where the Dauphin Charles was dallying away his time. Her Voices had bidden her assume the arms and the apparel of a knight; and the wealthiest inhabitants of Vaucouleurs had vied with each other in equipping her with warhorse, armor, and sword. On reaching Chinon, she was, after some delay, admitted into the presence of the Dauphin. Charles designedly dressed himself far less richly than many of his courtiers were appareled, and mingled with them, when Jean was introduced, in order to see if the Holy Maid would address her exhortations to the wrong person. But she instantly singled him out, and kneeling before him, said, "Most noble Dauphin, the King of Heaven announces to you by me, that you shall be anointed and crowned king in the city of Rheims, and that you shall be His vice-regent in France." His features may probably have been seen by her previously in portraits, or have been described to her by others; but she herself believed that her Voices inspired her when she addressed the King; [Proces de Jeanne d'Arc, vol. i. p. 56.] and the report soon spread abroad that the Holy Maid had found the King by a miracle; and this, with many other similar rumors, augmented the renown and influence that she now rapidly acquired.

The state of public feeling in France was not favorable to an enthusiastic belief in Divine interposition in favor of the party that had hitherto been unsuccessful and oppressed. The humiliations which had befallen the French royal family and nobility were looked on as the just judgments of God upon them for their vice and impiety. The misfortunes that had come upon France as a nation, were believed to have been drawn down by national sins. The English, who had been the instruments of Heaven's wrath against France, seemed now by their pride and cruelty to be fitting objects of it themselves. France in that age was a profoundly religious country. There was ignorance, there was superstition there was bigotry; but there was Faith—a Faith that itself worked true miracles, even while it believed in unreal ones. At this time, also, one of those devotional movements began among the clergy in France, which from time to time occur in national Churches, without it being possible for the historian to assign any adequate human cause for their immediate date or extension. Numberless friars and priests traversed the rural districts and towns of France, preaching to the people that they must seek from Heaven a deliverance from the pillages of the soldiery, and

the insolence of the foreign oppressors. [See, Sismondi vol. xiii. p. 114; Michelet, vol. v. Livre x.] The idea of a Providence that works only by general laws was wholly alien to the feelings of the age. Every political event, as well as every natural phenomenon, was believed to be the immediate result of a special mandate of God. This led to the belief that His holy angels and saints were constantly employed in executing His commands and mingling in the affairs of men. The Church encouraged these feelings; and at the same time sanctioned; the concurrent popular belief that hosts of evil spirits were also ever actively interposing in the current of earthly events, with whom sorcerers and wizards could league themselves, and thereby obtain the exercise of supernatural power.

Thus all things favored the influence which Joan obtained both over friends and foes. The French nation, as well as the English and the Burgundians, readily admitted that superhuman beings inspired her: the only question was, whether these beings were good or evil angels; whether she brought with her "airs from heaven, or blasts from hell." This question seemed to her countrymen to be decisively settled in her favor, by the austere sanctity of her life, by the holiness of her conversation, but, still more, by her exemplary attention to all the services and rites of the Church. The dauphin at first feared the injury that might be done to his cause if he had laid himself open to the charge of having leagued himself with a sorceress. Every imaginable test, therefore, was resorted to in order to set Joan's orthodoxy and purity beyond suspicion. At last Charles and his advisers felt safe in accepting her services as those of a true and virtuous daughter of the Holy Church.

It is indeed probable that Charles himself, and some of his counselors, may have suspected Joan of being a mere enthusiast; and it is certain that Dunois, and others of the best generals, took considerable latitude in obeying or deviating from the military orders that she gave. But over the mass of the people and the soldiery, her influence was unbounded. While Charles and his doctors of theology, and court ladies, had been deliberating as to recognizing or dismissing the Maid, a considerable period had passed away, during which a small army, the last gleanings, as it seemed, of the English sword, had been assembled at Blois, under Dunois, La Hire, Xaintrailles, and other chiefs, who to their natural valor were now beginning to unite the wisdom that is taught by misfortune. It was resolved to send Joan with this force and a convoy of provisions to Orleans. The distress of that city had now become urgent. But the communication with the open country was not entirely cut off: the Orleannais had heard of the Holy Maid whom Providence had raised up for their deliverance, and their messengers urgently implored the dauphin to send her to them without delay.

Joan appeared at the camp at Blois, clad in a new suit of brilliant white armor, mounted on a stately black war-horse, and with a lance in her right hand, which she had learned to wield with skill and grace…Her head was unhelmeted; so that all could behold her fair and expressive features, her deep-set and earnest eyes, and her long black hair, which was parted across her forehead, and bound by a ribbon behind her back. She wore at her side a small battle-axe, and the consecrated sword, marked on the blade with five crosses, which had at her bidding been taken for her from the shrine of St. Catherine at Fierbois. A page carried her banner, which she had caused to be made and embroidered as her Voices enjoined. It was white satin [Proces de Jeanne d'Arc, vol. i. p. 238.] strewn with fleur-de-lis; and on it were the words "JESUS MARIA," and the representation of the Savior in His glory. Joan afterwards generally bore her banner herself in battle; she said that though she loved her sword much, she loved her banner forty times as much; and she loved to carry it because it could not kill any one.

Thus accoutered, she came to lead the troops of France, who looked with soldierly admiration on her well-proportioned and upright figure, the skill with which she managed her war-horse, and the easy grace with which she handled her weapons.

Her military education had been short, but she had availed herself of it well. She had also the good sense to interfere little with the maneuvers of the troops, leaving those things to Dunois, and others whom she had the discernment to recognize as the best officers in the camp. Her tactics in action were simple enough…But while interfering little with the military discipline of the troops, in all matters of moral discipline she was inflexibly strict. All the abandoned followers of the camp were driven away. She compelled both generals and soldiers to attend regularly at confessional. Her chaplain and other priests marched with the army under her orders; and at every halt, an altar was set up and the sacrament administered. No oath or foul language passed without punishment or censure. Even the roughest and most hardened veterans obeyed her. They put off for a time the bestial coarseness which had grown on them during a life of bloodshed and rapine; they felt that they must go forth in a new spirit to a new career, and acknowledged the beauty of the holiness in which the heaven-sent Maid was leading them to certain victory.

Joan marched from Blois on the 26th of April with a convoy of provisions for Orleans, accompanied by Dunois, La Hire, and the other chief captains of the French; and on the evening of the 28th they approached the town…When it was day, the Maid rode in solemn procession through the city, clad in complete armor, and mounted on a white horse. Dunois was by her side, and all the bravest knights of her army and of the garrison followed in her train. The whole population thronged around her; and men, women, and children strove to touch her garments, or her banner, or her charger…

When it was known by the English that the Maid was in Orleans, their minds were not less occupied about her than were the minds of those in the city; but it was in a very different spirit. The English believed in her supernatural mission as firmly as the French did; but they thought her a sorceress who had come to overthrow them by her enchantments…the effect produced on their army by Joan's presence in Orleans, was proved four days after her arrival; when, on the approach of reinforcements and stores to the town, Joan and La Hire marched out to meet them, and escorted the long train of provision wagons safely into Orleans, between the bastilles of the English, who cowered behind their walls, instead of charging fiercely and fearlessly, as had been their wont, on any French band that dared to show itself within reach.

Thus far she had prevailed without striking a blow; but the time was now come to test her courage amid the horrors of actual slaughter. On the afternoon of the day on which she had escorted the reinforcements into the city, while she was resting fatigued at home, Dunois had seized an advantageous opportunity of attacking the English bastille of St. Loup: and a fierce assault of the Orleannais had been made on it, which the English garrison of the fort stubbornly resisted. Joan was roused by a sound which she believed to be that of Her Heavenly Voices; she called for her arms and horse…she rode out of the gate, and met the tide of her countrymen, who had been repulsed from the English fort, and were flying back to Orleans in confusion. At the sight of the Holy Maid and her banner they rallied and renewed the assault. Joan rode forward at their head, waving her banner and cheering them on. The English quailed at what they believed to be the charge of hell; St. Loup was stormed, and its defenders put to the sword, except some few, whom Jean succeeded in saving…on the following morrow it was resolved by the chiefs of the garrison to attack the English forts on the south of the river. For this purpose they crossed the river in boats, and after some severe fighting, in which the Maid was wounded in the heel, both the English bastilles of the Augustins and St. Jean de Blanc were captured. The Tourelles were now the only post which the besiegers held on the south of the river. But that post was formidably strong, and by its command of the bridge, it was the key to the deliverance of Orleans. It was known that a fresh English army was approaching under Falstolfe to reinforce the besiegers, and should that army arrive, while the Tourelles were yet in the possession of their comrades, there was great peril

of all the advantages which the French had gained being nullified, and of the siege being again actively carried on.

It was resolved, therefore, by the French, to assail the Tourelles at once, while the enthusiasm which the presence and the heroic valor of the Maid had created was at its height. But the enterprise was difficult. The rampart of the tete-du-pont, or landward bulwark, of the Tourelles was steep and high; and Sir John Gladsdale occupied this all-important fort with five hundred archers and men-at-arms, who were the very flower of the English army.

Early in the morning of the 7th of May, some thousands of the best French troops in Orleans heard mass and attended the confessional by Joan's orders; and then crossing the river in boats, as on the preceding day they assailed the bulwark of the Tourelles, "with light hearts and heavy hands." But Gladsdale's men, encouraged by their bold and skilful leader, made a resolute and able defense. The Maid planted her banner on the edge of the fosse, and then springing down into the ditch, she placed the first ladder against the wall, and began to mount. An English archer sent an arrow at her, which pierced her corselet and wounded her severely between the neck and shoulder. She fell bleeding from the ladder; and the English were leaping down from the wall to capture her, but her followers bore her off…In the meanwhile, the English in the bulwark of the Tourelles, had repulsed the oft-renewed efforts of the French to scale the wall. Dunois, who commanded the assailants, was at first discouraged, and gave orders for a retreat to be sounded, Joan sent for him and the other generals, and implored them not to despair…The faintness caused by her wound had now passed off, and she headed the French in another rush against the bulwark. The English, who had thought her slain, were alarmed at her reappearance; while the French pressed furiously and fanatically forward. A Biscayan soldier was carrying Joan's banner. She had told the troops that directly the banner touched the wall they should enter. The Biscayan waved the banner forward from the edge of the fosse, and touched the wall with it; and then all the French host swarmed madly up the ladders that now were raised in all directions against the English fort. At this crisis, the efforts of the English garrison were distracted by an attack from another quarter. The French troops who had been left in Orleans, had placed some planks over the broken part of the bridge, and advanced across them to the assault of the Tourelles on the northern side. Gladsdale resolved to withdraw his men from the landward bulwark, and concentrate his whole force in the Tourelles themselves. He was passing for this purpose across the drawbridge that connected the Tourelles and the tete-du-pont, when Joan, who by this time had scaled the wall of the bulwark, called out to him, "Surrender, surrender to the King of Heaven. Ah, Glacidas, you have foully wronged me with your words, but I have great pity on your soul and the souls of your men." The Englishman, disdainful of her summons, was striding on across the drawbridge, when a cannon-shot from the town carried it away, and Gladsdale perished in the water that ran beneath. After his fall, the remnant of the English abandoned all further resistance. Three hundred of them had been killed in the battle, and two hundred were made prisoners.

The broken arch was speedily repaired by the exulting Orleannais; and Joan made her triumphal re-entry into the city by the bridge that had so long been closed…Slowly and sullenly the English army retired; but not before it had drawn up in battle array opposite to the city, as if to challenge the garrison to an encounter. The French troops were eager to go out and attack, but Joan forbade it. The day was Sunday. "In the name of God," she said, "let them depart, and let us return thanks to God." She led the soldiers and citizens forth from Orleans, but not for the shedding of blood. They passed in solemn procession round the city walls; and then, while their retiring enemies were yet in sight, they knelt in thanksgiving to God for the deliverance which he had vouchsafed them.

…When Charles had been anointed King of France, Joan believed that her mission was

accomplished. And in truth the deliverance of France from the English, though not completed for many years afterwards, was then insured. ..

SYNOPSIS OF EVENTS BETWEEN JOAN OF ARC'S VICTORY AT ORLEANS, A.D. 1429, AND THE DEFEAT OP THE SPANISH ARMADA, A.D. 1588.

A.D. 1452. Final expulsion of the English from France.

1453. Constantinople taken, and the Roman empire of the East destroyed by the Turkish Sultan Mahomet II.

1455. Commencement of the civil wars in England between the Houses of York and Lancaster.

1479. Union of the Christian kingdoms of Spain under Ferdinand and Isabella.

1492. Capture of Grenada by Ferdinand and Isabella, and end of the Moorish dominion in Spain.

1492. Columbus discovers the New World.

1494. Charles VIII. of France invades Italy.

1497. Expedition of Vasco di Gama to the East Indies round the Cape of Good Hope.

1503. Naples conquered from the French by the great Spanish general, Gonsalvo of Cordova.

1508. League of Cambray, by the Pope, the Emperor, and the King of France, against Venice.

1509. Albuquerque establishes the empire of the Portuguese in the East Indies.

1516. Death of Ferdinand of Spain; he is succeeded by his grandson Charles, afterwards the Emperor Charles V.

1517. Dispute between Luther and Tetzel respecting the sale of indulgences, which is the immediate cause of the Reformation.

1519. Charles V. is elected Emperor of Germany.

1520. Cortez conquers Mexico.

1525. Francis I. of France defeated and taken prisoner by the imperial army at Pavia.

1529. League of Smalcald formed by the Protestant princes of Germany.

1533. Henry VIII. renounces the Papal supremacy.

1533. Pizarro conquers Peru.

1556. Abdication of the Emperor Charles V. Philip II. becomes King of Spain, and Ferdinand I. Emperor of Germany.

1557.[sic] Elizabeth becomes Queen of England.

1557. The Spaniards defeat the French at the battle of St. Quentin.

1571. Don John of Austria at the head of the Spanish fleet, aided by the Venetian and the Papal squadrons, defeats the Turks at Lepanto.

1572. Massacre of the Protestants in France on St. Bartholomew's day.

1579. The Netherlands revolt against Spain.

1580. Philip II. conquers Portugal.

CHAPTER X.
THE DEFEAT OF THE SPANISH ARMADA, A.D. 1588.

On the afternoon of the 19th of July, A.D. 158…the messengers and signals had been dispatched fast and far through England, to warn each town and village that the enemy had come at last. In every seaport there was instant making ready by land and by sea; in every shire and every city there was instant mustering of horse and man…But England's best defense then, as ever, was her fleet; and after warping laboriously out of Plymouth harbor against the wind, the lord-admiral stood westward under easy sail, keeping an anxious look-out for the Armada, the approach of which was soon announced by Cornish fishing-boats, and signals from the Cornish cliffs.

…Queen Elizabeth had found at her accession an encumbered revenue, a divided people and an unsuccessful foreign war, in which the last remnant of our possessions in France had been lost; she had also a formidable pretender to her crown, whose interests were favored by all the Roman Catholic powers; and even some of her subjects were warped by religious bigotry to deny her title, and to look on her as an heretical usurper. It is true that during the years of her reign which had passed away before the attempted invasion of 1588, she had revived the commercial prosperity, the national spirit, and the national loyalty of England. But her resources, to cope with the colossal power of Philip II., still seemed most scanty; and she had not a single foreign ally, except the Dutch, who were themselves struggling hard, and, as it seemed, hopelessly, to maintain their revolt against Spain.

On the other hand Philip II, was absolute master of an empire so superior to the other states of the world in extent, in resources and especially in military and naval forces, as to make the project of enlarging that empire into a universal monarchy seem a perfectly feasible scheme; and Philip had both the ambition to form that project, and the resolution to devote all his energies, and all his means, to its realization…Philip had also the advantage of finding himself at the head of a large standing army in a perfect state of discipline and equipment, in an age when, except some few insignificant corps, standing armies were unknown in Christendom. The renown of the Spanish troops was justly high, and the infantry in particular was considered the best in the world. His fleet, also, was far more numerous, and better appointed, than that of any other European power; and both his soldiers and his sailors had the confidence in themselves and their commanders, which a long career of successful warfare alone can create.

Besides the Spanish crown, Philip succeeded to the kingdom, of Naples and Sicily, the Duchy of Milan, Franche-Comte, and the Netherlands. In Africa he possessed Tunis, Oran, the Cape Verde and the Canary Islands; and in Asia, the Philippine and Sunda Islands and a part of the Moluccas. Beyond the Atlantic he was lord of the most splendid portions of the New world which "Columbus found for Castile and Leon." The empire of Peru and Mexico, New Spain, and Chili, with their abundant mines of the precious metals, Hispaniola and Cuba, and many other of the American Islands, were provinces of the sovereign of Spain.

…Alexander Farnese, Prince of Parma, captain-general of the Spanish armies, and governor of the Spanish possessions in the Netherlands was beyond all comparison the greatest military genius of his age. He was also highly distinguished for political wisdom and sagacity, and for his great administrative talents. He was idolized by his troops, whose affections he knew how to win without relaxing their discipline or diminishing his own authority. Pre-eminently cool and circumspect in his plans, but swift and energetic when the moment arrived for striking a decisive blow, neglecting no risk that caution could provide against, conciliating even the populations of the districts which he attacked by his scrupulous good faith, his moderation, and his address, Farnese was one of the most formidable generals that ever could be placed at the head of an army designed not only to win battles, but to effect conquests…Whatever diminution the Spanish empire might have sustained in the Netherlands, seemed to be more than compensated by the acquisition of Portugal, which Philip had completely conquered in 1580. Not only that ancient kingdom itself, but all the fruits of the maritime enterprises of the Portuguese had fallen into Philip's hands. All the Portuguese colonies in America, Africa, and the East Indies, acknowledged the sovereignty of the King of

Spain; who thus not only united the whole Iberian peninsula under his single scepter, but had acquired a transmarine empire, little inferior in wealth and extent to that which he had inherited at his accession. The splendid victory which his fleet, in conjunction with the Papal and Venetian galleys, had gained at Lepanto over the Turks, had deservedly exalted the fame of the Spanish marine throughout Christendom; and when Philip had reigned thirty-five years, the vigor of his empire seemed unbroken, and the glory of the Spanish arms had increased, and was increasing throughout the world.

One nation only had been his active, his persevering, and his successful foe. England had encouraged his revolted subjects in Flanders against him, and given them the aid in men and money without which they must soon have been humbled in the dust. English ships had plundered his colonies; had denied his supremacy in the New World, as well as the Old; they had inflicted ignominious defeats on his squadrons; they had captured his cities, and burned his arsenals on the very coasts of Spain. The English had made Philip himself the object of personal insult. He was held up to ridicule in their stage plays and masks, and these scoffs at the man had (as is not unusual in such cases) excited the anger of the absolute king, even more vehemently than the injuries inflicted on his power. [See Ranke's Hist. Popes, vol. ii. p. 170.] Personal as well as political revenge urged him to attack England. Were she once subdued, the Dutch must submit; France could not cope with him, the empire would not oppose him; and universal dominion seemed sure to be the result of the conquest of that malignant island.

There was yet another and a stronger feeling which armed King Philip against England. He was one of the sincerest and sternest bigots of his age. He looked on himself, and was looked on by others, as the appointed champion to extirpate heresy and re-establish the Papal power throughout Europe. A powerful reaction against Protestantism had taken place since the commencement of the second half of the sixteenth century, and Philip believed that he was destined to complete it. The Reform doctrines had been thoroughly rooted out from Italy and Spain. Belgium, which had previously been half Protestant, had been reconquered both in allegiance and creed by Philip, and had become one of the most Catholic countries in the world. Half Germany had been won back to the old faith. In Savoy, in Switzerland and many other countries, the progress of the counter-Reformation had been rapid and decisive. The Catholic league seemed victorious in France. The Papal Court itself had shaken off the supineness of recent centuries; and, at the head of the Jesuits and the other new ecclesiastical orders, was displaying a vigor and a boldness worthy of the days of Hildebrand or Innocent III.

Throughout continental Europe, the Protestants, discomfited and dismayed, looked to England as their protector and refuge. England was the acknowledged central point of Protestant power and policy; and to conquer England was to stab Protestantism to the very heart. Sixtus V., the then reigning pope, earnestly exhorted Philip to this enterprise. And when the tidings reached Italy and Spain that the Protestant Queen of England had put to death her Catholic prisoner, Mary Queen of Scots, the fury of the Vatican and Escurial knew no bounds.

The Prince of Parma, who was appointed military chief of the expedition, collected on the coast of Flanders a veteran force that was to play a principal part in the conquest of England. Besides the troops who were in his garrisons, or under his colors, five thousand infantry were sent to him from northern and central Italy, four thousand from the kingdom of Naples, six thousand from Castile, three thousand from Aragon, three thousand from Austria and Germany, together with four squadrons of heavy-armed horse; besides which he received forces from the Franche-Comte and the Walloon country. By his command, the forest of Waes was felled for the purpose of building flat-bottomed boats, which, floating down the rivers and canals to Meinport and Dunkerque, were to carry this large army of chosen troops to

the mouth of the Thames, under the escort of the great Spanish fleet. Gun-carriages, fascines, machines used in sieges, together with every material requisite for building bridges, forming camps, and raising fortresses, were to be placed on board the flotillas of the Prince of Parma, who followed up the conquest of the Netherlands, whilst he was making preparations for the invasion of this island. Favored by the dissensions between the insurgents of the United Provinces and Leicester, the Prince of Parma had recovered Deventer, as well as a fort before Zutphen, which the English commanders, Sir William Stanley, the friend of Babbington, and Sir Roland York, had surrendered to him, when with their troops they passed over to the service of Philip II., after the death of Mary Stuart, and he had also made himself master of the Sluys. His intention was to leave to the Count de Mansfeldt sufficient forces to follow up the war with the Dutch, which had now become a secondary object, whilst he himself went at the head of fifty thousand men of the Armada and the flotilla, to accomplish the principal enterprise—that enterprise, which, in the highest degree, affected the interests of the pontifical authority. In a bull, intended to be kept secret until the day of landing, Sixtus V., renewing the anathema fulminated against Elizabeth by Pius V. and Gregory XIII., affected to depose her…For some time the destination of the enormous armament of Philip was not publicly announced. Only Philip himself, the Pope Sixtus, the Duke of Guise, and Philip's favorite minister, Mendoza, at first knew its real object. Rumors were sedulously spread that it was designed to proceed to the Indies to realize vast projects of distant conquest. Sometimes hints were dropped by Philip's ambassadors in foreign courts, that his master had resolved on a decisive effort to crush his rebels in the Low Countries. But Elizabeth and her statesmen could not view the gathering of such a storm without feeling the probability of its bursting on their own shores. As early as the spring of 1587, Elizabeth sent Sir Francis Drake to cruise off the Tagus. Drake sailed into the Bay of Cadiz and the Lisbon Roads, and burnt much shipping and military stores, causing thereby an important delay in the progress of the Spanish preparations. Drake called this "Singeing the King of Spain's beard." Elizabeth also increased her succors of troops to the Netherlanders, to prevent the Prince of Parma from overwhelming them, and from thence being at full leisure to employ his army against her dominions.

Each party at this time thought it politic to try to amuse its adversary by pretending to treat for peace, and negotiations were opened at Ostend in the beginning of 1588, which were prolonged during the first six months of that year. Nothing real was effected, and probably nothing real had been intended to be effected by them. But, in the meantime, each party had been engaged in important communications with the chief powers in France, in which Elizabeth seemed at first to have secured a great advantage, but in which Philip ultimately prevailed…But Philip had an ally in France, who was far more powerful than the French king. This was the Duke of Guise, the chief of the League, and the idol of the fanatic partisans of the Romish faith. Philip prevailed on Guise openly to take up arms against Henry III…Meanwhile in England, from the sovereign on the throne to the peasant in the cottage, all hearts and hands made ready to meet the imminent deadly peril. Circular letters from the queen were sent round to the lord-lieutenants of the several counties requiring them "to call together the best sort of gentlemen under their lieutenancy, and to declare unto them these great preparations and arrogant threatenings, now burst forth in action upon the seas, wherein every man's particular state, in the highest degree, could be touched in respect of country, liberty, wives, children, lands, lives, and (which was specially to be regarded) the profession of the true and sincere religion of Christ: and to lay before them the infinite and unspeakable miseries that would fall out upon any such change, which miseries were evidently seen by the fruits of that hard and cruel government holden in countries not far distant. We do look," said the queen, "that the most part of them should have, upon this instant extraordinary occasion, a larger proportion of furniture, both for horseman and footmen, but especially horsemen, than hath

been certified; thereby to be in their best strength against any attempt, or to be employed about our own person, or otherwise. Hereunto as we doubt not but by your good endeavors they will be the rather conformable, so also we assure ourselves, that Almighty God will so bless these their loyal hearts borne towards us, their loving sovereign, and their natural country, that all the attempts of any enemy whatsoever shall he made void and frustrate, to their confusion, your comfort, and to God's high glory." [Strype, cited in Southey's Naval History.]

Letters of a similar kind were also sent by the council to each of the nobility, and to the great cities. The primate called on the clergy for their contributions; and by every class of the community the appeal was responded to with liberal zeal, that offered more even than the queen required. The boasting threats of the Spaniards had roused the spirit of the nation; and the whole people "were thoroughly irritated to stir up their whole forces for their defense against such prognosticated conquests; so that, in a very short time, all the whole realm, and every corner were furnished with armed men, on horseback and on foot; and these continually trained, exercised, and put into bands, in warlike manner, as in no age ever was before in this realm. There was no sparing of money to provide horse, armor, weapons, powder, and all necessaries; no, nor want of provision of pioneers, carriages, and victuals, in every county of the realm, without exception, to attend upon the armies. And to this general furniture every man voluntarily offered, very many their services personally without wages, others money for armor and weapons, and to wage soldiers: a matter strange, and never the like heard of in this realm or else where. And this general reason moved all men to large contributions, that when a conquest was to be withstood wherein all should be lost, it was no time to spare a portion." [Copy of contemporary letter in the Harleian Collection, quoted by Southey.]

…A camp was formed at Tilbury; and there Elizabeth rode through the ranks, encouraging her captains and her soldiers by her presence and her words. One of the speeches which she addressed to them during this crisis has been preserved; and, though often quoted, it must not be omitted here.

"My loving people," she said, "we have been persuaded by some that are careful of our safety, to take heed how we commit ourselves to armed multitudes for fear of treachery; but I assure you I do not desire to live to distrust my faithful and loving people. Let tyrants fear! I have always so behaved myself, that, under God, I have placed my chiefest strength and safeguard in the loyal hearts and good will of my subjects; and, therefore, I am come amongst you, as you see, at this time, not for my recreation or disport, but being resolved, in the midst and heat of the battle, to live or die amongst you all, to lay down for my God, for my kingdom, and for my people, my honor and my blood, even in the dust. I know I have the body but of a weak and feeble woman, but I have the heart and stomach of a king, and of a King of England too; and think it foul scorn that Parma, or Spain, or any prince of Europe, should dare to invade the borders of my realm; to which, rather than any dishonor shall grow by me, I myself will take up arms, I myself will be your general, judge, and rewarder of every one of your virtues in the field. I know already for your forwardness you have deserved rewards and crowns; and we do assure you, on the word of a prince, they shall be duly paid you. In the meantime, my lieutenant-general shall be in my stead, than whom never prince commanded a more noble or worthy subject, not doubting but by your obedience to my general, by your concord in the camp, and your valor in the field, we shall shortly have a famous victory over those enemies of my God, of my kingdom, and of my people."

We have minute proofs of the skill with which the government of Elizabeth made its preparations…Some of Elizabeth's advisers recommended that the whole care and resources of the government should be devoted to the equipment of the armies, and that the enemy, when he attempted to land, should be welcomed with a battle on the shore. But the wiser counsels… prevailed, who urged the importance of fitting out a fleet, that should encounter the Spaniards at sea, and, if possible, prevent them from approaching the land at all…If indeed the enemy had landed, we may be sure that be would have been heroically opposed. But history shows us so many examples of the superiority of veteran troops over new levies, however numerous and brave…

The ships of the royal navy at this time amounted to no more than thirty-six; but the most serviceable merchant vessels were collected from all the ports of the country; and the citizens of London, Bristol, and the other great seats of commerce, showed as liberal a zeal in equipping and manning vessels as the nobility and gentry displayed in mustering forces by land. The seafaring population of the coast, of every rank and station, was animated by the same ready spirit; and the whole number of seamen who came forward to man the English fleet was 17,472. The number of the ships that were collected was 191; and the total amount of their tonnage 31,985. There was one ship in the fleet (the Triumph) of 1100 tons, one of 1000, one of 900, two of 800 each, three of 600, five of 600, five of 400, six of 300, six of 250, twenty of 200, and the residue of inferior burden. Application was made to the Dutch for assistance; and, as Stows expresses it, "The Hollanders came roundly in, with threescore sail, brave ships of war, fierce and full of spleen, not so much for England's aid, as in just occasion for their own defense; these men foreseeing the greatness of the danger that might ensue, if the Spaniards should chance to win the day and get the mastery over them; in due regard whereof their manly courage was inferior to none."

…While [the] huge [Spanish] armada was making ready in the southern ports of the Spanish dominions, the Prince of Parma, with almost incredible toil and skill, collected a squadron of war-ships at Dunkirk, and his flotilla of other ships and of flat-bottomed boats for the transport to England of the picked troops, which were designed to be the main instruments in subduing England. Thousands of workmen were employed, night and day, in the construction of these vessels, in the ports of Flanders and Brabant. One hundred of the kind called hendes, built at Antwerp, Bruges, and Ghent, and laden with provision and ammunition, together with sixty flat-bottomed boats, each capable of carrying thirty horses, were brought, by means of canals and fosses, dug expressly for the purpose, to Nieuport and Dunkirk. One hundred smaller vessels were equipped at the former place, and thirty-two at Dunkirk, provided with twenty thousand empty barrels, and with materials for making pontoons, for stopping up the harbors, and raising forts and entrenchments. The army which these vessels were designed to convey to England amounted to thirty thousand strong, besides a body of four thousand cavalry, stationed at Courtroi, composed chiefly of the ablest veterans of Europe; invigorated by rest, (the siege of Sluys having been the only enterprise in which they were employed during the last campaign,) and excited by the hopes of plunder and the expectation of certain conquest. [Davis's Holland, vol. ii. p. 219.] And "to this great enterprise and imaginary conquest, divers princes and noblemen came from divers countries; out of Spain came the Duke of Pestrana, who was said to be the son of Ruy Gomez de Silva, but was held to be the king's bastard; the Marquis of Bourgou, one of the Archduke Ferdinand's sons, by Philippina Welserine; Don Vespasian Gonzaga, of the house of Mantua, a great soldier, who had been viceroy in Spain; Giovanni de Medici, Bastard of Florence; Amedo, Bastard of Savoy, with many such like, besides others of meaner quality." [Grimstone, cited in Southey.]

Philip had been advised by the deserter, Sir William Stanley, not to attack England in the first instance, but first to effect a landing and secure a strong position in Ireland; his admiral, Santa Cruz, had recommended him to make sure, in the first instance, of some large harbor on the coast of Holland or Zealand, where the Armada, having entered the Channel, might find shelter in case of storm, and whence it could sail without difficulty for England; but Philip rejected both these counsels, and directed that England itself should

be made the immediate object of attack; and on the 20th of May the Armada left the Tagus, in the pomp and pride of supposed invincibility, and amidst the shouts of thousands, who believed that England was already conquered. But steering to the northward, and before it was clear of the coast of Spain, the Armada, was assailed by a violent storm, and driven back with considerable damage to the ports of Biscay and Galicia. It had, however, sustained its heaviest loss before it left the Tagus, in the death of the veteran admiral Santa Cruz, who had been destined to guide it against England.

This experienced sailor, notwithstanding his diligence and success, had been unable to keep pace with the impatient ardor of his master. Philip II. had reproached him with his dilatoriness, and had said with ungrateful harshness, "You make an ill return for all my kindness to you." These words cut the veteran's heart, and proved fatal to Santa Cruz. Overwhelmed with fatigue and grief, he sickened and died. Philip II. had replaced him by Alonzo Perez de Gusman, Duke of Medina Sidonia, one of the most powerful of the Spanish grandees, but wholly unqualified to command such an expedition. He had, however, as his lieutenants, two sea men of proved skill and bravery, Juan de Martinez Recalde of Biscay, and Miguel Orquendo of Guipuzcoa.

The report of the storm which had beaten back the Armada reached England with much exaggeration, and it was supposed by some of the queen's counselors that the invasion would now be deferred to another year. But Lord Howard of Effingham, the lord high-admiral of the English fleet, judged more wisely that the danger was not yet passed, and, as already mentioned, had the moral courage to refuse to dismantle his principal ships, though he received orders to that effect. But it was not Howard's design to keep the English fleet in costly inaction, and to wait patiently in our own harbors, till the Spaniards had recruited their strength, and sailed forth again…On the 12th of July, the Armada having completely refitted, sailed again for the Channel, and reached it without obstruction or observation by the English.

The design of the Spaniards was that the Armada should give them, at least for a time, the command of the sea, and that it should join the squadron which Parma had collected, off Calais. Then, escorted by an overpowering naval force, Parma and his army were to embark in their flotilla, and cross the sea to England where they were to be landed, together with the troops which the Armada brought from the ports of Spain…Although the numbers of sail which the queen's government, and the patriotic zeal of volunteers, had collected for the defense of England exceeded the number of sail in the Spanish fleet, the English ships were, collectively, far inferior in size to their adversaries; their aggregate tonnage being less by half than that of the enemy. In the number of guns, and weight of metal, the disproportion was still greater. The English admiral was also obliged to subdivide his force; and Lord Henry Seymour, with forty of the best Dutch and English ships, was employed in blockading the hostile ports in Flanders, and in preventing the Prince of Parma from coming out of Dunkirk.

The orders of King Philip to the Duke de Medina Sidonia were, that he should, on entering the Channel, keep near the French coast, and, if attacked by the English ships, avoid an action, and steer on to Calais roads, where the Prince of Parma's squadron was to join him. The hope of surprising and destroying the English fleet in Plymouth, led the Spanish admiral to deviate from these orders, and to stand across to the English shore; but, on finding that Lord Howard was coming out to meet him, he resumed the original plan, and determined to bend his way steadily towards Calais and Dunkirk, and to keep merely on the defensive against such squadrons of the English as might come up with him.

It was on Saturday, the 20th of July, that Lord Effingham came in sight of his formidable adversaries. The Armada was drawn up in form of a crescent, which from horn to horn measured some seven miles. There was a south-west wind; and before it the vast vessels sailed slowly on. The English let them pass by; and then, following in the rear, commenced an attack on them. A running fight now took place, in which some of the best ships of the Spaniards were captured; many more received heavy damage; while the English vessels, which took care not to close with their huge antagonists, but availed themselves of their superior celerity in tacking and maneuvering, suffered little comparative loss. Each day added not only to the spirit, but to the number of Effingham's force. Raleigh, Oxford, Cumberland, and Sheffield joined him; and "the gentlemen of England hired ships from all parts at their own charge, and with one accord came flocking thither as to a set field, where glory was to be attained, and faithful service performed unto their prince and their country."

…The Spanish admiral also showed great judgment and firmness in following the line of conduct that had been traced out for him; and on the 27th of July he brought his fleet unbroken, though sorely distressed, to anchor in Calais roads. But the King of Spain, had calculated ill the number and activity of the English and Dutch fleets…the English and Dutch found ships and mariners enough to keep the Armada itself in check, and at the same time to block up Parma's flotilla. The greater part of Seymour's squadron left its cruising ground off Dunkirk to join the English admiral off Calais; but the Dutch manned about five-and-thirty sail of good ships, with a strong force of soldiers on board, all well seasoned to the sea-service, and with these they blockaded the Flemish ports that were in Parma's power. Still it was resolved by the Spanish admiral and the prince to endeavor to effect a junction, which the English seamen were equally resolute to prevent…

The Armada lay off Calais, with its largest ships ranged outside, "like strong castles fearing no assault; the lesser placed in the middle ward." The English admiral could not attack them in their position without great disadvantage, but on the night of the 29th he sent eight fire-ships among them…one of the largest galeasses ran foul of another vessel and was stranded. The rest of the fleet was scattered about on the Flemish coast, and when the morning broke, it was with difficulty and delay that they obeyed their admiral's signal to range themselves round him near Gravelines. Now was the golden opportunity for the English to assail them, and prevent them from ever letting loose Parma's flotilla against England; and nobly was that opportunity used. Drake and Fenner were the first English captains who attacked the unwieldy leviathans: then came Fenton, Southwell, Burton, Cross, Raynor, and then the lord admiral, with Lord Thomas Howard and Lord Sheffield. The Spaniards only thought of forming and keeping close together, and were driven by the English past Dunkirk, and far away from the Prince of Parma, who in watching their defeat from the coast, must, as Drake expressed it, have chafed like a bear robbed of her whelps. This was indeed the last and the decisive battle between the two fleets.

…It reflects little credit on the English Government that the English fleet was so deficiently supplied with ammunition, as to be unable to complete the destruction of the invaders. But enough was done to ensure it. Many of the largest Spanish ships were sunk or captured in the action of this day. And at length the Spanish admiral, despairing of success, fled northward with a southerly wind, in the hope of rounding Scotland, and so returning to Spain without a farther encounter with the English fleet. Lord Effingham left a squadron to continue the blockade of the Prince of Parma's armament; but that wise general soon withdrew his troops to more promising fields of action. Meanwhile the lord-admiral himself and Drake chased the vincible Armada, as it was now termed, for some distance northward; and then, when it seemed to bend away from the Scotch coast towards Norway, it was thought best, in the words of Drake, "to leave them to those boisterous and uncouth northern seas."

The sufferings and losses which the unhappy Spaniards sustained in their flight round Scotland and Ireland, are well known. Of their whole Armada only fifty-three shattered vessels brought back their beaten and wasted crews to the Spanish coast which they had quitted in such pageantry and pride…

SYNOPSIS OF EVENTS BETWEEN THE DEFEAT OF THE SPANISH ARMADA, A.D. 1588; AND THE BATTLE OF BLENHEIM, A.D. 1704.

A.D. 1594. Henry IV. of France conforms to the Roman Catholic Church, and ends the civil wars that had long desolated France.

1598. Philip II. of Spain dies, leaving a ruined navy and an exhausted kingdom.

1603. Death of Queen Elizabeth. The Scotch dynasty of the Stuarts succeeds to the throne of England.

1619. Commencement of the Thirty Years' War in Germany.

1624-1642. Cardinal Richelieu is minister of France. He breaks the power of the nobility, reduces the Huguenots to complete subjection; and by aiding the Protestant German princes in the latter part of the Thirty Years' War, he humiliates France's ancient rival, Austria.

1630. Gustavus Adolphus, King of Sweden, marches into Germany to the assistance of the Protestants, who were nearly crushed by the Austrian armies. He gains several great victories, and, after his death, Sweden, under his statesmen and generals, continues to take a leading part in the war.

1640. Portugal throws off the Spanish yoke: and the House of Braganza begins to reign.

1642. Commencement of the civil war in England between Charles I. and his parliament.

1648. The Thirty Years' War in Germany ended by the treaty of Westphalia.

1653. Oliver Cromwell lord-protector of England.

1660. Restoration of the Stuarts to the English throne.

1661. Louis XIV. takes the administration of affairs in France into his own hands.

1667-1668. Louis XVI. makes war in Spain, and conquers a large part of the Spanish Netherlands.

1672. Louis makes war upon Holland, and almost overpowers it, Charles II. of England is his pensioner, and England helps the French in their attacks upon Holland until 1674. Heroic resistance of the Dutch under the Prince of Orange.

1674. Louis conquers Franche-Comte.

1679. Peace of Nimeguen.

1681. Louis invades and occupies Alsace.

1682. Accession of Peter the Great to the throne of Russia.

1685. Louis commences a merciless persecution of his Protestant subjects.

1688. The glorious Revolution in England. Expulsion of James II. William of Orange is made King of England. James takes refuge at the French court, and Louis undertakes to restore him. General war in the west of Europe.

1691. Treaty of Ryswick. Charles XII. becomes King of Sweden.

1700. Charles II. of Spain dies, having bequeathed his dominions to Philip of Anjou, Louis XIV.'s grandson. Defeat of the Russians at Narva, by Charles XII.

1701. William III. forms a "Grand Alliance" of Austria, the Empire, the United Provinces, England, and other powers, against France.

1702. King William dies; but his successor, Queen Anne, adheres to the Grand Alliance, and war is proclaimed against France.

CHAPTER XI.
THE BATTLE OF BLENHEIM, 1704.

"The decisive blow struck at Blenheim resounded through every part of Europe: it at once destroyed the vast fabric of power which it had taken Louis XIV., aided by the talents of Turenne, and the genius of Vauban, so long to construct."— ALISON.

Though more slowly molded and less imposingly vast than the empire of Napoleon, the power which Louis XIV. had acquired and was acquiring at the commencement of the eighteenth century, was almost equally menacing to the general liberties of Europe…When Louis XIV. took the reins of government into his own hands, after the death of Cardinal Mazarin, there was a union of ability with opportunity, such as France had not seen since the days of Charlemagne. Moreover, Louis's career was no brief one. For upwards of forty years, for a period nearly equal to the duration of Charlemagne's reign, Louis steadily followed an aggressive and a generally successful policy. He passed a long youth and manhood of triumph.... But he lived on to see his armies beaten, his cities captured, and his kingdom wasted by disastrous war. It is as if Charlemagne had survived to be defeated by the Northmen, and to witness the misery and shame that actually fell to the lot of his descendants…When Louis XIV. began to govern, he found all the materials for a strong government ready to his hand. Richelieu had completely tamed the turbulent spirit of the French nobility, and had subverted the "imperium in imperio" of the Huguenots. The faction of the Frondeurs in Mazarin's time had had the effect of making the Parisian parliament utterly hateful and contemptible in the eyes of the nation. The assemblies of the States-General were obsolete. The royal authority alone remained. The King was the State. Louis knew his position. He fearlessly avowed it, and he fearlessly acted up to it. ["Quand Louis XIV. dit, 'L'etat, c'est moi:' il n'y eut dans cette parole ni enflure, ni vanterie, mais la simple enonciation d'un fait."—MICHELET, HISTOIRE MODERNE vol. ii. p. 106.]

Not only was his government a strong one, but the country which he governed was strong: strong in its geographical situation, in the compactness of its territory, in the number and martial spirit of its inhabitants, and in their complete and undivided nationality. Louis had neither a Hungary nor an Ireland in his dominions, and it was not till late in his reign, when old age had made his bigotry more gloomy, and had given fanaticism the mastery over prudence, that his persecuting intolerance caused the civil war in the Cevennes.

…While France was thus strong and united in herself, and ruled by a martial, an ambitious, and (with all his faults) an enlightened and high-spirited sovereign, what European power was there fit to cope with her, or keep her in check?

"As to Germany, the ambitious projects of the German branch of Austria had been entirely defeated, the peace of the empire had been restored, and almost a new constitution formed, or an old revived, by the treaties of Westphalia…"

As to Spain, the Spanish branch of the Austrian house had sunk equally low. Philip II. left his successors a ruined monarchy. He left them something worse; he left them his example and his principles of government, founded in ambition, in pride, in ignorance, in bigotry, and all the pedantry of state." [Bolingbroke, vol. ii. p. 378.]

It is not, therefore, to be wondered at, that France, in the first war of Louis XIV., despised the opposition of both branches of the once predominant house of Austria. Indeed, in Germany the French king acquired allies among the princes of the Empire against the emperor himself. He had a still stronger support in Austria's misgovernment of her own subjects…If, after having seen the imbecility of Germany and Spain against the France of Louis XIV., we turn to the two only remaining European powers of any

importance at that time, to England and to Holland…From 1660 to 1688, "England, by the return of the Stuarts, was reduced to a nullity." …when England, under her restored dynasty of the Stuarts, did take any part in European politics, her conduct, or rather her king's conduct, was almost invariably wicked and dishonorable…

Holland alone, of all the European powers, opposed from the very beginning a steady and uniform resistance to the ambition and power of the French king. It was against Holland that the fiercest attacks of France were made, and though often apparently on the eve of complete success, they were always ultimately baffled by the stubborn bravery of the Dutch, and the heroism of their leader, William of Orange. When he became king of England, the power of this country was thrown decidedly into the scale against France; but though the contest was thus rendered less unequal, though William acted throughout "with invincible firmness, like a patriot and a hero," [Bolingbroke, vol, ii, p.404.] France had the general superiority in every war and in every treaty: and the commencement of the eighteenth century found the last league against her dissolved, all the forces of the confederates against her dispersed, and many disbanded; while France continued armed, with her veteran forces by sea and land increased, and held in readiness to act on all sides, whenever the opportunity should arise for seizing on the great prizes which, from the very beginning of his reign, had never been lost sight of by her king.

…The empire, which now received the grandson of Louis as its king, comprised, besides Spain itself, the strongest part of the Netherlands, Sardinia, Sicily, Naples, the principality of Milan, and other possessions in Italy, the Philippines and Marilla Islands in Asia, and, in the New World, besides California and Florida the greatest part of Central and of Southern America. Philip was well received in Madrid, where he was crowned as King Philip V. in the beginning of 1701. The distant portions of his empire sent in their adhesion; and the house of Bourbon, either by its French or Spanish troops, now had occupation both of the kingdom of

Francis I., and of the fairest and amplest portion of the empire of the great rival of Francis, Charles V.

Loud was the wrath of Austria, whose princes were the rival claimants of the Bourbons for the empire of Spain. The indignation of William III., though not equally loud, was far more deep and energetic. By his exertions a league against the house of Bourbon was formed between England, Holland, and the Austrian Emperor, which was subsequently joined by the kings of Portugal and Prussia, by the Duke of Savoy, and by Denmark. Indeed, the alarm throughout Europe was now general and urgent. It was clear that Louis aimed at consolidating France and the Spanish dominions into one preponderating empire. At the moment when Philip was departing to take possession of Spain, Louis had issued letters-patent in his favor to the effect of preserving his rights to the throne of France. And Louis had himself obtained possession of the important frontier of the Spanish Netherlands, with its numerous fortified cities, which were given up to his troops under pretence of securing them for the young King of Spain. Whether the formal union of the two crowns was likely to take place speedily or not, it was evident that the resources of the whole Spanish monarchy were now virtually at the French king's disposal.

The peril that seemed to menace the empire, England, Holland, and the other independent powers, is well summed up by Alison: "Spain had threatened the liberties of Europe in the end of the sixteenth century, France had all but overthrown them in the close of the seventeenth. What hope was there of their being able to make head against them both, united under such a monarch as Louis XIV.?" [Military History of the Duke of Marlborough, p. 32.]

…The death of King William on the 8th of March, 1702, at first seemed likely to paralyze the league against France, for "notwithstanding the ill-success with which he made war generally, he was looked upon as the sole centre of union that could keep together the great confederacy then forming; and how much the French feared from his life, had appeared a few years before, in the extravagant and indecent joy they expressed on a false report of his death. A short time showed how vain the fears of some, and the hopes of others were." [Bolingbroke, vol. ii. p. 445.] Queen Anne, within three days after her accession, went down to the House of Lords, and there declared her resolution to support the measures planned by her predecessor, who had been "the great support, not only of these kingdoms, but of all Europe." Anne was married to Prince George of Denmark, and by her accession to the English throne the confederacy against Louis obtained the aid of the troops of Denmark; but Anne's strong attachment to one of her female friends led to far more important advantages to the anti-Gallican confederacy, than the acquisition of many armies, for it gave them MARLBOROUGH as their Captain-General…there are very few generals, of either ancient or modern times, whose campaigns will bear a comparison with those of Marlborough, either for the masterly skill with which they were planned, or for the bold yet prudent energy with which each plan was carried into execution…Marlborough's favor with the new queen by means of his wife was so high, that he was certain of obtaining the highest employment: and the war against Louis opened to him a glorious theatre for the display of those military talents, which he had before only had an opportunity of exercising in a subordinate character, and on far less conspicuous scenes.

He was not only made captain-general of the English forces at home and abroad, but such was the authority of England in the council of the Grand Alliance, and Marlborough was so skilled in winning golden opinions from all whom he met with, that, on his reaching the Hague, he was received with transports of joy by the Dutch, and it was agreed by the heads of that republic, and the minister of the emperor, that Marlborough should have the chief command of all the allied armies.

It must indeed, in justice to Marlborough, be borne in mind, that mere military skill was by no means all that was required of him in this arduous and invidious station. Had it not been for his unrivalled patience and sweetness of temper, and his marvelous ability in discerning the character of those with whom he had to act, his intuitive perception of those who were to be thoroughly trusted, and of those who were to be amused with the mere semblance of respect and confidence, had not Marlborough possessed and employed, while at the head of the allied armies, all the qualifications of a polished courtier and a great statesman, he never would have led the allied armies to the Danube. The Confederacy would not have held together for a single year…

War, was formally declared by the allies against France on the 4th of May, 1702…Marlborough had watched, with the deepest anxiety, the progress of the French arms on the Rhine and in Bavaria, and he saw the futility of carrying on a war of posts and sieges in Flanders, while death-blows to the empire were being dealt on the Danube. He resolved therefore to let the war in Flanders languish for a year, while he moved with all the disposable forces that he could collect to the central scenes of decisive operations. Such a march was in itself difficult, but Marlborough had, in the first instance, to overcome the still greater difficulty of obtaining the consent and cheerful co-operation of the Allies, especially of the Dutch, whose frontier it was proposed thus to deprive of the larger part of the force which had hitherto been its protection. Fortunately, among the many slothful, the many foolish, the many timid, and the not few treacherous rulers, statesmen, and generals of different nations with whom he had to deal, there were two men, eminent both in ability and integrity, who entered fully into Marlborough's projects, and who, from the stations which they occupied, were enabled materially to forward them. One of these was the Dutch statesman Heinsius, who had been the cordial supporter of King William, and who now, with equal zeal and good faith, supported Marlborough in the councils of the Allies; the other was the celebrated general Prince Eugene, whom the Austrian cabinet had recalled from the Italian frontier, to take the command of one of the Emperor's armies in Germany. To these two great men, and a few

more, Marlborough communicated his plan freely and unreservedly; but to the general councils of his allies he only disclosed part, of his daring scheme. He proposed to the Dutch that he should march from Flanders to the Upper Rhine and Moselle, with the British troops and part of the Foreign auxiliaries, and commence vigorous operations against the French armies in that quarter, whilst General Auverquerque, with the Dutch and the remainder of the auxiliaries, maintained a defensive war in the Netherlands. Having with difficulty obtained the consent of the Dutch to this portion of his project, he exercised the same diplomatic zeal, with the same success, in urging the King of Prussia, and other princes of the empire, to increase the number of the troops which they supplied, and to post them in places convenient for his own intended movements.

Marlborough commenced his celebrated march on the 19th of May. The army, which he was to lead, had been assembled by his brother, General Churchill, at Bedburg, not far from Maestricht on the Meuse: it included sixteen thousand English troops, and consisted of fifty-one battalions of foot, and ninety-two squadrons of horse. Marlborough was to collect and join with him on his march the troops of Prussia, Luneburg, and Hesse, quartered on the Rhine, and eleven Dutch battalions that were stationed at Rothweil. [Coxe's Life of Marlborough.] He had only marched a single day, when the series of interruptions, complaints, and requisitions from the other leaders of the Allies began, to which he seemed doomed throughout his enterprise, and which would have caused its failure in the hands of any one not gifted with the firmness and the exquisite temper of Marlborough…Marlborough reached the Rhine at Coblentz, where he crossed that river, and then marched along its right bank to Broubach and Mentz. His march, though rapid, was admirably conducted, so as to save the troops from all unnecessary fatigue; ample supplies of provisions were ready, and the most perfect discipline was maintained. By degrees Marlborough obtained more reinforcements from the Dutch and the other confederates, and he also was left more at liberty by them to follow his own course. Indeed, before even a blow was struck, his enterprise had paralyzed the enemy, and had materially relieved Austria from the pressure of the war. Villeroy, with his detachments from the French-Flemish army, was completely bewildered by Marlborough's movements; and, unable to divine where it was that the English general meant to strike his blow, wasted away the early part of the summer between Flanders and the Moselle without effecting anything…Marshal Tallard, who commanded forty-five thousand men at Strasburg, and who had been destined by Louis to march early in the year into Bavaria, thought that Marlborough's march along the Rhine was preliminary to an attack upon Alsace; and the marshal therefore kept his forty-five thousand men back in order to support France in that quarter. Marlborough skillfully encouraged his apprehensions by causing a bridge to be constructed across the Rhine at Philipsburg, and by making the Landgrave of Hesse advance his artillery at Manheim, as if for a siege of Landau. Meanwhile the Elector of Bavaria and Marshal Marsin, suspecting that Marlborough's design might be what it really proved to be, forbore to press upon the Austrians opposed to them, or to send troops into Hungary; and they kept back so as to secure their communications with France. Thus, when Marlborough, at the beginning of June, left the Rhine and marched for the Danube, the numerous hostile armies were uncombined, and unable to check him.

"With such skill and science had this enterprise been concerted, that at the very moment when it assumed a specific direction, the enemy was no longer enabled to render it abortive. As the march was now to be bent towards the Danube, notice was given for the Prussians, Palatines, and Hessians, who were stationed on the Rhine, to order their march so as to join the main body in its progress. At the same time directions were sent to accelerate the advance of the Danish auxiliaries, who were marching from the Netherlands." [Coxe.]

Crossing the river Neckar, Marlborough marched in a southeastern direction to Mundelshene, where

he had his first personal interview with Prince Eugene, who was destined to be his colleague on so many glorious fields. Thence, through a difficult and dangerous country, Marlborough continued his march against the Bavarians, whom he encountered on the 2d of July, on the heights of the Schullenberg near Donauwert. Marlborough stormed their entrenched camp, crossed the Danube, took several strong places in Bavaria, and made himself completely master of the Elector's dominions, except the fortified cities of Munich and Augsburg…Marlborough re-crossed the Danube, and on the 11th of August united his army with the Imperialist forces under Prince Eugene. The combined armies occupied a position near Hochstadt, a little higher up the left bank of the Danube than Donauwert, the scene of Marlborough's recent victory, and almost exactly on the ground where Marshal Villars and the Elector had defeated an Austrian army in the preceding year. The French marshals and the Elector were now in position a little farther to the east, between Blenheim and Lutzingen, and with the little stream of the Nebel between them and the troops of Marlborough and Eugene. The Gallo-Bavarian army consisted of about sixty thousand men, and they had sixty-one pieces of artillery. The army of the Allies was about fifty-six thousand strong, with fifty-two guns." [A short time before the War of the Succession the musket and bayonet had been made the arms of all the French infantry. It had formerly been usual to mingle pikemen with musketeers. The other European nations followed the example of France, and the weapons used at Blenheim were substantially the same as those still employed.]

…the chances of a battle seemed perilous, and the fatal consequences of a defeat were certain. The inferiority of the Allies in point of number was not very great, but still it was not to be disregarded; and the advantage which the enemy seemed to have in the composition of their troops was striking…Marlborough's words at the council of war, when a battle was resolved on, are remarkable, and they deserve recording. We know them on the authority of his chaplain, Mr. (afterwards Bishop) Hare, who accompanied him throughout the campaign, and in whose journal the biographers of Marlborough have found many of their best materials. Marlborough's words to the officers who remonstrated with him on the seeming temerity of attacking the enemy in their position, were "I know the danger, yet a battle is absolutely necessary; and I rely on the bravery and discipline of the troops, which will make amends for our disadvantages." In the evening orders were issued for a general engagement, and received by the army with an alacrity which justified his confidence.

The French and Bavarians were posted behind a little stream called the Nebel, which runs almost from north to south into the Danube immediately in front of the village of Blenheim. The Nebel flows along a little valley, and the French occupied the rising ground to the west of it. The village of Blenheim was the extreme right of their position, and the village of Lutzingen, about three miles north of Blenheim, formed their left. Beyond Lutzingen are the rugged high grounds of the Godd Berg, and Eich Berg, on the skirts of which some detachments were posted so as to secure the Gallo-Bavarian position from being turned on the left flank. The Danube protected their right flank; and it was only in front that they could be attacked. The villages of Blenheim and Lutzingen had been strongly palisadoed and entrenched. Marshal Tallard, who held the chief command, took his station at Blenheim: Prince Maximilian the Elector, and Marshal Marsin commanded on the left. Tallard garrisoned Blenheim with twenty-six battalions of French infantry, and twelve squadrons of French cavalry. Marsin and the Elector had twenty-two battalions of infantry, and thirty-six squadrons of cavalry in front of the village of Lutzingen. The centre was occupied by fourteen battalions of infantry, including the celebrated Irish Brigade. These were posted in the little hamlet of Oberglau, which lies somewhat nearer to Lutzingen than to Blenheim. Eighty squadrons of cavalry and seven battalions of foot were ranged between Oberglau and Blenheim. Thus the French position was very strong at each extremity, but was comparatively weak in the centre. Tallard seems to have relied on the swampy state of the part of the valley that reaches from below Oberglau to Blenheim, for preventing any serious attack on this part of his line.

The army of the Allies was formed into two great divisions: the largest being commanded by the Duke in person, and being destined to act against Tallard, while Prince Eugene led the other division, which consisted chiefly of cavalry, and was intended to oppose the enemy under Marsin and the Elector. As they approached the enemy, Marlborough's troops formed the left and the centre, while Eugene's formed the right of the entire army. Early in the morning of the 13th of August, the Allies left their own camp and marched towards the enemy. A thick haze covered the ground, and it was not until the allied right and centre had advanced nearly within cannon-shot of the enemy that Tallard was aware of their approach. He made his preparations with what haste he could, and about eight o'clock a heavy fire of artillery was opened from the French right on the advancing left wing of the British. Marlborough ordered up some of his batteries to reply to it, and while the columns that were to form the allied left and centre deployed, and took up their proper stations in the line, a warm cannonade was kept up by the guns on both sides.

The ground which Eugene's columns had to traverse was peculiarly difficult, especially for the passage of the artillery; and it was nearly mid-day before he could get his troops into line opposite to Lutzingen. During this interval, Marlborough ordered divine service to be performed by the chaplains at the head of each regiment; and then rode along the lines, and found both officers and men in the highest spirits, and waiting impatiently for the signal for the attack. At length an aide-de-camp galloped up from the right with the welcome news that Eugene was ready. Marlborough instantly sent Lord Cutts, with a strong brigade of infantry, to assault the village of Blenheim, while he himself led the main body down the eastward slope of the valley of the Nebel, and prepared to effect the passage of the stream.

The assault on Blenheim, though bravely made, was repulsed with severe loss; and Marlborough, finding how strongly that village was garrisoned, desisted from any further attempts to carry it, and bent all his energies to breaking the enemy's line between Blenheim and Oberglau. Some temporary bridges had been prepared, and planks and fascinas had been collected; and by the aid of these and a little stone bridge which crossed the Nebel, near a hamlet called Unterglau, that lay in the centre of the valley, Marlborough succeeded in getting several squadrons across the Nebel, though it was divided into several branches, and the ground between them was soft, and in places, little better than a mere marsh. But the French artillery was not idle. The cannon balls plunged incessantly among the advancing squadrons of the allies; and bodies of French cavalry rode frequently down from the western ridge, to charge them before they had time to form on the firm ground. It was only by supporting his men by fresh troops, and by bringing up infantry, who checked the advance of the enemy's horse by their steady fire, that Marlborough was able to save his army in this quarter from a repulse, which, following the failure of the attack upon Blenheim, would probably have been fatal to the Allies. By degrees, his cavalry struggled over the blood-stained streams; the infantry were also now brought across, so as to keep in check the French troops who held Blenheim, and who, when no longer assailed in front, had begun to attack the Allies on their left with considerable effect.

Marlborough had thus at last succeeded in drawing up the whole left wing of his army beyond the Nebel, and was about to press forward with it, when he was called away to another part of the field by a disaster that had befallen his centre. The Prince of Holstein-Beck had, with eleven Hanoverian battalions, passed the Nebel opposite to Oberglau, when he was charged and utterly routed by the Irish brigade which held that village. The Irish drove the Hanoverians back with heavy slaughter, broke completely through the line of the Allies…But at Blenheim their ardor in pursuit led them too far. Marlborough came up in person, and

dashed in upon their exposed flank with some squadrons of British cavalry. The Irish reeled back, and as they strove to regain the height of Oberglau, their column was raked through and through by the fire of three battalions of the Allies, which Marlborough had summoned up from the reserve. Marlborough having re-established the order and communication of the Allies in this quarter, now, as he returned to his own left wing, sent to learn how his colleague fared against Marsin and the Elector, and to inform Eugene of his own success.

Eugene had hitherto not been equally fortunate. He had made three attacks on the enemy opposed to him, and had been thrice driven back. It was only by his own desperate personal exertions, and the remarkable steadiness of the regiments of Prussian infantry which were under him, that he was able to save his wing from being totally defeated. But it was on the southern part of the battlefield, on the ground which Marlborough had won beyond the Nebel with such difficulty, that the crisis of the battle was to be decided.

Like Hannibal, Marlborough relied principally on his cavalry for achieving his decisive successes, and it was by his cavalry that Blenheim, the greatest of his victories, was won. The battle had lasted till five in the afternoon. Marlborough had now eight thousand horsemen drawn up in two lines, and in the most perfect order for a general attack on the enemy's line along the space between Blenheim and Oberglau. The infantry was drawn up in battalions in their rear, so as to support them if repulsed, and to keep in check the large masses of the French that still occupied the village of Blenheim. Tallard now interlaced his squadrons of cavalry with battalions of infantry; and Marlborough by a corresponding movement, brought several regiments of infantry, and some pieces of artillery, to his front line, at intervals between the bodies of horse. A little after five, Marlborough commenced the decisive movement, and the allied cavalry, strengthened and supported by foot and guns, advanced slowly from the lower ground near the Nebel up the slope to where the French cavalry, ten thousand strong, awaited them. On riding over the summit of the acclivity, the Allies were received with so hot a fire from the French artillery and small arms, that at first the cavalry recoiled, but without abandoning the high ground. The guns and the infantry which they had brought with them maintained the contest with spirit and effect. The French fire seemed to slacken, Marlborough instantly ordered a charge along the line. The allied cavalry galloped forward at the enemy's squadrons, and the hearts of the French horsemen failed them. Discharging their carbines at an idle distance, they wheeled round and spurred from the field, leaving the nine infantry battalions of their comrades to be ridden down by the torrent of the allied cavalry. The battle was now won. Tallard and Marsin, severed from each other, thought only of retreat. Tallard drew up the squadrons of horse which he had left in a line extended towards Blenheim, and sent orders to the infantry in that village to leave and join him without delay. But long ere his orders could be obeyed, the conquering squadrons of Marlborough had wheeled to the left and thundered down on the feeble army of the French marshal. Part of the force which Tallard had drawn up for this last effort was driven into the Danube; part fled with their general to the village of Sonderheim, where they were soon surrounded by the victorious Allies, and compelled to surrender. Meanwhile, Eugene had renewed his attack upon the Gallo-Bavarian left, and Marsin, finding his colleague utterly routed, and his own right flank uncovered, prepared to retreat. He and the Elector succeeded in withdrawing a considerable part of their troops in tolerable order to Dillingen; but the large body of French who garrisoned Blenheim were left exposed to certain destruction. Marlborough speedily occupied all the outlets from the village with his victorious troops, and then, collecting his artillery round it, he commenced a cannonade that speedily would have destroyed Blenheim itself and all who were in it. After several gallant but unsuccessful attempts to cut their way through the Allies, the French in Blenheim were at length compelled to surrender at discretion; and twenty-four battalions, and twelve

squadrons, with all their officers, laid down their arms, and became the captives of Marlborough.

"Such," says Voltaire, "was the celebrated battle, which the French call the battle of Hochstet, the Germans Plentheim, and the English Blenheim, The conquerors had about five thousand killed, and eight thousand wounded, the greater part being on the side of Prince Eugene. The French army was almost entirely destroyed: of sixty thousand men, so long victorious, there never reassembled more than twenty thousand effective. About twelve thousand killed, fourteen thousand prisoners, all the cannon, a prodigious number of colors and standards, all the tents and equipages, the general of the army, and one thousand two hundred officers of mark, in the power of the conqueror, signalized that day!"

Ulm, Landau, Treves, and Traerbach surrendered to the allies before the close of the year. Bavaria submitted to the emperor, and the Hungarians laid down their arms. Germany was completely delivered from France; and the military ascendancy of the arms of the Allies was completely established. Throughout the rest of the war Louis fought only in defense. Blenheim had dissipated for ever his once proud visions of almost universal conquest.

SYNOPSIS OF EVENTS BETWEEN THE BATTLE OF BLENHEIM, 1704, AND THE BATTLE OF PULTOWA, 1709.

A.D. 1705. The Archduke Charles lands in Spain with a small English army under Lord Peterborough, who takes Barcelona.

1706. Marlborough's victory at Ramilies.

1707. The English army in Spain is defeated at the battle of Almanza.

1708. Marlborough's victory at Oudenarde.

CHAPTER XII.
THE BATTLE OF PULTOWA, 1709.

...But though Russia remained thus long unheeded amid her snows, there was a northern power, the influence of which was acknowledged in the principal European quarrels, and whose good will was sedulously courted by many of the boldest chiefs and ablest councilors of the leading states. This was Sweden; Sweden, on whose ruins Russia has risen; but whose ascendancy over her semi-barbarous neighbors was complete, until the fatal battle that now forms our subject.

As early as 1542 France had sought the alliance of Sweden to aid her in her struggle against Charles V. And the name of Gustavus Adolphus is of itself sufficient to remind us, that in the great contest for religious liberty, of which Germany was for thirty years the arena, it was Sweden that rescued the falling cause of Protestantism; and it was Sweden that principally dictated the remodeling of the European state system at the peace of Westphalia.

From the proud pre-eminence in which the valor of the "Lion of the North" and of Torstenston, Bannier, Wrangel and the other Generals of Gustavus, guided by the wisdom of Oxenstiern, had placed Sweden, the defeat of Charles XII. at Pultowa hurled her down at once and for ever. Her efforts during the wars of the French revolution to assume a leading part in European politics, met with instant discomfiture, and almost provoked derision. But the Sweden, whose scepter was bequeathed to Christina, and whose alliance Cromwell valued so highly, was a different power...Finland, Ingria, Livonia, Estonia, Carelia, and other districts east of the Baltic, then were Swedish provinces; and the possession of Pomerania, Rugen, and Bremen, made her an important member of the Germanic empire. These territories are now all reft from her; and the most valuable of them form the staple of her victorious rival's strength...

The decisive triumph of Russia over Sweden at Pultowa was therefore all-important to the world, on account of what it overthrew as well as for what it established...Her rapid transition ...from being the prey of every conqueror to being the conqueror of all with whom she comes into contact, to being the oppressor instead of the oppressed, is almost without a parallel in the history of nations. It was the work of a single ruler; who, himself without education, promoted science and literature among barbaric millions; who gave them fleets, commerce, arts, and arms; who, at Pultowa, taught them to face and beat the previously invincible Swedes: and who made stubborn valor, and implicit subordination, from that time forth the distinguishing characteristics of the Russian soldiery, which had before his time been a mere disorderly and irresolute rabble.

The career of Philip of Macedon resembles most nearly that of the great Muscovite Czar: but there is this important difference, that Philip had, while young, received in Southern Greece the best education in all matters of peace and war that the ablest philosophers and generals of the age could bestow. Peter was brought up among barbarians, and in barbaric ignorance. He strove to remedy this when a grown man, by leaving all the temptations to idleness and sensuality, which his court offered, and by seeking instruction abroad. He labored with his own hands as a common artisan in Holland and in England, that he might return and teach his subjects how ships, commerce, and civilization could be acquired. There is a degree of heroism here superior to anything that we know of in the Macedonian king. But Philip's consolidation of the long disunited Macedonian empire, his raising a people which he found the scorn of their civilized southern neighbors, to be their dread, his organization of a brave and well-disciplined army, instead of a disorderly militia, his creation of a maritime force, and his systematic skill in acquiring and improving sea-ports and arsenals, his patient tenacity of purpose under reverses, his personal bravery, and even his proneness to coarse amusements and pleasures, all mark him out as the prototype of the imperial founder of the Russian power. In justice, however, to the ancient hero, it ought to be added, that we find in the history of Philip no examples of that savage cruelty which deforms so grievously the character of Peter the Great.

573

…at the time when Pultowa was fought, his reforms were yet incomplete, and his new institutions immature. He had broken up the old Russia; and the New Russia, which he ultimately created, was still in embryo. Had he been crushed at Pultowa, his mighty schemes would have been buried with him; and (to use the words of Voltaire) "the most extensive empire in the world would have relapsed into the chaos from which it had been so lately taken." It is this fact that makes the repulse of Charles XII. the critical point in the fortunes of Russia. The danger which she incurred a century afterwards from her invasion by Napoleon was in reality far less than her peril when Charles attacked her; though the French Emperor, as a military genius, was infinitely superior to the Swedish King, and led a host against her, compared with which the armies of Charles seem almost insignificant…

Peter had wisely abolished the old regular troops of the empire, the Strelitzes; but the forces which he had raised in their stead on a new and foreign plan, and principally officered with foreigners, had, before the Swedish invasion, given no proof that they could be relied on. In numerous encounters with the Swedes, Peter's soldiery had run like sheep before inferior numbers. Great discontent, also, had been excited among all classes of the community by the arbitrary changes which their great emperor introduced, many of which clashed with the most cherished national prejudices of his subjects. A career of victory and prosperity had not yet raised Peter above the reach of that disaffection, nor had superstitious obedience to the Czar yet become the characteristic of the Muscovite mind. The victorious occupation of Moscow by Charles XII. would have quelled the Russian nation as effectually, as had been the case when Batou Khan, and other ancient invaders, captured the capital of primitive Muscovy…

The character of Charles XII. has been a favorite theme with historians, moralists, philosophers, and poets. But it is his military conduct during the campaign in Russia that alone requires comment

here…the Swedish king, unlike his great predecessor Gustavus, knew nothing of the art of war, and was nothing more than a brave and intrepid soldier. Such, however, was not the light in which Charles was regarded by his contemporaries at the commencement of his Russian expedition. His numerous victories, his daring and resolute spirit, combined with the ancient renown of the Swedish arms, then filled all Europe with admiration and anxiety…But Charles at that time was solely bent on dethroning the sovereign of Russia, as he had already dethroned the sovereign of Poland, and all Europe fully believed that he would entirely crush the Czar, and dictate conditions of peace in the Kremlin…Charles himself looked on success as a matter of certainty; and the romantic extravagance of his views was continually increasing.

…Charles had not organized his war like Hannibal, on the principle of relinquishing all communications with home, keeping all his forces concentrated, and creating a base of operations in the conquered country. Such had been the bold system of the Carthaginian general; but Charles acted on no such principle, inasmuch as he caused Lewenhaupt, one of his generals who commanded a considerable detachment, and escorted a most important convoy, to follow him at a distance of twelve days' march. By this dislocation of his forces he exposed Lewenhaupt to be overwhelmed separately by the full force of the enemy, and deprived the troops under his own command of the aid which that general's men and stores might have afforded, at the very crisis of the campaign.

…Both sovereigns now prepared for the general action, which each perceived to be inevitable, and which each felt would be decisive of his own and of his country's destiny. The Czar, by some masterly maneuvers, crossed the Vorskla, and posted his army on the same side of that river with the besiegers, but a little higher up. The Vorskla falls into the Borysthenes about fifteen leagues below Pultowa, and the Czar arranged his forces in two lines, stretching from one river towards the other; so that if the Swedes attacked him and were repulsed, they would be driven backwards into the acute angle formed by the two streams at their junction. He fortified these lines with several redoubts, lined with heavy artillery; and his troops, both horse and foot, were in the best possible condition, and amply provided with stores and ammunition. Charles's forces were about twenty-four thousand strong. But not more than half of these were Swedes; so much had battle, famine, fatigue, and the deadly frosts of Russia, thinned the gallant bands which the Swedish king and Lewenhaupt had led to the Ukraine. The other twelve thousand men under Charles were Cossacks and Wallachians, who had joined him in that country. On hearing that the Czar was about to attack him, he deemed that his dignity required that he himself should be the assailant; and leading his army out of their entrenched lines before the town, he advanced with them against the Russian redoubts.

He had been severely wounded in the foot in a skirmish a few days before; and was borne in a litter along the ranks, into the thick of the fight. Notwithstanding the fearful disparity of numbers and disadvantage of position, the Swedes never showed their ancient valor more nobly than on that dreadful day. Nor do their Cossack and Wallachian allies seem to have been unworthy of fighting side by side with Charles's veterans. Two of the Russian redoubts were actually entered, and the Swedish infantry began to raise the cry of victory. But on the other side, neither general nor soldiers flinched in their duty. The Russian cannonade and musketry were kept up; fresh masses of defenders were poured into the fortifications, and at length the exhausted remnants of the Swedish columns recoiled from the blood-stained redoubts. Then the Czar led the infantry and cavalry of his first line outside the works, drew them up steadily and skillfully, and the action was renewed along the whole fronts of the two armies on the open ground. Each sovereign exposed his life freely in the world-winning battle; and on each side the troops fought obstinately and eagerly under their ruler's eye. It was not till two hours from the commencement of the action that, overpowered by numbers, the hitherto invincible Swedes gave way. All was then hopeless disorder and irreparable rout. Driven downward to where the rivers join, the fugitive Swedes surrendered to their victorious pursuers, or perished in the waters of the Borysthenes. Only a few hundreds swam that river with their king and the Cossack Mazeppa, and escaped into the Turkish territory. Nearly ten thousand lay killed and wounded in the redoubts and on the field of battle.

In the joy of his heart the Czar exclaimed, when the strife was over, "That the son of the morning had fallen from heaven; and that the foundations of St. Petersburg at length stood firm." Even on that battlefield, near the Ukraine, the Russian emperor's first thoughts were of conquests and aggrandizement on the Baltic. The peace of Nystadt, which transferred the fairest provinces of Sweden to Russia, ratified the judgment of battle which was pronounced at Pultowa. Attacks on Turkey and Persia by Russia commenced almost directly after that victory…

SYNOPSIS OF EVENTS FROM THE BATTLE OF PULTOWA, 1709, AND THE DEFEAT OF BURGOYNE AT SARATOGA, 1777.

A.D. 1713. Treaty of Utrecht. Philip is left by it in possession of the throne of Spain. But Naples, Milan, the Spanish territories on the Tuscan coast, the Spanish Netherlands, and some parts of the French Netherlands, are given to Austria. France cedes to England Hudson's Bay and Straits, the Island of St. Christopher, Nova Scotia, and Newfoundland in America, Spain cedes to England Gibraltar and Minorca, which the English had taken during the war. The King of Prussia and the Duke of Savoy both obtain considerable additions of territory to their dominions.

1714. Death of Queen Anne. The House of Hanover begins to reign in England. A rebellion in favor of the Stuarts is put down. Death of Louis XIV.

1718. Charles XII. killed at the siege of Frederickshall.

1725. Death of Peter the Great of Russia.

1740. Frederick II, King of Prussia, begins his reign. He attacks the Austrian dominions, and conquers Silesia.

1742. War between France and England.

1743. Victory of the English at Dettingen.

1745. Victory of the French at Fontenoy. Rebellion in Scotland in favor of the House of Stuart: finally quelled by the battle of Culloden in the next year.

1748. Peace of Aix-la-Chapelle.

1756-1763. The Seven Years' War, during which Prussia makes an heroic resistance against the allies of Austria, Russia, and France. England, under the administration of the elder Pitt (afterwards Lord Chatham), takes a glorious part in the war in opposition to France and Spain. Wolfe wins the battle of Quebec, and the English conquer Canada, Cape Breton, and St. John. Clive begins his career of conquest in India. Cuba, is taken by the English from Spain.

1763. Treaty of Paris: which leaves the power of Prussia increased, and its military reputation greatly exalted.

CHAPTER XIII.
VICTORY OF THE AMERICANS OVER BURGOYNE AT SARATOGA, A.D. 1777.

…All the physical essentials for national strength are undeniably to be found in the geographical position and amplitude of territory which the United States possess: in their almost inexhaustible tracts of fertile, but hitherto untouched soil; in their stately forests, in their mountain-chains and their rivers, their beds of coal, and stores of metallic wealth; in their extensive seaboard along the waters of two oceans, and in their already numerous and rapidly increasing population. And, when we examine the character of this population, no one can look on the fearless energy, the sturdy determination, the aptitude for local self government, the versatile alacrity, and the unresting spirit of enterprise which characterize the Anglo-Americans, without feeling that he here beholds the true moral elements of progressive might.

The ancient Roman boasted, with reason, of the growth of Rome from humble beginnings to the greatest magnitude which the world had then ever witnessed. But the citizen of the United States is still more justly entitled to claim this praise…

…The war which rent away the North American colonies of England is, of all subjects in history, the most painful for an Englishman to dwell on. It was commenced and carried on by the British ministry in iniquity and folly, and it was concluded in disaster and shame. But the contemplation of it cannot be evaded by the historian, however much it may be abhorred. Nor can any military event be said to have exercised more important influence on the future fortunes of mankind, than the complete defeat of Burgoyne's expedition in 1777; a defeat which rescued the revolted colonists from certain subjection; and which, by inducing the courts of France and Spain to attack England in their behalf, ensured the independence of the United States, and the formation of that trans-Atlantic power which, not only America, but both Europe and Asia, now see and feel.

Still, in proceeding to describe this "decisive battle of the world," a very brief recapitulation of the earlier events of the war may be…The five northern colonies of Massachusetts, Connecticut, Rhode Island, New Hampshire, and Vermont, usually classed together as the New England colonies, were the strongholds of the insurrection against the mother-country. The feeling of resistance was less vehement and general in the central settlement of New York; and still less so in Pennsylvania, Maryland, and the other colonies of the south, although everywhere it was formidably active. Virginia should, perhaps, be particularized for the zeal which its leading men displayed in the American cause; but it was among the descendants of the stern Puritans that the spirit of Cromwell and Vane breathed in all its fervor; it was from the New Englanders that the first armed opposition to the British crown had been offered; and it was by them that the most stubborn determination to fight to the last, rather than waive a single right or privilege, had been displayed. In 1775, they had succeeded in forcing the British troops to evacuate Boston; and the events of 1776 had made New York (which the royalists captured in that year) the principal basis of operations for the armies of the mother-country.

A glance at the map will show that the Hudson river, which falls into the Atlantic at New York, runs down from the north at the back of the New England States, forming an angle of about forty-five degrees with the line of the coast of the Atlantic, along which the New England states are situate. Northward of the Hudson, we see a small chain of lakes communicating with the Canadian frontier. It is necessary to attend closely to these geographical points, in order to understand the plan of the operations which the English attempted in 1777, and which the battle of Saratoga defeated.

The English had a considerable force in Canada; and in 1776 had completely repulsed an attack which the Americans had made upon that province. The British ministry resolved to avail themselves, in the next year, of the advantage which the occupation of Canada gave them, not merely for the purpose of defense, but for the purpose of striking a vigorous and crushing blow against the revolted colonies. With this view, the army in Canada was largely reinforced. Seven thousand veteran troops were sent out from England, with a corps of artillery abundantly supplied, and led by select and experienced officers. Large quantities of military stores were also furnished for the equipment of the Canadian volunteers, who were expected to join the expedition. It was intended that the force thus

collected should march southward by the line of the lakes, and thence along the banks of the Hudson river. The British army in New York (or a large detachment of it) was to make a simultaneous movement northward, up the line of the Hudson, and the two expeditions were to unite at Albany, a town on that river. By these operations all communication between the northern colonies and those of the centre and south would be cut off. An irresistible force would be concentrated, so as to crush all further opposition in New England; and when this was done, it was believed that the other colonies would speedily submit. The Americans had no troops in the field that seemed able to baffle these movements. Their principal army, under Washington, was occupied in watching over Pennsylvania and the south. At any rate it was believed that, in order to oppose the plan intended for the new campaign, the insurgents must risk a pitched battle, in which the superiority of the royalists, in numbers, in discipline, and in equipment, seemed to promise to the latter a crowning victory. Without question the plan was ably formed; and had the success of the execution been equal to the ingenuity of the design, the re-conquest or submission of the thirteen United States must, in all human probability, have followed; and the independence which they proclaimed in 1776 would have been extinguished before it existed a second year. No European power had as yet come forward to aid America. It is true that England was generally regarded with jealousy and ill-will, and was thought to have acquired, at the treaty of Paris, a preponderance of dominion which was perilous to the balance of power; but though many were willing to wound, none had yet ventured to strike; and America, if defeated in 1777, would have been suffered to fall unaided.

…Burgoyne had gained celebrity by some bold and dashing exploits in Portugal during the last war; he was personally as brave an officer as ever headed British troops; he had considerable skill as a tactician; and his general intellectual abilities and acquirements were of a high order. He had several very able and experienced officers under him,

Readings

among whom were Major-General Phillips and Brigadier-General Fraser. His regular troops amounted, exclusively of the corps of artillery, to about seven thousand two hundred men, rank and file. Nearly half of these were Germans. He had also an auxiliary force of from two to three thousand Canadians. He summoned the warriors of several tribes of the Red Indians near the western lakes to join his army…Burgoyne assembled his troops and confederates near the river Bouquet, on the west side of Lake Champlain…The army proceeded by water to Crown Point, a fortification which the Americans held at the northern extremity of the inlet by which the water from Lake George is conveyed to Lake Champlain. He landed here without opposition; but the reduction of Ticonderoga, a fortification about twelve miles to the south of Crown Point, was a more serious matter, and was supposed to be the critical part of the expedition. Ticonderoga commanded the passage along the lakes, and was considered to be the key to the route which Burgoyne wished to follow. The English had been repulsed in an attack on it in the war with the French in 1768 with severe loss. But Burgoyne now invested it with great skill; and the American general, St. Clair, who had only an ill-equipped army of about three thousand men, evacuated it on the 5th of July. It seems evident that a different course would have caused the destruction or capture of his whole army; which, weak as it was, was the chief force then in the field for the protection of the New England states. When censured by some of his countrymen for abandoning Ticonderoga, St. Clair truly replied, "that he had lost a post, but saved a province." Burgoyne's troops pursued the retiring Americans, gained several advantages over them, and took a large part of their artillery and military stores.

The loss of the British in these engagements was trifling. The army moved southward along Lake George to Skenesborough; and thence slowly, and with great difficulty, across a broken country, full of creeks and marshes, and clogged by the enemy with felled trees and other obstacles, to Fort Edward, on the Hudson river, the American troops continuing to retire before them.

Burgoyne reached the left bank of the Hudson river on the 30th of July. Hitherto he had overcome every difficulty which the enemy and the nature of the country had placed in his way. His army was in excellent order and in the highest spirits; and the peril of the expedition seemed over, when they were once on the bank of the river which was to be the channel of communication between them and the British army in the south….

The astonishment and alarm which these events produced among the Americans were naturally great; but in the midst of their disasters none of the colonists showed any disposition to submit. The local governments of the New England States, as well as the Congress, acted with vigor and firmness in their efforts to repel the enemy. General Gates was sent to take command of the army at Saratoga; and Arnold, a favorite leader of the Americans, was dispatched by Washington to act under him, with reinforcements of troops and guns from the main American army. Burgoyne's employment of the Indians now produced the worst possible effects. Though he labored hard to check the atrocities which they were accustomed to commit, he could not prevent the occurrence of many barbarous outrages, repugnant both to the feelings of humanity and to the laws of civilized warfare. The American commanders took care that the reports of these excesses should be circulated far and wide, well knowing that they would make the stern New Englanders not droop, but rage. Such was their effect; and though, when each man looked upon his wife, his children, his sisters, or his aged parents, the thought of the merciless Indian "thirsting for the blood of man, woman, and child," of "the cannibal savage torturing, murdering, roasting, and eating the mangled victims of his barbarous battles," [Lord Chatham's speech on the employment of Indians in the war.] might raise terror in the bravest breasts; this very terror produced a directly contrary effect to causing submission to the royal

578

army. It was seen that the few friends of the royal cause, as well as its enemies, were liable to be the victims of the indiscriminate rage of the savages;" [See in the "Annual Register" for 1777, p.117, the "Narrative of the Murder of Miss M'Crea, the daughter of an American loyalist."] and thus "the inhabitants of the open and frontier countries had no choice of acting: they had no means of security left, but by abandoning their habitations and taking up arms. Every man saw the necessity of becoming a temporary soldier, not only for his own security, but for the protection and defense of those connections which are dearer than life itself. Thus an army was poured forth by the woods, mountains, and marshes, which in this part were thickly sown with plantations and villages. The Americans recalled their courage; and when their regular army seemed to be entirely wasted, the spirit of the country produced a much greater and more formidable force." [Burke.]

While resolute recruits, accustomed to the use of fire-arms, and all partially trained by service in the provincial militias, were thus flocking to the standard of Gates and Arnold at Saratoga; and while Burgoyne was engaged at Port Edward in providing the means for the further advance of his army through the intricate and hostile country that still lay before him, two events occurred, in each of which the British sustained loss, and the Americans obtained advantage, the moral effects of which were even more important than the immediate result of the encounters. When Burgoyne left Canada, General St. Leger was detached from that province with a mixed force of about one thousand men, and some light field-pieces, across Lake Ontario against Fort Stanwix, which the Americans held. After capturing this, he was to march along the Mohawk river to its confluence with the Hudson, between Saratoga and Albany, where his force and that of Burgoyne were to unite. But, after some successes, St. Leger was obliged to retreat, and to abandon his tents and large quantities of stores to the garrison. At the very time that General Burgoyne heard of this disaster, he experienced one still more severe in the defeat of Colonel Baum with a large detachment of German troops at Benington,

whither Burgoyne had sent them for the purpose of capturing some magazines of provisions, of which the British army stood greatly in need. The Americans, augmented by continual accessions of strength, succeeded, after many attacks, in breaking this corps, which fled into the woods, and left its commander mortally wounded on the field: they then marched against a force of five hundred grenadiers and light infantry, which was advancing to Colonel Baum's assistance under Lieutenant-Colonel Breyman; who, after a gallant resistance, was obliged to retreat on the main army. The British loss in these two actions exceeded six hundred men: and a party of American loyalists, on their way to join the army, having attached themselves to Colonel Baum's corps, were destroyed with it.

Notwithstanding these reverses, which added greatly to the spirit and numbers of the American forces, Burgoyne determined to advance. It was impossible any longer to keep up his communications with Canada by way of the lakes, so as to supply his army on his southward march; but having by unremitting exertions collected provisions for thirty days, he crossed the Hudson by means of a bridge of rafts, and, marching a short distance along its western bank, he encamped on the 14th of September on the heights of Saratoga, about sixteen miles from Albany. The Americans had fallen back from Saratoga, and were now strongly posted near Stillwater, about half way between Saratoga and Albany, and showed a determination to recede no farther.

Meanwhile Lord Howe, with the bulk of the British army that had lain at New York, had sailed away to the Delaware, and there commenced a campaign against Washington, in which the English general took Philadelphia, and gained other showy, but unprofitable successes, But Sir Henry Clinton, a brave and skilful officer, was left with a considerable force at New York; and he undertook the task of moving up the Hudson to co-operate with Burgoyne. Clinton was obliged for this purpose to wait for reinforcements which had been promised from England, and these did not arrive till September. As soon as he received them,

Clinton embarked about 3,000 of his men on a flotilla, convoyed by some ships of war under Commander Hotham, and proceeded to force his may up the river, but it was long before he was able to open any communication with Burgoyne.

The country between Burgoyne's position at Saratoga and that of the Americans at Stillwater was rugged, and seamed with creeks and water-courses; but after great labor in making bridges and temporary causeways, the British army moved forward. About four miles from Saratoga, on the afternoon of the 19th of September, a sharp encounter took place between part of the English right wing, under Burgoyne himself, and a strong body of the enemy, under Gates and Arnold. The conflict lasted till sunset. The British remained masters of the field; but the loss on each side was nearly equal (from five hundred to six hundred men); and the spirits of the Americans were greatly raised by having withstood the best regular troops of the English army. Burgoyne now halted again, and strengthened his position by field-works and redoubts; and the Americans also improved their defenses. The two armies remained nearly within cannon-shot of each other for a considerable time, during which Burgoyne was anxiously looking for intelligence of the promised expedition from New York, which, according to the original plan, ought by this time to have been approaching Albany from the south. At last, a messenger from Clinton made his way, with great difficulty, to Burgoyne's camp, and brought the information that Clinton was on his way up the Hudson to attack the American forts which barred the passage up that river to Albany. Burgoyne, in reply, on the 30th of September, urged Clinton to attack the forts as speedily as possible, stating that the effect of such an attack, or even the semblance of it, would be to move the American army from its position before his own troops. By another messenger, who reached Clinton on the 5th of October, Burgoyne informed his brother general that he had lost his communications with Canada, but had provisions which would last him till the 20th. Burgoyne described himself as strongly posted, and stated that though the Americans in

front of him were strongly posted also, he made no doubt of being able to force them, and making his way to Albany; but that he doubted whether he could subsist there, as the country was drained of provisions. He wished Clinton to meet him there, and to keep open a communication with New York. [See the letters of General Clinton to General Harvey, published by Lord Albemarle in his "Memoirs of the Marquis of Rockingham," vol. ii. p. 335, ET SEQ.]

Burgoyne had over-estimated his resources, and in the very beginning of October found difficulty and distress pressing him hard.

The Indians and Canadians began to desert him; while, on the other hand, Gates's army was continually reinforced by fresh bodies of the militia. An expeditionary force was detached by the Americans, which made a bold, though unsuccessful, attempt to retake Ticonderoga. And finding the number and spirit of the enemy to increase daily, and his own stores of provision to diminish, Burgoyne determined on attacking the Americans in front of him, and by dislodging them from their position, to gain the means of moving upon Albany, or at least of relieving his troops from the straitened position in which they were cooped up.

Burgoyne's force was now reduced to less than 6,000 men. The right of his camp was on some high ground a little to the west of the river; thence his entrenchments extended along the lower ground to the bank of the Hudson, the line of their front being nearly at a right angle with the course of the stream. The lines were fortified with redoubts and field-works, and on a height on the bank of the extreme right a strong redoubt was reared, and entrenchments, in a horse-shoe form, thrown up. The Hessians, under Colonel Breyman, were stationed here, forming a flank defense to Burgoyne's main army. The numerical force of the Americans was now greater than the British even in regular troops, and the numbers of the militia and volunteers which had joined Gates and Arnold were greater still.

General Lincoln with 2,000 New England troops, had reached the American camp on the 29th of September. Gates gave him the command of the right wing, and took in person the command of the left wing, which was composed of two brigades under Generals Poor and Leonard, of Colonel Morgan's rifle corps, and part of the fresh New England Militia. The whole of the American lines had been ably fortified under the direction of the celebrated Polish general, Kosciusko, who was now serving as a volunteer in Gates's army. The right of the American position, that is to say, the part of it nearest to the river, was too strong to be assailed with any prospect of success: and Burgoyne therefore determined to endeavor to force their left. For this purpose he formed a column of 1,500 regular troops, with two twelve-pounders, two howitzers and six six-pounders. He headed this in person, having Generals Phillips, Reidesel, and Fraser under him. The enemy's force immediately in front of his lines was so strong that he dared not weaken the troops who guarded them, by detaching any more to strengthen his column of attack.

It was on the 7th of October that Burgoyne led his column forward; and on the preceding day, the 6th, Clinton had successfully executed a brilliant enterprise against the two American forts which barred his progress up the Hudson. He had captured them both, with severe loss to the American forces opposed to him; he had destroyed the fleet which the Americans had been forming on the Hudson, under the protection of their forts; and the upward river was laid open to his squadron. He had also, with admirable skill and industry, collected in small vessels, such as could float within a few miles of Albany, provisions sufficient to supply Burgoyne's Army for six months. [See Clinton's letters in Lord Albemarle, p. 337.] He was now only a hundred and fifty-six miles distant from Burgoyne; and a detachment of 1,700 men actually advanced within forty miles of Albany. Unfortunately Burgoyne and Clinton were each ignorant of the other's movements; but if Burgoyne had won his battle on the 7th, he must on advancing have soon learned the tidings of

Clinton's success, and Clinton would have heard of his. A junction would soon have been made of the two victorious armies, and the great objects of the campaign might yet have been accomplished. All depended on the fortune of the column with which Burgoyne, on the eventful 7th of October, 1777, advanced against the American position…Burgoyne pushed forward some bodies of irregular troops to distract the enemy's attention; and led his column to within three-quarters of a mile from the left of Gates's camp, and then deployed his men into line. The grenadiers under Major Ackland, and the artillery under Major Williams, were drawn up on the left; a corps of Germans under General Reidesel, and some British troops under General Phillips, were in the centre; and the English light infantry, and the 24th regiment under Lord Balcarres and General Fraser, were on the right. But Gates did not wait to be attacked; and directly the British line was formed and began to advance, the American general, with admirable skill, caused General Poor's brigade of New York and New Hampshire troops, and part of General Leonard's brigade, to make a sudden and vehement rush against its left, and at the same time sent Colonel Morgan, with his rifle corps and other troops, amounting to 1,500, to turn the right of the English. The grenadiers under Ackland sustained the charge of superior numbers nobly. But Gates sent more Americans forward, and in a few minutes the action became general along the centre, so as to prevent the Germans from detaching any help to the grenadiers. Morgan, with his riflemen, was now pressing Lord Balcarres and General Fraser hard, and fresh masses of the enemy were observed advancing from their extreme left, with the evident intention of forcing the British right, and cutting off its retreat. The English light infantry and the 24th now fell back, and formed an oblique second line, which enabled them to baffle this maneuver, and also to succor their comrades in the left wing, the gallant grenadiers, who were overpowered by superior numbers, and, but for this aid, must have been cut to pieces.

The contest now was fiercely maintained on both sides. The English cannon were repeatedly taken and retaken; but when the grenadiers near them were forced back by the weight of superior numbers, one of the guns was permanently captured by the Americans, and turned upon the English. Major Williams and Major Ackland were both made prisoners, and in this part of the field the advantage of the Americans was decided. The British centre still held its ground; but now it was that the American general Arnold appeared upon the scene, and did more for his countrymen than whole battalions could have effected. Arnold, when the decisive engagement of the 7th of October commenced, had been deprived of his command by Gates, in consequence of a quarrel between them about the action of the 19th of September. He had listened for a short time in the American camp to the thunder of the battle, in which he had no military right to take part, either as commander or as combatant. But his excited spirit could not long endure such a state of inaction. He called for his horse, a powerful brown charger, and springing on it, galloped furiously to where the fight seemed to be the thickest. Gates saw him, and sent an aide-de-camp to recall him; but Arnold spurred far in advance, and placed himself at the head of three regiments which had formerly been under him, and which welcomed their old commander with joyous cheers. He led them instantly upon the British centre; and then galloping along the American line, he issued orders for a renewed and a closer attack, which were obeyed with alacrity, Arnold himself setting the example of the most daring personal bravery, and charging more than once, sword in hand, into the English ranks. On the British side the officers did their duty nobly; but General Fraser was the most eminent of them all, restoring order wherever the line began to waver, and infusing fresh courage into his men by voice and example. Mounted on an iron-grey charger, and dressed in the full uniform of a general officer, he was conspicuous to foes as well as to friends. The American Colonel Morgan thought that the fate of the battle rested on this gallant man's life, and calling several of his best marksman round him, pointed Fraser out, and said: "That officer is General Fraser; I admire him, but he must die. Our victory depends on it. Take

your stations in that clump of bushes, and do your duty." Within five minutes Fraser fell mortally wounded, and was carried to the British camp by two grenadiers…Burgoyne's whole force was now compelled to retreat towards their camp; the left and centre were in complete disorder, but the light infantry and the 24th checked the fury of the assailants, and the remains of the column with great difficulty effected their return to their camp; leaving six of their cannons in the possession of the enemy, and great numbers of killed and wounded on the field; and especially a large proportion of the artillerymen, who had stood to their guns until shot down or bayoneted beside them by the advancing Americans.

Burgoyne's column had been defeated, but the action was not yet over. The English had scarcely entered the camp, when the Americans, pursuing their success, assaulted it in several places with remarkable impetuosity, rushing in upon the entrenchments and redoubts through a severe fire of grape-shot and musketry. Arnold especially, who on this day appeared maddened with the thirst of combat and carnage, urged on the attack against a part of the entrenchments which was occupied by the light infantry under Lord Balcarres. [Botta's American War, book viii.] But the English received him with vigor and spirit. The struggle here was obstinate and sanguinary. At length, as it grew towards evening, Arnold, having forced all obstacles, entered the works with some of the most fearless of his followers. But in this critical moment of glory and danger, he received a painful wound in the same leg which had already been injured at the assault on Quebec. To his bitter regret he was obliged to be carried back. His party still continued the attack, but the English also continued their obstinate resistance, and at last night fell, and the assailants withdrew from this quarter of the British entrenchments. But, in another part the attack had been more successful. A body of the Americans, under Colonel Brooke, forced their way in through a part of the horse-shoe entrenchments on the extreme right, which was defended by the Hessian reserve under Colonel Breyman. The Germans resisted well, and

Breyman died in defense of his post; but the Americans made good the ground which they had won, and captured baggage, tents, artillery, and a store of ammunition, which they were greatly in need of. They had by establishing themselves on this point, acquired the means of completely turning the right flank of the British, and gaining their rear. To prevent this calamity, Burgoyne effected during the night an entire change of position. With great skill he removed his whole army to some heights near the river, a little northward of the former camp, and he there drew up his men, expecting to be attacked on the following day. But Gates was resolved not to risk the certain triumph which his success had already secured for him. He harassed the English with skirmishes, but attempted no regular attack. Meanwhile he detached bodies of troops on both sides of the Hudson to prevent the British from recrossing that river, and to bar their retreat. When night fell, it became absolutely necessary for Burgoyne to retire again, and, accordingly, the troops were marched through a stormy and rainy night towards Saratoga, abandoning their sick and wounded, and the greater part of their baggage to the enemy.

…Burgoyne now took up his last position on the heights near Saratoga; and hemmed in by the enemy, who refused any encounter, and baffled in all his attempts at finding a path of escape, he there lingered until famine compelled him to capitulate…At length the 13th of October arrived, and as no prospect of assistance appeared, and the provisions were nearly exhausted, Burgoyne, by the unanimous advice of a council of war, sent a messenger to the American camp to treat of a convention.

General Gates in the first instance demanded that the royal army should surrender prisoners of war. He also proposed that the British should ground their arms. Burgoyne replied, "This article is inadmissible in every extremity; sooner than this army will consent to ground their arms in their encampment, they will rush on the enemy, determined to take no quarter." After various messages, a convention for the surrender of the army was settled, which provided that "The troops under General Burgoyne were to march out of their camp with the honors of war, and the artillery of the entrenchments, to the verge of the river, where the arms and artillery were to be left. The arms to be piled by word of command from their own officers. A free passage was to be granted to the army under Lieutenant-General Burgoyne to Great Britain, upon condition of not serving again in North America during the present contest."

The articles of capitulation were settled on the 15th of October: and on that very evening a messenger arrived from Clinton with an account of his successes, and with the tidings that part of his force had penetrated as far as Esopus, within fifty miles of Burgoyne's camp. But it was too late. The public faith was pledged; and the army was, indeed, too debilitated by fatigue and hunger to resist an attack if made; and Gates certainly would have made it, if the convention had been broken off. Accordingly, on the 17th, the convention of Saratoga was carried into effect. By this convention 5,790 men surrendered themselves as prisoners. The sick and wounded left in the camp when the British retreated to Saratoga, together with the numbers of the British, German, and Canadian troops, who were killed, wounded, or taken, and who had deserted in the preceding part of the expedition, were reckoned to be 4,689.

The British sick and wounded who had fallen into the hands of the Americans after the battle of the 7th, were treated with exemplary humanity; and when the convention was executed, General Gates showed a noble delicacy of feeling which deserves the highest degree of honor. Every circumstance was avoided which could give the appearance of triumph. The American troops remained within their lines until the British had piled their arms; and when this was done, the vanquished officers and soldiers were received with friendly kindness by their victors, and their immediate wants were promptly and liberally supplied. Discussions and disputes afterwards arose as to some of the terms of the convention; and the American Congress refused for a long time to carry into effect the article which provided for the return of Burgoyne's men to Europe; but no blame was imputable to General Gates or his army, who showed themselves to be generous as they had proved themselves to be brave…

SYNOPSIS OF EVENTS BETWEEN THE DEFEAT OF BURGOYNE AT SARATOGA, 1777, AND THE BATTLE OF VALMY, 1792.

A.D. 1781. Surrender of Lord Cornwallis and the British army to Washington.

1782. Rodney's victory over the Spanish fleet. Unsuccessful siege of Gibraltar by the Spaniards and French.

1783. End of the American war.

1788. The States-General are convened in France: beginning of the Revolution.

CHAPTER XIV.
THE BATTLE OF VALMY.

…France now calls herself a republic. She first assumed that title on the 20th of September, 1792, on the very day on which the battle of Valmy was fought and won. To that battle the democratic spirit which in 1848, as well as in 1792, proclaimed the Republic in Paris, owed its preservation, and it is thence that the imperishable activity of its principles may be dated.

Far different seemed the prospects of democracy in Europe on the eve of that battle…When France, in 1792, declared war with the great powers of Europe, she was far from possessing that splendid military organization which the experience of a few revolutionary campaigns taught her to assume…The army of the old monarchy had, during the latter part of the reign of Louis XV. sunk into gradual decay, both in numerical force, and in efficiency of equipment and spirit. The laurels gained by the auxiliary regiments which Louis XVI. sent to the American war, did but little

to restore the general tone of the army. The insubordination and license, which the revolt of the French guards, and the participation of other troops in many of the first excesses of the Revolution introduced among the soldiery, were soon rapidly disseminated through all the ranks. Under the Legislative Assembly every complaint of the soldier against his officer, however frivolous or ill-founded, was listened to with eagerness, and investigated with partiality, on the principles of liberty and equality. Discipline accordingly became more and more relaxed; and the dissolution of several of the old corps, under the pretext of their being tainted with an aristocratic feeling, aggravated the confusion and inefficiency of the war department. Many of the most effective regiments during the last period of the monarchy had consisted of foreigners. These had either been slaughtered in defense of the throne against insurrections, like the Swiss; or had been disbanded, and had crossed the frontier to recruit the forces which were assembling for the invasion of France. Above all, the emigration of the noblesse had stripped the French army of nearly all its officers of high rank, and of the greatest portion of its subalterns. More than twelve thousand of the high-born youth of France, who had been trained to regard military command as their exclusive patrimony, and to whom the nation had been accustomed to look up as its natural guides and champions in the storm of war; were now marshaled beneath the banner of Conde and the other emigrant princes, for the overthrow of the French armies, and the reduction of the French capital. Their successors in the French regiments and brigades had as yet acquired neither skill nor experience: they possessed neither self-reliance nor the respect of the men who were under them.

Such was the state of the wrecks of the old army; but the bulk of the forces with which France began the war, consisted of raw insurrectionary levies, which were even less to be depended on. The Carmagnoles, as the revolutionary volunteers were called, flocked, indeed, readily to the frontier from every department when the war was proclaimed, and the fierce leaders of the Jacobins shouted that the country was in danger. They were full of zeal and courage, "heated and excited by the scenes of the Revolution, and inflamed by the florid eloquence, the songs, dances, and signal-words with which it had been celebrated." [Scott, Life of Napoleon, vol. i c. viii.] But they were utterly undisciplined, and turbulently impatient of superior authority, or systematical control. Many ruffians, also, who were sullied with participation in the most sanguinary horrors of Paris, joined the camps, and were pre-eminent alike for misconduct before the enemy and for savage insubordination against their own officers.... Such phalanxed masses of fighters did the Carmagnoles ultimately become; but France ran a fearful risk in being obliged to rely on them when the process of their transmutation had barely commenced.

The first events, indeed, of the war were disastrous and disgraceful to France, even beyond what might have been expected from the chaotic state in which it found her armies as well as her government. In the hopes of profiting by the unprepared state of Austria, then the mistress of the Netherlands, the French opened the campaign of 1792 by an invasion of Flanders, with forces whose muster-rolls showed a numerical overwhelming superiority to the enemy, and seemed to promise a speedy conquest of that old battle-field of Europe. But the first flash of an Austrian saber, or the first sound of Austrian gun, was enough to discomfit the French. Their first corps, four thousand strong, that advanced from Lille across the frontier, came suddenly upon a far inferior detachment of the Austrian garrison of Tournay. Not a shot was fired, not a bayonet leveled. With one simultaneous cry of panic the French broke and ran headlong back to Lille, where they completed the specimen of insubordination which they had given in the field, by murdering their general and several of their chief officers. On the same day, another division under Biron, mustering ten thousand sabers and bayonets, saw a few Austrian skirmishers reconnoitering their position. The French advanced posts had scarcely given and received a volley, and only a few balls from the enemy's field-pieces had fallen among the lines, when two

regiments of French dragoons raised the cry, "We are betrayed," galloped off, and were followed in disgraceful rout by the rest of the whole army. Similar panics, or repulses almost equally discreditable, occurred whenever Rochambeau, or Luckner, or La Fayette, the earliest French generals in the war, brought their troops into the presence of the enemy.

Meanwhile, the allied sovereigns had gradually collected on the Rhine a veteran and finely-disciplined army for the invasion of France, which for numbers, equipment, and martial renown, both of generals and men, was equal to any that Germany had ever sent forth to conquer. Their design was to strike boldly and decisively at the heart of France, and penetrating the country through the Ardennes, to proceed by Chalons upon Paris. The obstacles that lay in their way seemed insignificant. The disorder and imbecility of the French armies had been even augmented by the forced flight of La Fayette, and a sudden change of generals. The only troops posted on or near the track by which the allies were about to advance, were the twenty-three thousand men at Sedan, whom La Fayette had commanded, and a corps of twenty thousand near Metz, the command of which had just been transferred from Luckner to Kellerman. There were only three fortresses which it was necessary for the allies to capture or mask—Sedan, Longwy, and Verdun. The defenses and stores of these three were known to be wretchedly dismantled and insufficient; and when once these feeble barriers were overcome, and Chalons reached, a fertile and unprotected country seemed to invite the invaders to that "military promenade to Paris," which they gaily talked of accomplishing.

At the end of July the allied army, having completed all preparations for the campaign, broke up from its cantonments, and marching from Luxembourg upon Longwy, crossed the French frontier. Eighty thousand Prussians, trained in the school, and many of them under the eye of the Great Frederick, heirs of the glories of the Seven Years' War, and universally esteemed the best troops in Europe, marched in one column against the central point of attack. Forty-five thousand

585

Austrians, the greater part of whom were picked troops, and had served in the recent Turkish war, supplied two formidable corps that supported the flanks of the Prussians. There was also a powerful body of Hessians, and leagued with the Germans against the Parisian democracy, came fifteen thousand of the noblest and bravest amongst the sons of France. In these corps of emigrants, many of the highest born of the French nobility, scions of houses whose chivalric trophies had for centuries filled Europe with renown, served as rank and file. They looked on the road to Paris as the path which they were to carve out by their swords to victory, to honor, to the rescue of their king, to reunion with their families, to the recovery of their patrimony, and to the restoration of their order. [See Scott, Life of Napoleon, vol. i. c. xi.]

Over this imposing army the allied sovereigns placed as generalissimo the Duke of Brunswick…Moving majestically forward, with leisurely deliberation, that seemed to show the consciousness of superior strength, and a steady purpose of doing their work thoroughly, the Allies appeared before Longwy on the 20th of August, and the dispirited and dependent garrison opened the gates of that fortress to them after the first shower of bombs. On the 2d of September the still more important stronghold of Verdun capitulated after scarcely the shadow of resistance.

Brunswick's superior force was now interposed between Kellerman's troops on the left, and the other French army near Sedan, which La Fayette's flight had, for the time, left destitute of a commander. It was in the power of the German general, by striking with an overwhelming mass to the right and left, to crush in succession each of these weak armies, and the allies might then have marched irresistible and unresisted upon Paris. But at this crisis Dumouriez, the new commander-in-chief of the French, arrived at the camp near Sedan, and commenced a series of movements, by which he reunited the dispersed and disorganized forces of his country, checked the Prussian columns at the very moment when the last

obstacles of their triumph seemed to have given way, and finally rolled back the tide of invasion far across the enemy's frontier.

The French fortresses had fallen; but nature herself still offered to brave and vigorous defenders of the land, the means of opposing a barrier to the progress of the Allies. A ridge of broken ground, called the Argonne, extends from the vicinity of Sedan towards the southwest for about fifteen or sixteen leagues…in 1792 it was thickly wooded, and the lower portions of its unequal surface were filled with rivulets and marshes. It thus presented a natural barrier of from four to five leagues broad, which was absolutely impenetrable to an army, except by a few defiles, such as an inferior force might easily fortify and defend. Dumouriez succeeded in marching his army down from Sedan behind the Argonne, and in occupying its passes, while the Prussians still lingered on the northeastern side of the forest line. Ordering Kellerman to wheel round from Metz to St. Menehould, and the reinforcements from the interior and extreme north also to concentrate at that spot, Dumouriez trusted to assemble a powerful force in the rear of the southwest extremity of the Argonne, while, with the twenty-five thousand men under his immediate command, he held the enemy at bay before the passes, or forced him to a long circumvolution round one extremity of the forest ridge, during which, favorable opportunities of assailing his flank were almost certain to occur…A pass, which was thought of inferior importance, had been but slightly manned, and an Austrian corps under Clairfayt, forced it after some sharp fighting. Dumouriez with great difficulty saved himself from being enveloped and destroyed by the hostile columns that now pushed through the forest…he resolved to cling to the difficult country in which the armies still were grouped, to force a junction with Kellerman, and so to place himself at the head of a force, which the invaders would not dare to disregard, and by which he might drag them back from the advance on Paris, which he had not been able to bar. Accordingly, by a rapid movement to the south…and after, with difficulty, checking several panics of his troops in which they ran by thousands at the sight of a few Prussian hussars, Dumouriez succeeded in establishing his headquarters in a strong position at St. Menehould, protected by the marshes and shallows of the river Aisne and Aube, beyond which, to the northwest, rose a firm and elevated plateau, called Dampierre's Camp, admirably situated for commanding the road by Chalons to Paris, and where he intended to post Kellerman's army so soon as it came up…The news of the retreat of Dumouriez from the Argonne passes, and of the panic flight of some divisions of his troops, spread rapidly throughout the country; and Kellerman, who believed that his comrade's army had been annihilated, and feared to fall among the victorious masses of the Prussians, had halted on his march from Metz when almost close to St. Menehould. He had actually commenced a retrograde movement, when couriers from his commander-in-chief checked him from that fatal course; and then continuing to wheel round the rear and left flank of the troops at St. Menehould, Kellerman, with twenty thousand of the army of Metz, and some thousands of volunteers who had joined him in the march, made his appearance to the west of Dumouriez, on the very evening when Westerman and Thouvenot, two of the staff-officers of Dumouriez, galloped in with the tidings that Brunswick's army had come through the upper passes of the Argonne in full force, and was deploying on the heights of La Lune, a chain of eminences that stretch obliquely from south-west to north-east opposite the high ground which Dumouriez held, and also opposite, but at a shorter distance from, the position which Kellerman was designed to occupy.

The Allies were now, in fact, nearer to Paris than were the French troops themselves; but, as Dumouriez had foreseen, Brunswick deemed it unsafe to march upon the capital with so large a hostile force left in his rear between his advancing columns and his base of operations. The young King of Prussia, who was in the allied camp, and the emigrant princes, eagerly advocated an instant attack upon the nearest French general. Kellerman had laid himself unnecessarily open, by advancing beyond Dampierre's Camp, which Dumouriez had designed for him, and moving forward across the Aube to the plateau of Valmy, a post inferior in strength and space to that which he had left, and which brought him close upon the Prussian lines, leaving him separated by a dangerous interval from the troops under Dumouriez himself. It seemed easy for the Prussian army to overwhelm him while thus isolated, and then they might surround and crush Dumouriez at their leisure.

Accordingly, the right wing of the allied army moved forward, in the grey of the morning of the 20th of September, to gain Kellerman's left flank and rear, and cut him off from retreat upon Chalons, while the rest of the army, moving from the heights of La Lune, which here converge semi-circularly round the plateau of Valmy, were to assail his position in front, and interpose between him and Dumouriez. An unexpected collision between some of the advanced cavalry on each side in the low ground, warned Kellerman of the enemy's approach. Dumouriez had not been unobservant of the danger of his comrade, thus isolated and involved; and he had ordered up troops to support Kellerman on either flank in the event of his being attacked. These troops, however, moved forward slowly; and Kellerman's army, ranged on the plateau of Valmy, "projected like a cape into the midst of the lines of the Prussian bayonets." [See Lamartine, Hist. Girond. livre xvii. I have drawn much of the ensuing description from him.] A thick autumnal mist floated in waves of vapor over the plains and ravines that lay between the two armies, leaving only the crests and peaks of the hills glittering in the early light. About ten o'clock the fog began to clear off, and then the French from their promontory saw emerging from the white wreaths of mist, and glittering in the sunshine, the countless Prussian cavalry which were to envelope them as in a net if once driven from their position, the solid columns of the infantry that moved forward as if animated by a single will, the bristling batteries of the artillery, and the glancing clouds of the Austrian light troops, fresh from their contests with the Spahis of the east.

...Serving under Kellerman on that day was one who experienced, perhaps the most deeply of all men, the changes for good and for evil which the French Revolution has produced. He who, in his second exile, bore the name of the Count de Neuilly in this country, and who lately was Louis Philippe, King of the French, figured in the French lines at Valmy, as a young and gallant officer, cool and sagacious beyond his years, and trusted accordingly by Kellerman and Dumouriez with an important station in the national army. The Duc de Chartres (the title he then bore) commanded the French right, General Valence was on the left, and Kellerman himself took his post in the centre, which was the strength and key of his position.

...Contrary to the expectations of both friends and foes, the French infantry held their ground steadily under the fire of the Prussian guns, which thundered on them from La Lune; and their own artillery replied with equal spirit and greater effect on the denser masses of the allied army. Thinking that the Prussians were slackening in their fire, Kellerman formed a column in charging order, and dashed down into the valley, in the hopes of capturing some of the nearest guns of the enemy. A masked battery opened its fire on the French column, and drove it back in disorder. Kellerman having his horse shot under him, and being with difficulty carried off by his men. The Prussian columns now advanced in turn. The French artillerymen began to waver and desert their posts, but were rallied by the efforts and example of their officers; and Kellerman, reorganizing the line of his infantry, took his station in the ranks on foot, and called out to his men to let the enemy come close up, and then to charge them with the bayonet. The troops caught the enthusiasm of their general, and a cheerful shout of VIVE LA NATION! taken by one battalion from another, pealed across the valley to the assailants. The Prussians flinched from a charge up-hill against a force that seemed so resolute and formidable; they halted for a while in the hollow, and then slowly retreated up their own side of the valley.

Indignant at being thus repulsed by such a foe, the King of Prussia formed the flower of his men in person, and, riding along the column, bitterly reproached them with letting their standard be thus humiliated. Then he led them on again to the attack marching in the front line, and seeing his staff mowed down around him by the deadly fire which the French artillery re-opened. But the troops sent by Dumouriez were now co-operating effectually with Kellerman, and that general's own men, flushed by success, presented a firmer front than ever. Again the Prussians retreated, leaving eight hundred dead behind, and at nightfall the French remained victors on the heights of Valmy.

All hopes of crushing the revolutionary armies, and of the promenade to Paris, had now vanished, though Brunswick lingered long in the Argonne, till distress and sickness wasted away his once splendid force, and finally but a mere wreck of it recrossed the frontier. France, meanwhile, felt that she possessed a giant's strength, and like a giant did she use it. Before the close of that year, all Belgium obeyed the National Convention at Paris, and the kings of Europe, after the lapse of eighteen centuries, trembled once more before a conquering military Republic.

...SYNOPSIS OP EVENTS BETWEEN THE BATTLE OF VALMY, 1792, AND THE BATTLE OF WATERLOO, 1815.

A.D. 1793. Trial and execution of Louis XVI. at Paris. England and Spain declare war against France. Royalist war in La Vendee. Second invasion of France by the Allies.

1794. Lord Howe's victory over the French fleet. Final partition of Poland by Russia, Prussia, and Austria.

1795. The French armies under Pichegru, conquer Holland. Cessation of the war in La Vendee.

1796. Bonaparte commands the French army of Italy and gains repeated victories over the Austrians.

1797. Victory of Jervis, off Cape St. Vincent. Peace of Campo Formio between France and Austria. Defeat of the Dutch off Camperdown by Admiral Duncan.

1798. Rebellion in Ireland. Expedition of the French under Bonaparte to Egypt. Lord Nelson destroys the French fleet at the Battle of the Nile.

1799. Renewal of the war between Austria and France. The Russian emperor sends an army in aid of Austria, under Suwarrow. The French are repeatedly defeated in Italy. Bonaparte returns from Egypt and makes himself First Consul of France. Massena wins the battle of Zurich. The Russian emperor makes peace with France.

1800. Bonaparte passes the Alps and defeats the Austrians at Marengo. Moreau wins the battle of Hohenlinden.

1801. Treaty of Luneville between France and Austria. The battle of Copenhagen.

1802. Peace of Amiens.

1803. War between England and France renewed.

1804. Napoleon Bonaparte is made Emperor of France.

1805. Great preparations of Napoleon to invade England. Austria, supported by Russia, renews war with France. Napoleon marches into Germany, takes Vienna, and gains the battle of Austerlitz. Lord Nelson destroys the combined French and Spanish fleets, and is killed at the battle of Trafalgar.

1806. War between Prussia and France, Napoleon conquers Prussia in the battle of Jena.

1807. Obstinate warfare between the French and Russian armies in East Prussia and Poland. Peace of Tilsit.

1808. Napoleon endeavors to make his brother King of Spain. Rising of the Spanish nation against him. England sends troops to aid the Spaniards. Battles of Vimiera and Corunna.

1809. War renewed between France and Austria. Battles of Asperne and Wagram. Peace granted to Austria. Lord Wellington's victory of Talavera, in Spain.

1810. Marriage of Napoleon and the Arch-duchess Maria Louisa. Holland annexed to France.

1812. War between England and the United States. Napoleon invades Russia. Battle of Borodino. The French occupy Moscow, which is burned. Disastrous retreat and almost total destruction of the great army of France.

1813. Prussia and Austria take up arms again against France. Battles of Lutzen, Bautzen, Dresden, Culm, and Leipsic. The French are driven out of Germany. Lord Wellington gains the great battle of Vittoria, which completes the rescue of Spain from France.

1814. The Allies invade France on the eastern, and Lord Wellington invades it on the southern frontier. Battles of Laon, Montmirail, Arcis-sur-Aube, and others in the north-east of France; and of Toulouse in the south. Paris surrenders to the Allies, and Napoleon abdicates. First restoration of the Bourbons. Napoleon goes to the isle of Elba, which is assigned to him by the Allies. Treaty of Ghent, between the United States and England.

1815. Napoleon suddenly escapes from Elba, and lands in France. The French soldiery join him and Louis XVIII. is obliged to fly from the throne.

CHAPTER XV.
THE BATTLE OF WATERLOO, 1815.

"Thou first and last of fields, king-making victory."—BYRON.

...One good test for determining the importance of Waterloo, is to ascertain what was felt by wise and prudent statesmen before that battle, respecting the return of Napoleon from Elba to the Imperial throne of France, and the probable effects of his success...Napoleon sought to disunite the formidable confederacy, which he knew would be arrayed against him, by endeavoring to negotiate separately with each of the allied sovereigns. It is said that Austria and Russia were at first not unwilling to treat with him. Disputes and jealousies had been rife among several of the Allies on the subject of the division of the conquered countries; and the cordial unanimity with which they had acted during 1813 and the first months of 1814, had grown chill during some weeks of discussions. But the active exertions of Tralleyrand, who represented Louis XVIII. at the Congress, and who both hated and feared Napoleon with all the intensity of which his powerful spirit was capable, prevented the secession of any member of the Congress from the new great league against their ancient enemy. Still it is highly probable that, if Napoleon had triumphed in Belgium over the Prussians and the English, he would have succeeded in opening negotiations with the Austrians and Russians; and he might have thus gained advantages similar to those which he had obtained on his return from Egypt, when he induced the Czar Paul to withdraw the Russian armies from co- operating with the other enemies of France in the extremity of peril to which she seemed reduced in 1799. But fortune now had deserted him both in diplomacy and in war.

On the 13th of March, 1815, the Ministers of the seven powers, Austria, Spain, England, Portugal, Prussia, Russia, and Sweden, signed a manifesto, by which they declared Napoleon an outlaw; and this denunciation was instantly followed up by a treaty between England, Austria, Prussia, and Russia (to which other powers soon acceded), by which the rulers of those countries bound themselves to enforce that decree, and to prosecute the war until Napoleon should be driven from the throne of France, and rendered incapable of disturbing the peace of Europe. The Duke of Wellington was the representative of England at the Congress of Vienna, and he was immediately applied to for his advice on the plan of military operations against France. It was obvious that Belgium would be the first battlefield; and by the general wish of the Allies, the English Duke proceeded thither to assemble an army from the contingents of Dutch, Belgian, and Hanoverian troops, that were most speedily available, and from the English regiments which his own Government was hastening to send over from this country. A strong Prussian corps was near Aix-la-Chapelle, having remained there since the campaign of the preceding year. This was largely reinforced by other troops of the same nation; and Marshal Blucher, the favorite hero of the Prussian soldiery, and the deadliest foe of France, assumed the command of this army, which was termed the Army of the Lower Rhine; and which, in conjunction with Wellington's forces, was to make the van of the armaments of the Allied Powers. Meanwhile Prince Swartzenburg was to collect 130,000 Austrians, and 124,000 troops of other Germanic States, as "the Army of the Upper Rhine;" and 168,000 Russians, under the command of Barclay de Tolly, were to form "the Army of the Middle Rhine," and to repeat the march from Muscovy to that river's banks.

The exertions which the Allied Powers thus made at this crisis to grapple promptly with the French emperor have truly been termed gigantic; and never were Napoleon's genius and activity more signally displayed, than in the celerity and skill by which he brought forward all the military resources of France, which the reverses of the three preceding years, and the pacific policy of the Bourbons during the months of their first restoration, had greatly diminished and disorganized. He re-entered Paris on the 20th of March, and by the end of May, besides sending a force into La Vendee to put down the armed rising of the royalists in that province, and besides providing troops under Massena and Suchet for the defense of the southern frontiers of France, Napoleon had an army assembled in the northeast for active operations under his own command, which amounted to between one hundred and twenty, and one hundred and thirty thousand men, with a superb park of artillery and in the highest possible state of equipment, discipline, and efficiency. [See for these numbers Siborne's History of the Campaign of Waterloo, vol. i. p. 41.]

The approach of the multitudinous Russian, Austrian, Bavarian, and other foes of the French Emperor to the Rhine was necessarily slow; but the two most active of the allied powers had occupied Belgium with their troops, while Napoleon was organizing his forces. Marshal Blucher was there with one hundred and sixteen thousand Prussians; and, before the end of May, the Duke of Wellington was there also with about one hundred and six thousand troops, either British or in British pay. [Ibid. vol. i. chap. 3. Wellington had but a small part of his old Peninsular army in Belgium. The flower of it had been sent on the expeditions against America. His troops, in 1815, were chiefly second battalions, or regiments lately filled up with new recruits. See Scott, vol viii. p. 474.] Napoleon determined to attack these enemies in Belgium. The disparity of numbers was indeed great, but delay was sure to increase the proportionate numerical superiority of his enemies over his own ranks. The French Emperor considered also that "the enemy's troops were now cantoned under the command of two generals, and composed of nations differing both in interest and in feelings." [See Montholon's Memoirs, p. 45.] His own army was under his own sole command. It was composed exclusively of French soldiers, mostly of veterans, well acquainted with their officers and with each other, and full of enthusiastic confidence in their commander. If he could separate the Prussians from the British, so as to attack each singly, he felt sanguine of success, not only against these the most resolute of his many adversaries, but also against the other masses, that were slowly laboring up against his eastern dominions.

The triple chain of strong fortresses, which the French possessed on the Belgian frontier, formed a curtain, behind which Napoleon was able to concentrate his army, and to conceal, till the very last moment, the precise line of attack which he intended to take. On the other hand, Blucher and Wellington were obliged to canton their troops along a line of open country of considerable length, so as to watch for the outbreak of Napoleon from whichever point of his chain of strongholds he should please to make it. Blucher, with his army, occupied the banks of the Sambre and the Meuse, from Liege on his left, to Charleroi on his right; and the Duke of Wellington covered Brussels; his cantonments being partly in front of that city and between it and the French frontier, and partly on its west their extreme right reaching to Courtray and Tournay, while the left approached Charleroi and communicated with the Prussian right. It was upon Charleroi that Napoleon resolved to level his attack, in hopes of severing the two allied armies from each other, and then pursuing his favorite tactic of assailing each separately with a superior force on the battle-field, though the aggregate of their numbers considerably exceeded his own.

The first French corps d'armee, commanded by Count d'Erlon, was stationed in the beginning of June in and around the city of Lille, near to the northeastern frontier of France. The second corps, under Count Reille, was at Valenciennes, to the right of the first one. The third corps, under Count Vandamme, was at Mezieres. The fourth, under Count Gerard, had its head-quarters at Metz, and the sixth under Count Lobau, was at Laon. [The fifth corps was under Count Rapp at Strasburg.] Four corps of reserve cavalry, under Marshal Grouchy, were also near the frontier, between the rivers Aisne and Sambre. The Imperial Guard remained in Paris until the 8th of June, when it marched towards Belgium, and reached Avesnes on the 13th; and in the course of the same and the following day, the five corps d'armee with the cavalry reserves which have been mentioned, were, in pursuance of skillfully combined orders, rapidly drawn together, and concentrated in and around the same place, on the right bank of the river Sambre. On the 14th Napoleon arrived among his troops, who were exulting at the display of their commander's skill in the celerity and precision with which they had been drawn together, and in the consciousness of their collective strength. Although Napoleon too often permitted himself to use language unworthy of his own character respecting his great English adversary, his real feelings in commencing this campaign may be judged from the last words which he spoke, as he threw himself into his traveling carriage to leave Paris for the army. "I go," he said, "to measure myself with Wellington."

…The 15th of June had scarcely dawned before the French army was in motion for the decisive campaign, and crossed the frontier in three columns, which were pointed upon Charleroi and its vicinity. The French line of advance upon Brussels, which city Napoleon resolved to occupy, thus lay right through the centre of the cantonments of the Allies.

…A glance at the map will show the numerous roads that lead from the different fortresses on the French northeastern frontier, and converge upon Brussels; any one of which Napoleon might have chosen for the advance of a strong force upon that city. The Duke's army was judiciously arranged, so as to enable him to concentrate troops on any one of these roads sufficiently in advance of Brussels to check an assailing enemy. The army was kept thus available for movement in any necessary direction, till certain intelligence arrived on the 15th of June that the French had crossed the frontier in large force near Thuin, that they had driven back the Prussian advanced troops under General Ziethen, and were also moving across the Sambre upon Charleroi.

…It was about three o'clock in the afternoon of the 15th, that a Prussian officer reached Brussels, whom General Ziethen had sent to Muffling to inform him of the advance of the main French army upon Charleroi. Muffling immediately communicated this to the Duke of Wellington; and asked him whether he would now concentrate his army, and what would be his point of concentration; observing that Marshal Blucher in

consequence of this intelligence would certainly concentrate the Prussians at Ligny. The Duke replied, "If all is as General Ziethen supposes, I will concentrate on my left wing, and so be in readiness to fight in conjunction with the Prussian army. Should, however, a portion of the enemy's force come by Mons, I must concentrate more towards my centre. This is the reason why I must wait for positive news from Mons before I fix the rendezvous. Since, however, it is certain that the troops MUST march, though it is uncertain upon what precise spot they must march, I will order all to be in readiness, and will direct a brigade to move at once towards Quatre Bras." [Muffling, p. 231.]

Later in the same day a message from Blucher himself was delivered to Muffling, in which the Prussian Field-Marshal informed the Baron that he was concentrating his men at Sombref and Ligny, and charged Muffling to give him speedy intelligence respecting the concentration of Wellington. Muffling immediately communicated this to the Duke, who expressed his satisfaction with Blucher's arrangements, but added that he could not even then resolve upon his own point of concentration before he obtained the desired intelligence from Mons. About midnight this information arrived. The Duke went to the quarters of General Muffling, and told him that he now had received his reports from Mons, and was sure that no French troops were advancing by that route, but that the mass of the enemy's force was decidedly directed on Charleroi. He informed the Prussian general that he had ordered the British troops to move forward upon Quatre Bras; but with characteristic coolness and sagacity resolved not to give the appearance of alarm by hurrying on with them himself....

Napoleon's operations on the 16th had been conducted with signal skill and vigor; and their results had been very advantageous for his plan of the campaign. With his army formed in three vast columns, [Victoires et Conquetes des Francais, vol. xxv. p. 177.] he had struck at the centre of the line of cantonments of his allied foes; and he had so far made good his blow, that he had affected the passage of the Sambre, he had beaten with his left wing the Prussian corps of General Ziethen at Thuin, and with his centre he had in person advanced right through Charleroi upon Fleurus, inflicting considerable loss upon the Prussians that fell back before him. His right column had with little opposition moved forward as far as the bridge of Chatelet.

Napoleon had thus a powerful force immediately in front of the point which Blucher had fixed for the concentration of the Prussian army, and that concentration was still incomplete. The French Emperor designed to attack the Prussians on the morrow in person, with the troops of his centre and right columns, and to employ his left wing in beating back such English troops as might advance to the help of their allies, and also in aiding his own attack upon Blucher. He gave the command of this left wing to Marshal Ney. Napoleon seems not to have originally intended to employ this celebrated General in the campaign. It was only on the night of the 11th of June, that Marshal Ney received at Paris an order to join the army. Hurrying forward to the Belgian frontier, he met the Emperor near Charleroi. Napoleon immediately directed him to take the command of the left wing, and to press forward with it upon Quatre Bras by the line of the road which leads from Charleroi to Brussels, through Gosselies, Frasne, Quatre Bras, Genappe, and Waterloo. Ney immediately proceeded to the post assigned him; and before ten on the night of the 15th he had occupied Gosselies and Frasne, driving out without much difficulty some weak Belgian detachments which had been stationed in those villages. The lateness of the hour, and the exhausted state of the French troops, who had been marching and fighting since ten in the morning, made him pause from advancing further to attack the much more important position of Quatre Bras. In truth, the advantages which the French gained by their almost superhuman energy and activity throughout the long day of the 15th of June, were necessarily bought at the price of more delay and inertness during the following night and morrow, than would have been observable if they had not

been thus overtasked. Ney has been blamed for want of promptness in his attack upon Quatre Bras; and Napoleon has been criticized for not having fought at Ligny before the afternoon of the 16th: but their censors should remember that soldiers are but men; and that there must be necessarily some interval of time, before troops, that have been worn and weakened by twenty hours of incessant fatigue and strife, can be fed, rested, reorganized, and brought again into action with any hope of success.

Having on the night of the 15th placed the most advanced of the French under his command in position in front of Frasne, Ney rode back to Charleroi, where Napoleon also arrived about midnight, having returned from directing the operations of the centre and right column of the French. The Emperor and the Marshal supped together, and remained in earnest conversation till two in the morning. An hour or two afterwards Ney rode back to Frasne, where he endeavored to collect tidings of the numbers and movements of the enemy in front of him; and also busied himself in the necessary duty of learning the amount and composition of the troops which he himself was commanding. He had been so suddenly appointed to his high station, that he did not know the strength of the several regiments under him, or even the names of their commanding officers. He now caused his aides-de-camp to prepare the requisite returns, and drew together the troops, whom he was thus learning before he used them.

… At five o'clock the Duke of Wellington and the Baron were on horseback, and reached the position at Quatre Bras about eleven. As the French, who were in front of Frasne, were perfectly quiet, and the Duke was informed that a very large force under Napoleon in person was menacing Blucher, it was thought possible that only a slight detachment of the French was posted at Frasne in order to mask the English army. In that event Wellington, as he told Baron Muffling, would be able to employ his whole strength in supporting the Prussians: and he proposed to ride across from Quatre Bras to Blucher's position, in order to concert with him personally the measures which should be taken in order to bring on a decisive battle with the French. Wellington and Muffling rode accordingly towards Ligny, and found Marshal Blucher and his staff at the windmill of Bry, near that village. The Prussian army, 80,000 strong, was drawn up chiefly along a chain of heights, with the villages of Sombref, St. Amand, and Ligny in their front. These villages were strongly occupied by Prussian detachments, and formed the keys of Blucher's position. The heads of the columns which Napoleon was forming for the attack, were visible in the distance. The Duke asked Blucher and General Gneisenau (who was Blucher's adviser in matters of strategy) what they wished him to do, Muffling had already explained to them in a few words the Duke's earnest desire to support the Field-Marshal, and that he would do all that they wished, provided they did not ask him to divide his army, which was contrary to his principles. The Duke wished to advance with his army (as soon as it was concentrated) upon Frasne and Gosselies, and thence to move upon Napoleon's flank and rear. The Prussian leaders preferred that he should march his men from Quatre Bras by the Namur road, so as to form a reserve in rear of Blucher's army. The Duke replied, "Well, I will come if I am not attacked myself," and galloped back with Muffling to Quatre Bras, where the French attack was now actually raging.

Marshal Ney began the battle about two o'clock in the afternoon. He had at this time in hand about 16,000 infantry, nearly 2,000 cavalry, and 38 guns. The force which Napoleon nominally placed at his command exceeded 40,000 men. But more than one half of these consisted of the first French corps d'armee, under Count d'Erlon; and Ney was deprived of the use of this corps at the time that he most required it, in consequence of its receiving orders to march to the aid of the Emperor at Ligny. A magnificent body of heavy cavalry under Kellerman, nearly 5,000 strong, and several more battalions of artillery were added to Ney's army during the battle of Quatre Bras; but his effective infantry force never exceeded 16,000.

When the battle began, the greater part of the Duke's army was yet on its march towards Quatre Bras from Brussels and the other parts of its cantonments. The force of the Allies, actually in position there, consisted only of a Dutch and Belgian division of infantry, not quite 7,000 strong, with one battalion of foot, and one of horse-artillery. The Prince of Orange commanded them. A wood, called the Bois de Bossu, stretched along the right (or western) flank of the position of Quatre Bras; a farmhouse and building, called Gemiancourt, stood on some elevated ground in its front; and to the left (or east), were the enclosures of the village of Pierremont. The Prince of Orange endeavored to secure these posts; but Ney carried Gemiancourt in the centre, and Pierremont on the east, and gained occupation of the southern part of the wood of Bossu. He ranged the chief part of his artillery on the high ground of Gemiancourt, whence it played throughout the action with most destructive effect upon the Allies. He was pressing forward to further advantages, when the fifth infantry division under Sir Thomas Picton and the Duke of Brunswick's corps appeared upon the scene. Wellington (who had returned to Quatre Bras from his interview with Blucher shortly before the arrival of these forces) restored the fight with them; and, as fresh troops of the Allies arrived, they were brought forward to stem the fierce attacks which Ney's columns and squadrons continued to make with unabated gallantry and zeal. The only cavalry of the Anglo-allied army that reached Quatre Bras during the action, consisted of Dutch and Belgians, and a small force of Brunswickers, under their Duke, who was killed on the field. These proved wholly unable to encounter Kellerman's cuirassiers and Pire's lancers; the Dutch and Belgian infantry also gave way early in the engagement; so that the whole brunt of the battle fell on the British and German infantry. They sustained it nobly. Though repeatedly charged by the French cavalry, though exposed to the murderous fire of the French batteries, which from the heights of Gemiancourt sent shot and shell into the devoted squares whenever the French horseman withdrew, they not only repelled their assailants, but Kempt's and Pack's brigades, led, on by Picton, actually advanced against and through their charging foes, and with stern determination made good to the end of the day the ground which they had thus boldly won…The arrival of the English Guards about half- past six o'clock, enabled the Duke to recover the wood of Bossu, which the French had almost entirely won, and the possession of which by them would have enabled Ney to operate destructively upon the allied flank and rear. Not only was the wood of Bossu recovered on the British right, but the enclosures of Pierremont were also carried on the left. When night set in the French had been driven back on all points towards Frasne; but they still held the farm of Gemiancourt in front of the Duke's centre. Wellington and Muffling were unacquainted with the result of the collateral battle between Blucher and Napoleon, the cannonading of which had been distinctly audible at Quatre Bras throughout the afternoon and evening. The Duke observed to Muffling, that of course the two Allied armies would assume the offensive against the enemy on the morrow; and consequently, it would be better to capture the farm at once, instead of waiting till next morning. Muffling agreed in the Duke's views and Gemiancourt was forthwith attacked by the English and captured with little loss to its assailants. [Muffling, p. 242.]

Meanwhile the French and the Prussians had been fighting in and round the villages of Ligny, Sombref, and St. Armand, from three in the afternoon to nine in the evening, with a savage inveteracy almost unparalleled in modern warfare. Blucher had in the field, when he began the battle, 83,417 men, and 224 guns. Bulow's corps, which was 25,000 strong, had not joined him; but the Field-Marshal hoped to be reinforced by it, or by the English army before the end of the action. But Bulow, through some error in the transmission of orders, was far in the rear; and the Duke of Wellington was engaged, as we have seen, with Marshal Ney. Blucher received early warning from Baron Muffling that the Duke could not come to his assistance; but, as Muffling observes, Wellington rendered the Prussians the great

service of occupying more than 40,000 of the enemy, who otherwise would have crushed Blucher's right flank. For, not only did the conflict at Quatre Bras detain the French troops which actually took part in it, but d'Erlon received orders from Ney to join him, which hindered d'Erlon from giving effectual aid to Napoleon. Indeed, the whole of d'Erlon's corps, in consequence of conflicting directions from Ney and the Emperor, marched and countermarched, during the 16th, between Quatre Bras and Ligny without firing a shot in either battle.

Blucher had, in fact, a superiority of more than 12,000 in number over the French army that attacked him at Ligny. The numerical difference was even greater at the beginning of the battle, as Lobau's corps did not come up from Charleroi till eight o'clock. After five hours and a half of desperate and long-doubtful struggle, Napoleon succeeded in breaking the centre of the Prussian line at Ligny, and in forcing his obstinate antagonists off the field of battle. The issue was attributable to his skill, and not to any want of spirit or resolution on the part of the Prussian troops; nor did they, though defeated, abate one jot in discipline, heart, or hope. As Blucher observed, it was a battle in which his army lost the day but not its honor. The Prussians retreated during the night of the 16th, and the early part of the 17th, with perfect regularity and steadiness. The retreat was directed not towards Maestricht, where their principal depots were established, but towards Wavre, so as to be able to maintain their communication with Wellington's army, and still follow out the original plan of the campaign. The heroism with which the Prussians endured and repaired their defeat at Ligny, is more glorious than many victories.

The messenger who was sent to inform Wellington of the retreat of the Prussian army, was shot on the way; and it was not until the morning of the 17th that the Allies, at Quatre Bras, knew the result of the battle of Ligny. The Duke was ready at daybreak to take the offensive against the enemy with vigor, his whole army being by that time fully assembled. But on learning that Blucher had been defeated, a different course of action was clearly necessary. It was obvious that Napoleon's main army would now be directed against Wellington, and a retreat was inevitable. On ascertaining that the Prussian army had retired upon Wavre, that there was no hot pursuit of them by the French, and that Bulow's corps had taken no part in the action at Ligny, the Duke resolved to march his army back towards Brussels, still intending to cover that city, and to halt at a point in a line with Wavre, and there restore his communication with Blucher. An officer from Blucher's army reached the Duke about nine o'clock, from whom he learned the effective strength that Blucher still possessed, and how little discouraged his ally was by the yesterday's battle. Wellington sent word to the Prussian commander that he would halt in the position of Mont St. Jean, and accept a general battle with the French, if Blucher would pledge himself to come to his assistance with a single corps of 25,000 men. This was readily promised; and after allowing his men ample time for rest and refreshment, Wellington retired over about half the space between Quatre Bras and Brussels. He was pursued, but little molested, by the main French army, which about noon of the 17th moved laterally from Ligny, and joined Ney's forces, which had advanced through Quatre Bras when the British abandoned that position. The Earl of Uxbridge, with the British cavalry, covered the retreat of the Duke's army, with great skill and gallantry; and a heavy thunderstorm, with torrents of rain, impeded the operations of the French pursuing squadrons. The Duke still expected that the French would endeavor to turn his right, and march upon Brussels by the high road that leads through Mons and Hal. In order to counteract this anticipated maneuver, he stationed a force of 18,000 men, under Prince Frederick of the Netherlands, at Hal, with orders to maintain himself there if attacked, as long as possible. The Duke halted with the rest of his army at the position near Mont St. Jean, which, from a village in its neighborhood, has received the ever-memorable name of the field of Waterloo.

Wellington was now about twelve miles distant, on a line running from west to east, from Wavre, where the Prussian army had now been completely reorganized and collected, and where it had been strengthened by the junction of Bulow's troops, which had taken no part in the battle of Ligny. Blucher sent word from Wavre to the Duke, that he was coming to help the English at Mont St. Jean, in the morning, not with one corps, but with his whole army. The fiery old man only stipulated that the combined armies, if not attacked by Napoleon on the 18th, should themselves attack him on the 19th. So far were Blucher and his army from being in the state of annihilation described in the boastful bulletin by which Napoleon informed the Parisians of his victory at Ligny. Indeed, the French Emperor seems himself to have been misinformed as to the extent of loss which he had inflicted on the Prussians. Had he known in what good order and with what undiminished spirit they were retiring, he would scarcely have delayed sending a large force to press them in their retreat until noon on the 17th. Such, however, was the case. It was about that time that he confided to Marshal Grouchy the duty of pursuing the defeated Prussians, and preventing them from joining Wellington. He placed for this purpose 32,000 men and 96 guns under his orders. Violent complaints and recriminations passed afterwards between the Emperor and the marshal respecting the manner in which Grouchy attempted to perform this duty, and the reasons why he failed on the 18th to arrest the lateral movement of the Prussians from Wavre to Waterloo. It is sufficient to remark here, that the force which Napoleon gave to Grouchy (though the utmost that the Emperor's limited means would allow) was insufficient to make head against the entire Prussian army, especially after Bulow's junction with Blucher…But the failure of Grouchy was in truth mainly owing to the indomitable heroism of Blucher himself; who, though he had received severe personal injuries in the battle of Ligny, was as energetic and ready as ever in bringing his men into action again, and who had the resolution to expose a part of his army, under Thielman, to be overwhelmed by Grouchy at Wavre on the 18th, while he urged the march of the mass of his troops upon Waterloo. "It is not at Wavre, but at Waterloo," said the old Field-Marshal, "that the campaign is to be decided;" and he risked a detachment, and won the campaign accordingly. Wellington and Blucher trusted each other as cordially, and co-operated as zealously, as formerly had been the case with Marlborough and Eugene. It was in full reliance on Blucher's promise to join him that the Duke stood his ground and fought at Waterloo; and those who have ventured to impugn the Duke's capacity as a general, ought to have had common-sense enough to perceive, that to charge the Duke with having won the battle of Waterloo by the help of the Prussians, is really to say that he won it by the very means on which he relied, and without the expectation of which the battle would not have been fought.

...the field of battle at Waterloo…[consists of] a valley between two and three miles long, of various breadths at different points, but generally not exceeding half a mile. On each side of the valley there is a winding chain of low hills running somewhat parallel, with each other. The declivity from each of these ranges of hills to the intervening valley is gentle but not uniform, the undulations of the ground being frequent and considerable. The English army was posted on the northern, and the French army occupied the southern ridge. The artillery of each side thundered at the other from their respective heights throughout the day, and the charges of horse and foot were made across the valley that has been described. The village of Mont St. Jean is situated a little behind the centre of the northern chain of hills, and the village of La Belle Alliance is close behind the centre of the southern ridge. The high road from Charleroi to Brussels (a broad paved causeway) runs through both these villages, and bisects therefore both the English and the French positions. The line of this road was the line of Napoleon's intended advance on Brussels.

There are some other local particulars connected with the situation of each army, which it is necessary to bear in mind. The strength of the British position did not consist merely in the occupation of a ridge of high ground. A village and ravine, called Merk Braine, on the Duke of Wellington's extreme right, secured his flank from being turned on that side; and on his extreme left, two little hamlets called La Haye and Papelotte, gave a similar, though a slighter, protection. Behind the whole British position is the extensive forest of Soignies. As no attempt was made by the French to turn either of the English flanks, and the battle was a day of straightforward fighting, it is chiefly important to ascertain what posts there were in front of the British line of hills, of which advantage could be taken either to repel or facilitate an attack; and it will be seen that there were two, and that each was of very great importance in the action. In front of the British right, that is to say, on the northern slope of the valley towards its western end, there stood an old-fashioned Flemish farm-house called Goumont, or Hougoumont, with out-buildings and a garden, and with a copse of beach trees of about two acres in extent round it. This was strongly garrisoned by the allied troops; and, while it was in their possession, it was difficult for the enemy to press on and force the British right wing. On the other hand, if the enemy could take it, it would be difficult for that wing to keep its ground on the heights, with a strong post held adversely in its immediate front, being one that; would give much shelter to the enemy's marksmen, and great facilities for the sudden concentration of attacking columns. Almost immediately in front of the British centre, and not so far down the slope as Hougoumont, there was another farm-house, of a smaller size, called La Haye Sainte, [Not to be confounded with the hamlet of La Haye at the extreme left of the British line.] which was also held by the British troops, and the occupation of which was found to be of very serious consequence.

With respect to the French position, the principal feature to be noticed is the village of Planchenoit, which lay a little in the rear of their right (I.E. on the eastern side), and which proved to be of great importance in aiding them to check the advance of the Prussians.

…As has been already mentioned, the Prussians, on the morning of the 18th, were at Wavre, which is about twelve miles to the east of the field of battle of Waterloo. The junction of Bulow's division had more than made up for the loss sustained at Ligny; and leaving Thielman with about seventeen thousand men to hold his ground, as he best could, against the attack which Grouchy was about to make on Wavre, Bulow and Blucher moved with the rest of the Prussians through St. Lambert upon Waterloo. It was calculated that they would be there by three o'clock; but the extremely difficult nature of the ground which they had to traverse, rendered worse by the torrents of rain that had just fallen, delayed them long on their twelve miles' march.

An army indeed, less animated by bitter hate against the enemy than was the Prussians, and under a less energetic chief than Blucher, would have failed altogether in effecting a passage through the swamps, into which the incessant rain had transformed the greater part of the ground through which it was necessary to move not only with columns of foot, but with cavalry and artillery. At one point of the march, on entering the defile of St. Lambert, the spirits of the Prussians almost gave way…The French and British armies lay on the open field during the wet and stormy night of the 17th; and when the dawn of the memorable 18th of June broke, the rain was still descending heavily upon Waterloo. The rival nations rose from their dreary bivouacs, and began to form, each on the high ground which it occupied. Towards nine the weather grew clearer, and each army was able to watch the position and arrangements of the other on the opposite side of the valley.

The Duke of Wellington drew up his army in two lines; the principal one being stationed near the crest of the ridge of hills already described, and the other being arranged along the slope in the rear of his position…The Duke formed his second line of cavalry. This only extended behind the right and centre of his first line. The largest mass was drawn up behind the brigades of infantry in the centre, on either side of the Charleroi road…The artillery was distributed at convenient intervals along the front of the whole line.

…On the opposite heights the French army was drawn up in two general lines, with the entire force of the Imperial Guards, cavalry as well as infantry, in rear of the centre, as a reserve.

…military critics have highly eulogized the admirable arrangement which Napoleon made of his forces of each arm, so as to give him the most ample means of sustaining, by an immediate and sufficient support, any attack, from whatever point he might direct it; and of drawing promptly together a strong force, to resist any attack that might be made on himself in any part of the field. [Siborne, vol. i. p. 376.] When his troops were all arrayed, he rode along the lines, receiving everywhere the most enthusiastic cheers from his men, of whose entire devotion to him his assurance was now doubly sure. On the northern side of the valley the Duke's army was also drawn up, and ready to meet the menaced attack.

Wellington had caused, on the preceding night, every brigade and corps to take up its station on or near the part of the ground which it was intended to hold in the coming battle. He had slept a few hours at his headquarters in the village of Waterloo; and rising on the 18th, while it was yet deep night, he wrote several letters to the Governor of Antwerp, to the English Minister at Brussels, and other official personages, in which he expressed his confidence that all would go well, but "as it was necessary to provide against serious losses; should any accident occur, he gave a series of judicious orders for what should be done in the rear of the army, in the event of the battle going against the Allies. He also, before he left the village of Waterloo, saw to the distribution of the reserves of ammunition which had been parked there, so that supplies should be readily forwarded to every part of the line of battle, where they might be required, The Duke, also, personally inspected the arrangements that had been made for receiving the wounded, and providing temporary hospitals in the houses in the rear of the army. Then, mounting a favorite charger, a small thorough-bred chestnut horse, named "Copenhagen," Wellington rode forward to the range of hills where his men were posted. Accompanied by his staff and by the Prussian General Muffling, he rode along his lines, carefully inspecting all the details of his position. Hougoumont was the object of his special attention. He rode down to the southeastern extremity of its enclosures, and after having examined the nearest French troops, he made some changes in the disposition of his own men, who were to defend that important post.

…The two great champions, who now confronted each other, were equals in years, and each had entered the military profession at the same early age…It is, indeed, remarkable that Napoleon, during his numerous campaigns in Spain as well as other countries, not only never encountered the Duke of Wellington before the day of Waterloo, but that he was never until then personally engaged with British troops, except at the siege of Toulon, in 1793, which was the very first incident of his military career. Many, however, of the French generals who were with him in 1815, knew well, by sharp experience, what English soldiers were, and what the leader was who now headed them. Ney, Foy, and other officers who had served in the Peninsula, warned Napoleon that he would find the English infantry "very devils in fight." The Emperor, however, persisted in employing the old system of attack, with which the French generals often succeeded against continental troops, but which had always failed against the English in the Peninsula. He adhered to his usual tactics of employing the order of the column; a mode of attack probably favored by him (as Sir Walter Scott remarks) on account of his faith in the extreme valor of the French officers by whom the column was headed. It is a threatening formation, well calculated to shake the firmness of ordinary foes; but which, when steadily met, as the English have met it, by heavy volleys of musketry from an extended line, followed up by a resolute bayonet charge, has always resulted in disaster to the assailants. [See especially Sir W. Napier's glorious pictures of the battles of Busaco and Albuera. The THEORETICAL advantages of the attack in column, and its peculiar fitness for a French army, are set forth in the Chevalier Folard's "Traite de la Colonne," prefixed to the first volume of his "Polybius," See also the preface to his sixth volume.]

It was approaching noon before the action commenced…at about half-past eleven o'clock, Napoleon began the battle by directing a powerful force from his left wing under his brother, Prince Jerome, to attack Hougoumont. Column after column of the French now descended from the west of the southern heights, and assailed that post with fiery valor, which was encountered with the most determined bravery. The French won the copse round the house, but a party of the British Guards held the house itself throughout the day. The whole of Byng's brigade was required to man this hotly-contested post. Amid shell and shot, and the blazing fragments of part of the buildings, this obstinate contest was continued. But still the English were firm in Hougoumont; though the French occasionally moved forward in such numbers as enabled them to surround and mask it with part of their troops from their left wing, while others pressed onward up the slope, and assailed the British right.

The cannonade, which commenced at first between the British right and the French left, in consequence of the attack on Hougoumont, soon became general along both lines; and about one o'clock, Napoleon directed a grand attack to be made under Marshal Ney upon the centre and left wing of the allied army. For this purpose four columns of infantry, amounting to about eighteen thousand men, were collected, supported by a strong division of cavalry under the celebrated Kellerman; and seventy-four guns were brought forward ready to be posted on the ridge of a little undulation of the ground in the interval between the two principal chains of heights, so as to bring their fire to bear on the Duke's line at a range of about seven hundred yards. By the combined assault of these formidable forces, led on by Ney, "the bravest of the brave," Napoleon hoped to force the left centre of the British position, to take La Haye Sainte, and then pressing forward, to occupy also the farm of Mont St. Jean. He then could cut the mass of Wellington's troops off from their line of retreat upon Brussels, and from their own left, and also completely sever them from any Prussian troops that might be approaching.

The columns destined for this great and decisive operation descended majestically from the French line of hills, and gained the ridge of the intervening eminence, on which the batteries that supported them were now ranged. As the columns descended again from this eminence, the seventy-four guns opened over their heads with terrible effect upon the troops of the Allies that were stationed on the heights to the left of the Charleroi road. One of the French columns kept to the east, and attacked the extreme left of the Allies; the other three continued to move rapidly forwards upon the left centre of the allied position. The front line of the Allies here was composed of Bylandt's brigade of Dutch and Belgians. As the French columns moved up the southward slope of the height on which the Dutch and Belgians stood, and the skirmishers in advance began to open their fire, Bylandt's entire brigade turned and fled in disgraceful and disorderly panic; but there were men more worthy of the name behind.

In this part of the second line of the Allies were posted Pack and Kempt's brigades of English infantry, which had suffered severely at Quatre Bras. But Picton was here as general of division, and not even Ney himself surpassed in resolute bravery that stern and fiery spirit. Picton brought his two brigades forward, side by side, in a thin, two-deep line. Thus joined together, they were not three thousand strong. With these Picton had to make head against the three victorious French columns, upwards of four times that strength, and who, encouraged by the easy rout of the Dutch and Belgians, now came confidently over the ridge of the hill. The British infantry stood firm; and as the French halted and began to deploy into line, Picton seized the critical moment. He shouted in his stentorian voice to Kempt's brigade: "A volley,

and then charge!" At a distance of less than thirty yards that volley was poured upon the devoted first sections of the nearest column; and then, with a fierce hurrah, the British dashed in with the bayonet. Picton was shot dead as he rushed forward, but his men pushed on with the cold steel. The French reeled back in confusion. Pack's infantry had checked the other two columns and down came a whirlwind of British horse on the whole mass, sending them staggering from the crest of the hill, and cutting them down by whole battalions. Ponsonby's brigade of heavy cavalry (the Union Brigade as it was called, from its being made up of the British Royals, the Scots Greys, and the Irish Inniskillings), did this good service. On went the horsemen amid the wrecks of the French columns, capturing two eagles, and two thousand prisoners; onwards still they galloped, and sabered the artillerymen of Ney's seventy-four advanced guns; then severing the traces, and cutting the throats of the artillery horses, they rendered these guns totally useless to the French throughout the remainder of the day. While thus far advanced beyond the British position and disordered by success, they were charged by a large body of French lancers, and driven back with severe loss, till Vandeleur's Light horse came to their aid, and beat off the French lancers in their turn.

Equally unsuccessful with the advance of the French infantry in this grand attack, had been the efforts of the French cavalry who moved forward in support of it, along the east of the Charleroi road. Somerset's cavalry of the English Household Brigade had been launched, on the right of Picton's division, against the French horse, at the same time that the English Union Brigade of heavy horse charged the French infantry columns on the left.

Somerset's brigade was formed of the Life Guards, the Blues, and the Dragoon Guards. The hostile cavalry, which Kellerman led forward, consisted chiefly of Cuirassiers. This steel-clad mass of French horsemen rode down some companies of German infantry, near La Haye Sainte, and flushed with success, they bounded onward to the ridge of the British position. The English Household Brigade, led on by the Earl of Uxbridge in person, spurred forward to the encounter, and in an instant, the two adverse lines of strong swordsmen, on their strong steeds, dashed furiously together. A desperate and sanguinary hand-to-hand fight ensued, in which the physical superiority of the Anglo-Saxons, guided by equal skill, and animated with equal valor, was made decisively manifest. Back went the chosen cavalry of France; and after them, in hot pursuit, spurred the English Guards. They went forward as far and as fiercely as their comrades of the Union Brigade; and, like them, the Household cavalry suffered severely before they regained the British position, after their magnificent charge and adventurous pursuit.

Napoleon's grand effort to break the English left centre had thus completely failed; and his right wing was seriously weakened by the heavy loss which it had sustained. Hougoumont was still being assailed, and was still successfully resisting. Troops were now beginning to appear at the edge of the horizon on Napoleon's right, which he too well knew to be Prussian, though he endeavored to persuade his followers that they were Grouchy's men coming to their aid.

Grouchy was in fact now engaged at Wavre with his whole force, against Thielmam's single Prussian corps, while the other three corps of the Prussian army were moving without opposition, save from the difficulties of the ground, upon Waterloo…Napoleon had witnessed with bitter disappointment the rout of his troops, foot, horse, and artillery, which attacked the left centre of the English, and the obstinate resistance which the garrison of Hougoumont opposed to all the exertions of his left wing. He now caused the batteries along the line of high ground held by him to be strengthened, and for some time an unremitting and most destructive cannonade raged across the valley, to the partial cessation of other conflict. But the superior fire of the French artillery, though it weakened, could not break the British line, and more close and summary measures were requisite.

It was now about half-past three o'clock; and though Wellington's army had suffered severely by the unremitting cannonade, and in the late desperate encounter, no part of the British position had been forced. Napoleon determined therefore to try what effect he could produce on the British centre and right by charges of his splendid cavalry, brought on in such force that the Duke's cavalry could not check them. Fresh troops were at the same time sent to assail La Haye Sainte and Hougoumont, the possession of these posts being the Emperor's unceasing object. Squadron after squadron of the French cuirassiers accordingly ascended the slopes on the Duke's right, and rode forward with dauntless courage against the batteries of the British artillery in that part of the field. The artillery-men were driven from their guns, and the cuirassiers cheered loudly at their supposed triumph. But the Duke had formed his infantry in squares, and the cuirassiers charged in vain against the impenetrable hedges of bayonets, while the fire from the inner ranks of the squares told with terrible effect on their squadrons. Time after time they rode forward with invariably the same result: and as they receded from each attack the British artillerymen rushed forward from the centers of the squares, where they had taken refuge, and plied their guns on the retiring horsemen. Nearly the whole of Napoleon's magnificent body of heavy cavalry was destroyed in these fruitless attempts upon the British right. But in another part of the field fortune favored him for a time. Two French columns of infantry from Donzelot's division took La Haye Sainte between six and seven o'clock, and the means were now given for organizing another formidable attack on the centre of the Allies…There was no time to be lost—Blucher and Bulow were beginning to press hard upon the French right. As early as five o'clock, Napoleon had been obliged to detach Lobau's infantry and Domont's horse to check these new enemies. They succeeded in doing so for a time; but as larger numbers of the Prussians came on the field, they turned Lobau's right flank, and sent a strong force to seize the village of

Planchenoit, which, it will be remembered, lay in the rear of the French right.

The design of the Allies was not merely to prevent Napoleon from advancing upon Brussels, but to cut off his line of retreat and utterly destroy his army. The defense of Planchenoit therefore became absolutely essential for the safety of the French, and Napoleon was obliged to send his Young Guard to occupy that village, which was accordingly held by them with great gallantry against the reiterated assaults of the Prussian left, under Bulow. Three times did the Prussians fight their way into Planchenoit, and as often did the French drive them out: the contest was maintained with the fiercest desperation on both sides, such being the animosity between the two nations that quarter was seldom given or even asked. Other Prussian forces were now appearing on the field nearer to the English left; whom also Napoleon kept in check, by troops detached for that purpose. Thus a large part of the French army was now thrown back on a line at right angles with the line of that portion which still confronted and assailed the English position. But this portion was now numerically inferior to the force under the Duke of Wellington, which Napoleon had been assailing throughout the day, without gaining any other advantage than the capture of La Haye Sainte. It is true that, owing to the gross misconduct of the greater part of the Dutch and Belgian troops, the Duke was obliged to rely exclusively on his English and German soldiers, and the ranks of these had been fearfully thinned; but the survivors stood their ground heroically, and opposed a resolute front to every forward movement of their enemies.

…All accounts of the battle show that the Duke was ever present at each spot where danger seemed the most pressing; inspiriting his men by a few homely and good-humored words; and restraining their impatience to be led forward to attack in their turn…But the Duke inspired all under him with his own spirit of patient firmness. When other generals besides Halkett sent to him, begging for reinforcements, or for leave to withdraw corps which were reduced to skeletons, the answer was the same: "It is impossible; you must hold your ground to the last man, and all will be well." He gave a similar reply to some of his staff; who asked instructions from him, so that, in the event of his falling, his successor might follow out his plan. He answered, "My plan is simply to stand my ground here to the last man." His personal danger was indeed imminent throughout the day; and though he escaped without injury to himself or horse, one only of his numerous staff was equally fortunate.

…Napoleon had stationed himself during the battle on a little hillock near La Belle Alliance, in the centre of the French position. Here he was seated, with a large table from the neighboring farm-house before him, on which maps and plans were spread; and thence with his telescope he surveyed the various points of the field. Soult watched his orders close at his left hand, and his staff was grouped on horseback a few paces in the rear. ["Souvenirs Militaires," par Col, Lemonnier-Delafosse, p. 407. "Ouvrard, who attended Napoleon as chief commissary of the French army on that occasion, told me that Napoleon was suffering from a complaint which made it very painful for him to ride."—Lord Ellesmere, p. 47.] Here he remained till near the close of the day, preserving the appearance at least of calmness, except some expressions of irritation which escaped him, when Ney's attack on the British left centre was defeated. But now that the crisis of the battle was evidently approaching, he mounted a white Persian charger, which he rode in action because the troops easily recognized him by the horse color. He had still the means of effecting a retreat. His Old Guard had yet taken no part in the action. Under cover of it, he might have withdrawn his shattered forces and retired upon the French frontier. But this would only have given the English and Prussians the opportunity of completing their junction; and he knew that other armies were fast coming up to aid them in a march upon Paris, if he should succeed in avoiding an encounter with them, and retreating upon the capital. A victory at Waterloo was his only alternative from utter ruin, and he determined to employ his Guard in one bold stroke more to make that victory his own.

Between seven and eight o'clock, the infantry of the Old Guard was formed into two columns, on the declivity near La Belle Alliance. Ney was placed at their head. Napoleon himself rode forward to a spot by which his veterans were to pass; and, as they approached, he raised his arm, and pointed to the position of the Allies, as if to tell them that their path lay there. They answered with loud cries of "Vive l'Empereur!" and descended the hill from their own side, into that "valley of the shadow of death" while the batteries thundered with redoubled vigor over their heads upon the British line. The line of march of the columns of the Guard was directed between Hougoumont and La Haye Sainte, against the British right centre; and at the same time the French under Donzelot, who had possession of La Haye Sainte, commenced a fierce attack upon the British centre, a little more to its left. This part of the battle has drawn less attention than the celebrated attack of the Old Guard; but it formed the most perilous crisis for the allied army…The French tirailleurs, who were posted in clouds in La Haye Sainte, and the sheltered spots near it, picked off the artillerymen of the English batteries near them: and taking advantage of the disabled state of the English guns, the French brought some field-pieces up to La Haye Sainte, and commenced firing grape from them on the infantry of the Allies, at a distance of not more than a hundred paces. The allied infantry here consisted of some German brigades, who were formed in squares, as it was believed that Donzelot had cavalry ready behind La Haye Sainte to charge them with, if they left that order of formation. In this state the Germans remained for some time with heroic fortitude, though the grape-shot was tearing gaps in their ranks and the side of one square was literally blown away by one tremendous volley which the French gunners poured into it. The Prince of Orange in vain endeavored to lead some Nassau troops to the aid of the brave Germans. The Nassauers would not or could not face the French; and some battalions of Brunswickers,

whom the Duke of Wellington had ordered up as a reinforcement, at first fell back, until the Duke in person rallied them, and led them on. Having thus barred the farther advance of Donzelot, the Duke galloped off to the right to head his men who were exposed to the attack of the Imperial Guard. He had saved one part of his centre from being routed; but the French had gained ground and kept it; and the pressure on the allied line in front of La Haye Sainte was fearfully severe, until it was relieved by the decisive success which the British in the right centre achieved over the columns of the Guard.

The British troops on the crest of that part of the position, which the first column of Napoleon's Guards assailed, were Maitland's brigade of British Guards, having Adams's brigade (which had been brought forward during the action) on their right. Maitland's men were lying down, in order to avoid as far as possible the destructive effect of the French artillery, which kept up an unremitting fire from the opposite heights, until the first column of the Imperial Guard had advanced so far up the slope towards the British position, that any further firing of the French artillerymen would have endangered their own comrades. Meanwhile the British guns were not idle; but shot and shell ploughed fast through the ranks of the stately array of veterans that still moved imposingly on. Several of the French superior officers were at its head. Ney's horse was shot under him, but he still led the way on foot, sword in hand. The front of the massive column now was on the ridge of the hill. To their surprise they saw no troops before them. All they could discern through the smoke was a small band of mounted officers. One of them was the Duke himself. The French advanced to about fifty yards from where the British Guards were lying down when the voice of one of the group of British officers was heard calling, as if to the ground before him, "Up, Guards, and at them!" It was the Duke who gave the order; and at the words, as if by magic, up started before them a line of the British Guards four deep, and in the most compact and perfect order. They poured an instantaneous volley upon the head of the French column, by which no less than three hundred of those chosen veterans are said to have fallen. The French officers rushed forwards; and, conspicuous in front of their men, attempted to deploy them into a more extended line, so as to enable them to reply with effect to the British fire. But Maitland's brigade kept showering in volley after volley with deadly rapidity. The decimated column grew disordered in its vain efforts to expand itself into a more efficient formation. The right word was given at the right moment to the British for the bayonet-charge, and the brigade sprang forward with a loud cheer against their dismayed antagonists. In an instant the compact mass of the French spread out into a rabble, and they fled back down the hill, pursued by Maitland's men, who, however, returned to their position in time to take part in the repulse of the second column of the Imperial Guard.

This column also advanced with great spirit and firmness under the cannonade which was opened on it; and passing by the eastern wall of Hougoumont, diverged slightly to the right as it moved up the slope towards the British position, so as to approach nearly the same spot where the first column had surmounted the height, and been defeated. This enabled the British regiments of Adams's brigade to form a line parallel to the left flank of the French column; so that while the front of this column of French Guards had to encounter the cannonade of the British batteries, and the musketry of Maitlands Guards, its left flank was assailed with a destructive fire by a four-deep body of British infantry, extending all along it. In such a position all the bravery and skill of the French veterans were vain. The second column, like its predecessor, broke and fled, taking at first a lateral direction along the front of the British line towards the rear of La Haye Sainte, and so becoming blended with the divisions of French infantry, which under Donzelot had been assailing the Allies so formidably in that quarter. The sight of the Old Guard broken and in flight checked the ardor which Donzelot's troops had hitherto displayed. They, too, began to waver. Adams's victorious brigade was pressing after the flying Guard, and now cleared away the assailants of the allied centre. But the battle was not yet won. Napoleon had still some battalions in reserve near La Belle Alliance. He was rapidly rallying the remains of the first column of his Guards, and he had collected into one body the remnants of the various corps of cavalry, which had suffered so severely in the earlier part of the day. The Duke instantly formed the bold resolution of now himself becoming the assailant, and leading his successful though enfeebled army forward, while the disheartening effect of the repulse of the Imperial Guard on the rest of the French army was still strong, and before Napoleon and Ney could rally the beaten veterans themselves for another and a fiercer charge. As the close approach of the Prussians now completely protected the Duke's left, he had drawn some reserves of horse from that quarter, and he had a brigade of Hussars under Vivian fresh and ready at hand. Without a moment's hesitation he launched these against the cavalry near La Belie Alliance. The charge was as successful as it was daring: and as there was now no hostile cavalry to check the British infantry in a forward movement, the Duke gave the long-wished-for command for a general advance of the army along the whole line upon the foe. It was now past eight o'clock, and for nearly nine deadly hours had the British and German regiments stood unflinching under the fire of artillery, the charge of cavalry, and every variety of assault, which the compact columns or the scattered tirailleurs of the enemy's infantry could inflict. As they joyously sprang forward against the discomfited masses of the French, the setting sun broke through the clouds which had obscured the sky during the greater part of the day, and glittered on the bayonets of the Allies, while they poured down into the valley and towards the heights that were held by the foe. The Duke himself was among the foremost in the advance, and personally directed the movements against each body of the French that essayed resistance. He rode in front of Adams's brigade, cheering it forward, and even galloped among the most advanced of the British skirmishers, speaking joyously to the men, and receiving their hearty shouts of congratulation. The bullets of both friends and foes were whistling fast round him; and one of the few survivors of his staff remonstrated with him for thus exposing a life of such value. "Never mind," was the Duke's answer; "Never mind, let them fire away; the battle's won, and my life is of no consequence now." And, indeed, almost the whole of the French host was now in irreparable confusion. The Prussian army was coming more and more rapidly forwards on their right; and the Young Guard, which had held Planchenoit so bravely, was at last compelled to give way. Some regiments of the Old Guard in vain endeavored to form in squares and stem the current. They were swept away, and wrecked among the waves of the flyers. Napoleon had placed himself in one of these squares…Napoleon cleared the throng of fugitives, and escaped from the scene of the battle and the war, which he and France had lost past all recovery. Meanwhile the Duke of Wellington still rode forward with the van of his victorious troops, until he reined up on the elevated ground near Rossomme. The daylight was now entirely gone; but the young moon had risen, and the light which it cast, aided by the glare from the burning houses and other buildings in the line of the flying French and pursuing Prussians, enabled the Duke to assure himself that his victory was complete. He then rode back along the Charleroi road toward Waterloo: and near La Belle Alliance he met Marshal Blucher. Warm were the congratulations that were exchanged between the Allied Chiefs. It was arranged that the Prussians should follow up the pursuit, and give the French no chance of rallying. Accordingly the British army, exhausted by its toils and sufferings during that dreadful day, did not advance beyond the heights which the enemy had occupied. But the Prussians drove the fugitives before them in merciless chase throughout the night. Cannon, baggage, and all the materiel of the army were abandoned by the French; and many thousands of the infantry threw away their arms to facilitate their escape. The ground was strewn for miles with the wrecks of their host. There was no rear-guard; nor was even the semblance of order attempted, an attempt at resistance was made at the bridge and village of Genappe, the first narrow pass through which the bulk of the French retired. The situation was favorable; and a few resolute battalions, if ably commanded, might have held their pursuers at bay there for some considerable time. But despair and panic were now universal in the beaten army. At the first sound of the Prussian drums and bugles, Genappe was abandoned, and nothing thought of but headlong flight. The Prussians, under General Gneisenau, still followed and still slew; nor even when the Prussian infantry stopped in sheer exhaustion, was the pursuit given up. Gneisenau still pushed on with the cavalry; and by an ingenious stratagem, made the French believe that his infantry were still close on them, and scared them from every spot where they attempted to pause and rest. He mounted one of his drummers on a horse which had been taken from the captured carriage of Napoleon, and made him ride along with the pursuing cavalry, and beat the drum whenever they came on any large number of the French. The French thus fled, and the Prussians pursued through Quatre Bras, and even over the heights of Frasne; and when at length Gneisenau drew bridle, and halted a little beyond Frasne with the scanty remnant of keen hunters who had kept up the chase with him to the last, the French were scattered through Gosselies, Marchiennes, and Charleroi; and were striving to regain the left bank of the river Sambre, which they had crossed in such pomp and pride not a hundred hours before.

…No returns ever were made of the amount of the French loss in the battle of Waterloo; but it must have been immense, and may be partially judged of by the amount of killed and wounded in the armies of the conquerors. On this subject both the Prussian and British official evidence is unquestionably full and authentic. The figures are terribly emphatic.

Of the army that fought under the Duke of Wellington nearly 15,000 men were killed and wounded on this single day of battle. Seven thousand Prussians also fell at Waterloo. At such a fearful price was the deliverance of Europe purchased.

…The overthrow of the French military power at Waterloo was so complete, that the subsequent events of the brief campaign have little interest. Lamartine truly says: "This defeat left nothing undecided in future events, for victory had given judgment. The war began and ended in a single battle." Napoleon himself recognized instantly and fully the deadly nature of the blow which had been dealt to his empire. In his flight from the battlefield he first halted at Charleroi, but the approach of the pursuing Prussians drove him thence before he had rested there an hour. With difficulty getting clear of the wrecks of his own army, he reached Philippeville, where he remained a few hours, and sent orders to the French generals in the various extremities of France to converge with their troops upon Paris. He ordered Soult to collect the fugitives of his own force, and lead them to Laon. He then hurried forward to Paris, and reached his capital before the news of his own defeat. But the stern truth soon transpired. At the demand of the Chambers of Peers and Representatives, he abandoned the throne by a second and final abdication on the 22d of June. On the 29th of June he left the neighborhood of Paris, and proceeded to Rochefort in the hope of escaping to America; but the coast was strictly watched, and on the 15th of July the ex-emperor surrendered himself on board of the English man-of-war the Bellerophon…

Robert E. Lee's Farewell Address to the Army of Northern Virginia

1865

After four years of arduous service, marked by unsurpassed courage and fortitude, the Army of Northern Virginia has been compelled to yield to overwhelming numbers and resources.

I need not tell the survivors of so many hard-fought battles who have remained steadfast to the last that I have consented to this result from no distrust of them; but feeling that valor and devotion could accomplish nothing that could compensate for the loss that would have attended the continuance of the contest, I determined to avoid the useless sacrifice of those whose past services have endeared them to their countrymen. By the terms of the agreement, officers and men can return to their homes and remain until exchanged.

You may take with you the satisfaction that proceeds from the consciousness of duty faithfully performed, and I earnestly pray that a merciful God will extend to you his blessing and protection.

With an unceasing admiration of your constancy and devotion to your country, and a grateful remembrance of your kind and generous consideration of myself, I bid you all an affectionate farewell.

"The Rough Riders Storm San Juan Hill, 1898"

"Roosevelt...made you feel like you would like to cheer."

Richard Harding Davis was a reporter who observed the charge up San Juan Hill. We join his account as American forces have massed at the bottom of the hill - the Spanish entrenched in a dominate position on its top. Behind the Americans, advancing troops have clogged the roads preventing an escape. The Americans appear to be stymied - unwilling to move forward and unable to retreat. Suddenly, Theodore Roosevelt emerges on horseback from the surrounding woods and rallies the men to charge:

"Colonel Roosevelt, on horseback, broke from the woods behind the line of the Ninth, and finding its men lying in his way, shouted: 'If you don't wish to go forward, let my men pass, please.' The junior officers of the Ninth, with their Negroes, instantly sprang into line with the Rough Riders, and charged at the blue block-house on the right.

I speak of Roosevelt first because, with General Hawkins, who led Kent's division, notably the Sixth and Sixteenth Regulars, he was, without doubt, the most conspicuous figure in the charge. General Hawkins, with hair as white as snow, and yet far in advance of men thirty years his junior, was so noble a sight that you felt inclined to pray for his safety; on the other hand, Roosevelt, mounted high on horseback, and charging the rifle-pits at a gallop and quite alone, made you feel that you would like to cheer. He wore on his sombrero a blue polka-dot handkerchief, a la Havelock, which, as he advanced, floated out straight behind his head, like a guidon. Afterward, the men of his regiment who followed this flag, adopted a polka-dot handkerchief as the badge of the Rough Riders. These two officers were notably conspicuous in the charge, but no one can claim that any two men, or anyone man, was more brave or more daring, or showed greater courage in that slow, stubborn advance than did any of the others.

. . .

I think the thing which impressed one the most, when our men started from cover, was that they were so few. It seemed as if someone had made an awful and terrible mistake. One's instinct was to call them to come back. You felt that someone had blundered and that these few men were blindly following out some madman's mad order. It was not heroic then, it seemed merely terribly pathetic. The pity of it, the folly of such a sacrifice was what held you.

They had no glittering bayonets, they were not massed in regular array. There were a few men in advance, bunched together, and creeping up a steep, sunny hill, the top of which roared and flashed with flame. The men held their guns pressed across their breasts and stepped heavily as they climbed. Behind these first few, spreading out like a fan, were single lines of men, slipping and scrambling in the smooth grass, moving forward with difficulty, as though they were wading waist high through water, moving slowly, carefully, with strenuous effort. It was much more wonderful than any swinging charge could have been. They walked to greet death at every step, many of them, as they advanced, sinking suddenly or pitching forward and disappearing in the high grass, but the others' waded on, stubbornly, forming a thin blue line that kept creeping higher and higher up the hill. It was as inevitable as the rising tide. It was a miracle of self-sacrifice, a triumph of bulldog courage, which one watched breathless with wonder. The fire of the Spanish riflemen, who still stuck bravely to their posts, doubled and trebled in fierceness, the crests of the hills crackled and burst in amazed roars, and rippled with waves of tiny flame. But the blue line crept steadily up and on, and then, near the top, the broken fragments gathered together with a sudden burst of speed, the Spaniards appeared for a moment outlined against the sky and poised for instant flight, fired a last volley and fled before the swift-moving wave that leaped and sprang up after them.

The men of the Ninth and the Rough Riders rushed to the blockhouse together, the men of the

Sixth, of the Third, of the Tenth Cavalry, of the
Sixth and Sixteenth Infantry, fell on their faces
along the crest of the hills beyond, and opened
upon the vanishing enemy. They drove the yellow
silk flags of the cavalry and the Stars and Stripes of
their country into the soft earth of the trenches,
and then sank down and looked back at the road
they had climbed and swung their hats in the air.
And from far overhead, from these few figures
perched on the Spanish rifle-pits, with their flags
planted among the empty cartridges of the enemy,
and overlooking the walls of Santiago, came,
faintly, the sound of a tired, broken cheer."
References:

Davis, Richard Harding, The Cuban and Porto
Rican Campaigns (1898); Freidel, Frank, The
Splendid Little War (1958); Morris Edmund, The
Rise of Theodore Roosevelt (1979).

Readings

"Glenwhorple"

A popular marching song for Highlander
regimental units during WWII.

1942-1945

The chorus is repeated after each verse.

There's a braw fine regiment as ilka mon should
ken,
They are deevils at the fechtin', they hate clured a
sicht o' men,
And ha'e suppit muckle whusky when the canteen
they gang ben,
The Hielan' men frae braw Glenwhorple.

Chorus

Heuch! Glenwhorple Hielan' men!
Great strong whusky-suppin' Hielan' men,
Hard- workin', hairy-leggit Hielan' men,
Slainte mhor Glenwhorple.

They were foonded by McAdam, who of a' the
men was fairst,
He resided in Glen Eden, whaur he pipit like tee
burst,
Wi' a fig leaf for a sporran, an'a pairfect Hielan
thairst,
Till he stole awe' the aipples free Glenwhorple.

When the waters o' the deluge drookit a' the
whole world oter,
The Colonel o' the Regiment his name was Shaun
McNoah,
Sae a muckle boat he biggit an' he sneckit up the
door,
an' he sailed awe from drooned Glenwhorple.

Then syne he sent a corporal, and gaired him find
the land,
He returned wi' an empty whusky bottle in his
hand,
Sae they kent the flood was dryin'; he was fu', ye
understand,
For he'd foond a public house abune the water.

When good King Solomon was ruler o' the Glen,
He had a hundred pipers and a thoosan' fechtin'
men,
An' a mighty fine establishment I hae no doot ye
ken,
For he kept a sicht o' wives in auld Glenwhorple.

Then there came a birkie bangster, who was
chieftain o' the Clan,
His name it was t'Wallace, an' he was a fechtin'
mon,
For he harried a' the border and awe' the Southron
ran,
Frae the dingin' o' the claymores o' Glenwhorple.

When the bonnie pipes are skirlin', an' the lads
are on parade,
I' the braw Glenwhorple tartan, wi' the claymore
an' the plaid,
When the Sergeant-Major's sober an' the Colonel's
no afraid,
O' seein' tartan spiders in Glenwhorple!

Eh, a bonnie sicht they mak', when the canteen
they gan ben,
then the morn's parade is o'er, she'll be fu' a'
drunken, men,
An' a thoosan' canty kilties will be stottin, doon
the Glen,
For they drink a power o' whusky in Glenwhorple.

Now the ladies o' the Regiment I hae no doubt ye
ken,
Are as brew and sassie lassies as you'll ere find in
the glen,
Though their legs are no so hairy they can keep up
with the men,
When it comes to suppin whisky in Glenwhorple.

When the monarch o' the islands founded a' the
colonies,
And they sent the Heilan' soldiers out across the
pitchaen seas,
Well they settled in the foothills and they called it
Calgary,
And they sired finer soldiers than Glenwhorple.

610

With the "Minutemen" we gather on the eve
o'labour's rest.
Though their shanks be clad with trews, their
heiland spirit is the best.
For more than fifty years now, we have put them
to the test,
marching side-by-side with soldiers of
Glenwhorple.

"Duty, Honor, Country"
General Douglas MacArthur:
Thayer Award Acceptance Address

West Point, NY
May 12, 1962

MacArthur Memorial Archives, Norfolk, VA
Record Group 25, Box 4, F, 3

"General Westmoreland, General Grove, distinguished guests, and gentlemen of the Corps!

As I was leaving the hotel this morning, a doorman asked me, "Where are you bound for, General?" And when I replied, "West Point," he remarked, "Beautiful place. Have you ever been there before?"

No human being could fail to be deeply moved by such a tribute as this [Thayer Award]. Coming from a profession I have served so long, and a people I have loved so well, it fills me with an emotion I cannot express. But this award is not intended primarily to honor a personality, but to symbolize a great moral code--the code of conduct and chivalry of those who guard this beloved land of culture and ancient descent. That is the animation of this medallion. For all eyes and for all time, it is an expression of the ethics of the American soldier. That I should be integrated in this way with so noble an ideal arouses a sense of pride and yet of humility which will be with me always: Duty, Honor, Country.

Those three hallowed words reverently dictate what you ought to be, what you can be, what you will be. They are your rallying points: to build courage when courage seems to fail; to regain faith when there seems to be little cause for faith; to create hope when hope becomes forlorn.

Unhappily, I possess neither that eloquence of diction, that poetry of imagination, nor that brilliance of metaphor to tell you all that they mean. The unbelievers will say they are but words, but a slogan, but a flamboyant phrase. Every pedant, every demagogue, every cynic, every hypocrite, every troublemaker, and I am sorry to say, some others of an entirely different character, will try to downgrade them even to the extent of mockery and ridicule.

But these are some of the things they do. They build your basic character. They mold you for your future roles as the custodians of the nation's defense. They make you strong enough to know when you are weak, and brave enough to face yourself when you are afraid. They teach you to be proud and unbending in honest failure, but humble and gentle in success; not to substitute words for actions, not to seek the path of comfort, but to face the stress and spur of difficulty and challenge; to learn to stand up in the storm but to have compassion on those who fall; to master yourself before you seek to master others; to have a heart that is clean, a goal that is high; to learn to laugh, yet never forget how to weep; to reach into the future yet never neglect the past; to be serious yet never to take yourself too seriously; to be modest so that you will remember the simplicity of true greatness, the open mind of true wisdom, the meekness of true strength. They give you a temper of the will, a quality of the imagination, a vigor of the emotions, a freshness of the deep springs of life, a temperamental predominance of courage over timidity, of an appetite for adventure over love of ease. They create in your heart the sense of wonder, the unfailing hope of what next, and the joy and inspiration of life. They teach you in this way to be an officer and a gentleman.

And what sort of soldiers are those you are to lead? Are they reliable? Are they brave? Are they capable of victory? Their story is known to all of you. It is the story of the American man-at-arms. My estimate of him was formed on the battlefield many, many years ago, and has never changed. I regarded him then as I regard him now—as one of the world's noblest figures, not only as one of the finest military characters, but also as one of the most stainless. His name and fame are the birthright of every American citizen. In his youth and strength, his love and loyalty, he gave all that mortality can give.

He needs no eulogy from me or from any other man. He has written his own history and written it in red on his enemy's breast. But when I think of his patience under adversity, of his courage under fire, and of his modesty in victory, I am filled with an emotion of admiration I cannot put into words. He belongs to history as furnishing one of the greatest examples of successful patriotism. He belongs to posterity as the instructor of future generations in the principles of liberty and freedom. He belongs to the present, to us, by his virtues and by his achievements. In 20 campaigns, on a hundred battlefields, around a thousand campfires, I have witnessed that enduring fortitude, that patriotic self-abnegation, and that invincible determination which have carved his statue in the hearts of his people. From one end of the world to the other he has drained deep the chalice of courage.

As I listened to those songs [of the glee club], in memory's eye I could see those staggering columns of the First World War, bending under soggy packs, on many a weary march from dripping dusk to drizzling dawn, slogging ankle-deep through the mire of shell-shocked roads, to form grimly for the attack, blue-lipped, covered with sludge and mud, chilled by the wind and rain, driving home to their objective, and for many, to the judgment seat of God.

I do not know the dignity of their birth, but I do know the glory of their death.

They died unquestioning, uncomplaining, with faith in their hearts, and on their lips the hope that we would go on to victory.

Always, for them: Duty, Honor, Country; always their blood and sweat and tears, as we sought the way and the light and the truth.

And 20 years after, on the other side of the globe, again the filth of murky foxholes, the stench of ghostly trenches, the slime of dripping dugouts; those boiling suns of relentless heat, those torrential rains of devastating storms; the loneliness and utter desolation of jungle trails; the bitterness of long separation from those they loved and cherished; the deadly pestilence of tropical disease; the horror of stricken areas of war; their resolute and determined defense, their swift and sure attack, their indomitable purpose, their complete and decisive victory—always victory. Always through the bloody haze of their last reverberating shot, the vision of gaunt, ghastly men reverently following your password of: Duty, Honor, Country.

The code which those words perpetuate embraces the highest moral laws and will stand the test of any ethics or philosophies ever promulgated for the uplift of mankind. Its requirements are for the things that are right, and its restraints are from the things that are wrong.

The soldier, above all other men, is required to practice the greatest act of religious training—sacrifice.

In battle and in the face of danger and death, he discloses those divine attributes which his Maker gave when he created man in his own image. No physical courage and no brute instinct can take the place of the Divine help which alone can sustain him.

However horrible the incidents of war may be, the soldier who is called upon to offer and to give his life for his country is the noblest development of mankind.

You now face a new world—a world of change. The thrust into outer space of the satellite, spheres, and missiles mark the beginning of another epoch in the long story of mankind. In the five or more billions of years the scientists tell us it has taken to form the earth, in the three or more billion years of development of the human race, there has never been a more abrupt or staggering evolution. We deal now not with things of this world alone, but with the illimitable distances and as yet unfathomed mysteries of the universe. We are reaching out for a new and boundless frontier.

We speak in strange terms: of harnessing the cosmic energy; of making winds and tides work for us; of creating unheard synthetic materials to supplement or even replace our old standard basics; to purify sea water for our drink; of mining ocean floors for new fields of wealth and food; of disease preventatives to expand life into the hundreds of years; of controlling the weather for a more equitable distribution of heat and cold, of rain and shine; of space ships to the moon; of the primary target in war, no longer limited to the armed forces of an enemy, but instead to include his civil populations; of ultimate conflict between a united human race and the sinister forces of some other planetary galaxy; of such dreams and fantasies as to make life the most exciting of all time.

And through all this welter of change and development, your mission remains fixed, determined, inviolable: it is to win our wars.

Everything else in your professional career is but corollary to this vital dedication. All other public purposes, all other public projects, all other public needs, great or small, will find others for their accomplishment. But you are the ones who are trained to fight. Yours is the profession of arms, the will to win, the sure knowledge that in war there is no substitute for victory; that if you lose, the nation will be destroyed; that the very obsession of your public service must be: Duty, Honor, Country.

Others will debate the controversial issues, national and international, which divide men's minds; but serene, calm, aloof, you stand as the Nation's war-guardian, as its lifeguard from the raging tides of international conflict, as its gladiator in the arena of battle. For a century and a half you have defended, guarded, and protected its hallowed traditions of liberty and freedom, of right and justice.

Let civilian voices argue the merits or demerits of our processes of government; whether our strength is being sapped by deficit financing, indulged in too long, by federal paternalism grown too mighty, by power groups grown too arrogant, by politics grown too corrupt, by crime grown too rampant, by morals grown too low, by taxes grown too high, by extremists grown too violent; whether our personal liberties are as thorough and complete as they should be. These great national problems are not for your professional participation or military solution. Your guidepost stands out like a ten-fold beacon in the night: Duty, Honor, Country.

You are the leaven which binds together the entire fabric of our national system of defense. From your ranks come the great captains who hold the nation's destiny in their hands the moment the war tocsin sounds. The Long Gray Line has never failed us. Were you to do so, a million ghosts in olive drab, in brown khaki, in blue and gray, would rise from their white crosses thundering those magic words: Duty, Honor, Country.

This does not mean that you are war mongers.

On the contrary, the soldier, above all other people, prays for peace, for he must suffer and bear the deepest wounds and scars of war.

But always in our ears ring the ominous words of Plato, that wisest of all philosophers: "Only the dead have seen the end of war."

The shadows are lengthening for me. The twilight is here. My days of old have vanished, tone and tint. They have gone glimmering through the dreams of things that were. Their memory is one of wondrous beauty, watered by tears, and coaxed and caressed by the smiles of yesterday. I listen vainly, but with thirsty ears, for the witching melody of faint bugles blowing reveille, of far drums beating the long roll. In my dreams I hear again the crash of guns, the rattle of musketry, the strange, mournful mutter of the battlefield.

But in the evening of my memory, always I come back to West Point.

Always there echoes and re-echoes: Duty, Honor, Country.

Today marks my final roll call with you, but I want you to know that when I cross the river my last conscious thoughts will be of The Corps, and The Corps, and The Corps.

I bid you farewell.

The Soldier's Creed

Reprinted with permission from the Official
Website of the United States Army
(http://www.army.mil)

I am an American Soldier.
I am a Warrior and a member of a team. I serve
the people of the United States and live the Army
Values.

I will always place the mission first.
I will never accept defeat.
I will never quit.
I will never leave a fallen comrade.

I am disciplined, physically and mentally tough,
trained and proficient in my warrior tasks and
drills. I always maintain my arms, my equipment
and myself.
I am an expert and I am a professional.
I stand ready to deploy, engage, and destroy the
enemies of the United States of America in close
combat.
I am a guardian of freedom and the American way
of life.
I am an American Soldier.

The Warrior's Code[i]
by Shannon E. French, Ph.D.

United States Naval Academy

"Warrior" should not be used to describe every individual who now fights, has ever fought, or prepares to fight a war. The term would have more strength if we reserved it to apply only to those war fighters who meet other criteria that may be less tangible, but are ultimately more significant, than that of taking up arms against an enemy. Before we call any collection of belligerents a culture of warriors, we should first ask why they fight, how they fight, what brings them honor, and what brings them shame. The answers to these questions will reveal whether or not they have a true warrior's code.

On the first day of the philosophy course I teach at the United States Naval Academy called, "The Code of the Warrior," I ask my students, who are midshipmen preparing for careers as officers in the U.S. Navy or Marine Corps, to reflect on the meaning of the word "warrior." To facilitate this, I give them an exercise that requires them to identify whether any of a list of five words are perfect synonyms for "warrior." They are then asked to write a brief explanation of why each of the five succeeds or fails as a synonym. The time constraint keeps their responses relatively raw, yet they are often surprisingly earnest or even impassioned.

The words I offer my students for their consideration are "murderer," "killer," "fighter," "victor," and "conqueror." I have found them consistently to favor the rejection of all five. The reasons they offer to account for why they dismiss each of these as synonyms for "warrior" regularly stress the idea that a true "warrior" has to be in some way superior to those who might qualify for the other suggested labels. Consider these representative comments from a variety of midshipmen:

MURDERER

"This word has connotations of unjust acts, namely killing for no reason. A warrior fights an enemy who fights to kill him."

KILLER

"A warrior may be required to kill, but it should be for a purpose or cause greater than his own welfare, for an ideal."

FIGHTER

"Simply fighting doesn't make a warrior. There are rules a warrior follows."

VICTOR

"Warriors will lose, too – and the people who win aren't always what a warrior should be."

CONQUEROR

"A conqueror may simply command enough power to overcome opposition. He can be very lacking in the ethical beliefs that should be part of a warrior's life."

Almost without exception, my students insist that a "warrior" is _not_ a "murderer." They even become emotional in the course of repudiating this (intentionally provocative) potential synonym. It is very important to them to be sure that I understand that while most warriors do _kill_ people, they never _murder_ anyone. Their remarks are filled with contempt for mere murderers:

➤ "Murder is committed in cold-blood, without a reason. A warrior should only kill in battle, when it is unavoidable."
➤ "Murder seems to me something that is done for an individual motive: a motive that has no real purpose or cause."
➤ "Murderers have no noble reason for their crimes."
➤ "While a murderer often kills innocent or defenseless people, a warrior restricts his killing to willing combatants. He may stray, but that is an error, not the norm."
➤ "This word has connotations of unjust acts, namely killing for no reason. A warrior fights an enemy who fights to kill him."
➤ "A murderer is someone who kills and enjoys it. That is not a warrior."
➤ "This term has very negative connotations associated with it because a murderer is one who usually kills innocent, unarmed people – while a warrior has honor in battle and does not take advantage of the weak."

- "A murderer murders out of hate. A warrior does not. He knows how to control his anger."
- "Murdering involves taking an innocent life, which does not make someone a warrior."
- "A warrior is not a murderer because a warrior has a code that he lives by which is influenced by morals which must be justified."
- "Warriors fight other warriors. Therefore they kill, not murder."
- "A murderer acts out of hate or personal selfishness."
- "'Murderer' lacks any implication of honor or ethics, but rather calls to mind ruthlessness and disregard for human life."
- "A murderer kills for gain, or out of anger. He does not allow victims a fair fight."
- "The term 'murder' represents an act done with malice. Warriors killed people in an honorable way."
- "'Murder' implies senseless and unjustified killing."
- "A murderer has no honor."

Clearly, my students do not regard the distinction between a warrior and a murderer as a trivial one. Nor should they. In fact, the distinction is essential.

Every human society on earth deems some behavior to be morally unacceptable, and murder is a good example of an act that is cross-culturally condemned. Whatever their other points of discord, the major religions of the world agree in the determination that murder (variously defined) is wrong. According to the somewhat cynical 17th-Century philosopher Thomas Hobbes, the fear of our own murderous appetites is what drove humans to form societies in the first place. We eagerly entered into a social contract in which certain rules of civilized behavior could be enforced by a sovereign power in order to escape the miserable, anarchic State of Nature where existence is a "war of every man against every man," and individual lives are "solitary, poor, nasty, brutish, and short."[ii] In other words, people want to live under some sort of system that at least attempts to make good the guarantee that when they go to sleep at night, they will not be murdered in their beds.

Unfortunately, the fact that we abhor murder produces a disturbing tension for those who are asked to fight wars for their tribes, clans, communities, cultures or nations. When they are trained for war, warriors are given a mandate by their society to take lives. But they must learn to take only certain lives in certain ways, at certain times, and for certain reasons. Otherwise, they become indistinguishable from murderers and will find themselves condemned by the very societies they were created to serve.

Whatever additional martial activities they may engage in, such as conquering foreign peoples, acquiring booty or expanding territory, warriors exist for one primary purpose. That purpose is to defend their communities from any forces that may seek to undermine the security of the social contract: from the "Barbarians at the Gate." The trick is that they must find some way to accomplish this goal without become the barbarians themselves.

Most projections into the haze of our prehistoric past suggest that early human societies were tribal, and that within these tribes a hunter class, charged with providing food for the tribe and protection from predatory animals, evolved into a warrior class having a broader mandate to protect the interests of the tribe generally against all threats, animal or human. Alterations in population sizes, migration, and the strained carrying capacity of certain regions of the earth caused more tribes to come in contact with one another and vie for resources. Inevitably, serious inter-tribal conflicts arose. Before long, a successful warrior class became essential to each tribe's survival. As more complex social-political systems developed and civilization advanced, the composition and exact duties of warrior classes around the globe underwent some changes. But their primary role remained constant: to protect and promote their culture's survival.

The survival of a society does not depend just upon the rescue of citizens or the retention of land. The survival of a culture depends as much, if not more, on the continued existence, recognition, and celebration of a coherent cultural self-conception – on the preservation of cultural identity – as it does on the continued existence of a sustained population or physical boundaries. Several cultures persist in the absence of any physical boundaries (e.g. nomadic cultures), and a culture can be destroyed or supplanted by means other than genocide or territorial conquest. A culture's identity is defined by its deepest values: the values that its citizens believe are worth defending, worth dying for. These are the values that shape a society's "way of life." And it is that "way of life" that warriors fight to maintain.

Warrior cultures throughout history and from diverse regions around the globe have constructed codes of behavior that establish that culture's image of the ideal warrior. These codes have not always been written down or literally codified into a set of explicit rules, yet they can be identified as they are carefully conveyed in some form to each succeeding generation of warriors. These codes tend to be quite demanding. They are often closely linked to a culture's religious beliefs and can be connected to elaborate (in some cases, death defying or excruciatingly painful) rituals and rites of passage. And in many cases they seem to hold the warrior to a higher ethical standard than that required for an ordinary citizen within the general population of the society that the warrior serves. The warriors themselves frequently police strict adherence to these standards; with violators being shamed, ostracized, or even killed by their peers.[iii]

But why to warriors need such a code? Why should a warrior culture want to restrict the actions of its members and require them to commit to lofty ideals? Might not such restraints cripple their effectiveness as warriors? What is wrong with, "All's fair in love and war?" Is winning not all that matters? Why should any warrior be burdened with concerns about honor and shame?

One reason for such warriors' codes may be to protect the warrior him- (or her-) self from serious psychological damage. The things that warriors are asked to do to guarantee their culture's survival are not always pleasant. There is truth in the inescapable slogan, "War is hell." The combination of the warriors' own natural disgust at what they must see in battle and the fact that what they must do on the battlefield seems so uncivilized, so against what they have been taught by their society, could make warriors feel tremendous self-loathing.

Warriors need a way to distinguish what they must do out of a sense of duty from what a serial killer does for the sheer sadistic pleasure of it. Their actions, like those of the serial killer, set them apart from the rest of society. Warriors, however, are not sociopaths. They respect the values of the society in which they were raised and which they are prepared to die to protect. Therefore it is important for them to conduct themselves in such a way that they will be honored and esteemed by their communities, not reviled and rejected by them. They want to be seen as proud defenders and representatives of what is best about their culture: as heroes, not "baby-killers."

By setting high standards for themselves, warriors can create a lifeline that will allow them to pull themselves out of the hell of war and reintegrate themselves into their society. A warrior's code may cover everything from the treatment of prisoners of war to oath keeping to table etiquette, but its primary purpose is to grant nobility to the warriors' profession. This allows warriors to retain both their self-respect and the respect of those they guard.

In the introduction to his valuable analysis of Vietnam veterans suffering from post-traumatic stress disorder (PTSD), *Achilles in Vietnam: Combat Trauma and the Undoing of Character*, psychiatrist Jonathan Shay stresses the importance of "Understanding … the specific nature of catastrophic war experiences that not only cause lifelong disabling psychiatric symptoms but can ruin good character."[iv]

Shay has conducted countless personal interviews and therapy sessions with American combat veterans as part of the Veterans Improvement Program (VIP). His work has led him to the conclusion that the most severe cases of PTSD are the result of wartime experiences that are not simply violent, but which involve what Shay terms the "betrayal of 'what's right'."[v] Veterans who believe that they were directly or indirectly party to immoral or dishonorable behavior (perpetrated by themselves, their comrades or their commanders) have the hardest time reclaiming their lives after the war is over. Such men may be tortured by persistent nightmares, may have trouble discerning a safe environment from a threatening one, may not be able to trust their friends, neighbors, family members or government, and may have problems with alcohol, drugs, child or spousal abuse, depression and suicidal tendencies. As Shay sorrowfully concludes, "The painful paradox is that fighting for one's country can render one unfit to be its citizen."[vi]

In a sense, the nature of the warriors' profession puts them at a higher risk for moral corruption than most other occupations because it involves exerting power in matters of life and death. Warriors exercise the power to take or save lives, order others to take or save lives, and lead or send others to their deaths. If they take this awesome responsibility too lightly - if they lose sight of the moral significance of their actions - they risk losing their humanity and their ability to flourish in human society.

In his powerful work, *On Killing: The Psychological Cost of Learning to Kill in War and Society*, Lt. Col. Dave Grossman illuminates the process by which those in war and those training for war attempt to achieve emotional distance from their enemies. The practice of dehumanizing the enemy through the use of abusive or euphemistic language is a common and effective tool for increasing aggression and breaking down inhibitions against killing. Grossman notes:

It is so much easier to kill someone if they look distinctly different than you. If your propaganda machine can convince your soldiers that their opponents are not really human but are "inferior forms of life", then their natural resistance to killing their own species will be reduced. Often the enemy's humanity is denied by referring to him as a "gook", "kraut", or "nip."[vii]

Like Shay, Grossman has interviewed many US veterans of the Vietnam War. Not all of his subjects, however, were those with lingering psychological trauma. Grossman found that some of the men he interviewed had never truly achieved emotional distance from their former foes, and seemed to be the better for it. These men expressed admiration for Vietnamese culture. Some had even married Vietnamese women. They appeared to be leading happy and productive post-war lives. In contrast, those who persisted in viewing the Vietnamese as "less than animals" were unable to leave the war behind them.

Grossman writes about the dangers of dehumanizing the enemy in terms of potential damage to the war effort, long-term political fallout, and regional or global instability:

Because of [our] ability to accept other cultures, Americans probably committed fewer atrocities than most other nations would have under the circumstances associated with guerrilla warfare in Vietnam. Certainly fewer than was the track record of most colonial powers. Yet still we had our My Lai, and our efforts in that war were profoundly, perhaps fatally, undermined by that single incident.

It can be easy to unleash this genie of racial and ethnic hatred in order to facilitate killing in time of war. It can be more difficult to keep the cork in the bottle and completely restrain it. Once it is out, and the war is over, the genie is not easily put back in the bottle. Such hatred lingers over the decades, even centuries, as can be seen today in Lebanon and what was once Yugoslavia.[viii]

The insidious harm brought to the individual warriors who find themselves swept up by such devastating propaganda matters a great deal to those concerned with the warriors' own welfare. In a segment on the "Clinical Importance of Honoring or Dishonoring the Enemy," Jonathan Shay describes an intimate connection between the psychological health of the veteran and the respect he feels for those he fought. He stresses how important it is to the warrior to have the conviction that he participated in an honorable endeavor:

> *Restoring honor to the enemy is an essential step in recovery from combat PTSD. While other things are obviously needed as well, the veteran's self-respect never fully recovers so long as he is unable to see the enemy as worthy. In the words of one of our patients, a war against subhuman vermin "has no honor". This is true even in victory; in defeat, the dishonoring absence of human themis [shared values, a common sense of "what's right"] linking enemy to enemy makes life unendurable.*[ix]

Shay finds echoes of these sentiments in the words of J. Glenn Gray from Gray's modern classic on the experience of war, *The Warriors: Reflections on Men in Battle*.[x] With the struggle of the Allies against the Japanese in the Pacific Theater of World War II as his backdrop, Gray brings home the agony of the warrior who has become incapable of honoring his enemies and thus is unable to find redemption himself:

> *The ugliness of a war against an enemy conceived to be subhuman can hardly be exaggerated. There is an unredeemed quality to battle experienced under these conditions, which blunts all senses and perceptions. Traditional appeals of war are corroded by the demands of a war of extermination, where conventional rules no longer apply. For all its inhumanity, war is a profoundly human institution (…). This image of the enemy as beast lessens even the satisfaction in destruction, for there is no proper regard for the worth of the object destroyed (…). The joys of comradeship, keenness of perception, and sensual delights [are] lessened (…). No aesthetic reconciliation with one's fate as a warrior [is] likely because no moral purgation [is] possible.*[xi]

It is not enough to ask, "Can our warriors still get the job done if they do not have a code?" We must also consider the related question: "What will getting the job done do to our warriors if they do not have a code?" Accepting certain constraints as a moral duty, even when it is inconvenient or inefficient to do so, allows warriors to hold onto their humanity while experiencing the horror of war - and, when the war is over, to return home and reintegrate into the society they so ably defended. Fighter who cannot say, "this far but no farther," who have no lines they will not cross and no atrocities from which they will shrink, may be effective. They may complete their missions, but they will do so at the loss of their humanity.

Those who are concerned for the welfare of our warriors would never want to see them sent off to face the chaotic hell of combat without something to ground them and keep them from crossing over into an inescapable heart of darkness. A mother and father may be willing to give their beloved son or daughter's life for their country or cause, but I doubt they would be as willing to sacrifice their child's soul. The code is a kind of moral and psychological armor that protects the warrior from becoming a monster in his or her own eyes.

It is easier to remain a warrior when fighting other warriors. When warriors fight murderers, they may be tempted to become the mirror image of the evil they hoped to destroy. Their only protection is their code of honor. The professional military ethics that restrain warriors – that keep them from targeting those who cannot fight back, from taking pleasure in killing, from striking harder than is necessary and that encourage them to offer mercy to their defeated enemies and even to help rebuild their countries and communities – are also their own protection against becoming what they abhor.

Legend has it that when a Spartan mother sent her son off to war she would say to him, "Come back with your shield or on it." If a warrior came back without his shield, it meant that he had laid it down in order to break ranks and run from battle. He was supposed to use his shield to protect the man next to him in formation, so to abandon his shield was not only to be a coward but also to break faith with his comrades. To come back on his shield was to be carried back either wounded or dead. Thus the adage meant that the young warrior should fight bravely, maintain his martial discipline, and return with both his body and his honor intact.

The warriors' mothers who spoke this line were not heartless monsters - far from it. It was spoken from great love. They wanted their children to return with their sense of self-respect still with them, feeling justifiably proud of how they had performed under pressure, not tortured and destroyed by guilt and shame. To come back with their shields was to come back still feeling like warriors, not like cowards or murderers. Everyone who cares about the welfare of warriors wants them not only to live through whatever fighting they must face, but also to have lives worth living after the fighting is done.

The warriors' code is the shield that guards our warriors' humanity. Without it, they are no good to themselves or to those with whom and for whom they fight. Without it, they will find no way back from war. My students are the warriors of the future. When they go into combat, I want them to be able to return from it intact in body and soul. I want all of them, every last one, to come back with their shields.

[i] *Note:* This paper is an earlier version of material later incorporated into the book **The Code of the Warrior: Exploring Warrior Values, Past and Present, by Shannon E. French** (Rowman & Littlefield Publishers, 2003). A version of this paper was also presented at the Joint Services Conference on Professional Ethics (JSCOPE) in 2001.
[ii] Thomas Hobbes, *The Leviathan* (New York: Collier Books, 1962), 100.
[iii] One relevant historical example comes from the Roman legions, where a man who fell asleep while he was supposed to be on watch in time of war could expect to be stoned to death by the members of his own cohort.
[iv] Jonathan Shay, *Achilles in Vietnam: Combat Trauma and the Undoing of Character* (New York: Simon & Schuster, 1994), xiii.
[v] Shay, *Achilles in Vietnam*, xiii.
[vi] Shay, *Achilles in Vietnam*, xx.

[vii] Dave Grossman, *On Killing: The Psychological Cost of Learning to Kill in War and Society* (Boston: Little, Brown, 1996), 161.
[viii] Grossman, *On Killing*, 163.
[ix] Shay, *Achilles in Vietnam*, 115.
[x] J. Glenn Gray, *The Warriors: Reflections on Men in Battle* (New York: Harper & Row, 1970), 152-53.
[xi] Gray, *The Warriors*, 152-53.

SECTION FOUR: HISTORICAL TIMELINE OF ENTRIES

Group	Beginning	Ending
Ancient and Classical World		
Akkadians	2200 BCE	2000 BCE
Egyptians	2133 BCE	100 BCE
Aryans	2000 BCE	800 CE
Peoples of the Sea	1218 BCE	1175 BCE
Hyksos	1786 BCE	1567 BCE
Charioteers	1700 BCE	331 BCE
Hittites	1680 BCE	1180 BCE
Assyrians	800 BCE	612 BCE
Hoplites	776 BCE	323 BCE
Scythians	750 BCE	225 BCE
Immortals	559 BCE	331 BCE
Persians	559 BCE	479 BCE
Romans	509 BCE	395 CE
Spartans	480 BCE	336 BCE
Celts	400 BCE	192 BCE
Sacred Band of Thebes	371 BCE	338 BCE
Macedonians	359 BCE	168 BCE
Zealots	6	73
Highlanders	100	---
Byzantines	330	1453
Vandals	350s	533
Goths	366	550
Huns	376	453
Franks	481	876
Shaolin Priests	497	1672
Dark and Middle Ages		
Lombards	560	773
Berserkers	700	1100s
Knights	702	1457
Vikings	793	1100s
Varangian Guard	839	1204
Magyars	896	---
Mamluks	909	1811
Normans	929	12th Century
Almoravids	1000	1100
Knights Templar	1097	1312
Knights Hospitallers	1113	1798
Condottieri	1159	1550
Samurai	13th	19th centuries
Longbowmen	1200	1500s
Mongols	1206	14th Century
Teutonic Knights	1276	1410

Group	Beginning	Ending
Janissaries	1330	1826
White Company	1361	1364
The Renaissance and Age of Exploration		
Hussites	1414	1436
Aztecs	1431	1522
Conquistadors	1492	1542
Cossacks	1500s	---
Plains Indians	1550	1881
Polish Winged Hussars	1605	1683
Swedes of Gustavus Adolphus	1618	1648
Cavaliers and Roundheads	1642	1646
Redcoats	1645	1881
Boers	1652	1902
Royal Marines	1664	---
Rangers	1670	---
Wild Geese	1691	1745
The Age of Revolutions		
Hessians	1700	1800
Prussians	1701	1871
Afghans	1747	---
British East India Company	1748	1857
Royal Americans	1755	---
Minutemen	1774	1775
United States Marines	1775	---
Submariners	1776	---
Irish Legion	1803	1815
Grande Armee	1804	1815
Marathas	1804-1806	and 1817-1818
Gurkhas	1816	---
Zulus	1816	1906
Ashanti	1820	1902
The Age of Empires to Twenty-First Century		
Texas Rangers	1823	---
Zouaves	1830	1891
French Foreign Legion	1831	---
Red Shirts	1834	1867
Dervishes, or Fuzzy-Wuzzy	1844	1885
Sikhs	1845	1947
San Patricio Battalion	1846	1847

Group	Beginning	Ending
Ever Victorious Army	1860	1864
Army of Northern Virginia	1861	1865
Hood's Texas Brigade	1861	1865
Irish Brigades	1861	1865
Iron Brigade	1861	1865
Mosby's Rangers	1861	1865
Stonewall Brigade	1861	1865
Terry's Texas Rangers	1861	1865
Buffalo Soldiers	1866	1951
Rough Riders	1898	1898
Boxers	1899	1900
Philipino Scouts	1899	1946
Goumiers	1908	1956
ANZACs	1914	1945
Czech Legion	1915	1920
Flying Circus	1915	1918
Lafayette Escadrille (Escadrille Americaine)	1915	1918
Storm Troops	1918	1918
Paratroopers	1919	---
Spetznaz	1920s	---
Arab Legion	1923	1956
Condor Legion	1936	1939
Lincoln Battalion	1936	1938
Waffen SS	1939	1945
Long Range Desert Group	1940	1943
Royal Air Force (Battle of Britain)	1940	1940
Flying Tigers (American Volunteer Group)	1941	1942
Special Air Service	1941	---
Tuskegee Airmen	1941	1945
Viet Minh	1941	1956
Afrika Korps	1942	1945
Chindits	1942	1945
Kamikazes	1942	1945
Alamo Scouts	1943	1945
Merrill's Marauders	1943	1944
Special Boat Service	1945	---
Green Berets	1952	---
SEALs	1962	---
Grenzschutzgruppe 9 (GSG-9)	1973	---
Delta Force	1977	---
Mujahidin	1979	---

SECTION FIVE: INDEX

Index

Page numbers in bold type refer to main reference.

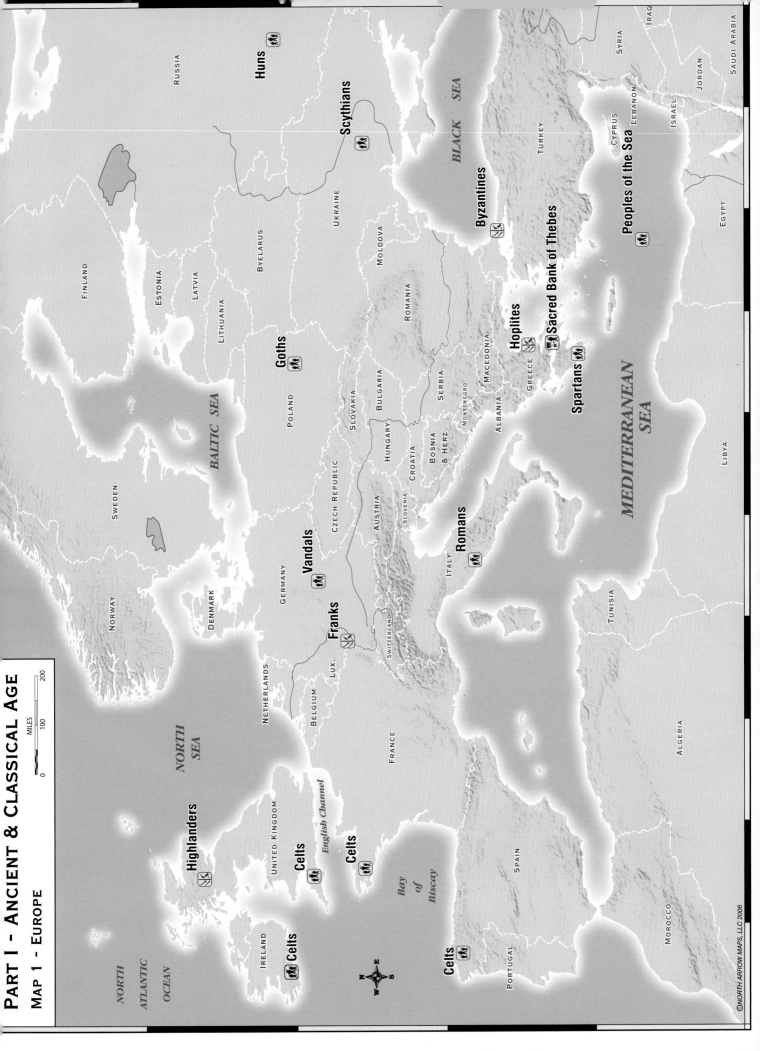

PART I - ANCIENT & CLASSICAL AGE
MAP 1 - EUROPE

MILES
0   100   200

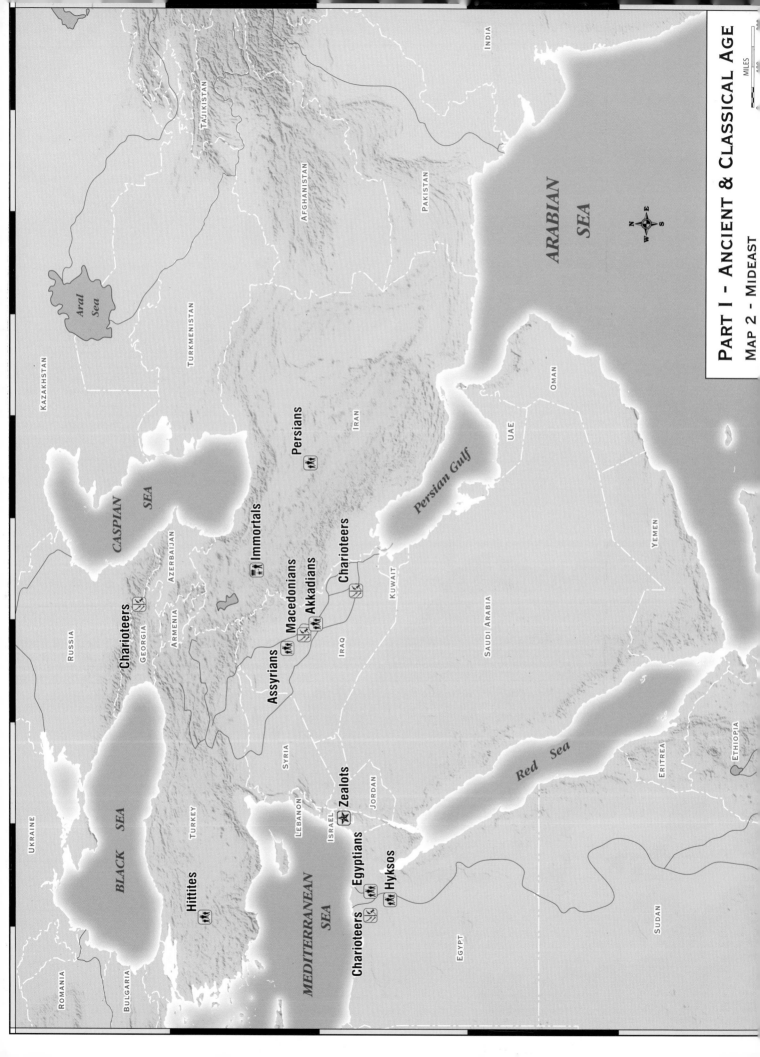

PART I - ANCIENT & CLASSICAL AGE
MAP 2 - MIDEAST

MILES

ARABIAN SEA

ARAL Sea

CASPIAN SEA

BLACK SEA

MEDITERRANEAN SEA

Red Sea

Persian Gulf

ROMANIA
BULGARIA
UKRAINE
RUSSIA
GEORGIA
ARMENIA
AZERBAIJAN
KAZAKHSTAN
TURKMENISTAN
TAJIKISTAN
AFGHANISTAN
PAKISTAN
INDIA
TURKEY
SYRIA
LEBANON
ISRAEL
JORDAN
IRAQ
IRAN
KUWAIT
SAUDI ARABIA
UAE
OMAN
YEMEN
EGYPT
SUDAN
ERITREA
ETHIOPIA

Hittites
Charioteers
Immortals
Persians
Macedonians
Akkadians
Charioteers
Assyrians
Zealots
Egyptians
Hyksos
Charioteers

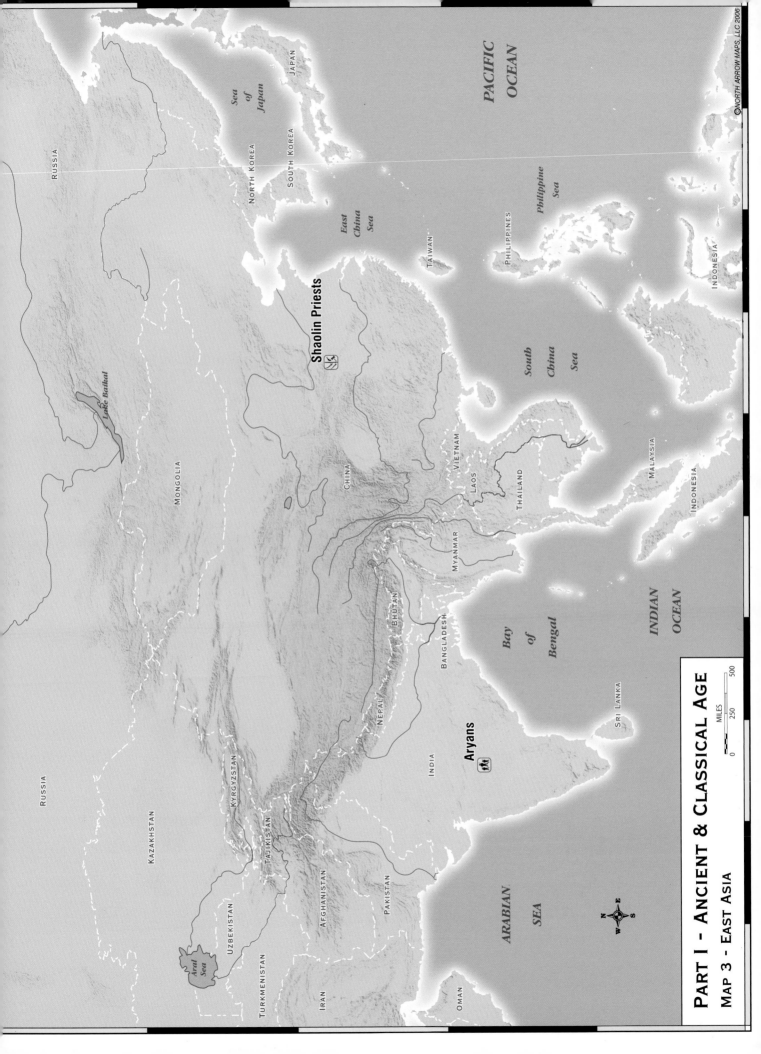

PACIFIC
OCEAN

RUSSIA

Sea
of
Japan

JAPAN

NORTH KOREA

SOUTH KOREA

East
China
Sea

Philippine
Sea

Lake Baikal

Shaolin Priests

TAIWAN

PHILIPPINES

INDONESIA

MONGOLIA

South
China
Sea

MALAYSIA

INDONESIA

CHINA

VIETNAM

LAOS

THAILAND

Aral
Sea

KAZAKHSTAN

KYRGYZSTAN

MYANMAR

BHUTAN

BANGLADESH

Bay
of
Bengal

INDIAN
OCEAN

UZBEKISTAN

TAJIKISTAN

NEPAL

TURKMENISTAN

AFGHANISTAN

INDIA

Aryans

SRI LANKA

IRAN

PAKISTAN

ARABIAN
SEA

N
W   E
S

OMAN

PART I - ANCIENT & CLASSICAL AGE
MAP 3 - EAST ASIA

MILES
0   250   500

©NORTH ARROW MAPS, LLC 2006

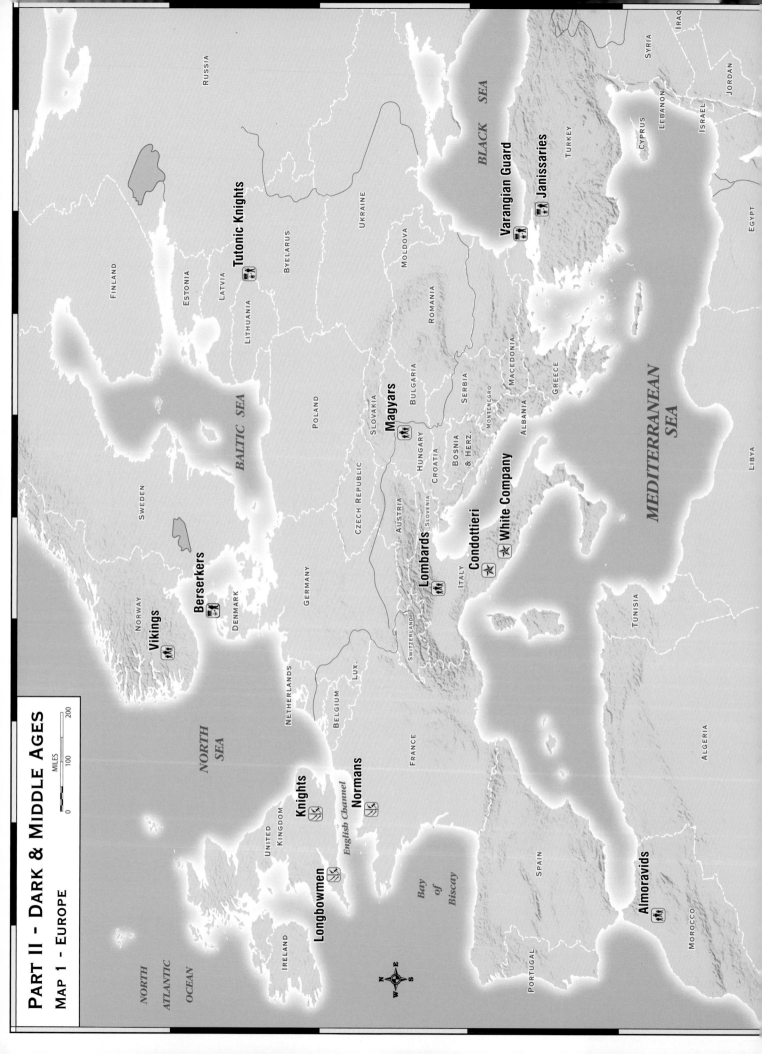

PART II - DARK & MIDDLE AGES
MAP 1 - EUROPE

MILES
0   100   200

NORTH ATLANTIC OCEAN

RUSSIA

FINLAND

Tutonic Knights

ESTONIA

LATVIA

BYELARUS

LITHUANIA

UKRAINE

BLACK SEA

Varangian Guard

Janissaries

TURKEY

SYRIA

IRAQ

JORDAN

ISRAEL

LEBANON

CYPRUS

EGYPT

LIBYA

MOLDOVA

ROMANIA

MACEDONIA

SERBIA

BULGARIA

Magyars

SLOVAKIA

HUNGARY

CROATIA

BOSNIA & HERZ.

MONTENEGRO

ALBANIA

GREECE

MEDITERRANEAN SEA

White Company

Condottieri

Lombards

ITALY

SLOVENIA

AUSTRIA

SWITZERLAND

CZECH REPUBLIC

POLAND

BALTIC SEA

SWEDEN

NORWAY

Vikings

Berserkers

DENMARK

GERMANY

NETHERLANDS

BELGIUM

LUX.

FRANCE

NORTH SEA

Knights

Normans

English Channel

UNITED KINGDOM

Longbowmen

IRELAND

Bay of Biscay

PORTUGAL

SPAIN

Almoravids

MOROCCO

ALGERIA

TUNISIA

N
W E
S

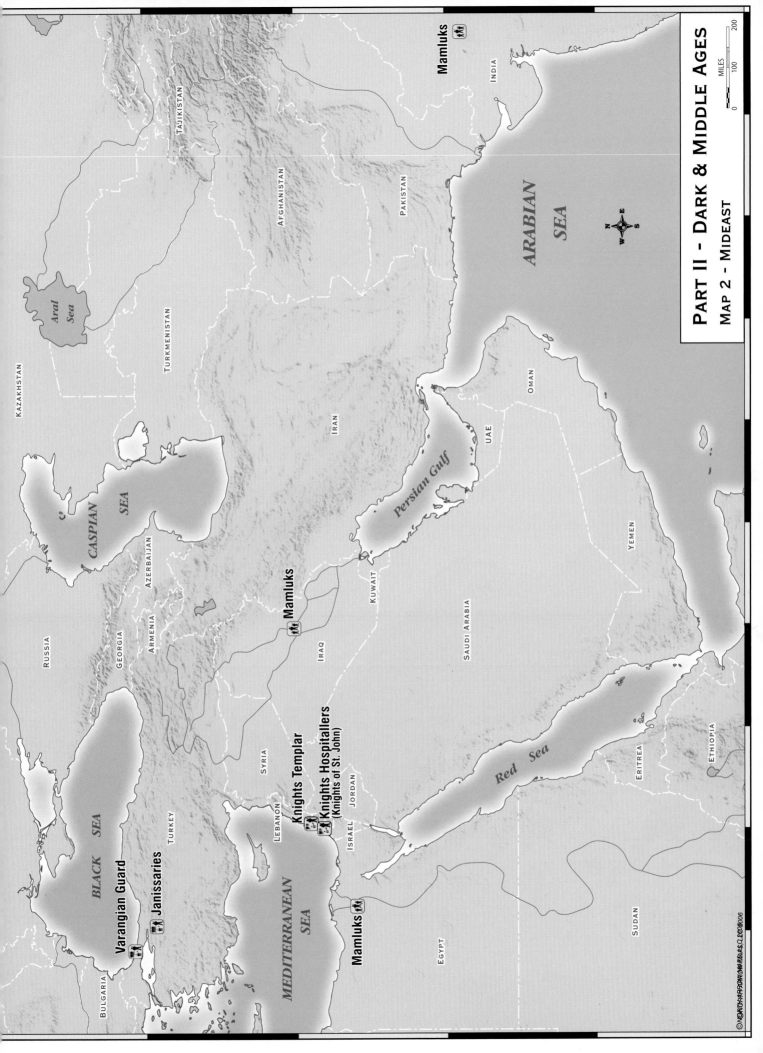

PART II – DARK & MIDDLE AGES
MAP 2 – MIDEAST

MILES
0   100   200

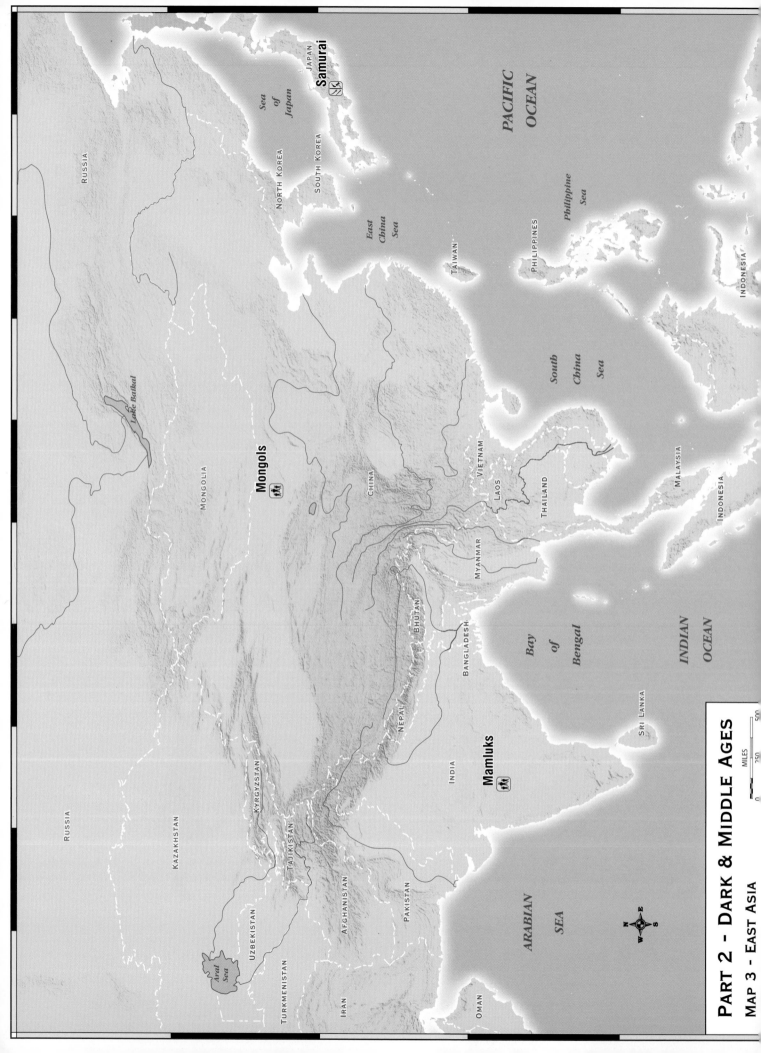

PART 2 - DARK & MIDDLE AGES
MAP 3 - EAST ASIA

MILES
0   250   500

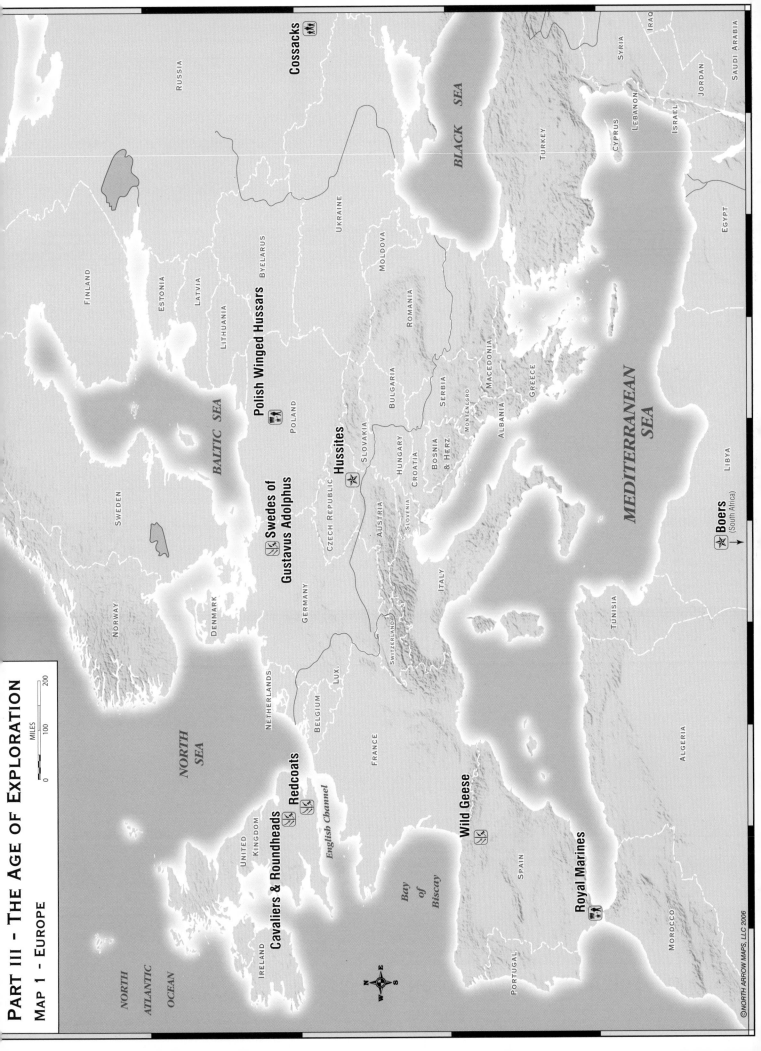

PART III - THE AGE OF EXPLORATION
MAP 1 - EUROPE

MILES
0   100   200

NORTH ATLANTIC OCEAN

NORTH SEA

BALTIC SEA

BLACK SEA

MEDITERRANEAN SEA

English Channel

Bay of Biscay

RUSSIA

FINLAND

SWEDEN

NORWAY

DENMARK

ESTONIA

LATVIA

LITHUANIA

BYELARUS

UKRAINE

MOLDOVA

ROMANIA

POLAND

GERMANY

CZECH REPUBLIC

SLOVAKIA

AUSTRIA

HUNGARY

SLOVENIA

CROATIA

BULGARIA

SERBIA

BOSNIA & HERZ.

MONTENEGRO

ALBANIA

MACEDONIA

GREECE

TURKEY

CYPRUS

SYRIA

LEBANON

ISRAEL

JORDAN

IRAQ

SAUDI ARABIA

EGYPT

LIBYA

TUNISIA

ALGERIA

MOROCCO

PORTUGAL

SPAIN

FRANCE

ITALY

SWITZERLAND

LUX.

BELGIUM

NETHERLANDS

UNITED KINGDOM

IRELAND

Cossacks

Polish Winged Hussars

Swedes of Gustavus Adolphus

Hussites

Cavaliers & Roundheads

Redcoats

Wild Geese

Royal Marines

Boers (South Africa) →

N E S W

©NORTH ARROW MAPS, LLC 2006

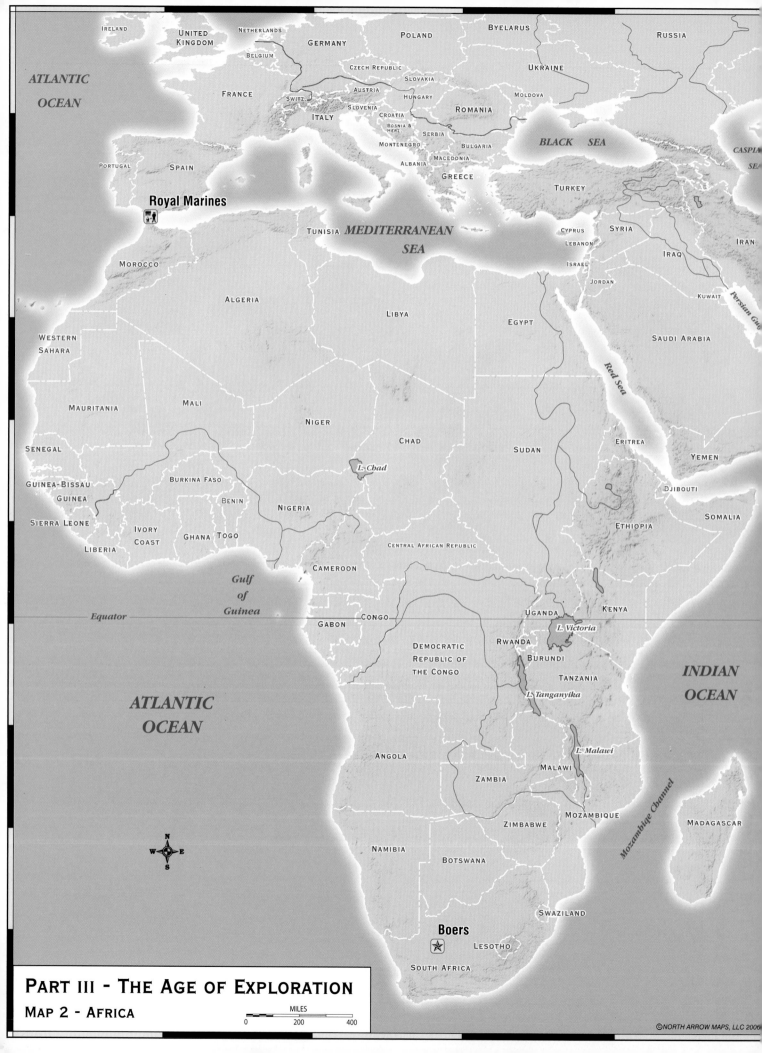

ATLANTIC OCEAN

IRELAND
UNITED KINGDOM
NETHERLANDS
BELGIUM
GERMANY
POLAND
BYELARUS
RUSSIA
CZECH REPUBLIC
SLOVAKIA
UKRAINE
FRANCE
SWITZ.
AUSTRIA
HUNGARY
MOLDOVA
ITALY
SLOVENIA
CROATIA
ROMANIA
BOSNIA & HERZ.
SERBIA
MONTENEGRO
BULGARIA
BLACK SEA
CASPIAN SEA
PORTUGAL
SPAIN
ALBANIA
MACEDONIA
GREECE
TURKEY

Royal Marines

TUNISIA
MEDITERRANEAN SEA
CYPRUS
SYRIA
LEBANON
ISRAEL
IRAN
IRAQ
MOROCCO
JORDAN
KUWAIT
Persian Gulf

WESTERN SAHARA
ALGERIA
LIBYA
EGYPT
SAUDI ARABIA
Red Sea

MAURITANIA
MALI
NIGER
CHAD
SUDAN
ERITREA
YEMEN

SENEGAL
L. Chad
DJIBOUTI

GUINEA-BISSAU
GUINEA
BURKINA FASO
BENIN
NIGERIA
ETHIOPIA
SOMALIA

SIERRA LEONE
IVORY COAST
GHANA
TOGO
CENTRAL AFRICAN REPUBLIC

LIBERIA
Gulf of Guinea
CAMEROON
UGANDA
KENYA

Equator
CONGO
L. Victoria

GABON
DEMOCRATIC REPUBLIC OF THE CONGO
RWANDA
BURUNDI

INDIAN OCEAN

ATLANTIC OCEAN
TANZANIA
L. Tanganyika

L. Malawi
ANGOLA
MALAWI
MOZAMBIQUE
Mozambique Channel
MADAGASCAR

ZAMBIA
ZIMBABWE

N W E S
NAMIBIA
BOTSWANA
SWAZILAND

Boers
LESOTHO
SOUTH AFRICA

PART III - THE AGE OF EXPLORATION
MAP 2 - AFRICA

MILES
0   200   400

©NORTH ARROW MAPS, LLC 2006

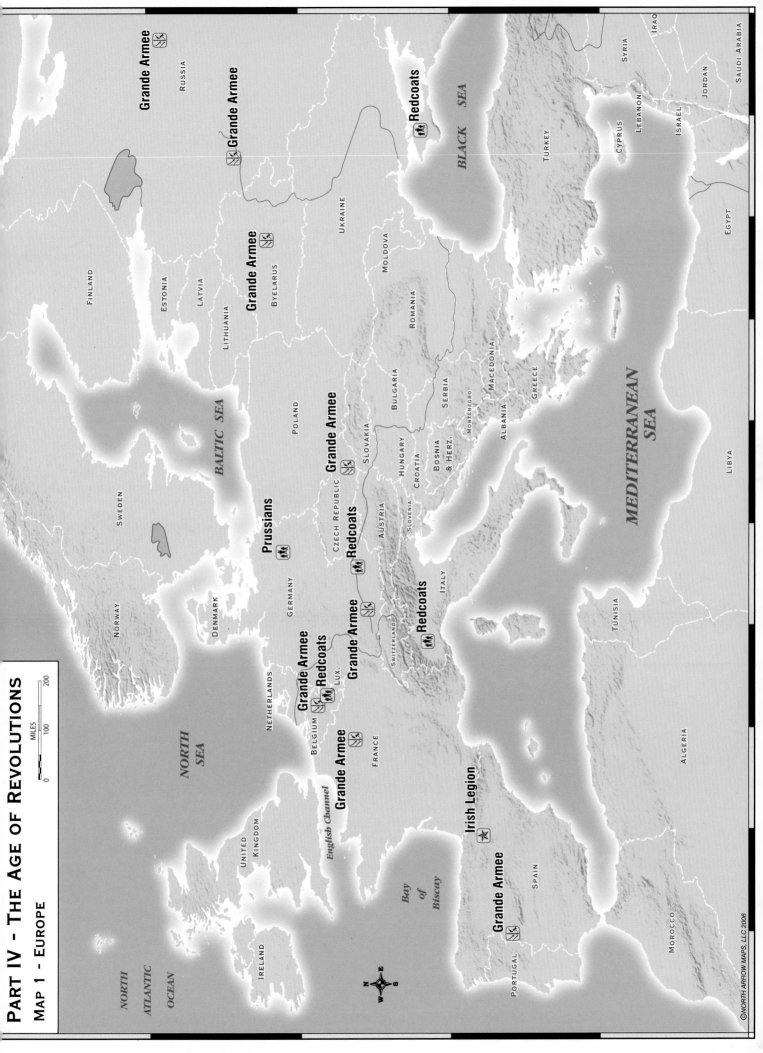

PART IV - THE AGE OF REVOLUTIONS
MAP 1 - EUROPE

MILES
0   100   200

Grande Armee

Grande Armee

Redcoats

RUSSIA

FINLAND

ESTONIA

LATVIA

LITHUANIA

Grande Armee

BYELARUS

UKRAINE

MOLDOVA

BLACK SEA

TURKEY

SYRIA

IRAQ

LEBANON

CYPRUS

ISRAEL

JORDAN

SAUDI ARABIA

EGYPT

LIBYA

BALTIC SEA

SWEDEN

POLAND

Grande Armee

Prussians

CZECH REPUBLIC

SLOVAKIA

HUNGARY

ROMANIA

SERBIA

BULGARIA

CROATIA

SLOVENIA

BOSNIA & HERZ.

MONTENEGRO

ALBANIA

MACEDONIA

GREECE

MEDITERRANEAN SEA

Redcoats

AUSTRIA

ITALY

Redcoats

NORWAY

DENMARK

GERMANY

Grande Armee

Redcoats

LUX.

Grande Armee

SWITZERLAND

NETHERLANDS

BELGIUM

FRANCE

Grande Armee

TUNISIA

ALGERIA

NORTH SEA

UNITED KINGDOM

English Channel

Bay of Biscay

Irish Legion

IRELAND

NORTH ATLANTIC OCEAN

N
W   E
S

SPAIN

Grande Armee

PORTUGAL

MOROCCO

©NORTH ARROW MAPS, LLC 2006

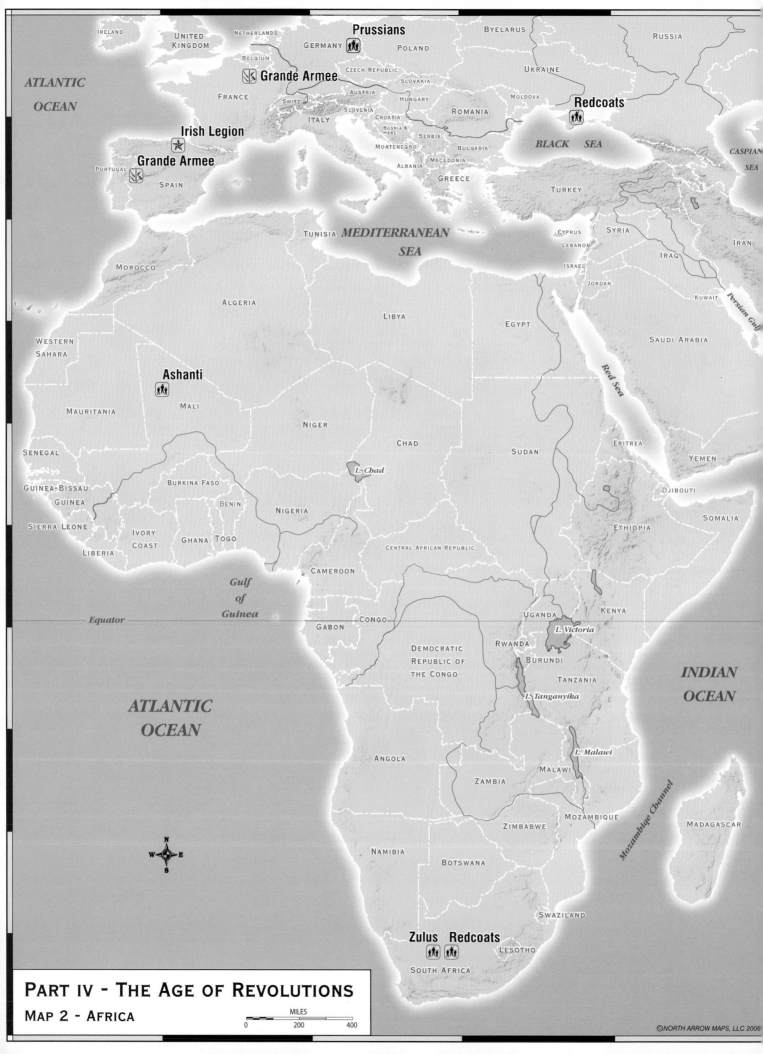

IRELAND · UNITED KINGDOM · NETHERLANDS · GERMANY · POLAND · BYELARUS · RUSSIA

Prussians

BELGIUM · CZECH REPUBLIC · UKRAINE

Grande Armee

FRANCE · SWITZ. · AUSTRIA · SLOVAKIA · HUNGARY · MOLDOVA

Redcoats

ITALY · SLOVENIA · CROATIA · ROMANIA

ATLANTIC OCEAN

BLACK SEA

CASPIAN SEA

Irish Legion

BOSNIA & HERZ. · SERBIA · MONTENEGRO · BULGARIA · MACEDONIA

Grande Armee

PORTUGAL · SPAIN · ALBANIA · GREECE · TURKEY

MEDITERRANEAN SEA

TUNISIA · CYPRUS · SYRIA · LEBANON · ISRAEL · IRAN · IRAQ · JORDAN · KUWAIT · *Persian Gulf*

MOROCCO

ALGERIA · LIBYA · EGYPT · SAUDI ARABIA

WESTERN SAHARA

Red Sea

Ashanti

MALI · NIGER · CHAD · SUDAN · ERITREA · YEMEN · DJIBOUTI

MAURITANIA

SENEGAL · *L. Chad* · SOMALIA

GUINEA-BISSAU · GUINEA · BURKINA FASO · BENIN · NIGERIA · ETHIOPIA

SIERRA LEONE · IVORY COAST · GHANA · TOGO

LIBERIA · CENTRAL AFRICAN REPUBLIC

CAMEROON

Gulf of Guinea · GABON · CONGO · UGANDA · KENYA

Equator · DEMOCRATIC REPUBLIC OF THE CONGO · RWANDA · *L. Victoria*

BURUNDI

TANZANIA

L. Tanganyika

ATLANTIC OCEAN

INDIAN OCEAN

ANGOLA · *L. Malawi*

MALAWI

ZAMBIA

ZIMBABWE · MOZAMBIQUE · MADAGASCAR

Mozambique Channel

NAMIBIA · BOTSWANA

SWAZILAND

Zulus **Redcoats**

LESOTHO

SOUTH AFRICA

N W E S

PART IV - THE AGE OF REVOLUTIONS
MAP 2 - AFRICA

MILES
0 — 200 — 400

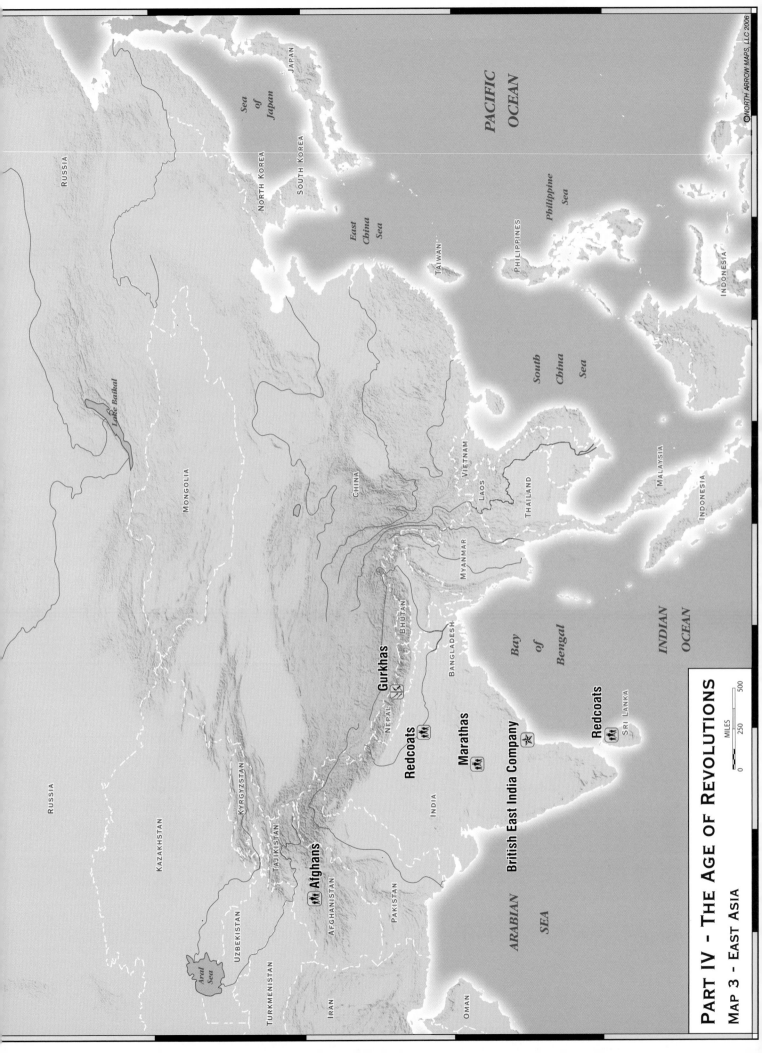

RUSSIA

Sea of Japan

JAPAN

NORTH KOREA

SOUTH KOREA

East China Sea

PACIFIC OCEAN

TAIWAN

Philippine Sea

PHILIPPINES

South China Sea

Lake Baikal

MONGOLIA

CHINA

VIETNAM

LAOS

THAILAND

MALAYSIA

INDONESIA

INDONESIA

Aral Sea

KAZAKHSTAN

KYRGYZSTAN

TAJIKISTAN

Afghans

AFGHANISTAN

PAKISTAN

MYANMAR

BHUTAN

Gurkhas

NEPAL

Redcoats

BANGLADESH

Bay of Bengal

Marathas

British East India Company

INDIA

Redcoats

SRI LANKA

INDIAN OCEAN

ARABIAN SEA

OMAN

IRAN

TURKMENISTAN

UZBEKISTAN

RUSSIA

PART IV - THE AGE OF REVOLUTIONS
MAP 3 - EAST ASIA

MILES

0   250   500

PART IV - THE AGE OF REVOLUTIONS

MAP 4 - THE AMERICA'S

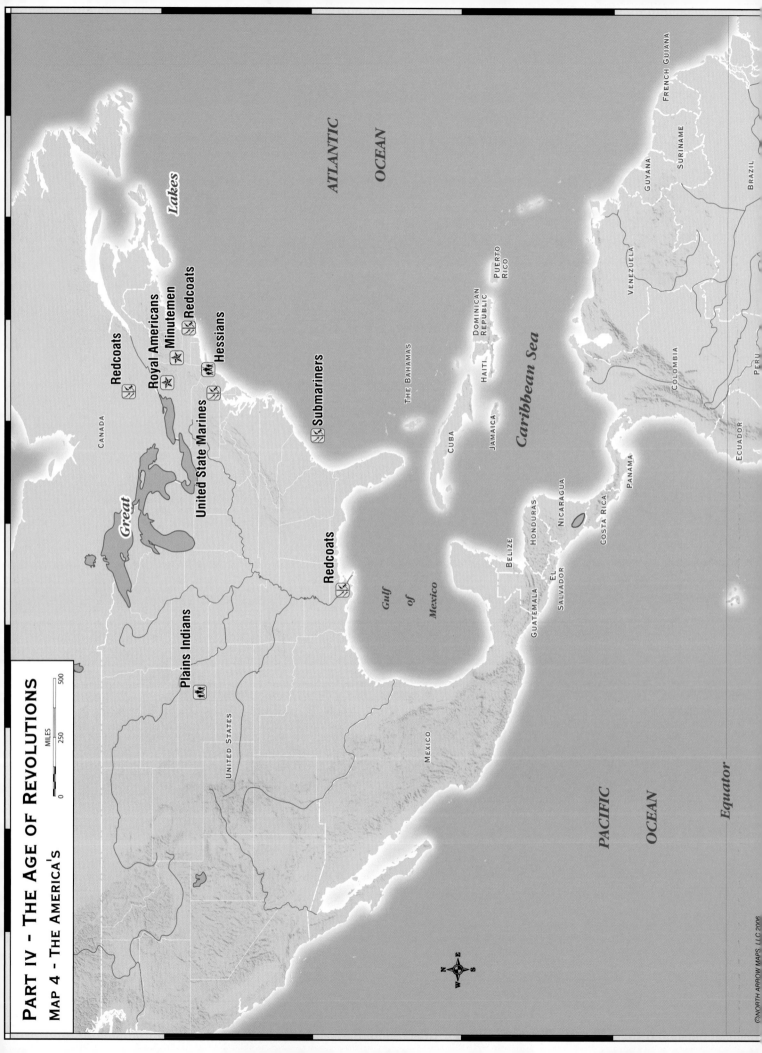

MILES

0   250   500

Redcoats

Royal Americans

Minutemen

Redcoats

Hessians

United State Marines

Submariners

Redcoats

Plains Indians

Great Lakes

CANADA

UNITED STATES

MEXICO

BELIZE

GUATEMALA

EL SALVADOR

HONDURAS

NICARAGUA

COSTA RICA

PANAMA

Gulf of Mexico

THE BAHAMAS

CUBA

JAMAICA

HAITI

DOMINICAN REPUBLIC

PUERTO RICO

Caribbean Sea

ATLANTIC OCEAN

PACIFIC OCEAN

Equator

COLOMBIA

VENEZUELA

GUYANA

SURINAME

FRENCH GUIANA

BRAZIL

ECUADOR

PERU

N
W   E
S

© NORTH ARROW MAPS, LLC 2006

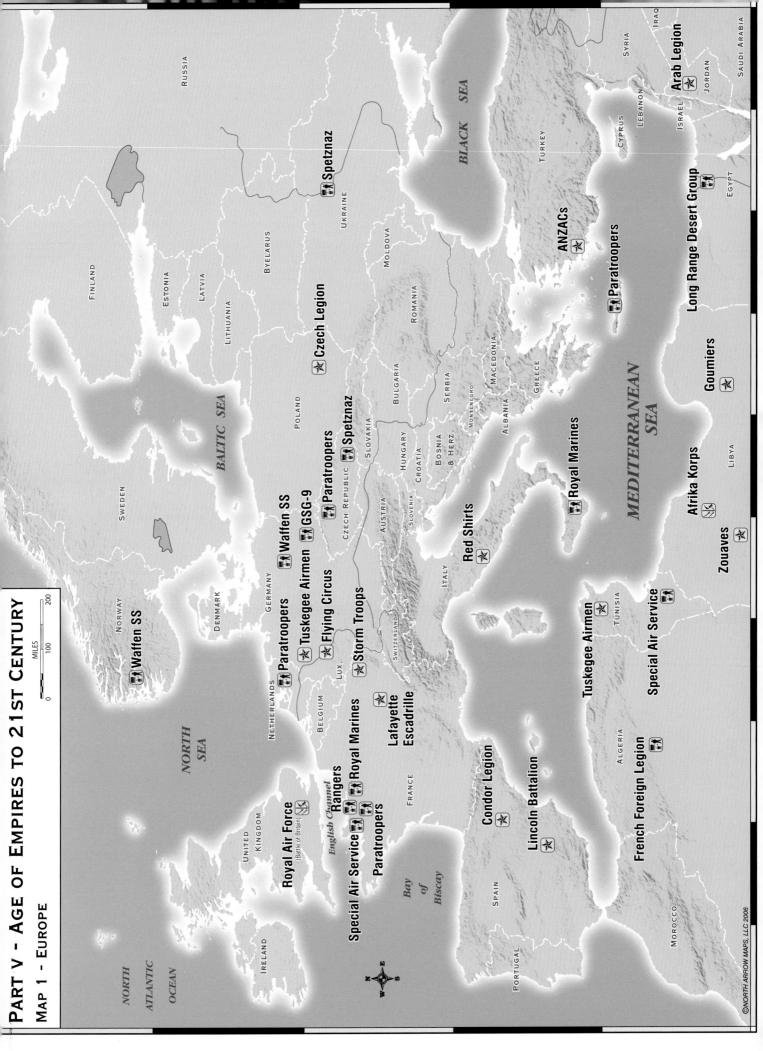

PART V - AGE OF EMPIRES TO 21ST CENTURY
MAP 1 - EUROPE

MILES
0   100   200

©NORTH ARROW MAPS, LLC 2006

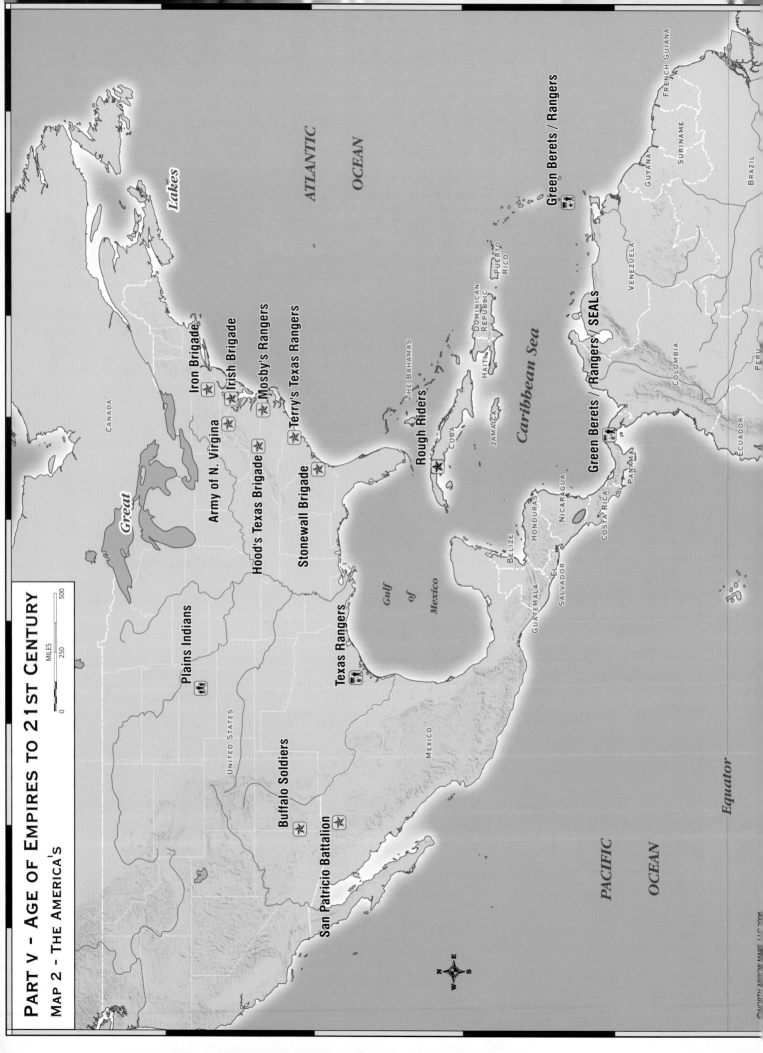

PART V - AGE OF EMPIRES TO 21ST CENTURY
MAP 2 - THE AMERICA'S

MILES

0   250   500

Lakes

Great

CANADA

ATLANTIC

OCEAN

UNITED STATES

Iron Brigade

Irish Brigade

Mosby's Rangers

Terry's Texas Rangers

Army of N. Virgina

Hood's Texas Brigade

Stonewall Brigade

Plains Indians

Buffalo Soldiers

San Patricio Battalion

Texas Rangers

Gulf
of
Mexico

MEXICO

THE BAHAMAS

Rough Riders

CUBA

JAMAICA

Caribbean Sea

HAITI

DOMINICAN
REPUBLIC

PUERTO
RICO

Green Berets / Rangers

SEALS

Green Berets / Rangers

BELIZE

GUATEMALA

HONDURAS

EL SALVADOR

NICARAGUA

COSTA RICA

PANAMA

VENEZUELA

COLOMBIA

GUYANA

SURINAME

FRENCH GUIANA

BRAZIL

ECUADOR

PERU

PACIFIC

OCEAN

Equator

N
W   E
S

© NORTH ARROW MAPS LLC 2006

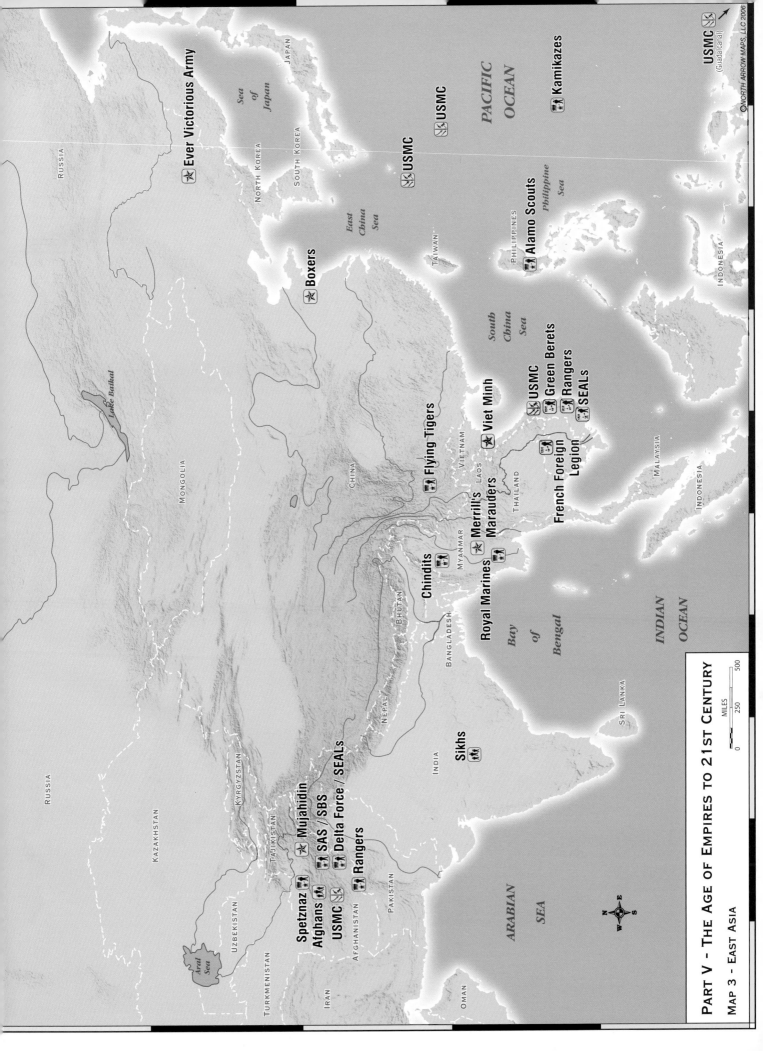

RUSSIA

Sea
of
Japan

JAPAN

★ Ever Victorious Army

NORTH KOREA

SOUTH KOREA

USMC

East
China
Sea

USMC

TAIWAN

PACIFIC
OCEAN

Kamikazes

Philippine
Sea

PHILIPPINES

Alamo Scouts

INDONESIA

★ Boxers

Lake Baikal

RUSSIA

MONGOLIA

CHINA

South
China
Sea

USMC
Green Berets
Rangers
SEALs

Flying Tigers

★ Viet Minh

VIETNAM

LAOS

MALAYSIA

KAZAKHSTAN

Merrill's
Marauders

French Foreign
Legion

INDONESIA

MYANMAR

KYRGYZSTAN

Chindits

THAILAND

Royal Marines

Bay
of
Bengal

INDIAN
OCEAN

TAJIKISTAN

Mujahidin

SAS / SBS

Delta Force / SEALs

Rangers

BHUTAN

BANGLADESH

Spetznaz
Afghans
USMC

NEPAL

Sikhs

SRI LANKA

UZBEKISTAN

AFGHANISTAN

PAKISTAN

INDIA

Aral
Sea

TURKMENISTAN

IRAN

ARABIAN

SEA

OMAN

N
W E
S

USMC
(Guadalcanal)

©NORTH ARROW MAPS, LLC 2006

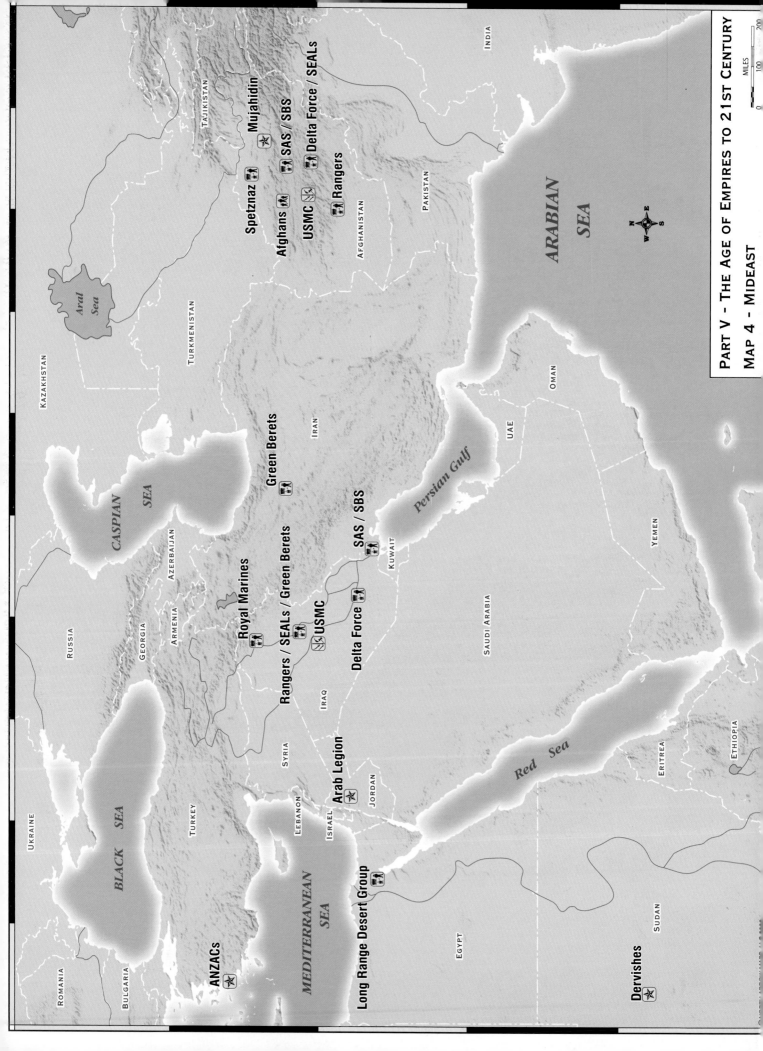

ROMANIA

BULGARIA

UKRAINE

RUSSIA

KAZAKHSTAN

ANZACs ✪

BLACK   SEA

Aral
Sea

GEORGIA

TURKEY

ARMENIA

AZERBAIJAN

TAJIKISTAN

Mujahidin ✪

Spetznaz 🔫

SAS / SBS 🔫

Delta Force / SEALs 🔫

Afghans 🔫   USMC 🔫   Rangers 🔫

CASPIAN

SEA

TURKMENISTAN

MEDITERRANEAN

SEA

LEBANON

SYRIA

Royal Marines 🔫

Rangers / SEALs / Green Berets 🔫 **USMC**

Green Berets 🔫

IRAN

AFGHANISTAN

PAKISTAN

Long Range Desert Group 🔫

ISRAEL

Arab Legion ✪

JORDAN

IRAQ

Delta Force 🔫

SAS / SBS 🔫

KUWAIT

Persian Gulf

UAE

OMAN

INDIA

EGYPT

Red   Sea

SAUDI ARABIA

YEMEN

ARABIAN

SEA

N
W ✤ E
S

SUDAN

ERITREA

ETHIOPIA

Dervishes ✪

MILES

0   100   200